THE

WAR OF THE REBELLION:

A COMPILATION OF THE

OFFICIAL RECORDS

OF THE

UNION AND CONFEDERATE ARMIES.

PREPARED, UNDER THE DIRECTION OF THE SECRETARY OF WAR,

BY

Lieut. Col. ROBERT N. SCOTT, Third U. S. Artillery,

AND

PUBLISHED PURSUANT TO ACT OF CONGRESS APPROVED JUNE 16, 1880.

SERIES I—VOLUME XVIII.

WASHINGTON:
GOVERNMENT PRINTING OFFICE.
1887.

28823

PREFACE.

By an act approved June 23, 1874, Congress made an appropriation "to enable the Secretary of War to begin the publication of the Official Records of the War of the Rebellion, both of the Union and Confederate Armies," and directed him "to have copied for the Public Printer all reports, letters, telegrams, and general orders not heretofore copied or printed, and properly arranged in chronological order."

Appropriations for continuing such preparation have been made from time to time, and the act approved June 16, 1880, has provided "for the printing and binding, under direction of the Secretary of War, of ten thousand copies of a compilation of the Official Records (Union and Confederate) of the War of the Rebellion, so far as the same may be ready for publication, during the fiscal year"; and that "of said number, seven thousand copies shall be for the use of the House of Representatives, two thousand copies for the use of the Senate, and one thousand copies for the use of the Executive Departments."*

This compilation will be the first general publication of the military records of the war, and will embrace all official documents that can be obtained by the compiler, and that appear to be of any historical value.

---

* Volumes I–V distributed under act approved June 16, 1880. The act approved August 7, 1882, provides that—

"The volumes of the Official Records of the War of the Rebellion shall be distributed as follows: One thousand copies to the Executive Departments, as now provided by law. One thousand copies for distribution by the Secretary of War among officers of the Army and contributors to the work. Eight thousand three hundred copies shall be sent by the Secretary of War to such libraries, organizations, and individuals as may be designated by the Senators, Representatives, and Delegates of the Forty-seventh Congress. Each Senator shall designate not exceeding twenty-six, and each Representative and Delegate not exceeding twenty-one of such addresses, and the volumes shall be sent thereto from time to time as they are published, until the publication is completed. Senators, Representatives, and Delegates shall inform the Secretary of War in each case how many volumes of those heretofore published they have forwarded to such addresses. The remaining copies of the eleven thousand to be published, and all sets that may not be ordered to be distributed as provided herein, shall be sold by the Secretary of War for cost of publication, with ten per cent. added thereto, and the proceeds of such sale shall be covered into the Treasury. If two or more sets of said volumes are ordered to the same address, the Secretary of War shall inform the Senators, Representatives, or Delegates, who have designated the same, who thereupon may designate other libraries, organizations, or individuals. The Secretary of War shall report to the first session of the Forty-eighth Congress what volumes of the series heretofore published have not been furnished to such libraries, organizations, and individuals. He shall also inform distributees at whose instance the volumes are sent."

The publication will present the records in the following order of arrangement:

The **First Series** will embrace the formal reports, both Union and Confederate, of the first seizures of United States property in the Southern States, and of all military operations in the field, with the correspondence, orders, and returns relating specially thereto, and, as proposed, is to be accompanied by an Atlas.

In this series the reports will be arranged according to the campaigns and several theaters of operations (in the chronological order of the events), and the Union reports of any event will, as a rule, be immediately followed by the Confederate accounts. The correspondence, &c., not embraced in the " reports " proper will follow (first Union and next Confederate) in chronological order.

The **Second Series** will contain the correspondence, orders, reports, and returns, Union and Confederate, relating to prisoners of war, and (so far as the military authorities were concerned) to State or political prisoners.

The **Third Series** will contain the correspondence, orders, reports, and returns of the Union authorities (embracing their correspondence with the Confederate officials) not relating specially to the subjects of the *first* and *second* series. It will set forth the annual and special reports of the Secretary of War, of the General-in-Chief, and of the chiefs of the several staff corps and departments; the calls for troops, and the correspondence between the National and the several State authorities.

The **Fourth Series** will exhibit the correspondence, orders, reports, and returns of the Confederate authorities, similar to that indicated for the Union officials, as of the *third* series, but excluding the correspondence between the Union and Confederate authorities given in that series.

ROBERT N. SCOTT,
Major Third Art., and Bvt. Lieut. Col.

WAR DEPARTMENT, *August* 23, 1880.

Approved:

ALEX. RAMSEY,
Secretary of War.

CONTENTS.

CHAPTER XXX.

(v)

CONTENTS OF PRECEDING VOLUMES.

VOLUME XVI.

CHAPTER XXVIII.

VOLUME XVII.

CHAPTER XXIX.

CHAPTER XXX.

OPERATIONS IN NORTH CAROLINA AND SOUTHEASTERN VIRGINIA.

AUGUST 20, 1862–JUNE 3, 1863.

SUMMARY OF THE PRINCIPAL EVENTS.*

Aug.	20–Sept. 10, 1862.—Army of the Potomac embarks for Aquia Creek and Alexandria, Va.†
	30, 1862.—Maj. Gen. Gustavus W. Smith, C. S. Army, assumes command of the defenses of Richmond, etc.
	Skirmish near Plymouth, N. C.
	31, 1862.—Skirmish at Franklin, Va.
Sept.	2– 3, 1862.—Expedition from Suffolk, Va.
	6, 1862.—Attack on Washington, N. C
	9, 1862.—Skirmish at Williamsburg, Va.
	17–20, 1862.—Operations at and about Shiloh, N. C.
	19, 1862.—The Confederate Department of North Carolina and Southern Virginia (Department of Virginia and North Carolina) constituted, under command of Maj. Gen. Gustavus W. Smith.
Oct.	3, 1862.—Skirmish on the Blackwater, near Franklin, Va.
	Affair on the Blackwater, near Zuni, Va.
	15, 1862.—Skirmish near Carrsville, Va.
	25, 1862.—Skirmish near Zuni, Va.
	29, 1862.—Skirmish on the Blackwater, Va.
	31, 1862.—Skirmish at Franklin, Va.
Nov.	1–12, 1862.—Expedition from New Berne, N. C., including skirmishes (2d) at Little Creek and Rawle's Mill.
	8, 1862.—Brig. Gen. W. H. C. Whiting, C. S. Army, assigned to command of the defenses of Cape Fear River, N. C.
	11, 1862.—Demonstration on New Berne, N. C.
	12–14, 1862.—Operations about Suffolk, Va., including skirmishes (12th) at Providence Church and (14th) at Blackwater Bridge, and Zuni, Va.
	16, 1862.—Skirmish at Gloucester Point, Va.
	17, 1862.—Affair near Carrsville, Va.
	18, 1862.—Skirmish at Franklin, Va.
	Skirmish at Core Creek, N. C.
	22, 1862.—Destruction of Salt-Works in Matthews County, Va.

---

*Of some of the minor conflicts mentioned in this "Summary" no circumstantial reports are on file.

†See Series I, Vols. XI and XIX.

Nov. 22, 1862.—Reconnaissance from Williamsburg, Va.

25, 1862.—Capture of the United States steamer Ellis, New River, N. C.

Dec. 1, 1862.—Skirmish at Beaver Dam Church, Va.

2, 1862.—Skirmish on the Blackwater, near Franklin, Va.

8-12, 1862.—Reconnaissances from Suffolk to the Blackwater and skirmishes at and about Zuni, Va.

10, 1862.—Attack on Plymouth, N. C.

11-15, 1862.—Reconnaissance from Yorktown to Gloucester, Matthews, King and Queen, and Middlesex Counties, Va.

11-20, 1862.—Expedition from New Berne to Goldsborough, N. C.

12, 1862.—Maj. Gen. Arnold Elzey, C. S. Army, assigned to command of the Richmond defenses, etc.

17, 1862.—Reconnaissance to Diascund Bridge and Burnt Ordinary, Va.

22, 1862.—Skirmishes near Windsor and at Joyner's Ferry, on the Blackwater, Va.

24, 1862.—The Eighteenth Army Corps constituted, under command of Maj. Gen. John G. Foster, U. S. Army.

27, 1862.—Skirmish at Elizabeth City, N. C.

28, 1862.—Skirmishes near Suffolk and at Providence Church, Va.

Jan. 7- 9, 1863.—Expedition from Yorktown to West Point and White House, Va.

8-10, 1863.—Expedition from Suffolk toward the Blackwater, Va.

9, 1863.—Skirmish near Providence Church, Va.

13, 1863.—Expedition from Yorktown to West Point, Va.

17-21, 1863.—Reconnaissance from New Berne to Pollocksville, Trenton, Young's Cross-Roads, and Onslow, N. C., and skirmishes (19th) at White Oak Creek and (20th) near Jacksonville.

19, 1863.—Scout from Williamsburg and skirmish at Burnt Ordinary, Va.

27-28, 1863.—Reconnaissances on the Neuse, Dover, and Trent Roads, N. C.

30, 1863.—Engagement at Deserted House, or Kelly's Store, near Suffolk, Va.

Feb. 1-10, 1863.—Expedition from New Berne to Plymouth, N. C.

2, 1863.—Destruction of Salt-Works at Wale's Head, Currituck Beach, N. C.

5, 1863.—Skirmish near Olive Branch Church, Va.

6-21, 1863.—The Ninth Army Corps, Maj. Gen. William F. Smith, U. S. Army, commanding, transferred from Army of the Potomac to Newport News, Va.

7, 1863.—Skirmish at Olive Branch Church, Va.

Skirmish near Edenton, N. C.

10, 1863.—Skirmish at Batchelder's Creek, N. C.

12-13, 1863.—Expedition from Batchelder's Creek and skirmish (13th) at Sandy Ridge, N. C.

13, 1863.—Skirmish near Washington, N. C.

17, 1863.—Maj. Gen. Samuel G. French, C. S. Army, temporarily in command of the Department of North Carolina and Southern Virginia.

18, 1863.—Two divisions of Longstreet's corps ordered from Army of Northern Virginia to defense of Richmond.

23, 1863.—Engagement at Fort Caswell, N. C.*

25, 1863.—Maj. Gen. Daniel H. Hill, C. S. Army, assumes command of troops in North Carolina.

26, 1863.—Lieut. Gen. James Longstreet, C. S. Army, assumes command of the Department of Virginia and North Carolina.

Mar. 1- 6, 1863.—Expedition from New Berne to Swan Quarter, N. C., and sk.r-mishes (3d and 4th) near Fairfield and Swan Quarter.

---

* The United States steamers Dacotah and Monticello engaged. See Annual Report of the Secretary of the Navy, December 7, 1863.

Mar. 6- 8, 1863.—Demonstration on Kinston, N. C., including skirmishes (7th) at Core Creek and near Dover.

6-10, 1863.—Expedition from New Berne to Trenton, Pollocksville, Young's Cross-Roads, and Swansborough, N. C.

7- 9, 1863.—Reconnaissance from Suffolk and skirmish (9th) near Windsor, Va.

7-10, 1863.—Expedition from Newport Barracks to Cedar Point, N. C.

7-14, 1863.—Expedition from New Berne to Mattamuskeet Lake, N. C.

8-16, 1863.—Expedition against New Berne, N. C., including skirmishes (13th-14th) at Deep Gully and attack (14th) on Fort Anderson.

10-13, 1863.—Demonstration on Plymouth, N. C.

13-16, 1863.—The Third Division, Ninth Army Corps, transferred from Newport News to Suffolk, Va.

17, 1863.—Maj. Gen. Ambrose E. Burnside, U. S. Army, assumes command of the Ninth Army Corps.

Skirmish near Franklin, Va.

19-26, 1863.—The First and Second Divisions, Ninth Army Corps, embark at Newport News for the Department of the Ohio.

23, 1863.—Skirmish at Winfield, N. C.

24, 1863.—Skirmish at Rocky Hock Creek, N. C.

25, 1863.—Affair at Norfolk, Va.

29, 1863.—Skirmish at Williamsburg, Va.

30, 1863.—Skirmish near Deep Gully, N. C.

30–April 20, 1863.—Siege of Washington, N. C., and pursuit of the Confederate forces.

Apr'l 1, 1863.—Lieutenant-General Longstreet's command reorganized, to consist of the Department of North Carolina (Maj. Gen. D. H. Hill commanding), Department of Southern Virginia (Maj. Gen. S. G. French commanding), and Department of Richmond (Maj. Gen. Arnold Elzey commanding).

Expedition from Yorktown to Smith's and Byrd's Plantations, Ware River, Va.

6, 1863.—Maj. Gen. E. D. Keyes, U. S. Army, temporarily in command of the Department of Virginia.

Skirmish at Nixonton, N. C.

7, 1863.—Expedition from Gloucester Point to Gloucester Court-House, Va.

9-14, 1863.—Operations against Gloucester Point, Va.

11, 1863.—Skirmish at Williamsburg, Va.

11–May 4, 1863.—Siege of Suffolk, Va.

12, 1863.—Reconnaissance from Gloucester Point to the vicinity of Hickory Forks, Va.

16, 1863.—Affair on the Pamunkey River, near West Point, Va.

27, 1863.—Expedition from Yorktown beyond Hickory Forks, Va.

27–May 1, 1863.—Expedition from New Berne toward Kinston, N. C., and skirmish (28th) at Wise's Cross-Roads.

May 3, 1863.—Skirmishes at Ashland and Hanover Station, Va.*

4- 5, 1863.—Skirmishes at Hungary Station, Tunstall's Station, Hanovertown Ferry, and Aylett's, Va.*

5, 1863.—Skirmish at Peletier's Mill, N. C.

7, 1863.—West Point, Va., occupied by the Union forces.

12-26, 1863.—Operations on the Seaboard and Roanoke Railroad and skirmishes (15th-16th) near Carrsville, Va.

15, 1863.—Capture of the steamers Emily and Arrow.

Expedition from West Point to Robinson's Plantation, King and Queen County, Va.

---

* Incidents of raid from Army of the Potomac. See Series I, Vol. XXV.

May 15-28, 1863.—Operations on the Norfolk and Petersburg Railroad and skir-
             mishes (17th) near Providence Church and (23d) at Antioch
             Church and Barber's Cross-Roads, Va.
      19-22, 1863.—Expedition from Gloucester Point into Matthews County, Va.
      20-23, 1863.—Demonstration on Kinston and skirmishes (22d) at Gum Swamp
             and (23d) at Batchelder's Creek, N. C.
      28, 1863.—The Confederate Department of North Carolina extended to em-
             brace Petersburg, Va., and the Appomattox River.
      31-June 1, 1863.—West Point, Va., evacuated by the Union forces.

SEPTEMBER 2-3, 1862.—Expedition from Suffolk, Va.

Report of Maj. Gen. John A. Dix, U. S. Army, commanding the Depart-
ment of Virginia.

FORT MONROE, VA., *September* 4, 1862.

On the evening of the 2d instant General Mansfield sent two companies of Dodge's cavalry, under Major Wheelan, to cut off a company
of rebel recruits on their way to Richmond.   The expedition was completely successful, the whole force, consisting of 2 officers, 65 soldiers,
and 44 white men, with 28 wagons and carts and 25 negroes, were
brought into Suffolk last night.   The negroes were tied when the party
were captured.

JOHN A. DIX,
Major-General.

Major-General HALLECK,
         General-in-Chief.

SEPTEMBER 6, 1862.—Attack on Washington, N. C.

REPORTS.*

No. 1.—Maj. Gen. John G. Foster, U. S. Army, commanding the Department of North
        Carolina.
No. 2.—Lieut. Col. Edward E. Potter, First North Carolina Infantry (Union).
No. 3.—Lieut. Col. John Mix, Third New York Cavalry.
No. 4.—Maj. Gen. Samuel G. French, C. S. Army.

No. 1.

Reports of Maj. Gen. John G. Foster, U. S. Army, commanding the De-
partment of North Carolina.

HEADQUARTERS DEPARTMENT OF NORTH CAROLINA,
            New Berne, N. C., September 7, 1862.

SIR: I have the honor to report that I have just received a communication from Colonel Potter, First Regiment North Carolina Union Volunteers, commanding at Washington, N. C., that the rebels attacked
that town yesterday morning with about 1,000 infantry, six companies

---

* For reports of Actg. Rear-Admiral S. P. Lee and Actg. Vol. Lieut. R. T. Renshaw,
U. S. Navy, see Annual Report of the Secretary of the Navy, December 1, 1862.

of cavalry, and one battery of artillery. Colonel Potter was at the time about leaving, in obedience to my orders, for Plymouth, N. C., with Colonel Mix, in command of five companies of cavalry and one battery of artillery, to co-operate with the Navy in attacking Hamilton, on Roanoke River. The attack of the rebels was made suddenly, and it appears they surprised the outer line of pickets, killing and wounding them, and, dashing into town, surprised the company of foot artillery in the barracks, stationed for garrison at the new field works, capturing from them four old brass 6-pounders, that were captured by us at New Berne.

Colonel Mix and Colonel Potter, hearing the firing, halted, and immediately returned into town, attacking the rebels vigorously, and after two and a half hours' hard fighting drove them from the town and beyond Tranter's Creek, 8 miles from town, taking 20 prisoners, many muskets, and about 30 horses.

The rebels left 12 dead and 12 wounded in the streets, carrying off many killed and wounded, some of which they had to leave by the roadside. It is reported that 30 dead bodies have been found up to time of last dispatch.

Our loss was 7 killed and 47 wounded, most of them slightly. Lieutenant Everett, adjutant of the cavalry, was shot in the knee. Colonel Potter had his horse shot under him.

An unfortunate disaster happened to the army gunboat Picket, causing her destruction. Just as the men were called to quarters the magazine blew up, undoubtedly from carelessness or accident, tearing the boat to pieces, instantly killing Capt. [Sylvester D.] Nicoll, the commander, and 19 men, and wounding 6 others.

The gunboat Louisiana, Captain Renshaw, U. S. Navy, rendered most efficient aid, throwing her shells with great precision, and clearing the streets through which her guns had range.

Our whole force in the fight at the time of the attack consisted of four companies of infantry, two of artillery, and five of cavalry, and was considerably outnumbered by the enemy.

I shall leave for Washington immediately to take such measures as may be necessary, and will send detailed list of the killed and wounded on my return.

I have the honor to be, very respectfully, your obedient servant,

                              J. G. FOSTER,
                              Major-General, Volunteers.

Major-General HALLECK,
   Commander-in-Chief, U. S. Army, Washington, D. C.

———

HEADQUARTERS DEPARTMENT OF NORTH CAROLINA,
      New Berne, N. C., September 12, 1862.

GENERAL: I have the honor to state, in addition to my brief report of the 7th of the attack on Washington, N. C., that, upon careful investigation of the circumstances and of the reports, that the affair, although undeniably a surprise at the outset, proves to have terminated in a very creditable display of gallantry by our troops. I find that all the men, infantry, cavalry, and artillery, recovering from their first surprise, drove the enemy from the town and 8 miles beyond.

We have knowledge of the loss of the enemy of 33 killed and about three times that number wounded. Our loss was 8 killed, 36 wounded, and 12 missing (as will be seen by list appended*), exclusive of those lost by the unfortunate blowing up of the army gunboat Picket. Owing to the death of the captain of the Picket, who was the only officer attached to the vessel, the list of killed and wounded has not been as yet made out.

I find that the explosion of the magazine of the Picket will not eventuate in the total loss of the vessel. The guns have already been recovered; the machinery can certainly be saved, and possibly the hull raised and repaired. If this be found impossible the machinery can be transferred to a canal-barge, and fit up a second gunboat as effective as the Picket.

The five companies of the Third New York Cavalry, and Battery H, Third New York Artillery, were very effective in driving the enemy from the streets. The two companies of the Twenty-fourth Massachusetts Volunteers and two companies of the First North Carolina Union Volunteers, under command of Col. E. E. Potter, First North Carolina, fought well and held their position.

I shall have the honor, in my next communication, to solicit the medal of honor for three most gallant men of the rank and file.

I have the honor to remain, general, very respectfully, your obedient servant,

J. G. FOSTER,
Major-General of Volunteers, Commanding.

Maj. Gen. H. W. HALLECK,
General-in-Chief, U. S. Army, Washington, D. C.

No. 2.

Report of Lieut. Col. Edward E. Potter, First North Carolina Infantry (Union).

HEADQUARTERS,
Washington, September 5 [6], 1862—12 m.

SIR: I have the honor to report that this town was attacked this morning at 4 o'clock by a force consisting, according to the reports of prisoners, of from 600 to 1,000 infantry, six companies of cavalry, and one battery of artillery. I had just started with Colonel Mix and his command for Plymouth, when the attack was made. A halt was ordered and we moved back into the town. A heavy firing of musketry was going on at the upper end of the town. As we turned into the main street some of the enemy's cavalry came charging down, using sabers and pistols freely. Some of them were knocked over and others turned back. The artillery was placed at the intersection of the streets, with the cavalry supporting it. I advanced up the main street with one piece of artillery and a squadron of cavalry to the infantry quarters, where a desultory firing was going on. The enemy had surprised the artillerymen at their quarters in the school-house, at the corner of Second and Bridge streets, and were there in very strong force. I placed the 12-pounder at the intersection of Main and Bridge. All the infantry, North Carolina and Massachusetts, supported the artillery. The firing here was very sharp. Nothing but a small lot separated our men from theirs, each firing from behind fences. Our piece did good execution, but the gunners were all shot, and I had to withdraw the gun and the

---

* Nominal list omitted.

infantry to give the Louisiana's guns a chance. The Louisiana opened at once, at my request, and did excellent service.

Cavalry skirmishing was going on in the mean time on the outskirts and in different streets. The enemy after a time began to retreat, taking with them, I am sorry to say, the four brass pieces which were in the yard of the academy. The cavalry pursued them several miles, but did not come up with them.

The most unfortunate event connected with the affair was the loss of the gunboat Picket. According to the report of the engineer her magazine exploded just as Captain Nicoll had ordered the men to quarters. It must have arisen from carelessness in opening the magazine. Captain Nicoll and 19 men were killed and 6 wounded. Our loss in the affair is as follows:

Company B, First North Carolina, Lieutenant Lyon: Two killed and 7 wounded.

Company D, Twenty-fourth Massachusetts: Two wounded.

Company B, Twenty-fourth Massachusetts: Four wounded.

Company G, Third New York Artillery: Two killed, 2 wounded, 4 missing.

Third New York Cavalry: Two killed and 25 wounded, slightly.

Company H, Third New York Artillery: One killed and 7 wounded.

The rebels left behind 12 killed and as many wounded, several mortally. We have also some 20 prisoners, and have taken several horses and a good many muskets.

The conduct of the men was generally good. In this hurried report I can make no mention of individual good conduct. Colonel Mix, with his cavalry, did excellently. Lieutenant Garrard made a very handsome charge. Lieutenant Lyon, of the North Carolina Volunteers, displayed great courage. Lieutenants Pendleton and Strong were with Colonel Mix during the fight. No casualties occurred among the officers, with the exception of Adjutant Everett, of the cavalry, shot in the knee. Several horses were shot from under their riders, among them my own.

Captain Murphy has returned after pursuing the enemy to Tranter's Creek. He reports that they carried off many dead and wounded. They have left some at a short distance from town. I shall make proper disposition for the defense of the town to-night. The Plymouth expedition is postponed.

Your obedient servant,

EDWARD E. POTTER,
Commanding Post.

Capt. SOUTHARD HOFFMAN,
Assistant Adjutant-General.

No. 3.

Report of Lieut. Col. John Mix, Third New York Cavalry.

SIR: I have the honor to report, for the information of the general commanding, the operations of my command on the 4th, 5th, and 6th instant:

In compliance with my instructions I shipped, on the 4th, one company (D) of the Third New York Cavalry and one battery (H) of the Third New York Artillery. They left this post at 11 p. m. and debarked at Washington, N. C., at 3 p. m. on the 5th. At 4 a. m. on the 6th a command, consisting of Companies D, G, I, and L, Third New York Cavalry, and Battery H, Third New York Artillery, with an aggregate of 263 men, formed for the expedition I had been ordered to make, and at 4.15 broke into column. Scarcely were the troops in column, the head of it having just reached the outskirts of the town, on the Plymouth road, when a rapid and continuous firing was heard to our left and rear. The column was counter-marched at the gallop, and the cavalry, in column of eights, ordered to charge and clear the different streets, which were now apparently full of small parties of the enemy's cavalry. The night was intensely dark, and between the darkness, fog, and dust it was impossible in many cases to distinguish friend from foe at half a dozen paces. The order to clear the streets was in each case most gallantly obeyed. Company L, Captain Garrard, charged First street, driving back a considerable body of cavalry to Bridge street, where he came upon a large body of infantry, and was compelled to retire; in doing this he cleared the cross-streets to his left. Company D, Captain Murphy, performed the same operation on Second street. Company G, Captain Hall, charged the length of Third street, driving back several small parties of cavalry, and, upon reaching the fence around the academy, found a large force of the enemy's infantry in position unfavorable to attack. Company H, Captain Willson, which was not to accompany the expedition, and consequently not out at the commencement of the fight, turned out and was in saddle and ready for action in an incredibly short space of time. The captain, hearing firing and loud cheers in direction of the academy, promptly proceeded with his company to ascertain the cause thereof, and found a large force of the enemy in possession of four brass guns, which had been left in park near the hospital, and over which accidental capture the rebels were giving vent to their exuberance of spirits in loud, continuous cheers and demoniac yells of "Death to the damned Yankees"; "No prisoners"; "No quarters," &c. The captain, nothing daunted by these friendly salutations, made a most gallant but unsuccessful attempt to recover the guns; dismounted a number of his men, under a severe fire, within 60 yards of the enemy, and attempted to tear down a fence to enable him to charge them, but could not succeed in making a sufficient opening for that purpose. Company I, Captain Jocknick, in the mean time had succeeded in driving a number of detached and very troublesome parties of enemy's cavalry from Third and Fourth streets, and had gone to the support of one of the guns of Battery H.

During the first hour of the *mêlée* the convalescents and sick men turned out largely, considering the number in hospitals. These were united with small scattering parties, who had become temporarily detached from their companies, by officers who were without commands, and did good service in clearing the cross-streets. Lieutenant Everett, acting adjutant, while conveying an order to a distant part of the command, encountered alone a party of the enemy's infantry on a side street, dashed past them, emptying, as he did so, the contents of his pistol among them. He was, in turn, fired into, receiving a serious wound in his right leg. The guns of Battery H, Captain Riggs, were promptly placed in position upon several cross-streets, and held in readiness to fire the moment that the enemy could be distinguished from among the confused mass in every direction. And I would here mention as an extraordinary fact, and as due entirely to the coolness and intrepidity of the officers and men of this battery, that in no instance did occur the mistake of firing upon our own people, and that in order to prevent such fatal mistake the enemy were allowed at times to approach within a few feet of the muzzles of the guns; then, when amid the dust, smoke, and fog the gray coats could be seen, the death-dealing contents of the pieces were hurled among them with such precision and effect as told them, plainer than could words have done, that Yankee guns, when manned, asked no quarter, but give unasked a (w)hole.

Our situation now began to assume a more tangible appearance. The river street and most of the cross-streets, for a distance of two or three blocks, had been, by means of rapid and successive cavalry charges, cleared entirely of the midnight assassins. Their cavalry had congregated upon the edge of the town and reformed for the attack. Their infantry had concentrated in two columns, one of which, with the assistance of one 6-pounder brass piece and a 3-pounder rifled gun, was endeavoring to turn our left flank, with the evident desire of getting between our forces and the gunboats. They were met at this point, and their object most completely foiled, by our infantry, consisting of two companies of the Twenty-fourth Massachusetts, two companies of the First North Carolina, one 12-pounder brass piece (Lieutenant O'Neil), and 20 cavalry, under Lieutenant Gouraud (which had been detailed as a provost guard for the expedition), all commanded in person by Colonel Potter, First North Carolina. At this point the fight was most severe, and continued without cessation for two hours and a half. Two sets of gunners having been shot away from the gun, it became necessary to haul it off, which was done without further loss. Our infantry in the mean time did good service with their rifles. The situation of Lieutenant Gouraud and his handful of mounted men at this point was aggravating in the extreme. Necessarily within supporting distance of the gun, he was greatly exposed to the raking fire of the enemy, and unable, from the inconsiderable numbers of his command and the position and strength of the enemy, to operate upon him. In this trying position the men evinced a most commendable degree of fortitude. One-fourth of their number having fallen victims to the enemy's missiles, the remaining few increased their enthusiasm for the charge, and made several effective dashes.

The enemy's second column of attack had advanced upon our center, and was composed of artillery and infantry, preceded by a squadron of cavalry. Their approach being observed, Company L, Captain Garrard, advanced boldly, and in close column, to the attack. His shout of "Come on," as he placed himself at the head of his men, was responded to by his daring followers with a yell and a rapid gallop that showed no want of confidence in their leader and themselves, and no fear of the solid column opposed to them. He met the enemy with a shock that told upon his columns, received the fire from their pistols, and vigorously responded with his sabers until finding that he was being surrounded by the enemy's infantry and in danger of being cut off he commanded his men to retire, which they did, gallantly cutting their way through the infantry—who were now in the rear of them—having had a brilliant hand-to-hand conflict with vastly-superior numbers, in which the horses of all the officers of the company had been shot and 9 men and 14 horses wounded, promptly retiring behind the gun commanded by Lieutenant Mercer, leaving the street clear for the operation of the piece, which opened a destructive fire upon the enemy, who had brought a 6-pounder to bear upon him. An interesting cannon duel now ensued, but soon terminated by the withdrawal of the

6-pounder and the disappearance of the enemy from that street. Thus the enemy had been thrice foiled. First, his attempt to surprise and massacre us was foiled by the existence of the expedition, and, subsequently, when in position, his attack upon our left and center was obstinately met, and, though not without difficulty and hard fighting, successfully repulsed.

Upon the first intimation of the retreat of the enemy our cavalry, which had necessarily been much scattered, was concentrated and sent in pursuit, and moving rapidly out upon the Greenville road, soon encountered a flag of truce with a rebel surgeon, who desired the privilege of attending to his wounded. This flag was a well-calculated subterfuge, under which the enemy gained considerable in their retreat, as the officer commanding the pursuing party felt it his duty to suspend operations until he could communicate with the commanding officer, who was at the rear. After disposing of this flag of truce our cavalry pushed out 9 miles on the Greenville road, encountering only a surgeon's flag over a party of 18 of the enemy's wounded, and upon returning discovered two ambulances in the road, which he captured. The dismounted men of the detachment of cavalry were under standing orders, in the event of an attack, to report to Lieutenant Chesebrough, who was temporarily disabled for mounted duty. These men arrived, with the Colt's revolving rifles, and were stationed in ambush, for the purpose of preventing the entrance of the enemy's cavalry upon the upper end of Main street, and were most successful.

In conclusion, sir, too much cannot be said in praise of the coolness of the officers and men of my command, who fought full three times or more their number four hours, under the most trying circumstances. Battery H, Third New York Artillery, did most creditably, and the result of this first meeting with the enemy promises them a brilliant future. I would especially commend to the notice of the commanding general, in consequence of most gallant conduct, Corpl. James R. Nicoll, Company I, Third New York Cavalry, and Corpl. William Smith, Battery H, Third New York Artillery (the latter since lost his leg, by amputation, in consequence of wounds), and would respectfully suggest that medals of honor, recently ordered by Congress, be presented to these two men.

I am, sir, very respectfully, your obedient servant,
J. MIX,
Lieutenant-Colonel, Third New York Cavalry.

Maj. SOUTHARD HOFFMAN,
Assistant Adjutant-General, Dept. of North Carolina.

No. 4.

Report of Maj. Gen. Samuel G. French, C. S. Army.

PETERSBURG, VA., *September* 7, 1862.

General Martin telegraphs me our troops had a sharp fight of three hours at Washington, N. C., this morning (6th), but could not hold the town. Our loss heavy. We brought out three brass field guns.
S. G. FRENCH.

General S. COOPER.

SEPTEMBER 9, 1862.—Skirmish at Williamsburg, Va.

Reports of Maj. Gen. John A. Dix, U. S. Army, commanding the Department of Virginia, and resulting correspondence and orders.

YORKTOWN, VA., *September* 9, 1862.

Colonel Campbell, of the Fifth Pennsylvania Cavalry, was attacked this morning at Williamsburg and disgracefully beaten, partly by bad management and partly by the cowardly conduct of some of his men. I am glad to say that others behaved with proper spirit. The colonel and some 6 or 7 other officers are prisoners. I have not yet been able to ascertain the extent of the loss.

JOHN A. DIX,
Major-General, Commanding.

Major-General HALLECK.

___

FORT MONROE, VA.,
September 10, 1862—6.30 p. m.

The loss yesterday in the attack on the Fifth Pennsylvania Cavalry was the colonel, 2 majors, and 5 other officers and 29 men captured; 1 officer and 55 men missing; 7 killed and 13 wounded. We took 2 prisoners, from whom I learn that the attacking party consisted of a mixed force of Georgians, South Carolinians, and Virginians, certainly not exceeding 300 men. One of the majors ran away, and if a court cannot be found who have courage enough to shoot him he should be dismissed the service. I will report on his case especially. What remains of the regiment, about 430 men in all, are at Williamsburg, the rebels having retired.

JOHN A. DIX,
Major-General.

Maj. Gen. H. W. HALLECK,
General-in-Chief.

___

WAR DEPARTMENT,
Washington, September 10, 1862.

Order immediately a court-martial on the cowards of Williamsburg. If no one has courage to have them shot report them here, so that we can ask the President to cashier them.*

H. W. HALLECK,
General-in-Chief.

Major-General DIX, *Fort Monroe, Va.*

___

WAR DEPARTMENT,
Washington, September 11, 1862.

Order a court if you have officers suitable. If not, get the facts in relation to the bad conduct of the officers and I will ask the President to cashier them.

What is the object of holding Williamsburg? Why not withdraw the garrison to Yorktown?

---

* See Dix to Halleck, September 12, in "Correspondence, etc.," *post.*

Colonel Williams' cavalry was sent to General Burnside when he had none for reconnoitering the enemy. I have none here to send you at present.

H. W. HALLECK,
General-in-Chief.

Major-General DIX, *Fort Monroe, Va.*

—

GENERAL ORDERS, ⎱   HEADQUARTERS SEVENTH ARMY CORPS,
    No. 19.   ⎰   *Fort Monroe, Va., September* 25, 1862.

I. Before a general court-martial, of which Maj. Gen. John J. Peck is president, convened at Yorktown, Va., pursuant to Paragraph III, Special Orders, No. 97, current series, from these headquarters, of September 11, 1862, was arraigned and tried—

Maj. JACOB P. WILSON, Fifth Regiment Pennsylvania Cavalry, upon the following charges and specifications:

CHARGE I.—*Misbehavior before the enemy.*

Specification.—In this: That he, Jacob P. Wilson, a major in the Fifth Regiment of Pennsylvania Volunteer Cavalry, in the service of the United States, while on duty with his regiment at or near Williamsburg, Va., did misbehave himself before the enemy, and did shamefully abandon his post and command and run away. This at or near said Williamsburg, and between said Williamsburg and Yorktown, Va., on or about the 9th day of September, 1862.

CHARGE II.—*Speaking words inducing others to misbehave themselves before the enemy and to run away and to shamefully abandon the post which he or they were commanded to defend.*

Specification.—In this: That he, said Jacob P. Wilson, major as aforesaid, being stationed with his regiment at or near said Williamsburg, which post he and they were commanded to defend, did speak words inducing members of his regiment, or some of them, to misbehave themselves before the enemy, to shamefully abandon said post, and to run away. This at or near Williamsburg, on or about September 9, 1862.

CHARGE III.—*Cowardice.*

Specification.—In this: That said Jacob P. Wilson, major as aforesaid, while stationed with his regiment at or near said Williamsburg, and before the enemy, did, in a cowardly manner, misbehave, abandon his post and command, and run away. This at or near Williamsburg, Va., on or about the 9th day of September, 1862.

PLEA.—*Not guilty.*

FINDING OF THE COURT.

I. Upon careful consideration the court finds the accused, Maj. Jacob P. Wilson, Fifth Pennsylvania Volunteer Cavalry, " Not guilty," of each and all of the charges and specifications, and thereupon acquits him.

II. The proceedings and finding of the court are approved. Major Wilson will resume his sword and return to duty.

The encounter at Williamsburg, on which the charges against Major Wilson are founded, was, under all its aspects, most disgraceful to the regiment to which he belonged. The force of the enemy was certainly not superior to ours. The commanding officer had full notice of the

intended attack and chose his own ground. The men were misman-
aged; wrong words of command were given, and, although some of the
officers and men behaved with becoming gallantry, the regiment broke,
most of them ran away, some of them as far as Yorktown, 13 miles
from their camp. The colonel, 6 other officers, and nearly 60 enlisted
men were taken prisoners; the camp was partially destroyed; they
were not rallied until the enemy had retired; and the whole affair exhibited a want of organization and discipline utterly discreditable to
the principal officers, who are responsible for the condition of the regiment. It can never regain its standing until this stain on its character
is effaced by worthier conduct in the face of the enemy.

While the commanding general approves the finding of the court in
acquitting Major Wilson of the charge of cowardice, the testimony
shows that he might with propriety be brought before another court,
on less serious charges of misconduct, and, if it is not thought advisable to do so, it is only for the reason that so many others are as deeply
involved as himself in the general delinquency.

III. The general court-martial, of which Maj. Gen. John J. Peck is
president, is dissolved.

By command of Major-General Dix:

D. T. VAN BUREN,
Assistant Adjutant-General.

SEPTEMBER 17-20, 1862.—Operations at and about Shiloh, N. C.

REPORTS.

No. 1.—Capt. Enos C. Sanders, First North Carolina Infantry (Union), of affair at
Shiloh, N. C., September 17, 1862.

No. 2.—Capt. William B. Avery, commanding U. S. gunboat Lancer, of affair near
Shiloh, N. C., September 20, 1862.

No. 1.

Report of Capt. Enos C. Sanders, First North Carolina Infantry (Union),
of affair at Shiloh, N. C., September 17, 1862.

HEADQUARTERS,
Shiloh, N. C., September 18, 1862.

SIR: Last night we were attacked, as we had all the force over to
Pasquotank holding a meeting, and stopped overnight, except the
gun's crew, which we sent back, all except 16 men—them we had with
us. We got word this morning, and with about 30 men have landed 6
miles below Shiloh. There are 3 men killed, 3 wounded, and 5 or 6
taken prisoners, and they have taken all the arms and ammunition we
had and stores and provisions. They were completely surprised. The
men that got away think their force was about 50 strong. Please send
us a gunboat and men immediately; send two howitzers and ammunition for the same. We can intercept them at the upper end of the
county. It is necessary to have a chance to get a re-enforcement at

Pasquotank. They got our guns and all our private property. We have the names of some of the rebels. Joseph Forbes was one of the leaders.

E. C. SANDERS,
Captain, First North Carolina Infantry.

Col. W. A. HOWARD.

No. 2.

Report of Capt. William B. Avery, commanding U. S. gunboat Lancer, of affair near Shiloh, N. C., September 20, 1862.

UNITED STATES GUNBOAT LANCER,
September 21, 1862.

SIR: I reached Shiloh at 4 p. m. Friday, 19th, at dark. I landed 60 men, taking with me Lieutenants Fowler and Moore, and leaving the vessel in charge of Acting Master Allen. Being joined by the two lieutenants [and] Sanders with 20 men, we started at 9.30 p. m. for the place where the rebels were last heard of; reached that place to learn they were last heard of 4 miles off, in a swamp near the "lake," as they term a sort of pond. The men were two-thirds of them in carts, and so, by changing, the 12 miles already passed did not fatigue them much.

We left for "the lakes" at 4.30 a. m., so our hopes of surprising them before light were dispelled. In the swamp we found the men had gone one way that morning, half an hour previous, and the things had been sent another the night previous, toward the house of one Willis Williams. We had been told that it was there they had been encamped; so I decided to push on after the things, expecting to find a portion of their force with them. After 3 miles' more march we reached it to find no one there, and to learn that the things had been sent there the night before and they would not receive them, and they were taken back. The first house from the school-house we learned that the carts had some men without arms, and one man lying down apparently hurt. We knew they must be the prisoners, and I immediately took Lieut. Enos C. Sanders and 20 of the best men and gave chase after them. They had two and a half hours the start, and we had been traveling all night. By following their tracks we knew the road they took, and by inquiring learned that we were gaining on them. We went across the battle-field and over the bridges across the river and canal.

About 1½ miles beyond the river we came on them just as they were halting for dinner. The road was straight for half a mile to them, and through a swamp, so we could not avoid being discovered by the guard, which numbered some 15 men, I am told. We made a dash for them, and without firing a shot they took their guns and fled to the swamp across a corn field, leaving the muskets and prisoners in our hands. I immediately returned and reached the main body of the men at 2 p. m., having gone 18 miles in four hours.

We then started for Shiloh, distant 12 miles, and reached it 6.30 p. m., and at 8 p. m. all were on board, having been gone twenty-four hours.

Besides the 7 prisoners from Shiloh they had 2 of my men who had straggled behind and met the rebels, who had come into the road. I went down some twenty minutes after. Had I been half hour later I should have met them. Had I been one hour earlier I should have surprised them before they started. Had I been so fortunate I should have saved some 40 or 50 miles travel for myself and 20 of the men with Lieutenant Sanders.

As to the howitzer I have heard of it in two or three places by report. The most probable one is that it is up in Currituck County, somewhere in a swamp. Until I had started after them I did not know they did not have it with them to take it to Richmond. If Lieutenant Sanders follows my advice and "takes time by the forelock" he can find that gun and the tents. He claims to have 50 or 60 fighting men, and with two-thirds of that number he can scour the whole country.

I am, sir, very respectfully,

WM. B. AVERY,
Captain, Commanding Lancer.

Col. WILLIAM A. HOWARD,
Commanding Marine Artillery and Post, Roanoke Island.

OCTOBER 3, 1862.—Skirmish on the Blackwater, near Franklin, Va.

REPORTS.*

No. 1.—Maj. Gen. John A. Dix, U. S. Army, commanding the Department of Virginia.
No. 2.—Maj. Gen. John J. Peck, U. S. Army, commanding at Suffolk, including affair near Zuni.
No. 3.—Col. J. K. Marshall, Fifty-second North Carolina Infantry.

No. 1.

Reports of Maj. Gen. John A. Dix, U. S. Army, commanding the Department of Virginia.

FORT MONROE, VA., *October* 3, 1862—9.30 p. m.

Last night General Peck, by my order and direction, sent a force of nearly 2,000 cavalry, artillery, and infantry from Suffolk to Franklin, on the Blackwater, intending to attack the enemy at that point this morning early, and if possible cripple the floating bridge he has thrown across the river. Between 2 and 3 this morning two scoundrels from New York, belonging to Dodge's Mounted Rifles, one of them an orderly at General Peck's headquarters, deserted to the enemy and were seen riding rapidly through our lines. Couriers were sent out to recall the troops and a strong force was dispatched to support them. I have not yet heard of their return. We have reconnoitered the enemy closely several times with no loss, except one horse killed and one man shot through the hand. Suffolk has been put in good condition, and we have no concern of attack. Two of the four new regiments you promised have arrived. They are very raw, but when I get the other two I shall feel entirely at ease at all points.

JOHN A. DIX,
Major-General.

Major-General HALLECK, *General-in-Chief.*

---

* For reports of Actg. Rear-Admiral S. P. Lee, Commander H. K. Davenport, Lieut. Commander C. W. Flusser, Acting Vol. Lieut. E. R. Colhoun, and Actg. Master C. A. French, U. S. Navy, see Annual Report of the Secretary of the Navy, December 1, 1862.

FORT MONROE, VA., *October* 5, 1862—12.46 p. m.

I planned an expedition, as I advised you, to destroy the floating bridge the enemy had thrown over the Blackwater at Franklin. We were to have had the co-operation of the gunboats from Albemarle Sound by order of Admiral Lee, but I think they must have met with obstructions, as they did not come. Our troops, less than 2,000 in number, under Colonel Spear, Eleventh Pennsylvania Cavalry, held the enemy, greatly superior in force, at bay at the river for several hours waiting for the gunboats. They behaved with great coolness, and, as we think, killed and wounded from 70 to 100 of the enemy. Our loss was 1 killed and 6 wounded and missing.

JOHN A. DIX,
Major-General.

General HALLECK, *General-in-Chief.*

—

FORT MONROE, VA., *October* 7, 1862.

Major-General Peck telegraphs me as follows:

Our affair at Franklin was of more importance than we judged. From an examina- tion of several persons who were on the other side of the Blackwater I learn that the enemy's loss was over 200.

JOHN A. DIX,
Major-General.

Maj. Gen. H. W. HALLECK, *General-in-Chief.*

———

No. 2.

Reports of Maj. Gen. John J. Peck, U. S. Army, commanding at Suffolk, including affair near Zuni.

SUFFOLK, *October* 4, 1862.

The gunboats were about 10 or 15 miles below Franklin yesterday. They fired a good many shots, but did not appear during the day. Had they not met obstructions they would have come up. They heard the enemy's guns doubtless, as I did. They have three heavy guns, one a 32-pounder, commanding the swinging bridge. Colonel Spear reports not less than 8,000 up and down the river. Yesterday they were massed near Zuni. Knowing the boats were on the way they will expect our concert and may mask Franklin. There is great uncertainty in operations with gunboats. Had they waited until the 9th our risk would have been much less. Now the move is adventured to Weldon and Petersburg it looks risky. The bridge can be rebuilt in a few hours, and the fords are low. I will carry out your instructions if you will send them.

JOHN J. PECK,
Major-General.

Major-General DIX.

—

SUFFOLK, *October* 4, 1862.

Have been out on the advance nearly all day. Troops all in. Spear had a nice fight. Loss, 1 killed and some 6 wounded and missing.
After full inquiry as to the affair I judge 70 to 100 of the enemy were

injured. Within a day or two the enemy has been disposed to hold our pickets away from the river. Yesterday he occupied Windsor with about 300 cavalry and some infantry. At dawn I pushed Dodge's cavalry in there, and to-day we have recovered nearly all the territory.

> JOHN J. PECK,
> *Major-General.*

General DIX.

—

> SUFFOLK, *October* 4, 1862.

My troops are in, but they have had service, being out two nights and a day, and need rest.

Colonel Spear left the vicinity of Franklin after midnight. No firing has been heard to-day, and I conclude boats did not reach that place. My last telegram may give some information not at hand when your last was received, and I wait your reply.

> JOHN J. PECK,
> *Major-General.*

General DIX.

—

> HEADQUARTERS,
> *Suffolk, Va., October* 9, 1862.

COLONEL: On the 2d instant I was advised that the rebel pickets had been advanced nearly to Carrsville at points some 4 or 5 miles from the Blackwater. This information, in connection with the possibility of the appearance of our gunboats, in consequence of certain propositions made by Major-General Dix, but not perfected, induced me to dispatch Col. S. P. Spear, of the Eleventh Pennsylvania Cavalry, with a section of Follett's battery and about 1,700 men, in the night to Carrsville, with instructions to make a thorough reconnaissance in the direction of Franklin and the Blackwater. He moved at 9 p. m. and reached Carrsville before daylight. Early on the 3d he commenced his advance and soon met the enemy's pickets. Some skirmishing ensued, the rebels falling back upon their support with a view of checking his advance. This was of no avail, and pickets and supports were all driven confusedly down to the bank and over the river.

Colonel Spear advanced cautiously, and was soon opened upon by a 32-pounder and other heavy guns in battery across the stream. After looking to the immediate safety of his command the colonel made a careful examination of the position, placed Whitney's section and two small howitzers in action at favorable points with proper supports, and sent out parties for observation on his flanks.

A furious cannonade continued for an hour, when the enemy ceased his fire and fell back to a new position where he could act in concert with newly-arrived and fresh troops.

At this juncture Graham's celebrated Petersburg battery and a rocket battery arrived, and the action was renewed on his part with great vigor. Shot, shell, grape, and rockets were fired in great profusion, but with little or no damage to our well-posted troops. The Thirteenth Indiana Regiment, under Lieutenant-Colonel Dobbs, was moved down to the bank on the right, where it opened so sharp and close a fire upon the rebels that they terminated the action by falling back out of range.

On learning that Colonel Spear had proceeded with less than 1,300 men, instead of 1,700, and that his ammunition was nearly exhausted, that the river could not be crossed, and the object of the expedition having been fully attained, I directed him to return, which he did without any disturbance from the enemy.

Particular mention is made of the gallantry and good conduct of Lieutenant-Colonels Stetzel, Dobbs, Maxwell, and Gray, and of Lieutenant Whitney. Colonel Spear has added to his former high reputation by his coolness and good management on this occasion.

The force consisted of detachments from the Eleventh Pennsylvania Cavalry, Ninety-sixth New York Volunteers, One hundred and third Pennsylvania Volunteers, and Thirteenth Indiana Volunteer Infantry, and a section of Follett's artillery, and the commander speaks in the highest terms of all his officers and men.

The loss was 2 killed, 5 wounded, and 1 missing, which was extremely small, in view of the great superiority of the enemy in numbers. The rebel loss has been reported from 75 to 200.

On the 3d instant several hundred of the enemy crossed the river in the vicinity of Zuni and occupied Windsor, having among other designs that of tearing up the Petersburg Railroad. At dawn of the 4th Colonel Dodge, a meritorious officer, was advanced with a portion of the New York First Mounted Rifles, who promptly occupied the place, and during the day forced the enemy across the Blackwater.

Characterized by that earnestness which is an essential element of success, these affairs are very gratifying, and fortify the confidence already reposed in the troops.

I remain, very respectfully, your obedient servant,

JOHN J. PECK,
Major-General, Commanding.

Col. D. T. VAN BUREN,
Assistant Adjutant-General, Seventh Corps.

No. 3.

Report of Col. J. K. Marshall, Fifty-second North Carolina Infantry.

HEADQUARTERS,
Franklin, Va., October 4, 1862.

GENERAL: After having rested the night before at New South Quay the enemy steamed up the river in their gunboats yesterday morning and commenced pouring shot and shell upon us at daybeak. They brought with them three boats, two of which were small, carrying two guns each; the other large, carrying four, one a 64-pounder. Soon after the shelling commenced I dispatched Lieut. [John M.] Alexander (commanding Company A, Fifty-second Regiment North Carolina Troops) with orders to commence firing upon them at Crumpler's Bluff so soon as the last boat should have passed. In obedience to orders he commenced a well-directed and effective fire upon them, and succeeded in silencing their guns for a short while, but they quickened their time and succeeded in reaching a point of the river edged on both sides by an apparently impassable marsh. Here they recommenced their work of throwing shot and shell in every direction, and in the mean time moving up by degrees in the direction of Franklin. Pending this condition of things I sent Capts. [John C.] McCain [and Eric] Erson, and Lieut. [James M.] Kincaid, of the Fifty-second Regiment, together with Capt. [James T.] Mitchell, of the Fifty-ninth Regiment, pickets, holding their respective commands, to the neighboring bluffs with instructions to meet the boats on their return. Col. [D. D.] Ferebee with a large portion of his command took position along the road, first, where the old wharf formerly stood, and Capt. [William] Sharp's company, of the same command, was sent to meet and fire upon the boats from any point they could suitable for such work, but they penetrated the marsh, which was very deep, and drove in between 60 and 80 sharpshooters which had been thrown out from the gunboats. Now a general fire commenced on both sides, in which Colonel Ferebee and his command took [part] to a very considerable extent, but the boats found the work too hot for them and were forced to recede, and continued to move back, though continually throwing out an occasional shell. As they passed the bluffs every man who showed himself on deck or at the port-holes was cut down. As they passed down the river Captain Norfleet with his men pursued them, killing all who could be seen. Here I will state that the pilot was hid from view and sand-bags were placed along the decks of the boats. As I stated before, the shelling commenced at daybreak and the boats remained in the river until 10.30 a. m.

Our loss is 2 wounded, viz, Private Stroup, of the Fifty-second Regiment, and Private Parker, of the Fifty-ninth Regiment.

About 1 p. m. a large force appeared across the river, consisting of four full regiments of infantry, one regiment of cavalry, and six pieces of artillery, with one or two sections of rocket guns. One of Captain Graham's pieces (rifle) was placed at the depot and the other carried to the bridge. For about two hours Captain Graham with his rifle piece at the depot and Lieutenant Britton at the bridge entertained them handsomely. At 3.30 or 4 o'clock they retired, leaving on the field a few overcoats and one horse.

The enemy must have lost a large number on their boats and lost some on the field, but how many I cannot say.

One yawl-boat was left in the river near one of the bluffs. The force brought in the afternoon was intended to co-operate with the gunboats, but came too late.

Very respectfully, your obedient servant,

J. K. MARSHALL,
Colonel, Commanding at Franklin.

General S. G. FRENCH,
Commanding Department of North Carolina.

OCTOBER 25, 1862.—Skirmish near Zuni, Va.

Report of Maj. Gen. John A. Dix, U. S. Army, commanding the Department of Virginia.

FORT MONROE, VA., *October* 27, 1862.

An expedition was sent from Suffolk on Saturday night to the Blackwater. It took a wrong road and did not arrive till noon, instead of daybreak, on Sunday. The cavalry swam the river, and some howitzers were sent over in canoes. The enemy were cleared from the bank of the river by our infantry. Much valuable information was obtained. Lieut. William Wheelan, of the Mounted Rifles, a very meritorious officer, was killed; our only casualty. We captured a sergeant and 4 men of a Georgia cavalry regiment. I have directed Major-General Peck to keep a part of his force in motion constantly, so as to accustom them to marching instead of rusting in camp.

JOHN A. DIX,
Major-General.

Major-General HALLECK, *General-in-Chief.*

OCTOBER 31, 1862.—Skirmish at Franklin, Va.

Report of Maj. Gen. John J. Peck, U. S. Army.

SUFFOLK, VA., *November* 2, 1862.

SIR: On Friday night, October 31, we surprised the enemy at Franklin about 4 a. m., and shelled him with 75 projectiles before he opened. As ordered, the command at once moved away and reconnoitered as far as Zuni, Isle of Wight, &c.

After withdrawing Follett's battery the enemy opened and kept up a fire on the woods until nearly 11 a. m., supposing we were there. Colonel Spear was in command of the advance, and thinks the execution was great. He reports five regiments there, one at Ivor, and a force at Wakefield, but numbers unknown; others scattered along the river. No accident on our side. Ferry was in command. Wessells is ill. Longstreet has been at Petersburg and may be at Wakefield, from which he can move to any threatened point.

JOHN J. PECK,
Major-General.

General JOHN A. DIX, *Fort Monroe.*

NOVEMBER 1–12, 1862.—Expedition from New Berne, N. C., including skirmishes (2d) at Little Creek and Rawle's Mill.

REPORTS.

No. 1.—Maj. Gen. John G. Foster, U. S. Army, commanding the Department of North Carolina.

No. 2.—Col. Thomas G. Stevenson, Twenty-fourth Massachusetts Infantry, commanding brigade, of skirmishes at Little Creek and Rawle's Mill.

No. 3.—Capt. Job Arnold, Fifth Rhode Island Infantry, of skirmishes at Little Creek and Rawle's Mill.

No. 1.

Report of Maj. Gen. John G. Foster, U. S. Army, commanding the Department of North Carolina.

HEADQUARTERS DEPARTMENT OF NORTH CAROLINA,
New Berne, N. C., November 12, 1862.

GENERAL : I have the honor to report that, agreeably to my letter of the 30th ultimo informing you of my intention to make an expedition through the eastern counties of this State and stating the object of the move, I left this post on the 31st ultimo, and have just arrived here on my return.

I am happy to inform you that although the original plan for the capture of the three regiments foraging in that section was, owing to the condition of the roads, frustrated, the expedition will be of great service to our cause in this department.

The First Brigade, under the command of Col. T. J. C. Amory, together with the artillery, cavalry, and wagon train, was marched from this point across the country to Washington. The balance of my forces, including the Second Brigade, Colonel Stevenson, and the Third Brigade, Colonel Lee, were embarked on transports and landed at Washington, where they were joined by Colonel Amory's command on Saturday evening, the 1st instant.

On Sunday (the 2d) all the forces, amounting to 5,000 men, including twenty-one pieces of artillery, left Washington under my command for Williamston. On the evening of the same day we encountered the enemy, posted in a strong position at a small creek, called Little Creek. I immediately ordered Colonel Stevenson, commanding the Second Brigade, who was then in the advance, to make all haste in driving them from the opposite side of the creek, and push on at once. The engagement lasted for one hour, when the enemy, being driven from their rifle-pits by the effective fire of Belger's Rhode Island battery, retired to Rawle's Mill, 1 mile farther on, where they made another stand in a recently-constructed field work. Belger's battery and two batteries of the Third New York Artillery were immediately ordered into position, and, after a spirited engagement of half an hour, succeeded in driving the enemy from their works and across a bridge, which they burned. That night, while the pioneers rebuilt the burned bridge, the forces bivouacked on the field and proceeded the next morning to Williamston, where we arrived about noon. We started from there, after a short rest, in pursuit of the enemy, bivouacking about 5 miles from that place.

On the following day we reached and occupied the fortifications at Rainbow Banks, 3 miles below Hamilton, and then pushed on to Hamilton. Here we expected to find some iron-clad boats said to be in process of construction at Hamilton, but discovered nothing of the kind.

On the 6th left Hamilton in pursuit of the enemy toward Tarborough, and encamped on the same night within 10 miles of that place. It was my intention to pursue the enemy to Tarborough, but the exhausted condition of my men, most of whom had been sick during the last two months and had not yet recovered their strength, and the provisions being entirely exhausted so that I had to subsist the command by foraging, as well as the fact that the enemy were being largely re-enforced by railroad, changed my plans, and on the following morning (the 7th instant) I countermarched the column, reaching Hamilton the same night, where we remained until the next morning, when we marched for Williamston in the midst of a severe snow-storm. At Williamston we remained a day in order to give the men an opportunity to rest.

At daylight the next day (10th instant) we started for Plymouth, where we arrived that night.

The following day the troops were all re-embarked for New Berne.

During the engagement at Rawle's Mill and at Hamilton we captured 5 prisoners, who were paroled at Williamston. The loss on our side consisted of 6 killed and 8 wounded.

The expedition was instrumental in saving the town and forces at Plymouth from destruction and capture, as I found upon my arrival at the place that the enemy's forces while lying in the vicinity, besides being engaged in foraging, had reconstructed a bridge over the creek, 3 miles outside the town, for the transportation of their artillery to the opposite bank. I also learned from information gathered on the spot that an immediate attack was to have been made on the place, but upon hearing of my advance from Washington and seeing the danger of their capture they beat a precipitate and hasty retreat.

The navy, under command of Commander H. K. Davenport, senior officer, co operated heartily with me during the whole time by sending five gunboats to Hamilton, and there placing four boat howitzers with their crews at my disposal.

I desire to mention particularly the efficient conduct of Colonel Stevenson, commanding the Second Brigade, and Colonel Potter, of the First North Carolina Union Volunteers.

I recommend that Colonel Stevenson, for his efficient services on this march and in the affair of Little Creek and Rawle's Mill, as well as previous services at the battles of Roanoke and New Berne, be promoted to the rank of brigadier-general, to date from November 3, 1862.

I have the honor to be, very respectfully, your obedient servant,

J. G. FOSTER,
Major-General, Commanding.

Maj. Gen. H. W. HALLECK,
General-in-Chief, U. S. Army, Washington, D. C.

No. 2.

Report of Col. Thomas G. Stevenson, Twenty-fourth Massachusetts Infantry, commanding brigade, of skirmishes at Little Creek and Rawle's Mill.

HDQRS. SECOND BRIGADE, DEPT. OF NORTH CAROLINA,
New Berne, November 15, 1862.

SIR: I have the honor to report the following as the result of the skirmishes in which my brigade was engaged on Sunday night, November 2, 1862:

At about dusk, as the advance guard, composed of the Marine Artillery, a company of the Tenth Connecticut, and a portion of cavalry, were crossing Little Creek, on the road from Washington to Williamston, they were suddenly fired upon by the enemy from the opposite side of the creek, concealed in the woods on the right of the road. The cavalry and infantry retired, the Marine Artillery opening fire. Two companies of the Forty-fourth were then ordered to deploy on the other side of the creek. In crossing, the enemy opened a brisk fire on them which was immediately returned with good effect, but their ammunition getting wet they were ordered to retire, which was done in good order, with a loss of 1 killed and 6 wounded. In the mean time Captain Belger's battery had taken position in a corn field on the left of the road and opened fire, the enemy returning with musketry and artillery, which the well-directed fire of Captain Belger's battery soon silenced. Two companies of the Forty-fourth Massachusetts were then ordered to the front, but the enemy again opened fire, killing 1 and wounding 1. I then ordered them to fall back. Captain Belger opened fire once more on the enemy and in a short time caused them to retreat.

The column then moved forward slowly, the road being blocked up by trees cut by the retreating enemy to retard our advance which for two hours was very slow. A breastwork was found on our left which had the appearance of having been hastily deserted. The advance, composed of the Twenty-fourth Massachusetts, soon came upon a bridge burning over the creek by Rawle's Mill. The Twenty-fourth, whilst extinguishing the flames, were fired upon by the enemy, with both musketry and artillery, in position on the opposite side of the creek parallel with the main road, the Twenty-fourth losing 1 killed and 2 wounded. Captain Belger soon got his battery in position, when he opened fire and completely routed the enemy.

Too much praise cannot be awarded Captain Belger and his command for the masterly manner in which his guns were maneuvered, and for the coolness and discipline displayed by all.

Very respectfully, your obedient servant,

THOS. G. STEVENSON,
Colonel, Commanding Second Brigade.

Maj. SOUTHARD HOFFMAN,
Assistant Adjutant-General.

No. 3.

Report of Capt. Job Arnold, Fifth Rhode Island Infantry, of skirmishes at Little Creek and Rawle's Mill, N. C.

HDQRS. FIFTH REGT. RHODE ISLAND VOLUNTEERS,
Camp Anthony, New Berne, N. C., November 13, 1862.

SIR: I beg leave to submit to you the following report of the part taken by the Fifth Rhode Island in skirmishes of Sunday, November 2, 1862:

At the commencement of the action we received orders to support Belger's Rhode Island battery. We formed in line to the right and rear of the battery, in the corn field to the right of the road. When the battery moved to take its position we filed down the road and formed a line about 20 paces in the rear of the battery in the field to the left of the road, our right resting toward the road, and there remained till ordered to follow the battery across the ford. We had nearly reached the road when we were ordered to remain to support a section of Belger's battery, left in its former position.

We then formed in line in rear of a rail fence to the left and rear of the pieces, our left resting on the woods. As soon as the battery was ordered forward we joined the main column, and, crossing the ford, proceeded with it up the road to the rifle-pits this side of Rawle's Mill, and remained within supporting distance of the battery while it was engaged in shelling the enemy. At about 1 o'clock we entered the rifle-pits and there remained until daylight. At one time the regiment was under quite heavy fire, and it gives me much pleasure to state that both officers and men, without exception, behaved with the most perfect coolness.

JOB ARNOLD,
Captain, Commanding.

Col. THOMAS G. STEVENSON,
Comdg. Second Brig., First Div., Dept. of North Carolina.

NOVEMBER 11, 1862.—Demonstration on New Berne, N. C.

REPORTS.

No. 1.—Col. Thomas J. C. Amory, Seventeenth Massachusetts Infantry, commanding
   Brigade.
No. 2.—Capt. J. Waldo Denny, Twenty-fifth Massachusetts Infantry.
No. 3.—Lieut. James M. Drennan, Twenty-fifth Massachusetts Infantry.
No. 4.—Lieut. Henry M. Richter, Twenty-fifth Massachusetts Infantry.
No. 5.—Capt. John F. Moschell, Third New York Cavalry.

No. 1.

*Report of Col. Thomas J. C. Amory, Seventeenth Massachusetts Infantry,
   commanding Brigade.*

HEADQUARTERS FIRST BRIGADE, FIRST DIVISION,
New Berne, N. C., November 12, 1862.

MAJOR : I have the honor to state, for the information of the general
commanding, that on yesterday evening a report reached me that a force
of the enemy, composed of infantry, artillery, and cavalry, estimated as
being a brigade of at least four or five regiments, had made its appearance in front of our pickets on the Trent road, about Jackson's house,
and was gradually advancing as our pickets retired in this direction,
their supposed intention being an attack on New Berne during the temporary absence of a portion of our forces. I had returned from Plymouth
with a portion of my brigade only a few hours previous, and Colonel
Kurtz, Twenty-third Massachusetts, supposing himself still in command
of the post, failed to communicate immediately to me the information
he had received of the enemy's advance, but meanwhile, as he afterward
reported to me, took the precaution to warn the gunboats and troops
here to be in readiness. Major Garrard, Third New York Cavalry, with
the two mountain howitzers, had also been sent out on the Neuse road.
   Toward 9 o'clock p. m. Colonel Kurtz, by my order, reported to me,
and at the same time Lieutenant-Colonel Mix, commanding Third New
York Cavalry, gave me an account of the disposition already made of
our forces, and confirmed the information I had previously received as
to the force of the enemy.
   At this time the only regiments which had returned from Plymouth
were the Seventeenth, Twenty-fourth, part of the Twenty-third, and
about 150 men of the Forty-fourth Massachusetts. None of the artillery had yet arrived.
   To make the best possible disposition according to my judgment of
the small force then at my disposal, I withdrew all the pickets on the
Trent road, picketing the line of the edge of woods in front of Fort Totten, extending the line from the Trent to the Neuse River, keeping
mounted patrols on the Neuse road as far as the cross-road to railroad,
withdrawing the remainder of cavalry with mounted howitzers. I was
unaware at this time that the railroad monitor was with the two companies of infantry at the bridge, 9 miles from town. As soon as possible I sent orders for this force to fall back, but in the mean time the
enemy had got between them and New Berne, having cut them off by
the cross-road from Trent road past the red house. At about 2 o'clock
a. m. these companies were attacked, 1 man killed and 2 wounded of the
Twenty-fourth Massachusetts, and the enemy dispersed by a shell thrown
from the monitor.

I recalled the company of the Seventeenth Massachusetts, stationed at Evans' Mill, 8 miles from here. They arrived this morning at the camp of the Seventeenth Massachusetts and have since then returned. I dispatched a locomotive and train at 1.30 a. m. for Captain Lee's battery (Rocket Battalion) and all the available force, consisting of four companies infantry and about 30 cavalry at Newport Barracks. They arrived at 8 o'clock this morning. The infantry and cavalry returned by the morning train; the battery remains waiting further orders.

The Ninth New Jersey, Fifth Rhode Island, and Belger's battery having arrived during the night with the gunboat Hunchback, I posted these troops at various points as reserves to the line of pickets with orders to the infantry in case of an attack to occupy the rifle-pits extending across the peninsula.

At daylight this morning I ordered out forces on the different roads to reconnoiter the position of the enemy, still supposing him to be in force somewhere in our front. The whole cavalry force under Lieutenant-Colonel Mix was ordered to scout the Neuse road as far as Batchelder's Creek.

The Twenty-third Massachusetts, under command of Major Chambers, advanced along the railroad as far as the bridge, and leaving one company to re-enforce those in charge of the monitor, returned this evening without having seen the enemy.

From all the information I have been able to obtain I am inclined to believe that the force of the enemy which came down upon our pickets was much smaller than at first supposed, perhaps not over 300 men, infantry and cavalry. Whether or not a larger force remained in their rear I have not been able to learn with certainty.

Our regular pickets have since been re-established, those on the Trent road, consisting of four companies Twenty-fifth Massachusetts, extending out as far as Jackson's. The enemy burned the negro houses opposite Jackson's house. I think if one or two light howitzers could be posted with the reserves of this force it would be well.

I would also beg leave to call the attention of the general commanding to the fact that none of the block-houses are yet armed with guns.

The earthwork at the head of county bridge, on Trent River, was manned partly by a platoon of the Seventeenth Massachusetts.

A permanent guard well drilled at the heavy guns would be an advantage.

I am, sir, very respectfully, your obedient servant,

THOS. J. C. AMORY,
First Division, New Berne, N. C.

Maj. SOUTHARD HOFFMAN,
Asst. Adjt. Gen., First Division, New Berne, N. C.

No. 2.

Report of Capt. J. Waldo Denny, Twenty-fifth Massachusetts Infantry.

HEADQUARTERS CAMP HARKNESS,
November 14, 1862.

SIR : On the morning of Tuesday, the 11th instant, by your permission I ordered a party of 50 men, under command of Lieut. J. M. Drennan, of Company F, of my command, to proceed by an indicated route to the red house, and thence to the Trent road, at a point near the

Grapevine House, so called, near the Deep Gully, and from that point to return to this camp. The report of that scout by Lieutenant Drennan is inclosed herein and made a part of this report; also report of Lieut. H. M. Richter, officer of the day, who rendered efficient service with a small force of pickets in defending our lines from the attack of the enemy.

Upon learning of the attack upon our lines at about 4 o'clock p. m. I immediately caused my command at this camp—Companies F, G, and K, of the Twenty-fifth Massachusetts Regiment—to fall in, and followed your command of cavalry to the scene of action, dispatching orders to Company H, encamped 1 mile below this camp, to follow with all haste. Upon reaching the corner of the road going to the rear of French's house I met a private of your command riding his horse back from the engagement upon a run. He cried out to me to halt, as the enemy were coming down fast and in force. Supposing the order came from you I halted my command and proceeded on the road alone, being mounted, until I reached Lieutenant Tew with a reserve infantry force, being those who in part composed the scouting party. This officer stated that his men were exhausted, and that my companies could be of service. I immediately ordered my command forward and approached the Rocky Run under a fire of shell from the enemy, and turned to the right from the Trent road to the rear of the position held by you with your command. I reported to you at this point, and immediately after ordered Captain Wageley, of Company G, to take up position on the left of the Trent road so as to cover the bridge by his fire.

After remaining in our position for fifteen minutes, upon information that the enemy were attempting to flank us on our right, I withdrew my command to the road in rear of French's house, holding position in the narrow belt of timber upon that road and the right of Trent road, when we were joined by your command, taking position on the road in our rear. I sent a messenger to Captain Wageley informing him of our change of position and ordering him to join us in case of any strong attack upon him from the front or any appearance of an attack upon our flanks.

At this point Lieutenant Foster, in command of Company H, Twenty-fifth Massachusetts Regiment, reported to me with his command. Holding this position for some time we finally retired from it, with your approval, to gain a stronger position near the wood west of Mr. Eubanks' house. This was a strong position, where I flanked two companies upon each side of the road, guarding the position so we could not be flanked on either side without our knowledge. Very soon, however, Major Garrard, of your regiment, who had arrived and assumed command, ordered me to retire with my command to our camp, where he ordered me to place two companies in the clearing at Mr. Whitford's house, on the other side of Blakely's Branch, to support a howitzer placed in the road at that point. He also ordered me to place two companies in the yard of the Harrison house, both of which orders were executed. In about thirty minutes Major Garrard informed me he had orders from Colonel Kurtz, in command at New Berne, to retire to that city, and ordered me to retire with my command, taking such valuables as we could carry. We withdrew in order and marched as far as the belt of woods on the Trent road, next to Fort Totten, where I was ordered to deploy my detachment, which I did. In a short time I received orders from Major Garrard to withdraw to the city with my command, which I did, taking quarters for the night at Camp Oliver.

The next morning, upon orders from Colonel Amory, commanding brigade, I returned to this camp, finding the tents unmolested.

Only two of my command were slightly wounded, one in the face and another in the left hand.

I desire to call attention particularly to the coolness and bravery of Lieutenant Drennan and the men under his command, who twice drove back an overpowering force of the enemy and held them in check for nearly or quite an hour and a half. I think the advance of the enemy would have been disastrous to us had it not been for the brave conduct of Lieutenant Drennan.

All the officers and men of my command behaved themselves gallantly under fire.

Respectfully, yours,

J. W. DENNY,
Captain, 25th Massachusetts, Commanding Detachment.

Captain MOSCHELL,
Third New York Cavalry, Commanding Post.

[Indorsement.]

Received November 15, 1862, 10 a. m., and approved. Forwarded to Colonel Amory, Seventeenth Massachusetts.

JNO. F. MOSCHELL,
Captain, Commanding Outpost.

No. 3.

Report of Lieut. James M. Drennan, Twenty-fifth Massachusetts Infantry.

CAMP HARKNESS, *November* —, 1862.

SIR: I have the honor to report that on Tuesday morning I caused to be detailed by your orders from the three companies in this camp a force of 50 men, 3 corporals, and 3 sergeants, with Lieutenant Tew, and started on a foraging expedition, traveling as near as possible the route indicated by you.

We met with little success until we arrived near the red house, where we came onto cattle and swine. We soon shot down and dressed what we wanted and started for camp, taking the road nearest to Deep Gully. Being in the enemy's lines we advanced with caution. Soon, or about 3 o'clock p. m., my advance guard reported a force of cavalry, which I discovered as the enemy's. I deployed part of my command as skirmishers in the woods, on both sides of the road, with the remainder under Lieutenant Tew as a reserve, and advanced immediately on the place we last saw them. I gave orders not to fire unless fired on. As we came out on the Trent road the enemy were leaving the house at the grapevine, near the gully, and made all speed for the latter place. I did not deem it prudent to follow them, for many reasons, but started for camp, throwing out an advance and rear guard. After stopping about fifteen or twenty minutes to rest about 1 mile this side, we resumed our march for camp, and had barely time to get inside our vedettes when they attacked in force, driving in the outpost.

I immediately ordered our wagons to camp, and with 6 men went to the front to give them check. My men labored under the disadvantage of having the bright sun in their eyes and on their pieces, but we drove them from the open field into the woods. They rallied. I sent for the remainder of the first platoon and deployed them as skirmishers. A

brisk fire was kept up for some time by both parties until the enemy
gave way and ran for the woods again. We followed them, driving
them back in the woods out of sight (but not out of hearing, as much
abusive language passed back and forth). We occupied the ground
held by them for about ten minutes. I judged their game was to draw
us on. I had previously heard the rumbling of artillery back of them,
and I fell back on the rise of ground to my first position in close order.
They charged down the road to the position they had occupied and I
had just left, and deployed again, I doing the same behind the fence in
my position. In this relative position the firing was brisk on both sides.
The enemy opened with two pieces of artillery and a heavy line of
skirmishers, throwing out a force on both my flanks. I remained as long
as I deemed it prudent, then fell back in good order on the Jackson
house, and finally crossed the creek and took up a position just this
side, removing the planks from the bridge, &c.

I remained in this last position until Captain Moschell's cavalry company came up and Lieutenant Richter, with the reserve pickets; also
your own command.

My force kept the enemy in check about one hour and a half in the
fight and I think three hours from the time we first saw them. The
men of my command behaved splendidly under fire and deserved much
credit.

You knowing so well the lay of the land I have not appended a dia-
gram.

Respectfully submitted.

J. M. DRENNAN,
Lieut. Comdg. Co. F, Twenty-fifth Regiment Mass. Vols.

Capt. J. W. DENNY,
Twenty-fifth Massachusetts Infantry.

No. 4.

Report of Lieut. Henry M. Richter, Twenty-fifth Massachusetts Infantry.

CAMP NEAR HARRISON'S HOUSE,
November 12, 1862.

SIR: Yesterday afternoon at about 3 o'clock I heard firing in front
of the outpost while I was visiting the pickets. I supposed the firing
came from the foraging party which had left camp in the morning at 8
o'clock, under command of Lieutenant Drennan, so I rode slowly back,
waiting for an increase or continuation of the firing. About a mile this
side of Jackson's house I heard heavy musketry, and was informed by
a messenger that the outpost was attacked by infantry, cavalry, and
artillery, while Lieutenant Drennan held the Jackson house with his
fatigue party. I at once dispatched all my pickets double-quick to the
bridge about 50 paces this side of Jackson's house, where I relieved
Lieutenant Drennan, who took the reserve, deploying my men 16 strong
as skirmishers and holding bridge and creek.

The enemy in front of me was infantry, covered by an elevation of
the ground, so that I had no object to fire on. The fire of the enemy
had no effect whatever, as my men laid low and were covered by trees.
We only fired a few shots at the enemy when he showed himself, with
what effect I cannot say.

Lieutenant Ebbs, of the Third New York Cavalry, informed me that the rebels were trying to flank me by the way of Taylor's house in strong force. I kept the creek about ten minutes longer, and as I could not see any re-enforcements on our side (the cavalry having taken another position not known by me) I went slowly in retreat across the field toward the roads, the enemy charging in line of battle at my former position, their shots having no effect on my men. At the same time the right of the enemy charged the bridge with cavalry, and placing a howitzer on a bluff on the right of the road they sent a few shells over us without doing any damage.

At French's gate I formed my squad in line on one side of the road to give you a chance to pass down with your fresh command, which was approaching me. As my men were tired out by running up to the place of action I took position in your rear, throwing out pickets to the right of the road toward French's house, which road leads to Taylor's, Lieutenant Drennan doing the same on the left of the road leading to the mill near Jackson's house. There I reported to you when the battalion fell back, and dismissed my pickets to their respective companies.

I am, sir, your obedient servant,

HENRY M. RICHTER,
First Lieut. Twenty-fifth Regt. Mass. Vols., Officer of the Day.
Capt. J. W. DENNY, *Commanding Battalion.*

No. 5.

Reports of Capt. John F. Moschell, Third New York Cavalry.

HEADQUARTERS OUTPOST ON TRENT ROAD,
Harrison's House, November 13, 1862.

On the 11th instant I authorized Lieutenant Drennan and Lieutenant Tew, of Twenty-fifth Massachusetts, to go out near the red house to get some fresh meat, they having failed to supply us any from the subsistence department at New Berne. On the way back they came across a force of rebels, with three cannon, some cavalry, and infantry. They kept them at bay from 2.30 p. m. until 3.30, and fell back to my cavalry vedettes; they fired at them, and, the infantry assisting them, kept them back until word was sent to me at this place. I immediately went to their assistance with the balance of my force. I also sent word down to the commanding officer at New Berne, Colonel Kurtz; he sent Major Garrard out with three more companies of cavalry and the two mountain howitzers belonging to the regiment, when I was relieved from command by him. He ordered my forces to fall back to camp and afterward to New Berne, leaving all the Government and private property belonging to the command. Fortunately the rebels did not come down any farther than the Jackson house.

As far as I could ascertain the enemy's force consisted of two companies of artillery, four of cavalry, and three or four regiments of infantry. It is reported they are out about 8 miles from New Berne, on the Trent road, now.

Respectfully reported.

I have the honor to be, yours, &c.,

JNO. F. MOSCHELL,
Captain, Third New York Cavalry, Comdg. Outpost.

Major-General FOSTER.

HEADQUARTERS OUTPOST AT HARRISON'S HOUSE,
On Trent Road, N. C., November 13, 1862.

COLONEL: I have the honor to make the following report for the information of the commanding general:

On Tuesday, the 11th instant, I gave Captain Denny permission to send Lieutenants Drennan and Tew, with 50 men, out beyond the lines toward the red house to get some fresh meat (the subsistence department having failed to supply them any for some time) for his detachment. On their way back they came across a force of the enemy which they drove back toward the Deep Gully about 3 o'clock p. m.

Lieutenant Drennan then came on toward camp, and when he arrived at our outpost, or vedettes, they were followed by the enemy's cavalry and some artillery, which they posted near, and fired a couple of shot with a 6-pounder. Lieutenant Drennan made a stand, together with our cavalry, and fired several rounds, but finally falling back to the Jackson Creek Bridge. One of the cavalry vedettes (Henry Rancier) was wounded in the calf of his leg (flesh wound).

Information being sent me that we were attacked on the outpost by cavalry, artillery, and infantry, I immediately proceeded with my company, and, ordering Captain Denny with his infantry detachment to follow, I arrived at the creek bridge just as Lieutenant Drennan had crossed, and a shot from the cannon striking near did not deem it prudent to take my whole force across.

Lieutenant Ebbs and a couple of my company went across to see what position they were in. I had four men tear up the planks of the bridge to make it impassable for the artillery to cross.

I formed my men on the right of the road and sent Lieutenant Ebbs with two or three men behind Mr. French's house to the road leading to the red house, and a couple to the road leading toward Taylor's to prevent a flank movement.

I also ordered Lieutenant Drennan to fall back a little, for his men and himself were completely jaded out. When Lieutenant Richter came up with a squad I ordered him to deploy on my right as skirmishers. Then I withdrew a little more on account of the enemy coming up in full force with infantry and forming in front of us, and their cavalry on their left, with a piece of artillery.

A piece of artillery at the Jackson house was worked with shell, which exploded over the left flank of my company. At this time (it getting quite dark) I ordered Captain Wageley and his company (G) on the left of the road to watch the bridge and to prevent their crossing at the mill, and ordered Captain Denny with the balance of the infantry to fall back to the junction of the road leading from Trent road to the red house this side Mr. French's house, and afterward fall back with my company to the house known as Ben. Ansley's, this side French's, but leaving nine mounted vedettes at three points (three in each place). At this place Sergeant Middaugh, in charge of Major Garrard's advance guard, came up. I ordered Captain Denny and the infantry to fall back and form on the right and left of the road at the 5-mile post, and ordered Lieutenant Ebbs to form my company in rear of them behind a skirt of pine timber. At this time Lieutenant Chamberlain came up and delivered a message from Major Garrard for me to have the infantry fall back to camp, and after the infantry fell back to camp to have my company fall back and cover their retreat. I posted at six different places with three mounted vedettes in a place, and after visiting them went back and reported to Major Garrard.

Major Garrard immediately ordered me to call in all my vedettes, which I immediately did.

One of the vedettes lost his revolving rifle in falling back; the strap broke and in the dark could not find it.

The men behaved well in every instance. Lieutenant Ebbs saw three regimental colors and three cannons drawn by mules, and four guidons.

I have the honor, colonel, to be, very respectfully, yours, &c.,

JNO. F. MOSCHELL,
Captain, Third New York Cavalry, Commanding Outpost.

Col. JOHN MIX,
Commanding Third New York Cavalry.

NOVEMBER 12–14, 1862.—Operations about Suffolk, Va., including skirmishes (12th) at Providence Church and (14th) at Blackwater Bridge and Zuni, Va.

Report of Maj. Gen. John J. Peck, U. S. Army, commanding at Suffolk.

SUFFOLK, *November* 14, 1862.

About 11 o'clock p. m. on the 12th Colonel Claiborne, with 300 men, attacked our picket of New York Mounted Rifles at Providence Church, and was repulsed, retiring to the Blackwater. Last evening the same picket was fired upon again. Colonel Dodge was sent out to reconnoiter, and reached Windsor about midnight. At dawn he moved for Blackwater Bridge; had a brisk skirmish; drove their guard over; crossed a few men; captured three tents complete, canteens, camp kettles, two muskets, and all the camp equipage of the guard of 30 men. Strong breastworks were discovered a short distance back from the ford. He then moved up to Joyner's Ford, which was barricaded; Next to Zuni, where a strong guard offered much resistance. After bringing up his howitzers they fell back. They have strong rifle-pits there, from which they kept up a sharp fire upon our dismounted skirmishers. All their cooking utensils, seven rifles, cartridge-boxes, a sword, and many other things, with two of the guard, fell into our hands. The loss of the enemy was much greater than ours, which is 5 wounded.

These affairs are very handsome, and follow close upon the two late ones near Zuni and Franklin.

I trust these operations will meet your approval.

JOHN J. PECK,
Major-General.

Major-General DIX,
Commanding Department of Virginia

NOVEMBER 16, 1862.—Skirmish at Gloucester Point, Va.

REPORTS.

No. 1.—Brig. Gen. Henry M. Naglee, U. S. Army, commanding at Yorktown.
No. 2.—Col. William W. H. Davis, One hundred and fourth Pennsylvania Infantry.

No 1.

Report of Brig. Gen. Henry M. Naglee, U. S. Army, commanding at Yorktown.

HEADQUARTERS,
Yorktown, Va, November 16, 1862.

COLONEL : I would respectfully report that at 4 o'clock this morning
a dash was made upon the picket line at Gloucester Point, and 1 man
of the One hundred and fourth Pennsylvania Volunteers was killed, 3
were wounded, and 3 made prisoners.

The picket was an advanced one of 12 persons, made by Colonel
Davis, beyond supporting distance from the main picket line, within
the last four days, and without my knowledge; and that, although advised at 11 p. m., five hours in advance, that the enemy were lurking
upon the road, no proper order was given to support the advance picket
or to withdraw it.

This attack was made after Captain Hall had gone over the same
road at midnight, as reported to you by this mail, and nothing was
seen or known by either of the movements of the other.

Very respectfully, &c.,

HENRY M. NAGLEE,
Brigadier-General, Commanding.

Col. D. T. VAN BUREN,
Assistant Adjutant-General, Fortress Monroe, Va.

No. 2.

Report of Col. William W. H. Davis, One hundred and fourth Pennsylvania Infantry.

HEADQUARTERS,
Gloucester Point, Va., November 16, 1862.

CAPTAIN: I have the honor to report that last night about 11 o'clock
I received information through a contraband that a force of rebel cavalry,
said to be 600 strong, was on the road to Gloucester, 2 miles in front of
my picket lines. I immediately sent two companies to strengthen the
pickets, and wrote a note to Major Hall, who with his force was still
within the lines, giving the information to him. He had left, however,
before my messenger reached his camp, and did not get the information
which might have proved valuable to him.

Things remained quiet until about 4 o'clock this morning, when a picket
stationed on the Gloucester road discovered a party of cavalry approaching them. When challenged they answered, first, "Federals," and then
"One hundred and seventh Pennsylvania Cavalry," and immediately
poured two volleys into the pickets drawn up in the road. Our loss is 1
killed, 3 wounded, and 3 missing. It is not known whether any loss was

sustained by the enemy, but a colored man who was near by thinks some of them were hurt. The man who was killed was first made prisoner, but was shot because he refused to mount behind a cavalryman. His body was left lying in the road, but was recovered and brought into camp this morning

A negro came to the lines this morning and states that the enemy was about 75 strong, and was concealed near the Hook store waiting for our cavalry to pass out. A corporal who lately deserted from the One hundredth New York Regiment was with the party of the enemy and directing their movements. The point where the attack was made is about a third of a mile outside the picket lines, and the men, 12 in number, were thrown out as an advance post. I am informed that when the enemy left the ground they announced that they intended to return to King and Queen County.

If I learn anything additional I will immediately communicate it to you.

I remain, very respectfully, your obedient servant,

W. W. H. DAVIS,
Colonel One hundred and fourth Pennsylvania Vols., Comdg.

Capt. GEORGE H. JOHNSTON,
Assistant Adjutant-General.

NOVEMBER 17, 1862.—Affair near Carrsville, Va.

Report of Maj. Gen. John J. Peck, U. S. Army.

SUFFOLK, *November* 17, 1862.

GENERAL: At noon Major Wetherill with 150 men came upon 400 cavalry half-way between Holland's Corners and Carrsville. He reported fighting and retiring slowly. From not hearing from him I infer that he is all right.

My expedition left at 1 o'clock to-day and I hope for results.

JOHN J. PECK,
Major-General.

Major-General DIX.

NOVEMBER 18, 1862.—Skirmish at Franklin, Va.

Reports of Maj. Gen. John J. Peck, U. S. Army, commanding at Suffolk.

SUFFOLK, *November* 18, 1862—1 p. m.

General Wessells reports that the enemy has been re-enforced at Franklin in infantry and artillery, and that he is strong there. The fords have been blocked, the approaches closed, and the crossing is bad. A smart skirmish at the river, with only a horse wounded. It looks like rain.

JOHN J. PECK,
Major-General.

General DIX, *Fort Monroe.*

SUFFOLK, VA., *November* 18, 1862.

GENERAL: I advised you this afternoon of the reports from Wessells. The boats broke last night *en route,* and they were not able to make the bridge support the artillery. During the morning the enemy were in order of battle back from where he proposed to cross. He has shelled their camps. About noon he moved down in front of Franklin and was shelling the place. They are superior in numbers, and he thinks have from eight to twelve pieces. Only one wounded. Have advised him to move in near the Deserted House and come in to-morrow. A larger infantry force is needed for this position to enable us to cross that river in the presence of the force there, and the supports that may be sent by two railways. They could easily have re-enforced from Weldon during the day or from Wakefield or Ivor.

JOHN J. PECK,
Major-General.

Major-General DIX, *Fort Monroe.*

NOVEMBER 22, 1862.—Reconnaissance from Williamsburg, Va.

Report of Maj. Gen. John A. Dix, U. S. Army, commanding the Department of Virginia.

FORT MONROE, VA., *November* 23, 1862.

A reconnaissance was made from Williamsburg yesterday toward the Chickahominy. Killed 2 and captured 6 of the enemy and took 11 horses. No loss on our side.

JOHN A. DIX,
Major-General.

Major-General HALLECK,
General-in-Chief.

NOVEMBER 25, 1862.—Capture of the United States steamer Ellis, New River, N. C.

*Report of Brig. Gen. W. H. C. Whiting, C. S. Army, commanding Defenses of Cape Fear River.**

HEADQUARTERS,
Wilmington, N. C., November 28, 1862.

GENERAL: I have the pleasure of reporting that Captain Newkirk, of the cavalry, and Captain Adams, with a section of a field battery, have destroyed a steam gunboat of the enemy on New River. Her crew escaped. Her armament, ammunition, small-arms, and many articles of value will be saved. The enemy attempted to fire her, but being of iron but little damage was done. Great credit is due to Captains Newkirk and Adams and their officers and men.

Very respectfully,

W. H. C. WHITING,
Brigadier-General, Commanding.

Maj. Gen. GUSTAVUS W. SMITH,
Commanding, &c., Richmond, Va.

---

* For reports of Commander H. K. Davenport and Lieut. William B. Cushing, U. S. Navy, see Annual Report of the Secretary of the Navy, December 1, 1862.

DECEMBER 2, 1862.—Skirmish on the Blackwater, near Franklin, Va.

REPORTS.

No. 1.—Maj. Gen. John A. Dix, U. S. Army, commanding the Department of Virginia.
No. 2.—Maj. Gen. John J. Peck, U. S. Army.

No. 1.

Reports of Maj. Gen. John A. Dix, U. S. Army, commanding the Department of Virginia.

FORT MONROE, VA., *December* 2, 1862.

An expedition sent out from Suffolk yesterday by Major-General Peck captured to-day the celebrated Petersburg Rocket Battery, which was taken from our army, and drove the enemy across the Blackwater at Franklin. We have thirty odd prisoners, and are picking up more in the woods. Many of the enemy killed and wounded; our loss trifling. I will furnish details by mail.

JOHN A. DIX,
Major-General.

Maj. Gen. H. W. HALLECK,
　General-in-Chief.

—

HDQRS. DEPT. OF VIRGINIA, SEVENTH ARMY CORPS,
Fort Monroe, Va., December 4, 1862.

GENERAL: I sent you a message the day before yesterday, by telegraph, in regard to an action near the Blackwater between a party of the enemy and a portion of the Eleventh Pennsylvania Cavalry, sent out from Suffolk by Major-General Peck the previous day. Colonel Spear, of that regiment, who commanded the expedition, returned last night, bringing back his entire force, consisting, in addition to a part of his own regiment, of portions of the Thirty-ninth Illinois, Colonel Osborn; Sixty-second Ohio, Colonel Pond; One hundred and thirtieth New York, Colonel Gibbs; Sixth Massachusetts, Colonel Follansbee; One hundred and third Pennsylvania, Lieutenant-Colonel Maxwell; two sections of Davis' Massachusetts Light Battery and one section of Howard's battery, Fourth U. S. Artillery; in all, about 3,100 men. The expedition was sent out in pursuance of the object, heretofore explained to you, of keeping a part of my force in constant motion, and also to ascertain the truth of information reported to Major-General Peck in regard to the movement of the enemy in the vicinity of Franklin. While Colonel Spear's force was breakfasting his pickets were driven in, and a charge was made by about 500 of the enemy's cavalry, with a section of a rocket battery. It was gallantly met by Colonel Spear, at the head of 300 of his regiment, and the enemy, thrown into confusion by his impetuous attack, recoiled, and was driven over his floating bridge at Franklin, which is protected by a battery of heavy guns. Ten or 12 of the enemy were killed and 20 were taken prisoners. We also captured 14 horses, a quantity of harness, 7 saddles, 42 rifles, 70 rockets of 12 and 15 pounds, and other minor articles. We sustained no loss either in men or horses. General Peck speaks in high terms of the gallantry of Colonel Spear, who has distinguished himself on more than one occasion by his prompt and spirited movements; and the colonel mentions with commendation

Major Stratton and Lieutenants Buttz and Roper, of his regiment. The enemy retreated so suddenly that our artillery and infantry were not brought into action. The enemy's floating bridge swings from one bank of the Blackwater, which is very narrow, to the other, and is withdrawn from our side as soon as his forces cross.

Col. J. R. Griffin and Major Boggs commanded the insurgents. General R. A. Pryor has just taken command at Franklin.

With the means of crossing, the enemy's position at Franklin might easily have been attacked, and in all probability carried.

I am, very respectfully, your obedient servant,

JOHN A. DIX,
Major-General.

Maj. Gen. H. W. HALLECK,
General-in-Chief.

No. 2.

Reports of Maj. Gen. John J. Peck, U. S. Army.

SUFFOLK, *December* 2, 1862.

Our expedition, of which I advised you yesterday, has been a great success. Spies were sent in and a trap was sprung, but the rebels were caught. They attacked the advance this morning beyond Carrsville. We repulsed them, capturing the famous Petersburg Rocket Battery, and drove the whole force over the river. We are now shelling Franklin, having no means of crossing.

General Roger A. Pryor in command at Franklin; Col. Joel R. Griffin commanding the cavalry and Major Boggs the artillery; thirty odd prisoners now, more being found in the woods; many of the enemy killed and wounded. Our loss trifling.

Colonel Spear led his cavalry most gallantly upon the enemy's advance.

JOHN J. PECK,
Major-General.

Major-General DIX, *Fort Monroe.*

—

SUFFOLK, *December* 2, 1862.

In view of operations elsewhere, and of the fact that Spear has no means of crossing except with much loss and some risk of failure, I have directed him to hold on and shell the place, coming in to-night. The victory is now complete, but a repulse in crossing would take off the edge. The rebels have been tearing up the rails, so that we are not able to-day to use more than 8 or 10 miles. Parties are out at work. Will we get any pontoons?

JOHN J. PECK,
Major-General.

Major-General DIX, *Fort Monroe.*

—

SUFFOLK, VA., *December* 3, 1862.

On the morning of the 1st, contrabands reported that the rebels were throwing up works near the railway, 4 miles this side of Franklin. I ordered Colonel Spear to proceed there during the night with portions of the Thirty-ninth Illinois, Colonel Osborn; Sixty-second Ohio, Colonel Pond; One hundred and thirtieth New York, Colonel Gibbs; Sixth Massachusetts, Colonel Follansbee; One hundred and third Pennsylvania, Lieutenant-Colonel Maxwell; two sections of Davis', one of Howard's artillery, and a portion of his cavalry—in all 3,100—for information, and to drive off any force that he found there.

No works were found, but while breakfasting his pickets were driven in and a furious charge was made by some 500 cavalry, with a section of a rocket battery.

Colonel Spear took 300 of his cavalry and gallantly led them upon the head of the column, which recoiled under this impetuous attack. Confusion ensued; many jumped off and fled into the woods, while others put about for Franklin.

The cannoneers and horses being disabled, the gallant Pennsylvanians made quick work with the battery, and chased the Georgian squadrons to their floating bridge under the guns of Franklin. Besides driving the enemy over the river and capturing his section, 10 or 12 were killed and 20 made prisoners. Fourteen horses, harness, 7 saddles, 42 rifles, 70 rockets of 12 and 15 pound, and other minor articles fell into our hands.

No portion of the artillery or infantry was called upon, and I am happy to say that no loss of men or horses was sustained. Col. J. R. Griffin and Major Boggs commanded. General R. A. Pryor had just assumed command and was making his reconnaissance toward Suffolk.

This brilliant affair entitles Colonel Spear to great credit and adds to his already high reputation. He mentions favorably Major Stratton and Lieutenants Buttz and Roper.

Very respectfully,

JOHN J. PECK,
Major-General.

Maj. Gen. JOHN A. DIX,
Commanding Department of Virginia, &c.

DECEMBER 8–12, 1862.—Reconnaissances from Suffolk to the Blackwater and skirmishes at and about Zuni, Va.

REPORTS.

No. 1.—Maj. Gen. John A. Dix, U. S. Army, commanding the Department of Virginia.
No. 2.—Maj. Gen. John J. Peck, U. S. Army, commanding at Suffolk, Va.
No. 3.—Capt. J. H. Sikes, Company D, Seventh Confederate States Cavalry.

No. 1.

Reports of Maj. Gen. John A. Dix, U. S. Army, commanding the Department of Virginia.

FORT MONROE, VA., *December* 8, 1862.

The troops in this department will be ready to move at short notice. Banks' expedition, which came here wanting large amounts of quartermaster, commissary, and ordnance stores, has drawn us very low, but fresh supplies have been ordered. In furtherance of Foster's movement a cavalry force from Suffolk was thrown down upon the Chowan, near the mouth of the Blackwater, to-day. At midnight to-night South Quay camp will be shelled. On Thursday a dash will be made on Ivor, near Zuni. All this with a view to keep the enemy busy and to draw off his attention, and, if possible, his troops from Weldon, &c.

JOHN A. DIX,
Major-General.

Major-General HALLECK,
General-in-Chief.

—

FORT MONROE, VA., *December* 12, 1862.

Some of our cavalry got across the Blackwater; captured a captain, a sergeant, and 11 privates and killed a considerable number of the enemy. Our loss, 1 killed and 11 wounded.

JOHN A. DIX,
Major-General.

Maj. Gen. H. W. HALLECK,
General-in-Chief.

—

HDQRS. DEPT. OF VIRGINIA, SEVENTH ARMY CORPS,
Fort Monroe, Va., December 13, 1862.

GENERAL: The demonstrations were made as promised. On Monday we had a considerable force near the mouth of the Blackwater, or its junction with Chowan. On Tuesday we shelled South Quay. On Thursday we were to have been at Zuni, but from the badness of the roads General Ferry did not get there till yesterday morning (Friday). There was sharp fighting during the day, but we did not succeed in crossing, except with a small part of our cavalry.

We killed a considerable number of the enemy, captured a captain, a sergeant, and 11 men, and drew a large force there—part, as we suppose, from Weldon. We had 1 man killed and 11 wounded.

I heard from General Peck last night, and he supposed the object of the demonstration accomplished. There was an article in the Northern papers, which went to Richmond, of course, stating that General Emory had sailed from this post to re-enforce you, and I fear this false report has induced the enemy to strengthen himself in your front.

Hoping to hear favorable news from you, I am, respectfully and truly, general, yours,

JOHN A. DIX,
Major-General.

Maj. Gen. J. G. FOSTER,
Commanding Department of North Carolina.

———

No. 2.

Reports of Maj. Gen. John J. Peck, U. S. Army, commanding at Suffolk, Va.

SUFFOLK, VA., *December* 8, 1862.

Besides giving Foster Wessells' old brigade I proposed making a series of demonstrations toward Blackwater for his benefit, if practicable.

Accordingly Colonel Dodge will be on the Chowan at noon this day, at Manny's Ferry, and give the impression that he is looking for a crossing. Only 14 miles from railway but 20 from Suffolk. About midnight South Quay camp will be shelled. Thursday night dash at Ivor or Franklin.

Had Wessells' old troops remained, proposed making clean thing of Franklin; but I am weaker than before. These new men do not know their facings, and their hearts are not in warfare, judging from their desertions. Can you loan me two old regiments for four or five days, to arrive light on Wednesday? We must not fail if we attempt on Franklin. Nottoway Bridge being done brings Weldon within two hours' time.

JOHN J. PECK,
Major-General.

Maj. Gen. JOHN A. DIX, *Fort Monroe.*

—

SUFFOLK, *December* 8, 1862.

I alluded to the arrival of two regiments at Franklin this morning. This is confirmed; also that a third one was sent down on Friday to Wakefield and marched across to Franklin. I have a man who left Petersburg on Friday. He says all the approaches are being fortified; that infantry and artillery were sent to Wakefield; that Jackson's infantry was falling back to Richmond. He was told that a brigade of Stuart's cavalry was coming to the Blackwater; that the troops of General French had been ordered this way. He heard that 5,000 had gone from here to Carolina.

JOHN J. PECK,
Major-General.

General DIX.

—

SUFFOLK, *December* 9, 1862.

We shelled the rebel camps about midnight at South Quay. Has been very cold; ice thick enough to bear a horse.

JOHN J. PECK,
Major-General.

Major-General DIX.

—

SUFFOLK, *December* 9, 1862.

We threw seventy odd shells into the South Quay camps with effect. Found the Chowan strongly picketed and watched. A brigade and 500 cavalry on the Lower Blackwater, below Franklin.

JOHN J. PECK,
Major-General.

Major-General DIX.

—

SUFFOLK, VA., *December* 12, 1862.

Ferry's command was all night on the route, in consequence of the numerous detentions, and had no sleep. The demonstrations since Monday having been very successful in drawing the very marked attention of the enemy, I have directed the return to-morrow of the commands. One captain, 1 sergeant, and 11 privates were captured on the other bank in the rifle-pits. Some of our horse got over. The river was high, not fordable, and filled with obstructions, so that they could not bridge it under fire. Our loss, 1 killed and 11 wounded. Enemy's loss considerable.

JOHN J. PECK,
Major-General.

Major-General DIX.   .

—

SUFFOLK, VA., *December* 12, 1862.

General Ferry's demonstration is having the effect of drawing troops in that quarter, so that on the whole line we shall greatly benefit General Foster. He reports the river all blocked with trees and other obstructions; long lines of rifle-pits heavily lined with sharpshooters. Brigade of cavalry has arrived at Ivor. This last was reported to me by a man I have, and is confirmed. Has not crossed. Sharp firing now.

JOHN J. PECK,
Major-General.

Major-General DIX.

—

SUFFOLK, VA., *December* 12, 1862.

Franklin has been heavily re-enforced. Pryor was at Carrsville on Tuesday, and remained with 5,000 infantry, with his advance near Holland's Corners. Spear is at Carrsville watching the flank of Ferry. This corroborates my information sent you from deserters and contrabands. Firing in direction of Zuni.

JOHN J. PECK,
Major-General.

Major-General DIX.

—

[Addenda.]

Memorandum of understanding between Captain Flusser and General Foster, December 6, 1862.

1st. Captain Flusser to furnish pilots for the Chowan River to the army transports.

2d. On the 11th to be in the Upper Chowan with one or two gunboats; more gunboats if he can furnish them. These are to be re-enforced by two or more army gunboats, to be under Captain Flusser's command.

3d. To communicate with Major-General Peck, commanding at Suffolk, by means of parties sent from Winfield. The letter to be so written that if it falls into the hands of the enemy he will think that the attack is to be made on the Blackwater in earnest instead of being a demonstration. The word "co-operate" will express this idea to General Peck in speaking of your assistance. This letter must be sent at once. The general impression to be given to those who may communicate to the enemy is that a serious attack is to be made on the Blackwater.

4th. The coal-schooner to be brought up by Captain Graves is to be sent back to Roanoke Island as soon as the immediate wants of the gunboats are satisfied.

5th. The demonstration on the Blackwater is to continue for one week from the 11th, unless Captain Flusser hears from General Foster to the contrary, and even then the strong show of force is to continue for a few days longer, and even until General Foster sends to inform him that the main attack is completed. The force then is to make some hostile demonstration on the 11th, to keep it up until the 19th, and then to maintain a hostile attitude until he hears from General Foster.

6th. General Foster will write to General Peck through the canal, but this is not to prevent Captain Flusser sending a letter also. The rough draught of a suitable letter is inclosed.

C. W. FLUSSER,
Lieutenant-Commander.
J. G. FOSTER,
Major-General, Commanding.

Memorandum of understanding between Major-General Peck and General Foster, December 2, 1862.

1. Wessells' brigade to be at the landing on the Chowan, near Gatesville, some time during the day or night of the 6th (weather permitting), the transports being there to receive them.

JOHN J. PECK,
Major-General.

2. It is probable that a movement will commence as follows, viz:
3. Get down at night to mouth of North River, Albemarle Sound.
4. Start them—the transports—to the Chowan.
5. Arrive at mouth of river (Chowan).
6. Come up river.
7. Embark.
8. Start for W.
9. Arrive at W.
10. Prepare for march.
11. Start out 8 miles.
12. March to K.
13. Attack K.
14. March toward G.
15. Make preliminary attack.
16. Forcible attack.
17.
18. } Pretty sure of being before G.
19.

J. G. FOSTER,
Major-General, Commanding.

—

SUFFOLK, VA., *December* 12, 1862.

Maj. Gen. J. G. FOSTER:

Yours of the 11th just received.* My troops left yesterday, and are fighting now.

Captain Flusser has misunderstood the tenor of my message. My intention was to release him from co-operation on F. [Franklin], as

---

* Not found.

that was not the point I had decided to strike. Lest the courier should be captured I could not specify the place on the Blackwater.

A copy of my communication of this date is inclosed, which will more fully inform you.

In haste,

> JOHN J. PECK,
> *Major-General.*

—

SUFFOLK, *December* 12, 1862.

Maj. Gen. J. G. FOSTER,
    Commanding Department of North Carolina:

The brigade of Wessells was ahead of time and reached you in good order and will do good service.

My pontoons did not arrive. I found the enemy re-enforcing F. after we took the Rocket Battery from him, and I resolved to strike elsewhere, and communicated to Captain Flusser my intentions.

Accordingly, on Monday, I sent parties to the Chowan to look for crossings, &c.; on Tuesday morning shelled South Quay, &c. These operations, as intended, brought additional force to F. and the lower river line.

At noon yesterday all my available force left for the demonstrations on the river. The command should have been across Blackwater at daylight, but has been delayed by the terrible condition of the roads, five hours having been required to move 4 miles.

At this hour (11 a. m.) firing is heard from the vicinity of Zuni, where the Petersburg Railroad crosses the Blackwater. Unless we draw very heavily from Weldon and Petersburg by rail some results should attend in addition to aiding your operations, the success of which I have much at heart.

Your favors of the 5th and 8th arrived at noon yesterday.

In haste, very truly,

> JOHN J. PECK,
> *Major-General.*

P. S.—Three thousand were reported in F. on the 2d, and now 12,000 at F. and vicinity. Heavy additions have been made all along the river up to Zuni.

—

SUFFOLK, VA., *December* 12, 1862.

Major-General FOSTER,
    New Berne, N. C.:

Have sent communications to you via Norfolk and Winfield, giving you some details of my series of demonstrations. When we parted the enemy had in Franklin about 3,000, and perhaps as many more in the vicinity, and I was inclined to strike there. Finding the river wide and deep below and no pontoons to be obtained, and re-enforcements arriving there, I was compelled to change my point of attack, and accordingly released Captain Flusser from his co-operation. Fearing capture of the messengers, I did not tell the captain where I should make the demonstrations.

On Monday I sent cavalry and artillery to the Chowan, at Manny's Ferry, with a view to draw the enemy's attention in that quarter, which was entirely successful. About 1 a. m. on Tuesday the camp in the vicinity of South Quay was shelled.

Yesterday I sent a large force, cavalry and artillery, in the vicinity of Carrsville and Franklin, and from Colonel Spear, commanding, I learn that some 12,000 men are in that immediate locality. His force is still in that quarter.

Besides the movement toward Franklin I sent yesterday noon every available man to demonstrate near the crossing of the Petersburg Railway and the Blackwater River. The command is still in that direction and has occupied the attention of the enemy very much, who have been re-enforcing by railway, &c., all day.

Truly, yours,

JOHN J. PECK,
Major-General.

No. 3.

Report of Capt. J. H. Sikes, Company D, Seventh Confederate States Cavalry.

SIR : According to your order I have the honor to transmit to you a report of the engagement my command had with the enemy at Joyner's Ford, Blackwater River, Virginia, on December 12:

I was ordered by Col. [W. C.] Claiborne to leave Ivor on the 10th and repair to Joyner's (distant 6 miles) with my company and take command at that place. About 1 o'clock on the morning of the 12th I received information that the enemy were moving in the direction of the ford in considerable force and to prepare for an early attack. My camp was about 1 mile west of the ford. I ordered my men into line. After inspection I marched to Joyner's house, 200 yards west of the ford. I there halted, dispatched to the guard (who were in the rifle-pit) the information I had received and that I had arrived at the house. After light sufficient had appeared we discovered the enemy had taken position in our front, and for 200 yards above and below the ford, behind trees, stumps, and logs, of which there are an abundance, it being a cypress swamp. Their artillery were in position on an eminence in a field some 400 yards from the river. I divided my company, taking 15 men with me in the rifle-pit (which was rudely and hastily constructed) and ordered Lieut. [P. A. S.] Morris [Company D], with 12 or 15 men, to deploy down the river below the ford to watch the enemy and report to me if they attempted to cross. I found 9 picket guard in the rifle-pit (Capt. [F. E.] Burke, of the same regiment). Immediately on my entering the rifle-pit the enemy opened upon us a heavy fire of small-arms. We replied with equally as good will, and, am proud to say, with a great deal better effect. After receiving their fire for some time and discovering superior numbers, I dispatched to Colonel Claiborne my condition. After an almost incessant fire for more than an hour from their infantry, and failing to dislodge us, they ceased firing for a short time for the purpose, as the New York Herald's correspondent states, of a novel cavalry charge. He states General Peck ordered two companies of infantry to be mounted behind two of cavalry, charge across the river, dismount the infantry, drive us from our position or force us to surrender. They formed in a field to our left and came down the public road (which runs at right angles with the river until within 200 yards of the ford, when it turns to the left and runs nearly parallel with the stream) in columns of fours in beautiful and almost perfect order. When they arrived opposite the rifle-pits and were in the act of forming platoons (as they could have crossed in columns of platoons, the ford being sufficiently wide) we opened a volley upon them which had the effect of emptying a number of saddles and throwing the whole into disorder. While attempting to reform we fired so rapidly upon them that without orders, so far as we could hear (and we were sufficiently near to hear every order distinctly, the river not being over 30 yards wide), they right-about and made the quickest possible time to get into the thick woods.

After the retreat of the cavalry the enemy, who were posted behind trees and stumps, poured a perfect volley of oaths and imprecations upon us, expressive alike of their cowardice and degradation. They soon renewed the attack with both infantry and artillery, and proving unsuccessful from their position, they moved two howitzers down the road within 100 yards of the rifle-pit and opened with shell and canister, which they kept playing, I suppose, for more than an hour, during which time we took chances and fired occasionally. About this time, fearing they would make another charge under the protection of their artillery, I dispatched 3 men to camps to secure our horses, as I was determined to hold the pass to the last extremity. I dispatched 2 also up the river to watch their movements. They soon returned with the information that the enemy were crossing above the ford. I immediately moved up the river with all my force except 3 men, whom I left in the rifle-pit with orders to fire as rapidly as possible. My object was to prevent their crossing until re-enforcements could arrive, which I was momentarily expecting. The stream divides just above the ford and forms a small island. They had only crossed one branch and had halted on the island and discovering our movements returned in their boats.

While I was preparing to meet them above they had effected a crossing below the ford by means of pontoon boats at a deep bend of the river under the cover of dense thicket. As soon as I discovered they had landed we started in double-quick for Joyner's house, as that was our only chance to make a stand, they having landed ten to our one. They discovered our design and rushed to cut us off, and succeeded in doing so. Our only chance for defense then was a rail fence diagonally to our right. The labor and exposure we had been subject to for eight or ten hours had very much exhausted us. We were nearly surrounded before arriving at the fence. The enemy halted and fired (one company). The result was one of my men was instantly killed. I received a severe wound in the muscles of the right shoulder. I also received a wound in the hand while in the rifle-pit, which caused considerable loss of blood. I fell on receiving the wound in the shoulder and my men halted around me, and in a few moments we were surrounded by three companies of the Thirteenth Indiana Regiment. We were immediately taken over the river and hurried in the direction of Suffolk. Soon after we had crossed the river our artillery came up and opened upon the enemy, which had the effect to hasten their move toward Suffolk.

Our loss was as follows: Killed—Private Thomas Barker; dangerously wounded—Corpl. W. R .Green; taken prisoners—Privates William H. Dean, G. W. Gafford, Thomas J. Hasty, Chandler Smith, M. B. Smith, Jackson C. Spinks, George W. Baily, A. M. Brady, Jeff. Whitehead, and W. B. Whitehead.

Lieutenant Morris' men were so posted down the river as only to bring 3 of his men in the action.

My whole force in the rifle-pit did not at any time exceed 24, making a total of only 27 actually engaged with the enemy. Before our capture my forces were greatly reduced by sending couriers and men to secure horses, &c.

I feel it but just to state here that more resolute and determined bravery could not have been shown than that which was exhibited by our little band in defending the ford for more than four hours against an enemy of an overwhelming force. Their forces cannot be accurately stated, but from their own published accounts they had at and near the ford eight regiments of infantry, two regiments of cavalry, and one battery of artillery. They report men killed and wounded out of five different regiments.

The enemy's loss has been variously estimated by citizens living on their side of the river. Some say they lost over 100 in killed and wounded. We may safely say from what we saw and heard while we were prisoners that their loss was all of 50 men killed and wounded.

The object of the enemy was very apparent from the fact they had a large train of wagons, fifteen or twenty pontoon-boats (a portion of which they burned on their retreat), quite a number of ambulances, and everything necessary for the advance of a well-appointed army.

Before closing this report I feel it due the officers in whose hands we fell to mention that we received every kindness we could expect. We lacked nothing for our comfort they could reasonably supply.

Very respectfully, your obedient servant,

J. H. SIKES,
Captain Company D, Seventh C. S. Cavalry.

Maj. Gen. S. G. FRENCH, *Commanding Department.*

[Indorsement.]

HEADQUARTERS,
Petersburg, Va., March 14, 1863.

Respectfully forwarded. This is a record of a very successful skirmish on the Blackwater, in which Captain Sikes and his men greatly distinguished themselves.

S. G. FRENCH,
Major-General, Commanding

DECEMBER 10, 1862.—Attack on Plymouth, N. C.

REPORTS.*

No. 1.—Capt. Barnabas Ewer, jr., Third Massachusetts Infantry.
No. 2.—First Lieut. Jonathan T. Mizell, Company C, First North Carolina Infantry (Union).
No. 3.—Maj. Gen. Samuel G. French, C. S. Army.

No. 1.

Reports of Capt. Barnabas Ewer, jr., Third Massachusetts Infantry.

PLYMOUTH, N. C., *December 10, 1862.*

SIR: At 4.30 o'clock this morning our pickets were driven in by a force (as near as we can estimate) of four companies of infantry and one of cavalry and four pieces of artillery. They came in immediately, driving all before them. Our forces (some 200 men), after making all the

---

* For reports of Lieut. Commander Flusser and Acting Volunteer Lieutenant Behm, U. S. Navy, see Annual Report of the Secretary of the Navy, December 7, 1863.

resistance possible, took refuge in the custom-house. The artillery was planted so as to fire upon us there, by which means considerable damage was done. The town was fired in many places, and this morning is pretty much destroyed, including the building used for headquarters and all things therein.

At the third discharge of the enemy's artillery the gunboat Southfield received a shot through the boiler, which disabled her, but her captain kept up as brisk firing as his crippled condition would allow. The gunboat Commodore Perry hearing the firing came to our assistance, but was too late, as the enemy had left.

At roll-call this morning some 30 men were missing; several are wounded, one dangerously. I am in hopes some of the missing will come in, but some are no doubt prisoners. A number of the enemy are known to have been shot, as they were seen to fall, but were carried away by their comrades.

Further particulars will be forwarded as soon as we can obtain them.

Respectfully, your obedient servant,

B. EWER, Jr.,
Captain, Commanding Post.

General FOSTER.

—

HEADQUARTERS,
Plymouth, N. C., December 11, 1862—7 p. m.

SIR: I send this in addition to my first (yesterday's) report of the attack upon this place. The attack was made by cavalry, infantry, and artillery, their combined force being greatly superior to our own. By their artillery they were enabled to cripple the only gunboat (Southfield) then near the town, and to inflict considerable injury upon the custom-house, where the greater part of our forces had taken refuge.

After the Southfield had drifted a short distance down the river she was met by the Commodore Perry, who towed her up, and the two boats now lie opposite the town. The rebels had already left after having been here over an hour.

The town is more than half burned. All the principal buildings on the street where the hotel was situated are gone. Everything in headquarters was burned, including the record of those who had taken the oath of allegiance, and some muster and pay rolls which were to be forwarded to other garrisons in this part of the State. Company I lost 15 missing, 1 of whom is doubtless killed, and 2 wounded, 1 dangerously.

All this day they have been stationed just outside the town, their pickets being within a mile of the river. We have not sufficient force to warrant an attack upon them, being simply able to perform guard and picket duty, and even this comes so often that it is seriously affecting the health of the men, and in my judgment the necessity of sending more men to assist in that duty is quite apparent, and if we are expected to do anything more than simply to stand watch over the site of the town a much larger force seems indispensable. The citizens are pretty generally fleeing, and not much besides negroes will soon be left. The gunboats are ready, however, and by their assistance we will try to give the rebels a reception worthy of the cause, should they again become the attacking party.

Very respectfully, your obedient servant,

B. EWER, Jr.,
Captain, Commanding Post.

General FOSTER.

[Indorsement.]

Write to Captain Flusser, asking for a statement of the way the troops behaved, &c.*

J. G. F.

—

HEADQUARTERS,
Plymouth, N. C., December 30, 1862.

SIR: I have to report that on the morning of December 10, a little before 5 o'clock, our pickets were driven in by a force consisting (as near as we can learn from apparently reliable sources) of at least 600 men, composed of infantry, cavalry, and artillery. After making all possible resistance our forces, of not more than 150 men in line, mostly infantry, retreated to the custom-house. This movement was made in accordance with the plan of defense which has always contemplated the firing by the gunboats upon the town if attacked by a large force. The artillery was planted so as to fire upon the gunboat. Only one boat (Southfield, Captain Behm) was here (although there are generally two and frequently more), and she arrived the day before. The captain was not acquainted with the avenues of approach to the town. The third shot from the artillery passed through the boiler of the boat, letting the steam out and crippling her. She slowly drifted down the stream, firing as she went.

The enemy proceeded to set fire to the town, and after an hour thus spent, during which our men annoyed them as they could, they hurriedly withdrew.

Three of Company I were wounded (one of whom has since died) and 15 are missing, one of whom is supposed to be dead and the others prisoners.

I herewith transmit Lieutenant Fogerty's report of his loss. I also send estimates of the loss sustained by each company.†

Several of the enemy were seen to fall, and loud calls were made for their ambulances. Several deserters have since arrived, who report that seven companies of the Seventeenth North Carolina Regiment composed the infantry.

I am, very respectfully, your obedient servant,
B. EWER, JR.,
Captain, Commanding Post.

Colonel RICHMOND.

[Inclosure.]

PLYMOUTH, *December* 30, 1862.

DEAR SIR: In obedience to your order I send you the correct list of the men wounded and taken prisoners in my company at the attack on Plymouth the night of the 10th. We had 1 man wounded, 3 taken prisoners, and none killed. This is a correct statement of the attack.

Your obedient servant,
THOMAS J. FOGERTY,
First Lieutenant, Comdg. First North Carolina Cavalry.

Captain EWER.

---

* See "Addenda," p. 48.   †Not found.

[Addenda.]

UNITED STATES STEAMER COMMODORE PERRY,
Plymouth, N. C., December 30, 1862.

Maj. Gen. J. G. FOSTER,
   Comdg. Dept. of North Carolina, New Berne, N. C. :

DEAR GENERAL: Admiral Lee wishes me to remove the guns from Cobb's Point and further demolish the battery, if you have no objection.

Concerning the behavior of the troops here the other day, I hear that Sergeant Clift and some of the North Carolinians behaved well. I found some of the Massachusetts men and some of the North Carolinians at the custom-house when I arrived.

Captain Ewer was on board the Southfield, 1½ miles down the river. I asked where his men were, and he said he did not know, but hoped most of them were in the swamp. The fact is, so soon as the Southfield fell back (which she ought maybe not to have done) Ewer got frightened, left his men, and went on board. The whole affair was disgraceful, and the more so, as it has since been ascertained that the attacking party, those who entered the town, did not exceed 200 men. I shall write you again to-morrow.

Kind regards to your staff.

Sincerely, yours,

C. W. FLUSSER,
Lieutenant-Commander.

No. 2.

Report of First Lieut. Jonathan T. Mizell, Company C, First North Carolina Infantry (Union).

PLYMOUTH, N. C., *December* 16, 1862.

SIR : I resume my seat for the purpose of informing you of the attack the rebels made upon our little village, and I should judge from all the information I can gather and from what I saw they numbered some 450 strong—300 infantry, 3 pieces of artillery, and 70 cavalry. About 4.30 o'clock they drove our pickets in with a volley from their infantry, and in fifteen minutes our company was in line, and as the odds were too great for our little force I deemed it most prudent to fall back in the rear of the custom-house, and before we could all get in the building they had planted their pieces of artillery on the wharf and had fired some three rounds at the Southfield, and the third fire disabled her boiler. After they found she was disabled and dropped down the river they moved their field pieces on the corner opposite headquarters, but not without loss of some men. They commenced to shell the custom-house, and as they passed down the street in small groups our men would let the lead fly at them to the best advantage, and I do assure you our little North Carolina volunteers behaved most nobly. They were calm and collected, much more so than I expected. Sergeant Clift was informed that the rebels lost 15 killed and 30 wounded, some mortally and some slightly, and the information he got yesterday corroborates the other statements we received. I heard they had four wagon loads of killed and wounded. Our men never received a scratch. The North Carolina cavalry lost 3 men prisoners and 1 wounded. Company I, of Massachusetts, lost 14 prisoners, 1 wounded, and 1 missing. One man on the Southfield lost a leg. We sustained considerable loss from fire. The best and most of the principal part of the town are burned up. The families of our men were left without a change of clothing, and they are in a distressed condition. Besides, we have lost all of our books, pay and muster rolls, and a quantity of clothing belonging to the men; some ammunition. They captured nothing from the Government, but pillaged private dwellings, &c. I believe I have given all of the particulars that I can think of at present.

I must speak of something else in your last communication. You wrote to send the names of the twelve men that are to be transferred to the cavalry company, and inclosed you will find them on a piece of paper, and when you write to me I would be glad if you will send me the original muster-roll, so we can get the time of enlistment of them, as all of ours were destroyed by fire in Sergeant Clift's house, with all of his property. Also please send me a morning-report book; monthly and weekly reports also. I should be glad to have a descriptive and company clothing book; and by complying you will greatly oblige.

Yours, respectfully, &c.,

J. T. MIZELL,
First Lieut., Comdg. Company C, First N. C. Infantry.

Col. E. E. POTTER.

P. S.—DEAR SIR: We have not yet received our equipments that were left at Roanoke Island, and as soon as I can make it convenient I shall dispatch Sergeant Clift for them. Please answer soon.

No. 3.

Report of Maj. Gen. Samuel G. French, C. S. Army.

PETERSBURG, VA., *December* 12, 1862.

Plymouth, N. C., was attacked by our forces under Lieut. Col. [John C.] Lamb, of the Seventeenth North Carolina Regiment, and captured on the 10th instant at 5 a. m. The enemy's loss severe; 25 prisoners and 75 negroes taken. Town reduced to ashes. We had 1 captain and 6 men wounded; none killed. The gunboat protecting the town was driven away disabled.

S. G. FRENCH,
Major-General.

General S. COOPER.

DECEMBER 11–15, 1862.—Reconnaissance from Yorktown to Gloucester, Matthews, King and Queen, and Middlesex Counties Va.

Report of Brig. Gen. Henry M. Naglee, U. S. Army.

HEADQUARTERS FIRST BRIGADE,
Yorktown, Va., December 16, 1862.

COLONEL: I would respectfully report that, being in command during the absence of General Keyes and believing a little active employment would be of service to the men, on the 11th instant, at 6.30 a. m., I ordered the Fifty-second Pennsylvania, Colonel Dodge; Eleventh Maine, Colonel Plaisted; the One hundredth New York, Colonel Dandy; the Fifty-sixth New York, Major Wheeler; Battery H, First New York,

Lieutenant M nk, and two squadrons of the Fifth Pennsylvania Cavalry, Major McCandless, to proceed to Gloucester Court-House, where I followed and arrived at 6 p. m.

The Fifth Pennsylvania Cavalry were thrown out at 1 a. m. of the 12th to the North End Mill, on the Piankatank River road, preparatory to the landing a few hours later of Captain Hall, with 90 of the Sixth New York Cavalry, below Matthews Court-House, where he had been conveyed and landed in an admirable manner by Capt. Foxhall Parker, under the protection of the crew and guns of the Mahaska, assisted by one company of the Independent Battalion of New York, Colonel Comfort.

The only opposition here made was by some 40 rangers, who immediately fell back, and continued to do so as Captain Hall approached, repeatedly dispersing into the woods and swamps whenever he charged upon them and as often reassembling.

After the cavalry arrived and reported to me, on the afternoon of the 12th instant, the Fifth was ordered to Wood's Cross-Roads and found the picket of the King and Queen Cavalry advanced to that place. The main road to Scuffletown was, on the morning of the 13th, thoroughly examined beyond that place, and after finding no enemy in force in that direction, with 40 of the Sixth New York and the cavalry of Major McCandless I pushed the reconnaissance in the direction of Buena Vista, the headquarters of the King and Queen Cavalry. At 2 miles from that place the Fifth Pennsylvania were held in reserve, and Captain Hall, with 30 men, was sent to feel the position of the King and Queen Cavalry. He soon came in contact with their pickets, but they gave way; he got within 300 yards of their main force, but they would not stand. After repeated attempts he got within 150 yards and dismounted; fired a volley, which wounding several, they again retreated. Hall mounted and pursued and ran them through their encampment and 2 miles beyond it to Centreville. I then directed the barracks, stables, and all of their commissary stores to be burned and some arms found on the premises to be brought away. It being now late in the afternoon, the One hundredth New York, Colonel Dandy, was ordered forward to Wood's Cross-Roads and the cavalry to bivouac for the night at that place.

On the following day, at 6 a. m., Major McCandless' cavalry and those of Captain Hall were sent into Middlesex County, some 6 miles beyond the Dragon Ordinary, to destroy a large tannery, which was manufacturing a large quantity of leather for the use of the rebel army, the machinery, buildings, and 2,000 tanned hides being destroyed. Several wagon loads of finished leather were brought away, with the proprietors of the establishment, whom, I would recommend, should take the oath not to aid the rebel army in future.

On the night of the 14th the One hundredth New York, followed by the Sixth New York Cavalry, retired from Wood's Cross-Roads, by the way of Belle Roy, while the rest of the command marched directly to Gloucester Point, followed by Major McCandless, and by 4 p. m. of the 15th instant, with the exception of the cavalry, all had returned to their encampments at Yorktown, without the loss of a man or an animal. We found irregular cavalry (rangers) formed in Matthews, Gloucester, King and Queen, and Middlesex. The most of them were not in uniform, and were engaged in catching runaway negroes and in forwarding supplies to Richmond. As soon as they were attacked they scattered, and it was impossible to pursue them. The only means I could advise to meet the difficulty was to take horses and arms from the citizens, which, from the effect immediately apparent, I believe the most effectual.

I found several large herds of hogs and sheep on the road to the commissariat at Richmond, and I did not hesitate to turn their direction toward our lines. With almost equal want of hesitation I directed my quartermaster to take horses, cattle, sheep, and cows from those who had an abundance, and report to me an accurate account of everything taken, and from whom taken, that a proper record be kept to meet any demands hereafter.

Among some 15 or 20 prisoners taken, one-half of them were of the army. I found Captain Seawell, a prominent citizen of the counties named that dragged Virginia into secession, and who I found engaged in forming new companies of rangers.

I take great pleasure in referring to the conduct of Captain Hall, who charged and ran five times his number of the King and Queen Cavalry through their encampment. His command marched over 90 miles, and performed their duties to my entire satisfaction.

Major McCandless deserves special notice, but I regret that I cannot include his command, some of whom procured whisky by threatening the families of private residences.

To Colonel Plaisted and his regiment I return unqualified thanks for the unexceptionable manner they performed every duty.

The military conduct of the rest of the command was good, but much censure is due to the officers and their men for petty thieving practiced upon the people of the country. The conduct of the Fifty-sixth New York was disgraceful in this respect, and I have arrested the commanding officer and shall prefer charges against him.

In conclusion I would report that the four days' reconnaissance to Matthews, Gloucester, King and Queen, and Middlesex was entirely successful, and that the objects for which it was made have been fully accomplished.

Very respectfully, &c.,

HENRY M. NAGLEE,
Brigadier-General.

Lieut. Col. D. T. VAN BUREN,
Assistant Adjutant-General, Department of Virginia.

DECEMBER 11–20, 1862.—Expedition from New Berne to Goldsborough, N. C.

SUMMARY OF THE PRINCIPAL EVENTS.

Dec. 11–12, 1862.—Skirmishes on the Kinston Road.
    12–15, 1862.—Naval operations on the Neuse River.
    13–14, 1862.—Skirmishes at Southwest Creek.
    14, 1862.—Engagement at Kinston.
    15, 1862.—Affair at White Hall Bridge.
    16, 1862.—Engagement at White Hall.
        Affairs at Mount Olive Station and Goshen Swamp.
    17, 1862.—Raid on Dudley Station.
        Engagement at Goldsborough Bridge.
        Skirmish at Thompson's Bridge.

REPORTS.*

No. 1.—Maj. Gen. John G. Foster, U. S. Army, commanding the Department of North Carolina.

No. 2.—Return of Casualties in the Union forces.

No. 3.—Capt. David A. Taylor, Third New York Light Artillery, Chief Signal Officer,

No. 4.—Col. James H. Ledlie, Third New York Light Artillery, Chief of Artillery, commanding Artillery Brigade, of operations December 11–17.

No. 5.—Capt. Edwin S. Jenney, Battery F, Third New York Light Artillery, of engagements at Kinston and White Hall, December 14 and 16.

No. 6.—Maj. Chas. Fitz Simmons, Third New York Cavalry, of operations Dec. 15 and 17.

No. 7.—Maj. Jeptha Garrard, Third New York Cavalry, of operations Dec. 15–17.

No. 8.—Capt. John F. Moschell, Third New York Cavalry, of operations Dec. 11–16.

No. 9.—Capt. Newton Hall, Third New York Cavalry, of operations December 12–16.

No. 10.—Capt. Ferris Jacobs, jr., Third New York Cavalry, of operations Dec. 13–14.

No. 11.—Capt. George W. Cole, Third New York Cavalry, of operations Dec. 12–16.

No. 12.—Col. Thomas J. C. Amory, Seventeenth Massachusetts Infantry, commanding First Brigade, First Division, of engagements at Kinston, White Hall, and Goldsborough Bridge, December 14, 16, and 17.

No. 13.—Lieut. Col. John F. Fellows, Seventeenth Massachusetts Infantry, of engagements at Kinston, White Hall, and Goldsborough Bridge, Dec. 14, 16, and 17.

No. 14.—Maj. John G. Chambers, Twenty-third Massachusetts Infantry, of operations December 11–16.

No. 15.—Col. Charles L. Holbrook, Forty-third Massachusetts Infantry.

No. 16.—Col. Charles R. Codman, Forty-fifth Massachusetts Infantry, of engagements at Kinston and White Hall, December 14 and 16.

No. 17.—Col. Augustus B. R. Sprague, Fifty-first Massachusetts Infantry.

No. 18.—Col. Thomas G. Stevenson, Twenty-fourth Massachusetts Infantry, commanding Second Brigade, of engagements at Kinston, White Hall, and Goldsborough Bridge, December 14, 16, and 17.

No. 19.—Lieut. Col. Robert Leggett, Tenth Connecticut Infantry, of engagement at Kinston, December 14.

No. 20.—Col. Horace C. Lee, Twenty-seventh Massachusetts Infantry, commanding Third Brigade.

No. 21.—Maj. Josiah Pickett, Twenty-fifth Massachusetts Infantry.

No. 22.—Lieut. Col. William S. Shurtleff, Forty-sixth Massachusetts Infantry.

No. 23.—Col. Charles A. Heckman, Ninth New Jersey Infantry, First Brigade, Second Division.

---

* For report of Commander A. Murray, U. S. Navy, see Annual Report of the Secretary of the Navy, December 7, 1863.

No. 24.—Maj. Abram Zabriskie, Ninth New Jersey Infantry.

No. 25.—Brig. Gen. Henry W. Wessells, U. S. Army, commanding Third B:igade, Peck's Division, of operations December 5–21.

No. 26.—Lieut. Col. Abijah J. Wellman, Eighty-fifth New York Infantry, of engagement at Kinston, December 14.

No. 27.—Col. Lewis C. Hunt, Ninety-second New York Infantry, of engagement at Kinston, December 14.

No. 28.—Capt. George W. Hinds, Ninety-sixth New York Infantry, of engagement at Kinston, December 14.

No. 29.—Col. Joshua B. Howell, Eighty-fifth Pennsylvania Infantry, of operations December 13–17.

No. 30.—Maj. Alexander W. Taylor. One hundred and first Pennsylvania Infantry, of engagement at Kinston, December 14.

No. 31.—Lieut. Col. Wilson C. Maxwell, One hundred and third Pennsylvania Infantry, of engagement at Kinston, December 14.

No. 32.—Lieut. Col. Horace A. Manchester, First New York Marine Artillery, of naval operations on the Neuse River, December 12–15.

No. 33.—Maj. Gen. Gustavus W. Smith, C. S. Army, commanding Department of North Carolina and Southern Virginia, of operations December 13–18.

No. 34.—Lieut. Col. Walter H. Stevens, C. S. Engineers, of operations December 16–17.

No. 35.—Brig. Gen. Nathan G. Evans, C. S. Army, commanding Brigade, of operations December 13–17.

No. 36.—Col. Peter Mallett, North Carolina Battalion, of engagement at Kinston, December 14.

No. 37.—Brig. Gen. Thomas L. Clingman, C. S. Army, commanding Brigade, of engagement at Goldsborough Bridge, December 17.

No. 38.—Lieut. Col. Stephen D. Pool, C. S. Artillery, of engagement at Goldsborough Bridge, December 17.

No. 39.—Brig. Gen. Beverly H. Robertson, C. S. Army, commanding Brigade, of engagement at White Hall, December 16.

No. 1.

Reports of Maj. Gen. John G. Foster, U. S. Army, commanding the Department of North Carolina.

HEADQUARTERS DEPARTMENT OF NORTH CAROLINA,
Kinston, December 14, 1862.

GENERAL : I have the honor to inform you that I left New Berne for this place on the 11th, but that owing to the bad roads and consequent delays to train, &c., I did not reach Southwest Creek (5 miles from this town) till the afternoon of the 13th. The enemy were posted there, but by a heavy artillery fire in front and vigorous infantry attack on either flank I succeeded in forcing a passage and without much loss.

This morning I advanced on this town and found the enemy strongly posted at a defile through a marsh bordering a creek. The position was so well chosen that very little of our artillery could be brought in play. The main attack therefore was made by the infantry, assisted by a few guns pushed forward on the roads. We succeeded, after five hours' hard fight, in driving the enemy from their position. We followed them rapidly to the river; the bridge over the Neuse at this point was prepared for firing and was fired in six places, but we were so close behind them that we saved the bridge. The enemy retreated precipitately by the Goldsborough and ———— roads. Their force was about 6,000 men, with twenty pieces of artillery. The result is we have taken Kinston, captured eleven pieces of artillery, taken 400 or 500 prisoners, and found a large amount of quartermaster's and commissary stores. Our loss will not probably exceed 200 killed and wounded.

I march to-morrow at daylight on Goldsborough. From that point I return to New Berne, whence I will make a more detailed report.

I am, general, with great respect, your obedient servant,

J. G. FOSTER.

Major-General HALLECK.

—

HEADQUARTERS DEPARTMENT OF NORTH CAROLINA,
New Berne, N. C., December 20, 1862.

GENERAL: Referring to mine of the 14th instant, from Kinston, I have the honor to inform you that I succeeded in reaching Goldsborough and in burning the railroad bridge of the Weldon and Wilmington Railroad at that point. The bridge at Mount Olive I also destroyed, and about 4 miles of track. I encountered and defeated the enemy at Kinston, White Hall, Thompson's Bridge, and Goldsborough.

My loss in killed, wounded, and missing will not exceed 400.* The enemy's loss I have not ascertained. I have taken nine pieces of artillery, about 500 prisoners, and destroyed some quartermaster's and commissary stores.

I am, with great respect, your obedient servant,

J. G. FOSTER.

Maj. Gen. H. W. HALLECK.

—

HEADQUARTERS DEPARTMENT OF NORTH CAROLINA,
New Berne, N. C., December 27, 1862.

GENERAL: Referring to my letters of December 10, 14, and 20, I have the honor to report that I left this town at 8 a. m. of the 11th with the following forces:

General Wessells' brigade of General Peck's division (kindly loaned to me), Colonel Amory's brigade, Colonel Stevenson's brigade, Colonel Lee's brigade—in all, about 10,000 infantry; six batteries Third New York Artillery, 30 guns; Belger's battery First Rhode Island Artillery, 6 guns; section of Twenty-fourth New York Independent Battery, 2 guns; section of Twenty-third New York Independent Battery, 2 guns—total, 40 guns; the Third New York Cavalry, about 640 men.

We marched the first day on the main Kinston road about 14 miles, when, finding the road obstructed by felled trees for half a mile and over, I bivouacked for the night, and had the obstructions removed during the night by the pioneers.

I pushed on the next morning at daylight. My cavalry advance encountered the enemy when about 4 miles from the bivouac of the previous night, and after a sharp but brief skirmish the enemy were routed with some loss. On arriving at the Vine Swamp road I ordered Captain Hall, with three companies of cavalry, to push on up the main Kinston road as a demonstration, while the main column proceeded by the Vine Swamp road to the left, thereby avoiding the obstructions and the enemy on the main road. Captain Hall encountered the enemy in some force, but after a severe fight whipped them, taking 18 prisoners and killing a number. The march of the main column was somewhat delayed by the bridge over Beaver Creek being destroyed. This was rebuilt, and I pushed on, leaving a regiment (Fifty-first Massachusetts) and a section of artillery (Twenty-third New York) at the bridge to hold it and to protect the intersection of the main road and the road I was on, to

---

* But see revised statement, p. 60.

support Captain Hall, and to prevent any force driving him back and occupying the cross-roads in the rear. The main column pushed on about 4 miles and bivouacked for the night. There was some cavalry skirmishing during the day.

On Saturday, the 13th, we again started, leaving the second main road, the one I was on, to the right, and leaving at this intersection the Forty-sixth Massachusetts and one section of artillery (Twenty-fourth New York) to hold the position, and feint on the second main road. We reached Southwest Creek, the bridge over which was destroyed, and the enemy posted on the opposite bank, some 400 strong, with three pieces of artillery. The creek was not fordable, and ran at the foot of a deep ravine, making a very bad position for us. I ordered a battery in as good a position as could be obtained, and under their fire the Ninth New Jersey, which had the advance, pushed gallantly across the creek by swimming, by fragments of the bridge and by a mill-dam, and formed on the opposite bank. At the same time the Eighty-fifth Pennsylvania, of General Wessells' brigade, forced a passage by the felling of trees and fording about half a mile below the bridge, and engaged the enemy's left, who thereupon retired and deserted his breastworks. I had ordered the Twenty-third Massachusetts, of Colonel Amory's brigade, to cross at the mill to support the Ninth New Jersey, and also crossed the remainder of General Wessells' brigade. Colonel Heckman, with the Ninth New Jersey, advanced and was fired upon, when about 1 mile from the creek, with canister and musketry. The regiment charged at double-quick, drove the enemy, took some prisoners, and captured a 6-pounder gun, caisson, &c., complete. General Wessells bivouacked on the farther side of the creek with the Ninth in the advance. The balance of the command, with the artillery, remained on this side of the creek. The Ninth New Jersey; Company K, Third New York Cavalry, and Morrison's battery Third New York Artillery, had quite a skirmish with the enemy, but drove him and encamped for the night. From the south side of the creek I sent a company of cavalry to strike and proceed up the Kinston road, No. 2 (I was on No. 3). The company proceeded up the road toward Kinston, and found the enemy posted by a bridge, which was prepared to be destroyed. The company charged them, and they retired with some loss, destroying the bridge. The enemy's force at this place was estimated at one regiment and four pieces of artillery. Major Garrard, with three companies of cavalry and one gun of Allis' section of artillery, proceeded on a reconnaissance on a road leading to White Hall. After following this road about 10 miles, and having met with no opposition, they rejoined the main column.

Sunday, the 14th instant, I advanced the column, and when about 1 mile from Kinston encountered the enemy in strong force. They were posted in strong position in the wood, taking advantage of the ground, which formed a natural breastwork. Their position was secured on their right by a deep swamp and their left was partially protected by the river. The Ninth New Jersey was deployed as skirmishers, and General Wessells' brigade, with Morrison's battery Third New York Artillery, was ordered to advance to the right and left of the road, the battery being sent to our extreme right supported by one of General Wessells' regiments. Colonel Amory's brigade was then advanced, the Seventeenth Massachusetts Volunteers being sent to support Colonel Heckman on the right, and two regiments (Twenty-third and Forty-fifth Massachusetts) advanced up the road. My artillery (three batteries) I posted in a large field on the right of the road and about three-fourths of a mile in rear of our line of attack, the only position they could be placed in. I then ordered Colonel Stevenson's brigade, with Belger's Rhode Island battery, forward. The Twenty-fourth Massachusetts supported this battery, and the Fifth Rhode Island, Tenth Connecticut, and Forty-fourth Massachusetts were ordered forward, the two former on the left of the road and the latter on the right, to support the regiments there in pushing the enemy and turning that flank.

The Tenth Connecticut advanced steadily to the extreme front, relieving two of Wessells' brigade, which were short of ammunition, and after receiving a terrible fire for some twenty minutes made a most gallant charge in conjunction with the Ninety-sixth Regiment New York Volunteers of General Wessells' brigade, which, with the advance already made (slowly, but surely) of the entire line, forced the enemy to retreat precipitately for the bridge over the Neuse, which they crossed, firing the bridge, which had been prepared for that purpose. Several regiments were so close, however, that about 400 prisoners were taken from the enemy. A line was formed to the river and the fire extinguished before great damage was done.

The Ninth New Jersey and Seventeenth Massachusetts Regiments and General Wessells' brigade were at once crossed, pushed into the town, and halted. I ordered the bridge to be at once repaired for the crossing of cavalry and artillery.

General Evans retired about 2 miles from town with his command and formed line of battle. I sent a flag of truce to inquire whether he proposed to surrender. He declined. I immediately prepared to attack him, but knowing that he had three light batteries and one section to start with, was unwilling to sacrifice my men, and waited for my artillery to cross. I ordered Batteries E and I, Third New York Artillery to shell the enemy with their 20-pounder Parrotts (four in number) from the opposite bank, and crossed Colonel Amory's brigade with all dispatch; but before I could attack the enemy they had retired, and it being by this time night I was unable to pursue; moreover, my object was accomplished.

The troops bivouacked in the field beyond the town that night; a provost guard was established for the protection of the town and all necessary precautions were taken. I sent Captain Cole, Company K, Third Regiment New York Cavalry, down the east bank of the Neuse to a work commanding the river. He reported it deserted, with six guns in position, and the work to be of great strength. I sent the company back with teams to bring up the guns and blow up the magazine. Captain Cole being unable to remove the two heavy guns, one 8-inch columbiad and one 32-pounder, destroyed them, and brought back four field pieces complete. These, with two others deserted by the enemy and the one taken by the Ninth New Jersey, I sent to New Berne, under escort of Captain Cole's company (K) Third New York Cavalry.

The next morning, the 15th, I recrossed the river and took the river road for Goldsborough. I left a strong guard of cavalry in the town, under Major Fitz Simmons, to make a demonstration on the Goldsborough road on that side of the river. Colonel Ledlie, Third New York Artillery, remained to destroy commissary and quartermaster's stores and burn the bridge. Major Fitz Simmons advanced some 9 miles in the direction of Goldsborough, when, hearing the whistle of a locomotive, he fired three shots in the direction of the sound, upon which the train immediately returned in the direction of Goldsborough. Colonel Ledlie, before leaving Kinston, destroyed a locomotive, a railroad monitor, &c.

I advanced without opposition to within 3½ miles of White Hall, where I halted for the night. I sent Major Garrard with three com-

] anies of cavalry to make a reconnaissance to White Hall He found one regiment and four guns on our side of the bridge over the Neuse, but they quickly retreated as he approached, firing the bridge effectually.

The next morning (16th) I ordered Major Garrard, with five companies Third New York Cavalry and one section of artillery Twenty-third New York, to proceed to Mount Olive, a station on the Wilmington and Weldon Railroad, 14 miles below Goldsborough. In passing White Hall *en route* tor Mount Olive his command was fired upon from the opposite side of the river. He placed his guns in position and returned the fire until the main column arrived, when he limbered up and proceeded toward Mount Olive, which point he reached without opposition. Here he destroyed the railroad track for about a mile. He then proceeded along the line of the railroad for 4 miles and destroyed the bridge over Goshen Swamp. The track between Mount Olive and the Goshen Swamp Bridge was torn up and burned in five places.

The column having arrived at White Hall and finding the bridge burned and the enemy in some force, with infantry and artillery on the other side, and this being the direct road to Goldsborough, I determined to make a strong feint, as if to rebuild and cross. The Ninth New Jersey and Colonel Amory's brigade were sent forward and posted on the bank of the river to engage the enemy. I then ordered up several batteries and posted them on a hill overlooking the enemy's intrenchments. They opened on and silenced, after an hour's firing, the enemy's guns. The enemy still maintained their admirable position with sharpshooters, but deeming my object accomplished I moved my command forward toward Goldsborough, leaving sharpshooters in rear to continue the fight. We bivouacked that night 8 miles from Goldsborough, encountering no further opposition.

On the morning of the 17th I advanced on Goldsborough. I ordered Major Fitz Simmons, with two companies of cavalry, to make a feint in the direction of Dudley Station and Everettsville. They scattered a small force of the enemy there in every direction, burned two trestlework culverts, destroyed a train of four railroad cars, water-station, depot, &c., as well as some small-arms, which they were not able to carry off, and captured a flag of the enemy. They then returned by a short cut to the main column. I also ordered Major Garrard, with four companies of cavalry and one section of artillery, to make a feint in the direction of a bridge over the Neuse, on our right, called Thompson's Bridge. He found the enemy in force, supposed to be one regiment of infantry and four pieces of artillery, and the bridge already burned. I then directed, in order to make the feint more complete and to further distract the enemy, one regiment (Forty-third Massachusetts) and Angel's battery Third New York Artillery to the support of the cavalry and engage the enemy, which they did, silencing, after an hour's brisk engagement, the enemy's fire.

Colonel Lee's brigade was in advance of the main column and came upon the enemy in small force on the edge of the wood lining the railroad track. Riggs' battery Third New York Artillery was placed in position and opened on them, when the enemy retired. The Ninth New Jersey and Seventeenth Massachusetts were ordered to strike the railroad track and follow it up direct to the bridge, which they were to burn. Three regiments of Colonel Lee's brigade were ordered to their support (the Twenty-fifth, Twenty-seventh, and Third Massachusetts); the remaining regiment was thrown on the left to protect our flank in that quarter. General Wessells' brigade was advanced and formed on the hill overlooking the track, &c.; three regiments were thrown to the left, and the remaining regiments in lines, to be available at any point. My artillery was brought forward and placed in position, firing to the front and left, principally at the bridge. The enemy replied with artillery from the other side of the river. Colonel Heckman advanced steadily up the track, fighting the enemy's infantry posted at the bridge and receiving a fire from the artillery in a monitor-car on the track of the bridge. After two hours he reached the bridge, and under a heavy fire Lieutenant Graham, Twenty-third New York Battery, acting as aide-de-camp to Colonel Heckman, fired the bridge. All who had previously attempted it were picked off, as was wounded Lieut. B. N. Mann, Seventeenth Massachusetts, who accompanied him.

I brought all my artillery to bear to prevent any effort to save the bridge, and, when the fire was doing its work, ordered a countermarch for New Berne, leaving Colonel Lee to form the rear guard. Colonel Lee was forming his brigade to leave the field, deeming the fight over, when three regimental colors were seen across the railroad track, the men protected by the embankment on which the track was laid. Colonel Lee placed Morrison's battery in position and recalled his regiments in line. The enemy advanced with cheers across the railroad, steadily in line, upon Colonel Lee's brigade. Morrison's battery opened on the advancing line with spherical case and with good effect, but they advanced steadily until within 300 yards of the battery, when, unable to stand the fearful loss they were sustaining from the battery, they broke and retreated. Their retreat was unexpectedly covered by a masked battery in the woods on our left. Belger's Rhode Island battery, which had been brought back, opened in reply to the battery and on two regiments which came in view, supporting their guns. Riggs' battery Third New York Artillery was placed on an eminence on our left and in line with the enemy, thus bringing a cross-fire to bear. They were thereby forced to retire, as was also a regiment in the woods on our right.

Colonel Lee, having orders not to attempt any further move, again formed his brigade and batteries and proceeded to join the column, which I had halted on hearing the firing from Colonel Lee.

This was a bold attempt of the enemy to entrap and secure Colonel Lee's brigade and Morrison's battery. Owing to the efficiency of Colonel Lee and Morrison's battery it was a disastrous failure. With a strong cavalry rear guard I then started on my return by the direct road, took and transported my sick and wounded men from White Hall and Kinston, carrying them all safely to this point.

On the 13th a fleet of small boats left New Berne, under Commander Murray, U. S. Navy, to attack the works on the river at Kinston, but owing to the lowness of the water in the river only one small boat, the Allison, under Colonel Manchester, Marine Artillery, was brought into action. The works being too strong she, after a gallant resistance, was obliged to retire, having, however, effected a good purpose by mystifying General Evans as to where the attack was to come from, and induced him to retain several regiments on the Kinston side of the Neuse, thus diminishing the force opposed to us.

In conclusion I take great pleasure in reporting on the conduct of the officers and men under my command. It was most excellent, and maintained fully their high reputation.

General Wessells' brigade, of General Peck's division, behaved like veterans, and reflected, by their drill, discipline, and steadiness under fire, the qualities of their commanding officer.

Colonel Heckman, of the Ninth New Jersey, was, with his admirable regiment, always in advance, and displayed the greatest courage and efficiency.

The Tenth Regiment Connecticut Volunteers, under Lieutenant-Colonel Leggett (as they always have done), behaved in the most gallant and dashing manner, making a charge under a fire which in twenty minutes killed and wounded 90 men out of 340.

Colonel Potter, of the First North Carolina Volunteers, acted on my staff, and was of the greatest aid and assistance to me by his coolness and observation.

I must particularly mention the conduct of Lieut. George W. Graham, Twenty-third New York Battery, acting as aide to Colonel Heckman. Throughout the entire march he was conspicuous for his venturesome courage, and at Goldsborough, in company with Lieut. B. N. Mann, Seventeenth Massachusetts Volunteers, advanced and fired the bridge under the fire of the enemy's infantry and artillery. He only escaped capture by jumping from the bridge down the bank. Lieutenant Mann was wounded.

The artillery force, under Colonel Ledlie, was well placed and well served, and the commanding officer and the batteries, without exception, did most excellent service.

The Third New York Cavalry, though not acting as a regiment, were in all cases prompt, brave, and efficient, as shown in the body of my report.

Much credit is due to Mr. H. W. Wilson, engineer, who, in charge of the pioneers and a force of contrabands, did most excellent service in building bridges, repairing roads, &c.

I inclose to General E. A. Hitchcock the lists of paroled prisoners, numbering 496.*

I herewith inclose lists of the killed, wounded, and missing, showing an aggregate of 90 killed, 478 wounded, and 9 missing.†

Among the killed I must mourn Colonel Gray, of the Ninety-sixth New York Regiment. He was killed at the head of his regiment at the Kinston Bridge. Though but a few days in this department he had already won the high esteem of all here.

In the charge of the Tenth Connecticut they lost Capt. H. A. Wells and Lieuts. W. W. Perkins, T. D. Hill, and J. C. Coffing, all good and excellent officers, who died doing a gallant duty.

For many details of distinguished services of individual officers I beg to refer to the brigade and regimental reports herewith inclosed.

I have the honor to be, very respectfully, your obedient servant,

J. G. FOSTER,
Major-General, Commanding Department.

Maj. Gen. H. W. HALLECK,
    General-in-Chief, U. S. Army, Washington, D. C.

—

GENERAL ORDERS, }   HDQRS. DEPT. OF NORTH CAROLINA,
    No. 81.   }   *New Berne, December* 26, 1862.

The commanding general desires to thank the troops under his command for the new proof of their courage and steadiness afforded by the recent expedition. The veteran brigade of General Wessells and the troops of this department alike did their duty as soldiers well.

By order of Maj. Gen. J. G. Foster:

SOUTHARD HOFFMAN,
Assistant Adjutant-General.

---

* Omitted.   † But see revised statement, p. 60.

GENERAL ORDERS, }   HDQRS. EIGHTEENTH ARMY CORPS,
    No. 18.   }   *New Berne, January* 15, 1863.

In consideration of and as a reward for their brave deeds at Kinston, White Hall, and Goldsborough, the commanding general directs that the regiments and batteries which accompanied the expedition to Goldsborough inscribe upon their banners those three victories:

Kinston, December 14, 1862.
White Hall, December 16, 1862.
Goldsborough, December 17, 1862.

The commanding general hopes that all future fields will be so fought that the record of them may be kept by inscription on the banners of the regiments engaged.

By command of Maj. Gen. J. G. Foster:

[SOUTHARD HOFFMAN,]
Assistant Adjutant-General.

No. 2.

*Return of Casualties in the Union forces.**

[Compiled from nominal lists of casualties, returns, etc.]

Command.	Killed.		Wounded.		Captured or missing.		Aggregate.
	Officers.	Enlisted men.	Officers.	Enlisted men.	Officers.	Enlisted men.	
10th Connecticut	3	8	6	83			100
3d Massachusetts				2			2
5th Massachusetts				7			7
17th Massachusetts		1	4	25		2	32
23d Massachusetts		12	2	53			67
24th Massachusetts		1		7			8
25th Massachusetts		1		3		1	5
27th Massachusetts		1		2			3
43d Massachusetts		2		1		1	4
44th Massachusetts		8		13			21
45th Massachusetts		18	1	58			77
46th Massachusetts		1		3			4
51st Massachusetts				2			2
9th New Jersey		5	1	85		4	95
3d New York Cavalry				6		4	10
3d New York Light Artillery, Batteries B, E, F, H, I, and K.		5	2	25			32
New York Light Artillery, 24th Battery (section)		1					1
New York Marine Artillery		1		2			3
85th New York				3			3
92d New York		3	1	15			19
96th New York	1		1	5			7
85th Pennsylvania		1		8			9
103d Pennsylvania		16	1	52			69
1st Rhode Island Light Artillery, Battery F		2		5			7
5th Rhode Island		1		3			4
Total	4	88	19	468		12	591

Officers killed: Capt. Henry A. Wells, Lieuts. William W. Perkins and Theron D. Hill, Tenth Connecticut, and Col. Charles O. Gray, Ninety-sixth New York, at Kinston, December 14.
Officers mortally wounded: Lieuts. John C. Coffing and John M. Simms, Tenth Connecticut.

---

* Embraces losses in skirmishes on the Kinston road, December 11 and 12; skirmishes at Southwest Creek, December 13-14; engagement at Kinston, December 14; engagement at White Hall, December 16; skirmish at Thompson's Bridge and engagement at Goldsborough Bridge, December 17.

No. 3.

Report of Capt. David A. Taylor, Third New York Light Artillery, Chief Signal Officer.

HDQRS. SIGNAL DETACHMENT, DEPT. OF N. C.,
New Berne, December 22, 1862.

SIR: Supplementary to the report already made out (but which I was unable to forward before this time), I forward the following report of the proceedings of the detachment under my command:

On the 11th day of December, 1862, I accompanied Maj. Gen. J. G. Foster on an expedition to Goldsborough, taking with me the following-named officers with their men, viz: Joseph Fricker, first lieutenant, Eighth Pennsylvania Volunteers, and acting signal officer; F. Schlachter, first lieutenant, Eleventh Connecticut Volunteers, and acting signal officer; Henry T. Merrill, second lieutenant, Seventeenth Massachusetts Volunteers, and acting signal officer; C. C. F. Keith, second lieutenant, Twenty-third New York Volunteer Artillery; Edward S. Moffatt, second lieutenant, Ninth New Jersey Volunteers, and acting signal officer; and N. S. Barstow, second lieutenant, Twenty-fourth Massachusetts Volunteers, and acting signal officer.

Unfortunately Lieutenants Merrill and Barstow were taken sick soon after the expedition marched, and consequently were unable to take an active part in any of the battles which were fought on this march.

On Sunday, the 14th instant, the battle of Kinston was fought. As the battle was fought in a thick swamp there was no possible opportunity for signaling until just at the close of the action, after the enemy was driven into the open ground and across the Neuse River Bridge, when I saw a favorable opportunity to charge upon and capture two regiments of rebels, and accordingly I signaled back to General Foster to send forward a light battery and the cavalry which were already across the bridge; but the general instead sent up a flag of truce and asked them to surrender, which of course they did not do, but succeeded in escaping, as before treating they demanded and obtained a half hour's time, during which time the Union forces should remain halted at Kinston. I was most of the time occupied in carrying orders and placing troops in position and was with my flagmen a fourth of a mile in advance of the leading regiment.

At night I accompanied a company of cavalry to the rebel batteries, 4 miles below Kinston, and assisted in bringing off four field pieces and destroying an 8-inch columbiad and a 32-pounder siege gun, which were in position in the batteries, and with which the enemy had in the early part of the day driven off our gunboats.

On the 16th instant General Foster fought the battle of White Hall, on the Neuse River. As soon as the battle commenced I placed my officers in the most prominent positions on the field, and accompanied by Private Jacob A. Reed, Company I, Third New York Artillery, went in with the leading regiment and examined the position of the enemy. After obtaining a close and accurate survey of their works and position, I opened a station under a severe fire of musketry and called for some field guns to be sent to me, which General Foster immediately forwarded. Upon their arrival I placed them in position and twice sighted the guns myself. The fire of the guns was very effectual,

driving the enemy out of the works they occupied; also completely rid-
dling a half-finished gunboat which the enemy had on the stocks upon
the opposite side of the river, and were occupying as a rifle-work at the
time.

While sending the message for the guns I was hit by a musket-shot
on the index finger of the right hand, but fortunately was not much
hurt My flag received three shots through it. Private Reed behaved
with great coolness all through the engagement. Toward the close of
the action I was ordered by General Foster to withdraw the artillery
and pick out and post as many sharpshooters as would cover the enemy's position, which I accordingly did, under one of the severest
musketry fires I have ever seen.

On the 17th instant General Foster fought the battle of Goldsborough.
The object of the action was to gain possession of the railroad bridge
over the Neuse River. The action was a double one, the first being in
the morning, the second in the evening. In the morning the rebels,
after a little skirmishing, retreated across the railroad bridge, but kept
up a sharp fire of musketry and artillery on our advance. I went immediately on to the railroad, placing Lieutenant Schlachter with General Foster and other officers with different brigadiers and artillery.
After getting on the railroad I went immediately forward of the skirmishers, and at every favorable point made close observations of the
enemy's position, and finding it impossible to cross the bridge I called
for artillery, which immediately came forward, took position, and commenced shelling the enemy with very decided effect.

After the bridge was carried and burned and our batteries had silenced
the enemy's fire, General Foster drew off his forces, supposing the battle was over; but after about three hours the enemy came on with two
brigades of infantry and one battery from some crossing of the river above
the bridge and commenced an attack upon our rear, of which Lieutenant
Keith immediately informed me by signal and I informed the general.
The battle now renewed was soon ended, with very severe loss to the
enemy and very slight loss to us.

On account of the exceedingly difficult nature of the country and the
inexperience of my officers less signaling was done than otherwise
would have been. Both officers and men behaved as became soldiers
and gentlemen, and when this detachment shall have had sufficient
field practice they will compare favorably with any that I am acquainted
with. I take this occasion to recommend to your favorable consideration Lieuts. C. C. F. Keith, E. S. Moffatt, F. Schlachter, and Joseph
Fricker as capable and efficient officers; and Privates Jacob A. Reed,
Company I, Third New York Artillery; Samuel N. Rogers, Company A,
Twenty-first Massachusetts Volunteers; William N. Baker, Company
D, Eighth Pennsylvania Reserve Volunteer Corps; Pulaski Hindes,
Company G, Ninth New Jersey Volunteers, and William J. Lindsay,
First Pennsylvania Rifles, as cool, brave, energetic men, always ready
for any undertaking, however desperate, attentive to their duties, intel-
ligent and capable, precisely the men needed in this corps, and I take
pleasure in recommending them to the department, and hope they will
receive a suitable promotion.

Although somewhat foreign to this report, I cannot refrain from mentioning the conduct of Privates H. P. Baker, Company E, Third New
York Artillery, and Lucius D. Craft, Company D, Eighth Pennsylvania
Rifles Volunteer Corps, who, just at the close of the battle of Kinston,
rode a mile or so to the left of the line of battle and captured and

brought in a major, a captain, and some 30 non-commissioned officers and privates. An act of rash bravery rarely equaled.

All which is respectfully submitted.

Very respectfully, your obedient servant,

DAVID A. TAYLOR,
Captain and Chief Acting Signal Officer, Dept. of N. C.

Maj. ALBERT J. MYER,
Signal Officer, U. S. Army.

No. 4.

Report of Col. James H. Ledlie, Third New York Light Artillery, Chief of Artillery, commanding Artillery Brigade.

HEADQUARTERS ARTILLERY BRIGADE,
New Berne, N. C., December 24, 1862.

SIR: I have the honor to submit the following report of the operations of this brigade in connection with the recent expedition:

The artillery under my command consisted of Batteries B, E, F, H, I, and K, Third New York Artillery; Battery F, First Rhode Island Artillery, and a section each of the Twenty-third and Twenty-fourth New York Independent Batteries.

Leaving New Berne December 11, at 7 a. m., marched 14 miles. About 5 p. m., December 12, the Twenty-third New York Independent Battery, Captain Ransom, was left, with the Fifty-first Massachusetts Volunteers, to guard the bridge over Beaver Creek, 13 miles from Kinston. Captain Ransom remained there until the 14th, when he moved toward Kinston, and, supported by a company of the Fifth Massachusetts Volunteers, was assigned to the defense of a bridge near there. On the 15th he rejoined the main column.

About 9 a. m. December 13 the right section of Battery B, Third New York Artillery, under Lieutenant Day, which had been sent in advance of the main column with a squadron of cavalry, engaged a force of the enemy at Southwest Creek and shelled an earthwork commanding the bridge. The remaining two sections of Battery B, under Captain Morrison, were shortly after brought up and fired about 40 rounds. Batteries E, F, H, and K, Third New York Artillery, were brought into position on the center and left of our line, but did not open fire.

December 14, the skirmishers of the Ninth New Jersey Volunteers having engaged the enemy, the right section of Battery B, Third New York Artillery, under Lieutenant Day, was sent forward and took position in the road leading to the river bridge. The remaining sections of the battery, under Captain Morrison, were posted in an open field on the right of the road and shelled the woods. Battery F, Third New York Artillery, Captain Jenney, came into battery on the left of the road, 200 yards in rear, and fired at the bridge at the distance of $1\frac{1}{4}$ miles, the direction and distance being given by a guide. Batteries E and I, Third New York Artillery, were ordered to the support of Captain Morrison, and a section of Captain Jenney's battery, under Lieutenant Birchmeyer, was then ordered to the support of Colonel Heckman, Ninth New Jersey, on the extreme right, and opened on the enemy with great effect. The remaining two sections of the battery were soon after sent to the support of Colonel Heckman, and, moving down within a short distance of the bridge, opened a destructive fire upon the enemy attempting to cross, effectually cutting off their retreat. Under cover of this fire a part of the cannoneers of Battery F, assisted by a few of the Tenth Connecticut, extinguished the fires which the enemy had kindled on the bridge. Battery B, Third New York Artillery, which was now moved forward and posted on the left, opened with canister on the woods, and Batteries E and I, Third New York Artillery, took position in a field on the right. At this time 41 privates and 2 commissioned officers, belonging to the enemy, surrendered as prisoners to Captain Morrison, of Battery B, who sent them to the rear under guard. About one hour later Batteries E and I moved forward to the bank of the river and shelled the enemy over the town. Action closed about 1 p. m.

Loss in artillery brigade at Kinston: Battery B, Third New York Artillery, 1 man wounded; Battery F, Third New York Artillery, 3 men wounded. Loss in horses quite heavy.

The Twenty-fourth New York Independent Battery, Capt. Lee, which had been ordered, December 13, up the main road to a point 7 miles from Kinston, encamped there with the Forty-sixth Massachusetts Volunteers.

On the morning of the 14th one piece, under Lieutenant Cady, was sent up the road with a detachment of cavalry, and opened on the enemy, who were behind intrenchments, with two pieces of artillery, at a point where Southwest Creek crosses the direct road to Kinston. The enemy retired after a brisk engagement of three-quarters of an hour, and after the battle of Kinston the Twenty-fourth Battery rejoined our main column, December 16.

The affair at White Hall, Tuesday, December 16, commenced about 9.30 a. m. by a skirmish between a detachment of the Third New York Cavalry, accompanied by the Twenty-third New York Independent Battery, Captain Ransom, and the enemy's sharpshooters. This skirmish lasted but a few minutes, after which the cavalry and battery moved forward past the enemy's position. Shortly after, the Seventeenth Massachusetts, Lieutenant-Colonel Fellows, having engaged the enemy, Battery F, Captain Jenney, Third New York Artillery, was posted on the hill-side directly opposite the enemy's works and opened fire. One gun of this battery burst at about the twentieth round.

At 10.30 a. m. Battery K, Captain Angel, Third New York Artillery, was sent to the support of Captain Jenney and posted on his right. The right section of Captain Jenney's battery, under command of Lieut. J. F. Dennis, was then sent forward and posted on the left of the bridge, across the river. Battery E, Third New York Artillery, Lieutenant Ashby commanding, and Battery F, First Rhode Island Artillery, Captain Belger, were shortly afterward put in position on the hill above Batteries F and K, Third New York Artillery, and opened fire. The Twenty-fourth New York Battery, Captain Lee, was then posted in the swamp on the right of our line. Battery I, Third New York Artillery, Lieutenant Thomas, was sent forward to the left of the bridge, and a section of Battery K, Third New York Artillery, under Lieutenant Mersereau, was also brought up to that point. Battery H, Third New York Artillery, Captain Riggs, was now placed at about the center of our line, on the bank of the river, and, together with Captain Belger's battery, which had been posted on the right of the bridge, opened upon the enemy at a point-blank range. The action terminated a little after 12 m., the enemy's batteries having been completely silenced.

I desire particularly to mention the gallant conduct of Lieut. J. F. Dennis, commanding the advanced section of Battery F, Third New

York Artillery, who maintained his position until his ammunition was exhausted, under a very severe fire from the enemy's sharpshooters, and worked at his guns himself after a large number of his men had been shot down.

The Twenty-third New York Independent Battery, Captain Ransom, after passing White Hall on the morning of the 16th, marched with the cavalry command of Major Garrard to Mount Olive, on the Wilmington and Weldon Railroad, and assisted in tearing up the railroad track, burning the trestle-work, and destroying the telegraph at that point. Thence, on the morning of the 17th, marched to Thompson's Bridge, on the Neuse, 9 miles below Goldsborough. At that point a brisk engagement ensued, during which two sections of Battery K, Third New York Artillery, Captain Angel, came to Captain Ransom's support. After thirty minutes the combined efforts of these batteries completely silenced the enemy's fire, both of musketry and artillery. About midnight they rejoined the main column.

Loss in artillery brigade at White Hall : Battery E, Third New York Artillery, 3 men wounded; Battery F, Third New York Artillery, 5 men wounded; Battery I, Third New York Artillery, 1 man wounded; Battery K, Third New York Artillery, 2 men killed, 5 men wounded; Battery F, First Rhode Island Artillery, 2 men killed, 2 men wounded; Twenty-fourth New York Independent Battery, 1 man killed. Loss in horses very heavy.

About 11 a. m. Wednesday, December 17, the skirmishers of the Seventeenth Massachusetts Volunteers and Ninth New Jersey Volunteers having engaged the enemy, Battery H, Third New York Artillery, Captain Riggs, was ordered to the front and posted on an elevation overlooking the railroad track. A few rounds of spherical case scattered the enemy, who took refuge in the woods. Battery B, Third New York Artillery, was then brought into position on the right of and close to the railroad track, and opened upon the bridge, which was visible at about 200 yards distance. Batteries E and I, Third New York Artillery, Maj. T. J. Kennedy commanding, now moved forward, opening upon the railroad monitor and the enemy's battery on the other side of the bridge. The effect of this concentrated fire was very destructive. The railroad bridge, which had been fired by Lieutenant Graham, aide-de-camp to Colonel Heckman, was torn down in about half an hour and the enemy's battery and monitor completely silenced. The batteries then retired, Captain Morrison taking position on an elevation commanding the whole open field. Between 3 and 4 p. m., after our forces, with the exception of Colonel Lee's brigade, had taken up the line of march, two regiments of the enemy's infantry formed across the railroad track, cheering and waving their colors, and charged upon Captain Morrison's battery. He opened upon them first with spherical case and then with double canister with deadly effect, literally mowing them down. Belger's Rhode Island battery was ordered up and opened fire to the left, where the woods were lined with rebel infantry. The enemy then opened a well-directed fire upon us from a concealed battery. Battery H, Third New York Artillery, Captain Riggs, was ordered to the support of Captain Belger and posted on his left, opposite the enemy's right flank. After an hour's vigorous cannonading the enemy's fire, both of musketry and artillery, was completely silenced by Captains Belger and Riggs, and, as night was closing in, orders were received to retire, which was done in the best order. One section of Battery H, under Lieutenant Clark, was left with the rear guard.

Loss in artillery brigade at Goldsborough: Battery B, Third New

York Artillery, 2 men wounded; Battery K, Third New York Artillery, 1 man wounded; Battery F, First Rhode Island Light Artillery, 3 men wounded. Loss in horses slight.

The officers of the various batteries, without exception, handled their commands with coolness and skill, and when all did so well it is difficult to particularize.

I desire to mention Majors Stone and Kennedy, who commanded the reserve artillery, for the prompt manner in which they brought their batteries into action, and the efficiency with which they were served; also the members of my personal staff, Lieut. Alexander H. Davis, Lieut. E. P. Peters, and Chaplain William Hart, volunteer aides-de-camp, who were constantly under fire during the engagements, for the promptness displayed by them in performing the various duties assigned them. Lieut. Frederick W. Prince, acting brigade quartermaster, was also indefatigable in his exertions.

JAMES H. LEDLIE,
Col., Comdg. Arty. Brig. and Chief of Arty., Dept. of N. C.

Maj. SOUTHARD HOFFMAN,
  Asst. Adjt. Gen., Department of North Carolina.

No. 5.

Report of Capt. Edwin S. Jenney, Battery F, Third New York Light Artillery, of engagements at Kinston and White Hall, December 14 and 16.

HDQRS. BATTERY F, THIRD NEW YORK VOL. ARTILLERY,
New Berne, N. C., December 21, 1862.

COLONEL: I have the honor to report that in accordance with your order my battery joined the First Brigade, commanded by Colonel Amory, and marched from New Berne Thursday, the 11th instant. On the 14th instant we arrived within 2 miles of Kinston, without anything occurring except the usual casualties of a march in an enemy's country. By your order my battery then came into battery in an opening on the left of the road for the purpose of shelling Kinston. After expending about 120 rounds of ammunition I ceased firing, by order of Major-General Foster, and sent my left section, commanded by Lieutenant Birchmeyer, to support Colonel Heckman's position, on our right flank, and, by your order, posted my other two sections about half a mile nearer Kinston, in a field on the right-hand side the road. Lieutenant Birchmeyer's position was about 600 yards in front of the rebel battery, which was upon the opposite side of the river, and which was defended by breastworks, the river and an open field being between. He held this position alone, and did fine execution, until his fuse-shells were expended, when the rest of my battery, by your order proceeded into the same position. After shelling the rebel battery for a short time the enemy retreated from that place, and Colonel Heckman commenced a flank movement toward the bridge.

The infantry marched directly across the field, while my battery, by order of Colonel Amory, crossed to the left, nearer the bridge, and commenced a vigorous fire of canister and shell upon the retreating enemy. About four rounds had been discharged when I observed the rebels were firing the bridge. I immediately moved my battery to the end of the bridge, arriving there before any other troops—by this movement cutting off the retreat of some of the enemy, who were yet upon this side of the river. Lieutenant Birchmeyer, commanding left section, and First Sergeant Van Heusen, commanding center section, brought forward their cannoneers with watering buckets, and, assisted by a very few volunteers from the Tenth Connecticut, extinguished the fire upon the bridge, Lieutenant Dennis supporting them by a rapid fire of canister from his section. My loss at this place was as follows: Three men wounded—James H. Dunlap, guidon, in the thigh; Alexander Fullerton, corporal, in the arm; Charles Baughman, private, in the breast; and 5 horses killed.

We encamped in Kinston, and the next morning we resumed our march. In the afternoon Lieutenant Dennis, with his section, was ordered forward with the cavalry to White Hall, where he opened fire upon a rebel gunboat in process of construction and succeeded in partially destroying it, when he returned to the battery, which was encamped with the division.

On the 16th instant we resumed the march, my battery being in the advance. When near White Hall I was ordered forward and opened fire upon a rebel battery, situated on the opposite side of the river, about 1,000 yards distant. My right section was posted upon the bank of the river, where the bridge had been burned, about 200 yards distant from the enemy's battery. I kept up a continuous fire until my ammunition was exhausted, when I retired by your order. During the hottest of the fire one of my guns burst, injuring no one.

My losses at this place are as follows: Six men wounded and 8 horses killed.*

Immediately after the engagement we moved on with the column.

Our ammunition being exhausted we did not participate in the engagement near Goldsborough.

We arrived at our camp on the 20th instant.

My total casualties are as follows: Nine men wounded; 13 horses killed.

I desire to call your attention to the meritorious conduct of First Sergt. Stephen Van Heusen, who commanded my center section, and behaved gallantly both at Kinston and White Hall. I beg leave to recommend him for promotion to a lieutenancy. My non-commissioned officers and privates fought bravely, and it would be difficult to discriminate between them.

I am, colonel, your very obedient servant,

EDWIN S. JENNEY,
Captain, Comdg. Battery F, Third New York Vol. Artillery.

Col. JAMES H. LEDLIE,
Commanding Artillery Brigade.

No. 6.

Reports of Maj. Charles Fitz Simmons, Third New York Cavalry, of operations December 15 and 17.

COLONEL: I have the honor to report that on the morning of the 15th instant I proceeded along the Goldsborough road from Kinston with

---

* Nominal loss omitted. Casualties embodied in revised statement, p. 60.

Companies B, E, and H, and one of Allis' mountain howitzers, all of this regiment. My instructions were to simply make a feint toward Goldsborough and to capture any of the stragglers that might be found. I was also cautioned not to delay any longer than it was necessary to allow the main column to recross the bridge at Kinston; then to countermarch and act as rear guard. After going 6 miles my advance, commanded by Lieutenant Greig, Company H, came up with 12 mounted vedettes of the enemy. After a brisk chase of 3 miles they got away; not, however, before one of them was wounded by the lieutenant. About 800 yards distant from the spot where I concluded the farther chase to be fruitless I imagined I heard the noise of an engine; and, as I thought the feint would be more effective if cannon shots were fired, I ordered the howitzer in position and fired five rounds of spherical case-shot. After the third discharge the engine whistled and went toward Goldsborough. I sent some men forward, under Captain Willson, of Company H, to reconnoiter. They took 2 prisoners, South Carolinians, who refused to give any information further than that the train came down from Goldsborough that morning with troops, and had retired upon finding us advancing.

I returned to Kinston without further casualties and joined the main column.

All of which is respectfully submitted.

CHAS. FITZ SIMMONS,
Major, Third New York Cavalry.

Lieut. Col. JOHN MIX,
Commanding Third New York Cavalry.

—

COLONEL: I have the honor to report that on December 17, instant, I was detached from the main column of General Foster's army, then *en route* to Goldsborough Bridge, with Company B, Captain Moschell, and Company C, Lieutenant Mayes, for the purpose of destroying the railroad at Dudley Station, a point 5 miles distant from Goldsborough Bridge, on the Goldsborough and Wilmington Railroad. Upon entering the town the enemy's pickets, some 20 in number, scattered right and left in the direction of Mount Olive and Goldsborough. I in pursuance of orders proceeded to tear up the track, destroying the rails by piling up and interspersing them with dry lumber found at the station. I also burned two trestle-work culverts, a train of four railroad cars, water-station, depot, and storehouse. In the storehouse were some 50 muskets and 10 sabers, of no great value, and having no means of transportation I threw them into the flames. With the arms was a rebel flag, "the Stars and Bars," which I took away with me.

Having remained at Dudley two hours, to be sure that no attempt which might be made to save the railroad would be successful, I returned by a short cut to the main column, which I found engaged with the enemy at Goldsborough Bridge.

All of which is respectfully submitted.

CHAS. FITZ SIMMONS,
Major, Third New York Cavalry.

Lieut. Col. JOHN MIX,
Commanding Third New York Cavalry.

No. 7.

Reports of Maj. Jeptha Garrard, Third New York Cavalry, of operations
December 15–17.

SIR: I have the honor to report that in obedience to orders from Maj. Gen. J. G. Foster I took three companies of the Third New York Cavalry and one section of Jenney's battery Third New York Artillery on the evening of December 15 and marched to White Hall, on the Neuse River. No enemy was found on the south side of the river. The artillery threw eight or ten shells into a skeleton gunboat on the opposite side. Private Butler, of Company C, Third New York Cavalry, volunteered to swim the river and set fire to the boat. He did swim over, though shot at three times, and returned safely. The command then marched to camp.

Very respectfully,

JEPTHA GARRARD,
Major, Third New York Cavalry.

Lieut. Col. JOHN MIX,
Commanding Third New York Cavalry.

—

SIR: I have the honor to report that in obedience to orders from Maj. Gen. J. G. Foster I marched, on December 16, with two guns of Ransom's battery Twenty-third New York Artillery and five companies of Third New York Cavalry, to Mount Olive Station, on the Goldsborough and Wilmington Railroad, 14 miles below Goldsborough. The railroad was destroyed at this point for about 1 mile. Four miles beyond this point, toward Wilmington, a bridge over the Goshen Swamp was destroyed, and between Mount Olive Station and this bridge the road was torn up and burned in five places.

The object of the march being fully accomplished the command returned to camp.

Very respectfully,

JEPTHA GARRARD,
Major, Third New York Cavalry.

Lieut. Col. JOHN MIX,
Commanding Third New York Cavalry.

—

SIR: I have the honor to report that on December 17, in obedience to orders from Maj. Gen. J. G. Foster, I marched, with four companies Third New York Cavalry and two guns of Ransom's battery Twenty-third New York Artillery, to Thompson's Bridge to burn said bridge. The bridge was found to be already burned by the enemy. The enemy was found to be in force (artillery and infantry) on the opposite side. Re-enforcements of four guns of Angel's battery Third New York Artillery and Forty-third Regiment Massachusetts, Colonel Holbrook, were sent to hold the place until further orders.

At 8 o'clock next morning the command rejoined the army.

I wish to mention Captain Jacobs, Company E, Third New York Cavalry, for good conduct in charging down to the bridge under fire.

Very respectfully,

JEPTHA GARRARD,
Major, Third New York Cavalry.

Lieut. Col. JOHN MIX.

No. 8.

Reports of Capt. John F. Moschell, Third New York Cavalry, of operations December 11–16.

HDQRS. COMPANY B, THIRD NEW YORK CAVALRY,
New Berne, N. C., December 20, 1862.

COLONEL: On the morning of the 11th instant I, in command of Companies A and B, of the Third New York Cavalry, as the advance guard, proceeded on the Trent road as far as the Deep Gully (some 9 miles) and halted for further orders. Orders coming, I went on some 5 or 6 miles farther, capturing one of the enemy's pickets without firing a shot, and found the road so blockaded as to impede the farther advance of the column until the obstructions were removed. Sending Lieutenant Chamberlin and 30 men of Company A, dismounted, in the woods as skirmishers they captured a man and horse of the enemy.

While waiting to have the pioneers remove the obstructions we were sent, under command of Lieutenant-Colonel Mix, to make a reconnaissance to the left of the main road about a mile. Returning we bivouacked for the night.

On the morning of the 12th I proceeded on the main road as far as the junction of the Kinston road, where Companies B and K, Third New York Cavalry, and two companies of the Ninth New Jersey formed the advance guard. We proceeded on the Kinston road some 3 miles and encountered a force of the enemy's cavalry about 100 strong, as the prisoners reported. I charged on them with Company B for about $1\frac{1}{4}$ miles, when, coming upon an ambush of some 150 infantry behind a ditch and rail fence in the pine wood, I ordered a retreat, and rallied a quarter of a mile this side of the ambush, at the corner of a road leading to a house on the right of the road.

I found 2 men wounded—Private Butler, slightly in the thigh with buck-shot (subsequently cut out by Surgeons Palmer and Douglas), and Private Kingsley, severely wounded in the thigh with a musket-ball—and 4 men missing, viz, Privates Brightman, Coon, Goodspeed (wounded), and Hart, said Butler's horse being killed and 9 horses missing. The cause of so many horses missing was a deep ditch filled with water, where the horses fell, throwing their riders, and recovering ran away into the enemy's lines.

We captured 1 lieutenant, 9 men, and 2 horses. We also killed 1 captain and 4 men, wounding 1 colonel (Baker) and several men.

Great credit is due to both officers and men, who showed personal bravery and efficiency in the charge. I cannot close this report without particular mention of Lieutenant Ebbs; also First Sergt. William B. Shearer and Corporal Kent and Farrier Allen. The sword of First Sergeant Shearer did not return to its sheath without vengeance on the enemy, as their arms and heads plainly show.

I have the honor, &c.,

JNO. F. MOSCHELL,
Captain, Commanding.

Col. JOHN MIX,
Commanding Third New York Cavalry.

—

On the morning of the 13th I was sent with Company B, Third New York Cavalry, on a reconnaissance on the Kinston and Trent road, where it branches off, some 9 miles from Kinston. I proceeded about

2 miles and came across 4 mounted pickets at a farm or plantation house. My vedettes fired upon them and succeeded in capturing a carbine and saddle, but the men and horses escaped across the field to the woods. I continued on this road some 3 miles and came in sight of 1 mounted and 2 foot pickets. The vedettes fired at them, one running one way, the other two the other way. Continuing on a mile farther we came upon several pickets at a bridge about 3 miles from Kinston. They fired upon my vedettes, who returned the fire.

Owing to limited instructions I returned the same road and joined the main column at the church, some 6 miles south of Kinston.

I have the honor to be, very respectfully, your obedient servant,

JNO. F. MOSCHELL.

No. 9.

Report of Capt. Newton Hall, Third New York Cavalry, of operations December 12–16.

SIR: I have the honor to report that on the afternoon of December 12 I was ordered by Major-General Foster, in command of the forces then marching against Kinston, to take three companies of the Third New York Cavalry, viz, Companies A, D, and G, with one piece of Lieutenant Allis' section of artillery, under his (Lieutenant Allis') command, and march forward on the direct road to Kinston, feeling the enemy and making as strong a demonstration as possible with my command. I was also ordered to retire after having made this demonstration, to build large camp fires for the night, and hold the road until commanded to retire. I immediately moved forward, throwing a platoon of Company A, under command of Lieutenant Chamberlin, armed with carbines, in front of the column, with orders to proceed cautiously and give immediate notice of the presence of the enemy. Proceeding in this manner about 2 miles our advance came upon two cavalry vedettes, dismounted, with their horses saddled, but unbridled, and tied near the road. We were so close upon them that they were unable to mount, and started off across the field for the wood on foot. A shot from a carbine caused them to halt and they were taken prisoners. We again moved forward, and, having gained the information that part of a company of infantry was stationed at a large white house within three-quarters of a mile of the rebel forces encamped at Wise's Cross-Roads, I determined if possible to surprise them. Moving with even greater caution than before, we had advanced, as I judge, nearly half the distance when our advance came unexpectedly upon two mounted pickets, and, charging forward upon the instant, captured them without noise or alarm. Sending them to the rear we again advanced, and when within about a mile of the main guard we came upon an infantry picket, and, learning from him the distance to the house, charged in a body. As our advance approached the rebel station the rebels rushed in alarm and confusion from the house, and as they endeavored to get into line fired a few shots at us, when, unable to withstand our onset, they fled.

The skirmish here lasted but a few minutes, our men using their carbines and revolvers freely, leaving, as was subsequently ascertained, 13 dead and dying rebels upon the ground and taking 11 prisoners, besides those previously captured, among whom was 1 commissioned officer. The men killed and 11 of the prisoners taken belong to the Twenty-second South Carolina Regiment; the others were a part of Major

Nethercutt's command. After I had secured the prisoners I ordered the house to be set on fire, which was done, and, firing a sl ell from the howitzer as a parting salute, I slowly retired 2 or 3 miles, built large camp fires, posted a strong guard, and encamped for the night, keeping the horses saddled and ready to mount at an instant's notice.

There was no alarm during the night, nor at any subsequent time while I remained on the road, which I did, having no order to retire, until the 15th, when I moved up to Kinston Bridge, and, learning there that messengers had been sent for me, proceeded with my command to within 4 miles of White Hall, where I encamped for the night.

The next morning as the command was passing White Hall it was fired upon by the rebel sharpshooters from the other side of the river. I immediately ordered forward the howitzer, under command of Lieutenant Allis, who opened upon them with shell and canister. After three rounds were received by them they ceased firing and we passed without further molestation, joining the main column the evening of the same day near Goldsborough, not having lost a man killed, wounded, or missing.

I omitted to mention that the prisoners taken, to the number of 20, were turned over to the Fifty-first Massachusetts Regiment, then acting as rear guard, previous to our leaving the Kinston road. This number, however, did not include 3 who were subsequently taken, among whom was a sergeant of Major Nethercutt's band, and were paroled at Kinston on our return, making the whole number of prisoners captured by us while absent from your command 23.

While finding nothing to censure and much to praise in the conduct of every officer and soldier of the command, I cannot but think that the conduct of Lieutenant Chamberlin and Sergeant Beecher, of Company A, who were in charge of the first platoon in the attack upon the rebel pickets, deserves especial commendation. Much of the success attending the attack can be attributed to the soldierly qualities and good conduct displayed by them.

I must not neglect to mention Lieutenant Allis and his howitzer, which was always ready when wanted, and did us good service at White Hall.

I might mention others, but when I say that the conduct of all would, I think, have fully met your expectations and merited your approval if you had been present, I have said enough.

I am, colonel, very respectfully, your obedient servant,

N. HALL,
Captain, Third New York Cavalry.

Lieut. Col. JOHN MIX.

No. 10.

Report of Capt. Ferris Jacobs, jr., Third New York Cavalry, of operations December 13 and 14.

NEW BERNE, N. C., *December* 21, 1862.

COLONEL: I have the honor to report that on the morning of the 13th instant, pursuant to an order from Major-General Foster, I proceeded with my command, of less than 50 men, on the road to the right of my camp until it intersected a road leading into the main highway from New Berne to Kinston about 1½ miles from the point of intersection.

Ascertaining a few minutes after my arrival that a squadron of cavalry had passed down the road toward New Berne about one hour before, I immediately dismounted my command and posted it, so as to cut off the retreat of the enemy, and sent a messenger to General Foster with the intelligence. He returned with a piece from Belger's battery and permission to remain as long as I thought necessary. I had also been told by a contraband here that the enemy had directed him to draw a load of corn into Kinston for them, threatening to kill him on their return if he did not do it. He was about to do so when I came on the ground.

After lying perdu for one and a half hours I took a small party and reconnoitered in the direction of Kinston, and after proceeding about three-quarters of a mile found a bridge in the midst of an almost impenetrable swamp and broken down, the stringers being cut off. Very naturally concluding that no cavalry force would attempt to return to Kinston on that road I returned to camp and reported as above to the general and yourself.

The next morning (14th instant), upon a written order from General Foster to again proceed to the above-mentioned intersection and "hold and occupy the place," with verbal permission to skirmish across the broken bridge if I found my force sufficient, I proceeded with my command of the day previous, and one piece (3-inch Parrott) from Captain Lee's battery, under Lieutenant Cady, to the intersection, posted the piece on a knoll about one-half mile from and overlooking the broken bridge and a breastwork and rifle-pits, which I had found lay behind the bridge on the opposite side of the run, and went forward with 30 cavalry to the point where the road enters the wood, and about 40 rods from the intrenchment. The skirmishers then went forward, under Lieutenant Richardson, through the morass to the run and engaged the enemy's skirmishers on the other side. The range was short, a few yards, and Lieutenant Richardson reported it to have been quite effective. I then (near noon) opened fire with the piece from the knoll, and continued to throw shell into the intrenchment, at short intervals, for about two hours; but finding that the enemy was too well sheltered to be materially damaged at that distance I moved the piece up to the edge of the wood and opened fire with grape and canister at a range of less than 40 rods. About 40 cavalry (mounted) were drawn up in line in advance and to the right of the piece, but sheltered by the wood and a slight acclivity. To this the enemy (who up to this time had only engaged the skirmishers) replied from the intrenchment with grape and canister. After exchanging 12 or 15 shots a few of the enemy's infantry appeared about the bridge as though preparing a crossing, and fearing a sudden charge of a superior force on my feebly-supported piece, I ceased firing and sent the piece back to the eminence it before occupied. Very soon the skirmishers reported that they had crossed the run into the intrenchment, found that the enemy had withdrawn, leaving behind a number of muskets (Valley Forge pattern), haversacks, knapsacks, &c.

Previous to this I had sent Lieutenant Richardson to burn a bridge half a mile up the run and on our right flank. This he did without opposition. Captain Lee, of the artillery, having arrived, together with two companies of the Fifth Massachusetts, upon consultation with him it was concluded, from the sound of the musketry, that General Foster had advanced and was at or near the Kinston Bridge. Captain Lee repaired the bridge, with the assistance of the infantry and without tools, in an almost incredibly short time. Cautiously advancing about one-fourth of a mile and no enemy being seen I gave Sergeant Gibbs, of Company E, permission to dash on with 5 men until he either encountered the enemy or ran on the Federal pickets. In less than half an hour he returned with the intelligence that he met the Federal pickets about 1 mile from the bridge we had just crossed and in sight of the town.

The citizens estimated the force of the enemy at 1,200 infantry and four pieces of artillery, and their loss at 6 or 7 killed and wounded. Five prisoners were captured, 4 from the infantry, who said their regiment was the Twenty-fifth South Carolina, numbering 850 men, and that they lost but 1 man. One said he belonged to Rhett's South Carolina Battery, and that they had four pieces at the bridge but could only get two in position. The prisoners also stated that their officers variously estimated our forces to be from 5,000 to 10,000 at that place.

All of which is respectfully submitted.

F. JACOBS, JR.,
Captain, Commanding Detachment.

Lieut. Col. JOHN MIX,
Commanding Third New York Cavalry.

No. 11.

Report of Capt. George W. Cole, Third New York Cavalry, of operations December 12–16.

SIR : Having been ordered to take the advance on the morning of December 12, nothing of importance occurred to my command till on the morning of the 13th, when I was ordered to make a charge via Sandy Foundation and obtain a bridge on Southwest Creek, about 5 miles from Kinston, to prevent the destruction of it and hold the position if possible. This I proceeded to do, capturing three pickets and thus surprising the rebels destroying the bridge, and by dismounting 12 of my men and advancing under partial cover obtained the first volley, but received in return a shower of canister from a gun placed back of the bridge, and musketry, which severely wounded Jack Costello, of Philadelphia (canister-shot through the head). We succeeded by rapid sharpshooting in keeping them from the bridge and gun (which as often as they endeavored to load we would pick them off) for over an hour, till relieved by the skirmishers of the Ninth New Jersey Regiment.

After the bridge was repaired General Wessells ordered me to report to Colonel Heckman, who ordered me to feel of the enemy. On advancing we were fired into by concealed enemies in force, and B. F. Chapman, of Syracuse, was severely wounded by a rifle-ball in the thigh. After sharp skirmishing the rebels fell back and we encamped on the field, advancing with the company of skirmishers in the morning, and, while the battle was raging, frequently changing position to the right and left, as the enemy's batteries got our range, till ordered by General Foster to make a detour to our right, capturing 4 prisoners, and, endeavoring to cross the bridge to make a charge in the rear of the flying column, I was ordered by you to return and charge up the river. I did as far as the ground permitted, and, as there was no appearance of any enemy or tracks, returned and crossed the bridge, being then

ordered to make a reconnaissance down the river and obtain information of a battery. About 3 miles from town we found a battery wagon
just deserted, and pushing on deployed as foragers, after examining
the position, and charged across the rifle-pits and through their works,
finding in the first works extensive barracks and a secure work containing four 10-pounder guns loaded, with limbers, and one long 32-
pounder ship-gun. A few hundred yards down we found a strong
bomb-proof and earthworks, on which was an 8-inch columbiad, still
warm, with lots of loaded shell, but no powder in magazine. Throwing
out skirmishers I hastened to spike the two heavy guns and to gallop
to town for teams to draw off the 10-pounders, and, obtaining these,
drew off in the night the four guns, securely spiking the other two and
setting on fire the carriages, magazine, barracks, &c., slowly covering
the retreat to Kinston of the teams and guns, starting in the morning
of the 15th for New Berne with seven guns, by order of General Foster.
After proceeding some 6 miles on the Neuse road my advance guard
observed a party of the enemy on a cross-road, and charging down with
a platoon I took 7 prisoners from a South Carolina and 1 from a North
Carolina Regiment, arriving safely in New Berne with guns and prisoners December 16, turning over guns to Lieutenant Prouty and prisoners to Captain Messinger.

I have the honor to submit the above report.

Respectfully, &c.,

GEO. W. COLE,
Captain Company K, Third New York Cavalry.

Lieut. Col. JOHN MIX.

No. 12.

*Report of Col. Thomas J. C. Amory, Seventeenth Massachusetts Infantry,
commanding First Brigade, First Division, of engagements at Kinston,
White Hall, and Goldsborough Bridge, December 14, 16, and 17.*

HDQRS. FIRST BRIG., FIRST DIV., DEPT. OF N. C.,
New Berne, N. C., December 21, 1862.

MAJOR: I have the honor to submit the following report of the part
taken by the brigade under my command in the several actions of the
14th, 16th, and 17th instant:

The First Brigade, consisting of the Seventeenth, Twenty-third, Forty-
third, Forty-fifth, and Fifty-first Massachusetts Regiments (the last three
being nine months' volunteers), marched from New Berne, with the army
under Major-General Foster, on the morning of the 11th instant. The
brigade numbered at this time nearly 3,500 men. Of these, about 100
were sent back on our second day out, being mostly convalescents from
hospital who were found unfit to continue the march.

On our arrival at Southwest Creek on the 13th I was ordered to form
my brigade in two lines on the left of the road, detaching one regiment
to line the bank of the creek, the passage of which was disputed by
the enemy. I sent forward the Twenty-third Massachusetts, which
crossed at the mill-dam, the bridge having been destroyed; this regiment remained on the opposite bank, and rejoined my command on the
march next morning. The Fifty-first Massachusetts had previously been

detached, with orders to remain at Beaver Creek, guarding our rear; this regiment rejoined my command on the evening of the 14th.

On approaching the battle-field of Kinston on the morning of the 14th, by order of the commanding general I detached the Twenty-third and Forty-third Massachusetts to the right and left of the road, respectively, in support of batteries. The Seventeenth was sent to the extreme right to support Colonel Heckman, Ninth New Jersey, in advance. While superintending this movement on the right the Twenty-third and Forty-fifth were ordered forward in the center, and opened fire in the wood, gradually advancing, as did the entire line, driving the enemy to the bridge. On the right I posted the Forty-third to cut off the forces of the enemy on the river road from the bridge, and a portion of these, some 60 in number, shortly afterward surrendered to Major Chambers, Twenty-third Massachusetts.

In this action the Forty-fifth suffered most severely, as indicated by their return of the killed and wounded, hereto annexed,* together with the reports of regimental commanders, to which I beg leave to refer for particulars. The different regiments of my brigade were, during most of the action, scattered through the wood or separated in support of batteries. All who came under my observation conducted themselves with commendable steadiness and gallantry.

In the action at White Hall on the 16th, my brigade being in advance, three of the regiments (the Seventeenth, Twenty-third, and Forty-fifth) were immediately engaged, with what effect could not be ascertained, as the enemy was posted in intrenchments on the opposite side of the river, which was not fordable. These regiments did their whole duty, remaining under fire as far in advance as possible, until I was directed to withdraw them in order to allow the artillery to occupy this position, which was done, and the guns of the enemy soon afterward silenced. In resuming the march from White Hall I was directed to detach the Seventeenth to re-enforce the advance guard, under Colonel Heckman, Ninth New Jersey. The remainder of my brigade took position in the rear of the column.

On the morning of the 17th I was further directed to detach a regiment with the battery which was to hold Thompson's Ford, 5 miles above, which order I complied with, sending the Forty-third Massachusetts under Colonel Holbrook.

In the engagement at Goldsborough Bridge the three remaining regiments of my brigade were not brought into action. Colonel Heckman, of the Ninth New Jersey, will doubtless report upon the conduct of the Seventeenth in that action. Their list of wounded proves them to have been completely engaged, and the successful accomplishment of the object of the expedition in the destruction of the railroad bridge is the only comment I need make on their efficiency.

When all did their duty well it seems unnecessary to mention names, but I feel compelled in this place to testify to the fidelity with which Dr. Galloupe, the senior surgeon of my brigade, discharged his duties. His efficiency at all times, and his care of the wounded, merits the highest praise.

I am, major, very respectfully, your obedient servant,

THOS. J. C. AMORY,
Col. Seventeenth Massachusetts Vols., Comdg First Brigade.

Maj. SOUTHARD HOFFMAN,
Assistant Adjutant-General, New Berne, N. C.

---

* See revised statement, p. 60.

No. 13.

Report of Lieut. Col. John F. Fellows, Seventeenth Massachusetts Infantry, of engagements at Kinston, White Hall, and Goldsborough Bridge, December 14, 16, *and* 17.

HDQRS. SEVENTEENTH MASSACHUSETTS VOLUNTEERS,
New Berne, N. C., December 22, 1862.

LIEUTENANT : I have the honor to forward the following report of the movements of the regiment under my command on the late expedition to Goldsborough :

As nothing of particular interest occurred until Sunday, the 14th instant, that is not already known to the cómmander of the brigade, I will commence at the time I was ordered to report to General Wessells. Soon after the battle of Kinston commenced General Wessells ordered me forward to support Morrison's battery, which was stationed on the right of the road and in great danger of attack from the enemy. In about half an hour the battery was withdrawn to another position, and I was ordered to the edge of the wood. Soon after I was ordered to advance to the right to support another battery at that place. I found the Ninth New Jersey, Colonel Heckman, preparing to advance, and as I received an order to do the same the two regiments proceeded together. I was then notified that the Ninth New Jersey and Seventeenth Massachusetts were to act together, under command of Colonel Heckman. We pushed on over the open space in front and soon reached the bridge, which we crossed together, being the first regiments to go over. We took several prisoners and then marched to the town, when I was ordered on provost duty. This order was afterward countermanded and the regiment was ordered to rejoin the brigade on the other side of the bridge. On the way back I was ordered by General Foster to remain, as the brigade was to advance, and after joining the brigade was again ordered on provost duty.

On Monday we were again ordered to march, the Seventeenth being in advance with the Ninth New Jersey, and this order of march was continued on Tuesday, the 16th. Upon approaching White Hall the Ninth New Jersey was fired upon and deployed upon the banks of the river, where we followed, and remained some two or three hours, the enemy firing upon us from the opposite bank. Attempts were made to find a ford, but the water was found to be from 8 to 12 feet deep. During this time Lieutenant Day and 11 men were wounded. Upon resuming the march the Seventeenth was in the advance.

The next morning, being yet in the advance, I sent forward two companies of skirmishers, Companies F and C, under command of Captain Fuller, and upon approaching the battle-ground they were attacked, but drove the enemy before them. The enemy appearing to be in force in a wood to the left, I received orders from Colonel Heckman to proceed by a road through the wood and obtain possession of the railroad. This was successfully accomplished, with the loss of but 1 man, Sergeant Hardy, of Company F.

My next order was to take the regiment upon the railroad and proceed toward the bridge and to take advantage of the banks of the road for the protection of the men. We advanced, after leaving two companies to observe the enemy, and were soon fired upon by artillery and infantry ; and to avoid the raking fire from the artillery the men were ordered to the banks of the railroad and thus continue the advance. Our march was necessarily by the flank, and upon arriving within 10 feet of the bridge a heavy fire from artillery and musketry in front and musketry from each side and in the wood was opened upon us, while the shells from our own guns fell and burst between us and the bridge. Not being willing to lose the men by the fire from our own side I again ordered them to the banks of the road and sent a messenger to the artillery to change the direction of their fire; but as the shells continued to fall in the same place I was compelled to go myself and represent to the officer in command of the guns that his fire was endangering our own men. As I returned, Morrison's battery came up and took position near the bridge, and I directed the captain's attention to the depot beyond, where a train of cars had just arrived with re-enforcements for the enemy. Directing his guns with much judgment he sent a shell directly into them and continued to keep up a vigorous and effective fire until the bridge was destroyed. He then retired and I drew off my men to support a battery which continued to play farther to the right. After the firing ceased and the battery retired I rejoined the Ninth New Jersey and marched with them from the field.

I cannot close this report without adding my testimony to the admirable conduct of the men of my command. While under fire no sign of faltering was observed among any of them. They behaved like veterans accustomed to such scenes, and deserve all praise for their steadiness and prompt obedience to orders.

Lieut. B. N. Mann, our former adjutant, deserves especial mention for his efforts to destroy the bridge, receiving in the attempt a severe wound.

Adjutant Cheever also behaved with coolness and bravery, being always at hand to attend to the execution of orders, and the officers and men generally performed their duty to my entire satisfaction.

Captain Fuller, with the companies left to watch the enemy, did great service in preventing a flank movement, and captured two of their cavalry who had ventured inside of the line of skirmishers.

Our loss upon the railroad was 18 wounded, and in view of our exposed position and the fire which was kept up upon us the smallness of the number seems marvelous. The wounded men are in good spirits, and one of them after his wound was dressed desired to go back to the scene of action.

Inclosed I send an official report of the killed and wounded: Killed, 1; wounded, 29. Aggregate, 30.*

Very respectfully, your obedient servant,

J. F. FELLOWS,
Lieutenant-Colonel, Comdg. Seventeenth Massachusetts Vols.

Lieut. E. T. PARKINSON,
A. A. A. G., First Brig., First Div., Dept. of N. C.

No. 14.

Report of Maj. John G. Chambers, Twenty-third Massachusetts Infantry, of operations December 11–16.

HDQRS. TWENTY-THIRD REGT. MASSACHUSETTS VOLS.,
Camp Pendleton, December 23, 1862.

SIR: In accordance with General Orders, Nos. 29 and 31, I left camp with my command on the morning of December 11 and took my posi-

---

* But see revised statement, p. 60.

tion in the general column. The regiment numbered 641 enlisted men and 20 commissioned officers, not including surgeons and quartermaster. Upon mustering for the march on the second day I found that about 100 of the enlisted men who had started had been unable to stand the fatigue of the march, and had been sent back to New Berne by the surgeons.

In the forenoon of the second day (12th instant) Private John H. Montgomery, of Company I, who had straggled from the ranks into the wood, was shot through the foot by one of the enemy's scouts.

About noon on the 13th instant, the enemy having been discovered in force at Southwest Creek, my command was among the various infantry regiments ordered forward. The position assigned me was one on the left of the main road, facing the creek. I then deployed a company of skirmishers to ascertain the course of the creek and if there was any enemy in the front. Shortly after, by order of Colonel Potter, I marched my regiment across the creek at the dam and was then ordered to report to General Wessells.

That night the regiment was placed on picket duty in a swamp about midway between the creek above mentioned and Kinston.

During the afternoon of this day Corpl. William K. Worth accidentally shot himself through the hand.

The next morning I received orders to report to Colonel Heckman for skirmish duty, but owing to an unavoidable delay in receiving extra ammunition the order was countermanded and I was again placed in your brigade, where I remained until shortly after the commencement of the action before Kinston, when I was again ordered to report to General Wessells. General Wessells next sent me to report to Colonel Howell, of the Eighty-fifth Pennsylvania Regiment. In accordance with his orders I formed my line in the swamp on the left of the road and about 70 paces in the rear of the Eighty-fifth.

Although subjected to a heavy fire, being in the second line, my men were kept lying down and thus escaped with but 2 wounded, and those not severely. While marching forward I discovered a number of the enemy making through the wood, and immediately sent out a detachment, to which 2 officers and 58 enlisted men, belonging to the Twenty-second South Carolina, surrendered. They had thrown away their arms. Had I been permitted I could, undoubtedly, have secured a larger number; but being in the second line and under the orders of the commander of the first I could not move forward without his sanction.

We left Kinston early on the morning of the 15th instant. Nothing unusual occurred on the road until about noon on the 16th instant, when, as we were approaching a place called White Hall, the firing in front denoted that we had again come upon the enemy.

The Seventeenth Massachusetts, having the right of the brigade, was the first regiment ordered in, and my regiment was immediately formed in line and shortly ordered forward. I marched it through a small piece of swamp under a heavy fire and came to the edge of the Neuse River, my left resting near where the bridge had been destroyed. The enemy were on the opposite bank, secreted behind trees and stumps, and opposite my left they had a log fort. I immediately commenced firing, which we continued until we had expended about 40 rounds of ammunition, when we were ordered out to give place to a battery which had been posted in the open space in our rear.

After the action at White Hall, our brigade being placed in the rear, we did not participate in the action near Goldsborough.

In both actions the officers and men of my command behaved admirably, each seeming to vie with the other as to who should best perform his duty.

Respectfully submitted.

J. G. CHAMBERS,
Major, Commanding Twenty-third Massachusetts Volunteers.

Col. T. J. C. AMORY,
Comdg. First Brigade, Department of North Carolina.

No. 15.

Report of Col. Charles L. Holbrook, Forty third Massachusetts Infantry.

HDQRS. FORTY-THIRD REGT. MASSACHUSETTS VOLS.,
Camp Rogers, December 23, 1862.

SIR: At your request I respectfully submit the following statement of such matters of importance as occurred in this regiment during the campaign from which we have just returned:

The regiment has taken no active part in any of the engagements, but at the battle of White Hall we lost 1 man.

On the march of the column toward Goldsborough this regiment was detached and ordered to Spring Bank Bridge, when four companies were detailed as skirmishers and the remaining companies bivouacked for the night. Captain Tyler, of Company I, had 1 man killed, and Captain Doane, of Company E, had 1 wounded. The regiment marched at 12.30 a. m. to join the column on their return from Goldsborough.

D. A. Jackson, private Company I, reports having been taken prisoner the second day out, and, after being stripped of everything and kept for half a day, he was paroled. He then marched beyond Kinston till he met the hospital wagons returning with the wounded from White Hall; he got in and rode back to Kinston. He returned to New Berne in one of the gunboats.

The men are suffering severely from their feet being badly blistered and the opinion of the surgeon is that they should have rest for three or four days, and, with your approval, I propose to dispense with all drills until after Christmas.

I have the honor to be, very respectfully, your obedient servant,
CHAS. L. HOLBROOK,
Colonel Forty-third Massachusetts Volunteers.

Lieut. E. T. PARKINSON,
Acting Assistant Adjutant-General.

No. 16.

Report of Col. Charles R. Codman, Forty-fifth Massachusetts Infantry, of engagements at Kinston and White Hall, December 14 and 16.

HDQRS. FORTY-FIFTH MASSACHUSETTS MILITIA,
December 22, 1862.

LIEUTENANT: I have the honor to report that eight companies of this regiment (two being on detached service) were engaged in two actions during the late expedition into the interior of North Carolina.

On the 14th instant, the regiment being on the march toward Kinston, I received orders from Major Hoffman, chief of the staff of the general commanding, to advance into the wood on the south side of the Neuse River to support the troops of Wessells' brigade, then engaged and said to be hard pressed. I was directed to act under General Wessells' orders. In compliance with this order the regiment proceeded along the road until directed by General Wessells to file to the right, when it proceeded to enter a wood, which, as afterward appeared, was exposed to a cross-fire from the enemy. Upon entering the wood the regiment opened fire upon the enemy, who were found to be in front and whose fire for a time was very sharp. The regiment continued to advance, occasionally lying down to rest and to avoid the enemy's fire when hottest, and finally, after penetrating the wood, it found that the enemy had fled.

I should add that the Tenth Connecticut Regiment, during one of the periods when this regiment was halted, advanced gallantly through the wood to its assistance, and both regiments penetrated the wood at nearly the same time.

The conduct of the troops was excellent throughout. The action continued for more than an hour, during which time the regiment suffered a loss of 1 corporal and 12 men killed, or who have died of their wounds, and 1 sergeant, 5 corporals, and 38 privates wounded.

On the 16th, in the battle near White Hall, this regiment was ordered by Colonel Amory, commanding the brigade, to form upon the White Hall road, to act as circumstances might require. By further order from Colonel Amory the men were directed to lie down. The regiment did not move from its place during the action except to take position a few feet in the rear of the road, but nevertheless met with some casualties, sustaining a loss of 1 sergeant and 3 privates killed, and 2 sergeants, 2 corporals, and 12 privates wounded. The conduct of the men was in this instance also admirable.

I beg to add that, from the statements of prisoners and from other circumstances, I am satisfied that in the battle of Kinston it was the fire of this regiment that first made untenable the position of the enemy upon the road on the south side of the Neuse River.

The present effective state of the eight companies now in camp at New Berne is 29 officers and 582 men, and of the companies at Morehead City and Fort Macon 4 officers and 181 men; a total of 33 officers and 763 men.

I have the honor to be, respectfully,

CHARLES R. CODMAN,
Colonel, Comdg. Forty-fifth Massachusetts Militia.

Lieut. E. T. PARKINSON,
A. A. A. G., First Brig., Dept. of North Carolina.

No. 17.

Report of Col. Augustus B. R. Sprague, Fifty-first Massachusetts Infantry.

HDQRS. FIFTY-FIRST MASSACHUSETTS VOLUNTEERS,
Foster Barracks, New Berne, N. C., December 21, 1862.

In obedience to Department General Orders, No. 77, and Brigade General Orders, No. 31, I reported, with my command, 778 rank and file, on the Trent road in light marching order at 7 o'clock on the morning of Thursday, 11th instant, remaining with the brigade *en route* till the afternoon of Friday, when we were detached, in company with two pieces of artillery, under command of Captain Ransom, to guard the Beaver Creek Bridge, the main road to Kinston, and the road to Trenton, in rear of the advancing column.

Receiving orders from Major-General Foster at 1.30 o'clock on Sunday morning to join the main force without delay, we marched at sunrise, having in charge 21 prisoners (taken by the cavalry on the main road to Kinston), which were turned over to the provost-marshal upon our arrival at Kinston on Sunday morning.

We advanced with the brigade on Monday morning, arriving at the scene of action at White Hall about 11 a. m. on Tuesday morning, and, though not participating in the engagement, were within range of the enemy's guns on the right of the artillery, which was engaged.

At this point, in obedience to orders of Major-General Foster, Lieutenant Sanderson, with a detachment, was detailed to examine the river below the bridge, to ascertain the practicability of fording it. After a careful examination of the river for nearly a mile he reported that it was not fordable.

Tuesday afternoon, passing up with the main column on the left bank of the Neuse, we bivouacked at night about 12 miles from Goldsborough.

On Wednesday we were detailed to guard the baggage train, from which duty we were relieved in the afternoon when the baggage train and troops were countermarched, after the burning of the railroad bridge by the advance, keeping our place on the return on Thursday, Friday, and Saturday.

We encamped on Saturday night near Deep Gully and arrived at our barracks, on the Trent, at 11 o'clock on Sunday morning, my men considerably jaded and foot-sore.

The orders in regard to pillaging and foraging were enforced, and the men suffered in consequence of an insufficient supply of meat.

Taking into consideration the fact that this regiment had been but a week in the field and received their arms only two days before they received marching orders, I have the honor to report that they behaved well during the entire march.

None were killed, 2 wounded, and none missing.

I have the honor to be, very respectfully, your obedient servant,

A. B. R. SPRAGUE,
Colonel Fifty-first Massachusetts Volunteer Regiment.

Lieut. E. T. PARKINSON, *A. A. A. G., First Brigade.*

No. 18.

Report of Col. Thomas G. Stevenson, Twenty-fourth Massachusetts Infantry, commanding Second Brigade, of engagements at Kinston, White Hall, and Goldsborough Bridge, December 14, 16, and 17.

HDQRS. SECOND BRIG., FIRST DIV., DEPT. OF N. C.,
New Berne, N. C., December 21, 1862.

SIR: I have the honor to report the following as the result of the part taken by the Second Brigade in the late expedition :

Agreeably to orders from headquarters this brigade joined the column the morning of December 11 on the Trent road, being third in position. Nothing of importance occurred until the morning of Sunday, December 14, when within a few miles of Kinston the advance was attacked by the enemy in force. The Tenth Connecticut and Forty-fourth Massachusetts were ordered into position on right of road in support of battery; the Fifth Rhode Island and Twenty-fourth Massachusetts on left of road to support Belger's battery. The Tenth Connecticut, Fifth Rhode Island, and Forty-fourth Massachusetts were then ordered forward to the advance.

The Tenth Connecticut made a gallant charge, under a very galling fire, on the enemy, who were rapidly retreating over the bridge which had been set on fire. The Tenth Connecticut poured in a very destructive fire, capturing a rebel stand of colors and a number of prisoners. By the exertions and gallant conduct of this regiment the bridge was saved, they being the first to cross. As soon as the fire on the bridge was put out our forces crossed, the enemy retreating in all directions. No more resistance being offered, my brigade bivouacked on the outskirts of the town.

Next morning we recrossed the river, continuing the line of march toward Goldsborough.

On the morning of December 16 the enemy made another stand at White Hall, occupying a strong position on the other side of the river, having burned the bridge. The Forty-fourth Massachusetts and Tenth Connecticut were ordered into position on the banks of the river, on the left of the road leading to the bridge. Belger's battery was then ordered to shell the woods, the enemy's sharpshooters being so completely concealed that the fire of our infantry had but little effect. The line of march was then taken up toward Goldsborough, the Fifth Rhode Island and a few sharpshooters of the Twenty-fourth Massachusetts being left behind to engage the rebel sharpshooters till the rear of the column had passed.

At noon on the 17th arrived at railroad bridge over the Neuse River. Captain Belger's battery was ordered to the front, and did signal service in repelling the charges of the enemy. I formed my brigade in line of battle on the hill on the left of the road. The enemy having been defeated, I was ordered to take up the line of march toward New Berne; had got but a few miles when I received orders to countermarch and support a piece of artillery posted on the Everettsville road, where I remained about an hour. I then received orders to march on once more toward New Berne, arriving here last evening (December 20).

I cannot close this report without referring, as I do with gratitude, to the manner in which Col. F. L. Lee, commanding the Forty-fourth Regiment Massachusetts Volunteer Militia; Lieut. Col. R. Leggett, commanding the Tenth Connecticut Volunteers; Maj. R. H. Stevenson, commanding the Twenty-fourth Massachusetts Volunteers; Captain Arnold, commanding the Fifth Rhode Island Volunteers, and Captain Belger, commanding the Rhode Island battery (which was attached to my brigade for the occasion), have seconded all my efforts throughout the whole expedition. Their prompt and efficient action has facilitated every movement which has been undertaken.

The valuable services of the Tenth Connecticut Volunteers at Kinston, as of Captain Belger's battery at White Hall and at Everettsville, were not rendered, I regret to say, without heavy loss, as indicated by the list of killed and wounded, which I transmit.*

THOS. G. STEVENSON,
Colonel, Commanding Second Brigade, First Division.

Maj. SOUTHARD HOFFMAN,
    Assistant Adjutant-General.

---

* Embodied in revised statement, p. 60.

No. 19.

Report of Lieut. Col. Robert Leggett, Tenth Connecticut Infantry, of engagement at Kinston, December 14.

I have the honor to report the part taken by this regiment in the action of December 14 and the losses sustained by it. According to an order received from General Foster I advanced my regiment over three regiments already formed in line in the woods. On reaching the second line the regiment came under a severe fire from the enemy, but went steadily forward to the first line, which was engaged with the enemy and somewhat in disorder. The regiment formed in line with the advance and opened fire upon the enemy. After being under fire about thirty minutes the fire of the regiment was directed to the bridge, across which the enemy were retreating and which they were endeavoring to burn. In some five minutes the enemy broke and my regiment moved at a double-quick down the road. A portion of the enemy formed in line of battle in a corn field on the opposite side of the bridge and opened fire on us as we came on. Immediately on taking the bridge, where we captured about 50 of the enemy, we extinguished the flames. As soon as the enemy found we had taken the bridge they broke up their line in disorder and opened on us from the ditches on each side of the road. The regiment remained at the bridge about thirty minutes, keeping up a continual fire upon the enemy, when we crossed the bridge, taking a number of prisoners behind the intrenchments and, pushing forward, formed in line of battle opposite the city and awaited orders. While in the woods the regiment sustained a loss of 90 killed and wounded, including a captain and lieutenant killed and 2 lieutenants wounded. At the bridge 1 lieutenant was killed, 1 severely wounded, and 6 or 8 rank and file wounded. In the action at White Hall we formed line of battle and advanced to the river on the left of the bridge, opening fire according to order received. The enemy made no response, and one company was detailed to go down the bank of the river in search of a ford. Finding none, volunteers were called for to swim the river and cut down two tall trees on that side, while two were being felled on this side, and at the same time a company was sent to find lumber to build a bridge. The regiment was at work forming a bridge when it received orders to fall back. No loss was suffered by the regiment at this place.

R. LEGGETT,
Lieutenant-Colonel, Comdg. Tenth Regiment Connecticut Vols.

No. 20.

Report of Col. Horace C. Lee, Twenty-seventh Massachusetts Infantry, commanding Third Brigade.

HDQRS. THIRD BRIGADE, DEPT. OF NORTH CAROLINA,
New Berne, N. C., December 21, 1862.

SIR: I have the honor to report the movements of the Third Brigade, consisting of the Third, Fifth, Twenty-fifth, Twenty-seventh, and Fortysixth Regiments, under my command, on the late expedition to Goldsborough:

We were in line, as ordered, on Thursday, December 11, at 7 o'clock, our position being with the baggage train in the rear. It was nearly

10 before we were in column. The nature of the roads for a few miles out from New Berne was such that our progress was quite slow. We arrived, however, at the camp assigned us, on the Trent road, at about 8 p. m.

Friday (12th) we marched through the day, the roads through the swamps gradually growing worse, the train being constantly delayed, until 10 p. m. I had before leaving camp in the morning ordered Colonel Richmond, of the Third Regiment, to detail five companies from his regiment to march beside the wagons and assist the teamsters. Just before dark I ordered the remaining five to fall back and assist in the same manner, as the roads in many places were almost impassable.

Saturday (13th) were in column and moving by 8 o'clock, having, by order from General Foster, detailed the Third Regiment, with a corps of pioneers, to march as the day before and assist the train. Arriving about 10 o'clock at a cross-road, up which the main body had passed, the Forty-sixth regiment, with a section of Lee's battery, was left so posted as to command the approach from the main road to Kinston. We arrived soon after noon at a field near a creek within a few miles of Kinston, where the advance had met and driven back a body of the enemy. We encamped here for the night, and dealt out to the men two days' rations and 20 rounds extra of ammunition.

Sunday (14th) leaving the Fifth Regiment to guard the baggage train, we moved up the Kinston road, the Forty-sixth falling into their position in line as we came, they having been, by order of General Foster, moved up from the post where they had been left and occupied one near us through the night. We soon heard firing from the front and learned that the advance had met the enemy near Kinston. When we arrived we found General Wessells' and Colonel Amory's brigades engaged and Colonel Stevenson's drawn up in two lines, supporting Belger's battery and one of the Third New York Artillery. We were soon ordered to relieve Colonel Stevenson's command, which moved forward, we occupying their position. While here the enemy retreated and we went forward into Kinston, encamping for the night.

Monday (15th) we were the third in column, General Wessells having charge of the train, following the First and Second Brigades. We recrossed the river, marched through the day, and encamped about 8 o'clock.

Tuesday (16th) we were not fairly out of camp when firing was heard in advance of us. We moved on as rapidly as possible and found the First Brigade engaged with the enemy at White Hall. The Second Brigade was soon ordered to the front, and we, under orders from General Foster, moved immediately on toward Goldsborough, having, as we passed, 3 men wounded, leaving a small detachment of the Twenty-fifth and Forty-sixth Regiments as sharpshooters. We encamped at sundown about 8 miles below Goldsborough.

Wednesday (17th) we were early in line. Colonel Heckman, with the Seventeenth Massachusetts and Ninth New Jersey acting as skirmishers, we moved forward and came within sight of the Wilmington Railroad.

About 11 o'clock a small body of the enemy could be seen upon a hill-side near by. Riggs' battery was put in position and a few shells thrown among them, when they disappeared. We immediately advanced. The Twenty-fifth and Twenty-seventh Regiments were moved forward in line on the left, the battery supported by the Third and Forty-sixth upon the right, the Fifth, which had now come up with us, remaining in column. Emerging from the wood I found Colonel Heckman advancing up the railroad, and sent forward to support him the Twenty-fifth and Twenty-seventh Regiments, and subsequently the Third. The Fifth I formed on the left in the wood, commanding a road running down from a mill on the other side of the railroad. Discovering the appearance of troops near there, 1 sent forward a company of skirmishers from the Fifth Regiment, who reported that cavalry and infantry were in sight within the wood but retired as they advanced. The bridge across the Neuse was soon seen to be on fire, and orders came to destroy as much of the road as possible. This being accomplished and the firing having ceased we received orders to form column and follow the main column *en route* to New Berne. Four regiments had already formed and passed, most of them across the creek, in their usual and regular order of march, leaving the Fifth to support the battery.

At this time a detachment of the Third New York Cavalry coming up moved down toward the burning bridge, a few approaching its immediate vicinity. The latter were fired upon apparently by a regiment of the enemy from the edge of the wood near the bridge. The cavalry then moved quickly to the brow of the hill, followed by Captain Morrison's battery, which had been stationed midway between the crest of the hill and the bridge. Two or three regiments (three colors were seen) then emerged from the wood and quickly formed a line of battle just behind the railroad track. Captain Morrison's battery then opened a rapid fire upon them with shell, grape, and canister. A portion of the enemy instantly, with loud cheers, charged up the hill toward the battery, and bore up steadily in the face of a well-directed and most destructive fire.

I immediately ordered the Fifth Massachusetts Regiment to support Morrison's battery, and recalled the regiments that had retired across the creek, and ordered up Belger's battery, which had been assigned to me on account of its having more ammunition left than Riggs'. Warned by the rapid fire of the battery and by the cheers of the enemy they came up rapidly, whereupon I posted the Twenty-seventh Massachusetts Regiment on the left to prevent a flank attack in that direction, and placed the Twenty-fifth Massachusetts in support, believing the main attack of the enemy was in this direction, where he was supported by artillery. On the right I disposed the Third Massachusetts Regiment to resist a flank movement in that direction, and the Forty-sixth Massachusetts was held in reserve so as to be readily available to support the weakest portion of the line.

The enemy meanwhile had been staggered by the crushing fire of the batteries, and at sight of my supporting regiments broke and fled in disorder to the wood. His retreat was covered by a heavy fire from the battery on his right, which inflicted on my command a loss of 3 killed and 19 wounded.

Hereupon I ordered the Twenty-seventh Regiment to file into the wood and to approach the enemy's left and open fire, which they did accordingly. At this time a section of Riggs' battery opened fire from the eminence near the building used as a hospital, and I received orders from General Foster to retire under cover of this fire unless closely pressed by the enemy. The advance of the Twenty-seventh was checked by the fire from Riggs' battery, but the regiment reached a point at which it could put in a few effective volleys. Simultaneously Captain Belger's Rhode Island battery took position near my center and replied to the enemy's battery with good effect, and also shelled the wood that covered his infantry.

The last effort of the enemy was made on my right. He extended his lines along the wood and threatened my flank, when I ordered the Third Massachusetts to open fire. They did so, but soon discontinued as the enemy retired.

The battery on my left being silenced and the enemy making no further demonstration, and having received information that the creek in our rear was rapidly rising, I ordered my command to withdraw. In crossing the creek the water was up to the waists of the men.

Before retiring the field was carefully searched and the bodies of our dead were brought off. Our position was such, being just at the crest of the hill, that our loss was quite small.

My column slowly and in proper order now rejoined the main body. We arrived at New Berne on Sunday.

It is perhaps unnecessary for me to say that the old regiments (Twenty-fifth and Twenty-seventh) sustained their previous well-earned reputation, officers and men doing their utmost not only to hold but to add to their laurels acquired in the old First Brigade. The new regiments did nobly, marching up steadily and firmly and maintaining their line and position without flinching even in the most exposed situations.

I received great assistance from my acting assistant adjutant-general, Bartlett, and my aides, Lieutenant Myrick, of the Fifth Regiment, and Lieutenant Marsh, of the Forty-sixth.

Respectfully, your obedient servant,

H. C. LEE,
Col. Twenty-seventh Mass. Regt., Comdg. Third Brig.

Maj. SOUTHARD HOFFMAN,
Assistant Adjutant-General.

No. 21.

Report of Maj. Josiah Pickett, Twenty-fifth Massachusetts Infantry.

HDQRS. TWENTY-FIFTH REGT. MASSACHUSETTS VOLS.,
Camp Oliver, New Berne, N. C., December 29, 1862.

SIR: I have the honor to forward you the following report of the part taken by the Twenty-fifth Regiment in the late expedition to Kinston and Goldsborough:

Arriving from Plymouth late on the afternoon of the 10th with six companies of my regiment, I found orders awaiting me to be ready to march at 7 o'clock on the morning of the 11th and assigning my regiment to the Third Brigade, under command of Colonel Lee. I left New Berne on the morning of the 11th with six companies of the regiment. Captain Moulton joined me at the Harrison place (our outpost on the Trent road) with the other four companies, making an effective force, exclusive of field, staff, and line officers, of 672 men. Nothing occurred in which the regiment or any of it took part worthy of note till Sunday, the 14th instant, when our forces arrived in front of and commenced the battle of Kinston. Receiving orders to support Battery H, Third New York Artillery, I formed my regiment in line of battle and took position upon the left of the battery. Receiving orders shortly afterward to support Belger's Rhode Island battery I moved forward and took position upon the left. In this latter position I remained until the battle was decided. I then moved forward, crossed the bridge, and bivouacked my regiment that night in Kinston.

On Monday, the 15th, the march was resumed.

On the 16th our forces were engaged at White Hall. My regiment, though within range of the enemy's guns, was not engaged, but marching by the flank through the fields in the rear of our batteries we took up the line of march for Goldsborough. At this time I was called upon to furnish sharpshooters for duty on the banks of the river in clearing the woods on the other side of the enemy's riflemen. About 100 of my men volunteered for this dangerous duty. After being posted they rendered effective service. One man was here shot through the head and severely wounded.

On the 17th the line of march was resumed, the Third Brigade having the advance. Late in the morning skirmishing with the enemy's pickets commenced, which continued until we came upon their main force posted this side of the railroad bridge crossing the Neuse River. I was ordered forward to be in readiness to support the Seventeenth Massachusetts and the Ninth New Jersey, who were sharply engaged with the enemy. I moved forward in line of battle, taking position on the right of the railroad in the rear of the Twenty-seventh Massachusetts and quite near our batteries. I remained in this position till the bridge was burnt and the railroad torn up, when my regiment was withdrawn from the field. In a short time the enemy again made his appearance, advancing in two lines of battle with evident design of charging upon and taking one of our batteries. Receiving orders to again move into the field I advanced by the flank at double-quick and was assigned position in the rear of the Twenty-seventh Massachusetts and on the left and supporting Belger's battery. I ordered my men to lie down, and though exposed to a severe fire from the enemy which we had no chance to return yet the men behaved with perfect coolness. While in this position we sustained a loss of 1 killed and 3 wounded. Night brought an end to the contest, and we were withdrawn, and took up the line of march for New Berne, which we reached on Sunday, the 21st, and went into camp on our old ground.

I cannot end without mentioning in terms of the highest praise the conduct of both officers and men during the whole expedition. On the march, in the bivouac, under fire, in everything that they were called upon to perform they showed all the qualities of the true soldier, and their conduct merits and receives my heartiest commendations.

I have the honor to be, your obedient servant,

JOSIAH PICKETT,
Major, Commanding.

Lieut. GEORGE W. BARTLETT,
Acting Assistant Adjutant-General, Third Brigade.

No. 22.

Report of Lieut. Col. William S. Shurtleff, Forty-sixth Massachusetts Infantry.

HDQRS. FORTY-SIXTH MASSACHUSETTS VOLUNTEERS,
New Berne, N. C., December —, 1862.

SIR: I have the honor to report that in pursuance of your Orders, No. 18, dated December 10, 1862, the Forty-sixth Regiment of Massachusetts Volunteer Militia left its camping ground and entered upon its place in line of march at 7 o'clock on the morning of Thursday, December 11, 1862, and, in company with the other regiments and being third in line of your brigade, were *en route* toward Kinston at about 9 o'clock a. m., continuing the march until about 10 o'clock p. m., when it went into camp about 13 miles from New Berne, on the Trent road. It recommenced its march in the same order at 9 o'clock on the morning of December 12, and nothing of note having transpired again encamped with the other regiments of yours and the preceding brigades about 28 miles from New Berne.

Our march was again resumed on the morning of Saturday, the 13th, at about 9 a. m., and continued for about an hour, when our regiment was detached from your brigade and left, with two pieces of Riggs' battery, Captain Lee, to guard and hold certain cross-roads and the approaches from the rear and front of the center road of the three roads leading to Kinston.

The artillery having been placed with excellent judgment and skill by Captain Lee in position to completely command the approach in front from Kinston, the Forty-sixth was drawn up in line of battle behind and in support. Pickets were thrown forward on the Kinston road and one company (F), under Captain Conwell, was detached and posted at two angles of a triangle, some 200 yards in our rear, formed by a cross by-road connecting the road on which our main body was posted and the road taken by the main body of the army, so that no approach upon either road could be made by the enemy without our receiving timely warning. We held this position until sundown, when I received orders from Major Hoffman to advance my command 4 miles nearer to Kinston up the road on which we were then posted, and to hold and occupy certain cross-roads indicated until further orders. This order we executed, making the march after nightfall. I detached Company D (Captain Grimes), to march some 50 yards in advance, and then threw forward 10 men, under Lieutenant Knapp, as an advance guard against surprise. Having arrived at the position indicated, the artillery was placed in position by Captain Lee, the infantry drawn up in line in support in the edge of the woods skirting the cross-road; the several roads thoroughly picketed; the main road in front and a cross-road leading to the right by Captain Grimes' company, divided so as to make three posts, in charge, respectively, of Captain Grimes, Lieutenant Knapp, and Lieutenant Bronson; the road in our rear picketed with two posts from Captain Kingsbury's company (B), and the road leading to the left and toward the position of the advance of the army, and the road in our immediate right and left front by detachments from Captain Lincoln's company (G). Our baggage train I brought forward and placed on our left, on the cross-road leading to the rear of the advance, and of course between our left and our pickets. The men were then ordered to lie upon their arms, and of course no camp fires were allowed. This position we occupied undisturbed until morning, our pickets bringing in one prisoner, whom I delivered to the care of the rear guard; and then, in pursuance of an order from Major Hoffman, received about midnight, we proceeded at 7 a. m. of the next day to rejoin the main body, arriving just in time to take our proper place in line, where we continued until, the advance becoming engaged near Kinston, we were sent by your orders forward to support a battery, not then, however, engaged. After the engagement at Kinston was over we under your orders resumed our former position in line, and entering Kinston encamped there with the rest of your brigade.

Resuming our march on the following morning (Monday) we preserved our place in line until, the advance being engaged at White Hall with the artillery, under your orders we passed forward following the Twenty-fifth Massachusetts and formed in line on its left, but were immediately after by you ordered into line of march again.

At this time some 50 men were detached, under orders purporting and believed to come from Major-General Foster, to remain at White Hall as sharpshooters. We then proceeded in our proper place and encamped about 6 p. m. Our detachment of sharpshooters all reported to the regiment before morning, with the exception of one, Chapin, of Company I, who was wounded by a rifle-ball from the enemy's sharpshooters in the arm, not dangerously. Our march was resumed in place on the following morning about half past 7 o'clock, and, upon arriving near the line of the Wilmington Railroad, your brigade engaging the enemy, we were ordered up and formed line in support of Belger's battery, in a position taken at first but at once changed before it engaged the enemy, we following it and supporting it in its new position on the brow of a hill commanding the railroad and woods around the railroad bridge. This position we occupied until, the bridge having been burned and the track torn up, the battery retired and we were ordered to follow it *en route* for New Berne.

Pending, however, forming the line for the march, the enemy reappearing to the right and front of our late position and threatening the battery left to cover our retiring force as well as our flank, we were ordered back and at once formed in rear of the Third Massachusetts. In this position we remained, the men lying down, being subjected to a somewhat annoying fire of the enemy's battery on our left, but without having any opportunity to engage any portion of his force, until under your orders (the enemy's batteries having been either silenced or withdrawn and his infantry retired) we resumed our place in line *en route* again for New Berne, having at the outset to ford a mill-stream rendered swift and deep by the raising of the flood-gates by the enemy, as we supposed. In this action, and while occupying our position after the renewal of the engagement, I regret to state that we had 1 man (one Wall, of Holyoke, Mass., a member of Company B) mortally wounded and 3 others wounded by the shell of the enemy, the details of which I give in paper marked A, appended hereto.* Continuing our march, we encamped with the rest of your brigade about 10 o'clock p. m. at our camping ground of the previous night, and, resuming our march on the following morning at 8 o'clock, reached camp at about 11 o'clock p. m. after a march toilsome and harassing to the men to the last degree.

Resuming our march at 8 o'clock a. m. on the following day, after a comparatively easy march of some 12 miles we encamped about 6 miles below Kinston, passing down the river road. Resuming our march in our place in line on the day following, at 8 o'clock a. m., we again encamped at 6 o'clock some 13 miles from New Berne, on the Trent road, and from this place our ambulances without halting were sent forward under charge of Maj. James H. Waterman, surgeon of our regiment, then in charge of the ambulance train, to New Berne, our wagons following at early morning in advance of the brigade. Resuming our march at 7 o'clock a. m. we arrived at New Berne and our camping ground about 2 o'clock p. m., the men very foot-sore and weary, otherwise in good condition and spirits. I am happy to be able to state that from my careful observation of the men under my command, both under the trials of toilsome marches and the excitement of anticipated engagement with the enemy, I believe you have in them a body upon whom you may with confidence rely should occasion require you to use them in any

---

* Nominal list omitted. See p. 60.

of the ways that the exigencies of the service may require. I am happy also to bear witness to the energetic and conscientiously careful discharge of duty on the part of Captain Lee, with whom I was associated, as I have stated, and to whom I am greatly indebted for valuable assistance and counsel on our solitary night march and bivouac, and who, I am glad to learn, on subsequent detached duty added to his reputation and performed valuable service.

I should deprive myself also of a pleasure if I omitted to call to your notice the fact that the adjutant of our regiment, James G. Smith, commencing the expedition suffering from a painful accidental shot wound in the leg, still insisted upon accompanying the regiment, and though having double duty to perform, in the absence of one of the field officers, still manfully endured all the toils of the march and the field and rendered me invaluable service in the management and control of the regiment. I should also state that Colonel Bowler accompanied the expedition until after the affair at Kinston, but was unable by reason of indisposition to assume command, and felt constrained by increasing illness to return to New Berne on the morning of the third of the expedition.

Very respectfully, your obedient servant,

WILLIAM S. SHURTLEFF,
Lieut. Col., Comdg. Forty-sixth Massachusetts Volunteers.

Col. HORACE C. LEE,
Commanding Third Brigade, First Division.

No. 23.

Report of Col. Charles A. Heckman, Ninth New Jersey Infantry, First Brigade, Second Division.

HDQRS. NINTH REGIMENT NEW JERSEY VOLUNTEERS,
Camp Reno, December 21, 1862.

SIR: I have the honor to report that in accordance with your order I on the morning of the 11th with my regiment took my position on the right of the column, which position it retained during the whole march.

On the second day, December 12, we came up with the advance guard of the enemy. I immediately deployed two companies as skirmishers, and drove the enemy back without loss on our side.

On the morning of December 13, at 11 a. m., we came up with the enemy, who had two guns in position on the west bank of Southwest Creek, supported by infantry. I here found Captain Cole, Third New York Cavalry, with his men dismounted, warmly engaged with the enemy. Lieutenant-Colonel Mix had placed Lieutenant Day's section of Morrison's battery in a good position and was sending shell into them rapidly. I immediately ordered Companies C, H, and G to cross the stream on the right, while with the remainder of the regiment I crossed at a mill-dam about a mile above on the left. On arriving at their works from their rear I found it deserted and the guns withdrawn. My whole command having joined me I stationed one company at the bridge and with the balance, having sent you word of my intention, proceeded up the road, and when about a mile from the creek was saluted by a round of canister from a 6-pounder and musketry. I charged on the double-quick and Yankee yell and secured one 6-pounder and caisson, killed 3, wounded several, and took 8 of the enemy prisoners. Skirmishing continued through the whole day, my loss being 1 wounded and 1 taken prisoner.

About 3 p. m. Captain Cole, Third New York Cavalry, reported to me, by order of General Wessells, to reconnoiter forward. We had proceeded about three-fourths of a mile when our advance guard was fired upon by volleys of musketry from both sides of the road, wounding 1 cavalryman. I ordered the cavalry to the rear and deployed as skirmishers three companies on each side of the road. The men advanced steadily and firmly under a heavy but wild firing of two regiments of infantry and two 6-pounders. Morrison's battery came to my assistance and drove the enemy into their stronghold. We bivouacked for the night.

On Sunday, December 14, the enemy was found posted about 1 mile this side of the village of Kinston in strong force. Four companies (C, D, E, and I) were sent forward as skirmishers. They were opened on by artillery and infantry, but stood their ground admirably, and doing great injury to the enemy by their well-directed fire. Again Morrison came forward with a section of his battery and opened briskly, a regiment having arrived to support the battery. With the remaining six companies I moved to the right to prevent being flanked from that direction. We came up with a regiment of them on our right front, engaged them, and in a few minutes forced them to retreat precipitately. I next discovered a regiment on my right flank. Captain ———, with a section of his battery (New York artillery), opened upon them with splendid effect, and prevented them from forming a junction with their main column. Being re-enforced by four regiments of Wessells' brigade (Eighty-fifth and Ninety-sixth New York, One hundred and first Pennsylvania, and the Seventeenth Massachusetts) I formed the Eighty-fifth, Lieutenant-Colonel Wellman, and the Ninety-sixth, Colonel Gray, in line of battle to the right, the Ninth New Jersey and Seventeenth Massachusetts facing to our original fronts. The Eighty-fifth and Ninety-sixth advanced rapidly about 400 yards, discovered the enemy behind a fence in the edge of the wood, and poured a volley into them, at which they fled in confusion, exposed to our fire. I then ordered the Ninety-sixth, supported by the Eighty-fifth, to advance, under cover of the wood, upon the bridge, and the Ninth New Jersey, supported by the Seventeenth Massachusetts, to advance in a direct line across the open ground to the same point. The One hundred and first remained to support the battery.

On arriving near the bridge, shell, canister, and musketry were opened upon us from the opposite bank of the river. Firing continued from both sides about twenty minutes.

I regret, sir, the necessity to report that at this point we lost the gallant Colonel Gray.

After the enemy's guns had been silenced and their forces dispersed the Ninth New Jersey, aided by the Seventeenth Massachusetts and Eighty-fifth New York, extinguished the flames of the burning bridge and crossed in the following order: Ninth, Seventeenth, and Eighty-fifth.

My regiment secured three 6-pounder brass guns, one stand of colors, and a number of prisoners and small-arms.

Loss, 2 killed, 32 wounded, and 1 missing.

I take pleasure in adding that the lamented Colonel Gray, Lieutenant-Colonel Fellows, Lieutenant-Colonel Wellman, and Major Zabriskie, with their commands, without exception, displayed marked bravery and coolness, and proved effectually their efficiency and gallantry.

As soon as the bridge was sufficiently repaired to permit the crossing of the artillery I received the order forward. We marched through the town, the Ninth having the advance and the Seventeenth Massachusetts following. We marched along the bank of the river, crossed the railroad, and bivouacked for the night about 2 miles from Kinston, on the Goldsborough road.

At 6 a. m., the 15th instant, received orders to return to the bridge. On arriving at the bridge we crossed and continued our march in the direction of White Hall. Nothing of interest occurred throughout the day, and at night bivouacked 3 miles from White Hall.

At 7 a. m., 16th instant, we were again in motion, the Ninth New Jersey in advance. Upon our arrival at White Hall my advance guard drew the fire of the enemy, who were strongly intrenched and fortified on the opposite side of the river, having previously burned the bridge to prevent our crossing. I immediately ordered the fences thrown down on each side of the road for the artillery to take their position. In the mean time I had ordered four companies to deploy as skirmishers, which they did, the entire length of our front, and the engagement soon became general. The remaining six companies of the Ninth were immediately ordered forward to support the skirmishers and, when an opportunity offered, to engage the enemy. The Ninth warmly engaged the enemy until their ammunition (60 rounds) was expended. The regiment was then ordered to retire and send for ammunition. The Seventeenth Massachusetts relieved us on the left and the Twenty-third Massachusetts on the right. While waiting for ammunition the columr was ordered forward. We received orders to wait for our supply and bring up the rear.

Our loss was 3 killed, 42 wounded, and 3 missing.

I then received orders to take the Seventeenth Massachusetts and proceed in advance toward Goldsborough Bridge. Bivouacked the night of the 16th about 5 miles from the bridge.

Morning of the 17th column again moving, Seventeenth Massachusetts in advance, Ninth New Jersey following. About 2 miles from the bridge commenced driving in the enemy's pickets. On coming in sight of the bridge saw a regiment of the enemy passing along the railroad. I immediately ordered the Seventeenth Massachusetts to send out skirmishers and advance on the left of the road and the Ninth New Jersey to deploy and advance on the right as far as the railroad. Found the enemy here in force on both sides of the river. The Seventeenth, on reaching the railroad, by my order left one company where the country road crosses the railroad and then marched down the railroad in the direction of the bridge. The company left in position on the country road were charged upon by a squadron of cavalry whom they repulsed, and captured 2 prisoners, without loss on our side. The Ninth advanced on the right of the Seventeenth to within 30 feet of the river and bridge. As soon as the artillery arrived on the ground I withdrew the Ninth New Jersey and Seventeenth Massachusetts to give the artillery position. Torches were sent us and orders to burn the bridge. I rode up to the Ninth New Jersey and called for volunteers to burn the bridge. Numbers volunteered instantly, but as I wanted but three, Lieutenant Graham, acting aide to me, and two privates, one of Company E, William Lemons, and ———, took the port-fires and started on their dangerous mission. The enemy were thickly posted on both sides of the river and all about the bridge, but the volunteers were successful, and we soon had the gratification of seeing flames and smoke ascending in columns, and the bridge was effectually destroyed. Our loss was 12 wounded.

The object of the expedition having been accomplished I received orders to countermarch and return. Had proceeded about 1 mile when firing was heard in our rear, and word came forward that our rear had been attacked. I immediately ordered the Ninth New Jersey into line of battle on the left of the road and he Seventeenth Massachusetts on the right. Soon after forming there I received orders to return to the scene of action, which I did, and posted my regiments on the right and left of the country road and left of Belger's battery, which was warmly engaged with the enemy. Remained in that position about thirty minutes, when we were relieved by a regiment of Wessells' brigade, and we started on our return and arrived at New Berne Saturday evening, 20th instant, having marched the last day 30 miles.

Officers and men displayed great coolness and bravery. The color-sergeant and color-guard behaved nobly.

I deem it my duty, however, to mention particularly Lieut. George Graham, of Rocket Battery, W. W. McChesney (citizen), volunteer aides, for valuable services rendered throughout the expedition.

I have the honor to be, general, very respectfully, your obedient servant,

C. A. HECKMAN,
Colonel.

General J. G. FOSTER,
Commanding Department of North Carolina.

No. 24.

Report of Maj. Abram Zabriskie, Ninth New Jersey Infantry.

HDQRS. NINTH REGIMENT NEW JERSEY VOLS.,
December 21, 1862.

SIR : I respectfully forward to you the report of the part taken by the regiment under my command in the expedition, under Major-General Foster, against Goldsborough :

We started from New Berne on the morning of December 11, this regiment holding the advance of the column, which position it retained during the whole march.

On the second day, December 12, we came up with the advance guard of the enemy. By your order two companies were sent forward as skirmishers, and continued steadily to drive the enemy back without any loss on our side.

On the morning of December 13, at 11 a. m., we came up with the enemy in a strong position on the west bank of Southwest Creek. Two of the companies were ordered to cross the stream on the right, while the remainder of the regiment crossed at a mill-dam about a mile above on the left. When we arrived at the breastwork thrown up by the enemy I found it deserted both by their artillery and infantry. However, discovering the enemy half a mile farther up the road, the regiment charged on them at a run, and succeeded in capturing a gun and caisson, 6-pounder, besides wounding 3 of the enemy and taking 6 or 8 prisoners. Skirmishing with the enemy continued through the whole day, our loss being 1 man wounded and 1 taken prisoner.

On Sunday, December 14, the enemy were found posted about 1 mile this side of the village of Kinston in strong force. Four companies (C, D, E, and I) were sent forward as skirmishers. They were soon opened on by artillery and infantry, but stood their ground admirably, holding the position they had taken and doing great injury to the enemy by their well-directed fire. The remaining six companies were sent on the right to flank the enemy's position. We came up with a regiment of them stationed in the wood on the right, and after a half hour's fight succeeded in forcing them to retreat precipitately. Then advancing by your order across the field to the road I opened fire with the head of column upon the enemy, who were retreating across the bridge, and succeeded in preventing their escape. After crossing the bridge we took three guns, one stand of colors, and numerous prisoners.

Our loss in this battle amounted to 2 killed, 32 wounded, and 1 missing.

Resuming our march, on the 16th we came up with the enemy on the other side of the Neuse River, at White Hall, posted behind breastworks and buildings. The whole regiment was deployed along the banks of the river, kept up a brisk fire for about two hours, and were at last relieved, our ammunition being expended and our loss being very heavy—3 killed, 42 wounded, and 3 missing.

We again came up with the enemy December 17, posted on the north side of the Neuse, at the railroad bridge near Goldsborough. The right wing of the regiment was deployed along the bank of the river on the right of the railroad, while the left companies were held in reserve. The whole regiment was at last drawn off, after the firing of the bridge, to make way for the artillery. December 17 we commenced our return march, and arrived in New Berne on Saturday, December 20.

There were so many instances of individual courage shown in the different battles that it is difficult to mention particular names. However, I cannot forbear mentioning with praise Captain Stewart, Lieutenant Brown, Captain McChesney, and Lieutenant Townley, not only for personal bravery but for their ability as commanders of their respective companies; and also the names of Privates William Lemons, Company E, and —— ——, who, with Lieutenant Graham, set fire to the railroad bridge near Goldsborough.

I inclose a list of the killed, wounded, and missing.*

I am, sir, very respectfully, your obedient servant,

ABRAM ZABRISKIE,
Major, Commanding.

Col. C. A. Heckman.

No. 25.

Report of Brig. Gen. Henry W. Wessells, U. S. Army, commanding Third Brigade, Peck's Division, of operations December 5–21.

HEADQUARTERS THIRD BRIGADE, PECK'S DIVISION,
New Berne, N. C., December 22, 1862.

MAJOR: I have the honor to report that pursuant to instructions from Major-General Peck I left Camp Suffolk, Va., on the 5th instant with my brigade, composed of the Eighty-fifth, Ninety-second, Ninety-sixth New York, and Eighty-fifth, One hundred and first, and One hundred and

---

*Embodied in revised statement, p. 60.

third Pennsylvania Volunteers, under orders to proceed to New Ferry, on the Chowan, near Gatesville, there to report to the commanding officer of the Department of North Carolina.

My command arrived at the point designated on the 6th instant, where it was met by Major-General Foster with transports for the brigade. The troops embarked on the following day, arriving at this station on the 9th. An expedition having been planned and organized to move in the direction of Goldsborough, the column was put in motion on the morning of the 11th, the advance taken by Heckman's Ninth New Jersey Volunteers, followed by my own brigade, to which was attached Morrison's battery Third New York Artillery.

No serious obstacles were interposed by the enemy until arriving at Southwest Branch, 6 miles from the town of Kinston, where it was found the main road crossing the creek was well watched and strongly guarded both by artillery and infantry. A skillful feint having been made toward this point, the main body moved by an upper road, crossing the creek about half a mile below on a mill-dam. The bridge was found to be partially destroyed and the enemy covering it with two guns and a force of infantry.

This position was at once reconnoitered by the Ninth New Jersey Volunteers with their usual intrepidity, and a crossing was effected by the mill, threatening the enemy's right. At the same time, by direction of the commanding general, I detached the Eighty-fifth Pennsylvania Volunteers, Colonel Howell, with orders to force a passage below the bridge, by felling trees or fording, and engage him on the right. This difficult duty was handsomely performed. Howell's skirmishers, led by Captains Hooker and Phillips, pushed boldly through the swamp, engaged the enemy's battery under a shower of grape, and by a well-directed fire of musketry drove the cannoneers from the ground, and Heckman's advance appearing simultaneously from the left the enemy fled, leaving one of his guns in our possession. The brigade in the mean time crossed at the mill, and being joined by the Twenty-third Massachusetts Volunteers moved forward about 3 miles and bivouacked for the night, the Ninth New Jersey Volunteers with Morrison's battery taking up a position about 1 mile in advance.

On the following day (December 14) the line of march was resumed at an early hour and in the usual order. Heckman's skirmishers were soon engaged with the enemy's outposts, and to support him I directed the Eighty-fifth Pennsylvania Volunteers to move through the wood on the left of the road with a view to act against the enemy's right. A section of Morrison's battery was also ordered forward, supported by the One hundred and third Pennsylvania Volunteers, Lieutenant-Colonel Maxwell, with directions to take a suitable position and open fire.

The Eighty-fifth New York, Lieutenant-Colonel Wellman, was then thrown forward and to the right of the road, with instructions to engage the enemy on the flank and press him vigorously toward the left. This regiment was soon followed by the One hundred and first Pennsylvania Volunteers, Major Taylor, and the Ninety-sixth New York Volunteers, Colonel Gray, with similar orders. In the mean time being informed that a portion of the Ninth New Jersey Volunteers were failing in ammunition I directed the Ninety-second New York Volunteers, Colonel Hunt, to move down the road to relieve or support Colonel Heckman as circumstances might require. All these movements were executed by the several regiments with alacrity and precision, deserving the highest praise. My whole brigade was now in position before the enemy's line; the firing was heavy and almost incessant; the wounded were being rapidly brought to the rear, and the enemy, concealed by the wood and posted behind an almost impassable swamp, maintained his position with stubborn obstinacy. At this time, and on my application to the major-general commanding, I was re-enforced in succession by the Seventeenth, Twenty-third, and Forty-fifth Massachusetts Volunteers. These fine regiments took their positions with the coolness and precision of veterans, and the whole line was then directed to advance and push the enemy at every point. The major-general commanding having arrived on the ground made further disposition of the troops and conducted the affair to a rapid and successful termination.

Under my orders to advance, the whole brigade, supported on the left by other regiments, moved gradually forward, converging toward the enemy's line of retreat, driving him from the church and throwing him back toward the bridge, over which the main body escaped, leaving several hundred prisoners in our hands.

The retreat of the enemy was closely followed by the Eighty-fifth and One hundred and third Pennsylvania Volunteers on the 'eft (the latter suffering severely in crossing the open field), while the Ninety-sixth and Eighty-fifth New York and One hundred and first Pennsylvania Volunteers charged from the right; the Ninety-second moved along the road in support of the battery. The bridge was fired in several places by the enemy and exposed to a destructive fire of artillery and musketry from the opposite bank, but every regiment, including those from other brigades, seemed to vie with each other in emulation, and pressed forward with unflinching determination.

That gallant officer, Colonel Gray, Ninety-sixth New York Volunteers, with his face to the foe and the colors of his regiment first on the bridge, fell mortally wounded in the hour of victory.

The flames were extinguished without serious injury to the bridge, and my brigade being reformed on the opposite bank of the river continued its march through the village of Kinston and bivouacked for the night on the Goldsborough road.

The steadiness of the troops during this short conflict gave me full confidence of success, and the conduct both of officers and men, with rare exceptions, merits the highest praise. For special acts of gallantry and good conduct I have the honor to refer you to the reports of regimental commanders herewith inclosed. Captain Stewart, assistant adjutant-general; Captains Webster and Hall, brigade quartermaster and commissary, and my aides, Lieutenants Beegle and Foot, rendered most important service. My orders were conveyed by these officers to every part of the field in the thickest of the fight with the most gratifying coolness and intelligence. Acting Brigade Surgeon Rush also deserves the highest commendation for the prompt and efficient manner in which the onerous duties of his department were conducted.

A list of casualties accompanies this report.*

My brigade, having recrossed the Neuse, accompanied the expedition toward Goldsborough, and its object having been fully accomplished by the destruction of the railway and bridge, the whole command returned to this station, arriving at New Berne on the 21st instant.

Respectfully, your obedient servant,

H. W. WESSELLS,
Brigadier-General of Volunteers, Commanding.

Maj. SOUTHARD HOFFMAN,
Assistant Adjutant-General, Dept. of North Carolina.

---

* Embodied in revised statement, p. 60.

No. 26.

*Report of Lieut. Col. Abijah J. Wellman, Eighty-fifth New York Infantry,
of engagement at Kinston, December 14.*

HDQRS. EIGHTY-FIFTH REGIMENT NEW YORK VOLS.,
New Berne, N. C., December 22, 1862.

CAPTAIN : I have the honor to report that at the engagement before
Kinston, which occurred on the 14th instant, the Eighty-fifth New York
Volunteers participated in the following manner :

Pursuant to an order received from General Wessells the aforesaid
regiment was led to the right of the position which was occupied by
the Union forces during the earlier stages of the battle, and reported to
Colonel Heckman, of the Ninth New Jersey Volunteers, as his support,
at 11 a. m. In accordance with instructions from Colonel Heckman my
regiment was then moved to the extreme right, for the purpose of a
flank demonstration. After proceeding 500 yards, preceded by two companies of my command deployed as skirmishers, a regiment of the enemy
was discovered 200 yards in advance, drawn up behind a fence at the
edge of the wood in which we were. My skirmishers moved quietly to
the right of the regiment and opened a brisk fire upon the enemy, which
was returned without effect. While the attention of the latter was thus
engaged my own line advanced quickly and poured in a volley, at which
the enemy fled in confusion, some of them across an open field exposed
to our fire.

Subsequently my regiment was directed to support the Ninety-
sixth New York Volunteers in an advance upon the bridge, where the
lamented Colonel Gray received a mortal wound. My line was formed,
immediately on our arrival at the bridge, along the bank of the river
with the left resting at the bridge, which was being swept by grape and
canister together with musketry from the opposite bank. A hot fire
from both sides continued for twenty minutes. After the enemy's guns
had been silenced and their forces dispersed, men from Captain Jenney's
battery, the Ninth New Jersey Volunteers, and my own regiment extinguished the flames of the burning bridge. The Ninth New Jersey Volunteers then crossed over closely followed by the Seventeenth Massachusetts, which latter regiment had just at that moment arrived and
had not participated in the capture of the bridge. Immediately after
the latter regiment followed my own, which thus had the honor of being the first of General Wessells' brigade which gained the opposite
bank.

We captured between 20 and 30 prisoners, besides a quantity of small-
arms.

I take pleasure in adding that both officers and men, without an exception, displayed much bravery and coolness.

I am, very respectfully and truly, your obedient servant,

A. J. WELLMAN,
Lieut. Col., Comdg. Eighty-fifth New York Vols.

Capt. ANDREW STEWART,
Assistant Adjutant-General, Wessells' Brigade.

No. 27.

Report of Col. Lewis C. Hunt, Ninety-second New York Infantry, of engagement at Kinston, December 14.

HDQRS. NINETY-SECOND NEW YORK VOLUNTEERS,
December 21, 1862.

CAPTAIN: I have the honor to report that my regiment took part in the battle of Kinston, on the 14th instant, as follows:

I was ordered by General Wessells to relieve the Ninth New Jersey, which had for some time been engaged and their ammunition reported as running low. I found them in a heavily-wooded swamp, passed their line of battle, and deployed the regiment as skirmishers. This was done under a heavy fire from the enemy, which, fortunately, passed overhead for the most part on account of the peculiar conformation of the ground and the usual tendency to overfire, but rained down the leaves and branches upon us. The swamp with its thick undergrowth was next to impassable, but the men floundered through the bog-holes, sometimes up to their middle, delivering their fire as they advanced. The point upon which we were operating seemed to be occupied by the enemy in large force, and I moved three companies from the right flank toward the right and front, hoping to find higher ground from which I might make a diversion in support of the main body. I accompanied them, wishing to ascertain the nature of the ground toward the right and whether other troops were assisting in the attack. I found higher and more open ground but no assisting forces. I then sent my adjutant, Lieutenant Ward, to General Wessells asking for re-enforcements. Returning to the main body I found it had moved off toward the left flank and had charged upon a body of the enemy near the junction of the roads, but was received with such a volley as compelled it to fall back. I then formed my men for another charge upon the enemy directly in front, hoping to gain a ditch near the fence which we might hold until re-enforced. I directed my men to run up in line without firing, which the enemy no sooner perceived than they poured in a volley which indicated a force of five times our number, but which, as before, passed mainly overhead.

My men were now completely exhausted with their two hours' work in the swamp. We had tried to get a foothold to the front and on both flanks but had failed for want of numbers. The enemy were reported to me by several as passing our right flank, and I judged it best to draw back to the higher ground in our rear where I knew the One hundred and third Pennsylvania to have been posted. Here I received through yourself authority from General Wessells to direct the movements of the several regiments in the neighborhood. Having had the opportunity of getting a good knowledge of the position and its requirements, I directed Lieutenant Colonel Maxwell, whose regiment (the One hundred and third Pennsylvania) was nearly twice as strong as mine, to advance through the swamp directly to the front, occupy the ditch, and, if possible, pass on beyond the fence. The men were fresh and went forward gallantly to the task before them, which I lightened as much as possible by sending forward the Eighty-fifth Pennsylvania, Colonel Howell, lying in the wood near by, and pointed out the direction of attack. I presumed that my adjutant had returned to the right flank with the re-enforcements I had sent him for, and so, while my men were resting in support of a section of Morrison's battery and on the ground previously occupied by the

One hundred and third, I sent forward four of my officers in different directions toward the front with General Wessells' orders that every regiment should press forward. They fulfilled their mission to my entire satisfaction, contributing, I have every reason to believe, to the flight of the enemy which soon after took place.

My officers behaved most creditably, with one exception, of which a special report will be made, and the regiment, as a whole, sustained the reputation which it earned at the Seven Pines as a part of Casey's division. This is paying as high a compliment as the regiment could desire.

Of the officers whom I happened to notice I would mention Lieutenant-Colonel Anderson, Adjutant Ward, Captain Cleary, and Lieutenant Cole for their coolness and gallantry. Captains Bice, Miller, and Merriman, and Lieutenant Babcock are highly spoken of. Sergeant Ball, of Company —, was especially active and zealous, and deserves promotion. Sergeant O'Neil and Private Pierce, of Company E; Private Sheridan, of D, and Color-bearer Sergeant Thompson are especially mentioned by their company commanders. Surgeon Edmeston followed the regiment into the swamp and attended the wounded under fire, and, for his zeal, energy, and consideration during the whole expedition, deserves the highest praise.

A special report of the casualties, amounting to 3 killed, 16 wounded, and none missing, is herewith forwarded.*

I have the honor to be, very respectfully, your obedient servant,

L. C. HUNT,
Colonel, Ninety-second New York Volunteers.

Capt. ANDREW STEWART,
Assistant Adjutant-General, Wessells' Brigade.

No. 28.

Report of Capt. George W. Hinds, Ninety-sixth New York Infantry, of engagement at Kinston, December 14.

HDQRS. NINETY-SIXTH NEW YORK STATE VOLUNTEERS,
Camp near New Berne, N. C., December 21, 1862.

SIR: I have the honor to report that on the 14th instant, when the brigade engaged the enemy in front of Kinston, N. C., in compliance with the orders of General Wessells, this regiment, under command of Col. Charles O. Gray, moved down the road leading to the bridge in front and filed into the wood and moved by the right flank several hundred yards to the right of the road, where it was formed into line of battle and rested lying down, while a company of skirmishers was sent forward to feel the enemy's position. Finding him in the corner of the wood to the right in some force we advanced in line of battle under fire, the Eighty-fifth New York Volunteers being on our left and One hundred and first Pennsylvania Volunteers as support, charging and cheering, the enemy retreating. As we advanced we commenced a rapid fire, which was discontinued after a few moments, the enemy getting out of range.

Soon receiving an order to advance we moved toward the river, feel-

---

* Embodied in revised statement, p. 60.

ing our way through the strip of wood leading to the road. Arriving at the road and seeing the enemy crossing the bridge in retreat we charged rapidly toward it, delivering a rapid fire and receiving a raking fire from artillery and musketry. Arriving near the bridge our regiment was cut in two by the Tenth Connecticut crossing our line of march. Col. Charles O. Gray, with two companies, charged up to the bridge, arriving, with the regimental colors, first upon the end of the bridge, where a portion of a rebel regiment was cut off, they throwing their guns upon the burning timbers and retreating to the left. At this moment our noble colonel was shot through the breast by a musket-ball, from which wound he soon died. Had it not been for this sad blow our regiment must have been the first to have crossed after the fleeing enemy.

Respectfully,

GEORGE W. HINDS,
Captain, Comdg. Ninety-sixth Regiment New York Volunteers.

Capt. ANDREW STEWART,
Asst. Adjt. Gen., Third Brigade, Peck's Division.

No. 29.

Report of Col. Joshua B. Howell, Eighty-fifth Pennsylvania Infantry, of operations December 13-17.

HDQRS. EIGHTY-FIFTH PENNSYLVANIA VOLUNTEERS,
Camp near New Berne, N. C., December 22, 1862.

CAPTAIN: I have the honor to report that on December 13 instant, while on the march on the recent expedition to Kinston, &c., at the Southwest Creek, when the firing at that place began I was ordered by the general to take my regiment to the right of the road leading to the bridge, and on the right of the battery attached to our brigade, to support the battery.

Soon after I had placed my regiment in the position ordered I was ordered by the general to send forward two companies as skirmishers, to examine the wood and swamps as far as the creek, to see if a crossing were practicable and to feel for the enemy. In obedience to the order I sent forward Companies B and D, under command of Captain Hooker (Company B), senior captain. Shortly afterward I was ordered to move the regiment forward and cross the creek if at all practicable, and attack and drive the enemy if we found them on that side of the road. By felling trees across the creek and with much difficulty and labor we effected a crossing. We had not only the creek to pass over but swamps on both sides of it. While crossing the creek we heard sharp and rapid firing in the advance of us, and on coming out on the road ascertained that the two companies (B and D), under Captain Hooker, on their approach to the road from the wood, had come in contact with a party of the enemy (First Mississippi Light Artillery), who had a piece planted on the road. They were promptly attacked by Captain Hooker and driven from their gun—repulsed with a loss of 4 men killed.

In the conflict our men received two discharges of grape and canister from the enemy before they were driven from their gun. The enemy were driven up the road, and in the earnestness of pursuit it was omitted, unfortunately, to leave any one in charge of the piece captured. The Ninth New Jersey, coming up immediately thereafter, took the piece into their possession, and from this circumstance might have the entire credit of having captured it awarded to them; whereas the credit of the capture belongs to the two companies of my regiment exclusively. I do not believe, however, that that gallant regiment would claim the credit to the prejudice of my companies. I wish to state here that the timely arrival of Captain Hooker with the companies and the gallant achievement in capturing the gun and driving the enemy manifestly saved that brave regiment (the Ninth New Jersey) from being seriously cut up.

I desire, captain, to communicate to the general, in the very highest terms of commendation and praise, the promptness and gallantry manifested by the brave officers and enlisted men engaged in that affair; and I also desire to do the same justice to the other gallant officers and enlisted men of my regiment for their untiring zeal and indefatigable industry and energetic efforts made and exhibited in effecting the crossing of the creek, overcoming difficulties that seemed almost insurmountable, and also for the rapid movement forward (exhausted as they were) after the crossing was effected.

On December 14 instant, at the battle of Kinston, I was directed by the general, at the very commencement of the fight, to deploy my regiment in line and move it forward through the woods and swamps which lay on the left of the road leading to Kinston. That order was promptly obeyed—as promptly as the almost impassable character of the ground admitted of. After getting through we came to the open field on the left of the road, on the line with the fire of the enemy and in advance of the fire from our side. We met with some of the enemy in our passage. I sent my adjutant back to inform the general of our position (having received an order to halt), and to ask for further orders. The adjutant returned with orders to return to the road and there support the battery which was under the command of Captain Morrison, which order was obeyed. I found, however, a part of the left wing of the One hundred and third Pennsylvania Volunteers directly in front of us. Our position was on the left of the battery and left of the road.

Shortly afterward, in obedience to an order of Lieutenant Beegle, aide to the general, I moved my regiment, deployed in line of battle, forward, preceded by a part of the left wing of the One hundred and third Pennsylvania Volunteers. On coming out of the wood and swamp we came to an open field in front of us, and there we received sharp, rapid, and continuous fire from the enemy. I should think we were under fire there for an hour. We returned their fire as rapidly. The firing on our part was splendidly done. We then moved rapidly forward across the field, driving the enemy from the wood in front of us and from the church. We passed through the wood to a large open field lying between the wood and the river.

The fire of the enemy during this time was very heavy, but the gallant officers and enlisted men of my regiment and of that part of the One hundred and third Pennsylvania Volunteers which was with us dashed forward, with a shout and with cheers, through the fire without flinching. When about midway over the field I discovered, by ascending a slight elevation which we were approaching, that my own regiment and the One hundred and third would be cut to pieces by pursuing that line, and that I could accomplish as much by moving to the right, which I did. We succeeded, as I have before stated, in driving the enemy from our front and from their position in the church.

It gives me the greatest pleasure to refer the general to the gallant conduct of my officers and enlisted men in this engagement and to be able to speak in the very highest terms of their coolness, firmness, and courage during the whole time of the fight.

In the engagement at White Hall and at the railroad bridge my regiment was under the eye of the general, and, although not actually engaged in the firing, it was in line of battle and within reach of the enemy's fire, and behaved with coolness and firmness, and ready and desirous to be led into the fights.

For the good conduct and soldierly bearing of my regiment on the march, going and returning, we have already received the commendation of our general; that, with the consciousness that we deserve it, is our highest reward. There was no straggling from my regiment of any account, and from all disgraceful acts and scenes done and perpetrated on that march their skirts are free.

A list of the casualties has already been furnished you.*

I have the honor to be, captain, respectfully, your obedient servant,
JOSHUA B. HOWELL,
Colonel Eighty-fifth Pennsylvania Volunteers.

Capt. ANDREW STEWART,
Assistant Adjutant-General, Wessells' Brigade.

No. 30.

Report of Maj. Alexander W. Taylor, One hundred and first Pennsylvania Infantry, of engagement at Kinston, December 14.

HDQRS. 101ST PENNSYLVANIA VOLUNTEERS,
New Berne, N. C., December 24, 1862.

CAPTAIN: As commander of the One hundred and first Regiment Pennsylvania Volunteers during the engagement near Kinston, on Sunday, the 14th instant, I have the honor to submit the following as my report:

When the firing commenced in the morning, by order of the general the One hundred and first Regiment was drawn up in line of battle on the right of the road near the wood. We remained in this position until ordered by the general forward and to the right of the road in rear of the Ninety-sixth New York.

Soon after, by order of Colonel Heckman, we were moved forward and to the left to the support of a battery of the Third New York Artillery. We remained with this battery until the close of the engagement.

During the entire engagement the conduct of the regiment was all that could have been desired.

Very respectfully, your obedient servant,
A. W. TAYLOR,
Major One hundred and first Pennsylvania Volunteers.

Capt. ANDREW STEWART,
Assistant Adjutant-General.

----

* Embodied in revised statement, p. 60.

No. 31.

Report of Lieut. Col. Wilson C. Maxwell, One hundred and third Penn sylvania Infantry, of engagement at Kinston, December 14.

HDQRS. 103D REGIMENT PENNSYLVANIA VOLUNTEERS,
Camp near New Berne, N. C., December 25, 1862.

SIR: I have the honor to report the action of the One hundred and third Regiment Pennsylvania Volunteers in the engagement at Kinston:

Sunday, December 14, at 9.40 a. m., I was ordered to move my regiment forward as a support to one section of Morrison's battery, having the right wing rest on the right and the left wing on the left of said section, with orders to direct our movement with the battery. After advancing gradually for over 50 rods with said battery we halted, when the Ninety-second New York Volunteers moved past us and filed off in front of the right wing of the One hundred and third. After remaining not more than one hour in advance they fell back across the right wing and reformed their line in our rear.

At this time Captain Stewart, assistant adjutant-general, came up and ordered me to move my regiment forward in advance of the battery. We moved forward through a swamp of thick undergrowth and water from 1 to 2 feet deep and about 20 rods wide. Immediately after crossing said swamp we received a volley of musketry from the enemy's line, which we then learned was but a few rods in our advance. We delivered a volley, lay down under cover of a small knoll, reloaded and fixed bayonets, rose, delivered another volley, and charged up over the bank. At this time an order from the Eighty-fifth Pennsylvania, which was moving up in rear of the left wing, demanded us to cease firing, as we were firing into our own men.

The enemy's fire in front of our left was immediately directed on our right, making, in connection with the fire from the strong line in front, a heavy cross-fire; also we were in danger of a fire in the rear from the Forty-fifth Massachusetts, whose line was immediately in rear of our right wing. Under this combined fire I gave the order to lie down, and from this position we again rose, charged after the enemy some 20 rods, when their fire was completely silenced. We were then ordered to halt and await the arrival of the battery. During this time the Ninety-sixth New York moved by the flank from our right and reached the bridge. From the time we first formed our line as a support to the battery until we reached the bridge was from 9.40 a. m. to 2 p. m. Our loss during this time out of 430 actually engaged was 14 killed and 58 wounded, some of the latter mortally. During the whole of this time all of the officers and men of the regiment behaved in an exemplary manner, showing entire coolness. I will mention that when we made our first charge the Tenth Connecticut overlapped our extreme right two companies; from the second charge we moved past their line, passing their left.

Accompanying this you will find a complete list of the killed and wounded, made from the surgeon's report.*

I have the honor to be, sir, very respectfully, your obedient servant,
W. C. MAXWELL,
Lieutenant-Colonel, Comdg. One hundred and third Pa. Vols.

Capt. ANDREW STEWART,
Asst. Adjt. Gen., Third Brigade, Peck's Division.

---

* See revised statement, p. 60.

No. 32.

Report of Lieut. Col. Horace A. Manchester, First New York Marine Artillery, of naval operations on the Neuse River, December 12–15.

HEADQUARTERS MARINE ARTILLERY,
New Berne, N. C., December 16, 1862.

SIR: In accordance with your instructions on the 12th instant, after waiting until 4 p. m. at Willis' Landing and learning that your boats could not reach me for want of water, I proceeded on board the steamer Allison, accompanied by the steamers Ocean Wave, Port Royal, Wilson, and North State, to ascend the Neuse River on a reconnaissance toward Kinston. At dusk I anchored in the neighborhood of Lee's Landing, about 20 miles from New Berne by the river, making all dispositions for defense in case of attack.

At daylight on the 13th got under way, and, with much difficulty and labor, worked our way up to within 2 miles of Kinston, meeting with but slight opposition from the guerrillas on shore, by whose fire 1 man of the Allison crew was seriously wounded. About 2 miles from Kinston, upon a turn in the river, we suddenly found our boats in face of a 10-gun battery, and penned up within the banks of the river, about 100 feet wide. I immediately ordered the Port Royal, Ocean Wave, and Wilson to retire, the North State not having arrived, and interposed the Allison between the battery, which had opened fire, and the boats. The boats had to be backed down, as the river would not admit their turning, and it occupied twenty or thirty minutes. We replied to the enemy's fire with one Parrott gun, the first fire being within canister range. These shells were exploded within the batteries with apparent effect, as the enemy ceased their fire for some time after.

It was sunset when the firing commenced, and it became dark so soon that I was scarcely able to get the boats under the protection of the trees before we were left to grope in total darkness. The enemy's shell exploded over and around us with but little damage. The Allison received three shots, one taking off the tip of the pilot-house; the next passing through the roof and through the smoke-stack, and the third cutting away some fender and light work. Our boats were moved in double line, hay, beef, bread, &c., being packed along the sides. The guns were put into battery on the decks and bags of oats spread over the decks. In this position we awaited until morning in expectation of the enemy's appearance. Several attempts were made to reconnoiter our position in the early evening, which were promptly defeated by the sentinel's fire. A reconnaissance was made on theirs by Lieutenant Doane, but little information gained.

Soon after taking up our position for the night we heard heavy firing a few miles to the westward of us, which continued about an hour.

At daylight in the morning, upon examination, I found the largest boat on the bottom, and that the water had fallen during the night over 19 inches. I immediately ordered a lighter boat to hitch on to the Ocean Wave and drag her off and then drop down the river to deeper water. This was a slow operation, as we had to go stern foremost, and our boats often grounded. The forenoon was consumed in getting 5 miles. Here we found the North State, and learned that a force of the enemy was about 3 miles below to dispute our passage down. We winded all our boats but the Ocean Wave and dropped down 2 miles farther when we succeeded in turning her. The North State was sent forward to find the enemy's position, the others following to shell them out. About a mile from an old dam, on a turn where the water was swift, we found the first party, who fled after one of their number had been tumbled into the river by a shot. Occasional firing was kept up by the enemy for 5 miles, when we came upon a party lodged behind a log house. They stood but one fire from our Parrotts and ran, leaving, as we learned, several of their number killed and wounded. Here we learned from a contraband that a party of 70 had crossed early that morning to obstruct the river at Oldfield Bank Landing, and that, by the addition of others, we might expect to meet 140 men there. We proceeded at once to the place, the enemy keeping up an occasional shot at us. Here we found them in possession of both sides of the river, and occupying the turn so as to fire into the stern of our boats. They opened on the Ocean Wave with a volley which was returned with interest, and the other boats, seeing their position for the fire, opened with grape and canister with such effect that the last boat coming up could find no one to fire at. The boats, after a brief delay, passed on to Street's Ferry, where, meeting the boats of the navy, reported to you.

In the last fight Edwin J. Perkins, of Marine Artillery, was killed, and another of that regiment and a member of the Signal Corps were seriously wounded.

Our loss was 1 killed and 3 severely and several slightly wounded. Of the enemy, 1 was shot from the bridge and fell into the water, and 2 were blown to pieces on the bank. At the log house 30 men are said to have been in it when two 30-pounder Parrotts, loaded with canister, were fired through it at a distance of 200 feet, and at the Oldfield Bank the fire of the Ocean Wave, North State, and Port Royal was direct and within 400 feet of the enemy.

The Ocean Wave and Allison are somewhat disabled, both by shot and contact with trees; the North State has lost her rudder. The other boats are in good order for use.

Respectfully,

H. A. MANCHESTER,
Lieutenant-Colonel, Commanding Marine Artillery.
Commander A. MURRAY, *U. S. Navy.*

No. 33.

Reports of Maj. Gen. Gustavus W. Smith, C. S. Army, commanding Department of North Carolina and Southern Virginia, of operations December 13–18.

PETERSBURG, VA., *December* 13, 1862.

The force at Suffolk is believed to be still strong and threatening. Evans has been fighting all day in advance of Kinston, principally artillery. We were retiring slowly, and at night the enemy were near the bridge at Kinston. Evans calls for re-enforcements. One regiment started from here at 8 o'clock and one more will start at 6 o'clock in the morning from this place and one from the Blackwater. I will probably not leave this place before to-morrow afternoon. Is there anything from Fredericksburg?

G. W. SMITH,
Major-General.

Hon. JAMES A. SEDDON,
Secretary of War.

GOLDSBOROUGH, N. C., *December* 15, 1862.

I arrived here at 3 p. m. The telegraph with General Evans is cut off. By latest information he was at Falling Creek, 6 miles this side of Kinston. Enemy now estimated at 30,000, and scouts report re-enforcements constantly arriving from New Berne. Governor Vance is here. He tells me that all accounts agree in stating that our troops behaved admirably in the engagement of yesterday.

G. W. SMITH,
Major-General.

Hon. JAMES A. SEDDON,
Secretary of War.

—

WELDON, N. C., *December* 15, 1862.

Your telegram is received.* I have ordered three regiments of Daniel's brigade, the three Mississippi regiments and two batteries from Richmond, one regiment from Petersburg, and one from the Blackwater and batteries to be sent as soon as possible to Goldsborough. Please ask the Quartermaster-General to do everything in his power to expedite their transportation. Evans retired this side the river about dark and burned the bridge. General Beauregard will send 5,000 infantry and three batteries.

G. W. SMITH,
Major-General.

Hon. JAMES A. SEDDON.

[Indorsement.]

Preparation has been made to send forward all the troops referred to in this dispatch as soon as they can be ready to-day. The three regiments of Daniel's brigade will march to Petersburg with the batteries and take rail from there. The Mississippi regiments will go by rail all the way; start at 12 m.

Respectfully,

A. C. MYERS,
Quartermaster-General.

—

GOLDSBOROUGH, N. C., *December* 16, 1862.

MY DEAR SIR: Your letter of Sunday reached me at this place last night. I received your telegram of Sunday night at Weldon, and from that place by telegraph ordered troops forward to this point—one regiment of infantry from the Blackwater, one from Petersburg, and six from Richmond, with three batteries of artillery, leaving on the Blackwater two regiments of infantry, two of cavalry, and several batteries; one regiment at Petersburg, a small guard at Weldon, and a guard at the battery at the obstructions in the Roanoke near Hamilton. I arrived here after 3 p. m. yesterday, and sent you by telegraph a statement of the condition of affairs. At 12 o'clock midnight it was reported that the enemy were passing up the river on the south side toward Dudley Station or this place. General Evans appealed strongly for cavalry, reporting that he had but one company. I had none, nor troops of any kind. I improvised, with the assistance of the Governor, who is here,

_____

* See Confederate correspondence. Communication from Seddon to Smith, dated December 14, 1862, *post.*

the best means we could for obtaining information from the south side of the river. There were no troops there whatever, the battalion picketing on that side below Kinston having been enveloped by the enemy. General French arrived about 7 o'clock this morning with one regiment from Petersburg, and has gone down to Bear Creek, about 12 miles, to join General Evans. During the night, not knowing when the troops from Petersburg might be expected to get here, I had ordered General Evans to send one regiment to a bridge 6 miles below here and one to this place to guard the railroad bridge and common-road bridge near the city. We can get nothing through the telegraph from Wilmington. Heavy firing is now heard distinctly upon the river below, supposed to be at White Hall Bridge, 15 miles below, or perhaps near the Six Mile Bridge. There is, as usual, great delay and difficulty in the railroad transportation. I hope soon to obtain information of the enemy's movements, and on the arrival of the troops from Richmond will endeavor to strike an effective blow. Banks' fleet is reported by General Whiting as certainly at Beaufort, but it is not known whether or not they have landed. They are within ten or twelve hours' sail of him. Troops from General Beauregard were to have arrived in Wilmington this morning early, but I have heard nothing from there to-day. We have no cavalry, no transportation, and are laboring under some other difficulties. My staff is not here. I am much pressed for time, and write in great haste. The troops are in good heart. I shall do my best to give a good account of the enemy.

Very respectfully and truly, yours,

G. W. SMITH,
Major-General.

Hon. JAMES A. SEDDON,
Secretary of War.

P. S.—A good many of Evans' troops were cut off and are now coming straggling in across the river. The heavy guns in the battery at the obstructions below Kinston had to be abandoned when General Evans fell back. They had previously beaten back the gunboats. The 200 men composing the garrison, with the field battery, retired toward the north and arrived here with their pieces last night. General Evans has not furnished me with an estimate of his losses.

—

GOLDSBOROUGH, N. C., *December* 16, 1862.

The enemy made this morning a serious attack at White Hall Bridge, on the right and rear of our position, this side of Kinston. At 2 p. m. a cavalry force, estimated at 500 or more, burned a turpentine stem at Mount Olive, at the railroad, 14 miles from here; injured the track and cut the telegraph poles. Extent of injury not known.

Later.—The enemy have been driven back from White Hall Bridge; his loss very severe, ours not so. They have abandoned Kinston. The bridges below here are burned. We are sadly in want of cavalry. None of the troops from Richmond have arrived.

G. W. SMITH.

Hon. JAMES A. SEDDON.

—

GOLDSBOROUGH, N. C., *December* 18, 1862.

The enemy yesterday made a sudden movement in large force upon the two bridges near this place, drove back our pickets, and succeeded in burning the railroad bridge. Several brigades were afterward passed over the county bridge. They attacked and drove the enemy back and saved the county bridge. The enemy were in very large numbers, their second position was a very strong one; night was at hand; only a portion of the troops from Richmond had arrived; none of the artillery and none of the cavalry from either Richmond or Petersburg. I did not consider it advisable to attack them again. The enemy retired during the night. The few mounted we have (about 60) have been sent out to ascertain their position and probable intentions. It was supposed that the whole force of the enemy was present. The force was certainly over 15,000. Without cavalry it is almost impossible to obtain accurate or prompt information of the enemy's movements or numbers. They are burning mills and houses and devastating the country in every direction. We have not transportation sufficient even for ammunition. I shall move as soon as possible.

G. W. SMITH,
Major-General.

Hon. JAMES A. SEDDON,
    Secretary of War.

—

HEADQUARTERS,
Goldsborough, N. C., December 29, 1862.

GENERAL: I have the honor to inclose copies of the reports of Brigadier-Generals Evans, Robertson, and Clingman, giving an account of the various affairs with the enemy in this vicinity in their recent bridge-burning and pillaging expedition from New Berne.

Brigadier-General Evans, with 2,000 men, held them in check at Southwest Creek, beyond Kinston, on the 13th, and on the 14th delayed their advance for some time and succeeded in withdrawing his force with small loss to the left bank of the Neuse River at Kinston. He held them at bay until the 16th, when they advanced on the opposite side of the river and made an attack at White Hall Bridge, about 18 miles below Goldsborough, in which they were driven back by General Robertson with severe loss. Small re-enforcements arrived from Petersburg and Wilmington on the 15th, one regiment of which was placed in position to cover the railroad bridge over the Neuse, near this place. A battalion of artillery, which had made a successful retreat from the works at the obstructions below Kinston after the enemy occupied the latter point in force, was stationed on this side of the river at the railroad bridge, and about half a mile above at the county bridge. On the 16th a regiment arrived from Wilmington and one from Petersburg, both of which were sent to the right bank of the river and placed under General Clingman's command to protect the two bridges.

On the morning of the 17th, having no cavalry and being unable to obtain information by other means, I directed Lieutenant-Colonel Stevens, of the Engineers, with two brigades and five pieces of artillery, to make a reconnaissance for the purpose of ascertaining the position and numbers of the enemy. General Evans' brigade had then reached Goldsborough by rail, and, remaining on board, only awaited the clearing of the track and watering of the engines to move by rail to the position already occupied by General Clingman with his three regiments, about 1½ miles beyond the railroad bridge. The capacity of the water-tanks being inadequate for the amount of transportation accumulated here at that time, the cars were delayed until after 12 o'clock for want of water, pending which the enemy appeared in force before General Clingman's three regiments and he withdrew across the county bridge to this side of the river. The artillery of the enemy was playing upon the railroad bridge, and Evans' brigade had at last to move forward by the county road and cross, if at all, the bridge half a mile above the railroad.

About 2 o'clock in the afternoon one bold and daring incendiary succeeded in reaching the bridge, and covered by the wire wall of the abutment, lighted a flame which soon destroyed the superstructure, leaving the masonry abutments and pier intact. At that time re-enforcements which I had ordered from Richmond were hourly expected. It was very important for us now to save the county bridge, the only means remaining of crossing the river in this vicinity. Evans' and Clingman's brigades were ordered to cross, supported by Pettigrew's brigade, and the Mississippi brigade, just coming in, was ordered to move forward at once.

The enemy were driven back from their position on the line of the railroad, but on account of the lateness of the hour, the nature of the ground, and the fact that our artillery, cavalry, and a large portion of the re-enforcements had not yet arrived, it was not advisable to attack their strong second position that evening. During the night the enemy made a hurried retreat to their fortifications and gunboats, moving with such celerity that it was useless to attempt pursuit with any other arm than cavalry, of which at that time, unfortunately, we had none. I passed over the railroad from the Neuse Bridge to Wilmington on the 24th and returned last night. The bridge is fast being repaired. At present we are subjected to the temporary inconvenience of transshipment across the county bridge, but in a very few days this will be remedied and everything restored to the former condition.

I regret that this grand army of invasion did not remain in the interior long enough for us to get at them. As it is, they burned the superstructure of two bridges, which cost originally less than $10,000 and can be replaced at once, and have utterly failed to attempt to take advantage of the temporary and partial interruption of our railroad line for the purpose of striking a decisive blow at any important point before we could thoroughly re-establish our communications with it.

I beg leave to call your attention to the reports of Lieut. Col. [W. H.] Stevens, C. S. Engineers, and of Lieutenant-Colonel Pool, as well as to those of the three brigadier-generals previously named.

Our loss is reported at 71 killed and 268 wounded, and about 400 missing. Most of the latter were taken prisoners at Kinston Bridge, and have since been returned paroled.

I am, general, very respectfully, your obedient servant,

G. W. SMITH,
Major-General, Commanding.

General S. COOPER,
Adjutant and Inspector General, Richmond, Va.

No. 34.

Report of Lieut. Col. Walter H. Stevens, C. S. Engineers, of operations December 16–17.

HEADQUARTERS,
Goldsborough, N. C., December 19, 1862.

GENERAL: I have the honor to submit the following report:

On the morning of Tuesday, the 16th instant, by your direction, I posted Lieutenant-Colonel Pool's battalion of North Carolina Troops (armed as infantry) at the railroad and county bridges over the Neuse near this place. Two pieces of artillery were placed commanding the railroad bridge, one at the county bridge, and two a short distance in the rear, enfilading a portion of the right bank of the river which flanked the position immediately at the bridge. These dispositions were completed at 7 a. m. About 10 a. m. I started with Colonel Cunningham without an escort to reconnoiter the right bank of the river from Dudley toward White Hall, having been led to believe that the enemy were or might be marching in that direction with a view of cutting the railroad. On arriving at Dudley, hearing nothing of the enemy, in company with Colonel Collier, of the county militia, I proceeded 4 or 5 miles on the road to White Hall, seeing nothing of the enemy. I soon saw a large smoke in the direction of Mount Olive. I rode immediately to Dudley and found a train of cars that started for Wilmington had turned back, finding the road was burned at Mount Olive. I took the train to this place to report to you the cutting of the road. On the way to Goldsborough I passed General Clingman's command on the roadside, near where the county road crosses the railroad.

Early the next morning I was directed to make an armed reconnaissance of the enemy with Generals Evans' and Clingman's commands. My instructions were to find the enemy, to sweep the county, guarding the flanks well, and if engaging the enemy the command should be so pressed as to fall back before being re-enforced, to fall back fighting and cross at the county bridge; or if pressed too closely to try that, to continue up the river, crossing higher up. A first-rate guide was furnished me.

General Clingman's command being on the road to Dudley, I informed General Evans that his command ought to go to Dudley by rail as soon as they could be embarked. As soon as the troops were fairly aboard I started with Captain Reinhart and a part of his cavalry company for Dudley. On reaching the county bridge I heard a few cannon-shot east of the railroad. On crossing the bridge I found a portion of General Clingman's command, Colonel Shaw commanding. I was informed by Colonel Shaw that the enemy were advancing in two columns, one by the railroad, the other by the White Hall road, and that one regiment (Colonel Marshall's) was posted at the railroad bridge on the right bank. General Clingman then came upon the ground and I recommended him to form his command with two pieces of artillery obliquely across the county road, covering the head of the bridge. I then proceeded to the front and right on the county road to a point where the road turns to cross the railroad on the way to Dudley. A steady fire of artillery was kept up by the enemy at the railroad bridge. I soon saw one regiment of the enemy get on the railroad track, soon another, and finally four in all; these, with four or six pieces of artillery, were all the troops I could see. They marched deliberately toward the railroad bridge, then double-quicked for a few instants, and finally disappeared from my view either in the woods or behind the railroad embankment. Immediately a sharp fire of musketry ensued. This very quickly ceased. I rode back to the county bridge and found General Clingman's command falling back, one regiment double-quicking on the road from the railroad bridge to the county bridge. I then met General Clingman, who said his men would not stay at the railroad bridge, and asked me if I thought he had better cross the bridge. I thought if the men would not stand they had better cross, and told him so.

Lieutenant Fuller, of Starr's battery, placed his guns in position with coolness and judgment, and worked them some moments with ability, only ceasing his fire when all of his command, save his support, were over the bridge. Captain Reinhart's cavalry were cool and staid by me until ordered over the bridge.

The command with the artillery were posted then upon the left bank. I then joined General Evans, who was near the bridge, and in a few seconds discovered the railroad bridge on fire At his request I immediately reported the fact to you. A short time after seeing you I accompanied you to the field. Clingman had recrossed and was on the right near the railroad. As I crossed in your company, Evans' command were crossing. He was starting a regiment in toward the railroad bridge when we crossed. I then accompanied you to the extreme right to Clingman's position, from whence I had informed you you could see the whole field. While with General Clingman a portion of his command had charged the enemy and rejoined his line while we were in company with him. Clingman's whole line then advanced, upon which we crossed to the left (General Evans' position). Upon reaching General Evans we found our whole line up to the railroad embankment. It was then dark and the firing had ceased. The large number of the enemy, strongly posted, with numerous artillery, the darkness and extreme coldness of the night, induced me to give my opinion in the council in favor of withdrawing to the right bank of the river, which was effected deliberately before midnight.

I have the honor to inclose the report of Colonel Pool.

Respectfully submitted.

W. H. STEVENS,
Lieutenant-Colonel of Engineers.

Maj. Gen. GUSTAVUS W. SMITH.

No. 35.

Reports of Brig. Gen. Nathan G. Evans, C. S. Army, commanding Brigade, of operations December 13–17.

KINSTON, N. C., *December 14,* 1862.

General Foster attacked Kinston yesterday with 15,000 men and nine gunboats. I fought him ten hours. Have driven back his gunboats. His army is still in my front. I have only four regiments, and will await his attack this morning. I think I can hold my position.

N. G. EVANS,
Brigadier-General.

General S. COOPER.

HEADQUARTERS EVANS' BRIGADE,
Near Goldsborough, N. C., December 20, 1862.

MAJOR: I have the honor to submit the following report of the action of the troops under my command in the recent engagements near Kinston, White Hall, and at the railroad bridge near this place:

On Saturday, the 13th instant, the enemy approached Kinston in considerable force and attacked the line of our forces under the immediate command of Col. James D. Radcliffe, North Carolina Troops, who had taken position on the west side of Southwest Creek. At 10 o'clock I arrived on the ground and assumed command, and ordered Colonel Radcliffe to take command of the left wing at the crossing of the upper Trent road. The enemy then was attacked at Hines' Mill while he attempted to cross the creek. After a sharp engagement of an hour I fell back toward the Neuse River, keeping line of battle and arresting his approach about 2 miles from Kinston Bridge. He then attacked in considerable force, but retired after an engagement of ten hours. I rested on my arms that night in this position, the enemy ceasing fire after nightfall.

On the morning of the 14th (Sunday), being informed by Colonel Radcliffe that the enemy was approaching his position, I directed him to open fire while I would attack his left. I ordered an immediate advance, and soon became engaged with my whole line with the enemy in heavy force—supposed to be about 20,000. The action lasted three hours, when, ascertaining his greatly-superior force, I retired with my command across the Neuse Bridge, when the enemy pursued with heavy fire, stormed the bridge, and drove me back to the town of Kinston, capturing about 400, including no [number of?] sick prisoners. Reforming my line, with the additional re-enforcements of Col. [S. H.] Rogers' Forty-seventh Regiment North Carolina Troops, in a commanding position in rear of the town, I again awaited the attack. About 3 p. m. Major-General Foster sent his staff officer (Colonel Potter) to summon me to surrender, which I promptly declined. In an hour he commenced shelling the town, but hesitated to renew his direct attack. Taking advantage of my position, I retired in column to Falling Creek, where the major-general commanding had forwarded me additional re-enforcements. At this point (a very strong position) I encamped for the night. Hearing early next morning that the enemy had recrossed the river and was advancing on White Hall in my rear, I immediately dispatched one regiment (the Eleventh North Carolina Troops, Col. [C.] Leventhorpe) and 600 dismounted cavalry, the whole under the command of Brig. Gen. B. H. Robertson, to proceed in haste and dispute his crossing at White Hall, while I would attack his rear toward Kinston. The report of Brigadier-General Robertson is herewith inclosed, marked A.* I here sent Colonel Rogers to march on Kinston, and held my other forces in readiness to move in either direction. Finding the enemy had retired across the river and burned the bridge, I ordered my whole command to Mosely Hall, a position where I could support General Robertson. At this point I met Major-General French, commanding department, who immediately assumed command and timely re-enforced Brigadier-General Robertson. My force engaged at Kinston consisted of the Seventeenth, Twenty-second, Twenty-third, and Holcombe Legion South Carolina Volunteers; Colonel Radcliffe's Sixty-first Regiment North Carolina Troops; Major Mallett's battalion; Capt. [R.] Boyce's light battery South Carolina Volunteers; Captains Bunting's and Starr's batteries North Carolina troops. Lieutenant-Colonel Pool, commanding North Carolina heavy artillery, commanded the intrenchments at the obstructions below Kinston and attacked the gunboats and held them in check while I regained my position in rear of the town. My whole force amounted to 2,014.

From Mosely Hall (after the repulse of the enemy at White Hall) I was directed by the major-general commanding the department to report to Goldsborough. On my arrival with my command was ordered by Maj. Gen. G. W. Smith to assume command of Brig. Gen. T. L. Clingman's brigade and make an armed reconnaissance of the enemy approaching the railroad bridge. I immediately ordered General Clingman to advance his brigade over the river by the county bridge and engage him; that I would support his left. On arriving beyond the bridge about a

---

* See report No. 39.

mile General Clingman became engaged with the enemy in heavy force. I directed Evans' brigade to advance to his support. On reaching the railroad I found the enemy drawn up in line of battle marching up to the railroad. I then directed my brigade to cross the railroad and engage the enemy, which was done in a spirited manner. I also herewith inclose General Clingman's report, together with a list of killed and wounded.

In conclusion I would call the attention of the major-general commanding to the gallant conduct and admirable judgment of Colonel Radcliffe, who had disposed his troops to dispute every advance of the enemy, and regret to add that, holding his position to the last of the fight, he was taken prisoner, but readily paroled. The following officers were observed by myself as conspicuous in the battles of Saturday and Sunday: Col. P. Mallett, North Carolina Troops; Capt. [M. G.] Zeigler, Holcombe Legion; Adjt. W. P. Du Bose, wounded while leading his regiment; Capt. [S. A.] Durham, [Company H], Twenty-third South Carolina Volunteers, wounded severely leading his regiment in action at the railroad.

To the promptness of General Clingman in obeying my orders I am particularly indebted for the repulse at the railroad near Goldsborough.

To my personal staff (Capt. A. L. Evans and First Lieut. Samuel J. Corrie, aide-de-camp) I am much indebted, both for the intrepidity and alacrity with which they obeyed my orders, both often leading troops in action. I recommend both to the especial attention of the major-general commanding. Col. John A. Baker, Forty-fourth [Forty-first] North Carolina Troops, deserves especial notice; though suffering with a slight wound, was very energetic as my assistant through the engagements of the two days.

Colonels Radcliffe and Mallett being paroled prisoners, the reports of their respective commands will be forwarded as soon as exchanged.

Herewith please find list * of killed and wounded in my brigade. The lists from the other commands have not been furnished me.

Very respectfully submitted.

N. G. EVANS,
Brigadier-General, Commanding.

Maj. S. W. MELTON,
Assistant Adjutant-General, Goldsborough, N. C.

No. 36.

Report of Col. Peter Mallett, North Carolina Battalion, of engagement at Kinston, December 14.

HEADQUARTERS EVANS' BRIGADE,
Wilmington, N. C., March 26, 1863.

GENERAL: I have the honor to forward the report of Col. P. Mallett, commanding battalion, of the action of his command at the battle of Kinston, N. C. I forward this report direct, as my report had been sent in some time since.

Very respectfully, your obedient servant,

N. G. EVANS,
Brigadier-General, Commanding.

General S. COOPER,
Adjutant and Inspector General, Richmond, Va.

---

* Not found.

[Inclosure.]

FAYETTEVILLE, N. C., *February* 20, 1863.

GENERAL: Confinement to my bed for the last two months will, I trust, be apology sufficient for the delay in reporting to you the part taken by my command in the battle near Kinston, on Sunday, December 14, [1862].

I arrived at Kinston by railroad Sunday morning at 7 o'clock and immediately reported to and was ordered by you to take position with my battalion (consisting of 19 officers and 460 men) in the rifle-pits on the east bank of Neuse River to support a South Carolina battery commanding the county bridge.

At 8.30 we were in position, and in a few moments musketry firing commenced on the left of the line of battle, which was formed on the west side of the river, and at 9 o'clock the first gun was fired by the artillery.

At 9.15 I received an order through one of your aides to march at double-quick across the bridge. Having crossed, I met you on the west side directing men pouring spirits of turpentine on cotton placed upon the bridge. You ordered me to take my command through the field on the right of the White Hall road and engage the enemy. We passed through the field under a fire of shell from the enemy (losing 1 man) to the distance of a quarter of a mile to a fence on the edge of a swamp, on the other side of which the enemy appeared to be in force. Here we engaged the enemy for some time, but the principal point of attack appeared to be the church known as Harriet's Chapel, on my left, where was stationed a section of Starr's battery, supported by the Sixty-first Regiment North Carolina Troops, under Colonel Radcliffe. At length the firing upon my part of the line ceased almost entirely. Being anxious to charge the enemy and drive him back, I sent Lieutenant Little to the section of artillery on my left to ascertain the real position of the enemy and of our forces, it being impossible to charge through the swamp in my front. About the time of Lieutenant Little's return (without any accurate information) I received by courier a written order from you, as follows:

COLONEL: Let me know if the enemy are in your front. If not, join me at the bridge.

At this time, there being no indication of the enemy in front, I drew off in good order and returned to the bridge, but to my surprise you were absent, leaving no order or instructions for me. Observing that the South Carolina battery commanding the bridge had been removed and the bridge apparently deserted, I concluded you were waiting for me on the east side, and retreating toward Kinston I proceeded across the bridge. In a few moments after crossing I was met by an officer of your staff with orders to go back. This order I promptly obeyed, marching again at a double-quick through the same field to my former position under a heavy fire of the enemy's artillery, and was almost immediately hotly engaged with his infantry. In about an hour I was re-enforced with 90 to 100 men from the Sixty-first North Carolina, commanded by Lieut. Col. [W. S.] Devane, who took position on my right. The enemy made a vigorous charge at this time on my left, and was as vigorously repulsed. Old veterans could not have met the foe with more coolness and determination than these newly-tried men. He appeared determined to force his way through my lines. At the church I ordered Lieutenant-Colonel Devane to re-enforce my left. He took his position promptly and did good service, and I here take pleasure in testifying to his coolness and undoubted bravery. With his assistance and the company of my right flank, commanded by Lieutenant McRae, also ordered to the left, we held the enemy in check some time. My ammunition now began to fail, and after sending repeatedly to the rear could not be replenished. Apprehending an attempt to turn my right also Captain McRae, acting as my lieutenant-colonel, was directed to observe closely and give me immediate notice of any advance in that direction. He reported the enemy in force, but no attempt was made to flank me owing, I suppose, to the impenetrable swamp between us.

At this time, having held the enemy in check for about three hours, looking in vain for re-enforcements, the section of artillery near the church retired, I since learn, for want of ammunition. Immediately after, Lieutenant-Colonel Devane sent me word that the enemy were flanking us on the left, and withdrew his men toward the bridge. Finding myself alone and the enemy pressing upon us I ordered a retreat, which was made in good order, the men continuing their fire with effect. At the bridge I intended to make another stand, but on approaching it found it on fire and crowded with men endeavoring to cross. A panic ensued. The enemy pressed upon us from two directions at double-quick in large force and the bridge the only means of escape. The greater portion of my command succeeded in crossing, while the other was driven back by the flames.

While endeavoring to keep the men back, fearing the bridge would fall every moment, I was wounded in the leg by a Minie ball and obliged to relinquish the command to Captain McRae, whose self-possession and bravery should not be left unnoticed. Being under a heavy cross-fire from an overwhelming force, my men and ammunition exhausted, and the bridge impassable, I advised Captain McRae to surrender. The enemy now directed his fire upon the retreating troops on the Kinston side, who spiritedly returned the fire with good effect, killing a colonel (Gray) and others near the bridge.

The enemy's force was between 20,000 and 25,000 men, with seventy-two pieces of artillery. General Foster admitted to me that we had repulsed three of his veteran regiments with a loss of 100 men; since ascertained to be about 250.

I regret to report the loss of two of my best officers, who fell at the close of the engagement: Lieut. J. J. Reid, commanding Company A, fell by my side near the bridge, and Lieut. J. H. Hill, commanding Company C, while retreating on the Kinston side. Both led their companies gallantly through the entire engagement. Braver or more gallant young men never drew a sword

Our loss was 7 killed, 22 wounded, 8 missing, and 175 taken prisoners.

After diligent search and inquiry for Adjt. E. N. Mann and Lieut. R. K. Williams I am reluctantly forced to include them in the list of killed.

Officers and men, nearly all of whom were under fire for the first time, behaved with the coolness, determination, and bravery of veterans.

It would be almost invidious to discriminate, but I cannot refrain from mentioning the conspicuous gallantry and bravery of Lieut. J. R. McLean, commanding Company F.

Inclosed please find a list of killed and wounded.*

Hoping I may be allowed to engage the enemy under more favorable circumstances, I am, general, your obedient servant,

PETER MALLETT,
Colonel, Commanding Battalion.

Brig. Gen. N. G. EVANS.

---

* Nominal list shows 12 killed and 34 wounded.

No. 37.

Report of Brig. Gen. Thomas L. Clingman, C S. Army, commanding Brigade, of engagement at Goldsborough Bridge, December 17.

HEADQUARTERS CLINGMAN'S BRIGADE,
December 21, 1862.

CAPTAIN: Before detailing the particulars of the affair of the 17th (Wednesday) I ought perhaps to state that I arrived at Goldsborough early on Tuesday morning, the 16th, accompanied by only the Eighth North Carolina Regiment, commanded by Col. [H. M.] Shaw. From Major-General Smith orders were received to pass to the south side of the Neuse River and take a position intermediate between Goldsborough and Dudley's Depot, on the line of the railroad. I selected a point where the railroad is crossed by the road from White Hall, along which the enemy were expected to approach, and which is about 1½ miles south of the railroad bridge. During the day I was re-enforced by the Fifty-first North Carolina Regiment, of my brigade, commanded by Lieut. Col. [William A.] Allen, just up from Wilmington. In the course of the night following the Fifty-second North Carolina Regiment, of Pettigrew's brigade, commanded by Col. [J. K.] Marshall, arrived with orders to report to me, but to be held in reserve in the rear of the other two regiments.

On the morning of the 17th, being informed by one of General Smith's staff that he desired particularly to hear from me, I returned with him on the locomotive to Goldsborough, and was instructed by General Smith to report to Brigadier-General Evans and with my brigade to accompany him in making a reconnaissance in force to ascertain the position and strength of the enemy. Within a few moments after receiving this order a dispatch was placed in my hands from my adjutant-general stating that the enemy were reported by our scouts as being in 3 miles of my position. This was read to General Evans while he was in the presence of General Smith, and he at once ordered me to go on and fight the enemy, saying that he would follow with his brigade to support me. On returning to my command I found that the enemy in heavy force, both of infantry and artillery, were advancing from the southeast across the open fields and also from the south along the line of the railroad, while their cavalry were seen approaching along the county road which passed in my rear. It ought to be stated that the county bridge is about half a mile above that of the railroad, and that the road crossing it was nearly parallel with the railroad. Between the two is a swamp, but infantry can pass along the bank of the river without much difficulty, and 1½ miles from the river the two roads are connected by a cross-road through a plantation. It being impossible with only three regiments to hold both the bridges and at the same time fight a large army, Colonel Marshall with the Fifty-second Regiment was stationed in front of the railroad bridge and Colonel Shaw with the Eighth, supported by a section of Starr's battery, was placed in the field in front of the county bridge; Colonel Allen with the Fifty-first was between the two to support either in case of need. The enemy soon opened heavily, both with artillery and musketry, against Colonel Marshall, evidently with a view of reaching the railroad bridge. I therefore carried the Fifty-first Regiment to his support and placed it on his right flank. So heavy, however, was the fire from the large force of the enemy that these regiments were broken and fell back. They were soon rallied and taken back to their positions. The increasing volleys of musketry and the rapid falling of shells from the numerous batteries of the enemy, in spite of all my efforts to keep them longer in position, caused them to give way a second time. It being obvious, indeed, that so small a force could not long maintain a contest against such heavy odds, they were formed in the rear and carried back in good order to the county bridge, and with the force stationed there recrossed the river. To defend the bridge the two guns of [J. B.] Starr's battery, [Company B, Thirteenth Battalion North Carolina Artillery], under the command of Lieut. [T. C.] Fuller, were placed near it, and Colonel Marshall's regiment lined the river bank below and Colonel Allen's occupied it above, while Colonel Shaw's was placed in the rear as a reserve. For the defense of the railroad there was placed in position on the north side of the river Colonel Pool's battalion with several pieces of artillery. After the above-stated disposition had been made, possibly an hour later, one of General Evans' staff informed me at the county bridge that he desired to see me. On my going back to the field where he was posted he told me that it was all important to hold the county bridge and that I must do it. I replied that I was satisfied the dispositions made were sufficient, and on my asking as to the defenses of the railroad bridge he declared that all was secure there, but renewed his order to me to hold the county bridge. Not long after my return to it I was informed that the railroad bridge was on fire. After it was burned the cannonade of the enemy ceased.

At a later period General Evans again sent for me, and on my going back to his station he ordered me to advance across the bridge with my entire command and attack the enemy and feel his strength. The Sixty-first North Carolina Regiment, of my brigade, commanded by Lieutenant-Colonel Devane, having by this time arrived, it with three already under my command and the two field pieces above mentioned were moved across the river. Skirmishers were thrown forward in all directions and the enemy was found to be posted from the river for $1\frac{1}{2}$ miles along the railroad in line of battle, well protected by the high embankment of the road in front of them. The regiments of Shaw and Devane and the two guns were moved along the county road while I carried as rapidly as possible the regiments of Marshall and Allen down the river bank and placed them in line within less than 300 yards of the enemy's right, but in a position where they were pretty well protected from the artillery. They were instructed to lie down, to make no reply to the enemy, and no attempt to pass the open field between them and the enemy until they should hear our attack on the right. As soon, however, as that occurred they were ordered to rise and with a shout to move forward at a run and carry, if possible, the embankment behind which the enemy were posted.

Rejoining the other two regiments I led them along the county road and from it by the cross-road through the open field against the enemy's left wing. I formed them in line of battle, the right of Colonel Shaw resting on the cross-road while his left and Colonel Devane's extended toward the enemy's center. One of the field pieces, unfortunately, from the giving way of the bridge, fell into a ditch and was not gotten out in time to take part in the action. The other piece moved along the road on the right of our line and was itself protected on its flank by skirmishers who covered the ground for several hundred yards. Before we reached the railroad, however, the enemy abandoned it and we occupied it without a struggle. The two regiments stationed near the river likewise advanced to it without loss, and, as I subsequently learned, General Evans' brigade soon filled up the center. After retreating from this position the enemy occupied a higher field in our front with a large number of cannon and heavy bodies of infantry drawn up in two lines with an interval of 100 or 200 yards between them. As soon as Lieutenant Fuller opened on them with his gun their artillery, which had previously directed its fire against our left where the regiments of Marshall and Allen were stationed, was shifted and its concentrated volleys were poured upon our right. Their position approached within 400 yards there, while from our left it was more than a half mile distant. With the large number of pieces they had in play it is a wonder they did not succeed in disabling a single gun. Notwithstanding the disparity of force and the loss of several of his men, Lieutenant Fuller, with the greatest gallantry, continued to reply until darkness put an end to the contest. During the evening the regiments of Colonels Marshall and Allen, by General Evans' order as I have since learned, made a charge against the enemy's position on the hill. They advanced most courageously, but were repulsed by heavy showers of grape and musketry. As they had to move across an open space of 1,000 yards, swept by heavy batteries supported by large masses of infantry, it was barely possible that they could carry such a position. Their prompt and daring attempt furnished the highest evidence of their courage and readiness to obey orders. Immediately after dark the enemy retreated with his entire army, and soon after we recrossed the river, the troops under my command following General Evans' brigade and bringing up the rear. The entire force at my disposition that day was rather below 2,000 men.

The loss was:

Command.	Killed.	Wounded.	Missing.
Marshall's regiment	11	58	10
Allen's regiment	6	43	8
Shaw's regiment	3	6	
Devane's regiment			
Total	20	107	18

I cannot give the casualties of Fuller's section precisely. I learn that the loss in the two first-named regiments occurred mainly in the charge above referred to; but for this we should have had the satisfaction of knowing that we had, with vastly inferior force, driven the enemy from a strong position and obliged his whole army to retreat almost without loss on our part.

In conclusion I take pleasure in saying that the officers and men in all the regiments behaved in a manner creditable to veteran troops.

Capt. Edward White, my assistant adjutant-general, and Capt. A. M. Erwin, my aide-de-camp, were energetic and prompt in carrying orders to all parts of the field.

Very respectfully, yours, &c.,

T. L. CLINGMAN,
Brigadier-General.

Capt. A. L. EVANS,
Assistant Adjutant-General, Evans' Brigade.

No. 38.

Report of Lieut. Col. Stephen D. Pool, C. S. Artillery, of engagement at Goldsborough Bridge, December 17.

GOLDSBOROUGH, N. C., *December* 19, 1862.

COLONEL: Soon after daybreak the morning of the 16th instant my command, consisting of Companies B, G, and H, Tenth North Carolina Troops, Company F, Fortieth North Carolina, and Starr's battery of artillery, took the positions assigned them on the north side of Neuse River commanding the immediate approaches to the railroad and county bridges.

Everything remained quiet until about noon of the 17th, when the enemy, occupying the south side of the river and east of the railroad, opened fire with evident design of destroying the bridge. To effect this their batteries employed for about two hours shell and solid shot, occasionally discharging shrapnel along the north bank of the river to dislodge any force there. The south bank of the river west of the railroad was occupied by a portion of Brigadier-General Clingman's brigade, the left of the Fifty-second North Carolina Troops, Colonel Marshall, resting against the bridge. Orders were sent me by Colonel Marshall not to open fire with the section of Starr's battery, commanding the bridge, until his troops retired. About 2 p. m. the Fifty-second broke and in confusion retired from the bridge, leaving the south of that important structure entirely undefended except by the forces on the north bank of the Neuse. Orders were immediately sent by me to Captain Starr to open fire with shrapnel on the mouth of the bridge to prevent the enemy if possible from entering and destroying it. The order was immediately obeyed. While the left of the Fifty-second was retiring I saw a small force of the enemy running down the railroad bank, shouting and yelling as if in pursuit. Suspecting their design to be to enter and destroy the bridge, I cautioned my men to be on the alert and as soon as they came within range to pour their fire into them. This was done so effectually that two were instantly killed; the others fled precipitately. Our fire having disclosed our exact position, the enemy opened upon us with a most severe fire of canister, shell, and shrapnel for about half an hour, our guns replying with rapidity and effect. During this fire my men on the banks of the river remained perfectly quiet, receiving the enemy's fire unflinchingly. Thinking they had dislodged us, the enemy sent forward 2 men to effect the destruction of the bridge by fire. I cautioned my men of the approach of the men, and as soon as they broke cover for the bridge fire was opened upon them. One fell back wounded, the other succeeded in reaching the projecting brick-work, where he was enabled to complete his work in perfect security from any fire from the north bank of the river. No effort was spared by my men to reach him with their fire. Different points of the bridge were selected, and shot after shot poured in in the vain hope of killing him. His work proved successful, and in less than ten minutes the entire southern and eastern faces of the bridge were in flames. Seeing the destruction completed, I gave orders to retire to the rear of the section of Starr's battery posted on the railroad. Subsequently my entire command was ordered to the county bridge; two pieces of the battery were placed in position. Companies B and F were posted on the west side of the bridge, while Companies G and H took position on the east—all on the north bank of the river. Here we remained during the night and until ordered to this point next day.

Late in the afternoon of the 17th one section of Starr s battery, in charge of First Lieut. T. C. Fuller, engaged the enemy south of the river, near the point where the county road crosses the railroad. All speak in terms of praise of the gallantry displayed here, and of the efficiency of Lieutenant Fuller's fire. The details of this engagement do not come within the scope of this report. Justice will be done by the brigadier-general commanding at that point.

I cannot close this report without expressing my admiration of the coolness with which my officers and men stood fire for more than two hours without an opportunity of returning it, and of the gallantry displayed by all of Captain Starr's officers and men engaged. Killed, 3; wounded, 6. Captain Starr received a slight wound on arm from fragment of spent shell.

I have the honor to be, colonel, yours, very respectfully,
                                   STEPHEN D. POOL,
         Lieutenant-Colonel, Commanding Battalion Artillery.

No. 39.

Report of Brig. Gen. Beverly H. Robertson, C. S. Army, commanding Brigade, of engagement at White Hall, December 16.

                                         HEADQUARTERS,
                     Goldsborough, N C., December 19, 1862.

CAPTAIN: I have the honor to report that in accordance with your order I left Mosely Hall, on the Goldsborough and Kinston Railroad, at 11.30 a. m., 15th instant, and, with Leventhorpe's regiment, portions of Ferebee's and Evans' regiments, and a section of artillery from [J. W.] Moore's [Third North Carolina] battalion, commanded by Lieut. [N.] McClees, proceeded to White Hall, on the Neuse River, to burn the bridge at that point and dispute the enemy's crossing should he attempt to turn our right. Having no cavalry I impressed a citizen guide and pushed forward to reconnoiter in advance of my command. Upon reaching White Hall I learned that the enemy had not made his appearance there. I then ordered my guide to scout toward Kinston to prevent surprise. One hour later my force arrived and I made rapid preparations for burning the bridge. Making a personal examination some miles to the front without finding the enemy, I returned to White Hall. Shortly afterward citizens, with jaded horses and apparently much excited, announced the enemy was advancing. I ordered Major Jackson and Lieut. [W. N.] Worthington to watch his movements, but they could not find him. I waited his approach until nearly dark and determined to recross and burn the bridge, according to my orders. The torch had scarcely been applied when the enemy's cavalry appeared with artillery. They shelled the woods until late at night, destroying the gunboat in process of construction on this side. Several men, taking off their clothes, attempted to cross the river by swimming, but were driven back by our sharpshooters. From the force displayed it was evidently his intention to cross the White Hall Bridge.

About 9 a. m. on the 16th a brisk picket skirmish commenced. I visited the bridge, and after giving the necessary instructions went back to order up the Thirty-first North Carolina Regiment, Col. [John V.] Jordan, which had arrived during the night, and which I placed in position as much sheltered as circumstances would permit. I then posted the artillery as well as the nature of the ground would admit and ordered both shell and solid shot to be fired. For some time previous the enemy had been firing from 12 to 18 pounders, some of immense caliber. Owing to a range of hills on the White Hall side the enemy had the advantage of position. The point occupied by his troops being narrow, not more than one regiment at a time could advantageously engage him. I therefore held Leventhorpe, Ferebee, and Evans in reserve, leaving the artillery, Thirty-first Regiment, and two picket companies in front. The cannonading from the enemy's batteries became so terrific that the Thirty-first Regiment withdrew from their position without instructions but in good order. I immediately ordered Colonel Leventhorpe forward. The alacrity with which the order was obeyed by his men gave ample proof of their gallant bearing, which they so nobly sustained during the entire fight, which raged with intensity for several hours after they became engaged. No veteran soldiers ever fought better or inflicted more terrible loss upor an enemy considering the numbers engaged. It was with difficulty they could be withdrawn from the field. Three times did they drive the Yankee cannoneers from their guns and as often prevent their infantry regiments from forming line in their front. In spite of the four hostile regiments whose standards waved from the opposite bank did these brave men continue to hold their ground, and finally drove the enemy in confusion from the field. More than 100 of their dead and wounded were left upon the river bank. The conduct of this regiment reflects the greatest credit upon its accomplished and dauntless commander.

Colonel Ferebee, of the Fifty-ninth Regiment, displayed the most signal coolness and courage. For several hours, with 18 men of the picket guard belonging to the Eleventh Regiment, he fought the enemy at close quarters, notwithstanding his own command was not in action.

The Fifty-ninth and Sixty-third Regiments, although in reserve, were nevertheless exposed to a galling fire from the enemy's artillery. A few were killed and a number wounded. Both officers and men behaved admirably.

The section of artillery was remarkably well served, Lieutenant McClees and his men remaining cool and collected.

My thanks are especially due to Maj. George Jackson, Capt. Charles H. Gordon, and Lieutenant Worthington, members of my staff, for their efficient services and their prompt delivery of orders under the heaviest fire.

The soldierly qualities displayed by Colonel Leventhorpe on the march and during the action, to which I can bear witness, strongly recommend him to the favorable consideration of the authorities.

About 70 stand of arms and a quantity of clothing were collected from the battle-field.

I regret having to report the death of Lieut. [W. N. M.] Means, Company E, Eleventh Regiment North Carolina Troops, and also First Sergeant Bristol, Company B, of the same regiment. They both fell like brave men in the faithful performance of their duty.

The loss of the enemy, though not accurately ascertained, is known to have been very heavy.

I herewith inclose a list* of killed and wounded on our side.

Very respectfully, sir, your obedient servant,

B. H. ROBERTSON,
Brigadier-General, Commanding.

Capt. A. L. EVANS,
    Asst. Adjt. Gen., Hdqrs. Evans' Brigade, in the Field.

---

* Nominal list shows 10 killed and 42 wounded.

DECEMBER 22, 1862.—Skirmishes near Windsor and at Joyner's Ferry, on the Blackwater, Va.

Report of Brig. Gen. Orris S. Ferry, U. S. Army.

SUFFOLK, *December* 23, 1862.

GENERAL : Lieutenant-Colonel Onderdonk, with 200 of Dodge's cavalry, had a skirmish with a force of the enemy, consisting of artillery, cavalry, and infantry, 4 miles beyond Windsor yesterday. Colonel Onderdonk was conveying the ballot-boxes to Smithfield, and this force was sent across from Zuni to intercept him. He succeeded in extricating himself with the loss of 4 horses, but no men. He captured 2 of the enemy, and believes that he killed a number with his rifles.

Lieutenant-Colonel Stetzel, of Spear's cavalry, yesterday made a reconnaissance to Joyner's Ford with four companies. He found the enemy there in considerable force, and had a sharp skirmish across the river. He captured 4 of their pickets and 1 horse, without loss to himself.

O. S. FERRY,
Brigadier-General.

Major-General DIX, *Fort Monroe.*

DECEMBER 28, 1862.—Skirmishes near Suffolk and at Providence Church, Va

Report of Brig. Gen. Orris S. Ferry, U. S. Army.

[DECEMBER 29, 1862.]

Colonel Gibbs, sent out by me at 3 o'clock p. m. yesterday toward Carrsville to occupy the enemy while Spinola's column was moving out, came in contact with the enemy's scouting parties a short distance beyond our pickets. He drove them back, capturing 9 of them, and bivouacked about 10 miles from here. The prisoners say that Pryor was at Carrsville with two brigades of infantry, two regiments of cavalry, and nine pieces of artillery. Colonel Gibbs returned at daylight this morning. I send the prisoners to the Fortress to-day.

On the Windsor road an attack was made on our vedettes at Providence Church at 4 o'clock p. m. yesterday. The vedettes were driven in, but the reserves attacked and repulsed the enemy, driving them back several miles to a main body of about 300 cavalry.

O. S. FERRY,
Brigadier-General.

Major-General DIX, *Fort Monroe.*

JANUARY 7-9, 1863.—Expedition from Yorktown to West Point and White House, Va.

Report of Maj. Gen. Erasmus D. Keyes, U. S. Army, commanding Fourth Army Corps.

HEADQUARTERS FOURTH ARMY CORPS,
Yorktown, Va., January 10, 1863.

SIR: I have the honor to submit the following report of a successful raid up the country between the Pamunkey and Mattapony Rivers and at the White House.

A detachment of cavalry of the Fifth Pennsylvania and Sixth New York Regiments, under Maj. W. P. Hall, and another of the One hundred and fifteenth New York Infantry, under Captain McKittrick, 300 in all, left Yorktown on the evening of the 7th instant in steamers cooperating with the strong naval forces on this station.

It was concerted with Capt. F. A. Parker,* commanding the gunboats on the York River, that he would clear out the Pamunkey and destroy the railroad station, &c., at the White House, while the infantry should hold West Point with the aid of a gunboat and the cavalry should sweep the roads and country on the left bank. Unfortunately, however, the water was too low to enable the vessel to reach the White House. Major Hall therefore crossed the river at that point in a skiff with a small party, burnt the ferry-boat, also a small steamer called the Little Magruder, two sloops loaded with grain, two barges, four pontoon boats, a storehouse containing a thousand bushels of wheat, &c., a quantity of whisky, soap, salt, &c.

The torch was then applied to the railroad depot, which contained freight for Richmond; the tank, the rolling stock, signal station, sutler's buildings, &c. When the destruction was complete the party recrossed the river.

On the left bank of the Pamunkey the cavalry captured and brought in 6 wagons and 2 carts, with 26 mules and 8 horses. The wagons were laden with "blockade goods," such as salt, black-lead, gum-shellac, buckles and rings, gutta-percha belting, bars of tin and iron, brass wire, 60 ounces of quinine, and a lot of gold lace, stripes, and stars for rebel uniforms.

The expedition got off without its destination being known or suspected by any person except Captain Parker and myself. The conduct of Maj. W. P. Hall, Sixth New York Cavalry, entitles him to special notice and praise. His success was complete, and he lost neither man nor horse.

It will not, I trust, be deemed out of place to say that the success of the land part of the expedition was largely indebted to Captain Parker's admirable management of his vessels. On this and many other occasions I have noticed the zeal and good judgment of that naval officer.

I have the honor to be, very respectfully, your obedient servant,

E. D. KEYES,
Major-General, Commanding Fourth Army Corps.

Major-General DIX,
Commanding Department of Virginia.

---

* For Commander Parker's report see Annual Report of the Secretary of the Navy, December 7, 1863.

JANUARY 8–10 1863.—Expedition from Suffolk toward the Blackwater, Va.

Report of Col. Samuel P. Spear, Eleventh Pennsylvania Cavalry.*

HDQRS. ELEVENTH PENNSYLVANIA VOL. CAVALRY,
Camp Suffolk, Va., January 12, 1863.

SIR: I have the honor to transmit the following report of the reconnaissance made by me, in obedience to instructions dated Headquarters, Suffolk, Va., January 7, 1863:

I left Suffolk on the morning of the 8th instant in command of the following force, viz: Howard's battery, six pieces; the One hundred and fifty-fifth, One hundred and twelfth, and One hundred and thirtieth New York Volunteers; the One hundred and sixty-fifth Pennsylvania Militia, and 600 of my own regiment (Eleventh Pennsylvania Cavalry), ambulances, &c., for the purpose of protecting General Ferry's embarkation on the river Chowan, some 37 miles from Suffolk. I encamped on the night of the 8th near Holland's Corners.

Next morning I started toward Carrsville, as the spirit of my instructions was such as to "leave much to my discretion," relative to the approach of the enemy from any quarter. At Carrsville I received valuable information from Mr. Whitehead, which afterwards proved to be correct, that Pryor was down in the vicinity of Barber's Cross-Roads with a large force. I at once got into position, supposing that my presence toward Somerton would no longer be necessary. After remaining here for about an hour a dispatch was received ordering me at once to Somerton (as per original instructions). I obeyed the order, countermarched, and had proceeded to the Quaker Church, on the Somerton road, when another dispatch was received directing re-enforcements to report to me, and Maj. Samuel Wetherill, with three companies of cavalry and the One hundred and sixty-fourth New York Volunteers, reported.

I encamped at the Quaker Church, and the next morning the Thirteenth Indiana, Lieutenant-Colonel Dobbs, reported, when, according to the dispatch, I proceeded with the entire force to Blanchard's Corners; thence to McClenna's Station; thence, via Deserted House, Western Branch Church, &c., to Windsor. At Windsor my advance, commanded by Lieut. John L. Roper, captured a dispatch, directed to General R. A. Pryor, in the hands of two Confederate cavalry. These prisoners, with their horses, were immediately sent to headquarters, and I will here remark that great credit is due to Lieutenant Roper for his prompt, energetic, and faithful performance of the important duty of leading the advance of such a large body of troops.

At this point (Windsor) I sent out detachments of cavalry in every direction to ascertain the direction of the enemy, and in about one hour discovered that he had retired on the road direct to Carrsville, passing over the same ground I occupied the previous day, and crossed the river at Franklin with his wagons, stores, troops, &c. I found Mr. Whitehead's information, relative to the strength and location of the enemy, to be correct, and was of the following strength, viz: Fourteen pieces of artillery, 1,500 to 2,000 cavalry, and about 6,000 infantry. I have put this at the lowest estimate; some have estimated his strength at 12,000 men, consisting of all arms.

At Windsor I encamped on the same ground occupied by Pryor the day previous, and sent a dispatch to headquarters for rations, forage,

---

* See also Peck to Dix, January 10, in "Correspondence, etc."

and other necessaries, which call was quickly and correctly responded to, which gave great comfort to both men and horses in a most tremendous rain-storm.

After a bivouac of about three hours, and the return of my detachments sent out in every direction, I had a consultation with all the commanders of the different arms which resulted in the determination to return to Suffolk; and it being in accordance with instructions I started at 5.50 p. m. on the Petersburg road via Providence Church, drawbridge, &c., on my return, and reported in person to the commanding general at 8 p. m. on the night of the 10th instant. I found that the new regiments of infantry lately arrived (One hundred and fifty-fifth and One hundred and sixty-fourth) used their entire three days' rations in two, and did not take with them their shelter-tents. I find these shelter-tents to be of indispensable use on reconnaissances, marches, &c., as they do for both blanket, bed, or tent, as the weather might demand.

It gives me great pleasure to report the fact of the valuable assistance rendered by Colonel Gibbs, commanding the infantry. Nearly the entire three days and nights he was constantly in the saddle, first at one point and then at another, encouraging his men, supplying their wants, and exhibiting sound judgment in all his orders, positions, and maneuvers, ever ready at a moment's warning to place the infantry, without noise or confusion, at any place required. Captain Howard, chief of artillery, was prompt and untiring in his duty and always ready to cheerfully execute all directions and orders in a true, spirited manner. He and his officers are all worthy of my best thanks. The cavalry, under command of Major Wetherill, were all that could be desired, caring well for their horses. They performed their arduous duty in such a manner as to prove beyond a doubt that in case of greater emergency their pride will always be "to horse," and their results a faithful execution of existing orders. Major Stratton, who first led the cavalry before the arrival of Major Wetherill, performed his duty in his usual thorough manner, and is to my command a very useful and valuable officer.

Colonel Dodge reported at the Deserted House with 200 cavalry, and very kindly offered his services in any manner I might suggest. His urbanity and politeness is worthy of emulation. The entire command, through rain, mud, and water, are deserving of my warmest commendation in expressing their readiness at any moment to execute any orders and under any circumstances.

I am, sir, very respectfully, &c.,

S. P. SPEAR,
Col. Eleventh Pennsylvania Vol. Cav., Comdg. Expedition.

Maj. B. B. FOSTER,
Assistant Adjutant-General.

JANUARY 9, 1863.—Skirmish near Providence Church, Va.

Report of Maj. Gen. John J. Peck, U. S. Army.

FORT MONROE, VA., *January* 15, 1863.

The Richmond papers are boasting that General Pryor repulsed our troops near Providence Church on the 9th instant. The following dispatch of the 10th from General Peck gives the true version of the affair. The attack was repulsed by our Mounted Rifles, under Maj. [James N.] Wheelan. It is due to the latter and to our troops that the truth should be known, and if you see no objection I would be glad to have the dispatch published:

The enemy crossed the Blackwater in considerable force and attempted yesterday to drive in our right at Providence Church. Infantry, cavalry, and artillery were employed by the rebels, but they were repulsed by Major Wheelan's New York Mounted Rifles. At dusk the enemy's advance was charged and driven back upon his support. At intervals through the night shells were thrown from rebel batteries.

JOHN J. PECK,
Major-General.

JOHN A. DIX,
Major-General, Commanding.

Maj. Gen. H. W. HALLECK,
General-in-Chief.

JANUARY 17–21, 1863.—Reconnaissance from New Berne to Pollocksville, Trenton, Young's Cross-Roads, and Onslow, N. C., and skirmishes (19th) at White Oak Creek and (20th) near Jacksonville.

REPORTS.

No. 1.—Col. Simon H. Mix, Third New York Cavalry.
No. 2.—Col. Augustus B. R. Sprague, Fifty-first Massachusetts Infantry.

No. 1.

Report of Col. Simon H. Mix, Third New York Cavalry.

NEW BERNE, N. C., *January* 22, 1863.

SIR: I have the honor to report that in obedience to orders I marched from New Berne on the morning of the 17th instant with eight companies of my regiment and proceeded a distance of about 12 miles up the south bank of the Trent River to Mill Creek, near Pollocksville, where a halt became necessary in consequence of the destruction of a bridge across that stream. The bridge was expeditiously rebuilt and my line of march resumed through Pollocksville a short distance on the road toward Trenton, where, at an angle of a thickly-wooded road, three shots in rapid succession were fired from an ambush on the advance guard of my column. A halt was immediately ordered, when it was discovered that the road was blockaded by trees felled across it for some distance in front. I communicated the fact to Colonel Amory, acting brigadier-general, in command of the expedition, who ordered me to encamp my regiment for the night.

The obstruction being removed at this point, I moved my regiment at 7 a. m. on the morning of the 18th, reaching Trenton, 13 miles distant from Pollocksville, about 11 o'clock a. m. Several points on the route, about midway between Pollocksville and Trenton, were blockaded by felled trees, and a large mill-dam, the flow from which crosses the road within a half mile of Trenton, was found to be cut, with the evident intention of flooding the road to prevent my passage into the town. The cut in the dam was repaired in season to prevent great delay in my march.

At Trenton I discovered some rebel cavalry, who retreated up the White Hall road toward Kinston. A strong blockade of felled trees across the road, densely wooded, and swamps on both sides prevented my pursuit. Immediate preparations were made for removing the blockade, and the bridge across the river at Trenton was burned and destroyed to the water's edge. The blockade of the road in the mean time having been removed I marched up the White Hall road about 6 miles and destroyed a bridge which crossed the Trent River at that point.

This accomplished and night arriving I countermarched my regiment to Trenton and encamped for the night. I countermarched to Trenton as a matter of necessity, inasmuch as the road leading to Comfort, as I ascertained, was blockaded to such an extent as to defy all farther progress in that direction.

On the morning of the 19th, at 7 o'clock, I marched from Trenton without obstruction to Young's Cross-Roads, taking a road southward, which intersects the main road from Trenton to Pollocksville, 4 miles from the latter place.

The distance from Trenton to Young's Cross-Roads by this route is 17 miles. I reached Young's Cross-Roads about noon and found the bridge across White Oak River, 1 mile below Young's Cross-Roads, on the road leading toward Jacksonville, destroyed, and a strong barricade erected on the opposite bank to oppose its reconstruction.

From this barricade my advance was fired upon without effect as it neared the stream. A howitzer was brought forward and the barricade stormed with canister, which had the effect to silence the enemy's fire and cause him to retreat from the position. In so great haste did the enemy retire that he left behind five sabers and a quantity of ammunition.

Preparations were made to rebuild the bridge across White Oak River, and my regiment, after carefully reconnoitering the adjacent roads, encamped at Young's Cross-Roads for the night. During the evening two contrabands came within our lines, who stated that they were with the enemy at the time of my firing into the stockade at White Oak River, and that the rebel officer in command received three severe wounds at the first fire of the howitzer. I retained these contrabands as guides, and procured from them reliable information.

The bridge across White Oak River was completed and crossed on the morning of the 20th instant at 10 o'clock. Leaving all my transportation behind at Young's Cross-Roads with the infantry, I pressed my regiment forward in the direction of Jacksonville with great rapidity.

Five miles from Young's Cross-Roads my advance guard met and surprised a company of rebel cavalry, about 50 in number, which was pursued at a gallop for nearly 12 miles by a portion of Major Cole's battalion, my regiment being kept up at supporting distance.

When within about 5 miles of Jacksonville, and about 20 distant from Young's Cross-Roads, our pursuit was checked by the destruction of a bridge across Big Northeast Run, a stream about 20 feet in width, which bridge had been previously arranged for speedy removal; a stockade had been erected about 100 yards on the opposite side of this stream, at the end of a deep, wooded gorge, from which a heavy volley of buck-shot was poured back upon our advance.

The howitzer was again brought to bear, the stockade cleared, and the bridge repaired. At this point I had 1 man killed and 1 seriously but not fatally wounded by the enemy's fire. My regiment again moved forward and reached the intersection of the road leading from Comfort to Jacksonville, 3 miles from the latter place, where I halted, after ascertaining that the bridge across New River at Jacksonville would be destroyed by fire on our approach and all communication with the enemy in that direction would be cut off, he having safely arrived on the opposite side.

After a short halt at this last-mentioned place, night approaching and a terrible storm of rain and wind setting in, I countermarched my regiment to Young's Cross-Roads, which point was reached at 10 p. m., where I again encamped for the night. My entire return march was through a heavy storm of wind and rain, which caused the road to become very heavy and difficult to travel.

I captured 3 prisoners between Young's Cross-Roads and Jacksonville, and also took of the enemy's transportation three wagons with three pairs of mules attached, and one mule-saddle, with holsters, pistols, &c. With one of the prisoners a horse was captured.

Believing my orders had been obeyed and carried out to the full extent of my ability to perform the same, on the morning of the 21st instant I returned with my command to New Berne, N. C., reaching that place at 3 o'clock p. m.

I am, sir, with great respect, your obedient servant,

[SIMON H. MIX,
Colonel, &c.]

Lieut. Col. SOUTHARD HOFFMAN,
Assistant Adjutant-General, Eighteenth Army Corps.

No. 2.

Report of Col. Augustus B. R. Sprague, Fifty-first Massachusetts Infantry.

FOSTER BARRACKS, *January* 21, 1863.

On the 17th instant, in conformity to Special Orders, No. 14, joining a portion of the First Brigade and a detachment of artillery and the Third New York Cavalry, I marched with seven companies of my command (Companies F, E, and G being on detached service) by Brice's Creek and the south side of the Trent River to Pollocksville, about 13 miles distant; arrived at 5 p. m. and went into bivouac for the night. On the morning of the 18th two companies, under the command of Major Harkness, marched with the main column toward Trenton, while I was ordered, with the five remaining companies and a detachment of cavalry, to guard the approaches and hold Pollocksville till the return of the main force. This was successfully accomplished, and upon the return of the main body at noon of 19th instant, I received instructions to move five companies to Young's Cross-Roads and hold that point till the arrival of the main column.

Without a guide we passed the spot known as Young's Cross-Roads (about 7 miles from Pollocksville), and coming suddenly upon White Oak Creek my advance guard received the fire of the enemy's outposts on the other side of the river, the bridge having been destroyed and a breastwork of logs formed for their protection. The advance, under the direct command of Lieutenant-Colonel Studley, returned the fire and the enemy retired.

In obedience to instructions we bivouacked at the cross-roads, and at evening were joined by the Third New York Cavalry. Soon after daylight, 20th instant, crossed White Oak River with a detachment and established an outpost on the Jacksonville road to guard the approaches while the bridge over the creek was being rebuilt. The main force, under Colonel Amory, arrived and a portion of the cavalry pressed forward to a point near Jacksonville and reported the enemy in force at that place. The object of the expedition accomplished, we left Smith's Mill on the morning of the 21st, passing through Pollocksville, and arrived at New Berne in the evening. A heavy rain during the preceding night made muddy roads and overflowing streams. William P. Kent, of Company I, who marched in apparent good health, was taken suddenly ill and died in an ambulance on the route.

I have the honor to be, very respectfully, your obedient servant,

A. B. R. SPRAGUE,
Colonel Fifty-first Massachusetts Regiment.

Lieut. E. T. PARKINSON,
A. A. A. G., First Brigade, Dept. of North Carolina.

JANUARY 19, 1863.—Scout from Williamsburg and skirmish at Burnt Ordinary, Va.

Report of Maj. William G. McCandless, Fifth Pennsylvania Cavalry.

HEADQUARTERS FOURTH ARMY CORPS,
Yorktown, Va., January 21, 1863.

GENERAL : I have the honor to forward the following report of a scout made on the 10th instant by Major McCandless, of the Fifth Pennsylvania Cavalry, sent out by Lieutenant-Colonel Lewis, commanding that regiment, under orders from myself:

I left camp with a scouting party, consisting of 120 men, at 9 o'clock a. m. When, beyond the picket, at the point where the roads diverge, I divided my command, sending one party by the York River with orders to join the main column at the Six Mile Ordinary and another party up the Jamestown road to the Chickahominy River with instructions to go by way of Centreville and join me at the Burnt Ordinary, while I proceeded with the remainder of my force directly up the Richmond road.

At the Six Mile Ordinary the party reported having seen nothing of the enemy. My strength was now about 80 men. With this number I went on up the Richmond road, and when arrived at Mrs. Pickett's gate, 9 miles from Williamsburg, I came upon the enemy's first post of 3 mounted men and at the brick church half a mile farther on discovered their reserve of 16 men, who were at once chased by my advance guard, under Lieutenant Vezin, as far as the Burnt Ordinary, at which point they were met by a force of the enemy's cavalry coming alongside the Centreville road, and who, dashing upon the head of the advance guard with a sudden swoop, succeeded in cutting off and capturing 4 of our men, who, in the excitement, had gotten 300 or 400 yards in advance, and then began instantly to draw up in line of battle. Lieutenant Vezin, seeing the fate of his men and perceiving that an instant's delay would give the enemy time to form, and notwithstanding the fact that he had but 13 men with him, ordered the rest of the advance guard to "draw saber and charge," which was done in the most gallant manner and in the face of a volley from the enemy's guns.

The flashing of our sabers in air and the shouts of the men as they charged upon the foe was more than the enemy could stand, and, breaking at once in every direction they fled precipitately, about 20 returning up the Centreville road and the balance taking the Diascund road, which party being the larger we pursued and succeeded in retaking 3 of our captured men, with their horses and arms, and in capturing 4 of the enemy, besides wounding one other, who, however, escaped through the woods, leaving his horse in our hands. I regret to have to report the loss by capture of Private McNeill and the injury of Private John Brown, who was shot in the side. We pursued the enemy 3 miles beyond the Burnt Ordinary, but their horses being fresh and fleeter than ours they all, with the exception of those above mentioned, made good their escape.

Having learned the force of the enemy to consist of one regiment of infantry and 500 cavalry stationed at Diascund Bridge I returned to camp by the Centreville road, and was joined on the road by the party who went to the Chickahominy River. They reported no enemy in sight on either side of that river.

The activity and energy of the officers and men of the Fifth Pennsylvania Cavalry and the uniform success which has attended their numerous scouts during the last three months are worthy of notice.

Very respectfully, your obedient servant,

E. D. KEYES,
Major-General, Commanding Corps.

Maj. Gen. JOHN A. DIX,
  Comdg. Seventh Army Corps and Dept. of Virginia.

JANUARY 27–28, 1863.—Reconnaissances on the Neuse, Dover, and Trent Roads, N. C.

Report of Col. John Richter Jones, Fifty-eighth Pennsylvania Infantry.

HDQRS. OUTPOSTS, CAMP FIFTY-EIGHTH REGT. PA. VOLS.,
January 28, 1863.

SIR: I have the honor to report that in order to close our lines effectually and at the same time to obtain information of the position of the enemy on my front, I yesterday dispatched strong parties on the Neuse and Dover roads; also on the railroad and on the Trent road. My directions were to feel the enemy, capturing his small parties and outposts but avoiding those which showed strength, and to obtain as much intelligence as possible. My several parties returned this evening.

On the Neuse and Dover roads the bridges over Core Creek were found broken down, and no posts on this side, and no parties met except one of a few men near the creek on the Neuse road, who retired hastily and escaped into the woods. There were no pickets on the Dover road crossing or the railroad, but a very small one at the Neuse, beyond the creek.

The railroad bridge at Core Creek was found standing, but the uprights are chopped nearly off close to the water, so as to fall readily. From the information obtained the enemy seem to have retired to Sandy Ridge, some 2½ miles beyond Core Creek, where they are fortifying themselves. They also have blocked up the cross-roads between the railroad and the Dover road. The force at Sandy Ridge is reported by residents of the vicinity to be two companies, and they also report that General Evans is in command at Kinston, but with what force they do not know or choose to say.

On the Trent road while a working party which I sent to finish blocking the roads on the flank of Deep Gully was thus engaged, the escort, Company K, of the Fifty-eighth Pennsylvania Volunteers, under Capt. Cecil Clay, moved in advance. On the Trent road, near the 14-mile post, a blockade was found obstructing effectually the passage of artillery and cavalry, and continuing more or less complete to beyond the eighteenth post. At the forks of the Trent road Captain Clay discovered a post of the enemy, which, by judicious arrangements, he surrounded and surprised, capturing the whole party—8 infantry and 2 cavalry. In this little affair, Captain Clay reports that good service was rendered by Lieutenant Wells (Company F), who, being with him for topographical purposes, had command of the squad which made the actual capture: also that his men behaved admirably.

The arms and horses taken will be turned over to the proper department. The prisoners, 10 in number, I send to headquarters under charge of Captain Clay.

Very respectfully, your obedient servant,

J. RICHTER JONES,
Colonel, Commanding Outposts.

Lieut. Col. SOUTHARD HOFFMAN,
Asst. Adjt. Gen., Eighteenth Army Corps.

JANUARY 30, 1863.—Engagement at Deserted House, or Kelly's Store, near Suffolk, Va.

REPORTS.

No. 1.—Maj. Gen. John J. Peck, U. S. Army.
No. 2.—Brig. Gen. Michael Corcoran, U. S. Army.
No. 3.—Col. Samuel P. Spear, Eleventh Pennsylvania Cavalry.
No. 4.—Col. William McEvily, One hundred and fifty-fifth New York Infantry.
No. 5.—Brig. Gen. Roger A. Pryor, C. S. Army.

No. 1.

Reports of Maj. Gen. John J. Peck, U. S. Army.

HEADQUARTERS UNITED STATES FORCES,
Suffolk, Va., February 4, 1863.

On January 29 information reached me that General Pryor had been encamped at Holland's Corners, 14 miles distant, with a force of all arms, the preceding night. Captain Ward, of the Eleventh Pennsylvania Cavalry, was promptly dispatched to procure reliable data and watch his movements. Late in the afternoon this most valuable and daring officer reported that General Pryor had gone in the direction of the Deserted House, with some 2,000 infantry, 500 cavalry, and a number of pieces of artillery. Parties were sent to the indicated point and returned about 8 p. m. with information of his arrival there. I at once organized a special force, consisting of the following: Eleventh Pennsylvania Cavalry, Colonel Spear; Follett's (Fourth U. S. Artillery) battery; Davis' (Seventh Massachusetts) battery; two mountain howitzers; the Thirteenth Indiana, Lieutenant-Colonel Dobbs; the Sixth Massachusetts, Colonel Follansbee; the One hundred and thirtieth New York, Lieutenant-Colonel Thorp; the One hundred and sixty-seventh Pennsylvania, Colonel Knoderer; the Sixty-ninth New York, Colonel Murphy, and the One hundred and fifty-fifth New York, Colonel McEvily; Colonel Gibbs commanding the infantry (amounting, by the morning reports of that day, to some 4,800 total), and placed it under the command of Brig. Gen. M. Corcoran.

He left about 1 a. m., with instructions to proceed cautiously, ascertain the locality of the enemy and force him from his position, inflicting all the loss possible. About 3.20 a. m. the cavalry came upon the rebel picket, driving it in and back upon the enemy's main line of battle. Follett's battery supported by the Thirteenth Indiana Regiment, and

two sections of Davis' battery, supported by the One hundred and thirtieth New York Regiment, were pushed forward to an open space in
front of the enemy by the light of the camp-fires. At 3.40 a. m. Follett
opened his fire and was immediately replied to by all the Confederate
artillery. Davis' battery joined in and the cannonade was continued
without cessation until 6 a. m. General Corcoran ordered the infantry to advance at 5.15 a. m., but the order was not promptly executed,
although given more than once. He says the One hundred and sixty-
seventh Pennsylvania became a confused mass, mixed up with other
regiments, and filled up the entire road, leaving it impassable and creating a temporary confusion among some other regiments in the rear.
At the request of the lieutenant-colonel it was sent to the rear to restore
confidence and reform.

About 6 a. m. one section of artillery was placed in the road, with the
Thirteenth Indiana on the right and the One hundred and thirtieth New
York on the left, supported by the Eleventh Pennsylvania Cavalry,
and the whole, under Colonel Spear, advanced upon the enemy. Other
regiments were formed in successive lines, supporting the movement.
Upon the approach of this determined mass the enemy faltered and
commenced his retreat. He was pursued vigorously until the troops
reached a thick wood and marsh. The One hundred and thirtieth New
York and cavalry were sent forward to reconnoiter and found the enemy well posted at the distance of 2 miles. A section of Davis' battery
and the Sixty-ninth New York took position on the road and opened
upon the enemy.

As it was now 10.15 a. m. a halt was ordered to give the men breakfast, while awaiting fresh supplies of ammunition and re-enforcements
called for after the opening of the engagement.

Soon after 11 o'clock Colonel Foster joined, with the One hundred and
twelfth New York and three pieces of the Second Wisconsin Battery,
and the ammunition, and was placed in command of the infantry. At
12 o'clock the plan of flanking by the Franklin road was given up and
an attack in front ordered. The One hundred and twelfth New York,
a section of Wisconsin guns, and two companies of cavalry were detailed to hold the Deserted House, and the command moved on again.

The enemy had commenced his retreat, but all possible haste was
made to overtake his fleeing battalions. At Pecosin Creek a sharp
skirmish occurred between the Thirteenth Indiana and the rear guard.
The cavalry followed 2 miles beyond Carrsville, when pursuit was discontinued. It being evident that no further stand would be made a
return to Deserted House was ordered.

At Carrsville Major Wheelan reported with six companies of Dodge's
Rifles and one howitzer and was assigned to duty. Later in the day a
section of the Second Wisconsin guns also joined. The whole command reached the Deserted House about 6 p. m. and Suffolk after midnight, having made a march of 32 miles in twenty-four hours and beaten
the enemy soundly.

Our loss was as follows: *

	Killed.	Wounded.	Missing.
Officers	2	9	
Privates	23	93	9
Total	25	102	9

* But see revised statement, p. 135.

The rebel loss must have been more than ours, judging from the indications of the field and roads and from the fact that 1,140 rounds of shot and shell were thrown from our batteries. Thirteen prisoners fell into our hands.

The Thirteenth Indiana is spoken of in very flattering terms; also the Sixty-ninth, One hundred and fifty-fifth, and One hundred and thirtieth New York.

The demoralization of the One hundred and sixty-seventh Pennsylvania, already spoken of, undoubtedly arose from a complication of unfavorable circumstances rather than from any determination to disobey orders. It had never been under fire, its position at the head of the column near the artillery (exposed to the enemy's fire for near two hours in the darkness without being engaged), and the fact that the colonel was desperately wounded and the lieutenant-colonel and major unhorsed were considerations well calculated to create temporary confusion. From this it recovered, and no complaint was made during the subsequent operations. This regiment should avail itself of the earliest opportunity to wipe out any suspicion that may have attached to its conduct at the Deserted House.

General Corcoran speaks in high commendation of Colonel Foster, of the Thirteenth Indiana, in command of the infantry; of Colonel Spear, commanding the cavalry; of Captain Follett, senior officer of artillery, and of Surgeon Hand, medical director. These are all officers of rare merit, who have won high reputation by their bravery, prudence, and fidelity.

Lieutenant-Colonels Dobbs and Thorp; Captain Davis, Lieutenants Hartwell, Devoll, and McCurdy (Seventh Massachusetts Battery); Lieutenants Whitney and Wilkeson (Fourth Artillery); Surgeons Dwyer and Nolan, Assistant Surgeons Spencer and Fawcett, Quartermaster Cooke, Captain Blodgett (assistant adjutant-general), and Aides-de-Camp Tracey, Hughes, and Winterbotham are particularly noticed for zeal, gallantry, and good conduct.

The troops that joined during the day are deserving of credit for the alacrity with which they responded to the call of duty.

The wounded, in kind and skillful hands, are doing well. Especial praise is due them for unflinching courage on the field and patient endurance of suffering.

The dead fell in the performance of high and stern duties assumed in behalf of a country menaced by the most cruel and wicked rebellion recorded in history. Nobly have they discharged all obligations, leaving bright examples of valor and fidelity for their fellow-soldiers and countrymen. Their families and friends have the deepest sympathies of the American people, and the precious and enduring recollections that their blood was poured out in the defense of constitutional liberty.

The artillery of the enemy equaled ours, while he had a chosen position and choice of ground in his retrograde movement. A flank move early in the day would probably have been decisive, and the victory full and complete. The action was prematurely brought on by the advance some two hours before daylight, during which time the usual supply of battery ammunition was nearly exhausted and the temper of the troops severely tried. Delays ensued and the enemy commenced his retreat.

Under all the circumstances it was a handsome affair, and the enemy will long remember his losses, disappointment, and narrow escape from capture.

General Corcoran and the troops are entitled to my warmest appro-bation for the brilliant achievement contributed by them to the cause of the Government.

Very respectfully, your obedient servant,

JOHN J. PECK,
Major-General.

Col. D. T. VAN BUREN,
Assistant Adjutant-General, Seventh Army Corps.

—

[Addenda.]

Return of Casualties in the Union forces engaged at the Deserted House, or Kelly's Store, Va., January 30, 1863.

[Compiled from nominal list of casualties, returns, etc.]

Command.	Killed.		Wounded.		Captured or missing.		Aggregate.
	Officers.	Enlisted men.	Officers.	Enlisted men.	Officers.	Enlisted men.	
13th Indiana Infantry			1	11			12
7th Massachusetts Battery		2		14			16
6th Massachusetts Infantry	1	3	2	5			11
69th New York Infantry [N. G. A.]		3	1	8		5	17
112th New York Infantry		1		1			2
130th New York Infantry	1	6	2	18		2	29
155th New York Infantry				2		3	5
164th New York Infantry		1		1		2	4
11th Pennsylvania Cavalry		1	1	18			20
165th Pennsylvania Infantry				5			5
167th Pennsylvania Infantry			1	9			10
4th U. S. Artillery, Battery D		4		8			12
Total	2	21	8	100		12	143

Officers killed.—Lieut. Edward D. Sawtell, Sixth Massachusetts; Capt. Rowley P. Taylor, One hundred and thirtieth New York.
Mortally wounded.—Col. Charles A. Knoderer, One hundred and sixty-seventh Pennsylvania.

—

SUFFOLK, *January 30, 1863.*

Three of Follett's guns have arrived; two of them disabled by ina-bility to get shells down; one of his limbers exploded. Our loss about 100. My extra force had arrived at the latest; also Colonel Foster. The enemy had fallen back from 3 to 4 miles since daylight, contesting different positions. I have repeatedly guarded against being led too far away in case of success. It has been a hard night and day, but I feel sure that we have a victory. One of the churches has been pre-pared for the wounded.

Prisoners say that battery horses were nearly exhausted and the guns were moved by hand at intervals. Some guns will probably be secured.

JOHN J. PECK,
Major-General.

Major-General DIX, *Fort Monroe.*

No. 2.

Report of Brig. Gen. Michael Corcoran, U. S. Army.

HEADQUARTERS CORCORAN'S IRISH LEGION,
Suffolk, Va., February 1, 1863.

MAJOR: I have the honor to report that, in compliance with orders received from Maj. Gen. John J. Peck, at 9.30 p. m. on Thursday the 29th ultimo I proceeded to take command of the troops designated for the expedition to attack the rebel force under General Roger A. Pryor.

Arriving at the point previously arranged for the rendezvous of our troops at 12 o'clock I found most of the regiments already on the ground or had passed them on their march thereto.

At 1 a. m. on Friday, the 30th, everything being in readiness I commenced the march in the order according to the annexed supplement. I continued the march until, arriving near the Nansemond County Poor House, I ordered a halt for about ten minutes, after which we proceeded on toward the Deserted House.

About 1 mile from the latter place our advance guard, at 3.20 a. m., met the enemy's pickets posted in strong force on the road and in the woods. They were promptly charged, some being killed and others taken prisoners. The charge was continued by two companies of Colonel Spear's cavalry up to the enemy's front, who were drawn up in line of battle. I pushed forward Captain Follett's battery of the Fourth U. S. Artillery, supported by the Thirteenth Regiment Indiana Volunteers, and two sections of Captain Davis' (Seventh Massachusetts) battery, supported by the One hundred and thirtieth New York Volunteers. They gained an open space in front of the enemy, whose camp-fires were burning. The other regiments of the command, which were in line of battle along the south side of the road, were ordered to lie down when the artillery firing commenced.

Captain Follett's battery first opened at 3.40 a. m. on the north side of the road, and the enemy immediately replied with twelve pieces, some of which were of a larger caliber than our own. Captain Davis took position on the south side of the road, and our own guns and the enemy's kept up an incessant and very rapid fire until 6 a. m.

At about 5.15 a. m. I gave orders for the infantry to advance. This order, twice repeated, was not promptly executed, through cause which I reported verbally to the major-general yesterday. On learning this I immediately ordered an advance a third time and went in person to the One hundred and sixty-seventh Regiment Pennsylvania Militia and sent orders to the regiments in the rear to advance in succession in the order of battle previously assigned. I found the One hundred and sixty-seventh without a single field officer. The colonel, I afterward learned with regret, was seriously, if not mortally wounded, and the lieutenant-colonel and major had their horses killed under them and were temporarily hurt. I asked if there was any officer present who would take command of the regiment. The adjutant promptly responded and used all exertions to get the men forward, but did not succeed. They became a confused mass, mixed up with other regiments, and filled up the entire road, leaving it impassable and creating a temporary confusion among some other regiments in the rear. The lieutenant-colonel came up to me about this time and requested permission to take his regiment to the rear in order to restore confidence and have them reformed. I became convinced this must be done, and

consequently ordered the Sixty-ninth Regiment New York National
Guards (who behaved throughout with admirable steadiness, although
suffering severely from the enemy's shell) and the One hundred and
fifty-fifth New York Volunteers to take position in line of battle about
800 paces in the rear and stop any of the command from retiring beyond that point. One company of Spear's cavalry was placed on the
road for a similar purpose. I rode down to see this order executed, and
on returning to the front in company with Colonel Spear, at 5.40 a. m.,
determined to charge the enemy with the bayonet, and ordered two
pieces of artillery to be placed on the road and formed the Thirteenth
Indiana and One hundred and thirtieth New York on the right and left,
strongly supported by Spear's cavalry. These orders were promptly
attended to, and at 6 a. m. they all moved forward under command of
Colonel Spear. I ordered up the other regiments and formed them in
successive lines of battle.

The enemy rapidly retreated at our apparent approach, and were
vigorously pursued until our infantry advance was stopped by thick
woods and marsh. On the concentration of our forces at this point I
ordered the One hundred and thirtieth New York Volunteers to be
thrown forward as skirmishers on each side of the road and a portion
of Spear's cavalry to reconnoiter on the road, who soon reported the
enemy's artillery strongly posted about 2 miles in front. Our skirmishers here were under the command of Lieutenant-Colonel Thorp,
and continued to advance steadily. The enemy on perceiving them
came forward with their peculiar yell to dislodge them, but were quickly
driven back with much loss. They tried this three times with the
same result. Lieutenant-Colonel Thorp acted bravely and exhibited
much coolness and good judgment. Two pieces of Captain Davis' battery, supported by the Sixty-ninth New York National Guards, meanwhile took position on the road and opened on the enemy.

It may be necessary for me to state that from 5.30 a. m. the remainder of our artillery were almost entirely without ammunition.
The men of the command had eaten nothing up to this time, 10.15 a. m.,
and had made a rapid march. I therefore ordered a halt for the purpose of giving them time for breakfast and awaiting fresh supplies of
ammunition. I consulted the colonels and chiefs of commands and
decided to endeavor to take the enemy in flank by moving along the
old Franklin road.

At about 11 a. m. Colonel Foster reported to me, and I immediately
placed him in command of the entire infantry. Soon after, the One
hundred and twelfth Regiment New York Volunteers and three pieces
of the Second Wisconsin Battery, with a fresh supply of artillery ammunition, reported. My thanks are due to these commands for the
prompt manner in which they marched to the scene of action and the
desire they manifested to join in the pursuit of the enemy. The two
howitzers attached to the Eleventh Pennsylvania Cavalry were present
and were brought to bear on the enemy while on their retreat in the
morning.

At 12 m. everything was in readiness and I altered the former determination and decided to attack the enemy in front, and again moved
forward for that purpose, leaving the One hundred and twelfth New
York Volunteers, two pieces of the Second Wisconsin Battery, and two
companies of Spear's cavalry to hold the Deserted House. The enemy
had commenced his retreat. We pursued with all possible haste toward
Carrsville. At Pecosin Creek the Thirteenth Indiana Volunteers, as
skirmishers, came up with their rear guard, strongly posted on the

opposite bank, and a sharp skirmish ensued. Our artillery was quickly placed in position and opened, receiving no reply. After a few minutes I ordered the artillery to cease fire and Colonel Spear to charge the enemy across the bridge, which he did in his usual gallant and fearless manner. He continued on nearly 2 miles beyond Carrsville and returned, reporting the enemy entirely out of sight.

I then concluded that all attempts to get them to engage were useless, and therefore farther pursuit unnecessary. Major Wheelan, with six companies of Dodge's New York Mounted Rifles, reported at this time and was immediately assigned to duty. We returned toward Suffolk, halting at the Deserted House at 6 p. m. to give the men time for rest and food.

Details were ordered to bury those of the enemy's dead who, in their flight, were left on the field, and among whom was a lieutenant, as indicated by his uniform.

We fired, according to Captain Follett's official report, 1,140 rounds of shot and shell, and the ground occupied by the enemy was strewn with dead soldiers, horses, broken rammers, sponges, knapsacks, and cartridge-boxes; and innumerable pools of blood on the roadside and in the woods gave full proof of the immense havoc our artillery created during the night engagement. I ascertained, from information received on the way to Carrsville, that 25 wagons were believed to have been impressed for the purpose, and were driven off filled with their killed and wounded. I visited a large farm house occupied by Mrs. Mulholland, which they had used as one of their hospitals. Both floors of the building were covered with blood and pieces of bone and flesh. My informant told me that 40 wounded had been there, among whom were 4 officers. A prisoner asserts that our first shell killed one of their colonels.

The Thirteenth Indiana Volunteers, with its accomplished lieutenant-colonel, I found ever ready to obey all orders promptly and cheerfully, and did signal service. Of the Sixty-ninth New York National Guards and the One hundred and fifty-fifth New York Volunteers, as they belong to my own command, I do not desire to speak as flatteringly as they deserve. What I have a right to say of Colonel Spear, commanding the cavalry, would scarcely add to his already high reputation as one of the most accomplished officers in the service, a thorough disciplinarian, and one who does not know what fear is. He led every charge in person, and I found him, his lieutenant-colonel, majors, adjutant, and other officers and entire command ever ready to perform every duty assigned them with the greatest alacrity. His perfect knowledge of the country was of incalculable service to me.

Colonel Foster is also too well known to the major-general for me to endeavor to elevate his military character beyond that very high standard he has already earned and attained. I must, however, state that he fully maintained this character and rendered me most efficient service from the time of his arrival.

Captain Follett, as chief of artillery, acted with great judgment, and himself and officers, as also Captain Davis and officers and the men of both batteries, cannot be spoken of too highly for their coolness and indomitable courage during such a severe engagement.

I was most ably assisted by Captain Blodgett, my assistant adjutant-general; Lieutenant Tracey, my aide-de-camp, and Lieutenants Hughes and Winterbotham, detailed on my staff. They carried my orders and messages everywhere under the most galling fire, and all are alike deserving of the highest praise and commendation. Captain Blodgett was slightly wounded in the left knee by a piece of shell.

I also desire to mention the excellent soldierly qualities of Private James

Collins, Company E, of Colonel Spear's regiment, who was detailed to me as orderly.

For specific accounts of meritorious conduct of subordinate officers who did not come under my own observation I beg leave to refer you to accompanying reports.

Dr. Hand, the medical director at this post, was present and directed the transportation of our wounded and relieved and prevented much suffering. Dr. Dwyer, surgeon of the Sixty-ninth, took charge of the building occupied as our hospital, and, with the assistance of Dr. Nolan, surgeon of the One hundred and fifty-fifth, and Assistant Surgeons Ewen, Spencer, Fawcett and others, rendered good service in that department.

Quartermaster Cooke, of the One hundred and fifty-fifth New York Volunteers, was placed in command of the transportation and gave most perfect satisfaction.

The number of prisoners taken by us has not been generally mentioned in the official reports to me, but I believe them to be about 30.

Our total loss is as follows:*

	Killed.	Wounded.	Missing.
Officers	2	9	
Non-commissioned officers	3	21	1
Privates	18	65	14
Total	23	95	15
Total casualties			133

The whole command arrived at headquarters in most excellent spirits at 1 a. m. on the 31st ultimo, making a march of 32 miles in about twenty-four hours.

I cannot close without returning my sincere thanks to Maj. Gen. John J. Peck, commanding this post, for the high honor he conferred on me in intrusting the command of this important expedition to me and leaving in his special orders and dispatches so very much to my own discretion. I endeavored to execute everything to the best of my ability, and hope that all I have done meets his approbation.

I am, major, with high respect, your obedient servant,

MICHAEL CORCORAN,
Brigadier-General, Comdg. at Battle of Deserted House, Va.

Maj. B. B. Foster, *Assistant Adjutant-General.*

[Supplement.]

Order of march of force under command of Brig. Gen. M. Corcoran, United States Volunteers, from signal station near Suffolk, Va., from 1 to 3.20 a. m. Friday, January 30, 1863:

Six companies Eleventh Pennsylvania Cavalry, under command of Col. Samuel P. Spear; Thirteenth Regiment Indiana Volunteers, under command of Lieut. Col. C. J. Dobbs; Battery D, Fourth U. S. Artillery, under command of Captain Follett, acting as chief of artillery; two sections Seventh Massachusetts Battery, under command of Captain Davis; One hundred and thirtieth Regiment New York Volunteers, under command of Lieutenant-Colonel Thorp; Ambulance Corps; Sixth Regiment Massachusetts Volunteers, under command of Colonel Follansbee; One hundred and sixty-seventh Regiment Pennsylvania Militia, under command of Colonel Knoderer; One hundred and fifty-fifth Regiment New York Volunteers, under command of Colonel Mc-

---

* But see revised statement, p. 135.

Evily; train; one section Seventh Massachusetts Battery, under command of Lieutenant ———; Sixty-ninth Regiment New York National Guards, under command of Colonel Murphy, and two companies Eleventh Pennsylvania Cavalry, under Major Cornog.

No. 3.

Report of Col. Samuel P. Spear, Eleventh Pennsylvania Cavalry.

HDQRS. ELEVENTH PENNSYLVANIA VOL. CAVALRY,
Camp Suffolk, Va., February 1, 1863.

SIR: Inclosed herewith I have the honor to transmit a list of the killed and wounded in an engagement in which my regiment was engaged for thirteen hours, being three hours and eleven minutes under a most tremendous fire of shot and shell from the enemy's heavy guns.

This is the fifth heavy engagement that the regiment has taken an active part in since October 1, 1862, in the vicinity of Blackwater.

The recent battle took place on the morning of the 30th of January, 1863, at the Deserted House, 9 miles west of Suffolk, Va. The enemy consisted of 16 pieces of heavy artillery, 1,200 cavalry, and 6 regiments of infantry. Our force was 12 pieces of artillery, 5 regments of infantry, and my regiment, the Eleventh Pennsylvania Cavalry. The cavalry opened the engagement by a charge on the enemy's pickets, and was from that moment till the end, as before stated, constantly in the hottest of the battle. Lieut. Col. George Stetzel and Majs. Samuel Wetherill and George T. Cornog were present with the regiment and rendered prompt and valuable services during the entire engagement. The non-commissioned officers and men performed their duty in excellent style, and during a crashing fire they proved an ornament to the service and an honor to their State. It will be seen by the inclosed list that Capt. Albert J. Ackerly had his horse killed by a piece of a shell, and that Capt. John B. Loomis and my adjutant, A. A. Menzies, had their horses instantly killed by a heavy shot. My own horse was seriously and perhaps mortally wounded by a shot in the breast.

Both officers and men are worthy of the highest commendation for their coolness, courage, and undaunted bravery.

I most respectfully request that permission may be granted to have inscribed upon the regimental colors the words, "Blackwater" and "Deserted House."

I am, sir, very respectfully, your obedient servant,
S. P. SPEAR,
Colonel, Eleventh Pennsylvania Volunteer Cavalry.

Hon. ELI SLIFER, *Secretary of State.*

No. 4.

Report of Col. William McEvily, One hundred and fifty-fifth New York Infantry.

SUFFOLK, VA., *January* 31, 1863.

SIR: In compliance with Special Orders, No. 31, from general headquarters, I herewith furnish for the information of the brigadier-general commanding a detailed account of the expedition in which the regiment under my command was engaged on the 30th instant:

In accordance with orders received the regiment fell in at 12 o'clock midnight and marched for the signal station on the South Quay road, a short distance from which, farther on, it came up with the rear of the rest of the forces composing the expedition, under command of Brigadier-General Corcoran, and proceeded with them to within about half a mile of the place known as the Deserted House, where the regiment was drawn up in line of battle, heavy firing in the front having announced that we had got up with the enemy and that an engagement had commenced. In this spot we remained within range of the rebel artillery, exposed to occasional danger from the discharge of shot and shell, the men of my command behaving with a coolness and self-possession seldom evinced by volunteers under a first fire.

Here a temporary confusion was created among the soldiers of my command by the One hundred and sixty-seventh Pennsylvania and the Sixth Massachusetts Regiments falling back in disorder upon them, but from this they soon recovered and remained steady in line until 6 a. m., when an order was received to advance, which was complied with, and the regiment was again formed in line of battle on the other side and within half a mile south of the Deserted House. At this time the companies were mustered to ascertain if any casualties had occurred, when it was found that there was 1 man of the One hundred and sixty-fourth Regiment (two companies of which were attached to my regiment in lieu of Companies D and K on duty at the time the regiment was ordered out, Company K being on picket duty and D detailed to garrison Fort Halleck) killed; 2 men of Company B, of my regiment, wounded, and 5 reported missing.

From this position we then followed the enemy, who was retreating, some 5 or 6 miles, when, in consequence of renewed firing in our front, the regiment was once more formed in line of battle, soon after which, the firing having ceased, I was ordered to return with my command to the Deserted House, where I arrived about 6 p. m. and remained till 9 o'clock, the men resting and refreshing themselves after the fatigue they had undergone. From here I was ordered to Suffolk, for which place I marched with my regiment and arrived at 1 a. m. on 31st instant.

I must particularly mention th valuable assistance rendered me throughout the whole time the engagement lasted by Major Flood, whose services principally conduced to the restoration of order and confidence when the regiment had been thrown into confusion by the One hundred and sixty-seventh Pennsylvania and Sixth Massachusetts Regiments.

I would also make favorable mention of Captain Byrne and the soldiers under him, whose anxiety to get into action was such that it was with difficulty they were restrained from charging on the rebel batteries. I should do an injustice to the gallant men composing the two companies of the One hundred and sixty-fourth Regiment attached to the One hundred and fifty-fifth if I omitted to mention the brave and steady manner in which they behaved.

From the bearing of all the officers and men engaged in the affair and the coolness and intrepidity displayed by them during the time it lasted, I feel confident that they possess all those qualities necessary to make good and efficient soldiers, and of their willingness to display the same whenever occasion offers.

I have the honor to be, sir, your obedient servant,

WM. McEVILY,
Col., Comdg. One hundred and fifty-fifth Regt. New York Vols.

Capt. J. J. BLODGETT, *A. A. G.*

No. 5.

Report of Brig. Gen. Roger A. Pryor, C. S. Army.

HEADQUARTERS FORCES ON THE BLACKWATER,
February 4, 1863.

CAPTAIN : I have the honor to submit the following report of the fight at Kelly's Store on the 30th ultimo :

With the design of subsisting my command as largely as possible within the enemy's lines, on the 25th ultimo I crossed the Blackwater on a foraging expedition.   The detachment consisted of the regiments of Cols. [Robert C.] Trigg, [J. J.] McMahon, and [Thomas] Poage ; 150 men of Col. [W. C.] Claiborne's [Seventh Confederate] Cavalry ; [Capt. J. C.] Coit's, and a section, respectively, of [Capt. S. T.] Wright's and [Capt. Louis H.] Webb's batteries.   Subsequently I directed Maj. [S. P.] McConnell to join me with a part of [H. A.] Edmundson's battalion and a section of S. Taylor Martin's battery.   The entire force did not exceed 1,800 of all arms.

The evening of the 25th I bivouacked at Somerton.   Informed of the presence of the enemy's cavalry at Gatesville, some 12 miles distant, I dispatched Lieut. Col. [V. H.] Taliaferro that night with 100 mounted men to beat up their quarters ; but they were appraised of his approach, and despite the celerity of his march they continued to escape by a circuitous route to Suffolk.

The 26th I moved from Somerton to Holland's Store, where I was detained three days by inclement weather.

On the 29th I resumed my march, and that evening about 5 o'clock I reached Kelly's Store, on the direct road from Franklin to Suffolk, distant from the former 12 miles, from the latter scarcely 9.   Apprehending a probable attack, I disposed my force in such manner as to be prepared for any contingency.   I preferred to approach Kelly's by the road from Kinsale Swamp, because it conducted toward the enemy by a direct instead of an oblique march, and because, being covered on either side by an extensive and impenetrable *pognosia*, it protected me against the possibility of a flank attack, except through certain obscure pathways, which a small force would suffice to block up.   At Kelly's the road divides— one fork leading directly to Suffolk, the other turning almost perpendicularly to the left and sweeping around by Ely's and Providence Church. A hundred or two paces from the store both roads are intersected by a swamp, but it opposes scarcely any obstruction to the passage of troops. The store stands in an open field of considerable extent, inclosed on either side by a thick pine growth reaching to both roads at the point where they traverse the swamp.   The wood in rear of the field, about 1 mile from the swamp, I occupied with the regiments of McMahon and Poage, deployed on both sides of the road.   One battalion of Trigg's regiment was in the pines on the left, a little in advance of Poage's, the other on the right, a little in advance of McMahon.   The batteries I destined to sweep the field in case the enemy should cross the swamp.   A section of 6-pounders I advanced to within 300 yards of the store, one gun being on either side of the road.   Some 400 yards to the rear and on either side of the road I placed a rifled piece and howitzer.   This was Coit's battery. Wright's section, consisting of a rifled gun and howitzer, was in position on the left of the road and in line with Coit's rearmost pieces.   Edmundson's battalion, with a section of Martin's and a section of Webb's batteries, were held in reserve some three-quarters of a mile in rear of the main body, and were so posted as to observe the two by-paths which there intersect the Kelly road, the one communicating with the railway and the other with the Carrsville road on the left. The cavalry were employed in outpost duty, a strong picket being stationed on both roads some distance beyond the swamp. A company of infantry was also placed on each road immediately at the swamp. Hardly were these dispositions completed when the vedettes in advance of the cavalry outposts encountered and drove back a small scouting party from Suffolk. Anticipating an attack during the night by a large force of cavalry, I prepared an ambuscade by posting 100 sharpshooters on the direct road a mile beyond the swamp. As was expected, about 3 o'clock the enemy's cavalry approached the men in ambush and received a volley which emptied many a saddle and threw the column into confusion. They rallied, however, and were saluted with another destructive fire. The infantry behind then engaged my skirmishers, who, being overpowered by numbers, were obliged to recross the swamp. Here they were again placed in ambush, and again they poured a deadly volley into the enemy's cavalry at a distance of 10 paces. Meanwhile the enemy's whole force pressed on across the swamp.

At this moment I reached the spot and immediately directed Captain Coit to open with his advance section. He was anticipated by the enemy, who had already gotten a couple of mountain howitzers in position. The ground being favorable to the action of the enemy's cavalry, I apprehended some peril to the pieces in advance, and accordingly after a few rounds I retired them on a line with the other sections. All my artillery, except the reserve under Captain Martin, was now engaged. The enemy, too, had brought up his batteries, and there ensued and was maintained for two hours as furious a cannonade as I have ever witnessed. It was now 4 o'clock precisely; by 6 o'clock the enemy's advance was decisively checked and all his guns silenced, except a single piece which discharged an occasional shot with feeble effect.

At this moment word was brought me from various sources that the cars were running and were accumulating troops in rear of my right flank. This information obliged me to move my main force to the point occupied by the reserve in order to prevent the enemy debouching on my flank and rear. Accordingly I directed the infantry to retire by successive battalions and the artillery by alternate sections. The movement was executed with perfect deliberation and without the least annoyance. The reserve, now become the advance, was re-enforced and arranged in a skirt of woods behind the field, about 400 paces in width, which the enemy in his approach would be obliged to traverse. Skirmishers were thrown forward to the right and left. The artillery was disposed on the edge of a field in such order as to rake the road and sweep every foot of the field. The position was sufficiently strong, and we awaited the approach of the enemy if he should prove in a mood to renew the fight. After the lapse of nearly an hour their cavalry appeared in the woods on the opposite side of the field. A single discharge of spherical case sent them scampering away. Next they brought up a howitzer, but after three rounds that also was disabled and withdrawn. Their infantry then issued from the woods across the field with the evident design of charging our batteries, but being confronted by our skirmishers and assailed by storm of case and canister they broke and ran in the utmost confusion, nor did they rally again. My line of skirmishers was advanced and scouts were sent forward to ascertain the enemy's presence, but they were not to be found. They were beaten and had fled toward Suffolk. Despite our inferior force and deficiency in cavalry I resolved on pursuit, and had issued orders accordingly, when I received the embarrassing information that the artillery ammunition was exhausted. In this circumstance no alternative was left me but to return toward our base of supply. After remaining on the field from 8 until 1 o'clock (five hours) without seeing or hearing of the enemy we retired leisurely, marching 3 miles in so many hours, and exempt from all interruption until we reached Kinsale Swamp, when the enemy's cavalry attempted a dash on our rear guard. He was promptly repulsed and severely chastised. We proceeded to Carrsville and bivouacked 6 miles from the field of battle.

The fortunate issue of this engagement, maintained against such superior force (the enemy's force being fully 8,000), I attribute to the favor of Providence and the superb valor of the troops of my command. For four hours the infantry lay under a terrific storm of shell, case, and canister, and yet hardly a man abandoned his place in the ranks. But the chief glory of the fight must be accorded to the artillery. To the rapidity and effect of their fire, the firmness with which they held their position and maintained the fight against more numerous and heavier batteries and under the menace of a charge by cavalry and infantry, is due the decisive repulse sustained by the enemy.

When all discharged their duty so admirably it is difficult to distinguish particular merit in individuals; but I could not acquit myself of injustice if I omitted to recall the services of Captains Coit, Martin, and Wright. By their gallantry and judicious conduct these officers imparted the noblest spirit and the greatest efficiency to their respective commands and contributed chiefly to the successful event of the day.

The casualties in the command were few, but among them I have to lament the death of Colonel Poage, of the Fiftieth, and Capt. [Thomas P.] Dobyns and Lieut. [John S.] Lacy, of the Fifty-fourth Virginia Volunteers, all courageous and capable officers. Persons with the best opportunities of information report the enemy's loss to exceed 300 in killed and wounded. My own dead and wounded were brought from the field, except the few who fell in the fight across the swamp and who were lost in the thickness of the woods and the darkness of the night.

In conclusion I have to commend the conduct of my staff: Of Capt. [W. H.] Whitner, assistant adjutant-general, whose zeal, gallantry, and intelligence are worthy of all praise; of my aide, Lieut. [C.] McCann, who exhibited his usual activity and reckless audacity of courage, and of Messrs. McMullen and Barnes, who were equally fearless and energetic in communicating my orders and directing their execution.

I have the honor to be, very respectfully, your obedient servant,

ROGER A. PRYOR,
Brigadier-General, Commanding.

Capt. GEORGE G. GARRISON,
Assistant Adjutant-General.

[Indorsement.]

HEADQUARTERS DEPARTMENT OF NORTH CAROLINA,
Goldsborough, N. C., February 10, 1863.

I have the honor to forward the report of General R. A. Pryor, inclosing with it the list of killed and wounded. It is with pleasure I call the attention of the War Department to the successful defense of the lines of the Blackwater. Although I have never been able to place an adequate force on the line, yet by defensive works and constant vigilance it has been held since July last against a force often five or six times our numbers. Three times in heavy columns they have tried to force a passage and have in each instance been repulsed, and our forces have constantly traversed the counties on the left bank and drawn therefrom most of their own supplies.   Col. C. Leventhorpe, the former commander of the lines, and General Pryor both deserve commendation for their successful defense of that frontier with their small commands.

S. G. FRENCH,
Major-General, Commanding.

[Addenda.]

Return of Casualties in the Brigade commanded by Brig. Gen. Roger A. Pryor, in engagement at Kelly's Store, Va.

[Compiled from nominal lists on file.]

Command.	Killed.			Wounded.			Aggregate.
	Officers.	Enlisted men.	Total.	Officers.	Enlisted men.	Total.	
50th Virginia Regiment, Col. Thomas Poage	1	......	1	1	6	7	8
63d Virginia Regiment, Col. J. J. McMahon	......	4	4	1	9	10	14
54th Virginia Regiment, Col. Robert C. Trigg	2	......	2	......	4	4	6
Coit's battery, Capt. J. C. Coit	......	1	1	1	5	6	7
Wright's battery, Capt. S. T. Wright	......	......	......	1	2	3	3
Martin's battery, Capt. S. T. Martin	......	......	......	......	1	1	1
Grand total							39

FEBRUARY 1–10, 1863.—Expedition from New Berne to Plymouth, N. C.

Report of Col. Francis L. Lee, Forty-fourth Massachusetts Infantry.

HDQRS. 44TH REGIMENT MASS. VOL. MILITIA,
Camp Stevenson, New Berne, February 14, 1863.

CAPTAIN : I have the honor to report that in obedience to order of January 31, 1863, I embarked my command on steamer Northerner and arrived at Plymouth, N. C., at 4 p. m. on February 2.

Upon landing I consulted with Major Bartholomew, Twenty-seventh Massachusetts Regiment, commander of the post, in regard to closing the lines; but learning from him that information of our arrival and probable force had undoubtedly been sent forward to the enemy even before our arrival, I deemed it unwise to interfere with existing arrangements in regard to passing the lines.

Learning that Commodore Flusser was absent, I proceeded in company with Major Bartholomew to inspect the location of his pickets and his preparations for defense, and found the pickets well placed, his precautions against surprise sufficient, and every advantage taken of the natural defenses of the town, the major having almost completed a ditch connecting the two swamps lying south of the town.   Inside of this ditch, which is about 6 feet in depth and about 15 feet wide, the earth is thrown up sufficiently high to afford shelter for sharpshooters. Major Bartholomew proposes to erect a small block-house where the Long Acre road crosses this ditch, and also one upon the Jamesville road at the crossing of the ditch.   My carpenters built draw-bridges for each of these roads, and I would respectfully suggest that two field howitzers would render the defense of these roads easy against any force likely to be brought against them, and that they are most earnestly desired by Major Bartholomew. I would also recommend a further supply of axes and shovels, as the want of these tools prevents Major Bartholomew from availing himself fully of the services of the contrabands in his command.

Upon the Long Acre road the picket is stationed at the ditch, about three-quarters of a mile from the custom-house, with an outer picket of 5 men half a mile in advance at the junction of the road with the Lee's Mill road. At this point there is a blockade of trees fallen across the road.

Upon the Columbia road the picket is established just west of the bridge, crossing Coneby Creek, about two miles from the custom house. This bridge is taken up each night and affords an easy and sure defense, as the creek is very deep.

Upon the Jamesville road the picket is at the ditch, about 1 mile from the custom-house, and a cavalry vedette is stationed about half a mile in advance.

Upon inquiring as to the probable force and location of the enemy, I learned from Major Bartholomew that he, in company with Commodore Flusser, had, on January 30, made a reconnaissance as far as Jamesville on the gunboat Commodore Perry, shelling the woods at various points but finding no signs of the presence of the enemy. It was the opinion of Major Bartholomew that the position and strength of the enemy was as follows: Two companies of the Seventeenth North Carolina Regiment at Rainbow Bluff with two field pieces; the remainder of that regiment, with four field pieces, in the vicinity of the bluff, anywhere between Hamilton and Williamston; four companies of infantry some 7 miles northwest of Washington, and the remainder of their regiment at or near Greenville; three companies of cavalry scouting anywhere between the Tar and Roanoke Rivers.

A cavalry scout to Ward's Bridge, some 4 miles from town, failed to discover any signs of rebel scouts, though they learned that parties of two or three cavalrymen had been seen in that vicinity within a week.

Commodore Flusser arrived on the evening of the 2d of February, and after consultation I arranged to go with my regiment on his three gunboats to Williamston, starting the next morning at 7 o'clock and landing at Williamston or Jamesville as might be thought best—the landing party to be supported by three boat howitzers and their crews, under command of Lieutenant Furness, of the Valley City. On the following morning a drifting snow-storm rendered any advance by land or water impossible; the impassable state of the roads also prevented an expedition to Windsor to confiscate bacon packed for rebel use.

On Friday, February 6, finding that no coal could be furnished to our transport by the Navy and that my pioneers were unable to supply the requisite quantity of wood, I was obliged to send out some 3 miles to buy and draw some dry wood belonging to Mr. Harrison, a loyal man living on the Long Acre road. Before starting the wagons Major Bartholomew told me that he had good reason to believe that many of the inhabitants upon that road had abused their protection papers by smuggling out salt in larger quantities than they needed for home consumption; that they had packed large stores of bacon intended for the use of the rebel troops; that he thought an examination and confiscation of a portion of their bacon, if found in such large quantities, would be desirable. I therefore took four of my companies and went some 13 miles out, taking on the way the horses, mules, and carts to transport the pork if found. I examined the farms of the persons suspected, and finding from two to three tons of bacon took from four of them 3,385 pounds, leaving much, for want of transportation, which I think would properly have been brought away. This bacon, with 22 horses and mules and 16 carts, I handed over to Major Bartholomew, leaving it to his judgment to return any of the horses and carts to persons in whose loyalty he had confidence, and directing him to see that quartermaster's receipts for the property taken should be given to the parties, in order that if they could rebut the testimony with regard to their sympathy and aid for the rebel cause they might receive payment from the Government.

On Sunday morning, being informed by the captain of our transport that unless we started then he would be obliged to lay at Plymouth until coal was found him, and my rations not being sufficient for over two days longer, I left Plymouth that afternoon, and after anchoring at Roanoke for coal, arrived here on the evening of Tuesday, February 10.

Yours, with respect,

FRANCIS L. LEE,
Colonel, Comdg. Forty-fourth Regt. Mass. Vol. Militia.

Capt. ANDREW STEWART,
Assistant Adjutant-General.

P. S.—Inclosed please find instructions received from headquarters relative to the movement above stated.

[Indorsement.]

HEADQUARTERS EIGHTEENTH ARMY CORPS,
New Berne, N. C., February 15, 1863.

Approved and respectfully forwarded.

H. W. WESSELLS,
Brigadier-General Volunteers, Commanding.

[Inclosure.]

HDQRS. DEPT. OF NORTH CAROLINA, 18TH A. C.,
New Berne, January 31, 1863.

Col. FRANCIS L. LEE,
Comdg. Forty-fourth Massachusetts Volunteer Militia:

COLONEL: You will embark your command to-morrow morning at 7 o'clock on the steamer Northerner and proceed directly to Plymouth, N. C.

The Massasoit will be at the wharf at the foot of Middle street for the purpose of transferring your regiment to the Northerner.

Upon your arrival at that place you will assume command of the post, and immediately after consultation with Captain Flusser, U. S. Navy, and Major Bartholomew, Twenty-seventh Massachusetts Volunteers, take the necessary steps to drive in the enemy's pickets.

It is reported here that the enemy is in force (about 1,000) at Jamesville. Should you find this report corroborated by the information you may receive at Plymouth, you will advance on that place and whip the enemy; and if upon consultation with the above officers it should be deemed advisable you are authorized to advance as far as Williamston.

It is necessary that the advance should be made very shortly after your arrival, so that the enemy may not receive information of your arrival at the place, and you are therefore advised to close the lines.

Captain Flusser, U. S. Navy, will furnish you with some boat howitzers and crews, and he, as well as Major Bartholomew, are strongly recommended to you from their long experience at the post.

Much of course must be left to your own discretion, and the greatest confidence is placed in your judgment and abilities. The general's desire is to drive the enemy back and prevent their annoying our forces at Plymouth.

Yours, very respectfully,

SOUTHARD HOFFMAN,
Assistant Adjutant-General.

FEBRUARY 2, 1863.—Destruction of Salt-Works at Wale's Head, Currituck Beach, N. C.

Report of Capt. Francis E. Porter, Eighth Massachusetts Infantry.

HEADQUARTERS,
Roanoke Island, February 5, 1863.

CAPTAIN: Pursuant to information received from you in your communication of December 29, 1862, of there being salt-works in operation on Currituck Beach, I on the 2d instant went with a force of 90 men on the United States steamer Halifax and succeeded in destroying the same, together with about 100 bushels of salt, without opposition. These same works are located at a place called Wale's Head and have before been destroyed by our forces, but were rebuilt and in full operation and, I should say, were manufacturing salt at the rate of about 50 bushels per day. My expedition was a perfect success.

Trusting my actions may meet your approbation, I am, captain, respectfully, your obedient servant,

F. E. PORTER,
Captain, Commanding Post.

Capt. JOHN F. ANDERSON,
Acting Assistant Adjutant-General, New Berne, N. C.

FEBRUARY 5, 1863.—Skirmish near Olive Branch Church, Va.

Report of Maj. Christopher Kleinz, Fifth Pennsylvania Cavalry.

CAMP MAGRUDER,
Near Williamsburg, February 5, 1863.

COLONEL: I have the honor to report that in obedience to instructions I proceeded this morning in command of the second and third squadrons, numbering in all 156 men, to make a reconnaissance of the country as far as Twelve Mile Ordinary. Arriving at Fort Magruder I was joined by 26 men, under Lieutenant Williamson, and from thence to William and Mary College; here I detached the third squadron, under Captain Stetson, with orders to take the Jamestown road and scout that portion of the country around by Green Spring farm; to come in by Centreville, and send me word as to his arrival down to the junction of the Centreville and Richmond roads, where I, with the remaining part of my force, was waiting.

During the interval I sent Lieutenant Williamson on with his command toward York River, some 5 miles, who on returning reported no sign of an enemy. On receiving word of Captain Stetson's arrival at Centreville I marched to Six Mile Ordinary, where I was joined by Captain Stetson, who reported no traces of the enemy in the direction from which he came.   With my whole force I now proceeded up the Richmond road to Mrs. Pickett's gate, where the advance guard came on the enemy's pickets, which they gallantly drove in, capturing 1 prisoner (and [who] in their hasty retreat left part of their arms, blankets, and a Virginia dinner at Olive Branch Church, where their reserve of 8 men was posted), and pursued them 2 miles beyond Twelve Mile Ordinary.

In accordance with instructions I halted my main force at the Ordinary, and finding no force near, and from information received believing none to be nearer than Diascund Bridge, I returned with my command and prisoners to camp.

I am, colonel, your obedient servant,

C. KLEINZ,
Major.

Lieutenant-Colonel LEWIS, *Comdg. Fifth Pa. Cav.*

FEBRUARY 6–21, 1863.—Transfer of Ninth Army Corps from the Army of the Potomac to Newport News, Va.

Itinerary of the Ninth Army Corps, Maj. Gen. William F. Smith, U. S. Army, commanding, February 6–28.*

February 6.—In accordance with orders from corps headquarters the Third Division struck tents on the Rappahannock River, near Falmouth, and proceeded by cars to Aquia Creek and thence by transports to Fort Monroe, where it arrived on the 10th; thence it proceeded to Newport News.

February 9.—The Second Division struck tents near Falmouth; took cars for Aquia Creek, and transports from thence to Newport News, where it arrived on the 11th. The artillery of this division, having been landed at Hampton on the 15th, joined at Newport News on the 21st.

February 10.—The First Division left camp on the Rappahannock and proceeded by cars and transports to Newport News.

FEBRUARY 7, 1863.—Skirmish at Olive Branch Church, Va.

REPORTS.

No. 1.—Maj. Gen. Erasmus D. Keyes, U. S. Army, commanding Fourth Army Corps.
No. 2.—Maj. Christopher Kleinz, Fifth Pennsylvania Cavalry.
No. 3.—Brig. Gen. Henry A. Wise, C. S. Army.
No. 4.—Col. William B. Tabb, Fifty-ninth Virginia Infantry.

No. 1.

Reports of Maj. Gen. Erasmus D. Keyes, U. S. Army, commanding Fourth Army Corps.

HEADQUARTERS FOURTH CORPS,
Yorktown, February 8, 1863.

GENERAL: A squadron of the Fifth Pennsylvania Cavalry, which left on a reconnaissance yesterday afternoon, encountered a force of

---

* From Corps Return for February, 1863.

rebel cavalry and infantry at Burnt Ordinary, about 25 miles above here. After a short conflict our squadron retired, having lost several officers and men. I will report in detail as soon as I learn the facts.

E. D. KEYES,
Major-General.

Maj. Gen. JOHN A. DIX, *Fort Monroe.*

—

YORKTOWN, *February* 9, 1863.

The report of particulars has not come in. I would rather delay a little than report an exaggerated loss before the stragglers return. Rumor now places it about 23. The officer in command exceeded his instructions by going to Burnt Ordinary when he was directed to go only to Six Mile Ordinary. I am going up to examine in person before I give the facts.

E. D. KEYES,
Major-General.

Major-General DIX.

—

HEADQUARTERS FOURTH CORPS,
Yorktown, February 10, 1863.

Lieut. George Smith and 5 privates reported missing in the reconnaissance of the 7th instant have come in. Lieutenant Williamson was killed and Captain Hagemeister and Lieutenants Reinmuller and Little were taken prisoners. Five rebel deserters have just come in.

Lee's brigade of cavalry is reported, on pretty good authority, to be in King William County, opposite the White House.

E. D. KEYES,
Major-General.

Major-General DIX, *Fort Monroe.*

———

No. 2.

Report of Maj. Christopher Kleinz, Fifth Pennsylvania Cavalry.

CAMP OF FIFTH PENNSYLVANIA CAVALRY,
Near Williamsburg, February 8, 1863.

COLONEL: I have the honor to make the following report: That during your absence yesterday from the regiment—the command having been turned over to me by you before leaving—three deserters from enemy came into our lines and delivered themselves to our pickets. They stated that several more were outside who desired to come in, but in consequence of the enemy having sent out patrols for the purpose of discovering and arresting them they were afraid to venture.

Shortly afterward two other deserters came in and delivered themselves up, and who corroborated the statement of the others, saying furthermore that 16 of their men likewise disposed were at Walker's Mill, 3 miles beyond and to the right of our pickets, on the Richmond road; also that they had heard of 20 of their own men patroling in front of our lines and in the immediate neighborhood in search of deserters, and of whom the men at Walker's Mill were in fear.

I deemed it necessary to send out a scout to ascertain if there was any truth in these statements. Accordingly a squadron, composed of Companies L and M, numbering 84 men, and commanded by Captain Faith, was sent out with instructions to take the road leading to Walker's Mill to the right at the Richmond road picket post, and from Walker's Mill to proceed to Six Mile Ordinary, and then return to camp via the Richmond road; in the event of meeting with the enemy's patrol, as previously mentioned, to capture them if possible.

I have been informed that Captain Faith proceeded as far as Six Mile Ordinary without discovering any trace of the enemy. He then ordered his advance guard to proceed 300 or 400 yards beyond, on the Richmond road, and halt. This the advance guard proceeded to do, when they discovered a small patrol in their front. The lieutenant commanding advance guard sent back to Captain Faith for orders. Captain Faith, in violation of orders received from me, ordered the lieutenant to charge and capture them if possible, and that he would support him.

The enemy fled on the approach of our men, and after being pursued for 2 miles they took a road leading to the right, our advance guard in hot pursuit. At this point Captain Faith threw out another advance guard, upon the direct road, endeavoring to cut off the enemy's retreat. Another body of rebels, being either infantry or dismounted cavalry, and secluded by a ravine along this part of the road, allowed our advance guard to pass them, and as the column was passing poured into them two or three volleys, emptying about twenty saddles. At the same time a small body came out of the woods and charged the rear of the column, throwing our main body into confusion, and owing to the unexpectedness of this fierce attack they could not be rallied until they had retreated to Six Mile Ordinary, a distance of from 2 to 3 miles. Here they rallied, charged, and dispersed the pursuing enemy; but in consequence of their horses being completely worn-out they were unable to take advantage of the change in our favor.

The number missing at present is 5 officers and 33 men; some of the latter are supposed to be in the woods, their horses having been shot and disabled. The enemy's loss, so far as I can ascertain, appears to be 5 killed and 15 wounded.

Immediately on hearing the firing I ordered out one battalion under Major McCandless to support Captain Faith. On reaching Williamsburg they met the retiring party and there halted for further orders. In the mean time you had arrived in camp and resumed command.

I am, colonel, very respectfully, your obedient servant,

C. KLEINZ,
Major.

Lieutenant-Colonel LEWIS,
Commanding Fifth Pennsylvania Cavalry.

[Indorsement.]

HEADQUARTERS PENNSYLVANIA CAVALRY,
Yorktown, February 9, 1863.

Respectfully forwarded to Major-General Dix, commanding department.

Captain Faith, who commanded the scouting party, is wounded in the face and speaks with difficulty.

The reconnaissance was not conducted properly, and was in violation of my general instructions. Lieutenant-Colonel Lewis, commanding

Fifth Pennsylvania Cavalry, had left for Yorktown on business but a short time before the party was sent out by Major Kleinz in consequence of the representations of the deserters.   I have heretofore regarded Cap-tain Faith as an enterprising officer, but he and Major Kleinz have in this instance both allowed themselves to be deceived.

Captain Faith was led into an ambush at a point near Nine Mile Or-dinary, which is about 21 m:les from Yorktown.

E. D. KEYES,
Major-General.

No. 3.

Report of Brig. Gen. Henry A. Wise, C. S. Army.

BRIGADE HEADQUARTERS,
Chaffin's Farm, Va., February 10, 1863—12 m.

GENERAL : The report of Col. [William B.] Tabb, [Fifty-ninth Vir-ginia Infantry,] is fully confirmed.   On Saturday, the 7th instant, at about 5 p. m., the enemy advanced in force (about 85 cavalry) up the Telegraph road and approached near the Olive Branch Church, below the Burnt Ordinary.   Colonel Tabb had about 100 infantry and about 150 cavalry.   When the enemy came within short range he fired one volley of infantry and charged with his cavalry, killing some 7 or 8 and wounding some 2 or 3, which were captured, and capturing 35 prisoners, with their horses, arms, accouterments, &c., and pursuing the enemy down to the Six Mile Ordinary, and there firing severely into them and putting them to rout.   Probably their wounded who escaped amounted to some 10 or 20 more.   Thus the colonel, without the loss or injury of a man or horse, succeeded in killing, wounding, and capturing some 50 or 60 of the enemy's cavalry—from a fifth to a fourth of his whole num-ber.   I send to you 35 prisoners, among whom are 1 captain and 2 lieutenants.   One lieutenant was killed.   These men are chiefly Ger-mans, of the rascally Fifth Pennsylvania Cavalry, who destroyed the records of Charles City County and who burned the buildings, library, &c., of the venerable William and Mary College.   I trust they will be dealt with accordingly.

Accompanying this is a note from Colonel Tabb.   I have approved of his request to retain the horses, arms, &c., for his cavalry.   They need them.

Very respectfully, your obedient servant,
HENRY A. WISE,
Brigadier-General.

Major-General ELZEY, *Commanding, &c.*

No. 4.

Report of Col. William B. Tabb, Fifty-ninth Virginia Infantry.

HEADQUARTERS,
Diascund Bridge, Va., February 7, 1863.

GENERAL : I left my encampment here at 10 a. m. to-day and with a detachment of six companies of cavalry and four of infantry (an aggre-gate force of 235) moved down the Telegraph road in the direction of

Williamsburg. At Olive Branch Church, 1 mile below the Burnt Ordinary, my advance guard came upon a detachment of the enemy's cavalry. The position being favorable I immediately disposed my force in
ambush and awaited their approach. When they had come within
close range I ordered a volley of musketry, and taking advantage of
their confusion charged them with my cavalry. They were easily
routed. The pursuit was continued as far as the Six Mile Ordinary.

The enemy lost 7 killed, 2 wounded, and 36 captured, with their
horses, arms, and equipments. In my command there are no losses or
casualties to report.

My original object was to penetrate the enemy's lines and gain the
rear of the guard force in Williamsburg. My intention having been
discovered, I decided to abandon it for the present and returned to my
intrenchments.

Very respectfully, your obedient servant,

W. B. TABB,
Colonel, Commanding.

Brig. Gen. H. A. WISE, *Commanding, &c.*

[Indorsement.]

FEBRUARY 8, [1863]—7.30 p. m.

I respectfully forward this excellent report of a successful skirmish
with the enemy without the least loss. Colonel Tabb deserves more
than a word of approval.* May I not send another battalion to re-
enforce him ?

HENRY A. WISE.

FEBRUARY 12–13, 1863.—Expedition from Batchelder's Creek and skirmish
(13th) at Sandy Ridge, N. C.

Reports of Col. John Richter Jones, Fifty eighth Pennsylvania Infantry.

HDQRS. OUTPOSTS, CAMP FIFTY-EIGHTH PA. VOLS.,
Batchelder's Creek, February 14, 1863.

SIR: I have the honor to report the result of an expedition made yesterday and the night before in order to ascertain the force of the enemy
on my front and also to abate their audacity.

At 8 p. m. Thursday evening I moved my effective men, leaving this
post in charge of those not capable of severe duty assisted by a company which I ordered up temporarily from the railroad crossing.

At Tuscarora I dispatched Captain Brown, of the Fifty-eighth, with
two companies, to move on the Neuse and Dover roads and scour the
country near the Neuse River, and also to co-operate generally with my
movement.

At "Jones' Clearing," 1 mile short of Core Creek, I dispatched one
company to seize the railroad bridge at the creek and to remain there in
order to co-operate with me when necessary; and at the same point I
moved by a road crossing the railroad southward, with seven companies.
Under guidance of an intelligent negro, on route partly over wood-paths
and through swamps, I reached the enemy's position on Sandy Ridge
at daybreak. Unfortunately, from the difficulty of the route, which was
almost impracticable even to infantry, it was later than I contemplated,
and before the camp was completely surrounded the enemy was alarmed,

* See report No. 3, p. 152.

rushed from their quarters and opened an irregular fire. I had ordered my men to capture the enemy with the bayonet, but my flank companies and some of the others fired also and a short action ensued. When the enemy ran, which was very soon, the proximity of the woods and the incompleteness of my arrangements saved most of them, but we captured 43, of whom 4 were wounded, and in addition one of them also was killed and left on the ground. Providentially none of my men were hurt, though for a time the enemy's fire was sharp.

After burning the tents, quarters, &c., and destroying the stores, &c., I returned by the Dover road. Their pickets behind Core Creek on the railroad and other roads being alarmed made their escape. Bridging Core Creek at the Dover road I reached my camp in the afternoon.

Meanwhile Captain Brown, with his two companies and a detachment of Company E, Third New York Cavalry, under Captain Jacobs, whom I had previously ordered to co-operate, had scoured the country along the Neuse, discovering a body of the enemy, 40 or 50 strong, whom they followed briskly but were unable to catch.

The enemy at Sandy Ridge were Companies C, Captain Davis, and D, Captain Robinson, Eighth North Carolina, and are reported as 180 or 200 strong. The party pursued by Captains Brown and Jacobs was Captain Avirett's company.

As soon as an inventory of the arms and property captured can be made I will order a return of them to the proper department.

As a general result, this expedition has swept away the enemy's posts on our front and enables us to occupy without opposition the line of Core Creek, if judged expedient, as in my opinion it is. In the march over an almost impracticable route, the distance made in twenty hours being at least 32 miles, and in the short action which ensued the conduct of my men was all that could be expected from soldiership of the highest grade.

Very respectfully, your obedient servant,

J. RICHTER JONES,
Colonel Fifty-eighth, Commanding Outposts.

Lieut. Col. SOUTHARD HOFFMAN,
Assistant Adjutant-General.

If not already ordered, please send me some cars to transport the prisoners to New Berne.

—

HDQRS. OUTPOSTS, CAMP FIFTY-EIGHTH PA. VOLS.,
Batchelder's Creek, February 19, 1863.

SIR: I have the honor to report that I have ordered to be turned in to the proper department captured ordnance and ordnance stores as per the annexed inventory. Also that I have on hand fourteen captured shot-guns, in more or less serviceable condition, or injured, which not falling under the classification of ordnance as known to the service, I propose distributing among the captors as a reward and an incitement, with the assent of headquarters, of course.

Also that I have turned into the proper department and taken a receipt therefor, as in my hands for the public service, captured horses, mules, and wagons, as per inventory.

Very respectfully, your obedient servant,

J. RICHTER JONES,
Colonel Fifty-eighth, Commanding Outposts.

Lieut. Col. SOUTHARD HOFFMAN,
Assistant Adjutant-General, Eighteenth Army Corps.

Inventory of ordnance and ordnance stores captured from the Confederates at Sandy Hill, N. C., February 13, 1863, by Col. J. R. Jones, commanding Fifty-eighth Regiment Pennsylvania Volunteers.

No.	Description.	Condition.	Caliber of gun.
35	United States muskets, Harper's Ferry and Springfield..	Serviceable.	.69
2	United States muskets, Harper's Ferry and Springfield..	Unserviceable	.69
1	Belgian rifle...	Serviceable...................	.54
1	North Carolina rifle...................................	......do	
20	Gun-slings	Unserviceable	
3	Bayonets........	Serviceable	
3	Bayonet-scabbards.....................................	......do...	
40	Cartridge-boxes	......do	
32	Cartridge-belts	......do	
1	Cap-pouch	......do	
2	Waist-belts	......do	
	Waist-belt plates.....................................		

The above is a correct inventory of ordnance and ordnance stores captured as above stated.

M. J. HADLEY,
Acting Ordnance Sergeant Fifty-eighth Regt. Pa. Vols.

FEBRUARY 13, 1863.—Skirmish near Washington, N. C.

REPORTS.

No. 1.—Lieut. Col. Luke Lyman, Twenty-seventh Massachusetts Infantry.
No. 2.—Capt. George F. Jocknick, Third New York Cavalry.

No. 1.

Report of Lieut. Col. Luke Lyman, Twenty-seventh Massachusetts Infantry.

HEADQUARTERS,
Washington, N. C., February 16, 1863.

DEAR SIR: I have the honor to report that on Friday last, 13th, the cavalry company stationed at this post crossed the bridge, drove in the enemy's vedettes, surprised their picket headquarters (where some 40 cavalry were stationed), and captured 7 men and 12 horses; one of the men was dangerously wounded and is now in our hospital. The horses I turned over to the post quartermaster (a poor lot); the saddles were retained by the cavalry company. The prisoners I will send to New Berne by the first opportunity, unless ordered to parole, and send them out the lines from this point. They belong to the Sixty-second Georgia State Troops, but are North Carolinians. If you wish me to parole them here please inform me.

Have I the authority—if not, will you give it to me—to appoint a board of appraisers? The surgeons would like to purchase of the Government one or two of the captured horses.

"All quiet along the lines."

I remain, very respectfully, your obedient servant,

LUKE LYMAN,
Lieutenant-Colonel, Commanding Post.

Lieutenant-Colonel HOFFMAN, *A. A. G.*

No. 2.

Report of Capt. George F. Jocknick, Third New York Cavalry.

WASHINGTON, N. C., *February* 14, 1863.

COLONEL: The monotony of the daily routine of military duties here for the last few weeks has at last been interrupted by a little affair which reflects much credit on all concerned.

Having ascertained that the enemy kept a picket station on the other side of the river, some 3 or 4 miles from this post, and were in the habit of pushing their vedettes close up to our lines, I sent yesterday First Lieutenant O'Brien with a detachment of 20 men of my company to intercept them and thus check their boldness for the future.

The command left here at 1 o'clock p. m. yesterday, and returned in less than two hours with 7 prisoners and the following amount of captured property: Twelve horses, 12 saddles, 5 bridles, 8 Enfield muskets, 1 Harper's Ferry musket, and 1 saber.

Lieutenant O'Brien reports that after proceeding about a mile the enemy's vedettes were discovered some distance in advance, when he immediately charged, determined to overtake them. The enemy after firing their pieces put spurs to their horses and retreated up the Greenville road at their utmost speed. A 3-mile race was the result, at the termination of which our lieutenant found himself with only a small part of his command in the very nest of their main guard—a troop of some 30 or 40 mounted and dismounted cavalry. Our men in the rear, retarded by gullies in the road, were pressing up rapidly. But so complete was the surprise that the enemy at once broke for the swamps, where they fired volley after volley, but without any effect whatever. One of the prisoners captured is mortally wounded, and how many more were left on the field cannot be ascertained.

We had no casualties on our side except the wounding of a horse rode by First Sergeant Richards.

Among the prisoners is a color-sergeant and an orderly-sergeant, both very intelligent men. The latter states that the troops engaged belonged to the Sixty-seventh Georgia Regiment, being a detachment of Captain Thompson's company, * under command of Lieutenant Holt. Our men, I am told, all behaved well and are much pleased that we at last have been able to retaliate in the open field for the many outrages committed on our pickets by skulkers in the swamps.

The horses captured are of pretty good breed, but in a miserable, worn-out condition; their backs covered with sores and ulcers. I shall turn them over with the rest of the property to the quartermaster at this post.

Respectfully submitting the above report, I have the honor to be, your obedient servant,

G. F. JOCKNICK,
Captain, Comdg. Company I, Third New York Cavalry.

Col. S. H. MIX,
Comdg. Third New York Cavalry, New Berne, N. C.

---

* Company E, Sixty-second Georgia.

MARCH 1-6, 1863.—Expedition from New Berne to Swan Quarter, N. C.,
and skirmishes (3d and 4th) near Fairfield and Swan Quarter.

Report of Capt. Colin Richardson, Third New York Cavalry.

NEW BERNE, N. C., *March 6,* 1863.

COLONEL: I have the honor to report that I left this place Sunday,
March 1, at 5 p. m., on board the steamer Escort with my company (F,
Third New York Cavalry) and the first howitzer of the battery attached
to the same regiment, also Company G, First North Carolina Volunteers, and proceeded to Rose Bay Bridge, not, however, without a great
deal of delay for the want of a pilot, as there was no one on either of
the two boats who was sufficiently acquainted with the place. I then
ordered Captain Brinkerhoff to make a reconnaissance with his boat
North State, who after a delay of four hours reported that he had found
the bridge. I ordered the scow alongside and disembarked the infantry
and howitzer and a portion of the cavalry, placing Lieutenant Joy in
command until my arrival.

On arriving with the balance and having resumed the command I
ordered a small guard on board the North State, with orders to the
captain of the same to destroy the bridge; I in the mean time proceeded along the north side of the lake for a distance of about 5 miles.
With much difficulty and delay we marched, the crossings of the road
having been torn up by the negroes, under the orders of one Henry
Cradle (whom I have brought back a prisoner), and having a protection
from Governer Stanly. I encamped for the night at the cross-roads.

Next morning at daybreak I resumed my march, encountering and
driving in the enemy's pickets. About 3 miles from Fairfield we drove
more of the enemy, and on arriving at the place I found it nearly deserted. I passed on about 2 miles farther, when I discovered a boat on
the lake; hailed it, but no attention was paid to the hail. I ordered
Lieutenant Burke to throw a shell across the bow of the boat, which
brought it to shore. I found in the boat two men without protections,
whom I ordered out of the boat, and placed in it a squad of infantry
under charge of a non-commissioned officer, to sail around to Lake Landing, with orders to save the bridge if possible. I then moved on and
encamped for the night 9 miles from Lake Landing.

The next morning (Wednesday) I resumed the march. After moving
about 5 miles I was fired upon by guerrillas from some houses on the
right of the road. Our men drove them from the houses into the woods.
I then deployed the infantry to the right and threw out cavalry skirmishers in front and rear and covered the infantry with the howitzer,
shelling the woods and dispersing the enemy in all directions. Having
rallied my command, I moved on toward Lake Landing, leaving Lieutenant Morse, with a party of cavalry, to burn their headquarters. I
proceeded without further interruption until arriving at the bridge,
which I found destroyed. I ordered the fences to be torn down and
used to rebuild the bridge. I then moved on and drove in mounted
pickets during the whole march from Lake Landing to within about 1½
miles of Swan Quarter, when I was attacked from the swamp on the
right of the road in front and rear by about 80 guerrillas and ordered
to surrender. A deep canal about 8 feet wide ran between me and the
attacking party. As my vedettes were passing, the guerrillas fired one
shot. Lieutenant Benson immediately charged with the first platoon
of cavalry and received a volley, killing 3 of my men and wounding

the lieutenant and several others. Six horses were killed and many wounded. I ordered the infantry to deploy into the woods as skirmishers, not, however, without some difficulty, and ordered Lieutenant Burke to unlimber his piece and give the enemy a few rounds of canister, supported by the second platoon of cavalry. Here Lieutenant Burke was wounded in the face, breast, and hand. The remainder of the enemy were dispersed and fled, having sustained a loss of many of their number, among whom was their captain killed and a lieutenant taken prisoner. After having my killed and wounded taken care of and placed in wagons and carts which I had captured, I moved on to Swan Quarter, and having learned that a force of 250 or 300 guerrillas was lying in ambush about 3 miles from Swan Quarter, on the road to Rose Bay, and deeming it inexpedient to encounter it with my weakened force, I dispatched Corporal Kent, Company F, Third New York Cavalry, and 3 men to sail in a small boat to the gunboat North State, ordering Captain Brinkerhoff to steam around to Swan Quarter Landing. The next morning, he having arrived, I embarked on board the steamer Escort, which had accompanied the gunboat. I arrived here at 4 p. m. to-day.

I beg leave to make honorable mention of Luther H. Farnsworth, Company I, Fifth Massachusetts Volunteers, who accompanied the infantry. He was cool and courageous, jumping through the canal and taking the extreme right, leading the platoon of infantry into the fight; also Lieutenant Morse, of the Third New York Cavalry, who was of great service in the rear, returning the fire of the enemy with effect and holding them in check.

My loss is as follows: Killed, 3; wounded, 2 lieutenants (Benson and Burke) and 12 men of my company and 1 of the First North Carolina Volunteers. One sergeant of my company has since died of his wounds.

I am, sir, respectfully, yours,

COLIN RICHARDSON,
Capt. Company F, Third New York Cav., Comdg. Expedition.

Lieut. Col. SOUTHARD HOFFMAN,
Assistant Adjutant-General.

MARCH 6-8, 1863.—Demonstration on Kinston, N. C., including skirmishe**s** (7th) at Core Creek and near Dover.

REPORTS.*

No. 1.—Col. Josiah Pickett, Twenty-fifth Massachusetts Infantry.
No. 2.—Col. J. Richter Jones, Fifty-eighth Pennsylvania Infantry.
No. 3.—Capt. Ferris Jacobs, jr., Third New York Cavalry.
No. 4.—Capt. James R. Chamberlin, Third New York Cavalry.
No. 5.—Brig. Gen. Junius Daniel, C. S. Army, commanding at Kinston.

No. 1.

Report of Col. Josiah Pickett, Twenty-fifth Massachusetts Infantry.

HDQRS. TWENTY-FIFTH REGT. MASSACHUSETTS VOLS.,
Camp Oliver, New Berne, N. C., March 12, 1863.

COLONEL: I have the honor to report that in compliance with orders issued by you on the 5th instant I proceeded with my command on the

---

* See also Capt. David A. Taylor's report, p. 170.

6th to the forks of the Trenton and Kinston roads, 17 miles distant from this place.

We reached our destination about 4 p. m. I immediately secreted my force from the observation of the enemy, between Jumping Run and Nethercutt's, my purpose being to make a demonstration on their outposts during the night. The expedition, consisting of three companies of infantry, under command of Captain Denny, with Captains Jacobs' and Chamberlin's companies of the Third New York Cavalry, left our bivouac at midnight, proceeding rapidly up the Kinston road a distance of 4 miles. The cavalry, leading the advance, encountered and were fired upon by the rebel pickets. They immediately made a most gallant charge of over a mile, the infantry following at double-quick, reaching Jones' house (their reserve picket post). Captain Jacobs succeeded in capturing two of the enemy's scouts, and in so doing was fired upon from an ambush, seriously wounding a sergeant and private of his company.

Ascertaining that their camp was alarmed, Captain Denny ordered the infantry in the advance and pushed on, receiving and returning their fire from various points. When within a short distance of their camp the infantry were deployed as skirmishers on each side of the road. The line moved up speedily, passing the barricade of trees, and when within a few rods of the rebels (intrenched by another barricade) received a heavy volley of musketry; this was returned, and after a sharp skirmish the rebels were routed and pursued for some distance, but escaped into the woods.

Pursuit being useless, and perhaps under the circumstances imprudent, Captain Denny ordered his men to return—burned their camp, destroying twelve tents, several log barracks, a large number of new knapsacks, arms, equipments, blankets, several boxes of new clothing, and in fact everything left by the rebels in their hasty departure.

Owing to their superior speed only 5 prisoners were taken, whom I forwarded under guard to headquarters. The force reported back to our bivouac with no loss, and only 2 wounded, at 6 a. m., having marched a distance of 16 miles and within 12 miles of Kinston. From muster-rolls found in the enemy's camp their force was estimated at 190 effective men. Ours numbered 130 infantry (which was the only force engaged after leaving Jones' house) and 80 cavalry.

I desire to acknowledge the gallantry, bravery, and endurance of both officers and men engaged in the affair. Considering their fatiguing march of the previous day, to march 8 miles after midnight, whip the rebels handsomely, and return by daybreak, very much credit is due them. Captain Denny is entitled to great praise for the able manner in which he conducted the expedition. The Third New York Cavalry sustained its brilliant reputation. To Captains Jacobs and Chamberlin I am under great obligation for their valuable co-operation and assistance. They left us on the morning of the 7th. During our stay at Nethercutt's scouting parties were sent out occasionally to observe the movements of the enemy.

On the morning of the 8th, Captain O'Neil discovered them in Trenton and exchanged shots across the river. Captain Harrington, from a reconnaissance on the Kinston road, returned with the intelligence that a large body of rebel cavalry had approached to within 1 mile of our pickets during the night. Receiving orders from you at 10 a. m. on the 8th to fall back to a more defensible position, I retired to the forks of the Trenton and Pollocksville roads, remaining there until the

10th at 2 p. m., when, by your orders, I returned to New Berne, leaving the four companies, under Captain Denny, in their former position, near Deep Gully.

I have the honor to be, very respectfully, your obedient servant,

JOSIAH PICKETT,
Colonel Twenty-fifth Regt. Massachusetts Volunteers.

Col. HORACE C. LEE,
Comdg. Second Brig., First Div., Eighteenth Army Corps.

No. 2.

Reports of Col. J. Richter Jones, Fifty-eighth Pennsylvania Infantry.

HDQRS. OUTPOSTS, CAMP FIFTY-EIGHTH PA. VOLS.,
March 8, 1863.

SIR : I have the honor to report that conformably to instructions I made a movement in connection with the general reconnaissance, but as the orders were not received in time, not in fact until the 7th, I was unable to operate in exact connection.

I left my camp at 8 o'clock the evening of the 6th (Friday) with the efficient men of the Fifty-eighth (about 500) and reached the neighborhood of Core Creek about 2 a. m. of the 7th, having also ordered a small detachment of Company H, Third New York Cavalry, to follow. Ascertaining that the line of the creek—relinquished after my expedition to Sandy Ridge—was again occupied by the enemy, I endeavored to cross at some unobserved point, but owing to the darkness of the woods and the depth of water in the swamps was unable. Being obliged to force a passage, I did so at the Dover road, just before daylight, by opening a heavy fire on the crest of the breastwork which defended the crossing, while a party rushed over the single string-piece, a round log, which remained on the bridge. The enemy fired sharply at first, but their fire was soon silenced, when they cried out that they surrendered, but on the consequent cessation of our fire they took the opportunity to retire under cover of the darkness before my men could reach their works.

I then rebuilt the bridge, which detained me until full daylight, and leaving a company in charge of it I moved forward, but the various posts of the enemy had been put on the alert by the firing, and the alarm had been propagated, perhaps, to Kinston by signal-rockets sent up immediately afterward.

About a mile beyond the creek my advance was fired on from a swampy thicket and woods flanking the road on both sides, and as the enemy stuck closely to cover it cost my skirmishers time and labor to dislodge them. In my subsequent advance at the forks of the Dover and the railroad depot roads I captured a camp recently and suddenly abandoned, apparently by two companies, containing rough shelter, blankets, knapsacks, spare clothing, &c., the blankets, &c., being good and new ; but I could find no enemy in force, and being informed by the negroes that they knew of none nearer than Rouse farm, 12 miles from the creek, and the driving of fugitives from thickets and swamps without definite object being useless labor, I concluded to return.

From the marks on the captured property the enemy whom I encountered belong to the Forty-third North Carolina and the Sixty-third North

Carolina Cavalry, but what numbers of either regiment were in front did not appear, the enemy keeping closely under cover and the country being thickly wooded. They are a different class of troops from those I have hitherto met, contesting successively every strong position and giving way only to my superior numbers. Their arms are also different, being, from the whistle of the bullets, the Minie or others of similar tone.

From the information of negroes it would seem that some general officer (General French, some of them say) visited their posts on Wednesday last, ordered the line of Core Creek to be reoccupied, and brought re-enforcements. Also yesterday, while I was on my return, the whistle of a locomotive was heard some distance up the railroad toward Kinston, and on the supposition that fresh troops might be brought up I took a strong position and awaited a couple of hours, but no show of increase of force being made I resumed my march.

On the whole, my movement effected nothing beyond driving back some of the enemy's posts and accustoming our men to *la petite guerre*. As to capturing their men, that will be difficult while they hold the line of Core Creek and impose on us the necessity of forcing a passage every time we cross.

Very respectfully, your obedient servant,

J. RICHTER JONES,
Colonel Fifty-eighth Pennsylvania Vols., Comdg. Outposts.

Lieut. Col. SOUTHARD HOFFMAN,
Assistant Adjutant-General, Eighteenth Army Corps.

—

HDQRS. OUTPOSTS, CAMP FIFTY-EIGHTH PA. VOLS.,
March 10, 1863.

SIR: In reference to the surrender of the enemy's picket in the breastwork on the Dover road beyond Core Creek I have the honor to report the following facts:

As soon as the sentinel at the enemy's works fired I opened a rapid fire from the two companies which had been previously placed under cover along the near bank of the creek. Our fire was answered immediately by about twenty pieces, and for a few minutes there was a brisk exchange of shots. Then the enemy's fire suddenly ceased. Standing a few yards from the bridge, which my storming party was endeavoring to cross, I heard my officers on the right and left give the command, "Cease firing; they've surrendered," and our fire almost immediately ceased. On inquiry afterward I was informed by officers and non-commissioned officers that they distinctly heard from the enemy's side of the creek the words, "We surrender; don't fire," several times repeated. It was very dark at the time and the passage of the bridge on the single remaining string-piece difficult, so that it cost my men some time to cross and form beyond the creek, and when they entered the enemy's works they were empty. As the ground rises rapidly to the rear of the breastwork it would have been hazardous to leave them if our fire had not ceased, and I attribute the escape of the picket to the cessation of our fire, consequent on the supposition of the surrender.

Very respectfully, your obedient servant,

J. RICHTER JONES,
Colonel, Commanding Outposts.

Lieut. Col. SOUTHARD HOFFMAN,
Assistant Adjutant-General, Eighteenth Army Corps.

No. 3.

Report of Capt. Ferris Jacobs, jr., Third New York Cavalry.

RED HOUSE, *March* 7, 1863.

Col. J. RICHTER JONES,
    Commanding Outposts :

COLONEL : I have the honor to report that pursuant to your permission I proceeded yesterday with my own and Captain Chamberlin's company up the Trent road, joined Colonel Pickett, Twenty-fifth Massachusetts, encamped at a concealed point near Nethercutt's, and at 12 o'clock at night marched with the two companies cavalry, and three companies infantry furnished by Colonel Pickett, to the Kinston forks (4 miles beyond Nethercutt's), the cavalry keeping pace with the infantry.

On the knoll immediately beyond the Kinston forks my advance vedettes were fired upon, whereupon I set the whole cavalry column in motion, charging at full speed up the Kinston road with the intention of capturing the reserve picket station of about 30 men. Not finding them at the place specified I continued the charge, without halting, to the house of one Jones, being about 3 miles from the place where we met the first picket. The infantry followed at double-quick and in a few minutes joined me.

At this place it was ascertained that we were within 1 mile of the enemy's camp, which was near the house of one Green. After a moment's consultation the line of march was again taken up, with cavalry in advance. At this moment, and while I was giving instructions to the vedettes, two mounted men approached, and upon being apprehended purported to have been sent out to ascertain the cause of the disturbance. About a quarter of a mile farther, on encountered a party of six infantry, who surrendered, and while the sergeant (Mosier) in charge of the advance was receiving their arms, four of them fired upon him, wounding him severely in the hip and 1 man in the arm. Four of six escaped. At this point I drew in the cavalry, threw out lines of skirmishers upon the flanks, and advancing quickly upon their camp received a severe fire from their barricaded camp in the direction of the skirmishers.

The skirmishers escaped by falling to the ground and covering themselves in a ditch a few rods in front of the enemy's breastwork of trees. Captain Denny, in command of the infantry, then pushed forward in fine style and after a few minutes' sharp firing entered the camp, the enemy escaping in a sort of chaparral so dense that a footman unopposed could barely have passed through.

The infantry companies under Captain Denny behaved exceedingly well. The enemy in their haste had left everything, even their knapsacks (which were new, having been issued to them three days previous), and 15 or 20 Enfield rifles which they had just received.

There were two streets of tents, about ten in each, and two officers' tents, and a commissary tent in addition. In short, they abandoned everything. After an examination of a few minutes I ordered the camp and its contents burned, which was done, producing quite a smart explosion of fire-arms, which had been concealed or overlooked.

Only one prisoner was captured here. The camp was exceedingly strong by natural position and artificial defenses, and could have been held by the same number of resolute men for hours against an army without artillery. There were two companies of the Forty-fifth North Carolina, commanded by Captains Rankin and Scales, and both were said by the prisoners to have been in charge of a major.

After the destruction of the camp I moved back to the house previously occupied as a reserve picket station, but since the late desertion the station had been removed to the woods near by, where a large picket-fire was burning when we advanced. The enemy had between their camp and the outpost from which we were fired upon 40 men on duty each day, all of whom, with the exception of the outpost vedette, were driven in, and escaped us without firing a shot or in any way alarming the main body. The reserve picket-station house was burned.

Reached the camp of the Twenty-fifth Massachusetts, at Nethercutt's, at daybreak. It is sufficient to say that the cavalry detachment behaved with more than the usual spirit and promptitude.

The affair is of but little importance except for the information gained or confirmed. It is also worthy of mention, perhaps, that the movement penetrated farther into the enemy's country in that direction than any other reconnaissance with exception of General Foster's advance on Goldsborough.

Trusting that you will pardon the particularity and diffusiveness of this report, I remain, with great respect, your obedient servant,

F. JACOBS, JR.,
Captain, Commanding Detachment.

[Appendix.]

COLONEL: I should have mentioned in the body of my report that the success of the movement mainly depended upon the accuracy of the information derived by Captain Chamberlin from the late deserters and other sources, and that it was upon Captain Chamberlin's suggestion that the attempt was made.

Yours, respectfully,

F. JACOBS, JR.

[Indorsement.]

I have the honor to forward Captain Jacobs' report of his spirited movement, made under my authorization in connection with the general movement.

Very respectfully,

J. RICHTER JONES,
Commanding Outposts.

No. 4.

Report of Capt. James R. Chamberlin, Third New York Cavalry.

HDQRS. COMPANY A, THIRD NEW YORK CAVALRY,
Trent Road, N. C., March 10, 1863.

COLONEL: I have the honor to submit the following report:

From information which I deem reliable I ascertained there were two companies of infantry (picked men), belonging to the Forty-fifth North Carolina Regiment, encamped on the Kinston road some 12 miles this side of Kinston, and I determined to surprise them.

After making a map of the country, with which I was somewhat familiar, I opened my plan to Capt. F. Jacobs, jr., Company E, Third

New York Cavalry, and proposed that we unite our two companies (A and E) and make an attempt on the rebel camp, to which he acceded. We accordingly provided our command with two days' rations, and left camp at noon on March 7, our whole command numbering 102 men, all told, Company A furnishing 48 and Company E 54 men.

At Major Nethercutt's (secesh) house we came across the Twenty-fifth Regiment Massachusetts Volunteers, commanded by Col. J. Pickett, which was acting as a corps of observation at that point. We bivouacked with them for a few hours. From a contraband whom I picked up I learned that the enemy had changed their camp and had received additional re-enforcements. Upon consultation with Captain Jacobs we determined to ask of Colonel Pickett two companies of infantry, and he very kindly assigned us three companies (A, C, and K), commanded by Captain Denny, Company K, Twenty-fifth Massachusetts Regiment, numbering about 130 men.

With this additional force we left Nethercutt's house at 12 o'clock that night. Upon reaching the Trenton Cross-Roads, a distance of 4 miles, we halted for the infantry to close up and then made our preparations for the attack, for it was only some one-fourth of a mile beyond this point that we expected to meet their first picket, and our plan was, after drawing his fire, the cavalry was to commence a charge at once and endeavor to capture their reserve picket station of 25 men, said to be some half a mile beyond. We placed some of our fleetest horses with the advance guard, which was commanded by Lieutenant Gibbs, of Company E, Third New York Cavalry, and after allowing a few moments of rest the column was again put in motion. Slowly and silently we moved along, every man intent on doing his duty, and determined not to be outdone by another. Presently we saw a flash, and then the sharp, shrill report of the rebel picket's rifle, with his ball whistling over the heads, unharmed, of our entire column. Hardly had the flash died away when the command "charge" was given, and instantaneously the whole column started like one man. On we flew, like the wind, the ground fairly quaking beneath our feet. The picket station reached, but not a rebel was found—they had heard the alarm and fled like thieves in the night. On we dashed to Hoble's house, a mile beyond, and again to Jones' house, still another mile, but found nothing. So impetuous had been our charge that we had completely cut through and cut off their advance guard, which I afterward learned was composed of 40 men.

While waiting here for the infantry to come up, which were to follow us at double-quick, and while Captain Jacobs was giving some instructions to the advance guard, up rode two rebel cavalrymen, evidently mistaking us for friends, and inquired, "What's the matter below?" Before these words had hardly left their lips several of Colt's "Love me quicks" were presented to their heads and they were "gobbled." One of them, in utter astonishment, remarked, "That's another damned Yankee trick." We learned from our prisoners that the rebel camp was about 1¼ miles beyond, but nothing definite as to its situation. After the infantry had arrived we determined to attack them with our combined force. Accordingly, Companies A and C, of the infantry, were placed in rear of our advanced guard, followed by the cavalry, while Captain Denny's company (K) was held in reserve, and in this order all again pressed forward. We had gone but a short distance when our advance guard met six rebel infantrymen, who had been sent out to ascertain what had become of their two mounted men. They all immediately surrendered, and while the two first were in the act of giving up their arms their comrades jumped into the woods and fired, wounding Sergeant Mosier and Private Morenus, of Company E, Third New York Cavalry. The infantry were then thrown out on the flanks as skirmishers, while the cavalry kept in the road. In a very few minutes we met the enemy's line of skirmishers and a brisk fire commenced. We adopted the "drop game" on them—that is, we fell down immediately after firing, loading our pieces on the ground; and after drawing their fire, which invariably passed over our heads, we would up and charge them again. In this manner we kept gradually pressing forward and soon reached their camp, which we found strongly barricaded on three sides. The rebels here attempted to make a final stand, but it was of short duration, for we carried their works by storm, they retreating in hot haste toward Kinston. In their camp we found several fine tents and any quantity of clothing, camp and garrison stores, arms and accouterments, and several packages (sent by express), containing coffee, tea, sugar, ham, and other delicacies of camp life, evidently showing that some of our claiming-to-be Union friends within our lines not only sympathized with but contributed to our enemies. We hastily gathered everything together and burned all, together with their camp, to the ground.

Not deeming it safe to remain long in such close proximity to Kistonn with such a small force we commenced our homeward march, reaching camp at daylight, having marched 16 miles and done our fighting in six hours, our entire casualties being the sergeant and private of Company E, as before mentioned.

I must not omit to say that both officers and men behaved themselves with great credit to their country, and never have I seen men fight with more determination or bravery.

We took 5 prisoners. Of the loss of the enemy I had no means of ascertaining, as the night was quite dark and we had no time to look after bereaved friends.

. I have the honor to be, colonel, your very obedient servant,

JAS. R. CHAMBERLIN,
Captain, Comdg. Company A, Third New York Cavalry.

Lieut. Col. GEORGE W. LEWIS,
Commanding Third New York Cavalry.

No. 5.

Report of Brig. Gen. Junius Daniel, C. S. Army, commanding at Kinston.

HEADQUARTERS,
Kinston, N. C., March 10, 1863.

GENERAL: I have the honor to acknowledge the receipt of yours of yesterday.

In the different skirmishes with the enemy on Saturday there were two infantry lost, supposed to be captured. I have since learned that there are two couriers missing, supposed to be captured. Major Winston lost a few tent-flies and a few blankets. I have learned from citizens that the enemy buried —— men on their retreat on the lower Trent road and that they had others wounded. On the Dover road citizens say there were several killed and some wounded. These reports come from citizens below and I think are reliable.

I would have made these statements sooner but my pickets are so far apart and on so many roads that I could not have done so sooner. I forgot to mention that one of my men deserted and made known to the enemy my signals, and it was in this way that they got upon the two infantrymen. Nothing of the enemy this morning. Generals Robertson and Pettigrew are here.

Very respectfully, &c.,

JUNIUS DANIEL,
Brigadier-General.

Maj. Gen. D. H. HILL,
   Commanding, Goldsborough, N. C.

MARCH 6-10, 1863.—Expedition from New Berne to Trenton, Pollocksville, Young's Cross-Roads, and Swansborough, N. C.

REPORTS.

No. 1.—Brig. Gen. Henry Prince, U. S. Army, commanding Expedition.

No. 2.—Capt. David A. Taylor, Third New York Light Artillery, Chief Signal Officer, of operations March 5-15.

No. 3.—Lieut. Joseph Fricker, Eighth Pennsylvania Reserve Infantry, Acting Signal Officer, of operations March 5-15.

No. 4.—Surg. Pitkin B. Rice, One hundred and thirty-second New York Infantry, Chief Medical Officer.

No. 5.—Lieut. Francis U. Farquhar, U. S. Corps of Engineers, Chief Engineer Eighteenth Army Corps.

No. 6.—Col. Silas P. Richmond, Third Massachusetts Infantry.

No. 7.—Col. Augustus B. R. Sprague, Fifty-first Massachusetts Infantry.

No. 8.—Lieut. Col. George W. Lewis, Third New York Cavalry.

No. 9.—Maj. Jeptha Garrard, Third New York Cavalry.

No. 1.

Report of Brig. Gen. Henry Prince, U. S. Army, commanding Expedition.

HDQRS. FIFTH DIVISION, EIGHTEENTH ARMY CORPS,
New Berne, N. C., March 11, 1863.

COLONEL: I have the honor to report that the reconnaissance in force, which I was directed to make by your letter of the 5th instant, was completed last evening by the return to New Berne and distribution to former quarters and commands of all the parts of my column. The instructions I received have been entirely carried out and the objects of the expedition fully accomplished.

It gives me pleasure to say that the most admirable spirit was manifested by every portion of the command. The desire to carry out the views of the Government, as made known through orders from time to time, was made strikingly apparent in all ranks, as was also the desire to have their determination to do so tested in the face of opposition, even to the death. At the same time their feeling toward the enemy was self-possessed and magnanimous, as was illustrated by instances of personal conduct. I will give a narrative of the expedition for the records of the department. A copy of my orders is subjoined (A).

The column formed as it passed over the bridge at Brice's Creek, at 8.30 a. m. on the 6th. We crossed the bridge, which we had to construct over Mill Creek, at 2.15 p. m., and bivouacked on ———— Creek, at McDaniel's plantation, at 4 p. m., at which place the train did not get fully up till near 12 o'clock at night. Leaving the train parked here, guarded by the Third Regiment Massachusetts Volunteers and a section of Riggs' battery, the column marched at 6.30 o'clock next morning in the same order. The cavalry arrived at Trenton at 8.45 a. m., followed by the *voltigeurs*, where I joined them immediately, sending back to halt the main body 2 miles in rear.

At 10 a. m. I sent from Trenton to General Spinola and Colonel Jourdan, commanding brigades, the message that "the bridges we were ordered to destroy have not been rebuilt since their former destruction; the enemy's cavalry have been scattered by a charge of ours; there is no body of the enemy on this side the Trent, and consequently the column will face-about and return to the wagons." The column marched in returning at 10.15 a. m.

At 11.45 a. m., having obtained all the information I could at Trenton and created the indefinite impression that I was going to Kinston or toward Richlands to look up their cavalry, I withdrew the cavalry to feed, without the limits of the town, and then continued the return march.

I arrived with the main column at McDaniel's at 1.30 p. m., and having previously sent orders to the train to hitch up, marched at 3.15 p. m. by a direct route to Young's Cross-Roads. The cavalry pushed on rapidly with its howitzer, followed more moderately by the *voltigeurs*. When nearing Young's Cross-Roads Colonel Lewis, being with the advance of the cavalry, discovered, as he supposed, the enemy's picket of two mounted men, and he charged to capture them. They proved to be one Lieutenant Sharp, aide-de-camp to General Whiting, and another lieutenant. Their start being a long one, they got off by plunging into and swimming the White Oak River, to the bank of which they were followed, where they fired upon their pursuers from the opposite side.

A party of cavalry, being sent up the Pollocksville road, drove some foot pickets into the swamp. Darkness came on before the infantry came up. We had withdrawn all but a small guard from the river to lay out the camp, which was to be on ground about a mile distant from the river, and a sentinel at the river being approached in the darkness from the direction of camp by six men, hailed them, at which they halted and cocked their guns. He called, "Turn out the guard," and instantly the persons scattered in the cover. This party was Captain Harris and five of his men, as we afterward learned. As soon as the infantry came up I sent two companies to deploy, under the guidance of Captain Farquhar, United States Engineers, who was directed by me to reconnoiter the river thoroughly in the neighborhood. He ascertained that a log below the bridge was the means that footmen had of crossing. The river was carefully watched for the rest of the night, that no more of the rebels should get back to their quarters. On the opposite side of the river there was a steady light of a small camp bearing southwest by the compass. I could not tell whether it was a bright camp light 5 miles off or a lesser one a mile. The train did not come up till 2.30 o'clock in the night, owing to holes wearing in the road over which the howitzer and caisson charged with the cavalry. One of my permanent orderlies, who happened to be stationed to show the way that the wagons should turn out, reports seeing, during the hour of intensest darkness (perhaps 7 o'clock), previous to the coming up of the infantry, bearing southwest, a light, probably a fire balloon, which rose and stood awhile, dipped several times, moved horizontally back and forth several times, then descended. Presuming from all these indications that a picket guard of the enemy intended to annoy the constructors of the bridge which I had to make here, I did not commence it till I had crossed a regiment, which I did soon after daylight in the morning.

Having deployed a company of skirmishers on the immediate bank of this side, I placed two Napoleon guns in position to command the opposite bank, and sent a regiment across in single file on the log. The regiment which performed this duty and formed its line beyond the swamp was the One hundred and thirty-second New York, Lieutenant-Colonel Hitchcock. The commander was ordered not to cross till three companies were over, and quite an emulation was excited among the captains as to who should go over first. Colonel Hitchcock ordered the left flank company forward, and its commander, Capt. George Micha, Company A, One hundred and thirty-second Regiment New York Volunteers, was first on the log and on the opposite bank. No opposition was made till the verge of the swamp was reached, when half a dozen shots of small-arms were exchanged.

At 10.30 a. m. the bridge was ready, and the column, with three days' rations, moved over it, leaving behind to guard the bridge and train the Third Regiment Massachusetts Volunteers, a battalion of the One hundred and sixty-eighth Pennsylvania Militia, two sections of Parrott guns, one section of Napoleon guns, and a company of cavalry, Colonel Richmond, Third Massachusetts, in command.

It being open country for the 4 miles to the next defile, Colonel Lewis was permitted to go on rapidly to it with the cavalry, followed within supporting distance by the *voltigeurs* of Major Garrard. The cavalry of the enemy were seen upon all flanks and in rear by these forces, cut off and scattered by our movements, and they were either left behind us or found some course other than the road we traveled to get away by.

We marched a mile or so beyond where the road forks off to Snead's Ferry, which the guide-post there says is 20 miles distant, and, finding a good position, bivouacked at 6.15 p. m.

In the morning I detached the cavalry to go back to the forks, take the Snead's Ferry road, and proceed on that route and toward Swansborough, taking into consideration the imminent prospect there of unfavorable weather, as far as he thought he could, and join or communicate with me in the evening. At 12 m., presuming that the cavalry were at or near Swansborough, I marched back to and halted at the forks of the road to Swansborough till 4 p. m., at which time the cavalry joined me. Lieutenant-Colonel Lewis' report of this scout is appended. It was now evident from our reconnaissance that all the forces of the enemy in this region were withdrawn behind the New River; that the bridge at Jacksonville had been destroyed and not yet rebuilt, and that there could be no point whatever in marching my column any farther away.

No enemy could be met with without going farther than the organization and supply of the command contemplated. There was nothing left undone which the expedition set out to do; nothing more whatever which my imagination could suggest as within our reach to be done. I therefore returned from this point at once to Young's Cross-Roads, reaching there at 6 p. m., and on the following day, the 10th, pursued the route to New Berne. Of course there were many incidents occurring having an interesting bearing on the *personnel* of our troops. At a time when I was in the front with the advance guard of the cavalry I saw a corporal and two vedettes, who were 100 yards out beyond me on the road, hail and receive the surrender of three mounted rebels, uniformed and armed. A bend in the road concealed from the rebels the danger they were approaching, and the corporal and vedettes, though ready, made no attempt to fire. It could not have been performed quieter on the stage, and the balanced self-possession which it indicates I regard as a quality of the command. Beyond this I am satisfied by this march that there is neither corruption of politics nor infamy-of-peace notions to taint the pure patriotism of the command. It is glowing with a desire to enforce, as the country's true soldiers, a decided policy of the Government for suppressing the rebellion.

Inclosed herewith please find (marked A, B, C, D, E, and F)* a copy of my instructions; report of Lieut. Col. G. W. Lewis, Third New York Cavalry, of scout toward the sea-board; receipt of department provost-marshal for seven prisoners, including a commissioned officer, sergeant, corporal, and four privates; report of property captured by the cavalry; report of property captured by the *voltigeurs*; copy of my orders† relating to the expedition.

I am, colonel, very respectfully, your obedient servant,

HENRY PRINCE,
Brigadier-General of Volunteers, Commanding.

Lieut. Col. SOUTHARD HOFFMAN,
Asst. Adjt. Gen., Eighteenth Army Corps, New Berne, N. C.

[Inclosure A.]

HEADQUARTERS EIGHTEENTH ARMY CORPS,
New Berne, N. C., March 5, 1863.

GENERAL: By direction of the major-general commanding I have the honor to submit, for your guidance, the following points:

You will proceed with your command to Trenton by the road on the south side of Trent River. On arriving there you are to destroy the Trenton Bridge and the White Hall Bridge. The enemy in this direction will be carefully observed. You will then countermarch your command to Pollocksville and Young's Cross-Roads. From this latter point, after leaving a strong rear guard for the protection of the wagon train and such force of artillery and infantry as you may deem needful to hold that point, you will push on toward Onslow. Observing the enemy in this direction you will take a strong position with the infantry and batteries of your command, and send all the mounted force at your command to scour thoroughly the country between the White Oak and New Rivers. From the information you may be able to obtain you will be able to determine as to the expediency of pushing the reconnaissance as far as Snead's Ferry, near the mouth of the New River.

The object of this expedition is to make a strong reconnaissance in the direction of Wilmington, to ascertain the roads, the crossings of the rivers and creeks, the position of the enemy, &c., and if possible to capture or break up two companies of cavalry supposed to be between the White Oak and New Rivers.

I am, general, very respectfully, your obedient servant,

SOUTHARD HOFFMAN,
Assistant Adjutant-General.

Brig. Gen. HENRY PRINCE,
Comdg. Fifth Division, Eighteenth Army Corps.

---

* Inclosures B, D, and E are Reports Nos. 8 and 9.
† They relate solely to the routine duties of troops on the march and are therefore omitted.

[Inclosure C.]

PROVOST-MARSHAL'S OFFICE,
New Berne, N. C., March 10, 1863

Received from Colonel Lewis, Third New York Cavalry, 7 prisoners, viz: William B. Pringle, Tenth North Carolina Volunteers; T. B. Snipes, Lieut. L. B. Williams, Josiah Tyson, and Wesley B. Mews, Sixty-third North Carolina Volunteers; Joseph Grey, deserter, and Z. M. Caston, citizen.*

GEORGE F. WOODMAN,
Department Provost.

No. 2.

Report of Capt. David A. Taylor, Third New York Light Artillery, Chief Signal Officer, of operations March 5–15.

HDQRS. SIGNAL DETACHMENT, EIGHTEENTH A. C.,
New Berne, N. C., March 16, 1863.

SIR: In pursuance to your orders, on the 5th instant I detailed two officers (Lieuts. Joseph Fricker and E. R. Blagden) to accompany the force commanded by Brigadier-General Prince on the late reconnaissance to Swansborough. At the same time I detailed First Lieut. N. S. Barstow to accompany the force under Colonel Sprague, at Newport Barracks, which was to advance on Swansborough by southern route, and Second Lieut. Henry T. Merrill to accompany the command of Colonel Pickett, who covered the right flank of General Prince's movement.

That the different forces might have a ready and certain mode of communication I drew up a rocket code of signals for the use of the officers on this expedition. The command of General Prince bivouacked near Pollocksville on the night of the first day's march; the command of Colonel Pickett bivouacked at the Trenton Cross-Roads, with a heavy picket force of the enemy in front, for the reason that Colonel Pickett was going to attempt a surprise of the enemy. Lieutenant Merrill did not answer the rockets sent up by General Prince, as the rockets would reveal the position of Colonel Pickett's force which it was necessary to keep concealed. At 3 a. m. of the 6th instant Colonel Pickett surprised a rebel picket, taking 5 prisoners and destroying their camp.

On the 7th instant Colonel Pickett fell back to the Pollocksville Cross-Roads to await the return of General Prince. General Prince marched directly to Swansborough, Colonel Sprague at the same time advancing to the same point and reaching there nearly the same time, when communication between the two commands was immediately opened by Lieutenants Fricker and Barstow.

On the return of the different forces there was no occasion for any signal communication between them. All parties arrived at New Berne in time to take part in the skirmish at Fort Anderson on the 14th. On the morning of March 14, immediately after the attack on Fort Anderson, Lieutenant Merrill and party was placed on board gunboat Shawsheen, Lieut. E. R. Blagden and party on the Hunchback, and Lieut. Joseph Fricker, on the evening of that day, on board the gunboat

---

* Discharged soldier from Thirty-fifth North Carolina Volunteers; has his discharge with him.

G. F. W.

Hetzel. As soon as the attack commenced Lieutenant Barstow signaled to Lieutenant Fricker that the enemy were in front of the fort in large force, with artillery, and asked for re-enforcements, to which was replied, "Hold out as long as you can; re-enforcements will come as quickly as possible." When the gunboats got into position their fire was directed by means of signals by Lieutenant Barstow, stationed at Fort Anderson, and Lieutenant Merrill, on board the Shawsheen. Lieutenant Merrill, from the paddle-box of the boat, was able to obtain a better view of the movements of the enemy than any one else. He so skillfully directed their fire that one of the enemy's pieces was for a time abandoned and their infantry driven back some distance. Had the garrison of Fort Anderson been strong enough to have made it safe a well-conducted sortie would have easily captured one or more of the enemy's guns.

On the morning of the 15th three boats went up the Neuse, accompanied by Lieutenants Fricker, Merrill, and Knox, who, by their signals, kept up a constant communication between the different boats to the entire satisfaction of the officers in command, who expressed themselves in terms of admiration at the ease, rapidity, and certainty with which every message was transmitted.

I am, sir, very respectfully, your obedient servant,

DAVID A. TAYLOR,
Captain and Acting Signal Officer in Charge.

Maj. Gen. J. G. FOSTER,
Commanding Eighteenth Army Corps.

No. 3.

Report of Lieut. Joseph Fricker, Eighth Pennsylvania Reserve Infantry, Acting Signal Officer, of operations March 5–15.

HDQRS. SIGNAL DETACHMENT EIGHTEENTH ARMY CORPS,
New Berne, March 18, 1863.

SIR: I have the honor to submit to you the following report of the expedition under the command of General Prince:

In obedience to your orders of March 5, 1863, I reported to General Prince for signal duty. Left New Berne at 8 o'clock, March 6, and proceeded 3 miles beyond Pollocksville; bivouacked for the night. According to arrangements made previous to starting I sent up two red rockets, the first at 9 o'clock p. m., the second at ten minutes past 9. The rockets were to indicate that "the advance of our column is here, and all quiet," but I received no reply from the other parties.

On the morning of the 7th we started and advanced on Trenton. We remained in Trenton a few hours, then started and bivouacked about 6 miles from Trenton that night There was nothing of any account took place, with the exception of taking a few of the enemy's pickets along the march.

On the 9th I received an order from General Prince to accompany the advance cavalry to Swansborough, a distance of 16 miles, which I did, accompanied by Flagmen W. J. Lindsay and H. P. Baker. When within 1 mile of Swansborough the cavalry charged into the town, myself and flagmen in the advance carrying a red signal flag. I immediately went down to the water's edge and called attention from the party on the opposite side of Bogue Inlet. It was replied to by Lieutenant Barstow, signal officer, who accompanied a party under command of Colonel Sprague, of the Fifty-first Massachusetts Volunteers. We sent several official messages; Lieutenant-Colonel Lewis, who was in command of the cavalry and to whom I was ordered to report by General Prince, sending messages across the inlet and receiving reply in return. . There was nothing worthy of note on our return to New Berne.

Immediately on returning to New Berne I went to my station on the south side of the Neuse River, a short distance from General Foster's headquarters. I remained there, communicating with Lieutenant-Colonel Anderson on the opposite side.

On Saturday, March 14, at 5.45 a. m. I received the following official message from the fort:

To General FOSTER:

The enemy have attacked our pickets with artillery and infantry. They are in large force. The colonel wants more men.

BARSTOW.

I immediately sent the message to General Foster. In a few minutes the general came and told me to send to Lieutenant-Colonel Anderson, who was then in command of the Ninety-second New York, to hold out as long as he could and not surrender unless he was compelled to.

I also received and sent a large number of messages from the fort asking for more troops and re-enforcements, which I replied to, by order from General Foster, that re-enforcements would be there in a short time and that the gunboats were getting in position. I also received messages directing the fire of the gunboats and stating the location of the enemy. I also received messages from the gunboats Hunchback, Lockwood, and Shawsheen.

On the evening of the 14th I was ordered on board the commodore's boat Hetzel; remained there until 9 a. m., March 15, when I was ordered on gunboat Allison to proceed up the Neuse River on a reconnaissance.

We went up the river to Street's Ferry, a distance of 12 miles. The enemy had retreated beyond this point. We found four of the enemy's pickets; they skedaddled. We then shelled the woods for an hour, and returned to New Berne the same day.

With great respect, I remain, your obedient servant,

JOSEPH FRICKER,
First Lieut., 8th Pa. R. V. C., and Actg. Sig. Officer 18th A. C.

Capt. D. A. TAYLOR,
Chief Acting Signal Officer, Eighteenth Army Corps.

No. 4.

Report of Surg. Pitkin B. Rice, One hundred and thirty-second New York Infantry, Chief Medical Officer.

HDQRS. FIRST BRIG., FIFTH DIV., EIGHTEENTH A. C.,
New Berne, March 12, 1863.

CAPTAIN: I have the honor to make the following report of the expedition just returned:

The division, commanded by Brig. Gen. Henry Prince, comprised of the two brigades commanded, respectively, by Brig. Gen. F. B. Spinola and Col. James Jourdan, together with two batteries of artillery, under the command of Major Stone, and four companies of cavalry, under the command of Lieutenant-Colonel Lewis, left New Berne on the morning of the 6th instant, and after marching over good roads with no difficult streams to cross, making 18 miles, bivouacked for the night in a large open field on high dry ground contiguous to an abundance of wood and excellent water.

The men of the several infantry regiments, viz, the One hundred and seventy-first, One hundred and fifty-eighth, One hundred and sixty-eighth, and One hundred and seventy-fifth Pennsylvania Militia, comprising Brigadier-General Spinola's command, and the One hundred and fifty-eighth and One hundred and thirty-second New York Volunteers, together with the Third Massachusetts Militia, commanded by Colonel Jourdan, bore the march exceedingly well; none sick; a few complaining of sore feet, occasioned by ill-fitting boots.

The second day the regiment left camp in light marching order, traveled 6 miles and returned to the camp of the previous night, the route being over a dry sandy road with no formidable streams to pass. After a halt of two hours, to enable the men to rest and prepare their rations, the march was resumed over a road about 3 miles of which was through low swampy ground. At 8 o'clock p. m., after accomplishing 22 miles, encamped on high dry ground adjacent to wood and running water. On this day's march the men suffered considerably from blistered feet; none, however, reported sick.

The next morning, March 8, at daybreak broke camp, and leaving the One hundred and sixty-eighth Pennsylvania and Third Massachusetts Militia as a guard to the wagon train, crossed White Oak River and traveled 14 miles; bivouacked in a pine grove 5 miles from the junction of the Swansborough and New Berne Cross-Roads, near to a full supply of good water. Next day at 1 p. m. resumed the line of march and returned to our former camping ground at White Oak River.

At 7 o'clock on the morning of the 10th the column took up its direction homeward. During the early part of the day the roads were excellent, but heavy rain setting in about noon rendered them heavy and the march very fatiguing; nevertheless the various regiments reached their camps about 8.30 p. m., and no stragglers reported.

The entire march was performed in good order and unattended with any casualty; very few men were sufficiently sick to be conveyed in ambulances; the principal complaint was sore feet, the result of chafing, confined almost entirely to those who wore heavy boots. The contrast in this respect between the boot and Government shoe was very marked and exhibited the superiority of the latter and absolute necessity of every infantry soldier substituting it for the boot on the march. Frequent bathing with cold water afforded great relief, and on the last day's march of 22 miles but little complaint was heard. The rations provided for the regiments were abundant and of excellent quality. Fresh beef was furnished three days out of five.

This report is written on the second day after the return of the troops, and the effects of the march on the physical condition and health of the men appear to be more beneficial than otherwise. The sick reports from the various regiments this morning are even less than usual.

Respectfully submitted.

P. B. RICE,
Surgeon.

Capt. S. W. WALDRON,
   Assistant Adjutant-General.

No. 5.

Report of Lieut. Francis U. Farquhar, U. S. Corps of Engineers, Chief
Engineer Eighteenth Army Corps.

HEADQUARTERS EIGHTEENTH CORPS D'ARMÉE,
New Berne, March 12, 1863.

SIR: I have the honor to report that in accordance with your orders I joined the command of Brigadier-General Prince on the 6th instant.

The command moved along the Pollocksville road on the south side of the Trent. After passing Brice's Creek the general direction of the road was a very little north of west. As far as Mill Creek the road was only tolerable, but after the rain it was very bad. We found it necessary to build the bridge across Mill Creek, which occasioned a halt of the advance guard of two hours. After passing the creek the road was firm and good. From Pollocksville the road bore nearly west. Our first day's march ended at the Mill Creek, near McDaniel's plantation. On the 7th the march was resumed toward Trenton. With the exception of the crossing of the creek near McDaniel's the road was good. The creek near Trenton could not well be forded by field artillery when the creek is high. The Trenton Bridge was destroyed, as was also the White Hall Bridge. From reliable information we learned that there was a bridge known as the Quaker Bridge, and another bridge above White Hall and below Tuckahoe Creek. There is also a small neighborhood bridge known as Wilcox's Bridge, about 6 miles from Trenton. However, these bridges are not absolutely necessary, as at the ordinary height of water the stream is fordable in many places above Trenton.

The road from New Berne to Trenton affords many good places for camping, especially after passing Mill Creek, water and wood being abundant. At Trenton the command countermarched and returned to McDaniel's plantation, where we had camped the previous night. From thence we took a road bearing south by east for 5 miles and southeast for 3, which brought us to Young's Cross-Roads. This road passed for the greater part through an extensive pocoson. The road was bad in some places. About Young's Cross-Roads the ground was good for camping. Here our day's march ended. The bridge across White Oak River was destroyed, and would have been rebuilt during the night, but the troops and negroes were very tired, having marched nearly 22 miles, and the enemy's pickets were on the other side of the stream. On the morning of the 8th instant the troops crossed at 6.45. By 9.30 the bridge was finished. The general direction of the road toward Jacksonville south by one-half east. The country is slightly undulating. On the west side of the road for 8 or 9 miles is an extensive pocoson, from which flow many small tributaries of the White Oak River. Through this semi-swamp run many roads, at most times impracticable for wagons, but through which with great toil infantry might march. About 4½ miles from White Oak River there is a church known as "The Tabernacle," near which the road forks, the left fork leading direct to Swansborough, the distance to latter place being 13 miles; the right-hand road leads to Jacksonville, the distance being 16 miles. About 4 miles from this fork the road again forks, the right-hand fork leading to Jacksonville, the left direct to Snead's Ferry, passing through Piney Green. Near this latter fork the command bivouacked for the night.

The next morning, with the cavalry for an escort, I made a reconnaissance to Swansborough. We took the Snead's Ferry road as far as Piney Green; then we turned to the left toward Swansborough. From Piney Green to Swansborough the distance is 12 miles, and to

Snead's Ferry 15 miles. The roads are quite good, being of sand, but the country is flat, and in wet seasons would not afford good camping grounds. Swansborough is a small place, easily defended, and can be approached by vessels drawing 8 feet of water. After spending two hours at Swansborough, during which time communicated with General Potter, we countermarched for 2¾ miles, when we took the right-hand road and joined the infantry at Morton's, near "The Tabernacle." We then marched on to Young's Cross-Roads, where we bivouacked for the night.

The next morning we marched for New Berne via Pollocksville.

Accompanying this report is a sketch of the roads passed over.*

Hoping that the information gained may be useful, I have the honor to be, general, your obedient servant,

FRANCIS U. FARQUHAR,
Second Lieut. U. S. Engrs., and Chief Engr. 18th Corps d'Armée.

Maj. Gen. J. G. FOSTER.

No. 6.

Report of Col. Silas P. Richmond, Third Massachusetts Infantry.

HDQRS. THIRD REGT. MASSACHUSETTS VOL. MILITIA,
Camp Jourdan, New Berne, N. C., March 12, 1863.

COLONEL: I have the honor to make the following report of the part taken by myself and command in the recent expedition under the command of General Prince:

On the evening of the 5th instant I received orders to march at 6 o'clock on the following morning with three days' cooked rations.

March 6.—Formed regimental line at 6 a. m., and almost immediately after joined a column consisting of Prince's division and took up the line of march toward Pollocksville. I marched 24 officers and 529 men. After crossing the Trent River I received an order detailing myself and command to the responsible and laborious position of escort to the subsistence train, which consisted of nearly 100 wagons heavily laden. I made the following distribution of my regiment: Two companies in advance, four companies in the center, and three companies in the rear of the train. We made good progress for about 6 miles, after which we encountered bad places in the road, which caused much delay and hard labor, but we finally succeeded in bringing the whole train to the place of bivouac at about 10 p. m. This was on the McDaniel's plantation, 4 miles beyond Pollocksville. The distance marched this day was said to be 18 miles.

March 7.—Early this morning I received orders to park the train in the best possible position, and with my regiment, a section of Morrison's battery, and a platoon of cavalry remain and defend it. I sent out the cavalry as patrols and five of my companies as pickets in different directions, holding the remainder of my command in a position near the train, which I had parked near the center of a broad field. During the morning the main column marched to Trenton and returned without meeting any opposing force. Nothing of importance happened at the place of bivouac during the absence of the commanding general. At 3 p. m. the whole force took up the line of march toward Young's Cross-Roads. My regiment was detailed to march in the rear of the train and a company of cavalry in my rear. The roads were exceedingly bad, and I had to detail a large number of my men to go forward and assist in getting the wagons over the bad places. The train moved very slowly,

---

* Omitted as unimportant.

the teams being frequently stuck. We arrived at the place of bivouac
(Young's Cross-Roads) with the whole train at 3 a. m. on the morning
of the 8th, having marched about 10 miles.

March 8.—My regiment with the One hundred and sixty-eighth Pennsylvania Volunteers, Belger's battery, and a small company of cavalry,
the whole being under my command, were detached from the column
and ordered to hold this place while the main column moved on toward
Swansborough. The larger portion of the subsistence train was left with
us. My whole force amounted to 1,120 men. I immediately parked the
train in a large field near White Oak River, threw out strong infantry
pickets with cavalry patrols beyond on the different roads, disposed of
the remainder of my force to the best of my judgment for defense, and
awaited the result. The remainder of the day passed very quietly.

March 9.—The night passed without any occurrence of importance, as
also did the day until 6 p. m., when the main column returned, the advance reporting to have been to Swansborough without meeting the
enemy in force. During the absence of the general my cavalry patroled
the roads as far as Pollocksville in the rear and some 9 miles to the right
on the opposite side of White Oak River, and also about 15 miles on the
road to Peletier's Mill, meeting no opposing force or signs of the enemy.
The whole column again bivouacked here for the night.

March 10.—Had the train straightened out and my regiments in line
before 7 a. m., but had to wait some time for the First Brigade, they
having the advance, my regiment coming next in column, the train following, and the remainder of the Second Brigade in the rear. The column moved at about 8 a. m., taking the direct road to Pollocksville. On
arriving at the last-named place, in accordance with orders I halted my
regiment and the train until all the force in the rear had passed on; we
then moved on. Colonel Jourdan destroyed the bridge after we crossed.
It now commenced to rain very heavily and continued to do so about
two hours. This rendered the roads very bad indeed. My regiment
was distributed through the train in the same manner as on the first
day out. We moved very slowly and with much hard labor in assisting
the train. The head of the train reached New Berne about 9 o'clock,
but the rear did not get in until after 11 p. m. The distance marched
this day was 22 miles.

Both my officers and men were very much exhausted with their constant exertions to assist the train along. There were no severe casualties in my command during the expedition. I am pleased to say that
although my command occupied the hardest and most responsible position during the entire expedition, yet there was but very little complaint, the men, with but few exceptions, doing their duty nobly.

All of which is respectfully submitted.

S. P. RICHMOND,
Colonel, Commanding Third Massachusetts.

Col. J. JOURDAN, *Comdg. 2d Brig., 5th Div., 18th A. C.*

No. 7.

Report of Col. Augustus B. R. Sprague, Fifty-first Massachusetts Infantry.

HDQRS. FIFTY-FIRST MASSACHUSETTS REGIMENT,
Beaufort, N. C., March 11, 1863.

COLONEL: In obedience to instructions from department headquarters I left Newport Barracks on the morning of the 7th instant with

Companies B, C, D, H, and I, of my regiment, a section of Lee's battery, Lieutenant Cady, and Captain Moschell's company of Third New York Cavalry.

Passing through the pocoson around the head of Big Broad Creek we arrived at Cedar Point, opposite Swansborough, some 18 miles from Newport, about 4 o'clock on the afternoon of the 7th.

The steamer Wilson did not make her appearance at the mouth of the White Oak River as arranged, and as no other transportation could be procured to cross the river (about 1½ miles wide at this place) the troops went into bivouac in the woods at Cedar Point. On the morning of the 8th, the Wilson not having arrived, I accompanied Captain Moschell's company of New York cavalry on a reconnaissance up the east side of White Oak Creek to a point called Dorton's Ferry (about 16 miles distant from the Point by road), about 6 miles from Smith's Mill, or Young's. *En route* we passed over Pettiford's, Hadnot's, and Hunter's Creeks; examined Dorton's Ferry, long since abandoned as a thoroughfare and entirely impracticable as such in consequence of the extended marsh over which a road must necessarily be built to the river bank. The marsh which borders the river at this point is nearly a mile in width and the river in the vicinity about 200 feet broad.

There is no ferry or ford between the Point and the mouth of the White Oak River. We returned to Cedar Point, arriving at the camp soon after dark.

On the morning of the 9th communicated with Lieutenant-Colonel Lewis, who had reached Swansborough, coming down on the other side of the river with a detachment of Third New York Cavalry.

At 6 o'clock a. m., 10th instant, left Cedar Point and returned to Newport Barracks.

Saw nothing of the enemy during our advance and absence, and am convinced that they do not cross White Oak River in force, and that Swansborough has only been occupied by some 15 or 20 of the enemy as an outpost.

Brigadier-General Potter, chief of staff, joined me in the expedition, and I respectfully refer to him in the matter of details, relative to ferry, fords, depth and width of rivers, &c., in conformity to original instructions.

I have the honor to be, very respectfully, your obedient servant,

A. B. R. SPRAGUE,
Colonel Fifty-first Massachusetts Regiment.

Lieut. Col. SOUTHARD HOFFMAN,
Assistant Adjutant-General, Eighteenth Army Corps.

No. 8.

Reports of Lieut. Col. George W. Lewis, Third New York Cavalry.

HEADQUARTERS THIRD NEW YORK CAVALRY,
New Berne, N. C., March 11, 1863.

GENERAL: I have the honor to report that in obedience to the following order, viz—

HEADQUARTERS FIFTH DIVISION, EIGHTEENTH ARMY CORPS,
Bivouac in Field, March 9, 1863—6 a. m.

Lieutenant-Colonel Lewis, with the cavalry and *voltigeurs,* will reconnoiter upon the road leading from this point to Snead's Ferry, and will pass from it toward

Swansborough, going as far on both routes as he may consider prudent, taking into consideration the threatening state of the weather, so as to join the main body by night or communicate with it.

By command of Brigadier-General Prince:

S. W. WALDRON, JR.,
Captain and Assistant Adjutant-General—

I started with four companies of my regiment and one mounted howitzer and 150 mounted men, under Major Garrard, in the direction of Swansborough, which road intersects the road to Jacksonville via Snead's Ferry at Piney Green, 11 miles from Jacksonville and 13 from Swansborough. Halting at Piney Green I sent a detachment up the road to Snead's Ferry, 2 miles or more; they reporting nothing in that direction, I moved on to Swansborough, arriving there at 11 a. m., communicating with General Potter, at Hill's plantation, directly opposite Swansborough, through Lieutenant Fricker, the signal officer accompanying my command. General Potter immediately crossed to Swansborough in a small boat.

After remaining at Swansborough nearly three hours I took up the line of march and joined the left of the column, under your command, at the forks of the road, 5 miles from Young's Cross-Roads, at 5 p. m.

During the march we captured three Confederate soldiers, one a paroled prisoner named Caston, who was not yet exchanged; one by the same name who claims to have been recently discharged, and Private William B. Pringle, Tenth North Carolina Volunteers, who was visiting Swansborough on a furlough.

On my advance I captured several citizens, taking them to Swansborough, but returning them to their homes on my return. I ascertained by inquiries all along the route that the rebel pickets had left the day before for Jacksonville.

I am, general, with great respect, your most obedient servant,

G. W. LEWIS,
Lieutenant-Colonel, Commanding Third New York Cavalry.

Brigadier-General PRINCE,
Commanding Fifth Division, Eighteenth Army Corps.

—

HEADQUARTERS THIRD NEW YORK CAVALRY,
New Berne, N. C., March 12, 1863.

GENERAL: I have the honor to report the following list of property taken by my command during the recent march, viz:

Horses	6
Light wagons	3
Cavalry sabers and belts	3
Jack	1
Jennies	2

Very respectfully, your obedient servant,

G. W. LEWIS,
Commanding Third New York Cavalry.

Brigadier-General PRINCE,
Commanding Fifth Division, Eighteenth Army Corps.

No. 9

Report of Maj. Jeptha Garrard, Third New York Cavalry.

HEADQUARTERS VOLTIGEURS,
——, —, 1863.

List of property taken on march made by General Prince's division by Maj. Jeptha Garrard, commanding *voltigeurs:*

Horses... 2
Colt 1
Buggies.. 2
Harness for buggy 1

JEPTHA GARRARD,
Major, Third New York Cavalry, Comdg. Voltigeurs.

Captain WALDRON, JR.,
   Assistant Adjutant-General, Prince's Division.

MARCH 7-9, 1863.—Reconnaissance from Suffolk and skirmish (9th) near Windsor, Va.

Report of Col. Charles C. Dodge, First Battalion New York Mounted Rifles.

HEADQUARTERS MOUNTED RIFLES,
Suffolk, Va., March 9, 1863.

SIR : I have the honor to submit the following report of a late reconnaissance at Smithfield, Blackwater, &c.:

In accordance with instructions from general headquarters I started with about 450 of my command and one field howitzer on the evening of the 7th instant for the Isle of Wight Court-House, and thence to Smithfield, where I remained till about 9 a. m. on Sunday, the 8th instant.   No enemy were discovered, although the day before Lieutenant-Colonel Taliaferro was reported there with a small party.   He had undoubtedly returned across the river by Broadwater or Proctor's Bridge. Making the cross-roads my headquarters, strong scouting parties carefully reconnoitered the vicinity for a circle of 10 miles, but met no enemy.   The inhabitants of this district assured us that since Pryor's raid there some two months ago no large force has visited the town.   A few mounted rebels occasionally appear, but do not remain any time.   I am confident all that district, including Surry Court-House, may be safely considered free from them.   From Smithfield we proceeded via Benn's Church to Chuckatuck, where we spent the night.   Every effort was made to gain information as regards the enemy and their visits to this place, and our exertion satisfied me that, excepting on one or two occasions, never more than two or three Confederate soldiers had dared to enter the peninsula.   These persons came to see their relations, &c., and seldom have done any one an injury.   I believe, however, forage, bacon, &c., have been sent from there to Zuni and Petersburg in times past, but none whatever can be found now, and the disadvantage of this therefore exists no longer.   The guerrillas have burned down the only bridges leading direct from Chuckatuck toward Suffolk or Windsor.

On the a. m. of the 9th instant we were obliged to make a detour of some miles, improvise a bridge, and proceed toward Barber's Cross-

Roads and Windsor, arriving about 10 a. m.   Parties were at once sent out toward Blackwater Bridge and Zuni.   The former had not proceeded far when its advance guard, in turning a sharp bend in the road, suddenly came upon the advance of a small force of the enemy *en route* for Windsor.   Shots were exchanged, and my advance at once ordered to charge.   This they did well, the main column supporting them at as close a distance as possible.   At our first fire, however, the enemy, whom we learned to be some 50 of Claiborne's Confederate cavalry (Seventh Regiment), turned and fled precipitately.   Lieut. Thomas Freeborn, with Squadron D, pursued them at his utmost speed, driving them vigorously, the entire column following at the gallop; but as they had some half a mile the start of us and fresh horses it was impossible to come up with them, although we followed to within half a mile of Blackwater Bridge at the most rapid gait in our power.   They crossed the river at once upon the pontoon bridge there.   Lieutenant Freeborn and Major Wheelan succeeded, however, in capturing four men and horses, with several rifles, shot-guns, &c., which the enemy had thrown away in their flight.   The prisoners are in the hands of the provost-marshal, awaiting such examination and disposition as you may decide.   Believing it imprudent to attempt to force the bridge, considering the force we knew to be there and the wearied condition of our men and horses, we returned with our captures to Windsor.   The party going toward Zuni went to within sight of the river banks, but met no force on this side, although pickets, as usual, were discovered on the other.

Thus the entire section of country which I guard has been most carefully reconnoitered, and, I trust, to the general's satisfaction.   The conduct of my men has been everything that could be desired, and all of the regimental officers and men are but the more eager from the experience of to-day to meet the enemy in a fair fight, that they may then prove, as they have often before, the injustice of late reports circulated by malicious parties concerning the demoralization, &c., of the Mounted Rifles.   Not a man has been lost, nor, I can safely say, a pennyworth of property destroyed.

I have the honor to remain, general, very respectfully, your obedient servant,

CHARLES C. DODGE,
Colonel, Commanding.

Maj. B. B. FOSTER,
    Assistant Adjutant-General.

MARCH 7–14, 1863.—Expedition from New Berne to Mattamuskeet Lake, N. C.

Report of Col. David B. Morris, One hundred and first Pennsylvania Infantry.

HDQRS. ONE HUNDRED AND FIRST REGT. PA. VOLS.,
New Berne, N. C., March 17, 1863.

SIR: I have the honor to submit the following as my report of the expedition under my command around Lake Mattamuskeet, Hyde County, North Carolina.

In obedience to instructions from corps headquarters of March 7 I embarked the troops under my command, viz, One hundred and first and One hundred and third Regiments Pennsylvania Volunteers, Company F, Third New York Cavalry, and one piece and caisson Third New York Artillery, on the afternoon of 7th instant, on board the Northerner and Escort. Accompanied by the North State and two scows, we proceeded to Swan Quarter, Hyde County, arriving at 7 o'clock a. m., 8th instant, and the gunboat Allison at once proceeded to Rose Bay Bridge to prevent its reconstruction.

After eight or ten hours delay, caused by the captain of the steamer Northerner failing to go nearer than about 13 miles to the landing, we commenced debarking the troops in the afternoon of the 8th instant. Seven companies of infantry and one platoon of cavalry, with howitzer, under command of Lieutenant-Colonel Armor, One hundred and first Pennsylvania Volunteers, were debarked and marched to Swan Quarter, 1½ miles from the landing, arriving about 5 o'clock p. m. The remainder of the troops debarked at 11 o'clock on the morning of the 9th and proceeded to Swan Quarter. Acting on the advice of Captain Richardson, Third New York Cavalry, we then advanced in two columns, one in a southwest direction, under command of Colonel Morris, the other in a northwest direction, under command of Lieutenant-Colonel Armor, forming a junction at Mason's house at the earthwork, distant about 8 miles from Swan Quarter, where we bivouacked for the night, after posting our picket. During the night our picket captured 1 man (Thomas Voliva), attempting to fire upon the picket.

We resumed the line of march at 6.30 o'clock a. m., 10th instant, proceeding around the lake from north to east, marching 25 miles, and bivouacked for the night on Spencer's farm. At 6 o'clock a. m., 11th instant, resumed the march; arrived at Swan Quarter about 6 o'clock p. m., having marched 30 miles. During the 10th and 11th it rained almost incessantly, consequently the roads were very bad. No armed force at any point was to be seen.

A few stragglers, whose names were on the guerrilla muster-roll, were captured and brought to New Berne. A few others, supposed to belong to the company, were also brought with us—11 in all. They are now in the hands of the provost-marshal at New Berne.

About 60 citizens were made prisoners, but released at Swan Quarter upon taking the oath of allegiance. From the best information that could be obtained the band of guerrillas in this county were scattered about in small parties of from 6 to 8, through the almost impassable swamps.

Quite a number of horses, oxen, and carts were captured, but the greater part were abandoned, not deeming them of sufficient value to warrant the delay of transportation and expense of subsistence. On the morning of the 12th instant Captain Richardson, with 300 men and all available transportation, was sent out 7 miles, to the farm of Judge Donald, for the purpose of bringing in a quantity of cotton, corn, and bacon.

The following is an approximate list of all the property turned over to the proper authorities : Seventeen horses; 13 buggies; 1 yoke oxen; 1 schooner, Snow Squall, of Washington, of about 35 tons burden ; 8 cart-loads cotton (small portion unginned), not baled ; about 1,500 pounds bacon ; about 400 bushels corn ; about 40 slaves, who followed us to the landing. We embarked on the 13th instant and arrived at New Berne on 14th instant. The only buildings burned by my order were the outbuildings of a farm-house near Fairfield, in which we found a rebel officer's coat, ammunition, &c. I regret to state that a small mill at Swan Quarter was fired and burned, and also a barn filled with corn adjoining Spencer's farm was burned by an unknown party; also a number of stacks of fodder on the farm of Judge Donald was burned without my order.

I would also call attention to a lack of proper discipline among the line officers of the One hundred and third Regiment Pennsylvania Volunteers. They seem to have little or no control over their commands, and lack energy to enforce proper discipline. To this there are some exceptions.

The One hundred and First Regiment Pennsylvania Volunteers also lacks discipline, which I attribute to my long absence from it, but which in the course of time I will bring about again. As an instance of insubordination in the One hundred and third Regiment Pennsylvania Volunteers, while embarking on board the Northerner from the steamer Escort the officers and men, contrary to repeated orders, rushed forward before the boat could be made fast to such an extent as to endanger life and to render it impossible for the officers of the boat to manage her. Having repeated the order for the men to remain in their places and await orders, and all to no effect, I seized a gun and fired down the side of the boat for the purpose of deterring the men, but with no intention of injuring any one. At the moment of firing a man rushed forward and was slightly injured.

My thanks are due the officers of the Escort, North State, Lockwood, and Allison for their valuable assistance.

I am, sir, very respectfully, your obedient servant,

D. B. MORRIS,
Colonel, Commanding Expedition.

Lieut. Col. SOUTHARD HOFFMAN,
Assistant Adjutant-General.

—

[Addenda.]

NEW BERNE, *March* 28, 1863.

Major-General FOSTER, *Commanding, &c.:*

GENERAL: I deeply regret to be compelled, in the last hours of my stay here, to distress you by complaints of the outrages of our forces in the last expedition to Hyde County. In numerous instances, well authenticated, they entered and robbed the houses of loyal men, destroyed furniture, insulted women, and treated with scorn the protections which by your advice I had given them. Can I give to people whose loyalty is not and has never been questioned any assurance that you can see them protected?

As matters now stand the loyal men and women, aged and infirm, outside of our lines are the most unfortunate and oppressed in our country; both sides pillage and rob them. I know you have uniformly rebuked these atrocities, but your words have been treated like my protections.

I invoke for the people referred to such interposition as your sense of duty and humanity will suggest.

With high respect and regard, yours, &c.,

ED. STANLY.

[Indorsement.]

MARCH 29, 1863.

Referred to Colonel Morris for report.

J. G. FOSTER,
Major-General.

MARCH 8–16, 1863.—Expedition against New Berne, N. C., including skirmishes (13th–14th) at Deep Gully, and attack (14th) on Fort Anderson.

REPORTS.*

No. 1.—Maj. Gen. John G. Foster, U. S. Army, commanding the Department of North Carolina.

No. 2.—Capt. David A. Taylor, Third New York Light Artillery, Chief Signal Officer.

No. 3.—Lieut. Nathaniel S. Barstow, Twenty-fourth Massachusetts Infantry, Acting Signal Officer, of attack on Fort Anderson.

No 4.—Itinerary of the First Division, Eighteenth Army Corps, Brig. Gen. Innis N. Palmer, U. S. Army, commanding, March 7–15.

No. 5.—Col. Josiah Pickett, Twenty-fifth Massachusetts Infantry, Second Brigade, of skirmishes at Deep Gully.

No. 6.—Brig. Gen. Henry Prince, U. S. Army, commanding Fifth Division, of operations March 15–16.

No. 7.—Maj. Gen. Daniel H. Hill, C. S. Army, commanding Expedition.

No. 8.—Maj. John C. Haskell, C. S. Army, commanding Artillery.

No. 9.—Brig. Gen. John J. Pettigrew, C. S. Army.

No. 10.—Brig. Gen. Richard B. Garnett, C. S. Army.

No. 11.—Brig. Gen. Junius Daniel, C. S. Army.

No. 12.—Brig. Gen. Beverly H. Robertson, C. S. Army, commanding Cavalry.

No. 1.

Reports of Maj. Gen. John G. Foster, U. S. Army, commanding the Department of North Carolina.

HEADQUARTERS EIGHTEENTH ARMY CORPS,
New Berne, N. C., March 15, 1863.

GENERAL: The enemy are retiring from an attack on this town, which was intended to have been strong, but was feeble, very feeble, in all places except on a work on north side of Neuse River, directly opposite the town. At that point the enemy opened a brisk artillery fire from seventeen pieces, which continued about three hours. They retired a short distance and remained threatening the work till this morning, when they retired. The whole force of the enemy, from deserters, was 13,000 infantry and cavalry and thirty-nine pieces of artillery. I am sending parties out in all directions to harass the enemy's retreat. The attack was on the 14th, the anniversary of the taking of the town, and the supposition is that they intended to recapture the town on that day.

I remain, general, very respectfully, your obedient servant,

J. G. FOSTER,
Major-General, Commanding.

Major-General HALLECK,
　　General-in-Chief.

———

HEADQUARTERS EIGHTEENTH ARMY CORPS,
New Berne, N. C., March 15, 1863.

GENERAL: Referring to my telegram of this date I have the honor to report that on the evening of the 13th the enemy appeared in force on the Trent road, driving in our picket posts on that road; the force on

---

* For reports of Actg. Rear-Admiral S. P. Lee and Commander A. Murray, U. S. Navy, see Annual Report of the Secretary of the Navy, December 7, 1863.

the road was heavily re-enforced and ordered to retire slowly, and fight if they were pressed.

At daylight of the 14th General Pettigrew, with a force of 7,000 men and seventeen pieces artillery, attacked a small work on north side of the Neuse River, occupied by the Ninety-second New York Volunteers, Lieutenant-Colonel Anderson.* They opened a fire from all their pieces on the work and held their infantry in reserve for assault. Colonel Anderson was summoned to surrender several times, which he declined doing. Referring to me for orders, I instructed him to defend and hold the work. The Navy gunboats were in an unfortunate position to be of much assistance at first, owing to one being aground and the other two damaged. They were, however, towed to position by tugs, and, assisted by a battery of rifled guns on this side of the Neuse, compelled General Pettigrew to withdraw his artillery and infantry, merely remaining in a threatening position till this a. m., when he finally retired. On south side of Trent River the enemy advanced to within 6 miles of New Berne, but have withdrawn. The attack was to have been made with vigor enough by General Pettigrew to have taken Camp Anderson, which would have enabled him to have planted rifled batteries at that point, whence he might have driven the gunboats from the river and shelled the town, during which a strong attack was to have been made on Trent and Neuse roads. Our pickets held them on Trent road, although they were ordered to fall back to my defenses where I proposed making the fight.

The whole affair, meant to be effective and strong, was ineffective and weak, inflicting no damage and accomplishing no object.

The force of the enemy was about 13,000 to 14,000 infantry and cavalry and thirty-nine pieces of artillery. Our loss was only 2 killed and 4 wounded.

Referring to my letter of March 2, I beg to say that recent information shows General Longstreet with his corps to be on the Blackwater, and not southwest, as reported.

I am, general, very respectfully, your obedient servant,

J. G. FOSTER,
Major-General, Commanding.

Maj. Gen. H. W. HALLECK,
    General-in-Chief U. S. Army, Washington, D. C.

No. 2.

Report of Capt. David A. Taylor, Third New York Light Artillery, Chief Signal Officer.

HEADQUARTERS SIGNAL DETACHMENT,
        New Berne, March 18, 1863.

SIR: Inclosed I forward you copies of the reports of Lieutenants Merrill † and Barstow, containing an account of their signal operations at and in the vicinity of New Berne during the late movements, and of the action which took place here on the 14th instant.

I can truly say that both Lieutenants Merrill and Barstow are by far too modest in describing their own share of the work.

---

* The casualties in the Ninety-second New York Infantry were 3 men wounded and 3 men missing; 1 man reported as killed, March 13.
† Not found.

The position occupied .by Lieutenant Barstow was one of extreme danger; every tent and house within the works at Fort Anderson was riddled by shot and shell, and the parade literally blown up by the enemy's artillery. Both Lieutenant Barstow and his flagman (Marsh) were struck by spent pieces of shell, but fortunately received no injury of any account. It is but justice to Lieutenant Merrill to state that but for him the gunboat on which he was placed would have done more damage to our troops than the enemy, as either through the stupidity, excitement, or drunkenness of its commanding officer they were going to open fire on the only place where the garrison of the fort were covered from the fire of the enemy. Lieutenant Merrill having taken position on the paddle-box had a fine view of the field and the roads by which the enemy must come to assault the place, and the moment the head of their columns showed themselves gave directions, distances, and elevations to the gunners, and that so accurately that some of the rebel guns were for a time abandoned and their infantry driven back. He and Lieutenant Barstow together directed the fire of the gunboat Hunchback and the batteries on shore on the south side of the Neuse.

With a corps of such officers as Lieutenant Merrill I would be willing to undertake anything.

It was impossible for these officers to get their reports ready in time, or these copies would have accompanied my own report of the same transaction, lately mailed to you.

I remain, sir, very respectfully, your obedient servant,

DAVID A. TAYLOR,
Captain and Acting Signal Officer.

Maj. A. J. MYER, *Signal Officer, U. S. Army.*

No. 3.

Report of Lieut. Nathaniel S. Barstow, Twenty-fourth Massachusetts Infantry, Acting Signal Officer, of attack on Fort Anderson.

HEADQUARTERS SIGNAL DETACHMENT,
New Berne, March 16, 1863.

SIR: On the 13th instant, in pursuance to orders of Captain Taylor, I reported for signal duty to Lieutenant-Colonel Anderson, at Fort Anderson, on the north side of the Neuse River, New Berne, N. C.

On the morning of the 14th instant, just before daylight, the fort was attacked by General Pettigrew with two brigades of infantry and seventeen pieces of artillery.

By order of Colonel Anderson I sent the following message to Major-General Foster:

The enemy are in front of us in large force, with artillery; we want men.

Answer:

Re-enforcements shall be sent as soon as possible.

After sending this message, by the severity of the enemy's fire I was compelled to change my position, and took a more sheltered place.

From Colonel Anderson to General Foster:

Send more men, send them quickly.

Answer:

Hold out as long as you can; lie close; men are coming.

This message was several times repeated, each time by order of Colonel Anderson in his extreme anxiety for re-enforcements. I sent several messages to the gunboats, directing their fire, such as, "Fire higher," "Fire to the left," "Fire to the right," &c., but having no blank book with me at the time could not record them.

I wish to recommend to your notice my flagman, Timothy S. Marsh, Company D, Twenty-first Massachusetts Volunteers, who throughout the whole affair behaved with admirable coolness under a fire the severest I ever saw.

I have the honor to remain, yours, very respectfully,

N. S. BARSTOW,
Lieutenant and Acting Signal Officer.

Capt. D. A. TAYLOR,
Chief Acting Signal Officer.

No. 4.

*Itinerary of the First Division, Eighteenth Army Corps, Brig. Gen. Innis N. Palmer, U. S. Army, commanding, March 7-15.**

March 7.—In accordance with orders from Headquarters Eighteenth Army Corps, five companies of the Fifty-first Massachusetts Volunteer Militia, of the First Brigade, marched from Newport Barracks to Cedar Point, opposite Swansborough, on White Oak River, where they bivouacked. Here the infantry remained while a reconnaissance, under General Potter, chief of staff Eighteenth Army Corps, was made some 16 miles farther on into the enemy's country. On the return of the reconnoitering party the infantry returned to Newport Barracks, arriving on the 10th instant.

March 13.—In anticipation of an attack upon New Berne three regiments of the Second Brigade, viz, the Fifth Massachusetts Volunteer Militia, Twenty-fifth Massachusetts Volunteers, and the Forty-sixth Massachusetts Volunteer Militia, were sent to Deep Gully, on the Trent road. On arriving at the Gully it was found that the enemy had crossed and were strongly posted. Bivouacking for the night, preparations were made for a morning attack. At daylight the movement commenced and the fire of the skirmishers had just opened, when orders were received to retire to New Berne, leaving one regiment, the Twenty-fifth Massachusetts Volunteers, to hold the enemy in check. This was done.

March 14.—The regiment at Deep Gully was re-enforced this a. m. by the Forty-sixth Massachusetts Volunteer Militia, of the Second Brigade. An attack on New Berne being apprehended, the Forty-third Massachusetts Volunteer Militia and other forces, under command of Col. T. J. C. Amory, marched 18 miles on the Kinston road on a reconnaissance, but, the enemy having retired, returned on the 16th to camp.

March 15.—The enemy commenced falling back, closely followed some 15 miles by the Forty-sixth Massachusetts Volunteer Militia; but the road being rendered impassable at this point by the retreating force the Forty-sixth retraced their steps toward New Berne.

---

* From Returns of the Division and First and Second Brigades for March, 1863.

No. 5.

Report of Col. Josiah Pickett, Twenty-fifth Massachusetts Infantry, Second Brigade, of skirmishes at Deep Gully.

HDQRS. TWENTY-FIFTH REGT. MASSACHUSETTS VOLS.,
Camp Oliver, New Berne, N. C., March 15, 1863.

SIR : I have the honor to report that on the 13th instant, at 5.30 p. m., I started with six companies of my regiment for the outpost near Deep Gully, that place being attacked by the enemy and being held by the other four companies of my regiment with a part of the Third New York Cavalry. I arrived at the disputed ground soon after dark and learned that the enemy were in strong force in our front, with infantry, cavalry, and artillery, a distance of half a mile. By order of Colonel Lee, commanding the brigade, I divided my regiment, placing a wing on either side of the Trent road, throwing out a strong picket to guard against surprise, and remained on our arms until morning.

At daybreak I moved forward a company as skirmishers and they immediately engaged the enemy's line. General Palmer taking command, I was ordered forward with my regiment, supported by the Fifth and Forty-sixth Regiments Massachusetts Volunteers, with a section of Riggs' and one piece of Belger's batteries. Musketry firing was kept up for nearly three hours. The city being attacked in our rear, the regiments supporting me were withdrawn for its defense, and i was left, with my regiment and two pieces of artillery, to take care of the enemy as best I could. Having special orders from General Palmer not to expose the pieces, I blockaded the road and fell back to a better position at the Jackson House and awaited their advance. They soon began to shell the woods around and kept it up at intervals during the day, but did not advance. At 4 p. m. I sent out one company, under command of Captain Harrington, to observe the movements and position of the enemy if possible. He went as far as Deep Gully and found them falling back and exchanged shots with them at that place. I was relieved by the Forty-third Regiment Massachusetts Volunteer Militia at 6 p. m. on the 14th, and returned to camp at New Berne with a loss of 1 man wounded and 1 missing.

Respectfully submitted.

JOSIAH PICKETT,
Colonel Twenty-fifth Regiment Massachusetts Volunteers.

GEORGE W. BARTLETT,
A. A. A. G. Second Brig., First Div., Eighteenth Army Corps.

No. 6.

Report of Brig. Gen. Henry Prince, U. S. Army, commanding Fifth Division, of operations March 15–16.

HDQRS. FIFTH DIVISION, EIGHTEENTH ARMY CORPS,
New Berne, N. C., March 16, 1863.

COLONEL : Pursuant to orders, verbally communicated to me by the commanding general, my division moved out yesterday on the road south of the Trent River to feel the enemy, who had just then been reported from the front to have probably crossed in large force to that side. At half past 1 o'clock the regiments left their camps, and at twenty minutes to 6 the command bivouacked 3½ miles this side of Mill Creek. The ground and road being very bad and wet for 3 miles forward and the moon being absent made it impracticable to go farther. We found a picket of the enemy 2 miles in front, and our own picket, a mile in front, reports three shots fired into it in the night.

We advanced at daylight to-day. We approached Mill Creek as if to find it occupied. Meeting no opposition we took possession of the opposite bank at 8 a. m. I pushed on at once with the infantry to Pollocksville and there learned that Robertson with his cavalry left that place yesterday at 1 o'clock p. m., going to Kinston.

Having a picket on the Trent, this side of Mill Creek, I communicated by it with the gunboat North Star, the captain of which placed himself under my orders. This was prior to the advance from Mill Creek. I directed the boat to proceed to Pollocksville, where she arrived soon after the troops, when I ordered her to return to New Berne.

Satisfied that the enemy were beyond reach and that no troops were left in that vicinity, I marched my command back to their quarters at New Berne.

The One hundred and fifty-eighth Pennsylvania Militia was detailed last evening for the advance guard in the morning, and Colonel McKibbin commanded it, although after being detailed his horse had fallen upon him and fractured the fibula of one of his legs. He returned in the gunboat from Pollocksville. He expressed himself as ably seconded in the duties of the morning by Lieutenant-Colonel Troxel and Major Hale, of his regiment.

Very respectfully, your obedient servant,

HENRY PRINCE,
Brigadier-General Volunteers, Commanding.

Lieut. Col. SOUTHARD HOFFMAN,
A. A. G., Hdqrs. Eighteenth Army Corps, New Berne. ·

No. 7.

Report of Maj. Gen. Daniel H. Hill, C. S. Army, commanding Expedition.

GOLDSBOROUGH, N. C., *March* 16, 1863—10 p. m.

Have just this moment arrived from below. Our expedition was partly successful. I went with Daniel's brigade on the lower Trent road to New Berne, and sent Robertson around on the upper Trent road to cut the railroad. Pettigrew was to bombard the shipping and barracks from the other side. The result was highly satisfactory on our road.

On Friday we drove them to their first line of works at Deep Gully, 8 miles from New Berne. This was a very strong position naturally, and strengthened by earthworks. It was defended by five companies and two pieces of artillery. General Daniel in person charged it and captured it with four companies. We held it that night and I sent an order to Robertson to cut the railroad the next day.

At daylight Saturday morning the Yankees made a feeble attempt at a recapture of Deep Gully. General Pettigrew opened at the same time, but I soon discovered that he had been repulsed, as the firing was plainly that of the heavy guns of a gunboat. After repulsing the

Yankees at Deep Gully I would have pursued them to their next stronghold, at Rocky Run, 3 miles nearer New Berne, but as Pettigrew had been silenced, and there were three shorter roads to Kinston than the one I was on, I fell back to a point opposite Trenton. Remained there Sunday and until noon to-day. No pursuit by the Yankees. Our loss has been slight.

General Pettigrew reports:

The absence of the Whitworth ruined us. The 20-pounder Parrotts are worse than useless. One burst, killing 4 men and wounding 4; another broke its axle. The shells of all of them burst just at the mouth of the gun. I hope never to see them again.

Robertson sent me out a lieutenant, who partly cut the railroad. He sent out a colonel, who saw some Yankees and came back. Robertson did not go himself. We must have a better man. Garnett did not start until Sunday. I have sent Pettigrew to Greenville to protect him if necessary. I propose to go over there myself in a few days. I fear Garnett has seriously compromised himself by his long delay. If it be true, as your scout reports, that the Yankees have been so heavily re-enforced at New Berne they may attempt to cut Garnett off. Had the Whitworth been sent the gunboat would have been beaten and New Berne would have been at Pettigrew's mercy. Then if my original plan had been carried out of moving Ransom on the Sound road to the rear of New Berne I think we would have gained the town, or at least have caused a very salutary alarm. The spirit manifested by Whiting has spoiled everything. My order of assignment says: "General D. H. Hill is assigned to the command of all the troops in North Carolina." If I am to be cut down to two brigades I will not submit to the swindle.

So far as I can judge there will be no movement at Charleston until Hooker gets out of the mud. Then there will be a general movement on Fredericksburg, Petersburg, the North Carolina Railroad, and Wilmington. We ought to have been clearing out North Carolina while Hooker was mud-bound. This I urged three months ago, but I was unheeded. It is not yet too late to do something and I am anxious to go to work. I started out with my throat in a terrible fix and thought it might cost me my life. Thank God, I am no worse.

Foster ought to be ashamed of letting one brigade run him into his rat-hole.

I have received nothing but contemptuous treatment from Richmond from the very beginning of the war, but I hope they will not carry matters so far as to perpetuate a swindle.

You were greatly mistaken in supposing that I was indifferent about the Whitworth. I told you that it was too late to get it, but that it was worth all the guns I had. I had tried the Parrotts, and their shells all burst prematurely.

If the Yankee re-enforcements are as large as your scout represents them they will establish an inland communication between New Berne, Washington, and Plymouth, and thus have their cordon of forts complete from Suffolk down. A glance at the map will show how seriously this would embarrass us. For my part I could get no information from New Berne.

With great respect,

D. H. HILL,
Major-General.

[General LONGSTREET.]

No. 8.

Report of Maj. John C. Haskell, C. S. Army, commanding Artillery.

HEADQUARTERS ARTILLERY,
March 16, 1863.

CAPTAIN: I have the honor most respectfully to submit the following report of the artillery under my command:

1st. Having on March 8, in obedience to orders from Maj. Gen. D. H. Hill, marched from Goldsborough with a portion of the reserve artillery, I bivouacked at Falling Creek, 26 miles from Goldsborough, 8 from Kinston.

2d. On the night of the 8th at this place I received orders to report to Brig. Gen. J. J. Pettigrew, and from him orders to move on to Kinston with the rifle guns of my command, which consisted of four 20-pounder Parrott guns of the Macon Light Artillery, under command of Lieut. [C. W.] Slaten, and one 3-inch rifle of the Montgomery Light Artillery, under command of Lieutenant Davis. Having reported there with the above-mentioned guns, I was joined by the following batteries: Captain Wyatt's, with two 12-pounder Napoleons (bronze), one heavy 12-pounder (bronze), and one 10-pounder Parrott; Capt. [J.] Graham's, of one 3-inch rifle, one 12-pounder howitzer, and two 6-pounders (bronze), and a section of Captain Graham's battery (attached to Daniel's brigade), of two 3-inch rifles. With this artillery I marched in rear of the brigade and trains about 21 miles from Kinston and halted for the night. About a mile from the camping ground I was delayed for over three hours by a portion of the brigade wagon train, and when they moved out, one of my guns, a 3-inch rifle, broke through a corduroy bridge, letting the piece down into the water; all the other guns of the command escaped. Two being behind this were delayed until this gun could be pried out and the bridge repaired. All the guns then crossed except the last two. The horses of the first of these took fright and pulled one side of the gun-carriage over the edge of the bridge. The water underneath being some 4 feet deep, with great difficulty the wheels were taken off the carriage and the gun dismounted. To do this, however, it was found necessary to cut away part of the bridge, and before it could be repaired and the guns gotten to camp it was near daylight and the men and horses were much jaded.

At 7 a. m. on the 10th the artillery resumed the march in the same position as the day before and marched as far as Palmetto Creek, which was crossed by all the artillery except the 20-pounder battery, the first gun of which crushed in the bridge and was drawn out by hand with great difficulty. The bridge was then repaired in about three hours and the rest of the train passed over and moved on, allowing the brigade commissary wagons to pass in front. In this order the march was continued until within about 3 miles of the camping place for the night, when the artillery was stopped by the brigade wagon train, which had stalled in the middle of a stream. The wagons were removed by about 10 o'clock that night, when all the light guns and one 20-pounder crossed, I getting over about 11.30 o'clock. The rest of the 20-pounders were behind the commissary wagons, which did not cross until about 2 the next evening, as the stream was impassable and had to be bridged. If this battery had crossed the night before I do not think they could have advanced farther, as the horses were broken down. After crossing, the artillery again moved forward and arrived within about 2 miles of Barrington's Ferry and halted with all the guns except the 10-pounder Parrott of Captain Wyatt's battery, which I had placed in position under Lieutenant Rives at Pettiford's Ferry to enfilade the work at Barrington's Ferry and fire at the gunboats when expedient. This gun fired a number of rounds at the encampment and redoubt, the effect of which could not be seen, and eight at a gunboat, four of which Lieut. [Charles M.] Rives thinks took effect, when she hauled off out of range.

The artillery, with the exception of this piece, was moved forward just about daybreak, and I was directed by General Pettigrew to place them in position so as to play upon the earthwork at the ferry and the gunboats upon the river. In obedience to this order I placed the guns of Captains Wyatt's and Graham's batteries in position about 400 yards from the work, and directed them to open fire with shell and case-shot, which they did, throwing the shell and case-shot with great precision in the work. After some rounds Captain Wyatt commenced firing solid shot from some of his guns to batter down the breastwork. It was soon found unavailing and stopped. As soon as the batteries of Captains Wyatt and Graham commenced firing I ordered up the rifle guns and placed them in position on the right and left of these batteries, giving them orders to direct their fire against the gunboats, except a section of 3-inch rifles under Lieut. Aldon Alexander, which was placed upon the extreme right, with orders to fire upon the earthwork at a point where it seemed weakest. Though the guns were worked well and fired accurately the effect was small. The rest of the rifle guns fired at the gunboat, which was distant 1¾ miles, with but little effect. Although they struck her several times it was impossible, with the very inferior ammunition with which they were supplied, to shoot accurately enough to strike any vital part unless by chance. After the firing had continued about an hour the first piece of the 20-pounders burst, mortally wounding 1 man and severely wounding 2 others. About half an hour after this, by the direction of General Pettigrew, the guns were gradually withdrawn and taken back about 1 mile, with the exception of the smooth guns of Captains Wyatt's and Graham's batteries, which were kept close to be moved up if necessary. About 3 p. m. they were withdrawn and moved back to the halting place of the night before and halted there until about 12 o'clock at night of the 14th, when the artillery moved again until it arrived at the ground where I had encamped the night of the 12th, and halted there until about 12 m. on the 15th; then again moved to Swift Creek and took position to repel an attack which was anticipated.

During the march it was found necessary to dismount and leave one of the 20-pounder Parrotts, as the axle, which had an old crack in it, was found on examination to have broken in two during the fire of the 14th and could not be replaced. It was hidden, so that it might be sent for hereafter. I would most respectfully recommend that the 20-pounders be taken from the Macon Light Artillery, as it is a good company and deserves better than to have its members wounded and killed by defective guns.

I would beg leave, most respectfully, to call to the favorable consideration of the general, Lieut. Aldon Alexander, who on the march down gave invaluable aid by his skill as an engineer and untiring energy in commanding, which would without him have been the cause of much greater delay than was experienced. All the men and officers behaved coolly and well.

The following were the casualties: Macon Light Artillery had 1 man mortally wounded, 2 severely; Lieutenant Alexander's section had 1 man wounded by a shell from the enemy, not dangerously. The remaining batteries lost none killed and none wounded. From Captain Graham's battery there is 1 missing.

I am, captain, very respectfully, your obedient servant,

JOHN C. HASKELL,
Major, Commanding Artilery.

Capt. [N. C.] HUGHES,
Assistant Adjutant-General.

No. 9.

Report of Brig. Gen. John J. Pettigrew, C. S. Army.

HEADQUARTERS PETTIGREW'S BRIGADE,
Greenville, N. C., March 17, 1863.

GENERAL: The expedition intrusted to me having failed in accomplishing the hoped-for result, I submit the following statement of the causes:

I left Goldsborough on the 9th instant (Monday) with the portion of my brigade there stationed and arrived at Kinston on Tuesday afternoon. That night I received your instructions to take the two rifled guns of General Daniel, the four 20-pounder Parrotts of the reserve artillery, and the Whitworth gun in case it arrived, and to proceed to Barrington's Ferry; to get my guns in position without observation if possible; to open a concentrated fire upon the enemy's work, which it was thought would so demoralize the enemy as to induce an almost bloodless surrender. I was then to open on the Yankee shipping and barracks. It was important that the bombardment should begin on Thursday. The distance was 57 miles, and the heavy rain of Tuesday and Wednesday had swollen the swamps and put the roads in very bad condition. Many of the bridges broke down under the 20-pounders, all causing great delay, but I wrote you that I hoped to carry the work by moonlight on Friday morning with the bayonet, which I preferred, as the enemy in New Berne then would not know the result and I might thus be enabled to intrench the guns before the gunboats attacked. The infantry reached the camp, 8 miles from Barrington's, at dark, and I intended to start at midnight for the ferry, but a swamp some 3 miles in rear of the halt changed under the train into a quicksand. The men vainly worked all night in the freezing water to repair it. It was necessary to bridge the whole swamp in a new place, which was done under the superintendence of Lieutenant Koerner, of the Topographical Engineers, who offered his services and greatly aided me. About 3 p. m. Friday the bridge was finished. The infantry arrived at the ferry early in the night, but the 20-pounders having mired, the artillery was detained until late in the morning.

In a reconnaissance made by me and Major Haskell and my aides during the afternoon, Pettiford's Ferry had appeared a suitable point for attacking the gunboats and perhaps for enfilading the work. A rifled gun, under Lieutenant Rives, was placed there before daylight. The Twenty-sixth Regiment (Col. [H. K.] Burgwyn), assisted by Captain Whitford's Rangers, were to capture or drive in the enemy's pickets. The Twenty-sixth supported by the Forty-fourth Regiment, if necessary, were to carry the work. I hoped then to intrench the 20-pounders and drive away the gunboats and the enemy from his intrenchments in front of New Berne. The first part of this programme was excellently well carried out; 3 of the enemy's pickets were captured; the bridges within the enemy's lines were repaired. At 400 yards we came for the first time in view of the work. The result of what I had heard of the character of the work and learned from my reconnaissance of the previous day, and from what I now saw before me, was as follows:

It was a simple *pan coupé*, situated on a slight elevation, the height of the interior crest being 8 or 9 feet and the ditch in front 6 by 8 feet. It was flanked by a swamp of 3 or 4 miles on the right and a swampy creek on the left, so that it could only be approached in front. The road ran down to its center and then along the ditch of the left half. The garrison was composed of a two-years' regiment, about 250 or 300 strong.

It was now broad daylight. The presumption was the garrison would fire one round, costing us 50 or 100 men. I therefore decided to display my force, demoralize them by a heavy fire, and demand a surrender, thus saving my own men and not unnecessarily killing theirs. The light batteries deployed finely into battery at 400 yards from the work and opened upon it a rapid and well-directed fire. After a few minutes I demanded a surrender by Lieut. [Louis G.] Young, my aide-de-camp. This was a mistake on my part and I regret it very much, but it had no effect upon the principal object of the movement. They declined surrendering without consulting General Foster, &c. The firing was then recommenced. I now devoted my attention to the 20-pounders. I regret to say that their performance was execrable—fully as bad as the experiments at Goldsborough led us to fear. A gunboat lay opposite us at the wharf in New Berne, about 1½ miles distant, getting up steam and firing upon us, in which she was aided by field guns, probably Whitworths from the sound of the missiles. Half of the shells from the 20-pounders burst just outside of the guns. They turned over in the air and were perfectly harmless to the enemy. At length the axle of one of these guns broke and it became unserviceable. Then another burst, wounding 3 men, 1 of them mortally. These four 20-pounders were our sole agents for accomplishing the object of the expedition. It was now painfully evident that they were worse than useless. Of the six guns composing the battery two had burst at Fredericksburg, one here, a fourth was disabled by the breaking of an axle-tree. The ammunition was fully as bad as the guns. The light guns would have been effective against gunboats in an ordinary-sized river, but the Neuse at New Berne is so wide as to enable them to remove a mile or two distant. Other boats with heavy guns were coming round from the Trent. The principal object of the expedition having then utterly failed it seemed to me folly longer to expose the men and *matériel* of the artillery. The only question was whether I should carry the work before withdrawing. The Twenty-sixth had been in waiting ever since daylight and would have done it in five minutes. The advantage of so doing would have been the capture of some 300 two-years' men, with their arms. The work we could not hold. The disadvantage was the probable loss of a certain number of men 60 miles from our hospitals. I decided against it. It cost me a struggle, after so much labor and endurance, to give up the *éclat*, but I felt that my duty to the country required me to save my men for some operation in which sacrifices would be followed by consequences, not in capturing two-years' men and holding temporary possession of breastworks, however brilliant the operation might be. I therefore withdrew the whole command except the Twenty-sixth Regiment, which remained within about 500 yards of the place in order to cover the withdrawal of Captain Whitford's men. I cannot too highly express my admiration of the manner in which they stood the furious shelling of the enemy without flinching. The rest of the command was about a mile distant.

In the afternoon, the enemy having received re-enforcements, I thought he might sally out, so I drew up in line parallel to the fire of the gunboats, the right resting some three-quarters of a mile from the work. While in this position the enemy's scouts were perceived advancing, doubtless to discover our position, but they disappeared as soon as our skirmishers showed themselves. The shelling of the gunboats continued all day. The two rifled guns at Pettiford's Ferry replied, and, I have every reason to think, disabled one.

Later in the afternoon I withdrew to my camp. During the night the sounds of drums, bugles, and bands in New Berne announced that their forces had retreated from General Daniel's front; but as we heard nothing from his guns after 12 m. I concluded that he had not pursued. The whole force in New Berne could thus be thrown upon my rear at very short notice, so the next day (Sunday) I fell back 8 miles, within striking distance of Swift Creek. I then received your order to proceed to Greenville.

It will thus be seen, general, that the not capturing of the fort was owing to myself, for which I have given my reasons, good or bad. The failure of the effort to drive the gunboats out of New Berne and the troops from their intrenchments was owing solely to the utter worthlessness of the 20-pounder Parrotts, which had hung around our necks like a millstone during the march and failed us in the vital moment. My attack was partly effective in withdrawing the troops from General Daniel's front, and had I been supplied with four Whitworth guns I firmly believe you might have slept in New Berne that night.

For details of the artillery I refer to the report of Major Haskell, who discharged his whole duty.

I was greatly indebted throughout to that gallant and efficient officer Captain Whitford.

I cannot refrain from bearing testimony to the unsurpassed military good conduct of those under me. In seven days they marched 127 miles, waded swamps, worked in them by night and day, bivouacked in the rain, sometimes without fire, never enjoyed a full night's rest after the first, besides undergoing a furious shelling, and discharging other duties. All this without murmuring or even getting sick.

The loss of the enemy I have no means of ascertaining. Several boat-loads of apparently dead or wounded men were sent over to New Berne.

Our casualties were caused by the bursting of the 20-pounder and by the shells from the gunboats. The fort did not return our fire at all. Including concussions and other trivial injuries they amount to 23, distributed as follows:

Killed	2
Seriously wounded (2 mortally since died)	7
Slightly wounded	14
Total	23

Among the wounded is the adjutant-general of the brigade, Capt. [N. C.] Hughes, whose face was injured by sand thrown into it by the striking of a shell upon the ground nearly in front of him.

We left the fragments of the 20-pounder that burst on the field in front of the work at Barrington's Ferry. They could not have her taken off without a wagon.

Very respectfully, your obedient servant,

J. J. PETTIGREW,
Brigadier-General, Provisional Army, Confederate States.

Maj. Gen. D. H. HILL,
Commanding Department of North Carolina.

[Inclosure.]

GOLDSBOROUGH, N. C., *March* 10, 1863.

[Brig. Gen. J. J. PETTIGREW:]

I wish you to take all the rifled guns in your own brigade, Daniel's, and the reserve artillery, and the Whitworth gun from Wilmington (if arrived) and move with your brigade to the neighborhood of Barrington's Ferry. Get all your guns in position, if possible, without observation and open a concentrated fire upon the enemy's work at the ferry. It is thought that this can be reduced; if so, push up your guns to it after its fall and open upon the Yankee shipping and barracks. It is important that this bombardment shall begin on Thursday, and your brigade must move part of the way to-morrow. It is proper for you to know that there is to be a combined movement from the James to the Cape Fear, and you are to begin it. Upon your success depends very much the success of the scheme. The condition of Contentnea Creek or the roads below may prevent your march, or there may be other objections which I do not understand. If so, wait until you see me; hope to be down to-morrow. I most earnestly hope, however, there will be no obstacle in the way. I have written to General Garnett, at Greenville, that you would begin on Thursday. Everything is intrusted to your skill, prudence, and good management.

With great respect,

D. H. HILL,
Major-General.

No. 10.

Report of Brig. Gen. Richard B. Garnett, C. S. Army.

HEADQUARTERS GARNETT'S BRIGADE,
Tarborough, N. C., March 11, 1863.

GENERAL: I have the honor to make the following report, which I deem important you should be in possession of:

My last regiment has just arrived. My troops have been very much delayed on the route, owing to want of concert among the railroad agents. I did not receive your letter of instructions until about 1 o'clock to-day, which was the first reliable information I had of my destination. Being entirely ignorant of the country in which I was ordered to operate, I consulted with the post quartermaster, Captain Brown, who informed me that he had done business in Hyde County for many years. He was of the opinion that it had been very much stripped by the Yankees, and introduced to me a Mr. Blount, of the Forty-first North Carolina Regiment, whom he represented as a very trustworthy man and a native of Beaufort, the adjoining county to Hyde. Mr. Blount gives me the following information, which he obtained in Hyde County while endeavoring to get out a horse belonging to him:

The Yankee troops have destroyed the following bridges: Pungo Bridge, 100 yards long; Wilkerson Creek Bridge, 40 yards long; Broad Creek Bridge, 60 yards long, and Rose Bay Bridge, 20 yards long. (All of these except the first are in Hyde County, and must be rebuilt before wagons can pass over the only accessible road through the county. This last fact is confirmed by Captain Brown.) Mr. Blount was told by Dr. Milton Selby and Mr. Davis (gentlemen of high standing in Hyde) that the Federal troops had lately made several raids into the county (one about a week since), destroying and carrying off large quantities of bacon (about 15,000 pounds from a Mr. Bell), besides wantonly killing beef-cattle and other stock. The number of the enemy in their last expedition was about 1,500, Mr. Blount reports ten gunboats on the Sound, two of which he saw in Pungo River.

I have but few mechanics in my command and no building-tools except axes. It would be almost impossible to build a bridge over the Pungo River if attacked by the gunboats, which would probably be the case, as the water is some 20 feet deep and the work would necessarily occupy several days. With regard to the other bridges I can form no idea, being ignorant of the facility for getting timber, &c., in their neighborhood. You can judge, seeing the distance I would have to march and the detention I would meet with from the causes above stated, whether the concert you mentioned with other troops could be carried out.

I shall leave for Greenville to-morrow morning, which place I cannot reach until the next day. As the information may modify your views, I am desirous of hearing from you as soon as possible. You will therefore oblige me very much by replying by the bearer.

Very respectfully, your obedient servant,

R. B. GARNETT,
Brigadier-General, Commanding.

Maj. Gen. D. H. HILL, *Commanding.*

No. 11.

Report of Brig. Gen. Junius Daniel, C. S. Army.

HEADQUARTERS,
Kinston, N. C., March 11, 1863.

GENERAL: Your letters of instructions have been received and delivered. General Robertson left yesterday; General Pettigrew this morning; Major Haskell is about leaving. I am very anxious that you should come down to-day. You are aware that there are four roads from this place to New Berne besides the railroad. I do not think I can advance in any force or with wagons over any other than the lower Trent. The bridges are destroyed on Neuse and Dover roads and it will require a day or two to build them. You are also aware that unless General Robertson operates between the Trent and White Oak that the upper Trent road will be left open to the enemy. I think I understood from General Robertson that his orders were to operate on south side of Trent, allowing him to go beyond the White Oak I presume

The only news from the enemy is that of the 8th. The enemy's cavalry went to Swansborough from Smith's Mill, where they met some of their men in boats. The cavalry returned to Smith's Mill on the 9th.

Very respectfully, &c.,

JUNIUS DANIEL,
Brigadier-General.

Maj. Gen. D. H. HILL,
Commanding at Goldsborough, N. C.

No. 12.

Report of Brig. Gen. Beverly H. Robertson, C. S. Army, commanding Cavalry.

HEADQUARTERS CAVALRY BRIGADE,
March 21, 1863.

MAJOR: I have the honor to report, for the information of the major-general commanding, that on Monday, the 9th instant, in obedience to his written instructions, and immediately after their receipt, I moved with six squadrons of my command—three from the Fifty-ninth and the remainder from the Sixty-third Regiment North Carolina Troops, in all about 500 men—to the south side of Trent River; thence toward Jacksonville, the enemy having been reported advancing in that direction.

Upon my arrival at Huggins' farm I was informed by Capt. [T. W.] Harris, [Company E, Sixty-third North Carolina Troops, or Fifth Cavalry], on picket duty in that vicinity, that the Yankees had recrossed the White Oak River and probably returned to New Berne. Learning next morning (Thursday) that they were reported in force at Trenton, I at once started for that point via Comfort, in the vicinity of which I encamped the same night.

Early on the following day, in order to protect Daniel's right and reconnoiter the country, I proceeded to Pollocksville, where it was stated the enemy had their pickets stationed and were strongly fortified. Upon my arrival there I ascertained the Yankees had crossed Mill Creek several days previous and destroyed the bridge over that stream, which, on account of the recent rains, I found impassable for cavalry, at least in that vicinity. I therefore returned to McDaniel's Mill and encamped, leaving McIntire's squadron on picket at Pollocksville and Mill Creek, with orders to hold those places at all hazards. With a view to carrying out the instructions of the major-general commanding, I detached a party under command of Lieut. W. J. Wiley, Company F, Sixty-third Regiment, with directions to move rapidly and cut the railroad between Sheppardsville and New Berne. I provided the party with a few axes and sent with it the only good guide I had—Private Dennis, Forty-first Regiment North Carolina Troops. With the bulk of my force I determined either to head Mill Creek and operate in the enemy's rear nearer New Berne or move upon Sheppardsville. Upon reaching Richard Oldfield's I was informed by a most respectable, intelligent, and loyal citizen (well known to many of my officers), and perfectly familiar with that section of country, that but few cavalry could be advantageously used there. I therefore decided to detach a good squadron, with instructions to strike a blow at or near Evans' farm, about 7 miles from New

Berne. With his usual alacrity Col. [P. G.] Evans, [Sixty-third North Carolina Troops, or Fifth Cavalry], who is perfectly acquainted with that neighborhood, volunteered to command it and selected Capt. [E. F.] Shaw's squadron. With the remainder of my command I moved on toward Sheppardsville, reaching Peletier's Mill, 20 odd miles distant, before sunset. After gaining from reliable sources all the information I could relative to the enemy's strength, position, &c., I made arrangements to attack Sheppardsville early next day (Sunday), or at least to occupy the enemy's attention at that point while Colonel Ferebee, who promptly offered his services for the purpose, would destroy the railroad above Newport Creek, taking the left-hand road beyond Kennedy's Mill. During the night official dispatches were received, both from the major-general commanding and from Colonel Evans, whose contents induced me to abandon my plan. By reference to the map you will perceive that I had reached a point 25 or 30 miles in front of Smith's Mill, on White Oak, following the only road by which it was possible for me to return.

Colonel Evans having been compelled to fall back over Mill Creek my position was by no means desirable, since in the event of the enemy's advance to the fork of the road at Smith's Mill I should have been forced to cut my way through or swim the White Oak at Swansborough. Some time before day Lieutenant Wiley's party returned and reported they had torn up the railroad track at a point 3 miles above Sheppardsville. From the proximity of the enemy's forces they were compelled to wait until after night to commence operations. I was highly gratified with the promptness and efficiency displayed by Lieutenant Wiley and party.

Colonel Evans had not advanced more than 6 or 7 miles beyond Mill Creek before he encountered a large force of the enemy's cavalry, with which he skirmished awhile, resulting in the loss of one horse killed on our side and disabling one of the enemy's. The colonel then ordered a charge, but the road was in such condition that the horses mired down and two men were dismounted. The shouting, however, had the effect of routing the Yankees, but the colonel did not deem it prudent to pursue, as his rear was much exposed. A prisoner whom we captured reported a large force in that vicinity, as did also a loyal citizen.

Colonel Evans speaks in the highest terms of the coolness and gallantry of Captain Shaw and Lieut. John C. Hines, of Company C. He also mentions the good conduct of Sergt. Lewis H. Darden, whose horse was killed under him; Privates Thomas O. Bunting, Richard H. Lee, Charles Butler, Thomas M. Ferrill, Walter J. Moore, George M. Tatum, George Vaun, Cornelius Timothy, Isaac W. Grist, and Corpl. W. F. Culbreth, all of whom volunteered to go to the front and watch the enemy.

I am pleased to state that my whole command during the march continued in excellent spirits despite the weather, and seemed anxious to engage the foe. My movements were seriously interrupted and impeded by the scarcity of forage, of which there is not sufficient to supply the wants of the few citizens remaining in those counties.

I am greatly in need of a good battery, and respectfully ask that one be ordered to me without delay.

Very respectfully, your obedient servant,

B. H. ROBERTSON,
Brigadier-General.

Maj. ARCHER ANDERSON,
    Asst. Adjt. Gen., Hdqrs. Dept. of N. C., Goldsborough.

MARCH 10–13, 1863.—Demonstration on Plymouth, N. C.

Report of Maj. Walter G. Bartholomew, Twenty-seventh Massachusetts Infantry, commanding Post.

PLYMOUTH, N. C., *March* 13, 1863.

GENERAL : I have the honor to report that on the 10th instant, at about 3 o'clock p. m., the enemy made their appearance, about 50 strong, within rifle-shot of our outpost. I immediately ordered the garrison to take position in line of the inside pickets and sent a company out as skirmishers, who proceeded about 2 miles and found they were in force one-half mile farther on. I reported to Captain Flusser, of the gunboat Perry, but the enemy not making any further demonstrations at that time did not open upon them. After standing an hour in a drenching rain another alarm was given. As the enemy advanced and fired upon our pickets the gunboats commenced to shell them, and they retired. They made their appearance again about 10 in the evening so close to our lines that we could hear them speak distinctly. At a signal from the boats the pickets were drawn in, and they were again shelled, as I learn, with good effect, as several were reported killed and wounded. We were under arms the remainder of the night but were not molested. In the morning I sent a party to reconnoiter, who went as far as Corpeur's blacksmith's shop, which had been used as a picket post, and burned it in sight of the enemy, and ascertained their strength to be about 800 men of the Seventeenth North Carolina Regiment.

This morning (the 13th), about 2 o'clock, three rockets were sent up by the enemy and were answered by two blue ones several miles up the river. Thus we are still in doubt as to what they intend to do, but expect to meet them with determination whatever way they come. Both officers and men behaved with their usual gallantry, and expressed much disappointment that the affair should end so quietly.

I am, general, your very obedient servant,

W. G. BARTHOLOMEW,
Major, Commanding Post.

MARCH 17, 1863.—Skirmish near Franklin, Va.

REPORTS.

No. 1.—Maj. Gen. John J. Peck, U. S. Army.
No. 2.—Col. Samuel P. Spear, Eleventh Pennsylvania Cavalry.

No. 1.

Report of Maj. Gen. John J. Peck, U. S. Army.

SUFFOLK, VA., *March* 17, 1863.

DEAR SIR : Colonel Spear was delayed from four to five hours, and reached the vicinity of Franklin about 9 o'clock. He charged with cavalry, capturing one lieutenant, but his men failed to get over the earthworks, ditches, &c. He made a second charge with like results. He shelled them with effect. He went down toward South Quay and is now returning. Major Stratton led a charge and was twice wounded, but only slightly. Lieut. [G. B.] Knight and one man missing. Lieut. [S. L.] Monday is badly wounded. It was a bold dash for cavalry, and impressed the rebels with the idea that our men were in earnest.

JOHN J. PECK,
Major-General.

General DIX.

No. 2.

Report of Col. Samuel P. Spear, Eleventh Pennsylvania Cavalry.

HDQRS. ELEVENTH PENNSYLVANIA VOL. CAVALRY,
Camp Suffolk, Va., March 18, 1863.

SIR: I have the honor to submit the following report of a reconnaissance made by me in the direction of Franklin, &c.:

On the evening of the 16th I received orders from the commanding general, through his assistant adjutant-general, to make a thorough investigation of the ground occupied by a supposed force on the Blackwater, and opposite to, on this side of the river from Franklin. I accordingly left Suffolk in command of 350 cavalry and four pieces of Davis' battery, and, proceeding very cautiously, arrived at and found the enemy's outer pickets at Hebron Church, half a mile from Carrsville and 4½ miles this side of Franklin. They at once fled to the woods, and undoubtedly, by a pathway, gave information of my approach. I advanced, and at a point 1 mile this side of Franklin found a small picket; captured a first lieutenant in charge and sent him at once to your headquarters. Here I ordered a charge of three companies, under Maj. F. A. Stratton, and he gallantly made the same, in which, immediately under the breastworks of the enemy, he lost his horse and full equipments. Some of his men were wounded and Lieut. Samuel L. Monday was badly wounded in the abdomen. The party under command of Major Stratton, after examining the enemy's defenses, &c., and in accordance to orders, returned and joined my main body. Captain Davis was then directed and threw about eighteen shells directly into the enemy's lines, which must have done great destruction.

I then ordered cease firing and made a second charge of three companies, under Maj. George T. Cornog, which was done in such a manner as to merit my thanks. The enemy's intrenchments, masked battery, and rifle-pits were so constructed as to be impassable for cavalry, and while no results could be gained by me, enabled him to a very great advantage.

The fortifications, rifle-pits, &c., are about 200 yards from Blackwater River and running nearly parallel with it, and it is estimated, by a minute examination, that one regiment of infantry, about 250 cavalry, two 10-pounder rifled guns, and one section of rocket battery is the strength of the enemy on this side of the river at that point.

Inclosed please find a list of wounded and missing,* and see note of some since returned. Lieutenant Knight must, I think, have been thrown from his horse, and is probably now a prisoner unhurt.

It gives me pleasure to commend highly the conduct of Majs. Franklin A. Stratton and George T. Cornog for their prompt, energetic, and spirited manner in conducting their respective charges, and unless

---

* Not found. Regimental returns report 1 officer and 2 men wounded, and 1 officer and 11 men missing.

these movements had been made it would have been impossible to have given a correct or even a slight account of the enemy's defenses, strength, &c.

Lieut. Samuel L. Monday was seriously wounded* while in the performance of his duty, and I regret exceedingly this serious injury to an excellent and promising officer.

Capt. Phineas A. Davis is deserving of great cred t for his portion of duty in the reconnaissance, and officers and men all behaved well.

Having performed the duty assigned me, I returned to camp at 7 last evening.

While I regret exceedingly the loss in missing I am positive that I could not have carried out my instructions with less casualties.

Very respectfully, your obedient servant,

S. P. SPEAR,
Colonel Eleventh Pennsylvania Cavalry.

Maj. B. B. FOSTER,
Assistant Adjutant-General.

MARCH 23, 1863.—Skirmish at Winfield, N. C.

REPORTS.

No. 1.—Maj. Gen. John A. Dix, U. S. Army, commanding the Department of Virginia.
No. 2.—Maj. Gen. John G. Foster, U. S. Army, commanding the Department of North Carolina.
No. 3.—Maj. Gen. John J. Peck, U. S. Army.

No. 1.

Report of Maj. Gen. John A. Dix, U. S. Army, commanding the Department of Virginia.

FORT MONROE, VA., *March 29, 1863.*

On the 23d the enemy, with three companies Forty-second North Carolina and a guerrilla force, under command of Colonel Brown, Forty-second North Carolina, attacked the post at Winfield, on the Chowan, below Gatesville. Lieutenant McLane, with part of a company of the First North Carolina Volunteers, took refuge in a block-house, and after an hour and a half's fighting repulsed the enemy. The next day General Foster came up from Plymouth with three companies, which were landed and sent in pursuit. Four companies of the Eleventh Pennsylvania Cavalry were sent from Suffolk the same day by General Peck. Some of Colonel Brown's command succeeded in crossing the Chowan. The residue were overtaken by General Foster's companies, and after a skirmish were dispersed and scattered in the swamps. Our troops were trying to hunt them up at last accounts. This morning the enemy attacked Williamsburg with infantry and cavalry, and were repulsed by the Fifth Pennsylvania Cavalry, under Colonel Lewis. They had retreated an hour ago. All was quiet at Williamsburg, and Colonel Lewis had re-established his pickets.

JOHN A. DIX,
Major-General.

Major-General HALLECK, *General-in-Chief.*

---

* Died of his wounds March 18, 1863.

No. 2.

Report of Maj. Gen. John G. Foster, U. S. Army, commanding the Department of North Carolina.

CHOWAN RIVER, STEAMER JOHN FARON,
March 25, 1863.

GENERAL: The rebels attacked the post at Winfield on the morning of the 23d at daybreak. Lieutenant McLane, with the portion of his company (of the First North Carolina Volunteers) that had not left him, took refuge in the block-house, and after one and a half hours' fighting repulsed the enemy, whose force consisted of three companies of the Forty-second North Carolina and a guerrilla force, all under the command of Colonel Brown, of the Forty-second North Carolina. I was at Plymouth at the time and ran up with three companies, landed them, and started them in pursuit, at the same time patroling the river with my boat to prevent their recrossing and also sending for some cavalry to General Peck, at Suffolk, to scour the country and pick up stragglers. Some of Colonel Brown's command succeeded in recrossing, but the remainder were overtaken by our companies at Rocky Hock Creek yesterday morning and attacked, and after a short skirmish scattered into the swamps.

Four companies of your fine regiment, the Eleventh Pennsylvania Cavalry, arrived at night, too late to do much scouting, but will to-day try to force out these fugitive rebels. You can, if you choose, send a brief epitome of this small affair to General Halleck.

If you still entertain the idea of holding the country north of the Albemarle, now garrisoned by very small parties, I shall be happy to vacate whenever you find it convenient to replace my small garrisons or to establish others more convenient for you. I think the post at Winfield should be maintained to intercept smuggling across the Chowan River.

With great respect, very truly, yours,

J. G. FOSTER,
Major-General, Volunteers.

General JOHN A. DIX,
    Comdg. Seventh Army Corps, Fort Monroe, Va.

No. 3.

Reports of Maj. Gen. John J. Peck, U. S. Army.

SUFFOLK, VA., *March* 23, 1863.

The post at Winfield, N. C., was attacked this morning by a considerable force of guerrillas in the absence of the gunboat. One of the pickets came in. I at once ordered Major Stratton to go down with a party of cavalry and render any assistance in his power.

JOHN J. PECK,
Major-General.

General DIX.

SUFFOLK, VA., *March* 24, 1863

A communication from General Foster's headquarters reached me this morning. The gunboats had arrived at Winfield from Plymouth and relieved the garrison after all their barracks were burned. They crossed 8 miles below. Yesterday I sent a strong party, under Major Stratton, and hope we may be able to cut off and capture some of them. Shall follow them up.

JOHN J. PECK,
Major-General.

General Dix.

—

SUFFOLK, VA., *March 25, 1863.*

Major Stratton reached Winfield at 8 a. m., in excellent time. The gunboat had been back with four companies of infantry and left again prior to his arrival. The infantry were in pursuit. The rebels moved off toward Edenton. Some heavy guns were heard in that direction.

JOHN J. PECK,
Major-General.

Major-General Dix.

———

MARCH 29, 1863.—Skirmish at Williamsburg, Va.

REPORTS, ETC.*

No. 1.—Brig. Gen. Richard Busteed, U. S. Army, commanding at Yorktown, and orders.
No. 2.—Lieut. Col. William Lewis, Fifth Pennsylvania Cavalry.
No. 3.—Brig. Gen. Henry A. Wise, C. S. Army.
No. 4.—Col. William B. Tabb, C. S. Army.
No. 5.—Capt. G. A. Wallace, C. S. Army.

No. 1.

Report of Brig. Gen. Richard Busteed, U. S. Army, commanding at York-town, and orders.

YORKTOWN, *March 30, 1863.*

I sent you this morning the report of Colonel Lewis, who is now here. Our casualties were 5 wounded, 6 missing, and 2 murdered. The boots were stolen from off our dead.

The enemy's loss in killed and wounded, according to the most reliable accounts, is at least 18. He came with a train of wagons and four field pieces, and was guided into the town by citizens of Williamsburg at three different points.

I will send you to-morrow three of the enemy's force, who deserted to us. I have the pleasure to report everything quiet now.

RICHARD BUSTEED,
Brigadier-General, Commanding.

General Dix.

—

HEADQUARTERS FOURTH ARMY CORPS,
Yorktown, Va., March 29, 1863.

Colonel LEWIS:

I received on Thursday from General Dix a telegram that Williamsburg must not be destroyed unless actually taken possession of by the

———

* See also Dix to Keyes, May 26, 1863, in "Correspondence, etc.," *post.*

enemy, and then not unless absolutely necessary for our own safety. You must be guided by these rules in all that you do.

                    RICHARD BUSTEED,
        Brigadier-General, Commanding the Forces at Yorktown.

ORDERS.]   FOURTH ARMY CORPS,
                            Yorktown, Va., March 29, 1863.

COMMANDING OFFICER,
        Williamsburg, Va.:

The attack of the enemy on our lines at Williamsburg this (Sabbath) morning was accompanied by circumstances of so aggravated a character as to call for prompt and severe punishment to those most implicated. Conclusive evidence has been furnished to the commanding general that the attack was aided, if not planned, by citizens of Williamsburg and carried to a successful end by them and their abettors outside the lines; that the enemy were led into the city by one or more citizens, and that when once in they were enabled by the aid of the citizens and their own overwhelming force to occupy the most advantageous points for attack and defense; that upon their occupation of the city they were assisted by the citizens in their attack upon our forces, who were fired upon from the houses lining the streets, the dead bodies of the murdered being despoiled and stripped, their boots pulled off their feet; that the stores of their sympathizers within the city were thrown open to their advantage and their horses loaded with packs prepared for their arrival. To provide against a repetition of the outrage, the commanding general directs:

1st. That all the privileges to all store-keepers in the city of Williamsburg to purchase and sell goods are revoked.

2d. That all citizens in the city of Williamsburg and vicinity who are willing to take the oath of allegiance to the Government of the United States will present themselves to the provost-marshal of Williamsburg for the purpose of taking such oath on or before the 1st day of April, 1863.

3d. That all citizens in the city of Williamsburg and vicinity who are not willing to take the oath of allegiance to the Government of the United States, excepting the servants and employés of the Eastern Lunatic Asylum of the State of Virginia, will prepare themselves and their families to be placed beyond the lines now occupied by the armed forces of the said Government by the 2d day of April, 1863.

4th. The greatest publicity possible will be given to this order and the cause leading to its issue, and the end to be accomplished by its enforcement will be communicated to all concerned.

By order of Brigadier-General Busteed, commanding post:

                    C. C. SUYDAM,
                    Assistant Adjutant-General.

                    YORKTOWN, VA., *March 30, 1863.*

Col. WILLIAM LEWIS,
        Commanding Fifth Pennsylvania Cavalry:

General Dix directs that the order I issued to you to-day shall not be enforced. You will therefore consider it as revoked. Notify the provost-marshal at Williamsburg.

                    RICHARD BUSTEED,
                    Brigadier-General, Commanding.

HDQRS. DEPT. OF VIRGINIA, SEVENTH ARMY CORPS,
Fort Monroe, March 31, 1863.

Maj. Gen. E. D. KEYES,
Commanding, Yorktown, Va. :

GENERAL: In view of the raid on Williamsburg on Sunday last, and rumors of complicity on the part of the inhabitants with the assailants, you will give orders as follows:

1st. No persons will be allowed to go to Williamsburg from any point south of Fort Magruder without taking the oath of allegiance.

2d. No citizen of Williamsburg will be permitted to go to Yorktown or to any place south of Fort Magruder without taking the oath of allegiance.

3d. No person will be allowed to trade in Williamsburg without first taking the oath of allegiance.

4th. No further supplies will be allowed to be taken to Williamsburg for the use of the inhabitants, except the produce of the neighboring farms, until further orders.

An investigation will be made into the circumstances alleged to have occurred at the time of the attack, and if the parties accused of aiding and abetting it are detected and reasonable presumption of their guilt is shown they will be brought before a military tribunal and punished according to the laws of war.

The objections to the order issued by General Busteed are:

1st. If the enemy should come in overwhelming force and dispossess us of Williamsburg the order would be an idle threat.

2d. It assumes without investigation that the reports of complicity with the enemy are true and that all the inhabitants are implicated, whereas we must ascertain who is guilty and leave the innocent undisturbed.

3d. It has not been the policy of the Government in towns which are occupied as outposts, and which may only be temporarily held as such, to apply the tests imposed by General Busteed's order; but on the contrary to leave the people unmolested if they continue in the quiet pursuit of their customary occupations and give no aid or comfort to the enemy.

4th. An order of such extensive scope as that of General Busteed, who was only temporarily in command in your absence, should not have been issued without authority of the commanding general of the department.

Should it be found that any house in Williamsburg was occupied by the enemy with the consent of the owner for the purpose of firing upon our troops it will be razed to the ground.

JOHN A. DIX,
Major-General.

No. 2.

Report of Lieut. Col. William Lewis, Fifth Pennsylvania Cavalry.

HEADQUARTERS FIFTH PENNSYLVANIA CAVALRY,
Near Williamsburg, Va., March 29, 1863.

COLONEL: I have the honor to report that at about 5 a. m. this day a body of infantry, 100 strong, drove in our pickets near Lipscomb's farm and advanced into Williamsburg while a large force of cavalry, estimated at 1,000 in number, advanced on the Richmond road, having with them four pieces of artillery and a number of wagons. The cavalry engaging the attention of Lieutenant Wenzel, of Company C, who with 26 of his men were stationed on the Richmond road, the infantry succeeded in getting in his rear. Lieutenant Wenzel, finding himself cut off, drew saber and charged through their infantry to join Captain Stetson, in command of reserve pickets, but in so doing had 2 men killed and himself and 3 others wounded; 9 men additional were dismounted and are missing. Lieutenant Wenzel behaved with great gallantry. He gives a very clear account of the whole affair, and is positive as to the strength of enemy, as he allowed them to approach within 500 yards before retreating. Their battery was planted at the college ready for action. On ascertaining their strength Captain Stetson, with picket reserve, fell back and joined the regiment in line of battle near Fort Magruder under my command. Before receiving contrary orders from your headquarters I ordered Captain Bayley, in command of Fort Magruder, to shell the enemy out of the town, which was accomplished after firing about 12 rounds from a 6-pounder. Our picket line was then reestablished, the enemy still holding a position in the woods about one-half mile beyond Williamsburg. One 24-pounder was then run from Fort Magruder and preparations made for an advance, with the idea of clearing our picket line, whereupon the enemy retired. In this affair we lost 7 horses besides the men previously named. The enemy lost in killed and wounded 12 men, whom they carried away in their wagons, and 4 deserters.

After quiet was restored I returned to camp with my command, and arrived here at 11 a. m.

Very respectfully, your obedient servant,

WM. LEWIS,
Lieutenant-Colonel, Commanding.

Lieut. Col. C. C. SUYDAM,
  Asst. Adjt. Gen., Fourth Army Corps, Yorktown, Va.

[Indorsement.]

HEADQUARTERS FOURTH ARMY CORPS,
Yorktown, Va., March 29, 1863.

Respectfully forwarded.

The within report is furnished to the major-general commanding the department for his information. I am, however, not satisfied with its completeness, and have directed Lieutenant-Colonel Lewis to report to me in the morning that I may obtain a more full and detailed account of the occurrences of this morning.

RICHARD BUSTEED,
Brigadier-General.

———

No. 3.

Report of Brig. Gen. Henry A. Wise, C. S. Army.

MARCH 31, 1863.

*   *   *   *   *   *   *

Colonel Tabb, on March 29 instant, made a descent upon the Federals at Williamsburg. The result of the expedition was the capture of the town and the killing and capturing of about 15 of the enemy without loss on the part of Colonel Tabb. Some time since, as has been reported already, Colonel Tabb captured some 36 Federal cavalry. The cavalry on the Peninsula are doing good duty and are actively employed. They are doing all that can be done with them.

Very respectfully,

HENRY A. WISE,
Brigadier-General.

No. 4.

Report of Col. William B. Tabb, C. S. Army.

HEADQUARTERS,
Diascund Bridge, Va., March 30, 1863.

CAPTAIN: I have to report the failure of my attempt to capture Fort Magruder. My plan of operations was as follows:

The whole command moved together to Petitt's farm, between 3 and 4 miles from Williamsburg, on the Telegraph road. Here 100 infantry, under Capt. G. A. Wallace, were detached. Captain Wallace was directed to gain the rear of Fort Magruder by a detour to the left through Petitt's and Lipscomb's farms, passing between the pickets at Capitol Landing Bridge and Williamsburg, and to surprise the fort before daybreak. The main body moved to within 1½ miles of Williamsburg. The report of Captain Wallace's guns was to be the signal for a general advance. Signals were concerted by which I could be apprised of the success or failure of the assault. Had the fort been carried Captain Wallace would have been re-enforced there and a detachment sent to King's Mill; if he failed the main body was to form in line of battle at the east end of the town, and Captain Wallace, falling back over ground protected from the guns at the fort and inaccessible to cavalry, would come up by the Capitol Landing road, enter Williamsburg in my rear, and so rejoin the main body. Partly through the blunders of guides, in whose efficiency I have every reason to rely, and partly through straggling among the men by which the command was divided and time lost in getting it together, Captain Wallace's detachment was two hours going not quite 4 miles. They reached Capitol Landing road after daybreak and came in full view of the enemy's pickets. All thought of capturing the post by surprise had now to be abandoned, and an open assault would have involved a sacrifice altogether disproportionate to the advantage to be gained. Captain Wallace prudently forbore to make the attack, and, signaling me to that effect, moved up toward Williamsburg on the Capitol Landing road. The main body moving rapidly forward drove the picket and provost guard back on Captain Wallace, who, without loss, killed and wounded 4 and made 11 prisoners. I will forward Captain Wallace's report.

The failure to capture Fort Magruder involves the failure of the expedition to King's Mill. The most direct road looking from Williamsburg to King's Mill passes over two mill-dams, both of which have been cut, making the road impassable for cavalry. The only other road passes within close range of Fort Magruder. The citizens of Williamsburg inform me, however, that nothing could be gained by going there; the negroes have all been removed.

Large smokes were observed at Fort Magruder and Whittaker's Mill. Mr Douglas, the superintendent of the lunatic asylum, who was watching from the tower, reported that the enemy were burning their stores.

I am still confident that the enterprise is easily practicable, but in this connection I will write again.

Very respectfully, your obedient servant,

W. B. TABB,
Colonel, Commanding.

Capt. J. H. Pearce,
Assistant Adjutant-General.

No. 5.

Report of Capt. G. A. Wallace, C. S. Army.

Diascund Bridge, Va., *March* 30, 1863.

Sir : I beg to hand you here my report of the expedition intrusted to me :

The object being the capture of Fort Magruder by surprise, I left you at a point on the Telegraph road about 3 miles from Williamsburg, at 2 a. m. yesterday. I took with me two guides, Companies F and A, Fifty-ninth Virginia Regiment, and Capt. [J. C.] Hill's company, of Forty-sixth Virginia Regiment, numbering 102 muskets. It was thought by your guides that we could reach the point from which I was to make the assault on the fort before daylight, but the guides whom you gave me, though they knew the direction, seemed to know nothing of any path. We were led over a very rough country—through ploughed fields, over fences, deep and wide ditches, through a swamp that took the men over knee-deep, and through some timber with very thick undergrowth. Owing to all this our progress was very slow; as it was, the darkness caused Company A, Fifty-ninth Regiment, and Captain Hill's company to be separated from my command, and at daylight I reached the open country about 1 mile from the fort with Company F, Fifty-ninth Regiment, only. I sent back one of the guides to find the two lost companies and when he returned with them it was so light that we could be seen, and were undoubtedly seen from Williamsburg. I determined therefore to push on. On reaching a point near the Capitol Landing road we discovered three of the enemy, mounted, coming from Williamsburg. They having discovered who we were turned their horses, and I ordered a volley to be fired on them. I then determined, being discovered, to make my way through Williamsburg to form a junction with you on the Telegraph road, if not at Williamsburg itself. A few minutes after the first I fired the second volley, as the signal agreed on, and was proceeding over the old field toward the town when we were threatened by a body of cavalry on our left. I immediately formed line of battle and advanced at double-quick and in good order. They seeming to advance, I halted and fired several rounds. Having dispersed them I marched by the flank to the town. Another large body of cavalry in the mean time was discovered in a field on our left, who followed **us** to the town. When I struck the main street, up which I filed my force, this last body followed. In the mean time we captured 4 prisoners, horses, arms, &c., and fired on several who would not surrender.   I then discovered about 30 or 40 cavalry forming ahead of us at College Place.   Having thus the enemy to contend with at each end of the street I formed my men on the right side of Main street, when the body at College Place advanced in a charge.   We held our fire until they were close to us.   Our fire broke and confused them.   We killed 3 men at this fire and wounded several and took 7 prisoners who were not wounded, besides killing and capturing the like number of horses, arms, &c.   I continued to move, but made another stand immediately at College Place upon discovering that the enemy in my rear moved after us.   While in this position the enemy in the rear retired and your force then appeared.

This ends my report except to say I feel sorry your main object failed.

The enemy's loss in killed and wounded will be at least 13 and prisoners 11.   We did not lose a man.   Our men acted very bravely.

I am, colonel, very respectfully, your obedient servant,

G. A. WALLACE,
Captain, Commanding.

Col. W. B. TABB,
Commanding Forces near Diascund, Va.

MARCH 30, 1863.—Skirmish near Deep Gully, N. C.

*Extract from " Record of Events" of Second Brigade, Fifth Division, Eighteenth Army Corps.**

Five companies of this brigade picketed that portion of our lines running from red house to Trent River, in the vicinity of Deep Gully, at which place, on March 30, a slight skirmish with the enemy's pickets occurred, on which occasion Private Fosdick, Company C, One hundred and fifty eighth New York Volunteers, was wounded and captured by the enemy.

---

* From Return for month of April, 1863.

MARCH 30-APRIL 20, 1863.—Siege of Washington, N. C., and pursuit of the Confederate forces.

SUMMARY OF THE PRINCIPAL EVENTS.

Mar.   30, 1863.—Skirmish at Rodman's Point, Pamlico River.
          Washington invested by the Confederate forces under Maj. Gen. Daniel H. Hill.

April   1, 1863.—Engagement at Rodman's Point.*
         2, 1863.—Engagement at Hill's Point, Pamlico River.*
       4-5, 1863.—Engagement at Rodman's Point.*
         9, 1863.—Action at Blount's Creek.
      13-21, 1863.—Expeditions from New Berne to Swift Creek Village.
        15, 1863.—Siege raised.
        16, 1863.—Affairs at Hill's and Rodman's Points.
      16-21, 1863.—Expedition from New Berne toward Kinston
      17-18, 1863.—Skirmishes at Core Creek.
      17-19, 1863.—Expedition from New Berne to Washington
        19, 1863.—Skirmish at Big Swift Creek.
        20, 1863.—Skirmish at Sandy Ridge.

REPORTS, ETC.†

No. 1.—Maj. Gen. John G. Foster, U. S. Army, commanding the Department of North Carolina.

No. 2.—Capt. David A. Taylor, Third New York Light Artillery, Chief Signal Officer.

No. 3.—Brig. Gen. Edward E. Potter, U. S. Army, commanding at Washington, of operations April 16-17.

No. 4.—Itinerary of the First Division, Eighteenth Army Corps, Brig. Gen. Innis N. Palmer, U. S. Army, commanding, April 7-25.

No. 5.—Brig. Gen. Henry M. Naglee, U. S. Army, commanding Second Division, of Expedition from New Berne to Washington, April 17-19.

No. 6.—Brig. Gen. Charles A. Heckman, U. S. Army, commanding First Brigade, of Expedition from New Berne to Washington, April 17-19.

No. 7.—Itinerary of the Fourth Division, Brig. Gen. Henry W. Wessells, U. S. Army, commanding, March 15-April 13.

No. 8.—Brig. Gen. Henry Prince, U. S. Army, commanding Fifth Division, of operations on the Pamlico, April 4-6, and Expedition from New Berne toward Kinston, April 16-21, with resulting correspondence.

No. 9.—Col. Silas P. Richmond, Third Massachusetts Infantry, of operations April 7-10 and April 16-21.

No. 10.—Capt. John M. Willson, Third New York Cavalry, of skirmish at Sandy Ridge, April 20.

No. 11.—Col. J. Richter Jones, Fifty-eighth Pennsylvania Infantry, of skirmish at Sandy Ridge, April 20.

No. 12.—Brig. Gen. Francis B. Spinola, U. S. Army, commanding Provisional Division and First Brigade, Fifth Division, of operations on the Pamlico, April 1-4; action at Blount's Creek, April 9, and Expeditions from New Berne to Swift Creek Village, April 13-21.

No. 13.—Itinerary of the Second Brigade, Fifth Division, Col. James Jourdan, One hundred and fiftieth New York Infantry, commanding, April 7-22.

No. 14.—Brig. Gen. Robert Ransom, jr., C. S. Army, of skirmish at Sandy Ridge, April 20.

---

* Between Union gunboats and Confederate batteries.
† For reports of Actg. Rear-Admiral Lee, Commanders Davenport and Renshaw, Lieutenant-Commander McCann, Acting Volunteer Lieutenants MacDearmid and Graves, and Acting Masters Saltonstall and Boomer, U. S. Navy, see Annual Report of the Secretary of the Navy, December 7, 1863. See also D. H. Hill to Beauregard, April 20, 1863, in "Correspondence, etc.," post.

No. 1.

Reports of Maj. Gen. John G. Foster, U. S. Army, commanding the Department of North Carolina.

FORT WASHINGTON,
Washington, N. C., April 3, 1863.

GENERAL: I have the honor to report that hearing of an approaching attack on this place by D. H. Hill's *corps d'armée*, I started from New Berne at 2 o'clock on Sunday, March 29, ordering re-enforcements to follow at once.

In consequence of the transport getting aground at the mouth of the river the troops did not arrive before the enemy succeeded in investing the place by placing batteries on the river banks and on the roads leading from the town.

I found here a garrison of only sixteen companies of infantry, one company of artillery, and 25 cavalry—1,200 men in all. The enemy opened fire on our advance posts on Monday night and on Wednesday morning at daybreak opened from batteries of rifled guns on the opposite side of the river.

One gunboat, the Commodore Hull, received ninety-eight shots from a battery of Whitworth guns. I put up batteries on this side of the river to reply to and draw the fire of three guns from the gunboat; at the same time I sent word to General Palmer to send troops to take the batteries on the river by landing and attacking the batteries, while the gunboats (also to be sent) attacked them in front.

Owing to the lack of transports—the most of our vessels being absent at Hilton Head—the force brought and which arrived under General Prince on Tuesday and Friday, below the Hill's Point Battery, was not sufficient to cope with the enemy's force supporting the battery. I therefore directed him to send a regiment or two through the blockade in boats and then return to New Berne and march across to this place, attacking the enemy in the rear and raising the siege. I am, however, anxious lest the disposable force now left in New Berne may not be sufficient to effect this object, and therefore ask, respectfully but earnestly, that re-enforcements be sent immediately to New Berne in force not less than 5,000 men. It will also aid me very much to have General Dix and a force from Suffolk to join two regiments at Plymouth and make a demonstration from that place. This should not, however, interfere with the rapid sending of troops to New Berne, as their want is very urgent. I am quite confident that I can hold out here till the place is relieved. I shall not leave until that time, as I consider my presence absolutely necessary. The firing on both sides has been continued at intervals since Wednesday, but without material injury or effect.

I would most respectfully but earnestly renew my application to have the detachment of the Eighteenth Army Corps now at Hilton Head returned to this department to replace the troops that now may be sent from General Dix's department to meet the present emergency. I can effect more with those men than with superior numbers of other troops, and their discipline and efficiency are fast being impaired by the inactivity and unfortunate circumstances surrounding them at Port Royal.

I am confident that heavy operations will be necessary in this State, and that the most desperate efforts are and will continue to be made to drive us from the towns now occupied. I trust therefore that you will regard my application for the immediate return of this detachment as tending to meet a necessity of the war.

Referring to the pressing necessity for immediate re-enforcements to relieve me at this place, I would respectfully suggest that the 5,000 men be sent temporarily from General Dix's command and with the utmost expedition.

I understand, from an officer who came through the blockade, that General Palmer has already made the above request in substance of General Dix.

I have honor to be, very respectfully, your obedient servant,

J. G. FOSTER,
Major-General, Commanding.

Maj. Gen. H. W. HALLECK,
    Commander-in-Chief U. S. Army, Washington, D. C.

—

NEW BERNE, N. C., VIA FORT MONROE, VA.,
                    April 23, 1863—3 p. m.

I left New Berne on the morning of the 18th with a force to raise the siege at Washington. Our advance of cavalry, with Brigadier-General Naglee, came upon the enemy's rear-guard of cavalry near Washington, and, after driving it several miles, routed it, capturing their battle-flag and taking a surgeon and 5 men prisoners, killing and wounding several. The cavalry were still following their retreat yesterday. I found that the main body withdrew from before Washington with the artillery on the night of the 15th. General Potter immediately leveled their batteries in front of the town, and after occupying Hill's and Rodman's Points made a dash after the retiring force, capturing 2 officers and a drum-major. Everything is now secure.

J. G. FOSTER,
Major-General.

Maj. Gen. H. W. HALLECK,
    General-in-Chief.

—

HDQRS. DEPT. OF NORTH CAROLINA, 18TH ARMY CORPS,
                New Berne, N. C., April 30, 1863.

GENERAL: I have the honor to make the following report in relation to the siege of Washington, N. C.:

Learning an attack was to be made upon Washington I left here, with several members of my staff, for that place, arriving there at 7.30 a. m. on March 30. The garrison of the place was eight companies of the Forty-fourth Massachusetts Volunteer Militia, eight companies of the Twenty-seventh Massachusetts Volunteers, two companies of the First North Carolina (Union) Volunteers, one company of the Third New York Cavalry, and one company of the Third New York Artillery. After making an examination of the works and giving necessary orders as to strengthening them I at once sent out a reconnaissance of one company of the Forty-fourth Massachusetts Volunteer Militia, one piece of artillery, and a few cavalrymen to ascertain if the enemy held the cross-roads 3 miles from Washington. When about 1½ miles from the town the party was fired upon by the enemy in some force. They returned and reported.

I also sent one company of the First North Carolina (Union) Volunteers, Captain Lyon, and one 12-pounder Wiard to occupy Rodman's Point, on the south side of Pamlico River and 1½ miles below the town. This company landed at the Point, and, having thrown out pickets, erected an earthwork in which they placed the field piece. That night their pickets were driven in and the company driven to their boats. At daylight the next a. m. the enemy advanced to the beach and forced the boats off, wounding Captain Lyon and 9 men. At sundown our pickets on the Jamesville road were driven in by the enemy's cavalry.

Tuesday, March 31, a cutter of the United States gunboat Commodore Hull was sent down the river after a scow upon which were some men of the First North Carolina who had been driven from Rodman's Point the previous night. When opposite Hill's Point it was opened upon by a battery of four rifled guns. It was also fired upon by a battery at Swan's Point. At 12 o'clock midnight a schooner, in charge of Mr. Gilbert, was dispatched to New Berne with orders for re-enforcements. The enemy sent in a flag of truce to open communication with the commanding officer. I refused to receive any flag of truce.

April 1.—At daylight this morning the gunboat Commodore Hull was opened upon by a battery at Rodman's Point (opposite which she was lying in order to prevent the erection of a battery) and from one a little above which had been thrown up during the night. The Hull got aground opposite the battery, but maintained a gallant fight during the day, though with no result. At night she floated off and returned to town.

April 2.—The gunboats below the barricade were seen engaging the Hill's Point Battery. The movements of the enemy indicating the erection of his siege batteries, I caused traverses to be erected along the line of our intrenchments, merlons to be placed on the fort, the door of the magazine to be casemated, the ditches to be enlarged and flooded by means of dams, and the whole garrison generally was steadily kept at work strengthening the defenses; 10,000 rations were put in the fort, with the intention of holding it to the last extremity even were other portions of the line forced by the enemy's column. A redoubt was built on the right flank of our works, near Block-house No. 4, bearing on Rodman's Point, upon which were mounted three guns. Another redoubt was erected, covering the marsh on the right of the fortifications. At night a schooner loaded with ammunition and commissary stores ran the batteries, as small boats had previously done.

April 3.—At daylight the enemy opened fire upon the gunboats from a battery abreast the town and near the New Berne road, which they had erected during the night. This battery was silenced by the gunboats. A redoubt was erected at the end of the bridge crossing the Tar River and in the town, for the purpose of sweeping the bridge and also the streets of the town in case the enemy should succeed in forcing an entrance, and in it was placed one 6-pounder gun. The work was erected and to be manned by Captain Jocknick with his company of cavalry, dismounted. I ordered a party of this company of cavalry, under Lieutenant O'Brien, to cross the river in boats and endeavor to capture the gun on the marsh opposite the steamer Louisiana, which had been silenced by the gunboats. It was found impracticable to reach its position, owing to the intervening swamps.

April 4.—This morning the gunboat Ceres, Lieutenant MacDearmid, ran the blockade with a good supply of ammunition.   At noon General Potter embarked on the gunboat Ceres, with two companies of the Twenty-seventh Massachusetts and one company of the Third New York Cavalry (dismounted) for the purpose of driving the enemy from Rodman's Point and occupying the position ourselves.   The Ceres got aground nearly opposite the battery, and it being impossible to accomplish the desired object the men were landed in small boats on the Washington side of the river, below Block-house No. 4, and thence returned to the town.

April 5.—The Ceres, after being exposed to the fire of the battery for twelve hours, to which she gallantly replied until her ammunition was exhausted, floated off at night and came up to the town.

April 6.—An abatis was placed in front of our battery on the Plymouth road and on the borders of the creek bounding our right flank.

April 7.—A battery of two guns opened from the woods beyond the creek upon Fort Hamilton.   A battery (Fort Ceres) was built on the left of Block-house No. 1 and one 30-pounder Parrott mounted upon it and manned by officers and men from the Ceres for the purpose of commanding the approach to the town by way of the river from above, it having been heard that the enemy intended coming down in scows protected by cotton bales.

April 8.—The enemy fired all day at the gunboats and Fort Hamilton, to which the fort did not reply for want of ammunition.   One gun was placed in battery on the south side of the river opposite the gunboats, but was silenced by them.   At dark I commenced works on Castle Island, situated in the middle of the river opposite the town.

April 9.—This morning I discovered the enemy had built four batteries, Nos. 1, 2, 3, and 4, in front and to the right of the fort, and were mounting guns.   We opened fire on them to disturb the working parties.   I was obliged to abandon the attempt to continue the work on Castle Island by daylight, owing to the fire of the enemy's batteries across the river.   Two small schooners, with Lieutenant-Colonel McChesney, First North Carolina (Union) Volunteers, and Master McKeever on board, arrived from below, bringing ammunition.

April 10.—At 8.30 a. m. the enemy opened fire upon the fort from Batteries Nos. 1, 2, 3, and 4, one gun in each.   The fire was returned by three 32-pounders from the fort and by a 32-pounder in the battery on the Jamesville road.   After firing for somewhat over an hour the enemy withdrew their guns from sight and ceased firing.

April 11.—The enemy opened fire upon the fort and the lines at 7.30 a. m. from all their batteries.   The fort and the gun on the Jamesville road replied.

April 12.—At 9 a. m. the enemy opened fire from Batteries Nos. 1, 2, 3, 4, and from a new one (No. 5) at the right of their former batteries. We replied, and the enemy withdrew their guns from sight after an hour's firing.   The gunboats Hull and Eagle, discovering the enemy repairing the battery opposite them with cotton bales, opened upon it, set the cotton on fire, and drove the gunners from their posts.

April 13.—The enemy endeavored to replace a gun in the work on the cotton battery, but were forced by the gunboats to abandon the undertaking.   Learning the enemy had small armed boats and scows in the river for the purpose of capturing our dispatch boats and interrupting communication between the town and the gunboats below, Captain MacDearmid, of the Ceres, and Captain Gouraud, aide-de-camp, started upon a schooner with a boat howitzer to clear the river.   The schooner was fired into by the enemy's boats; she replied, and drove the boats ashore. The batteries at Rodman's and Hill's Points opened upon her also, striking her, but without damage.

That night the steam-transport Escort, with hay bales placed on her guards and decks as a protection, ran the batteries. There also arrived two small schooners with ammunition and commissary stores. The Escort had on board the Fifth Rhode Island Volunteers, Col. H. T. Sisson, and a plentiful supply of ammunition and commissary stores. She had 60 shots fired at her from the batteries but was not struck.

April 14.—The Fifth Rhode Island Volunteers were properly placed on the line of works. At 12 m. the enemy opened fire with all their batteries and were replied to by all of ours. After an hour's firing they withdrew their guns from sight. Regarding everything as safe in the town, and the re-enforcements and men, with the supplies of ammunition and provisions, as ample until I could raise the siege, I determined to run the blockade and place myself at the head of the relieving force in order to insure more efficiency in its conduct. I therefore embarked on board the Escort for the purpose of running the batteries at night, but the pilot could not distinguish the necessary marks to proceed by and therefore waited for daylight. I left Brig. Gen. E. E. Potter, chief of staff, in command of the place in my absence.

April 15.—At daylight the Escort started and ran the batteries. She was fired at one hundred times by the Rodman's and Hill's Point batteries and struck forty times, but with no material injury. The pilot, Padrick, a brave and skillful man, was killed by a rifle-shot. At 6 a. m. all the enemy's batteries (Nos. 1, 2, 3, 4, 5, and 6, the last opening for the first time) opened and continued a heavy firing for an hour.

April 16.—At daylight 5 deserters from the enemy (conscripts of the Eighth Virginia) arrived in Washington and reported that the enemy had retired from our front and were retreating on Greenville. General Potter immediately sent out the entire force of cavalry (one company) to harass their rear and at the same time a force of contrabands was employed to level the enemy's batteries in front. Fort Hamilton fired a number of shots into the Rodman's Point Battery. There being no reply it was surmised that the battery had been abandoned. The gunboats Eagle, Ceres, and Hull thereupon steamed down and opened upon the battery, which eliciting no response, the Ceres, without orders, sent a boat on shore to take possession. As the boat neared the land three volleys of musketry were fired into her by the enemy concealed in the intrenchments. The engineer of the Ceres was killed and 2 men were wounded. The gunboats then renewed the attack, rapidly shelling the battery. The gunboats below were now seen shelling the Hill's Point Battery, which they soon passed, and reported it to be evacuated.

At this time the enemy having also retired from the Rodman's Point Battery, it was taken possession of by a party from the gunboat Eagle. Five companies of the Fifth Rhode Island Volunteers, under Lieutenant-Colonel Tew, with one 12-pounder and one 6-pounder, were sent down in the Ceres to occupy the battery. They immediately commenced the construction of intrenchments to hold the position. There was found in one of the batteries at Rodman's Point the carriage of a 32-pounder barbette gun in perfect order; also fragments of several exploded guns. Toward evening three companies of the Forty-fourth Massachusetts Volunteer Militia, with one 12-pounder Wiard and one 6-pounder, were sent to occupy the Hill's Point Battery in connection with three companies of the Forty-third Massachusetts Volunteer Militia from below. They intrenched themselves there. The pickets of the enemy occasionally appeared through the night, but in the morning they had entirely disappeared from the vicinity.

In the mean time I returned to New Berne and proceeded to organize operations so as to effectually raise the siege. To distract the enemy I directed General Prince to march up the railroad as far as he could toward Kinston and make a vigorous attack, continuing it for several days. At the same time I crossed the Neuse with all my available force and marched directly toward Blount's Creek, the point where General Spinola was repulsed in the first attempt to relieve the siege, sending at the same time General Spinola, with his brigade, to make an attack on the enemy at Swift Creek, which is on the direct road between New Berne and Washington. The movement toward Kinston with this latter movement, together with the enemy's information of the accession of strength of Heckman's brigade and the fact that after fourteen days of close siege of Washington General Hill had failed to obtain a single advantage or to advance one step nearer his object, in all probability caused him to retreat.

On arriving at Blount's Creek I found it abandoned. General Naglee, with detachments of two companies of cavalry, pushed on in advance toward Washington. He succeeded in capturing 5 of the enemy's rear guard by a brilliant dash on them made by himself, Captain Johnston, assistant adjutant-general; Captain Cochen, and Captain Gouraud, aide-de-camp.

The next morning, April 19, he pushed on, with the cavalry, and fought the enemy's rear guard, driving them from breastwork to breastwork and finally forcing them to retire, taking some prisoners, killing and wounding some, and capturing the battle-flag of the Seventh Confederate Cavalry (Georgia).

The column pushed on, arriving at Washington Sunday evening, April 19. After making necessary dispositions at Washington I returned to New Berne to make general dispositions for the defense of the department, which I will report. General Hill has returned up the country with his forces and all our posts are now relieved from pressure.

I take advantage of this opportunity to say that the garrison of Washington—the Twenty-seventh Massachusetts Volunteers, Forty-fourth Massachusetts Volunteer Militia, two companies of the North Carolina (Union) Volunteers, one company of the Third New York Cavalry, and one company of the Third New York Artillery—behaved nobly; and regarding the intrenchments which by their cheerful and zealous labor I had been enabled to throw up, together with the courage shown in all cases, I believe they could have successfully resisted an assault of all the forces under General Hill at the Point. I must also acknowledge the timely assistance of the Fifth Rhode Island Volunteers, brought up on the Escort by Colonel Sisson.

I have the honor to be, general, very respectfully, your obedient servant,

J. G. FOSTER,
Major-General, Commanding.

Maj. Gen. H. W. HALLECK,
General-in-Chief, U. S. Army, Washington, D. C.

Return of Casualties in the Union forces during the siege of Washington, N. C., March 30–April 16, 1863.

[Compiled from nominal lists of casualties, returns, etc.]

Command.	Killed.		Wounded.		
	Officers.	Enlisted men.	Officers.	Enlisted men.	Aggregate.
27th Massachusetts Infantry				10	10
43d Massachusetts Infantry				2	2
44th Massachusetts Infantry			1	3	4
1st North Carolina Infantry, Company B		1	1	6	8
3d New York Light Artillery, Battery G				1	1
Total		1	2	22	25

No. 2.

Report of Capt. David A. Taylor, Third New York Light Artillery, Chief Signal Officer.

HEADQUARTERS SIGNAL DETACHMENT,
New Berne, N. C., April 21, 1863.

SIR : I have the honor to forward you a report of the late operations of this detachment connected with the siege of Washington, N. C.:

On the 9th instant, at my solicitation, Lieutenant-Colonel Hoffman, assistant adjutant-general of this department, ordered me to open communication between Washington and the gunboats in the Pamlico River, below Washington. On the morning of the 10th instant, in company with Lieut. J. B. Knox, acting signal officer, I started from New Berne, and that evening met the gunboats 12 miles below Washington. I directed Lieutenant Knox and men to report to Captain McCann, commanding gunboat fleet in Pamlico River, and always to be on the boat at the blockade near Hill's Point.

That night, in company with Lieutenant-Colonel McChesney, First North Carolina Infantry, and Lieutenant Josselyn, of the Navy, and accompanied by my flagmen, Jacob A. Reed, Company I, Third New York Artillery, and Horace P. Baker, Company E, Third New York Artillery, I went up to Washington in a row-boat and reported to Maj. Gen. J. G. Foster.

In making arrangements for the opening of communication, Captain McCann agreed to always have a boat on the river within sight of Washington, and Lieutenant Knox had to entirely depend upon the boats to place him in a position from which he could communicate with me. Notwithstanding his agreement, Captain McCann did not have a boat at the point designated until the second day, and then only for a couple of hours, during which time Lieutenant Knox was unable to find my flag, and it was not until the third day that he saw it; after which communication was kept up at all times when the gunboats were at the proper stations.

Whenever my flag was raised at Washington a cross-fire from the southwest and the north was opened upon it by the enemy.

On the 16th, while signaling to Lieutenant Knox from No. 4 block-house at Washington, Private Reed, standing on the parapet of the battery, flagged three messages of some length under a very severe fire of shell and shrapnel from the enemy's batteries at Rodman's Point and Blount's house. Many of the shell and shrapnel burst very close, dropping pieces immediately around him, but Reed never once left his position until I had done signaling. Reed has several times before this behaved in an equally admirable manner, and I take pleasure in again recommending him to your favorable notice, and hope he may receive a suitable promotion. He is sober, intelligent, discreet, and brave, and has been kept in the ranks solely for the reason that he has been detached from his company and serving in a separate command.

Very respectfully, your obedient servant,

DAVID A. TAYLOR,
Captain and Acting Signal Officer.

Maj. Gen. J. G. FOSTER,
Commanding Eighteenth Army Corps.

No. 3.

Reports of Brig. Gen. Edward E. Potter, U. S. Army, commanding at Washington, of operations April 16–17.

WASHINGTON, N. C., *April* 16, 1863.

GENERAL: The enemy evacuated the batteries in our front last night and retreated toward Greenville by the Jamesville road. Five deserters came in this morning at 5 o'clock, who brought the information. They stated the force under General Garnett on this side of the river to be about 4,000 men and that they received orders last night to withdraw in order to re-enforce the army in Virginia.

I sent Captain Jocknick out on a reconnaissance to learn the whereabouts of the enemy. He followed them 4 or 5 miles, but they had crossed Tranter's Creek at Gainer's Bridge. Suspecting that there was a general movement I requested Captain Renshaw this morning to send a gunboat to Rodman's to discover whether any of the guns had been left there. The Ceres and the Eagle went down and shelled the Point but received no reply. A sergeant of the Forty-third Massachusetts volunteered to go down and ascertain the condition of affairs. He went with 10 or 15 men of that regiment on a schooner. When they had reached the Point a small boat put off from her to land as did also one from the Ceres. This was contrary to my wish and instructions. When they had got quite close to the shore the rebels opened a sharp fire of musketry, killing the third engineer of the Ceres and wounding 2 men of the Forty-third. The boats were all got off. Being convinced that the force at the Point was very small I determined to send five companies of Fifth Rhode Island to occupy it this afternoon.

In the mean time the gunboats had come up from below and threw a large quantity of 9-inch shells into Rodman's. I sent the five companies on the Ceres and in a flat protected by hay bales. On the flat was a 6-pounder. Master McKeever went down on a schooner armed with a boat howitzer. He was the first to land. The whole force landed without opposition. Hill's Point is also evacuated. I shall send three companies to occupy it along with the two companies of the Forty-third Massachusetts now below.

I have had all the batteries on the ridge in our front leveled to-day.

I have just received intelligence that the rebel cavalry have appeared on the Jamesville road.

Please send me word what other disposition you wish made of the force under my command, and what will be your plans under the altered circumstances.

       Very respectfully,

                           EDWARD E. POTTER,
                              Brigadier-General, Commanding.

Maj. Gen. J. G. FOSTER,
    Commanding Eighteenth Army Corps.

—

              OFF HILL'S POINT, *April* 18, 1863—2 p. m.

GENERAL: We occupied Rodman's Point last evening with five companies of the Fifth Rhode Island, a 6-pounder smooth-bore, and a navy howitzer. There was some skirmishing between the rebel pickets and our own; one of them (the rebels) was killed and 3 prisoners taken—a captain, drum-major, and a private. Later I sent three companies of the Forty-fourth with a field piece to Hill's Point. Here they were to be joined by the detachment of the Forty-third lying in the river. I have visited both places to-day. They have commenced throwing up works at both places and will soon be in an excellent condition for defense. A gunboat lies off each Point. At Rodman's the rebels left behind them a 32-pounder carriage. Their cavalry came down on the Jamesville road yesterday evening only with a view of picking up stragglers, as I was told by 5 deserters who came in this morning. The enemy are in full retreat, and their show of resistance yesterday was to enable them to get off their guns which were probably troublesome in the muddy roads. Our pickets have been out to-day nearly to the cross-roads, as I am told by the lieutenant-colonel of the Fifth Rhode Island, and have seen nothing of them. If we had had sufficient force to pursue them I think some of their guns might have been taken. I shall continue the work on the castle, and also those laid out between Block-houses Nos. 3 and 4. A large supply of ammunition came up this morning.

       Very respectfully, your obedient servant,

                           EDWARD E. POTTER,
                              Brigadier-General, Commanding.

Major-General FOSTER,
    Commanding Eighteenth Army Corps.

A dispatch from General Naglee addressed to you arrived yesterday, which I opened.

———

No. 4.

*Itinerary of the First Division, Eighteenth Army Corps, Brig. Gen. Innis N. Palmer, U. S. Army, commanding, April 7–25.**

April 7.—The Forty-third and Seventeenth Massachusetts Regiments, of the First Brigade, and Fifth Massachusetts, of the Second Brigade, together with other troops of the Eighteenth Army Corps, crossed the Neuse River, and under General Spinola marched to the relief of the besieged garrison at Washington, N. C.

———

* From Division Return for April, 1863.

April 9.—Arrived at Blount's Creek, found the enemy strongly in-trenched; engaged them, but finally withdrew, and returned to New Berne. Immediately after the return of the column the Forty-third Massachusetts, of the First Brigade, went on board of transports and proceeded toward Washington, N. C. After lying off the rebel bat-teries in the Pamlico River for seven days returned to New Berne.

April 17.—The Seventeenth Massachusetts Volunteers, of the First Brigade, and the Fifth Massachusetts Volunteer Militia and two com-panies of the Forty-sixth Massachusetts Volunteer Militia, of the Second Brigade, forming a part of the force under the immediate command of General Foster, crossed the Neuse River and marched on Washington, N. C., arriving there on the 20th instant, without meeting the enemy; distance 35 miles.

April 22.—Returned to New Berne by transports.

April 25.—The Forty-fifth Massachusetts Volunteer Militia (First Bri-gade) relieved from duty as provost guard of the city of New Berne, complimented by Major-General Foster for the efficient and soldierly manner in which the duty had been performed.

No. 5.

Report of Brig. Gen. Henry M. Naglee, U. S. Army, commanding Second Division, of Expedition from New Berne to Washington, April 17–19.

HEADQUARTERS NAGLEE'S DIVISION,
New Berne, N. C., April 21, 1863.

COLONEL: I would respectfully report that the advance, consisting of Heckman's brigade, a detachment of the Third New York Cavalry, and one light howitzer, crossed Blount's Creek on the afternoon of the 18th of April, after a march of 22 miles.

Here I learned that the forces of the enemy under General Hill had retired in the direction of Greenville; that a rear guard still held the crossing of this road with that leading from New Berne direct to Wash-ington, and that the road was picketed and held by the Second Geor-gia Cavalry. We proceeded without opposition until we were about crossing the Chocowinity Creek, where, by a bold cavalry dash, we cap-tured 5 of the enemy, and it being night withdrew to the right bank and held the bridges at the mills, that at the main road having been destroyed. Our pickets at both bridges were fired upon repeatedly during the night; returning the fire, killed several of the enemy at the main-road crossing.

On the morning of the 19th we were under arms by 4 a. m., and at 6 found the enemy occupying the field works commanding the bridges and mill-dam. A force was sent across the dam while a mounted one was pushed across the bridges, and both attacked in a spirited manner and drove the enemy from the breastworks.

Again they formed and occupied another line of works about 1 mile from the last, and again were dispossessed of them.

At the long line of works crossing the New Berne and Washington roads, 3 miles from the latter place, they again showed a determination to resist our progress. We approached cautiously and determinately, and without hesitation attacked them. The horse of an officer was shot and threw his rider, and a charge was ordered, which resulted in the capture of the captain of the Second Georgia Cavalry and the speedy retreat of his men and soon after of all the force. It now became a spirited race until near the crossing, where the enemy turned into the road toward Greenville, and where the howitzer was ordered into battery and opened with such effect that all organization was abandoned and the Second Georgia Cavalry threw down its colors and scattered in confusion. General Foster having ordered that I should not pursue beyond this point I ordered the cavalry to bivouac, that Heckman's brigade should do the same as soon as he should come up, and that all should await further orders.

I am happy to notice the services and gallant conduct of my assistant adjutant-general, Capt. George H. Johnston, and that of Capts. George E. Gouraud and Cochen, who assisted in a charge which captured more of the enemy than the number of those that engaged them on our side.

The efficient conduct of Lieutenant Beecher, of the Third New York Cavalry, attracted my attention.

We killed several of the enemy and made a number of prisoners.

Very respectfully, &c.,

HENRY M. NAGLEE,
Brigadier-General.

Lieut. Col. SOUTHARD HOFFMAN,
Assistant Adjutant-General, Eighteenth Army Corps.

No. 6.

Report of Brig. Gen. Charles A. Heckman, U. S. Army, commanding First Brigade, of Expedition from New Berne to Washington, April 17–19.

HEADQUARTERS HECKMAN'S BRIGADE,
New Berne, N. C., April 21, 1863.

SIR: I have the honor to make the following report of the part taken by two regiments of my brigade during the recent expedition to Washington, N. C.:

Friday (17th instant) having received orders to cross the Neuse River with my command and take the advance, I proceeded on the road toward Washington as far as Penify's plantation, distance from New Berne 7 miles, the road for a great part of the way being of the most horrid character.

The column not having closed up, I placed Belger's battery, commanded by Lieutenant Simpson, in position, and my two regiments of infantry and a squadron of cavalry, commanded by Lieutenant Beecher, in line to support them. I then ordered the troops to bivouac for the night.

At daylight on the morning of the 18th formed line and commenced the march without interruption until we arrived at Swift Creek road at 10 a. m. Learning that the road to Swift Creek was blockaded for a number of miles I continued on the direct road to Blount's Creek Mill. At 12 m., the main column being some distance in the rear, I halted to rest and allow the column to close up. After a halt of about two hours I was joined by General Naglee and staff, when we immediately pushed forward and reached Blount's Creek about 3.30 p. m. Found the bridge over the creek destroyed, but with very little labor the pioneers constructed a passage through the mill. Received orders from General

Naglee to halt the column when it arrived, bivouac, and move forward early in the morning, the general proceeding in the direction of Washington, accompanied by his staff. As soon as the cavalry arrived and had fed their horses I ordered them to follow, which they did, coming up with the general about 8 miles from our encampment.

At 5.30 a. m., column again in motion, received orders that upon arriving at the road leading to Hill's Point to take one regiment of infantry and ascertain if the fort was occupied, and, if so, by whom. Accompanied by my staff and followed by the Ninth New Jersey Volunteers I rode into the fort and found it occupied by detachments of the Forty-third and Forty-fourth Regiments Massachusetts Volunteers.

At 12 m. received orders to continue the march toward Washington, leaving the Ninth New Jersey and Twenty-third Massachusetts at Hill's Point. Placed the Seventeenth Massachusetts in advance, and arrived at Washington at 3 p. m. The Ninth New Jersey Volunteers arrived by boat from Hill's Point at 5 p. m. Left on steamer Escort for New Berne, N. C., on the 20th and reached here at 6 a. m. 21st.

I am, general, very respectfully, your obedient servant,

C. A. HECKMAN,
Brigadier-General, Commanding Brigade.

Lieut. Col. SOUTHARD HOFFMAN,
Assistant Adjutant-General, Eighteenth Army Corps.

No. 7.

Itinerary of the Fourth Division, Eighteenth Army Corps, Brig. Gen. Henry W. Wessells, U. S. Army, commanding, March 15–April 13. [*]

March 15.—The Forty-fourth Regiment Massachusetts Volunteer Militia received marching orders and proceeded to Washington, N. C., by transport, where they remained until April 22, when they returned to New Berne.

March 30.—Companies A and G went on a scout, and, falling into an ambuscade, returned to Washington, with a loss of 3 men wounded and prisoners and Captain Richardson wounded. The rebels the next day blockaded the Pamlico River and laid siege to the town, keeping up a continuous firing until the 16th, when they withdrew their forces and abandoned the siege.

April 13.—Colonel Sisson, with the Fifth Rhode Island Regiment, succeeded in running the enemy's batteries, re-enforcing the garrison at Washington without loss.

No. 8.

Reports of Brig. Gen. Henry Prince, U. S. Army, commanding Fifth Division, of operations on the Pamlico, April 4–6, and Expedition from New Berne toward Kinston, April 16–21, with resulting correspondence.

HDQRS. FIFTH DIVISION, EIGHTEENTH ARMY CORPS,
New Berne, N. C., April 13, 1863.

COLONEL: My last formal dispatch was dated April 3, at which time I was present at department headquarters here. I left next morning

---
[*] From Division Return for April, 1863.

(4th inst.) for the Pamlico River and arrived at Blount's Bay at 8 p. m. In addition to the gunboats which I left there—the Lockwood, Allison, and sloop Granite—I found the Southfield, Whitehead, and Seymour. The Ceres, which arrived on Thursday evening, had during that night buoyed out the passage through the barricade, and, while engaging the battery about 3 o'clock the same night, passed through. The enemy probably withheld their fire supposing that the Ceres would be impaled, and must have been surprised to see her steam off up the river. On the following night they removed the buoys placed by Captain MacDearmid. The evening of the 4th Dr. Rice left in a row-boat with dispatches for General Foster. By him I informed the general of my views of the state of things at the barricade, and the impossibility of taking the battery by landing.

On the morning of the 5th I had Colonel Dyer's regiment (One hundred and seventy-fifth Pennsylvania) on board the schooner Annie L. Edwards (with part of Ransom's battery), to be towed to Washington by the gunboat Lockwood, Captain Graves, who volunteered for the purpose. They were under way, approaching the barricade in gallant style, when Dr. Rice's boat and another belonging to the Southfield arrived from Washington, and the officers of the Navy on board of them said that there was not water enough above for the Lockwood, so I stopped them and turned them back.

The Northerner arrived with the following troops on board: The One hundred and first Pennsylvania, Colonel Morris, 350 strong; the Fifth Massachusetts, Colonel Peirson, 500 strong; making the whole number here, artillery and infantry, 2,500 men. In the afternoon the Hunchback, Captain McCann, arrived, having been detained by boisterous weather. The Hunchback, Southfield, and Whitehead made a combined attack on the battery at 6 p. m. The battery replied with but three shots, which passed near the Hunchback.

As soon as dark came on (in order that the enemy might not observe) I began preparing the Emilie steamer, by disposing bales and boxes of clothing and three bales of cotton to protect the boiler, for the reception of a regiment, intending to place her in charge of Captain Wells, of the Seymour, who said he would make the effort to run her up to Washington. Later, toward 10 p. m., a dispatch arrived from General Foster. The dispatch in the morning directed as follows:

If you find it to be too risky to land and take the batteries, content yourself with sending me through two regiments, with a plentiful supply of ammunition for the guns (32-pounders, 6-pounder Wiards, 6-pounder smooth-bores, and 3-inch guns); then, leaving the gunboats to take care of Hill's Point battery, return at once to New Berne and, taking every man that can possibly be spared (five regiments are enough for the safety of New Berne), march across the country from Fort Anderson to Washington. I am quite sure that you will only meet ten regiments on the way, and them you can overcome. The road from Fort Anderson to Swift's Creek is bad but the rest is good. You can also go by the way of Street's Ferry, but it involves the bridging of Batchelder's Creek and the crossing of the Neuse River and Swift's Creek. It is better to corduroy 5 miles of the road from Fort Anderson.

And the dispatch of this evening says:

If you cannot send the two regiments through without delaying the main demonstration and attack from New Berne send only one, or leave it to be sent, and push the other matter. It is my belief that the battery at Hill's Point will be abandoned when our force approaches the cross-roads 3½ miles from here on the road to New Berne.

The project of sending a steamer crowded with men was proposed for discussion between the higher navy officers and some of my staff, and as my ideas of its impropriety were not shaken I countermanded the orders given to the Emilie and ordered the One hundred and fifty-eighth Pennsylvania, Lieutenant-Colonel Troxel, to embark at once in the schooners Annie L. Edwards and Flambeau, these vessels to be towed to Washington by the Allison and Phœnix, commanded, respectively, or guided, by McKeever and De Camarra, of the Louisiana and Hunchback, both of whom volunteered for the purpose.

The following is a copy of the orders to the troops:

SPECIAL ORDERS, }   HEADQUARTERS,
    No. 1.   }   Blount's Bay, April 5, 1863—12 p. m.

The One hundred and fifty-eighth Regiment Pennsylvania Volunteers will embark to-night in the two transports, in which it is to run the batteries of the enemy, to join the commander of the Eighteenth Army Corps in the defense of Fort Washington. The steamers Allison and Phœnix will tow the transports through.

By order of Brig. Gen. Henry Prince:

ALBERT ORDWAY,
First Lieutenant and Acting Assistant Adjutant-General.

The plan was as follows: When the vessels were ready they were to run up to the Hunchback and there receive the orders to start from Captain McCann, who was to have the passage through the barricade marked and was to engage the battery with all the gunboats.

Myself and staff were up all night attending to this, and at 4 o'clock, having called General Spinola for the purpose, we stood on the upper deck of the Escort to see them pass.

At this hour they had reached the Hunchback, near the barricade, and were stopped by Captain McCann, because, as he afterward reported to me, he thought it would be daylight when they would be passing the upper (Rodman's Point) battery.

At 6 o'clock on the morning of the 6th I left for New Berne, having given orders to each transport that was to accompany me and each one that was to remain. At evening I arrived at New Berne.

On the 7th I appointed Major Frankle chief of staff for an expedition which I expected to conduct, and I passed the day with my staff examining persons who knew the country between the Neuse and Washington and endeavoring to form a plan of operations conformable thereto and to General Foster's wishes.

During the day I was quite ill and constantly retching, to the interruption of the investigation. This was increased about 9 p. m. on learning that the Allison and Phœnix had arrived here and brought the schooners with the regiment I hoped had reached General Foster.

I received from department headquarters a list of the troops that would be over the Neuse in the course of the night and available for a march, and I organized them into brigades and constructed an order of march.

Early on the 8th I awoke with a blinding headache and sickness, and sent an officer of my staff with the organization and order of march at once to General Palmer, with the message that I was too ill to attend to any duty.

Indisposition has prevented my making this report before.

I have the honor to be colonel, very respectfully, your obedient servant,

HENRY PRINCE,
Brigadier-General of Volunteers.

Lieut. Col. SOUTHARD HOFFMAN,
    A. A. G., Hdqrs. Eighteenth A. C., New Berne, N. C.

N. B.—I have inadvertently omitted to say that in the night of the 5th instant I sent through the barricade in an open boat all the 6-pounder and 3-inch guns' ammunition which arrived in the Northerner.

APRIL 16, 1863—7.30 p. m.

I am 4 miles from Core Creek, having stopped at dark, working till that time bringing along rails and laying them down. I shall drive in the pickets on this road to-night with a company, reconnoitering to the bridge.

Colonel Jones, with his own and the Eighth Massachusetts, will go to the crossings on the Dover road and beat up the enemy's quarters on the other side of the creek, if possible, in course of the night.

In the morning early I shall go ahead. It is thought the enemy's pickets are watching us.

Yours,

HENRY PRINCE.

Lieut. Col. SOUTHARD HOFFMAN,
    Assistant Adjutant-General.

—

HDQRS. FIFTH DIVISION, EIGHTEENTH ARMY CORPS,
New Berne, N. C., April 22, 1863.

COLONEL: Pursuant to instructions, dated Headquarters Eighteenth Army Corps, New Berne, April 16, 1863, I advanced on that day in the direction of Kinston with Col. J. Jourdan's command, consisting of five companies of the One hundred and fifty-eighth Regiment New York Volunteers, nine companies of the One hundred and thirty-second Regiment New York Volunteers, nine companies of the Third Regiment Massachusetts Volunteers, and four companies of the Eighth Regiment Massachusetts Volunteers, with four pieces of Riggs' battery, and with Col. J. Richter Jones' command, consisting of the Fifty-eighth Regiment Pennsylvania Volunteers and 21 enlisted men of Company H, Third New York Cavalry.

In the evening I re-enforced Colonel Jones with a battalion of the Eighth Massachusetts Volunteers and directed him to follow the Dover road and take possession of its crossing of Core Creek. The main column followed the railroad, which required some repairing as we went along, and encamped about 4 miles from Core Creek. Camping places being very sparse, the route does not admit of much choice in this respect. I sent forward immediately Captain O'Connor, of Company G, One hundred and fifty-eighth Regiment New York Volunteers, with his company, to reconnoiter to the railroad crossing of Core Creek. He found a picket there of about 25 men; exchanged a volley with them and drove them to the other side. Colonel Jones marched his command in the night to Core Creek and endeavored to cross at a blind ford, but failed on account of the depth of water from recent rains. He then bivouacked near Dover Crossing.

The next morning Colonel Jourdan advanced over Core Creek, at the railroad crossing, with all the force not already stated to be with Colonel Jones, excepting the Third Regiment Massachusetts Volunteers and the battery held in reserve and some companies on picket. He extended to the right, after crossing, to the Dover road. Colonel Jones, finding Nethercutt's men opposed to his crossing, forced the passage, and in a smart skirmish, in which he followed them 3 miles, drove them beyond reach.

In this skirmish we lost 1 man killed and 4 wounded, all of the Fifty-eighth Regiment Pennsylvania Volunteers. Three of the enemy left on the ground were buried by the victors. A large party worked all this day upon the railroad bridge and laying down sleepers and rails beyond to a considerable distance.

In the course of the day I received the further instructions to "assume an offensive and strongly defensive position on the line of Core Creek and hold the same until further orders." At night the troops were withdrawn to the right bank, on the railroad and on the Dover road, with pickets out on the left bank.

On the 18th Colonel Jourdan with the same forces crossed the rail-road bridge and advanced something over a mile to the Core Creek Switch, whence a road leads to the Dover road, intersecting it at three-quarters of a mile from the Dover Crossing and about 1½ miles from the switch. He extended his command to the Dover road and held the point of junction with it in force. At the same time Colonel Jones passed down Core Creek on the west side to take in rear any party at the Neuse road crossing of Core Creek. This operation occupied the whole day, the troops not getting back into their camps till some time after dark. Four rebel cavalry only were found at the Neuse Cross-ing, who were captured, with their arms and horses. The party then crossed the creek, having to construct means of crossing for their ambulance, and returned, by the road on the east side, to the Dover Crossing. The next day, Sunday, the troops were not disturbed in their bivouac.

On Monday morning, having fully concerted the operation with Colonel Jones and Colonel Jourdan, I directed these zealous and ener-getic officers to advance, maintaining a constant communication with each other until the long sand ridge should be fully explored. The troops of the two camps moved at the same time. The left wing ex-tended to the Dover road and scoured to the right and left of the rail-road through most difficult ground; the right advanced by the open country bordering the Dover road and dashed first into the Sandy Ridge region, when they were opposed by skirmishers. The noise of this con-flict was the first communication the left was able to obtain with the right, although nearly abreast with it. The enemy's pickets on the railroad retired along the track, firing, thus giving distant notice of our progress there. Arriving at the Biddle road, an avenue 1 mile long from the long sand ridge to the railroad, while the skirmish was going on, Colonel Jourdan moved rapidly to the right upon it, with a bat-talion, and in support. The affair concluded on the Dover road about a mile in advance of the avenue. At that place the Sandy Ridge de-clines into a swamp, and the last end of it was roughly intrenched. The rapid movement and severe fire of the excellent skirmishers of the Fifty-eighth Pennsylvania and gallant charge of 17 cavalry of company H, Third New York Cavalry, under Sergeant Dow, leaping the intrench-ments, drove the main body of the rebels into the swamp, and detained a commissioned officer and 27 enlisted men of the Forty-ninth North Carolina Regiment in our hands as prisoners.

Our loss in this skirmish was 7 enlisted men of the Fifty-eighth Pennsylvania Volunteers and 1 of Company H, Third Regiment New York Cavalry, wounded. Three horses of the same cavalry party were killed.

On Tuesday, pursuant to orders from Headquarters Eighteenth Army Corps, my column returned to the New Berne lines and resumed their former positions.

I have to acknowledge myself under obligations to Colonel Jones, of the Fifty-eighth Regiment Pennsylvania Volunteers, and Colonel

Jourdan, commanding the Second Brigade of my division, for their untiring energy and intelligence; also to Major Fitz Simmons and Lieutenant Greig, Third Regiment New York Cavalry, who joined my staff for the expedition, the former as chief of staff and the latter as aide-de-camp.

No opportunity offered for the use of artillery; but in it, and, I may add, throughout the entire command, the very best kind of spirit was made evident to me.

Inclosed please find a report of Colonel Jones.

I am, colonel, very respectfully, your obedient servant,

HENRY PRINCE,
Brigadier-General of Volunteers, Commanding.

Lieut. Col. SOUTHARD HOFFMAN,
Asst. Adjt. Gen., Eighteenth Army Corps, New Berne, N. C.

—

HDQRS. FIRST DIVISION, EIGHTEENTH ARMY CORPS,
New Berne, N. C., April 24, 1863.
Maj. Gen. J. G. FOSTER,
Comdg. 18th Army Corps, Dept. of N. C., New Berne, N. C.:

GENERAL: I have the honor to acknowledge the receipt of your communication of yesterday, in which you inquire whether, during your recent absence at Washington, N. C., the question as to your power to give commands from that place was raised by any one, and, if so, by whom and under what circumstances.

It is natural for one to infer from this interrogatory that you have heard that the question was raised, and I think it but justice to myself and others to state that in no official manner was this done. But as you inquire if this matter was spoken of in "such consultations and conversations between commanding officers as would naturally under such circumstances take place and influence actions," I think it proper to add that the only remark that came under my own observation, and that could be considered by any one as at all calculated to raise the question of your power, was a remark uttered in private conversation by General Prince on the morning of the 10th instant (I think), and this occurred in this way: Several officers, including myself, were standing on the pavement near your quarters. General Prince said:

Here is a question. General Foster is shut up in Washington with a small command. He is unable or unwilling to leave there. Is he then in command of the department, or who is then in command?

The above is the substance of the remark, as I understood it. I paid no attention to it at the time, as I was very much occupied in getting ready to leave for the blockade. I left the place where the conversation was going on while General Prince was conversing, and I do not even now recollect the persons who were there but I think General Wessells was. This was not calculated to "influence (my) actions." General Prince certainly never advised with me, officially or privately, as to the power of the commanding general while in Washington, and the remark was simply an idle one, which I thought it better not to make at that time, and I regret the necessity for ever speaking of it.

I am, sir, very respectfully, yours,

I. N. PALMER,
Brigadier-General, Commanding First Division.

HEADQUARTERS DISTRICT OF THE PAMLICO,
Washington, N. C., April 26, 1863.

Maj. Gen. J. G. FOSTER,
Comdg. Eighteenth Army Corps, Dept. of N. C.:

GENERAL: Your letter of the 21st instant* was received by me on the 22d. You say:

The siege of Washington being raised, my duty to our country, to yourself, and to myself requires some explanation of past events.

I will endeavor to answer *seriatim* the queries which follow this passage satisfactorily to our country, to yourself, and to myself.
The passage which I will first consider is as follows:

Learning that an attack was to be made on Washington, I left on March 29 for that place and arrived there on the 30th. April 1, I wrote to General Palmer suggesting three ways of raising the siege and expressing my preference for the first, which was to land a strong force at a point below Hill's Point Battery, take that battery in reverse, march up in rear of Rodman's Point, and join me at Washington Bridge. What effort, if any, was made to carry out my orders as above quoted? Was any reconnaissance made by your order for the purpose of learning the strength and position of the enemy, on the result of which you reported to me that it was impracticable to land and take the batteries?

On the 1st day of April the following letter from General Palmer, commanding the department in your absence, was received by me:

HEADQUARTERS EIGHTEENTH ARMY CORPS,
New Berne, April 1, 1863.

Brigadier-General PRINCE, *New Berne, N. C.:*

GENERAL: Information is just received from General Foster from Washington, N. C., that that place is about to be attacked by the enemy in force. The re-enforcements under General Spinola have not been able to get to Washington, as the rebels have established a battery at Hill's Point, near the blockade below that city. General Foster has directed that you proceed immediately to that vicinity to take such measures for the reducing of this battery as your good judgment may dictate, and you will get the re-enforcements to their destination if possible.

The gunboats from here are ordered to proceed immediately to that point and they will be under way in an hour or two. The steamer North Shore will be placed at your disposition. She takes a supply of ammunition for 32-pounder and Wiard guns with her. The gunboats from Plymouth have also been sent for, and they will be down as soon as possible.

I send you the letter of General Foster for your information.

General, very respectfully, your obedient servant,

I. N. PALMER,
Brigadier-General, Commanding.

With the above came a letter from General Potter, of which the following is a copy:

WASHINGTON, N. C., *March 31, 1863—12 n*

Brigadier-General PALMER, *Commanding:*

GENERAL: The rebels are about to attack us in strong force. They sent in a flag of truce this morning for the purpose of having the women and children removed. The flag was not received. The regiments and battery that were to follow us have not arrived; cause supposed to be the fire from a battery which the rebels have planted at Hill's Point where they formerly had one. We can hold out for two or three days. General Foster wishes you to send up at once all the gunboats that can be spared, and, if possible, 400 rounds of 32-pounder shot and shell, and 200 rounds of 12-pounder Wiards. He also wishes either yourself or General Prince to come up and to act according to your own discretion in attacking the battery at Hill's Point.

If the gunboats cannot succeed in silencing the battery in question it will rest with you or General Prince to decide as to the advisability of landing your infantry and flanking the battery.

I am, very respectfully, your obedient servant,

EDWARD E. POTTER,
Chief of Staff.

---

* The only copy of this letter found is in letterpress-book, and is illegible.

I remember reading also a letter from you stating that there were three means of relieving Washington.

I left New Berne, on the North Shore, at 2.45 in the afternoon of that day and arrived at the fleet, off Bath in Pamlico River, at 2.45 the following morning. (The 2d, not the 4th.) General Spinola was in command there. I sought him immediately and talked with him of the situation of matters. He instantly showed me an order he had issued for landing some troops at daybreak for the purpose of storming the Hill's Point Battery. No reconnaissance had been made, and I did not see that his plan contemplated one, and asked him if he proposed to make it without any. He replied that he had no intention to attempt his plan without one and should make a reconnaissance first in the morning. I then approved this course and directed the reconnaissance to be made. This was done according to my detailed instructions. The officer in command of the party that made it reported verbally to my satisfaction. There were present about 1,600 men, artillery and infantry, and the two little armed steamers, Lockwood and Allison, and a sailing sloop with a heavy gun on board, which vessels vainly endeavored to interest the Hill's Point Battery.

I informed myself, by the examination of many different persons and by personal observation, of the precise nature of the situation of Hill's Point Battery and of all the ways by which it could be approached and all the places where landing was not naturally obstructed and where it was obstructed by nature. And, as enjoined so forcibly in my instructions, I permitted myself to be governed solely by my judgment in deciding that a landing could not be effected with any means at my command. Nothing has occurred to shake this opinion or modify it. Time and light all confirm it. When I had formed it fully I did all I could to make it immediately known to you and to General Palmer. At evening on the 3d of April I left the river for New Berne, to go and return as quickly as possible, for the purpose of conferring with General Palmer. I carried the following dispatch with me to General Palmer, having written it to send:

PAMLICO RIVER, N. C., *April 2,* 1863.

Col. SOUTHARD HOFFMAN,
    Asst. Adjt. Gen., Eighteenth Army Corps, New Berne, N. C.:

COLONEL: The battery on Hill's Point is very strong. The gunboats we have (the Allison and Lockwood) make no impression on it. Its geometrical position, considered with the relative situation of the enemy's forces, make it unassailable except by gunboats.

Whether 5,000 troops landed on this river or marched from New Berne would be immaterial; no less would be able to reach the battery and get away again if unsuccessful.

Landing therefore with me is out of the question as things stand. Blount's Creek is impassable, and at the bridge is a camp of 1,000 men. There is no way of my command getting out of the triangle formed around the battery by the water and the road. I shall lie here and threaten, and if a strong force of gunboats comes the battery can be fully tested.

Large vessels (gunboats) cannot find their way through the blockade, the buoys being up and the piles being cut off 2 feet under water, and while they are beleaguered the well-served eight guns (some Whitworths) could destroy them. I shall attempt to send some ammunition to Washington to-night in a small boat, hugging the northern shore; but it will be a trifle, I know. The officers of the gunboats will consider well while near the battery the feasibility of one running through, but I feel confident they will decide adversely to the attempt. If General Dix sends 5,000 men we may relieve Washington. If the large gunboats come they may succeed.

In order to remain here, coal is necessary. I send a tug to bring us a schooner containing it. As every steamer will be out of coal in thirty-two hours, whatever else fails let the tugs bring some coal-vessel.

    Yours, respectfully,

                                        HENRY PRINCE,
                                    Brigadier-General, Volunteers.

And on the same day I endeavored to express myself better and more clearly in a communication to your headquarters, a copy of which I sent through the barricade to you, which is as follows:

NEW BERNE, *April* 3, 1863.

Lieutenant-Colonel HOFFMAN:

COLONEL: The above sketch (for correction of which I refer to the map of North Carolina by Topographical Bureau) is to indicate the relative situation of points referred to in the following statement : General Foster, with two regiments, a company of cavalry, and a company of artillery (1,200 men), and three gunboats is at Washington. He is invested on the north side of the river by the brigades of Pettigrew and Garnett, as he states in his letter to General Prince of April 2, 1863. On the south side is D. H. Hill with two brigades, according to General Foster's information, same letter ; but other information, to which he probably has not access, indicates a stronger force.

The enemy have at Rodman's Point a battery with which they are destroying the gunboats. At Hill's Point the enemy have a fine battery of six or eight guns. A barricade formerly constructed by the enemy extends from Hill's Point to Swan Point ; the barricade consists of a double row of piles cut off 2 feet under water. Instead of destroying the barricade our vessels made a passage through it 60 feet wide, and marked the passage with buoys. The enemy having removed the buoys, it is not possible in the expanse of the river to know where the passage is running. The battery therefore perfects the blockade and also the investment of the small force of ours at Washington.

Having been up myself to the front of the Hill's Point Battery and felt it with some small gunboats, and having reconnoitered the shore there and obtained carefully sifted information, I can add something to the above statement.

Blount's Creek has a long bridge where the road crosses, and is impassable below. The bridge is partly removable, and at it is a force 1,000 strong of the enemy ever since these operations commenced. Above the bridge the swamp is impassable. In reconnoitering the shores of Blount's Bay I found the enemy's pickets of infantry on its west shore, all along, and infantry and cavalry on its east shore. This shows the enemy to be on the alert there ; and having seen lying there transports filled with troops two nights and a day before I arrived there they are in anticipation of a landing. The enemy therefore on the south side of the river are in force to defend the Hill's Point Battery.

It is believed by me from my reconnaissance that the nature of the position west of Blount's Creek does not admit of the gunboats rendering any assistance to troops that have landed save while they are on the immediate shore ; the entire bank is high, rugged, and wooded. Any force landed there places itself at once in a state of siege from which there is no retiring excepting under most adverse circumstances. A march upon the shore itself would expose the troops to a fire from the bluff which they could not fairly return.

As I am about to return to the position I shall use all the means I can to obtain further knowledge of the enemy, and if an opportunity to land occurs I shall do it. Up to this time since the first arrival of the troops near Blount's Bay the high wind and low water would have prevented any descent before as well as after my arrival. If anything can be done by the combined forces of army and navy assembled at the barricade you may be assured that no pains will be spared to do it.

It is understood at the headquarters of the Eighteenth Army Corps that the enemy's regiments in this region are full, and it is not unlikely that two brigades of D. H. Hill's command number ten regiments.

Very respectfully, your obedient servant,

HENRY PRINCE,
Brigadier-General, Volunteers.

I returned to Blount's Bay the next day. In the trip I had seen the Southfield and two other gunboats from Plymouth on their way to Blount's Bay, where they arrived before me, and I left the Hunchback, from New Berne, detained by the weather in the mouth of the Neuse. The passage of the Sound was rendered very difficult, and was constantly being interrupted during the most of the time I was up in the Pamlico River by the high wind. The first re-enforcements arrived on the 5th. There were then in all 2,500 men there ; clearly not enough to attempt the operation of forcing the crossing of Blount's Creek, which cannot be more correctly described now that our troops have it in possession than it was by me then.

The instructions contemplate a fair trial of the large class of gunboats. The Hunchback did not succeed in reaching Blount's Bay until the afternoon of the 5th. On that day I received your instructions to leave the river to the care of the gunboats, and left early the next morning. I do not think a full test of what the gunboats could do with the battery had then been made, but supposed it would be. There were no means of landing troops at Blount's Bay under fire, and it was of no use to collect them unless the troops could get there. It seems not to have been possible up to the time I quit there to get a sufficient force from New Berne to fight the brigade of 4,500 men, which was the least force that could be reasonably deemed to be supporting the Hill's Point Battery.

To recapitulate: I arrived at the forces on the Pamlico River at 3 o'clock on the morning of the 2d of April. An order had been issued for troops to land at daylight and storm the Hill's Point Battery. I countermanded this order—my greatest service yet rendered to the country in any one act. I ordered an armed reconnaissance, in which I explained every detail of the mode in which it should be conducted in the events that I imagined might occur. It was completed to my satisfaction. I reconnoitered the region carefully myself. I ascertained the nature of it with the most irrefragable accuracy, as well as the position of the enemy, whose force I correctly estimated. I sifted justly the mass of information I obtained on all these subjects, and thus saw the situation clearly and positively. The stormy night of the 3d of April and the day of the 4th I traversed the waters of Pamlico Sound to New Berne and back. On the 5th of April I received your orders to quit the river with the 2,500 men that were there in my command, excepting one regiment to be sent by the naval force to you, and I accordingly left early on the morning of the 6th of April for New Berne.

And now as to the question of landing. The notes written by you from Washington, such as I saw, cannot be regarded technically as orders. Their style suggested the idea to me that you did not so regard them yourself, as they are not sufficiently coherent with each other or sufficiently definite in themselves, it seems to me, to be considered such. In the paragraph of your letter which I am now considering you said: "I wrote to General Palmer suggesting three ways," &c., and "expressing my preference for the first," &c. You then said: "What effort, if any, was made to carry out my orders as above quoted?" I think from this that you do not always regard them as orders. They are in fact, as you style them yourself, your suggestions and preferences from your point of view at the moment of writing. Undoubtedly you would not consider them orders in the case of failure of anything done in pursuance of them.

In one addressed to General Palmer you say that the first plan was described to be "to land a strong force below (no place being particularized) Hill's Point Battery, take that battery in reverse, march up in rear of Rodman's Point, and join me at the bridge."

In one addressed to me, dated April 2, you say:

The batteries must be taken in succession, to do which it is necessary to land under cover of the gunboats and to assail the battery in its flank or rear at the same time that the gunboats assail it in front. The battery will probably be supported by a brigade, which you must whip. If you have not troops enough send at once to Palmer with orders from me to load any steamer or sail-vessel with troops enough to do the business surely—

At this stage I visited General Palmer, who said that he was using all the transportation—

If the gunboats arrive before more troops arrive you can make the attempt to land under their cover.

But the class of gunboats that were expected to affect the battery did not arrive till the 5th April.

In another addressed to me you said that after the Hill's Point Battery was taken the troops ought to re-embark in order to proceed to the Rodman's Point Battery on transports.

The letter of General Potter, chief of your staff, says:

> He (General Foster) also wishes either yourself or General Prince to come up and to act according to your own discretion in attacking the battery at Hill's Point. If the gunboats cannot succeed in silencing the battery in question it will rest with you or General Prince to decide as to the advisability of landing your infantry and flanking the battery.

Thus I have shown most clearly that it rested solely on my judgment and responsibility to decide whether the landing of troops near the Hill's Point Battery should be made, and I shall proceed to show that I decided correctly.

D. H. Hill was known to be on the south side of the Pamlico River with at least two brigades of rebels. I derived this knowledge not only from you but from other sources of information. From your headquarters I learned that the rebel regiments about here were all full, each brigade consisting of five regiments, numbering, say, 4,500 men.

But as the Hill's Point Battery was the key of the whole investment it would be taking a short-sighted view of the generalship of the rebels to suppose that they could not concentrate all their force that was south of the river in its defense; and when we were nearest to being able to land, when we had in all 2,500 men at Blount's Bay, I knew, by ocular observation, that they were concentrated for the defense of that battery against a landing. The indications were conclusive. This is now rendered a demonstrated certainty by our troops having marched over the ground and witnessed their freshly-vacated camps there since the raising of the siege of Washington.

To land west of Blount's Creek would have been to place one's self where the formation of the shore line refused to permit the gunboats to render any assistance to the infantry landed. No point juts out upon which the gunboats might fire without firing over (that is, into) our troops. No place whatever can be named west of Blount's Creek below the battery where the gunboats could assist the retreat. The troops therefore would have to depend upon themselves and the intrenchments they might make after landing. From the mouth of Blount's Creek to Hill's Point Battery is 2½ miles of shore line, forming a uniform and gentle curve of which Hill's Point is the culmination merely. The general level of the land along there is 40 feet above the river, the bank of which is bluff. A landing west of Blount's Creek would be on this curve of 2½ miles in length. Inside of it lies encamped the supporting brigade of rebels—their pickets everywhere on the curve; their main body not over 2 miles distant from any part of it.

I will suppose that the other brigade south of the river is distributed at Blount's Creek Bridge, Swift Creek Village, Rodman's Point, the cross-roads, and a point between the cross-road and Swift Creek.

I will suppose that we could land 500 men in row-boats, stern-wheelers, &c., at a time. Let us see how the landing would proceed:

The transport full of troops draws as near to the shore as she can. She is then half a mile off (or she remains beyond the range of musketry, which would make the time longer). Each trip to land 500 takes twenty minutes, and, if no contingency prolongs it, the transfer of the whole to land takes one hour and two-thirds. Meantime the rebels have been called to arms by the fire of their pickets, and being not over

2 miles distant they are at the landing place in an hour after the landing begins and besiege it before the landing is complete. The two
principles, without the observance of which the operations should not be
attempted, are, first, a secure retreat, and, second, some prospect of
taking the battery. Any one can decide the question.

I should have been willing with 5,000 troops, having assured myself
of your clearly expressed approbation of doing so, as my letters already
quoted show, to have attempted what I have described, because I think
our soldiers, with a superior *morale* arising from the holiness of their
cause, are superior in battle to the rebel rank and file, more steady and
persevering, more coolly determined on retaining a reserve of energy
and a few unwasted cartridges for final exhibition, and to sweep the
field.

To land east of Blount's Creek would have been safe and under the
cover of the gunboats; but then there would have been between the
column and the battery the obstacle of an unfordable creek, watchfully
guarded, with a single bridge partly removable and occupied in force.
It is evident that 2,500 men would not have forced the crossing of
Blount's Creek if they had landed on the east side of it and remained
in a condition to go farther. In fact the entire available force of this
department, all the infantry, cavalry, and artillery that could be marched
from New Berne, in precise total 6,400 men, went there on the 9th of
April, and after experimenting on it marched back to New Berne again
with their killed and wounded, because they could not force it without
a too great cost of men. As landing or marching there would have
brought the forces to the same identical place, it is therefore demonstrated that my judgment was correct in pronouncing it to be out of
the question to get on the flank or rear of Hill's Point Battery by landing east of Blount's Creek, for there is no way of turning Blount's Creek,
as a swamp at the head of it, beginning at the bridge, covers an area
10 miles long and 6 miles wide, and the only pocoson road through it
is impassable.

Landing east or west was, as I wrote to you, out of the question, then,
with my forces. I sincerely hope I have rendered it as plain to the country and to yourself as it has long been to me.

The next paragraph of your letter is as follows:

Nothing being done on the Pamlico River in accordance with my plan No. 1, I wrote
on the 5th of April ordering you to take command of all the available forces and
march across the country to Washington. Why did you not go in command?

This question is answered, I think, fully in my reports to your headquarters of April 13, 1863, rendered for the purpose of answering it. If
you will suggest any deficiency in the explanation as there given I will
supply it with pleasure. I believe, in preparing myself for the march, I
foresaw every difficulty likely to occur in the march and all the places
where it was possible there would be any opposition, and made up my
mind how I could persistently endeavor to meet the one and overcome
the other.

Was any counsel of war held as to the expediency of marching across the country?

None that I have heard of. But this extraordinary question is entitled to more consideration than is supplied by a full answer. I did not
ask the opinion of any officer or officers whatever in respect to marching to Washington. At one time General Palmer, Colonel Hoffman
(the assistant adjutant-general of the department) at another, and General Spinola at another time were in my quarters, a few moments each,
at the time when myself and my confidential personal staff were gath-

ering and collating information from persons of all colors respecting the country between New Berne and Washington and were discussing in the most perfect privacy whatever subjects in connection therewith it pleased us to mention, it having been stated by me to them that nothing which was uttered that day by them or by me should be considered an opinion, but as a mere suggestion to thought and memory. No reserve was observed when the persons named were in, and no other person was treated with any part of such confidence. I am forced to suppose that this working with my staff is the foundation of the question, if it has any, strange as it may seem, because I cannot imagine any other.

Did you, publicly or privately, in consultation with the commanding officer, give your opinion, similar to that expressed to me in a letter, that the garrison at Washington were in an eel-pot and the mouth closed, and so convey the impression that it was inexpedient to incur much risk in endeavoring to raise the siege, accepting the surrender as a foregone conclusion, and that the troops that should march to my rescue would in all probability be cut off?

I have never held such opinions, and have never expressed any such to you or to any one. I never had impressions resembling such as you mention above and never conveyed any such to any one, publicly or privately. If I had done so publicly, as I have no right to do, the information would be at your service; if privately, as I have the most perfect right to do to a commanding officer, it would be sacred with him. There were two commanding officers whom I consulted with, General Palmer, commanding the department in your absence at Washington, with whom I was bound to consult as the commanding officer; the other was General Spinola, whom I relieved in command on the Pamlico River, which fact placed me on similar terms with him to a certain degree. I was habitually frank with them, and if my frankness is partly exposed I submit to you that it is not my fault. They are proper persons for my freest intercourse on public matters. The ideas I may have expressed on those matters to the commanding officer of the department in the form of advice, crude surmises, or partly conceived thoughts for the purpose of eliciting an exchange of impressions, or for persuasion, or conversation merely in that intercourse, the freedom of which is equally sanctioned by discretion and honor and the good of the service, are not subject to interrogatories, in which they are liable to misconstruction, for the public eye. It is my freedom to express myself according to the inclination of the moment or the final decision of my judgment to the officer in command, with whom I am in customary association, on the current affairs which engage us, untrammeled by the supposition that either he or his confidential staff officer will expose my remarks anywhere. I shall only hold myself responsible to the public for what I so say when it is properly imparted to the public, and then I will substantiate the correctness of the motives actuating my words in the broadest, highest, and purest meaning of a motive; for I will never speak by any other, however agreeable it might be for me to do so. I shall not, therefore, here review my and their ideas exchanged in private conversations. Doing so imperfectly would be as unjust to them as it would be to me. I may say in general, however, that in discussing a proposed military operation I habitually make every supposition of success or failure, and more especially of failure, that my ingenuity can devise, as the only means of preparing myself or assisting any one else to prepare properly and fully to conduct it.

The eel-pot simile I used only in the sense in which I used it to you, viz, as suggesting the manner in which I presumed the rebels regarded

Washington. I never so regarded it myself, but on the contrary always expressed as my firm opinion, in the most public manner and with the intention to diffuse it, that you could come out whenever you pleased and also bring your command, with perhaps some loss, and that I fully shared your confidence of success. I used this simile discreetly with some of those persons interested in running the barricade for you, in connection with such remarks as that the enemy let the Ceres go by without firing at her and probably would let anything else go in, to encourage these persons in making the passage of the blockade.

Was the question raised regarding my authority to give orders? If so, when, by whom, and under what circumstances?

The question was not raised that I know of regarding your authority to command the troops in North Carolina. If I had any talk on the topic it was in private with General Palmer or General Spinola, and was either for my own or their amusement and not for any other purpose. If in your meaning of the words of the inquiry you are of the opinion that the circumstances in which you were at Washington of themselves raised the question, you must admit that I would have been absent-minded not to think of it.

Trusting that I have fulfilled the promise with which I began, I am, general, very respectfully, your obedient servant,

HENRY PRINCE,
Brigadier-General, Volunteers.

—

HEADQUARTERS EIGHTEENTH ARMY CORPS,
New Berne, May 8, 1863.

Brig. Gen. HENRY PRINCE,
Comdg. District of the Pamlico, Washington, N. C.:

GENERAL: I have the honor to acknowledge the receipt of your letter of April 26 in reply to mine of the 21st.

It is of course desirable in all military operations that the pros and cons should be fully weighed and the operation contemplated be made as certain as possible; that as a rule. But exigencies do occur when it is a duty to act even though the risk of failure is greater than the chance of success; this as an exception; and under this latter hypothesis I consider the attempt to relieve Washington to have been. I can therefore only regret that the attempt to storm Hill's Point was not made, the more so, as a reconnaissance made by Captain Douglas, of the Fifth Rhode Island Volunteers, showed that Hill's Point might have been carried. Information shows that only one brigade was within near reaching distance of that Point.

I fear that your judgment against the feasibility of attacking the place was too generally disseminated, and that the effect on subordinate officers and men was to discourage and seriously impair the *morale* so essential to success.

This is written, general, to acknowledge your report, and to express my regrets that your views were not mine; or, rather, that you did not recognize the emergency as one justifying and calling for some risks and greater efforts than were made.

I remain, general, respectfully, yours,

J. G. FOSTER,
Major-General, Commanding.

HEADQUARTERS DISTRICT OF THE PAMLICO,
Washington, N. C., May 10, 1863.

Maj. Gen. J. G. FOSTER,
Commanding Department of North Carolina:

GENERAL: Perfectly coinciding with you in the generalities of your letter of May 8, 1863, respecting the subject of landing at Hill's Point, the reasons I have assigned in my letter to you of the 26th of April, 1863, forbid my drawing the same special inference from them, and the hypothesis which you there state that you consider applicable to the case needs no other commentary than is furnished by the result of the siege.

There is no manner in which my judgment could have affected the *morale* of the troops. I am confident that it was never otherwise than well affected by me. After the fleet returned from the Pamlico, when the troops were crossing the Neuse for the purpose of marching to Washington, in which expedition they expected me to lead them, no regiment passed my house that did not rend the air with unanimous cheers. No cause whatever has existence for the fear you express, and I do most solemnly avow before my Maker that no valid reason can be assigned for it.

As I believe that an examination of the reconnaissance referred to by you as made by Captain Douglas, Fifth Rhode Island Volunteers, will deprive the remark you predicate upon it of all force, I beg that you will cause me to be furnished with an account of it.

Respecting the "one brigade" immediately in support of the battery it is but just to say that it was Pettigrew's, containing six full regiments, nominally 5,400 men, and that it was re-enforced by Claiborne's cavalry and by artillery. But D. H. Hill had two brigades on the south side of the river besides three unattached North Carolina regiments. Hill's Point Battery was the key of the investment. All military men will agree that he could therefore concentrate his main body in its defense. No doubt can exist of it. But this is of no moment in the argument. Pettigrew's brigade is sufficient for my purposes.

I have in vain endeavored to reach with my perceptive faculties the object of this correspondence. Has the interest of the country suffered? Or, on the other hand, has everything terminated according to the utmost blessing of the Almighty? The siege of Washington is raised in the best possible manner. The enemy acquired no advantage whatever over us in the course of it. Everything has resulted in the utter defeat and overthrow of his plans. Nothing could be better. Your name is the theme of every newspaper correspondent. And yet this correspondence is entered upon with me, in which there seems to be an elaborate effort to give currency to facts which have no existence by asserting them interrogatively, and in which, notwithstanding the favorable result of the siege, you now even go so far as to say "I can therefore only regret that the attempt to storm Hill's Point was not made," plainly regretting that an unnecessary and imminent risk of another Ball's Bluff was not run by landing 2,500 men in the face of Pettigrew's brigade, although such landing would have been in opposition to your own instructions given in writing to me. In this regret, which is uttered with such poetical sincerity, neither our country nor myself can possibly participate.

General, it is clear to the most common apprehension that the "hypothesis," the "fear," and the "regret" expressed in this letter have no existence in your mind; and I am sure that the reconnaissance which shows that Hill's Point Battery could have been taken by my 2,500 men will prove equally fictitious.

Very respectfully, general, your obedient servant,

HENRY PRINCE,
Brigadier-General Volunteers, Commanding District.

No. 9.

Reports of Col. Silas P. Richmond, Third Massachusetts Infantry, of operations April 7–10 and 16–21.

CAMP JOURDAN,
New Berne, N. C., April 11, 1863.

SIR: The following is a correct report of the part taken by myself and command in the recent reconnaissance in force under Brigadier-General Spinola.

April 7, 6.30 p. m.—Received orders to march immediately with three days' cooked rations, and seven in bulk to follow. My command left camp at 7 p. m., marched to Foster's Wharf, and there embarked on the steamer Allison, which took us across the Neuse River. We landed near Fort Anderson and bivouacked for the night. I had with me 24 officers and 517 men.

April 8.—Waited during the morning for the remainder of the troops to cross over. The troops were temporarily brigaded anew, my regiment being put in the First Brigade, under command of Acting Brigadier Amory. The whole column was under General Spinola, and consisted of three brigades of five regiments each with a small force of cavalry and artillery. The column moved at 1.30 p. m., my regiment having the left of the First Brigade. We marched in a northerly direction. The roads for the most part were very good and the column moved fast. We made no halts for rest. We passed New Hope School-House about sunset, taking the road to the left. We marched until 9 p. m., then bivouacked by the road side. Distance marched, 15 miles.

April 9.—Our brigade moved at 6.30 a. m., in the same order as yesterday. Marched back on the same road about 4 miles; then took a cross-road, which led into the main road to Core Point, and continued on in the latter; halted a short time for dinner and then marched on until 3 p. m., when we got in close proximity to Swift Creek, and the enemy's pickets were met—2 of them captured and the rest driven in. The enemy almost immediately opened on us with batteries on the other side of the creek. Our batteries moved to the front and engaged the enemy for about two hours, without any apparent effect. The enemy's shell, though few in number, were excellently aimed, every one causing some loss on our side. Ammunition being nearly all expended the order was given to retire, which we did in good order, marching back to the cross-roads near New Hope School-House and then bivouacked for the night, it being then about 9 p. m., and having marched during the day about 30 miles.

April 10.—The column was put in motion at about 7 a. m., Colonel Amory's brigade having the lead and marching left in front, which brought my regiment in advance. Reached the ferry near Fort Anderson at 10.30 a. m., and after a little delay we were transported across the river, reaching New Berne at 12 m., having marched in all about 55 miles in less than forty-eight hours from the time of leav ng Fort Anderson. I brought my men all safely into camp although they were more completely tired out than at any previous time during the campaign.

Respectfully submitted.

S. P. RICHMOND,
Colonel, Commanding Regiment.

S. A. ILSLEY,
A. A. A. G., Second Brigade, Eighteenth Army Corps.

HDQRS. THIRD REGT. MASSACHUSETTS VOL. MILITIA,
Camp Jourdan, New Berne, N. C., April 23, 1863.

COLONEL: On the morning of the 16th instant I received orders to have my command formed ready to march, with three days' cooked rations, seven in bulk, and 100 rounds of ammunition per man. The necessary preparations were immediately made and line formed.

A large number of both officers and men were on the sick list, consequently the column marched was less in number than at any previous time. I was too unwell to leave camp, and the regiment went under the command of Lieutenant-Colonel Barton.

The following is a copy of report to me:

CAMP JOURDAN,
New Berne, N. C., April 22, 1863.

Col. S. P. RICHMOND:

COLONEL: I have the honor to make the following report of the part taken by the Third Regiment in the late expedition under General Prince toward Kinston, N. C.:

Formed regiment line at 1C.30 on the morning of April 16 and marched with 448 men and 23 officers to the depot at New Berne; embarked on the cars at 2.45 p. m.; proceeded to a point 4 miles beyond Batchelder's Creek and bivouacked for the night.

On the morning of the 17th formed line at 7.30 and embarked on the cars and proceeded up the railroad and halted at the Jones plantation, a point near Core Creek; disembarked and formed line of battle. Three companies were ordered to report to Colonel Jourdan. Sent forward Companies C, B, and H. Regiment rested on their arms during the day and bivouacked here for the night.

18th.—All quiet through the night. Three companies were ordered to report to Colonel Jourdan. Sent forward Companies D, F, and A. Orders received to hold the regiment in readiness to act as a reserve. Sent out Company E on picket. Regiment halted here for the night.

19th.—All quiet through the night. Company G ordered on the cars to guard the train and ammunition. Regiment remained inactive through the day and bivouacked here for the night.

20th.—All quiet through the night. Three companies were ordered to report to Colonel Jourdan. Sent forward Companies K, E, and G. About 9 o'clock firing was heard at the front. Received orders to go on board the cars as a support to the battery. Moved forward to Core Creek and halted. At 2 o'clock returned to our former position and bivouacked here for the night.

21st.—All quiet through the night. Regiment remained inactive until 3 o'clock when orders were received to prepare to march. Embarked on the cars at 6 o'clock and returned to New Berne, reaching camp at 7 p. m. Whole distance traveled, 34 miles. No casualties.

All of which is respectfully submitted.

JAMES BARTON,
Lieutenant-Colonel Third Regiment Mass. Vol. Militia.

During the absence of the main portion of the regiment those remaining in camp improved in health considerably, but I am sorry to say that our sick list is still very large. Company I returned from detached service on the 20th instant, and last evening we had a dress-parade in which all the companies belonging to the regiment participated.   It was a very pleasing reunion to us, it being the first time at which all the companies have had an opportunity to form on the same line since the first day of our arrival in this department.

I remain, colonel, most respectfully, your obedient servant,

S. P. RICHMOND,
Colonel, Commanding Regiment.

Col. J. JOURDAN,
Comdg. Second Brig., Fifth Div., Eighteenth Army Corps.

No. 10.

Report of Capt. John M. Willson, Third New York Cavalry, of skirmish at Sandy Ridge, April 20.

PICKET STATION, NEUSE ROAD,
April 22, 1863.

SIR: I have to report to you that in the skirmish with the enemy April 20, 1 man was wounded and 3 horses killed and 1 revolver lost. Seventeen of my command were engaged, under the command of Sergt. Henry Dow.   I was sick and could not take command.

I am, respectfully, yours,

JOHN M. WILLSON,
Captain, Third New York Cavalry, Commanding Station.

Col. S. H. MIX,
Commanding Third New York Cavalry.

No. 11.

Report of Col. J. Richter Jones, Fifty-eighth Pennsylvania Infantry, of skirmish at Sandy Ridge, April 20.

HDQRS. FIFTY-EIGHTH REGIMENT PENNSYLVANIA VOLS.,
Camp at Core Creek, April 20, 1863.

SIR: I have the honor to report that I advanced on the Dover road this morning according to arrangements.   No enemy were found this side of Sandy Ridge, but at the junction, or just beyond the causeway running from the railroad, fire was opened on my skirmishers.   I had three companies deployed, which drove the enemy gradually back, they making a stand at every strong position.   Near the upper end of the ridge, where it is not more than 100 yards wide, they had a breastwork of logs and earth reaching across to the swamps on both flanks, which they endeavored to hold and defended with great resolution.   Finding the front likely to cost me many men, I deployed two more companies on the right and left flanks, with directions to force their way through the swamps.   Those swamps were barely passable by woodmen, but my men succeeded in advancing on the flank of the breastwork, when they raised a shout, at which the enemy abandoned it, and fled into the swamp to the rear of the ridge.

I cannot speak too highly of the conduct of my officers and men, of their coolness and steadiness under fire, and of their perseverance in pushing the enemy.   The enemy opposed to us were one company of

Nethercutt's battalion and three companies of the Forty-ninth North Carolina, Lieutenant-Colonel Flemming, and they numbered, one of the prisoners says, 225. We found one of the enemy dead on the field (whom we buried decently), 2 wounded and took 27 prisoners.

Our loss is 8 wounded, one of whom belongs to Company H, Third New York Cavalry, which company behaved gallantly and lost 3 horses. The breastwork where the enemy made their final stand is at the upper end of the ridge, about 6 miles by the Dover road from Core Creek; beyond, that road runs principally through swamps to its junction with the railroad.

Very respectfully, your obedient servant,

J. RICHTER JONES,
Colonel Fifty-eighth Regiment.

Captain WALDRON,
Assistant Adjutant-General.

No. 12.

Reports of Brig. Gen. Francis B. Spinola, U. S. Army, commanding Provisional Division and First Brigade, Fifth Division, of operations on the Pamlico, April 1–4; action at Blount's Creek, April 9, and of Expeditions from New Berne to Swift Creek Village, April 13–21.

HEADQUARTERS SPINOLA'S BRIGADE,
Washington, N. C., May 12, 1863.

COLONEL: In obedience to verbal orders, received at 4 o'clock on the morning of March 31, for me to have two regiments of my brigade ready to embark from the wharf at Fort Spinola at daybreak and for myself and staff to accompany them to Washington, N. C., where I would report to General Foster, I have the honor to report, viz:

I immediately proceeded to execute the order. The One hundred and seventy-first and One hundred and seventy-fifth Regiments Pennsylvania Militia, the first commanded by Colonel Bierer and the second commanded by Colonel Dyer, were at the wharf at the appointed time. At 6 a. m. the steamer Emilie, with a schooner in tow, started with the One hundred and seventy-fifth Regiment and the right wing of the One hundred and seventy-first Regiment, and at 10 o'clock the same morning the steamer John Farron started, with schooner in tow, the left wing of the One hundred and seventy-first Regiment being on the Farron and three pieces of Ransom's battery, with caissons, limbers, and 200 rounds of ammunition for each gun, together with Captain Ransom and his company, being on the schooner; myself and staff on the Faron.

I proceeded down the Neuse River and at 2 p. m. came up with the steamer Sylvan Shore, lying at anchor inside of the light-house at the mouth of Neuse River. I gave the captain orders to proceed at once to the steamer Thomas Colyer, then aground on a shoal about 8 miles from the light-house, and take the One hundred and fifty-eighth Regiment Pennsylvania Militia from on board of her and proceed with it to Washington, N. C., with all dispatch.

The One hundred and fifty-eighth Regiment had started for Washington on March 29 under orders from Headquarters Eighteenth Army Corps. I subsequently ascertained that the steamer Sylvan Shore could not accommodate all of the regiment, and at 3 o'clock of the same day

I overtook the steam-tug Alert and sent her, together with the stern-wheel steamer Wilson, after the remainder of the One hundred and fifty-eighth Regiment. After the regiments had all been taken from the Colyer I put part of them on the John Farron and a portion of them on the schooner with the artillery, and directed the tug to take the schooner in tow and reach Washington with her as soon as possible.

At 4.30 p. m. passed Brant Island Shoals Light-House, and at 7 o'clock passed the light-house at the entrance to Pamlico River. At 7.20 o'clock met the steamer North Shore. The officer aboard informed me that he was bound to New Berne with dispatches from General Foster to General Palmer, and that the rebels had erected batteries on Mull's and Hill's Points, on the Pamlico River, and that it was General Foster's orders not to proceed any farther up the river until gunboats should arrive to convoy the transports by the batteries. I proceeded to within about 5 or 6 miles of Mull's Point, and at 9.30 o'clock came to anchor. Our approach was signaled by the enemy from a point about 10 miles below Mull's Point. The signals were very distinct and continued at intervals throughout the night.

On Wednesday morning, April 1, the gunboat Lockwood passed by a little before daylight, and proceeded to within 1 mile of Hill's Point and came to anchor.

At 6 o'clock on the morning of April 1 I got the steamer Farron and other transports under way and proceeded up the river, and at 9 o'clock again anchored within 2½ miles of the Hill's Point Battery.

At 10 o'clock I visited the gunboat Lockwood and learned from Mr. Hicks, who commanded her, that there were five guns mounted on the battery on Hill's Point; that he had been directly under the battery and had seen and counted the guns. Mr. Hicks expressed his willingness to do anything in his power to assist the transports in running by the batteries, whereupon I requested him to proceed within range and open fire upon it, which he did, taking his vessel directly under it and continuing to fire for an hour and a half without any reply from the enemy.

At 2.30 p. m. Captain Gouraud, of General Foster's staff, and Lieutenant Cole, of my staff, volunteered to run by the blockade in a small boat and proceed to Washington with dispatches for General Foster. They got safely by the Hill's Point Battery, and after proceeding a few miles up the river met Master's Mate McKeever, of the gunboat Louisiana, who was on his way down with dispatches from General Foster. Captain Gouraud and Lieutenant Cole returned again to the steamer.

Master's Mate McKeever said that no boat drawing 6 feet of water could reach Washington, as the tide was lower than it had been for a year. This statement was also confirmed by the pilot of the gunboat Lockwood, who asserted to his knowledge that it had never before been so low; all the transports required more than 6 feet of water; while Mr. Hicks, commanding the gunboat, gave it as his opinion that he believed it impossible for any of the transports to pass the batteries, as the channel was only about 80 feet in width and all the buoys had been removed by the enemy.

At 7.30 p. m. I sent the steamer Sylvan Shore to New Berne for additional gunboats and ammunition of the kind required for the guns at Washington, that aboard of the transports not being of the character required for the gunboats and artillery at that place. The stern-wheel steamer Wilson arrived and reported at 9.30 p. m.

Lieutenant Cole, of my staff, and Master's Mate McKeever started in a small boat to run the blockade, with dispatches for General Foster, and got safely through, and returned at 7.15 o'clock on the morning of April 2 with dispatches from General Foster.

After arriving in front of the rebel batteries and remaining there all day, and finding it quite impossible to run the transports by the batteries at that time or until additional gunboats should arrive so as to hold the enemy's guns in check while the vessels were passing, and after having carefully examined in person the shore from the mouth of Blount's Creek to within a short distance of Hill's Point, having likewise made the necessary soundings along the shore to ascertain the depth of water between the above-named points with a view to select the most suitable place to land, I decided to have the troops put ashore and storm the works on Hill's Point, and to that end issued the following orders on the afternoon of April 1, 1863:

SPECIAL ORDERS, }   HEADQUARTERS ABOARD JOHN FARON,
    No. 1.   }   Pamlico River, N. C., April 1, 1863.

I. Colonel Dyer, commanding the One hundred and seventy-fifth Regiment Pennsylvania Militia, will disembark his regiment on the steamer Wilson and land them near the mouth of Blount's Creek and storm the battery on Hill's Point at daylight to-morrow morning.

II. Colonel Bierer, commanding the One hundred and seventy-first Regiment Pennsylvania Militia, will hold that portion of his command that is now aboard the steamer Émilie in readiness to disembark at daylight to-morrow morning to support Colonel Dyer, who is to storm the battery on Hill's Point.

III. Lieutenant-Colonel Troxel, commanding the One hundred and fifty-eighth Regiment Pennsylvania Militia, will hold that portion of his command that is now aboard the steamer Emilie, and a sufficient number in addition from aboard the schooner to make his command 300 men in all, in readiness to disembark at daylight to-morrow to act in conjunction with Colonel Bierer's command as support to Colonel Dyer, who is to storm the battery on Hill's Point.

IV. Lieut. Thomas Low, in command of three guns of the battery, now aboard the schooner Annie L. Edwards, will be ready to go into action with his guns at daylight to-morrow morning. He will act in concert with the captain of the gunboat Lockwood. The schooner will be towed into action by a propeller.

By command of Brigadier-General Spinola:

                                   L. HANLEY,
                          Captain and Assistant Adjutant-General.

I also made a thorough and careful examination on the evening of April 1 of the approaches by water to Bath, on the north side of the river, with a view of landing there and marching to Washington in case I failed in taking the battery on Hill's Point.

At 2 o'clock on the morning of April 2 the steamer North Shore arrived with Brig. Gen. Henry Prince and staff aboard. The foregoing orders were not executed, as General Prince took command of the forces, and all movements from that time until he left again for New Berne were under his direction and will, I presume, be embodied in his report.

At 6 p. m. on the 2d instant the steam-tug Alida left for New Berne, and at 8 o'clock the same evening General Prince and staff started for New Berne on the steamer North Shore, which again left me in command.

April 3 I loaded eight small boats with ammunition, and although it was blowing almost a gale of wind, which rendered the undertaking of running the blockade extremely hazardous in addition to passing the enemy's batteries, yet I experienced no difficulty in finding a sufficient number of volunteers from aboard the gunboats to man all the small boats, and at 9 p. m. this little fleet started, under the command of Lieutenant Williams, of my staff, and reached the garrison in safety. Upon consultation with Captain MacDearmid, of the gunboat Ceres, he volunteered to buoy out the channel and run his boat past the batteries.

Accordingly at 10 o'clock on the night of April 3 he started to place the buoys, and at 12 o'clock reported that he had succeeded and was then ready to run his boat through if I desired it. I accordingly had the Ceres brought alongside of the Farron and put on board of her all the ammunition her magazine could hold.

At 2.45 o'clock on the morning of April 4 Captain MacDearmid started with his gunboat and passed all the batteries in safety, the Hill's and Swan's Point Batteries firing at him as long as he was within range of their guns.

At 4 o'clock on the morning of April 4 I received a dispatch from General Foster for General Prince. It was of an important character, and I concluded to forward it at once to General Prince at New Berne. Accordingly I had the 600 troops on the Farron transferred to the two schooners that had Ransom's battery aboard, and started the steamer at 6 o'clock in the morning for New Berne with a letter to General Palmer, asking that all the small boats, together with the surf boats and launches that could be procured at New Berne, might be sent down by the steamer on her return, as I had become satisfied that the garrison could be re-enforced by passing the blockade with these boats in the night, in case all other plans failed. The steamer returned but the boats did not come.

At 2 o'clock three additional gunboats arrived, the Southfield, White-head, and Seymour. Their several commanders expressed a desire to render all the assistance in their power toward relieving the garrison, and wished to know my desires in the matter; whereupon I requested that they would at once engage the battery on Hill's Point, which they did at a distance of about 1,000 yards, and nothing could have been more accurate than the firing of the Southfield and one or two others of the boats, from the effect of which I became entirely satisfied that the battery could be passed in safety.

After ascertaining that the buoys put down by Captain MacDearmid had not been disturbed, and as soon as dark set in, I had the whole of Ramson's battery, including officers and men, transferred to the schooner Nellie D., and the six guns placed in position on the schooner's deck. I likewise transferred the whole of the One hundred and seventy-fifth Regiment Pennsylvania Militia, under command of Colonel Dyer, num-bering 600 men, on the same schooner, and had made arrangements for the gunboat Lockwood to take aboard the ammunition that had reached me for the gunboats and batteries at Washington, and also to take the schooner in tow and run the blockade with her before daylight on the following morning. The above arrangements were made by the regi-mental and battery commanders in pursuance of the following orders:

SPECIAL ORDERS, }   HEADQUARTERS ABOARD THE THOMAS COLYER,
    No. 2.   }   *Pamlico River, near Hill's Point, N. C., April 4,* 1863.

I. Col. Samuel A. Dyer, commanding One hundred and seventy-fifth Regiment Pennsylvania Militia, will immediately transfer his command from the schooner ——— to the schooner Nellie D. that has Ransom's battery aboard, for the purpose of running the blockade by the rebel batteries on Hill's and Swan's Points and Rod-man's Quarters and re-enforcing General Foster at Washington.

II. The utmost caution must be exercised in keeping the men between decks while passing the batteries.

III. Captain Ransom, commanding battery, will transfer the guns of his battery, together with caissons, ammunition, and men, from the schooner ——— to the schooner Nellie D., and have all his guns placed in position and ready for action on the deck of the schooner Nellie D., so as to assist in fighting his way past the batteries.

IV. The captain of the schooner Nellie D. will receive aboard his vessel Colonel Dyer's regiment of infantry and the balance of Ransom's battery.

V. Captain Graves, of the gunboat Lockwood, is requested to receive aboard his boat the ammunition sent from New Berne for General Foster, and lay his vessel alongside the schooner Nellie D. for the purpose of towing her past the batteries and through the blockade to Washington between now and daylight.

By command of Brigadier-General Spinola, commanding:

L. HANLEY,
Captain and Assistant Adjutant-General.

Everything was in readiness to make the move under the above orders when General Prince and staff arrived in the steamer Escort at about 11 p. m., April 4, and assumed command, after which the execution of the foregoing orders devolved upon him. The arrangements for running the blockade with the gunboat and schooner were not carried out, although the schooner had weighed anchor and the gunboat had made fast to her and both were under way when General Prince countermanded the orders and the schooner again came to anchor. I had made all the above arrangements under the belief that the favorable moment to re-enforce the garrison had arrived, as there were 2 or 3 feet more water in the river than there had been at any time since my arrival. I ascertained this fact by soundings made under my own personal supervision. The reason for countermanding the orders under which the arrangements had been made for the schooner Nellie D. and gunboat Lockwood to run the blockade I have no doubt will be fully explained in General Prince's report.

All the officers and men of my brigade were both willing and anxious to incur any risk or to encounter any danger necessary to relieve the beleaguered city, and no troops in the army could have manifested a greater willingness to make any necessary sacrifice to re-enforce the garrison and to relieve it from the perils that surrounded it.

I cannot close this report without bearing testimony to the gallant conduct of the Navy while acting in conjunction with my command, particularly Captain MacDearmid, of the gunboat Ceres. The conduct of the several commanders of the gunboats engaged was all that could have been expected of them. They manifested great bravery, coupled with a willingness to do all in their power to relieve the garrison.

I have the honor to be, very respectfully, your obedient servant,

F. B. SPINOLA,
Brigadier-General.

Lieut. Col. SOUTHARD HOFFMAN,
Assistant Adjutant-General, Eighteenth Army Corps.

HDQRS. ON FIELD AT LITTLE SWIFT CREEK,
April 8, 1863—Wednesday night, 11 o'clock.

GENERAL: In pursuance to your instructions of to-day the column under my command started at 3 o'clock p. m. and arrived at this place at 8 o'clock p. m., The advance guard met the enemy's pickets about 7 miles from Fort Anderson. They retreated without returning fire, and about half an hour later we heard their alarm guns. From information entirely reliable I learn that the enemy, 6,000 infantry and 1,000 cavalry, are in a strong fortified position at Walter Ruff's farm, on the road leading to Blount's Creek. I also learn from the same source that the enemy occupy both sides of Swift Creek Bridge. There are other forces on the road leading to Kinston, but I could not learn their position or strength. It is to be presumed that the enemy is in strong position and force at the cross-roads near Washington. Should I proceed to Washington on the Swift Creek road I feel assured that I will be attacked in the rear by the forces above named on Ruff's farm, and would also be harassed on my left flank by the forces stationed on the Kinston roads. In case I fail to drive the enemy from the cross-roads near Washington and am compelled to retreat it can only be done with a large sacrifice, if at all. From all the information I have received it establishes the strength of the enemy not less than 20,000, under Hill, Pettigrew, and Garnett. The majority of the information fixes the enemy's strength at 22,000, and it is therefore supposable that we will have to encounter at least 10,000 under Hill at the cross-roads near Washington. that being the main position of the enemy. It appears to me now that the only possible successful way to relieve the garrison is to take the battery at Hill's Point, and in that way raise the blockade.

We are constructing the bridge over Little Swift Creek to-night.

I shall have a consultation to-night with the brigade commanders, artillery, and cavalry. It is my intention to start from here in the morning for Blount's Creek, and engage the enemy there, and drive them, if possible, beyond the battery on Hill's Point with a view of taking it. Should I not be successful I shall retreat to Fort Anderson, as I am satisfied it is utterly impossible to march on Washington by the Swift Creek route without endangering my entire command. In the event of having to retreat it will be necessary that transportation be ready to convey the command across the Neuse River. Send forward immediately the forage wagons and wagons with officers' baggage; the other wagons leave till you hear further from me.

I am, general, very respectfully, your obedient servant,

F. B. SPINOLA,
Brigadier-General.

Brig. Gen. I. N. PALMER.

—

HEADQUARTERS GENERAL SPINOLA'S COMMAND,
NEAR NEW HOPE SCHOOL-HOUSE,
Thursday Evening, April 9, 1863—11.30 o'clock.

GENERAL: I have the honor to communicate that I started at 7 o'clock this morning from Little Swift Creek with my command and marched to Ruff's Mill, at the head of Blount's Creek, a distance of 15 miles. Two miles from this place we met and exchanged fire with the enemy's picket, which was continued till we reached the cross-roads, 1 mile from Ruff's Mill. I followed the enemy with the intention of crossing Blount's Creek, in order to make my way to Washington, as I have already indicated in my last letter to you. I found, however, the enemy's position almost impregnable, owing to the thickness of swamp woods on the north side of Blount's Creek, and also to the strong earthworks on the south side of the creek, behind which the enemy were 2,000 strong. I will also mention that these earthworks are thrown up close to the bridge, which was destroyed by the enemy previous to my arrival there. The earthworks were partly dug in the ground and partly thrown up, so that they could only be reached by depressing our pieces. In the enemy's works were six pieces mounted, which I judge to be 12-pounder howitzers, [which] were served with great skill. Behind these fortifications, at a distance of about a half mile, were also 3,000 of the enemy, the whole 5,000 being under the command of General Pettigrew. I also learn from reliable sources that the roads from Blount's Creek to Washington and Hill's Point are entirely occupied by the enemy, and I learn by positive evidence that there are two brigades encamped at and near the cross-roads in front of Washington, under the immediate command of General Hill. The engagement was commenced by a company of the Third New York Cavalry with a mountain howitzer. The howitzer, under command of Lieutenant Burke, and the company of cavalry, under the command of Captain ———, were under the direction of Major Garrard, Third New York Cavalry, temporarily detailed on my staff. The cavalry detachment constituted part of Colonel Amory's brigade, who engaged the enemy at the bridge for nearly two hours. Owing to the condition of the ground it was impossible to develop a large force against the enemy, and therefore only two regiments of infantry, the Seventeenth and Forty-third Massachusetts Volunteers, two sections of Captain Belger's battery, and one section of 32-pounder howitzers, under command of Lieutenant ———, together with the cavalry above named, were actually engaged. Though we succeeded in silencing the enemy's battery, yet we were unable to drive them from their position, as our infantry and artillery fire were without much effect upon them, owing to the nature of their earthworks and the position of our guns. It was equally impossible to enfilade their works or to cross or ford the creek at any other point, and, as stated above, the bridge being destroyed we were unable to charge the enemy or build the bridge under their heavy musketry fire. Seeing that it was impossible to cross the creek, I was obliged to return, and did so at 5 o'clock this afternoon, in regular order, without being molested in any way by the enemy.

I take pleasure in stating that Colonel Amory's conduct during the march and engagement was of the most creditable character, as was also Major Frankle's, Major Garrard's, and Major Stone's, temporarily detailed on my staff. The Seventeenth Massachusetts Volunteers, under command of Lieutenant-Colonel Fellows, is especially deserving of notice; while all the officers and men of the command manifested an anxious determination to reach Washington at all hazards and relieve the garrison there, but failed to do it for the reason that they could not perform impossibilities.

I deplore the necessity of stating the casualties of officers and men during the engagement, which was very slight considering the nature of our engagement. Captain Belger was wounded in the hip, the ball passing through his thigh and killing his horse; Lieutenant Roberts, Seventeenth Massachusetts, left arm broken by a Minie ball; 2 men of Battery F, First Rhode Island Artillery, 1 slightly, the other severely; 5 men of Seventeenth Massachusetts, 1 severely.

I shall leave this place for New Berne to-morrow morning, feeling conscious that I have done all that was in my power to comply with the requests of General Foster as well as to carry out your instructions.

I am, general, very respectfully, your obedient servant,

F. B. SPINOLA,
Brigadier-General.

Brig. Gen. I. N. PALMER.

———

CAMP AT NEW HOPE SCHOOL-HOUSE,
Tuesday, April 14, 1863.—5 p. m.

GENERAL : Pursuant to instructions received last night I left Fort Anderson with my command at 10.30 a. m. and arrived at this place at 4 p. m. At the forks of the road, about 8 miles from Fort Anderson, I sent the whole detachment of cavalry (but 10) and the cavalry howitzer on the road leading to the right, which terminates at the road leading to Blount's Creek and about 1 mile from the school-house. I expected the enemy's pickets to be posted at this place in strength, and therefore instructed the commandant of the cavalry to march quickly over the road in order, if possible, to cut them off from their main force; in the mean time our main column marched on the direct road here. I am happy to inform you that Captain Chamberlin, commanding the cavalry, has faithfully performed the duty assigned him by succeeding in cutting off and capturing two cavalry pickets stationed here. From our prisoners we have received information that the enemy occupied Blount's Creek with 6,000 infantry and one regiment of cavalry, and from that to the cross-roads leading to Washington they have 15,000 infantry and three regiments of cavalry stationed. They are fortified in every available position with about one hundred and fifty pieces of artillery.

I also learn that the stringers of the bridge across Blount's Creek are cut, which, if so, will prevent our crossing there.

The prisoners belong to Colonel Claiborne's regiment, Seventh Confederate Cavalry, newly arrived from the Blackwater. They state that there are 50,000 rebel soldiers stationed around Washington. I have sent the cavalry in two parts to scour the roads leading to Blount's Creek and Swift Creek. The latter road I have our pioneers employed in clearing what we blockaded in our last march here, as I intend leaving here at daylight in the morning and march toward Swift Creek, leaving a portion of my command to occupy our present position until we return.

I am, general, very respectfully, your obedient servant,
F. B. SPINOLA,
Brigadier-General.

Brigadier-General WESSELLS,
Commanding Eighteenth Army Corps.

—

HEADQUARTERS SPINOLA'S BRIGADE,
Washington, N. C., May 15, 1863.

COLONEL : In obedience to orders received from Headquarters Eighteenth Army Corps, directing that my brigade should be at Foster's Wharf at 2 a. m. on April 8 for the purpose of crossing the Neuse River, I have the honor to submit the following report:

The brigade reached the place designated a quarter of an hour before the time specified, and in two hours were all over the river. They bivouacked near the old rebel fort on the road leading to the New Hope School-House.

At between 1 and 2 o'clock on the morning of April 8 I called upon Brig. Gen. Henry Prince at his headquarters to ascertain if there were any specific instructions to be issued in regard to the expedition and to learn what time he had fixed on for the column to commence moving. I believe that General Prince was to command the expedition, as he had been ordered by General Foster to proceed with it to the relief of the garrison at Washington, N. C., which was then invested by the enemy.

I found General Prince in a state of mind denoting that he was very much exercised in regard to the propriety of making the contemplated march, and he freely expressed his opinion to me that the expedition could not succeed, that it must be a very great failure, for he did not believe that any of those who accompanied it would return, as we would all be captured, and that it was like making the rebels a present of all the artillery.

General Prince at this interview also invited me to volunteer to take the command of the expedition, which I declined in the most positive and unmistakable language. I was entirely willing to take my chance with others of either falling upon the field or being taken prisoner, but my own good sense promptly told me that the size of the expedition and the importance of its trust forbade one of my limited military experience from assuming its command, except under positive orders from my superior officers, and then, in obedience to a willing heart, I could only promise to do the best I could to accomplish the object of the expedition.

At about 10 a. m. on April 8 a messenger called at my room and told me that General Palmer desired to see me at once. I immediately proceeded to his headquarters, when he informed me that the command of the expedition would fall upon me. This was the first intimation I had received that this important trust would be placed under my charge. I expressed my astonishment at it, and told General Palmer that I could not assume the command unless I received a written order to that effect, which he assured me I should have before starting.

I have deemed it due to truth and the interest of the service that these facts should be stated in this report, as they form a link in the history of the efforts made to relieve the invested garrison.

I then crossed the river, and shortly after reaching the other side was handed the following order:

FORT ANDERSON, NEUSE RIVER,
April 8, 1863.

Brig. Gen. F. B. SPINOLA,
  U. S. Volunteers, New Berne, N. C.:

GENERAL: The forces for the relief of Washington are hereby placed under your command, and a list of them is furnished to you. General Foster, commanding this department, has given positive instructions that all the available force at New Berne shall march to Washington to his relief. You will perceive that this order has been implicitly obeyed as far as placing the troops at your disposition is concerned.

You have informed me that you have read the orders sent to General Prince by General Foster. As these are the only instructions I have seen I can only direct you to bear in mind the letter of General Foster and exercise your best judgment in carrying out his views. The sole object of the expedition is to get the troops into Washington, now invested by the enemy, and I feel confident that everything that can be done will be effected.

Please to keep me informed of the state of affairs as you proceed. Look well to the roads leading into your route from the direction of Kinston. Should you be obliged to build a bridge at Swift Creek it should be protected, for the supplies for your command may not be able to start until to-morrow.

I will not anticipate a failure to get through, but should you be obliged to return (for I shall send for you if this place is attacked by any force that I think will be able to overcome the force left here) let the return movement be conducted with order and great care.

I am, general, very respectfully, your obedient servant,

I. N. PALMER,
Brigadier-General, Commanding.

on the receipt of which I directed the column to be ready to move at 3 o'clock that afternoon. I organized the several regiments comprising the command into three brigades, of five regiments each, and assigned to each brigade its proper portion of artillery, and also gave the cavalry the necessary instructions to govern them on the march.

The First Brigade was put under the command of Colonel Amory, of the Seventeenth Massachusetts Volunteers, and comprised the following infantry and artillery: The Seventeenth Massachusetts Volunteers, two 32-pounder howitzers, Forty-third Massachusetts Volunteers, One hundred and first Pennsylvania Volunteers, Ninety-sixth New York Volunteers, Third Massachusetts Volunteers, and Belger's battery.

The Second Brigade was commanded by Colonel Lee, and consisted of the following-named infantry and artillery : The Eighty-fifth New York Volunteers, One hundred and third Pennsylvania Volunteers, Riggs' battery, Fifth Massachusetts Volunteers, Eighth Massachusetts Volunteers, and One hundred and thirty-second New York Volunteers.

The Third Brigade was under the command of Colonel Bierer, and included the following regiments of infantry and pieces of artillery : Two pieces of artillery, One hundred and seventy-fifth Pennsylvania Militia, One hundred and fifty-eighth New York Volunteers, One hundred and seventy-first Pennsylvania Militia, One hundred and fifty eighth Pennsylvania Militia, and Fifth Rhode Island Volunteers.

The following official statement, purporting to show the true strength of the command, was also furnished me by General Palmer on the day the expedition was to leave, and it is the one referred to in General Palmer's order :

Official statement of troops that can be furnished Brig. Gen. H. Prince, U. S. Volunteers, commanding Expedition, April 8, 1863.

	Men.
Eighty-fifth New York Infantry	445
One hundred and third Pennsylvania Infantry	471
Fifth Massachusetts Infantry	593
Eighth Massachusetts Infantry	271
One hundred and fifty-eighth New York Infantry	245
One hundred and thirty-second New York Infantry	555
Third Massachusetts Infantry	674
Seventeenth Massachusetts Infantry	591
Forty-third Massachusetts Infantry	701
One hundred and first Pennsylvania Infantry	395
Ninety-sixth New York Infantry	278
One hundred and seventy-first Pennsylvania Infantry	600
One hundred and fifty-eighth Pennsylvania Infantry	600
One hundred and seventy-fifth Pennsylvania Infantry	600
Fifth Rhode Island Infantry	388
Total infantry	7,407

Artillery, 16 guns.
Cavalry, two squadrons, 400 men.

By command of Brig. Gen. I. N. Palmer, commanding:

J. A. JUDSON,
Captain and Assistant Adjutant-General.

It is evident that this statement was prepared with the understanding that General Prince was to command. It represents the strength of the expedition to be 7,807, exclusive of the artillery, which was 316, as shown by a field report made at the time of starting, which would make the whole force 8,123; while the field report received from each brigade, together with the artillery and cavalry, half an hour before starting, showed the whole force to be but 6,465, instead of 8,123, a difference of 1,658 less than that shown by the official statement.

The column moved promptly at 3 o'clock, and reached Little Swift Creek at 8 o'clock the same evening, having marched between 14 and 15 miles. The advance guard met the enemy's picket about 7 miles from Fort Anderson. They retreated without returning fire. Half an hour later three heavy guns were heard in the direction of Swift Creek Village, which I took for alarm guns of the enemy. From information of a character that seemed entirely reliable I learned that six regiments of infantry (about 6,000 men), under command of General Pettigrew, and one regiment of cavalry, under command of Colonel Claiborne, numbering about 1,000 men, were encamped at Walter Buff's farm, on the road leading to Washington and Hill's Point, where it crosses Blount's Creek. From various sources I learned that the enemy were also in large force at Swift Creek Village and occupied both sides of the bridge, as well as the roads leading to Kinston and Greenville; but I could not learn their exact strength, except that they occupied five or six different camps. The fact that the enemy were in force at the cross-roads·in front of Washington was also confirmed by both contrabands and prisoners in a manner that left no doubt in my mind that the strength of the enemy on the south side of Pamlico River and vicinity, and all of which were within supporting distance of each other, could not have been less than 12,000 or 15,000 men, although it was fixed by all the information received at a much greater number. With these facts before me, and after a consultation with the brigade commanders together with the chief officer of artillery, who were unanimous in their expressions of opinion that the column had better return to New Berne, as in their judgment an absolute failure would be the result of the expedition if we proceeded by this route, I therefore concluded not to go by the way of Swift Creek Village.

The infantry of the enemy at this place was strongly intrenched and had thrown up earthworks for their artillery which commanded all the direct approaches to the village, although from the evidence received their strength in the village proper was not as great as mine, and if I had attacked them there and driven them out of the place they could have retreated toward the cross-roads in front of Washington and joined the forces located at that point. Still, to have pursued this course and pushed on toward Washington by this route would have exposed my left flank to the assault of the enemy, who were encamped in considerable force on the roads leading toward Kinston and Greenville, while Pettigrew would certainly have crossed Blount's Creek and attacked my rear, for I had no way of protecting it except by dividing my force and it was not large enough to admit of that being done, particularly so as I would have been compelled to have met at the cross-roads and in my front a force very much larger than my own and well intrenched.

Thus hemmed in on three sides by an active foe, with an impenetrable swamp on my right, it would have left me but a small chance of success and no opportunity whatever of falling back in the event of a repulse at the cross-roads, the consequence of which would have been either the annihilation of my command or its capture, to avoid which I decided to try and reach Washington by the way of Blount's Creek road, and if possible drive the enemy back, so as to reach Hill's Point and capture that battery and thus raise the blockade. In making this march I could completely cover my rear and flanks by removing the bridges across Little Swift Creek and blockading the roads over which I was to pass before reaching the main road leading to Blount's Creek, all of which I did, although I could not have protected my rear and flanks by the same means if I had taken the Swift Creek road, as it would have cut off my only means of retreat in the event of a repulse, as well as to have completely destroyed all communication with New Berne, which I was directed to protect and keep open for the accommodation of the wagon and ammunition train, which could not start until one day after the main body of the troops.

I further deem it of interest that the following communication, received from General Palmer while on the march, should be introduced in this report, as it is confirmatory of my own information in regard to the strength and position of the enemy:

NEW BERNE, N. C., *April 9, 1863—8 a. m.*

Brig. Gen. F. B. SPINOLA,
  United States Volunteers:

GENERAL: Yours, written at 11 p. m. yesterday, I have received. An hour before I received your letter I heard from Captain McCann, commanding the gunboats on the river near the blockade, the same information concerning the force and position of the enemy. Your suggestions as to the mode of relief for Washington, taking all things into consideration, appear to be good. I cannot trammel you with orders. Your own good judgment must dictate your course. Your suggestion concerning the transportation and the wagons to be forwarded shall be adopted.

  Very respectfully, yours,

I. N. PALMER,
  Brigadier-General, Commanding.

On the morning of April 9 I moved back from Little Swift Creek toward the New Hope School-House, which I reached at 9 o'clock, halted the column, fed the artillery horses (the forage having just reached me at this point), and at 10 o'clock started for Blount's Creek, a distance of 11 miles, which place I reached at about 3 o'clock in the afternoon. After marching 2 miles we met and exchanged fire with the enemy's pickets, which was continued until we reached the cross-roads 1 mile from Ruff's Mill, which is located near the head of the creek. I here halted the column for about fifteen minutes while I made a reconnaissance of the approaches to the bridge which led over the creek. I here found the enemy in force and strongly intrenched. I moved forward Colonel Amory's brigade, with two 32-pounder howitzers under the command of Lieutenant Folk, and the 12-pounder Napoleon battery under command of Captain Belger. The approaches to the creek by the main road were through a dense wood with marsh on the left, the ground to the right being a little higher but heavily timbered, while the edge of the stream could not be reached owing to its swampy nature, together with the growth of heavy timber and underbrush which rendered it impassable, so that it was impossible to reach the creek below the bridge except toward its mouth, a distance of 5 or 6 miles, and there it could not be crossed without the aid of pontoon bridges or flats decked over, neither of which I had been provided with.

As we approached, the enemy opened fire on the column from the opposite bank of the creek and the engagement was immediately commenced by Company —, Third New York Cavalry, Captain Pond, which was dismounted and deployed as skirmishers, with a mountain howitzer under command of Lieutenant Burke, the howitzer and cavalry being under the direction of Major Garrard, Third New York Cavalry. The advance line of skirmishers was also engaged at the same time with the cavalry and howitzer companies.

The enemy on the opposite bank of the creek, which is not fordable and crossed only by a bridge which they had rendered impassable by tearing off the planking, were concealed on the higher ground occupied by them. I accordingly had the skirmishers, the howitzer, and cavalry companies withdrawn, and opened fire with canister from the two 32-pounder howitzers, to which I soon added four pieces of Belger's battery, the enemy replying in the same manner with grape, canister, and shell. The engagement continued for an hour and three-quarters in this way.

Having silenced the enemy's guns and dismounted one of them, and finding it utterly impossible under the circumstances to cross the creek, I ordered the infantry to fall back and the artillery gradually withdrawn, with a squadron of cavalry in their rear.

No property of any description was left behind. The return march was made without the least confusion or interruption of any kind and without any molestation from the enemy. The column proceeded as far as the New Hope School-House and bivouacked for the night, and returned to New Berne the next day.

The casualties of officers and men were 11 wounded, none killed, which was very slight considering the nature of the engagement. Captain Belger was wounded in the leg, the ball passing through his thigh and killing his horse under him; in the Seventeenth Massachusetts Volunteers, Lieutenant Roberts and 7 men; in the artillery, 2 men besides Captain Belger.

It is impossible to ascertain the loss of the enemy. Several prisoners were taken. As our fire was well sustained, it doubtless did good execution.

The Seventeenth Massachusetts Volunteers and the Forty-third Massachusetts Militia were the only part of my infantry engaged, and the conduct of both officers and men was all that could be desired, as was also that of the artillery and cavalry engaged.

I take great pleasure in stating that the conduct of Colonel Amory, commanding brigade; Lieutenant-Colonel Lewis, of the cavalry; Lieutenant-Colonel Fellows, commanding Seventeenth Massachusetts, together with Captain Belger, of the artillery, during the march and engagement, was not only cool and brave but of the most creditable character, particularly while under fire; as was also that of Major Garrard, of the Third New York Cavalry; Major Frankle, of the Seventeenth Massachusetts Volunteers, and Major Stone, of the Third New York Artillery, the last-named officers having been temporarily detailed on my staff.

I am, colonel, with respect, your obedient servant,

F. B. SPINOLA,
Brigadier-General.

Lieut. Col. SOUTHARD HOFFMAN,
Assistant Adjutant General, Eighteenth Army Corps.

—

HEADQUARTERS SPINOLA'S BRIGADE,
Washington, N. C., May 18, 1863.

COLONEL: I have the honor to submit the following report:
At 5 p. m. on April 13 I received the following order:

NEW BERNE, N. C., *April* 13, 1863.

Brigadier-General SPINOLA,
Commanding Brigade:

GENERAL: You will cross the Neuse with your brigade with as much expedition as practicable, and make from Fort Anderson a careful reconnaissance in the direction of Washington, for the purpose of ascertaining the condition of the country and to divert the attention of the enemy from their attempt on our position at Washington. A squadron of cavalry and a section each from Belger's, Riggs', and Ransom's batteries are ordered to accompany you.

Major Garrard, an officer of intelligence and familiar with the country, will report to you in person for such duty as you may require.

The road to the New Hope School-House and that toward Swift Creek Village should be carefully examined, and in all movements care should be taken to secure your flanks and rear by occupying strong and unassailable positions. Much is left to your discretion, it being understood that General Foster's desire is for us to occupy or divert the attention of the enemy from his front.

The quartermaster's department is ordered to furnish the necessary transportation. Three days' rations will be taken in the haversacks, and additional supplies sent to you at Fort Anderson on your requisition.

It is desirable that you move with all your effective force and issue strict orders against straggling, marauding, destruction of property, and the wanton practice of firing the woods along the line of march.

Communicate frequently with these headquarters.

Respectfully, your obedient servant,

H. W. WESSELLS,
Brigadier-General of Volunteers, Commanding.

I immediately ordered the necessary rations prepared for the march, and at 8 o'clock on the evening of April 13 reached Foster's Wharf, and the brigade crossed over the Neuse River. At 11 o'clock we reached the old rebel fort 1 mile beyond Fort Anderson and bivouacked for the night.

At daybreak on the morning of April 14 the brigade took up its line of march toward the New Hope School-House, which place we reached early in the forenoon. Having marched 10 miles I halted the column to allow the men to rest and prepare their dinner, after which I carefully examined by strong detachments all the roads leading to this place for a distance of 7 or 8 miles, except the one leading to Swift Creek.

After the return of the various detachments, it being late in the day and the men considerably fatigued, I ordered the brigade to bivouac for the night.

There was no enemy in any force on any of the roads examined except pickets, 5 of whom I captured, 3 of them belonging to Claiborne's cavalry and 2 of them to Whitford's battalion. It was my intention to have moved on toward Swift Creek Village and attack the enemy at that place, but before reaching Little Swift Creek I received the following explanatory instructions from the general commanding:

HEADQUARTERS EIGHTEENTH ARMY CORPS,
New Berne, N. C., April 14, 1863.

Brigadier-General SPINOLA:

SIR: I am directed by the general commanding to inform you that it will be impossible to send you more cavalry. The general is afraid that you may have misunderstood his orders. His desire is that you should simply make a thorough reconnaissance, not an attack, and that you should be particular to keep your rear strongly protected so in case you want additional supplies it will not be necessary to send a guard with the train. Each road in your rear should be left strongly guarded. The general desires you to communicate with him in writing as often as possible.

I am, general, very respectfully, your obedient servant,

JOHN F. ANDERSON,
Major and Assistant Adjutant-General.

At daylight on the morning of April 15 the brigade moved toward Swift Creek by the old road across Little Swift Creek. I found the road blockaded and the bridge over the creek destroyed. I commenced a reconstruction of the bridge, but before I had completed it I received an order from General Wessells to return to New Berne, which I did that night.

I gained on this reconnaissance no additional information in regard to the position and force of the enemy, all the proofs establishing their strength, as heretofore reported, from 18,000 to 25,000, and chiefly encamped at and near Swift Creek Village, the cross-roads in front of Washington, at Blount's Creek, and on the north side of Washington. The brigade on reaching Fort Anderson bivouacked for the night and remained there until April 18.

I have the honor to be, colonel, very respectfully, your obedient servant,

F. B. SPINOLA,
Brigadier-General.

Col. SOUTHARD HOFFMAN, *A. A. G., Eighteenth Army Corps.*

Itinerary of the First Brigade, Fifth Division, Eighteenth Army Corps, March 31-April 21, 1863.*

March 31.—The One hundred and seventy-first, One hundred and fifty-eighth, and One hundred and seventy-fifth Regiments Pennsylvania Militia, of this brigade, left New Berne on steamboats and transports, to re-enforce General Foster at Washington, N. C. Found the river block aded by rebel-batteries on both sides, which were attacked by our gun boats, but failed to raise the blockade, and we had to return to New Berne, where we arrived April 6.

April 8.—The same three regiments left New Berne on another expedition by land to Washington, and went as far as Blount's Creek, where we had an artillery engagement. The bridge over the creek being torn up and the creek not fordable, we returned to New Berne, where we arrived on the night of the 10th instant.

April 13.—The whole brigade crossed the Neuse River and went on a reconnaissance.

April 14.—Marched toward Swift Creek and Washington, N. C. At New Hope School-House we captured 2 rebel cavalry pickets. We then marched toward Little Swift Creek, but by orders of General Wessells we returned to Fort Anderson on the night of the 15th and bivouacked there until the 18th, when the brigade again left for Swift Creek Village, clearing the blockade on the roads and building three bridges on our march.

April 19.—In the afternoon we met the enemy's pickets and drove them across Big Swift Creek that night.

April 20.—We crossed into the village. Finding no rebels there we returned to New Berne, where we arrived on the night of April 21.

No. 13.

Itinerary of the Second Brigade, Fifth Division, Col. James Jourdan, One hundred and fiftieth New York Infantry, commanding, April 7-22.*

The principal incidents of the history of this brigade during the month ending April 30 are as follows:

April 7.—The regiments of this brigade, under the immediate command of Col. F. J. Coffin, of the Eighth Massachusetts Volunteer Militia (I being absent from the department by authority of the major-general commanding), formed a part of the force which marched under command of Brig. Gen. F. B. Spinola for the purpose of relieving the garrison at Washington, N. C.; said force failing to accomplish the object for which it marched, returned to New Berne April 10. Nothing worthy of special mention occurred on the occasion referred to.

April 17.—This brigade again moved in the direction of Kinston, under my immediate command, together with other forces under the general direction of Brig. Gen. Henry Prince, commanding Fifth Division, Eighteenth Army Corps, and after passing Core Creek scoured the country to within about 10 miles of Kinston, skirmishing continually, and, by proper co-operation with other forces, succeeded in compelling the enemy to retire precipitately from an intrenched camp on a place known as Sandy Ridge, leaving in our hands between 30 and 40 prisoners, and after accomplishing the object for which it marched, returned to New Berne on April 22.

---

* From Brigade Return for April. 1863.

No. 14.

Report of Brig. Gen. Robert Ransom, jr., C. S Army, of skirmish at Sandy Ridge, April 20.

HEADQUARTERS,
Kinston, N. C., April 21, 1863.

GENERAL: Your note of to-day is received. I have started five different parties to vicinity of Morehead City and New Berne. Whitford reports the Yankees retiring from Swift Creek; says Foster declares he will give you a hard fight, which will do to write in the history of the war. In an hour after your telegram came I started a regiment and four pieces of artillery to Coward's Bridge. I have now here sixteen field pieces. I kept [A. D.] Moore, [Company E, Tenth North Carolina Volunteers, or First Artillery], as I deemed his battery of importance. Yesterday there was another skirmish on Sandy Ridge; three companies of the Forty-ninth and about 70 of [Maj. J. H.] Nethercutt's men, [Eighth North Carolina Battalion]. The enemy was first driven back, but got a strong re-enforcement and in turn we had to retire. We had 1 killed, 6 wounded, and 12 or 14 missing. Three horses were killed by our men belonging to the field officers. We went forward to in sight of Core Creek after the fight. To hold Core Creek would require at least two regiments. I cannot afford to fritter away strength. We shall soon know if the enemy is going to come this way. I should have to fight him on Southwest [Creek] or not at all until he gets to the river. We are working on Southwest. If I have time will destroy the works over the bridge. For three days I have been getting sick, and am now hardly able to write this. If morning finds me no better this place will need your presence or some one else. I have no horses. Where are the Wheeler horses? I heard that the men were permitted to sell them or send them home. If an attack be made here we cannot well have too many guns. I am almost ill.

Yours, respectfully and truly,

R. RANSOM, JR.,
Brigadier-General.

General D. H. HILL.

P. S.—I have just heard (9 p. m.) that the enemy is rebuilding the railroad; finished to Core Creek, and were working this side with very large force.

APRIL 1, 1863.—Expedition from Yorktown to Smith's and Byrd's Plantations, Ware River, Va.

REPORTS.

No. 1.--Maj. Gen. Erasmus D. Keyes, U. S. Army.
No. 2.—Second Lieut. William S. Andrews, Ninth New York Infantry, Acting Signal Officer.

No. 1.

Report of Maj. Gen. Erasmus D. Keyes, U. S. Army.

HEADQUARTERS FOURTH ARMY CORPS,
Fort Yorktown, Va., April 7, 1863.

GENERAL: I have the honor to forward the following extract from the report of Lieut. Com. J. H. Gillis, commanding United States steamer Commodore Morris, to Admiral Lee, of an expedition into Gloucester County by the land and naval forces on this station. Commander Gillis had on the 31st ultimo made an examination of the country bordering on Ware River and found stored there large quantities of grain for the Southern Army. I extract from his report as follows:

I therefore embarked my men, and with Mr. Smith as prisoner returned to Yorktown; immediately communicated with General Keyes, informed him of the circumstances, and, his views coinciding with mine as to the necessity of either bringing off or destroying the grain, I determined to return to Ware River on the following morning, the 1st instant, and on informing General Keyes that a rebel cavalry force was stationed at Gloucester Court-House, and that our operations, if we went without a considerable force, would not be likely to remain undisturbed, he immediately placed at my disposal as many men, cavalry or infantry, whichever I thought would be best, as I thought would be necessary. I took 100 infantry, and with these and the Delaware, which I fortunately met on my way down York River and directed to accompany me, I yesterday morning returned to the plantation of Mr. Smith and commenced removing a quantity of wheat, of which there was about 1,000 bushels, but had not gotten off more than 250 bushels before the alarm was given that the cavalry were approaching. The men were immediately formed and we prepared to give them a warm reception as they charged down upon us, and a few well-directed shots caused a wavering in their ranks, and a cheer and a charge on the part of both sailors and soldiers turned an attack into a retreat, and they fled until out of range of our muskets, when they halted and appeared to be holding a consultation, but just at this time a shot was fired from the 100-pounder rifle on board this ship, which struck right in their midst, and they again took to flight and disappeared around a bend of the road. On going down the road some distance I discovered indications of the effect of our firing, there being quite a quantity of blood in the road, showing that some of the party had paid pretty dearly for their temerity.

I would state that when we were seen approaching, the overseer's son was sent off, and I had not the least doubt, when I learned that such was the case, that he had been sent to bring a force sufficient to cut us off, not expecting to meet any more than had landed the day before, and they were doubtless very much surprised on seeing so large a force. They succeeded in capturing 2 of our pickets in their charge, but had not time to take them off, when they in their turn were charged upon, and the consequence was that we did not lose a man. Knowing that it would take me a long time to remove the grain, and that the enemy would have ample time to bring down a strong force upon us, I determined to destroy it, and therefore set fire to all but one of the buildings, in which there were at least 1,500 bushels of corn; that I left for the use of the family and the hands on the plantation.

After seeing the fires well under way I embarked my force without further molestation and started to return. Arriving opposite to the house of a man by the name of Byrd, who is an officer in the rebel army, and who had left his property in charge of an old negro servant, I landed a party, who found that there was a large quantity of corn stored in his barns, and these were also set fire to; and, although the party were on shore but a few moments, they came very near being captured, the cavalry making a dash down upon them under cover of the smoke of the burning buildings; but I discovered them in time to throw a shell from one of the howitzers, which exploded in their midst and they fled without accomplishing their object. I destroyed at this latter place, as near as could be estimated, 1,000 bushels of wheat and 3,000 bushels of corn, making altogether some 22,000 to 23,000 bushels of grain that the rebels have thus been deprived of.

I have the honor to be, very respectfully, your obedient servant,
E. D. KEYES,
Major-General, Commanding Fourth Army Corps.

Brig. Gen LORENZO THOMAS,
Adjutant-General, U. S. Army.

No. 2.

Report of Second Lieut. William S. Andrews, Ninth New York Infantry,
Acting Signal Officer.

ON BOARD U. S. STEAMER COMMODORE MORRIS,
Off Yorktown, Va., April 3, 1863.

CAPTAIN: I have the honor to report to the Signal Officer of the Army, having directed the fire of this vessel (from the shore) by signals on a small body of the enemy at head of Ware River, near Gloucester Court-House, Va., on the 1st instant.

On the 31st of March, Captain Gillis, of the Commodore Morris, discovered a large quantity of grain stored in barns at the head of Ware River. It was determined either to remove it or destroy it, and on the next day, the 1st, we returned to Ware River with two companies of infantry on board the Morris, and the gunboat Delaware in company.

Captain Gillis expected interruption from the rebel cavalry that infests Gloucester and Matthews Counties to the number of about 200. I accompanied him ashore for the purpose of communicating with the Morris in case of necessity, relying on one of my flagmen, Private George H. Walker, whom I left on board, to read the signals.

The party landed; soldiers and sailors numbered about 200. The men all landed between 11 and 12 a. m. and set to work carrying the grain to the boats and loaded a schooner brought for that purpose. The infantry posted pickets and made the usual preparations for defense in case of attack. A number of messages were sent to gunboat between that time and 1 p. m. At about that time a cavalry force of the enemy were seen approaching our pickets. I immediately signaled the Morris that the enemy approached, and by Captain Gillis' order directed them how to fire. The first shot fired from the boat fell in the midst of the rebels, emptying one saddle. They retired precipitately several hundred yards, leaving two of our pickets, whom they had already captured, and whom in their flight they attempted to kill. The gunboats continued to fire; constantly directed by signals as the enemy changed positions, the Delaware firing in the same direction as the Morris. Our men now advanced up the road at a double-quick, firing one or two volleys. The enemy retired into the edge of a piece of woods, about 1,000 yards distant from our position, which the gunboats continued to shell, still directed by signals. In consequence of the interruption by the enemy the plan of removing the grain was abandoned and the barns were fired. When they were burned we returned to the vessels, all the force being embarked by 3.30 p. m.

The following is an extract from the report of Lieutenant-Commander Gillis, commanding United States steamer Morris, to Acting Rear-Admiral Lee, commanding North Atlantic Blockading Squadron, which I am permitted to make:

> I would state that I received most important aid from Lieutenant Andrews, of the Signal Corps, as by his assistance I was enabled to direct the aiming of the guns on board this vessel. All my messages were transmitted with the greatest celerity, almost as rapidly as they could have been given had they been delivered orally, and with entire accuracy, and this, too, during the excitement of a sudden attack.

I desire to call especial attention to the coolness and efficiency of Private George H. Walker, signal flagman. For some months I have known of Walker's capacity to read. He obtained the code over a year ago through the negligence and carelessness of an officer instructed at Annapolis. For a long time I promised the severest punishment to my men if caught attempting to read or to obtain any portion of the code, but finding that officers senior to myself not only tolerated but encouraged their men to do so, I spoke to them of it, and was informed that the matter was well known to Major Myer. Since being at Yorktown, therefore, I have allowed Walker to read, and have been astonished at his intelligence, superior to that of some officers I have worked with. Lieutenant Benson and myself abbreviated all ordinary messages to at least one-fourth their length if sent in full; but Walker seldom has trouble to read them. In directing the fire of the Morris on the 1st instant I at first partially spelled out the messages, using only the more suggestive abbreviations, such as eny, enemy; apch, approach, &c. But desiring to work more quickly I used the abbreviations fll, ef, of, fo, ect, and was somewhat astonished at Walker's receiving them all instantly and correctly without once calling for a "repeat." He has never heretofore received the official abbreviations from me, but I have now given them to him, as I deem myself justified in doing, as I am liable at any time to have occasion to use them with him.

I desire to recommend Private Walker for promotion. I intended to have recommended him for appointment as sergeant under the new organization of the Signal Corps, and now I consider that he has doubly earned his chevrons. Walker has been with me since June 25, 1862, and I have had ample opportunity of knowing his capacity.

The accompanying plan * will explain the relative positions of the forces engaged in the affair of the 1st instant. The outline of the sketch was enlarged from a chart.

I have the honor to remain, very respectfully, your obedient servant,
WM. S. ANDREWS,
Second Lieut. Ninth N. Y. Vols. and Acting Signal Officer.

Capt. LEONARD F. HEPBURN,
Acting Signal Officer, Washington, D. C.

P. S.—Since this report was written information has been received at Major-General Keyes' headquarters that during the firing from the gunboats, directed by signals, on the 1st, the enemy lost 4 killed and 3 wounded.

Our forces sustained no loss whatever.

---

* Not found.

APRIL 6, 1863.—Skirmish at Nixonton, N. C.

Report of Capt. Enos C. Sanders, First North Carolina (Union) Infantry.

WASHINGTON, N. C., *May* 1, 1863.

I started on the steamer Massasoit for New Berne and arrived at midnight. Took the same boat on the 2d instant for Plymouth. I made application for transportation at New Berne, and the quartermaster, Lieutenant-Colonel Biggs, ordered the Massasoit to go the whole trip with me; but as his orders did not reach the captain of the steamer I went to Plymouth, where I arrived on Sunday, the 3d instant. Saw Commander Charles Flusser that evening; he was to send a gunboat as convoy to the steamer Massasoit, which I had already procured the use of, to go as far as Roanoke with me.

After getting the men that I was after (but afterwards the general decided to send a gunboat and a company of infantry), on the morning of the 4th I started at 5 a. m. on the United States gunboat Southfield, Captain Behm commanding, with a company of the Eighty-fifth New York Infantry, Lieutenant Whitney commanding. Arrived at Halley's Landing at 9 a. m.; the wharf had been burned by the Confederates. I landed with the company, and, on making inquiries, found that the men of Company E were encamped in the woods 10 miles from that place, and as it was uncertain about the force of the enemy in that vicinity I did not think it prudent to go into the country. We then started for the Pasquotank River, where we arrived at 5 p. m. We landed at the mouth of the river and marched to Shiloh, a distance of 10 miles, where we went aboard of the gunboat at 10 p. m. I sent word to the men to be ready the next day to go with me.

On the morning of the 5th we went to Elizabeth City; landed and got the family of William Wright; went to Shiloh; the schooner Patty Martin had arrived; went to Jones' Mill; landed; marched to Old Trap; found some of the men collected there, but the others, not knowing of our presence, could not be found. We stayed till morning, and then went on board with 7 of my men, as follows: Peter, Stephen, Cornelius, and Nicholas Burgess, Ithean and Wilson Duncan, and Dempsey Wright. We crossed over to the Pasquotank side; landed and got the family of Joseph Morgan. There were four men in that county belonging to my company; one, John Cartwright, came with us; one could not be found, and the other two were, one sick and one wounded. We went aboard at dark.

On the morning of the 6th the Southfield started for Roanoke at 2 a. m. I started for Nixonton, on Little River, at daylight with the schooner Patty Martin and my men, numbering 17. We arrived at the landing of Thomas Moss' place at 5 p. ma.; came to anchor; sent a boat ashore with 6 men, with orders not to land till they found all right; a large flat at the landing looked suspicious. As the boat approached the land they saw a handkerchief waived in the window of Mrs. Moss' house. They put about and pulled for the schooner, when they were fired upon by the guerrillas. They returned the fire from the boat, and we commenced a brisk fire from the schooner, which was kept up till the boat came alongside, when we got under way and headed down the river.

We had used nearly all the ammunition we had. There was no one hurt on our side, although the boat was within 40 yards of the shore when fired upon. The vessel was struck several times. We got to the mouth of the river at sunset, where we found the United States steamer

Whitehead, Captain French commanding. We went back to Nixonton in the morning; got the family of Mr. Moss, and started for Roanoke Island. I landed at Croatan for the family of J. W. Harrison, but the weather was so heavy he could not get on board. Stopped at Roanoke till 10 p. m.; got under way and sailed for Washington, where we arrived at 6.30 a. m., on Sunday, May 10.

I labored under the difficulties of having a gunboat of too much draught of water, whose commander was very anxious to get to Roanoke, and therefore would not give me time to do my business as I could if I had had the command of the expedition myself.

I left 11 men in Camden, 3 in Pasquotank, and 2 in Elizabeth City. It was impossible to get word to them in so short a time, as they have to keep hid in the woods most of the time.

Yours, respectfully,

E. C. SANDERS,
Captain, Company D, First North Carolina (Union) Vols.

APRIL 7, 1863.—Expedition from Gloucester Point to Gloucester Court-House, Va.

Report of Col. A. H. Grimshaw, Fourth Delaware Infantry.

CAMP GILPIN,
Gloucester Point, April 9, 1863.

GENERAL: I have the honor to report that in obedience to your order of — instant I left this post at 7 a. m. on Tuesday, the 7th instant, with a detail from the Fourth Delaware Volunteers and three companies of the One hundred and sixty-ninth Pennsylvania Drafted Militia, the squadron of the Second Massachusetts Cavalry attached to this command, and a detachment of cavalry under Major Hall, of the Sixth New York. The party proceeded up the main road to Gloucester Court-House. At Abingdon Meeting-House I left one company of One hundred and sixty-ninth Pennsylvania Drafted Militia to prevent any communication with the enemy's pickets.

Beyond Hickory Fork Major Hall was ordered to proceed to the right, and after destroying any grain he might find, to join the column at or near Gloucester Court-House. With regard to the particulars of the destruction of grain I refer to Major Hall's report, which I have directed him to send directly to your headquarters.

No mail was found at Gloucester Court-House ready to be sent south. A few letters, which I have handed to General Keyes, were found. These confirm the account of the late fight with and defeat of Lee's cavalry.

In accordance with the instructions of the general commanding the Fourth Army Corps I made preparations to return to Gloucester Point on the 7th, since the re-enforcements from the gunboat had not landed, and the signal—one rocket—was not received by the boat. The distance to the station of the boat being evidently greater than we had supposed, Major Hall proceeded by the Bell Roy road, making a detour toward the York River, so as to destroy a quantity of grain in a barn beyond Gloucester Court-House, of which we obtained information at Gloucester Court-House. The major rejoined the column at Hickory Fork. The force marched during thirteen hours 32 miles. The men and horses returned in good spirit and condition. The roads were muddy and obstructed by numerous collections of water.

I inclose a report of Lieutenant Toner, quartermaster of Fourth Delaware Volunteers, of the amount of material seized and placed in his charge; also a note from Major Crowninshield.*

Allow me to speak of the good conduct of the men and the promptness of the officers accompanying the expedition. Major Hall was active and efficient and rendered me especial service by his advice and experience. Lieutenant-Colonel Tevis, Fourth Delaware, and Major Crowninshield, with Captain Paul, all contributed, each in his position, to the success of the movements.

I did not destroy the grain at Tabb's farm, because it is within such a short distance that a very small force can transport it to this post.

Very respectfully, your obedient servant,

A. H. GRIMSHAW,
Colonel, Commanding Post.

Major-General KEYES, *Yorktown, Va.*

APRIL 9-14, 1863.—Operations against Gloucester Point, Va.

Report of Col. D. J. Godwin, C. S. Army.

HEADQUARTERS,
King and Queen Court-House, Va., April 15, 1863.

GENERAL: In obedience to your order of the 7th instant I proceeded on Thursday, the 9th, with all the force under my command then armed and equipped, to the enemy's fortifications at Gloucester Point. I arrived in the neighborhood of the Point Thursday evening. By daybreak on Friday morning I appeared in front of his works and remained there during the day, making demonstrations at several different points. I appeared alternately as infantry and cavalry, and so maneuvered my troops as to represent a heavy force. I drove in his pickets early on Friday morning, killing 1, wounding another, and captured 2 unhurt. I had 2 men wounded, 1 badly, the other only slightly. I kept up these demonstrations Saturday, Sunday, Monday, and Tuesday until 12 m., at which time I returned to my camp, leaving behind, however, two full companies to watch the enemy's movements. The enemy's force at the Point consisted of two infantry regiments, one battalion of cavalry, and two field batteries. I am satisfied that my demonstrations had the effect of diverting his force from the Peninsula. I found it utterly impossible to attack him behind his works with success, and therefore decided not to do so. His fortifications at the Point are strong and thorough.

My officers behaved with great gallantry and my men with marked firmness.

I have the honor to be, general, very respectfully, your obedient servant,

D. J. GODWIN,
Colonel, Commanding.

Maj. Gen. ARNOLD ELZEY,
Commanding Department of Richmond, Va.

P. S.—Capt. Robert Tomlin, a volunteer aide, who behaved with distinguished gallantry, I regret to say, was severely wounded in the leg

---

*Not found.

APRIL 11, 1863.—Skirmish at Williamsburg, Va.

REPORTS, ETC.

No. 1.—Maj. Gen. Erasmus D. Keyes, U. S. Army.
No. 2.—Brig. Gen. Rufus King, U. S. Army, commanding at Yorktown, with resulting correspondence.

No. 1.

Reports of Maj. Gen. Erasmus D. Keyes, U. S. Army.

FORT MONROE, VA., *April* 11, 1863.

Our communication with Fort Magruder is re-established. The enemy have retired beyond. They destroyed some camp and garrison
equipage of the Fifth Pennsylvania Cavalry and a small amount of
hospital stores. No other loss reported. Wise and his whole force are
near Williamsburg. I have ordered Colonel West to hold the strong
line of defense below the city at all hazards. It would be very injurious
to give it up.

E. D. KEYES,
Major-General.

Maj. Gen. H. W. HALLECK,
General-in-Chief.

—

NORFOLK, VA., *April* 11, 1863—8 p. m

The enemy was fairly repulsed at Williamsburg to-day. Our pickets
are in the edge of the city, and the line of Fort Magruder, strengthened
by another regiment, is now guarded from York River to James River.
We lost no men. Found two dead rebels, but they had time, when our
shots fell, to carry off dead and wounded. While the affair at Williamsburg was closing the rebels attacked Peck's pickets at Suffolk, and a
deserter just in from there reports that 50,000 men are close upon our
lines. I have ordered all our troops to hold their ground without regard to the number of the enemy.

E. D. KEYES,
Major-General.

Maj. Gen. H. W. HALLECK,
General-in-Chief.

———

No. 2.

*Reports of Brig. Gen. Rufus King, U. S. Army, commanding at Yorktown,
with resulting correspondence.*

YORKTOWN, *April* 11, 1863—7.45 a. m.

The enemy appeared in front of Williamsburg this morning about 6
o'clock. Our pickets fell back in good order to Fort Magruder. Colonel
West has opened fire on the town and is now firing. Force of the enemy
not yet known.

RUFUS KING,
Brigadier-General.

Major-General KEYES, *Fort Monroe.*

YORKTOWN, *April* 11, 1863—8.20 a. m.

The enemy in large force, cavalry, artillery, and infantry, have passed through Williamsburg and are moving on Fort Magruder. Another force of infantry, reported 500 strong, have got on this side of the fort. They have captured and destroyed the camp of the Fifth Pennsylvania, burned the hospital, and paroled the patients. I have ordered the Sixth New York to fall back toward Yorktown. All communication with Colonel West is cut off. The troops here are under arms. If it be possible I shall send re-enforcements to Colonel West; not, however, so as to endanger this post. Can a boat be sent up at once?

RUFUS KING,
Brigadier-General.

Major-General KEYES, *Suffolk*.

—

YORKTOWN, *April* 11, 1863—12.30 p. m.

I have just received a letter from Colonel West. He is all right and safe in Fort Magruder. He reports Wise in front with his entire command. The road is open between this point and Fort Magruder. I have sent cavalry up to patrol the road and keep me advised of all movements. Except the camp and property of the Fifth Pennsylvania and some hospital stores we have lost nothing.

RUFUS KING,
Brigadier-General.

Major-General KEYES, *Fort Monroe*.

—

YORKTOWN, *April* 11, 1863—2.30 p. m.

We have reopened communications with Fort Magruder. Colonel West has just telegraphed that everything is safe there; that the enemy are retreating, but still occupy Williamsburg, and that we have lost nothing but what was captured in the cavalry camp. He asks for a fresh regiment of infantry. I shall send him Colonel Johnson's regiment, and will bring over the Fourth Delaware to replace them, if need be.

RUFUS KING,
Brigadier-General.

Major-General KEYES, *Fort Monroe*.

—

HEADQUARTERS DEPARTMENT OF VIRGINIA,
Fort Monroe, April 11, 1863.

Brigadier-General KING,
    Commanding, Yorktown:

If the enemy are in rear of Williamsburg he can only be there in very small force, so I wish you to send up Colonel Johnson's regiment to clear them out and communicate with West. If there be two gunboats on the station you can bring over the Fourth Delaware, who are plucky. If West has provisions and ammunition he can hold against 10,000 men, and the enemy can't spare that number; so he must hold on. I have asked Admiral Lee to send a gunboat up James River. During the day the gunboat should move up and down between Yorktown and West's Landing.

E. D. KEYES,
Major-General

HEADQUARTERS DEPARTMENT OF VIRGINIA,
Fort Monroe, April 11, 1863.

Brigadier-General KING, *Yorktown :*

I have directed a stern-wheel steamer for West to be sent up if one can be had.

If West does not waste his ammunition he ought to do five times as much damage to the enemy as he receives. I cannot understand how the 500 got below Fort Magruder. Did they cross the James River ?

Do all you can to supply West and to encourage him and his men to fight.

E. D. KEYES,
Major-General.

—

HEADQUARTERS DEPARTMENT OF VIRGINIA,
Fort Monroe, April 11, 1863.

Brigadier-General KING, *Yorktown :*

Order Colonel West to cease firing on Williamsburg unless he knows the enemy are present there in arms. He will waste his ammunition. That town must be held as a shield, and it must not be destroyed except in accordance with my orders.

E. D. KEYES,
Major-General.

—

[APRIL 12, 1863.]

Brigadier-General KING:

The line of defense at Fort Magruder ought not to be given up lightly. You ought not bring away anything from Gloucester Point. You may, however, use your discretion about sending another regiment of infantry toward Williamsburg.

E. D. KEYES,
Major-General.

—

YORKTOWN, *April* 12, 1863—9 a. m.

Colonel West telegraphs that all is quiet as yet at the front; that the enemy are in large force on the other side of the town. He recommends abandoning the town and establishing his pickets on this side, as his force is not strong enough to guard the Peninsula. We have taken 10 prisoners, one of them an officer, who corroborates the rumor of yesterday that Wise has issued orders to take the forts at all hazards.

RUFUS KING,
Brigadier-General.

Major-General KEYES, *Fort Monroe.*

—

YORKTOWN, *April* 12, 1863—11.35 a. m.

Major Chamberlin, who has just come in from Fort Magruder, brings me a verbal communication from Colonel West to the effect that he thinks his position insecure and the line too extended to be successfully defended. From prisoners and deserters he learns that Wise, who is in command of the enemy's force, has 4,000 infantry, 500 or 600 cavalry, and 6 or 8 pieces of artillery; that his orders from Richmond are to take and hold Williamsburg and Fort Magruder, and that he expresses his determination to do so. The prisoners say that their attack yester-day would have succeeded if the infantry that came around in rear of our cavalry camp had not been too late. They also report that Longstreet was to have attacked Suffolk and Fitzhugh Lee Gloucester at the same time that Wise assailed our front. Colonel West thinks that it will be difficult to hold his position without more infantry. He would also like two more 12-pounders. Unless he can be thus re-enforced he advises an abandonment of the present line and the establishment of a new and shorter one, say in the neighborhood of the brick hospital. A tug-boat came down James River as far as King's Mill Landing yesterday and went up again. Wise, with his troops, is still at Williamsburg await-ing re-enforcements, as is said, though the attack may be renewed at any moment. All quiet thus far to-day.

RUFUS KING,
Brigadier-General.

Major-General KEYES.

—

YORKTOWN, April 12, 1863—4 p. m.

Colonel West telegraphed an hour ago that the enemy were reported to be advancing, and that his troops were under arms; but as we have heard no firing, the report was probably unfounded.

Fourteen rebel prisoners, two of them lieutenants, have arrived here from Fort Magruder. They will be sent to Fort Monroe in the morning.

Are we to continue to supply the patients in the insane asylum at Williamsburg?

RUFUS KING,
Brigadier-General.

Major-General KEYES, <i>Norfolk.</i>

—

HEADQUARTERS DEPARTMENT OF VIRGINIA,
April 12, 1863—4 p. m.

Brigadier-General KING, <i>Yorktown, Va.:</i>

Until you receive further dispatches from me, do as circumstances re-quire; but I do not advise sending up any artillery to Williamsburg. I think it will be far more dangerous to withdraw from that line than to hold it.

E. D. KEYES,
Major-General.

P. S.—Keep me advised by telegraph.

—

YORKTOWN, VA., April 12, 1863.

I do not think the line of defense now established will be given up. Colonel West is confident that he can hold his ground. No change will be made at Gloucester Point unless unforeseen circumstances require it. I shall keep a gunboat lying off Queen's Creek, which will communi-cate with Colonel West.

Three more prisoners were brought in to-night and others on the way. Everything quiet.

RUFUS KING,
Brigadier-General.

Major-General KEYES.

YORKTOWN, *April* 12, 1863—10.20 p. m.

I have just received a dispatch from Fort Magruder. All quiet there, but an attack on the redoubts is expected in the morning. Colonel West suggests that a gunboat stationed off College Creek, in James River, would prevent the enemy from turning his left and thus probably enable him to keep his line unbroken.

RUFUS KING,
Brigadier-General.

Major-General KEYES, *Norfolk.*

—

YORKTOWN, *April* 12, 1863—9 a. m.

Colonel WEST, *Fort Magruder:*

Do as you think best about drawing your pickets in closer to the forts. Keep me advised of any change in the situation of affairs and of your wants. General Keyes telegraphs from Norfolk that the line between Williamsburg and Yorktown must be held at all hazards.

RUFUS KING,
Brigadier-General.

—

FORT MAGRUDER, *April* 12, 1863.

Lieut. Col. C. C. SUYDAM:

I did not understand by your last dispatch whether Colonel Johnson's regiment is to remain here or return. He wants to know so as to provide himself and fix camp where they are. There are no bridges on King's and College Creeks. The enemy did not cross the creek; they stole down along College Creek and so around by the Brick Church road. They cannot do it again without my knowledge.

ROB'T M. WEST,
Commanding Advance Brigade.

—

APRIL 12, 1863.

Colonel WEST:

Colonel Johnson's regiment will remain with you for the present. He had better get five days' supplies.

C. C. SUYDAM,
Assistant Adjutant-General.

APRIL 11–MAY 4, 1863.—Siege of Suffolk, Va

SUMMARY OF THE PRINCIPAL EVENTS.

April   11, 1863.—Confederate forces, under command of Lieut. Gen. James Longstreet, advance upon Suffolk.

               Skirmish on the South Quay Road, near the Blackwater.

    12–13, 1863.—Skirmishes on the Edenton, Providence Church, and Somerton Roads.

    14, 1863.—Engagement at the mouth of West Branch and near the Norfleet House, Nansemond River.

    15, 1863.—Engagement near the Norfleet House.

               Skirmish on the Edenton Road.

    17, 1863.—Skirmishing generally along the lines.

    19, 1863.—Capture of Battery Huger, Hill's Point.

    23, 1863.—Affair at Chuckatuck.

    24, 1863.—Skirmish on the Edenton Road.

May   1, 1863.—Skirmish at South Quay Bridge.

  2 4, 1863.—Confederate forces retire from Suffolk.

    3, 1863.—Skirmishes near Hill's Point and Reed's Ferry, Nansemond River.

               Skirmish at Chuckatuck.

               Reconnaissance on the Providence Church Road.

    4, 1863.—Skirmish at Leesville.

REPORTS, ETC.*

No. 1.—Maj. Gen. John A. Dix, U. S. Army, commanding the Department of Virginia, with congratulatory orders.†

No. 2.—Abstract from "Record of Events" in the Department of Virginia, April 11–May 4.

No. 3.—Capt. Charles L. Davis, Eighty-second Pennsylvania Infantry, Chief Signal Officer.

No. 4.—Maj. Gen. John J. Peck, U. S. Army, commanding at Suffolk.†

No. 5.—Return of Casualties in the Union forces.

No. 6.—Brig. Gen. Michael Corcoran, U. S. Army, commanding First Division, Seventh Army Corps.

No. 7.—Maj. Alexander G. Patton, First New York Mounted Rifles, of skirmish on the Edenton Road, April 15.

No. 8.—Itinerary of the First Brigade, Brig. Gen. Henry D. Terry, U. S. Army, commanding, April 11–30.

No. 9.—Col. Robert S. Foster, Thirteenth Indiana Infantry, commanding Second Brigade.

No. 10.—Lieut. Col. John McConihe, One hundred and sixty-ninth New York Infantry.

No. 11.—Itinerary of the Third Brigade, Col. Mathew Murphy, One hundred and eighty-second New York Infantry, commanding, April 9–May 3.

No. 12.—Col. William McEvily, One hundred and fifty-fifth New York Infantry.

No. 13.—Itinerary of the Reserve Brigade, Col. David W. Wardrop, Ninety-ninth New York Infantry, commanding, April 24–May 1.

No. 14.—Brig. Gen. Charles C. Dodge, U. S. Army, commanding Southeast Front.

---

* For reports of Actg. Rear-Admiral S. P. Lee, Lieuts. W. B. Cushing and R. H Lamson, and Actg. Master C. H. Brown, U. S. Navy, see Annual Report of the Secretary of the Navy, December 7, 1863.

† See also dispatches between Keyes, Dix, Hooker, and Peck, April 11–May 4, and Dix's and Peck's telegrams to Halleck, in "Correspondence, etc.," *post.*

No. 15.—Brig. Gen. George W. Getty, U. S. Army, commanding Third Division, Ninth Army Corps.

No. 16.—Col. Harrison S. Fairchild, Eighty-ninth New York Infantry, command ng First Brigade.

No. 17.—Col. William R. Pease, One hundred and seventeenth New York Infantry.

No. 18.—Brig. Gen. Edward Harland, U. S. Army, commanding Second Brigade.

No. 19.—Col. John E. Ward, Eighth Connecticut Infantry, of the capture of Battery Huger, April 19.

No. 20.—Col. Griffin A. Stedman, jr., Eleventh Connecticut Infantry.

No. 21.—Col. Arthur H. Dutton, Twenty-first Connecticut Infantry, commanding Third Brigade.

No. 22.—Maj. Hiram B. Crosby, Twenty-first Connecticut Infantry.

No. 23.—Brig. Gen. George H. Gordon, U. S. Army, commanding Reserve Division, of operations May 1–4.

No. 24.—Maj. Gen. Samuel G. French, C. S. Army, commanding the Department of Southern Virginia.

No. 25.—Maj. L. M. Shumaker, C. S. Artillery, Chief of Artillery, of the capture of Battery Huger, April 19.

No. 26.—Maj. F. J. Boggs, C. S. Artillery, of the capture of Battery Huger, April 19.

No. 27.—Maj. James Dearing, C. S. Artillery, of the capture of Battery Huger, April 19.

No. 28.—Capt. Robert M. Stribling, Fauquier Artillery, of the capture of Battery Huger, April 19.

No. 29.—Lieut. Col. John A. Jones, Forty-fourth Alabama Infantry, of the capture of Battery Huger, April 19.

No. 30.—Col. John K. Connally, Fifty-fifth North Carolina Infantry, of the capture of Battery Huger, April 19.

No. 31.—Maj. Gen. George E. Pickett, C. S. Army, commanding Division, of skirmish on the Edenton Road, April 24.

No. 1.

Reports of Maj. Gen. John A. Dix, U. S. Army, commanding the Department of Virginia, with congratulatory orders.

FORT MONROE, VA., *April* 19, 1863.

I deem it due to the forces at Suffolk to notice briefly their gallant conduct during the last six days. On Tuesday General Peck's right was attacked and the enemy's advance was gallantly met by Colonel Foster's light troops, driving him back to the line of his pickets; Anderson's division was engaged at the same time on the water front with our gunboats and batteries, and suffered materially. On Wednesday a rebel battery of 20-pounder rifled guns was effectually silenced, and an attack on the Smith Briggs, an armed quartermaster's boat, was repulsed. Repeated attempts have been made on our lines but have all been foiled. The storming of the enemy's battery near the West Branch of the Nansemond by General Getty and the gunboats under Lieutenant Lamson of the Navy, and the capture of six guns and 200 prisoners closes the operations of the six days against the enemy's large force very satisfactory.

JOHN A. DIX,
Major-General.

Maj. Gen. H. W. HALLECK,
    General-in-Chief.

HDQRS. DEPT. OF VIRGINIA, SEVENTH ARMY CORPS,
Fort Monroe, Va., May 23, 1863.

GENERAL : In the latter part of September last the town of Suffolk was threatened by the enemy, who had concentrated a large force on the Blackwater. Brigadier-General Ferry, who commanded at Suffolk, made the best practicable arrangement of his troops to meet the enemy's advance, but the place was entirely without intrenchments. It had been occupied from the time the enemy evacuated Norfolk, but without any definite purpose, except as an advanced position from which the country east of the Blackwater and Chowan and between the James River and Albemarle Sound might be watched and the land communication be kept up between Norfolk and North Carolina east of the Dismal Swamp.

I suggested last autumn the relinquishment of this position on account of some inherent objections to it, since explained in my letter of May 10th instant, and the occupation of a more defensible line nearer Norfolk. It was decided at that time to hold it, and Major-General Peck, whom I ordered to take command at Suffolk on September 22, and in whose experience, discretion, and military skill I had entire confidence, immediately commenced the execution of a system of intrenchments planned by himself, which the physical conformation of the place and the contiguous country necessarily rendered very extensive. For six months a portion of the troops under his command were diligently engaged in the construction of these works.

With a view to have them fully occupied and to inure them to more active service I directed him to keep about one-third of his force constantly in motion and to harass the enemy on the Blackwater by all practical means. My directions were carried out with good judgment and with very satisfactory results. Frequent expeditions were made; the enemy was repeatedly attacked. In nearly every rencounter the advantage was on our side; prisoners were taken, munitions of war were captured, and a rocket battery fell into our hands. While engaged in these labors and active movements General Peck, by constant attention, brought his command to an excellent state of discipline.

On April 11 the enemy suddenly advanced with a large force, commanded by Lieutenant-General Longstreet, which had been quietly assembled on the Blackwater, intending to take Suffolk by assault; but finding the place well prepared for defense, after repeated unsuccessful attempts on our lines in all of which he was signally repulsed, he sat down before it and commenced an investment according to the most approved principles of military science. The details of all the operations of the siege, which terminated at the end of twenty-two days by his retreat in the night, are fully given in the report of Major-General Peck, which I have the honor to transmit herewith.

When the enemy appeared before Suffolk I was in the city of New York with leave of absence for a few days on a surgeon's certificate of disability.

On the following day (Sunday, April 12) I received a dispatch informing me of the enemy's presence and I left the same evening, reaching Suffolk on Tuesday morning, the 14th. From this time I was every alternate day at Suffolk and on the Nansemond River, where the gunboats belonging to the blockading squadron of Admiral Lee were engaged with the enemy's batteries, being thus enabled to bear testimony from personal observation to the good conduct of all concerned in resisting the enemy's advance. The large force of the enemy, amounting to some 35,000 men, and the character of the Upper Nansemond—running back to the rear 7 miles with a very narrow channel and affording very extraordinary facilities for cutting off our communications with Norfolk—rendered incessant vigilance necessary to defeat his purpose, and unremitting labor to cover weak points with additional works. The successful termination of the investment is due in a great degree to the industry of Major-General Peck in putting his position in a state of defense, the judicious arrangements made to repel attacks upon his works, and his unslumbering vigilance from the advance of the enemy's forces to their final retreat; and I desire to acknowledge his great promptitude in carrying out all my suggestions and orders and his good judgment in the far more numerous exigencies in which he acted on his own discretion.

To his officers and men the highest praise is due for their gallantry in the face of the enemy and their zealous devotion to all their duties, including the construction of extended and heavy intrenchments—the least attractive but often the most essential service of an army in the field. Particular reference is due to Brigadier-General Getty, who was placed in charge of the Nansemond, the most vulnerable part of our line, and under whose direction a portion of our force was thrown across the river and a battery of five guns carried by storm.

My thanks are due to Admiral Lee, who co-operated by means of his gunboats in preventing the enemy from crossing the Nansemond, and to Lieutenants Cushing, Lamson, and Harris, who displayed great coolness, gallantry, and good judgment in the management of their vessels. Lieutenant Lamson deserves particular mention as having suggested the capture of the battery on the river and having aided General Getty in carrying the plan into execution. I desire to refer to the report of Major-General Peck for a more particular mention of the services of his officers and men.

I have the honor to be, very respectfully, your obedient servant,

JOHN A. DIX,
Major-General.

Maj. Gen. H. W. HALLECK,
General-in-Chief.

—

GENERAL ORDERS, } HDQRS. DEPT. OF VIRGINIA, SEVENTH A. C.,
No. 32.   }   *Fort Monroe, Va., May 6, 1863.*

The major-general commanding congratulates Major-General Peck and the troops under his command at Suffolk on the sudden retreat of the enemy to the Blackwater, after a close investment of the place for more than three weeks by a superior force led by some of the most distinguished generals in the service of the insurgents. The enemy has sustained a loss of five guns, and not less than 1,500 men in prisoners, killed, wounded, and deserters, while ours is limited to a comparatively small number of killed and wounded. For this result the highest praise is due to Major-General Peck, through whose untiring industry and good judgment during the last six months the place has been strongly fortified, and through whose watchfulness it has been held during the investment. The same high praise is due to the troops under his command and to their officers. Their courage and vigilance, their firmness in resisting the enemy's attacks, their gallantry in assaulting him in his works on repeated occasions deserve the heartfelt thanks which the major-general commanding hereby tenders to them.

The major-general commanding avails himself of the occasion to acknowledge the gallant and efficient co-operation of the gunboats sent by Admiral Lee into the Nansemond, under Lieutenants Cushing and Lamson, in silencing the enemy's batteries, in resisting the enemy's attempts to cross the river, and especially the assistance lent by the latter to General Getty in capturing five of the enemy's guns.

By command of Major-General Dix:

D. T. VAN BUREN,
Assistant Adjutant-General.

No. 2.

Abstract from "Record of Events" in Department of Virginia, April 11-- May 4.*

April 11.—The enemy advanced upon Suffolk, Va., from Blackwater, drove in our pickets, capturing the outpost of cavalry on South Quay road, and was not checked until within artillery range, when he was driven back.

April 12.—He advanced on the Somerton road, but was repulsed, retiring hastily, and our infantry pickets were posted on the original lines.

April 13.—The enemy concentrated along the Nansemond, erected heavy batteries, and succeeded in blockading the river; he failed in all his attempts to effect a crossing. The gunboats and our batteries were almost incessantly engaged and several times silenced the enemy's batteries.

April 19.—The enemy opened on the gunboats from Fort Huger. A plan was immediately agreed upon by General Getty and Lieutenant Lamson, U. S. Navy, to cross the river and attack the fort. The gunboats and batteries opened upon it impetuously. In the mean time a detachment from the Eighty-ninth New York Volunteers and from the Eighth Connecticut crossed on the gunboat Stepping Stones and stormed the fort, and were highly successful, capturing five pieces of artillery, two 20-pounder Parrotts and three 12-pounder howitzers; also 129 prisoners, including 9 officers.

April 20.—Major Stratton, Eleventh Pennsylvania Cavalry, visited Elizabeth City, N. C., and found it abandoned by our forces.

April 27.—A reconnaissance in force was made upon the enemy's right flank on the Edenton road, also on the Somerton, and after some skirmishing the enemy was driven from his rifle-pits back upon his main line. Two transports ran the blockade under the volunteer pilotage of Lieutenants Rowe and Horton, Ninety-ninth New York Volunteers. Many shots were fired by the enemy, but little damage was done to the steamers.

April 28, 29, *and* 30.—Skirmishing on the river between our gunboats and the enemy.

The following re-enforcements arrived during the month:

April 12.—Ninth New York Volunteers, assigned to Getty's division.

April 14.—Nineteenth Wisconsin Volunteers, assigned to Getty's division (transferred April 28).

April 16 *and* 17.—Two brigades assigned to Abercrombie's division, consisting of eight regiments; one regiment transferred to General Corcoran's division.

April 18.—One hundred and seventeenth New York Volunteers, as-

---

* From Returns of Seventh Army Corps for April and May, 1863.

signed to General Getty, and One hundred and sixty-ninth New York Volunteers, assigned to General Corcoran.

April 19.—Detachment of the Third New York Volunteers and the First Delaware, Sixteenth and Nineteenth New York Batteries.

April 17.—The Ninth Vermont was assigned to General Getty and transferred, April 24, to the Reserve Brigade. The Twenty-sixth Michigan and One hundred and fifty-second New York assigned to General Corcoran.

April 22.—The Tenth New Jersey was assigned to General Corcoran and the One hundred and eighteenth New York assigned to Reserve Brigade.

The following officers were killed and wounded during the month:

April 8.—Captain Bowdish, commissary of subsistence; killed by accident on the railroad.

April 12.—Lieut. Col. Edgar A. Kimball, Ninth New York Volunteers; killed by Brig. Gen. M. Corcoran while on duty.

April 23.—Capt. John E. White, Ninety-ninth New York Volunteers; wounded by rebel sharpshooters.

April 24.—Surg. James Wilson, Ninety-ninth New York Volunteers; wounded by rebel sharpshooters. Second Lieut. B. Conron, Thirteenth Indiana Volunteers; killed in skirmish on Somerton road. Col. C. Buell, One hundred and sixty-ninth New York Volunteers; wounded in skirmish on Somerton road. Maj. Alonzo Alden, One hundred and sixty-ninth New York Volunteers; wounded in skirmish on Somerton road.

April 15.—Capt. J. McAnally, One hundred and fifty-fifth New York Volunteers; wounded in the skirmish on Edenton road.

April 24.—Second Lieut. T. J. Cantwell, One hundred and sixty-fourth New York Volunteers; wounded in the skirmish on Edenton road.

May 1.—The Ninety-ninth New York Volunteers had a skirmish with the enemy on South Quay road, near Suffolk. Loss: killed, 4; wounded, 42.

May 2.—Two companies of the Third Pennsylvania Artillery reported.

May 3.—Reconnaissance on the Petersburg road by General Getty; enemy driven from their rifle-pits on their main line. Loss, killed and wounded, 60. After dark the enemy abandoned the siege of Suffolk, retiring in haste toward the Blackwater.

May 4.—Colonel Foster commenced pursuit after the enemy, coming on the rear guard at Leesville, which were dispersed and most of them captured. General Corcoran pursued them on the Edenton road, General Terry on the South Quay road, and a cavalry detachment on the Petersburg road, but all were unable to come across any force. Many prisoners were captured, mostly stragglers (about 250), including 4 officers. One hundred and thirty signified their willingness to take the oath of allegiance and were sent North.

No. 3.

Report of Capt. Charles L. Davis, Eighty-second Pennsylvania Infantry, Chief Signal Officer.

OFFICE OF CHIEF SIGNAL OFFICER, DEPT. OF VA.,
Fort Monroe, Va., May 9, 1863.

COLONEL: I have the honor to submit the following report of the operations of the Signal Corps in the siege of Suffolk, lasting from April 11 to May 2:

For some months past I have had a signal station on a tree near the crossing of the Seaboard and Roanoke and Norfolk and Petersburg Railroads, to which the pickets on the South Quay and Carrsville roads were instructed to report for orders in case of attack. Through this station the commanding general at Suffolk was kept informed of movements on the front toward the Blackwater.

This station stood at the junction of two roads, on each of which a company of cavalry was stationed 1,200 yards in advance.

At 3.30 p. m. April 11 a contraband reported to the officer (Lieutenant Thayer) on duty at this station that the enemy was advancing in force on both roads and only a few miles distant. Through the extraordinary promptness of this officer this information was immediately transmitted to General Peck by Lieutenant Strong, who received it by signals at Suffolk. A few minutes afterward Lieutenant Thayer (noticing the cavalry soldiers coming in at a furious rate, riding barebacked) sent to General Peck by signals the message, "Pickets driven in. Re-enforcements needed."

In the absence of a commissioned officer to command the infantry pickets Lieutenant Thayer took command and made such disposition of them as he thought necessary to check the advance of the enemy's vanguard and prevent the cutting off of the cavalry pickets on the South Quay road.

This action he immediately reported by signals to General Peck, and while so doing the enemy opened fire with their sharpshooters on Lieutenant Thayer and his flagmen (Privates A. H. Eames and W. J. Mott), who were located in the top of a high tree performing their duty, and so remained until the arrival of a regiment of cavalry, when Lieutenant Thayer was ordered to abandon his post and come in.

On the 12th I was notified by telegraph that signal supplies and officers were needed at Suffolk. The supplies were promptly sent, and I received orders from the commanding general of the department to proceed there at once, taking with me such officers as could be spared from elsewhere.

Communication was immediately opened by Captain Tamblyn between the signal tower (which had been previously erected in the town of Suffolk for this very emergency) and the fronts, commanded by Generals Terry, Corcoran, and Dodge. These lines of communication were constantly employed in transmitting intelligence as to the movements of the enemy.

On the morning of the 13th a message was received from Lieutenant Strong, on General Terry's front, that the enemy had established a signal station at the junction of the Seaboard and Roanoke and Norfolk and Petersburg Railroads and were signaling. This information I immediately gave to General Peck, and was directed by him to ascertain from Captain Lee whether he could shell the enemy from their position, and if so, direct him to do it. Captain Lee, from his gunboat in the Nansemond River, immediately opened his fire, and being entirely unable to see where his shot struck on account of the intervening woods he was directed in his firing by signals. The point where each shot struck, with directions as to change of range, was given him through signals by Lieutenant Thayer, who noted the effect of each shot from the tower in Suffolk and transmitted the same to Captain Lee by signals. After firing a number of shots, most of which struck well, Lieutenant Thayer signaled to Captain Lee that the enemy's signal station was abandoned.

On the 14th Lieutenant Young, stationed at headquarters of General Corcoran, at Fort Union, together with numerous other messages, trans mitted the information from General Corcoran to General Peck that the enemy had attacked on the Somerton road. Promptly orders were returned to General Corcoran to open fire. These messages were transmitted while the shells of the enemy were falling around them and evidently directed at the signal flag of Lieutenant Young, who, with his flagman (Private J. W. Brown), exhibited great coolness during the attack.

These lines of communication were kept open and transmitting much valuable information until the 16th, when, the enemy threatening to cross the Nansemond River and attack our right and rear, General Peck directed communication to be opened with General Getty's front and the forces on the Nansemond. Captain Tamblyn was therefore directed to break up communication with the other fronts, as of less importance, and open a line down the Nansemond River. This was accomplished in a very short time, and the line was constantly used in transmitting important, and, in some cases, confidential messages between the different stations. This line was composed of four stations, and the officers and men operating them were all so constantly on duty, night and day, sleeping and eating only when a short leisure would permit, that without relief some of them must have succumbed had not matters taken a change.

This line of communication was kept open and (until the raising of the siege and departure of the enemy) was continually useful.

A field telegraph train would have been of eminent utility in this locality, and I shall have one or more of these trains at my disposal in a few days.

In closing this report I wish to state that officers and men all stood up to their duty nobly and when nearly worn-out with fatigue by watching and working night and day and under fire of the enemy. To Capt. W. Tamblyn, acting signal officer, the senior officer of that part of my detachment at Suffolk, great credit is due for his faithful supervision of affairs.

Lieuts. A. M. Thayer, R. P. Strong, George F. Young, and H. R. Murray, acting signal officers, deserve special mention for having stood faithfully to their duties under the fire of the enemy's sharpshooters.

Flagmen A. H. Eames, W. J. Mott, C. H. Treadwell, and J. W. Brown performed their duties faithfully, even when the flag they held in their hands was the special mark of the enemy.

I inclose herewith a map, showing the different lines of communication had by signals. The small red flags indicate the stations and the dotted lines the lines of communication had at different times.

All of which is respectfully submitted.

I have the honor to be, colonel, very respectfully, your obedient servant,

CHARLES L. DAVIS,
Captain and Chief Signal Officer, Department of Virginia.
Lieut. Col. LOUIS H. PELOUZE, *Assistant Adjutant-General.*

No. 4.

Reports of Maj. Gen. John J. Peck, U. S. Army, commanding at Suffolk.

HEADQUARTERS UNITED STATES FORCES,
Suffolk, Va., May 5, 1863.

COLONEL: On September 22, 1862, I was ordered to Suffolk, with about 9,000 men, to repel the advance of Generals Pettigrew and French from the Blackwater, with 15,000 men. No artificial defenses were found nor had any plan been prepared. Situated at the head of the Nansemond River, with the railways to Petersburg and Weldon, Suffolk is the key to all the approaches to the mouth of the James River on the north of the Dismal Swamp. Regarding the James as second only in importance to the Mississippi for the Confederates and believing that sooner or later they would withdraw their armies from the barren wastes of Northern Virginia to the line of the James and attempt the recovery of Portsmouth and Norfolk as ports for their iron-clads and contraband trade, I prepared a system, and on the 25th commenced Fort Dix. From that time until the present I spared no pains for placing the line of the river and swamp in a state of defense. My labors alarmed the authorities at Richmond, who believed I was preparing a base for a grand movement upon the rebel capital, and the whole of the Blackwater was fortified, as well as Cypress Swamp and Birchen and Chipoak Rivers. This line rests upon the James near Fort Powhatan.

About February 26 Lieutenant-General Longstreet was detached from Lee's army and placed in command of the Department of Virginia, with headquarters at Petersburg. Of his corps, 15,000 were on the Blackwater and 15,000 between Petersburg and the river, near the railway. This distribution enabled him to concentrate in twenty four hours within a few miles of Suffolk and looked threatening. Reports were circulated and letters written to the effect that Longstreet was in South Carolina and Tennessee with all his forces with the view of throwing me off my guard.

My information was reliable, and I fully advised the department of the presence of this force, and on March 14 Getty's division (Ninth Corps) reported for duty. Early in April deserters reported troops moving to the Blackwater, that many bridges were being constructed, and that a pontoon train had arrived from Petersburg.

On the 6th I was advised that General Foster was in great need of troops and asked to send him 3,000. I replied that no soldiers ought to leave the department, but I would spare that number provided they could be supplied at short notice.

On the 10th, at 4.30 p. m., as the troop train was leaving, I was informed of the contents of a captured mail by General Viele to the effect that General Longstreet would attack me at once with from 40,000 to 60,000; that he had maps, plans, and a statement of my force, and that General Hill would co-operate.

On the 11th Hood's division followed up my cavalry, returning from Blackwater on the South Quay road, and about 4 p. m. captured, without a shot, the cavalry outposts. Others followed on other roads and a surprise in open day was attempted. The signal officers, under Captain Tamblyn, rendered most signal service. Lieutenant Thayer held his station for a long time in spite of the riflemen about him.

On the 12th, about noon, Pickett's division advanced on the Somerton and Jenkins' on the Edenton road, and a large column on the river by the Providence Church road. Much fine skirmishing took place on all these roads, but the pickets were pressed back and the enemy was not checked until he came within artillery range. He sustained some loss and fell back a few miles to his line of battle.

On the 13th the enemy skirmished with our light troops on all the approaches. On the Somerton, Colonel Foster handled him very roughly, driving him back and restoring his picket line at sundown. On the river the contest was sharp and long, but the batteries and gunboats held the enemy at bay.

On the 14th Lieutenant Cushing, U. S. Navy, was hotly engaged for several hours with a large force at the mouth of the West Branch. His loss was severe, but the enemy suffered much and had some artillery dismounted. The enemy opened a ten-gun battery near the Norfleet house for the purpose of destroying the gunboats and of covering a crossing. Lieutenant Lamson, with the Mount Washington, West End, and Stepping Stones, engaged the battery for some hours in the most gallant manner, but was compelled to drop down to the West Branch. The Mount Washington, completely riddled and disabled, grounded, as did the West End, and both were towed off by the Stepping Stones. The rudder of the Alert was broken. Several batteries on the river were opened with fine effect and others were pushed with all dispatch toward completion. More or less skirmishing and artillery fire on all portions of the lines. In the night the Smith Briggs, lying near my headquarters, was attacked, but Captain Lee and the guns of the draw-bridge repulsed the enemy.

On the 15th the force between Suffolk and West Branch was reported by the best authorities at 10,000, with a pontoon train under the immediate command of General French. About noon our batteries, under the direction of General Getty, below the mouth of Jericho Creek, were warmly engaged with the Norfleet battery. Four of the rebel 20-pounder rifles were dismounted and the battery was silenced. A party sent out on the Edenton road captured the camp equipage of one regiment. Fear of an ambuscade prevented taking of many prisoners.

On the 17th Major Stratton, with a force of cavalry, held South Mills, which is the key to nearly all the approaches from North Carolina on the south side of the Dismal Swamp. There was much skirmishing on all the avenues of approach with some field artillery. General Terry's front was much annoyed from the first day by the near approach of riflemen. Under his orders the enemy was signally punished.* General French's engineer was taken prisoner by Lieutenant Cushing's pickets. He was laying out works and had a map of Suffolk, which he tore to pieces.

On the 18th the enemy was very active in throwing up new batteries and rifle-pits along the river. A heavy one was in progress near the mouth of West Branch on Hill's Point. Admiral Lee, U. S. Navy, ordered all the boats out of the Upper Nansemond, lest they should be destroyed, leaving the whole defense of the river to the land forces. The admiral was urged to reconsider his orders. Upon my representation the order was temporarily suspended.

On the 19th, about dusk, General Getty and Lieutenant Lamson executed most successfully a plan which had been agreed upon for crossing the river and capturing Battery Huger at the mouth of the West Branch. The Eighty-ninth New York and Eighth Connecticut were taken over on the Stepping Stones. Five pieces of artillery, 9 officers, and 120 soldiers were captured. It was well conceived and ably conducted, and reflects great honor on the combined arms. Lieutenant Lamson suggested the enterprise, landed with four of his howitzers, and played a brilliant part. Captain Stevens was conspicuous for his gallant conduct in this affair and deserves mention; also Lieutenants McKechnie and Faxon, aides of General Getty.

On the 20th Major Stratton visited Elizabeth City, N. C., and found

---

* Return of Terry's brigade, First Division, Seventh Army Corps, for April, 1863, gives the following casualties in this affair of the 17th: Three privates killed and 10 wounded.

it abandoned by our troops. He found General Longstreet's pickets in the vicinity of Sandy Cross.

On the 21st the command was highly honored by a visit from Major-General Halleck, Commander-in-Chief, accompanied by Major-General Dix.

On the 22d a heavy rain-storm commenced, suspending all fatigue labors, but adding materially to the strength of the swamp on the left flank.

On the 24th a demonstration was made upon the enemy's right flank, on the Edenton road, under General Corcoran and Colonels Foster and Spear, while a feint was made on the Somerton by Colonel Buehler. The enemy was driven in confusion from all his advance points and rifle-pits back upon his main line of defense behind the dam and swamp at Darden's Mill. A force estimated at about 1,500 was believed to be massed on that front. The object of the move was attained and the command withdrawn. Colonels Beach, Drake, and Murphy had provisional brigades, and handled them extremely well; Captain Simpson commanded the artillery.

On the 25th information was received of the arrival of heavy artillery from Petersburg. Troops were reported on this side of the Chowan, on the way from General Hill, under General Garnett.

On the 27th Major Stratton occupied Camden Court-House and burned a ferry-boat of the enemy's. Rebels were very active at night, chopping, moving troops, and signaling. A new battery of three guns was opened by them below the Norfleet Battery. Chopping parties were broken up by the Redan and Mansfield Battery. They reoccupied the Hill's Point Battery in the night. The steamers Commerce and Swan, under the volunteer pilotage of Lieutenants Rowe and Horton, of the Ninety-ninth New York Volunteers, ran down past the batteries in the night, but not without many shots. These officers are entitled to much credit for this service.

On the 28th Suffolk was visited by a heavy storm. A rebel work for several guns was discovered on the river.

On the 29th the Hon. Secretary of State, W. H. Seward, paid a visit, in company with Major-General Dix, to this command.

On the 30th, early in the morning, the enemy opened with one Whitworth, one 30 and one 35 pounder Parrott. Toward night they opened fire upon the Commodore Barney, and the battery was silenced by the Barney (Lieutenant Cushing, U. S. Navy) and Captain Morris, battery in Fort Stevens.

May 1.—There was a sharp skirmish on General Terry's front about 5 p. m.* The enemy, re-enforced largely, was held in check from the guns of Nansemond, South Quay, and Rosecrans with considerable loss. Another brigade from North Carolina was reported to have joined Longstreet.

May 3.—A reconnaissance in force was made by Generals Getty and Harland on the enemy's left flank. The troops crossed at 9 a. m., at the draw-bridge, under the fire of Battery Mansfield, the Onondaga, and the Smith Briggs, and seized the plateau near Pruden's house in spite of sharpshooters in the rifle-pits, orchards, and woods. The advance was slow, every inch being hotly contested. The movement resulted in bringing heavy re-enforcements for the enemy. His numbers and artillery failed to check the troops. By night the enemy was massed

---

* Return of the Seventh Army Corps, Department of Virginia, for the month of May, 1863, gives the loss in this affair as follows: Four killed and 42 wounded, all of the Ninety-ninth New York Infantry.

on his strong lir e of intrenchments and under the fire of a numerous
artillery. The purpose of the movement having been attained, the
troops were directed to remain on the ground awaiting events.

In conjunction with the above, Major Crosby crossed the Nansemond
near Sleepy Hole with the Twenty-first Connecticut, a section of the
Fourth Wisconsin Battery, and eleven mounted rifles. At 4 a. m. pushed
on and occupied Chuckatuck, driving out 300 rebel cavalry. He skirmished all the way to Reed's Ferry, capturing 16 prisoners, and then
returned to the river under cover of the gunboats. At the same time
Colonel Dutton crossed in boats and occupied Hill's Point with the
Fourth Rhode Island, a portion of the One hundred and seventeenth
New York, and a detachment from the Commodore Barney. He advanced some distance, but was met by a superior force posted strongly
in the woods, and after much skirmishing returned upon Hill's Point,
from which the enemy could not dislodge him.

I again take pleasure in acknowledging the valuable services of Lieutenants Cushing, Lamson, and Harris, U. S. Navy. These officers rendered every assistance in their power in crossing the river. Lieutenant
Cushing sent a boat howitzer and detachment with the Fourth Rhode
Island, under Colonel Dutton.

I regret to state that Colonel Ringold, of the One hundred and third
New York, lost his life from two wounds while leading on his men in
the most gallant manner. He was a meritorious officer.

May 4.—About 9 p. m. on the 3d the enemy commenced retiring
upon the Blackwater. His strong line of pickets prevented deserters
and contrabands from getting through with the information until he had
several hours the start. Generals Corcoran and Dodge were promptly
in pursuit on the Edenton road while Colonel Foster followed upon the
Somerton. By 6 a. m. Colonel Foster was pressing the rear of a formidable column on the old road near Leesville. He was compelled, from the
smallness of his force, to wait for the command under General Corcoran
and could not again strike the column before it reached the river.
The cavalry of Colonels Spear and Onderdonk were pushed on numerous roads, and rendered valuable services in procuring information and
capturing prisoners.

Thus ends the present investment or siege of Suffolk, which had for
its objects the recovery of the whole country south of the James extending to the Albemarle Sound in North Carolina, the ports of Norfolk and Portsmouth, 80 miles of new railroad iron, the equipments of
two roads, and the capture of all the United States forces and property
with some thousands of contrabands.

General Longstreet finding that an assault at the outside upon works
defended by one-half his own force would be expensive and uncertain,
and having failed in turning either flank, decided to besiege the place
and asked for re-enforcements; probably not less than two divisions
joined from General Hill. The works constructed are on the most
extensive scale and in the most approved manner.

The rules and regulations prescribed by military authorities for the
conduct of siege operations have been observed. Some idea may be
formed of this so-styled foraging expedition when I state that not less
than 10 miles of batteries, covered-ways, and rifle-pits have been
thrown up; most of the artillery was protected by embrasures; the
parapets were from 12 to 15 feet in thickness and well revetted, while
the covered ways were from 8 to 10 feet. Longstreet had a wire laid
from the Blackwater, and telegraphed arrangements throughout his
lines.

RESULTS.

We have taken five pieces of the famous Fauquier Artillery, about 400 prisoners, some rifles, and camp equipage. Probably 500 or 600 have been killed and wounded and 500 have deserted, making a total loss of at least 1,500.

Our own killed is 44; wounded, 202, and missing, 14. Total, 260.*

All the *morale*, prestige, and glory belong to the patient and brave officers and men of the Federal Army.

Besides these brilliant results, this command has held the masses of the enemy around Suffolk in order that General Hooker might secure the crowning victory of the war, and it is entitled to a share of the glory that may accrue to his arms. My thanks are due all officers and soldiers who have worked cheerfully and patriotically on these fortifications. They now see that their labors are not in vain.

The truth of history requires that I should state that a small portion of the One hundred and twelfth New York became homesick and discontented, and said that they came to fight and not to dig. This feeling was seized upon by politicians, and since the adjournment of the Senate I have been advised that efforts were made to defeat my confirmation in consequence thereof. Soldiers who love their country will cheerfully perform any duty assigned them; men who know how to build fortifications will know how to defend or assault them. It should not be forgotten that the principal rebel successes have been behind intrenchments, as at Manassas, Fredericksburg, Richmond, Vicksburg, Charleston, &c.

It is an unpleasant duty to state that most of the Ninth New York, Colonel Hawkins, left this command on the 3d, by expiration of their term of service, while their comrades were actively engaged with the enemy. It can be regarded only as an unfortunate termination of a hitherto brilliant career of service.

To Generals Corcoran, Terry, Dodge, and Harland, and Colonels Dutton and Gibbs, commanding fronts or lines; Colonels Spear and Onderdonk, of the cavalry; Colonels Gurney and Wardrop, commanding reserves, and Captain Follett, chief of artillery, I am under very great obligations for the able, faithful, judicious, and cheerful discharge of every duty incident to their important positions.

General Getty was intrusted with the river line below the Onondaga Battery, the key of the position and about 8 miles in length—a very difficult line to defend against an enterprising enemy acquainted with every by-path and guided by owners of the soil. His responsibilities were of the highest order, and the labors of his troops were incessant. Under his vigilant supervision everything was done that could be for the security of the right flank, and the enemy was foiled in all plans for crossing.

Col. R. S. Foster, of Indiana, commanding brigade and a portion of the front, added fresh laurels to the high reputation which he established in West Virginia and on the Peninsula. He was at home in grand skirmishes, and the enemy always recoiled before him.

General Gordon reported three days before the conclusion of the siege and was assigned to the command of the Reserve Division. His long and varied experience rendered his judgment of great value, and I regret that he has been called to another field.

My thanks are due General Viele, of Norfolk, for the prompt transmission of important intelligence and for the alacrity with which my calls were responded.

---

* But see revised statement, p. 288.

Captain Ludlow, quartermaster at Norfolk, deserves mention for his untiring efforts in forwarding the main bulk of supplies for the army.

The medical department, under the able management of Dr. Hand, was in excellent working order and equal to every emergency. The wounded were promptly cared for and spared all unnecessary suffering. The commissary department was admirably managed by the late Captain Bowdish, and since his death by Captain Felt.

Colonel Murphy commanded brigade; Colonel Drake, Fort Union; Colonel Hawkins, Fort Nansemond; Captain Sullivan, Fort Halleck; Colonel Davis, the Draw-Bridge Battery; Colonel Worth, Battery Mansfield; Colonel Thorp, the Redan and Rosecrans; Captain Johnson, Battery Monday; Colonel England, Battery Montgomery; Colonel Pease, Battery Stevens, and Colonel McEvily, Fort Dix, with ability, and their troops were always ready for the enemy.

Major Stratton, Eleventh Pennsylvania Cavalry, was at South Mills watching the operations of the troops from Carolina. By his discretion and energy the rebels were prevented from penetrating the Dismal Swamp.

Captain Tamblyn, Lieutenants Seabury, Young, Thayer, Strong, and Murray, of the Signal Corps, have been indefatigable day and night and of the greatest service in their department. Captain Davis shares the above commendation for the few days he was here.

The conduct of Lieutenant-Colonel Nixon, Ninety-ninth New York; of Captain Morris, Lieutenants Hasbrouck, Hunt, Whitney, and Beecher, of the artillery; Lieutenants James, Grant, Macardle, Soederquist, and Burleson, on engineer duty; of Lieutenant Buttz, assistant provost marshal, and of Major Wetherill, was conspicuous. Major Stewart, of the Engineer Corps, joined for a few days, evincing the same lively interest which characterized his valuable services on the Peninsula.

The command is mainly indebted to the provost-marshal, Major Smith, of the One hundred and twelfth New York, for the good order and cleanliness which has prevailed in town and camp.

The co-operation of the gunboats, under Lieutenants Cushing, Lamson, and Harris, U. S. Navy, sent by Admiral Lee, has been very effective, and I take great pleasure in acknowledging the gallant services of their officers and crews. The army gunboats Smith Briggs and West End, commanded by Captain Lee and Lieutenant Rowe, proved invaluable. The Smith Briggs was for many days the only boat above the West Branch, in consequence of the order of Admiral Lee.

My personal staff have all earned a place in this record by their zeal, fidelity, and unremitting labors day and night, increased by injuries which I sustained from the fall of my horse. Their claims to promotion were established long before the siege of Suffolk. Maj. B. B. Foster, assistant adjutant-general; Capt. George S. Dodge, quartermaster; Lieuts. Charles R. Stirling and James D. Outwater, aides-de-camp; Lieut. A. B. Johnson, ordnance officer, and Lieut. James D. Mahon, judge advocate.

Doubtless many names have been omitted, but discrimination is impossible where all have done so well.

For the conclusion is reserved the agreeable duty of testifying to the cordial and efficient support I have ever received from Major-General Dix. No request or suggestion has ever escaped his attention, and most of my requirements have been anticipated by his liberal and comprehensive policy.

Very respectfully, your obedient servant,

JOHN J. PECK,
Major-General.

Col. D. T. VAN BUREN, *A. A. G., Dept. of Va.*

GENERAL: My excuse for this trespass upon your most valuable time is that I have been unofficially advised that Admiral Lee has endeavored to depreciate the importance of Longstreet's campaign against me.

This is very singular, for he did not visit Suffolk during the nine months I was in command, and saw nothing of my system of fortifications or of Longstreet's, the development of which was from 9 to 10 miles. His headquarters were at Newport News, some 30 miles from mine. His views were based entirely upon the impressions of young and inexperienced subordinates, whose vision was limited to short distances beyond the gunboat decks.

On April 20, thirteen days before the conclusion of the siege, he ordered all the boats to Hill's Point for safety, 7 miles from Suffolk, against which I protested, and some sharp correspondence ensued. Besides the distance the densely-wooded banks of the Nansemond were unfavorable for forming a judgment of the numbers and labors of the enemy, everywhere screened in timber. The whole country was one vast forest, out of which I had to cut a field of fire for my artillery. Admiral Lee thinks that Longstreet brought a force of negroes for building his extensive line of works. On his arrival the negroes ceased to come into my lines, and parties were sent out to bring them in for information, but without success.

After his repulse on May 3 and night retreat some blacks escaped from Franklin and informed me that all the contrabands, except servants and drivers, were left at Franklin, across the Blackwater, to prevent their escape. They also stated that they prayed very loud that "Massa Longstreet might be whipped by you folks."

Captain Lamson, one of the most gallant officers in the U. S. Navy, commanded the flotilla in the Upper Nansemond, and was on the staff of the acting admiral. He says he made a complete examination, during two days, of Longstreet's lines after his retreat, and changed his opinion and so told the admiral; he estimated the rebel force from 35,000 to 50,000. Major-General Dix was over my lines, including the Nansemond, every alternate day, and had favorable opportunities for judging; he says some 35,000. General Gordon states that the works he examined could not have been made by less than 30,000.

Major-General Keyes concluded my situation was so critical that I ought to evacuate the lines to save the troops from capture. On my positive refusal he called for two corps. He estimated 40,000 prior to Hill's arrival.

A mail, with several hundred letters, was taken, showing that Hill was to co-operate, and that they had a statement of my force, artillery, and a map of the works.

General Hooker telegraphed that his reliable spy in Richmond advised that Jeff. Davis had ordered Hill to leave North Carolina and join Longstreet at Suffolk. All prisoners, deserters, and Union people agreed as to this co-operation.

About April 26 a division arrived from Little Washington, having crossed the Chowan near Gatesville. General Hill joined with his entire command on May 1, by way of Weldon, Franklin, and Holland's Corners. Hill's letter to Longstreet, asking orders, is in my possession.

General Dix employed a spy to visit the armies of Longstreet and Lee in February and March. He was two weeks in Longstreet's lines and longer in Lee's. Through a friend in the War Office in Richmond he was allowed entire freedom in the camps and sold his goods to officers and men on credit. He reported 28,000 to 30,000 in March in my general front and one hundred and nine regiments, of some 84,000, in the army of Lee. Then 28,000, with the forces of Hill from North Carolina, represent generally the mass opposed to me. My effective force for some days was 14,928. I asked for one division only. For a few days I had about 29,000 effectives on a line from below Hill's Point, on the river, extending across to the Dismal Swamp of at least 15 miles in length, with a detachment of the same at South Mills, 30 miles distant, the key to the southern approaches of the swamp.

The campaign will be clear when it is stated that Hill was to make noisy and furious demonstrations in Carolina, for the purpose of inducing General Foster to call for troops from Virginia. Accordingly, Pettigrew appeared in the vicinity of New Berne and Hill attacked or cannonaded Washington.

Our casualties were 6 at New Berne, but I have failed to learn that any occurred at Washington. Ten thousand were asked for General Foster, and I was called upon to contribute from my 15,000 on the 10th April. Against my judgment I consented to send 3,000, and they were on the troop train. Longstreet was advised of this detachment in a few hours and advanced that very night. With your approval I brought back the 3,000 at dusk, and very luckily for our affairs in that quarter.

The operations about Suffolk, ending May 4, were suddenly eclipsed in the night of general gloom and painful anxiety which attended Hooker's great disaster at Chancellorsville. Attention was not again awakened upon that field, and the campaign has been imperfectly understood by the public.

I desire to thank you for the liberal support sent me at Suffolk.

With sentiments of respect, your obedient servant,

JOHN J. PECK.

Major-General HALLECK,
    Commander-in-Chief, Washington, D. C.

[Inclosure.]

From the Philadelphia Enquirer, April 24, 1863.

THE GALLANT CAMPAIGN AT SUFFOLK.

Having in our recent articles traced the progress of the war in the Southwest, in Tennessee, and in North Carolina, we follow them up this morning by a review of the short and exciting campaign about Suffolk. This campaign, in presence of some of the vast events of the war, appears to be nothing more than an episode, but in our judgment it is entitled to considerable prominence. It must be remembered that the military authorities charged with the occupation of Norfolk established an important post at a considerable distance to the southwest of that city—at Suffolk, where the Petersburg and Norfolk Railroad intersects the Seaboard and Roanoke Railroad, leading to Weldon, N. C. Suffolk is also at the head of navigation on the Nansemond River, which empties into the James River near its mouth. From this post the National troops were enabled to operate to a distance in the interior of the south side of Virginia, keeping the country comparatively clear of guerrillas, contraband traders, and spies, and thus more effectually guarding Norfolk.

For a long while the rebel leaders at Richmond permitted this occu pancy by the Union forces to pass without interference, although it was exceedingly unpalatable to their adherents in the country occupied. Within the last two or three weeks, however, for reasons that may appear in the sequel, they detached a heavy force, under their pet general—Longstreet—to recover Suffolk and to bring Norfolk once more under the sway of the rebellion. The movement commenced about the same time with that of General Hill against General Foster's garrison at Washington, N. C., and the two were unquestionably intended to co-operate with each other.

Having massed some 38,000 men behind the Blackwater River General Longstreet began the execution of his plan on the 10th instant by crossing his grand army over that stream by means of five pontoon bridges.

On the next night his advance drove in our pickets in front of Suffolk, and the situation of our forces began to look serious.

The rebel plan was to cut the Nansemond River some 6 miles or so below Suffolk, on our right flank, while another force was to be thrown against the Norfolk Railroad, on our left flank and rear, and, thus surrounded, General Peck's entire army and the city of Norfolk were to fall a rich and easy prize into the hands of the enemy. It so happened, however, that two matters over which the rebel chieftains could exercise but little control interfered to defeat the scheme. In the first place General Peck, who was in command of the National force, was entirely too vigilant, too active, and too enterprising for General Longstreet; and in the second place General Foster's resolute resistance against Hill at Washington, N. C., where the latter stubbornly persisted in holding out after his adversary claimed that he was hopelessly cut off, prevented Hill from coming up in time to execute his share of the grand achievement. Nevertheless, General Longstreet went at his plan with energy, and from April 11, when he first drove in our pickets, until Tuesday last he kept up an incessant series of attacks of the most harassing and vexatious character to General Peck's troops. He rushed his squadrons of cavalry against our lines in one place and established batteries of field artillery to sweep the Nansemond River at others. He maneuvered to overwhelm us here and flank us there, and in every way endeavored to penetrate our lines, but was baffled in every attempt by the watchfulness, activity, endurance, skill, and courage of General Peck and his brave companions in arms.

Among those who were conspicuous on our side General Getty, Colonel Foster, of the light troops, and Lieutenant Lamson, of the Navy, are mentioned by General Dix; Colonel Foster having repelled an assault upon the right, and General Getty, with Lieutenant Lamson, having stormed, in the most gallant manner, a troublesome battery of six guns, which they captured, with 160 prisoners.

Thus repulsed at every point, Longstreet appears to have abandoned his enterprise, at least for the present, for the latest advices state that skirmishing ceased on the 21st.

Now, what is the importance of this defeated movement of Longstreet's? To get an intelligent answer to that question we have only to look at contemporaneous operations on the James River. For several weeks past the rebels have been quite busy fortifying its banks just as they have fortified the Mississippi. They are casemating Fort Powhatan, and have three batteries thoroughly finished. They are taking up the obstructions at Fort Darling. They know the value of water communication to us, and of what priceless advantage it is to them to be able to prevent our passage. This is the lesson they have learned at Vicksburg, Port Hudson, Fort Pemberton, and at Charleston.

If they fortify the James down to its mouth it is closed for our purposes and left free for theirs. It brings their iron-clads, now lying idle at Richmond, clear down to Hampton Roads, where they may lie in wait and have their opportunities always in sight. To complete this grand scheme of operations Norfolk is wanted, and then, with their iron-clads, that city would be an open port until we could complete another fleet of monitors to close it up again. We tried to develop all this some days ago. Moreover, there are indications that the rebel leaders intend to defend Richmond with a much smaller army than that hitherto devoted to that purpose, and upon a line much nearer to that city than the Rappahannock. That is the reason why there is so much activity in strengthening the works immediately in front of Richmond. They know that we can scarcely assail that city by the land route, for that compels a long line of communications, which experience tells them they can break up with a small and active body of cavalry; hence another reason for fortifying the James and closing the water approaches against our iron-clads. All these considerations make the campaign about Suffolk a rather important feature of the war and not a mere episode. It appears to be over for the present, but we trust that the vigilance, activity, and skill which have thus far baffled the enemy will continue to be exerted, and that General Peck will have supports at hand. Longstreet's withdrawal may only be temporary, to wait the tardy arrival of Hill from North Carolina.

The Richmond Examiner of November 27, 1863, has the following in its leading editorial upon Lieutenant-General Longstreet and his Knoxville and Suffolk campaigns, which are pronounced as parallel failures. The liberal admissions by the rebel press at the time and now respecting the Suffolk operations are highly creditable to the command of Major-General Peck, and ought to satisfy those who sought to underrate that campaign:

Perhaps the result might have been different if Longstreet and his corps of the Virginia army had been in line. His operations in East Tennessee afford little compensation for the reverse at Chattanooga, nor have the late bare and scanty news from that quarter sustained the high hope which the public justly based on the first intelligence briskly forwarded by General Bragg. His telegram declared that Longstreet's cavalry had pursued the enemy into Knoxville, that the infantry was close up, and it was natural to suppose that the next news would be that of Knoxville's recapture; but the next news from Longstreet contained a mention of intrenching, which suggested disagreeable reminiscences of Suffolk. Since then little or nothing has been heard from Longstreet unless we are to receive the unofficial story of the telegraph this morning to be trustworthy. Oh, that it may be so! His pressure on Burnside has undoubtedly quickened Grant's attack on Bragg, while the absence of his whole corps from the Confederate line at the time of Sherman's arrival in the Federal host has given the enemy a great opportunity. It was during the parallel campaign of Longstreet against Suffolk that Hooker made his *coup* at Chancellorsville; but he found there Jackson, while Grant had to do with Bragg alone.

HDQRS. ARMY AND DISTRICT OF NORTH CAROLINA,
New Berne, N. C., December 25, 1863.

GENERAL: I have the honor to make the following supplementary report as a part of my report of operations during the siege of Suffolk in April and May last:

The name of Col. J. P. McMahon, One hundred and sixty-fourth New York, should have been in the paragraph commencing with "Colonel Murphy, commanding brigade."

My right flank rested upon the Upper Nansemond for some 8 miles, a narrow, shallow, and tortuous stream, offering great facilities to an enterprising enemy for crossing and cutting the communications with Norfolk. Including this the whole line extending to the Dismal Swamp was from 12 to 15 miles in length; besides a force in observation was requisite at South Mills, 30 miles distant, the key of the southern approaches to the swamp. In view of these and other objections I advised the withdrawal of the troops to a new and short line near Portsmouth after the reduction of the rebel and Union fortifications.

The advance of Pettigrew toward New Berne and of Hill upon Little Washington were only feints (our casualties being less than a dozen at both places) made by order of Longstreet some days before the date fixed for his own advance upon Suffolk for the purpose of inducing the authorities in North Carolina to call on Virginia for re-enforcements. As designed, 10,000 were asked for North Carolina, of which I was contributing 3,000 on the 10th. The information reached Longstreet at Franklin, and he crossed the Blackwater that night.

Major-General Hooker kindly telegraphed that he had advices that General Hill would join Longstreet. The time when the North Carolina troops arrived is material. Major Stratton, of the cavalry, reported the fact on the 20th, and I did the same on the 25th, some of them being captured. Major Stratton was correct, for Major-General Foster advised that the enemy retired from Little Washington on the evening of the 15th, and that the deserters said the cause was that they were ordered to re-enforce the army in Virginia.

May 4, while in full pursuit of the columns of Longstreet and Hill toward the Blackwater, an order was received to dispatch General Gordon with a large force to West Point. Ten thousand additional were also ordered to be held in readiness to move at a moment's notice, leaving but the ordinary small garrison intact at Suffolk and of course ending offensive operations.

On May 4 prisoners were taken representing forty odd regiments and independent commands, which gives some idea of the organization and masses of the enemy. The many miles of earthworks thrown up by the rebels were constructed by the troops. Lest the contrabands should come into my lines the bulk of them were left on the other side of the Blackwater.

It is proper to remark that the forces under my command from September to April, 1863, were rated by the public at twice and even thrice the actual numbers.

I am, very respectfully, your obedient servant,

JOHN J. PECK,
Major-General.

Brig. Gen. LORENZO THOMAS,
Adjutant-General, U. S. Army.

[Indorsement.]

HEADQUARTERS DEPARTMENT OF THE EAST,
New York City, January 21, 1864.

Respectfully forwarded.

The withdrawal of the troops to a line nearer Norfolk was suggested by me after the investment of Suffolk and was ordered by the General-in-Chief.

JOHN A. DIX,
Major-General.

No. 5.

Return of Casualties in the Union forces.

[Compiled from nominal lists of casualties, returns, etc.]

Command.	Killed.		Wounded.		Captured or missing.		Aggregate.
	Officers.	Enlisted men.	Officers.	Enlisted men.	Officers.	Enlisted men.	
CORCORAN'S DIVISION.							
Brig. Gen. MICHAEL CORCORAN.							
Terry's Brigade.							
Brig. Gen. HENRY D. TERRY.							
26th Michigan*							
130th New York		1		5			6
152d New York*							
1st Battalion New York Sharpshooters		1		4			5
167th Pennsylvania				1			1
11th Rhode Island*							
Total Terry's brigade		2		10			12
Foster's Brigade.							
Col. ROBERT S. FOSTER.							
13th Indiana				1			1
6th Massachusetts*							
112th New York*							
169th New York		1	3	4			8
165th Pennsylvania		1		4			5
166th Pennsylvania				15		1	16
Total Foster's brigade		2	4	23		1	30
Murphy's Brigade.							
Col. MATHEW MURPHY.							
10th New Jersey*							
155th New York			1	4			5
164th New York		1	1	8			10
170th New York*							
182d New York†							(*)
Total Murphy's brigade		1	2	12			15
Total Corcoran's division		5	6	45		1	57
GETTY'S DIVISION.							
Brig. Gen. GEORGE W. GETTY.							
First Brigade.							
Col. RUSH C. HAWKINS.							
10th New Hampshire*							
9th New York*							
89th New York		3	1	9			13
103d New York	1	2	2	15			20
117th New York*							
Total First Brigade	1	5	3	24			33

*No loss reported.
† Or Sixty-ninth New York National Guard Artillery.

Return of Casualties in the Union forces—Continued.

Command.	Killed.		Wounded.		Captured or missing.		Aggregate.
	Officers.	Enlisted men.	Officers.	Enlisted men.	Officers.	Enlisted men.	
Second Brigade.							
Brig. Gen. EDWARD HARLAND.							
8th Connecticut		4		16			20
11th Connecticut		2	1	3			6
15th Connecticut		1		4			5
16th Connecticut		3	2	18			23
Total Second Brigade		10	3	41			54
Third Brigade.							
Col. ARTHUR H. DUTTON.							
21st Connecticut		1		3			4
13th New Hampshire	1	2	2	14			19
25th New Jersey	1	1		13			15
4th Rhode Island		1		4			5
Total Third Brigade	2	5	2	34			43
Light Artillery.							
1st Pennsylvania, Battery A*							
5th U. S., Battery A				3			3
Total Light Artillery				3			3
Total Getty's division	3	20	8	102			133
GURNEY'S DIVISION.							
Col. WILLIAM GURNEY.							
Second Brigade.							
Col. BURR PORTER.							
22d Connecticut							
40th Massachusetts							
141st New York							
Total Second Brigade							
Third Brigade.							
Col. ROBERT S. HUGHSTON.							
127th New York							
142d New York							
143d New York							
144th New York							
Total Third Brigade							
Total Gurney's division†							
RESERVE BRIGADE.							
Col. DAVID W. WARDROP.							
99th New York		13	4	54			71
118th New York*							
9th Vermont*							
19th Wisconsin*							
Total Reserve Brigade		13	4	54			71

* No loss reported.
† No loss. "Not under fire."

Return of Casualties in the Union forces—Continued.

Command.	Killed.		Wounded.		Captured or missing.		
	Officers.	Enlisted men.	Officers.	Enlisted men.	Officers.	Enlisted men.	Aggregate.
CAVALRY.							
1st New York Mounted Rifles				4		1	5
11th Pennsylvania*							
Total cavalry				4		1	5
LIGHT ARTILLERY.							
Capt. FREDERICK M. FOLLETT.							
1st Delaware Battery							
7th Massachusetts Battery							
16th New York Battery							
19th New York Battery							
4th U. S., Battery D							
4th U. S., Battery L							
2d Wisconsin Battery							
4th Wisconsin Battery							
Total Light Artillery*							
HEAVY ARTILLERY.							
Capt. JOHN A. BLAKE.							
2d Battalion, Third Pennsylvania*							
UNASSIGNED.							
3d New York (Battalion)*							
Grand total	3	38	18	205		2	266

* No loss reported.

Officers killed.—Col. Benjamin Ringold, One hundred and third New York; Capt. Lewis H. Buzzell, Thirteenth New Hampshire; and Chaplain Francis E. Butler, Twenty-fifth New Jersey.

No. 6.

Report of Brig. Gen. Michael Corcoran, U. S. Army, commanding First Division, Seventh Army Corps.

HDQRS. FIRST DIVISION, SEVENTH ARMY CORPS,
Suffolk, Va., May —, 1863.

MAJOR: In compliance with orders from headquarters I respectfully submit the following report as to the operations on the Edenton and Somerton roads and the line of defenses under my command, extending from Fort Nansemond to Fort Halleck, during the late investment of this place by the enemy:

On Saturday, April 11, it being reported that the enemy was advancing against this place, I immediately repaired to my front and had all the troops placed under arms and ready for action. The enemy did not, however, advance within sight, and this condition of affairs remained until Monday afternoon following, when an advance was made by the enemy on the Somerton road. He opened upon us with artillery. The guns of Forts Union, Nansemond, and McClellan replied with such effect as to very soon silence theirs and drive the enemy back. Some skirmishing ensued, in which detachments from the Thirteenth Indiana and One hundred and twelfth New York Volunteers and One hundred and sixty-fifth and One hundred and sixty-sixth Pennsylvania Militia took part and deserve great credit for their actions on that occasion. Our picket lines were re-established that afternoon.

On Wednesday, the 15th, Col. J. P. McMahon, of the One hundred and sixty-fourth Regiment New York Volunteers, went out on the Edenton road for the purpose of reconnoitering the enemy's position. He brought with him three companies of infantry, one from the One hundred and sixty-fourth, One hundred and fifty-fifth, and One hundred and seventieth Regiments respectively, two companies of cavalry of the First New York Mounted Rifles, under the command of Major Patton, and one howitzer. They started out just before daylight, drove in the enemy's pickets, and engaged the Seventeenth Virginia Regiment, capturing 4 prisoners and killing and wounding several. They found that the enemy were in considerable force a short distance from his outposts.

On the same day Colonel Spear, of the Eleventh Pennsylvania Cavalry, went out on the Somerton road with a small force, consisting of four companies of infantry, two from the One hundred and sixty-fifth and One hundred and sixty-sixth Pennsylvania Militia respectively, two pieces of the Seventh Massachusetts Battery, one company of his own regiment, with guns, and three companies of cavalry, and made an attempt to charge their rifle-pits, but this movement was not as successful as was anticipated it would be. Small parties were from time to time afterward sent out on the several roads, also in the direction of the Dismal Swamp and along the Jericho Canal, but nothing of interest occurred. The object of the parties sent in the latter direction was to discover if the enemy were endeavoring to get through in that locality, but no evidence of any such attempt could be discovered.

On April 24 an expedition, which had been for some time in contemplation, went out under my command on the Edenton road. It consisted of about 5,000 infantry, 500 cavalry, and 10 pieces of artillery. I assigned Col. R. S. Foster to the command of the infantry; Colonel Spear had charge of the cavalry, and Captain Simpson of the artillery. A small party went out at the same time on the Somerton road to engage the attention of the enemy there and co-operate with us on the Edenton road if necessary. We advanced about 4 miles and met the enemy's outposts. The pickets retired, and we found the enemy's advance behind rifle-pits. Our artillery opened, and after considerable firing on both sides the enemy was driven from his position and our skirmishers occupied it. The firing still continued a short time, and finally the enemy fell back some distance and ceased firing. In accordance with my instructions I gave instructions not to follow, and we slowly returned to camp. As full reports of this and the other affairs above alluded to have already been furnished I refrain from giving any extended or detailed account of them.

On the 2d instant, about 11 p. m., we received information from two deserters that the enemy was retreating from our front, and I immediately went in person to the major-general commanding and reported the information and that I had ordered a force out on the Edenton and Somerton roads. The major-general having approved of my action I started out myself, ordering an additional force to follow. Colonel Foster went on the Somerton road and General Dodge on the Edenton. I accompanied the latter. He crossed over to the Somerton and met the force under Colonel Foster at Leesville; we advanced some distance farther, and as it was then apparent that the enemy were beyond reach I ordered the troops to return, except a few cavalry left for the purpose of picking up the enemy's stragglers. On the march we captured a large number of prisoners, arms, &c.

From the commencement of the affair the officers and men evinced the most commendable disposition to do their whole duty, always on the alert and ever ready to obey all commands of their superior officers.

The works, which at the beginning were unfinished, by unceasing exertions were soon completed, while other works of defense were also as rapidly and cheerfully erected. The woods in front were cleared to a great extent by slashing parties, who were at work at times night and day. The pickets maintained their ground, except upon two or three occasions when they were forced to retire by overpowering numbers, and deserve great praise for their courage and vigilance; in fact the desire exhibited by the troops to meet the enemy either inside or outside the works gave undoubted assurance that the enemy would have been encountered, had he attempted to carry out his intention of attacking this place, with as courageous and determined a resistance as could possibly be made by gallant men. I feel called upon to state that I was ably assisted throughout the whole time by General Dodge and Colonel Foster, who, respectively, commanded portions of my front, and that they were always at the post of duty and carried out their instructions upon all occasions promptly and cheerfully. I send their reports herewith.

I remain, major, your most obedient servant,

MICHAEL CORCORAN,
Brigadier-General, Commanding.

Maj. B. B. FOSTER,
Assistant Adjutant-General.

—

HEADQUARTERS DIVISION,
Fairfax Court-House, Va., December 14, 1863.

MAJOR: I beg leave to state that I understand I inadvertently omitted to give in my report of the operations at Suffolk, Va., an estimate as to the probable strength of the enemy during the investment, and therefore request that the following supplement may be appended to said report:

From information received from deserters the strength of Longstreet's forces at his approach ranged between 32,000 to 45,000, none under the former, which was corroborated by the statement of a man claiming to have been in the commissary department, who reported that 34,000 rations had been issued at the Blackwater when Longstreet was preparing to cross.

During the first three days not less than 40 prisoners and deserters were examined, whose statements convinced me that the strength of the enemy at that time was not less than 32,000. The deserters from Pickett's division established the fact that many of the regiments had just been filled up to 900 men; some were very weak, but the average seems to have been about 500.

Many of the deserters had run great risks to reach our lines, and, being either of Northern birth or Irishmen, were anxious to give accurate information.

It is certain that the whole of Longstreet's grand corps, comprising the entire divisions of Pickett, Hood, and French, were engaged in the first advance on Suffolk, as well as Jenkins' division, of the Blackwater troops, who took position on the Edenton road on the fourth day of the siege.

The disposition of the rebel force during the first two weeks of the siege was, in my opinion, as follows: Jenkins' (probably 4,000 strong) mainly in position on the Edenton road near Darden's Mill; Pickett's division (of four brigades) on the Somerton road, his right meeting Jenkins' left in the woods between the Edenton and Somerton; Hood's division on the South Quay, connecting with Pickett opposite Fort Nansemond; French on the Providence Church road and river line.

During the pursuit of the enemy, on the morning of their retreat (May 4), we ascertained beyond the possibility of a doubt that on May 1 or 2 two brigades of North Carolina troops (Garnett's and another) joined Pickett, and encamped with him on the Somerton. During that pursuit nearly 300 prisoners were captured from forty different regiments, all of which had been encamped on the Edenton and Somerton roads, and were from Jenkins' and Pickett's divisions and the two North Carolina brigades exclusively.

These prisoners rather increased than diminished the previous estimates of the enemy's strength and confirmed fully the statements of deserters and people residing in the vicinity.

The vast and formidable lines of the enemy's works could not have been constructed in twenty-three days by less than 35,000 troops, considering the constant state of activity in which they were kept by the movements of our forces. Our own troops were incessantly engaged in fatigue duty, and certainly performed less than one-fourth of the labor done by the enemy.

I am convinced by the foregoing facts that the enemy under command of Longstreet during the investment of Suffolk was not less than 34,000 men, exclusive of Hill's re-enforcements.

I am, major, yours, very respectfully

                        MICHAEL CORCORAN,
                                Brigadier-General.

Maj. B. B. FOSTER,
    Assistant Adjutant-General.

No. 7.

Report of Maj. Alexander G. Patton, First New York Mounted Rifles, of skirmish on the Edenton road, April 15.

                  CAMP FIRST MOUNTED RIFLES,
                      Suffolk, Va., April 18, 1863.

GENERAL: I have the honor to report that at 3 o'clock on the morning of the 15th instant I left this camp to make a reconnaissance on the Edenton road, to attack the enemy, and, if possible, to ascertain his force. My command consisted of Company E, Captain Gregory; Company M, Captain Masten, and one howitzer, in charge of Corporal McConnoll, of Company D, all of this regiment. At Fort Dix I was joined by Colonel McMahon with two companies of infantry.

We proceeded cautiously for some 2½ miles, when, having approached near to the enemy's pickets, I directed one shot to be fired from the howitzer; Captain Gregory to charge down the road with his company, Captain Masten supporting him, the howitzer party having directions to advance at quick-time with the infantry, supported by a detail from our picket guard under Captain Poor commanding Company D. The road was found to have been barricaded no less than eight times, but such was the rapidity of our movement that the outer sentry at the enemy's camp was captured.

Charging upon the right of the enemy they were found to be drawn up in line of battle in the woods, and the advance fell back to await the arrival of the remainder of the party, which on coming up was formed in an open field on the right of the road and in front of the enemy. Company D was then deployed as skirmishers on the edge of the woods to cover our right and a charge made upon the right of the enemy, which was met by a galling fire and we were forced to fall back. At about the same moment the infantry rushed forward, cheering, and attacked their left, and by their rapid and effective fire, in conjunction with that of the howitzer opening on their right, forced them to fall back through their camp on the cross-roads leading just —— miles to the Somerton road. At this point we charged again, driving the enemy some distance, but losing 2 men of Company D, whom (the enemy at length having received re-enforcements of infantry and artillery) we were forced to leave in their hands.

Having accomplished the object of the movement and destroyed the camp of the enemy we fell back leisurely, without annoyance, the enemy appearing to be too much crippled to attempt any offensive operations.

Our loss in the affair was 2 men wounded and prisoners from Company D, and 1 wounded; and 1 man wounded in the howitzer party, and 18 horses killed and wounded.

I have to acknowledge the efficient aid rendered me by Colonel McMahon and the infantry under his command, and to present to your notice Corporal McConnoll, who handled the howitzer in the most efficient manner.

I have the honor to be, general, very respectfully, your obedient servant,

A. G. PATTON,
Major, First New York Mounted Rifles.

Brig. Gen. M. CORCORAN.

No. 8.

Itinerary of the First Brigade, Brig. Gen. Henry D. Terry, U. S. Army, commanding, April 11-30.*

April 11, *Saturday.*—The enemy appeared before and invested Suffolk. The brigade immediately took position in the trenches and have remained there ever since.

April 17, *Friday.*—A reconnaissance was sent out, consisting of six companies of the One hundred and thirtieth New York Volunteers, two companies of the Ninety-ninth New York Volunteers, and one company of the New York State Sharpshooters, for the purpose of ascertaining the force of the enemy in front. They were found in force in rifle-pits with large reserves. The loss sustained was as follows: Killed, 2 pri-

---

* From Return of Brigade for April, 1863.

vates of the Ninety-ninth New York Volunteers and 1 private of the One hundred and thirtieth New York Volunteers; wounded, 4 privates of the Ninety-ninth New York Volunteers, 5 privates of the One hundred and thirtieth New York Volunteers, and 1 private of the eighth company New York State Sharpshooters.

No. 9.

Report of Col. Robert S. Foster, Thirteenth Indiana Infantry, commanding Second Brigade.

HEADQUARTERS FOSTER'S BRIGADE,
Suffolk, Va., May 9, 1863.

CAPTAIN : In pursuance of circular from your headquarters I have the honor of submitting the following report of the part taken by my command during the twenty-three days of the investment of Suffolk :

Upon receiving information on Saturday, April 11, of the approach of the enemy I immediately visited my command and found them occupying their respective positions previously assigned. Every arrangement was made to secure as strong a defense as possible. No evidence of the enemy's appearance on my front until Sunday.

On Monday, the 13th, the pickets on the Somerton road were driven in by a force of infantry and cavalry, the pickets maintaining their ground as long as possible. The enemy opened on us with artillery, and immediately the guns from Forts Union, Nansemond, and McClellan responded and silenced their guns. At 3.30 p. m. I sent out a party of skirmishers, accompanying them myself, consisting of details from the Thirteenth Indiana, One hundred and twelfth New York Volunteers, and One hundred and sixty-fifth and One hundred and sixty-sixth Pennsylvania Militia. They advanced rapidly and drove the enemy's skirmishers back to their reserve at Brothers' house, on the Somerton road. I then established my old picket line, extending from the right of Fort Union to Fort Nansemond, and have maintained said line throughout the siege.

Too much praise cannot be given to the detachments from the above-mentioned regiments in their skirmishing on that day. At the earnest solicitations of Colonel Spear, Eleventh Pennsylvania Cavalry, I sent out two pieces of the Fourth Wisconsin Battery, under Captain Vallee, supported by one company of the One hundred and sixty-fifth Pennsylvania Militia. After having fired a few rounds I recalled them. In the morning I ordered the houses on the Somerton road near the reserve picket station burned, which was accomplished. The enemy used the white house of Brothers as a shelter, and I was anxious to destroy it if possible. To this end I dispatched on several occasions a party of skirmishers to effect this object, but the overpowering force of the enemy prevented.

On Wednesday Colonel Spear (with orders from General Corcoran) took command of a small party, consisting of two companies of the One hundred and sixty-fifth Pennsylvania Militia, two companies of the One hundred and sixty-sixth Pennsylvania Militia, two pieces of the Seventh Massachusetts Battery, one company of his own regiment, with guns, and three companies of cavalry, and made an attempt to charge their rifle-pits at Brothers' house, but without success.

On Thursday, April 16, a party of skirmishers, under Lieutenants

Wallick and Conron, of the Thirteenth Indiana, were sent out. They exchanged a few shots with the enemy, but found them too strong to make any advance.

On the succeeding day I sent Lieutenants Zent and Conron with a party of the Thirteenth Indiana to flank the works at the white house if possible. After a sharp engagement they were obliged to withdraw. In this encounter Lieutenant Conron received a wound from which he died a few days after. He was a brave and gallant officer, and sacrificed his life in his zeal to accomplish my desire. In all these skirmishes the men and officers from the different regiments behaved in a gallant and praiseworthy manner, and one name I wish particularly to mention: Private Bircham, Company F, Thirteenth Indiana Volunteers.

On Saturday, the 18th, an unusual quietude prevailed on the picket lines. The pickets of the One hundred and twelfth New York exchanged newspapers with the enemy's pickets and received the assurance they would not be fired on as pickets. The Thirteenth Indiana was ordered to report to General Getty at the small-pox hospital.

On Sunday a portion of my command was ordered to be in readiness to form a part of an expedition on the Edenton road, and I also organized a party to push out on the Somerton road to co-operate with the former party. Said expedition was postponed and did not go out until the succeeding Friday.

The forces from my front consisted of the Eleventh, Fifteenth, and Sixteenth Connecticut and the Thirteenth Indiana, under command of Colonel Beach, Sixteenth Connecticut; the One hundred and sixty-ninth New York and five companies of the One hundred and twelfth New York forming a part of Colonel Drake's command. I was intrusted with the command of infantry. A report has already been furnished of the result of the expedition.* I have kept large details from the different regiments at work during the whole time building new works and strengthening the old, chopping the trees on the front, and in every way doing all I could to make our means of resistance as successful as possible. Upon hearing of the enemy's departure, early on Monday morning, and under General Corcoran's directions, I started in pursuit of the enemy, the result of which has already been furnished you officially.

During the time, I have had the following regiments on my front: The One hundred and sixty-ninth New York was added to my brigade on April 17. In addition to my brigade the Eleventh, Fifteenth, and Sixteenth Connecticut and One hundred and forty-third, One hundred and twenty-seventh, and One hundred and eighteenth New York have occupied a portion of my front at different periods. The Seventh Massachusetts, First Delaware, Sixteenth New York, and Fourth and Second Wisconsin Batteries also constituted at different times a part of my command. All the above commands exerted themselves to the discharge of their duties in an acceptable and praiseworthy manner, at all times meeting every detail with promptness and in every way discharging their duties in a soldierlike manner. During the time, in the different expeditions and skirmishes, the enemy met with a heavy loss, as subsequent events prove.

ROBT. S. FOSTER,
Colonel, Commanding Brigade.

Capt. J. J. BLODGETT,
   Assistant Adjutant-General.

* Return of the Second Brigade, Third Division, Seventh Army Corps, for the month of April, 1863, shows a loss in this affair of 3 killed and 11 wounded.

No. 10.

Report of Lieut. Col. John McConihe, One hundred and sixty-ninth New York Infantry.

HEADQUARTERS 169TH NEW YORK VOLUNTEERS,
Camp Griswold, Suffolk, Va., May 8, 1863.

ADJUTANT: In pursuance of your circular, dated May 7, requiring commanders of regiments to prepare and send in an official report of the part taken by their respective commands in the scenes of the past twenty-three days, I beg leave to report that the One hundred and sixty-ninth Regiment New York State Volunteers left Martindale Barracks, Washington, D. C., on the morning of April 15, with orders to go to Norfolk, reporting *en route* at Fort Monroe. We were transported by the steamer John Warner to Norfolk, Va., arriving there on the 16th instant. The same day we were transported by rail to Suffolk, Va., arriving there late in the night, and on the morning of April 17 we were, by order of General Peck, attached to Acting Brigadier-General Foster's brigade, and occupied a camp near the breastworks on the Somerton road. From this date up to April 24 we continued to furnish fatigue parties to work on the fortifications.

On April 24 the regiment was placed in the Second Provisional Brigade, Col. J. C. Drake commanding, and moved out on the Edenton road with the other forces, and took part in the reconnaissance in force made by General Corcoran on that occasion. The regiment was placed far in advance of all others in support of Captain Follett's battery (D, Fourth U. S. Artillery), and unflinchingly faced a continuous and unabating shower of shell, grape, and canister from the well-directed fire of the enemy until orders were received to retire, the object of the reconnaissance having been accomplished. The colonel (Clarence Buell) was severely wounded by a piece of shell, and Lieutenant Hughes, of Company A, was badly injured in the leg by a shell; E. H. Brock, of Company H, was instantly killed, the back and top of his head being carried away by a shell; Major Alden's horse was wounded in the neck by a shell and the major bruised; Corporal Noyes, Privates Falen, Fogarty, and Kennely were wounded.

On April 28 Captain Vaughn, of Company F, was detailed for the purpose of making a reconnaissance through the Jericho Canal, which expedition was eminently successful, being made through an overflowed swamp, almost impenetrable on account of the depth of the water and the nature of the vines, brush, and timber, and at a time when the rain fell unceasingly for the two days (the 28th and 29th) that the said company was absent.

On May 3 the regiment stood under arms on Main street during the day, being ordered to act as a reserve, in conjunction with the Thirteenth Indiana Regiment, under Colonel Dobbs, to a force which crossed the Nansemond at the foot of said street, and attacked the enemy on the Providence Church road. During the night the regiment occupied Fort Peck and the rifle-pits on the left of said fort at the foot of Main street.

Monday, the 4th, the regiment returned to camp, and has been engaged in doing picket duty and furnishing fatigue parties.

I am, very respectfully,

JOHN McCONIHE,
Lieutenant-Colonel, Commanding.

Lieut. S. E. MARVIN, *A. A. A. G., Gen. Foster's Brigade, Suffolk, Va.*

No. 11.

Itinerary of the Third Brigade, Col. Mathew Murphy, One hundred and eighty-second New York Infantry, commanding, April 9–May 3.

In accordance with General Orders, No. 22, from Headquarters United States Forces, Suffolk, Va., issued April 9, 1863, Brigadier-General Corcoran assumed command of the First Division, Seventh Army Corps; whereupon the senior colonel, Mathew Murphy, assumed, by right of rank, command of the Irish Legion, and immediately issued his General Orders, No. 5, to that effect, appointing Lieut. J. Townsend Connolly, of the Sixty-ninth Regiment, his acting assistant adjutant-general, and established his headquarters at Fort Dix, on the southeast front of our lines, facing the Edenton road.

April 11.—The enemy invested Suffolk and soon after (the next day or so) worked around gradually from the South Quay, when our pickets were first driven in to the Jamestown and Edenton roads. Immediately on the first alarm the long roll was beaten, and the troops deployed in line along the breastworks, running right and left from Fort Dix. Their relative conditions continued as follows until the siege was raised: The Sixty-ninth Regiment defending works in front of its camp, on the right of the line; the One hundred and sixty-fourth Regiment next in line and first on the left of the said fort; the One hundred and fifty-fifth at first marched up from their camp in reserve and formed along the works, bivouacking at night between the One hundred and sixty-fourth and One hundred and Seventieth Regiments, and on the left of the One hundred and sixty-fourth.

April 15.—No action was taken offensively on the part of this Legion against the enemy until the 15th instant, when a small force was sent out on the Edenton road to reconnoiter. This force consisted of one company from the One hundred and fifty-fifth Regiment (Company I), one company from the One hundred and seventieth, and one company from the One hundred and sixty-fourth (Company C), together with a squadron of cavalry from the First New York Mounted Rifles, and one 6-pounder, the whole force under the command of Colonel McMahon, of the One hundred and sixty-fourth Regiment, Major Patton having charge of the cavalry and gun. It started from Fort Dix at 2.30 a. m., and, after marching 2½ miles out on the Edenton road, drove in the enemy's mounted pickets, followed them as rapidly as possible to ——— Mill, where they found a rebel regiment drawn up in line of battle to receive them. The enemy were posted in the rear of a large field, on the right of the road covering a cross-road, which led across the mill-dam to the Somerton road. Here a conflict ensued of half an hour's duration, when the enemy retreated, taking up his second position on the opposite side of the mill-pond. A few well-directed shots from the 6-pounder gun drove him from this place, when re-enforcements arrived to the enemy. Colonel McMahon, after advising with Major Patton, deemed it best to retire, the object of the reconnaissance being accomplished, the entire camp equipage of the enemy captured, besides some provisions and 3 prisoners. Our loss was 9 men wounded and 3 killed—12 in all. A list of casualties that have occurred in the entire brigade has been forwarded through the proper channels, with names, nature, &c.; hence it will be better not to recapitulate here, as our space is limited. From this date (15th) until the 24th the brigade was engaged night and day

---

* From Return of the Corcoran Irish Legion, Seventh Army Corps, for month of April, 1863.

in building intrenchments, digging and slashing, cutting trees to give full range to the guns, &c.

April 23.—The Tenth New Jersey was assigned to this Legion, when the One hundred and fifty-fifth returned to camp in reserve and the Tenth New Jersey took its place between the One hundred and sixty-fourth and One hundred and seventieth Regiments.

April 24.—The brigade accompanied General Corcoran on the grand reconnaissance in force of that date. Marching from Fort Dix down the Edenton road, double column closed in mass, it brought up the rear of the column and marched with it until halted in a large field on the right, and formed line of battle to the right, while the artillery, cavalry, and skirmishers in front carried on the affair. Only one regiment was marched from this line (the One hundred and sixty-fourth, Colonel Mc-Mahon) previous to halting and forming line; it was sent to the front, under orders of General Corcoran, to support a line of skirmishers. In this regiment occurred our only loss. While occupying the enemy's rifle-pits 15 men were wounded (1 mortally) and all borne off the field, when the order was given to fall back. The remaining regiments did not engage the enemy, and consequently lost none. The column started from Fort Dix at about 2 p. m. and returned about 6 p. m. From this date until May 3 none of the regiments were engaged on other duty than fatigue, picket, &c.

May 3.—The One hundred and seventieth Regiment accompanied General Getty on his reconnaissance in force across the Nansemond River, on the Smithfield road. An account of the proceedings in May will be deferred to the report of that month.

No. 12.

Report of Col. William McEvily, One hundred and fifty-fifth New York Infantry.

HDQRS. 155TH REGT. N. Y. STATE VOLS.,
CORCORAN LEGION, 1ST DIV., 7TH ARMY CORPS,
Suffolk, Va., May 11, 1863.

In compliance with orders received I here forward, for the information of the brigadier-general commanding southeast front during the time of the investment of Suffolk by the enemy, a detailed account of the operations of the One hundred and fifty-fifth Regiment New York Volunteers, under my command :

An alarm from the apprehended approach of the rebels in force commenced in the afternoon of April 11, and five companies of the regiment were sent to man the breastworks and four ordered to garrison Fort Dix.

From April 11 to 19 the regiment remained doing duty on the line of breastworks, on which latter date all but three companies returned to camp, where an order was received to be in readiness for an advance against the enemy, but this order was not carried into effect as anticipated.

On the morning of April 14 Company I, with detachments from other regiments under the command of Col. J. P. McMahon, One hundred and sixty-fourth Regiment New York Volunteers, had a skirmish with the enemy, and behaved with great gallantry, coolness, and determination, driving the rebel forces, though superior in number, back on their line of intrenchments. Captain McAnally and Privates Michael Dennison, John Glennon, John Gallivan, and John Leary were wounded in this fight.

On the 21st the regiment was ordered out for a reconnaissance, and proceeded as far as the breastworks, where it remained from 10 a. m. to 1.30 p. m., when the order was countermanded, and the regiment, after relieving the companies then in Fort Dix, with others returned to camp.

Nothing of importance transpired until April 24, when the regiment prepared to move to Fort Halleck, according to an order received the day previous, but did not go on account of a second order countermanding it and requiring the regiment to at once get ready to go on a reconnaissance, which it did, starting at 2 p. m. and returning at 6 p. m., having marched out about 3 miles on the Edenton road. No casualties occurred, the regiment not being called into action. The regiment remained in camp till the 26th, on which day Colonel McEvily received an order from Brigadier-General Dodge charging him with the defense of Fort Dix and the battery adjoining.

Until May 2 nothing momentous occurred. At 10 o'clock in the evening of that day the long roll was beat, and the regiment marched up to Fort Dix, when, under command of General Corcoran, it went out on the Edenton road and re-established our pickets that had been driven in, went close to the enemy's lines and then returned, arriving in camp at 2 a. m.

At 3.45 o'clock on May 4 the regiment, with other troops, started out in pursuit of the enemy, who were retreating, marching past their fortifications on the Edenton road and turning off on the Somerton road, and was ordered to halt and hold the cross-roads known as Holland's Corners; the remainder of the force, the One hundred and sixty-fourth New York Volunteers, Sixty-ninth New York National Guard, and Company A, Thirteenth Indiana, together with a number of other regiments, went ahead in pursuit. Quite a number of prisoners here gave themselves up into our hands, and many were captured and sent back by the forces ahead. Toward evening all the troops returned to the Corners, and reported the enemy across the Blackwater River, since which the usual routine of regimental and garrison duties have been resumed.

During the period of the investment of Suffolk by the enemy, unfortunately no opportunity occurred for the regiment to distinguish itself, although both officers and men showed by their cheerful discharge of every duty their willingness and anxiety to render every possible aid toward the discomfiture of the enemy.

I am, lieutenant, respectfully, your obedient servant,

WILLIAM McEVILY,
Colonel, Commanding Regiment.

Lieut. J. T. CONNELLY, *Acting Assistant Adjutant-General.*

No. 13.

Itinerary of the Reserve Brigade, Col. David W. Wardrop, Ninety-ninth New York Infantry, commanding, April 24–May 1. *

This brigade was formed and Colonel Wardrop assigned to the command by Special Orders, No. 106, dated April 24, 1863, from Head-

---

*From Returns of the Reserve Brigade, Seventh Army Corps, for the months of April and May, 1863.

quarters, Suffolk, Va., Major-General Peck commanding. It then consisted of the Ninth Vermont Volunteers, Nineteenth Wisconsin Volunteers, Ninety-ninth New York Volunteers, One hundred and eighteenth New York Volunteers, and the One hundred and fifty-second New York Volunteers. By Special Orders, No. 109, dated April 26, 1863, from Headquarters, Suffolk, Va., the One hundred and fifty-second New York Volunteers was detached from the brigade and attached to General Terry's brigade. During the siege of Suffolk all the regiments have been actively employed in manning the rifle-pits and strengthening the fortifications and other duties of the defense. The following officers have been wounded by sharpshooters during the month, but before the formation of the brigade:

April 23.—Capt. John E. White, commanding Company G, Ninety-ninth New York Volunteers; thigh and arm, slightly.

April 24.—James Wilson, M. D., surgeon Ninety-ninth New York Volunteers; chest, slightly.

May 1.—At the beginning of the month the various regiments composing the brigade were posted in different parts of the defenses, under the immediate orders of the commanders of the several fronts on which they were stationed.

On the afternoon of the 1st the Ninety-ninth New York Volunteers, then under orders of Brigadier-General Terry, was sent out to reconnoiter the enemy's rifle-pits. The enemy was found in strong force and the regiment was obliged to retire. Loss, 13 killed (or died of wounds) and 31 wounded. Two officers, Capt. James H. Hart and Capt. Charles E. Cartwright, were wounded; both slightly.

No. 14.

Report of Brig. Gen. Charles C. Dodge, U. S. Army, commanding Southeast Front.

HEADQUARTERS SOUTHEAST FRONT, FORT DIX,
Suffolk, Va., May 7, 1863.

CAPTAIN: In accordance with circular just received I have the honor to submit the following report of operations upon this (southeast) front, extending from Forts Union to Halleck, inclusive, since Saturday, April 1, when I first assumed command:

As at that time the enemy were already in our immediate front and the general disposition of our force complete, it only remained for me to carry out the orders received from Brigadier-General Corcoran, commanding front defenses, to watch closely, and, if advisable, counteract any movement of the enemy; to make every preparation in my power for the defense of my line; to keep the troops constantly on the alert and ready for immediate service; to finish as rapidly as possible the various works then in process of erection, or which thereafter might be decided upon, including a large amount of slashing, &c. These orders were diligently complied with.

It seeming advisable to ascertain the force and intentions of the enemy upon this immediate front, a detachment, under command of Colonel McMahon, One hundred and sixty-fourth Regiment New York Volunteers, and consisting of three companies of infantry, a squadron of cavalry (the First New York Mounted Rifles), and a mountain howitzer, was advanced at daylight on the morning of the — ultimo, and vigor-ously engaged the rebel outposts, driving them quite back upon their reserves, who retired nearly a mile to the old mill, about 5 miles from this place. At this time about 3,000 men were reported on the Edenton road and vicinity.

The rebels at once commenced throwing up a redan and strong breast-works completely commanding the road and approaches to their posi-tion. Rifle-pits for the protection of their outposts were also con-structed. It was not considered advisable to attempt to prevent this as our forces were at that time too much engaged upon important duty under General Getty. Slight skirmishing between the outposts con-tinued daily, with, however, but 2 casualties upon our part. Scouts were continually out, and every exertion was made to keep us fully informed of whatever the enemy might be attempting. Occasional de-serters from their ranks aided us greatly in this respect.

On the — a force of some 200 infantry and an equal number of cav-alry, under the command of Col. S. P. Spear, Eleventh Pennsylvania Cavalry, endeavored to again feel the enemy on our front, but was unable to drive them from their rifle-pits, which were uncommonly de-fensible.

On the — most of the troops along this front were detailed by the brigadier-general commanding for a reconnaissance in force under his own command. During his absence it became my duty to dispose, as advantageously as possible along General Corcoran's front, such fresh troops as had been ordered up to defend the line in place of those re-lieved, and to prepare for any emergency that might occur upon either the Edenton or Somerton roads, upon which our forces were engaged. General Corcoran reported the enemy re-enforced to about 6,000 or 8,000 men and eight pieces of artillery on the Edenton road.

From the — ultimo to the 2d instant nothing of moment occurred along this front, and our men were kept most busy at the various fatigue work necessary.

About 11 o'clock on the evening of the 3d instant the officer of the day reported with two deserters, who informed us that the enemy were rapidly withdrawing their forces and *en route* for the Blackwater. The troops were at once ordered under arms and the report forwarded to headquarters south front. Investigation and additional deserters soon confirmed the first report, and with a column of about 150 cavalry, four pieces of light artillery, and three regiments of infantry I started, by command of Brigadier-General Corcoran, in pursuit. Advancing rap-idly but cautiously we soon arrived at the enemy's earthworks, which were found quite deserted. Pushing on, a small cavalry detachment was sent to Cypress Chapel, on the Edenton road, where several rebel officers and men were secured, and with the main body we moved by the first available road over to the main Somerton road, and leaving a force at the cross-roads pushed on to Leesville, where we united with Colonel Foster's column, which, starting simultaneously with ourselves and having some 5 miles less distance to travel, had reached that point in advance of us and succeeded in picking up large numbers of strag-glers and a portion of the enemy's rear guard as prisoners.

Brigadier-General Corcoran then assuming command of the united forces, we advanced some distance toward Holland's Corners, where, upon consultation, it was decided that no advantage could be gained by push-ing the infantry farther, as our advanced scouts and others reported the main force of the enemy already over the river and occupying their strong earthworks there. Cavalry, however, was thrown forward to

Holland's Corners, Carrsville, Deserted House, &c. and succeeded in bringing in some 40 or 50 prisoners. The entire column was then returned to Suffolk and the troops resumed the usual regimental and general duties.

During the time that I have been in command of this part of General Corcoran's front occasional but immaterial changes have occurred in the troops and their dispositions.

I have but few casualties to report, a list of which has been forwarded. Much arduous labor has been accomplished, which can but prove satisfactory to the general commanding.

I am happy to say in conclusion that with scarce an exception officers and men, under every circumstance of exposure, fatigue, and danger, have exhibited such cheerful endurance, earnest faithfulness, and eager desire to meet the enemy as must always insure them success, while it merits the admiration and gratitude of the commanding generals.

Very respectfully, your obedient servant,

CHARLES C. DODGE,
Brigadier-General.

Capt. J. J. Blodgett,
Assistant Adjutant-General.

No. 15.

Report of Brig. Gen. George W. Getty, U. S. Army, commanding Third Division, Ninth Army Corps.

HDQRS. THIRD DIVISION, NINTH ARMY CORPS,
Suffolk, Va., May 12, 1863.

SIR: On April 11, the alarm of the enemy's approach being given, in compliance with the orders of the major-general commanding, the troops of this division were called out under arms. The pickets along the northeastern front were strengthened; two companies of the Tenth New Hampshire were placed in Fort Halleck, where they remained until May 10; the troops under Colonel Dutton engaged in fortifying the river; the Twenty-first Connecticut and five companies of the Thirteenth New Hampshire at Fort Connecticut; the Fourth Rhode Island, One hundred and third New York, and the remainder of the Thirteenth New Hampshire at Fort Stevens were called in. Three companies, however, of the Thirteenth New Hampshire were ordered to remain at Fort Connecticut, with orders to observe the river, resist any attempt of the enemy to cross until the last moment, and then to fall back to Suffolk over the corduroy bridge across Broer's Creek, taking up the bridge. The troops remained under arms and on the alert during the night. The Second Brigade strengthened the south front between Forts Union and McClellan, and remained in this position until April 28, with the exception of the Eighth Connecticut Volunteers, which, on the 14th, was ordered to the river front, where it has since remained.

On the 18th General Harland was assigned to the command of the front from Fort Halleck to Battery Onondaga, and on the 28th the Eleventh and Fifteenth Regiments Connecticut Volunteers, and on the 29th the Sixteenth Connecticut Volunteers, reported to him.

On the 12th Col. A. H. Dutton, commanding the Third Brigade, was placed in command of the line of defenses included between Forts Jericho and Halleck, and at once set to work throwing up rifle-pits and fortifying his position. Under Colonel Dutton's supervision the front between Fort Halleck and Battery Onondaga was very materially strengthened. Rifle-pits were thrown up, covering all the approaches by the Portsmouth road, and a second line on the west bank of Jericho Creek and Fort Dutton, on the left of Fort Jericho, was thrown up. He was relieved on April 18 by Brigadier-General Harland and assigned to the command of the river defenses between the mouth of Jericho Creek and Dr. Council's. The Eighty-ninth Regiment New York Volunteers was placed in Fort Montgomery, where it remained until May 6 with the exception of temporary absences.

On the 13th the Fourth Regiment Rhode Island Volunteers was ordered to report to Brigadier-General Corcoran and was stationed by him behind the breastworks on the left of Fort Union. It occupied this position until May 1, when it was relieved by the Ninth Vermont and placed on the line of river defenses near Fort Connecticut, where it now is. The One hundred and third New York was stationed on the 13th instant behind the breastworks to the left of Fort Union, a position which it held until May 6. The Ninth Regiment New York Volunteers was placed in Fort Nansemond, where it remained until relieved and sent North on May 3.

It is my painful duty in this connection to animadvert upon the course pursued by the Ninth Regiment New York Volunteers, who for the first time in their military history turned their backs upon the enemy, and, deaf to the appeals of the commander of the department, persisted in returning home, when every consideration of patriotism, honor, and pride called upon them to remain and share the dangers of battle with their comrades in the field. Most deeply do I regret that a regiment whose career since they entered the service two years ago has been most brilliant should at the close sully their glorious reputation by such an act; but it is due to truth to say that in my opinion the fault lies chiefly with the officers, and most of all with the commanding officer, whose whole course in this affair seems to have been actuated by personal pique and caprice.

On April 14, reconnoitering along the river, I discovered a battery of the enemy at Norfleet's farm, which in an engagement that morning with our gunboats had disabled the Mount Washington and repulsed the remainder. I found that this battery mounted four guns—two 20-pounder Parrotts and two brass 12-pounders; that it commanded completely a point directly opposite and extending out some distance from this side, and that a large party of the enemy was at work strengthening the battery and throwing up additional works and rifle-pits. I immediately sent for guns and troops, negroes and tools, which arrived in the course of the afternoon.

During the night I filled the point with sharpshooters to dispute the passage of the enemy in case he attempted to cross, and posted the Tenth New Hampshire and a section of artillery to check his farther advance in case he succeeded in driving our sharpshooters and effecting a lodgment on the point. Their position was strengthened with rifle-pits during the night. Two positions were selected for batteries, one near the base of and a little to the right of the point, since named Battery Kimball, distant some 1,200 yards from the enemy's battery, the other on the left side of the point, at the mouth of Broer's Creek, distant 900 yards from the enemy's battery, and since named Battery Morris.

The works were pushed vigorously during the night. Battery Morris, constructed by Captain Beger, Second Wisconsin Battery, who, with three guns of his battery (10-pounder Parrotts), had been sent to me by the order of the commanding general, was completed and the guns placed in position before 2 a. m.   Battery Kimball was completed about midnight.   Two 20-pounder Parrott guns, under Captain Morris, Ninth Regiment New York Volunteers, and one 3-inch gun of the Fourth Wisconsin Battery, also under his charge, were placed in position.   Both batteries were screened by trees and underwood.

At daylight the next morning Captain Beger, cutting away the trees which intercepted his fire, opened on the enemy's battery, firing percussion-shell from one gun, fuse-shell from a second, and case-shot from the third.   In a few moments the enemy replied, firing briskly.   Several of the 20-pounder shells passed through and through the frail parapet of Battery Morris.   As soon as his whole attention was engaged with Battery Morris and the position of his guns ascertained from their fire, the screen was thrown aside from Battery Kimball and Captain Morris opened fire from all his guns, directing his whole fire on one piece of the enemy, and successively on two others, silencing all three in turn, Captain Beger meanwhile keeping up a hot and well-directed fire from his three guns in Battery Morris.   At the end of two hours the enemy's fire slackened and became very feeble.   In another hour he was entirely silenced.

During the action our sharpshooters, who had been placed on the point and on an island in the marsh to the right, kept up a fire which must have proved very annoying to the enemy's gunners, since it provoked one or two discharges of canister.   The following night he withdrew his guns.

The only casualties were 3 drivers of Battery A, Fifth United States Artillery, wounded, 1 mortally.   One of the 20-pounder Parrotts threw off its muzzle after firing twelve rounds and was replaced by a 3-inch gun from the Fourth Wisconsin Battery, a section of which had been sent to me and was kept in reserve.

The three days following every nerve was strained to put the river in a thorough state of defense.   The military road already completed to Fort Connecticut was extended to Fort Stevens.   Batteries and rifle-pits were thrown up on all the exposed points.   The troops, as fast as they arrived, were sent into the trenches, and on the 18th the following was the disposition of the troops along the line of the river:

Lieut. G. B. Easterly, Fourth Wisconsin Battery, at Battery Kimball, with one 20-pounder Parrott and two 3-inch guns; Thirteenth New Hampshire Volunteers, with one company of sharpshooters, holding position next below the mouth of Jericho Creek; Captain Beger, Second Wisconsin Battery, with two guns, in Battery Morris, supported by one company of the Twenty-fifth New Jersey Volunteers; Lieutenant Crabb, with one section of light 12-pounders; Lieutenant Schulz, with one section of 10-pounder Parrotts; the Tenth New Hampshire Volunteers, Ninth Vermont Volunteers, one company of the Twenty-fifth New Jersey Volunteers, and four companies of the Nineteenth Wisconsin Volunteers, under the command of Colonel Donohoe, Tenth New Hampshire Volunteers, holding position of Fort Connecticut, from Broer's Creek to Dr. Council's; Captain Morris, with two 20-pounder Parrotts in Battery Stevens, supported by Colonel Pease, One hundred and seventeenth New York Volunteers; Major Wheelan on the right of Colonel Pease, with four companies of Mounted Rifles. and five gunboats between the mouth of Broer's Creek and a point half a mile below Dr. Council's landing.   Gunboats below West Branch; number not known.   Two regiments of infantry, the Eighth Connecticut and Nineteenth Wisconsin Volunteers, six companies, and one section of artillery in reserve.

On the 14th instant the enemy had planted a battery in the earth-works on Hill's Point, and, in the engagement that ensued between them and our naval forces in the river, almost entirely destroyed the gunboat Mount Washington.　After this action five gunboats returned to the Upper Nansemond, above Hill's Point, and it became evident that their safety required that this battery should be silenced, for the channel of the river runs within 50 yards of Hill's Point, and the action of the 14th showed conclusively that it would be almost certain de-struction for any boat to attempt to run past.　It was therefore with a view to deliver our gunboats from a dangerous position, as well as to annoy the enemy and to gain possession of an important point for future operations, that an expedition to cut out the battery was under-taken.　The plan of operation, as arranged with Lieutenant Lamson, U. S. Navy, commanding flotilla, was as follows: Five hundred men were to embark on the gunboat Stepping Stones at Dr. Council's land-ing, proceed down the river, land on Hill's Point just above the bat-tery, and charge the works with the bayonet.　Lieutenant Lamson volunteered to land four boat howitzers to co-operate in this movement, and at his request was furnished with 40 men to man the drag-ropes.

At 5.30 p. m. on April 19, detachments of 130 men from the Eighth Connecticut and 140 men from the Eighty-ninth New York embarked on the Stepping Stones at Dr. Council's landing.　A canvas screen, which effectually concealed the men, was drawn up all around the deck, and the boat pushed off and steamed rapidly down the stream.　As she approached the battery not a shot was fired or a sound heard to indi-cate the presence of the enemy.　He was waiting, with all his guns double-shotted with canister, until the vessel should come abreast and within 50 yards of his battery.　At 300 yards above the battery Lieu-tenant Lamson headed his boat inshore, but striking on a spile she glanced off, and, borne on the ebb-tide, was on the eve of shooting in front of the battery, when Lieutenant Lamson, with admirable presence of mind, reversed the paddle-wheels and backed her aground.　The men jumped off from both ends of the boat up to their waists in mud and water, scrambled hastily ashore, and with a cheer dashed for the battery.　In an instant Lieutenant Lamson had landed his howitzers and followed.　The enemy, apprised of our approach by the cheers, opened a hot fire of musketry, and was enabled even to reverse and fire one of his guns; but seeing himself cut off, and receiving one or two discharges of canister from Lamson's howitzers, he surrendered. The capture of 5 guns, 7 officers, and 130 men, the liberation of the five gunboats above, and the occupation of a point of vital importance to the enemy and an admirable point of operations for us were the results of one of the most brilliant achievements of the war.　Our loss was 4 killed and 10 wounded.

The battery taken, our whole attention was turned to fortifying the position and preparing for attack.　The boat howitzers were placed in battery just above the landing place in a position to sweep the plain in front over which the attacking party must pass, rifle-pits were com-menced, and pickets thrown out.　Col. A. H. Dutton was placed in com-mand.　Five companies of the Tenth New Hampshire Volunteers, a detachment of 60 men of the Ninth Vermont, Colonel Pease, One hun-dred and seventeenth New York, with four companies of his regiment, and Lieutenant Crabb, Battery A, Fifth U. S. Artillery, with gun de-tachments to man the captured pieces, were sent over to re-enforce the position, and by morning a formidable line of rifle-pits and batteries was erected.

The boat howitzers were withdrawn and re-embarked on the arrival of Lieutenant Crabb. Contrary to expectation the morning dawned without an attack. A section of Battery A, Fifth U. S. Artillery, under the command of Lieutenant Murray, and the remainder of the One hundred and seventeenth New York were sent across. The day was spent in fortifying and strengthening the position. No demonstration was made by the enemy during the day with the exception that in the morning a line of skirmishers advanced across a field and afterward withdrew.

In compliance with the order of the major-general commanding, given upon my representations, the position was evacuated on the night of the 20th. The movement began soon after dark. The artillery, intrenching tools, surplus ammunition, &c., were embarked on the Stepping Stones, and the troops ferried across and landed on the marsh opposite by the West End and by small boats. The picket line was held to the last moment, and at 12.30 o'clock the last load crossed over undisturbed by the enemy, who during the whole evacuation scarcely fired a shot or gave the least annoyance.

After the capture of Hill's Point Battery nothing of special importance occurred until May 3. The enemy's sharpshooters caused considerable annoyance to our pickets and working parties; nevertheless the works were pushed vigorously, every available man being sent into the trenches.

On the 18th the enemy opened fire from two heavy guns in sunken batteries on the West Branch, a few hundred yards above Hill's Point; but the capture of Hill's Point on the 19th exposed them to a similar fate and necessitated their withdrawal. They were withdrawn on the night of the 19th.

On the 24th the Ninth Vermont, Eighth Connecticut, and the Nineteenth Wisconsin Volunteers were ordered by the major-general commanding to report to General Dodge to take part in a reconnaissance under direction of General Corcoran. They returned the following morning.

On the 27th instant a new battery of the enemy was discovered some distance west of Norfleet's house, and on the morning of the 28th it opened fire on the Swan and Commerce, two unarmed steamers which passed down the river from Suffolk.

On April 30 the enemy opened fire from a battery of three heavy guns at Le Compte's house on the West Branch. After a short engagement with the gunboats and the two 20-pounder Parrotts, under Captain Morris, in Fort Stevens, the battery was silenced.

On May 2 I received orders to make a reconnaissance on the Providence Church road the following day.

The operations of the 3d instant constituted a reconnaissance designed to ascertain the number and position of the enemy's force and his movements. They were threefold. The main force was to advance on the Providence Church road, while two expeditions were to cross the Nansemond below at different points, seize Reed's Ferry, and feel the enemy's left. The One hundred and third and Eighty-ninth Regiments New York Volunteers, supported by the Twenty-fifth New Jersey and Thirteenth New Hampshire, crossing the bridge over the river, deployed as skirmishers on the right and left of the road and advanced, driving the enemy back from position to position until he took refuge in his rifle-pits and batteries. Hasbrouck's battery followed along the road, and, with the assistance of Davis' battery, kept silent the enemy's artillery. Major Wheelan, with four companies of the Mounted Rifles, followed

Hasbrouck's battery but was not brought into action. The Connecticut regiments, Eleventh, Fifteenth, and Sixteenth, under General Harland, followed and supported the advance, relieving the advance regiments as they exhausted their ammunition and holding the ground already gained; Colonel Onderdonk's cavalry, the One hundred and forty-third, One hundred and forty-fourth, and One hundred and seventieth Regiments New York Volunteers, constituted the reserve, under the command of Colonel McIvor, of the One hundred and seventieth Regiment New York Volunteers.

The enemy was found strongly posted at the forks of the Providence Church and Reed's Ferry roads. An earthwork on his left rested on a swamp, from which strong rifle-pits extended across his whole front and rested on his right on a branch of the river. It will be seen that the position could not be turned, and to carry it a direct assault had to be made on the front, which, even if successful, must inevitably have resulted in a great sacrifice of life. It was determined, therefore, on consultation with the major-general commanding, that the objects of the reconnaissance, in revealing the position and force of the enemy, were attained as far as was possible under the circumstances, and therefore nothing remained but to withdraw with as little loss as possible. Accordingly, the rifle-pits on the enemy's side next the draw-bridge were manned by the One hundred and seventieth New York Volunteers, and the whole force was rapidly and quietly withdrawn without the loss of a man. The movement was completed by 9 p. m. and the bridge taken up.

We lost in this engagement Col. Benjamin Ringold, of the One hundred and third Regiment New York Volunteers, a most gallant and valuable officer, who fell at the head of his regiment late in the afternoon.[*]

Meanwhile the Fourth Rhode Island Volunteers crossed in boats at Hill's Point at daylight and advanced across the field toward the woods, but, encountering a superior force of the enemy advantageously posted in the woods, they were compelled, after considerable skirmishing, to withdraw upon Hill's Point, from whence they were withdrawn to this side the following night. The Fourth Rhode Island was assisted by a boat howitzer from the Commodore Barney and by a detachment of the One hundred and seventeenth New York Volunteers. The Twenty-first Connecticut, a section of Vallee's battery, Fourth Wisconsin, and a sergeant and 10 men from the Mounted Rifles, under command of Major Crosby, of the Twenty-first Connecticut, crossed the river near Sleepy Hole, with the assistance of the gunboats, and advanced to Chuckatuck, where they drove out some 300 of the enemy's cavalry, part of which retreated on the route leading to Isle of Wight and the remainder on the road leading to Everett's Bridge, some 3 miles above Reed's Ferry. Skirmishing all the way, they pushed forward to Reed's Ferry, which they occupied after a brisk skirmish, in which they captured a lieutenant and 15 men. Being unable to communicate with our forces on the left, the Fourth Rhode Island, or the main advance, Major Crosby, moved down the left bank of the West Branch to the Nansemond and took up an intrenched camp, from which he was withdrawn the following day. He lost 2 killed and 4 wounded.

On May 5 the commanding general published General Orders, No. 31, announcing the retreat of the enemy.

On the 7th, Field Orders, No. 14, were issued, disposing the troops of this division as follows, which positions they now occupy: The Second

---

* Return of the Seventh Army Corps, Department of Virginia, for the month of May. 1863, gives the following casualties in this affair: Sixty killed and wounded.

Brigade, General E. Harland, from Fort Halleck to the mouth of Jericho Canal; the Third Brigade, Col. A. H. Dutton, on the river, from the mouth of Jericho Creek to Battery Stevens; the First Brigade, Col. H. S. Fairchild, in reserve along the line of Suffolk County road from Jericho Canal to Calhoun's; the artillery in the batteries along the river.

The amount of work performed by troops on this line, taken in connection with the great amount of picket duty necessitated by the extent of the line and the incessant watchfulness imposed by the presence of the daring and enterprising enemy in great force, is astounding. On the front, from Fort Halleck to Battery Onondaga, there have been thrown up 3,434 yards of rifle-pits and 308 yards of parapet, 7 feet high and 7 feet in thickness on top. On the river line, 4,398 yards of rifle-pits, 1,944 feet of parapet, with an average height of 8 feet and thickness of something over 10 feet on top, were constructed. In addition to which some 10 miles of entirely new roads, including several bridges over impassable creeks and marshes and miles of corduroying, were made. Much of the work was done under the fire of the enemy's sharpshooters, who proved exceedingly annoying during the whole course of the siege. These results could not have been obtained had I not had the efficient support of Colonels Dutton and Pease, commanding the upper and lower defenses respectively, and their officers and men. Both of these officers worked day and night.

Colonel Dutton, in addition to his duties as a commanding officer, was also obliged to assume those of an engineer, and personally laid out and constructed many of the most important works on this line.

Lieutenant Murray, of Battery A, Fifth U. S. Artillery, was also of great service in constructing works. Fort Lamson and a battery next below Dr. Council's was laid out by him.

The services of Colonel Derrom, in constructing roads and bridges, were of the utmost value. Without the bridge constructed by him across Broer's Creek it is doubtful whether the line of the river could have been held with the small force at my disposal.

Colonel Stevens, also, of the Thirteenth New Hampshire, is deserving of credit. Both Colonels Stevens and Derrom displayed zeal, judgment, and courage on the 3d instant.

The whole deportment of the troops was excellent; with a single exception there was no complaint. Every order was obeyed with the utmost cheerfulness, and the same men who came off picket duty in the morning went on fatigue duty at night without a murmur.

The artillery is especially deserving of great credit. Captain Morris, Ninth New York Volunteers, with a battery of 20-pounder Parrotts, with the assistance of three 10 pounder Parrotts of Captain Beger's battery, silenced most effectually the enemy's battery at Norfleet's, and afterward rendered good service in silencing his batteries at Le Compte's.

The services of the signal officers, Lieutenants Thayer and Murray, were great, and rendered always cheerfully and promptly.

I cannot close this report without acknowledging the important services rendered by the naval forces co-operating in the river, a tribute which they have richly merited. Lieutenants Cushing and Lamson and the officers and men of their commands have shown that in their country's service they know no fear, and that the old breed of naval heroes is not extinct; but to Lieutenant Lamson in particular, whose gallantry exhibited in his engagements at Norfleet's and at Hill's Point has been fully equaled by the willingness and desire he has shown on all occasions to co-operate with the land forces and to do everything for the good of the service, my thanks are due. But in acknowledging the services of meritorious officers I must not omit those of my own staff. To their services I am myself a witness, and with great pleasure am I able to state that in every emergency they have responded to the call made upon them with alacrity and willingness. Captain Gardner, assistant adjutant-general; Lieutenants McKechnie and Faxon, aides-de-camp; Dr. Humphreys, medical director, and Lieutenant Herbert, ordnance officer, did their whole duty, and in this is comprised everything.

Capt. Hazard Stevens, assistant adjutant-general, whose distinguished services and conduct have been acknowledged in previous reports, was particularly conspicuous throughout the operations above recited. On all occasions, whether in the discharge of his legitimate duties in the trenches, reconnoitering, or on the field under the enemy's fire, he evinced an earnestness and devotion worthy of emulation and deserving the highest praise.

I append lists* of officers and men of the Eighty-ninth New York and Eighth Connecticut Volunteers, who participated in the storming of the enemy's battery at Hill's Point; also reports of brigade, battery, and regimental commanders. Lists of casualties already transmitted.†

I am, sir, very respectfully, your obedient servant,

GEO. W. GETTY,
Brigadier-General, Commanding Division.

Maj. B. B. Foster,
Assistant Adjutant-General, Suffolk, Va.

No. 16.

Report of Col. Harrison S. Fairchild, Eighty-ninth New York Infantry, commanding First Brigade.

HDQRS. FIRST BRIG., THIRD DIV., NINTH ARMY CORPS,
Near Suffolk, Va., May 7, 1863.

SIR: In compliance to circular orders from Headquarters, Third Division, dated May 5, 1863, I have the honor to submit the following report:

On the evening of April 11, by your orders, I sent two companies of the Tenth New Hampshire to Fort Halleck, and on the morning of the 12th the remaining eight companies of this regiment were sent to relieve the Eighty-ninth New York Volunteers, on picket at the Jericho Canal, and the Eighty-ninth Regiment ordered to Fort Montgomery.

On the 13th the Tenth New Hampshire Volunteers was relieved by the Thirteenth New Hampshire Volunteers and returned to camp. On the afternoon of April 13 the One hundred and third Regiment New York Volunteers was sent to the front, on the right of Fort Union, and the Ninth New York Volunteers was held in reserve between Forts Union and McClellan until evening and then sent to Fort Nansemond. On the same afternoon the eight companies of the Tenth New Hampshire Volunteers were sent to the Nansemond River, below Jericho Canal, near the small-pox hospital. This disposition of the regiments

---
* Not found. † Embodied in revised statement p. 286

of the brigade, and subsequently placed under different commanders other than the brigade commander, remained so until April 23, when Col. R. C. Hawkins assumed command of this brigade by Special Orders, No. 100, dated Headquarters Third Division, April 23, 1863.

On Saturday, May 2, by Special Orders, No. 109, dated Headquarters Third Division, May 2, 1863, I again assumed command of the brigade, but having no command assigned me on the front with any portion of the brigade, consequently not being in a position personally to observe the actions of the several regiments, I can only submit reports of the regimental commanders, giving an account of their operations, and a list of casualties in each regiment, which are herewith inclosed.*

General, I have the honor to be, yours, very respectfully,

H. S. FAIRCHILD,
Colonel, Commanding.

General GEORGE W. GETTY,
Commanding Third Division, Ninth Army Corps.

No. 17.

Reports of Col. William R. Pease, One hundred and seventeenth New York Infantry.

HDQRS. ONE HUNDRED AND SEVENTEETNH N. Y. VOLS.,
Calhoun's Point, Va., April 19, 1863—11.30 a. m.

GENERAL : I have the honor to report about 10.15 a. m. to-day a new rebel battery, opposite Stevens' battery at this Point, opened fire on the gunboat below here. They fired two or three shots before the boat replied. The boats from above moved down to a point opposite this camp and opened fire. Stevens' battery opened as soon as possible and very satisfactorily. A new battery of the enemy, heretofore unknown to us, below the old battery, opened the fire, and we believe that it has been pretty effectually silenced. I filled the rifle-pits, dug last night, with sharpshooters, and a brisk fire has been kept up on their sharpshooters. The enemy have not replied to the fire of the battery on this Point. They have not fired for the last forty minutes. The gunboats are firing occasionally. All is well. No casualties known.

Very respectfully, general, your obedient servant,

W. R. PEASE.

General GETTY,
Commanding Third Division.

HEADQUARTERS,
Calhoun's Point, Va., April 21, 1863.

CAPTAIN: I have the honor to report that at 6 o'clock p. m. yesterday I received an order from the commanding general to hold the One hundred and seventeenth New York Volunteers and a section of the Fourth Wisconsin Battery in readiness to march to the landing at Dr. Council's house and embark for Hill's Point in case the party sent against the enemy's work at that place were successful. The place was

---
* Embodied in revised statement, p. 286.

carried about 7 o'clock p. m., and this command marched immediately. On arriving at Dr. Council's no boat was ready to take the command over. About 10 o'clock p. m. Captain Vallee received an order to return with his section of artillery to Calhoun's Point. The One hundred and seventeenth New York Volunteers, 720 strong, remained in the road until about 12 p. m., and received an order to report to Colonel Donohoe, Tenth New Hampshire Volunteers, about 1½ miles above Dr. Council's. The regiment reported as ordered, and about 2.30 p. m. on the 20th an order was sent to send four companies of the One hundred and seventeenth New York Volunteers back to Dr. Council's house to embark for Hill's Point. A special order was received from the commanding general for the colonel of the One hundred and seventeenth New York Volunteers to take command of the four companies of his regiment and accompany them to Hill's Point. Companies D, F, H, and K were the companies sent over; they arrived at 4 o'clock p. m. and began to intrench. A detail was made from the companies to furnish skirmishers. The skirmishers were deployed and exchanged shots with the enemy, in which First Sergt. William Casselman, Company D, One hundred and seventeenth New York Volunteers, was severely wounded in the right leg by a rifle-ball from the enemy's skirmishers. The first fire applied to the building on Hill's Point was set by Second Lieut. D. B. Magill, One hundred and seventeenth New York Volunteers, who volunteered to perform the service. At 10 o'clock a. m. on the 20th the remainder of the regiment arrived and reported and were set to work intrenching. At 3 o'clock p. m. the order to evacuate the Point was issued. The embarkation commenced on one of the gunboats, and after landing about 400 men on the marsh opposite Hill's Point the small boats were substituted, and the crossing of all was completed about 12.30 a. m. on the morning of the 21st. All reached their old camp in safety.

I am, captain, very respectfully, your obedient servant,

W. R. PEASE,
Colonel, Comdg. One hundred and seventeenth N. Y. Vols

Capt. HAZARD STEVENS,
   Asst. Adjt. Gen., Third Division, Ninth Army Corps.

HDQRS. ONE HUNDRED AND SEVENTEENTH N. Y. VOLS.,
Calhoun's Point, Va., April 22, 1863—8.30 a. m.

CAPTAIN: I have the honor to report all quiet on this end of the line. No movement of the enemy discovered last night; no evidences of any parties working during the night. If we could have the use of a 12-pounder boat howitzer it would be very effective indeed in preventing the enemy from placing artillery in the battery on the opposite shore. Captain Morris informs me that the howitzer can be obtained from Captain Cushing, on the gunboat. I have a four-gun battery nearly completed, and respectfully request that the remainder of Captain Vallee's pieces be sent down. There was no movement of the gunboats during the night.

Very respectfully, captain, your obedient servant,

W. R. PEASE,
Colonel, Comdg. One hundred and seventeenth N. Y. Vols.

Captain STEVENS,
   Assistant Adjutant-General.

HEADQUARTERS CALHOUN'S POINT, VA.,
May 1, 1863.

CAPTAIN: I have the honor to report the gunboats all below Hill's Point. They were fired upon while moving down about 7 o'clock p. m. yesterday. The officer in command of the picket at Hill's Point last night reports that about 9.40 p. m. his sentinels saw men approaching in small parties of 2 and 3, and our men who were on guard in advance of the rifle-pits opened fire upon them. The enemy returned it and continued to advance, increasing in numbers. Our sentinels fell back, firing, and the men behind the rifle-pit opened fire; but the enemy still advanced and greatly outnumbered our party. Our men took to the boats and on reaching the boats not a piece was loaded to give the signal agreed upon in case they were obliged to retreat. The officer in command, Lieutenant Magill, then fired three shots from his revolver, which was the signal, and all put off. They reached the opposite bank in safety a few minutes past 10 o'clock p. m. There was no firing from the enemy after the boats reached the shore, but in going they fired several volleys. There is nothing in reference to the enemy's batteries since 7 o'clock p. m. yesterday. The 30-pounder Parrott has not arrived.

Very respectfully, your obedient servant,

W. R. PEASE,
Colonel, Commanding.

Capt. HAZARD STEVENS,
Asst. Adjt. Gen., Third Division, Ninth Army Corps.

—

HEADQUARTERS CALHOUN'S POINT, VA.,
May 4, 1863—8.45 p. m.

CAPTAIN: I have the honor to report that I this morning sent Lieutenant Risley, of the One hundred and seventeenth New York Volunteers, with 30 men of his regiment, across the river with orders to advance as far as possible, and gain such information as he could of the movements of the enemy. He landed and sent a party of his men out as skirmishers, advancing slowly; seeing some indications of the enemy, I ordered him to return to the rifle-pits until I could send for one of the gunboats to come up and protect his left flank and rear. At 1.30 p. m., there being no indications that we were to receive any assistance from the gunboat, I directed Lieutenant Risley to advance slowly and go as far as he could. He started and found no impediment to his progress; he passed four batteries in the woods along the marsh on the right bank of the West Branch all bearing on the river. He reports that the enemy kept the right bank of the West Branch very strongly picketed. He passed on to the battery on the hill at Le Compte's house. The position is a very strong one; an excavation made behind a fence, revetted with timbers and two embrasures; rifle-pits on the right and rear of the buildings. Lieutenant Risley sent a citizen and a negro, both of whom I sent to headquarters of the division.

Very respectfully, your obedient servant,

W. R. PEASE,
Colonel, Commanding.

Capt. HAZARD STEVENS,
Asst. Adjt. Gen., Third Division, Ninth Army Corps.

No. 18.

Report of Brig. Gen. Edward Harland, U. S. Army, commanding Second Brigade.

HDQRS. [SECOND BRIG.,] THIRD DIV., NINTH ARMY CORPS,
Suffolk, Va., May 6, 1863.

CAPTAIN: I have the honor to submit the following report of the movements of the troops of this brigade from April 11 to the present time:

On the afternoon of April 11 the brigade was placed under arms in consequence of the approach of the enemy. I received orders from General Peck to hold my command in readiness to support either General Terry or Colonel Foster, who had commands, respectively, on the right and left of Fort Nansemond.

The troops remained under arms during the night, and on the morning of the 12th, by order of General Peck, I sent the Eighth and Sixteenth Regiments Connecticut Volunteers to occupy a portion of the breastworks on the right of Fort Union. About noon of the same day I received verbal instructions from Brigadier-General Corcoran to take command of the line of defenses between Forts Union and McClellan.

On the morning of the 14th the entire brigade was posted along the line of breastworks under my command. That evening, by order of General Peck, I sent the Eighth Connecticut to report to General Getty for instructions, since which time the regiment has not been under my command.

On April 18 I was ordered to take command of the line of defenses extending from Fort Halleck to Battery Onondaga. The Eleventh and Fifteenth Regiments reported to me on April 28 and the Sixteenth on the 29th.

Nothing of any importance occurred until May 3, when, with the Eleventh, Fifteenth, and Sixteenth Regiments, I took part in the reconnaissance on the Providence Church road. The regiments crossed the Nansemond at the draw-bridge at about 9 o'clock on the morning of May 3. Immediately after the brigade had crossed the bridge the One hundred and third and Eighty-ninth New York, in the advance, engaged the enemy's pickets. The brigade halted, and remained in this position until about 12 m., when I crossed the river to confer with General Getty, and received orders from him to send one regiment to support the One hundred and third New York, which was reported to be without ammunition, and also to return and take the general direction of the movement.

I recrossed and sent the Sixteenth Connecticut, under command of Colonel Beach, up to the support of the One hundred and third Regiment, and having reached said regiment relieved it. After relieving the One hundred and third the Sixteenth engaged the enemy and moved forward a short distance until the right of the regiment rested on the bank of the river. This position was held by the regiment until night, when the troops were withdrawn to the other side of the river.

Soon after sending the Sixteenth Connecticut to support the One hundred and third New York I received word from Colonel Derrom, commanding the Twenty-fifth New Jersey, on the right of the road, that he needed support; also word to the same effect from Colonel Stevens, commanding the Thirteenth New Hampshire, which was on the left of the road. I sent the Fifteenth Connecticut, under Colonel Upham, to re-enforce the right, and the Eleventh Connecticut, under Colonel Stedman, to re-enforce the left.

The reports of the commanders of these different regiments are herewith forwarded, by which it will be seen that their positions did not vary materially during the rest of the day. The general position remained the same throughout the day, with the exception that part of the artillery took up a more advanced position about 5 p. m., by order of General Getty. About the same time I placed the One hundred and forty-third New York, one of the regiments held in reserve in the orchard, on the left of the road. The regiment was deployed in a direction parallel to the line of battle, the right resting about 100 yards in rear of the left of the advance while the left of the regiment rested on a bay that set back from the river.

About sunset Captain Stevens, of General Getty's staff, informed me that General Getty wished me to withdraw the troops to the other side of the river as soon as I could, under cover of night; that he desired the pickets withdrawn last, and that he wished one section of Howard's battery and one of Davis' battery to remain until the bulk of the troops had crossed. Captain Stevens indicated the positions which General Getty desired those sections of batteries to occupy. He also stated that General Getty wished me to direct Colonel Derrom, of the Twenty-fifth New Jersey, to make a detail of men from his regiment to take up the bridge after the troops had all crossed, and to superintend the work himself. I sent one staff officer to give the necessary orders to the troops on the right of the road and another to those on the left. Before these staff officers returned Lieutenant Faxon, aide-de-camp of General Getty informed me that General Getty wished to see me at General Peck's headquarters. I found General Getty, who told me that he had given orders that four pieces of Davis' battery instead of two were to remain to protect the troops in falling back, and that Colonel Davis, of the —— Regiment, would superintend the taking of the bridge instead of Colonel Derrom, and that he wished me to have a detail of men sufficient for that purpose report to Colonel Davis at the bridge. General Getty further directed me to place one of the regiments which had been held in reserve during the day in the rifle-pits on the left bank of the river, to serve as a rear guard. I went to the other side of the river to superintend the withdrawal of the forces.

After the troops had all crossed the river except the One hundred and seventieth New York, which was then marching from the rifle-pits (where it had been placed to serve as a rear guard to the bridge), I saw Lieutenant Faxon, who informed me that it was not General Getty's intentions that the troops should be withdrawn until further orders were received from him; that he had heard that the enemy were retreating, and if so he wished to be in a position to follow them up in the morning. The movement had then been conducted so far that in a few minutes all the troops would be across. I therefore did not order the crossing to cease, but waited until the last had crossed and then reported in person to General Getty that the troops were across and that Colonel Davis was commencing to take up the bridge. General Getty repeated what Lieutenant Faxon had informed me—that it was not his intention to have the forces withdrawn until ordered by him. As the rumor that the enemy were retreating proved to be true it is to be regretted that this singular misunderstanding should have arisen.

I forward herewith regimental reports of the movements of the different regiments in this brigade from April 11 to April 30, and reports of the commanders of the Eleventh, Fifteenth, and Sixteenth Regiments of the part taken by their respective regiments in the reconnaissance of the 3d instant. Lists of casualties have already been forwarded.*

I am, captain, very respectfully, your obedient servant,

EDWARD HARLAND,
Brigadier-General, Commanding.

CHARLES T. GARDNER,
Assistant Adjutant-General.

No. 19.

Report of Col. John E. Ward, Eighth Connecticut Infantry, of the capture of Battery Huger, April 19.

HDQRS. EIGHTH REGIMENT CONNECTICUT VOLS.,
Suffolk, Va., May 6, 1863.

GENERAL: I have the honor to submit the following report of the part taken by my regiment in the capture of the rebel battery at Fort Huger, April 19, 1863.

On the afternoon of April 19, in accordance with orders from General Getty, I marched from my bivouac with six companies (130 men) of my regiment and embarked on the gunboat Stepping Stones, in company with Lieutenant-Colonel England and about 150 men of the Eighty-ninth New York Volunteers. We were landed at Hill's Point, in the rear of Fort Huger, a little before sunset, immediately charged upon the works, and after a very short struggle captured the fort, with five pieces of artillery, a large quantity of ammunition, and about 130 prisoners, including 7 officers. Having taken possession we immediately proceeded to place the captured guns in position to resist any attempt of the enemy to retake the Point, and commenced intrenching ourselves as well as possible with the means at our disposal.

Re-enforcements, including the other four companies of my regiment, soon arrived, and all were employed during the night in constructing rifle-pits, removing ammunition from the fort, and performing picket duty. At about 10 o'clock our pickets stationed a short distance outside the fort were attacked and driven in, but were immediately reposted and held their position until the regiment was relieved at noon the following day.

The loss of my regiment in this affair was 1 killed, 4 severely wounded, and several others very slightly injured. A list* of the names of the killed and wounded is forwarded herewith.

Very respectfully, yours,

J. EDWARD WARD,
Colonel Eighth Regiment Connecticut Volunteers.

Brig. Gen. J. D. WILLIAMS,
Adjutant-General State of Connecticut.

---

* Embodied in revised statement, p. 287.

No. 20.

Reports of Col. Griffin A. Stedman, Jr., Eleventh Connecticut Infantry.

HDQRS. ELEVENTH CONNECTICUT VOLUNTEERS,
May 3, 1863.

SIR: I have the honor to report that the Eleventh Regiment Connecticut Volunteers crossed the Nansemond River at the draw-bridge this morning, being part of the Second Brigade, Third Division. About midday it was ordered to the front to support the Thirteenth New Hampshire Volunteers, which was skirmishing on the left of the new Providence Church road. By order of Colonel Stevens, in charge of the troops in that place, the regiment was deployed and became a part of the line of skirmishers. After advancing some distance into the woods (50 rods) the line halted, by command of Colonel Stevens, and remained in that position until withdrawn by command of Brigadier-General Harland. During this time the line was within 20 yards of the enemy and exchanged shots constantly.

Casualties: Capt. Randall H. Rice, Company A, wounded in leg and in the arm; both wounds serious. Private John Bracken, Company F, wounded in the abdomen; Private Samuel Bassett, Company A, wounded in the knee; and Private Auguste Didier, Company I, missing; he was sent forward and did not return; supposed to have been shot or captured. The regiment marched with 220 enlisted men and 20 officers, and returned to camp without a straggler.

Respectfully, your obedient servant,
GRIFFIN A. STEDMAN, JR.,
Colonel Eleventh Connecticut Volunteers.

Lieut. H. P. GATES,
Acting Assistant Adjutant-General, Second Brigade.

HDQRS. ELEVENTH CONNECTICUT VOLUNTEERS,
Suffolk, Va., May 5, 1863.

SIR: In compliance with Special Orders, No. 78, dated Headquarters Second Brigade, Third Division, Ninth Army Corps, May 1, 1863, I have the honor to submit the following report of the operations of this regiment from April 11 to April 30:

At the time of the alarm the regiment was ordered under arms and remained so until the evening of April 12, when the men were allowed to go to their quarters for the night.

On the morning of the 13th it was ordered to the parapet, on Foster's front, between Forts Union and McClellan.

On April 24 it composed a part of a reconnoitering force on the Edenton road, under Brigadier-General Corcoran. During this reconnaissance the regiment was deployed as skirmishers. Casualties were 1 man killed and 1 wounded.

On the 28th ultimo it was relieved from duty on Foster's front and received orders to report to Brigadier-General Harland, on the river front, where it still remains.

Respectfully, your obedient servant,
GRIFFIN A. STEDMAN, JR.,
Colonel Eleventh Connecticut Volunteers.

Lieut. H. P. GATES,
Acting Assistant Adjutant-General.

No. 21.

Report of Col. Arthur H. Dutton, Twenty-first Connecticut Infantry, com
manding Third Brigade.

HDQRS. THIRD BRIG., THIRD DIV., NINTH ARMY CORPS,
Suffolk, Va., May —, 1863.

CAPTAIN: I have the honor to submit the following report of recent operations:

Early in the month of April my command was constituted as follows: The Fourth Rhode Island and Thirteenth New Hampshire Volunteers, stationed on the Norfolk and Petersburg Railroad, three-quarters of a mile north of Suffolk; the Twenty-fifth New Jersey Volunteers, on Jericho Creek, three-quarters of a mile northwest of the above, and the Twenty-first Connecticut Volunteers, on the Nansemond River, 3 miles below Suffolk. The latter regiment had just commenced the work now known as Fort Connecticut, and on April 8 was joined by three companies of the Thirteenth New Hampshire, under Major Storer.

On the 10th ultimo, information having been received that the enemy was advancing from the Blackwater, I was ordered to proceed, with the Fourth Rhode Island, the Thirteenth New Hampshire, and the One hundred and third New York, to a point on the Nansemond opposite the mouth of Western Branch, fortify the position, open direct communication with the Twenty-first Connecticut, and hold the entire line between the said point and the mouth of Jericho Creek, to prevent any crossing of the enemy. Below this point the river was safely held by gunboats. The command arrived at the point designated about midnight. At sunrise the work on the fortifications commenced; trees were felled, rifle-pits made, Battery Stevens commenced, and Lieutenant Bruce, of my staff, reconnoitered a site for a military road to the camp of the Twenty-first Connecticut. A road was already in progress from the latter camp direct to Jericho Creek, and only awaited the completion of a trestle bridge over Broer's Creek, under charge of Colonel Derrom, Twenty-fifth New Jersey.

On the evening of the 11th, however, orders were received to return instantly to Suffolk. No means of transportation being at hand, it became necessary to leave a considerable quantity of baggage and a small guard. The battalion of Major Storer was retained at Fort Connecticut, with instructions to maintain a strict watch on all sides to prevent a crossing of the enemy, if possible, and, if forced to retreat, to do so by way of the new road, destroying camp equipage, &c., and demolishing the trestle bridge. No attack being made, on the following day our position was strengthened. I was assigned to the command of the line of defense included between Forts Halleck and Jericho. On this line I threw up rifle-pits and posted the troops in the most advantageous manner for concentration upon any given point, while at the same time I held myself in readiness to support General Corcoran, on my immediate right, should his be the line attacked. Not thinking it safe to send a train of wagons for the abandoned baggage, I dispatched two or three at a time to Battery Stevens, and by this means transferred everything in safety from that point to my headquarters. Six men from the Fourth Rhode Island remained there permanently to observe the enemy. The baggage of the Twenty-first Connecticut was transferred by hand over Broer's Creek and thence by wagons to its camp.

On the 12th the Fourth Rhode Island was assigned to the command of Brigadier-General Corcoran.

On the 13th the Nineteenth Wisconsin was assigned to my command, and on the day following the Ninth Vermont also reported to me.

On the 15th my line of defense was extended to Battery Onondaga. at the mouth of Jericho Creek It may suffice here to remark that all points of the defenses have been constantly strengthened each day since the commencement of the siege, all soldiers, including pickets, being required to labor day and night on the intrenchments.

On Tuesday, the 14th, the enemy having, from a battery nearly op posite the small-pox hospital, engaged and damaged the naval forces on the river, I was ordered to reconnoiter positions for counter batteries and superintend their construction.   Under the supervision of the general commanding division I constructed Batteries Kimball and Morris, the Tenth and Thirteenth New Hampshire and Eighth Connecticut bivouacking near at hand as supports.

Early on the morning of the 15th these batteries, consisting of two 20-pounder Parrotts, two 3-inch rifled guns, and three 10-pounder Parrotts, being detachments from the Second and Fourth Wisconsin and Morris' Independent Batteries, opened fire, and by 10 o'clock the rebels ceased to reply.

On the 17th the Ninth Vermont Volunteers proceeded to Fort Connecticut.   Meantime the military road from Suffolk to Fort Stevens had been completed by the Twenty-fifth New Jersey Volunteers, five companies of which regiment were in camp at Broer's Creek.

On April 18 General Harland superseded me in command of the troops on the Jericho, and I was assigned to duty on the 19th on the line of the Nansemond, making my headquarters at Fort Connecticut.

On the evening of the 19th the rebel battery of five guns at Hill's Point was captured by detachments from the Eighth Connecticut and the Eighty-ninth New York.   The following is an account of the capture of the Hill's Point Battery on the Nansemond River:

Shortly before sunset the gunboats on the river and the four rifled guns at and near Battery Stevens (two 20-pounder Parrotts, Captain Morris, and two 3-inch ordnance guns, Captain Vallee) opened a terrific fire upon the rebel battery.   Meantime detachments from the Eighty-ninth New York, Lieutenant-Colonel England, and the Eighth Connecticut, Colonel Ward, embarked on the gunboat Stepping Stones, Lieutenant Lamson, at a point about a mile above the battery.   Protected by the artillery fire the gunboat boldly steamed down the river and ran close to the shore, about 200 yards above the rebel work—the shore at the point being an abrupt bluff.   Immediately the troops disembarked, wading to their waists in water, ascended the bluff, and with loud cheers charged on the rear of the fort.   Meantime the gunboat's crew had landed four boat howitzers, placed them in position, and opened on the fort. The enemy, taken completely by surprise, were able to discharge but two or three volleys of musketry and one gun, when our troops entered the work and captured the entire party, consisting of 7 officers and 130 men, with five brass guns and a large supply of ammunition.

I was now directed by Brigadier-General Getty to assume command of the post and put it in a state of defense during the night.   The force at my disposal for this purpose consisted of detachments of the Eighth Connecticut, Eighty-ninth New York, Tenth New Hampshire, and Ninth Vermont, in all about 700 men. The soldiers, although fatigued and fasting, worked with a most commendable zeal to intrench themselves, as we fully expected an attack in the morning.

To the two detachments first named especial credit is due. They had been under arms nearly all day , had most gallantly captured the battery in the evening; had been a considerable time without food, and were drenched with the water through which they were forced to wade in landing, yet not a murmur was heard from them throughout.

I forward herewith a sketch from memory, showing the location of the rebel battery and the works thrown up for our own defense. Half an hour before daylight our preparations were nearly complete and the troops in position. The artillery was massed on the left, covering the point of disembarkation, three guns being in Battery A and one how-itzer in Battery D. All were loaded with canister and directed to sweep the plain by which the enemy must approach. One howitzer was disabled, the trail of the carriage being broken. My design was to defend the entire line if possible, and if forced to abandon a portion to withdraw the troops on the right across the ravine and concentrate my entire force upon the left, which, besides being the strongest position, also covered the communication with the naval forces.

At early daylight a line of the enemy's skirmishers was discovered advancing about 1,000 yards distant. They covered themselves behind trees and fences and a few were observed entering a house a few hundred yards in front of our left.

About this time the One hundred and seventeenth New York, Colonel Pease, and a section of Gilliss' battery (A, Fifth U. S. Artillery) arrived and were duly posted, the latter in Battery C and subsequently in Battery B.

It now became apparent that the enemy did not meditate an attack, but contented himself with annoying our pickets by occasional scattering shots. I accordingly gave direction that the house above alluded to should be fired and the woods shelled. This being accomplished we were troubled no more.

During the day (20th) our troops continued to strengthen the defenses, but in the afternoon orders were received to evacuate the place. This was done by the assistance of the naval forces. The intrenching tools, artillery, limber-chests, &c., were placed aboard the gunboat Stepping Stones before dark, quakers being substituted in the batteries; but during the process the ebbing tide left the steamer aground, and fears were entertained that the enemy might attack us before she floated again, in which event the destruction of the vessel and the loss of much material might have resulted. Immediately after dark, however, the process of ferrying the troops across the river in row-boats commenced and was safely accomplished by midnight; meantime the steamer was got off in safety. The evacuation was thus completed without the loss of a man or a single article of property.

In this connection I cannot forbear paying a tribute to the valor and energy of the naval forces under Lieutenant Lamson. This gallant officer has at all times shown himself most willing to render invaluable assistance to the land forces with men and material, fearlessly imperiling the safety of himself, his men, and his vessels.

The day following the evacuation of Hill's Point I was assigned to the command of all the troops on the Nansemond from Jericho Creek to Dr. Council's place. They consisted of the Tenth New Hampshire Volunteers, the Twenty-first Connecticut Volunteers, the Thirteenth New Hampshire Volunteers, the Eighth Connecticut Volunteers, the Twenty-second Connecticut Volunteers, the Ninth Vermont Volunteers, Gilliss' battery (A, Fifth U. S. Artillery), three guns of Beger's (Second Wisconsin) battery, four guns of Vallee's (Fourth Wisconsin) battery, one 20-pounder Parrott (unassigned), and four guns captured from the enemy. The Thirteenth New Hampshire replaced the Nineteenth Wisconsin, which regiment, by command of General Getty, has been sent to Suffolk for disgraceful conduct. The infantry and artillery was advantageously posted along the river and the fortifications advanced daily. No action occurred previous to May 3 except continual firing between opposing batteries and pickets.

On the night preceding May 3, as a part of a combined movement, I was directed to send the Fourth Rhode Island Volunteers across the Nansemond at Hill's Point in row-boats, to march thence at daybreak and occupy the Suffolk and Smithfield road near its junction with the Providence Church road, communicating with the Twenty-first Connecticut at Reed's Ferry, on the West Branch; also to cross the Twenty-first Connecticut some 3 miles lower down with a section of Vallee's battery and a squad of cavalry. This force was to advance to Chuckatuck and communicate with the Fourth Rhode Island at Reed's Ferry.

The latter force crossed, as directed, under command of Major Crosby, and marched to Chuckatuck, his progress being constantly impeded by the enemy's skirmishers, who resisted his advance with tenacity although in small force. Reaching Chuckatuck he did not consider it safe to send a detachment to Reed's Ferry, and therefore proceeded to that place with his entire column. Not meeting the Fourth Rhode Island at that point, as expected, and having no other means of communicating with co-operative forces—the Reed's Ferry Bridge being burned—he marched down the West Branch to the Nansemond, losing some half a dozen men. His march was impeded from beginning to end by the enemy's skirmishers, but his movements were continued regardless of obstacles. His regiment behaved with great gallantry. While already nearly exhausted with fatigue and picket duty it performed in twelve hours a march of 18 miles, 8 miles of which were through an enemy's country, drove its opponent before it, and brought in 16 prisoners, including 1 officer. For further details of Major Crosby's march I refer to his graphic report, herewith forwarded.

Meantime Lieutenant-Colonel Buffum, with the Fourth Rhode Island, 250 strong, occupied the opposite shore before daybreak, but not being familiar with localities disembarked by mistake half a mile above Hill's Point. I had urged upon him the importance of taking a guide, which, however, he declined to do, pleading a perfect understanding of the position. I joined his command at daybreak and instantly saw the misfortune that might have resulted from his error had the enemy occupied Hill's Point in any force, as, by holding the intrenchments there thrown up by me on April 20, they might have easily kept us away. We, however, immediately occupied the place, driving out about a dozen rebels. I now formed line of battle, threw out skirmishers, and advanced. Immediately the enemy opened fire from behind fences and trees. We drove them about three-quarters of a mile, to the edge of a forest which completely environed the position from shore to shore. Here their fire was so rapid that I halted to study the position. I drew their fire in volleys two or three times to determine their force, which I estimated at from 200 to 400. Between me and them there was a quarter of a mile of open ground, over which we could not have advanced without tremendous loss. I then threw skirmishers into the timber on the right and there also discovered the enemy in greater or less force. It seemed therefore that to advance farther would insure my being cut off from Hill's Point and perhaps captured. I therefore fell back and proceeded to the gunboat Barney to consult with Captain Cushing. Here it was reported that the enemy had 500 men at Le

Compte's house, about half a mile to the right of my advance, between me and Reed's Ferry.

It now occurred to me that if the main advance from Suffolk was successful the force opposed to me would be intercepted between General Getty, the West Branch, and myself, and I accordingly resolved to attract their attention by continual skirmishing. Captain Cushing kindly supplied me with a boat howitzer and a detachment of sailors. Colonel Pease, One hundred and seventeenth New York, also sent me, at my request, 100 men, and I once more advanced, driving the enemy to the skirt of the woods. Skirmishing continued for a couple of hours, when the enemy brought artillery and opened fire upon me. My howitzer having expended its ammunition I again retired with slight loss.

During the engagement the officers of the regiment behaved with great coolness and bravery, and there were individual instances of gallantry among the men, but I regret to state that the mass of the men exhibited an aversion to exposing themselves, a willingness to retreat, and a contempt for good order that I scarcely expected in a regiment of two years' experience and which has five battles inscribed upon its flag.

At about 3 p. m. I received a dispatch from Major Crosby announcing his success. I therefore meditated a joint movement of the two regiments upon the enemy near Le Compte's house, which I was assured would result successfully though involving considerable loss; but learning that the Twenty-first Connecticut was utterly exhausted and without food for man or horse I concluded to await orders from the general commanding. After dark, by order of General Getty, I withdrew the troops from Hill's Point, bringing over also some valuable pieces of timber, which I found useful the following day.

On the 4th the enemy retired altogether from our front, and I withdrew Major Crosby's force. The horses and artillery were embarked by the aid of an improvised floating wharf which I constructed out of row-boats and loose timber.

Ever since the commencement of the siege I have been generally well seconded by the officers and soldiers under my command. All have nobly done their duty, but some have done more. Among these I take pleasure in mentioning Maj. H. B. Crosby, of the Twenty-first Connecticut, who has always shown himself a zealous, industrious, brave, and trustworthy officer. I would also specially commend Colonel Derrom, Twenty-fifth New Jersey, to whose ability as an engineer the service is much indebted; Colonel Donohoe, of the Tenth New Hampshire, to whom I am indebted for valuable co-operation in superintending the river defenses; Major Storer, of the Thirteenth New Hampshire; Captains Brown and Reed, of the Fourth Rhode Island, and Lieutenant Bruce, of my staff, for their faithful and soldierly deportment in the various trying scenes in which they separately participated. I am indebted for repeated and valuable favors to Lieutenants Cushing and Lamson, U. S. Navy, commanding flotilla. I also take pride in calling the attention of the general commanding to the general admirable behavior in action of the three new regiments of my brigade. I transmit herewith a list of casualties in my brigade.*

I have the honor to be, very respectfully, your obedient servant,

A. H. DUTTON,
Colonel, Commanding.

Capt. CHARLES T. GARDNER,
Assistant Adjutant-General.

---

* Embodied in revised statement, p. 287.

No. 22.

Report of Maj. Hiram B. Crosby, Twenty-first Connecticut Infantry.

HDQRS. TWENTY-FIRST REGT. CONNECTICUT VOLS.,
Suffolk, Va., May 5, 1863.

LIEUTENANT: I have the honor to report that in compliance with orders from the general commanding I crossed the Nansemond on Sunday, at 4 o'clock in the morning, May 3, having under my command the Twenty-first Regiment Connecticut Volunteers, a section of the Fourth Wisconsin Battery under Lieut. Martin McDevitt, and a sergeant with 10 men of the First New York Mounted Rifles. My orders were to march to Chuckatuck and from thence to Reed's Ferry, opening communication with the Fourth Rhode Island on my left.

The troops were under way for Chuckatuck at 4.30 o'clock Sunday morning, the distance being 2½ miles. My skirmishers came upon the line of rebel pickets about half a mile from the Nansemond, their fires still burning. The rebel pickets fell back to Chuckatuck as we advanced. When within half a mile of the village we saw a company of rebel cavalry drawn up in the main street leading into the village. I ordered Lieutenant McDevitt to open fire upon them with artillery, and the rebels, after a few rounds, retired to the farther side of the village, at the junction of the Reed's Ferry and Isle of Wight roads. I advanced the skirmishers to the village and moved up the column. Appearances indicated that the enemy would make a stand at that point, but they again retired, a portion of their force taking the Isle of Wight road, but the greater number retiring by the Reed's Ferry road.

As soon as my command were in the village I sent Sergeant Trowbridge, of the Mounted Rifles, and his detachment of cavalry to reconnoiter the road leading to the Isle of Wight, and also ordered Captain Spittle, acting major of the Twenty-first, with Companies A and K, to skirmish along the Reed's Ferry road. From the accounts given by contrabands at this point the enemy's cavalry were estimated at about 300 strong, and that they had a camp at Isle of Wight and also on the Reed's Ferry road. I ordered Lieutenant McDevitt to put the artillery in position to command both roads until they could be reconnoitered. On discovering that the enemy intended to make no resistance at this point the column was moved ahead on the Reed's Ferry road. Captain Spittle came upon the camp on this road about half a mile beyond Chuckatuck. The enemy had but just left; their camp-fires still burning. About a mile beyond Chuckatuck the roads branch off, one leading to Reed's Ferry the other to Everett's Bridge. The foot-prints indicated that the enemy's cavalry had retired by the latter road, but as the two roads ran near together for quite a distance I halted the column at this point, put the guns in position commanding both roads, and ordered Captain Spittle to reconnoiter them. The enemy were then reported nowhere in sight.

The column was at once set in motion along the Reed's Ferry road, with the exception that Lieutenant McDevitt, with one piece of artillery and a sufficient support, was left behind to command the Everett's Bridge road until an advance was secured. The column had moved but an eighth of a mile in advance when I ordered Sergeant Trowbridge to make a reconnaissance on the Everett's Bridge road for about

50 rods, passing over the same ground which our skirnishers had pre viously gone over. The cavalry had gone but a short distance when the enemy, who had suddenly returned, opened fire upon them, killing 1 and wounding 2 of their number. Lieutenant McDevitt opened upon them at once and shelled them back toward Everett's Bridge.

The column was delayed at this point about half an hour, but there being no signs of the enemy's returning I advanced the skirmishers rapidly on the Reed's Ferry road, and again set the column in mo tion.

Our march was necessarily slow, owing to the thick underbrush through which the skirmishers were obliged to make their way. On approaching the West Branch we again discovered the enemy's pickets. The skirmishers, under Captain Spittle, Captain Shepard, and Captain Belden, advanced gallantly and were soon engaged. The artillery was moved up with supports and opened fire at once, commanding the oppo site bank of the creek, where the enemy had two companies of sharp shooters as a support. The skirmish at this point was short and spirited, resulting in our capturing 1 lieutenant, 3 sergeants, 2 cor porals, and 10 privates of the enemy. Our loss was 3 wounded, 1 of whom died some two hours afterward as we were without surgical aid.

We encamped Sunday night on the Nansemond, near the ferry, and under protection of the gunboats. On the next morning Captain Spittle was sent out with Companies A and K to reconnoiter, and returned, bringing 2 deserters, who were dispatched to the general commanding. He further reported that the enemy, on the opposite side of the West Branch from us, commenced their retreat on the evening previous at 8 o'clock, and that the most of their forces had retired before midnight, burning behind them the bridge at Page's Mill.

I am under great obligations to Flag-Officer Captain Cushing and also to Captain Lamson. Acting Master's Mate Lawrence rendered me great assistance in giving information where to post the artillery so as to be of service to our troops engaged with the enemy on the other side of the creek, and also took quite an active part in the skirmish. My thanks are due to the officers of the regiment for their prompt and hearty co-operation.

The patience and courage of the men, after the fatigue of the past ten days, is deserving of especial praise.

I take pleasure in mentioning the gallant conduct of Lieutenant Mc Devitt, of the Fourth Wisconsin Battery, and the prompt and efficient manner in which both he and his men performed their duty.

The detachment of New York Mounted Rifles, under Sergt. [James L.] Trowbridge, are also deserving of great praise, for, though few in number, they were of the greatest assistance.

The casualties are as follows : Company K, killed, Private Alfred J. Freeman; Company A, wounded, Private Hiram C. Loomis; Com pany K, Private Lyndes C. Bushnell.

I am, lieutenant, very respectfully, your obedient servant,

HIRAM B. CROSBY,
Major, Commanding.

Lieut. G. A. BRUCE,
Acting Assistant Adjutant-General, Third Brigade.

No. 23.

Report of Brig. Gen. George H. Gordon, U. S. Army, commanding Reserve Division, of operations May 1–4.

HEADQUARTERS GORDON'S DIVISION,
Folly Island, S. C., October 21, 1863.

GENERAL: Constant service in the field has delayed a report of my participation in the memorable siege of Suffolk, Va., during portions of the months of April and May in the present year. Reporting to Major-General Dix, commanding the Department of Virginia, on April 29, I was ordered to join you at Suffolk, Va., to assume command of a division of troops within the almost closely-invested town. I reported on May 1 and was assigned to the command of the Reserve Division, consisting of two brigades, the Second and Third, of what was formerly Abercrombie's division, the Second, commanded by Col. Burr Porter, of the Fortieth Massachusetts Regiment, consisting of his own regiment, the Twenty-second Connecticut, One hundred and forty-first New York, and Eleventh Rhode Island Regiments; the Third, commanded by Col. William Gurney, of the One hundred and twenty-seventh New York Regiment, consisting of that regiment and the One hundred and forty-second, One hundred and forty-third, and One hundred and forty-fourth New York Regiments; in all, eight regiments, numbering over 5,000 officers and men. The siege had continued for some days before my arrival. I found the enemy holding a belt of woods that surrounded the town in front and flank from the Nansemond on the right to the Dismal Swamp on the left. His rifle-pits covered his line far to the front, while his sharp-shooters annoyed not only our gunners at their pieces but the men in their encampments.

All had been done that skill could suggest to strengthen your position. An outer and inner line of forts protected the front; strong inclosed works defended the flanks, the whole connected by a line of intrenchments for infantry protected by ditches and abatis. The woods cleared from your front gave a full sweep to the artillery. Every precaution by artificial works, by the advantages of strong natural sites, and by a judicious disposition of the troops to repel an assault, seemed to me to have been taken. The sudden flight of the enemy from the front on the night of May 3, thus raising the siege, placed my division at the disposal of the commander of the department, by whom I was immediately ordered on the important duty of occupying, holding, and fortifying West Point as a military base for future operations. The removal of the enemy from our front developed the whole of his operations and gave me a good opportunity of judging, from the extent and character of his works, the force which threatened your position.

It was well known that Generals Longstreet and Hill, of the rebel service, had united their forces in front of Suffolk. Without taking into consideration the reports of deserters and facts revealed by reconnaissances, special as well as in force, but simply judging from the amount of labor performed in completing their lines of investment, the besieging force could not have been less than 30,000. Everywhere in front, from the Nansemond to the swamp, they had thrown up heavy intrenchments for infantry. On all the roads batteries for artillery, in embrasure, well revetted, with ditches wide and deep, and abatis skillfully laid and thickly interwoven, rendered a sortie almost hopeless. Not only one line of such defenses covered the enemy's front but on some roads three, four, and even five parallel lines of formidable works were formed, indicating in the clearest manner a strengthened base from which the approaches were to be made and upon which the enemy could retire if forced back in their attack.

These works were made with great skill and of great strength. The parapet for infantry defense could have resisted the heaviest rifle caliber, being not less than 12 feet thick. Apart from lines of earthworks for offensive operations there were also temporary structures in process of erection, covered sheds to protect supplies, and every evidence of preparations for the reduction of the fortifications of Suffolk.

While thankful for the movement of the Army of the Potomac, which gave the disappointed rebel commanders an opportunity of withdrawing from your front, as every humane soldier should be at being spared the sacrifices of an unnecessary conflict, regret will mingle with triumph that he who came strong in the conviction of an easy victory did not try your metal, but, satisfied with a glance, turned from the offensive to the defensive and finally stole away in the night, under pressure of a strong reconnaissance of your forces, which drove him from his rifle-pits back to his first line of defenses.

I am, general, very respectfully, your obedient servant,

GEO. H. GORDON,
Brigadier-General of U. S. Volunteers.

Maj. Gen. JOHN J. PECK,
Commanding, North Carolina.

No. 24.

Reports of Maj. Gen. Samuel G. French, C. S. Army, commanding the Department of Southern Virginia.

HDQRS. DEPARTMENT OF SOUTHERN VIRGINIA,
Near Suffolk, Va., April 22, 1863.

SIR: I respectfully submit to the lieutenant-general commanding the following report respecting the loss of the guns of Stribling's battery:

On the morning of the 15th instant I started from my camp on the South Quay road, at the request of Lieutenant-General Longstreet, to endeavor to destroy the gunboats of the enemy in the Nansemond River. Stribling's, Bradford's, and [J. C.] Coit's batteries were taken down. Only one gunboat could be seen, and she was lying behind the point of land below the mouth of the Western Branch of the Nansemond. The batteries were put in position in the hope she would move up, but a storm coming on and the near approach of night induced me to withdraw the guns. The engineer informed me that he and other officers had selected two sites for batteries—the one near the left of General Hood's line of battle, in which there was in a work constructed a battery of field artillery and an infantry force for protection; the other was the work built for the defense of the river when we held Suffolk, and that in it was an infantry force, but no artillery. I directed Maj. L. M. Shumaker, my chief of artillery, on the night of the 16th to take from some houses on a farm near by materials to construct platforms, and before morning to put the guns of Stribling's battery in the work. This he accomplished.

The next morning three gunboats attempted to pass up. One succeeded, but was severely damaged, when the other two turned back. I had selected the site for pits for two 32-pounders, and on the night of the 18th they were completed and the guns placed in position. For the protection of these guns in the pits I asked that three companies of infantry be sent, designing to use them, however, to guard also the road where all the camps were, but the lieutenant-general ordered down the Fifty-fifth North Carolina Regiment, Colonel Connally commanding.

On Sunday, the 19th, the situation of affairs was thus: Bradford's battery was in the new work, with instructions from my chief of artillery, while the work was defended by troops from Hood's division, and by his officers they were posted, relieved, and got their orders. In the Hill's Point Battery were Stribling's battery, with my instructions; the work defended by two companies of infantry, under instructions from the officers placing them there. The 32-pounders were in position and a company of the Fifty-fifth North Carolina near by, while the other companies were a supporting force to either of these last two batteries. All the batteries were to receive further support from General Hood's command if required, and all my officers were so informed, and couriers were left there to communicate such intelligence to General Law, who was on the extreme left, if his aid should be required. The river as low down as the mouth of the West Branch was guarded by the troops of General Hood, and reported, of course, to their commanders. I was ill on Sunday and could not ride down the river, but sent Col. G. A. Cunningham. There were four gunboats above the work on Hill's Point and three below, and five or six land batteries and sharpshooters on the opposite side of the river.

About 10 a. m. the four gunboats above and the land batteries opened a sharp fire on the Hill's Point work, and two gunboats from below moved up to aid them, when the 32-pounders opened fire on them, and after a spirited engagement one was slightly injured and both were driven back. The fire on the work, however, continued until near 4 p. m., when it ceased. Major Shumaker then communicated with Captain Stribling, and although it was reported that the gunboats had troops on board his note does not intimate that he apprehended an attack by a force of the enemy landing for that purpose.

About 4 p. m. Colonel Cunningham instructed Colonel Connally to support the batteries, and this was, as he states, about an hour and a half before the guns were lost. In that time he might have been near the work, so far as distance is concerned, but I have my doubts if any regiments could have passed the wide plain and rendered any real support under the fire that was or could have been brought to bear on their approach. The manner of attack appears to have been to have sent one gunboat down as though she was going to pass the work to engage the attention of the men in the fort, while from the other boats a force of about 500 men was landed. It appears to me that if the garrison was surprised, they were negligent; if not surprised, they did not offer a sufficient resistance.

I inclose herewith papers marked—

A—Order detailing Colonel Connally's regiment, by direction of the general commanding.

B—Copy of orders given Colonel Connally.

C—Colonel Connally's report.*

D—Maj. L. M. Shumaker's report.†

E and F—General French's orders to Major Shumaker.

G—Major Shumaker's note to Captain Stribling after the cannonade ceased.

---

*See Report No. 30.   † See Report No. 25.

H—Captain Stribling's answer; shows he apprehended no land attack.

J—Report of property lost by the capture.

K—Report of Major Boggs, of the artillery.*

As before stated, I was ill in camp, which was some 9 or 10 miles distant from Hill's Point. As soon as I heard that the attack had been made and the report that the .guns had been captured by the enemy I started for the purpose of retaking the work. On arriving there, about 1 a. m. on the morning of the 20th, I found on the ground Major-General Hood, General Law, and General Robertson, with his brigade. The night was dark, the ground unknown to the troops, the enemy's pickets out in advance of the work, and to have retaken the work by crossing the open plain under the fire of seven gunboats stationed near the fort, that of the land batteries, and that of the enemy in the work was believed would involve a sacrifice of men of more value to us than the fort if recaptured. The enemy, as you are aware, the night following evacuated the work. The report shows that 93 men, all the horses, harness, running-gear of cannons, limbers of guns, fuse, wagons, &c., were not in the work, and that the loss was only the five guns and most of the ammunition chests.

You are perhaps aware that on neither of those works could any labor be performed in the day-time, owing to the opposite bank being strongly occupied by the enemy, and I do not think the parties in the fort had time to prepare embrasures for the guns looking to the rear in anticipation of a land attack.

Very respectfully, your obedient servant,

S. G. FRENCH,
Major-General, Commanding.

Maj. G. Moxley Sorrel,
Assistant Adjutant-General.

[Indorsement.]

HEADQUARTERS,
Near Suffolk, Va., April 25, 1863.

Respectfully forwarded.

There seems to have been a general lack of vigilance and prompt attention to duties on the part of most of the parties connected with this affair. General French seems to be under the impression that General Hood's command was expected to protect the batteries. Such was not the expectation, and his conclusion that General Hood's command was expected to protect them seems strange, as the batteries were under his control exclusively, and he was twice ordered to take the Fifty-fifth North Carolina, the largest in this army, for that purpose. General Hood naturally and properly considered himself relieved from responsibilities with the river batteries when they were especially assigned to the charge of General French. His (General Hood's) division was on our left, and was ready, of course, to resist any general attack of the enemy; but the staff officers of General French should have made all of their reports to General French, that he might have made the necessary arrangements to resist any landing by the enemy. The slight loss of Colonel Connally's regiment while lying within 600 yards of the old fort will hardly justify the conclusion that nothing could live through the enemy's artillery fire. The attack was made about sunset, or a little later. The cannonade being more brisk than any that we had previously had with the gunboats, I took out my watch and

---

* See Report No. 26.

counted the number of shots per minute. In no instance did they exceed thirteen to the minute; the average, I think, was about eight. Of the thirteen shots that could have been fired at a command charging across the field after night it is not likely that more than four could have taken effect, and those ought not to be expected to destroy more than 2 men per shot. So I think it reasonable to conclude that the fort and battery could have been recaptured with the loss of 75 men. Many of the officers were of limited experience, however, and I have no doubt acted as they thought best. I do not know that any of them deserve particular censure. This lesson, it is hoped, will be of service to us all. The command at the fort seems to have been completely surprised, and is probably less excusable than other parties in the affair.

JAMES LONGSTREET,
Lieutenant-General, Commanding.

[Inclosure A.]

SPECIAL ORDERS, }　　　HEADQUARTERS FRENCH'S COMMAND,
　　No. 3.　　 }　　　　　　　　　　　　　　　*April* 17, 1863.

I. Brig. Gen. J. R. Davis will detail three companies of the Fifty-fifth North Carolina Troops, Col. J. K. Connally, to proceed immediately to Norfleet's house, on the Reed's Ferry road, to report to Maj. L. M. Shumaker for duty in guarding the batteries located in that vicinity. One day's rations will be taken. The remainder of the regiment will march to the same place to-morrow morning for permanent duty on the river.

*　　*　　*　　*　　*　　*　　*

By command of Maj. Gen. S. G. French:

GRAHAM DAVES,
Assistant Adjutant-General.

General J. R. DAVIS, *Commanding, &c.*

[Inclosure B.]

SPECIAL ORDERS, }　　　HEADQUARTERS FRENCH'S COMMAND,
　　No. 7.　　 }　　　　　　　　　　　　　　　*April* 18, 1863.

I. Col. J. K. Connally, commanding Fifty-fifth North Carolina Troops, will detail two companies from his regiment for picket duty to-night, one to take post near the fish-house (Le Compte's) to prevent a landing by the enemy. In case a landing should be attempted, the boats will be permitted to reach the shore before being fired upon. This company will furnish a picket force of 4 men (in charge of a corporal) to take position on the Reed's Ferry road half a mile below Le Compte's house. Prompt information will be given of an advance of the enemy in force, but care will be taken not to give false alarms. The second company will take post near the battery now erecting (Smoot's). This company will furnish a party to assist in loading the wagons with forage and provisions from Riddick's farm. In case of attack Colonel Connally will hold his regiment in readiness to support the artillery and will maintain his position until the last.

*　　*　　*　　*　　*　　*　　*

By command of Maj. Gen. S. G. French:

GRAHAM DAVES,
Assistant Adjutant-General.

[Inclosure E.]

APRIL 19, 1863.

Major SHUMAKER:

I will have this matter of forage attended to. I hope you may succeed in sinking those infernal gunboats that have shown no consideration for women or children. If you cripple one and can use the field batteries against her do so. I felt too ill from the medicine I took to come down this morning. Keep me advised.

Yours, truly,

S. G. FRENCH,
Major-General.

[Inclosure F.]

HEADQUARTERS, *April* 19, 1863.

Major SHUMAKER:

Let me know what the result of the heavy cannonade now going on. Show this to Colonel Connally and have him post his regiment to repel any landing of infantry against the batteries. They had better move down near the battery of Stribling. The countersign is "Morgan" for to-night.

Yours, truly,

S. G. FRENCH,
Major-General.

[Inclosure G.]

MOORE'S HOUSE, *April* 19, 1863.

CAPTAIN: Let me know the result of the enemy's fire to-day. We have information that the boat you disabled day before yesterday has been towed down the river, sunk about to her gunwales. Citizens from the other side of the river saw her. She will not trouble you again soon. I go up to headquarters to-night and wish to take a report to the general.

L. M. SHUMAKER,
Major and Chief of Artillery.

[Inclosure H.]

BATTERY AT HILL'S POINT, VA.,
April 19, 1863.

MAJOR: The enemy has shelled us steadily for about three hours from gunboats lying up the river. There are four of them, and from their movements I think they are preparing to run down at least one of them. The lower boats have been otherwise occupied. There are no casualties, and we will be prepared to give them a warm reception should any attempt to run down. Our embrasures are now widened, so that we will be able to give the boat three shots from each gun as they run by.

With respect,

R. M. STRIBLING,
Captain, Commanding Battery.

[Indorsement.]

This note was written just before the work was attacked by the party that landed and carried the work.

S. G. FRENCH,
Major-General.

[Inclosure J.]

CAMP NEAR SUFFOLK, VA., *April* 20, 1863.

Maj. L. M. SHUMAKER:

SIR : In obedience to your order, received this morning, I have the honor to make the following report of the condition of Stribling's battery. The battery was captured by the enemy yesterday evening, when the loss was as follows:

Commissioned officers 4
Non-commissioned officers 8
Privates 47
12-pounder guns 3
24-pounder howitzers 2
Chests with 12-pounder ammunition 9
Chests with 24-pounder ammunition 6

The present condition of the battery is as follows:

Commissioned officers present for duty 1
Non-commissioned officers present for duty 7
Privates present for duty 83

Aggregate present 91

Public horses 93
Wagons 3
Ambulances 1
Forges 1
Limbers to guns 5
Running-gear to caissons 5
Chests of 12-pounder gun ammunition 3
Chests of 24-pounder howitzer ammunition 2

REMARK.—In addition to the number of men stated above as present for duty there are 6 privates absent sick, who may reasonably be expected to join their company within a few weeks.

With respect, your obedient servant,

GRAY CARROLL,
Lieutenant, Commanding Stribling's Battery.

—

HEADQUARTERS DEPARTMENT OF SOUTHERN VIRGINIA,
May 25, 1863.

GENERAL : During the three weeks that Lieutenant-General Longstreet kept the enemy confined within Suffolk there was an effort made to remove the iron from the Seaboard and Roanoke Railroad. Commencing near Suffolk, the engineer department succeeded in taking up about 3 miles of the rails and removed it toward Franklin and deposited it at or near a place known as Beaver Dam, where it could be protected by the forces near Franklin. After we withdrew from Suffolk the enemy discovered the effort made to secure the iron on our part, and soon marched to Carrsville with a force of between 9,000 and 10,000 infantry, 30 pieces of artillery, and cavalry, and immediately fortified their position and commenced taking up the track and removing it toward Suffolk. General Jenkins assembled all the available forces, and with about 3,000 men crossed over and drove in all their advanced lines behind their intrenchments and kept them there for near three days, causing them to abandon the road this side of Carrsville, and thus enabled our forces to save the road to that point, except a few hundred yards, and the iron brought from near Suffolk. The enemy would not leave his works to attack us, and with our small force had we driven him from his intrenchments it would have been a victory barren of results and involving a heavy sacrifice of men on our part. All this time while confronting him we were removing the iron as rapidly as possible. The road destroyed, the enemy fell back and immediately with his whole force assumed a position at Windsor, on the Norfolk and Petersburg Railroad, and simultaneously moved up the Chowan with gunboats above the Nottoway River.

Leaving some force to attack the gunboats in case they came up I assembled about 3,000 men and on Saturday afternoon crossed the Blackwater at the Blackwater Bridge by means of pontoons and moved in the direction of Windsor. I found the enemy again with all his force in a thick woods, his lines running from the railroad to across the Blackwater road. His outposts and advanced lines were rapidly driven in, and I assumed a line of battle in hopes he would move to the attack. This he did not do, and after dusk I withdrew to the right bank of the river. There were no results that seemed in anywise attainable that would have justified me in attacking the enemy, outnumbering us fourfold.

While over the river information was received that the enemy's gunboats had moved up the Meherrin and taken possession of Murfreesborough, N. C. General Jenkins the same night moved to Franklin, and with his forces was directed to operate against the gunboats. I do not know what forces Maj. Gen. D. H. Hill has in North Carolina to guard those streams.

It is to me a source of great regret that so little of the iron from the two railroads referred to was taken up during the time General Longstreet was at Suffolk. I am sure had there been any concert or a proper concert of action in the departments the bridge over the Blackwater could have been built, and by constructing a small curve at the crossing of the roads near Suffolk trains could have been run from Petersburg to Franklin via Suffolk and both roads taken up. Had a bridge been thrown across the Zuni before General Longstreet moved and during the month he was making preparations, every bar of iron could have been secured while we were there at Suffolk.

Yours, very respectfully,

S. G. FRENCH,
Major-General, Commanding.

General S. COOPER,
Adjutant and Inspector General.

[Indorsement.]

ENGINEER BUREAU, *June 9,* 1863.

Respectfully returned to the honorable Secretary of War.

No effort was spared to remove the iron from the Norfolk and Petersburg road and from the Seaboard road while General Longstreet was in command; but his efforts, assisted by the engineers under his control, were given to the collection of supplies for the army, these being considered of the first importance. Everything possible with the engineers has been done to save the iron in question, and I am now able to report that a large part of the iron from the Seaboard Railroad is on the right bank of the Blackwater.

J. F. GILMER,
Colonel of Engineers and Chief of Bureau

No. 25.

Report of Maj. L. M. Shumaker, C. S. Artilley, Chief of Artillery, of the capture of Battery Huger, April 19.

HEADQUARTERS,
Near Ely's, Va., April 21, 1863.

GENERAL: In obedience to your order I have the honor to report that on the morning of the 19th I directed Major Boggs to send Capt. [D. L.] Smoot, [Alexandria Light Artillery, or Company E, Eighteenth Battalion Virginia Artillery], with his two 30-pounder Parrott guns, into the works constructed for him to the west of Hill's Point Battery, occupied by Captain Stribling. Captain Smoot got into position just before daylight, and I directed Major Boggs to order him not to unmask or fire until the boats above Hill's Point attempted to come down or those below attempted to pass up. I also directed him to send Captain Bradford, with his four heavy 12-pounders, to relieve Capt. [S. T.] Martin, [Battery B, Twelfth Virginia Battalion], then occupying Major Henry's position with four 12-pounder howitzers, and to instruct him not to fire at anything but a gunboat, and only then when they came within short range, stating that your orders to me were to sink the boats if possible. Captain Stribling's battery was placed in the work at Hill's Point after I had explained the position and character of the work to both General Longstreet and yourself.

On Thursday night, the 16th, I had thoroughly inspected the work, and, finding the platforms burned away, took the heavy siding from a corn-crib on the Riddick farm to make floors for the carriages. These floors did not raise the guns sufficiently to fire over the parapet, constructed originally for guns of heavy caliber, mounted on barbette carriages. I ordered Captain Stribling to cut embrasures for all his pieces, which was done as far as could be that night and finished the succeeding night, so that on the morning of the 19th I had three batteries in position on the Nansemond River, to wit: Bradford's at Norfleet's Landing, Major Henry's position; Captain Stribling's, consisting of two 24-pounder howitzers and three 12-pounder Napoleons, at Hill's Point, in a very strong earthwork; and Captain Smoot, with two 30-pounder Parrott rifles, to the west of and about two-thirds of a mile from Hill's Point, where the river widens and a semicircular bluff bounds a large marsh.

On the morning of the 17th there were three gunboats above Hill's Point and below Norfleet's Landing, and five below Hill's Point lying below the mouth of the West Branch of the Nansemond River. About 10 o'clock three of these attempted to pass up by the battery at Hill's Point, and one of them succeeded in passing; the others were driven back, one of them severely damaged, as she was towed down the river afterward, disabled, and thought by the citizens to be sinking.

Thus, on the morning of the 19th there were four gunboats above Hill's Point and three below. About 10 o'clock Colonel Cunningham came down from headquarters (as I understood from himself and Lieutenant Etting) to relieve me, and he at once took charge and went around to Smoot's position. Shortly afterward the 30-pounder guns opened, and then commenced a general firing from all the gunboats and two of the enemy's land batteries, four of the boats and two batteries firing upon Hill's Point, the others directing their fire upon Smoot's position and occasionally shelling the woods where our sharpshooters were. About 4 o'clock there was a general cessation of firing, and I sent a messenger to Captain Stribling with a note inquiring into the casualties, a copy of which is herewith inclosed, with Captain Stribling's indorsement thereon.* About 1 o'clock Major Boggs informed me that the gunboats above Hill's Point had moved farther up the river, their decks covered with troops, and Captain Martin also reported to me that a large body of infantry (he thought a regiment, if not more) had passed his position (Norfleet's Landing) the day before, moving down the river. These facts I mentioned to General Law immediately after being informed of them, he having come to Moore's house where I then was.

Shortly after receiving Stribling's reply to my note I received a note from you giving me general directions, and I determined not to return to camp. About sunset I saw the boats in motion above Hill's Point, and from the signal whistles I judged that one or more of them intended to try to pass the batteries. I dispatched a messenger to Captain Smoot to hold himself ready, and held Coit's two 3-inch rifled guns to dash out whenever I could make them available in sinking any boat that we might disable. In a short time I heard a volley of musketry, then a few scattering shots, and then loud and continued cheering. In a few moments a messenger informed me that the enemy had landed a large body of infantry from three boats above Hill's Point, and had charged and taken the position. I immediately sent Major Boggs to inform Colonel Connally, who at once moved his regiment down. I then sent a courier to General Law, one to General Hood, and one to yourself. The courier to General Law returned, bringing me word from him that he could not send us assistance, and I at once directed Major Boggs to order Captain Bradford out from his position and sent Captain Smoot an order to get his guns and ammunition out into the road as soon as possible. I then ordered Coit's two light guns forward and went toward the fort or work as far as the farm-houses to ascertain the position of affairs. I soon became satisfied that any attempt to retake the guns with the force we had must fail, and that neither infantry nor artillery could cross the plateau under the cross-fire of seven gunboats and two land batteries, with an unknown body of infantry filling the work and lining the river bank. I therefore returned to the Reed's Ferry road to await your coming and to direct the movements of the remaining batteries. Your note directing me to have Connally post his regiment to support Stribling's battery and to prevent the landing of troops was not received until 8 o'clock, an hour or more after the position had been taken.

I herewith inclose Major Boggs' and Lieutenant Carroll's† reports, and copies of the various notes, directions, &c., referred to above.

In conclusion, general, I have the honor to ask for a court of inquiry as well to verify the facts stated in the foregoing report as to have a record answer to any charge of neglect of duty, either expressed or implied.

Very respectfully,

L. M. SHUMAKER,
Major and Chief of Artillery.

Maj. Gen. S. G. FRENCH,
Commanding Division.

P. S.—It may be proper to state that the work is a heavy earthwork, fronting down the river, with heavy traverses between the guns, the

---

* See Inclosures G and H to Major-General French's report, No. 24.
† See inclosure J to Major-General French's report, No. 24.

right gun being the only one able to fire across the river at right angles. The guns could not be fired to the rear, as there was rising ground immediately in rear of and higher than the work itself, and it was behind this in rear of the work that the landing was effected, there being no pickets, as I understood, on the river above to give information.

No. 26.

Report of Maj. F. J. Boggs, C. S. Artillery, of the capture of Battery Huger, April 19.

- PROVIDENCE CHURCH. VA., *April* 21, 1863.

MAJOR: In response to your call for a detailed report of the occurrences on the 19th I regret to say I have but an imperfect recollection of more than general affairs. Captain Smoot went into battery on the night of the 18th. On the 19th I went to the point below him, in view of the gunboat, to watch the effect of his shot if he should open. The instructions I gave him as received from you were to wait until a boat attempted to pass Stribling's position, or, if no attempt was made to pass, to wait for the boat to take a nearer position, as on the day before. I was not a little surprised to hear Smoot's guns open, as the boat, I thought, had not gone up far enough. The shots, however, were good. One, I am confident, struck on the starboard side in front just under the hurricane deck. During the night succeeding you ordered Smoot, in my presence, to come out cautiously, removing his guns first by hand, which he did, and last night succeeded in getting out his caissons. The orders given by me and from you to Stribling were to fire at nothing but a gunboat on attempting to pass or within short range, which order was strictly obeyed.

On the 18th, about 8 o'clock, three boats from below came up in line of battle and opened a terrific fire on Stribling's position, the rear boats continuing the fire while the first boat passed. Lieutenant Marshall informed me in the evening that two shots were fired at the leading boat, one taking a damaging effect. Seven shots were fired at the second boat, five taking effect and the sixth striking down the flag-staff. Several citizens of my acquaintance informed me that she was towed below in a sinking condition. I witnessed this fight also, and heard the crash of timber from the shots on the second boat.

On the evening of the 19th, about sunset, I was standing with you and Mr. Waterbury in Mrs. Moore's yard when we heard heavy firing and cheering, which, on investigation, we found to be the shout of the enemy in the capture of Stribling's battery. I immediately communicated your order to Colonel Connally to carry down his regiment, which order was executed. Coit's section was also carried in. The shelling was terrific, and I do not believe a dog could have made the trip from Riddick's quarters to the fort. In the morning of this day, while I was watching the effect of Smoot's battery, I observed three boats above the fort, one a large side-wheel vessel, this one, at least, loaded with troops. This information I communicated to you, and expressed my fears to several officers (I think to you) that there would be an effort to land troops. Capt. [James A.] Shingleur was there and saw the vessels and troops. Just after the report reached us of the capture of Stribling's battery you remarked that you had sent to General Law, but that he informed you he had not the troops to spare. I think you remarked you had also sent to General Hood. Without delay, as I thought, Generals Hood and Law, and shortly after General French, were at the cross-roads and dispositions of infantry made. Bradford's battery was occupying the works above Henry's, and were ordered out by you through me, and I had succeeded in getting out all the pieces but one. General Hood ordered it back again, where it remained until last night, when everything was brought out in safety. The orders given to and obeyed by Captain Bradford were to fire at nothing but boats in passing or the enemy at short range. One wheel in this battery was shattered and the muzzle molding of one gun struck by the shot of the enemy. This battery, as well as the Hill's Point Battery, was commanded, the former by three, the other by two, land batteries over the river, and both by large bodies of sharpshooters.

F. J. BOGGS,
Major, Commanding.

Maj. L. M. SHUMAKER, Chief of Artillery.

No. 27.

Report of Maj. James Dearing, C. S. Artillery, of the capture of Battery Huger, April 19.

APRIL 21, 1863.

GENERAL: Your letter recommending me a quartermaster was received just as we were starting on to Suffolk, and this is the first opportunity I have had of replying. I sent up a recommendation approved by General Pickett and General Longstreet about a week or ten days before receiving your letter, and hope every day to see the "phiz" of my quartermaster. I have two medical officers with my battalion, one ordnance officer, one adjutant, and a lieutenant acting as quartermaster.

I had just succeeded in getting Capt. [M. C.] Macon four Napoleons, giving him a battery of four Napoleons and two Parrotts, and also getting him 50 conscripts. Capt. [W. H.] Caskie was in a fair way to get four Napoleons, and I was hard at work to obtain a rifle Parrott battery, if possible, for Capt. [J. G.] Blount, when we were ordered to this side of the Blackwater. Soon after getting here—that is within 1½ miles of Suffolk—Major-General French came down, and having no command (though being the ranking major-general here), General Longstreet finally gave him the command of all the artillery. General French immediately took two of my batteries—Captain Stribling's and Captain Bradford's, which had been assigned me at Petersburg, composed of four 12-pounder brass pieces—and sent them away down on Nansemond River, some 15 miles from me, putting Captain Stribling between two streams just where they unite and both of them navigable for gunboats, giving Captain Stribling only two companies of infantry as a support. The enemy came up in front, on both flanks, and in rear, and captured Captain Stribling, his battery of three Napoleons, and two 24-pounder brass howitzers, and 56 of his men. The caissons, with the chests taken off, and the horses were half a mile back and escaped. Lieut. [G.] Carroll also escaped, not being present. He has some 90 odd men and the horses yet remaining. All of the best of the horses General French has turned over to some other batteries. I do think it very trying to have one's command thus split up and captured, especially in such a way as this has been done. If it is a military necessity to separate battalions no one will more cheerfully acquiesce than myself; but this has proven itself not to be such an one, for General French has hastened to remove all batteries remaining near that point to some safe inland position.

I have been working hard and straining every point to fully equip and man my battalion, and was flattering myself that I was succeeding pretty well when this drawback comes upon me. It does seem that it is but a poor inducement for one to get a fine battalion if he is to have nothing to do with commanding it in times of peril—if it is to be placed in traps to be captured without fighting. I had hoped that I might have the honor of commanding my own battalion on a battle-field, there to share its honors, victories, or defeats; but it seems otherwise. I had no idea of accepting a sinecure when I became a field officer of artillery, and when my battalion is needed I wish to carry it into battle myself.

I have received both of the papers recommending officers for Caskie's battery. He has one vacancy for a lieutenant, and I should much prefer Lieut. [S. F.] Chapman to [L.] Booker. I sent Captain Caskie himself back to Richmond to see if he could hasten the filling of the requisition for his guns. I have written to him on the subject and am expecting an answer daily. Some charges against Lieut. [T. B.] McCurdy, of the same battery, came down to-day, and I have just ordered him back to report to Colonel Crutchfield for trial. He appears to be an indifferent and worthless officer and talks of resigning. I hope he may, if my impressions prove true.

I hope, general, you will allow me to have the Parrott gun Captain Caskie turned over to Colonel Crutchfield. I am greatly in need of rifles, and wish much to have a rifle battery, and besides really think I am justly entitled to that gun. The battery was sent to me without horses or guns, though it had both, and both ought rightfully to have been sent—at least all he had. My horses are doing well, and if Captain Stribling had his battery and I had the Parrotts for Captain Blount I would be satisfied.

Believe me, general, your obedient servant,

JAMES DEARING,
Major, Commanding Battalion.

Brig. Gen. WILLIAM N. PENDLETON,
Chief of Artillery, Army of Northern Virginia.

P. S.—I forgot to mention that Lane's Whitworth gun burst in North Carolina, and that both of his 20-pounder Parrott guns have been disabled down here; one, elevating screw was broken; the other gun was cracked, I believe.

[Indorsement.]

HDQRS. ARTILLERY CORPS, *April 27, 1863.*

Respectfully forwarded to the commanding general for his information, and to express the anxiety of the undersigned lest much care in adjusting our artillery organization be frustrated by change of system in those temporarily serving elsewhere. Major Dearing's views and feelings seem reasonable and soldier-like. It is hoped they may be in the main approved by General Lee and Lieutenant-General Longstreet.

Respectfully submitted.

W. N. PENDLETON,
Brigadier-General and Chief of Artillery.

P. S.—No reflection whatever upon General French is intended by the undersigned, who has a favorable and very kind recollection of General F. Unaware, however, of the difficulties incident to the rupture and readjustment of recent battalion organizations, he may not quite fully appreciate the importance of not permanently weakening a battalion as such. To encourage these efficient young battalion com manders seems practically wise. The other points mentioned by Major D. are attended to.

Respectfully,

W. N. P.

No. 28.

Report of Capt. Robert M. Stribling, Fauquier Artillery, of the capture of Battery Huger, April 19.

PETERSBURG, VA., *May* 6, 1863.

GENERAL : In reply to your request of this morning I have the honor of making the following report of the capture of my battery on the Nansemond River on the evening of April 19 :

About 11 p. m., April 16, my battery was placed in position in the old fort on Hill's Point by Major Shumaker, chief of artillery, with orders from him to fire upon any boats running up or down the river that might attempt to pass the fort, and to fire under no other circum stances except when the fire would be undoubtedly with effect, but to keep the men under cover as well as possible. Lieutenant-Colonel Coleman, of General Law's brigade, was in the fort with some infantry when I went into position. The next morning the enemy opened upon the fort from gunboats below and above, and also from a land battery upon the opposite shore. About 11 a. m. three boats attempted to run by the fort—one ran aground about 600 yards below, and only one succeeded then in passing; we fired upon it and made several holes through it. Toward sunset the boat which had been aground got off and passed by; we made seven holes through her, and I understood permanently disabled her. Saturday was a day of comparative quiet, no shots of any consequence being fired at the fort and we not firing at all.

Early Sunday morning firing commenced from the gunboats and about 1 p. m. became quite furious and continued so until between sundown and dark, when, upon a signal, all firing ceased, and immediately one of the boats above ran near the shore and rapidly landed two or more regiments about 400 yards above the fort. They double-quicked by the flank across the neck of land, thereby cutting off all communication. They then faced to the front, discharged their pieces, and charged upon the fort. The pieces which had been turned toward the land and the infantry supports (two companies, numbering about 60 men, and commanded by Captain Bozeman, of Forty-fourth Alabama Regiment, General Law's brigade) opened upon them and held them in check. They soon, however, flanked the fort on either side and entered it through a swamp and over the parapets on the river side and in rear of the guns. We were hastened off with the greatest rapidity and put on board the boat.

About 2 o'clock on the night of the 16th the pickets stationed up the river fell back to the fort, reporting that the enemy had landed in large force above. Notice was immediately sent through one of my sergeants to General Law. In the mean time Lieutenant-Colonel Coleman advanced his skirmishers up the river and found no enemy at the points indicated. They had re-embarked, as I learned after my capture. My sergeant returned and reported that a regiment was in the woods, about three-quarters of a mile distant, having been sent down to our support. When the enemy landed on the evening of the 19th there was no picket or lookout up the river; no gun was fired or no notice whatever served of their approach, and as the shore was heavily wooded we could see nothing from the fort. I had been led to suppose that the banks of the river were picketed and that I would receive notice of the approach of a land force, and also that there was a regiment in supporting distance. The construction of the fort was of such a nature that I could not use my guns with full effect against a land force, though it was admirably adapted to resist an attack from the gunboats and to blockade the river at that point.

I neglected to state that while the gunboat was aground during the morning of the 17th no gun in the fort could be brought to bear upon it on account of the narrowness of the embrasure which had been hastily cut out the night before. That night they were widened sufficiently to give command of the point.

I am, general, with great respect, your obedient servant,

R. M. STRIBLING,
Captain Fauquier Artillery.

[Maj. Gen. S. G. FRENCH.]

P. S.—It might be well to add that on the night of the 16th, when the alarm was given, Lieutenant-Colonel Coleman told me that he had orders to notify General Law should any force cross the river, and that he had no courier. As my sergeant had a horse I offered him to the colonel, and he was sent by his order.

[Indorsement.]

Stribling's guns were lost because the infantry placed in the work as a garrison by Generals Hood and Law, and from whom they received all orders, were captured. When Hood's infantry garrison surrendered the guns were captured. Why not inquire how it was the garrison found in the fort was captured?

S. G. FRENCH.
Major-General, Commanding.

No. 29.

Report of Lieut. Col. John A. Jones, Forty-fourth Alabama Infantry, of the capture of Battery Huger, April 19.

Names of the companies and their strength captured in the fort at Hill's Point, on the Nansemond River, April 19, all from the Forty-fourth Alabama Regiment.

	Officers.	Non-commissioned officers.	Privates.	Aggregate.
Company A	4	6	18	28
Company B	1	6	36	43
Total	5	12	54	71

JNO. A. JONES,
Lieutenant-Colonel, Comdg. Forty-fourth Alabama Vols.

No. 30.

Report of Col. John K. Connally, Fifty-fifth North Carolina Infantry, of the capture of Battery Huger, April 19.

APRIL 22, 1863.

SIR: I have the honor to state that in compliance with Special Orders, No. 3, Headquarters French's Command, dated April 17, three compa-nies from my regiment marched on Friday night, the 17th, to Norfleet's house, on the Reed's Ferry road, and on Saturday morning, the 18th, reported to Major Shumaker for duty, as specified in the order. The fort intended for the reception of the two 32-pounder rifled pieces which my regiment was to support not having been completed, a detail of 60 men was, by order of Major Shumaker, made from the three companies to finish it. This having been done on Saturday evening, the 18th, the guns were placed in position during the night.

On Saturday morning, the 18th, I moved with the seven remaining companies of my regiment to Norfleet's house, and some time during the evening communicated with Major Shumaker, who advised me to place 4 men and a corporal at Le Compte's house, 4 men and a corporal at Reed's Ferry, 4 men and a corporal at a point nearly equi-distant between Le Compte's house and the ferry, and a company at Moore's house to support the three points mentioned. He also advised me to place a company near the gate at the entrance of the field in which the battery of 32-pounder pieces was situated to support it. In addition to this advice I received an order from General French in exact accordance with the major's advice, except that the company placed at Moore's should be placed at Le Compte's house. In posting my men I obeyed General French's order to the letter except as to placing a company at Le Compte's house. This I did not do because Major Shumaker told me that he was thoroughly acquainted with the posts mentioned, and that it was better to place the company at Moore's, which I did.

On Sunday evening, the 19th, Colonel Cunningham rode up to my quarters some time between 4 and 6 o'clock and told me in substance— I do not remember his language—that General French wished me to support the batteries. The order was general, and I immediately or-dered Lieutenant-Colonel Smith and Maj. [A. H.] Belo to go and ascer-tain the position of the batteries, the number of men necessary for their support, the ground to be occupied by the support, and to report to me as early as possible. They had not been gone more than an hour or an hour and a half when I heard loud cheering in the direction of the river. A few moments afterwards an officer (I know not who) rode up and reported that Stribling's battery had been charged by the enemy and captured. I immediately ordered my regiment under arms, left one company at Moore's house to support the three posts mentioned above, two companies at the gate referred to to support the battery of 32-pounder pieces, and with the seven other companies proceeded as rap-idly as possible to the house nearest Stribling's battery, which was in the fort known as the Old Fort. There I came up with Capt. [L. R.] Ter-rell, General Law's assistant adjutant-general, with two companies from the Forty-eighth Alabama Regiment. I inquired of the captain what he was doing there, and learned that he had been sent by General Law with the two companies mentioned to relieve the two companies which were in the fort when it was captured. He stated that he had arrived too late—that the fort had been taken before he could render assistance. I had never been to the fort, knew nothing of its position or the grounds around it, and asked Captain Terrell if he could give me any information concerning it, telling him that I intended to charge and retake the guns. He stated that he had been to the fort and knew all about its position; that it was situated on a point of land extending down to the river, and that there was a deep ravine or marsh in its front over which my men could not possibly charge. In addition to this the fort was defended by six gunboats—three above and three below—and two land batteries across the river. I intended to charge and retake the fort, if possible, but upon learning its position and defense from Captain Terrell knew that it would be worse than folly to make the attempt. Wishing, however, to ascertain if it was still occupied by the enemy I moved up to within some 500 or 600 yards of the fort, formed line of battle, and ordered the men to lie down. I then ordered Lieutenant-Colonel Smith, with two companies deployed as skirmishers, to advance until fired upon, then to fall back upon the regiment. He had not advanced more than 50 or 60 yards before he was fired upon by the enemy's skirmishers, and, as ordered, fell back. The fire of my skirmishers discovered to the enemy the position of the regiment, when they opened upon me a heavy cross-fire from the six gunboats and two batteries. I immediately withdrew my regiment out of range of their grape-shot, and, thinking they would probably advance with the intention of capturing the battery of 32-pounder pieces in my rear, formed a second line of battle about half a mile from the Old Fort, threw forward skirmishers under command of Major Belo, and, although shelled from the gunboats, awaited patiently the enemy's advance until, I suppose, about 1 a. m., when General Law came up and told me that I was too far in advance and to fall back upon the skirt of woods some quarter of a mile in my rear; also to draw in my line of skirmishers. I obeyed General Law's orders. This, as stated above, was about 1 o'clock. At daylight, or very soon thereafter, General Hood came up and placed me under command of General Robertson, with whom I remained until near sundown, when I was ordered by General Hood, through General Robertson, to rejoin my brigade. General Law not attempting to retake the fort during the night of the 19th, and General Hood not attempting it on the 20th, establishes the fact that the attempt would have been injudicious, and that I was fortunate in meeting with Captain Terrell, whose statement relative to its position and defense alone prevented my making it.

It will be seen, major, from this report that I did not have any men in or near the fort when it was captured; that it was attacked so soon after Colonel Cunningham left me that I could not possibly have placed men in position for its support; that when captured two companies from General Law's brigade were moving forward to relieve the two companies which were in it, and that I moved with all possible dispatch to recapture the fort, had it been possible.

As I was the commanding officer on the field at the time, I deem it my duty to give Captain Terrell's statement concerning the action of the two companies under his command, which was that all the men in the two companies deserted him except nine. I do not know the names of the nine men who remained with the captain or I would give them, thinking they deserve favorable notice.

The fire upon my regiment, as you may well imagine, was very heavy indeed, yet both officers and men received it unflinchingly and with veteran-like steadiness. Lieutenant-Colonel Smith, Major Belo, and Adjt. [H. T.] Jordan behaved with the utmost coolness and gallantry. I had 10 men wounded (1 mortally) and 1 man missing, supposed to have been killed.

I am, major, very respectfully, your obedient servant,

JNO. K. CONNALLY,
Colonel Fifty-fifth Regiment North Carolina Troops.

Major DAVES.

[Indorsements.]

CAMP NEAR SUFFOLK, VA., *April* 22, 1863.

I do not know the precise hour the instructions were given Colonel Connally, but think it was earlier than 4 p. m. They would have been delivered in the forenoon, but Colonel Connally was absent from camp with General Law. I had left the batteries and arrived at camp before the attack was made.

Respectfully,

GEO. A. CUNNINGHAM.

HEADQUARTERS,
Near Suffolk, Va., April 22, 1863.

Colonel Connally is in error, perhaps, in regard to the time he saw Colonel Cunningham and received his instructions.

S. G. FRENCH,
Major-General.

No. 31.

Report of Maj. Gen. George E. Pickett, C. S. Army, commanding Division of skirmish on the Edenton Road, Va., April 24.

HEADQUARTERS PICKETT'S DIVISION,
April 26, 1863.

MAJOR: I have the honor to inclose report* of Col. [J. B.] Magruder, of the Fifty-seventh Virginia, commanding on the Whitemarsh road, of the skirmish which took place on his front on the 24th instant. Since his report has been handed in 4 of the pickets thought to be prisoners have returned. They took refuge in the swamps upon the advance of the enemy. They report from what was overheard that the officers had great difficulty in making their men come up to the mark. Simultaneously with the attack on the Whitemarsh road the enemy advanced in my immediate front, opening fire from one of their redoubts near the point of the pond with three rifled guns; also from a redoubt in our right front, and from a section of artillery which they brought out in front of my advanced pickets. Their picket line, which was re-enforced, tried to advance under cover of this heavy artillery fire, but were easily repulsed by my pickets, who maintained their position and did not call on the reserve regiment which I had sent up to support if necessary.

I am sorry to report that two very valuable officers of the Fourteenth Virginia were very seriously wounded—Capts. [William D.] Tompkins, [Company B], and [P.] Poindexter, [Company I]. They were shot while

---

* Not found.

in the execution of their duty with the most advanced of the scouts. Also two men of the Twenty-ninth Virginia, Corse's brigade, slightly wounded.

The officers and men engaged all acted with great coolness and readiness, and it is evident the enemy was badly hurt.

I am, major, very respectfully, your obedient servant,

GEO. E. PICKETT,
Major-General, Commanding.

Maj. G. MOXLEY SORREL,
Asst. Adjt. Gen., Dept. of Virginia and North Carolina.

APRIL 12, 1863.—Reconnaissance from Gloucester Point to the vicinity of Hickory Forks, Va.

Report of Lieut. Col. Charles C. Tevis, Fourth Delaware Infantry.

CAMP GILPIN, GLOUCESTER POINT, VA.,
April 12, 1863.

COLONEL: In pursuance of your orders I marched a detachment of 150 men (infantry), taken from the Fourth Delaware Regiment, to the points indicated in your instructions to me. I felt all the woods between York River and the main county road as far up as Timber Neck Creek, and then took what is called the Pine Swamp road until its intersection with the Bell Roy road, about 1½ miles above Hickory Fork.

All the country was carefully examined by my line of skirmishers, and indications of the recent presence of the enemy were found, particularly at a small Methodist chapel called Providence Chapel, about 3 miles beyond our lines. All the inhabitants concurred in stating that about 200 cavalry (Captains Littleton's, Clopton's, and Allen's companies), under Colonel Godwin and Major Vaughan, had been down since Friday morning, and had returned about 6 p. m. to-day to King and Queen's Court-House, where they are encamped. I found a considerable quantity of grain in the mill belonging to Coleman Roberts, on the Bell Roy road, and as the rebels are in the habit of picketing there to bait their horses, and as the owner confessed to correspondence with their leaders, I burned the mill. My detachment returned by the main county road, only halting to destroy a grist and saw mill belonging to Prosser Tabb, near Hickory Fork, in which large quantities of flour have been lately ground for the use of the Richmond army. I would especially call attention to Charles Curtis, at Wilson's Creek, who receives stores for the rebels and who had rented the last-mentioned mill.

I have the honor to forward, too, the papers taken from two cavalry soldiers belonging to the Fifth Virginia Cavalry, whom I captured, and who were empowered by the rebel general, Stuart, to collect horses for his regiments. The men and officers of my command did their duty well. i would speak particularly of the services of Lieut. John J. Toner, regimental quartermaster, and of Dr. Hopkins, regimental surgeon, who were of material assistance to me in the capture of the prisoners.

Very respectfully,

CHARLES CARROLL TEVIS,
Lieutenant-Colonel Fourth Delaware Volunteers.

Col. A. H. GRIMSHAW,
Fourth Delaware Volunteers, Commanding Post.

APRIL 16, 1863.—Affair on the Pamunkey River, near West Point, Va.

Report of Maj. Peyton Wise, Forty-sixth Virginia Infantry.

HEADQUARTERS,
White House, Va., April 19, 1863.

GENERAL: I have just returned from Taylor's Quarter, 2 miles from West Point, to which place I was called on Thursday evening last by occurrences of which the following shall be a report. Permit me only to premise that this should have been sent to you earlier, but that a dispatch which reached me at the place just named, and other reports which came to me tending to show that you had retired from Williamsburg, left me in ignorance of your whereabouts. On Thursday evening last a dispatch reached me by courier from Capt. [G. W.] Abbitt (stationed at Taylor's Quarter, on the Pamunkey River, with his own company and that of Capt. [G. D.] Huffman and a section of artillery under Lieutenant Hudgin) that two gunboats were descried in York River slowly approaching West Point. I immediately telegraphed this fact to General Elzey, and then, after sending an order to Captain Haynes (stationed at Canton, in King William County, near Mattapony River, with a company of cavalry) to scout the Mattapony River down to its mouth, with a view to watch out for and prevent, as far as possible, any attempted landing of the enemy above us on that river, or any raid of gunboats, I proceeded directly to Taylor's Quarter. This was the scene of the little action which I shall relate to you. The two gunboats referred to were steam propellers, one of large size, the other of dimensions not so great but respectable, and both conveying troops. The fact that they bore troops is distinctly vouched for by citizens at West Point, who were not only close enough to both to see with ease what was on board of them but were not so far removed from the smaller of the two as that they could not hear voices on it. The larger of the gunboats lay off abreast the point and near the opposite shore, on which is the "brick house." The smaller one passed West Point up into the Pamunkey about half a mile. At this distance she was opened upon by our artillery, which consisted of two small guns (of the Blakely pattern) with round shot. The first shot was ineffectual, but the second and third, following in quick succession, went tearing and crashing right through her. It is supposed that she was struck twice afterward, but certain it is that after an action of about three-quarters of an hour she retired, evidently with the greatest difficulty and very badly damaged. As she repassed West Point groans and screams of the most heart-rending description, heard with the utmost distinctness at the Point, told not only of damage done to vessel but that her crew had experienced the effect of the iron hail. When this gunboat rejoined her consort they both steamed down York River and have not been heard of since. Next day at as early an hour as possible General Elzey was informed of what had been done. Col. [R. T. W.] Duke was informed of it with equal promptness by his pickets (Capt. [J. C.] Hill's company) at Eltham, who were witnesses of the whole transaction. I shall leave you to judge, sir, what was the destination of the troops on board of these vessels, but to enable you to form as correct a judgment as possible permit me to state that I am now firmly convinced that the only object of the small gunboat in entering the Pamunkey River was the capture of a large schooner which was pushing its way down the river and was near Eltham. The larger one, too, went toward the Brick House Landing and lay near it. Can these troops have been destined to flank you? If my command, while performing the special service assigned to it, has been indeed instrumental in protecting your rear, you need scarcely my assurance that no one is more grateful for it than your obedient servant,

PEYTON WISE,
Major, Commanding, &c.

Brig. Gen. HENRY A. WISE, *Commanding, &c.*

APRIL 27, 1863.—Expedition from Yorktown beyond Hickory Forks, Va.

Extract from "Record of Events" of Seventh Army Corps. *

April 27.—Lieutenant-Colonel Tevis, Fourth Delaware Volunteers, with a detachment from his regiment and a detachment from the Second Massachusetts Cavalry, went some distance above Hickory Forks, destroyed a large amount of stores of the rebel army, consisting of grain, cotton, bacon, flour, salt, coffee, sulphur, powder, flints, percussion-caps, and quinine; also collected and drove within the lines 57 head of horned cattle, 260 sheep, and 8 horses and mules.

APRIL 27–MAY 1, 1863.—Expedition from New Berne toward Kinston, N. C., and skirmish (28th) at Wise's Cross-Roads.

REPORTS.

No. 1.—Brig. Gen. Innis N. Palmer, U. S. Army, commanding Expedition.
No. 2.—Col. George H. Peirson, Fifth Massachusetts Infantry.
No. 3.—Lieut. Col. Luke Lyman, Twenty-seventh Massachusetts Infantry.
No. 4.—Col. Charles L. Holbrook, Forty-third Massachusetts Infantry.
No. 5.—Col. Charles R. Codman, Forty-fifth Massachusetts Infantry.
No. 6.—Col. J. Richter Jones, Fifty-eighth Pennsylvania Infantry.

No. 1.

Reports of Brig. Gen. Innis N. Palmer, U. S. Army, commanding Expedition.

HDQRS. FIRST DIVISION, EIGHTEENTH ARMY CORPS,
Core Creek, Dover Road Crossing, N. C., April 28, 1863—9 p. m.

COLONEL: About midday to-day the weather cleared up a little and a demonstration was made, having for its object principally the capture of any of the enemy who might be on Sandy Ridge. Colonel Amory, with two regiments (the Seventeenth and Forty-fifth), was ordered to march up the railroad as rapidly as possible to the point where the railroad and Dover road cross. Colonel Jones, with his own regiment (the Fifty-eighth Pennsylvania) and the Twenty-seventh Massachusetts, was ordered up the Dover road. The arrangement was that the two columns

---

* From Return for month of April, 1863.

should meet at the junction mentioned. I recollected what General Foster had told me about making the demonstration with infantry, and also about giving Colonel Jones a command. All the other forces were held in readiness to move in any direction. Nothing was found on the ridge, the intrenchments nearest Core Creek having been abandoned. The forces arrived at the junction nearly at the same time and there found intrenchments with a force to defend them. A sharp skirmish took place, when the enemy were driven out, leaving 2 men dead and 1 wounded. They retired up the railroad in the direction of Kinston. Their line of retreat they had taken care to keep open and it was impossible to get behind them.

The wounded man found in the enemy's works is with Colonel Jones' command, which has not yet arrived in camp. I will get all the information I can from him as soon as he arrives here and communicate further with you to-morrow.

Our loss is 1 man killed and 6 wounded.

This skirmish took place some 10 miles this side of Kinston. The only information I have been able to obtain thus far in regard to the enemy's position, &c., at Kinston is from a negro, who says, "They have plenty men, plenty guns, plenty forts."

We have provisions enough for to-morrow. If more provisions are sent some wagons should be sent to transport them, for the roads are very bad between here and the railroad. I have had them repaired as far as possible to-day.

Very respectfully, your obedient servant,

I. N. PALMER,
Brigadier-General, Commanding.

Lieut. Col. SOUTHARD HOFFMAN,
Assistant Adjutant-General, Eighteenth Army Corps.

—

HDQRS. FIRST DIVISION, EIGHTEENTH ARMY CORPS,
Core Creek Railroad Crossing, April 29, 1863.

COLONEL : The rebel works carried yesterday are 8 miles from Kinston. They command the railroad and the Dover road. They were erected last week and have four embrasures. General Ransom, with his brigade (six regiments), is 2 to 4 miles nearer Kinston. General Hill has another division in that vicinity, at different points, where there are other defenses. I cannot tell the condition of the bridge at Kinston; the wagon-road bridge is good. I think we have impressed them with the belief at Kinston that the whole Union force in this vicinity is to be hurled on them. I send down 2 wounded men and 2 dead (one of the Fifty-eighth Pennsylvania and one of the Forty-fifth Massachusetts); both the wounded are of the Forty-fifth. One Confederate wounded also goes down. It was a hard day's work yesterday. The commands returned at midnight. The roads are dreadful.

Very respectfully, yours,

I. N. PALMER,
Brigadier-General.

Lieut. Col. SOUTHARD HOFFMAN,
Assistant Adjutant-General, Eighteenth Army Corps.

P. S.—Yours of 6 a. m. to-day received. The position of the forces around Kinston are undoubtedly as I have given above.

HDQRS. FIRST DIVISION, EIGHTEENTH ARMY CORPS,
New Berne, N. C., May 2, 1863.

COLONEL : In accordance with instructions from department head-quarters of April 26, 1863, on the morning of the 27th instant I embarked my division upon the cars, and at 3 p. m. all the command were at Batchelder's Creek. The First Brigade, Colonel Amory commanding, was sent forward on the railroad to Core Creek. In accordance with my orders he took possession of the bridge at that point and sent a force immediately across the creek to the switch but found nothing. His command bivouacked on the railroad immediately behind the creek, while the remainder of the command, consisting of the brigade of Colonel Lee, the Fifty-eighth Pennsylvania Volunteers, Colonel Jones, one section of Riggs' battery, and a company of the Third New York Cavalry, moved up a cross-road to the Neuse road, and from thence to the Dover-road Crossing of Core Creek, behind which we encamped. Thus was the command posted on two different roads, some 2½ miles apart, with a good cross-road connecting.

Immediately after my arrival at the Dover-road Crossing I sent a force across the creek and beyond to feel the enemy's pickets, but the party found nothing.

At midnight it commenced to rain very heavily and continued until noon of Tuesday, the 28th instant. At the conclusion of the storm the whole country seemed flooded—the roads in a horrible condition; still I determined to make a movement on Sandy Ridge so that the enemy might at least be kept on the alert, even if we effected no captures or fought no fight. I felt confident, however, that we should find some of the enemy's troops at the crossing of the Dover road with the railroad, and perhaps some few in the intrenchments at the easterly portion of Sandy Ridge. I therefore ordered the following movements :

Colonel Amory, with two regiments (the Seventeenth Massachusetts Volunteers and the Forty-fifth Massachusetts Volunteer Militia), was ordered to march up the railroad as rapidly as possible to the point where the railroad and Dover road cross. I will here say that Colonel Amory, who has been ill for some time, was not able to go with the brigade, inasmuch as it was impossible to march horses on the railroad. He therefore returned to the bivouac, leaving Colonel Codman, of the Forty-fifth Massachusetts Volunteer Militia, in command.

Colonel Jones, with his own regiment (the Fifty-eighth Pennsylvania) and the Twenty-seventh Massachusetts Volunteers, Lieutenant-Colonel Lyman, one company of the Forty-fourth Massachusetts Volunteer Militia, and two companies of the Third New York Cavalry was ordered forward on the Dover road, the understanding being that the two columns should join hands at the above-mentioned crossing. In accordance with orders from the commanding general the artillery was not taken beyond Core Creek. All the other troops were held in readiness to move in any direction. Colonel Jones moved cautiously, and finding the intrenchments on Sandy Ridge abandoned he pushed on with his column beyond the ridge, seeing nothing of the enemy until the head of the column arrived within 100 yards of the crossing, when he was suddenly saluted with a volley of musketry from the opposite side of the railroad. Supposing that there was a chance the party might be a portion of Colonel Amory's column he took measures to discover the truth, and found the enemy posted in rifle-pits, several hundred feet in length, and entirely concealed in the thick brush. Some 75 yards in rear was found another line of heavy earthworks of some 500 or 600 feet front, with an embrasure looking down the Dover road, but without a gun. Both these lines were parallel to the railroad and strongly protected on the flanks by marsh and thick underbrush, which was taken advantage of by the enemy's sharpshooters.

Colonel Jones immediately opened fire upon the enemy's works, gradually advancing, and was making preparations to turn both flanks of the position at the same moment, when a brisk fire was opened from down the railroad from the column of Colonel Amory's brigade under Colonel Codman. After delivering one volley two companies dashed down the track with fixed bayonets and took possession of the work. This decided the affair, the enemy retiring in disorder up the railroad toward Kinston, leaving 4 killed and 2 wounded (1 mortally) on the ground. One of the wounded was brought in.

The force of the enemy is variously estimated; probably about 300 men. He had no artillery. It was impossible to get in the rear and capture this force, for they had taken care to keep the line of retreat perfectly clear. After destroying the enemy's camp, both columns returned to their respective camps.

The following day (the 29th instant) I directed that one regiment of Colonel Amory's brigade be sent up the railroad beyond Core Creek to support a fatigue party, which was to make a show of repairing the railroad. The Forty-third Massachusetts was sent upon this duty, and on this and the day following succeeded in putting the road in good condition for a distance of $2\frac{1}{2}$ miles beyond the creek.

During the day of the 29th two cavalrymen, with some of the infantry and artillery, went out a short distance from camp, when they were attacked by a party of guerrillas. The two cavalrymen were killed. They had permission from their commanding officer to leave camp. The other men, I have no doubt, were on a pillaging expedition, and I am rather sorry that they were not the sufferers. Cavalry and infantry were immediately sent in pursuit. They brought in several prisoners, evidently citizens. A careful examination of these men convinced me that they could not be the perpetrators of the deed. I therefore released them, with the admonition that if anything of the kind again occurred in their neighborhood they would be held responsible.

On the 30th a general move was made on different roads in such a way as to create the impression that all the roads leading to Kinston were filled with troops advancing on that place, and I have no doubt that the enemy at Kinston believed it. The column on the railroad worked at the repairs with a will, while the occasional whistle of the cars undoubtedly conveyed the idea that troops were coming up from New Berne. Colonel Lee, with a portion of the Twenty-seventh and Forty-sixth Massachusetts Regiments, was sent to reconnoiter the road leading from a point a mile or two across Core Creek (Dover-road Crossing) to the Neuse road, while Colonel Jones, with the cavalry only, moved by still another path to strike the Neuse road higher up. The Fifth Massachusetts, Colonel Peirson, of the Second Brigade, moved down the Dover road toward the point at which the skirmish took place on the 28th instant. Colonel Lee went through to the Neuse road, a distance of about 6 miles, and returned, finding nothing but the traces of a small party which had been in the neighborhood a day or two before. Colonel Jones, with the cavalry, moved to a cross-road in front of the one followed by Colonel Lee and struck the Neuse road at Biddle's, a point some 6 miles from Core Creek. Here he expected to find a picket, which he hoped to capture, but on arriving he found they had fallen back. He then pushed on toward Moseley's Creek. The inhabitants informed him that a brigade of infantry, with artillery, was strongly intrenched at Moseley's Creek, but on arriving at that point he found the whole force had retired toward Kinston on hearing of the skirmish of Tuesday.

The position at Moseley's Creek Colonel Jones reports to be quite strong. The creek here has two branches, behind each of which the rebels had thrown up earthworks. The first line is some 400 feet long, with one embrasure looking down the road. The front is broken into bastions and a rifle-pit is placed in the rear. The second work has two embrasures, more extensive than the other, flanking arrangements, broader and deeper water in front, and is altogether a formidable affair. The camps in rear of these works Colonel Jones burned and destroyed.

From the information procured by Colonel Jones I have no doubt the enemy drew in all their forces on all the roads leading to Kinston after the advance and skirmish by the two columns on the 28th instant.

Colonel Peirson, with his command, made a successful reconnaissance down the Dover road, resulting in some useful information in regard to the character of the country and road, location of cross-roads, houses, &c., as will be seen by the accompanying sketch. On arriving within about 1½ miles of the intrenchments on the railroad Colonel Peirson drove in the enemy's pickets and reconnoitered their position, which he reports was occupied by a strong force; what number it was impossible for him to discover.

On receipt of Special Orders, No. 125, from Headquarters Eighteenth Army Corps, on the 1st instant, I immediately returned to New Berne with my division, by railroad, sending Colonel Jones, with his regiment and the cavalry, around by the Neuse road and Batchelder's Creek.

The whole command behaved very well. The commanding officers of regiments, &c., showed themselves energetic in the discharge of their duties. To Colonel Jones, of the Fifty-eighth Pennsylvania, I am indebted for much valuable information regarding the country, its inhabitants, &c. Energetic, untiring, and zealous, he has shown himself the man for his place as commandant of the outposts in front of New Berne.

I have the honor to be, colonel, very respectfully, your obedient servant,

I. N. PALMER,
Brigadier-General.

Lieut. Col. SOUTHARD HOFFMAN,
Assistant Adjutant-General, Eighteenth Army Corps.

No. 2.

Report of Col. George H. Peirson, Fifth Massachusetts Infantry.

HDQRS. FIFTH REGT. MASSACHUSETTS VOL. MILITIA,
Fort Peirson, New Berne, N. C., May 3, 1863.

SIR: In obedience to orders received, dated Core Creek, April 30, I respectfully submit the following report of the reconnaissance made by me on that day:

We left camp about 9 a. m. and moved on the Dover road, taking notes and gaining, as far as possible, information concerning that road, the cross-roads on either side, as well as the nature of the country. We met with no opposition until we arrived within 1½ miles of the enemy's position, at what is called Wise's Cross-Roads. We were there fired upon by seven of the enemy's pickets, who were driven into the woods. We then advanced cautiously, skirmishing with the different pickets on the road, until we arrived near to the enemy's works, which command the railroad and the Dover road, about 10 miles from our camp. After reconnoitering about one and a half hours and drawing their fire I found the enemy in strong force. I then retired, agreeably to my instructions.

Accompanying this report I send a sketch of the roads, &c., through which I passed, which I hope will prove satisfactory to you.

Respectfully, yours,

GEORGE H. PEIRSON,
Colonel, Comdg. Fifth Regt. Massachusetts Volunteer Militia.

Capt. J. A. JUDSON,
Asst. Adjt. Gen., First Division, Eighteenth Army Corps.

P. S.—I omitted to state that on my approaching the enemy's works he fired several buildings situated just in front of him, probably to prevent my taking shelter behind them.

No. 3.

Report of Lieut. Col. Luke Lyman, Twenty-seventh Massachusetts Infantry.

HDQRS. TWENTY-SEVENTH REGT. MASS. VOLS.,
Camp Potter, New Berne, N. C., May 2, 1863.

DEAR SIR: I have to report the part taken by this regiment in the battle at Wise's Cross-Roads on Tuesday, April 28:

At 12 m. of that day I received orders to report with my regiment to Colonel Jones, of the Fifty-eighth Regiment Pennsylvania Volunteers, which I did immediately. We moved about 1 o'clock, the Fifty-eighth Regiment leading the column. When about 2 miles out Companies D and E were thrown forward as skirmishers on the left of the road and two companies of the Fifty-eighth Regiment on the right. No obstructions were met with except the enemy's pickets, who retreated upon our approach, until reaching the cross-roads. Here the skirmishers found about one regiment of the enemy behind earthworks. They engaged them promptly, and in less than one hour's fighting, averaging 20 to 25 rounds to a man, charged their works and drove them out, Company D being the first to mount the parapet, receiving a volley as they did so from the retreating enemy who had covered themselves behind a second line of earthworks but left them immediately after delivering a volley. The remaining companies of the regiment were not brought into action.

Our casualties were small, only 2 being wounded, and they slightly; none killed.

I was not in a position to witness the action and therefore cannot speak personally of the behavior of the companies engaged, but I am pleased to place on record in this form the opinion of Colonel Jones, who was in front and in direct command. He volunteered to say to me on our return that these companies behaved nobly.

Respectfully submitted.

LUKE LYMAN,
Lieutenant-Colonel, Commanding Regiment.

Col. HORACE C. LEE,
Comdg. Second Brig., First Div., Eighteenth Army Corps.

No. 4.

Report of Col. Charles L. Holbrook, Forty-third Massachusetts Infantry.

HDQRS. FORTY-THIRD MASSACHUSETTS VOLUNTEERS,
Camp Rogers, N. C., May 2, 1863.

COLONEL: In accordance with orders received Wednesday evening, 29th ultimo, this regiment left the camp of the brigade on Thursday morning at 6 o'clock and marched about 5 miles on the railroad toward Kinston, halting near where the pioneer corps was engaged in repairing the road. The regiment bivouacked in the woods, and returned to the camp of the brigade yesterday morning, and at 1 p. m. embarked on the train and returned to New Berne.

On Thursday scouting parties were sent out in different directions and pickets posted, and nothing of importance transpired after leaving the camp of the brigade. At the suggestion of General Palmer large fires were built in the woods in and about our camp on Thursday night.

I have the honor to be, very respectfully, your obedient servant,

CHAS. L. HOLBROOK,
Colonel Forty-third Massachusetts Volunteers.

Col. T. J. C. AMORY,
Commanding Brigade.

No. 5.

Report of Col. Charles R. Codman, Forty-fifth Massachusetts Infantry.

HDQRS. FORTY-FIFTH MASSACHUSETTS VOL. MILITIA,
Camp Massachusetts, near New Berne, N. C., May 1, 1863.

LIEUTENANT: In compliance with orders from brigade headquarters I have the honor to submit a report of the part taken by the troops under my command on the expedition up the railroad on April 28:

On the evening of April 27, the brigade being then at Core Creek, on the railroad, I received orders from Colonel Amory, commanding the brigade, to send two companies of this regiment, under a field officer, to proceed up the railroad the next morning early and endeavor to ascertain the strength of the enemy, with orders, however, not to drive in the enemy's pickets or to engage in any action.

Early on the morning of the 28th the companies of Captains Minot and Tappan were placed under the orders of Major Sturgis, and that officer was directed to carry out the above instructions. The companies left camp before 7 o'clock and proceeded upon their destination. At the same time, in compliance with orders from Colonel Amory, Captain Bumstead's company was directed to proceed to the cross-roads leading to the Dover road, with instructions to explore that road and to communicate with Brigadier-General Palmer, whose column was on the Dover road.

At about 12 o'clock I received orders from Colonel Amory to proceed with the rest of the regiment and the Seventeenth Massachusetts Volunteers (Lieutenant-Colonel Fellows commanding) up the railroad to overtake Major Sturgis, and to push on to the cross-roads nearest to the junction of the Dover road with the railroad, with discretionary orders to proceed to the junction. I was instructed to intercept any parties of the enemy that might be driven down this cross-road by General Palmer's column.

The troops immediately started upon the expedition, and upon reaching the cross-roads I found Major Sturgis who reported the enemy in some force in the neighborhood of the junction. That officer had carried out his instructions with the most scrupulous fidelity, having carefully concealed his force from the enemy, so as to give them no warning of our approach, and thus preventing them from receiving re-enforcements, the presence of which at a later period of the day might have been embarrassing. As his men were much exhausted I directed him to leave one company at the point at which I overtook him and to order the others to follow the column slowly. The column then proceeded, driving in the enemy's vedettes and pickets. This duty was performed by Company B, Forty-fifth Regiment, Captain Churchill, the pickets being uniformly posted behind log barricades and uniformly driven out by flanking parties from Company B.

Upon arriving at the cross-roads and learning that General Palmer's column, under Colonel Jones, Fifty-eighth Pennsylvania Volunteers, was pushing up the Dover road, I determined to proceed to the junction. Company F, Captain Daland, was ordered to relieve Company B, in the advance, and the column then pushed forward, one company of the Seventeenth Massachusetts Volunteers being left at the cross-roads. As we approached the junction Lieutenant-Colonel Peabody, in charge of the advance, sent me word that there was an earthwork across the railroad. I immediately ordered a halt and determined to make no attack until Colonel Jones arrived, not knowing what might be the wish of the brigadier-general commanding. The breastwork had no ditch in front, and I inferred that the enemy had no artillery, as they might have used it with effect before this time if they had had any in position. In a few moments the enemy fired a volley from the breastwork upon the advance of Colonel Jones, which was immediately returned, and I then made dispositions for an attack. The breastwork was thrown up across the track and extended some distance to our left. It also ran along the track, crossing the Dover road. I immediately ordered Captain Daland to open fire with his company, stationed on the railroad and deployed as skirmishers on the right and left, which was done very vigorously. I then deployed the companies of Captains Wales and Homans of the Forty-fifth, and subsequently two companies of the Seventeenth, as skirmishers on the left of the railroad, with orders to advance, firing. The firing of these companies was rapid and energetic, and that of the enemy, which was sharp for a time, soon slackened.

A favorable opportunity was then presented for a charge, and as night was approaching it was necessary to decide the affair at once. Company A, Captain Denny, of the Forty-fifth, having the colors of the regiment, had been held in reserve, and was now ordered to fix bayonets and prepare to advance. It came up gallantly along the railroad in column of platoons, supported by a company of the Seventeenth, and as it approached the work the first platoon fired a volley, and then, stooping down, the second fired over the heads of the first. The company then rushed forward with the bayonet, the whole line of skirmishers charging at the same time, and the colors of the regiment were planted upon the work, the enemy giving way. I then communicated with Colonel Jones, and in accordance with orders the whole command marched back to camp.

In this affair the troops under my command sustained a loss of 1 man killed, Private H. M. Putney, of Company F, Forty-fifth Massachusetts (shot through the head), and 2 wounded seriously, Corpl. G. C. Richards, Company E (in the thigh), and Private J. F. Ames, Company K, Forty-fifth Massachusetts Volunteer Militia (in the cheek). One man, Corpl. [William D.] Leatherby, Company K, of the Forty-fifth, received a slight wound in the thigh, and Captain Murdoch, also of the Forty-fifth, acting on the staff of Colonel Amory, received a contusion from a glancing ball. Four of the enemy's dead were found behind the breast-work. The number of his wounded cannot of course be ascertained.

The conduct of the troops throughout this affair was perfectly good. Where all behaved well it would be invidious to particularize. I will only say that I am much indebted to Lieutenant-Colonel Fellows, commanding the Seventeenth Massachusetts Volunteers, for judicious advice and hearty support.

Very respectfully, your obedient servant,

CHARLES R. CODMAN,
Colonel Forty-fifth Massachusetts Volunteer Militia.

Lieutenant PARKINSON,
A. A. A. G., First Brig., First Div., Eighteenth Army Corps.

No. 6.

Reports of Col. J. Richter Jones, Fifty-eighth Pennsylvania Infantry.

HDQRS. FIFTY-EIGHTH REGT. PENNSYLVANIA VOLS.,
Camp at Batchelder's Creek, N. C., May 1, 1863.

SIR: In reference to the forward movement ordered on Tuesday, April 28, with a view to strike any force of the enemy on Sandy Ridge and vicinity on the Dover road, I have the honor to report that I marched at the time designated by you, with the Fifty-eighth Pennsylvania Volunteers, the Twenty-seventh Massachusetts Volunteers, one company of the Forty-fourth Massachusetts, and two companies of the Third New York Cavalry. Expecting to find, as on all previous occasions, an enemy on Sandy Ridge, I moved cautiously, a line of skirmishers in the advance, composed of one company of the Fifty-eighth and one company of the Twenty-seventh, supported by two other companies of the same regiment, the cavalry 300 yards in rear of the first line, the main column 400 yards farther to the rear.

Finding no enemy on the Ridge, which ends about 5½ miles from Core Creek, I advanced beyond, on the road through the pocoson. That road runs principally through swamps, with an occasional oasis of dry ground, and, being chiefly covered with water or very wet mud, is heavy and difficult. It was thus late before we emerged on the drier country toward the railroad crossing. When approaching that point, on the supposition that the column which you had ordered to move on the railroad some two hours earlier than I started must be already in position at the crossing, I allowed my main column to halt and rest, and proceeded with my advanced line and the cavalry. When less than 100 yards from the crossing a sharp fire, converging on the Dover road, was opened from beyond the railroad. My advanced line immediately took cover and began to return the fire; but, supposing our friends necessarily at the crossing and that it must be them firing under mis apprehension, I ordered all whom my voice could reach to cease firing, and also ordered the guidon of the cavalry to be brought forward and waved, so as to manifest our true character beyond mistake. The volley with which the guidon was saluted manifested clearly the true character of the fire on us, and I immediately deployed my two reserve companies on the flanks of the two already in line; sent hastily for my main column, and directed Captain Pond, who volunteered to act as aide, to ascertain the whereabouts of our railroad column; at the same time I endeavored personally to detect the position of the enemy and the character of his defense. Scarcely a man was visible, but his fire in front came from beyond the railroad, while his wings were advanced under cover of woods and brush, the ground in his front being entirely open or affording very imperfect shelter. As soon as my main body approached I detached three companies to deploy as skirmishers and move by a flank on the right of the enemy's line of fire so as to enfilade it, and then to sweep at right angles to the rear and along his line.

Just as this movement commenced, and while I was detaching three other companies to move around his left, a brisk fire was opened from a direction which I felt sure must come from our railroad friends, which Captain Pond, who just then returned, placed beyond doubt. They were advancing at right angles with the enemy's line, who, being at the same time pressed in front by the companies of the Fifty-eighth and Twenty-seventh, soon gave way and retired in disorder. The true character of the enemy's position and defenses now appeared. We found several hundred feet of rifle-pit breastworks on the rear of and parallel with the railroad, but entirely concealed by low bushes and brush, without flank faces, however, though flanked by bushes and woods. This way a kind of outwork, about 75 yards to the rear, is the principal defense, a heavy earthwork of 500 or 600 feet front and embrasure looking down the Dover road, flank faces, and altogether a strong fortification, especially as a swamp on the right, at short musketry range with open ground between, renders a flank movement difficult. Considering the character of the enemy's works it is difficult to imagine why they abandoned them on so feeble a defense, especially as they seemed fully manned with additional men advanced on the flanks of the outer line. It is equally astonishing that our loss in carrying those works could be so small, being 1 killed and 1 wounded of the companies of the Fifty-eighth and none injured of the Twenty-seventh; 1 killed and 3 wounded of the line which advanced on the flank. The four companies in front, however, fought deployed as skirmishers, and took advantage of whatever cover the ground afforded. As to the enemy's loss, 4 were reported to me as dead on the ground, 1 as mortally wounded—since died, I understand—and 1 wounded was brought a prisoner with us, the other wounded having been carried off by themselves.

In this affair the men behaved remarkably well. Those of the Fifty-eighth and Twenty-seventh I can speak of on personal knowledge; the others on information I received on the ground.

The number of the enemy I have no means of estimating, except from their fire, which was that of four or five companies. The people of the neighborhood said there was a regiment there, but I doubt it. They also stated that there was a brigade, with a battery, at Wise's Forks, 2 miles in the rear, which may be true.

Having destroyed the enemy's camp and effected the object of the expedition, I returned leisurely by the Dover road to our bivouac behind Core Creek.

Very respectfully, your obedient servant,

J. RICHTER JONES,
Colonel Fifty-eighth Regiment.

Captain JUDSON, *Assistant Adjutant-General.*

HDQRS. FIFTY-EIGHTH REGT. PENNSYLVANIA VOLS.,
Camp at Batchelder's Creek, N. C., May 1, 1863.

SIR: In reference to the reconnaissance ordered by General Palmer yesterday on the Neuse road in front of Core Creek I have the honor to report:

I proceeded with Companies — and G, Third New York Cavalry, commanded by Captain Pond, in the aggregate about 90 men, toward the Neuse, making a long detour in order to get into the rear of and surprise the cavalry picket at Biddle's, about 6 miles beyond Core Creek. The picket was not there, having been withdrawn on Tuesday evening on the news of the fight on the Dover road. Being unsuccessful in this collateral affair, I moved forward on the Neuse road toward Moseley's Creek. According to the information obtained at Biddle's there was a brigade of infantry, with artillery, at Moseley's Creek, but as I advanced the number reported continually decreased until, about a mile this side, I was told that the enemy had retired entirely after the fight of Tuesday. Advancing cautiously, with part of the cavalry dismounted and deployed as skirmishers, I verified the report and found the position abandoned. The position at Moseley's Creek is naturally strong, there being two branches of the creek, about 50 yards apart, and the works which I found there are two lines of breastworks, one behind each branch. The first line, about 400 feet long, is in part a heavy earthwork with an embrasure, covering the road, but principally a lighter work, good only against musketry, but with a deep rifle-pit in the rear; it has also flanking and enfilading faces. The second work is much heavier; has two embrasures; more flanking fire; broad and deeper water in front, and is altogether a formidable defense. In the rear of the works I found three separate camps, which I burned and destroyed. From the information I received it seems that the enemy (a brigade of infantry without artillery) retired precipitately on Wednesday evening. As my arrangements to return the same day did not allow me to follow the fugitives, I was obliged to rest satisfied with the reports of the people in the neighborhood that there were no regular posts of the enemy short of Kinston, and that Kinston itself was 7 or 8 miles distant. From the trepidation everywhere apparent I have no doubt of my having been able to advance within sight of that place without opposition, and I would have done so if other circumstances had allowed. On my route the inhabitants expressed their opinion freely that the Southern troops had abandoned them, and generally they asked me for written protection.

Having accomplished fully the object of the reconnaissance I returned and reached the bivouac, behind Core Creek, about 9 p. m.

The cavalry are entitled to great praise for this arduous march of 36 miles through a country supposed to be filled with enemies and affording continual opportunities for ambuscade, and with the prospect of ultimately confronting a brigade. They did their duty unflinchingly, and the admirable arrangements made by Captain Pond prevented the scattered guerrillas whom we saw occasionally from using the advantages of the swamps and thickets against us.

Very respectfully, your obedient servant,

J. RICHTER JONES,
Colonel Fifty-eighth Pennsylvania Volunteers.

Captain JUDSON,
Assistant Adjutant-General.

MAY 12–26, 1863.—Operations on the Seaboard and Roanoke Railroad, Va., and skirmishes (15th and 16th) near Carrsville.

REPORTS.

No. 1.—Maj. Gen. John A. Dix, U. S. Army, commanding the Department of Virginia.
No. 2.—Maj. Gen. John J. Peck, U. S. Army, commanding at Suffolk.

No. 1.

Report of Maj. Gen. John A. Dix, U. S. Army, commanding the Department of Virginia.

FORT MONROE, *May* 16, 1863—1 p. m.

Colonel Foster is covering our work, which is in good progress on the railroad near Carrsville. He has been engaged with the enemy more or less. For two days a lively artillery fire has been kept up on our workmen. Yesterday the enemy advanced within canister range, but was driven back with considerable loss. On our side a caisson was riddled, a horse killed, and 9 men wounded.

The iron is arriving in Norfolk. When we get on the other road we shall probably have some sharp fighting.

JOHN A. DIX,
Major-General.

Maj. Gen. H. W. HALLECK,
    General-in-Chief.

—

[Addenda.]

Extract from "Record of Events" of Seventh Army Corps.*

May 12.—Forces under Col. R. S. Foster went to Carrsville to cover working parties employed in taking up the rails on the railroad between Suffolk and the Blackwater.

May 16.—Surgeon Hand, medical director, and Captain Stevenson captured by the guerrillas getting in rear of the troops.

*   *   *   *   *   *   *

May 26.—The expedition commenced returning to their camp, the object of their mission being entirely accomplished; 36 miles of railroad were secured.

*   *   *   *   *   *   *

———

No. 2.

Reports of Maj. Gen. John J. Peck, U. S. Army, commanding at Suffolk.

MAY 15, 1863.

Colonel Foster reports good progress up to daylight. The enemy fired about sixty shot and shell down the railway between 5 and 7 p. m. no material damage. An attempt on his picket line failed.

JOHN J. PECK,
Major-General.

Major-General DIX.

———

* From Return for the month of May, 1863.

MAY 16, 1863.

The work on the road has proceeded slowly from the damage done by the rebels; besides, Colonel Foster's troops have been engaged more or less for two days. The enemy has kept up a lively artillery fire on the track most of the time. Yesterday they advanced upon his position within canister range, not suspecting his amount of artillery, and were driven back with much loss. One of Davis' caissons is riddled with bullets; 1 horse killed, 9 slightly wounded. Our loss is very slight. Have deemed it best to press the work, making that the object rather than engaging the enemy at that distance. Colonel Foster has managed thus far with great judgment.

JOHN J. PECK,
Major-General.

Maj. Gen. JOHN A. DIX.

—

MAY 18, 1863.

In the skirmish of Saturday General Jenkins' loss was 17 killed and about 30 or 40 wounded; ours none, or very slight.

JOHN J. PECK
Major-General.

General DIX.

MAY 15, 1863.—Capture of the Steamers Emily and Arrow.

REPORTS.

No. 1.—Capt. Francis E. Porter, Eighth Massachusetts Infantry.
No. 2.—Capt. W. Dewees Roberts, Eleventh Pennsylvania Cavalry.

No. 1.

Report of Capt. Francis E. Porter, Eighth Massachusetts Infantry.

GENERAL: I have just learned that the steamers Emily and Arrow were captured by guerrillas, at Currituck Canal, on Friday.
Yours, respectfully,

F. E. PORTER,
Captain, Commanding Post.

Brig. Gen. H. W. WESSELLS.

[Indorsement.]

DISTRICT OF ALBEMARLE,
Plymouth, N. C., May 17, 1863—7 p. m.

Respectfully referred to Headquarters Department of North Carolina. Two gunboats from Captain Flusser's squadron will start in two hours for Roanoke and Currituck, using the North Shore as a tender. One hundred and fifty infantry will embark in the boats, to attempt the recapture or destruction of the Arrow and Emily. I am not in possession of the details. The gunboats are the Commodore Perry and Valley City.

H. W. WESSELLS,
Brigadier-General Volunteers, Commanding.

No. 2.

Report of Capt. W. Dewees Roberts, Eleventh Pennsylvania Cavalry.

CAMDEN COURT-HOUSE AND SHILOH, N. C.,
May 17, 1863.

MAJOR : I have the honor to make the following report from the expedition sent out yesterday afternoon to intercept the party supposed to have captured the Emily and Arrow.

The Pasquotank Guerrillas crossed the Pasquotank River about 5 miles below Elizabeth City on Friday morning, the 15th instant. About 4 o'clock in the afternoon they captured one of the above-named boats in Currituck Canal, and with her pushed out into North River, where they captured the other boat, taking her crew prisoners. They then landed their prisoners, and, under a sufficient guard, appear to have taken them across the lower end of Camden County to near Shiloh and from thence across the Pasquotank River to Elizabeth City, where they arrived on the morning of the 16th instant (yesterday). Hearing of a Federal force in the vicinity, under Lieutenant Titus, they again went down the river and landed on the south side of the Pasquotank. The captured boats seem to have been taken down the Albemarle Sound and up the Chowan River. The rebel crew declared their intention of so doing, but if overtaken by our forces they would then destroy the boats.

The party capturing these boats seem to have been about 40 of the Pasquotank Guerrillas, Captain Elliott commanding, and were guided by Captain Sanderlin, of the Camden Guerrillas. None of the Camden company, except the captain, were engaged in the capture.

I have received this information from several persons living in the vicinity of Currituck Bridge, and the statements of all being the same I deem it entirely reliable.

I am, very respectfully, your obedient servant,

W. DEWEES ROBERTS,
Captain, Eleventh Pennsylvania Volunteer Cavalry.

Maj. F. A. STRATTON,
Commanding at South Mills, N. C.

[Indorsements.]

HEADQUARTERS, *South Mills, N. C., May* 17, 1863.

Respectfully forwarded to Brigadier-General Viele.

Captain Roberts was sent with one company of cavalry and a howitzer to intercept the captors of the Emily and Arrow immediately upon the receipt of General Viele's dispatch on yesterday, but the notice was not soon enough to enable my party to intercept the rebels. Lieutenant Titus and one company was also out in the vicinity of Elizabeth City where the rebels landed, but hearing of his presence there they re-embarked and escaped, probably through the Sound.

FRANKLIN A. STRATTON,
Major, 11th Pa. Cav., Comdg. Detachment at South Mills, N. C.

HEADQUARTERS, *Norfolk, Va., May* 18, 1863.

Respectfully forwarded for the information of the major-general commanding the department.

I sent a dispatch to Major Stratton, at South Mills, as soon as I learned that the Emily and Arrow had been captured.

EGBERT L. VIELE,
Brigadier-General, Commanding.

MAY 15, 1863.—Expedition from West Point to Robinson's Plantation, King and Queen County, Va.

Report of Brig. Gen. George H. Gordon, U. S Army.

HEADQUARTERS UNITED STATES FORCES,
West Point, Va., May 16, 1863.

GENERAL: Last night I sent out a small expedition to capture if possible—if not, destroy— many hundred bushels of grain which a negro reported to be in a barn. Running up the left bank of the York River, about 2 miles below the mouth of the Mattapony, Captain Babcock, of the gunboat Morse, carried my infantry to its destination and co-operated with his men and boats. The grain was found stored in a large granary; it was in bulk. The distance inland was about 1 mile. It was found impossible to carry the grain away; therefore the building, with its contents, was destroyed. Captain Motley, of my staff, who accompanied the expedition, estimates the amount of grain destroyed at over 600 bushels. The barn was very large and a very fine one, securely locked and barred. The negro, who proved a faithful guide, says the proprietor, Mr. Robinson, has been in the habit of shipping grain to Richmond; that he sent a schooner load just before my arrival.

I am satisfied that the occupation of this Point by our forces and the river by the gunboats will compel rebels to resort to land travel, if that be possible, to transport the large amounts of grain now on the river bank awaiting transportation to Richmond.

The company of infantry I sent out was Captain Wheeler's, of the One hundred and forty-second Regiment New York Volunteers, Colonel Curtis.

I am indebted to Captain Babcock, of the Morse, for information that led to the capture of this grain.

I am, general, very truly, your obedient servant,

GEO. H. GORDON,
Brigadier-General, Comdg. U. S. Forces, West Point, Va.

Maj. Gen. JOHN A. DIX,
Fort Monroe, Va.

MAY 15-28, 1863.—Operations on the Norfolk and Petersburg Railroad and skirmishes (17th) near Providence Church and (23d) at Antioch Church and Barber's Cross-Roads, Va.

REPORTS.

No. 1.—Maj. Gen. John A. Dix, U. S. Army, commanding the Department of Virginia.

No. 2.—Maj. Gen. John J. Peck, U. S. Army, commanding at Suffolk.

No. 3.—Itinerary of the Reserve Brigade, Department of Virginia, Brig. Gen. Isaac J. Wistar, U. S. Army, commanding, May 15–28.

No. 1.

Report of Maj. Gen. John A. Dix, U. S. Army, commanding the Department of Virginia.

FORT MONROE, VA., *May* 24, 1863.

The enemy, with two regiments of infantry and two field pieces, attacked a detachment of our forces under General Dodge, on the Petersburg Railroad, 5 miles this side of Zuni, yesterday, and was promptly and handsomely repulsed. The rails we are removing are very heavy, but they will all be at Suffolk by Thursday.

> JOHN A. DIX,
> *Major-General.*

Maj. Gen. H. W. HALLECK,
  General-in-Chief.

No. 2.

Reports of Maj. Gen. John J. Peck, U. S. Army, commanding at Suffolk.

MAY 17, 1863.

General Dodge does not think there is any large force about Smithfield. Major Patton had taken 5 men and 6 horses; when returning, his rear guard was surprised and driven on the command, and in the fight a bridge broke, letting down about 12 of his party, making confusion. The prisoners escaped.

> JOHN J. PECK,
> *Major-General.*

Major-General DIX.

MAY 18, 1863.

General Dodge went out with all the force of cavalry, about 140, to Smithfield. On the return of the party, Major Patton was attacked by about 300 in a swamp and had a heroic fight. He was wounded in three places and his horse wounded several times. His men did well.

> JOHN J. PECK,
> *Major-General.*

General DIX.

MAY 18, 1863.

I sent General Dodge to Scott's Mill and he made a very bold reconnaissance with only about 140 men. It was on the return that the attack was made on the Cypress Mill road, 3 miles from Providence Church—not on our maps. Major Patton fought well. His move was signaled and they were ready for him.

> JOHN J. PECK,
> *Major-General.*

General DIX.

MAY 20, 1863.

Major Stratton reports the affair at Newby's Bridge as highly creditable on the part of Lieutenant Titus and his small detachment. Lieutenant Beatty, so severely wounded and left, has been brought in and is doing well. They had 5 killed and a number wounded, while our loss was 4 wounded.

> JOHN J. PECK,
> *Major-General.*

Major-General DIX.

MAY 24, 1863.

At the same moment of attacking the advance at Antioch Church a demonstration was made at Barber's Cross-Roads, where a regiment is watching the approaches centering there. Both failed, and the enemy was repulsed with considerable loss. At the church we lost 1 captured and 3 wounded, and captured a few prisoners.

Every rail beyond Windsor is removed.

JOHN J. PECK,
Major-General.

Major-General Dix.

No. 3.

Itinerary of the Reserve Brigade, Department of Virginia, Brig. Gen. Isaac J. Wistar, U. S. Army, commanding, May 15–28.

May 15.—By direction of Major-General Peck, Colonel Wardrop was sent, with the Ninety-ninth New York Volunteers and Nineteenth Wisconsin Volunteers, to assist in protecting working parties engaged in tearing up the tracks of the railroad between Suffolk and the Blackwater.

May 20.—The Ninth Vermont Volunteers and the One hundred and eighteenth New York Volunteers were sent, by order of Major-General Peck, on the same duty, under the command of Brigadier-General Dodge.

May 26.—The Nineteenth Wisconsin Volunteers returned, and May 27 the other regiments; but the Ninety-ninth New York Volunteers were ordered out again immediately.

May 28.—The Ninety-ninth New York Volunteers returned to camp.

MAY 19–22, 1863.—Expedition from Gloucester Point into Matthews County, Va.

REPORTS.

No. 1.—Maj. Gen. Erasmus D. Keyes, U. S. Army, commanding Fourth Army Corps.

No. 2.—Col. Judson Kilpatrick, Second New York Cavalry, commanding Cavalry Brigade.

No. 3.—Lieut. James H. Gillis, U. S. Navy.

No. 1.

Report of Maj. Gen. Erasmus D. Keyes, U. S. Army, commanding Fourth Army Corps.

HEADQUARTERS FOURTH CORPS,
Fort Yorktown, Va., May 23, 1863.

SIR: I have the honor to report that a combined expedition left Gloucester Point on the night of the 19th instant and returned yesterday morning under the following instructions :

A combined expedition will set out to-night for Matthews County. The cavalry and a section of artillery, supported by 200 infantry, to leave Gloucester Point at 10

---

* From Return for May, 1863.

a. m., will be under the immed.ate orders of Col. J. Kilpatrick, commanding cavalry brigade. The gunboats and ferry-boat, under the command of Lieutenant-Commander Gillis, U. S. Navy, will have on board 200 infantry subject to the orders of Lieut. Col. C. C. Suydam, of my staff. A small supply of intrenching tools will be on board, with some extra ammunition for the field artillery. The infantry will carry 100 rounds of ammunition per man, and all the troops will have two days' cooked rations.

Colonel Kilpatrick will consult with Lieutenant-Commander Gillis and Lieutenant-Colonel Suydam in regard to the movement necessary to insure prompt and effective co-operation. Besides inflicting as much injury as possible on armed enemies the detachments of the expedition will capture and bring in all animals and supplies needful to our troops that may be found, but will not wantonly burn or pillage anywhere.

E. D. KEYES,
Major-General, Commanding Fourth Army Corps.

The cavalry was from the New York Harris Light and Twelfth Illinois. The artillery was commanded by Captain Mink, of the First New York Volunteer Artillery, and the two battalions of infantry were from the One hundred and Sixty-ninth Pennsylvania Drafted Militia and the Fourth Delaware, commanded, respectively, by Majors Smyth and La Motte.

The expedition was conducted with spirit by the officers, and the men behaved well. Only some straggling parties of the enemy were seen. One guerrilla was killed and 2 of our men were wounded. About 300 horses and mules were captured, besides about 150 head of horned cattle and the same number of sheep. A small amount of grain was brought in, and a large amount of grain and forage collected for the rebel Government was destroyed. Five mills stored with grain and flour were burned.

I have the honor to be, sir, your most obedient servant,

E. D. KEYES,
Major-General, Commanding Fourth Army Corps.

Maj. Gen. JOHN A. DIX,
Commanding Department of Virginia.

No. 2.

Report of Col. Judson Kilpatrick, Second New York Cavalry, commanding Cavalry Brigade.

HEADQUARTERS CAVALRY BRIGADE,
Fort Yorktown, Va., May 22, 1863.

GENERAL: I have the honor to report the entire success of the expedition under my command sent out by you on the morning of the 20th instant.

I left Gloucester Point at 1 a. m.; reached Gloucester Court-House at daylight; passed down into Matthews County, and communicated with Lieutenant-Colonel Suydam, in command of the forces sent by water, at 9 a. m., at the head of North River.

Having posted pickets across the neck from North River to Piankatank, I proceeded to Matthews Court-House without opposition, and again communicated with Lieutenant-Colonel Suydam. I returned to

Gloucester Court-House on the evening of the 21st, having scouted the whole of Matthews and a portion of Gloucester Counties, finding only straggling parties of the enemy.

The entire expedition returned at 8 a. m. this morning, without the loss of a man. Two men of the Second New York were wounded by a guerrilla; the guerrilla was killed. We captured and brought with us 300 horses and mules, 150 head of beef cattle, and the same of sheep. Large quantities of grain and forage collected for the rebel Government were destroyed.

The officers and men of the command deserve great credit for the prompt and soldierly manner in which every order was obeyed and duty performed.

Respectfully submitted.

J. KILPATRICK,
Colonel, Commanding Cavalry Brigade.

Maj. Gen. E. D. KEYES,
Commanding Fourth Army Corps.

No. 3.

Report of Lieut. James H. Gillis, U. S. Navy.

U. S. GUNBOAT COMMODORE MORRIS,
Off Yorktown, Va., May 22, 1863.

SIR: I have to report that at the request of Major-General Keyes I have acted in conjunction with Brigadier-General Kilpatrick, by covering his operations in Matthews County. The object of the expedition was to mount all the dismounted men under his command.

On the morning of the 20th instant I took on board 100 men from the Fourth Delaware Volunteers, under Major La Motte, and with the Winnisimmet in company, she having on board 100 of the same regiment, proceeded to North River, where we arrived at 5.30 a. m. I remained at this place until communication was had with General Kilpatrick, and in the evening I went into East River to cover his operations there. I remained at this place until about 9 o'clock the next morning and then started for the rendezvous on North River. After I arrived some horses were brought on board the Winnisimmet and we lay quiet all day waiting to hear from the different squads that had been sent out. At 6 o'clock, all being ready for a departure, I took on board 200 of the Fourth Delaware and started for Yorktown, where I arrived at 12.30 last night.

About 250 horses, 150 head of cattle, and a large number of sheep were captured by the land forces in their march across the country.

General Kilpatrick and Lieutenant-Colonel Suydam, in obedience to orders issued to them, destroyed all the property which they considered useful to the rebels.

Very respectfully, your obedient servant,

J. H. GILLIS,
Lieutenant, Commanding.

B. C. CHETWOOD,
Lieut. Col. and Inspector General, Fourth Army Corps.

MAY 20–23, 1863.—Demonstration upon Kinston, N. C., and skirmishes (22d) at Gum Swamp and (23d) at Batchelder's Creek.

REPORTS.

No. 1.—Maj. Gen. John G. Foster, U. S. Army, commanding the Department of North Carolina.

No. 2.—Col. J. Richter Jones, Fifty-eighth Pennsylvania Infantry, of skirmish at Gum Swamp.

No. 3.—Itinerary of the First Division, Eighteenth Army Corps, Brig. Gen. Innis N. Palmer commanding, May 20–23.

No. 4.—Col. George H. Peirson, Fifth Massachusetts Infantry, commanding Second Brigade.

No. 5.—Col. Josiah Pickett, Twenty-fifth Massachusetts Infantry.

No. 6.—Col. Silas P. Richmond, Third Massachusetts Infantry, Second Brigade, Fifth Division, of operations May 23.

No. 1.

Reports of Maj. Gen. John G. Foster, U. S. Army, commanding the Department of North Carolina.

HEADQUARTERS EIGHTEENTH ARMY CORPS,
New Berne, N. C., May 22, 1863.

GENERAL : I have the honor to report that, finding the enemy's troops were constantly being drained from this department for Virginia, and finding that I could safely make a demonstration toward Kinston and capture the enemy's picket regiment, I ordered Col. J. Richter Jones, commanding outpost (Fifty-eighth Pennsylvania Volunteers), to endeavor to surround the enemy at Gum Swamp, and, if capturing it, to make a demonstration as if attacking in force, carefully guarding a safe and sure retreat. I re-enforced him with four regiments, four pieces of artillery, and three companies of cavalry, and I am happy to say that so far the plan has been successfully carried out. Colonel Jones surrounded the Fifty-eighth North Carolina, attacking them on four sides, and succeeded in capturing between 200 and 300 prisoners.

I forward this meager account by this opportunity, and will have the honor to send the further details as soon as they are ascertained.

Colonel Jones is some 7 miles from Kinston, threatening that place. His retreat, should he be forced to fall back, is perfectly secure.

In my previous letters I omitted to mention, owing to the press of business and the fact that I was just going on a tour of inspection, a very successful little affair of four companies Third New York Cavalry, under Lieutenant-Colonel Lewis, about the 7th of this month.* They were ordered to make a circuit from New Berne to the White Oak River via Pollocksville and Young's Cross-Roads and return by the way of Newport. Colonel Lewis, learning where a company of the enemy's cavalry were, which had gone from Kinston to endeavor to cut the railroad communication between this point and Beaufort, charged them and succeeded in killing 2, capturing 14, and taking 36 horses, and without the loss of a man killed or wounded on our side.

I have the honor to be, very respectfully, your obedient servant,
J. G. FOSTER,
Major-General, Commanding.

Maj. Gen. H. W. HALLECK,
General-in-Chief, U. S. Army, Washington, D. C.

---

* Reference probably to skirmish at Peletier's Mill, May 5.

HEADQUARTERS EIGHTEENTH ARMY CORPS,
New Berne, N. C., June 2, 1863.

GENERAL : Referring to my brief report of May 22, I have the honor to report that, learning from Col. J. Richter Jones, commanding outpost, that he deemed it possible to capture the enemy's outpost regiments at Gum Swamp, 8 miles from Kinston, I ordered Colonel Lee's brigade, consisting of the Fifth, Twenty-fifth, Twenty-seventh, and Forty-sixth Massachusetts Regiments, three pieces of Riggs' battery, and a battalion of cavalry, to report to him.

Colonel Jones ordered the Fifth, Twenty-fifth, and Forty-sixth, with the artillery and cavalry, under command of Colonel Peirson, Fifth Massachusetts, to advance up the railroad and Dover roads to attack the enemy's works in the front, while the Fifty-eighth Pennsylvania Volunteers and the Twenty-seventh Massachusetts Volunteers, under the immediate command of Colonel Jones, took a path through the swamp to reach the rear of the enemy's position.

The main column, under Colonel Peirson, met the enemy's pickets at daylight of the 22d, and, driving them in, commenced an attack on the front. Colonel Jones, with his command, owing to the character of the road they had taken (the men having to go by single file), did not arrive at the desired place until 9 a. m. On arriving in rear of the enemy's position Colonel Jones deployed such portions of his command as could be used to advantage, opened fire, and advanced. The enemy fired a few desultory volleys, then broke and fled in great confusion, taking to the swamps, and escaping by paths known only to themselves. On hearing the firing of Colonel Jones' command Colonel Peirson advanced his command and entered the works in front. After securing the prisoners (165) and spoils, demolishing the enemy's works and resting his men, Colonel Jones made a demonstration and show of advance on Kinston. At dusk the same evening his pickets were driven in and he found himself attacked by the enemy in force and with artillery. He, in obedience to orders, at once retired, followed by the enemy, and reached our outpost line without loss. Colonel Lee's brigade was put on cars in waiting and returned to their camps.

The enemy, mortified at the success of Colonel Jones, and being strongly re-enforced from Goldsborough, attacked our outpost line on the p. m. of the 23d. I sent out a supporting force to Colonel Jones and the enemy were repulsed at every point, but with great loss to us and the service in the death of Colonel Jones, who was shot through the heart as he was leading on two companies of his regiment to dislodge the enemy from a position he had taken up. By the death of Colonel Jones a most brave, zealous, and able officer has been lost to the service and to this department.

I have the honor to inclose a list of casualties and a list of prisoners and articles captured.

I have the honor to be, very respectfully, your obedient servant,

J. G. FOSTER,
Major-General, Commanding.

Maj. Gen. H. W. HALLECK,
General-in-Chief, U. S. Army, Washington, D. C.

[Inclosure.]

Killed	2
Wounded	5
Missing	1
Total	**8**

Prisoners	16~
Horses	28
Ambulances and teams	3
Baggage wagons	2
Muskets and equipments	80
12-pounder howitzer with limber	1
Rounds of ammunition	11,000

No. 2.

Report of Col. J. Richter Jones, Fifty-eighth Pennsylvania Infantry, of skirmish at Gum Swamp.

CAMP AT GUM SWAMP, EIGHT MILES FROM KINSTON,
May 22, 1863—12 m.

SIR : I have the honor to report that my attempt to cut off the enemy's troops at Gum Swamp has partially succeeded.

I made the detour successfully with the Fifty-eighth Pennsylvania and Twenty-seventh Massachusetts, and attacked the enemy in the rear; but, owing to my defective knowledge of the ground, he was able to defend himself some time under cover of a swamp, and when finally broken his men mostly escaped.

However, we captured 165 prisoners, and almost took General Ransom himself, who was accidentally at the post. The enemy's regiments engaged were the Fifty-sixth North Carolina and Twenty-fifth North Carolina, and on our part the Fifty-eighth Pennsylvania and Twenty-seventh Massachusetts. Our loss is small—2 wounded, of the Fifty-eighth. Of the enemy, I have 6 wounded reported to me.

Our [I] propose reconnoitering Wise's Cross-Roads this afternoon, and to-morrow returning to our old lines. A particular report hereafter.

Very respectfully, your obedient servant,

J. RICHTER JONES,
Commanding Outposts.

Lieut. Col. SOUTHARD HOFFMAN,
Assistant Adjutant-General, Eighteenth Army Corps.

No. 3.

Itinerary of the First Division, Eighteenth Army Corps, Brig. Gen. Innis N. Palmer commanding, May 20–23.*

May 20.—The Twenty-fifth and Forty-sixth Regiments, of the Second Brigade, which were commanded by Colonel Peirson, of the Fifth Massachusetts Volunteer Militia, in accordance with orders from Headquarters Eighteenth Army Corps, moved at midnight to Batchelder's Creek, the commanding officer of the detachment reporting to Col. J. R. Jones, of the Fifty-eighth Pennsylvania, commanding outpost.

May 21.—The remainder of the Second Brigade (accompanied by Lieutenant Horton, acting commissary of musters, and Lieutenant Allen, aide-de-camp on the division staff), consisting of the Twenty-seventh

---

* From Return for May, 1863.

Massachusetts Volunteers and the Fifth Massachusetts Volunteer Militia, was transported by railroad to White's house, about 1 mile from Core Creek, where they were afterward joined by the remainder of the brigade and the Fifty-eighth Pennsylvania, with some cavalry and artillery. At dusk the Twenty-seventh was sent, with the Fifty-eighth Pennsylvania, both under the immediate command of Colonel Jones, of the Fifty-eighth Pennsylvania, by an unfrequented path to the rear of the enemy's outpost, at Gum Swamp, some 8 miles from Kinston, N. C. At midnight the remainder of the column moved up the Dover road (to which they had previously marched from the railroad) to attack the enemy in front.

May 22.—At daybreak the advance of the United States troops on the Dover road encountered the enemy's pickets and drove them in. The main body then came up and annoyed the enemy with desultory skirmish firing until about 10 a. m., when Colonel Jones (who had succeeded in reaching the enemy's rear) made a dash upon their position, and, in conjunction with the troops in front, succeeded in capturing 165 prisoners. Our column now slowly retired, closely followed by the enemy with cavalry and artillery. He shelled our rear for some time, but without effect, and about 9 p. m. our troops bivouacked behind Core Creek.

May 23.—At daylight our pickets were attacked, but the enemy's advance was driven back by a few well-directed shell. A move was then made toward the railroad, but it was soon discovered that the enemy had crossed Core Creek, on the line of the railroad, and were reoccupying in force. Accordingly Colonel Jones, wishing to avoid another action, made his way through a dense swamp, striking the railroad several miles below White's house, and, taking the cars awaiting there, returned to New Berne about 5 p. m. The prisoners on their arrival were paroled by the following staff officers of this division: Captain Judson, assistant adjutant-general; Lieutenant Horton, acting commissary of musters; Lieutenant Allen, acting aide-de-camp. The pickets at Batchelder's Creek were shortly after attacked, and the Forty-fifth Regiment Massachusetts Volunteer Militia, of the First Brigade, was sent out.

No. 4.

Report of Col. George H. Peirson, Fifth Massachusetts Infantry, commanding Second Brigade.

HDQRS. SECOND BRIG., FIRST DIV., EIGHTEENTH A. C.,
New Berne, N. C., May 27, 1863.

By reason of the lamented death of Col. J. Richter Jones, Fifty-eighth Pennsylvania Volunteers, a most gallant, earnest, devoted, and loyal-hearted soldier and patriot, and the commander of the late expedition to the enemy's outpost, known as Gum Swamp, it devolves upon the undersigned, being the senior officer present, to make as complete a report thereof as possible for the information of the commanding general. The forces comprising the expedition consisted of Lee's brigade (Twenty-fifth, Twenty-seventh, Fifth, and Forty-sixth Massachusetts Regiments), under the immediate command of the undersigned; the Fifty-eighth Pennsylvania Volunteers, under command of Lieutenant-Colonel Curtiss; three pieces of Battery H, Third New York Artillery, under

command of Lieut. John D. Clark; and four companies of the Third
New York Cavalry and Allis' battery, under command of Captain
Jacobs.

The Twenty-fifth and Forty-sixth Regiments, with the artillery, left
New Berne at midnight of the 20th instant and arrived at Batchelder's
Creek at daybreak on the morning of the 21st.

The Twenty-seventh and Fifth Regiments arrived at Batchelder's
Creek by rail at 8 o'clock on the 21st, and soon after the cavalry reported near the creek, on the Neuse road. Colonel Jones then took
command, sent forward by rail the Twenty-seventh and Fifth Regiments
to White's house, in the vicinity of a mile from Core Creek; the cavalry and artillery by the Dover road, and subsequently, on the return of
the train, transported the remaining infantry to White's house. From
there, about 5 o'clock, the Twenty-seventh Regiment was sent up the
railroad to a depot on Core Creek, there to halt and await further orders. The remaining regiments marched to Core Creek, on the Dover
road, where we joined the Fifty-eighth Pennsylvania, previously sent
forward by Colonel Jones.

The object of the expedition was to surround and capture a rebel
regiment at Gum Swamp, the outpost of the enemy, 8 miles from Kinston. I have now the honor to state in detail, so far as I am able, the
means taken to accomplish it.

It was decided to send two regiments by an unfrequented and circuitous path to the enemy's rear, while the main column moved up and
occupied the enemy's attention and prevented his escape in front; both
columns were to arrive at the enemy's intrenchments as near daybreak
as possible on the morning of the 22d, and thus make a joint attack
front and rear. Accordingly, at dusk on the 21st, Colonel Jones
moved at the head of his column, consisting of the Fifty-eighth Pennsylvania and Twenty-seventh Massachusetts, which he subsequently
joined at the depot, and stealthily proceeded, under cover of the night
and by direction of a faithful guide, to gain the enemy's rear.

Not being able to state from personal knowledge the movements and
doings of this column I quote so much of the reports of Lieutenant-
Colonels Lyman and Curtiss as appertains to this:

FROM THE REPORT OF LIEUTENANT-COLONEL LYMAN.

At 8 o'clock Colonel Jones, with his regiment, joined us, when the march commenced. We left the railroad to our right and took a path through the woods and
swamp running, in its general direction, parallel with the railroad and I should judge
from 1 to 3 miles from it. The path was almost impenetrable for a large part of the
way, and it was with great difficulty we succeeded in getting through. The guide
is deserving of great praise for bringing us out at the point indicated, showing a
thorough knowledge of the country. We arrived at a point about 1 mile in rear of
the enemy's works at 7 o'clock in the morning, only halting during the night to clear
our way. The march was necessarily slow and very tedious; the distance was said
to be 14 miles; in my opinion it was much farther. Here the men were allowed to rest
for a half hour to eat their breakfast. Moving on to within a short distance of the
breastwork Colonel Jones ordered me to send four companies to hold the Dover road
to prevent an attack upon our rear by the enemy coming from Kinston. I detailed
Companies B, C, G, and K, under command of Captain Caswell, and sent them as
directed; three more companies of the regiment were ordered to advance and take
possession of the railroad at a point above the works. Companies H, I, and D were
sent forward under command of Captain Sanford. The remaining companies of the
regiment were held in reserve for the support of Captain Sanford under my own orders.
Captain Sanford came upon the enemy almost immediately, directly in front of his
advance; they having retreated from their works and taken position behind the railroad embankment, he attacked them immediately. A brisk musketry fire was kept up
for a short time on both sides, when Captain Sanford ordered a charge with the bayonet, which was done in splendid style, the enemy retreating to the woods, our men

following and taking a number of prisoners. As soon as a charge was made I took the reserve farther to the left, so as to cut off the enemy's retreat upon the railroad above Captain Sanford's position. Most of the prisoners were taken between and in front of these two detachments.

FROM THE REPORT OF LIEUTENANT-COLONEL CURTISS.

The two regiments turned off to the left of the railroad into a kind of path, which was not often traveled. We pursued the wanderings of this path, streams, swamps, swales, and ditches, where it seemed impossible for man to pass. The great difficulty of moving, except by single file, prevented our arrival at the works until about 10 o'clock a. m., when Colonel Jones, who commanded the expedition, directed that two companies from the Fifty-eighth, then under my command, to wit, Company I, under the command of Lieut. W. W. Wells, and Company K, to be sent forward, under the command of Capt. Cecil Clay. These companies immediately deployed as skirmishers and advanced cautiously, under cover of the wood, until they arrived at a cleared field near the railroad and within plain view of the enemy's works. Both companies quickly opened fire, and then under a double-quick charged upon the enemy, capturing one piece of artillery while the officer in charge was endeavoring to discharge it upon us. Company I, commanded by Lieutenant Wells, arrived at the piece, having the shortest distance to go, a little in advance of Company K, which was making with all possible speed to capture the piece. The enemy fled terror-stricken, after discharging their pieces, in all directions into the adjacent swamps, except the rebel lieutenant commanding the artillery, who was vainly endeavoring to discharge his piece upon our advancing column, but which was wrested from him and captured, together with six horses, which had become detached from the piece, and with their drivers were endeavoring to flee.

The other column, under my own immediate command, moved from Core Creek at midnight on the 21st, and at daybreak encountered the enemy's pickets about 1 mile from their intrenched position at Gum Swamp. The column moved up steadily to within 500 or 600 yards of the intrenchments and were there deployed—the Twenty-fifth on the extreme right, the Fifth on the extreme left, and the Forty-sixth in support of the artillery in the center; the cavalry were placed within supporting distance in the rear. My object was simply to attract the attention of the enemy and as far as possible to keep them in ignorance of our real intention. Accordingly I ordered each regiment to send forward skirmishers and draw the fire of the enemy, keeping themselves protected as much as possible. Desultory firing was thus kept up for several hours, with trifling damage to ourselves and probably to the enemy. About half past 9 or 10 rapid firing was heard in the rear of the enemy. Judging that Colonel Jones had succeeded in reaching the desired position, I moved forward the Twenty-fifth Massachusetts on the right and the Fifth Massachusetts on the left, and ordered them to be prepared, if necessary, to charge the intrenchments. The Forty-sixth Massachusetts were ordered to support the Twenty-fifth, advancing farther to the front; Colonel Pickett, commanding Twenty-fifth, prudently threw forward skirmishers to ascertain if the works were abandoned. The skirmishers reporting that the enemy had left their first line I ordered forward the regiments rapidly to gather up the fruits of the victory. On entering the work we met detachments of the Twenty-seventh Massachusetts and Fifty-eighth Pennsylvania bringing in prisoners, many of whom they had captured by brilliantly charging them.

Detached squads were sent into the swamps to hunt out and capture those of the enemy who were there concealed; many prisoners were taken in this manner.

The force of the enemy, from the information received from prisoners, appears to have been between 600 and 700. The escape of so many was principally owing to the fact that the detachment of the Fifty-eighth Pennsylvania sent down the Dover road to attack directly in the rear routed the enemy before another detachment of the Twenty-seventh Massachusetts had reached the railroad on the left.

Colonel Jones, as soon as he could communicate with our column, ordered forward the cavalry, but the enemy, before the cavalry could overtake them, had proceeded too far to be cut off.

The whole force remained at and near these works until after 5 o'clock p. m., many of the men employed in demolishing the works, the others being allowed to rest. At this time our pickets were attacked by artillery and infantry and driven in. The Twenty-seventh and Fifty-eighth, then in bivouac on the other side of the creek, joined the main column, and a disposition was made of the whole force to resist an attack. After opening with artillery upon the enemy, who were in considerable force on the railroad, the column slowly retired, one piece of Battery H being in the rear of the infantry and one company of cavalry, under command of Captain Willson, covering the rear of the column. The enemy closely followed and opened with artillery upon our column, fortunately doing no harm, to which Lieutenant Clark replied with a few shots. Another column, apparently of considerable strength, moved down the railroad on the right. At 10 o'clock p. m. we crossed Core Creek and encamped for the night, being undisturbed by the enemy. A little after daybreak on the morning of the 23d the enemy's skirmishers engaged ours at the creek, but a few shell from our artillery silenced their skirmish firing altogether.

Colonel Jones had previously determined to move his command in two columns from Core Creek, the one on the Dover road to Batchelder's Creek and the other by the cross-roads to the railroad and thence by cars to New Berne. In the opinion of Colonel Jones the enemy were not posted in any very considerable strength at this creek, and hence he did not deem it necessary to vary from his previous plans. Accordingly Colonel Jones, with the artillery, cavalry, and Fifty-eighth Pennsylvania, guarding the prisoners and baggage train, moved leisurely down the Dover road to Batchelder's Creek without the least molestation from the enemy. The main column (Lee's brigade), under my immediate command, took the cross-road leading to the railroad, distant some 3 miles. Colonel Pickett, being at the head, sent forward one company as an advance guard, with orders to proceed to the railroad and report the condition of things there. In a few moments messengers came back from Lieutenant Hunt, Twenty-seventh Regiment, who had been left with 20 men at the Core Creek railroad bridge, with the information that the enemy had driven in his pickets and that three regiments were coming down the railroad track with the very evident intention of commanding the road, or, at all events, of attacking our left and rear before we could reach the cars. Judging that it was most wise under the circumstances to avoid a collision with the enemy, inasmuch as a victory even would have been a sacrifice of men and barren of any substantial benefits, and the more certainly to prevent their getting between our column and the cars, then in waiting in the vicinity of White's house, on consultation with Colonel Pickett, Twenty-fifth Massachusetts, and my staff officers, Captain Bartlett and Lieutenant Myrick, I determined to strike in a diagonal direction through the woods to the left and thus reach the cars in the shortest time. Unfortunately we were obliged to pass through a dense, briery-tangled, and dismal swamp, so common in the low marshy lands in this part of the country. Our progress was thus somewhat delayed, but in due time the whole column safely crossed and took the cars for New Berne.

The subsequent attack by the enemy at Batchelder's Creek on the afternoon of the 23d, which resulted in the death of Colonel Jones, not being within the limits or against the forces of my command, I have no report concerning this to make. Most of the commanders who have made their reports to me unite with their commands in deploring the loss the department and the service have sustained in his death. As a soldier he was brave, stout-hearted, and untiring in his efforts; as a man, earnest, magnanimous, honorable, and devoted to his duty. He was never appalled by danger or overcome by incapacitating fear, but always sought to deal heavy and sturdy blows against the enemies of his country.

I desire to mention in favorable terms the forces under my command. The Twenty-seventh and Fifty-eighth Regiments are deserving of praise for the patience with which they bore the fatigues of the night march and the gallant manner in which they charged upon and captured so many of the enemy. Lieutenant-Colonel Lyman speaks in approving terms of his officers and men. Lieutenant-Colonel Curtiss specially mentions Captain Clay, Company K, and Lieutenant Wells, Company I, for their energy, skill, and gallantry. I commend the Twenty-fifth Massachusetts for their high state of discipline and for the promptness and zeal which they displayed on all occasions. The Fifth and Forty-sixth Massachusetts manifested great enthusiasm to distinguish themselves and add to their character as regiments; had serious work been required of them I have no doubt they would have done it with spirit and determination. *

I have the honor to report the following number of prisoners and the following list of captured property as the fruits of the expedition : One hundred and sixty-five prisoners, 28 horses, 10 mules, 2 baggage wagons, 3 ambulances, 10 sets single harness, 6 artillery harness (complete), 11 saddles, 3 saddles (artillery), 9 bridles, 80 muskets, 80 sets of equipments, 11,000 rounds of ammunition, 1 12-pounder howitzer with limber.

I have the honor also to state the casualties in tabular form :

	Killed.	Wounded.	Missing.	Remarks.
5th Massachusetts				
25th Massachusetts		3	1	Slightly wounded. Missing man last seen at Core Creek.
27th Massachusetts	2	1		1 killed, left in hands of enemy; 1 died of wounds, May 29 ; 1 slightly wounded in leg.
46th Massachusetts		1		Slightly wounded.
3d New York Cavalry				
3d New York Artillery (Battery H)				
58th Pennsylvania				
Total	2	5	1	

I have the honor to transmit an elegant and accurate map of the defenses at Gum Swamp, drawn by Sergt. Charles Brigham, Company K, Fifth Regiment Massachusetts Volunteer Militia.†

I am, colonel, very respectfully, yours,

GEORGE H. PEIRSON,
Colonel, Commanding.

Lieut. Col. SOUTHARD HOFFMAN, *Assistant Adjutant-General.*

---

* Medal of honor awarded to Sergt. Andrew S. Bryant, Company A, Forty-sixth Massachusetts, for gallantry in this action.
† Not found.

No. 5.

Report of Col. Josiah Pickett, Twenty-fifth Massachusetts Infantry.

HDQRS. TWENTY-FIFTH REGT. MASSACHUSETTS VOLS.,
Camp Oliver, New Berne, N. C., May 25, 1863.

SIR: I have the honor to submit the following report of the part taken by the Twenty-fifth Regiment Massachusetts Volunteers in the late expedition to Gum Creek:

I left my camp in this city at 12.30 o'clock on the morning of the 21st. My orders were to proceed to Batchelder's Creek and report for orders to Colonel Jones, Fifty-eighth Regiment Pennsylvania Volunteers. I reached Batchelder's Creek a little after daylight and immediately reported. Having some hours in which to rest my men, I placed them in the woods on the right of the road leading to the camp of the Fifty-eighth Regiment Pennsylvania Volunteers. At about 3 p. m. I placed my regiment aboard a train of cars in waiting and moved up the railroad about 8 miles in the direction of Core Creek. There we disembarked and joined the other regiments of the Second Brigade, the Twenty-seventh Massachusetts Volunteers and the Fifth Massachusetts Volunteer Militia. We then marched to Core Creek and bivouacked until 11.30 o'clock.

At 12 o'clock we took up the line of march for Gum Creek, my regiment in the advance. After crossing the bridge at Core Creek I threw forward Company K, Capt. J. Waldo Denny commanding, as an advance guard. We moved on quietly, meeting no opposition from or seeing any signs of the enemy until about 4 o'clock in the morning of the 22d, when our advance guard met the enemy's pickets, exchanged shots with them, and drove them in. Advancing cautiously, we were soon in the neighborhood of the enemy's camp. By order of Colonel Peirson I filed my regiment into the field to the right of the road and took position on the left flank of the enemy, forming line of battle. I sent out Company K, Capt. J. Waldo Denny, and Company E, Capt. Thomas O'Neil, as skirmishers and to discover and report the position of the enemy. Captains Denny and O'Neil soon sent word that they were within sight of a long line of earthworks and had exchanged shots with the enemy. I instructed them to engage him closely, so as to draw if possible his attention from his flanks and rear. This they succeeded in doing admirably. Our skirmishers exchanged their first shots with the enemy at his earthworks at about 6.30 o'clock. At 10 o'clock we heard firing in the rear of the enemy, which indicated the approach of Colonel Jones in that direction. I immediately strengthened my line of skirmishers by throwing forward Company A, Captain Goodwin, and moved forward my regiment in line of battle. Company A was soon over the earthworks. The enemy, outflanked and attacked in the rear, had fled precipitately to the woods and swamps, and I had the pleasure in a few moments of seeing my regimental colors planted upon their intrenchments. At 5 p. m. the enemy, no doubt re-enforced from Kinston, moved down the railroad and commenced shelling the woods.

The object of the expedition having been accomplished, after our artillery had thrown a few shells at them, we took up the line of march for Core Creek; my regiment, with Company —, of the Third New York Cavalry, and one piece of artillery from Battery —, Third New York Artillery, formed the rear guard. The enemy followed us, occasionally shelling the woods. They, however, did us no damage, and we arrived safely at Core Creek at about 10.30 that night. We bivouacked here without fires for the night.

At 6.30 o'clock on the morning of the 23d we took up the line of march for the railroad, there to take the cars for Batchelder's Creek. The column had been in motion but a few moments when the enemy's advance guard fired upon our troops from the other side of the creek. Our artillery soon dispersed them, and, being in the advance, I threw forward one company as advance guard, with orders to proceed to the railroad and report the condition of things there. In a few moments messengers came in with information that the enemy had driven in the pickets of the Fifty-eighth Pennsylvania Volunteers, who were stationed upon the railroad, and that they were moving down in force (three regiments), with the very evident intention of striking our left flank and rear before we could reach the cars. In order to prevent this movement, which would have proved very disastrous to us, by order of Colonel Peirson I filed the head of the column to the left into the woods, intending to run parallel with the railroad for some distance and then to strike it far enough down as to enable us to bring our whole force into position and give them battle. The head of the column struck into a swamp, which at first seemed but little likely to impede our march, but ere long it became almost impenetrable and seemed interminable; without guides and in endeavoring to reach the railroad, we lost our way. Finally a pocket-compass was obtained, and in a short time we struck the railroad some distance below where we intended to and about 2 miles above Tuscarora Depot. Here we met the cars, and the men were picked up as they came out of the woods, and without any further occurrence of importance were conveyed to New Berne. I reached my camp between 3 and 4 p. m. Saturday, the 23d.*

I have the honor to be, respectfully, yours,

JOSIAH PICKETT,
Colonel, Comdg. Twenty-fifth Regt. Massachusetts Vols.

Capt. GEORGE W. BARTLETT,
A. A. A. G., Second Brig., First Div., Eighteenth A. C.

No. 6.

Report of Col. Silas P. Richmond, Third Massachusetts Infantry, Second Brigade, Fifth Division, of operations May 23.

HDQRS. THIRD MASSACHUSETTS VOLUNTEER MILITIA,
Camp Jourdan, near New Berne, N. C., May 25, 1863.

COLONEL: I have the honor to make the following report of the movement of my command during the late disturbance at the outposts:

At 4 p. m. on the 23d instant I received orders to have my command in readiness to march at a moment's notice with 60 rounds of ammunition.

At 7 p. m. about 200 rebel prisoners were committed to my charge, and at the same time news came that Colonel Jones, Fifty-eighth Pennsylvania, was killed at Batchelder's Creek, and that his regiment, together with Lee's brigade, had been driven in with some loss.

At 8 p. m. I received orders to march immediately. I did so, having written instructions to govern my movements. Being obliged to leave

---

* Nominal list of casualties shows 3 men wounded and 1 missing.

a strong guard over the rebel prisoners, I had with me only 25 officers and 453 men. I took the Neuse road and proceeded to a point beyond its intersection with the railroad, and halted in a convenient position for communication with our force on the Neuse road, near Batchelder's Creek, and also with our force on the railroad near the same creek. We there rested on our arms during the remainder of the night.

Just after daylight on the 24th, by order of General Palmer, I sent Company A, of my command, forward to the junction of the Neuse and Washington roads to support a section of Howell's battery.

At 9.30 a. m., report having been received from the outposts that the enemy had retired, I received orders to return with my command to camp at New Berne, leaving the outposts as they were. The day was extremely hot and the roads very dusty, therefore we marched very slowly. Reached camp about noon. No severe casualties.

Respectfully submitted.

S. P. RICHMOND,
Colonel, Commanding Regiment.

Col. J. JOURDAN,
    Comdg. Second Brig., Fifth Div., Eighteenth Army Corps.

MAY 31–JUNE 1, 1863.—Evacuation of West Point, Va.

Report of Brig. Gen. George H. Gordon, U. S. Army, with itinerary of his division, May 4–June 1.

YORKTOWN, VA., *June* 1, 1863.

GENERAL: I have the honor to report the successful removal of the force under my command from West Point, without the loss of a single man or the abandonment of a single dollar's worth of Government property. About 7 p. m. this evening, just twenty-four hours after the movement commenced, I removed the planking of the wharf and sailed from the post.

I am, sir, yours, truly,

GEO. H. GORDON,
Brigadier-General.

Major-General DIX.

—

Itinerary of the Second Division, Fourth Army Corps, May 4–June 1.[*]

May 4.—At Suffolk, Va., Brig. Gen. George H. Gordon assumed command of the division [formerly Abercrombie's].

May 5.—Broke up camp and moved by rail to Norfolk the same night.

May 6.—Embarked on transports for Fort Monroe.

May 7.—Sailed for West Point, and on arriving there immediately commenced throwing up fortifications for defense, consisting of a line of intrenchment extending from the Mattapony to the Pamunkey. The Fortieth Massachusetts was thrown out to the front on picket while the rest of the division worked constantly and well on the intrenchments. Six earthworks, mounting fifteen guns, and having embrasures

---

[*] From "Record of Events" on Return for May, 1863.

for twenty-six, and making a complete circle of fire, were thrown up and made very strong by ditches and abatis. Parties were sent out into the surrounding country, who destroyed or brought away large quantities of grain, seized horses, mules, bacon, &c., and great numbers of negroes were brought in.

May 31, *Sunday.*—Commenced to embark for Yorktown, which was continued without interruption from the enemy until everything was safely on board of the transports and taken to Yorktown.

CORRESPONDENCE, ORDERS, AND RETURNS RELATING SPECIALLY TO OPERATIONS IN NORTH CAROLINA AND SOUTHEASTERN VIRGINIA FROM AUGUST 20, 1862, TO JUNE 3, 1863.

UNION CORRESPONDENCE, ETC.

FORT MONROE, *August* 20, 1862—10 a. m.

Maj. Gen. E. D. KEYES,
　Commanding Fourth Corps, Yorktown, Va. :

Your corps is to halt at Yorktown until further orders. If you have passed beyond the vicinity of that place when this reaches you, you will at once return to Yorktown and there await further orders, which may not reach you for some days.

GEO. B. McCLELLAN,
Major-General.

HEADQUARTERS ARMY OF THE POTOMAC,
　Fort Monroe, August 20, 1862.

General E. D. KEYES,
　Commanding Fourth Army Corps, Yorktown :

The commanding general directs that you remain with your corps in the immediate vicinity of Yorktown until further orders. You will probably remain for several days.

General Heintzelman was directed to send one or two regiments to occupy Gloucester Point; as General Heintzelman's corps is about embarking you will please hold that Point with one or two regiments from your command until you embark.

R. B. MARCY,
Chief of Staff.

HEADQUARTERS ARMY OF THE POTOMAC,
　Fortress Monroe, August 21, 1862.

Maj. Gen. E. D. KEYES, *Yorktown :*

Supplies of every necessary character for the troops can be obtained at Yorktown. There is no necessity for any officers to visit Fortress Monroe to obtain them.

The general commanding directs that you confer with Lieut. Col. B. S. Alexander, and furnish from your command the necessary details of working parties to carry out his views with regard to the defense of

Yorktown. The general commanding further directs that you send a brigade to Williamsburg for a few days to cover this work. The general desires you to take the general command and control of the operations.

Exhibit this to General Van Alen.

R. B. MARCY,
Chief of Staff.

HEADQUARTERS ARMY OF THE POTOMAC,
Fort Monroe, Va., August 21, 1862—10.30 p. m.

Maj. Gen. E. D. KEYES,
Commanding Fourth Army Corps, Yorktown, Va.:

I am instructed by the commanding general to say that, owing to the great emergency which exists at this time, it is necessary that you should furnish working parties for the defenses of Yorktown at the earliest moment that tools can be obtained.

The engineer officer in charge will call upon you when the details are required.

R. B. MARCY,
Chief of Staff.

HEADQUARTERS ARMY OF THE POTOMAC,
Fort Monroe, August 22, 1862—3 p. m.

Maj. Gen. E. D. KEYES, *Yorktown, Va.:*

As a temporary measure, please place one of your field batteries in the work at Gloucester Point.

Please push the work laid out by the engineer officers with the utmost rapidity. I hope to have new troops to relieve your men by the time transports are ready for your corps. Please detail some of your artillery officers and non-commissioned officers to instruct the garrison you found under General Van Alen in the use of heavy guns, and have them prepare tables of ranges, &c., for them. I trust to your zeal and activity in this very trying moment.

They are fighting now on the Rappahannock. A general engagement is probably going on now.

GEO. B. McCLELLAN,
Major-General.

HEADQUARTERS ARMY OF THE POTOMAC,
August 22, 1862.

Maj. Gen. E. D. KEYES,
Commanding Fourth Army Corps:

The duty intrusted to your corps, while it is no doubt disagreeable, is of the utmost importance. I fully realize how severe a tax it is upon men who have fought so gallantly and worked so hard as your corps to require them now to go upon fatigue duty. I feel sure, however, that if they know that the work I now call upon them to perform is necessary they will perform it cheerfully. You will please detail as large working parties as the tools available will permit to perform the work laid out by the engineer officers.

It is a matter of vital importance that the details should be furnished and the work done in the shortest possible time.

I have taken all the necessary steps to have your command relieved by new troops at the earliest practicable moment.

It is imperatively necessary that the work required should be pushed with the utmost vigor. You will be held responsible that this work is pushed with all the rapidity possible with the means at your command, and hold your command in readiness to move at the shortest notice.

If you judge it necessary, send two regiments or an entire brigade of infantry to Williamsburg to cover your operations.

Please push as far as possible the instruction of the old garrison in heavy artillery practice, and give me in full your views as to the best method of holding Williamsburg and the force necessary for that purpose.

Send a couple of squadrons of cavalry to Goucester to patrol and examine the country on the left bank of the York.

If you think it advisable, send a much larger force of cavalry there for temporary duty. While we have a large cavalry force comparatively idle it may be well to occupy a large portion of it in clearing out the country on that side of the York River.

If you think it best to occupy a point near Williamsburg by infantry, hold Fort Magruder and destroy the adjacent works.

Very respectfully, your obedient servant,

GEO. B. McCLELLAN,
Major-General, Commanding.

FALMOUTH, *August* 26, 1862.
(Received 2.40 p. m.)

Major-General HALLECK:

Please inform me when you can send say 5,000 new troops to Yorktown. If they can be supplied within three days can order forward Couch's division, now at Yorktown, with the means of transportation at our disposal. Your reply involves the question of retaining or discharging several large transports, for which we are paying a high price. I shall be glad to have your answer at once, as I propose returning shortly to Aquia Creek, to proceed thence to Alexandria.

GEO. B. McCLELLAN,
Major-General.

WASHINGTON, *August* 26, 1862.

Major-General McCLELLAN, *Falmouth:*

Five thousand new troops can be sent to Yorktown as soon as you can spare transports for that purpose. They can be embarked at Alexandria.

H. W. HALLECK,
General-in-Chief.

NAVY DEPARTMENT,
August 29, 1862.

Hon. E. M. STANTON,
Secretary of War :

SIR : The large naval force in the James River being no longer required there, directions are about being given to send the vessels to
other points, where their presence is most essential.

If Newport News is to be held by the Army I respectfully suggest
that half a dozen 200-pounder rifled Parrott guns be mounted there as
a means to assist in keeping blockaded the iron-clad vessels now building at Richmond.

Very respectfully,

GIDEON WELLES.

---

*Abstract from Monthly Return of the Department of Virginia (Seventh Army Corps),
Maj. Gen. John A. Dix commanding, for the month of August, 1862 (headquarters
Fort Monroe, Va.).*

Command.	Present for duty.		Aggregate present.	Aggregate present and absent.	Aggregate present and absent last monthly return.	Pieces of field artillery.
	Officers.	Men.				
Department Headquarters, Maj. Gen. John A. Dix.....	17	2	19	19	19	......
Fort Monroe, Maj. Joseph Roberts...................	14	300	455	493	506	10
Camp Hamilton, Brig. Gen. Henry W. Wessells.....	109	1,895	2,227	3,916	964	6
Newport News, Maj. Reuben V. King	31	529	598	782	81	......
Norfolk, Brig. Gen. Egbert L. Viele.................	86	1,639	2,061	2,261	2,308	6
Suffolk, Brig. Gen. J. K. F. Mansfield...............	228	4,861	5,792	7,178	4,597	6
Total.....................................	468	9,224	11,133	14,630	8,456	28
Fourth Army Corps, Maj. Gen. Erasmus D. Keyes......	7	......	7	10	......	......
Williamsburg, Va...............................	56	1,041	1,256	1,527	......	20
Williamsburg, Va...............................	......	......	......	......	1,237	......
Yorktown, Va	147	2,624	3,222	5,499	......	......
Yorktown, Va	23	630	751	806	1,795	......
Gloucester Point, Va	4	104	110	152	......	4
Total.....................................	237	4,399	5,346	7,994	3,032	24
Fort Wool, Capt. Ira Winans, detachment Ninety-ninth New York Volunteers.	3	65	70	86	166	......
Sewell's Point, Capt. John C. Lee, detachment Ninety-ninth New York Volunteers.	1	70	80	92	95	......
Grand total................................	726	13,760	16,648	22,821	11,768	52

Troops in the Department of Virginia, commanded by Maj. Gen. John A. Dix, August 31, 1862.

FORT MONROE, VA.

Maj. JOSEPH ROBERTS, Fourth U. S. Artillery, commanding.

Detachment Regulars.
Detachment 99th New York Infantry.
Batteries Wis. Light Artillery (2d and 4th).

CAMP HAMILTON, VA.

Brig. Gen. HENRY W. WESSELLS commanding.

FOURTH ARMY CORPS.

92d New York.
96th New York.
85th Pennsylvania.
101st Pennsylvania.
103d Pennsylvania.

SEVENTH ARMY CORPS.

11th Pennsylvania Cavalry, Company C.
5th Maryland.
7th Battery New York Light Artillery.

NEWPORT NEWS, VA.

Maj. REUBEN V. KING, Eighty-fifth New York, commanding.

85th New York.
11th Pennsylvania Cavalry, Company M.

NORFOLK, VA.

Brig. Gen. EGBERT L. VIELE commanding.

Detachment 1st New York Mounted Rifles.
99th New York (6 companies).
58th Pennsylvania.
19th Wisconsin.
4th U. S. Artillery, Battery D.

SUFFOLK, VA.

Brig. Gen. J. K. F. MANSFIELD commanding.

SEVENTH ARMY CORPS.

Brig. Gen. MAX WEBER.

1st Delaware.
3d New York.
4th New York.
13th New York.
25th New York.

SEVENTH ARMY CORPS.

1st New York Mounted Rifles.
11th Pennsylvania Cavalry.
4th U. S. Artillery, Battery L.

FOURTH ARMY CORPS.

Brig. Gen. ORRIS S. FERRY.

39th Illinois.
13th Indiana.
62d Ohio.
67th Ohio.

FORT WOOL.

Capt. IRA WINANS commanding.

Detachment 99th New York.

SEWELL'S POINT.

Capt. John C. LEE commanding.

Detachment 99th New York.

FOURTH ARMY CORPS.

Maj. Gen. ERASMUS D. KEYES commanding.

YORKTOWN, VA.

FOURTH ARMY CORPS.

Second Division.

Maj. Gen. JOHN J. PECK commanding.

SEVENTH ARMY CORPS.

Brig. Gen. JAMES H. VAN ALEN comdg.

Independent Battalion New York Vols.
Detachment 4th Pennsylvania Cavalry.
7th Battery Massachusetts Light Artillery.
Detachment 1st New York Artillery.

WILLIAMSBURG, VA.

3d Battalion 6th New York Cavalry.
5th Pennsylvania Cavalry.
Reserved artillery.

GLOUCESTER POINT, VA.

Maj. J. WATTS DE PEYSTER commanding.

Battery New York Artillery (Fourth Army Corps).

Abstract from Monthly Return of the Department of North Carolina, Maj. Gen. John G. Foster commanding, for the month of August, 1862.

Command.	Present for duty.		Aggregate present.	Aggregate present and absent.	Aggregate present and absent last monthly return.
	Officers.	Men.			
First Brigade.					
Col. T. J. C. AMORY.					
17th Massachusetts Volunteers, Lieutenant-Colonel Fellows. 23d Massachusetts Volunteers, Col. John Kurtz............ 25th Massachusetts Volunteers, Maj. Josiah Pickett........ 27th Massachusetts Volunteers, Col. H. C. Lee..............	92	2,545	3,477	3,836	3,638
Second Brigade.					
Col. T. G. STEVENSON.					
10th Connecticut Volunteers, Lieut. Col. B. S. Pardee........ 24th Massachusetts Volunteers, Lieut. Col. F. A. Osborn.... 9th New Jersey Volunteers, Col. C. A. Heckman.......... 5th Rhode Island Volunteers, Capt. Job Arnold............	40	1,186	1,555	1,792	1,785
Grand total.................................	132	3,731	5,032	5,628	5,423

WASHINGTON, D. C., *September 2, 1862.*

Major-General DIX, *Fort Monroe:*

The great danger of Washington renders it necessary that the remainder of Keyes' corps be sent here as rapidly as possible; at least all of it that you can spare.

The entire army of the enemy is before us, and the fighting has been daily for a week with varying results.

H. W. HALLECK,
General-in-Chief.

HEADQUARTERS FOURTH CORPS,
Yorktown, Va., September 3, 1862.

Brig. Gen. S. WILLIAMS,
Adjutant-General, Army of the Potomac:

SIR: I have the honor to inclose herewith the proceedings of a board of officers convened at this place by my orders to examine and report upon the condition of the defenses of Yorktown and what is necessary to place them on a proper footing.

In regard to the force necessary the report of the board corresponds pretty nearly with my letter of 27th ultimo * on the same subject. It would be well to place three gunboats in York River; one or two should be kept moving continually, otherwise this fine river will be greatly used for the comfort of the enemy, and perhaps for our annoyance.

I remain, respectfully, your most obedient servant,

E. D. KEYES,
Major-General, Commanding Fourth Corps.

---

* Not found.

[Inclosure.]

GENERAL ORDERS, ⎰　　　　　　　HEADQUARTERS FOURTH CORPS,
　　No. 86.　⎱　　　　　　　　*Yorktown, August* 29, 1862.

A board of officers, to be composed of Maj. Gen. John J. Peck, Brig. Gen. William H. Emory, Col. John C. Dodge, Fifty-second Pennsylvania Volunteers, will convene at Yorktown to-morrow morning at 10 o'clock.

The board will examine and report upon the present armament of Yorktown, its condition, and the amount and condition of the ammunition on hand; the present state of the ramparts, magazines, and other appliances. The board will also give an opinion as to what is necessary, in addition to the means on hand, to place Yorktown in a suitable condition for defense.

By order of Major-General Keyes:

　　　　　　　　　　　　　　　OSWALD JACKSON,
　　　　　　　　　　　　　　　　　Aide-de-Camp.

　　　　　　　YORKTOWN, VA., *August* 30, 1862.

The board met pursuant to the foregoing order, all the members named being present, and adjourned to make the examination preliminary to the following report:

　　　　　　　YORKTOWN, VA., *August* 31, 1862.

The board report the condition of the armament is as follows:

There are forty-two garrison pieces of various caliber in position at Yorktown; none at Gloucester Point. Most of these pieces are out of adjustment from the settling of the earth and warping of the platforms and other wood-work connected with the mounting of the pieces, so as to make it difficult and in some cases wholly impracticable to work them.

Of the ammunition.

Inclosed is a list of the ammunition, which is wholly insufficient and not well assorted.

The present state of the ramparts at Yorktown.

The extent of the covering line, independent of the shore line, is about 1 mile. The interior revetment is good. The exterior ditch and exterior face of the work is in many places so much washed away and defaced as to form but little impediment to an assaulting column. The whole ditch and the ramparts, exterior and interior, and a considerable portion of the inclosure of the work is overgrown with noxious weeds, and the earth is saturated with human fæces and decaying animal matter.

The condition of the magazines.

All except two are damp and unfit for use.

The exterior lines and approaches.

Two divisions, Peck's and Couch's, were left here to level the approaches and exterior works commanding this fort and cut down the forest. Before doing anything of any consequence (working a thousand shovels and picks one day and a half), two brigades of Peck's division and the whole of Couch's division were ordered away, and the mass of the work yet to be done in the removal of these obstacles to a proper defense of Yorktown cannot be better described than by stating the number of days' labor it would take. The number of troops here is as follows : Five regiments, First Brigade, Second Division, 1,900 ; Independent Battalion, 500 ; and there are 250 negro laborers. From this force must necessarily be deducted the old and new guards, 250 men, and the regiment detailed to man the guns, 370 men, leaving a total of 2,000 men to work, if unmolested by the enemy ; and it is estimated that it will take this force thirty days to accomplish the work of destroying the approaches and restoring the slopes and ditches of the work itself. These estimates are independent of the work at Gloucester Point, where two regiments of the First Brigade are stationed and where the picket and fatigue duty is sufficient to occupy their attention.

Of what is necessary.

The plan of the board of engineers, a copy of which is in possession of Major-General Peck, a member of this board, and which has been approved by General McClellan and herewith submitted, contains, in the opinion of the board, all the suggestions necessary to place Yorktown in a state of defense. But in the opinion of the board the force now left here is wholly inadequate to accomplish this work within the time when the enemy is likely to attack this work, if it is attacked at all ; and of the armament suggested in that plan of defense, none has been sent.

The board recommend that armament be at once sent, and urgently recommend that an ordnance officer be sent to mount that armament and direct the readjustment of the pieces now here.

The board is of the opinion that when the work is in a state of defense contemplated by the engineers, the garrison necessary to hold it and the approaches should consist of one regiment of cavalry, one regiment of artillery, and 4,000 infantry, if of old troops ; if of new levies, from 6,000 to 8,000 infantry.

There is at present but one gunboat at this place. In the opinion of the board two more are necessary—one on each of the flanks of the work, and the third to pass up and down the river and break up the trade between Richmond and the rich counties of Gloucester and Matthews, on the eastern side of the river.

In this connection it is proper to state that the height and abruptness of the bank of the river at Yorktown will diminish the aid that might otherwise be expected from their co-operation in the defense of the work.

There is with the garrison at Gloucester Point a field battery of four pieces, and in this fort two field batteries of four guns each, but it is not known whether the two batteries at this place are a part of the garrison.

JOHN J. PECK,
Major-General.
W. H. EMORY,
Brigadier-General.
JOHN C. DODGE, Jr.,
Colonel Fifty-second Pennsylvania Volunteers.

HEADQUARTERS FOURTH CORPS,
Yorktown, September 3, 1862.

The proceedings of the board of which Major-General Peck is president are approved. The board is dissolved.

E. D. KEYES,
Major-General, Commanding Fourth Corps.

[Indorsement.]

The report of the board of officers seems to be based upon the idea that Yorktown may be attacked by a very large force, and consequently recommends additional armament and much engineering work.

With my limited knowledge of Yorktown I of course do not know exactly what is most expedient to be done; but it strikes me that the forty-two pieces of artillery now there, and a garrison increased by new troops to bring it up to one regiment of artillery, one regiment of cavalry, and three of infantry, in all about 4,000 men, are all-sufficient for any probable attack.

An ordnance officer should be sent to Yorktown to unspike guns, adjust platforms, and overhaul ordnance and ordnance stores, and General Keyes should be directed to apply his whole available force to leveling the exterior works and approaches and repairing the defenses as suggested by the board of engineers which examined the works.

An additional gunboat for patroling York River, and in case of attack in co-operating in the defense of Yorktown, would be desirable.

G. W. CULLUM,
Brigadier-General, Chief of Staff.

[Sub-inclosure.]

Memorandum of guns and ammunition at Yorktown, Va.

8-inch columbiads	17
32-pounder guns	8
42-pounder gun	1
24-pounder guns	4
9-inch Dahlgren Navy guns	4
7-inch Navy howitzers	4
8-inch siege howitzer	1
8-inch mortar (spiked)	1
68-pounder rifle gun (spiked)	1
10-inch gun	1

Ammunition.

Powder (barrels)	100
8-inch cartridges	400
32-pounder cartridges	250
24-pounder cartridges	150
42-pounder cartridges	150
8-inch shells filled, in magazine	300
8-inch shells, to be filled	200
8-inch shells, bad	681
10-inch shells, bad	35
10-inch shells, good	75
32-pounder shells, bad	125
42-pounder shells, bad	22
9-inch Dahlgren, good	60
24-pounder shells, bad	300
12-pounder shells, bad	20
100-pounder rifle shells, bad	24
24-pounder grape	20
32-pounder grape	70
32-pounder canister	100
32-pounder shot	121
8-inch shot	242
8-inch grape	218
10-inch shot	15
24-pounder shot	125
42-pounder canister	8

WAR DEPARTMENT,
Washington, September 3, 1862.

Maj. Gen. JOHN A. DIX, *Fort Monroe, Va. :*

If last division of General Keyes' corps has not commenced to embark suspend the order till I can send new troops to replace them.

H. W. HALLECK,
General-in-Chief.

FORT MONROE, VA.,
September 3, 1862—2 p. m.

Maj. Gen. H. W. HALLECK,
General-in-Chief :

Averell's brigade of cavalry was embarking when I received your
dispatch of last evening. The embarkation will be completed to day
and to-morrow. I will send you a detailed account of the entire force
on the Peninsula and at Norfolk and Suffolk to-morrow. Your dispatch
of this morning is received.

JOHN A. DIX,
Major-General.

WAR DEPARTMENT,
Washington, September 3, 1862.

Major-General DIX, *Fort Monroe, Va. :*

As the embarkation has commenced, my dispatch of this morning
will be of no effect. I will send you fresh troops as soon as possible to
replace those sent up here.

H. W. HALLECK,
General-in-Chief.

HEADQUARTERS SEVENTH ARMY CORPS,
Fort Monroe, Va., September 4, 1862.

Hon. E. M. STANTON,
Secretary of War :

SIR: Immediately after I was placed in command of the troops at
this post and in the vicinity I called the attention of the Government
to the destitute condition of the 20,000 people of Norfolk, arising from
the interruption of their commercial intercourse while the rebels were
in possession of the city, and the system of exclusion which was adopted
after it was captured by us and which I found in force. I recommended a total change of regimen on grounds of humanity as well as
policy. I thought it due to ourselves as generous conquerors to put
an end to the restrictions, which under the insurgents were a matter of
constraint but which we continued as a matter of choice, and to afford
a free ingress to the necessaries and comforts of life of which the inhabitants were in extreme need. My recommendations were adopted
only to a limited extent. Eight vessels were permitted by the Secretary
of the Treasury to proceed there with cargoes. Nearly three months
have elapsed, and the people are even more destitute than they were
when they came under our dominion. The suspension of business to a
great extent necessarily compels them to live on what they have saved
instead of their daily earnings, which are for the most part cut off, and
they are constantly becoming by the consumption of their savings less

able to pay high prices. Besides, the non-intercourse we are keeping up has, by excluding supplies, rendered the city entirely destitute of many of the essential articles of subsistence; they are not to be had at any price. This infliction, and it is a serious one, falls on the loyal as well as the disloyal, and it is certainly not calculated to add to the number of our friends or diminish the number of our enemies. I advised a liberal treatment for all, punishing where any open hostility to the Government was shown.

I do not understand that this view of the subject was disapproved by the Government; but from a communication recently received from the Treasury Department a difficulty is supposed to exist in the fact that Norfolk is within the section of the country affected by the blockade.

It is respectfully suggested that since the capture and occupation of Norfolk by the military forces of the United States the principles of public law applicable to blockaded ports are no longer in force there. It is not a case of complete conquest, in which we must look to our Constitution and laws for the authority which we exercise, but it is a case in which the place is held by the right of military occupation, in which we are exercising the powers given by the laws of war, and in which we may further accord to the inhabitants privileges not strictly conferred by those laws. Rear-Admiral Goldsborough, who lies in the harbor in the Minnesota, is not there to enforce the blockade, but to enforce the military occupation.

That this is the view taken by the Government I cannot doubt, for certainly the right to grant the permits given by the Secretary of the Treasury to introduce eight cargoes of merchandise for general traffic is not to be found in the laws of blockade, which imply a naval force on the part of one belligerent and a closed port on the part of another.

I do not overlook the fact that Norfolk is a recovered possession, and that we hold it theoretically to be now, and always to have been, a part of the United States. But we do not act on this assumption, for if we did we should extend our civil jurisdiction over it and set in motion the customary machinery of administration. On the contrary, we govern it by military force and treat it for all practical purposes as a conquest.

Under the rule of military occupation, therefore, we may, without being questioned by neutrals, admit any intercourse with our own citizens, or any portion of them, essential to the maintenance of our authority or to the preservation and comfortable support of those whom we have subjected by our power. It is on this principle, I suppose, that the limited right to trade has been conferred in a few instances on particular individuals.

I beg leave further to suggest whether permits of this description, granted to afford to the inhabitants of the town or district thus subjected and held by force the means of subsistence, should not be given by the military commander; whether they can with propriety come from the Secretary of the Treasury, who is at the head of a civil department and whose functions in respect to revenue and commerce are wholly inapplicable to conquered territories governed by the laws of war. It seems to me that the other function is incident to the right of military occupation and not to be defended on any other grounds.

Should this view of the subject be concurred in I respectfully request that I may be authorized to grant permits to vessels to go to Norfolk with such supplies as I deem indispensable to save the inhabitants from suffering by hunger and cold, and that Rear-Admiral Goldsborough be directed to respect the permits thus granted by me.

In regard to the justice of this measure there are considerations, already briefly alluded to, which address themselves to us with great force. The people of Norfolk are cut off by our occupation of the place from their former sources of supplies. We have surrounded them by a cha n of sentinels and have interdicted trade with the insurgent States from which they could always draw at some price the necessaries they needed. They are in worse condition in this respect now than they were under the Confederates; and it is submitted whether, on every principle of justice to them and to ourselves, we should not allow them the privilege of obtaining what they need from the loyal portions of the Union. It seems to me that we are bound to do this or to let them pass through our lines into the insurgent States.

The inclosed letter from Brigadier-General Viele, the military governor of Norfolk, states the case with great brevity and force, and I commend it to the attention of the Government.

I have the honor to be, very respectfully, your obedient servant,

JOHN A. DIX,
Major-General.

[Inclosure.]

NORFOLK, VA., *September* 2, 1862.

Major-General DIX,
Commanding, &c., Fort Monroe :

GENERAL : There are two questions connected with the administration of affairs in this city and Portsmouth which have become a source of embarrassment to me. The one is the procurement of supplies for those who have the means, and the other the supplying of those who have not the means.

We are, in point of fact, holding here in custody about 20,000 people; we must either let them feed themselves or we must feed them.

The opening of the port for a restricted trade seems to me to be a measure of necessity to save the Government from great annoyance. Food must be allowed to come in or the people will starve. If food is allowed to come in the products of the surrounding country must be allowed to go out to pay for it. Again, there is a large class of persons here who have no means whatever to purchase food if it were here; these are mostly willing to go away to the neighboring counties and to North Carolina if allowed to do so. They are helpless women and children, who are begging daily at my headquarters for food. Those who are too poor to go or who have no friends may be supported by levying contributions upon those who have the means.

I have always considered that the only point to be attained here was perfect tranquillity. This has been secured so far; in order to continue it the steps I have referred to appear to be necessary.

Very respectfully, your obedient servant,

EGBERT L. VIELE,
Brigadier-General.

FORT MONROE, VA.,
September 5, 1862—2 p. m.

Maj. Gen. H. W. HALLECK :

The whole efficient force in the Department of Virginia is about 18,000, distributed as follows: Suffolk, 5,300; Norfolk, 2,300; Newport News, 100; Hampton, 2,300; Camp Hamilton, 900; Fort Monroe, 600; Yorktown, 5,100; Williamsburg, 1,300. The different corps of which this force is composed have about 3,000 absent. Sick not included in the above statement. A small regiment has been transferred to Newport News from Hampton, not affecting the aggregate.

JOHN A. DIX,
Major-General.

FORT MONROE, *September* 5, 1862—4 p. m.

Major-General HALLECK:

Major-General Keyes is very desirous of leaving Yorktown with his reserve artillery to resume the command of Couch's division, and is willing to take and train another division from the new forces now coming into the field. I should be very glad to retain him, but cheerfully consent to the arrangement if it meets with your approval, as it will obviate the necessity of sending new troops here and enable me to retain Major-General Peck, a very good officer, and his division, which is well trained, and of which two brigades, Ferry's and Wessells', have been already incorporated with the forces here and at Suffolk. General Keyes informs me that he trained Couch's division and is quite willing to train another. His reserve artillery can be spared if I can keep Peck's division.

JOHN A. DIX,
Major-General.

PRIVATE.]   SUFFOLK, VA., *September* 5, 1862.

Major-General HALLECK,
   Commanding Army, Washington City:

GENERAL: A deserter, on whom I can rely, says there are but about 15,000 men at Richmond. The brigades of Generals Ransom and Martin are stationed below Richmond, opposite Fort Darling.

There is a brigade at Petersburg. The Merrimac No. 2 (Richmond) is about finished and has her bow gun in. She is commanded by Captain Pegram, and her crew are from the old Merrimac. She draws 11 feet of water, and has a double sheathing of iron, separated by a course of timber. The iron is reported to be thicker than that of the old Merrimac.

I have thought the above information might be of some service to you. I have already written the Secretary of the Navy to the same effect as to the Merrimac.

The man also stated that all the troops of Stonewall Jackson amounted to about 200,000. He left Richmond about a week since, and says that Generals Lee, Ewell, Mahone, Colston, Armistead, Wright, Longstreet, and the two Hills are with Jackson.

The enemy will never attack this place, which is naturally strong, so long as pressed on the side of Richmond. I repeat, there are three old regiments here—the First Delaware and Third and Fourth New York Volunteers—well drilled, and been in service for about fourteen months and have never fired a gun at the enemy. They will average 800 men, and many men and officers have been in the Mexican war. Three green regiments could readily take their places here, and these could, by return boats, proceed up the Potomac to the Army of Virginia.

I am ready at all times myself to take any command you will think it to the interest of the country to give me, and believe I can do more than I can here.

25 R R—VOL XVIII

You will excuse this private letter; an official one on tl is subject might by some be thought out of place.

Very truly and sincerely, your obedient servant,

JOS. K. F. MANSFIELD.

HEADQUARTERS SEVENTH ARMY CORPS,
Fort Monroe, Va., September 7, 1862.

Brig. Gen. O. S. FERRY,
    Commanding at Suffolk, Va.:

I wish to complete a reconnaissance in the vicinity of the Dismal Swamp. It will be under the direction of Capt. William Heine, who is engaged in constructing military maps of the district south and west of Suffolk. It will be necessary to send with him two companies of infantry, a company of cavalry or mounted riflemen, and a section of artillery, with two mountain howitzers, under a discreet and efficient field officer. It will probably be necessary to pass around the Dismal Swamp, returning on the east side. The men must have rations for eight days, and they must take with them their tents and the smallest practicable amount of camp equipage. During the first two or three days it will be well to send two or three companies of cavalry out on the road nearest to the Blackwater, in the direction of Somerton and Winton, as a cover to the movement. A number of wagons, sufficient to carry the provisions, forage, and tents, will be sent with them, and an ambulance for the use of the engineers. At this season the men should be covered at night, and if possible their tents should be pitched under the shelter of trees and their march should be suspended during the heat.

The movement will conform to the requirements of Captain Heine, who is charged with the reconnaissance; but the command of the escort, and all that relates to the control of the men, will be under the direction of the senior officer, who will be enjoined to enforce the strictest discipline. The inhabitants of the country will be protected against all disturbance, and the least violation of their property will be visited with the most extreme rigor of the law. Should it be necessary to procure supplies from the district through which the movement is made the commanding officer will endeavor to obtain them by agreement with the parties, or, if compelled to take them, he will give receipts on public account and render a return to me of the articles taken, with the names of the owners.

Everything will be in readiness on Monday, so that the party will move early on Tuesday morning, and I trust to you to make such arrangements as to insure the object of the expedition, and at the same time to carry out my wishes, which will be creditable to those who are engaged in it.

If you have not mountain howitzers we can send them from here. Answer immediately.

JOHN A. DIX,
Major-General.

WAR DEPARTMENT,
Washington, September 7, 1862.

Major-General DIX, *Fort Monroe, Va.:*

Send to Washington as promptly as possible the First Delaware and the Third and Fourth New York Regiments, now at Suffolk.

H. W. HALLECK,
General-in-Chief.

FORT MONROE, VA., *September* 8, 1862.
Major-General HALLECK:

I shall send your order for the First Delaware and Third and Fourth New York to Suffolk. You are perhaps not aware that these regiments are the flower of command, and my main reliance if Suffolk is to be defended. I should be glad, at all events, to be allowed to send the Fifth Maryland instead of the Third New York. I want the latter here if I cannot have Gibson's artillery.

JOHN A. DIX,
Major-General.

WAR DEPARTMENT,
Washington, September 8, 1862.
Maj. Gen. JOHN A. DIX, *Fort Monroe, Va.*:

Make the change of regiments you proposed. Bring away from Suffolk all extra arms.

H. W. HALLECK,
General-in-Chief.

SPECIAL ORDERS,) HDQRS. OF THE ARMY, ADJT. GEN.'S OFFICE,
No. 229.   )   *Washington, September* 8, 1862.

*   *   *   *   *   *   *

IV. Brig. Gen. J. K. F. Mansfield, U. S. Volunteers, is relieved from duty in the Army of Virginia, and will report in person to Major-General McClellan.

*   *   *   *   *   *   *

By command of Major-General Halleck:

E. D. TOWNSEND,
Assistant Adjutant-General.

FORT MONROE, *September* 9, 1862.
Major-General HALLECK:

The Fourth New York, First Delaware, and Fifth Maryland have left here for Washington in the steamers Louisiana, J. A. Warner, and State of Maine.

JOHN A. DIX,
Major-General.

U. S. FLAG-SHIP MINNESOTA,
September 9, 1862.
Major-General DIX:

GENERAL: The naval force here has recently been so greatly reduced that I have no additional gunboat to spare for York River.

S. P. LEE,
Acting Rear-Admiral.

FORT MONROE, *September* 9, 1862.
Hon. E. M. STANTON,
Secretary of War:

Five hundred and twenty-five prisoners of war sent from Alexandria were delivered at Aiken's Landing and 604 of ours returned. They are paroled on both sides. I sent the latter last evening to Washington. Mr. Ould makes an earnest request that General Thomas will give him an interview. There are 5,000 of our prisoners at Richmond, which they wish us to take. Every steamboat here is employed in moving the three regiments from Suffolk to Washington, called for Sunday.

I have just received a dispatch from General Keyes, at Yorktown, informing me that our pickets have been driven in at Williamsburg. I fear Colonel Campbell has been compelled to retire, as the rebels are in possession of the telegraph station at Williamsburg. I am just leaving for Yorktown to be back to-night. I do not think it safe to take any more troops from this quarter unless we retire from Yorktown and Suffolk. I cannot even get another gunboat for Yorktown from Admiral Lee. I earnestly request that one or two more may be sent from the Potomac.

JOHN A. DIX,
Major-General.

WASHINGTON, September 10, 1862.

Hon. GIDEON WELLES,
        Secretary of the Navy :

SIR : General Dix telegraphs that the withdrawal of most of his forces to Washington leaves Yorktown too weak, and earnestly requests that one or two more gunboats be sent from the Potomac.

Very respectfully, your obedient servant,

H. W. HALLECK,
General-in-Chief.

FORT MONROE, VA., September 10, 1862.
(Received 10.30 a. m.)

Maj. Gen. H. W. HALLECK,
        General-in-Chief:

I have just returned from Yorktown, and find a dispatch from General E. D. Keyes, received since I left, saying that he is required to embark Peck's division for Alexandria. This leaves my force so reduced that it is impossible to hold Suffolk or Yorktown and protect the 7,000 sick here and in the vicinity. To retain them would be to invite attack. I propose therefore to fall back from Suffolk to Norfolk, and to destroy the guns at Yorktown and abandon it. I shall not have any infantry at Suffolk, and at Yorktown only 800 men.

JOHN A. DIX,
Major-General.

WAR DEPARTMENT,
Washington, September 10, 1862.

Major-General DIX, Fort Monroe, Va. :

When General McClellan asked for Peck's division he was to send you 5,000 new troops to take their place. This he was probably prevented from doing by General Wool stopping troops to guard the railroads. General Mansfield thinks the forces left at Suffolk sufficient. We must not at present abandon either Yorktown or Suffolk, and you must retain troops sufficient to hold them till others arrive. Stop any new troops coming from the North. It is understood that several regiments are coming by water from New York. The Boston troops should be at Fort Monroe to-day. It is believed that the entire force of the enemy is before us here, and that not more than 10,000 or 15,000 Home Guards were left at Richmond. If you have reliable information different you must retain more troops.

> H. W. HALLECK,
> *General-in-Chief.*

> WAR DEPARTMENT,
> *Washington, September* 10, 1862.

Major-General DIX, *Fort Monroe, Va. :*

The Merrimac, with two regiments from Boston, is bound to this place. If you can stop her at Fort Monroe keep those regiments for your command.

> H. W. HALLECK,
> *General-in-Chief.*

> FORT MONROE, VA.,
> *September* 10, 1862—4 p. m.

Maj. Gen. H. W. HALLECK,
> *General-in-Chief:*

When General McClellan was between this fort and Richmond, and before the occupation of Suffolk, General Wool had 14,978 men, of whom 12,847 were effective, for the defense of the fort, Newport News, and the immediate district of country, exclusive of General Peck's division. My force is but 5,326 men, of whom only 4,108 are effective, and with this I have not only the same district which General Wool had, but Norfolk, Suffolk, and Yorktown in addition.

I have reliable information that an attack on Suffolk is meditated. A brigade went down from Petersburg to defend it a few days ago, and from that point the railroad communication is open to the Blackwater at Franklin, or Carrsville, 20 miles from Suffolk. I have at Suffolk to-day only 2,900 effective men. When General Mansfield had a much larger force, and McClellan was between us and Richmond, he pressed me for re-enforcements. He certainly cannot know that the Third and Fourth New York and the First Delaware, the best regiments, have been withdrawn. They numbered over 2,300 men.

General Keyes advises me this morning that he has information from various sources establishing the fact that the rebels are in considerable force of artillery, cavalry, and infantry at Barhamsville, 18 miles from Williamsburg. There are numerous evidences of activity on his part in various directions, and if we hold Suffolk and Yorktown I certainly ought to have 20,000 men. This was the smallest number thought by General McClellan to be sufficient for the purpose.

I earnestly request that the sick, except those belonging to regiments here, may be sent North. September is the worst season, and the new hospitals are so miserably constructed as to be unfit for convalescents in storms, which are frequent at this season. But the great objection is in having so large a number of sick in a district exposed to attack and not covered by defensive works.

> JOHN A. DIX,
> *Major-General.*

HEADQUARTERS,
Washington, N. C., September 10, 1862.

Capt. SOUTHARD HOFFMAN,
      Assistant Adjutant-General:

DEAR HOFFMAN: Captain Jocknick made a reconnaissance yesterday to Tranter's Creek. Upon reaching the bridge he discovered that it was undergoing repairs, and going on it to examine more closely was fired on by a concealed force. Only two of his men were slightly wounded. There is good reason to believe that the enemy are collected in considerable numbers, and that they are repairing the bridge for a speedy attack on this place. Their force, according to negro and " secesh" authority, is set down at from 2,000 to 6,000. I have 43 of the Marine Artillery in the fort and Captain Wall's company of the Third New York, some 30 men. The block-house at the east end of the town is finished but there is no gun for it. The one on the Greenville road is going up rapidly. Two guns are immediately needed for these houses. Please send them at once.

Private Hahn, of Captain Jocknick's company of cavalry, ordered to New Berne, was detailed by General Foster to act as editor of the New Era. Colonel Mix's order is for Captain Jocknick to take all his men, detached or otherwise; so Hahn will go. I told him he would have to make application to you or the general if he is to return here.

Lieutenant McLane, of the First North Carolina, went to New Berne on sick leave. His brother writes that he is just recovering and that the surgeon says that a short visit to a Northern climate is necessary for his recovery. I mention the case for the general's consideration.

      Yours, very truly,

                              EDWARD E. POTTER,
                                    Commanding Post.

————

                              FORT MONROE, VA., September 11, 1862.

Maj. Gen. H. W. HALLECK,
      General-in-Chief:

Colonel Williams' regiment of cavalry was ordered here at my special request for service under my command. On its arrival General McClellan ordered it, without landing, to Aquia Creek, promising me another regiment. I have not been furnished with one, and, moreover, five companies of the Fourth Pennsylvania Cavalry, on duty here, have been taken away. I have only 500 cavalry at Williamsburg. Another regiment is indispensable.

                              JOHN A. DIX,
                                    Major-General.

————

                              FORT MONROE, VA., September 12, 1862.

Maj. Gen. H. W. HALLECK,
      General-in-Chief:

A court, for the trial of Major Wilson, was ordered before your dispatches were received.* It will meet on Monday next.

I have had a steamer out for two days watching for the Merrimac and other transports, with troops from Boston and other Northern cities, but none have been found, and the newspapers announce that the Mer-

————————————
                        * See p. 11.

rimac has reached Alexandria. I cannot hold Williamsburg with 500 cavalry. I have kept them there the last four days with the hope that they might do something to retrieve the character of the regiment. I will withdraw them to Yorktown. In abandoning Williamsburg we leave to the mercy of the insurgents some good Union men, whom we induced, by assurances of protection, to come out for us. I fear I shall get no troops here unless you send them direct from the North to report to me.

JOHN A. DIX,
Major-General.

UNITED STATES FLAG-SHIP MINNESOTA,
Norfolk, Va., September 12, 1862.

Maj. Gen. JOHN A. DIX, U. S. A.:

GENERAL: I have the honor to inform you that in order to strengthen our position at Yorktown I have diverted the gunboat Valley City, now undergoing repairs at Fortress Monroe, from her intended destination on the blockade off Wilmington, where her services are much needed, and to-morrow, when her repairs will probably be finished, she will proceed to assist the United States gunboat Chocura in her present operations in York River.

I am, very respectfully, your obedient servant,

S. P. LEE,
Acting Rear-Admiral.

HEADQUARTERS SEVENTH ARMY CORPS,
Fort Monroe, Va., September 12, 1862.

Hon. E. M. STANTON,
Secretary of War:

SIR: The contraband negroes who have been permitted to collect in great numbers at this fort and in this vicinity have always been and are now a very great source of embarrassment to the troops in this garrison and in the camps hereabouts and to the white population in this neighborhood. In case the fort should be invested or approached by the enemy's forces I should feel obliged to ship them all to the North.

This disposition, it seems to me, ought to be made of them without needless delay, and, if possible, with the concurrence of the authorities of the State or States to which they may be sent. To this end I respectfully ask permission and authority from the War Department to communicate and make arrangements with the Governors of Massachusetts and other Northern States with a view to the transfer to those States of all colored men, women, and children now under the superintendence of Mr. C. B. Wilder, at Old Point Comfort and its vicinity, amounting to about 2,000.

I have the honor to be, with great respect, yours,

JOHN A. DIX,
Major-General.

YORKTOWN, VA., September 12, 1862.

Maj. Gen. H. W. HALLECK,
General-in-Chief:

Having been placed in charge of the engineering operations at this place and Gloucester by General McClellan I deem it my duty to report that the armament directed by him is held at Fort Monroe for orders from Washington.* They are needed.

JOHN J. PECK,
Major-General.

———

WAR DEPARTMENT,
Washington, September 12, 1862.

Major-General DIX, *Fort Monroe, Va.:*

General Casey was directed some days ago† to send you four new regiments from this place. A part has already gone. If with these and the troops coming by water you cannot hold Suffolk, of course it must be given up. Yorktown ought certainly to be held. General Peck telegraphs here for armament from Fort Monroe. All such matters are under your direction.

H. W. HALLECK,
General-in-Chief.

———

FORT MONROE, VA., *September* 13, 1862.

Maj. Gen. H. W. HALLECK,
General-in-Chief :

The One hundred and thirtieth New York has just arrived and will go to Suffolk. It is very raw, not even knowing the manual of arms. The rebels had 1,500 men repairing the Petersburg Railroad to the Blackwater, and I have no doubt contemplate an early movement on Suffolk. The loss of my three best regiments at that point is unfortunate at this moment. No effort will be spared to maintain our position there.

JOHN A. DIX,
Major-General.

———

WAR DEPARTMENT,
Washington, September 14, 1862.

Major-General DIX, *Fort Monroe, Va.:*

Issue such ordnance stores as you deem necessary for the good of the service, either for Yorktown or elsewhere. This is not a time to delay for formalities.‡

H. W. HALLECK,
General-in-Chief.

———

WAR DEPARTMENT,
Washington, September 15, 1862.

Major-General DIX, *Fort Monroe, Va.:*

Four new full regiments have been sent to you from here. Nothing is yet heard of the Merrimac. General Wool has been directed not to issue any more passes to cross our lines. You will exercise your dis-

———

* See Halleck to Dix, September 14.
† On September 10.
‡ See Peck to Halleck, September 12, p. 391.

cretion in the case you report, but I am decidedly of opinion that at the present time persons from Baltimore should not be permitted to go into Virginia

H. W. HALLECK,
General-in-Chief.

SEPTEMBER 17, 1862.

General DIX:

The Morse, our lightest draught, is ordered up the Nansemond.

S. P. LEE,
Acting Rear-Admiral.

UNITED STATES FLAG-SHIP MINNESOTA,
Norfolk, Va., September 17, 1862.

Maj. Gen. JOHN A. DIX, *Commanding, &c.:*

GENERAL: When the rebels evacuated Norfolk they left a steam gunboat on the stocks in this city and the necessary material provided for her, part of which came from the navy-yard. Admiral Goldsborough arranged with General Viele, now absent, to have the hull so far completed as to allow of launching the gunboat, with the view of towing it to the Washington Navy-Yard, there to be finished and equipped. The only expense to be incurred here would be for the labor, which the admiral assumed to defray. It is desirable to have this object carried out as speedily as possible. I have therefore to request that you will be so good as to cause the quartermaster who has control both of Mr. Burroughs and the building yard to require Mr. Burroughs to hasten the launching of this gunboat, which can be done, I am informed, in eight or ten days.

I have the honor to be, general, respectfully, yours,

S. P. LEE,
Acting Rear-Admiral.

WASHINGTON, *September* 18, 1862.

Major-General DIX:

The two regiments at the Patuxent are subject to your orders. General Banks thinks that one can be spared.

H. W. HALLECK,
General-in-Chief.

UNITED STATES FLAG-SHIP MINNESOTA,
Norfolk, Va., September 18, 1862.

Maj. Gen. JOHN A. DIX,
Commanding Seventh Army Corps, Fortress Monroe, Va.:

GENERAL: The president of the Norfolk Gas Company recently applied to me, through General Viele, to send a quantity of shingles to the North. This application was promptly referred to the Navy Department, and in reply I am instructed that "no traffic in shingles, cotton, tobacco, or other articles can be permitted in the region blockaded."

I have the honor to be, general, very respectfully, yours,

S. P. LEE,
Acting Rear-Admiral.

UNITED STATES FLAG-SHIP MINNESOTA,
Norfolk, Va., September 18, 1862.

Maj. Gen. JOHN A. DIX, U. S. A.,
Commanding Seventh Army Corps, Fortress Monroe, Va.:

GENERAL : The instructions from the Navy Department, of which I informed you to-day, make it necessary that I immediately direct the naval vessels on guard duty not to allow any steamer or sailing vessel to pass in or out of this harbor and these waters unless she is in the service of the Army or the Navy, and has nothing on board except the United States mail or United States troops and public property, viz, Army or Navy stores and supplies.

In respect to all Army transports I respectfully request that you will cause each to be supplied with an official certificate stating the name of the transport; that she is in the service of the Army, and that she has nothing on board for traffic. Such a certificate should be left with the officer of the Navy guard vessel by every steamer or vessel passing either way.

I further request to be informed of the name and official position of the officer at Norfolk and at Fort Monroe whom you may authorize to issue these certificates. All vessels without such certificate will be liable to detention.

Whilst I desire to carry out my instructions with fidelity I need not assure you of my further wish to do so in accordance with your official convenience.

I have the honor to be, general, very respectfully, yours,
S. P. LEE,
Actg. Rear-Admiral, Comdg. N. Atlantic Blockading Squadron.

HEADQUARTERS SEVENTH ARMY CORPS,
Fort Monroe, Va., September 19, 1862.

Actg. Rear-Admiral S. P. LEE,
Commanding North Atlantic Blockading Squadron :

ADMIRAL : I have the honor to acknowledge the receipt of your two communications of the 18th instant. I have directed the provost-marshal, Capt. William E. Blake, to give the certificates you require. I shall, however, call the attention of the Government to the instructions you have received from the Navy Department and ask that some action may be had on my communication of the 4th instant to the Secretary of War, of which I inclose a copy. You may be assured that until some proper system of intercourse with Norfolk is established, so that the people may receive what they need for their subsistence and comfort, I shall interpose no obstacle to the execution of those instructions; but, on the contrary, shall do all in my power to aid you in carrying them out.

I am, very respectfully, your obedient servant,
JOHN A. DIX,
Major-General.

HEADQUARTERS SEVENTH ARMY CORPS,
Fort Monroe, Va., September 19, 1862.

Actg. Rear-Admiral S. P. LEE,
Commanding North Atlantic Blockading Squadron :

ADMIRAL : Since writing to you this morning I have received the regulations concerning internal and coastwise intercourse, of which I inclose a copy,* and under which I think we may accomplish the object I had in view in my communication of the 4th instant to the Secretary of War, though I should have preferred the arrangement I suggested.

I am, very respectfully, your obedient servant,

JOHN A. DIX,
Major-General.

WAR DEPARTMENT,
Washington City, September 19, 1862.

Maj. Gen. JOHN A. DIX,
Commanding at Fort Monroe, Va.:

GENERAL: The Secretary of War directs me to acknowledge the receipt of your communication of the 12th instant, in which you state that the contraband negroes which have been permitted to collect at Fort Monroe and in its vicinity have been and now are a very great source of embarrassment to the troops in the garrison and neighboring camps, and that in the event that the fort should be invested or approached by the enemy's forces you should be obliged to ship them all North. In view of these circumstances you request permission and authority to communicate and make arrangements with the Governors of Massachusetts and other Northern States with a view to a transfer to those States of all colored men, women, and children now under the superintendence of Mr. C. B. Wilder at Old Point Comfort and its vicinity, amounting to about 2,000.

In reply the Secretary instructs me to say that the permission to enter into a correspondence and the authority to make arrangements with the executives of the several Northern States for the purpose indicated is granted and conferred upon you agreeably to your request.

Very respectfully, your obedient servant,

P. H. WATSON,
Assistant Secretary of War.

WAR DEPARTMENT,
Washington, September 19, 1862.

Major-General DIX, *Fort Monroe, Va.:*

Send up all of Peck's division, which you can replace with the new troops. His division will be filled up here.

H. W. HALLECK,
General-in-Chief.

FORT MONROE, VA., *September 20, 1862.*

Maj. Gen. H. W. HALLECK,
General-in-Chief:

I was all day at Suffolk yesterday, expecting an advance from the Blackwater, where the rebels had sent down a considerable force from Petersburg. I have two of Peck's brigades there and three of the new regiments—perfectly raw. One never had had arms in their hands till they reached there yesterday. At Yorktown and Gloucester I have only Emory's brigade; here only one regiment; at Camp Hamilton one regiment, and at Newport News only 500 men. It would be very unsafe to withdraw any of Peck's division at this moment. I have at Suf-

---

* Not found.

folk the great bulk of my force. The rebels have finished the railroad from Petersburg to the Blackwater. The secessionists were cooking for them at Suffolk night before last with the assurance that they were to be there yesterday. I beg you to let Peck's division remain at present. He is superintending the armament of Yorktown. I have not a single artillery, ordnance, or engineer officer for that post.

JOHN A. DIX,
Major-General.

HEADQUARTERS SEVENTH ARMY CORPS,
Fort Monroe, Va., September 20, 1862.

Maj. Gen. H. W. HALLECK,
General-in-Chief:

GENERAL: I requested by telegraph that General Peck's division might not be taken away from me at present, assigning, briefly, the reasons. I do so now more in detail.

My aggregate force present on the 10th instant was as follows:

Fort Monroe	520
Camp Hamilton	3,330
Newport News	518
Norfolk	2,021
Suffolk	3,454
Yorktown and Gloucester	3,868
Williamsburg	817
	14,528
Deduct sick	1,384
	13,144
Add four new regiments, about	3,400
Total	16,544

Since the 10th I have, in order to meet a threatened movement against Suffolk, augmented my force there to about 8,500, and left at Camp Hamilton only one regiment.

Suffolk.—This is at the moment my most important position. The enemy has just finished the railroad from Petersburg to the Blackwater, 20 miles from Suffolk, and on Tuesday and Wednesday moved a considerable body of infantry to that point. There was a force of cavalry and artillery in the vicinity before. On Thursday I went to Suffolk with reasonable assurance that there would be an advance on us, and examined the preparations made for defense by General Ferry.

The gauge of the Norfolk and Petersburg Railroad is 5 feet, and the gauge of the Norfolk and Weldon, or Seaboard, 4 feet 8½ inches. Having no locomotives for the former we altered the gauge to 4 feet 8½ inches from Norfolk to Suffolk, connecting the two roads at the latter point by a Y, so as to use the equipment on either road at pleasure. Since the enemy have completed their road from Petersburg to the Blackwater I have been altering the gauge from Suffolk to Blackwater, so as to render it useless to them and advantageous to us if we wish to throw a force down from Suffolk, thus enabling us to control this communication as far as the Blackwater. We are out some 6 miles, and are altering 3 miles a day. When you decided to hold Suffolk I determined to make it as effective as possible, and this change of gauge may be of great importance if we are in force again in this quarter and in North Carolina. To effect this object I must have troops, and the number I now have there may be indispensable to enable me to hold the place against attack. I have ordered a reconnaissance in force to be made to-day in the direction of the Blackwater.

Yorktown.—The armament is now in progress. General Peck is super-intending it. I have no one who can do it so well. Indeed, I have for duty but one engineer under my command; only one ordnance officer, who has charge of the arsenal here, and only one artillery officer, who has been until recently the commanding officer of this post. The scien-tific corps of the army have been absorbed by other commands. I may be obliged to send General Peck to Suffolk if an advance is made by the enemy.

The intrenchments constructed by the Confederates at Yorktown are very strong, but were intended for a large force. It is not proposed to hold the place with more than 4,000 men, and therefore some out-works not intended to be occupied are in progress of demolition. The arma-ment will be completed as rapidly as possible, and with the present force and the guns already in position the place could hold out against greatly superior numbers.

Gloucester.—General McClellan, before he left here, ordered Glouces-ter to be armed. I do not propose to execute the order until we have completed the armament of Yorktown and until I have 20,000 effective men, for I do not think a smaller number sufficient to protect my ex-tended lines.

This position is auxiliary to Yorktown in controlling the navigation of the York River. It is commanded by Yorktown Heights, but it might, nevertheless, in the hands of an enemy, be a source of annoyance.

Newport News.—This post was abandoned in June last by order of General McClellan. Everything was removed except the sick and a company of cavalry, as a guard. Since then the sick have been increased and I have added a very small regiment of infantry.

The Secretary of the Navy requested that we would mount two or three 200-pounder guns to aid the gunboats in defending themselves against the new Merrimac, but we have no 200-pounders, and unless I have a competent force there the enemy might, if we were to obtain them, use them against us. There are some earthworks, a good deal dilapidated, for defense against an inland attack, but they require about 3,000 men to man them. All the guns were removed.

Newport News as a station defends nothing. The channel of the James River is wide. A vessel drawing from 17 to 18 feet can pass out at a distance of 1½ miles, although the deeper part of the channel is near the land. Its occupation as a post was always of questionable utility.

Williamsburg I consider of no importance, except as an advance post for watching a movement of the enemy from the Chickahominy. By holding it we are able to push our vedettes farther out. It is too dis-tant from Yorktown (13 miles), but I have only a small cavalry force there. It is under a brave and vigilant officer, who I think will take care of himself. I need for—

	Men.
Fort Monroe	1,000
Camp Hamilton	2,000
Yorktown	4,000
Gloucester	1,000
Williamsburg	800
Norfolk	3,000
Newport News	500
Suffolk (at present)	8,000
Total	20,300

If we fall back from Suffolk we must have a larger force at Norfolk.

With no other force in the Department of Virginia I think the above estimate the lowest number by which the several places occupied by us can be held against the forces which the enemy can easily send against us.

If Peck's division is taken from me I shall have but 9,000 effective men left, and of these more than one-third are entirely raw—for the most part unacquainted even with the manual of arms.

I am, very respectfully, your obedient servant,

JOHN A. DIX,
Major-General.

FORT MONROE, VA., *September* 20, 1862.

Maj. Gen. H. W. HALLECK,
General-in-Chief:

I have just received a dispatch from Captain Rodgers, of the Galena, informing me that 2,000 troops came from Petersburg the day before yesterday and 3,000 yesterday to the Blackwater; that from 8,000 to 10,000 are assembled now, and that 15,000, recently arrived, are on the south side of the James River, in the vicinity of Richmond. This accords with my information from other sources.

JOHN A. DIX,
Major-General.

HEADQUARTERS SEVENTH ARMY CORPS,
Fort Monroe, Va., September 21, 1862.

Hon. SALMON P. CHASE,
Secretary of the Treasury:

SIR: Captain Slicer, of the revenue service, has written to you in regard to some shipments by the schooner Geranium from Baltimore to this post, under a regular clearance from the custom-house. I gave a permit to the shippers to bring certain enumerated articles for the people at Back River and the vicinity. But a quantity of other articles not embraced in my permit were allowed to be shipped by the collector; among them are 3,000 percussion caps. These articles were intended for a neighborhood where there is at this season a good deal of game, and the inhabitants ought not to be deprived of the privilege of shooting. I propose to detain them to be sold here to individuals, for their personal use, under special permits and in such small quantities as to make it clear that they are not intended for traffic. Back River is about 7 miles from the fort.

There are also, not embraced in my permit, 84 gross of matches—12,096 boxes. In Baltimore they may have cost $75. In Richmond they would bring 75 cents a box—$9,072. Such a quantity imported for a small neighborhood, taken in connection with the difference of price, shows that they were intended for sale where the enormous profit is to be obtained. These I propose also to detain.

As the custom-house officers have cleared these articles, and as there is no irregularity, there seems to be no reason for holding the vessel or the residue of the cargo. She has been detained by Captain Slicer, and the only question is whether the articles referred to shall be stopped here. This question I suppose need not embarrass me, as the clearance was for this post, and there is no reason why the articles not included in my permit should be allowed to go farther.

I think it very important that the trade with Norfolk and Portsmouth and the district immediately adjoining my command should be regulated by permits given by me as the commander of the military department. Through my provost-marshals and other subordinates I can ascertain the wants of every neighborhood, and indeed of every family, and thus be able to limit the supply to their reasonable wants. Collectors at a distance have no such knowledge, and a privilege intended to meet real necessities may be perverted, as it often is, to purposes of traffic with disloyal districts and individuals.

I am, very respectfully, your obedient servant,

JOHN A. DIX,
Major-General.

WASHINGTON, D. C., *September* 21, 1862.

Major-General DIX, *Fort Monroe:*

The ordering up of Peck's division was at General McClellan's urgent request. In the advance of the enemy's army against this place and Maryland he did not deem it necessary on the Peninsula. If you require it, keep it and discharge the transports.

H. W. HALLECK,
General-in-Chief.

SUFFOLK, *September* 21, 1862.

Major-General DIX:

I have reason to believe that the infantry and artillery of the enemy have gone to Franklin, and that a bridge is constructed there. Their numbers are reported at 8,000 to 10,000, besides those heretofore at Franklin. Five hundred of their cavalry are reported on this side there.

O. S. FERRY,
Brigadier-General.

UNITED STATES FLAG-SHIP MINNESOTA,
Off Newport News, Va., September 23, 1862.

Maj. Gen. JOHN A. DIX,
Comdg. Seventh Army Corps, Fort Monroe, Va.:

GENERAL: I have the honor to transmit herewith for your information a copy of my instructions to officers on guard duty, enforcing the blockade of Norfolk and of these waters; also a number of printed certificates for vessels (other than the mail or troop steamers) passing in and out, to leave at the guard vessel. This certificate is prepared on one side for the signature of Captain Blake, as arranged with you, and on the other side for the signature of the master of the vessel; the first stating that the vessel is in the service of the army exclusively, and both declaring that she has no article but only proper supplies for the army on board.

The mail boats from Baltimore and Norfolk and troop transports will not be required to stop for inspection, as they are understood to have a responsible army police on board and will not be allowed by you to violate the blockade.

I will thank you to inform me what steps you have taken or may take to insure this result.

I have the honor to be, general, respectfully, yours,

S. P. LEE,
Actg. Rear-Admiral, Comdg. N. Atlantic Blockading Squadron.

[Inclosure.]

Instructions for officers on guard duty.

No vessel must be allowed to pass inward except the mail steamer and transports with troops without stopping at the guard vessel and delivering a certificate signed by Capt. W. E. Blake, provost-marshal, at Fort Monroe, that the vessel is in the employ of the War Department and has supplies for the army only on board. Vessels without such certificates must be taken charge of and the circumstances immediately reported to the admiral or senior officer present.

Outward-bound vessels, other than those before excepted (mail steamers, &c.), must stop at the guard vessel and leave a certificate signed by ——, stating the vessel to be empty (in ballast) or has supplies for the army only on board.

Vessels attempting to pass without such certificate must be taken charge of and reported as before directed.

A boarding-book must be kept, and the names of all vessels passing the guard vessels in or out be entered therein, with the date, by whom owned, name of master, tonnage, and cargo. A weekly return, showing the foregoing, must be made to the admiral or senior officer present.

S. P. LEE,
Actg. Rear-Admiral, Comdg. N. Atlantic Blockading Squadron.

———

FORT MONROE, VA., *September 23, 1862.*

Maj. Gen. H. W. HALLECK,
　　　General-in-Chief:

The enemy have completed their bridge at Carrsville, on the Norfolk and Seaboard Railroad, and have crossed a part of their force. They must have on the Blackwater 12,000 men, and for two or three days they have been concentrating them at Carrsville, one day's march from us. A column has left Richmond in the direction of Williamsburg, but I can get no definite information as to its numbers. The new Merrimac is expected down the river in ten days. There is nothing to cope with her but the Monitor. The Galena is no better than a wooden gunboat. If anything befalls the Monitor everything about us may be smashed up, our 12,000 men at Norfolk and Suffolk cut off from us, and our communication with Washington and Baltimore closed. The Ironsides was here, but has been withdrawn. There certainly ought to be another efficient armor-clad steamer sent here promptly.

JOHN A. DIX,
Major-General.

SUFFOLK, *September* 23, 1862.

Major-General DIX:

Arrived in good season. Have been over most of the approaches. The work is being pushed. No report as yet from Colonel Spear's reconnaissance.

JOHN J. PECK,
Major-General.

———

SUFFOLK, *September* 23, 1862.

Major-General DIX:

I have received a report from Colonel Spear, commanding reconnaissance, to this effect: He found first picket of enemy 3 miles this side Franklin; drove them. Proceeded a mile farther and met the enemy in some force at junction of South Quay and Franklin roads; enemy fell back. One mile from Franklin, cavalry and infantry picket; drove that and proceeded half mile farther. Enemy opened with artillery; reconnaissance halted and reconnoitered vicinity. Five thousand infantry at Franklin on both sides river; 2,000 at South Quay; 1,200 at Preston's Ferry. Floating bridge across Blackwater; [can] cross cars or artillery. Strict guard kept.

JOHN J. PECK,
Major-General.

———

WASHINGTON, D. C., *September* 24, 1862.

Maj. Gen. JOHN A. DIX, *Fort Monroe:*

The defense of the points occupied by you is necessarily left to your discretion. You will retain Peck's division and I will send you as soon as possible four more new regiments. The calls of General McClellan for re-enforcements and the tardy movements of new troops render it difficult to satisfy all demands.

I do not insist upon your holding all points now in your possession. In that matter you must be guided by the best interests of the country.

H. W. HALLECK,
General-in-Chief.

———

HEADQUARTERS DEPARTMENT OF NORTH CAROLINA,
New Berne, N. C., September 24, 1862.

Maj. Gen. H. W. HALLECK,
General-in-Chief U. S. Army, Washington, D. C.:

GENERAL: I have the honor to say that some time since I made a formal application to the honorable Secretary of War for more troops for this department. This application was made previous to the great answer made by the loyal States to the President's call for troops.

I learn now that large numbers of new regiments are pouring into Washington, and beg your attention, therefore, to my request for more troops, and in this connection I beg leave to say that, seeing the turn affairs are taking in Virginia and Maryland, the occupation in force of this department may be most advantageous to the campaign. The advantages of this post for drilling and perfecting new regiments are very great. The place is healthy now, wood is in great abundance, water sufficient, and subsistence and quartermaster's supplies are easily obtained from New York, both to this point and to Beaufort, from which point the railroad is in good order and running.

I have some eight regiments of infantry here of old troops, divided into two brigades, commanded by most excellent officers (acting briga-dier-generals), Colonels Amory and Stevenson, and with other excellent colonels could readily drill any number of new regiments you might send. My artillery force (Third New York Artillery) is good. They number five light batteries, with twenty-eight pieces; Rhode Island Battery, with six pieces; Rocket Battalion, with eight pieces. My siege train ready for transportation, though at present on shipboard, with supply of ammunition, consists of four 30-pounder Parrott guns; in addition to which I can land for the investment of any sea-coast place ten 32's (long), on ship-carriages. My cavalry force is one good and efficient regiment, Third New York Cavalry.

My knowledge of the country in this region, derived from being sta-tioned here as engineer officer in charge and more lately in command of this department, enables me to use the small force at my disposal to advantage, which advantages would of course be greatly increased by having a much larger force at my disposal.

Hoping you will see fit to send me additional troops, I am, with great respect, your obedient servant,

J. G. FOSTER,
Major-General.

FLAG-SHIP MINNESOTA,
Newport News, September 24, 1862.

Maj. Gen. JOHN A. DIX,
Commanding Seventh Army Corps, &c.:

GENERAL: The schooner A. S. Pearcy, recently attempting to leave Norfolk under a permit from the provost-marshal with a cargo of mer-chandise, was stopped, and the case referred to the Navy Department. In reply I am instructed not to allow any vessel to import or export merchandise into Norfolk, Elizabeth River, or any part of the country blockaded; that Beaufort, N. C., is the only port open for general traffic within the limit of the North Atlantic Squadron; that what are called permits from any officer, except the Secretaries of the War, Treasury, and Navy, authorizing the ingress or egress of any vessel in violation of the blockade are not to be regarded; that the schooner Pearcy, with merchandise from Norfolk for Baltimore, must not be allowed to depart; that there must be no favoritism or license for trade given to any one or more of our own countrymen within the blockaded region, or to im-port or to export merchandise, which would justly be considered as evasive of the blockade and in bad faith; that no officer of the Army or Navy is authorized to grant permits, and that all vessels engaged in illegal traffic must be seized; that such as under the authority of the War or Navy Departments may be engaged to carry supplies to the Army or Navy will take no return cargo; that the blockade is intended to interdict all trade whatever with the country blockaded during its continuance and should be rigidly enforced.

In communicating to you the foregoing I am happy to acknowledge your assurance of your disposition to aid me, as you essentially may, in giving effect to the policy of the Department, although you entertain a different view of the subject.

I have the honor to be, general, most respectfully, yours,
                                          S. P. LEE,
                                       Acting Rear-Admiral.

P. S.—Commodore Livingston can give return freights of Government property from the Norfolk navy-yard to Northern navy-yards to quite a number of the vessels bringing army supplies here. It will be advantageous to them and to the Government interests if you will be so good as to have them so informed.

HEADQUARTERS SEVENTH ARMY CORPS,
Fort Monroe, Va., September 24, 1862.

Lieut. Com. C. W. FLUSSER, U. S. N.:

SIR: The accompanying letter from [to] Acting Rear-Admiral Lee will explain to you the earnest desire I feel to have two or three gunboats sent up the Chowan and Blackwater Rivers as far as Franklin, where the enemy has concentrated a considerable force for the purpose of attacking Suffolk. I have at the latter place a sufficient force to co-operate with you in the attack on Franklin in driving the enemy away and destroying the bridge which he has recently constructed over the Blackwater at that place, which is the crossing of the Seaboard Railroad. There is deep water as high as Franklin, but I do not know the character of the Blackwater above its junction with the Chowan. I consider the expedition a very important one, and trust there may be no obstacle to its accomplishment.

If the gunboats can go up, please let me know when they will [reach] Franklin and I will have my force there.

I am, very respectfully, yours,
                                          JOHN A. DIX,
                                           Major-General.

[Inclosure.]

HEADQUARTERS SEVENTH ARMY CORPS,
Fort Monroe, Va., September 24, 1862.

Actg. Rear-Admiral S. P. LEE,
Commanding North Atlantic Blockading Squadron:

ADMIRAL: I had last evening an earnest request from Major-General Peck, commanding at Suffolk, that two or three gunboats should be sent up the Chowan and Blackwater Rivers as far as Franklin, where the enemy have a force of from 10,000 to 12,000 men. If this can be done I think we shall be able to disperse this force and destroy the bridge at that place.

I have sent my aide, Major Dix, with this dispatch, and will be glad to receive your answer by him.

I have received your communication of yesterday and will give it my early attention.

I have the honor to be, your obedient servant,
                                          JOHN A. DIX,
                                           Major-General.

HEADQUARTERS SEVENTH ARMY CORPS,
Fort Monroe, Va., September 25, 1862.

Actg. Rear-Admiral S. F. LEE,
Commanding North Atlantic Blockading Squadron:

ADMIRAL: I have sent the passes designed for Norfolk to Capt. J. H. Liebenau, provost-marshal, who will sign them for vessels coming from that port. Captain Blake will sign passes for vessels going from this post.

The mail and transport vessels are subjected to a strict examination, and nothing is permitted to go in them except supplies for the army or articles belonging to individuals not designed for traffic. An account of everything carried in these vessels is kept by the captain of the port. By these precautions there can be no traffic with Norfolk except such as is carried on under the regulations which I sent to you.

I am, very respectfully, your obedient servant,
JOHN A. DIX,
Major-General.

HEADQUARTERS SEVENTH ARMY CORPS,
Fort Monroe, Va., September 25, 1862

Actg. Rear-Admiral S. P. LEE,
Commanding North Atlantic Blockading Squadron:

ADMIRAL: I have deferred answering your communication of the 17th instant in order to obtain all the facts in regard to the steam gunboat on the stocks in Norfolk. General Viele, on a reference of the matter to him, says:

Admiral Lee is laboring [under] a misapprehension. The private ship-yard of one Nash was seized by my order for Government purposes, and it has been and now is used by the quartermaster for repairing vessels used by the army for transportation. In the yard and on the stocks is a vessel completed, intended for the insurgents by this man Nash. I directed the quartermaster to complete the vessel sufficient for launching.

On mentioning the fact to Admiral (then Commodore) Goldsborough he offered the use of a gunboat to tow the vessel to Washington. That is all the understanding there was in the matter.

This subject was brought to my attention in the month of August. I was not aware that General Viele had done anything in regard to it, and on a statement of facts by Captain Ludlow, the quartermaster at Norfolk, I ordered him to have the vessel planked up so that she could be launched and towed to Baltimore, where I proposed, with the consent of the War Department, to have her finished. I inclose a copy of Captain Ludlow's report to me, stating the facts at my request.* The work has been done by my order; and I directed him further to place in her, if it should be found suitable, a boiler left by the insurgents.

I am, very respectfully, your obedient servant,
JOHN A. DIX,
Major-General.

UNITED STATES FLAG-SHIP MINNESOTA,
Newport News, Va., September 25, 1862.

Maj. Gen. JOHN A. DIX, U. S. A.,
Commanding Seventh Army Corps, Fort Monroe, Va.:

GENERAL: The Navy Department informs me that timely notice

---

* Not found.

should be given to the inhabitants of Norfolk, &c., in order that those of them might leave who should avoid personal exposure to our fire, whilst defending the place if attacked by the rebel forces.

I submit to you that in order to avoid all embarrassments to an efficient defense arising from delay in giving this notice, we should, as soon as you think it necessary to do so, give such public notice to the inhabitants of Norfolk and Portsmouth, to foreign consuls and their families therein residing, as may be proper.

I invite your advice and co-operation in the premises and submit herewith the within for your consideration and amendment. I think the matter demands our immediate attention.

I have the honor to be, general, your obedient servant,

S. P. LEE,
Actg. Rear-Admiral, Comdg. N. Atlantic Blockading Squadron.

[Inclosure.]

Official notice is hereby given to all non-combatants, foreign consuls, &c., that the present threatened attack by the rebel forces on Suffolk, an outpost of Norfolk and Portsmouth, Va., makes it necessary to notify them that if they shall continue to reside in these towns they will do so at their own peril, and must take the consequences that may ensue from the exposure they will encounter during the defense of Norfolk and Portsmouth by the military and naval forces of the United States.

JOHN A. DIX,
Major-General.

S. P. LEE,
Actg. Rear-Admiral, Comdg. N. Atlantic Blockading Squadron.

To be communicated through General Viele to the authorities and inhabitants of Norfolk and Portsmouth, to each foreign consul, and to be published in the Norfolk Union newspapers.

HEADQUARTERS SEVENTH ARMY CORPS,
Fort Monroe, Va., September 25, 1862.

Actg. Rear-Admiral S. P. LEE,
Commanding North Atlantic Blockading Squadron:

ADMIRAL: I have had the honor to receive your communication of this morning in regard to the threatened attack of the rebels on Suffolk. The question of giving the notice of which you inclose a draught is a very important and delicate one and I desire time to consider it. There has been as yet no movement this side of the Blackwater, and it appears to me that an advance should precede such a notice, which would induce a large number of the inhabitants of Norfolk to leave and devolve on us the obligation of passing them through our lines. If we intended to make the attack there would be no question as to the propriety of giving the notice.

I am, very respectfully, your obedient servant,

JOHN A. DIX,
Major-General.

UNITED STATES FLAG-SHIP MINNESOTA,
Off Newport News, Va., September 26, 1862.

Maj. Gen. JOHN A. DIX, U. S. A.,
    Comdg. Seventh Army Corps, Fort Monroe, Va.:

GENERAL: I have the honor to acknowledge the receipt of your reply to my communication of the 25th, relative to giving notice to the foreign consuls and to the inhabitants of Norfolk to prepare them in the event of an attack on Norfolk, now threatened by the concentration of rebel forces in the vicinity of Suffolk, the outpost of Norfolk. Should the enemy march upon the town, and under shelter of it attack the troops and gunboats, the latter, stationed in the harbor to assist in maintaining our occupation of the place, would be obliged to fire upon it.

By giving timely notice to the women and children, the consuls, &c., we shall feel free to fire, should it become necessary to do so. By hesitation and delay, lest we put to some inconvenience the inhabitants, of whom the influential, if not the larger part, appear hostile to the General Government, we may entail on ourselves the disagreeable alternative, in the event of a sudden attack, of firing upon a town whose people have not had the benefit of a previous and proper notice. A premature warning would be better for them and for us than none at all, and might possibly have the effect of inducing the enemy, at the instance of the inhabitants, to desist from any attempt against our position there.

I therefore propose that the terms of a notice shall at once be arranged to your satisfaction and signed by me, so that you may date, sign, and publish it, whenever in your good judgment it shall be proper to do so.

I have the honor to be, general, very respectfully, yours,

S. P. LEE,
Actg. Rear-Admiral, Comdg. N. Atlantic Blockading Squadron.

HDQRS. DEPT. OF VIRGINIA, SEVENTH ARMY CORPS,
Fort Monroe, September 27, 1862.

Maj. Gen. H. W. HALLECK:

GENERAL: Soon after I took command here I presented to the Government the case of the inhabitants of Norfolk, who were then and are now more grievously affected by the commercial restrictions imposed on them.

On the 4th instant I presented their case a second time to the War Department, reiterating my views, and contending that Norfolk, not being a blockaded port, is not subject to the laws of blockade, but that it is held by military occupation and governed by the laws of war, and that neutral nations cannot call us to account for any commercial intercourse we may think proper to allow for the comfort of our troops or of the inhabitants who are dependent on us, and for whose wants every dictate of justice and humanity calls on us to provide.

The state of things here is deplorable. The people are suffering for want of almost all the necessaries of life. They pay to-day $16 per barrel for flour. Through our interdiction of trade we have shut them out both from the North and the South, and they are actually worse off than they were under the insurgents. I confess I do not understand the policy, if there is any. The permission was asked the other day to take a cargo of coal there for the gas company, and it was refused by the Secretary of the Treasury. There have been two or three murders recently and dark streets will facilitate the perpetration of crime. Permits have been given to particular individuals to take cargoes there in a few instances for general traffic, and in direct violation of the laws of blockade, if the blockade exists. But the Secretary of the Navy has instructed Admiral Lee not to allow any traffic in tobacco, shingles, or other products of the labor of the inhabitants with the places from which merchandise has been introduced under the permits referred to, and as they have no money they cannot as a general rule avail themselves of the benefits of this partial reopening of trade. Special permits are a source of the most unconscionable extortions. A man was permitted to take 250 tons of coal the other day, and the city being nearly destitute he sold for $15 a ton what cost him about $6. The Secretary of the Navy has instructed Admiral Lee not to allow anything to pass except supplies for the army on permits from General Dix. There is a revenue cutter here in charge of a discreet and vigilant officer who is exercising the appropriate function of suppressing illicit trade; but the Navy Department assumes that the admiral is there to enforce a blockade as if the place belonged to an enemy, whereas it is in our possession, held by military occupation, and should be governed by the commander of the military forces until the laws of the United States are fully extended over it. How can it be said to be a blockaded port when the United States mail is carried to and fro daily and a post-office established for general correspondence without restriction? I earnestly ask your attention to my letter of the 4th instant to the Secretary of War.

The permits given at Washington to particular individuals to trade at Norfolk, for want of proper information, have been granted in some instances to unworthy persons. One was obtained not long ago by an individual who was turned out of the quartermaster's department at this post for fraud and who was recently found with a large quantity of quinine destined unquestionably for Richmond.

You may have heard that articles are smuggled through Norfolk to Richmond. No doubt a pound of tea and a pair of boots may reach there occasionally. Smuggling exists wherever a large profit is to be made. But these leaks at Norfolk and everywhere else do not amount to an appreciable sum. Tea has risen in three months from $15 to $20 a pound at Richmond, and other articles in proportion, showing how little has been gained by contraband trade.

If the War or Treasury Departments are unwilling to trust to the military commander the power of granting permits to carry to Norfolk what is necessary to save the people from absolute suffering, but prefer to retain it, it should be delegated to a special agent here, who will know precisely what is needed, and who can, through the information he will gain, confine supplies to proper limits and the privilege of trading to honest hands.

I hope you will be able to spare half an hour from your urgent duties to consider this matter. Between the Treasury Department, whose province it is to regulate peaceful commerce, and the Navy Department, which fancies it is enforcing a blockade, the unfortunate inhabitants of Norfolk and Portsmouth (one-third of them loyal) are in danger of starvation, and the military authorities, which have the nominal control, bear all the responsibility and the odium.

I am, very respectfully, your obedient servant,

JOHN A. DIX,
Major-General.

HDQRS. DEPT. OF VIRGINIA, SEVENTH ARMY CORPS,
Fort Monroe, Va., September 27, 1862.

Maj. Gen. JOHN J. PECK, *Commanding at Suffolk :*

GENERAL : I have ordered Captain Davis' battery to you from Yorktown. I will direct General Viele, in case of any sudden emergency,
to execute any order you may give him. His force is small, and I do
not wish it disturbed except in an exigency so pressing as to render
consultation with me dangerous.

The Morse draws so much water that she cannot safely go higher up
the Nansemond. Admiral Lee has promised me another gunboat of
less draught, and I will ask him to put her under your orders so that
she can take the place of the West End in case of need.

I trust the telegraph line will be completed to-day so that our com
munications may be more regular.

I am, very respectfully, your obedient servant,

JOHN A. DIX,
Major-General.

———

FLAG-SHIP MINNESOTA,
Newport News, September 28, 1862.

Maj. Gen. JOHN A. DIX, *Comdg. Seventh Army Corps :*

GENERAL : I have the honor to transmit herewith blank certificates
for the use of army transports outward bound from Yorktown and
vicinity, to be presented to the naval guard vessel in York River. I
beg you will cause these to be sent to the provost-marshal at Yorktown.

I have the honor to be, general, very respectfully, yours,

S. P. LEE,
Acting Rear-Admiral.

———

UNITED STATES FLAG-SHIP MINNESOTA,
Newport News, Va., September 27, 1862.

Maj. Gen. JOHN A. DIX, U. S. A.,
Commanding Seventh Army Corps, Fort Monroe, Va. :

GENERAL : I have to request that all army transports, before attempting to pass in or out through the blockade of James River or to
and from the Nansemond River, may be directed to stop and show to
the senior naval officer off Newport News the authority and object for
their passing the blockade. It will not answer to allow any vessel or
steamboat, though hoisting a white flag, to pass unquestioned and unknown.

I have the honor to be, general, very respectfully, yours,

S. P. LEE,
Actg. Rear-Admiral, Comdg. N. Atlantic Blockading Squadron.

———

HDQRS. DEPT. OF VIRGINIA, SEVENTH ARMY CORPS,
Fort Monroe, Va., September 28, 1862.

Actg. Rear-Admiral S. P. LEE,
Commanding North Atlantic Blockading Squadron :

ADMIRAL : I supposed all vessels going into the James River or the
Nansemond reported. Colonel Ludlow, one of my aides, who went to
Aiken's Landing with flag of truce twice, told me he reported to Cap-
tain Rodgers on both occasions, before you came from Norfolk. The

last flag that went up a few days ago was a boat from Washington in charge of an officer from that city. He was not aware, I presume, of the rule. I will give the necessary directions to the captain of the port here, who has the supervision of all vessels arriving or leaving.

I am, very respectfully, your obedient servant,

JOHN A. DIX,
Major-General.

HDQRS. DEPT. OF VIRGINIA, SEVENTH ARMY CORPS,
Fort Monroe, Va., September 29, 1862.

Maj. Gen. H. W. HALLECK:

GENERAL: In my letter of the 27th instant I stated that permits to trade in Norfolk had been given to improper persons. Yesterday Mr. Noyes, the person I alluded to as having been turned out of the quarmaster's department for fraud and having been found with a large quantity of quinine in Norfolk sent to him surreptitiously, arrived here, with a permit from General Wadsworth to trade, with a very heavy invoice of merchandise—among other items 2,000 tons of coal. I am very happy to know that such a supply of necessaries is to go to Norfolk for the relief of the people, but I greatly regret that it is in such hands. At the same time the quartermaster has received for examination from Mr. Tucker, Assistant Secretary of War, a fraudulent claim against the Government from this same man.

There also arrived here yesterday a man named Ward with supplies for the Marine Corps, purchased by him on a permit from the Secretary of the Navy. He refused to take the oath of allegiance, and I stopped the goods. I sent him with the assistant provost-marshal to General Viele, who reports as follows:

"This man Ward is a rebel scoundrel, who was imposed upon the provost-marshal by Captain McCawley (Marines), who is certainly very much in fault in the matter. The man's antecedents are bad. He has made a fortune in contracts for the insurgents. I think a man named Kirby, a renegade Englishman, is the agent in the matter."

If there had been a proper system of supervision here in regard to permits to trade these cases would not have occurred.

I think this will show the importance of trusting the matter of granting permits to the commander of the military department or of having a special agent of the War or Treasury Departments here. In that case Capt. James Millward, jr., the captain of the port here, would be a proper person, and his duties would be performed under my supervision. He keeps an account of all supplies received for the inhabitants around here, and is thus able to tell at any moment what any family needs. The same system through subordinates might be extended to Norfolk.

I am, very respectfully, your obedient servant,

JOHN A. DIX,
Major-General.

HDQRS. DEPT. OF VIRGINIA, SEVENTH ARMY CORPS,
Fort Monroe, Va., September 29, 1862.

Actg. Rear-Admiral S. P. LEE,
Commanding North Atlantic Blockading Squadron:

ADMIRAL: We had advices yesterday from the Blackwater. The enemy have not crossed, nor can I ascertain that they have been re-enforced. I think there is not an armed insurgent within 40 miles of Norfolk, unless it be some lurking squads, or perhaps companies, in the Dismal Swamp. In the mean time we have strengthened Suffolk so as to feel confident of resisting any force the enemy can have on the Blackwater.

I have fully considered the matter of the proposed notice to the people of Norfolk and the foreign consuls residing there, and regret to differ in opinion with you in regard to the policy of giving it at the present time. I am not sure that we can say that Suffolk is threatened until there is an advance of the enemy's forces, and I do not think the people of Norfolk should be disturbed unnecessarily. The hostile attack should be imminent. A notice of twenty-four hours is all that is needed in case of an attack or intended bombardment, and where we are merely acting on the defensive a longer one cannot be expected of us.

I have express orders not to allow any one to pass through our lines without the permission of the Secretary of War. If the proposed notice is to have any effect at all it will be to induce the wealthier portions of the people to leave, and they are in general opposed to us. The poor, among whom are all the loyal part of the population, have not the means of leaving. The result would therefore be to drive off those who sympathize with the insurgents and diminish the objection on the part of their forces to attack the place. I should, moreover, feel greatly embarrassed by applications to pass our lines. I am constantly refusing them now to parties who wish to go to Richmond. The proposed notice would insure a renewal of these applications and impose on me the obligation to grant them as well as others which might be made, while I am prohibited from doing so.

There is another consideration: I do not like at this time to acknowledge that we are acting on the defensive. The enemy, as I see from the Richmond papers, have been expecting an attack on Petersburg, and they think we have been very heavily re-enforced at Suffolk. The notice would be an acknowledgment that we have not the means of making an aggressive movement, and it might encourage such a movement against us.

These objections, as you see, relate chiefly to time. The form of the notice you inclosed to me is entirely unobjectionable. The only suggestion that occurs to me is the addition of the following words at the close, viz: "In case these places shall be assailed."

If you will, as you proposed in your letter of the 26th, send me such a notice, signed by yourself, I will use it when I think it necessary.

I am, very respectfully, your obedient servant,

JOHN A. DIX,
Major-General.

HDQRS. DEPT. OF VIRGINIA, SEVENTH ARMY CORPS,
Fort Monroe, Va., September 30, 1862.

Lieut. Com. C. W. FLUSSER,
Commanding U. S. Steamer Commodore Perry:

SIR: In consequence of some unexpected obstacles we cannot be ready until about the 10th proximo. I will give you three days' notice.

The bridge has not been reconstructed at Franklin for the Roanoke and Seaboard Railroad, but a floating bridge has been thrown across the Blackwater at that point.   A large force has been sent down from Petersburg, but we think the bulk of it is at Zuni, the crossing of the Petersburg road.   We are quite strong at Suffolk.

Respectfully, yours,

JOHN A. DIX,
Major-General.

Abstract from Return of the Department of Virginia, Maj. Gen. John A. Dix commanding, for September 30, 1862.

Command.	Present for duty.		Aggregate present.	Aggregate present and absent.	Pieces of field artillery.
	Officers.	Men.			
Department staff.	16	3	21	....	....
Fort Monroe (Col. S. M. Alford)	24	586	774	859	....
Camp Hamilton (Col. A. Conk)	47	1,090	1,227	1,431	10
Newport News (Maj. R. V. King)	29	419	541	752	....
Norfolk (Brig. Gen. E. L. Viele)	116	2,329	2,906	3,780	6
Suffolk (Maj. Gen. J. J. Peck)	380	7,796	9,386	11,957	20
Yorktown (Maj. Gen. E. D. Keyes)	231	4,533	5,918	8,168	28
Total	843	16,756	20,773	26,947	64

Abstract from Return of the Department of North Carolina, Maj. Gen. John G. Foster commanding, for September 30, 1862.

Command.	Present for duty.		Aggregate present.	Aggregate present and absent.	Remarks.
	Officers.	Men.			
First Brigade (Col. T. J. C. Amory).	81	2,591	3,594	3,929	At New Berne, with detachment at Newport Barracks.
Second Brigade (Col. T. G. Stevenson).	81	2,059	2,745	3,263	At New Berne, with detachment at Beaufort.
Cavalry (Lieut. Col. John Mix).	32	666	838	917	At New Berne.
Artillery (Col. J. H. Ledlie).	40	819	1,122	1,700	At New Berne.
Detachments	5	266	303	343	At Fort Macon, Morehead City, Newport Barracks, and Plymouth.
Total	239	6,401	8,602	10,152	

UNITED STATES FLAG-SHIP MINNESOTA,
Off Newport News, Va., October 1, 1862.

Maj. Gen. JOHN A. DIX, U. S. A.,
Comdg. Seventh Army Corps, Fort Monroe, Va.:

GENERAL: Your communication of the 29th was received yesterday.
You think the notice proposed by me on the 25th not now necessary, as your outpost at Suffolk has been sufficiently strengthened and as you believe there is not now an armed insurgent, excepting perhaps some lurking companies in the Dismal Swamp, within 40 miles of Norfolk. The situation was different when I communicated with the Department

in reference to the notice. Then you had just informed me that the enemy was concentrating and threatening to attack Suffolk with a force double our own there in numbers; that you had suggested to General Halleck to withdraw the troops from Suffolk, which he declined to do; that to prevent the enemy from getting between Suffolk and Norfolk you desired, and I stationed, a gunboat in the Western Branch of the Nansemond; and General Viele had recently informed me that he had arranged to barricade and defend Norfolk or a part of the town embracing the custom-house. I cheerfully accept your opinion that the proposed notice is not necessary at the present time. The alteration you propose in the notice, viz, that the consuls, women, and children should leave, " in case these places shall be assailed," would, I respectfully suggest, render the notice inoperative; would not relieve these non-combatants, who would be between two fires, and might occasion complaint on the part of foreign governments.

As you also think a notice of twenty-four hours would be sufficient and that no notice is now necessary, I presume the matter had better be deferred until from your official sources of information, which are better than mine, you think it time to act; of which I hope you will duly inform me.

I have the honor to be, general, very respectfully, yours,

S. P. LEE,
Actg. Rear-Admiral, Comdg. N. Atlantic Blockading Squadron.

P. S.—A steamboat with a white flag hoisted ran this blockade, up James River, to-day.

HDQRS. DEPT. OF VIRGINIA, SEVENTH ARMY CORPS,
Fort Monroe, Va., October 1, 1862.

Actg. Rear-Admiral S. P. LEE,
   Commanding North Atlantic Blockading Squadron:

ADMIRAL: I have the honor to inclose a copy of the notice you sent me.

I also inclose a copy of a letter from the Secretary of the Treasury in regard to a vessel detained at Norfolk. You will observe that the right of the military commander to clear a vessel from a blockaded port—the vessel having arrived there under a proper clearance—is distinctly admitted. This will relieve the question of supplies for Norfolk of a good deal of difficulty. The Secretary of the Treasury has just granted a permit for a very large quantity of necessaries—among other items, 2,000 tons of coal. The inhabitants have no money, or at least none which the importers will take. They must therefore pay in the products of their labor—tobacco, shingles, sweet potatoes, &c. Under the decision of the Secretary of the Treasury they may do so; and I trust, as the right to regulate commerce resides in the Treasury Department, that you will not consider your instructions from the Secretary of the Navy as conflicting with this decision. This rule has always been recognized heretofore. On the return of a vessel entering Norfolk under the authority of the Treasury Department, with merchandise, I have authorized her to be cleared, with a cargo of agricultural products, to any port of entry in a loyal State. Were it otherwise the permit to carry necessaries there would be a mockery. The case of the Marblehead is precisely in point, for she was regularly cleared for Norfolk, and is laden with staves, &c., for a return cargo. The Secretary, you will notice, does not decide her case as a special one but states the rule which covers it.

The Delaware, which has taken the place of the Morse, is precisely what we want. With the West End, a heavy tug which I have armed, we shall have an efficient river defense. I do not know what instructions you have given the commander of the Delaware, and I will be much obliged to you if you will request him to act in conjunction with the West End, under the direction of Major-General Peck, who will be advised of all exigencies as they arise and know how to meet them.

I am, admiral, very respectfully, your obedient servant,

JOHN A. DIX,
Major-General.

UNITED STATES FLAG-SHIP MINNESOTA,
Off Newport News, October 2, 1862.

Maj. Gen. JOHN A. DIX, U. S. A.,
Comdg. Seventh Army Corps, Fortress Monroe, Va. :

GENERAL : Your communication of the 1st instant is received. I do not see that the letter of the Secretary of the Treasury to Mr. Cutting respecting the schooner Marblehead allows anything more than that she may be cleared without a cargo of merchandise. This view is consistent with my instructions of September 18 from the Secretary of the Navy, which I read to you, and the substance of which I wrote to you on the 23d ultimo. The conclusion you arrive at and the course you propose seem to me to be clearly in conflict with my orders. Your communication and this reply will, however, be referred to the Department for its consideration and decision.

I have the honor to be, general, very respectfully, your obedient servant,

S. P. LEE,
Actg. Rear-Admiral, Comdg. N. Atlantic Blockading Squadron.

UNITED STATES FLAG-SHIP MINNESOTA,
Off Newport News, October 3, 1862.

Maj. Gen. JOHN A. DIX, U. S. A.,
Comdg. Seventh Army Corps, Fort Monroe, Va.:

GENERAL : My instructions to the commanding naval officer in the Nansemond River are to go up as near as he can to the West Branch of that river and prevent the enemy from crossing there ; to endeavor to intercept rebel mails passing along there and between Norfolk and Richmond, and to avail himself of such information as General Peck, from his position, may be enabled to give, in order to facilitate a co-operation with General Peck's forces, or otherwise, as may be best, against the enemy. I hope General Peck will communicate freely with our gunboat.

I sent the Morse to-day to relieve the Delaware, the latter to go outside awhile. The Morse is the more efficient vessel of the two, as she is a double-ender and does not have to turn in that narrow stream, in doing which I fear the Delaware has got aground as she has not yet returned.

I have the honor to be, general, very respectfully, yours,

S. P. LEE,
Actg. Rear-Admiral, Comdg. N. Atlantic Blockading Squadron.

SUFFOLK, *October* 3, 1862--10 p. m.

Major-General DIX:

Spear was induced to go on to Franklin in consequence of supposed gunboat firing. He has held the enemy at bay all day with his little force, doing them much harm. For the night, he is occupying Beaver Dam Church. He has positive orders to fall back upon Wessells, 10 or 12 miles from here, toward Western Branch Church. Enemy's pickets, infantry and cavalry, reported at Windsor; probably result of deserter's information. Gunboats have not reached Franklin. Spear has done splendidly.

> JOHN J. PECK,
> *Major-General.*

HEADQUARTERS DEPARTMENT OF VIRGINIA,
Fort Monroe, Va., October 3, 1862.

Actg. Rear-Admiral S. P. LEE,
Commanding North Atlantic Blockading Squadron:

ADMIRAL: I very much regret that last steamer sent with flag of truce to Aiken's Landing should have passed you without reporting. It was sent off in great haste, on a direction from the Secretary of War, with an officer who had never before been on that service. I have taken such measures as I trust will effectually prevent any such failure to report hereafter.

I have the honor to acknowledge the receipt of your communication of yesterday, and am, very respectfully, admiral, your obedient servant,

> JOHN A. DIX,
> *Major-General.*

HEADQUARTERS DEPARTMENT OF NORTH CAROLINA,
New Berne, N. C., October 3, 1862.

Maj. Gen. H. W. HALLECK,
Commander-in-Chief U. S. Army, Washington, D. C.:

GENERAL: I have the honor to inform you that everything is quiet throughout this department, and as I am in the habit of making constant armed reconnaissances very little picket firing even is at the outposts.

The health of the troops is not particularly good just now (we have some 1,500 sick), but is improving, and expect that cold weather will soon bring them up.

Our hospital arrangements we have perfected to a great degree here, Beaufort, and Portsmouth, and we think they will compare most favorably with any United States hospitals elsewhere.

During our stay here we have formed and equipped, mounted and drilled, five light batteries from the Third New York Artillery. My requisitions for this object on the Ordnance Department have met generally prompt and full attention; the men are good, the officers take hold, and the batteries are, I think, quite efficient. I am now reorganizing the batteries (2) of the New York Rocket Battalion, and for this purpose have required for six Napoleons and the necessary number of horses, which we hope will be promptly filled; also requisitions for cavalry horses to mount recruits and remount men whose horses have been killed in service or by an epidemic which broke out in the summer.

I had the honor to make a brief statement of my force in my letter of

September 24, and to request re-enforcements of infantry to be sent if it was expected of me to go into active service during the cool weather now rapidly approaching. Further reflection on this subject has convinced me of the propriety of my request, and especially as regards new egiments, and I beg leave to reurge this matter and to further say that, even if it is not intended that I should make any decided movement, this place presents very great facilities as a camp of instruction for a very large body of troops and would be more available for operations on the flank of the enemy should that be rendered necessary by their retreat from Richmond or from any other cause. Even if thirty or forty new regiments be sent I will devote my personal time to drilling and perfecting them in their duties. I have several old colonels who are abundantly able to assist me in training the regiments in battalion and brigade movements.

I take measures to be fully informed through deserters, spies, &c., of the enemy's strength, preparations for defense, and movements in this department.

Between this point and Raleigh there are about 8,000 men, principally infantry, two regiments of cavalry, and a small force of light artillery. In the country between the Tar and Roanoke Rivers there is a movable force of about 3,000 men, threatening Washington and Plymouth, and fearing to attack either.

My informant says that a permanent guard of one regiment is kept at Weldon Bridge; but there are other supporting bodies that could be concentrated to the amount of 5,000 or 10,000 men before I could reach there. This, of course, is independent of any force that might be sent from Richmond or Petersburg.

At Wilmington and in the defenses at the mouth of the Cape Fear River are about 3,000 men. The extent and strength of the defenses at the mouth of the Cape Fear have been largely increased of late. On Federal Point, north of New Inlet, a long line of batteries has been erected, inclosing in their limits the light-house and terminating beyond in a large and strong work called Fort Fisher. The number of guns mounted are thirty-six, several of which are of so great caliber as to throw shot farther than any guns carried by the present blockading squadron. The force of the fort is now actively engaged in erecting a large bomb-proof casemate battery of six heavy guns. Across New Inlet is Turk's Island, on which there is a battery of six guns. At the mouth of the Cape Fear River, Fort Caswell has been strengthened, but to what extent I am unable to say; the sand-hills, however, within range of its guns, have been leveled, so as to afford no shelter.

Fort Johnston consists of, in addition to the original block-house, a battery of at least three guns. Ascending the river the defenses are, first, Fort Saint Philip, at Old Brunswick, mounting nine guns, bearing on the river—open gorge. On the east side are three batteries: First, Lazaretto Battery, mounting three guns; second, Fort French, a bomb-proof, mounting three guns; third, Fort Ellis, mounting seven guns. The first battery is about 7 miles from Wilmington; the second is within 500 yards of the first, and the third 3½ miles from the first, and are all open gorge. There are also small batteries protecting the roads to Masonborough Inlet.

Epaulements for the purpose of sheltering field pieces are thrown up at intervals from Fort Fisher to Masonborough Inlet. The pieces usually sent on the beach are two heavy breech-loading English rifled guns, saved from the wreck of the Modern Greece. I have late information that Masonborough Inlet is extensively used by light-draught vessels in running the blockade. At last dates there were there forty-three light schooners. I have informed the naval commanders of that fact. There are also some salt-works at that place and on the adjoining waters. The distance is too great for an expedition from here, unless the same expedition were to attack Wilmington itself. I have destroyed all the salt-works within reach of me, as per previous report.

I am advancing the defenses of this town, and they are now strong enough to require a siege to take, I think. The defenses of Washington, which were not mounted or garrisoned at the time of the recent attack, are now both, and are sufficiently strong to offer very great resistance to an attempt at a *coup de main*.

I am erecting block-houses at all the lesser exposed points on the line of the railroad, &c. Many are finished and the rest are progressing well.

I omitted to mention, in speaking of Wilmington, that yellow fever has broken out there and bids fair to become an epidemic. The inhabitants have fled the town; the telegraph office is closed, and all work on the iron-clad gunboats now building there is suspended. Concerning these gunboats I have some information which I deem accurate, and which I will give in brief as you may desire to communicate the same to the Navy Department: They are 150 feet in length, 35 or 40 feet beam, and will draw some 14 feet water. They are simply intended for river defense and are not designed to cross the bar. The engines are from the Modern Greece and the Uncle Ben. They are not yet set in. Five weeks' work will be necessary to finish the first and three months for the second. They are to be plated with railroad iron and built after the pattern of the Merrimac No. 1.

I am, with great respect, your obedient servant,

J. G. FOSTER,
Major-General.

SUFFOLK, *October* 5, 1862.

General DIX:

Although I supposed the 9th would be the day, yet I felt anxious about matters in the direction of Franklin; the more so as the enemy was advancing his picket line some 4 or 5 miles from the river; hence I sent Spear for information upon which to base action. He was at Franklin from an early hour till after midnight. Longer delay under the circumstances would have been risky. My information about the obstructions led me to doubt their ability to co-operate. Sent a party to the South Quay region last night to return via Wianoke and Somerton with information of the boats; will aid if possible. We have acted in good faith, and, as you remark, no blame can attach to us. I shall strive to reflect your views, and trust my efforts will command your approval.

JOHN J. PECK,
Major-General.

UNITED STATES FLAG-SHIP MINNESOTA,
Off Newport News, October 5, 1862.

General JOHN A. DIX, U. S. A.,
Commanding Seventh Army Corps, Fortress Monroe, Va.:

GENERAL: I regret to have to inform you of a violation of the blockade by the schooner Caspar Heft, chartered on the 1st instant by Cattell

& Moore, to take a load of shingles from Suffolk to Philac elphia, and with a permit, dated October 1, from General Viele's assistant adjutant-general, the provost-marshal of Norfolk, to Cattell & Moore to send this schooner to Suffolk to load with shingles.   Lieutenant Babcock, of the Morse, reports that this schooner is in ballast and that her master informed him that these shingles are for a private speculation and not for the army or navy.   I had the honor to read to you my instructions from the Department on this subject and to communicate to you the substance of them on the 22d ultimo.   Under these instructions I cannot recognize this permit or allow this trade.

I have the honor to be, general, your obedient servant,

S. P. LEE,
Actg. Rear-Admiral, Comdg. N. Atlantic Blockading Squadron.

WASHINGTON, D. C., *October* 6, 1862.

Major-General DIX, *Fort Monroe:*

GENERAL: Your communications of the 27th and 29th ultimo in regard to trade with Norfolk have been submitted to the Secretary of War, and I am directed to reply that trade with that post is under the general control of the Secretary of the Treasury.   Nevertheless, as commanding officer of the department, you have full authority to compel all vessels to report to you for inspection, and to take such other measures as may be necessary to prevent frauds.

Very respectfully, your obedient servant,

H. W. HALLECK,
General-in-Chief.

UNITED STATES FLAG-SHIP MINNESOTA,
Off Newport News, Va., October 6, 1862.

Maj. Gen. JOHN A. DIX, U. S. A.,
Commanding Seventh Army Corps, Fort Monroe, Va. :

GENERAL: Your communication to me of the 1st instant, and its inclosure, with my reply in copy, were referred to the honorable Secretary of the Navy.   In reply thereto the Department writes that my decision in the matter is correct and in conformity with instructions and the law of blockade; that there must be no traffic—no return cargo; that supplies may be conveyed to the troops but not to the people of Norfolk and Virginia.

I respectfully request your aid in your department in putting a stop to all further attempts to violate the blockade and the instructions of the Department, which I have had the honor to communicate to you.

I have the honor to be, general, very respectfully, yours,

S. P. LEE,
Actg. Rear-Admiral, Comdg. N. Atlantic Blockading Squadron.

HDQRS. DEPT. OF VIRGINIA, SEVENTH ARMY CORPS,
Fort Monroe, Va., October 6, 1862.

Actg. Rear-Admiral S. P. LEE,
Commanding North Atlantic Blockading Squadron :

ADMIRAL: I have the honor to acknowledge the receipt of your communication of this date, and to say in reply that I shall do all in my power hereafter, as I have heretofore, to aid you in preventing any commercial intercourse with Norfolk except such as is permitted by the Secretary of the Treasury under special permits granted in conformity to the printed regulations concerning internal and coastwise intercourse, of.which I sent you a copy. I have not, since I received those regulations, granted permission to any vessel or any merchandise to leave this post for Norfolk except in compliance with them.

The terms of instructions quoted by you as having been received by the Navy Department are so broad that I desire in order to understand the interpretation you put on them to make a few inquiries for my own guidance. They state that "supplies may be conveyed to the troops but not to the people of Norfolk."

Do you understand this declaration to include supplies of merchandise cleared for Norfolk under the regulations referred to and intended for the people and not for the troops?

The instructions also declare "that there must be no traffic—no return cargo." Do you understand that you are to prevent the traffic carried on under special permits from the Secretary of the Treasury and in conformity to the regulations?

The Marblehead was allowed to return from Norfolk with a cargo under a permit and under a rule prescribed by the Secretary of the Treasury. If another vessel with a "return cargo" should, under this rule, be cleared for a Northern port by a permit from the commander of the military department, would you consider it your duty to stop her under your instructions from the Navy Department?

If, under your instructions, "no traffic" is allowed, what "trade" in or shipments of cotton or other merchandise, conducted in pursuance of said regulations, are referred to and authorized by the order of the Secretary of the Navy, page 8 of the pamphlet edition of the regulations?

A gentleman has exhibited to me a permit from the Secretary of the Treasury, on the certificate and request of the Secretary of War, to carry a large quantity of supplies to the people of Norfolk. Among other items are 2,000 tons of coal, of which only 160 tons have been delivered. Do you consider your instructions as requiring you to stop the remaining 1,840 tons of coal and the other supplies enumerated in the permit?

I make these inquiries not only because I desire to understand your own views distinctly, but because the instructions you have received, if taken literally, seem to me to be inconsistent and in conflict with the regulations which both the War and Navy Departments have sanctioned. In a word, I do not see how any traffic should be provided for and regulated if "no traffic" is allowed.

I am, very respectfully, your obedient servant,

JOHN A. DIX,
Major-General.

HDQRS. DEPT. OF VIRGINIA, SEVENTH ARMY CORPS,
Fort Monroe, Va., October 8, 1862.

Hon. E. M. STANTON,
Secretary of War:

SIR: The condition of the people of Norfolk and Portsmouth is such as to demand the immediate and decisive action of the Government. It is fully set forth in my letter to you of the 4th September and in my letter to Major-General Halleck of the 27th. There is this difference, however, that their sufferings for want of the necessaries of life are constantly and rapidly increasing. A fortnight ago flour was $16 a barrel; it is now $25. We have shut them out from the sources of supply both North and South.

The Treasury Department, on the 28th of August last, prescribed "Regulations concerning commercial intercourse with insurrectionary States and sections." The Secretaries of War and Navy by separate orders called on the officers of the Army and Navy to respect and carry out these regulations. On the other hand the Secretary of the Navy, notwithstanding this direction to naval officers, has instructed Admiral Lee to allow no traffic whatever.

It is not impossible that this conflict in the Secretary's own orders has arisen from the construction given by him to regulation 3, which forbids any "clearance or permit whatsoever to any port, place, or section affected by the existing blockade except for military purposes." If it be so, he is in conflict with the Secretary of the Treasury and the Secretary of War, who are jointly (the former at the request of the latter) granting such permits for traffic with Norfolk, though to an extent too limited to meet the wants of the people.

I desire, in the first place, to suggest that Norfolk and Portsmouth are not blockaded ports; that they lack the fundamental condition of a blockade—hostile possession. That this is the view taken by the Treasury and War Departments I cannot doubt, for they would otherwise have been restrained by regulation 3 from granting any permits or clearances. The fact that they are granting such permits and clearances shows conclusively that they do not regard them as blockaded. The laws of blockade, therefore, have no application to them. I have insisted uniformly that it is a case of military occupation, and that those places are governed by the commander of the military forces under the laws of war; that it is his province to allow so much commercial intercourse as is necessary for the comfort of the troops and of the inhabitants, subject to such restrictions as the Government should think proper to impose on him, and that neutral nations can raise no question in regard to such intercourse under the laws of blockade.

The Secretary of the Navy has also instructed Admiral Lee to allow no return cargo to be cleared from Norfolk in the vessels sent there with supplies for the people. These instructions are also in direct conflict with those of the Secretary of the Treasury. On application to the latter a few days since he authorized the schooner Marblehead to be cleared from Norfolk with a cargo of staves and headings, and in the same paper the right to the military commander to clear vessels on the return voyage was distinctly recognized and conceded. It is respectfully submitted that any other rule would be a mockery. The inhabitants of Norfolk and Portsmouth have no money—nothing, at all events, which importers from the loyal States will take—and a denial of the privilege of giving in exchange and sending away the products of their own labor is equivalent to a denial of all supplies. I therefore respectfully ask the decision of the Government on the following points:

1st. Is Norfolk a blockaded port, or is it a place held by military occupation and governed by the laws of war?

2d. Is it not open to the traffic provided for in the regulations of the Secretary of the Treasury of the 28th August?

3d. When supplies under the authority of the proper departments are sent to Norfolk is not the military commander at liberty to grant clearances to the vessels carrying such supplies with a return cargo of the products of the labor of the inhabitants or other merchandise to any port in a loyal State?

4th. May not the commander of the military department under the laws of war authorize the introduction into Norfolk of such necessaries of life as are required to save the inhabitants from suffering by hunger and cold?

When these questions are decided I respectfully request that the naval commander may receive such instructions as to prevent any conflict or misunderstanding with the commander of the military forces. I request, further, as a matter of more pressing necessity, that such instructions may be given to him as to obviate the existing conflict with the Treasury and War Departments.

In the mean time I desire to apprise you that as I put on the regulations of the 28th of August, which have your sanction, a construction entirely different from that apparently given to them by the Secretary of the Navy, under which he has instructed Admiral Lee to allow no traffic with the people of Norfolk, I shall consider it my duty if supplies come here with your permit and that of the Secretary of the Treasury to allow them to go to Norfolk, notwithstanding the seemingly conflicting instructions referred to from the Secretary of the Navy.

I am, sir, very respectfully, your obedient servant,

JOHN A. DIX,
Major-General.

UNITED STATES FLAG-SHIP MINNESOTA,
Off Newport News, Va., October 8, 1862.

Maj. Gen. JOHN A. DIX, U. S. A.,
Commanding Seventh Army Corps, Fort Monroe, Va.:

GENERAL: I have the honor to acknowledge the receipt yesterday of your communication dated the 6th instant.

I see no difficulty in executing my instructions from the Navy Department (the substance of which I have communicated to you under dates of September 18 and 23 and October 4) in connection with the printed regulations to which you refer.

Permits given by the Secretaries of the Treasury, War, or Navy will be respected, but not if given by any other officer.

No vessel will be allowed to pass the guard vessel with merchandise until her permit and manifest have been examined by me—in my absence, by the senior officer—and found to be duly authorized. A vessel attempting to pass under an unauthorized permit will be seized and the facts reported to the Navy Department.

Vessels with army supplies will be passed under a certificate from headquarters that they contain only army supplies and no merchandise; this certificate to be left with the guard vessel.

In either case the papers justifying admission will be forwarded to the Navy Department.

By my communication to you of October 6 you were informed that the Navy Department, after seeing a copy of your letter dated October 1, and of its inclosed copy of Secretary Chase's letter of September 27 to Mr. E. H. Cutting, decided that the Marblehead was not authorized to take a return cargo. The report made to me from the guard vessel, whose commander has since been detached from the squadron, was that the Marblehead passed out in ballast. I am now surprised to learn from your letter of October 6 that this vessel "was allowed to return from

Norfolk with a cargo, under a permit and under a rule prescribed by the Secretary of the Treasury."

I know not who gave such a permit. Neither it, nor a rule for it, can be found in the above-mentioned copy of Secretary Chase's letter to Mr. Cutting. The proceeding was a manifest violation of the blockade; it is my duty to state the facts to the Department.

I beg leave to suggest that the War or Treasury Department can best explain any part of the printed instructions not distinct to you.* Perhaps embarrassment arises from considering that the port of Norfolk, the blockade of which has never been raised by proclamation of the President, is to be regarded as on the same footing as the ports of Beaufort and New Orleans.

I have the honor to be, general, very respectfully, yours,

S. P. LEE,
Actg. Rear-Admiral, Comdg. N. Atlantic Blockading Squadron.

HDQRS. DEPT. OF VIRGINIA, SEVENTH ARMY CORPS,
Fort Monroe, Va., October 9, 1862.

Actg. Rear-Admiral S. P. LEE,
Commanding North Atlantic Blockading Squadron :

ADMIRAL : I have the honor to acknowledge the receipt of your communication of the 8th instant, in reply to mine of the 7th, and am happy to know that the instructions of the Secretary of the Navy, declaring that "no traffic" should be permitted with Norfolk, is not considered as interfering with traffic by permits given under the regulations concerning coastwise intercourse, &c.

In regard to the schooner Marblehead the permit to pass was given at Norfolk in the letter of the Secretary of the Treasury of the 27th of September, written in reply to one from Mr. Cutting asking a clearance for the vessel and a return cargo, as was stated by him, although the return cargo is not mentioned in the Secretary's answer. I have sent to Washington to ascertain whether it was mentioned in Mr. Cutting's letter which the Secretary acknowledges.

The Marblehead was cleared before any notice of the view taken by the Secretary of the Navy was received. Why she was reported to you as cleared in ballast I cannot imagine.

I have brought the whole subject of traffic with Norfolk before the Government and trust that it will be disposed of in some satisfactory mode. Among other questions I have specifically referred to is that of return cargoes. In the mean time I shall act in strict conformity to the regulations.

I have just learned that a permit was granted yesterday in my absence, at the request of General Viele, to a schooner laden with coal and lumber for Norfolk, and that the captain of the guard boat after allowing her to pass sent to Norfolk to recall her. I have directed that she be sent back as he requests. I have not seen her papers, but believe that the permit was improperly granted by Captain Millward. The schooner came here with a regular clearance for Norfolk, as I am informed, but the permit of the Secretary of the Treasury was wanting. I shall see that there is no recurrence of this irregularity.

I am, very respectfully, your obedient servant,

JOHN A. DIX,
Major-General.

P. S.—I have, on reflection, thought best to notice briefly the suggestion in your letter "that the War or Treasury Departments can best

explain any part of the printed instructions not distinct to me." I be
lieve I have a perfectly distinct understanding of them. The questions
I proposed to you were made for the purpose of ascertaining how you
understood them, with a sincere desire to obviate all misunderstanding
between us in carrying them out, and if we disagreed to ask the de
cision of the proper authority.

The grounds I have taken with the Government are briefly these:

1st. That Norfolk is not a blockaded port; that it lacks the funda
mental condition of a blockade—hostile possession.

2d. That if it were a blockaded port the traffic allowed under the
regulations concerning coastwise intercourse is in violation of the laws
of blockade recognized by civilized States. No nation can shut out
neutrals from intercourse with a blockaded port and allow intercourse
with it to its own people.

3d. That Norfolk not being a hostile possession, but held as a mili
tary occupation, we are free to allow so much traffic as is necessary for
military purposes and to prevent those whom we have subjected to our
power from suffering by hunger or cold—a duty dictated by the com
monest principles of humanity, and that it is on those conditions only
that the traffic allowed under the regulations can be justified.

I do not state these views with the desire or expectation of influ
encing your own, but to advise you frankly of the grounds I have taken.
I deem this frankness due to the relations between us.

I have instructed the provost-marshal at Norfolk to issue no permits
for vessels with return cargoes or to vessels desirous of exporting do
mestic or other products until the decision of the Government is
known.

UNITED STATES FLAG-SHIP MINNESOTA,
Off Newport News, October 10, 1862.

General JOHN A. DIX, U. S. A.,
Commanding Seventh Army Corps, Fortress Monroe, Va.:

GENERAL: The steamer John A. Warner passed up this morning
under a flag of truce and in charge of an army officer, who was recog
nized by the boarding officer from this ship. I will feel obliged to you if
the officers in charge of steamers on this duty would exhibit written
authority to me from your headquarters, as they generally do.

Very respectfully, yours,

S. P. LEE,
Actg. Rear-Admiral, Comdg. N. Atlantic Blockading Squadron.

UNITED STATES FLAG-SHIP MINNESOTA,
Off Newport News, October 10, 1862.

Maj. Gen. JOHN A. DIX, U. S. A.,
Commanding Seventh Army Corps, Fort Monroe, Va.:

GENERAL: I have the honor to acknowledge the receipt to-night of
your communication of the 9th instant.

The words "no traffic," to which you refer, related to such unauthor
ized traffic as in the case in hand—that of the schooner Marblehead—
but did not revoke my previous instructions to respect the permits of
the Treasury, War, and Navy Departments. I have seen but one duly-
authorized permit, viz, that given by the War Department, at the in-

stance of the Peruvian minister, to the agents of the Peruvian Government to reship from Norfolk the guano belonging to that Government, which permit was immediately respected by me.   If Mr. Cutting applied for, and the Treasury Department did not give him, a permit to take a return cargo in the Marblehead, it was a virtual refusal of such a permit by that Department instead of being a permit to take a return cargo as construed and carried out by General Viele.   The Secretary of the Treasury only ruled that the Marblehead—the vessel only—might be "cleared" (have permission to sail), not with a cargo, and did not, I respectfully submit, authorize her being cleared, as she was, with a return cargo, under a military permit purporting to be based on a rule of the Treasury Department, which cannot be construed from the copy you sent me of Mr. Chase's letter to Mr. Cutting of September 27. This military permit for a return cargo was, I beg leave to remind you, in conflict with my instructions from the Navy Department, which I had the honor to communicate to you on the 23d–24th of September, six days previous to the sailing of the Marblehead.

It appears that the schooner Conrad Fox, which you say came to Fortress Monroe loaded with coal and lumber for Norfolk, did not, as you were informed, come to Fortress Monroe " with a regular clearance for Norfolk." The captain of this schooner informed Captain Case to-day that he has no clearance or manifest, as there was no custom-house at Havre de Grace to issue them.   Besides her enrollment and license for coasting trade she has nothing but a bill of lading, dated Havre de Grace, September 27, 1862, for 85 tons of coal and 5,000 feet of cullings, to be delivered to Kimberly & Bros., at Norfolk, Va.   On the back of this bill of lading are the following indorsements:

HEADQUARTERS,
Norfolk, Va., October 8, 1862.

Permission is hereby given to Messrs. Kimberly & Bros. to receive from Fortress Monroe 85 tons of coal, per schooner Conrad Fox.
By order of Brigadier-General Viele:

J. H. LIEBENAU,
Assistant Adjutant-General and Provost-Marshal.

Approved and permitted.

JAMES MILLWARD,
Captain of Port, &c.

Lumber is included in the above permit from Norfolk.

EGBERT L. VIELE,
Brigadier-General.

Whilst the Conrad Fox had no special permit from the Treasury, War, or Navy Departments to trade, and not even the usual custom-house clearance, the military facilities shown by these indorsements were, I regret to find, given to her to trade here in violation of the instructions of the Government, which I had duly and seasonably communicated to you.   The Conrad Fox was boarded by an officer from the Victoria (guard vessel), near Norfolk, on the 8th, and her papers examined and found informal.   When this officer returned and made his report to the commander of the Victoria the latter immediately dispatched a boat to bring the Conrad Fox back, but she got to the wharf at Norfolk before the boat could reach her, when the provost-marshal interfered and claimed control of the vessel.   He delivered her up on the 9th instant, by your order, and I am relieved by your assurance that there shall be " no recurrence of this irregularity."   I am gratified that the provost-marshal at Norfolk has your instructions "to issue no permits to vessels with return cargoes or to vessels desirous of exporting domestic or other products until the decision of the Government is known."

Whilst wishing to avoid all discussion about the policy of the block-ade here, in my reply of the 8th to yours of the 7th instant I endeavored to meet the scope of your questions by stating what my instructions, which I had some time before communicated to you, required me to do.

Allow me in conclusion to thank you for the frankness with which you have communicated to me your views, and to say that whatever may be the determination of the Government upon the points you have presented it will be my duty and effort at all times to carry out faithfully my instructions from the Department, and in the manner the most convenient to the administration of your branch of the public service.

I have the honor to be, general, very respectfully, yours,

S. P. LEE,

Actg. Rear-Admiral, Comdg. N. Atlantic Blockading Squadron.

HEADQUARTERS,
Washington, October 10, 1862.

DEAR HOFFMAN: I inclose a copy of a letter sent by flag of truce, and copy of an order issued with regard to the shooting of vedettes or pickets, and the paroles of two wounded prisoners sent outside the lines. The letter and order were in accordance with instructions from General Foster.

*   *   *   *   *   *   *

Yours, truly,

EDWARD E. POTTER.

[Inclosures.]

HEADQUARTERS,
Washington, N. C., October 9, 1862.

Commanding Officer Confederate Forces nearest Washington :

SIR: I send by flag of truce, of which Captain Willson, Third New York Cavalry, is the bearer, Surgeon Stone and two paroled prisoners.

By the advice and suggestion of Major-General Foster, commanding the Department of North Carolina, I avail myself of this opportunity to inquire whether the inhuman and murderous practice of shooting pickets and vedettes is countenanced by the officers of the Confederate Army.

Brigadier-General Martin in conversation with General Burnside, and Captain Tucker while here a few days ago as the bearer of a flag of truce, both denounced this custom and agreed to use their best endeavors to put an end to it. Notwithstanding this agreement and these denunciations two of our vedettes were yesterday murdered in the most cold-blooded manner.

I desire to know whether these acts are committed by the authority and with the approval of officers. If such outrages be not checked I shall be compelled to resort to retaliation of the severest character.

I am, sir, your obedient servant,

EDWARD E. POTTER,
Colonel, Commanding Post.

GENERAL ORDERS, }
No. 6.   }

HEADQUARTERS,
Washington, October 8, 1862.

In order to check the inhuman and cowardly practice on the part of the enemy of shooting our vedettes and pickets it is hereby ordered that

whenever these outrages shall be committed by persons secreted near houses or on plantations the premises in question shall be at once laid waste and destroyed.

By order of Col. Edward E. Potter, commanding post:

J. W. ATWILL,
Acting Adjutant.

UNITED STATES FLAG-SHIP MINNESOTA,
Off Newport News, October 11, 1862.

Maj. Gen. JOHN A. DIX,
Commanding Seventh Army Corps, Fortress Monroe:

GENERAL: I am just informed by Lieutenant-Commander Babcock, U. S. Navy, commanding the gunboat Morse on guard duty at Norfolk, that yesterday he detained the schooner Chesapeake, going into Norfolk for repairs, under a "permit" signed by "James Millward, Captain Port and Harbor Master, Fortress Monroe, Va.," and by your command.

I respectfully suggest to you that this vessel was not going in with army supplies, and, as she is not known to be in distress, that it would be better, rather than have her pass the blockade, that she should be sent to Baltimore for any convenient repairs she may need. I will direct Lieutenant-Commander Babcock to return her papers and send her to you.

The boarding officers understood that, according to the arrangement between you and myself, the necessary certificates to pass vessels were to come from your headquarters and to be signed by Captain Blake, your assistant adjutant-general. Lieutenant-Commander Babcock had not, I presume, heard of the other officer or office above mentioned.

Allow me further to suggest, in connection with the matter of repairing outside vessels at Norfolk, that, owing to the difficulty of getting hands there to repair the gunboat Barney I was obliged to send her to her station unfinished after a fortnight's detention, and this notwithstanding that the United States quartermaster at Norfolk, Captain Ludlow, has always been very obliging, [tendering] us the facilities for repairs at the ship-yards in Norfolk, which are all under his control. As there are no facilities for repairing the United States gunboats at the Gosport Navy-Yard, owing to the destruction by the enemy of the work-shops, I beg that the facilities for repairs at the ship-yards under army control at Norfolk may be reserved as far as practicable for the use of the Navy.

I have the honor to be, general, very respectfully, yours,

S. P. LEE,
Actg. Rear-Admiral, Comdg. N. Atlantic Blockading Squadron.

UNITED STATES FLAG-SHIP MINNESOTA,
Off Newport News, Va., October 11, 1862.

Maj. Gen. JOHN A. DIX,
Commanding Seventh Army Corps, Fortress Monroe:

GENERAL: Lieutenant-Commander Babcock, of the gunboat Morse, on duty at Norfolk, reports that the master of the Pioneer, mail-boat between Fortress Monroe and Norfolk, says that he has been in the habit for some time, by your permission, of carrying merchandise in considerable quantities between the two places, and, as I understand, for purposes of traffic. The same officer reports to me that he is informed that

agents from Baltimore are in the habit of going to Norfolk in the mail-boat Pioneer, getting vegetables, fruit, &c., which they take to Fortress Monroe and ship immediately to be sold in Baltimore on private speculation. I beg that you will be so good as to inquire into this matter and forbid traffic on board these mail-boats, which are under your control. You are aware that the mail-boats have not been required in passing to leave the usual certificate at the guard vessel, because it was understood that they were under good military police and would not therefore violate the blockade. If, however, they are engaged in trade the usual official certificate will be necessary as in case of vessels passing the blockade with army supplies.

I have the honor to be, general, very respectfully, yours,

S. P. LEE,

Actg. Rear-Admiral, Comdg. N. Atlantic Blockading Squadron.

HDQRS. DEPT. OF VIRGINIA., SEVENTH ARMY CORPS,
Fort Monroe, Va., October 11, 1862.

Actg. Rear Admiral S. P. LEE,
Commanding North Atlantic Blockading Squadron:

SIR: I have the honor to inclose the copy of Mr. Cutting's letter on which the schooner Marblehead was cleared "with her cargo" by the direction of the Secretary of the Treasury, a copy of whose letter you have. In the latter, a rule is prescribed for like cases.

I have therefore to advise you that I shall on application clear with return cargoes from Norfolk vessels which go there with permits from the Secretary of the Treasury, in conformity with the regulations concerning coastwise intercourse, &c.

I am, very respectfully, your obedient servant,

JOHN A. DIX,
Major-General.

UNITED STATES FLAG-SHIP MINNESOTA,
Off Newport News, Va., October 11, 1862.

Maj. Gen. John A. DIX, U. S. A.,
Commanding Seventh Army Corps:

GENERAL: I have the honor to acknowledge the receipt this afternoon of your communication of this date, inclosing a copy of Mr. Cutting's letter of September 27, 1862, to the Secretary of the Treasury.

There is an inaccuracy in Mr. Cutting's letter which requires a prompt correction at my hands. Mr. Cutting came on board to inquire if his vessel (not vessels) with lumber could pass the guard vessel. I had but recently assumed the command, and not being familiar with the state of affairs, inquired of Commander Case, captain of the fleet, for information about the matter, and was informed in reply that Admiral Goldsborough had allowed Mr. Cutting's vessels to pass, and Commander Case said he believed Mr. Cutting was one of several firms who were trading here under a permit from the Secretary of the Treasury. It was upon this understanding of the case that I assented not to interrupt what seemed usual and proper. But it is incorrect in Mr. Cutting to assert that I "granted" him the "privilege" of trading. I never meant to do any such thing.

On the 18th of September I received instructions from the Secretary

of the Navy, in reply to the application of the gas company, "that no traffic in shingles, cotton, or tobacco could be permitted" here. I immediately sent Commander Case and Mr. Saltonstall on shore to inform General Viele of the Department's answer to the gas company, and directed them to inform Messrs. Catlett & Moore and Mr. Cutting that trade here was not allowed.

Commander Case learned from the provost-marshal that Mr. Cutting had gone North the evening before, and the provost-marshal said he could not direct Commander Case where he could find Messrs. Catlett & Moore, but he would notify them of this order of the Department.

The Marblehead sailed under a military permit, purporting to be under sanction of the Treasury Department, on the 30th of September. Commander Case has read and indorsed this statement.

In reply to your notice to me "that you shall, on application, clear with return cargoes from Norfolk vessels which go there with permits from the Secretary of the Treasury, in conformity with the regulations concerning coastwise intercourse," &c., I have to inform you that it will be my duty, under my instructions, to pass any vessel into Norfolk with a cargo of merchandise showing me a permit therefor from the Secretary of the Treasury, and that it will also be my duty, under instructions, to seize any vessel passing out of Norfolk with a cargo of merchandise under a permit from you.

In your comunication to me of the 9th instant you say: "I have brought the whole subject of traffic with Norfolk before the Government, and trust it will be disposed of in some satisfactory manner;" and you also say in the same communication: "I have instructed the provost-marshal at Norfolk to issue no more passes to vessels with return cargoes or to vessels desirous of exporting domestic or other products until the decision of the Government is known." I sincerely trust, general, that you will adhere to this considerate course. You know my instructions and my duty to obey them.

I have the honor to be, general, very respectfully, yours,

S. P. LEE,
Acting Rear-Admiral.

SPECIAL ORDERS, }	HDQRS. OF THE ARMY, ADJT. GEN.'S OFFICE,
No. 290.	}	*Washington, October* 11, 1862.

*	*	*	*	*	*	*

II. Brig. Gen. James H. Van Alen, U. S. Volunteers, is hereby relieved from duty at Yorktown, Va., and will report in person without delay to the General-in-Chief.

By command of Major-General Halleck:

E. D. TOWNSEND,
Assistant Adjutant-General.

HDQRS. DEPT. OF VIRGINIA, SEVENTH ARMY CORPS,
Fort Monroe, Va., October 12, 1862.

Actg. Rear-Admiral S. P. LEE,
North Atlantic Blockading Squadron:

ADMIRAL: Lieutenant-Commander Babcock is entirely mistaken in supposing that the Pioneer has been engaged by my permission in carrying merchandise in considerable quantities between Norfolk and this post for purposes of traffic. The only articles allowed to go in the mail-boat are sutlers' goods for the military forces, or goods in small quantities, having the requisite permits from the Treasury Department. I have given the strictest orders to the captain of the port, Capt. James Millward, and am assured by him that they are rigidly enforced. I will thank you to recognize him as authorized to give permits to vessels and merchandise going to Norfolk with the requisite permission from the Treasury Department.

I am also assured by Captain Millward that no vegetables nor fruit are brought here in the Pioneer and shipped direct to Baltimore to be sold on speculation. The only articles of that description brought here from Norfolk are for the use of the troops and the population in the vicinity of the fort.

Captain Millward was appointed captain of the port by Major-General Wool before the capture of Norfolk. His duty is to board all vessels coming here or departing, and to supervise generally all that is done in the harbor.

I am, very respectfully, your obedient servant,

JOHN A. DIX,
Major-General.

UNITED STATES FLAG-SHIP MINNESOTA,
Off Newport News, Va., October 15, 1862.

Maj. Gen. JOHN A. DIX, U. S. A.,
Commanding Seventh Army Corps, Fort Monroe, Va.:

GENERAL : I have the honor to inform you that a guard steamer has been stationed at a convenient distance from Fortress Monroe for the purpose of enforcing the blockade.

I would respectfully request you to cause the masters of all vessels in the employ of the army to leave a certificate on board of her similar to that left on board the guard steamer at Norfolk by vessels so employed.

I have the honor to be, general, very respectfully, yours,

S. P. LEE,
Actg. Rear-Admiral, Comdg. N. Atlantic Blockading Squadron.

UNITED STATES FLAG-SHIP MINNESOTA,
Off Newport News, Va., October 15, 1862.

Maj. Gen. JOHN A. DIX, U. S. A.,
Commanding Seventh Army Corps, Fortress Monroe, Va.:

GENERAL : Your letter of the 6th instant, making certain specific inquiries relative to my interpretation of and proposed course of conduct under my blockading instructions from the Department, was, with my reply thereto of the 8th, submitted to the Navy Department for its decision.

The Department approves of my letter of the 8th instant to you of my course in regard to traffic and the ingress and egress of vessels as correct and in conformity with my instructions and duty, and instructs that until the blockade is raised or modified it must be strictly maintained.

The honorable Secretary of the Navy says:

> That there is distress in Norfolk and the whole insurrectionary region I doubt not. The object of the blockade is to destroy their traffic while in rebellion. The relief is in the hands of the people who have only to be loyal to be relieved. The case is not one of sympathy but of duty.

The honorable Secretary, under date of October 13, also says:

> The rule which General Dix applies to Norfolk, denying that it is a blockaded port, would exempt any port and the whole coast, with the exception of Wilmington and Charleston, from blockade, for all are held by military occupation.

I have the honor to be, general, very respectfully, yours,

S. P. LEE,
Actg. Rear-Admiral, Comdg. N. Atlantic Blockading Squadron.

TREASURY DEPARTMENT,
October 16, 1862.

The Hon. SECRETARY OF WAR:

SIR: I have the honor to transmit herewith, for your information and such action as you may think necessary, copy of a letter this day received from Maj. R. W. Shenk, of the One hundred and thirty-fifth Regiment Pennsylvania Volunteers, relative to abuses of flag of truce boats on the James River.

With great respect,

S. P. CHASE,
Secretary of the Treasury.

[Inclosure.]

ON BOARD STEAMER KENNEBEC,
Annapolis Bay, October 15, 1862.

Hon. SALMON P. CHASE,
Secretary of the Treasury:

DEAR SIR: I respectfully call your attention to certain facts which have come to my notice, and which as an officer of the United States Government I feel my duty to make known to you. Flags-of-truce boats are now and have been to a great extent used, in addition to their lawful mission, to pass contraband goods and other articles through the lines at Aiken's Landing on James River. I predicate my belief upon this: First, a trunk was placed on board of the John A. Warner, purporting to pass upon the permission of a lady going South and placed by accident on board of said boat, then under my command. Upon examination I found no single article of woman's apparel, but cloths, quinine, mathematical instruments, a large quantity of silk, thread, needles, &c. I retained and will turn it over to the proper authorities at Washington on my return. Second: I was approached at the landing by a certain Col. Blanton Duncan, of Kentucky, now engraver of the notes of the Confederate Treasury, who desired me to enter into arrangements to pass goods suitable to his business and other avocations from the boat through the lines, and mentioned in connection the assistance of a prominent officer of the rebel Government. Duncan assured me that he had such arrangements with officers connected with flag-of-truce boats, and mentioned a firm in Washington where the articles could be supplied; also giving me a list of them.

No doubt many other violations could be discovered if ordinary watchfulness were instituted. I write the above in order, if the Department desires, to take some action to prevent the same. I have had charge of flag-of-truce boats during the past two weeks, and return to Aiken's Landing to-morrow morning, and if any new evidence comes to my notice the same will be promptly made known to you. I return to Washington on the 20th instant.

I am, very respectfully, your obedient servant,
R. W. SHENK,
Major, One hundred and thirty-fifth Pa. Vols., Comdg.

———

NAVY DEPARTMENT,
October 16, 1862.

Hon. E. M. STANTON,
Secretary of War:

SIR: Admiral Lee, commanding the North Atlantic Blockading Squadron, informs the Department that considerable quantities of merchandise are carried in the mail steamers which pass daily between Fortress Monroe and Baltimore and between Fortress Monroe and Norfolk. Unless some measures are adopted to prevent it the practice will lead to difficulty, for while the blockade continues Admiral Lee has no alternative but to enforce it in good faith. He suggests that—

It would be a partial remedy if the War Department would order Generals Wool and Dix not to allow any merchandise or articles for traffic to be shipped on these mail steamers plying between Fortress Monroe and Norfolk and between Fortress Monroe and Baltimore; it would be an effectual remedy and a more natural state of things if these steamboats were under navy control.

I would respectfully recommend that the recommendations of Admiral Lee in regard to orders to Generals Wool and Dix be given by the War Department.

Very respectfully,
GIDEON WELLES,
Secretary of the Navy.

———

WAR DEPARTMENT,
Washington City, D. C., October 17, 1862.

Hon. GIDEON WELLES,
Secretary of the Navy:

SIR: The Secretary of War directs me to acknowledge the receipt of your communication of the 16th instant relative to the report of Admiral Lee, commanding the North Atlantic Blockading Squadron, that merchandise is daily transported in the mail steamers between Fortress Monroe and Baltimore and between Fortress Monroe and Norfolk, and suggesting orders for a more stringent enforcement of the blockade. In reply I am instructed to inform you that copies of your communication have been transmitted to Major-Generals Dix and Wool for their information.

I have the honor to be, your obedient servant,
P. H. WATSON,
Assistant Secretary of War.

HDQRS. DEPT. OF VIRGINIA, SEVENTH ARMY CORPS,
Fort Monroe, Va., October 18, 1862.
Actg. Rear-Admiral S. P. LEE,
Commanding North Atlantic Blockading Squadron:

SIR: I have the honor to acknowledge the receipt, on my return from Washington, of your three communications, one of the 11th and the other two of the 15th instant.

In regard to permits for vessels with return cargoes from Norfolk, I do not see how I can properly refuse to grant one if application is made to me under the decision of the Secretary of the Treasury. If you deem it your duty under the instructions of the Secretary of the Navy to seize a vessel having such a permit I can have no possible objection. It is a conflict between two Departments of the Government, for which neither of us is responsible. I trust, however, that no such case will arise until some proper disposition is made of the whole subject. But individuals have rights which I am bound to respect, and if any one brings himself clearly within the class of cases disposed of by the Secretary of the Treasury, who has the general regulation of commerce, I cannot put him off because the Secretary of the Navy takes a view of the question of blockade which I conceive to be at variance with all the received rules of international law. I had the honor to reply personally to the arguments quoted from one of his letters to you in your communication of the 15th.

The instructions you have given to the commander of the gunboat stationed under the guns of this fort are embarrassing the public service exceedingly. A vessel laden with coal and lumber, purchased by the ordnance officer for public use, was stopped yesterday and detained the whole day for certificates, greatly to my annoyance.

Vessels cleared to this post, unless it is regarded as a blockaded port ought not to be detained; and I believe such an interference with the military administration of this command to be entirely without precedent. It certainly was so under your two predecessors, and I consider it altogether inconsistent with the comity due from one service to the other. If you deem it your duty, under the instructions of the Secretary of the Navy, to place a gunboat under the guns of this fort, the headquarters of a military department, and subject it to all the restrictions of an enemy's port in order to enforce the blockade, I shall bring the matter before the Government without delay. If you do not, then I respectfully request that the gunboat may be anchored above the fort, and that commercial intercourse with this post may be left, as it always has been heretofore, under the control of the Treasury Department and the military authorities. All vessels coming here are boarded and their papers and cargoes examined by the officers of the revenue cutter, and they are visited again by the captain of the port, to whom they are required to report on shore and who also examines their papers. To subject them to a third visitation appears to me to be superfluous and a needless vexation. I state these facts not as having any bearing on the graver objections I have made to the system of visitation at this post, but to show that it is called for by no considerations of public necessity.

The sloop A. C. Broderick was cleared from this post for Baltimore with 51 bushels of wheat, 19 hides, 100 pounds rags, 2,000 pounds of iron, and 160 bushels of oysters, and has been stopped by your gunboat. Unless you regard Fort Monroe as blockaded I respectfully submit that there is nothing in the instructions of the Navy Department which you communicated to me to warrant the detention of this vessel. The property belongs to persons within our lines, and as the military commander here I claim the right to clear vessels to any port in a loyal State, subject to the usual custom-house inspection. I respectfully ask if you consider this post as blockaded, and if not I will thank you to furnish me with a copy of the instructions under which the detention is made that I may make a proper representation to the Government.

I am, very respectfully, your obedient servant,

JOHN A. DIX,
Major-General.

UNITED STATES FLAG-SHIP MINNESOTA,
Off Newport News, Va., October 18, 1862.

Maj. Gen. JOHN A. DIX, U. S. A.,
Commanding Seventh Army Corps, Fortress Monroe, Va. :

GENERAL : Lieutenant-Commander Babcock, commanding guard vessel below Norfolk, reports that he has, under his instructions, detained the schooner Elizabeth English, as, excepting her enrollment and license, she had only a bill of lading, showing that she contained 330 tons of coal purporting to be shipped by the United States War Department at Philadelphia on the 2d instant, and signed David English, who or whose office is not known here.

The master of the army tug which was towing the schooner up informed the commanding officer of the guard vessel that he asked the assistant quartermaster and provost-marshal at Fortress Monroe for the usual certificates (viz, that the vessel is in the employ of the army and has only supplies for the army on board), and that they told him he did not want any such a certificate and should not have any.

If the Elizabeth English is in the employment of the army, and has supplies for the army only on board, I will thank you to have the usual and proper certificate to that effect sent to Lieutenant-Commander Babcock for me. If she is not in the employment of the army, and her cargo is not exclusively for the use of the army, you would oblige me by letting me know it. I beg to observe that no inconvenience will be experienced by your department if the usual and proper certificate is always sent with the vessel having army supplies on board.

The commanding officer of the guard vessel below Norfolk also reports to me that he has vainly endeavored to obtain from some of the steam-tugs passing to and fro between Fortress Monroe and Norfolk such a certificate as would show that they are in the employment of the army and are only so employed. This was according to the understanding between us, as shown by my communication to you of September 18 and your reply of September 19. I respectfully request that you will now favor me with a list of the names of all the steam-tugs in the employment of the army plying between Fort Monroe and Norfolk, so that when once known to the guard vessel in the Elizabeth River there may be no difficulty about their passing afterward without stopping, provided they are not towing vessels, especially such as are not in the employment of the army and whose cargoes are not duly certified.

I have the honor to be, general, very respectfully, yours,

S. P. LEE,
Actg. Rear-Admiral Comdg. N. Atlantic Blocking Squadron.

P. S.—The commanding officer of the gunboat Wyandotte, on guard duty off Fort Monroe, reports that he yesterday detained the schooner

John Francis, loaded with merchandise and articles for traffic. The John Francis was bound from Fort Monroe to Yorktown under a permit signed, by your command, by Captain Millward, of the army. Her manifest, written in a large folio book, consists of miscellaneous merchandise, owned by B. F. Voorhees (name not legibly written). This afternoon a certificate was brought to me signed, by your command, by Captain Millward, saying that this cargo of goods (not army supplies) is solely for the use of the Sixth [Fourth?] Army Corps, under the command of Maj. Gen. E. D. Keyes, at Yorktown. The bearer of this certificate states that Mr. Voorhees, who swears in the manifest that he is the owner of the cargo, is not a sutler in the army but a general trader at Fort Monroe.

The certificate does not state, as is usual, that this vessel is in the employ of the army and has only supplies for the army on board. I am not informed that Mr. Voorhees has a permit to trade from either the Treasury, War, or Navy Departments. I decline under the circumstances to accept the certificate as sufficient to justify this vessel passing the blockade with her cargo of goods.

I have reported the facts to the Navy Department.

Very respectfully, yours,

S. P. LEE.

WASHINGTON, *October* 18, 1862—10.25 a. m.

Major-General DIX:

It was resolved in Cabinet yesterday that the Norfolk trade should be placed under your personal direction, in the manner proposed when you were here.

Clearances for which you ask admission into the port will be granted by the Treasury Department, and all exports permitted by you will be allowed by the Navy to pass. Your own attention personally is requested and your own signature to permits required.

EDWIN M. STANTON,
Secretary of War.

UNITED STATES FLAG-SHIP PHILADELPHIA,
Hampton Roads, Va., October 20, 1862.

Maj. Gen. JOHN A. DIX, U. S. A.,
Commanding Seventh Army Corps, Fort Monroe, Va.:

GENERAL : I have the honor to acknowledge the receipt of your communications of the 18th and 19th instant. In regard to permits for vessels with return cargoes from Norfolk you are aware that the decision of the Navy Department is adverse to your making any such clearance. I do not know of any conflicting decision of the Secretary of the Treasury. The North Atlantic blockade extends from the Piankatank River, on the western shore of Virginia, to the coast of South Carolina, excepting the harbor of Beaufort, the blockade of which has been raised by proclamation of the President. Within these limits I am required to maintain a strict blockade and to prevent all traffic, except under a permit from the Secretary of the Treasury, War, or Navy. My instructions to the gunboat off Fort Monroe are only to carry out my orders from the Government, and her station is safe and convenient for that purpose. Fort Monroe has never been declared a port of entry; it is situated within the blockaded region, and all vessels in the employment of the army with only army or supplies of any kind or public property on board pass freely and frequently not only to Fort Monroe but to all other points here in the occupation of the army, on a certificate from your headquarters; or, in case of a vessel coming from a Northern port, on a certificate from the United States quartermaster there, stating, in a very few words, that such is the character of the vessel and cargo. It is impossible therefore that the public service should thereby be embarrassed exceedingly, or at all; but the contrary is the case—the public service is benefited to the extent that supplies are thus kept out of the insurrectionary region.

You say: "A vessel laden with coal and lumber, purchased by the ordnance officer for public use, was stopped yesterday and detained the whole day, greatly to my annoyance." You refer doubtless to the Conrad Fox, which had violated the blockade, got to Norfolk without a permit from either the Treasury, War, or Navy Departments, but under an unauthorized permit from army officers (which I am expressly ordered not to respect), and with a cargo of coal and lumber brought from Havre de Grace without any clearance, for Kimberly & Bros., traders at Norfolk. The Navy Department released this vessel on the ground that she acted on supposed authority, but forbade her to land or receive cargo. To prevent any further violation of the blockade by her she was towed just outside the lower gunboat and released to go where she pleased outside the blockade, but the Conrad Fox instead of going away anchored immediately, and your ordnance officer bought her cargo. As soon as the usual certificate was sent to the guard vessel, showing that the cargo of this vessel had now become army supplies, she was permitted to pass in to unload, as I am informed by the officer commanding the guard vessel. If there was any delay about sending off the usual and necessary certificate to the gunboat it was wholly unnecessary, as you have already complained "that she is stationed under the guns of this fort"—the necessary situation of the men-of-war, our own and foreign, at anchor here—where one of your many steam-tenders might communicate with her in fifteen or twenty minutes. You wish me to remove this gunboat from her anchorage outside and below the fort to an anchorage inside and above the fort, that commercial intercourse may go on. This would be to violate my orders to maintain the blockade strictly until it is modified or raised ; to this end the gunboat must be stationed where she can conveniently intercept and board vessels, and when these have merchandise for traffic detain them to be reported to the Department. When vessels with army supplies have passed the blockade and are inside discharging, I see no objection to their visitation and search by both the military authorities and the revenue officers, as gross irregularities may be detected and prevented by such additional precautions.

Since the receipt of your communication of the 19th (although I had previously reported the case of the John Francis to the Department), informing me that her cargo of goods is sent at the request of General Keyes to be sold within the fortifications at Yorktown for the use of his command there, I have directed the gunboats to let her pass.

I have the honor to be, general, very respectfully, yours,

S. P. LEE,

Actg. Rear-Admiral, Comdg. N. Atlantic Blockading Squadron.

HDQRS. DEPT. OF VIRGINIA, SEVENTH ARMY CORPS,
Fort Monroe, October 21, 1862.

Maj. Gen. H. W. HALLECK,
General-in-Chief:

GENERAL: I have an arrangement with a man who has the means of obtaining accurate information in regard to affairs in Richmond and the districts lying upon the James River, the Chickahominy, and the Blackwater. I have no secret-service fund, but I allow him to carry some articles for peddling in the districts referred to and to bring back tobacco. He has crossed the lines without suspicion four times in his wagon, and will leave here in two or three days.

The forces of the enemy in Richmond and the country on this side are as follows:

At Franklin, on the Blackwater, under General French	4,000
At Zuni, on the Blackwater, under General Pettigrew	5,000
At Wakefield, 8 miles from Zuni, under General Anderson	2,000
At Petersburg one regiment, about	800
At Richmond	7,000
Between the James and Chickahominy, under General Wise, including a cavalry regiment just arrived from Georgia	7,000
Between Richmond and White House two regiments, just sent there, about	1,500
Total	27,300

From other and less reliable sources I get nearly the same result.

My informant says there is no intention of moving down the Peninsula in force until the naval armament is complete. The Richmond (and the new Merrimac) has taken out her boilers, which were found too small, and others are in course of construction. He thinks she cannot be ready for a month.

I shall be advised of any intended general movement unless my man falls under suspicion and is not allowed to go at large. He has a pass from the Government at Richmond to peddle in Henrico County, and has no difficulty in crossing the lines and reaching me by way of Williamsburg.

I am, very respectfully, your obedient servant,

JOHN A. DIX,
Major-General.

HDQRS. DEPT. OF VIRGINIA, SEVENTH ARMY CORPS,
Fort Monroe, Va., October 22, 1862.

Actg. Rear-Admiral S. P. LEE,
Commanding North Atlantic Blockading Squadron:

SIR: I have the honor to inclose a dispatch received by telegraph from the Secretary of War.* Will you please advise me whether it has been communicated to you; also whether it will be considered by you as sufficient to warrant the passage of vessels from the Nansemond and Yorktown, with exports, under my permits?

I am, very respectfully, your obedient servant,

JOHN A. DIX,
Major-General.

---

* See of October 18, p. 433.

HDQRS. DEPT. OF VIRGINIA, SEVENTH ARMY CORPS,
Fort Monroe, Va., October 22, 1862.

HON. E. M. STANTON,
Secretary of War:

SIR: I received yesterday Mr. Watson's letter of the 17th instant inclosing a copy of a communication of the Secretary of the Navy of the 16th concerning the carrying of merchandise in the mail steamers plying between this post and Baltimore in one direction and Norfolk in the other. The Secretary says he is informed by Admiral Lee that considerable quantities of merchandise are carried on these steamers, and suggesting as a partial remedy that Generals Wool and Dix should be ordered not to allow any merchandise or articles for traffic to be shipped on these steamers, and as an effectual remedy that they should be put under navy control.

If Admiral Lee intends to intimate that merchandise is illicitly carried on these steamers and in violation of any law, either of revenue or blockade, I take it upon myself to say that he is laboring under a very great error; that every article which is brought here from Baltimore is examined, and if it has not the proper custom-house permit is sent back or detained; that every article put on board the mail steamer for Norfolk comes within one of the two classes, of supplies for the army or merchandise, usually in very small quantities passed regularly through the custom-house at Baltimore with permits for Norfolk, and if there is any violation of established regulations the fault is with the Treasury Department, and this I will not presume. The captain of the port here keeps a register of every packet and its contents coming from Baltimore or going to Norfolk, with the name of the party receiving it, and everything is carefully examined. Every possible precaution is taken to prevent abuse, and, as I believe it can be shown, with entire success.

The officers under my command, as well as those belonging to the revenue department placed here by the Secretary of the Treasury, are as anxious as those of the navy to arrest all illicit traffic and intercourse with the insurgents, and I believe they have performed, and will continue to perform, their duty with quite as much faithfulness and efficiency. I see no reason on this score for putting these mail steamers under navy control; and on every other there are insuperable objections to such an arrangement. They are employed by the Quartermaster's Department. Those which run between this post and Baltimore under a contract with that Department are specially designed to carry troops and supplies for the army in addition to the mails, and I see no more propriety in putting them under navy control than in placing a naval transport under army control. The Secretary of the Navy has not in his communication approved this suggestion of Admiral Lee; but I deem it nevertheless my duty to my command to state to you my objections to it.

In regard to orders to General Wool and myself I take it for granted the Government does not object to the transportation by the mail steamers of merchandise for this post or Norfolk under the customary sanctions of the Treasury Department. There are several persons in addition to the sutler who have permission to trade with the garrison and with the people in this vicinity. Such an order would compel them to employ a sailing vessel every time they had a small quantity of necessaries to bring here. This morning some ice, flour, and other articles came down by the mail steamer, having gone through the regular custom-house formalities, for our sutler, Mr. Moody; for Mr. Kimberly, who supplies the hospital, and some other persons. Every article is subjected to the most rigid scrutiny. If it is intended to interfere with the trans portation of supplies—a measure I consider entirely uncalled for and unwise—the order should be addressed to the Baltimore custom-house and not to General Wool. It is unnecessary to state, for you know the fact, that there is a very considerable population outside of the fort under the protection of the Government, and that there are some 3,000 colored persons here who require their little comforts. I allow a colored man to go to Baltimore occasionally and bring here supplies for these people. All these supplies necessarily obtained in small quantities would be cut off if Admiral Lee's recommendation to allow no merchandise to be brought by the mail boat were adopted.

Having disposed of this matter I deem it my duty to call the attention of the Department to what I consider an unwarrantable interference with my command by Admiral Lee. This will be best illustrated by presenting the cases in which he has detained vessels having supplies for the army or employed in services connected with it.

1st. Mr. J. B. Braham, a contractor for hides and fat with the commissary of subsistence at Suffolk, sent a vessel here from New York to receive these articles, which had been accumulating for some time, with 20 sacks of salt for their preservation. The vessel, the schooner Alexander, was cleared for this port at New York. The permit was approved by the commissary of subsistence, Major-General Peck, and myself, and the papers were found correct by the revenue officers. My approval was in these words, as will be seen by the papers:

The duty of the Government to allow the purchaser of its property to take it away is so very clear that the captain of the port will give a permit to the Alexander to go to Suffolk to receive the hides (and with the salt—20 sacks—necessary to preserve them), subject to the approval of Admiral Lee.

Strictly, I had a right to send the vessel to her destination to perform a service connected with my department, but out of courtesy to the admiral, and with a sincere desire to maintain in all things a friendly understanding with him, I made the permit subject to his approval. It was rejected; and the contractor sent the vessel back to New York, leaving the articles he had purchased to spoil in the hands of the Government. The papers are annexed, marked A.*

2d. The sloop A. C. Broderick was loaded at Fort Monroe with 51 bushels of wheat, 19 hides, 100 pounds of rags, 2,000 pounds of iron, and 160 bushels of oysters. The goods were owned by persons within our lines, and they were cleared, under a permit from me, for Baltimore, where they were to be subject to the custom-house inspection usual in such cases. I exercised this right as the military commander here, and insisted that the commander of the naval forces could not with propriety interfere with it. The vessel has been stopped against my remonstrance. She is still detained, and the oysters have been thrown overboard.

There are other cases in which vessels have been detained, and in several instances greatly to my annoyance, but as they have been released I do not deem it necessary to state them. But I desire to call the attention of the Department to the fact that a gunboat has been stationed below the fort for the purpose of boarding every vessel that enters the Roads, when the service could be just as well performed between this post and Newport News. It is entirely unnecessary for the purpose of the blockade of the James River and Nansemond, as all vessels coming to this post are boarded by the revenue officers who are on duty here and by the captain of the port. While the naval forces were under the command of Commodore Stringham, Admiral Golds-

---

* Not found.

borough, and Admiral Wilkes no such system of visitation was insti·
tuted, and there is no reason why it should be adopted now. On the
18th instant I called the attention of Admiral Lee to the subject in a
letter, of which the following is an extract :

Vessels cleared to this post [unless it is regarded as a blockaded port] ought not
to be detained, and I believe such an interference with the administration of this
command to be entirely without precedent. It certainly was so under your two
predecessors, and I consider it altogether inconsistent with the comity due from one
service to the other. If you deem it your duty, under the instructions of the Secretary
of the Navy, to place a gunboat under the guns of this fort, the headquarters of a
military department, and subject it to all the restrictions of an enemy's port in order
to enforce the blockade, I shall bring the matter before the Government without delay.
If you do not, then I respectfully request that the gunboat may be anchored above
the fort, and that commercial intercourse with this post may be left, as it always has
been heretofore, under the control of the Treasury Department and the military authorities. All vessels coming here are boarded and their papers and cargoes examined by the officers of the revenue cutter, and they are visited again by the captain
of the port, to whom they are required to report on shore and who also examines their
papers. To subject them to a third visitation appears to me to be superfluous and
a needless vexation. I state these facts not as having any bearing on the graver objections I have made to the system of visitation at this post, but to show that it is
called for by no considerations of public necessity.

To this remonstrance I have received the following reply :

You wish me to remove the gunboat from her anchorage outside or below the fort to
an anchorage inside and above the fort, that commercial intercourse may go on. This
would be to violate my orders to maintain the blockade strictly until it is modified
or raised; to this end the gunboat must be stationed where she can conveniently
intercept and board vessels, and where these have merchandise for traffic detain them
to be reported to the Department.

In another part of this communication Admiral Lee says :

The North Atlantic blockade extends from the Piankatank River, on the western
shore of Virginia, to the coast of South Carolina, excepting the harbor of Beaufort, N.
C., the blockade of which has been raised by proclamation of the President. Within
these limits I am required to maintain a strict blockade and to prevent all traffic,
except under a permit from the Secretary of the Treasury, War, or Navy.
My instructions to the gunboat off Fort Monroe are only to carry out my orders
from the Government, and her station is safe and convenient for that purpose. Fort
Monroe has never been declared a port of entry ; it is situated within the blockaded
region.

From the whole tenor of this reasoning it is manifest that the admiral
deems it his duty to enforce the blockade against this post. Though
within the blockaded region it is a military station, occupied by the
Government forces, and lacks the essential condition of a blockade—
hostile possession. What I insist on is that the commercial intercourse
with it shall be carried on under the usual custom-house regulations,
and that the planting of a gunboat under the walls of the fort to examine vessels going to it (for vessels going into the Roads can be as
well examined higher up) is altogether unprecedented, uncalled for,
and now practiced for the first time since the war commenced, although
the naval forces on this station have been commanded by three of the
most distinguished and experienced officers in the naval service.
It is with great regret that I feel constrained to trouble you with
these matters. I have endeavored by friendly correspondence with Admiral Lee to adjust them ; and I might have rested still longer in the
hope of success had not the communication of the Secretary of the Navy
been referred to me. The whole matter, however, concerns the War
Department quite as deeply as myself, involving as it does a question
of authority and of comity between the military and naval services.
I am, very respectfully, your obedient servant,

JOHN A. DIX,
Major-General.

UNITED STATES FLAG-STEAMER PHILADELPHIA,
Hampton Roads, Va., October 25, 1862.
Maj. Gen. JOHN A. DIX, U. S. A.,
Commanding Seventh Army Corps, Fort Monroe, Va.:

GENERAL: I have the honor to acknowledge the receipt of your communications of the 20th and 23d instant, inclosing lists of the thirty-five steamers now in the employment of the army in the Department of Virginia, any of which I suppose are liable to be discharged at any time. In respect to those which are employed inside of Fortress Monroe their certificates once left with the blockading vessel below Norfolk are sufficient; but in respect to those (except the mail-boats) coming from or going to Baltimore or to and from the North, I have respectfully to request that you will have them ordered to stop at the Wyandotte, the outside guard vessel on blockade for Hampton Roads, &c., and leave the usual certificate from your headquarters or from the proper officer detailed by you for that duty, or from the quartermaster at the post whence they came, stating that the steamer in question is then in the employment of the Government and has only army supplies on board or is in ballast, as the case may be. This will occasion but a few moments' delay and will prevent violations of the blockade. The guard vessel has omitted all steamers from her report, an irregularity which will be corrected immediately. It is obvious that my instructions can be carried out with fidelity, and yet without inconvenience to your branch of the public service, with your co-operation.

I have the honor to be, general, very respectfully, yours,
S. P. LEE,
Actg. Rear-Admiral, Comdg. N. Atlantic Blockading Squadron.

———

UNITED STATES STEAMER PHILADELPHIA,
Hampton Roads, Va., October 25, 1862.
Maj. Gen. JOHN A. DIX,
Commanding Seventh Army Corps:

GENERAL: I inclose a copy of a report of the 24th instant from the commanding officer of the United States gunboat Wyandotte, stationed on blockade duty off Fortress Monroe, showing that whilst thus engaged in the performance of duty her officers were, when on quarter-deck of that vessel, deliberately fired at several times by one of your sentinels and narrowly escaped being shot. Whilst I confidently expect you will consider that the magnitude of this crime calls for a prompt trial by court-martial and exemplary punishment, I respectfully request to be informed of the course you deem it your duty to adopt that I may acquaint the Department thereof, in connection with my report of this grave affair.

I have the honor to be, general, very respectfully, yours,
S. P. LEE,
Actg. Rear-Admiral, Comdg. N. Atlantic Blockading Squadron.

———

HDQRS. DEPT. OF VIRGINIA, SEVENTH ARMY CORPS,
Fort Monroe, Va., October 25, 1862.
Actg. Rear-Admiral S. P. LEE,
Commanding North Atlantic Blockading Squadron:

ADMIRAL: I have received your communication of this morning, with a report from the commanding officer of the Wyandotte, stating that her officers were deliberately fired on by one of the sentinels at this post. It is the first intimation I have received from any quarter of th extraordinary occurrence. I shall take immediate measures to brin; the offender before a court-martial, that he may be punished in the mos' exemplary manner. I should not have waited for a request from yoɪ to that effect had I been aware of the occurrence before yóur communi cation was received.

I am, very respectfully, your obedient servant,
JOHN A. DIX,
Major-General.

UNITED STATES FLAG-STEAMER PHILADELPHIA,
Hampton Roads, October 25, 1862.

Maj. Gen. JOHN A. DIX, U. S. A.,
Commanding Seventh Army Corps, Fortress Monroe, Va.:

GENERAL: I received yesterday afternoon your communication of October 22, inclosing a copy of a telegram to you from the honorable the Secretary of War, dated the 18th instant, informing you of the con- clusion of the Cabinet to place the Norfolk trade under your personal direction in the manner proposed by you when you were in Washington.

In reply to your inquiry I beg leave most respectfully to say that I have not received from the Navy Department the instructions referred to by the Secretary of War in his telegram of the 18th, but on the con- trary I have received a dispatch from the honorable the Secretary of the Navy, dated October 22 (four days later than the date of Secretary Stanton's to you), approving of the detention of the schooner John Francis, loaded with merchandise for Yorktown, with a permit from you.

Under these circumstances I deem it my duty to transmit a copy of your letter and its inclosure to the honorable Secretary of the Navy, and to await the orders of the Navy Department before attempting to deviate from my present positive instructions.

I have the honor to be, general, very respectfully, yours,
S. P. LEE,
Actg. Rear-Admiral, Comdg. N. Atlantic Blockading Squadron.

FORT MONROE, VA., October 25, 1862.

Hon. E. M. STANTON,
Secretary of War:

Admiral Lee informs me that he has no notice from the Secretary of the Navy of the decision of the Cabinet as to trade with Norfolk. I have communicated to him your dispatch of the 18th, but he has directions from the Navy Department as late as the 22d which seem to be in conflict with it. I am giving permits to bring out staves and other articles, and the vessels are stopped by his orders.
JOHN A. DIX,
Major-General.

HEADQUARTERS DISTRICT OF NORTH CAROLINA,
Raleigh, October 25, 1862.

Maj. Gen. J. G. FOSTER, U. S. A.,
Comdg. Department of North Carolina, New Berne, N. C.:

GENERAL: Your letter of the 18th instant was received a few days ago. I send inclosed herewith a list of men belonging to Company K,

Thirty-first Regiment North Carolina Troops, who are within your lines. These men were paroled on Roanoke Island, and I respectfully request you to send them beyond your lines.

Lieut. Col. S. D. Pool, Tenth Regiment, will send a list of the men absent from his command within your lines. I would thank you to send them out as promised in your letter of the 18th.

I received on the 20th a letter written by Colonel Potter, U. S. Army, commanding at Washington, dated the 9th instant, asking if the "practice of shooting pickets and vedettes is countenanced by officers of the Confederate Army." He stated in that letter that "two of our vedettes were yesterday murdered in the most cold-blooded manner." The practice of shooting pickets is not countenanced by officers of the Confederate States Army, but when pickets are surprised by a superior force and surrender demanded they are liable to be shot if they attempt to escape. I have investigated the case reported by Colonel Potter and find that the vedettes referred to by him were surprised . and ordered three times to halt and surrender before they were fired on. The statement made by the Washington paper of the 11th instant in regard to the affair acknowledges that they were halted once, which should have been sufficient, considering the force.

I am satisfied that the conduct of a detachment of the Third New York Cavalry at Mr. Woods', near Core Creek, was as reported to you, and I would be glad to know the result of your investigation of the matter, and what has been done with the guilty parties.

I am, very respectfully, your obedient servant,

J. G. MARTIN,
Brigadier-General.

P. S.—Your letter of the 22d instant is received. The one sent to the Governor was delivered.

SUFFOLK, *October* 26, 1862.

Major-General DIX:

Colonel Dodge reports that Longstreet has arrived at Petersburg with 30,000 men, which force is now occupying Waverly (7 miles from Wakefield), Wakefield, Berlin, and Franklin. He also reports considerable force on the Seaboard and Roanoke road, probably within 15 miles of Fanklin.

The railroad at Ivor has been repaired and busy for two days carrying troops. This information, save as to the numbers, agrees in the main with reports of deserters and contrabands whom I have examined. Twenty thousand troops may be there, and perhaps more.

JOHN J. PECK,
Major-General.

HDQRS. DEPT. OF VIRGINIA, SEVENTH ARMY CORPS,
Fort Monroe, Va., October 27, 1862.

Actg. Rear-Admiral S. P. LEE,
Commanding North Atlantic Blockading Squadron:

ADMIRAL : I have the honor to inclose a copy of a report from Colonel Alford, the commanding officer of the post, in regard to the supposed firing on the gunboat lying off the fort by a sentry.

It appears that a private belonging to the guard, but not posted as a sentinel, went outside of the water battery, and, in violation of positive orders, fired his musket three times at some ducks a short distance from the shore. I have examined the man myself, and am satisfied from his statement that it was an act of mere carelessness, and that it did not occur to him that any one on board of the gunboat would be in danger. Indeed he says, what I have no doubt is true, that he was not thinking of the gunboat at all. The occurrence is very much regretted by Colonel Alford and myself, and, as you will perceive, the guilty party had been imprisoned for trial by court-martial before any attention had been called to the transaction.

I am, very respectfully, your obedient servant,

JOHN A. DIX,
Major-General.

UNITED STATES FLAG-STEAMER PHILADELPHIA,
Hampton Roads, October 27, 1862—8 p. m.

Maj. Gen. JOHN A. DIX, U. S. A.,
Commanding Seventh Army Corps, Fortress Monroe, Va. :

GENERAL: I beg leave to refer you to the dispatch of this date from General Lockwood at Drummondtown, just received through your telegraphic office.

The Coast Survey chart does not show that a gunboat can approach Drummondtown, which the general map shows is situated about half-way between the bay and sea-coast. I will cheerfully send a gunboat, if it can get where the Belvidere is, for moral effect and to accompany such a detachment of troops as you may deem it proper to send to the assistance of General Lockwood, but I shall need instructions from Washington, which you or General Wool may solicit, to justify the use of naval force, the necessity of which I think may be obviated by such military measures as you have the ready means of taking.

I have the honor to be, general, very respectfully, yours,

S. P. LEE,
Actg. Rear-Admiral, Comdg. N. Atlantic Blockading Squadron.

NAVY DEPARTMENT,
October 27, 1862.

Hon. E. M. STANTON,
Secretary of War:

SIR: I have the honor to inclose herewith an extract from a dispatch, dated the 24th instant, received from Actg. Rear-Admiral S. P. Lee, commanding the North Atlantic Blockading Squadron, in which he ventures to express his views in favor of abandoning Yorktown and Norfolk.

I am, respectfully, your obedient servant,

GIDEON WELLES,
Secretary of the Navy.

[Inclosure.]

UNITED STATES FLAG-STEAMER PHILADELPHIA,
Chesapeake Bay, October 24, 1862.

Hon. GIDEON WELLES,
Secretary of the Navy, Washington, D. C. :

SIR: * * * We occupy this unimportant and untenable position (Yorktown) at considerable expense. I am confirmed in my former belief that our best course would be to abandon this position after destroying all the military works at and near Yorktown, whether erected by the rebels or ourselves, which could encourage a future occupation even with field pieces by the former, especially for the purpose of annoying the gunboats, which are sufficient to keep the blockade and police of these waters. I would apply the same rule to all the rebel works near Norfolk, and would hold no military occupation of any place in this vicinity outside Fortress Monroe except such as might be necessary to protect our present occupation of the Gosport Navy-Yard. This would allow a large force, of from 20,000 to 30,000 (now scattered and making, as it were, a frontier line, liable to attack in detail), to be concentrated for the effectual prosecution of a campaign, and it would leave our gunboats free to move about and preserve a strict blockade instead of occupying positions rendered necessary only by the positions of the army.

I have the honor to be, &c.,

S. P. LEE,
Actg. Rear-Admiral, Comdg. N. Atlantic Blockading Squadron.

WASHINGTON, *October* 28, 1862—7 p. m.
Major-General DIX:

The Secretary of State desires to have a personal interview with you respecting Norfolk trade, about which there is difficulty with the Navy Department, and that in the mean time you grant no more permits either for exports or imports.

You will please come here at your earliest convenience, and suspend all permits.

EDWIN M. STANTON,
Secretary of War.

UNITED STATES FLAG-STEAMER PHILADELPHIA,
Hampton Roads, Va., October 28, 1862.
Maj. Gen. JOHN A. DIX, U. S. A.,
Commanding Seventh Army Corps, Fortress Monroe, Va.:

GENERAL: Our troops in the Sounds have at some important points no works, and are protected there by the vessels. In view of the threatened attack in that quarter the light-draught and heavy battery of the Southfield, which vessel has for some time been undergoing very slow repairs at Norfolk, make her services absolutely necessary in the Sounds at this time. I have urgently to request that you will cause all the force at Norfolk which can be effectually employed to be assigned to her, with a view to her immediate completion.

I will thank you for an answer to this.

I have the honor to be, general, very respectfully, yours,

S. P. LEE,
Actg. Rear-Admiral, Comdg. N. Atlantic Blockading Squadron.

HDQRS. DEPT. OF VIRGINIA, SEVENTH ARMY CORPS,
Fort Monroe, Va., October 29, 1862.
Actg. Rear-Admiral S. P. LEE,
Commanding North Atlantic Blockading Squadron:

ADMIRAL: I have not thought it profitable to continue the discussion with you of the blockade at this post, as you assure me that in all you have done and are doing you are carrying out the orders of the Navy Department. I shall therefore address what I have to say to the Secretary of War, that all questions arising here may be adjusted at Washington.

I have endeavored to give you all the aid in my power in carrying out your instructions, and shall continue to do so, for I am as anxious as you can possibly be to prevent illicit traffic with the States or parts of States in actual insurrection against the Government of the United States, and I agree with you that those instructions may be carried out without inconvenience to the branch of the public service with which I am connected.

I respectfully suggest that as you have a complete list of all the steamers in the employ of the army here they should be allowed to pass freely from this post to Norfolk, Suffolk, Yorktown, and Newport News. They will all be provided with certificates from the chief quartermaster of the Seventh Army Corps, Lieut. Col. C. W. Thomas. The authentic list sent to you by me is a certificate from myself that the steamers named in it are actually in the employ of the army.

It is desirable that the certificates given by Colonel Thomas should be retained by the captains of the steamers. If any steamer is discharged, Colonel Thomas' certificate will be taken from the captain, and I will notify you immediately, in order that you may strike the steamer from your list. On the other hand, if any new steamer is chartered, I will give you the like immediate notice, that you may add it to the list.

All steamers passing the Wyandotte and not being on your list will be directed to stop and exhibit their certificate. I respectfully suggest that the steamers on your list, of which the commander of the Wyandotte should be provided with a copy, ought not to be required to stop. The delay is often inconvenient, independently of all other considerations. I am going to Washington this morning on the Metamora, on a summons from the Secretary of War, and it will be neither convenient nor consistent with my position as the commander of the department to be stopped by the guard boat, when the commander is aware that the Metamora is in the service of the army and that is the boat I use when I leave the post in performance of my military duties.

I am, very respectfully, your obedient servant,

JOHN A. DIX,
Major-General.

SUFFOLK, *October* 29, 1862.

Major-General DIX:

Colonel Dodge, who commanded the cavalry that crossed, gave the information that I reported from the other side. It was in every one's mouth and so confidently talked that he thought it was only a question of estimates. He says 20,000; they saying 30,000. Longstreet's name has never been used over there until last week. Deserters and conscripts reported to me that Longstreet was on his way early in the week, but I did not believe it. One says he saw a division on its way for Longstreet. When I asked the sergeant if Longstreet was there he said it would not be proper to answer. He and other persons spoke of French and Pettigrew freely. This population all asking to go away of late is suspicious. A heavy picket was at Carrsville last night.

JOHN J. PECK,
Major-General.

FORT MONROE, VA., *October* 29, 1862.

General PECK, *Suffolk:*

General Keyes reported a force of about 800 cavalry as approaching Williamsburg. They intended attacking this morning, but one of their pickets was captured by ours last night, and since then nothing has been done by them except picking up straggling negroes. No infantry are mentioned as being with them.

D. T. VAN BUREN,
Assistant Adjutant-General.

———

HDQRS. DEPT. OF VIRGINIA, SEVENTH ARMY CORPS,
Fort Monroe, Va., October 30, 1862.

Hon. SALMON P. CHASE,
Secretary of the Treasury:

SIR: I have received this evening your letter and the papers prepared by you concerning trade with Norfolk, and I feel a good deal of embarrassment in regard to the certificate. There are in Norfolk, Princess Anne, and Nansemond Counties, which we have taken possession of and cut off from Southern sources of supply, 40,000 inhabitants. We must feed them, and they can only be fed from the North. Can I certify that the supplies they need—food, fuel, clothing (for they must be warmed and clothed as well as fed)—are "required for military purposes?" Will not this extended traffic be complained of as a violation of the law of blockade if we admit that Norfolk is blockaded?

I regret that the Government has taken this view of the subject, for I feel with you the exceeding embarrassment to which it subjects us.

I have insisted that it was a case of military occupation and not of blockade; that you cannot blockade your own ports or a port you have taken from an enemy; that the act of capture *ipso facto* terminates the blockade and puts you in military possession with a totally different code of law for yourself as well as neutrals. You may make it as to them a closed, but it is no longer a blockaded, port. In most modern treaties, I believe, certainly in some, there is a chapter on military occupation, stating the consequences that flow from it. I conversed with Major-General Halleck on the subject, in Washington, ten days ago, and he concurred with me fully. I also conferred with the President, Secretary of State, and Secretary of War, and understood the latter to assent to my positions, and the two former to be at least impressed by my suggestions. I was very anxious to see you and called both at your office and your house, but was disappointed.

My reasoning is briefly this:

1st. Norfolk is not a blockaded port, as it lacks the fundamental condition of a blockade—hostile possession.

2d. If it is a blockaded port, the traffic allowed under the regulations concerning "coastwise intercourse" is in violation of the laws of blockade recognized by all civilized States. A government cannot shut out neutrals from trade with a blockaded port and allow intercourse with such port to its own people.

3d. Norfolk not being an enemy's port, but held by military occupation, we are free to allow such traffic as is necessary to maintain the possession and to prevent those whom we have subjected to our power from suffering by hunger and cold, a duty enjoined by every consideration of humanity. It is on these conditions only that the traffic proposed to be allowed can be justified.

On the theory of military occupation the answer to inquiries from the representatives of foreign governments seems to me very simple and conclusive. The Treasury Department gives no permits to trade; general trade is not restored; the place is governed by martial law, and it rests with the commander of the forces to authorize, by special permits, the introduction of such supplies as are indispensable for the troops and the people they hold in subjection and no more. In the exercise of this authority he may in his discretion grant permits to others than our own citizens; it is a matter over which, as the military commander, he has the entire control, subject to the interposition of the Government for the correction of abuse.

On the other hand, if it is a blockaded instead of being simply a closed port, you can only reach your object by certifying that the supplies necessary to the sustenance of 40,000 people are required for military purposes or something equivalent. If the population were but a tithe of that for which we are to provide, though the principle would not be changed, the amount of necessaries sent to them might not attract attention. But in this case they can hardly fail to be noticed; and I do not see how you are to maintain your ground on the hypothesis of a blockade according to the received principles of international law.

I have made these hasty suggestions under a strong sense of the embarrassment I feel in regard to the certificate I am required to give. If you can resolve my doubts I shall be greatly relieved. But the solution of the whole difficulty in regard to Norfolk seems to be so easy under one view of the question and so beset with complications under the other that I cannot rest satisfied without stating to you the conclusions to which my reflections have brought me.

I do not see that any possible difficulty can arise within the blockaded region under this solution of the question of trade with Norfolk. Whenever you are blockading the enemy's ports or territory the law of blockade controls; whenever you get actual possession and hold by military occupation the commander of the forces governs under the laws of war.

If the question is settled beyond the possibility of reconsideration I beg to be immediately advised, as the people of Norfolk are suffering for want of the necessaries of life. In any case a speedy determination is for the same reason exceedingly desirable.

If the question is not an open one, will it not be sufficient for me to certify that the shipment, &c., is "required for the purposes of my command in this military department?"

I am, very respectfully, your obedient servant,

JOHN A. DIX,
Major-General.

SUFFOLK, VA., *October* 30, 1862.

Major-General DIX:

No longer any doubt of Longstreet's arrival at Petersburg with one division last week. It comes from all quarters and from parties who have no knowledge of each other. It has just come from two of the Surry Court-House pickets—deserters. It is only a question as to the numbers and positions of them. Will shell something at 2 this night.

JOHN J. PECK,
Major-General.

HEADQUARTERS DEPARTMENT OF NORTH CAROLINA,
October 30, 1862.

Maj. Gen. H. W. HALLECK,
General-in-Chief, U. S. Army, Washington, D. C.:

GENERAL: I have the honor to report that I am about to start on an expedition, for the following purposes:

Information was sent me from Plymouth by the navy that three regiments had left from the neighborhood of Plymouth to go down into Washington and Hyde Counties, for the purposes of foraging and obtaining conscripts. These counties form a bag, the mouth of which is between Washington and Plymouth. If I am not too late (as the information was forty hours in reaching me) I hope to engage and capture this force. Should I accomplish that I shall push on for Hamilton, on the Roanoke River, and endeavor to take that place. Should the forces in the counties above named have escaped I will push on at once for the same place. · I am led to make this attempt from information (received from the Navy) that two iron-clad gunboats were being constructed there, and these, of course, it is essential to destroy.

I shall take the following force, to rendezvous at Washington, N. C.: Belger's Rhode Island battery, six pieces; four batteries of the Third New York Artillery, sixteen pieces; about 130 of the Third New York Cavalry, and about 4,000 infantry, made up of detachments from the regiments under my command, and shall go in command myself.

I learn, and I believe reliably, that Governor Vance, of this State, has gone to Richmond, for the purpose of demanding of the Confederate Government the return to the State of all the troops from North Carolina, and that as an earnest of his success several regiments have been already ordered here; so with my force this is my only opportunity to strike a blow.

The New York papers gave a very accurate statement of the three regiments from Massachusetts arrived at this post, so of course my present force is well known to the enemy.

As soon as I return I shall have the honor of reporting my operations and the results.

I am, general, with great respect, your obedient servant,

J. G. FOSTER,
Major-General, Commanding.

UNITED STATES FLAG-STEAMER PHILADELPHIA,
Hampton Roads, Va., October 31, 1862.

Maj. Gen. JOHN A. DIX, U. S. A.,
Commanding Seventh Army Corps, Fortress Monroe, Va.:

GENERAL: I have the honor to acknowledge the receipt of your communication of the 29th instant.

I am gratified by your conclusion to adjust the question of blockade with the authorities at Washington, and very truly regret that you did not find it profitable to do so sooner.

I have always informed you of the text of my orders on this subject from the Secretary of the Navy, to whom I have regularly communicated our correspondence.

Having endeavored faithfully to discharge my duty, under very clear orders to maintain the blockade strictly, I have the satisfaction of knowing that my conduct has been fully approved by the Department in every case where military permits to trade have been given in violation of the blockade. In this connection I beg leave to inform you that in reply to my dispatch, inclosing a copy of yours of the 19th instant with a copy of a dispatch of the Secretary of War to you of the 18th instant respecting trade at Norfolk, the Secretary of the Navy informs me that he is expecting a communication from the Treasury or War Department specifying details of a proposed arrangement for permits, and until it is received that he has no new instructions to give in regard to the blockade.

In reference to the detention of the William Penn the Navy Department, under date of the 29th instant, approves my course and instructs me as follows:

Until the blockade is raised or broken or publicly modified it must be enforced in good faith by the navy. Fort Monroe is not a port of entry, and clearances are not to be made from that point, which is, like Norfolk, subject to blockade. If the Secretary of War or Treasury have seized or obtained possession of staves or tobacco, or any other articles which belong to the Government, and either of them have authorized such articles to be exported, you will recognize their authority. But permits from any officer for general traffic or exports on private account are unknown to the Department intrusted with the blockade and cannot be recognized.

In reply to my communication of the 24th instant you suggest, in substance, that all the steamers in the employ of the army, as shown by the authentic list you have sent me, should pass the blockade without stopping even at the outer guard vessel; that Colonel Thomas, chief quartermaster here, will give certificates to each steamer, which she shall retain while so employed, and when she is discharged Colonel Thomas' certificate will be taken from the captain, and you will immediately notify me, that she may be erased from the list you have sent; and if any new steamer is chartered you will give me like immediate notice, that she may be added to the list; and that all steamers not on the official list will be directed to stop at the outer guard vessel and show their certificates.

I cheerfully accept this proposition, and shall submit our correspondence on the subject and my action in relation thereto for the consideration and decision of the Navy Department.

In respect to the Metamora I beg leave to say that as soon as you informed me she was in your personal service the gunboat on guard duty was promptly instructed on the subject. Had the gunboat on blockade, while ignorant of the fact that you were on board the Metamora, stopped her, I am sure you would, on reflection, not have felt offended, as military men do not take offense at the proper challenge of a sentinel. Yesterday I was not allowed to go on the ramparts of Fort Monroe, though I was in uniform and had made myself known, without a permit from one of your officers, and then I was, and very properly, I believe, challenged by a sentinel and stopped until I exhibited my pass. I saw in this only military propriety and felt no infraction of dignity was intended.

I have the honor to be, general, very respectfully, yours,

S. P. LEE,
Actg. Rear-Admiral, Comdg. N. Atlantic Blockading Squadron.

HEADQUARTERS DISTRICT OF NORTH CAROLINA,
Raleigh, November 1, 1862.

Maj. Gen. J. G. FOSTER, U. S. A.,
    Comdg. Department of North Carolina, New Berne, N. C.:

GENERAL: Your letters of the 24th and 28th ultimo are received. I "appreciate the many difficulties in the way of finding, identifying, and collecting individuals scattered" within your lines and your promptness in sending them when found.

I respectfully request that hereafter all communications by flag of truce will be by land as heretofore, as I shall feel constrained to decline receiving flags of truce by boats sent up the river.

I inclose herewith a letter to the Hon. Edward Stanly and two others, which I would thank you to forward.

I am, very respectfully, your obedient servant,

J. G. MARTIN,
Brigadier-General.

FORT MONROE, *November* 3, 1862.

Hon. E. M. STANTON:

I have just learned that Major-General Wool has gone to Accomack County with a large force. Two companies of Wilkins' regiment of Maryland Home Guards refused to land at Pungoteague on Wednesday last. I sent over my gunboat on a call from General Lockwood, but before it arrived the malcontents had returned to their duty. The regiment was raised expressly to serve in Maryland; hence the discontent, which was, however, very brief.

JOHN A. DIX,
Major-General.

HDQRS. DEPT. OF VIRGINIA, SEVENTH ARMY CORPS,
Fort Monroe, Va., November 3, 1862.

Actg. Rear-Admiral S. P. LEE,
Commanding North Atlantic Blockading Squadron:

ADMIRAL: I believe I have never urged on you any matter a compliance with which would have been a violation of your instructions from the Navy Department. It is only in cases which I considered within your discretion that I have ventured to press on you my own views. They are now in possession of the Government and, I have no doubt, will be satisfactorily disposed of.

The permits given by me, which the Secretary of the Navy in his letter to you on the 29th ultimo says "cannot be recognized," were in accordance, in some instances, with a special authority from the Secretary of the Treasury, and in others with a general authority emanating from the same Department. I shall of course give no more until this conflict of opinion and action is reconciled.

In regard to the occurrence alluded to in your letter of the 31st ultimo within the fort, it is proper to state that there is a permanent rule, adopted long ago, that no officer can go upon the ramparts without the permission of the officer of the day, unless he is accompanied by the commanding general or one of his staff. The rule is applicable to all officers, whether belonging to the garrison or not, or whether of the Army or Navy. The case would be precisely similar if I had gone on board of one of your vessels without announcing myself.

But in the case of the harbor I respectfully suggest that it is entirely different. I have from the beginning objected to the blockade of this fort by a gunboat stationed under its guns as entirely unprecedented, unnecessary, and in disregard of the comity and friendly understanding which should exist between your service and mine, and which I am most anxious to preserve.

Knowing your instructions, when I found the Metamora wanted for another purpose, and when I decided to go to Washington in the City of Hudson, the Norfolk mail-boat, I sent on board the Wyandotte to advise the commander that I should pass in the last-named steamer, and that I was in haste to obey a summons from the Secretary of War. While objecting to the arrangement in my communications with you, I have nevertheless been careful not to act in contravention of it; and I now repeat, and appeal to your courtesy in making the request, that the Wyandotte may be stationed above the Baltimore Wharf, and that this fortress, the headquarters of the department, may be relieved from a system of visitation to which it was never before subjected. I should not make the request if I did not feel a perfect assurance that every public object in view could be as effectually accomplished, and that it is a matter entirely in your own discretion.

I am, very respectfully, your obedient servant,

JOHN A. DIX,
Major-General.

UNITED STATES FLAG-STEAMER PHILADELPHIA,
Hampton Roads, Va., November 4, 1862.

Maj. Gen. JOHN A. DIX, U. S. A.,
Commanding Seventh Army Corps, Fortress Monroe, Va.:

GENERAL: I have the honor to acknowledge the receipt of your two communications of yesterday.

The witnesses on board the Wyandotte, in the case of Private Gill, have been directed to obey the summons of the judge-advocate.

Considering your request for the removal of the Wyandotte as a virtual proposition to raise the blockade of these waters in violation of my instructions from the Navy Department, I have respectfully to inform you that I have referred your application to that Department for instructions.

I have the honor to be, general, very respectfully, yours,

S. P. LEE,
Actg. Rear-Admiral, Comdg. N. Atlantic Blockading Squadron.

TREASURY DEPARTMENT,
November 6, 1862.

Maj. Gen. JOHN A. DIX, *Fort Monroe:*

GENERAL: I have read your letter of the 27th [30th] ultimo, and the subject has been again considered by the President and the Cabinet. I am myself strongly inclined to adopt your views in regard to military occupation, but would not the certificate now required, or one in substance the same, be equally necessary in case that Norfolk, Princess Anne, &c., were regarded not as blockaded but as militarily occupied? At any rate for the present it is not decided to change the existing regulation. The subject is reserved for further consideration. The certificate and request mentioned in my letter will still be required as conditions for the clearances. I see no special objection, however, to substituting for the words "military purposes" the words "for the purpose of my military command," as suggested by you, in conversation, though I prefer the former phrase, which I regard as equivalent in meaning

I prefer it simply because those words have hitherto been used in the certificates from the War Department.

With the very highest respect and esteem, I remain, dear general, truly, yours,

S. P. CHASE.

HDQRS. DEPT. OF VIRGINIA, SEVENTH ARMY CORPS,
Fort Monroe, November 7, 1862.

Hon. SALMON P. CHASE, *Secretary of the Treasury:*

Your letter of the 6th is just received. The Secretary of War has directed me to give no permits at present to take anything to or from Norfolk. Those I gave previously under your instructions have been dishonored by Admiral Lee, under instructions from the Secretary of the Navy. The Government owes it to me, to itself, and to the people of Norfolk, who are starving with hunger and cold, to do something. I am willing to give any certificate which will insure these people food, fuel, and clothing. The loyal portion of the people of Norfolk and the Government employés not in the army are all suffering. Even the officers, who do not draw rations, are paying enormous prices for all the necessaries of life.

JOHN A. DIX,
Major-General.

WAR DEPARTMENT,
Washington City, D. C., November 8, 1862.

Hon. GIDEON WELLES, *Secretary of the Navy:*

SIR: Will you have the goodness to inform me whether instructions have been given to Admiral Lee to pass staves and other products from Suffolk and Norfolk, on the permit of Major-General Dix, to go North for the purchase of supplies?

The accompanying telegram from General Dix is the occasion for the inquiry.

Yours, truly,

EDWIN M. STANTON,
Secretary of War.

[Inclosure.]

FORT MONROE, *November 8, 1862.*

Hon. E. M. STANTON, *Secretary of War:*

Am I authorized to permit the people of Norfolk and Suffolk to send North staves and other products to pay for supplies, and has the Secretary of the Navy instructed Admiral Lee to pass them?

JOHN A. DIX,
Major-General.

HDQRS. DEPT. OF VIRGINIA, SEVENTH ARMY CORPS,
Fort Monroe, Va., November 8, 1862.

Maj. Gen. J. G. FOSTER,
Commanding Department of North Carolina:

GENERAL: When in Washington last week I was told by Major-General Halleck that re-enforcements had been sent to you and that you might perhaps move on Goldsborough or some point farther north, possibly Weldon, and cut the railroad connection between Richmond and the Southeastern Atlantic States. To reach Weldon you would have a long march, unless you ascend the Tar or Roanoke Rivers under the cover of gunboats; but I suppose in either case troops might be drawn from Petersburg or its vicinity to oppose you. I think it would be in my power to defeat such a purpose by making a strong demonstration of an attack on some point between Weldon and Petersburg. The enemy has a considerable force, which I can at least hold in check and neutralize on the Blackwater, near which it is embodied. If you have any movement in contemplation it will afford me great pleasure to co-operate with you, and it may be in my power to do so more effectually than I have above suggested.

I am, very respectfully, your obedient servant,

JOHN A. DIX,
Major-General.

NAVY DEPARTMENT,
November 9, 1862.

Hon. E. M. STANTON, *Secretary of War :*

SIR: In reply to your inquiry of the 8th instant I have the honor to inform you that this Department has issued no instructions to Acting Rear-Admiral Lee to allow exports from Suffolk or Norfolk or any other place within the limits of the blockade confided to him.

He is not authorized to recognize permits of any one but the Secretary of the Treasury and Secretary of War. I am not aware that the blockade enforced by the North Atlantic Blockading Squadron has in any respect been modified except by the President's proclamation opening the port of Beaufort.

I am, respectfully, your obedient servant,

GIDEON WELLES,
Secretary of the Navy.

WASHINGTON, *November 12, 1862.*

Maj. Gen. JOHN A. DIX :

By direction of the Secretary of War I send the following orders of the President :

EXECUTIVE MANSION,
Washington, November 12, 1862.

Ordered, first, that clearances issued by the Treasury Department for vessels or merchandise bound for the port of Norfolk, for the military necessi ies of the department, certified by the military commandant at Fort Monroe, shall be allowed to enter said port ; second, that vessels and domestic produce from Norfolk, permitted by the military commandant at Fort Monroe for the military purposes of his command, shall on his permit be allowed to pass from said port to its destination to any port not blockaded by the United States.

A. LINCOLN.

JOHN TUCKER,
Assistant Secretary of War.

WAR DEPARTMENT,
Washington City, November 13, 1862.

Maj. Gen. JOHN A. DIX,
Commanding, Fort Monroe, Va.:

GENERAL: In view of the numerous applications made to this Department for permits to trade with Norfolk, Portsmouth, and Suffolk, and the large aggregate amount of goods embraced in the schedules (almost if not quite enough to supply Richmond as well as Norfolk and its neighborhood), the Secretary of War deems it proper to suggest that in acting upon applications for licenses to ship goods to those places care should be taken to scale them down so as to limit the supplies imported to the actual necessities of the inhabitants. Unless this be done the places named will again become depots of supplies for the rebels at Richmond. An estimate of the population of Norfolk, Portsmouth, and Suffolk, counting four children or negroes as the equivalent of one adult citizen, will enable you readily to determine approximately, by the application of the army ration and clothing tables, the quantities of articles required by the inhabitants to supply their necessities.

Very respectfully, your obedient servant,

P. H. WATSON,
Assistant Secretary of War.

UNITED STATES STEAMER HETZEL,
Off New Berne, N. C., November 13, 1862.

Maj. Gen. J. G. FOSTER, U. S. A.,
Commanding Department of North Carolina:

GENERAL : I respectfully beg leave to offer for your consideration the following copy of a dispatch, dated November 4 instant, and received this day from Acting Rear-Admiral Lee, viz:

I have official information that the rebel gunboat No. 290 is on the coast. She may have consorts. Notify the vessels under my command in the Sounds of this and promptly give the intelligence to General Foster.

I have the honor to be, very respectfully, your obedient servant,

H. K. DAVENPORT,
Commander and Senior Officer in Sounds of North Carolina.

SUFFOLK, *November 14, 1862.*

Major General DIX, *Fort Monroe:*

I am surprised that General Foster did not advise you of his operations, as we could at that time have threatened about the Blackwater. His movement will cause some concentration of troops, which may perhaps extend to the Blackwater region.

A Georgia deserter, who left the company near Surry Court-House last night, says Longstreet's troops are coming to Suffolk. His lieutenant said that he saw 15,000 of them, and that they were barefooted and very destitute of clothing.

JOHN J. PECK,
Major-General.

SUFFOLK, VA., *November 14, 1862.*

Major-General DIX :

With your approval will have 4,000 infantry, 1,000 cavalry, and battery of artillery 4 miles above Franklin before dawn of Tuesday. Propose to cross cavalry and about 1,500 infantry, with one rifled cannon and two mountain howitzers, under Spear and Foster. Wish to clear all the neck to Nottoway if possible, and reach Jerusalem with cavalry.

This will have much effect on pending operations about Weldon and Petersburg. Can you not give me Jourdan's regiment? Shall send Wessells in command. If weather should be unfavorable will delay. Getting boats ready for a bridge.

JOHN J. PECK,
Major-General.

HDQRS. DEPT. OF VIRGINIA, SEVENTH ARMY CORPS,
Fort Monroe, Va., November 15, 1862.

P. H. WATSON, Esq.,
Assistant Secretary of War:

I have just received your communication of the 13th instant.

Please say to the Secretary of War that his wishes have been in every particular anticipated:

1st. I had an estimate made two weeks ago of the principal articles needed for the population within our lines at Norfolk and vicinity. I am reducing it to greater precision by an actual enumeration of the in-habitants, considerably diminished in number by the war since the last census.

2d. I have opened a set of books in which are to be entered, under their proper heads, each article and the quantity of each article for which permits are granted and also the quantities actually received, so that the footings of each day will exhibit the aggregate of both.

No effort will be spared to prevent abuse.

I am, very respectfully, your obedient servant,

JOHN A. DIX,
Major-General.

WAR DEPARTMENT,
Washington City, November 15, 1862.

Maj. Gen. JOHN A. DIX,
Commanding, Fort Monroe, Va.:

GENERAL: A letter was addressed to you by this Department, under date of the 13th instant, in relation to permits to trade with Norfolk, Portsmouth, and Suffolk. The Secretary of War directs me to inform you that as the action of which you will be duly advised is contemplated there will be no necessity for compliance on your part with the suggestions contained in the communication above referred to.

Very respectfully, your obedient servant,

P. H. WATSON,
Assistant Secretary of War.

FORT MONROE, *November* 15, 1862.

Major-General PECK:

I approve of your plan. If you cross only 1,500 cavalry they must be free from all incumbrances, so as to move rapidly, and you should have the residue of your force ready to move to their support if assailed by superior numbers. Try to make the officers and men feel that they are equal to double their numbers, as I believe they are.

JOHN A. DIX,
Major-General

FORT MONROE, *November* 15, 1862.

Major-General PECK, *Suffolk:*

I approve entirely of your movements on the Blackwater. These little successes encourage our men and habituate them to the fire of the enemy. The weather is fine. Keep a portion of your troops in motion, but let them be careful and not be surprised. The immense number of cross-roads require the utmost vigilance. Finish the railroad bridge as soon as possible.

JOHN A. DIX,
Major-General.

NOVEMBER 16, 1862.

Maj. Gen. JOHN A. DIX, *Fort Monroe:*

A few days since I telegraphed that Longstreet's troops had passed Petersburg, some 15,000. A deserter from Surry Court-House learned this from one of his officers, who had been to the city. A special dispatch from Washington to Philadelphia Inquirer on the 14th confirms the report by news from Culpeper. Foster's operations do not appear to have been entirely successful. They can concentrate so rapidly the chances are in their favor.

JOHN J. PECK,
Major-General.

HEADQUARTERS DEPARTMENT OF VIRGINIA,
Fort Monroe, Va., November 17, 1862.

His Excellency ABRAHAM LINCOLN,
President of the United States:

SIR: I feel a strong sympathy in behalf of the people of the Eastern Shore of Virginia—Accomack and Northampton Counties. When I sent an armed force against them, giving them assurances of protection and promising them the enjoyment of all the rights of loyal citizens, they laid down their arms. They have at no time since been in rebellion against the United States; on the contrary, they have united themselves to Western Virginia; they have had two elections, and they have sent strong Union men to the Legislature and Congress. In all things they have fulfilled the conditions on which I pledged to them equality in rights and privileges with the people of the loyal States. When you issued your proclamation in July last, designating the States and parts of States that were to be deemed loyal and omitting these two counties, I thought to write to you begging that they should be added to the number thus designated. I write now to make the request in order that they may be relieved from the penalties of disloyalty, and that the taint of disaffection may not rest upon a community in which no such feeling exists excepting in individual cases which may unfortunately be found everywhere. They are entitled to exemption by their loyal conduct during the last year, and the effect of such a declaration from you at this time could not fail to have a beneficial effect in other quarters. But it is chiefly as an act of justice to them that I urge it, and I am sure you will appreciate the earnestness with which I press it when you consider the relation in which I stand to them.

I have the honor to be, very respectfully, your obedient servant,

JOHN A. DIX,
Major-General.

HDQRS. DEPT. OF VIRGINIA, SEVENTH ARMY CORPS,
Fort Monroe, Va., November 17, 1862.

Maj. Gen. H. W. HALLECK, *General-in-Chief:*

GENERAL: I return herewith the letter of the Secretary of the Treasury of the 16th ultimo, with a copy of a letter from Maj. R. W. Shenk, One hundred and thirty-fifth Pennsylvania Volunteers, of the 15th, which I received yesterday.* Major Shenk charges that the " flag-of-truce boats are now and have heretofore been to great extent used, in addition to their lawful mission, to pass contraband goods and other articles through the lines at Aiken's Landing on James River." He states two grounds for his charge : First, that a trunk containing cloths, &c., was placed by accident on board of the boat under his command; and, second, that he was approached by a certain Col. Blanton Duncan, of Kentucky, to enter into an arrangement to pass goods, &c. On these grounds he brings a general accusation against the officers in charge of flag-of-truce boats, accusing not only them but the authorities here with want of " ordinary watchfulness." Why did he not report these facts to me on his return from Aiken's Landing that I might institute proper inquiries to detect and punish the frauds and the neglect which he charges upon officers here ? Why send his charges to the Secretary of the Treasury, who could at best only refer them to me for examination and report. Major Shenk was not placed in charge of a flag-of-truce boat by my order. He came here from Washington. It is probable that the trunk to which he refers was put on board his boat there, and that no one was in fault but himself; but he was placed under my control, and it was his duty to have reported to me on his return from Aiken's Landing, the more so as he was detained here by me and sent several times up the James River. He not only neglected his duty but brought a totally unfounded accusation, as I believe, against others.

I venture to say that flags of truce have never been used with a more careful regard to their sacred character than at this post. I have always selected the most discreet and vigilant officers and placed them under the most rigid instructions. So careful have I been not to violate them that I refused permission to one of the principal officers at this post to send some mourning garments to a little girl, his niece, in Richmond, that she might notice in the customary mode the death of a near relative. Passengers have only been allowed to take their wearing apparel, except in a single instance, in which a French lady of advanced age had permission to take some claret for her own use. Confederate prisoners have not been permitted to take anything with them but their ordinary baggage, and articles in their possession not coming within this restriction have been uniformly taken from them. The only instance in which I have allowed anything to be sent to Aiken's Landing was for Mr. Aiken himself. He had been very kind to our sick officers and men, and I allowed him to purchase in Baltimore four boxes of tin to repair his roof, 1,000 cigars, and a dozen pocket handkerchiefs, all for his own use. I have been thus particular because Major Shenk, who appears to have had more zeal than discretion or just conception of his own duty, has been guilty of a breach of trust in failing to report to me the facts stated in his letter, and has done a great injustice to the officers in charge of flag-of-truce boats by bringing accusations against them implying either fraud or gross negligence.

I am, sir, very respectfully, your obedient servant,

JOHN A. DIX,
Major-General.

---

* See p. 429.

HEADQUARTERS DEPARTMENT OF NORTH CAROLINA,
New Berne, November 18, 1862.
Maj. Gen. H. W. HALLECK,
General-in-Chief U. S. Army, Washington, D. C.:

GENERAL : Referring to my report of recent reconnaissance, I have the honor to make the following statements :

The enemy have much increased their force and their activity in this State. We have engaged at different times in one way and another seven old regiments, viz, the Eighth, Tenth, Seventeenth, Twenty-sixth, Thirty-first, Fifty-first, and Fifty-ninth ; and I am informed by what I consider reliable authority that Governor Vance has had a difficulty or quarrel with President Davis as regards conscripts, the consequence of which is that the Governor is raising or has raised two brigades of conscripts within assisting distance of Goldsborough. Their artillery force I think to be inferior to mine as yet. There were at Tarborough sixteen pieces, and I found threatening this town on my return ten other pieces. These, with the supporting force, retired on my return. And in the same connection I would state that I heard near Tarborough of the appointment of General Longstreet to the command of this department. This report has since been confirmed, both here and in the Richmond papers. In addition, Governor Vance in person was with the forces at Tarborough.

I would respectfully remark that the above simple statements prove the reliability of my opening paragraph, and, in addition, show the determination of the enemy to withstand my advances in their rich country of the eastern counties, and also, if possible, to diminish my hold on that section. On the other hand the weakening influences of the past malarious season has so weakened the strength of my old regiments that for hard, active service I have scarcely available one-half their nominal strength at the moment. The new regiments (nine-months' men) arrived here, viz, the Third, Fifth, Forty-third, Forty-fourth, Forty-fifth, and Forty-sixth Massachusetts, are good troops but are new, and some never have had their arms, and I should wish some drill before trusting them in a fight.

Admiral Lee has been here, and with him I have had a full and free talk, and am happy to say that he fully coincides with me in my views as to co-operation and as to force required.

Referring to the above simple statements I would most respectfully suggest that if possible I should be allowed at once 10,000 old troops in addition to the few new troops ordered here, and would express my hopes and wishes that those old troops should be the men of the Ninth Army Corps, with whom I have been associated and of which corps I was the senior officer under General Burnside.

The sooner I have the force the sooner I will endeavor to perform my plans, and, I think, the views of Government, viz, the cutting of the railroad (Weldon and Wilmington) and the taking of Wilmington and the works at New Inlet and the mouth of the Cape Fear River.

I most respectfully request, in addition to the officer recommended for promotion to brigadier-general, that three regular brigadier-generals be sent me, and as a matter of choice I would suggest General Gillmore, and if none be available now appointed, call your attention to Captains Prime, Morton, and Casey, of the Engineer Corps, and Lieutenant-Colonel Biggs or Capt. D. W. Flagler, Ordnance Corps, as most acceptable to me. I would also ask an engineer officer, of which I have none, and an ordnance officer. I have received from General Dix a letter as to his co-operation with me in any attempt to cut the railroad communications, and would say that such co-operation would be most desirable, as proved at Tarborough, where the re-enforcements came even from Petersburg. I can act and he assist if the line be cut south of Weldon, and he act and I assist if at Weldon, which point he can reach more easily than I.

I have the honor to be, general, very respectfully, your obedient servant,

> J. G. FOSTER,
> *Major-General, Commanding.*

SUFFOLK, VA., *November* 18, 1862.

Major-General DIX, *Fort Monroe :*

In consequence of our several repeated attacks upon Franklin, Zuni, &c., the rebel authorities have been led to the belief that my force is large and that I have designs upon their communications. My belief is that they are bringing back all the forces taken away.

> JOHN J. PECK,
> *Major-General.*

SUFFOLK, *November* 18, 1862.

General DIX :

You will see that the Richmond papers of October 29, and since, are calling attention to movements on Weldon from Suffolk.

They also give it out that they are driven out of Franklin after a severe fight. See Petersburg Express 27th, in Philadelphia Inquirer of 17th.

> JOHN J. PECK,
> *Major-General.*

WASHINGTON, D. C., *November* 18, 1862.

Major-General DIX, *Fort Monroe :*

Please give me your best opinion as to the number of the enemy now at Richmond and also at Petersburg.

> A. LINCOLN.

FORT MONROE, *November* 18, 1862—2 p. m.

His Excellency the PRESIDENT :

My only reliable information in regard to the enemy's forces in Richmond and vicinity of Petersburg comes from a man who has not been here for four weeks. It was then 11,000 on and near the Blackwater, north of Franklin or Carrsville; at Petersburg, 700; at Richmond, 7,000; between the James and Chickahominy, 7,000; and near White House, 1,500; total, 27,200. This is my latest information. The forces at different points frequently vary, and I place little reliance on reports brought to me by deserters, stragglers, and negroes.

I sent 4,000 men to the Blackwater yesterday, intending to cross. While writing this dispatch information is sent to me by Major-General Peck, from Suffolk, that the expedition found the enemy re-enforced in artillery and infantry at Franklin (Carrsville on the maps) and the fords blocked. A sharp skirmish was going on across the river, which is very narrow higher up. The enemy is on this side of the Blackwater, and our pickets are engaged almost every night. The moment I can get any reliable information as to the force in Richmond and Petersburg I will forward it. I have reason to believe that the force specified in the district embraced in the enumeration at the beginning of this dispatch is reduced rather than increased. In twelve hours it can be concentrated either at Richmond or Petersburg.

JOHN A. DIX,
Major-General, Commanding.

FORT MONROE, VA., *November* 18, 1862.
General H. W. HALLECK,
General-in-Chief:

I have just received the following dispatch from Major-General Peck, at Suffolk, viz:

A communication has just been received by the surgeon of the One hundred and thirty-second New York, from headquarters Banks' expedition, medical director, ordering immediately certain reports about officers, ambulances, &c. It came direct. I ask for explanation and for instructions. We need more troops here, and can hardly afford to lose this regiment.

JOHN J. PECK,
Major-General.

Independently of the impropriety of asking information from my subordinates, except through me, I must request that this regiment may not be taken from me. Indeed, General Casey has only sent me three of the four regiments he was ordered to send. I have sent 4,000 men to the Blackwater to-day, with a view to cross. Our vessels have been fired on almost every night for a week. At Gloucester yesterday we lost 6 men in killed and wounded and 3 taken prisoners. We captured 3 and did about the same damage to the enemy.

JOHN A. DIX,
Major-General, Commanding.

WASHINGTON, *November* 19, 1862.
Maj. Gen. JOHN A. DIX:

No orders have been given to my knowledge for any part of your command to report to Major-General Banks.

H. W. HALLECK,
General-in-Chief.

NOVEMBER 19, 1862.
Major-General DIX, *Fort Monroe:*

Wessells remained all night at Beaver Dam Church, a short distance from Franklin, and moved at dawn.

The rebels were telegraphing over the country with various colored lights until long after midnight.

JOHN J. PECK,
Major-General.

SUFFOLK, *November* 19, 1862.

Major-General DIX:

The cars were running from Petersburg to Zuni all last night, and it is presumed with additions of force. This information has just come in, and I doubt not accounts for the signals. Probably intending to strike here in the absence of one-half of my force, or strike Wessells in the flank. Colonel Dodge is going out toward Zuni to watch any movements.

JOHN J. PECK,
Major-General.

SUFFOLK, *November* 19, 1862.

Major-General DIX:

A courier is just in from the commander of Winfield, N. C., and of the gunboat there; states 200 rebel infantry crossed Chowan and are threatening the region. Lieutenant Etheridge is near the gunboat with his party and has destroyed their boats. They attacked the camp last night.

Wessells is in with his force.

JOHN J. PECK,
Major-General.

SUFFOLK, *November* 19, 1862.

Major-General DIX:

The Weldon road is now in complete order to the Nottoway, 5½ miles from Franklin. I have positive information that they are building the bridge across that river.

JOHN J. PECK,
Major-General.

HDQRS. DEPT. OF VIRGINIA, SEVENTH ARMY CORPS,
Fort Monroe, Va., November 19, 1862.

Maj. Gen. H. W. HALLECK,
General-in-Chief:

GENERAL: I have the honor to inclose six telegraphic dispatches from Major-General Peck.*

I wrote to General Foster soon after I saw you in Washington, offering to co-operate with him, and promising at least a demonstration on the Blackwater which might produce a diversion in his favor. I have had no answer from him and have acted on the presumption that my letter never reached him, although in sending expeditions to the Blackwater I have been influenced also by the desire to accustom my troops to marching, bivouacking, &c., and to the fire of the enemy.

I inclose a map of the district between Suffolk and the Blackwater, on which the roads are carefully drawn.†

Will you please let the President see the accompanying telegraphic dispatches, which may throw a little light on my dispatch to him yesterday?

I am, very respectfully, your obedient servant,

JOHN A. DIX,
Major-General.

---

* Probably those of 18th and 19th, pp. 458–460.   †Not found.

HEADQUARTERS DEPARTMENT OF VIRGINIA,
November 22, 1862.

Hon. E. M. STANTON:

SIR: 1 have received your order appointing Dr. Le Grand Russell "special commissioner to take charge of the colored refugees from the enemy at Fortress Monroe and its vicinity," and shall do all in my power to aid him in the proper discharge of his duties.

The peculiar phraseology of the order suggests the propriety of stating that all the negroes here are not refugees from the enemy. On the contrary, there are a number who are fugitives from the service of Union men, who have been persecuted by the secessionists for their fidelity to the Government of the United States, and a few who belong to persons residing in districts which have never been in possession of the insurgents. Some Union families in this neighborhood have lost all their negroes, whom I have, in obedience to the act of Congress, refused to give up. It will be troublesome to separate one class from the other, and assuming that the order was not intended to make any distinction, I shall, unless otherwise directed, put Dr. Russell in charge of both.

I avail myself of the opportunity of stating that under your authority I opened negotiations with the Governors of the States of Maine, Massachusetts, and Rhode Island, with a view to provide a temporary asylum for the contrabands here until the Government could make some permanent provision for them. The proposition was received with such marked disfavor by Governor Andrew, of Massachusetts, that I decided, notwithstanding a very kind and prompt response from Governor Sprague, of Rhode Island, to retain them here and make suitable provision for them for the winter. Accordingly I withdrew the sick from the hospital at Newport News and sent over a thousand of the colored fugitives there. But the very day they were removed from their encampment, where they were dying rapidly, I was advised that the Irish Legion, under General Corcoran, would arrive on the following day. Their tents had been so injured in New York by a storm on the eve of their departure that they were obliged to be put under cover, and, having no place for them but Newport News, I was compelled to remove the colored people again. They were sent to Craney Island, and the quartermaster is, under my instructions, erecting barracks for them. They will all be covered in the course of the coming week.

I am, very respectfully, your obedient servant,

JOHN A. DIX,
Major-General.

FORT MONROE, VA., *November* 23, 1862.

Major-General HALLECK,
General-in-Chief:

A reconnaissance was made from Williamsburg yesterday toward the Chickahominy. Killed 2 and captured 6 of the enemy and took 11 horses. No loss on our side.

JOHN A. DIX,
Major-General.

HEADQUARTERS DEPARTMENT OF VIRGINIA,
Fort Monroe, Va., November 24, 1862.

His Excellency ABRAHAM LINCOLN,
President of the United States :

SIR: I have had the honor to receive your letter of the 20th instant* in regard to the counties of Accomack and Northampton, or what is usually called the Eastern Shore of Virginia, and am gratified to learn from you that there is no objection to a recognition of their loyal condition. The reasons which make them so anxious on the subject are two:

1st. An unwillingness to be classed with the insurrectionary districts, considering it a stain upon their character and unjust to them, as they have given repeated evidences of their loyalty; and

2d. A desire to be exempt, as they claim they are entitled to be, from the penalty of 50 per cent. in addition to the taxes to be raised to support the Government, &c. This penalty is imposed by the concluding clause of section 1 of the act of June 7, 1862, chapter 98, of the laws of 1862. This is a "practical difficulty" from which they ask to be relieved.

They are perfectly willing to pay their share of the taxes like other loyal districts.

I am, very respectfully, your obedient servant,

JOHN. A. DIX,
Major-General.

FORT MONROE, VA., *November* 24, 1862.

Major-General HALLECK, *General-in-Chief:*

I have just received the following dispatch from General Naglee, at Yorktown:

My salt expedition to Matthews County has been a perfect success. Destroyed seventy-three large cast-iron boiling vessels of nine establishments and over one thousand bushels of salt. We are indebted to Capt. Foxhall Parker, commanding the naval branch of the expedition, for very effective service.

JOHN A. DIX,
Major-General.

FORT MONROE, *November* 24, 1862.

Major-General HALLECK, *General-in-Chief:*

I send you by this evening's boat, via Baltimore, Mr. Bernard, who is just from General G. W. Smith's office in Richmond. He has very valuable information. He is from Utica. He confirms my statement of 21st October as to the number of troops in the district, including the Blackwater, Petersburg, Richmond, and south toward the Chickahominy, about 27,000, though the distribution is not the same.

JOHN A. DIX,
Major-General.

UNITED STATES STEAMER SHAWSHEEN,
Off Winfield, N. C., November 24, 1862.

Lieut. C. W. FLUSSER, *Commanding, Albemarle Sound:*

SIR: As there are many reports in circulation which appear to be reliable, some of them at least, I deem it my duty to inform you of them. Part of Small's men are still on this side lurking about; Hill's com-

---

* Not found.

pany is reported to be in Gates County and a portion of the Nansemond Cavalry there, as two companies of paroled Roanoke prisoners that have been exchanged, now organized, and before crossing the lines intend to co-operate with the forces that have crossed the river and make an attack on this place and also to clean the counties of all the produce that they can get hold of and convey it across the river. The principal part of the citizens are very much enraged at those people coming across here committing such acts as they have since coming over.

Longstreet's force of 45,000 men is reported at Weldon. It is to be lamented that we have not taken that important place before this.

I saw and read a letter written in Raleigh by one of the convention men, wherein he says if Weldon falls into our possession that Virginia will have to come into the Union and North Carolina with her. He says their only hope is in the Conservative Democratic party North, but adds that there is little hope from them, as they are anxious for prosecuting the war, and it is so long before they come into power that death and starvation stare the Confederate Army in the face. He says their troops are in a deplorable condition, neither shoes, clothing, nor tents. He says he converses with the best men in the Confederacy from the President down. He says they called a convention of the State Council, which consists of seven members, and only three of them met; they waited three days and no other members met. He adds that this is the first time since the world was made that such a convention was called and not responded to.

To-day I was down across the river and met one of four men who can control the Legislature, and he says remove the bayonets from North Carolina and there would be a Noah's deluge for the State to come into the Union. I will not mention his name, but you can depend upon this.

There is a move on the tapis now of vital importance to the State which would develop itself on the fall of Weldon, for which they are all anxious to see. This man's assertion is substantiated by other good authority and may be depended upon. If you think this worth noticing I hope you will make it known to the proper authorities, and if there is going to be anything done in this direction it should be done immediately, as much dependence is placed on the support received from these counties, and a small force would defeat their movements in this quarter. I hope, as many others do, that something will be done; most all are willing to take the oath.

I went down the river yesterday (Sunday) and captured eleven boxes of tobacco, which are very valuable. To-day we captured a fine mule and cart that was in waiting to convey some goods, no doubt, into the country. Have destroyed all the boats on the opposite side of the river; they seem perfectly willing to destroy them. The difference in feeling toward our cause now and what it was two months ago is very apparent.

I was down to the mouth of Chowan to-day. I have one more trip to make down that way to-morrow or next day.

I have twelve tons of coal yet on hand.

One of Small's men was killed in the attack the first night by a shell. The pickets were fired on the next night after the Lockwood left, but we did not fire any from the boat, but embarked all but a guard. Our men are all in pretty good health.

I will send this by a small boat furnished by Lieutenant Etheridge.

I do not think of anything more of importance. Remember me to all friends.

Very respectfully, your obedient servant,

THOS. J. WOODWARD,
Acting Volunteer Lieutenant, Commanding.

SUFFOLK, *November* 25, 1862.

General DIX:

I have a deserter from one of Wise's regiments at Drewry's Bluff.   He says Wise's brigade has orders to come over to the Petersburg road in case of our advance.   This man was carried to Ivor and escaped again. A six-gun battery and one regiment of infantry came there from Petersburg last week.   They told him that 15,000 were at Weldon, and that we had 25,000 here.

I hope for a dash soon.   The river is high and a bridge is necessary; am making one.

JOHN J. PECK,
Major-General.

HDQRS. DEPT. OF VIRGINIA, SEVENTH ARMY CORPS,
Fort Monroe, Va., November 26, 1862

Brig. Gen. M. CORCORAN,
Commanding, Newport News :

GENERAL : A complaint has been made to me that the colored people who are to go to Craney Island have been forced to remain all night on the wharf without shelter and without food ; that one has died, and that others are suffering with disease, and that your men have turned them out of their houses, which they have built themselves, and have robbed some of them of their money and personal effects.   You will inquire promptly into these complaints and redress the wrongs which have been committed, if they are truly represented to me.   You will also see that the means are provided for burying the dead, and that these people are furnished with food by the commissary until they can be sent from Newport News.   A boat will be sent as soon as possible. These people are in our care and we are bound by every principle of humanity to treat them with kindness and protect them from exposure and injury in their persons and property.

Respectfully, yours,

JOHN A. DIX,
Major-General.

SUFFOLK, VA., *November* 26, 1862.

Major-General DIX, *Fort Monroe :*

Have organized an attack upon Ivor with at least 5,000.   The move would have been this day save rain and mud.   Our reconnaissances show that every bridge is down and all the fords are blocked by slashing the approaches.   We will have much to cut away on both sides.

The Banks command in your waters is calling the attention of the Government [enemy?] to the Suffolk line, and they may re-enforce. Have you any data ?

JOHN J. PECK,
Major-General.

FORT MONROE, *November* 26, 1862.

Major-General PECK:

My last advices from Richmond, very recent, are that they have no fears of an advance on the Suffolk line, but are fortifying slowly from Petersburg to Richmond.

JOHN A. DIX,
Major-General.

FORT MONROE, *November* 27, 1862.

Major-General PECK:

I have just received a letter from General Foster, at New Berne, saying he may ask my co-operation in an important movement about the 5th of December. Has your expedition gone? A week ago General French was at Petersburg with 4,000 men. I have nothing later.

JOHN A. DIX,
Major-General.

SUFFOLK, *November* 27, 1862.

Major-General DIX:

Mud and water have delayed our move. The enemy are signaling between here and the Blackwater.

JOHN J. PECK.

FORT MONROE, *November* 27, 1862.

Major-General PECK:

Perhaps it would be as well to wait till I hear from General Foster. In that case I will send an officer to him to-morrow. What do you think?

JOHN A. DIX,
Major-General.

HDQRS. DEPT. OF VIRGINIA, SEVENTH ARMY CORPS,
Fort Monroe, Va., November 27, 1862.

Maj. Gen. J. G. FOSTER,
Commanding Department of North Carolina:

GENERAL: I only received this evening your letter of the 14th instant. It is now too late for me to meet you, but if you will send by Lieutenant Mabie, who will take this dispatch to you, any communication which will indicate your wishes I will endeavor to meet them. I have not a large force at Suffolk, but sufficient to make a diversion on the Blackwater. The enemy are now turning their attention to the Suffolk route to Petersburg. They have recently put the railroad from the latter city to the Blackwater in order, but I have changed the gauge on this side so that they cannot use it. They are repairing the bridge on the Seaboard Railroad over the Nottoway so that they can re-enforce on the Blackwater from Weldon. I can attack at Franklin, where the Seaboard Railroad reaches the Blackwater (Carrsville on the maps), or at Zuni, where the Petersburg Railroad strikes the same river; or if I can aid you by a different movement let me know and I will do all in my power.

I had an expedition organized under Major-General Peck to move on Zuni to-morrow with 5,000 men, but since the receipt of yours have countermanded it in order to make the time suit you.

I am, respectfully and truly, yours,

JOHN A. DIX,
Major-General.

HEADQUARTERS DEPARTMENT OF NORTH CAROLINA,
Petersburg, Va., November 27, 1862.

General J. G. FOSTER, U. S. A.,
New Berne, N. C.:

DEAR SIR : During the march of the army under your command up
the valley of the Roanoke River, in the early part of this month, many
wanton acts of destruction of private property and many depredations
were committed by the troops under your command.

Negroes were forcibly abducted from their owners; many isolated
houses in the villages of Hamilton and Williamston were willfully
burned; parlors of private residences were used for stables; family car
riages were taken to your camps, abandoned, and destroyed; houses of
peaceful citizens were forcibly entered, doors and windows broken and
all the furniture destroyed; bedding was carried into the streets and
burned; women were insulted by your soldiers and robbed of all the
money and valuables on their persons, and all their clothing and that
of their children, except what they had on, was cast into the fire or torn
to pieces.

In general terms, your soldiers committed many robberies and prac
ticed a wanton and malicious destruction of private property.

Having been over a portion of your line of march and examined these
evidences of destruction I reported them to my Government, and I an
instructed to address you and inform you that such outrages are con
sidered as forfeiting the right of yourself and officers to be treated as
prisoners of war, and to inquire of you whether these outrages were
committed with your knowledge and sanction.

The action to be taken in the case will depend on the answer you may
make, and if no answer be returned in ten days after the delivery of
this letter it will be considered by the Government that you admit and
hold yourself responsible for the acts charged.

Very respectfully, your obedient servant,

S. G. FRENCH,
Major-General, Commanding.

WASHINGTON, D. C., *November* 29, 1862.

Major-General DIX, *Fort Monroe, Va.* :

Several regiments of Pennsylvania drafted militia will be sent to you
as soon as transportation can be procured.

H. W. HALLECK,
General-in-Chief.

HEADQUARTERS DEPARTMENT OF VIRGINIA,
Seventh Army Corps, Fort Monroe, Va., November 29, 1862.

Maj. Gen. H. W. HALLECK,
General-in-Chief:

GENERAL: I received the day before yesterday a letter from Major
General Foster, dated the 14th instant, at New Berne, in reply to mine
suggesting a co-operation between his forces and mine in a movement
against the enemy, and I immediately sent an officer to him in order to

prevent any further delay in communicating with him. I find myself much hampered for want of the means of crossing the Blackwater. The bridges are all destroyed from Zuni to Franklin, and the fords blocked by slashing and other obstructions. The river is narrow and deep and we are in want of pontoons.

I sent Mr. Joseph Francis, the inventor of the metallic life-boat, to the Quartermaster-General yesterday with a model of his corrugated-iron pontoon wagon. It is a wagon, pontoon, and boat, dispensing with the cumbersome pontoon train which carries nothing, and enables an army to cross streams with its baggage train without delay and to pass over its heavy artillery with rapidity and safety. The pontoon wagon floats with 2,400 pounds in it and holds up its carriage. I am very desirous of having twenty of these wagons. They can be fitted as bodies to the carriages of the common wooden wagons which we have here, and enable us to accomplish all our objects without adding to our baggage train. Mr. Francis has the means of constructing them at once at the factory of the corrugated-iron life-boats at Greenpoint, N. Y. He has just returned from Russia, and has had the satisfaction of seeing his pontoon wagon, after long-continued and severe tests, adopted by Great Britain and all the German States. I am satisfied that I can with twenty of them render valuable service in this quarter, and at the same time make a trial which will save the Government millions of dollars and thousands of lives by dispensing entirely with the heavy and expensive wooden pontoon train and giving our armies the means of crossing currents when pursued or pursuing, without delay.

I am, very respectfully, your obedient servant,

JOHN A. DIX,
Major-General.

Abstract from Return of the Department of Virginia, Maj. Gen. John A. Dix commanding, for November 30, 1862.

Command.	Present for duty.		Aggregate present.	Aggregate present and absent.	Pieces of field artillery.	Remarks.
	Officers.	Men.				
Fort Monroe, Col. S. M. Alford..	22	620	819	857	....	
Camp Hamilton, Col. A. Conk...	43	1,112	1,331	1,390	12	
Norfolk, Brig. Gen. E. L. Viele..	131	2,599	3,227	3,809	6	
Suffolk, Brig. Gen. J. J. Peck....	476	9,431	12,027	14,224	20	
Yorktown, Maj. Gen. E. D. Keyes.	242	4,784	6,285	7,809	28	Outposts at Gloucester Point and Williamsburg.
Total......................	914	18,546	23,689	28,089	66	

Troops in the Department of Virginia, Maj. Gen. John A. Dix commanding, November 30, 1862.

Fort Monroe.

Col. SAMUEL M. ALFORD.

3d New York.

Camp Hamilton.

Col. ANTHONY CONK.

139th New York.
11th Pennsylvania Cavalry, Company C.
Batt'n Pennsylvania Heavy Arty., Co. C.
2d and 4th Wisconsin Batteries.

Norfolk and vicinity.

Brig. Gen. EGBERT L. VIELE.

99th New York.
148th New York.
158th New York.
19th Wisconsin.
11th Pennsylvania Cavalry, Company M.
7th New York Battery.

Suffolk and vicinity.

Maj. Gen. JOHN J. PECK.

Ferry's brigade, Fourth Corps.
Wessells' brigade, Fourth Corps.
Foster's brigade, Seventh Corps.
Spinola's brigade, Seventh Corps.
1st New York Mounted Rifles.
11th Pennsylvania Cavalry.
7th Massachusetts Battery.
4th U. S. Artillery, Batteries D and L.
99th New York, Company I (detachment).

Yorktown and vicinity.

Maj. Gen. ERASMUS D. KEYES.

Naglee's brigade, Fourth Corps.*
Reserve Artillery, Fourth Corps.
6th New York Cavalry (battalion).
5th Pennsylvania Cavalry.
1st New York Artillery, Batteries F and H.

Abstract from Return of the Department of North Carolina, Maj. Gen. John G. Foster commanding, for November 30, 1862.

Command.	Present for duty.		Aggregate present.	Aggregate present and absent.
	Officers.	Men.		
First Brigade (Col. T. J. C. Amory)	137	3,456	4,417	4,782
Second Brigade (Col. T. G. Stevenson)	113	3,083	3,802	4,181
Third Brigade (Col. Horace C. Lee)	148	3,408	4,141	4,880
Unassigned	101	2,426	3,209	4,110
Total	499	12,373	15,569	17,959

Organization of troops in the Department of North Carolina, Maj. Gen. John G. Foster, U. S. Army, commanding, November 30, 1862.

First Brigade.

Col. T. J. C. AMORY.

17th Massachusetts, Lieut. Col. J. F. Fellows.
23d Massachusetts, Maj. J. G. Chambers.
43d Massachusetts, Col. Charles L. Holbrook.
45th Massachusetts, Col. Charles R. Codman.
51st Massachusetts, Col. A. B. R. Sprague.

Second Brigade.

Col. T. G. STEVENSON.

10th Connecticut, Maj. Robert Leggett.
8th Massachusetts Militia, Col. F. J. Coffin.
24th Massachusetts, Lieut. Col. F. A. Osborn.
44th Massachusetts Militia, Col. F. L. Lee.
5th Rhode Island, Maj. George W. Tew.

---

* Composition of brigades not indicated on original return.

Third Brigade.	*Unassigned.*
Col. HORACE C. LEE.	25th Massachusetts, Maj. Josiah Pickett.
	3d New York Cavalry, Col. S. H. Mix.
3d Massachusetts, Col. S. P. Richmond.	3d New York Artillery, Col. J. H. Ledlie.
5th Massachusetts, Col. G. H. Peirson.	23d New York Battery, Capt. A. Ransom
27th Massachusetts, Lieut. Col. Luke Lyman.	24th New York Battery, Capt. J. E. Lee.
	1st Rhode Island Artillery, Battery F
46th Massachusetts, Col. George Bowler.	Capt. James Belger.
9th New Jersey, Col. C. A. Heckman.	1st U. S. Artillery, Battery C, Lieut. C.
	Hook.

FORTRESS MONROE, VA., *December* 1, 1862.

General H. W. HALLECK,
Commander-in-Chief U. S. Army, Washington, D. C.:

GENERAL: I have just arrived here to confer with General Dix in regard to co-operating in offensive movements against the enemy. I shall return early to-morrow morning unless you wish me to remain longer to give me some special orders.

J. G. FOSTER,
Major-General, Volunteers.

WAR DEPARTMENT,
Washington, December 1, 1862.

Maj. Gen. J. G. FOSTER,
Fort Monroe, Va.:

I have no special instructions to give. Possibly the Secretary of War may have to-morrow.

H. W. HALLECK,
General-in-Chief.

YORKTOWN, *December* 1, 1862.

Major-General PECK, *Suffolk:*

I expect an officer from General Foster to-night. If not too late you had better defer any strong demonstration till he arrives.

JOHN A. DIX,
Major-General.

SUFFOLK, *December* 2, 1862.

Major-General DIX, *Fort Monroe:*

The interview with General Foster to-day was all that could be desired. He is an old friend, and we canvassed matters fully. Have memoranda which will govern moves for some days. I proposed to demonstrate strongly on a given day, which he did not expect, and which pleased him very much.

I very much desire that the new troops should arrive before Wessells' brigade moves.

JOHN J. PECK,
Major-General.

FORT MONROE, *December* 3, 1862.

Major-General PECK, *Suffolk:*

With Jourdan's regiment you will have five new ones and over 3,000 additional troops. The Pennsylvania regiments are of the very best material. Has Colonel Spear returned? Did he command the expedition? How many men had he? How many prisoners have you taken?* When was the rocket battery taken from our army? Give me details at once; I wish to write General Halleck.

> JOHN A. DIX,
> *Major-General.*

FORT MONROE, *December* 4, 1862.

Major-General PECK, *Suffolk:*

The new regiments are designed to be a part of your command. Make requisitions for all they need. They did not land here, and I supposed them fully supplied. The shoes, &c., wanted by General Wessells were sent ear.y this morning by steamer Arago. Make requisitions for better tents. ⌐ have been promised arms from Washington, but cannot get them.

> JOHN A. DIX,
> *Major-General.*

HEADQUARTERS DEPARTMENT OF NORTH CAROLINA,
New Berne, N. C., December 4, 1862.

Maj. Gen. S. G. FRENCH,
    Comdg. Department of North Carolina, Petersburg, Va.:

GENERAL: Your favor of November 27 I have the honor to acknowledge. I had previously received from General Martin a letter on the same subject, and as my answer to him covers most of the ground in yours I beg leave to inclose a copy. I beg to say in relation to postscript of your letter that not a negro, to the best of my belief, was forcibly abducted from his owner, and indeed I only suffered those to follow who insisted upon so doing. There were fifteen houses (says General Martin) burned at Hamilton; the fact I deplore. At Williamston two were burned from a defect in the flue of the chimney, as shown by investigation, and one small house pulled down to prevent the spread of the fire. Members of my staff were in each house and none of them saw horses in the parlors, though in one or two instances on piazzas; family carriages (not over three) may have been taken to transport sick men, not to destroy or abandon. That houses of peaceful citizens with the families in occupancy were entered, women and children insulted and robbed, I do not believe, as the provost-marshal heard nothing of the kind so gross as you report. In respect to that part of your letter as to the treatment of any officers not as prisoners of war, I would say that if after my letter your Government proposes to act on that principle I beg that you will have me informed for the regulation of my own course.

Very respectfully, your obedient servant,

> J. G. FOSTER,
> *Major-General, Commanding.*

---

* See p. 36.

[Indorsement.]

RICHMOND. VA., *December* 10, 1862.

Respectfully forwarded for the information of the War Department.

G. W. SMITH,
Major-General.

[Inclosure.]

HEADQUARTERS DEPARTMENT OF NORTH CAROLINA,
New Berne, N. C., December 4, 1862.

Brig. Gen. J. G. MARTIN,
Commanding, &c.:

GENERAL: Your letter of November 25,* inclosing an extract from the Boston Traveller, describing the alleged depredations of the army under my command in their late march up the country, I have received. In reply to your request to know whether these things were done by my order I have to state that draught animals, and in some cases carriages to be used as ambulances, beeves and pigs to subsist my men when short of provisions, and forage to subsist cavalry horses and draught animals were taken by my order. Every other species of depredation was not only not done by my orders but against them and against the strongest efforts to prevent them. On the march we found all the towns almost entirely abandoned by their inhabitants, the houses in some cases cleared of their furniture, in others partly, and in some not at all. I quartered my troops in the abandoned houses only. The principal cause of the depredations which I know were committed was, I think, that so many houses contained apple brandy, and which escaped the eye of the provost-marshal. I trust sincerely that in the future marches in this State you will be pleased to find a marked improvement in all these respects, and I earnestly recommend that you urge all peaceable citizens to remain on their estates, as that course will aid me greatly in protecting their property.

I have the honor to remain, general, your obedient servant,

J. G. FOSTER,
Major-General, Commanding.

GENERAL ORDERS, }
No. 64. . }

HDQRS. DEPT. OF NORTH CAROLINA,
New Berne, December 4, 1862.

A portion of the Marine Artillery having forfeited their right to any benefits from the investigating court now sitting on their case by their disgraceful and mutinous conduct in refusing work, threatening to seize an armed United States boat, threatening to abandon a post of the United States left under their care, and other conduct most subversive to good order and military discipline, it is ordered that these men be distributed as follows : To Battery C, First United States Artillery, at Fort Macon, 50 men; to Third New York Volunteer Artillery, to be distributed by Colonel Ledlie, 100 men, the balance, as may be hereafter ordered, to the volunteer regiments in this department. They will be paid, clothed, and fed according to the army regulations for the corps to which they are assigned, and it is hoped by the commanding general that the opportunity thus given them to redeem themselves by good order and honorable service under the flag of the United States will

---

* Not found.

be appreciated by the men and induce them to endeavor to become proficient, orderly, and efficient, as they are brave men.

II. That portion of the regiment which have not supported this rebellious movement but have stood to their duty will be retained under their present organization, and will be distributed to the different armed transports. They will receive, in addition to the pay of infantry soldiers, rations, and clothing, the following extra-duty pay: To those rated as experts or mechanics (including petty officers, engineers, and such other especially meritorious men as may be so rated), 40 cents a day extra; able seamen and all first-class men, 25 cents per day extra. Those men not able to do seamen's duty, boys, landsmen, &c., will receive no extra pay. Recruiting for the regiment will cease until further orders.

By command of Major-General Foster:

> SOUTHARD HOFFMAN,
> *Assistant Adjutant-General.*

GENERAL ORDERS, }   DECEMBER 4, 1862.
    No. 65.   }

General Orders, No. 63,* is hereby amended so as to read: " All the artillery in the department "—consisting of the Third Regiment New York Volunteer Artillery; Company C, First United States Artillery; Battery F, First Rhode Island Artillery; Twenty-third Independent Battery New York Volunteer Artillery; Twenty-fourth Independent Battery New York Volunteer Artillery—" is hereby formed into an artillery brigade, and will be under command of Col. James H. Ledlie, Third New York Volunteer Artillery."

By command of Major-General Foster:

> SOUTHARD HOFFMAN,
> *Assistant Adjutant-General.*

SUFFOLK, VA., *December 5, 1862.*

Maj. Gen. H. W. HALLECK,
        General-in-Chief:

If Col. D. A. Russell, of Massachusetts Volunteers, is appointed a brigadier I would be glad to have him in my command; is highly responsible, and I have but one general graduate of West Point and I have loaned him to General Foster with his brigade, an officer with whom I co-operate most heartily. Unless I can have experienced men I would rather have none, preferring to extemporize. The affair near Franklin on the 2d was very fine. No part of the army has worked harder than this, and I have been able to make the authorities at Richmond believe that my force was from 25,000 to 50,000 men. Richmond Whig, of November 27, numbers it at 33,000.

> JOHN J. PECK,
> *Major-General.*

WASHINGTON, D. C., *December 6, 1862.*

Major-General DIX:

Who is now in command at Norfolk?

> EDWIN M. STANTON.

---

* Of December 2, 1862. The above differs from that only in enumerating the organizations embraced in the brigade.

WAR DEPARTMENT,
Washington, December 6, 1862.

Major-General DIX, *Fort Monroe, Va.:*

The Adjutant-General informs me that Jourdan has been restored. You speak of sending a brigade of your troops to General Foster; by whose authority is this done? General Foster asked for more troops, but they were refused by the War Department. All available troops will immediately be wanted in your department.

H. W. HALLECK,
General-in-Chief.

FORT MONROE, VA., *December* 6, 1862.

Maj. Gen. H. W. HALLECK,
General-in-Chief:

When in Washington, on October 30, you desired me to communicate with General Foster and to co-operate with him in harassing the enemy. I wrote to him, but he being absent did not receive my letter for some time and his answer did not reach me till November 27. I advised you of these circumstances by letter of the 29th ultimo and that I had sent an officer to him. He came here immediately, and on conferring with him I agreed to let him have a brigade for ten days to attack Goldsborough and cut the railroad at that place. I directed General Peck to meet him at Norfolk and arrange the time. The brigade under General Wessells left Suffolk yesterday to march to Gates' Ferry, near Gatesville, where transports will be ready to receive it. I shall regret greatly if in this I have mistaken your wishes or exceeded my authority. It is not too late to recall General Wessells, if it be thought best and if I receive your order at once. I did not know General Foster had been refused troops by the Secretary of War.

JOHN A. DIX,
Major-General.

WAR DEPARTMENT,
Washington, December 7, 1862.

Maj. Gen. JOHN A. DIX, *Fort Monroe, Va.:*

The temporary detachment of the brigade to assist General Foster is approved. Have all your other troops ready to move by the time the brigade returns or before. The transportation will be mainly by water.

H. W. HALLECK,
General-in-Chief.

HDQRS. DEPT. OF VIRGINIA, SEVENTH ARMY CORPS,
Fort Monroe, Va., December 7, 1862.

Maj. Gen. H. W. HALLECK,
General-in-Chief:

GENERAL: The officer who returned with the flag-of-truce boat from City Point last evening reports great activity on the part of the enemy in the whole district of country lying between Petersburg and Richmond. This accords with other advices. Numerous works are in process of construction between these points. He lay two days at City

Point awaiting the movements of Mr. Ould, the commissioner for the exchange of prisoners, and distinctly heard the trains moving on the railroad both by night and day. It may be that the enemy are concentrating troops at Petersburg in anticipation of a landing on our part on the south side of James River. I feel a good deal of confidence that I shall in case of an offensive movement in the direction of Norfolk receive timely advices unless my agent is detected and arrested.

I am, very respectfully, your obedient servant,

JOHN A. DIX,
Major-General.

SUFFOLK, *December* 7, 1862.

General DIX:

Wessells arrived at noon on the 6th; reports no transports there; a barren waste, stripped of almost everything; no cattle there. He will get along without difficulty through the 7th. F. [Flusser?] will be there to-day unless some terrible storm sweeps the coast.

JOHN J. PECK,
Major-General.

SUFFOLK, *December* 7, 1862.

Major-General DIX:

Colonel Spear's estimate was between 7,000 and 8,000 at and in the vicinity of Franklin, along the river. To-day an old contraband came in from a plantation just this side of Franklin to get his liberty. He says two regiments have arrived by the engine from Weldon and some artillery recently; also that the Nottoway bridge is complete.

JOHN J. PECK,
Major-General.

FORT MONROE, VA.,
December 8, 1862—1 p. m.

Hon. E. M. STANTON,
Secretary of War:

Your inquiry in regard to the commander at Norfolk induces me to inform you that I have ordered an election of a member of Congress in that district and have charged General Viele with some of the necessary arrangements. I will write by mail to-morrow.*

JOHN A. DIX,
Major-General.

FORT MONROE, *December* 8, 1862.

Major-General PECK:

I have but one old regiment here, and that is the only force in the fort. You must do your best with the troops you have. Have all your forces ready to move on short notice. Have a thorough inspection of arms, clothing, and equipage. Have also an abundant supply of ammunition. Make requisitions for all deficiencies as soon as possible.

JOHN A. DIX,
Major-General.

---

* Correspondence in relation to that election will appear in Series III.

United States Steamer Cambridge,
Beaufort, N. C., December 8, 1862.

Maj. Gen. J. G. Foster,
Comdg. U. S. Army Forces, Dept. of North Carolina:

General: I glean the following information from the masters of the lately seized schooners Brilliant and J. C. Roker, to wit: There is at Nassau intending to run the blockade a small screw steamer, the Lizzie, belonging to Wilmington. Said steamer would be ready about the last of November or soon after.

Fort Fisher, at New Inlet, is considered the stronger fort compared with Caswell. There are forty guns mounted, including one 8-inch Columbiad (rifled) and two Whitworth guns. The fort is built of cabbage-wood, filled in with sand 14 feet thick. At Brunswick, up Cape Fear River, there is a strong work, and some 5 miles below Wilmington there is a stronger fortification in process of building.

The channels are all obstructed, with only a narrow passage, which is reported easily stopped when necessity requires, being defended by batteries on either side.

The iron-clads are to be perfected whenever iron is landed, intended mainly for river defense.

In my opinion the present moment is the best time to attack Wilmington and the adjacent forts. The longer the enterprise is delayed the more difficult it will prove to be, as a large number of men are kept at work strengthening the fortifications. I believe the troops should be landed in the vicinity of Fort Caswell, although Masonborough Inlet should be examined in this connection, but a military reconnaissance will determine the relative advantages of the two places.

At the last accounts there were about 4,000 troops in the vicinity of Wilmington. The yellow fever has entirely disappeared.

Salt is selling at $150 (Confederate money) per sack, or about $60 per bushel, and everything else in proportion, which is a proof that the blockade has been effectual. Gold is exchanged at the rate of $2.25 Confederate scrip for $1 in gold.

Let me repeat that the golden moment for action has arrived.

About 700 persons died from yellow fever in October and November out of a population of about 2,500.

The impression is that if Fort Caswell is taken Fort Fisher will be abandoned.

I am, sir, very respectfully, your obedient servant,

WM. A. PARKER,
Commander.

GENERAL ORDERS, }   [December 9, 1862.?]
    No. 76.   }

Being about to move once more the general commanding must again call attention to the conduct of the troops in pillaging, straying from the ranks, &c., and further orders that no one leave the ranks; that all foraging, unless by special order [from] division headquarters, and pillaging is strictly prohibited; and brigade, regimental, and company commanders will see that the orders are carried out, and that no scenes of disgrace like those of Hamilton be permitted.

Major Frankle is provost-marshal for the march.

By command of Major-General Foster:

SOUTHARD HOFFMAN,
Assistant Adjutant-General.

HDQRS. DEPT. OF VIRGINIA, SEVENTH ARMY CORPS,
Fort Monroe, Va., December 10, 1862.

Brig. Gen. M. C. MEIGS,
Quartermaster-General, U. S. A.:

GENERAL: The gunboat was launched to-day at Norfolk and was named General Jesup, after one of your predecessors. Captain Ludlow thinks he can complete her in forty days. I will see that she is properly armed and manned. She is a beautiful, and I trust will be a useful, vessel.

The amount (about $6,000) expended on her before she came into our hands was contributed by the ladies of Norfolk under the *régime* of the insurgents.

I am, very respectfully, your obedient servant,

JOHN A. DIX,
Major-General.

SUFFOLK, *December* 10, 1862.

Major-General DIX:

I am sorry that a move is expected so soon. Unless I have some rest I fear I shall break down altogether and be of no use. Foster will be at the place designated on the 20th. He said he expected to keep Wessells for a move to Wilmington. If so he will be gone till January. Troops are being inspected, requisitions made, and everything supplied. The instruction is crowded as rapidly as possible. Ferry knows all my views and plans and what kind of transportation will be needed on moving from here.

JOHN J. PECK,
Major-General.

FORT MONROE, *December* 10, 1862.

Major-General PECK:

What can I do if you go away? You are entitled to go, and permission would be granted if you ask it. General Halleck advises me that my command must be ready to move the moment Wessells returns, perhaps before, say by the 20th. I send you twenty iron wagons. They are not the improved pattern. They are intended to float and hold up their running gear. When detached from the carriages they are pontoons. Try them in the Nansemond.

JOHN A. DIX,
Major-General.

HEADQUARTERS DEPARTMENT OF NORTH CAROLINA,
New Berne, N. C., December 10, 1862.

Maj. Gen. H. W. HALLECK,
Commander-in-Chief U. S. Army, Washington, D. C.:

GENERAL: I have the honor to report that I am about to take the field again against the enemy in the direction of Goldsborough.

The information that I have received is to the effect that the enemy's Government is turning its attention to the importance of guarding the lines of communication to the south, and, if possible, of recovering some portion of the eastern portion of this State, the rich products of which would at this time be very valuable as supplies to their commissariat.

Two brigades have already arrived to re-enforce the troops already in the State for this purpose. I think by timely action I may disappoint their expectation, and shall therefore move on Kinston to-morrow morning at daybreak. I hope to defeat two brigades that are known to be there before assistance can arrive from Wilmington or Weldon or Tarborough. Succeeding in this, I shall push on to Goldsborough, destroy its railroad bridge, and another bridge across a swamp 10 miles south of Goldsborough, and then return to New Berne to prepare for an immediate attack on Wilmington.

I sincerely trust that the re-enforcements asked for in my letter of the 18th November, together with the officers of experience required to command brigades, may be sent me as soon as the exigencies of the service will permit.

My present force of infantry, consisting of 9,000 men capable of marching and fighting, 6,000 of whom are new—nine months' men—is too weak to give a good support to my forty pieces of artillery and to afford a fair chance of success against the older troops of the enemy in front of us. I have therefore found it necessary to borrow from General Dix the services for a time of General Wessells' brigade, consisting of six regiments (2,200 men). These regiments were kindly promised me at the time I telegraphed to you from Old Point Comfort, and met me according to appointment on the night of the 6th instant on the Chowan River, where I received them on board my transports and brought them to this place, arriving yesterday.

General Peck has agreed to make a simultaneous attack on the Blackwater, from Suffolk, in which our gunboats are to co-operate.

Even if I do not succeed in my expectations I hope my movement may be useful as a demonstration in favor of the Army of the Potomac.

I have the honor to be, very respectfully, your obedient servant,

J. G. FOSTER,
Major-General, Commanding.

———

FORT MONROE, VA., *December* 11, 1862.

Major-General HALLECK, *General-in-Chief:*

Major-General Peck is in great danger of breaking down unless he can have rest for twenty days. None can feel his loss at this time half so much as myself, for he has been all that I could ask in putting Suffolk in a state of defense and in preparing the troops for the field. But, feeling that it is absolutely necessary for him to have a respite, I respectfully ask it for him, and I telegraph in order that it may commence at once, if approved.

JOHN A. DIX,
Major-General.

———

SUFFOLK, *December* 12, 1862.

Major-General DIX:

Will end it here; will remain. We are very thin in numbers here. Ferry left at noon yesterday for Zuni, &c. Was to have been across at daylight. Writes the roads are in horrible condition. Was five hours moving 4 miles near Windsor. It is almost impossible to move in this country for the swamps and —— roads.

Any particulars from Fredericksburg? Captain Flusser writes that the enemy burned about two-thirds of Plymouth.

JOHN J. PECK,
Major-General.

FORT MONROE, VA., *December* 12, 1862.

Major-General HALLECK:

Major-General Peck telegraphs that his expedition to Zuni found the roads very bad. Our troops have not succeeded in crossing. The enemy has been strongly re-enforced. Sharp firing has been going on all day across the river. General Peck says the demonstration is hav- ing the effect of drawing troops to this quarter, so that on the whole line we shall greatly benefit General Foster. I have a dispatch from General Foster this morning informing me that he should leave New Berne at daybreak yesterday. Wessells was with him. He says the enemy in his front has been strengthened, and he expects a hard fight. The Pennsylvania regiments are arriving with wretched arms.

JOHN A. DIX,
Major-General, Commanding.

SUFFOLK, *December* 12, 1862.

Major-General DIX:

We have captured a rebel captain and 12 men; wounded and killed a good many of the enemy. The cars are running actively on the Petersburg road.

JOHN J. PECK,
Major-General.

FORT MONROE, *December* 12, 1862.

Major-General PECK:

I have twenty days' leave for you. Please come to me as soon as you can safely in reference to movements on the Blackwater.

JOHN A. DIX,
Major-General.

FORT MONROE, *December* 12, 1862.

Major-General PECK, *Suffolk:*

Nothing new from Fredericksburg. Burnside is in possession.
Have you received my dispatch notifying you of your leave of absence?
You say the cars are running actively on the Petersburg road. You mean the enemy, of course. Cannot we use the road from Suffolk down to the river at Windsor?

JOHN A. DIX,
Major-General.

SUFFOLK, *December* 12, 1862.

Major-General DIX:

If all is favorable through the night from the Blackwater I will run down in the morning and see you, as per your telegram of this date.

JOHN J. PECK,
Major-General.

SUFFOLK, *December* 12, 1862.

Major-General DIX:

Your telegram in respect to leave is received. You requested me to come down as soon as I could safely, which I construed as business relative to which you desired to see me before I availed myself of the leave. Is this right, or did you wish me to stop as I passed North?

We have drawn a large force to the river since the arrangement with General Foster. If all is quiet I will visit you and return here to-morrow. We cannot use the road much beyond Windsor. I meant the enemy's cars.

JOHN J. PECK,
Major-General.

FORT MONROE, *December* 12, 1862.

Major-General PECK, *Suffolk:*

I did not wish you to come here till you are on your way home. It would be a loss of time to come and go back to Suffolk. But I am anxious that you should take your leave as soon as you safely can. How long do you propose to let Ferry remain at the river? Where were the captain and wounded men captured? Foster left New Berne yesterday morning. The enemy have retired behind their breastworks at Fredericksburg. Burnside's main force is over and a fight is expected to-morrow.

JOHN A. DIX,
Major-General.

WAR DEPARTMENT,
Washington, December 13, 1862.

Major-General DIX, *Fort Monroe, Va.:*

A severe battle all day near Fredericksburg. A part of the enemy's line carried. Can you not make a diversion by a demonstration on Richmond? If so, no time should be lost.

H. W. HALLECK,
General-in-Chief.

FORT MONROE, VA., *December* 13, 1862.

Major-General HALLECK:

In view of General Burnside's movements, as well as General Foster's, I am doing all my means will allow to make a diversion. On Tuesday I went to Gloucester and reviewed the troops. Having been at Yorktown last week I arranged with General Naglee to make a demonstration in Gloucester County as far as the court-house, and farther on if he found it safe to do so. I have this moment received the following dispatch from him, dated in King and Queen County:

I have just scattered the King and Queen County cavalry and burned their barracks and camp. Have taken a large herd of hogs and sheep intended for the rebel commissariat. Shall be to-morrow at Saluda, near Urbana.

My only fear is that he is going too far, as the insurgents use their railroad from Richmond to the White House. He has four regiments of infantry, a battery, and three squadrons of cavalry. Major-General Peck has just left here, and will see you to-morrow morning. The enemy has a larger force on the Blackwater than we have at Suffolk. The Pennsylvania troops are perfectly raw, and have arms that are unfit for use. It would not do to put them in the field at present. General Peck will explain more fully. I will do all I can to keep the enemy occupied in this quarter. With the exception of the Pennsylvania Militia, my force fit for duty is only about 19,000, in the absence of Wessells' brigade, and I have a line of 70 miles in extent to protect.

JOHN A. DIX,
Major-General.

HDQRS. DEPT. OF VIRGINIA, SEVENTH ARMY CORPS,
Fort Monroe, Va., December 13, 1862.

Hon. E. M. STANTON:

SIR: Complaints have been made by those who take a strong interest in the condition of fugitives from service here, usually denominated "contrabands," that their labor since they have been employed by the United States has not been fully paid for. There are other grounds of complaint also, and with a view to remove them I desire to make the following suggestions, viz:

1st. The labor of these persons was not paid for until November 1, 1861, at which time a system of compensation was adopted under Major-General Wool. Before that time a large number of them had been employed and supplied with food and clothing. If the payment of wages was right after November 1 it would have been equally right before that time. The only difficulty is in ascertaining the exact amount of labor performed. Up to July 4, 1861, an accurate account was kept, and at the rate of $10 per month per man they were then entitled to $970. From July 4 to November 1, 1861, no rolls were kept, and the amount of labor performed during the interval is uncertain. There are, however, some data for an estimate. The numbers employed July 4 and November 1 are known, and by assuming a mean number a proximation to the truth may be reached. I do not put this mean higher than 200. At the above rate of compensation they would have earned $2,000 per month for the respective months of July, August, September, and October—deducting four days from the first-named month—and amounting in the aggregate to $7,741.95.

While Captain Tallmadge, quartermaster (recently deceased), was charged with the employment and compensation of these persons some arrearages accumulated, which, for reasons that need not be mentioned, remain unpaid. On the 1st of March, 1862, there was due to them the sum of $1,171.75. Their earnings during the month of March amount to the sum of $2,450. Both these sums should be paid. Many of the persons who performed the labor on account of which these arrears accrued are no longer here and many of them will not be found. It is therefore respectfully suggested that after waiting a reasonable time (say six months) for the claimants to present themselves, the balance unclaimed shall become a fund for the relief and support of the poor who are fugitives from service.

There is admitted to be due from the subsistence department $152. There is also due from the hospital department the sum of $880 for the services of 220 colored nurses during the months of November and December, 1861, and January and February, 1862. In these two cases there will be the same difficulty in ascertaining the persons to whom the money is due, and the same disposition is recommended. The payment of these amounts requiring the order of the Secretary of War, as do also the three bills forwarded with an explanatory letter by the commanding general of this department October 9, 1862, said three bills amounting in the aggregate to $1,479.34, I respectfully ask for such an order.

There are arrears now due for several months, which, like those that have accrued in the military service, are unpaid; but they are within the authority of the quartermaster and will be paid when he is in funds without any further order. The amount of these arrears, December 1, is about $16,590.91, making, with the sums before mentioned, an aggregate of $31,435.95 now due for contraband labor.

2d. In order to remove the contraband women and children from contact with the camps—a contact injurious to both—they have been transferred to Craney Island, where quarters are in preparation for them, and where they will be required to furnish such labor as they are able to perform in picking oakum, fishing, &c. It is respectfully asked that the needful authority be given to supply rooms for schools and places of worship at moderate expense for them. The Government having adopted the policy of receiving these fugitives, and, by implication, promised them protection and security, it is respectfully submitted that some provision should be made for their intellectual and religious as well as for their physical wants.

I am, very respectfully, your obedient servant,
JOHN A. DIX,
Major-General.

HEADQUARTERS DEPARTMENT OF NORTH CAROLINA,
Petersburg, Va., December 13, 1862.
Maj. Gen. J. G. FOSTER,
Commanding U. S. Forces, New Berne, N. C.:

GENERAL: Your letter of the 4th instant, inclosing a copy of one addressed by you to General J. G. Martin, has been received.

War, even when conducted by the acknowledged rules of Christian nations, inflicts so many evils on society that they should not be increased by the lawless acts of soldiers.

It affords me much gratification to learn that the acts of depredation referred to in my letter "were not only not done by your orders but against them and against your strongest efforts to prevent them," and it is to be hoped no future cause for complaints will be given by your forces.

Very respectfully, your obedient servant,
S. G. FRENCH,
Major-General, Commanding.

WASHINGTON, *December* 14, 1862.
Maj. Gen. J. G. FOSTER,
Commanding, &c., Department of North Carolina:

GENERAL: Your letter of the 10th is just received. At the present time it is not possible to send you any of the re-enforcements asked. If you should be unable to make any considerable advances into the interior it is hoped, nevertheless, that you will keep employed a large force of the enemy by your demonstrations. Later in the season we shall probably be able to give you additional troops. That, however, must depend upon the condition of affairs elsewhere.

Very respectfully,
H. W. HALLECK,
General-in-Chief.

FORT MONROE, VA., *December* 14, 1862.

P. H. WATSON, *Assistant Secretary of War:*

The arms brought here by the Pennsylvania drafted militia are for the most part the altered flint-lock musket, caliber .69. They were reported to me unfit for service. Lieutenant Baylor will inspect those at Newport News to-day and at Suffolk to-morrow, and a special report will be made. I do not desire any fancy arms, or even rifled muskets. Safe and serviceable rifled Springfield smooth-bores, caliber .69, are perfectly satisfactory.

JOHN A. DIX,
Major-General.

WASHINGTON, *December* 14, 1862.

Maj. Gen. JOHN A. DIX:

Have fully talked over with General Halleck affairs, as you desired. He says he wants us to occupy the enemy on the Blackwater and keep as many of them there as possible. He thinks we have done all we could with the means there. Attacks and demonstrations so as to keep the enemy busy and alarmed. The four regiments you spoke of he wishes me to say are for you, and to make such disposition as you deem best.

If you decide to give them to me I would suggest that their removal to Suffolk will be much to their advantage.

At Willard's until morning.

JOHN J. PECK,
Major-General.

YORKTOWN, VA., *December* 15, 1862.

Colonel VAN BUREN:

I completed my reconnaissance yesterday.

Dispersed the rangers in Middlesex. Destroyed a large tannery employed by the rebel government, and returned with 15 prisoners at 2 this a. m.

NAGLEE.

SPECIAL ORDERS, } HDQRS. OF THE ARMY, ADJT. GEN.'S OFFICE,
No. 394.   }   *Washington, December* 15, 1862.

*   *   *   *   *   *   *

IV. Brig. Gen. R. Busteed, U. S. Volunteers, will immediately report for duty to Maj. Gen. John A. Dix, U. S. Volunteers, at Fort Monroe, Va.

By command of Major-General Halleck:

E. D. TOWNSEND,
Assistant Adjutant-General.

WAR DEPARTMENT,
Washington, December 16, 1862.

Maj. Gen. JOHN A. DIX, *Fort Monroe, Va.:*

General Banks organized his own command and it was supposed he had taken Corcoran's brigade. He failed to report what troops he took with him. As the brigade is in your department it will be considered under your command.

H. W. HALLECK,
General-in-Chief.

WASHINGTON, *December* 16, 1862.

Major-General DIX:

General Burnside's army recrossed the Rappahannock during the night, and the pontoon bridges have been taken up. Raining hard there.

A. STAGER.

FORT MONROE, *December* 17, 1862.

General FERRY, *Suffolk:*

Have you tried the iron wagon-bodies to ascertain if they will answer the purpose of pontoons? I have ordered four new regiments of Pennsylvania Militia to you.

JOHN A. DIX,
Major-General.

SUFFOLK, *December* 17, 1862.

Major-General DIX:

Have tried the pontoons. They will not work. Will make full report by messenger to-morrow.

O. S. FERRY,
Brigadier-General.

FORT MONROE, *December* 18, 1862.

Brigadier-General FERRY:

I sent for Colonel Spear to ascertain the truth of reports in regard to rebel forces at Franklin. I have long desired to cross and capture or disperse them. I think it can be done. If you agree with me send Foster with 3,400 cavalry, Spear's regiment, and 300 of Dodge's rifles, and Howard's or Follett's artillery, with a section of Davis'. As soon as possible I will make a diversion above Smithfield. Spear left at 11 for Suffolk. See him as to details of proposed movement. I did not send for you because I did not wish you to leave Suffolk. Let me hear from you.

JOHN A. DIX,
Major-General.

SUFFOLK, *December* 18, 1862.

Major-General DIX:

I think the movement proposed by you might now succeed, and unless otherwise directed by you will send out the expedition to-morrow. You will get reports from me this afternoon of the last scouting parties.

O. S. FERRY,
Brigadier-General.

FORT MONROE, *December* 18, 1862.

Brigadier-General FERRY:

Let your expedition go to-morrow night. If there is time I will land force in Burwell's Bay, above Smithfield, to-morrow night. Send me the West End at once. Let me know to-night if you can get ready to-morrow night.

JOHN A. DIX,
Major-General.

SUFFOLK, *December* 18, 1862.

Major-General DIX:

The West End has gone to Norfolk for coal and will arrive there about this time or a little later.

O. S. FERRY,
Brigadier-General.

SUFFOLK, *December* 18, 1862.

Major-General DIX:

I have this evening a report from my post at Providence Church that the enemy are this side the Blackwater, near Isle of Wight Court-House, in force. I am sending out a detachment to reconnoiter. I do not think it advisable to undertake the other expedition till the detachment returns and reports the facts.

O. S. FERRY,
Brigadier-General.

SUFFOLK, *December* 18, 1862.

Major-General DIX:

The report about a rebel force at Isle of Wight is not well founded. I have examined the parties from whom it was derived. Colonel Spear has not returned yet. I based my opinion of the possibility of taking Franklin upon his former reports. I have this evening talked with Colonel Foster, who was out with Wessells. I think you should see him before ordering an expedition. I will send him to the fort to-morrow if you think best. He is a brave, experienced, and judicious officer.

O. S. FERRY,
Brigadier-General.

FORT MONROE, *December* 19, 1862.

Brigadier-General FERRY:

Let me know if Colonel Foster is coming here; if not, when you send out the expedition. No time should be lost, as Burnside's retreat leaves Lee's army at liberty, and in a few days you may have 20,000 or 30,000 men on the Blackwater. My force is ready.

JOHN A. DIX,
Major-General.

SUFFOLK, *December* 19, 1862.

Major-General DIX:

Colonel Foster is on the way to you now with dispatches from me.

O. S. FERRY,
Brigadier-General.

FORT MONROE, *December* 19, 1862.

Major-General PECK:

Colonel Spear is confident he can cross 2 miles above South Quay with 3,500 infantry, 1,000 cavalry, and eight pieces of artillery and take Franklin. General Ferry thinks 5,000 infantry necessary. What think you? Answer immediately. I shall make a diversion from Smithfield the day before.

JOHN A. DIX,
Major-General.

SUFFOLK, VA., *December* 19, 1862.

Major-General DIX:

The expedition talked of, to be successful, should have six good pontoons, 5,000 infantry, two batteries of artillery, and 1,000 cavalry. The fords are not to be relied on; making bridges of felled trees will not do for artillery. We cannot spare the above number of infantry suitable for the undertaking at present and have not the pontoons. I will write you my views to-morrow.

O. S. FERRY,
Brigadier-General.

———

FORT MONROE, *December* 20, 1862.

Brigadier-General FERRY:

Can you not improvise some pontoons? There should be no delay. I will be very glad to have you lead the expedition, but no time should be lost in moving.

JOHN A. DIX,
Major-General.

———

SUFFOLK, [WASHINGTON,] *December* 20, 1862.

Major-General DIX:

Spear reported 12,000 about Franklin. If Foster and Burnside have relieved the recent excess on our front, an attack is desirable; would hazard nothing. Not less than 5,000 ought to be sent; 7,000 would be better. As the troops are benefited by such duty we should always [send] enough. McClenna's Crossing is about the point. Great excitement in public mind since the late disaster.

JOHN J. PECK,
Major-General.

———

FORT MONROE, *December* 20, 1862.

Brigadier-General FERRY:

How many infantry have you fit for the expedition? I can give you some from this post and Yorktown, but in that case I must send you an officer ranking Colonel Foster, and abandon the diversion toward Zuni and Wakefield.

JOHN A. DIX,
Major-General.

———

SUFFOLK, VA., *December* 20, 1862.

Major-General DIX:

I can furnish 1,000 cavalry; that is enough. I can make the 5,000 infantry by putting in two of the newest regiments. I can put General Spinola in command with Foster to lead the advance. I can issue my orders at 9 o'clock forenoon and have the column in march at 3 o'clock afternoon of the same day, which is the usual hour.

O. S. FERRY,
Brigadier-General.

FORT MONROE, *December* 20, 1862.

Brigadier-General FERRY:

The expedition is one of importance and great delicacy, and if our forces succeed in crossing will need a commanding officer experienced in the management of troops. I will give General Spinola an early opportunity of seeing active service, but think another occasion will be better for him and us.

JOHN A. DIX,
Major-General.

Abstract from Tri-monthly Return of the Department of Virginia (Seventh Army Corps), Maj. Gen. John A. Dix commanding, for December 20, 1862 (headquarters Fort Monroe, Va.).

Command.	Present for duty.		Aggregate present.	Aggregate present and absent.	Aggregate last return.	Pieces of field artillery.	Present for duty equipped.					
							Infantry.		Cavalry.		Artillery.	
	Officers.	Men.					Officers.	Men.	Officers.	Men.	Officers.	Men.
Headquarters Fort Monroe.— Maj. Gen. John A. Dix	17	......	17	17	17	....	......	......	......	......	......	......
Fort Monroe.—Col. S. M. Alford:												
3d New York Infantry.....	26	633	805	858	831	....	29	711	......	......	......	......
Attached garrison..........	......	......	27	27	27	....	......	......	......	......	......	......
Total......................	26	633	832	885	858	....	29	711	......	......	......	......
Camp Hamilton.—Col. Anthony Conk:												
Infantry....................	34	723	831	855	856	....	35	764	......	......	......	......
Cavalry.....................	3	76	85	86	83	....	......	......	3	76	......	......
Artillery...................	16	415	497	584	433	12	......	......	......	......	17	427
Total......................	53	1,214	1,413	1,525	1,372	12	35	764	3	76	17	427
Newport News.—Brig. Gen. M. Corcoran:												
Infantry....................	110	2,542	3,004	3,108	2,702	....	112	2,644	......	......	......	......
Norfolk.—Brig. Gen. E. L. Viele:												
Infantry....................	132	2,406	3,072	3,584	3,583	....	130	2,523	......	......	......	......
Cavalry.....................	1	36	55	82	82	....	......	......	1	36	......	......
Artillery...................	4	140	151	195	197	6	......	......	......	......	4	140
Total......................	137	2,582	3,278	3,861	3,862	6	130	2,523	1	36	4	140
Suffolk.—Maj. Gen. J. J. Peck:												
Infantry....................	554	10,581	12,889	15,790	12,059	....	568	11,100	......	......	......	......
Cavalry.....................	69	1,467	2,099	2,344	2,351	4	......	......	71	1,745	......	......
Artillery...................	9	393	452	495	497	18	......	......	......	......	9	412
Total......................	632	12,441	15,440	18,629	14,907	22	568	11,100	71	1,745	9	412
Yorktown.—Maj. Gen. E. D. Keyes:												
Infantry....................	285	5,504	6,979	8,886	5,897	....	303	6,039	......	......	......	......
Cavalry.....................	36	947	1,060	1,168	1,174	....	......	......	36	858	......	......
Artillery...................	17	394	477	678	679	28	......	......	......	......	19	417
Total......................	338	6,845	8,516	10,732	7,750	28	303	6,039	36	858	19	417
Grand total..............	1,313	26,257	32,500	38,757	31,468	68	1,177	23,781	111	2,715	49	1,396

Troops in the Department of Virginia, commanded by Maj. Gen. John A.
Dix, December 20, 1862.

Fort Monroe, Va.

3d New York Infantry.

Newport News, Va.

69th New York [N. G. A.].
155th New York.
164th New York.
170th New York.
175th New York (detachment).

Suffolk, Va.

13th Indiana.
39th Illinois.
6th Massachusetts.
112th New York.
130th New York.
132d New York.
158th New York.
62d Ohio.
67th Ohio.
58th Pennsylvania.
85th Pennsylvania (battalion of).
158th Pennsylvania.
165th Pennsylvania.
166th Pennsylvania.
167th Pennsylvania.
168th Pennsylvania.
171st Pennsylvania.
174th Pennsylvania.
175th Pennsylvania.
176th Pennsylvania.
177th Pennsylvania.
1st New York Mounted Rifles.
11th Pennsylvania Cavalry (ten companies).
7th Massachusetts Battery.
4th U. S. Artillery, Battery D.
4th U. S. Artillery, Battery L.

Camp Hamilton, Va.

139th New York.
11th Pennsylvania Cavalry, Company C.
Roberts' Pennsylvania Heavy Artillery (three companies).
2d Wisconsin Battery.
4th Wisconsin Battery.

Norfolk, Va.

99th New York.
148th New York.
173d Pennsylvania.
19th Wisconsin.
11th Pennsylvania Cavalry, Company M.
7th New York Battery.

Yorktown, Va.

11th Maine.
56th New York.
81st New York.
98th New York.
100th New York.
Independent Battalion, New York (Enfans Perdus).
52d Pennsylvania.
104th Pennsylvania.
169th Pennsylvania.
172d Pennsylvania.
178th Pennsylvania.
179th Pennsylvania.
6th New York Cavalry (two companies).
5th Pennsylvania Cavalry.
1st New York Light Artillery, Battery F.
1st New York Light Artillery, Battery H.
8th New York Battery.
1st Pennsylvania Light Artillery, Battery E.
1st Pennsylvania Light Artillery, Battery H.
5th U. S. Artillery, Battery M.

DETACHED.

Wessells' Brigade.*

85th New York.
92d New York.
96th New York.
85th Pennsylvania.
101st Pennsylvania.
103d Pennsylvania.

FORT MONROE, *December* 21, 1862.

Major-General HALLECK, *General-in-Chief:*

Two sailing vessels have arrived here from New York to take Corcoran's brigade to General Banks. Two more, I learn, are coming.

---

* NOTE FROM RETURN.—Belongs to the command at Suffolk, but is now on detached service in North Carolina.

Two of them will be needed—one to take the sick and convalescents left here and another to take horses now here belonging to the expedition. As Corcoran is not to go, what shall be done with the two other transports when they arrive?

JOHN A. DIX,
Major-General.

WASHINGTON, D. C., *December* 21, 1862.

Major-General DIX, *Fort Monroe, Va.:*

The convalescents, stores, horses, &c., belonging to General Banks' expedition will be sent forward. It will be determined in the course of two or three days whether Corcoran's brigade will go or not. In the mean time the two transports for that purpose will await orders. Give us all the information you can about the enemy's movements.

H. W. HALLECK,
General-in-Chief.

FORT MONROE, VA., *December* 21, 1862.

Maj. Gen. H. W. HALLECK, *General-in-Chief:*

My man has arrived from Richmond. General Anderson's division, reported 13,000 strong, from Hanover County; the division of one of the Hill's, from the direction of Fredericksburg, 9,000 strong, and Hood's, from Richmond Fair Grounds, about 8,000 strong, have all gone south from Richmond since Monday, the 15th. Fifty-three pieces of artillery, some of which came from the direction of Fredericksburg, were sent across Mayo's Bridge toward Petersburg on Wednesday night. It was reported at Richmond that a large force was coming up the James River to land at City Point, and this may have led to the movement of artillery. On Wednesday night the Richmond iron-clad got her commissary stores on board. There has been great activity in Richmond the last week in the movement of troops through the city in a southerly direction, but my informant could not say where they went after leaving the city; heard that one brigade went toward the Blackwater; thinks the rest went to Weldon. He left Richmond Thursday. I have found his former statements accurate.

JOHN A. DIX,
Major-General.

SUFFOLK, VA., *December* 21, 1862.

Major-General DIX:

Give me the pontoons and I will take command of the expedition and leave General Spinola in command here during my absence, or I will see the colonels and get them to volunteer to serve under Colonel Foster cheerfully.

O. S. FERRY,
Brigadier-General.

HEADQUARTERS FOURTH CORPS,
Yorktown, December 21, 1862.

Col. D. T. VAN BUREN, *Assistant Adjutant-General:*

SIR: Since my return I have sent three reconnoitering parties, one of which captured three horses and some prisoners. Captain Parker has been up at West Point and sent a scout to the White House. The enemy has not been discovered in force, but there are indications of an intention to attack Williamsburg. I have taken precautions to bar the movements of the enemy, and I would like to have the opinion of Major General Dix as to the propriety of posting a regiment of infantry at Fort Magruder, below Williamsburg.

I have made two thorough inspections of the four regiments of Pennsylvania drafted militia, which have just arrived here, and found them all perfectly green. One of those regiments, the One hundred and seventy-second, I have assigned to duty at the heavy guns on the ramparts, and will lose no time in fitting all for service. At the present time none of them are in a condition to meet the enemy.

It is reported to me that the destruction of the salt-works in Matthews County was not complete. I have arranged with Captain Parker to go with a gunboat and 100 infantry and 50 cavalry on Wednesday next and complete that work.

I am much in want of an energetic brigadier, who understands tactics.

I have the honor to be, sir, your most obedient servant,

E. D. KEYES,
Major-General, Commanding Fourth Corps.

UNITED STATES FLAG-SHIP PHILADELPHIA,
Hampton Roads, December 21, 1862.

Maj. Gen. JOHN A. DIX,
Commanding Seventh Army Corps:

GENERAL: The department directs that the complement of the Colorado shall be filled up with contrabands, owing to the impossibility of shipping men. It will advance the public interest if you will be so good as to give such orders as will enable Captain Goldsborough, of the Colorado, to receive and ship thirty-two able-bodied contrabands.

I have the honor to be, general, very respectfully, yours,

S. P. LEE,
Actg. Rear-Admiral, Comdg. N. Atlantic Blockading Squadron.

FORT MONROE, VA., *December 23, 1862.*

Maj. Gen. H. W. HALLECK,
General-in-Chief:

I have just arrived from New Berne. My expedition was a perfect success.* I burned the railroad bridge at Goldsborough and Mount Olive and tore up several miles of the track of the Wilmington and Weldon Railroad. We fought four engagements, viz, at Southwest Creek, Kinston, White Hall, and Goldsborough, and whipped the enemy handsomely each time. The force of the enemy is now largely increased in North Carolina from Fredericksburg, rendering the second step in my plan of operations of doubtful execution unless I am pretty largely re-enforced. Can I communicate freely on this point by telegraph or shall I come to Washington for the purpose ? I have a steamer here and can be there in ten hours.

J. G. FOSTER,
Major-General.

_____
* See "Expedition from New Berne to Goldsborough, N. C.", December 11–20, 1862.

WASHINGTON, D. C., *December* 23, 1862.

Maj. Gen. J. G. FOSTER, *Fort Monroe:*

Consult fully with General Dix and then come to Washington.

H. W. HALLECK,
General-in-Chief.

UNITED STATES FLAG-STEAMER PHILADELPHIA,
Hampton Roads, Va., December 23, 1862.

Maj. Gen. JOHN A. DIX, U. S. A.,
Commanding Seventh Army Corps, Fortress Monroe:

GENERAL: The Belvidere, steamer, with supplies for the army, was stopped by the guard vessel below Norfolk because she was not on the certified list of the army steamers furnished by you and had not the certificate from the quartermaster, Colonel Thomas, as proposed by you and agreed to by me. On learning the facts I ordered that the Belvidere should pass up to Norfolk. Will you be good enough to issue such instructions as will prevent a recurrence of the inconvenience arising from the omission to comply with the simple and easy arrangement made at your instance and which the guard vessels have been instructed to comply with?

I have the honor to be, general, very respectfully, yours,

S. P. LEE,
Actg. Rear-Admiral, Comdg. N. Atlantic Blockading Squadron.

WAR DEPARTMENT,
Washington, December 24, 1862.

Maj. Gen. JOHN A. DIX, *Fort Monroe, Va.:*

It is decided that you send 12,000 men to General Foster's command. Those for whom you have transports will be sent to Beaufort and the others marched across to the Chowan. Please answer immediately how many you can send by sea. The troops should be good ones, leaving the new ones in the forts. I hope to send you a couple of regiments from here. This movement must be made in all haste. As soon as General Foster comes in I will telegraph again.

H. W. HALLECK,
General-in-Chief.

FORT MONROE, VA., *December* 24, 1862.

Maj. Gen. H. W. HALLECK,
General-in-Chief:

If I can take the two sailing vessels intended to carry Corcoran's brigade to General Banks I can send 3,500 men to Beaufort by sea. I can also send 1,800 by barges through the canal to Albemarle Sound. My force from Suffolk can move to-morrow, if necessary, but it shall not reach the Chowan River till the means of transportation are there. The steamers here are, with two exceptions, river crafts and not fit to go to sea. There will be no inconvenience in using the two transports of Banks' expedition temporarily, as I can retain his convalescent and sick at present. The troops will take tents and camp equipage. Shall those which go by water take rations?

JOHN A. DIX,
Major-General.

WAR DEPARTMENT,
Washington, December 24, 1862.

Major-General DIX, *Fort Monroe, Va.:*

General Foster thinks that the troops which go by land should go to Gates' Ferry, on the Chowan River, the place where Wessells' brigade embarked.

H. W. HALLECK,
General-in-Chief.

———

WAR DEPARTMENT,
Washington, December 24, 1862.

Major-General BURNSIDE, *Falmouth, Va.:*

General Foster wishes a brigadier-general—a regular officer of experience. Can you give him one? Please answer. Troops that fought at Fredericksburg are now in North Carolina.

H. W. HALLECK,
General-in-Chief.

———

FORT MONROE, *December* 24, 1862.

Brigadier-General FERRY:

Have your brigades—Spinola's and Gibbs'—ready to march at a moment's warning.

JOHN A. DIX,
Major-General.

———

FORT MONROE, *December* 24, 1862.

Major-General KEYES, *Yorktown:*

Have Naglee's brigade ready to move by water at a moment's warning.

JOHN A. DIX,
Major-General.

———

SUFFOLK, *December* 24, 1862.

Major-General DIX:

Is there no way in which at least partial payment can be made to these men before leaving? Gibbs and Spinola both report their men destitute. In my own the families of the men are really suffering, and it seriously affects the spirits of the men in the command.

O. S. FERRY,
Brigadier-General.

———

FORT MONROE, *December* 24, 1862.

Brigadier-General FERRY:

I have written to Washington repeatedly in regard to the payment of the troops. The answer is that after the 1st of January they will be paid up to November 1.

JOHN A. DIX,
Major-General.

GENERAL ORDERS,) WAR DEPARTMENT, ADJT. GEN.'S OFFICE,
No. 214.) Washington, December 24, 1862.

By direction of the President the troops in North Carolina will constitute the Eighteenth Army Corps, and Maj. Gen. J. G. Foster is assigned to the command.

By order of the Secretary of War:

L. THOMAS,
Adjutant-General.

SPECIAL ORDERS,) HDQRS. OF THE ARMY, ADJT. GEN.'S OFFICE,
No. 410.) Washington, December 24, 1862.

* * * * * * *

IV. Brig. Gen. I. N. Palmer, U. S. Volunteers, is assigned to duty
with the command of Maj. Gen. J. G. Foster, U. S. Volunteers, Department of North Carolina, and will report in person without delay.

* * * * * * *

By command of Major-General Halleck:

E. D. TOWNSEND,
Assistant Adjutant-General.

WAR DEPARTMENT,
Washington, December 25, 1862.

Major-General DIX, Fort Monroe, Va.:

General Foster left here last evening; and, if not detained by the fog,
will be with you this forenoon to arrange details. He saw the Commissary-General yesterday about rations. The troops sent to Beaufort
should take supplies with them unless he directs differently.

H. W. HALLECK,
General-in-Chief.

FORT MONROE, VA., December 25, 1862.

Maj. Gen. H. W. HALLECK,
General-in-Chief:

As you wished me to make the movement in haste I am getting all
the transportation I can find. The Cahawba arrived this morning from
New York with provisions for Alexandria. She will carry 1,500 troops.
I am transferring her cargo to two river steamers and shall send it
without delay to Alexandria. I have transportation enough for at least
6,000 troops ready. The International, one of the sailing-vessel transports from New York, got aground on Smith's Island Shoal yesterday.
I sent out a strong tug to her last night. If she can be got off she will
carry 1,000 more troops. General Foster not arrived.

JOHN A. DIX,
Major-General.

HEADQUARTERS FOURTH ARMY CORPS,
Yorktown, Va., December 25, 1862.

Col. D. T. VAN BUREN,
Asst. Adjt. Gen., Department of Virginia, Yorktown, Va.:

COLONEL: In reply to the circular of December 22, 1862, from Headquarters Department of Virginia. I have the honor to report that the

earthworks at Yorktown and Gloucester Point have never been author-itatively named. The officers at Gloucester Point, however, have called the work after myself, Fort Keyes, and I would beg leave to suggest for the work here the name of the major-general commanding the department. May I be informed if these names will be recognized?

Besides the work at Yorktown and Gloucester the only other work is Fort Magruder, about 1½ or 2 miles below Williamsburg, garrisoned by a company of the Fifth Pennsylvania Cavalry.

The armament of these works is as follows:

Fort Magruder.—One 24-pounder howitzer, four 12-pounder howitzers, one 6-pounder (iron) carriage, one coffee-mill (Union repeating).

At Yorktown.—Nine 8-inch columbiads, fifteen 20-pounder Parrotts, one 8-inch siege howitzer, eight 32-pounders, iron (smooth), four 10-inch mortars, five 12-pounder howitzers (brass), ten 3-inch ordnance guns (light batteries), two 100-pounder Parrotts, one coffee-mill (Union repeating), fourteen 12-pounder brass Napoleons (light batteries), one 42-pounder, iron (smooth), five 30-pounder Parrotts, one 32-pounder carronade, one 32-pounder (light ship gun), one 10-inch columbiad.

At Gloucester Point.—The only armament consists of one battery (four guns) of 3-inch ordnance guns.

Very respectfully, your obedient servant,

E. D. KEYES,
Major-General, Commanding Corps.

———

HDQRS. DEPT. OF VIRGINIA, SEVENTH ARMY CORPS,
Fort Monroe, Va., December 26, 1862.

His Excellency ABRAHAM LINCOLN,
President of the United States :

SIR : In your order authorizing me to permit the people of Norfolk to send to the loyal States the products of their labor the Nansemond River was not included. Suffolk is at the head of navigation, and the river is used by us in transporting our supplies to our troops there. There are oysters, shingles, and other articles on the river belonging to Northern people as well as to the people of Norfolk, and wanted in the loyal States. May I ask the extension of my authority to permit these articles to go North, by a new order from you, that of November 12 not being construed by Admiral Lee to cover these cases.

The inclosed papers, which I beg to have returned to me, show the hardship of the cases referred to.* I take the liberty to annex the order I need for your consideration, and am, very respectfully, your obedient servant,

JOHN A. DIX,
Major-General.

[Inclosure.]

EXECUTIVE MANSION.

Ordered, That the order of the 12th of November, in regard to trade with Norfolk, be extended to Suffolk and the Nansemond River, so far as the commander of the department shall deem necessary for military purposes.

———

* Not found.

FORT MONROE, VA., *December* 26, 1862.

Maj. Gen. H. W. HALLECK,
General-in-Chief:

General Foster left last evening for New Berne The troops commence embarking at Yorktown to-day. The transports will be obliged to return from Beaufort and take another load, as General Foster can only take 4,000 from the Chowan. The International is lost near Smith's Island. Her cargo will be saved. My force fit for duty is less than 25,000 men. I shall have but 12,000 left. I shall have but 5,000 at Suffolk and 2,500 at Yorktown. On the Blackwater there is a large force, and since Naglee's expedition the rebels have occupied Gloucester County, and General Keyes writes me they are menacing Gloucester Point. Twenty thousand men is the smallest number that can be relied on to hold Williamsburg, Yorktown, Gloucester, this fort, Norfolk, and Suffolk. I earnestly request that I may be re-enforced before the troops for General Foster's command get away. They embrace nearly every regiment that has been under fire. I lose, also, General Naglee and General Ferry, my only brigadiers who have had any experience in the field, except General Viele, who cannot at this moment be spared from Norfolk. I asked for the promotion of Colonel Alford, of the Third New York Volunteers, to the rank of brigadier. He will be needed at once. If General Lockwood can be spared from the Eastern Shore of Virginia I should like to have him. My new troops need experienced generals.

JOHN A. DIX,
Major-General.

SUFFOLK, *December* 26, 1862.

Major-General DIX, *Fort Monroe:*

There are reported for duty this morning in my brigade, 3,324; in Spinola's, 3,411; in Gibbs' (including 250 of Wessells' men), 3,057. Hence it appears that by adding one regiment to either of the brigades the 7,000 ordered will take but two brigades. Which two shall I send? Please answer soon as possible.

O. S. FERRY,
Brigadier-General.

FORT MONROE, *December* 26, 1862.

Brigadier-General FERRY:

Take Spinola's and add to it a regiment of 600 men, and put Wessells' men in your brigade. Naglee has many sick, and I must take 7,500 from your command.

JOHN A. DIX,
Major-General.

SPECIAL ORDERS, ⎰ HDQRS. OF THE ARMY, ADJT. GEN.'S OFFICE,
No. 414.   ⎱   *Washington, December* 26, 1862.
*   *   *   *   *   *   *

VI. Brig. Gen. H. D. Terry, U. S. Volunteers, will report for duty to Maj. Gen. John A. Dix, U. S. Volunteers, Fort Monroe, Va.

By command of Major-General Halleck:

E. D. TOWNSEND,
Assistant Adjutant-General.

SUFFOLK, *December* 27, 1862.

Major-General DIX:

Reports are reaching me from Carrsville and Windsor of the appearance of the enemy in force on this side the river. I have sent out scouting parties with orders to report as rapidly as possible.

O. S. FERRY,
Brigadier-General.

HEADQUARTERS EIGHTEENTH ARMY CORPS,
New Berne, N. C., December 27, 1862.

Maj. Gen. S. G. FRENCH,
Comdg. Dept. of North Carolina, Petersburg, Va.:

GENERAL: Your favor of [13th] instant I received to-day. I most fully agree with you that war is most horrible in the misery and ruin it must cause, even when carried on according to the acknowledged rules of Christian nations, and therefore beg to call your attention to and ask if it was by your approval that in the recent attack on Plymouth many houses and other buildings were fired, and to that extent families ruined and rendered homeless; that only want of time prevented other damage being done. I would also call your attention to the case of Mrs. Phelps, who was shot dead by a Confederate soldier. On occupying the town of Kinston recently the streets were found in many cases full of burning cotton, naval stores, &c., a destruction of property which I do not know your approval or disapproval of. The effect was that one house was set on fire, and that it was only by the greatest effort of officers and soldiers that a large portion of the town was saved from destruction.

Trusting that by our united efforts the war within our departments may be robbed of some of its horrors, I am, general, very respectfully, your obedient servant,

J. G. FOSTER,
Major-General, Commanding.

HDQRS. DEPT. OF VIRGINIA, SEVENTH ARMY CORPS,
Fort Monroe, Va., December 29, 1862.

Maj. Gen. J. G. FOSTER,
Commanding Department of North Carolina:

GENERAL: Four thousand troops left Suffolk yesterday morning for Winfield; they will arrive to-day. Four thousand five hundred left and will leave within twenty-four hours, commencing at sunset last evening, by water. The remaining 3,500 will be sent as rapidly as transports arrive—part to-morrow and the rest, I think, by the 2d of January; perhaps before. I send you every old regiment I have except one, which is in this fort.

One hundred tons ammunition leave to-morrow for Beaufort. Two thousand shovels and spades and the sand bags are here and will go with the ammunition. Part of the wagons and ambulances go with the troops; the rest will be sent in time.

I believe nothing has been left undone. The bearer will receive any commands you may have for Washington or me.   Let me know if I can do anything here.

Wishing you a success equal to that at Goldsborough, I am, respectfully and truly, yours,

JOHN A. DIX,
Major-General.

P. S.—I found a change in the troops at Suffolk necessary.   You will get—

1. Ferry's brigade, including 300 of Wessells' men................................ 3,600
2. Spinola's brigade 4,000
3. Naglee's brigade 4,080
4. Independent Battalion, New York 250
                                                                                      ─────
                                                                                      11,930

Some convalescents will carry the number, I think, above 12,000.

FORT MONROE, VA., *December* 29, 1862.

Maj. Gen. H. W. HALLECK,
General-in-Chief:

General Foster's arrangement with me was to have everything in North Carolina by the 4th proximo, before which day he could not be ready to land and prepare the troops to march.   The day for marching was fixed for the 8th.   I think it proper to advise you of these arrangements and of what I have done.   I have just sent a special messenger to him with the following information:

Four thousand troops left Suffolk for Chowan River yesterday morning; 4,500 left and to leave by water yesterday and to-day; remaining 3,500 leave as fast as transports arrive—part to-morrow and the rest by January 2 at farthest.   One hundred tons ammunition, 2,000 spades and shovels, and 10,000 sand-bags leave to-morrow.   Part of wagons and ambulances go with troops; the rest in time.

JOHN A. DIX,
Major-General.

FORT MONROE, VA., *December* 29, 1862.

Maj. Gen. H. W. HALLECK,
General-in-Chief:

Colonel Gibbs was sent out early yesterday morning toward the Blackwater to occupy the attention of the enemy while a force of 4,000 men for General Foster went down to the Chowan.   The colonel fell in with the enemy's scouts a short distance from our pickets, drove them, and captured 9.   They report Pryor 4 miles on this side of the Blackwater with two brigades of infantry, two regiments of cavalry, and nine pieces of artillery.   I send Corcoran's brigade from Newport News to Suffolk to-day.   General Ferry will leave Suffolk with 3,500 men as fast as transportation can be furnished, commencing this evening.   The Fourth Delaware and One hundred and fifteenth New York have arrived at Yorktown, where my infantry was reduced to 1,700 by the withdrawal of Naglee's brigade.   Two or three good regiments in addition to those I have would enable me to drive Pryor across the Blackwater, unless he is re-enforced.   To give success to General Foster's movements I beg to suggest that General Burnside should press the enemy incessantly.

JOHN A. DIX,
Major-General.

WASHINGTON, D. C., *December* 30, 1862.

Major-General BURNSIDE, *Falmouth:*

General Dix telegraphs that in order to succeed in his own and Foster's operations it will be necessary that you occupy and press the enemy so as to prevent large detachments.

H. W. HALLECK,
General-in-Chief.

FORT MONROE, VA., *December* 30, 1862.

Maj. Gen. H. W. HALLECK,
General-in-Chief:

When I telegraphed you in regard to my force I had before me the last return from Suffolk, which did not embrace the four last-arrived Pennsylvania regiments, so that after sending 12,000 men to Foster my aggregate for duty was 15,500 instead of 12,000. The addition of the Fourth Delaware and One hundred and fifteenth New York, now here, gives me an effective force of 16,900.

JOHN A. DIX,
Major-General.

DECEMBER 30, 1862.

Major-General DIX, *Fort Monroe:*

The ship at Norfolk draws 14½ feet of water. No vessel drawing more than 9 feet can enter the harbor of my destination. The captain of the ship has sealed orders and no other. I fear he will carry my regiment away from its destination. My men have but three days' rations from this morning. If the vessel is to sail, much more will be needed; if to be towed by steam-tugs, they will still require more than they have.

O. S. FERRY,
Brigadier-General.

DECEMBER 30, 1862.

Major-General DIX, *Fortress Monroe:*

I have turned over the command of this post to General Corcoran, who ranks me. I have sent the Sixty-seventh Ohio Regiment, 610 men, and the convalescent sick, and officers of the quartermaster's department of Spinola's brigade, numbering in all nearly 200 more, together with the ammunition and camp and garrison equipage of the Sixty-seventh Ohio, to Norfolk this morning to embark on the transport expected there this morning according to your dispatch of yesterday. When can I expect more transports, and how many?

O. S. FERRY,
Brigadier-General.

HEADQUARTERS EIGHTEENTH ARMY CORPS,
New Berne, N. C., December 31, 1862.

Maj. Gen. S. G. FRENCH,
Comdg. Department of North Carolina, Petersburg, Va.:

GENERAL: I have the honor to inclose copy of a letter addressed to me by His Excellency Edward Stanly, Military Governor of North Carolina. The letter explains itself, and I have merely to request an answer from you whether the acts complained of by the Governor have your sanction; and whether, as he desires to know, the negroes mentioned will be returned to their master? I also beg leave to inclose a slip from the Raleigh Standard in relation to the prisoners recently paroled and released by me at Kinston and other places between here and Goldsborough, and request to know whether these men are compelled to perform the duties therein stated contrary to their parole of honor. Some time during the latter part of November Surgeon Hunt, post surgeon at Washington, N. C., while taking a ride outside of our lines, was fired upon by parties in ambush and killed immediately. His person was rifled, and, among other things, a watch was taken from him which his relatives are very anxious to obtain possession of. If it is within your power will you please have this watch returned?

I remain, general, very respectfully, your obedient servant,

J. G. FOSTER,
Major-General, Commanding.

[Inclosure.]

DEPARTMENT OF NORTH CAROLINA,
New Berne, N. C., December 29, 1862.

Maj. Gen. J. G. FOSTER,
Commanding, &c. :

GENERAL: I have been informed that a portion of the forces of the enemies of the United States recently invaded the county of Washington and, among other depredations committed upon innocent citizens, they seized and carried away against their consent and against the consent of their owners a large number of slaves. From the home of Mr. M. Bowen they took away several of his negroes who had been faithful to him, and whom he protected and humanely supported. This outrage has not the defense attempted for the African slave trade, "that it brought uncivilized beings under the influence of Christianity and civilization." This robbery takes civilized beings from their families and homes; it deprives a kind master of his property and punishes slaves for their fidelity to him. I cannot believe the good people of North Carolina will justify such conduct. To the barbarous and willful burning of the town of Plymouth by the enemy your attention has already been called, and of that nothing more need be said. As the voice of civil authority outside of our lines has no longer any potency, I solicit your intervention with those commanding the forces of the so-called Confederate States, that we may ascertain by what rules this war is to be conducted, and whether those negroes to whom I have referred are to be delivered up to those to whom their services may be due.

I have the honor to be, &c.,

ED. STANLY,
Military Governor, &c.

Abstract from Return of the Department of Virginia, Maj. Gen. John A. Dix commanding, for the month of December, 1862 (headquarters Fort Monroe, Va.).

Command.	Present for duty.		Aggregate present.	Aggregate present and absent.	Aggregate present and absent last monthly return.	Pieces of field artillery.
	Officers.	Men.				
Fort Monroe, Va.—Maj. Gen. J. A. Dix and staff........	17	3	20	20	20	......
Fort Monroe.—Col. S. M. Alford:						
3d New York Infantry	25	643	809	836	830	......
Attached garrison......................			27	27	27	......
Camp Hamilton.—Col. A. Conk:						
139th New York Infantry.....................	33	704	817	854	872	......
Two batteries and three companies artillery......	16	455	537	669	433	12
One company cavalry......................	2	75	84	85	85	......
Norfolk, Va.—Brig. Gen. E. L. Viele and staff...........	6		6	7	8	......
Infantry.................................	128	2,579	3,093	3,487	3,520	......
Artillery.................................	3	131	150	195	199	6
Cavalry.................................	1	39	55	82	82	......
Suffolk, Va.—Major-General Peck and staff...........	6		6	8	7	......
Brigadier-General Corcoran's brigade..............	124	2,630	2,952	3,050		......
Col. R. S. Foster, First Provisional Brigade.......	173	3,158	3,830	4,572	1,979	......
Col. A. Gibbs, Second Provisional Brigade.........	89	1,906	2,430	2,870		......
Lieut. D. J. Bailey, detachment Company I, Ninety-ninth New York Infantry.	2	50	57	59	59	......
Brigadier-General Ferry's brigade					3,723	......
Brigadier-General Wessells' brigade...............					3,959	......
Brigadier-General Spinola's brigade...............					1,792	......
Cavalry.................................	64	1,569	2,097	2,169	2,188	4
Artillery.................................	10	396	456	494	517	18
Yorktown.—Maj. Gen. E. D. Keyes and staff...........	10		10	10	10	......
Infantry.................................	182	3,175	3,819	4,568	5,933	......
Artillery.................................	18	403	478	674	686	28
Cavalry.................................	36	843	1,054	1,162	1,180	......
Grand total........................	945	18,759	22,787	25,898	28,109	68

SUMMARY.

	Officers.	Men.	Aggregate present.	Aggregate present and absent.	Aggregate present and absent last monthly return.	Pieces of field artillery.
General, and staff officers, &c...................	39	3	42	45	45	......
Infantry...	756	14,845	17,807	20,296	22,667	......
Artillery...	47	1,385	1,648	2,059	1,862	64
Cavalry...	103	2,526	3,290	3,498	3,535	4
Total..	945	18,759	22,787	25,898	28,109	68

NOTE.—Brigadier-Generals Ferry, Wessells, and Spinola, with their respective brigades, were transferred to the Department of North Carolina, and the following regiments were added to the force at Suffolk: One hundred and sixty-fifth, One hundred and sixty-sixth, One hundred and sixty-seventh, One hundred and sixty-eighth, One hundred and fifty-eighth, One hundred and seventy-first, One hundred and seventy-fourth, One hundred and seventy-fifth, One hundred and seventy-sixth, One hundred and seventy-seventh Pennsylvania Militia, and One hundred and fifty-eighth New York Volunteers.

Brigadier-General Naglee's brigade transferred to Department of North Carolina, and replaced by the One hundred and sixty-ninth, One hundred and seventy-second, One hundred and seventy-eighth, One hundred and seventy-ninth Pennsylvania Militia, One hundred and fifteenth New York Volunteers, and the Fourth Delaware.

Abstract from Monthly Return of the Department of North Carolina, Maj. Gen. John G. Foster commanding, for the month of December, 1862 (headquarters New Berne, N. C.).

Command.	Present for duty.		Aggregate present.	Aggregate present and absent.	Aggregate present and absent last monthly return.
	Officers.	Men.			
Eighteenth Army Corps (Maj. Gen. J. G. Foster)........				15	....
First Division (Brig. Gen. H. W. Wessells)...............	201	3,996	5,962	7,087	3,226
Naglee's brigade..........................	195	3,700	4,380	5,802	....
Heckman's brigade.........................	96	2,236	2,847	3,759	3,860
Amory's brigade...........................	120	2,850	3,510	3,683	3,851
Lee's brigade.............................	108	2,802	3,526	3,879	3,908
Artillery.................................	58	1,400	1,732	2,230	2,175
Cavalry (Mix's)...........................	43	658	860	930	939
Total........	821	17,642	21,917	27,385	17,959

Organization of troops in the Department of North Carolina (Eighteenth Army Corps), Maj. Gen. J. G. Foster, U. S. Army, commanding, December 31, 1862.*

FIRST DIVISION.

Brig. Gen. HENRY W. WESSELLS.

First Brigade.

Brig. Gen. LEWIS C. HUNT.

85th New York, Lieut. Col. A. J. Wellman.
92d New York, Lieut. Col. Hiram Anderson, jr.
96th New York, Capt. George W. Hinds.
85th Pennsylvania, Col. J. B. Howell.
101st Pennsylvania, Lieut. Col. D. M. Armor.
103d Pennsylvania, Lieut. Col. W. C. Maxwell.

Second Brigade.

Col. THOMAS G. STEVENSON.

10th Connecticut, Lieut. Col. Robert Leggett.
24th Massachusetts, Lieut. Col. F. A. Osborn.
44th Massachusetts, Col. F. L. Lee.
5th Rhode Island, Maj. George W. Tew.

UNATTACHED.

Amory's Brigade.

Col. T. J. C. AMORY.

17th Massachusetts, Lieut. Col. J. F. Fellows.
43d Massachusetts, Col. C. L. Holbrook.
45th Massachusetts, Col. C. R. Codman.
51st Massachusetts, Col. A. B. R. Sprague.

Lee's Brigade.

Col. H. C. LEE.

5th Massachusetts, Col. George H. Peirson.
25th Massachusetts, Maj. Josiah Pickett.
27th Massachusetts, Lieut. Col. Luke Lyman.
46th Massachusetts, Col. George Bowler.

---

* The division and unattached brigades were organized and the commanders assigned by General Orders, No. 84, Headquarters Eighteenth Army Corps, December 28, 1862. The regimental commanders in First Division are given as stated in that order.

Heckman's Brigade.

Brig. Gen. CHARLES A. HECKMAN.

3d Massachusetts, Col. Silas P. Richmond.
8th Massachusetts, Col. Fred. J. Coffin.
23d Massachusetts, Maj. John G. Chambers.
9th New Jersey, Maj. Abram Zabriskie.

Artillery.

Brig. Gen. JAMES H. LEDLIE.

3d New York (eleven companies), Maj H. M. Stone.
23d New York Battery, Capt. A. Ransom.
24th New York Battery, Capt. J. E. Lee.
1st Rhode Island, Battery F, Capt. J. Belger.
1st U. S., Battery C, Lieut. C. Hook.

CAVALRY.

Third New York, Col. S. H. MIX.

DETACHMENT FOURTH ARMY CORPS.

Naglee's Brigade.*

Brig. Gen. HENRY M. NAGLEE.

11th Maine, Col. H. M. Plaisted.
56th New York, Lieut. Col. J. J. Wheeler.
81st New York, Col. J. J. De Forest.
98th New York, Col. Charles Durkee.
100th New York, Col. George B. Dandy.

Independent New York Battalion, Lieut. Col. Felix Comfort.
52d Pennsylvania, Col. John C. Dodge.
104th Pennsylvania, Lieut. Col. T. D. Hart.

HEADQUARTERS FIRST BRIGADE,
Morehead City, N. C., January 1, 1863.

Lieut. Col. D. T. VAN BUREN, *Fortress Monroe:*

COLONEL: I would respectfully report the arrival at this port of tl.e steamer Cahawba, with the Eleventh Maine and Ninety-eighth New York. We found entering the harbor just before us the Kennebec, with the Eighty-first New York, and that the Belvidere had discharged the One hundredth New York. Off Hatteras we parted our hawser and left the ship Montebello. Soon thereafter the wind shifted to the west and afterward to the northwest, which will insure her prompt arrival. The two monitors behaved admirably, and although we had quite a heavy blow they stood it with no apparent difficulty. At daylight of the 31st, when we saw them last, the storm had abated and the indications were all very favorable.

I have to report to General Foster at 1 p. m.

Very respectfully, &c.,

HENRY M. NAGLEE,
Brigadier-General.

FORT MONROE, VA., *January 1,* 1863.

General VIELE, *Norfolk:*

I learn that a leading citizen of Norfolk has been trying to incite the soldiers of the Ninety-ninth New York to murder negroes. If there is such a feeling existing the procession which is to take place to-day must be watched and, if necessary, stopped, not only on account of the feeling referred to but for the security of the negroes themselves.

JOHN A. DIX,
Major-General.

---

* First Brigade, Peck's division.

NORFOI K, *January* 1, 1863.

Major-General DIX:

I have taken every precaution to prevent disturbances to-day. I know the procession will be a source of deep mortification to the insolent secessionists here, but I have not felt like pleasing them by stopping it. It will be certainly very harmless as far as the negroes are concerned. If I knew the name of the person you refer to I would arrest him.

EGBERT L. VIELE,
Brigadier-General.

NORFOLK, *January* 1, 1863.

Major-General DIX:

The procession passed off without any disturbance. There were about 4,000 persons in it.

EGBERT L. VIELE,
Brigadier-General.

FORT MONROE, VA.,
January 2, 1863—4 p. m.

Major-General HALLECK, *General-in-Chief*, and
General M. C. MEIGS, *Quartermaster-General:*

I have been exceedingly unlucky in regard to transports for troop to North Carolina. The New York and Georgia, after being loaded were given up as unseaworthy. The Belvidere returned from Beaufor the day before yesterday for a second load, broken down, and has gon to Baltimore for repairs. The Connecticut was loaded with wagon and horses, and came down from Yorktown this morning, but her crew refused to go to sea. On examination she also proves unseaworthy and I am now trying to get the John Brooks to take them. She ha just arrived for service at Washington, and her captain objects to goin to sea, as her boilers are on her guards. The weather is very fine an I think she will go. In that case the Connecticut will take her place a Washington. Ten thousand troops have gone; there are 2,000 to ge The Cahawba should have been back last night with a transport sailin vessel in tow. If they get in to-night there will be time to meet Genera Foster's arrangements. I thought you ought to know the insufficienc of your steamboats for emergencies.

JOHN A. DIX,
Major-General.

HDQRS. DEPT. OF VIRGINIA, SEVENTH ARMY CORPS,
Fort Monroe, January 3, 1863.

Maj. Gen. J. G. FOSTER,
Commanding Department of North Carolina:

GENERAL: We have been very unfortunate in transports. We hav had to unload two, and two others returned here from Beaufort broke down. To-night I send you 1,000 men in the Cahawba; to-morrow, 8(in the Expounder. There will be but 100 or 200 left; these I expect send to-morrow night.

The aggregate force I have set apart for you is 14,000. You w have 12,000 effectives. I retain the sick.

I believe everything has been done that was possible. If our transports had not failed every man would have been with you to-day. As it is, the last will only be two days behind.

Wishing you every success, I am, yours, truly,

JOHN A. DIX,
Major-General.

UNOFFICIAL.]   HDQRS. DEPT. OF VIRGINIA, SEVENTH A. C.,
Fort Monroe, January 3, 1863.

[Major-General HALLECK:]

MY DEAR GENERAL: When I came here I undertook to examine all cases of disloyalty and misdemeanors of all sorts, but I was compelled to give it up. To relieve myself of this labor, impossible for me to perform, I appointed a provost judge, who has tried all such cases and sentenced to punishment. All capital cases have been referred to military commissions. Those which have been brought before him are cases of theft, rioting, &c. The criminals were both black and white. The highest penalty he has ever inflicted is imprisonment for sixty days. My authority to issue such an order has been questioned. To me it seems very clear. There is no civil magistrate in this county, or, indeed, in any part of the territory constituting my department. I should be glad, if I am right, to be fortified by your opinion, which I only ask for my own satisfaction. A single word in reply will oblige me.

I am, dear sir, truly, yours,

JOHN A. DIX,
Major-General.

[Inclosure.]

GENERAL ORDERS, }   HEADQUARTERS ARMY CORPS,
No. 6.   }   *Fort Monroe, Va., June 27, 1862.*

Capt. John A. Bolles, aide-de-camp, is hereby appointed provost judge, and as such authorized and ordered to hold a court for the trial of all cases, civil and criminal (not military), that may arise within the limits of this command and be brought before him, under such rules and regulations as he may establish; said court to be held at such times and places within this command as he may designate.

Captain Bolles will appoint one or more provost clerks, whose duty it will be, under his direction, to issue all orders, writs, and processes requisite to the prompt and efficient administration of justice, and also to preserve full and accurate records of the proceedings of said court. The several provost-marshals and their deputies to whom such orders, writs, and processes are directed will execute the same, without delay, in accordance with the precepts therein contained, and the same will be respected and obeyed as orders from these headquarters.

Full authority is given to Captain Bolles as provost judge to hear and try all causes, civil and criminal (not military), which may come before him, and to determine and decide the same as far as may be conformable with the established laws of the United States and of the several States applicable thereto, and where such laws are not applicable or are not sufficient for the ends of justice, according to his best judgment and understanding of the principles of justice, equity, and good conscience, subject in all cases to appeal from his decisions to the major-general of the army corps.

By command of Major-General Dix:

D. T. VAN BUREN,
Assistant-Adjutant-General.

FORT MONROE, VA., *January* 3, 1863.

M. C. MEIGS, *Quartermaster-General:*

The Expounder has just returned in good order and leaves again to-morrow. If I can have the Spaulding by to-morrow night I can close up in time for General Foster, leaving nothing undone. The storm which destroyed the monitor and crippled two of our steamers took two of our sailing-vessel transports from their tugs. One was recovered and the other is no doubt safe. Over 10,000 troops have reached their destination. One thousand go to-morrow morning and 800 to-morrow night.

JOHN A. DIX,
Major-General.

———

SUFFOLK, *January* 3, 1863.

Major-General DIX, *Fort Monroe:*

Ferry reports an increase of field artillery on the Blackwater to four full batteries. He says they have a shot-proof battery of two heavy guns at Franklin, made of railroad iron; also a four-gun work at Black-water Bridge, on each side of the river, from which point they can flank and threaten our columns moving on Franklin or Zuni. Have you any sand-bags to spare for our works?

JOHN J. PECK,
Major-General.

———

FORT MONROE, *January* 4, 1863.

Major-General PECK, *Suffolk:*

General Foster's transports are at Winfield. If it is thought best let the rest of the troops march there with three days' rations. If not, send down one or two companies of cavalry with an order to the transports to return to New Berne. In the latter case advise me, that I may send a topographical officer to take some notes.

JOHN A. DIX,
Major-General.

———

SUFFOLK, *January* 4, 1863.

Major-General DIX, *Fort Monroe:*

After consultation, Ferry will march in the morning to the point indi-cated in your telegram. I deem it best to send a squadron along. Will send more women [cavalry?] if you think best.

JOHN J. PECK,
Major-General.

———

FORT MONROE, *January* 4, 1863.

Major-General PECK, *Suffolk:*

I think a squadron enough. You are the best judge from the infor-mation you possess. General Foster passed through here to-day to Washington, and will be at New Berne on Wednesday night. He says the road to Winfield is not through Gatesville, but through Sunbury and Mintonsville.*

*   *   *   *   *   *

JOHN A. DIX,
Major-General.

———

* Some matters of detail omitted.

FORT MONROE, *January* 4, 1863.

Major-General PECK, *Suffolk:*

How many men have been sent from Suffolk, including Spinola's command, which marched to the Chowan, and the Fifty-eighth Pennsylvania, which went to Norfolk this morning?

JOHN A. DIX,
Major-General.

SUFFOLK, *January* 4, 1863.

Major-General DIX, *Fort Monroe:*

Six thousand seven hundred and four have gone, independent of Wessells; 1,200 to go.

JOHN J. PECK,
Major-General.

HEADQUARTERS EIGHTEENTH ARMY CORPS,
New Berne, N. C., January 5, 1863.

Maj. Gen. JOHN A. DIX,
Commanding Department of Virginia:

GENERAL: Your dispatch to Major-General Foster, who is absent, was delivered this 10 a. m.

The troops referred to by you, "Naglee's brigade," have all arrived, the only loss being one mule that jumped overboard on the night of the storm of December 30. Of General Ferry's brigade, the One hundred and seventy-fourth Pennsylvania and the Sixty-second Ohio have arrived. The Passaic, although badly strained, is under repair, and the prospects of rendering her immediately serviceable are entirely satisfactory.

The Montauk arrived off the harbor of Beaufort yesterday morning, when the coast pilot, in foolishly attempting to enter, ran aground upon the outer bar. I am most happy to advise you that the vessel floated as the tide flooded and came in without harm, having made the voyage in the most satisfactory manner.

I am, truly, yours,

HENRY M. NAGLEE,
Brigadier-General, Commanding.

SUFFOLK, *January* 7, 1863.

Major-General DIX:

General Ferry is at Holly Springs, near Winfield. No transports are there, and he is out of rations, which I am sending him. The transports sailed for New Berne Monday. What shall he do?

JOHN J. PECK,
Major-General.

WELDON, N. C., *January* 7 [6], 1863.

Maj. Gen. J. G. FOSTER, U. S. A.,
Comdg. Eighteenth Army Corps, New Berne, N. C.:

GENERAL: I have the honor to acknowledge the receipt of your communication of the 31st ultimo and a copy of a letter addressed to you by Edward Stanly, who signs himself Military Governor of North Car-

olina. In relation to prisoners of war when they have been paroled
can say that never to my knowledge have they been, nor have I eve
heard of their having been, employed in the performance of any dut
for the Government. As my Government has so faithfully respecte
the parole of prisoners I am the more astonished that you should hav
brought a merely hearsay rumor that came to the ears of the editor
the Raleigh Standard to my notice, when an order was issued from th
War Department of the United States requiring, as I remember, parole
prisoners to instruct recruits, garrison fortresses in the rear of the arm
and guard prisoners. While our press—as the extract you send m
shows—would denounce such violations of a parole of honor, I hav
seen yours teeming with the demand that the prisoners you have cal
tured and paroled should be sent to Minnesota to repel the Indians the
at war with your people. You ask me to answer whether the acts con
plained of by Governor Stanly have my sanction, "and whether, as h
desires to know, the negroes mentioned will be returned to their ma
ter?" His allegation is that our forces recently invaded the county
Washington and, among other depredations committed upon innocer
citizens, we seized, carried away, against the consent of their owners,
large number of slaves; that from the house of Mr. M. Bowen we too
away several of his negroes who had been faithful to him and whom h
protected and humanely supported; that this outrage has not the d
fense attempted for the African slave trade—"that it brought uncivilize
beings under the influence of Christianity and civilization;" that th
robbery takes civilized beings from their families and homes; it d
prives a kind master of his property and punishes slaves for the
fidelity to him. It is true our forces did invade the county of Wash
ington, and the officer in command did report to me that he brough
out with him some negroes. Mr. Stanly is a representative of th
United States Government, and I take it for granted speaks by a
thority, and if it be the determination of your Government to delive
up to their owners the 100,000 slaves you have stolen from their kin
and humane masters I am sure my Government will immediately caus
this one little act of "robbery" to be discountenanced and cause th
negroes to be restored, and thus return to their kind masters the
property; and to this end I will transmit to the proper authority you
communication and Mr. Stanly's letter.

As it is an acknowledged principle among Christian nations to r
spect private property on land I am sure my Government will hail th
as an evidence that hereafter you will cease to deprive private citizer
of their private property. I deplore as much as Mr. Stanly does th
taking of civilized beings from their families and homes and deprivin
owners of their property, and I would it were the only robbery of th
kind that has occurred; but so many have been committed by the force
of the United States that it is now regarded as legitimate and prope
"fit and necessary war measure." As Mr. Stanly says the voice of civ
authority outside your lines has no longer any potency, you may re
assured I will do all in my power to have those negroes delivered up
those to whom their services may be due, and will in every way di
countenance and forbid negro stealing, and in this I am sure both yo
and the good people of North Carolina will justify me.

I do not think the town of Plymouth was barbarously and willfull
burned, but, as reported to me, a house was fired in which your troo
made a stand and from which they fired on our troops. Such thing
will happen in war, and often for no cause except the spirit of destru
tion, as seen on the banks of the Mississippi, the Potomac, Roanok

Rappahannock, and the James Rivers, where cities, towns, and private residences, as a rule, have been burned or battered down by your land and naval forces.

I regret very much that in this street fight a woman was killed. It was first brought to my knowledge by a letter which was received from you, and it should be regretted that accidents of the same kind occurred from the batteries of General Burnside when they opened on the city of Fredericksburg.

Surgeon Hunt was riding with a party of soldiers when he was killed, and in the official report to me he was called and believed to be a lieutenant in command of a scouting party. I will at once, general, write to the captain of the company to which the attacking force belonged and do all in my power to find the watch, and if successful will send it to you that you may place it in the hands of his relatives.

I am, general, very respectfully, your obedient servant,

S. G. FRENCH,
Major-General, Commanding.

FORT MONROE, *January 7, 1863.*

Major-General PECK, *Suffolk:*

General Foster is here and is leaving for New Berne. Will send the transports back immediately. The officer in charge was to have awaited your orders. I fear they cannot be back till Saturday. If you cannot keep Ferry supplied with rations he must forage on the country. Send him a courier. It may be necessary to keep the enemy's attention occupied in the direction of Franklin so that Ferry may not be molested. I expect to send you more troops shortly. Rosecrans' victory is complete.

JOHN A. DIX,
Major-General.

SUFFOLK, *January 8, 1863.*

Major-General DIX:

Spear was still near Holland's at 6 p. m., and reports a very large force of the enemy going down toward Windsor to-day.

JOHN J. PECK,
Major-General.

UNITED STATES FLAG-SHIP MINNESOTA,
Hampton Roads, Va., January 8, 1863.

Maj. Gen. JOHN A. DIX, U. S. A.,
Commanding Seventh Army Corps, Fort Monroe:

GENERAL: I have to acquaint you with the fact that I was prevented from entering the gate in front of headquarters this evening by the sentinel on post there. I complain not of the sentinel, but of the order under which he represented that he acted after I had announced my name and station.

I am, sir, respectfully, your obedient servant,

S. P. LEE,
Actg. Rear-Admiral, Comdg. N. Atlantic Blockading Squadron.

FORT MONROE, VA., *January* 9, 1863.
Maj. Gen. H. W. HALLECK,
 General-in-Chief:

The enemy appeared yesterday in considerable force on this side of
the Blackwater, and has been attacking our pickets about 12 miles from
Suffolk with all arms since morning. The Richmond papers mention
that a large number of our troops have been withdrawn and sent to
North Carolina, and it would not be surprising if the enemy should concentrate a heavy force and attack us, unless the Army of the Potomac
can keep him busy.

         JOHN A. DIX,
          Major-General.

FORT MONROE, VA., *January* 9, 1863.
Maj. Gen. H. W. HALLECK,
 General-in-Chief:

The One hundred and fifteenth New York, which you sent me last
week, is ordered to the Department of the South by Secretary of War,
for burning the barracks at Chicago.* The regiment is at Yorktown,
where I am weak, and I do not wish to take any troops from Suffolk to
supply its place. Can you not send me another regiment?

         JOHN A. DIX,
        Major-General, Commanding.

NEW BERNE, N. C., *January* 9, 1863.
Lieut. Col. SOUTHARD HOFFMAN,
 Assistant Adjutant-General, Eighteenth Army Corps:

COLONEL: I have the honor to submit to you the report of Maj. George
W. Cole, of this regiment, of a reconnaissance made by him toward
Core Creek; also in regard to the alarm at our picket station at the
brick-yard, near railroad bridge, on the evening of the 7th instant.

I am, colonel, very respectfully, your most obedient servant,

         SIMON H. MIX,
   Colonel, Commanding Third New York Volunteer Cavalry.

[Inclosures.]

NEW BERNE, *January* 8, 1863.
Col. S. H. MIX,
 Commanding Third New York Volunteer Cavalry:

COLONEL: I have the honor to report having obeyed the order and
proceeded to the fork of the Dover and Neuse roads. I sent detachments to the bridges on Core Creek, and also to Street's Ferry. Lieutenant Hall, of Company G, went within 30 feet of the bridge on the
Dover road, learning that a company of Whitford's were holding the
rifle-pits beyond and were daily coming across—several yesterday.

Captain Pierce went within 300 yards, or near it, of the bridge on the
Neuse road; found no pickets in sight, but learned that Captain Avirett, of Alabama, with about 90 men, was holding the pits on the Neuse,
and that some 20 of his men were passing the road a few hours before,

---

        * Cipher.

Sergeant Garrett, with a squad of men, went to Street's Ferry and exchanged thirty or forty shots across the river with some of the enemy posted there. He also burned a picket station on this side of the river but destroyed no boats. Meanwhile I thoroughly scoured the country on the right of the railroad, from Core Creek to Batchelder's, finding none of the enemy or any sign of their being encamped. Having accomplished the order, and having no forage to last over night, I marched (after feeding at the bridge) my command to their respective camps, where they are at 5 p. m. this day in excellent condition. I believe from what I can learn there are less than 500 of the enemy holding the country at and beyond Core Creek. Found the roads beyond Batchelder's Creek very good, but this side very bad indeed.

Respectfully,

GEO. W. COLE,
Major, Third New York Volunteer Cavalry.

NEW BERNE, *January 9,* [1863.]

Col. S. H. MIX,
Commanding Third New York Volunteer Cavalry:

COLONEL: I have the honor to report, in obedience to orders, in regard to the alarm at the brick-yard picket camp near railroad bridge, in charge of Captain Doane, Forty-third Massachusetts Regiment, on the night of January 7:

I was with my command at the railroad bridge, and at about 10 o'clock several muskets were fired at the station of Captain Doane, and messengers sent to find the cause stated, through Captain Whytal, commanding post, that Captain Doane "had seen the enemy"—saw bayonets glisten; they were coming out in the open field—and that Captain Doane requested the cavalry sent down, &c. Having been consulted by Captain Whytal in regard to firing the monitor, I thought it not worth while, but he, knowing the parties, must judge. Presently I heard her four shots; one shell exploded. I then sent Lieutenant Sheldon, Company K, Third New York Cavalry, and Captain Pond, Company M, to make personal examination, and they reported "no sign of an enemy," as I supposed at first from the character of the firing; about thirty or forty shots in all. All was then quiet.

Respectfully,

GEO. W. COLE,
Major, Third New York Volunteer Cavalry.

FORT MONROE, VA., *January 10, 1863.*

Maj. Gen. H. W. HALLECK,
General-in-Chief:

I have sent the following to General Peck at Suffolk:

I have reliable information from Richmond that 10,000 infantry, 600 cavalry, and two batteries of artillery, with from 150 to 200 wagons left Richmond on Tuesday last, crossing the James River. The wagons would indicate that they were not going far south. It will be well to set inquiries on foot in the direction of the Blackwater, and warn Colonel Spear of the possibility of his being assailed by a superior force.

JOHN A. DIX,
Major-General, Commanding.

SUFFOLK, VA., *January* 10, 1863.

Major-General DIX, *Fort Monroe:*

Reports from the front state the enemy's force in the region of Windsor at 6,000, with six pieces—probably from four to six. Spear advanced so far toward Somerton yesterday that he could not possibly get to the position indicated until ten or twelve hours after the time. He must now be near Windsor with 4,000, and ten pieces.

JOHN J. PECK,
Major-General.

UNITED STATES FLAG-SHIP MINNESOTA,
Newport News, Va., January 10, 1863.

Maj. Gen. JOHN A. DIX, U. S. A.,
Commanding Seventh Army Corps, Fortress Monroe, Va.:

GENERAL: Your reply to my communication of Thursday evening was received yesterday, and I am very much gratified by the kind terms in which you express your regret at the occurrence referred to.

I desire to thank you for referring to me the letter of the master of the steamer Champion on the 31st ultimo, and to state that Commander Foxhall A. Parker, senior naval officer in York River and vicinity, reported to me in reply to my inquiries with regard to the supposed violation of the blockade at Mob Jack Bay, as observed by Captain Low, that vessels in heavy weather or when wind-bound have been accustomed to make a harbor of that bay under the protection of the guns of the United States steamer Crusader. Hence probably the error of Captain Low. Commander Parker is confident from his knowledge of the blockade in that vicinity that nothing larger than a canoe has succeeded in running that blockade since November 19, and even then under favor of night or thick weather.

I will always be glad to hear of any attempt to evade or violate the blockade. In this spirit I beg to inform you that the officer commanding the United States steamer Stepping Stones reported to me under date of the 3d as follows:

The most popular route for transportation of goods and information from Norfolk and Portsmouth appears to be by the Dismal Swamp road and Chowan, and by this route a surprising quantity of goods are smuggled into the enemy's lines.

I have the honor to be, general, very respectfully, yours,

S. P. LEE,
Actg. Rear-Admiral, Comdg. N. Atlantic Blockading Squadron.

SUFFOLK, VA., *January* 10, 1863.

Major-General DIX:

General Pryor is in command. We have captured messengers with a dispatch for him from Franklin, informing him that a column of 6,000 was approaching, referring to our moves yesterday.

JOHN J. PECK,
Major-General.

SUFFOLK, VA., *January* 10, 1863.

Major-General DIX:

The following is correct: Pryor has on this side 14 pieces, 7,000 infantry, and 1,500 cavalry. He crossed at Franklin, learning that we were moving there with about the same force. He told his friends that he would be in Suffolk by the middle of the week.

Those batteries ought to be here at once. When may I look for them?

JOHN J. PECK,
Major-General.

SUFFOLK, VA., *January 10, 1863.*

Major-General DIX,
Seventh Army Corps:

Our main column reached Windsor about 11 a. m. and has been joined by a portion of New York Mounted Rifles by way of Providence Church. The enemy falling back; our troops in pursuit.

JOHN J. PECK,
Major-General.

WAR DEPARTMENT,
Washington, January 10, 1863.

Major-General BURNSIDE, *Falmouth, Va.:*

General Dix reports that a large force of the enemy has crossed the Blackwater and attacked his pickets at Suffolk.

H. W. HALLECK,
General-in-Chief.

FORT MONROE, VA.,
January 11, 1863—7.30 p. m.

Maj. Gen. H. W. HALLECK,
General-in-Chief:

Major-General Foster desires me to say that he requires the services of a company of Sappers and Miners, regulars, if possible, and when ready to embark, if it is not generally known where they are destined, he would like to have them sent to Beaufort to report to the commanding officer for orders.

JOHN A. DIX,
Major-General.

FORT MONROE, VA.,
January 11, 1863—8 p. m.

M. C. MEIGS, *Quartermaster-General:*

Major-General Foster desires me to say that on consultation with Admiral Lee it was found that the naval vessels would be fully occupied in towing the monitors, and that they could not be relied on for the transportation of troops. He had therefore requested Colonel Thomas officially to take up any transportation he thought proper to replace the navy transports, and it would have your sanction. He says he will require 20,000 sand-bags and 2,000 shovels and spades in addition to those sent to him. He wishes them sent to the quartermaster or commanding officer at Beaufort.

JOHN A. DIX,
Major-General.

SUFFOLK, *January* 11, 1863.

Maj. Gen. JOHN A. DIX, *Fort Monroe:*

A Union man, who gives information from the Blackwater, says that Pryor had 12,000 and that another general was with him. The impression is that he designed an attack here at night, when a portion was absent. Our line is, by survey, over 9 miles.

JOHN J. PECK,
Major-General.

SPECIAL ORDERS, }   HDQRS. EIGHTEENTH ARMY CORPS,
No. 11.   }   *New Berne, January* 11, 1863.

*   *   *   *   *   *

III. General Naglee, commanding Second Division, will take the necessary steps to have his command prepared to move. The division will proceed to Beaufort, N. C., by rail, and will there be embarked. The baggage and camp equipage of the command will be taken to Beaufort by the troops. Twelve hours' notice will be given when the division is to start.

IV. General Wessells, commanding Fourth Division, will take the necessary steps to have his command prepared to move. The division will proceed to Beaufort, N. C., by rail, and will there be embarked. The baggage and camp equipage of the command will be taken to Beaufort by the troops. Twelve hours' notice will be given when the division is to start.

*   *   *   *   *   *

By command of Maj. Gen. J. G. Foster:

[SOUTHARD HOFFMAN,]
Assistant Adjutant-General.

GENERAL ORDERS, }   HDQRS. EIGHTEENTH ARMY CORPS,
No. 14.   }   *New Berne, January* 12, 1863.

The following-named officers* are announced as constituting the staff of the major-general commanding, and will be obeyed and respected accordingly:

Brig. Gen. Edward E. Potter, chief of the staff; Lieut. Col. Southard Hoffman, assistant adjutant-general; Capt. James H. Strong, aide-de-camp and assistant adjutant and inspector general; Maj. J. L. Stackpole, judge-advocate; Maj. John F. Anderson, senior aide-de-camp; Maj. Edward N. Strong, aide-de-camp; Capt. George E. Gouraud, aide-de-camp; Capt. Louis Fitzgerald, aide-de-camp; Capt. Daniel Messinger, provost-marshal; Lieut. Col. Herman Biggs, chief quartermaster; Capt. J. C. Slaght, assistant quartermaster; Capt. Henry Porter, assistant quartermaster; Capt. William Holden, assistant quartermaster; Capt. J. J. Bowen, assistant quartermaster; Lieut. Col. —— ——, chief commissary; Lieut. Joseph A. Goldthwaite, acting commissary of subsistence; Surg. F. G. Snelling, medical director; Lieut. F. U. Farquhar, United States Engineer Corps, chief engineer; Lieut. M. F. Prouty, acting ordnance officer; Lieut. J. Myers, United States Ordnance Corps, ordnance officer.

By command of Maj. Gen. J. G. Foster:

[SOUTHARD HOFFMAN,]
Assistant Adjutant-General.

---

* Amended in General Orders, No. 20, January 15, 1863, so as to include Capt. D. L. Taylor as chief signal officer.

Fort Monroe, Va., *January* 13, 1863.
Maj. Gen. H. W. Halleck,
            General-in-Chief:
  The flag of truce just arrived from City Point reports great activity
on the railroad south of Richmond. Cars were heard running all Sunday night; whether on the road to the Blackwater or Weldon is not
quite certain. I have reports from two sources of the arrival of a heavy
force at Zuni and of 12,000 men near Smithfield, on the James River.
General Peck is trying to ascertain the truth.

                                        JOHN A. DIX,
                                               Major-General.

Fort Monroe, Va., *January* 13, 1863.
Maj. Gen. H. W. Halleck,
            General-in-Chief:
  I have just received the following:

                              Suffolk, Va., *January* 13, 1863.
  We have just learned from reliable women whose friends from the country have
been in since Saturday that Pryor had 12,000 men, and that he was expecting more
troops; that they would have Suffolk anyhow. Generally these reports do not disturb my attention, but now it is proper to notice them.

                                        JOHN J. PECK,
                                            Major-General.
                                        JOHN A. DIX,
                                Major-General, Commanding.

                              Suffolk, Va., *January* 13, 1863.
Major-General Dix:
  Spear reports Pryor to have recrossed, strengthening the river front,
which is the weakest by far now. In all probability the gunboats would
be crippled early.

                                        JOHN J. PECK,
                                            Major-General.

                              Fort Monroe, *January* 13, 1863.
Major-General Peck, *Suffolk:*
  I understand from your dispatch that Pryor is on the other side of
the Blackwater. But I do not understand what you mean when you
say the gunboats would in all probability be crippled early.

                                        JOHN A. DIX,
                                            Major-General.

                              Suffolk, Va., *January* 13, 1863.
Major-General Dix:
  I intended saying that our water front is the weakest, and that I am
strengthening it, lest the boats should be crippled early in case of a
heavy attack. Their machinery is, of course, exposed.

                                        JOHN J. PECK,
                                            Major-General.

HDQRS. FIFTY-EIGHTH REGIMENT, PA. VOLS., U. S. A.,
Camp Batchelder's Station, January 13, 1863.

Lieut. Col. SOUTHARD HOFFMAN,
  Assistant Adjutant-General :

SIR: I have the honor to report that while examining in person yesterday the position at Tuscarora Station I discovered a small party of rebel guerrillas in the neighborhood. As soon as practicable I sent one of my companies (K, under Lieutenant Clay) with orders to move in the woods to the rear of the enemy and punish them for their audacity. Unfortunately my men were discovered too soon, upon which the guerrillas formed (to the number of about 50), but broke and ran before Lieutenant Clay could approach nearer than a quarter of a mile. It being almost dusk, pursuit through the woods was impracticable.

On the facts being reported to me I ordered two companies to be ready to move at 2 a. m. (when the moon would be up) and a third company at 4 a. m. The former (Companies B and I, Captains Metcalf and Buyers) were directed to move through the woods, a half mile on the flank of the railroad, some 5 or 6 miles, until in the rear of the position where the rebels were probably bivouacked, then to sweep the woods backwards to that position. The other company (A, Captain Brown) was directed to take post near the station, so as to intercept fugitives seeking the Tuscarora road. The officers were also directed in case the guerrillas should be seen anywhere to follow them rapidly as far as Core Creek.

My men have not yet returned, but having no guide and being obliged to move by the compass, their success in catching those perfectly acquainted with the country is doubtful.

At dusk and until about 10 p. m. there was a large fire on the railroad at some miles distance beyond Tuscarora; whether a signal or the burning of a culvert I have no means as yet of detecting.

In connection with my duties here I also report that on examination and inquiry I find the Trent road good now and likely to continue practicable for transportation. Also that I could post another infantry regiment advantageously on that line, not only on account of the importance of the line itself but also in order to allow me gradually to cover the country in my front and encourage and protect the transportation of turpentine to and within our lines. With the same view I propose as soon as practicable to rebuild the bridge on the Neuse road, over Batchelder's Creek, stationing there a strong infantry picket.

On the whole I think a few days will suffice to teach the enemy that they have no business east of Core Creek, and cannot safely venture across.

Very respectfully, your obedient servant,
  J. RICHTER JONES,
  Col. Fifty-eighth Regiment Pa. Vols., Comdg. Picket Line, &c.

SPECIAL ORDERS, }   HDQRS. EIGHTEENTH ARMY CORPS,
  No. 13.   }   *New Berne, January 13, 1863.*

*   *   *   *   *   *   *

XX. General Ferry, commanding division, will take the necessary steps to have the brigade of Colonel Osborn prepared to move. The brigade will proceed to Beaufort, N. C., by rail, and will there be embarked. The baggage and camp equipage of the command will be taken to Beaufort by the troops. Twelve hours' notice will be given when the brigade is to start.

*   *   *   *   *   *   *

By command of Maj. Gen. J. G. Foster:

> [SOUTHARD HOFFMAN,]
> *Assistant Adjutant-General.*

UNITED STATES FLAG-SHIP MINNESOTA,
Newport News, Va., January 13, 1863.

Maj. Gen. JOHN A. DIX, U. S. A.,
Commanding Seventh Army Corps, Fort Monroe, Va.:

GENERAL: Under the condition of my instructions from the Navy Department I have instructed the commanding officer of the guard vessel off Fortress Monroe to give permits to loyal citizens who will give security not to go up the creeks in, or to violate the rules of, this blockade, to take up oysters in Willoughby's Bay, Elizabeth River below Norfolk, Craney Island Flats, Hampton Bar, and York River below the guard vessel. My instructions necessarily prohibit oystering in Back River, Nansemond River, James River above Newport News, Western Branch of Elizabeth River, and all the creeks in this blockade. With the last boarding returns from the Mystic is your permit to the schooner Franklin to ship oysters from Back River to Baltimore. I have called Lieutenant-Commander Arnold's attention to this as being in conflict with his instructions, and I respectfully request that you will not give permits to vessels to ship oysters except within the limits specified.

I have the honor to be, general, very respectfully, yours,

> S. P. LEE,
> *Actg. Rear-Admiral, Comdg. N. Atlantic Blockading Squadron.*

FORT MONROE, VA.,
January 14, 1863—3.30 p. m.

Maj. Gen. H. W. HALLECK,
General-in-Chief:

A transport is on the way here to take the One hundred and fifteenth New York Volunteers, now at Yorktown, to the Department of the South. I renew the request for another regiment in its place. I should like very much two or three regiments more at Suffolk, and they will be indispensable if the enemy should attack with a large force.

> JOHN A. DIX,
> *Major-General, Commanding.*

HEADQUARTERS FOURTH CORPS,
Yorktown, January 14, 1863.

Major-General DIX,
Commanding Department:

Yesterday I went to West Point in the gunboat Mahaska to reconnoiter. Some 40 or 50 rebel cavalry were seen on the right bank of the Pamunkey, near its mouth. I took along a squad of cavalry and 100 infantry and captured and brought in 27 head of cattle about 3 miles above West Point.

> E. D. KEYES,
> *Major-General.*

SPECIAL ORDERS,)   HDQRS. EIGHTEENTH ARMY CORPS,
No. 14.   )   *New Berne, January 14, 1863.*

I. The following rules and regulations for the embarkation of the troops under marching orders will be observed, and commanding officers of divisions, brigades, and regiments will see that the same are strictly adhered to.

The order of embarkation will be as follows: First, General Naglee's division; second, General Wessells' division; third, General Ferry's division.

The vessel will be ordered to the wharf, and immediately on her arrival the troops, baggage, and camp equipage destined for her will be placed on board with as little delay as possible, when the vessel will immediately leave the dock and anchor in the harbor. The baggage and camp equipage of the regiments will be placed on board the same vessel with the troops. The baggage for the men will consist only f their tents (shelter tents, if possible), knapsacks, and cooking utensils (camp kettles); that of the officers of only one trunk, valise, or carpet-bag and mess kit; no heavy mess chests will be allowed. The men will be provided with three days' cooked rations, in haversacks, and 40 rounds of ammunition, in cartridge-boxes, before leaving New Berne; 40 rounds of additional ammunition for each man, in boxes, will also be placed on the vessel.

After embarkation the inclosed extracts from the Army Regulations will be strictly enforced, and in addition a guard must be placed over the fresh water, so that it may only be used for cooking (by order of the proper authority) and for drinking. Officers and men must alike use salt water for washing purposes. Signal officers will be sent to each division and brigade headquarters. The flag designating the headquarters of the commanding general will be a white castle on a blue ground.

The Union-jack at foremast, with the corps flag underneath (or division or brigade flag underneath, in case of division or brigade signals), shall be the signal for weighing anchor and starting in the following order: General Naglee's division, General Wessells' division, General Ferry's division.

Steamers will tow such sailing vessels as may be designated by the quartermaster. The signal for anchoring will be the American flag at the fore; if in a fog, two whistles from the flag-ship, repeated at intervals of one minute each. This signal will be repeated by the flag-ships of each division and brigade. At this signal the vessels will near each other and anchor in line.

In case stranding or any other case of distress the signal will be the American flag, Union down; at this signal the light-draught boats and tugs will be at once sent to the aid of the vessel in distress.

As far as practicable the vessels will keep together, but if separated will obey their sealed orders.

*   *   *   *   *   *   *

By command of Maj. Gen. J. G. Foster:
                              [SOUTHARD HOFFMAN,]
                                   Assistant Adjutant-General.

———

SUFFOLK, *January* 15, 1863.

Major-General DIX:

Nearly every person at the North, including officers, except at Army headquarters, rates us at from twice to thrice our present numbers, and expects results proportionally. The detachment of Corcoran's will be ready to leave when required. It has been in one of the forts. What do you think of the map I sent you?

JOHN J. PECK,
Major-General.

FORT MONROE, VA., *January* 15, 1863.

Maj. Gen. H. W. HALLECK, *General-in-Chief:*

I have just received the following from Suffolk:

A large force of the enemy left Carrsville during the day. They reported they were to be joined by other troops. The people there said they were going to Suffolk. Have sent out to ascertain their movements. A deserter from Weldon has just arrived. He left Monday morning; says several thousand infantry passed through on three days of last week for Franklin.

Also from Yorktown:

I send the following telegram, just received from Lieutenant-Colonel Lewis: "Can I have another regiment of infantry at once? If I can, I will hold Fort Magruder against odds; if not, I must continue to hold it as an outpost as long as I can."

E. D. KEYES,
Major-General.

JOHN A. DIX,
Major-General.

FORT MONROE, *January* 15, 1863.

Major-General KEYES, *Yorktown:*

I have nothing to give you. You must do the best you can. If your force is not sufficient to hold Fort Magruder it should be abandoned when the proper time comes. I am ordered to send one of your regiments away, but shall retain it till another comes.

JOHN A. DIX,
Major-General.

HEADQUARTERS FOURTH ARMY CORPS,
Yorktown, Va., January 15, 1863.

Major-General DIX,
Commanding Department of Virginia:

SIR: The news contained in the telegram which I forwarded you to-day is in exact accordance with the opinion expressed in my last letter to you, that the rebels would shortly attack Williamsburg and the camp of the Fifth Pennsylvania Cavalry, 4 miles below that town.

My present command of conscript regiments of infantry, mostly armed with flint-lock muskets altered to percussion, will not allow me to endeavor to resist a strong force at Fort Magruder. I must therefore regard that and all the positions held by the Fifth Pennsylvania Cavalry as outposts to be given up on the approach of a large mass of the enemy. If I had another full regiment of infantry I could hold that line (of Fort Magruder) long enough to inflict much greater damage on the enemy than enough to balance the advantages they would gain, if successful; but I cannot do so now. I trust, therefore, that another regiment will be sent me if possible.

I remain, very respectfully, your most obedient servant,

E. D. KEYES,
Major-General.

HDQRS. DEPT. OF VIRGINIA, SEVENTH ARMY CORPS,
Fort Monroe, Va., January 15, 1863.

Maj. Gen. J. G. FOSTER,
    Commanding Eighteenth Army Corps.

GENERAL: I send my aide-de-camp, Major Dix, to you, to advise you that 20,000 sand-bags and 2,000 shovels and spades have been ordered to you from New York. Major-General Halleck advises me that there is no company of Sappers and Miners which you can have. Everything has been sent to you except a few ambulances. I trust the steamer Convoy has arrived. It is the only one that has come here suitable to the service. From her light draught and great capacity I trust you will find her just what you want. If anything more is required I shall be happy to forward it.

With my best wishes for your success, I am, respectfully, your obedient servant,

JOHN A. DIX,
Major-General.

GENERAL ORDERS, }   HDQRS. EIGHTEENTH ARMY CORPS,
    No. 22.   }   *New Berne, January* 15, 1863.

The commanding general learns with deep regret of the insubordinate conduct of the Ninety-sixth New York Volunteers on the night of the 13th instant. It is the duty of commanding officers to use every effort to promote the comfort of the troops, their prompt payment, &c. This has been done. The commanding general has asked for, and is in hourly expectation of receiving, funds to pay those who have not been paid for a long time. The course of the soldier, if any neglect is shown in his case, is to make a respectful petition or remonstrance on the matter, but to obey. The recent acts of the Ninety-sixth were mutinous, and such as all good soldiers should be ashamed to have shared in. The only effect can be to lay the men open to trial for mutiny and consequent punishment, and cannot hasten, certainly, their desires. The duty of a regimental officer is to use his efforts to put down any attempt at insubordination, mildly if he can, by force and arms if he must. The officers of the Ninety-sixth and those regiments to which the mutineers went lamentably failed in their duties as commanders, or the breach of discipline referred to would have been promptly punished.

The commanding general hopes that no officer or soldier will again so fail in his duty. Another offense will surely meet its punishment.

By command of Major-General Foster:

[SOUTHARD HOFFMAN,]
Assistant Adjutant-General.

FORT MONROE, VA.,
January 16, 1863—7.30 p. m.

Major-General HALLECK,
    General-in-Chief U. S. Army:

Colonel Ludlow just returned from City Point. He learned that six regiments were sent from Petersburg to the Blackwater on Monday and Tuesday last. General Pryor is 7 miles this side, and there is no doubt that he has been strongly re-enforced.

JOHN A. DIX,
Major-General.

HDQRS. DEPT. OF VIRGINIA, SEVENTH ARMY CORPS,
Fort Monroe, Va., January 16, 1863.

Actg. Rear-Admiral S. P. LEE,
Commanding North Atlantic Blockading Squadron :

ADMIRAL : There are indications of activity on the part of the enemy above Yorktown and also on the Blackwater. General Pryor has crossed the river and is 7 miles on this side. I am so weakened by reenforcing General Foster in North Carolina that I can only act on the defensive. There are rumors in Norfolk of a raid from the direction of the Dismal Swamp, and General Peck telegraphs me this evening that our pickets have been fired on between Suffolk and Deep Creek. General Viele is very anxious to have a small gunboat, or, as he says, "an additional small gunboat sent up to remain near the draw-bridge," that he may look after the threatened raid in other directions. You will oblige me if you can comply with his request. The secessionists in Norfolk have been in high spirits for several days, and we hear in many quarters that some movement against us is intended.

I am, very respectfully, your obedient servant,

JOHN A. DIX,
Major-General.

UNITED STATES FLAG-SHIP MINNESOTA,
Newport News, January 16, 1863.

Maj. Gen. JOHN A. DIX :

GENERAL : I have sent another gunboat to Norfolk and have no additional gunboat to spare for that or any other purpose.

Respectfully, yours,

S. P. LEE,
Acting Rear-Admiral, &c.

SUFFOLK, VA., *January* 16, 1863.

Major-General DIX, *Fort Monroe :*

A severe storm of wind and rain has continued from last night and little can be done of any variety of work. Parties of cavalry are out on all the avenues of approach. Nothing has been reported since my last telegram. General Viele advised of rumors prevailing there of raids upon the railway and I sent out a party on the track last night.

JOHN J. PECK,
Major-General.

SUFFOLK, VA., *January* 16, 1863.

Major-General DIX, *Fort Monroe :*

The guerrillas attacked the pickets about 4.30 p. m., wounding 2. They were driven some miles and dispersed. I do not think they will repeat the experiment. Doubtless they acted under instructions from Pryor. Pryor moved away and we do not know his position ; supposed to be near Holy Neck Church. We captured two of his men, of the Fiftieth Virginia. He has several old regiments from Northwestern Virginia.

JOHN J. PECK,
Major-General.

FORT MONROE, *January* 16, 1863.

Major-General PECK, *Suffolk:*

It seems difficult to believe that there are between you and Deep Creek any except guerrillas belonging to the counties of Virginia and North Carolina to the east and south of you. If you think otherwise it is important to ascertain. There is no doubt a very bad feeling in that direction growing out of the trouble at Elizabeth City, where, I am told, the officer in command of the North Carolina native troops has armed 200 negroes.

JOHN A. DIX,
Major-General.

SUFFOLK, VA., *January* 16, 1863.

Major-General DIX:

Mr. Nash, Federal surveyor from Norfolk County, represents that a force of 20,000 or 25,000 is on the Blackwater; that 3,000 of Stuart's cavalry will make a raid through the swamp and attack Portsmouth and Norfolk. He says his information is from a reliable source. He stated that he had communicated this matter to General Viele. Who is Mr. Nash? I give it as it comes to me.

JOHN J. PECK,
Major-General.

HEADQUARTERS EIGHTEENTH ARMY CORPS,
New Berne, January 17, 1863.

Major-General HALLECK,
General-in-Chief U. S. Army, Washington, D. C.:

GENERAL: I regret to say I have not been able to embark as soon as I expected, owing to the non-arrival of siege ammunition and water, but am now embarking, and I will continue until I am all ready and then start at once.

I shall leave everything in safe condition here under General Prince, with at least 12,000 infantry, artillery, and cavalry. I consider this ample, for a short time at least.

I consider it necessary that I should go with the force going, as many of the troops are old men with me, and my experience in disembarking, &c., is extensive, so I can see them disembarked safely. I shall communicate the result of this as soon as possible.

If it is found that the work is heavier than I now anticipate I shall leave my troops safe and return at once to Hampton Roads for re-enforcements. I do not think it safe to leave less than 12,000 men in this department at present.

I am, however, confident of success, and shall do everything in my power to insure an early and satisfactory result.

The amount of solid shot for the siege guns arrived up to this time is not sufficient, and I have written to General Ripley on this subject, urging him to hurry it forward.

I remain, general, very respectfully, your obedient servant,

J. G. FOSTER,
Major-General, Commanding.

FORT MONROE, *January* 17, 1863.

Major-General PECK, *Suffolk:*

Mr. Nash is a very good man. Ascertain, if you can, specifically what his reliable information was, from whom derived, &c.

Colonel Ludlow returned last night from City Point. Reports that six regiments went from Petersburg to the Blackwater on Monday and Tuesday. Can it be possible that Pryor is trying to get around by way of the Dismal Swamp to cut off your connection with Norfolk? It would be a very dangerous experiment for him.

JOHN A. DIX,
Major-General.

SUFFOLK, VA., *January* 17, 1863.

Major-General DIX, *Fort Monroe:*

Your telegram relating to six regiments leaving for Blackwater on Monday and Tuesday is noticed. Deserters say that several regiments passed from Weldon to Franklin last week. If so, they must be very strong there. Most likely the 10,000 you advised of with teams would be incorporated for a grand advance. Their extraordinary exertions for subsistence and forage induces the belief of additions. Mr. Nash left before your telegram arrived. I wish you could see him.

JOHN J. PECK,
Major-General.

FORT MONROE, *January* 17, 1863.

Hon. E. M. STANTON, *Secretary of War:*

I have just received the following:

SUFFOLK, *January* 17, 1863.

There is a great and increasing discontent in the regiments that have not been paid for several months, in consequence of the sufferings of families. Unless steps are taken to remove the cause of complaint I fear the spirit and usefulness of the troops will be materially impaired. Will you please communicate this to the Hon. Secretary of War?

JOHN J. PECK.
Major-General, Commanding.

JOHN A. DIX,
Major-General.

FORT MONROE, *January* 18, 1863.

Major-General PECK, *Suffolk:*

Do you know where Pryor is? Have you any reliable intelligence from the enemy, either as to his force or his movements?

JOHN A. DIX,
Major-General.

SUFFOLK, VA., *January* 18, 1863.

Major-General DIX:

It is my impression that Pryor recrossed Blackwater during the late storm, which was very severe. Patrols report nothing of his moves this morning. Reports are contradictory and not as satisfactory as is desirable. Parties are watching the avenues leading toward Edenton and the Swamp.

JOHN J. PECK,
Major-General.

UNITED STATES FLAG-SHIP MINNESOTA,
Newport News, Va., January 19, 1863.

Maj. Gen. JOHN A. DIX, U. S. A.,
Commanding Seventh Army Corps, Fort Monroe, Va.:

GENERAL: I respectfully refer to you the inclosed extracts from a report from Lieutenant Flusser, commanding United States steamer Commodore Perry, dated at Winfield, Chowan River, January 5, 1863,* and relating to an extensive illicit trade carried on between Norfolk and Richmond. This mischievous trade ought to be discontinued.

I have the honor to be, general, very respectfully, yours,
S. P. LEE,
Actg. Rear-Admiral, Comdg. N. Atlantic Blockading Squadron.

———

UNITED STATES FLAG-SHIP MINNESOTA,
Off Newport News, Va., January 19, 1863.

Maj. Gen. E. D. KEYES, U. S. A.,
Commanding at Yorktown:

GENERAL: It gave much pleasure to receive yours of the 14th and to learn from it that you appreciate Commander Parker's character for caution and enterprise—qualities so valuable and possessed by him in such degree as to claim my confidence in what he may attempt in an emergency and there is not time to confer previously with me. He is there to co-operate with you in measures for the advancement of the public interest, and in this regard needs no new instructions from me.

I have the honor to be, general, very respectfully, yours,
S. P. LEE,
Actg. Rear-Admiral, Comdg. N. Atlantic Blockading Squadron.

———

SUFFOLK, VA., *January* 19, 1863.

Major-General DIX, *Fort Monroe*:

Our parties have been over all the roads and report no force in their routes. Their pickets were found at Windsor and Carrsville yesterday.
JOHN J. PECK,
Major-General.

———

FORT MONROE, VA., *January* 19, 1863.

Maj. Gen. H. W. HALLECK,
General-in-Chief:

I send a letter from General Foster. I sent Major Dix, one of my aides, two days ago with latest intelligence. A dispatch goes to General Ripley. Everything here for General Foster has been sent:

GENERAL: I have been much delayed in the preparations of my transports, and therefore have not got off as soon as I expected. The solid-shot ammunition for the siege guns has not yet arrived in sufficient quantity, neither have any of the water-schooners which were to be sent from Baltimore with the Dispatch. However, I am doing the best that I can and am embarking at Beaufort. The embarkation will occupy three or four days, and then I shall sail.
J. G. FOSTER,
Major-General.

JOHN A. DIX,
Major-General.

———

* Not found.

GENERAL ORDERS, }   HDQRS. EIGHTEENTH ARMY. CORPS,
    No. 26.   }   *New Berne, January* 19, 1863.

Lieut. Col. Francis Darr is hereby announced as chief commissary of subsistence on the commanding-general's staff, and will be obeyed and respected accordingly.

By command of Maj. Gen. J. G. Foster:

                    SOUTHARD HOFFMAN,
                        Assistant Adjutant-General.

————

HDQRS. DEPT. OF VIRGINIA, SEVENTH ARMY CORPS,
            Fort Monroe, Va., January 20, 1863.

Actg. Rear-Admiral S. P. LEE,
    Commanding North Atlantic Blockading Squadron:

ADMIRAL: I have the honor to acknowledge the receipt of your letter of yesterday with an extract from a report from Lieutenant-Commander Flusser in regard to an illicit trade carried on between Norfolk and Richmond. I shall refer it to General Viele, and take prompt measures with a view to the detection of the parties engaged in this traffic. Will you please direct Lieutenant-Commander Flusser to report the nature of the goods destroyed and the names of the persons who were engaged in smuggling them within the Confederate lines? If he will hereafter take into custody and deliver to the officer in command at Roanoke Island any parties engaged in illicit trade, that they may be sent to me, I will see that they are punished; or if he will advise you of any such arrests I will send for the parties wherever they may be. The most rigid rules have been adopted at Norfolk in regard to goods permitted to leave the city. Not a sack of salt is allowed to go out without a permit, and the name of the person to whom it is given is registered. The same rule is enforced in regard to all other articles. In one case $3,000 worth of goods were allowed to be taken into Princess Anne County for sale. The person to whom the permit was given, in violation of his engagement, took them to North Carolina. We followed him and captured him and the property a few miles from the point on the Chowan from which Lieutenant-Commander Flusser writes. He is now in Fort Norfolk, where I shall keep him, and the property will be sold at auction for the benefit of the poor.

Every effort has been made to prevent illicit traffic; but in view of the lawlessness of a large number of the parties engaged in trade in Norfolk—all of whom, by the by, have taken the oath of allegiance—I decided two days ago to grant no more permits to take goods there at present, excepting for the use of the troops.

I am, very respectfully, your obedient servant,

                    JOHN A. DIX,
                        Major-General.

————

UNITED STATES FLAG-SHIP MINNESOTA,
        Newport News, January 20, 1863.

Maj. Gen. JOHN A. DIX,
    Commanding Seventh Army Corps, Fortress Monroe:

GENERAL: I respectfully submit for your further information regarding the traffic between Norfolk and Richmond a copy of the report to me from Lieutenant Flusser, commanding United States steamer Commodore Perry, dated Elizabeth City, January 13, and an extract from another report of his of the same date respecting further trade from Norfolk.

I have the honor to be, general, very respectfully, yours,

S. P. LEE,
Actg. Rear-Admiral, Comdg. N. Atlantic Blockading Squadron.

SUFFOLK, VA., *January* 20, 1863.

Major-General DIX:

Major Stratton made a fine reconnaissance toward Blackwater. At Carrsville he found a picket of 9 men, capturing 2 of them. Thinks the enemy's main force on the other side. Prisoners are on the way ·in. A good deal of signaling on the Somerton. Shall have that quarter examined very closely to-morrow. Pickets of some strength found at Windsor.

JOHN J. PECK,
Major-General.

HEADQUARTERS EIGHTEENTH ARMY CORPS,
New Berne, N. C., January 20, 1863.

Maj. Gen. H. W. HALLECK,
General-in-Chief U. S. Army, Washington, D. C.:

GENERAL: The transports from this place have all left, but are de layed by the low water on the Swash, at Hatteras.

Naglee's division is embarked at Beaufort. The other divisions will embark as soon as their transports reach Beaufort. I shall sail as soon as all are on board, probably by Friday or Saturday. I have just received information from a spy, who has been within the enemy's lines and conversed with their soldiers, to the effect that the rebel force in this State has been largely increased from the army in Virginia; that Wilmington has been re-enforced; that the main body intended to be thrown by railroad either to Weldon or Wilmington is at Goldsborough, and that Weldon is not strongly guarded, the rebels relying on the force in front on the Blackwater, under Pryor, and on the proximity of the reserve at Goldsborough.

The rebels report their force in the State to be 200,000, which is manifestly grossly exaggerated. The rebel soldiers reported to the spy that 75,000 men were at Goldsborough. I think this also is exaggerated; that there may be 75,000 men all told in the State is probable, since they could venture to withdraw even more than that number from the Army of Virginia, in consequence of the presumed inactivity of our army on the Rappahannock. They have full information of the condition of the army on the Rappahannock from our own newspapers, and are much cheered by the reports and evidently do not fear any movements from that quarter.

Colonel Amory's brigade is now out on a strong reconnaissance on the south bank of the Trent River. This advance was impeded by felled trees and burnt bridges. The rebels burnt all the bridges over the Trent River and all over the creeks on the south route from Trenton to Jacksonville (or Onslow). The cavalry (Third New York) are sweeping all the country between the White Oak and New Rivers, hoping to capture some of the rebel cavalry.

Contrabands report that the enemy fell back from Onslow on the 18th in the direction of Wilmington. The destruction of bridges and obstruction of roads indicates an apprehension of our forces being on the advance in that direction.

I shall take every precaution in my power to leave everything safe at this place and shall spare no efforts to make the expedition a perfect success. I think I can assure you that there will be no failure if you will give me further re-enforcements in case I find them indispensable.

I am not apprehensive about the reported concentration of forces at Goldsborough, for I hardly think that the rebels will venture on an attack while their own towns are in danger, and certainly not if any signs of movement are made by the Army of the Rappahannock.

I have the honor to be, general, with great respect, your obedient servant,

> J. G. FOSTER,
> *Major-General, Commanding.*

> HEADQUARTERS DEPARTMENT OF NORTH CAROLINA,
> *New Berne, January 20, 1863.*

Maj. Gen. J. G. FOSTER, *Commanding, &c.:*

GENERAL: I am informed by several gentlemen, residents of Elizabeth City, that there are in that town about 250 negroes armed and daily drilled by officers of the Army of the United States. I also learn that Captain Sanders is in command.

If the President commands this, officers of the Army are expected to obey.

In his proclamation "that such persons (slaves) of suitable condition will be received into the armed service of the United States, to garrison forts, positions, stations, and other places, and to man vessels of all sorts in said service," he has not ordered, as far as I can hear, that every subordinate officer at every post can receive negroes into the service without some regulations from headquarters.

Is every provost-marshal or captain to judge of the "suitable condition" of the negroes?

Are no instructions to be given that they are not to be sent out into the field or allowed to go on foraging excursions, committing pillage and robbery at discretion?

My attention has been called already to several instances of this kind. I have promised to and do invoke your assistance to prevent if possible the most deplorable calamities that will fall upon our loyal citizens and upon the negroes if superior discretion and experience do not now control them.

I most earnestly solicit your attention to this matter, and that I may be authorized to inform our loyal fellow-citizens that no inexperienced subordinate shall without your sanction, and until proper restraints are provided, incur the danger of a servile war.

Very respectfully, &c.,

> ED. STANLY,
> *Military Governor.*

> DEPARTMENT OF NORTH CAROLINA,
> *New Berne, January 20, 1863.*

Major-General FOSTER, *Commanding, &c.:*

GENERAL: I have just received a letter from Edenton of date the 6th instant informing me that a band of negroes and soldiers, armed, visited

SUFFOLK, VA., *January 21, 1863.*

Major-General DIX:

The prisoners say that large additions have been made to the force on Blackwater—several new Virginia regiments and some Louisiana and Tennessee; that the force is larger than ever before; a camp of five regiments at Jerusalem. It accords with the general tenor of reports from prisoners, deserters, &c.

JOHN J. PECK,
Major-General.

———

SUFFOLK, VA., *January 22, 1863.*

Major-General DIX:

It has seemed to me that the Confederates have thrown some extra force on the Blackwater, with a view of holding as much force here as possible and then of sending it to North Carolina, if called for. I cannot believe that they will at this wet season undertake a movement by way of South Mills on Portsmouth. Pryor's command has been somewhat increased and materially improved by exchanges of his new regiments for old ones. This may explain the departure from Petersburg of the troops reported by Colonel Ludlow, and also a statement of one of the deserters from Weldon that troops were passing both ways on the Seaboard road. Having these views I have not asked for any troops, reserving that action until something positive reaches me, but all the time adding to the strength of the position.

JOHN J. PECK,
Major-General.

———

SUFFOLK, *January 23, 1863.*

Major-General DIX:

Major Stratton with a suitable force will leave in the morning, unless very stormy, to make a thorough examination of the Dismal Swamp, passing in at Deep Creek and going out at South Mills. He will be four or five days, and will procure information.

JOHN J. PECK,
Major-General.

———

SUFFOLK, *January 24, 1863.*

Major-General DIX:

About Monday I propose sending some 4,000 or 5,000 to Blackwater, under Corcoran or Foster, if weather favors. It leaves this place very weak, but I want to feel of them in some manner.

JOHN J. PECK,
Major-General.

———

FORT MONROE, VA.,
January 26, 1863—9 a. m.

Maj. Gen. H. W. HALLECK, *General-in-Chief:*

One of my aides returned late last night from General Foster. He was detained on his way back by violent gales. Left New Berne on the 20th. Naglee's brigade was embarked at Beaufort; other divisions awaiting transports expected to move on the 23d or 24th. Rebels in North Carolina had been largely re-enforced from the army in Virginia, and Wilmington has been re-enforced. Main body of the enemy was at Goldsborough. Weldon was not strongly guarded, the rebels relying on Pryor's force on the Blackwater to protect that point. General Foster thinks there may be 75,000 rebel troops in North Carolina. This is the substance of a dispatch from him, which will go to you by this evening's mail.

• I have reason to believe that a portion of the force on the Blackwater ten days ago has been sent to Goldsborough by way of Weldon.

Some 4,000 or 5,000 men will be sent to-day from Suffolk to the Blackwater to reconnoiter, and ascertain, if possible, what force Pryor has. The One hundred and fifteenth New York has been sent to the Department of the South from Yorktown.

JOHN A. DIX,
Major-General.

FORT MONROE, VA., January 27, 1863.

Maj Gen. H. W. HALLECK,
      General-in-Chief:

The Richmond Inquirer of this morning has the following:

GOLDSBOROUGH, N. C., January 25, 1863.

A respectable refugee, just arrived from Beaufort, reports the Abolitionists' fleet, ninety-two sail, including two monitors and six other iron-clads, in Beaufort Harbor. Also that 52,000 Abolitionists are encamped at Morehead City and Carolina City. General Robertson has just returned to Kinston from a reconnoitering expedition through Jones and Onslow Counties. He reports that a company of cavalry, Captain Perkins, surprised a party of Abolitionists last Friday at Big Northeast Bridge, near Jacksonville, Onslow Court-House, killing 1 captain and 5 privates and routing the balance. No loss on our side.

JOHN A. DIX,
Major-General.

YORKTOWN, January 27, 1863.

Major-General DIX :

Colonel Lewis telegraphs an attempt was made this morning to capture our pickets. About 12 shots were fired by the enemy, but no one hurt or captured. All is again quiet, the enemy having retired. Last night at about 9 p. m. it was reported from Gloucester Point that the enemy was approaching our pickets there. Nothing further this morning. I respectfully call your attention again to the increase of my force, which is necessary.

E. D. KEYES,
Major-General.

HDQRS. FIFTY-EIGHTH REGT. PENNSYLVANIA VOLS.,
Camp at Batchelder's Creek, January 27, 1863.

Lieutenant-Colonel HOFFMAN,
      Assistant Adjutant-General:

SIR : I have the honor to report that immediately on receiving the orders to ignore passes and close our lines I made arrangements and gave directions for carrying them into effect.

34 R R—VOL XVIII

Also to-day I have put strong parties on the Neuse, the Trent, and the railroad with instructions to stop all passengers.

From information received yesterday I believe the enemy have returned from Core Creek, on the railroad and Neuse road, but I shall verify that fact to-day.

I learn also that the enemy at Goldsborough are apprehensive of an advance from New Berne simultaneous with our naval expedition.

Very respectfully, your obedient servant,

J. RICHTER JONES, •
Commanding Outposts.

SUFFOLK, *January* 29, 1863.

Major-General DIX:

Major Stratton has returned. He seized and brought in 42 large sacks of salt. The other capture by Dodge's men is large; it is said there are many loads. Have just ordered out fifteen teams and a force to protect them. Pryor came over Sunday night perhaps with a view to the securing of this property.

JOHN J. PECK,
Major-General.

BEAUFORT, N. C., *January* 30—11.30 a. m.,
Via Fort Monroe, Va., February 8, 1863.

Maj. Gen. H. W. HALLECK,
General-in-Chief:

The constant and strong southerly winds (amounting at times to gales) that have prevailed for the past ten or fifteen days have prevented our sailing, although most of the troops have been on board ready to sail more than a week. Yesterday the wind shifted to the northwest, and as everything looked favorable I started the fleet. Nearly all got over the bar before dark, with a fair start down the coast. The wind, however, shifted back to the southwest after dark, and blew strongly, preventing the few remaining vessels going to sea. It is still blowing hard (11.30 a. m). This will interfere very much with the progress of the fleet, and may scatter it considerably. As soon as the wind will permit I shall start with the remaining vessels. So long a continuance of southerly gales is very unusual.

J. G. FOSTER,
Major-General, Commanding.

FORT MONROE, VA., *January* 30, 1863.

His Excellency ABRAHAM LINCOLN,
President United States:

No iron-clads have left for two days. The Weehawken is at Norfolk; the Patapsco is here, waiting for favorable weather, and the Nahant is at Newport News. I have just telegraphed to General Halleck our success in a fight with Pryor.

JOHN A. DIX,
Major-General.

FORT MONROE, VA., *January 30, 1863.*

Maj. Gen. H. W. HALLECK, *General-in-Chief:*

General Peck telegraphs that our victory is complete, and that Pryor passed through Carrsville in full retreat at 3 p. m., 6 miles from the Deserted House, where our forces attacked him just before daylight.

> JOHN A. DIX,
> *Major-General.*

FORT MONROE, VA., *January 30, 1863.*

Major-General HALLECK, *General-in-Chief:*

Following just received from Suffolk:

Major-General DIX:

My last dispatch should be corrected by later dispatches. As yet he says the enemy are in position.

> JOHN J. PECK,
> *Major-General.*
> JOHN A. DIX,
> *Major-General, Commanding.*

FORT MONROE, VA., *January 30, 1863.*

Major-General HALLECK, *General-in-Chief:*

Pryor fell back 3 or 4 miles, contesting the ground in his retreat. General Peck gives me no details, but thinks we have a victory, and that we shall secure some of the enemy's guns. Our loss about 100.* The roads are very deep, and our men have had a hard time in getting through them.

> JOHN A. DIX,
> *Major-General.*

SUFFOLK, VA., *January 30, 1863.*

Major-General DIX:

Have just received a report from a party I sent out to the vicinity of Carrsville for information to the effect that the cars have been running briskly to Franklin since afternoon.

> JOHN J. PECK,
> *Major-General.*

HDQRS. DEPT. OF VIRGINIA, SEVENTH ARMY CORPS,
Fort Monroe, Va., January 31, 1863.

Actg. Rear-Admiral S. P. LEE,
Commanding North Atlantic Blockading Squadron:

ADMIRAL: Will you oblige me by sending an officer to confer with General Viele, at Norfolk, in regard to illicit trade? The privilege of trading has been abused, and I am desirous of surrounding it with all possible safeguards. I have given no permits to introduce goods into Norfolk since the 17th instant, and think I shall confine commercial transactions there hereafter to retail dealers.

I have the honor to be, very respectfully, yours,

> JOHN A. DIX,
> *Major-General.*

---

* But see revised statement, p. 135.

HDQRS. DEPT. OF VIRGINIA, SEVENTH ARMY CORPS,
Fort Monroe, Va., January 31, 1863.

Maj. Gen. E. D. KEYES,
  Commanding, &c., Yorktown, Va.:

GENERAL: A limited supply of efficient arms (Enfield rifles) has been received at the arsenal at this place. You will therefore make proper requisitions for such regiments as are most in need of such arms.

By command of Major-General Dix:

D. T. VAN BUREN,
Assistant Adjutant-General.

Abstract from Tri-monthly Return of the Department of Virginia (Seventh Army Corps), Maj. Gen. John A. Dix commanding, for January 31, 1863 *(headquarters Fort Monroe, Va.).*

Command.	Present for duty. Officers.	Present for duty. Men.	Aggregate present.	Aggregate present and absent.	Aggregate last return.	Pieces of field artillery.	Infantry. Officers.	Infantry. Men.	Cavalry. Officers.	Cavalry. Men.	Artillery. Officers.	Artillery. Men.
*Headquarters Fort Monroe.—*Maj. Gen. John A. Dix	17		17	17	17							
*Fort Monroe.—*Col. S. M. Alford:												
Infantry	22	618	789	836	836		28	687				
Attached garrison			25	25	25							23
Total	22	618	814	861	861		28	687				23
*Camp Hamilton.—*Col. Anthony Conk:												
Infantry	29	659	780	824	825		35	700				
Cavalry	3	73	80	86	86				3	74		
Artillery	9	279	321	337	422						10	281
Total	41	1,011	1,181	1,247	1,333		35	700	3	74	10	281
*Norfolk.—*Brig. Gen. E. L. Viele:												
Infantry	129	2,422	3,033	3,458	3,470		131	2,608				
Cavalry	2	39	58	82	82							
Artillery	4	135	149	190	192	6			2	51	4	137
Total	135	2,596	3,240	3,730	3,744	6	131	2,608	2	51	4	137
*Suffolk.—*Maj. Gen. J. J. Peck:												
Infantry	361	7,079	8,663	9,946	10,189		361	7,079				
Cavalry	67	1,568	2,085	2,328	2,329	4			70	1,773		
Artillery	17	620	709	761	765	30					17	650
Total	445	9,267	11,457	13,035	13,283	34	361	7,079	70	1,773	17	650
*Yorktown.—*Maj. Gen. E. D. Keyes:												
Infantry	162	2,505	3,028	3,523	4,444		163	2,650				
Cavalry	43	853	1,044	1,155	1,157				45	942		
Artillery	16	383	466	663	669	28					19	413
Total	221	3,741	4,538	5,341	6,270	28	163	2,650	45	942	19	413
*Point Lookout, Md.—*Maj. J. C. Brown: Detachment Independent Battalion New York Volunteers.	5	150	184	200	200		5	152				
Grand total	886	17,383	21,431	24,431	25,708	68	723	13,876	120	2,840	50	1,504

Abstract from Tri-monthly Return of the Eighteenth Army Corps, Department of North Car olina, Maj. Gen. John G. Foster commanding, for January 31, 1863 (headquarters New Berne, N. C.).

Command.	Present for duty.		Aggregate present.	Aggregate present and absent.	Aggregate last return.	Present for duty equipped.			
						Infantry.		Cavalry.	
	Officers.	Men.				Officers.	Men.	Officers.	Men.
Eighteenth Army Corps, Maj. Gen. J. G. Foster.	19	....	19	19	19	......	......	......	......
First Brigade, First Division, Col. T. J. C. Amory.	129	2,750	3,454	3,627	3,657	123	2,776	......	......
Second Brigade, First Division, Col. H. C. Lee.	112	2,751	3,532	3,843	3,851	......	......	......	......
Second Division, Brig. Gen. H. M. Naglee.	......	......	......	6,787	6,798	......	......	......	......
Third Division, Brig. Gen. O. S. Ferry.	26	564	711	5,807	5,807	......	......	......	......
Fourth Division, Brig. Gen. H. W Wessells.	153	3,008	3,653	6,321	6,376	153	3,008	......	......
Fifth Division, Brig. Gen. H. Prince.	231	4,615	5,438	7,074	7,100	239	4,874	......	......
1st North Carolina Union Volunteers, Capt. C. A. Lyon.	19	432	496	532	534	......	......	......	......
Artillery brigade, Brig. Gen. J. H. Ledlie.	26	779	1,006	2,216	2,085	......	......	......	......
3d New York Cavalry, Col. S. H. Mix.	40	586	747	933	935	......	......	44	630
Grand total..............	755	15,485	19,056	37,159	37,162	515	10,658	44	630

HEADQUARTERS EIGHTEENTH ARMY CORPS,
Beaufort, S. C., February 2, 1863.

Maj. Gen. H. W. HALLECK,
   General-in-Chief U. S. Army, Washington, D. C.:

GENERAL: I arrived here last night and entered the harbor this morning. All of my steamers are safe except one, the Pilot Boy, which became disabled off Georgetown, S. C., and was left at anchor. I have sent the tug Freeborn to take her back to Beaufort, N. C.

All the sailing vessels of the fleet are within a few leagues of this harbor, and will probably be in safely to-morrow.

The monitors Nahant and Weehawken have not arrived. The supply of ammunition for the iron-clads is not sufficient, and more has to be sent before operations can be begun. The naval preparations will not be completed within two weeks from this time. I shall therefore be obliged to disembark my command to preserve their health until these preparations are completed. In the mean time I shall probably make a movement to distract the enemy's attention, and also make a short trip to New Berne, N. C., to ascertain the condition of affairs there.

If any change of plan is ordered by you resulting from these delays please to have it sent to New Berne by bearer of dispatches within twelve days from this time.

I have the honor to be, very respectfully, your obedient servant,
               J. G. FOSTER,
               Major-General, Commanding.

WAR DEPARTMENT,
Washington, February 2, 1863.

Major-General DIX, *Fort Monroe, Va.:*

The Ninth Army Corps has received orders to report to you at Fort Monroe.

H. W. HALLECK,
General-in-Chief.

UNITED STATES FLAG-SHIP MINNESOTA,
Newport News, February 2, 1863.

Maj. Gen. JOHN A. DIX, U. S. A.,
Commanding Seventh Army Corps, Fortress Monroe:

GENERAL: I have directed the guard vessel off Fort Monroe not to allow George Bush or his schooner, Elizabeth Bush, to pass the blockade again. He has, he says, been in the habit, under a permit from you, to take old rags, scrap-iron, and hides from Hampton to Philadelphia, bringing nothing back. By his own admission he has been in the habit of visiting Chuckatuck in his boat without authority, and as such communications are manifest violations of the blockade I have deemed it advisable to secure the public interest by cutting off his means of carrying information, letters, or property in the manner above indicated.

I have the honor to be, general, very respectfully, yours,

S. P. LEE,
Acting Rear-Admiral.

SUFFOLK, VA., *February* 2, 1863.

Major-General DIX:

Unusual activity of the enemy reported to-day. Two hundred cavalry at Windsor; a large force at Carrsville, with an intermediate party. Have parties out.

JOHN J. PECK,
Major-General.

FORT MONROE, *February* 3, 1863.

Major-General PECK, *Suffolk:*

Within a week I expect to be largely re-enforced. I am anxious that Pryor shall not escape again. If he advances I suggest whether all the motive power of the railroad cannot be used to throw a force in his rear by a sudden movement.

JOHN A. DIX,
Major-General.

SUFFOLK, *February* 3, 1863.

Major-General DIX:

Very glad to learn of the expected troops. When Pryor comes I will hope to bag him. He tears up the road this side of Carrsville as often as I repair it, so that I could not use hand-cars. Supposed he was bagged the other day. He was where flanking was practicable on both flanks. Our people used up their ammunition before dawn and lost time waiting for more. Meantime enemy fell back.

JOHN J. PECK,
Major-General.

UNITED STATES FLAG-SHIP MINNESOTA,
Newport News, Va., February 6, 1863.

Maj. Gen. JOHN A. DIX, U. S. A.,
Commanding Seventh Army Corps, Fortress Monroe, Va.:

GENERAL: Yours of the 31st ultimo was duly received. Pressing engagements have prevented an earlier reply to it. I have no authority to regulate or sanction the privilege of trading at Norfolk by surrounding it with safeguards. It will be satisfactory to me to receive and to give the utmost attention to any written communication you may now or at any time make to me which will enable me to stop illicit trade at Norfolk or elsewhere within the limits of the North Atlantic Blockading Squadron. The new fleet captain has just entered upon his duties and is not familiar with the situation of affairs here.

I have the honor to be, general, yours, respectfully,

S. P. LEE,
Actg. Rear-Admiral, Comdg. N. Atlantic Blockading Squadron.

HDQRS. DEPT. OF VIRGINIA, SEVENTH ARMY CORPS,
Fort Monroe, Va., February 7, 1863.

Actg. Rear-Admiral S. P. LEE,
Commanding North Atlantic Blockading Squadron:

ADMIRAL: It was at General Viele's request that I asked you to send him an officer with whom he might confer in regard to some additional safeguards in regard to trade. The general thought he might obtain valuable suggestions from an officer of the Navy. That was all he had in view. The occasion which made such a conference desirable has now passed by.

I have the honor to be, very respectfully, yours,

JOHN A. DIX,
Major-General.

SUFFOLK, VA., *February 8, 1863.*

Major-General DIX:

My scouting party went to Carrsville in the night. Captain Roberts reports the arrival of a battalion at Franklin of cavalry armed with sabers, rifles, and revolvers. Two companies were at Carrsville and Holland's yesterday, returning via South Quay. The contraband says there was much rejoicing at Franklin, and the troops turned out on the arrival.

JOHN J. PECK,
Major-General.

SUFFOLK, *February 8, 1863.*

Major-General DIX:

Very intelligent contraband escaped this morning. Has a family here. His master resides 1 mile from Franklin. Yesterday he overheard him and officers talking in the field. Pryor has been re-enforced by Georgia and Louisiana troops; will have 8,000 this week. General Colston has dropped down to Zuni from Petersburg with 12,000; both are coming here in a few days. His account is very honestly given. It looks very plausible. Pryor has been receiving aid; this is confirmatory.

JOHN J. PECK,
Major-General.

SUFFOLK, VA., *February* 8, 1863.

Major-General DIX:

If there is any truth in the information conveyed in my last telegram the force under Colston must be same reported as being camped 8 miles from Petersburg last week; the amounts correspond. Their plan is probably a dash for a few days, while not imperatively called for elsewhere.

Several men have deserted to the enemy.

JOHN J. PECK,
Major-General.

FORT MONROE, *February* 8, 1863.

Major-General PECK:

The Ninth Army Corps is ordered here. One brigade has arrived. I will let them take position at Newport News at present, ready to be thrown in any direction. Keep up your reconnaissances and advise me of any hostile movement.

JOHN A. DIX.

WAR DEPARTMENT,
Washington, February 9, 1863—4 p. m.

Major-General DIX, *Fort Monroe, Va.:*

The Ninth Army Corps, ordered to your command, will be used as you may deem proper. It, however, should be kept together as much as possible. A portion of it may be ordered farther south immediately.

H. W. HALLECK,
General-in-Chief.

NEW YORK, *February* 9, [1863.]

General M. C. MEIGS:

I think there will be no difficulty in accomplishing in New York what we talked of Saturday, for any number of men less than 12,000. If you wish I will send you a detailed report in cipher early to-morrow. It will take a few days to get things ready. You can see General Halleck.

A. E. BURNSIDE.

FORT MONROE, VA.,
February 10, 1863—3 a. m.

Maj. Gen. H. W. HALLECK,
General-in-Chief:

I send a dispatch just received from General Peck. I have telegraphed to the President the news in yesterday's Richmond papers, just received. The Ericsson left two hours ago with her three sub-

marine tows, and is going at the rate of 4 miles an hour. Will you
please advise Secretary of the Navy? Wind west; weather beautiful.

SUFFOLK, VA., *February* 10, 1863.

Major-General DIX :

A contraband from Weldon says very strong and extensive earthworks are constructed on the approaches. He heard that Pettigrew contemplated a raid across
the river, while Pryor would occupy us with his command. A Massachusetts lady
came from Weldon yesterday on her way North. She said that the enemy had 50,000
men near the railroad that could be concentrated at Wilmington, Goldsborough, or
Weldon in a few hours. I give these items as in connection with others that you may
have, that their proper value may be arrived at.

JOHN J. PECK,
Major-General.

JOHN A. DIX,
Major-General.

———

NEW YORK, *February* 10, 1863.

Major-General HALLECK, *General-in-Chief:*

I telegraphed to General Meigs yesterday in regard to obtaining
vessels in New York, and can give you details in cipher if you wish it.*

A. E. BURNSIDE,
Major-General.

———

WASHINGTON, *February* 11, 1863.

Maj. Gen. AMBROSE E. BURNSIDE, *New York:*

Expedition postponed for the present.

H. W. HALLECK,
General-in-Chief.

———

SUFFOLK, *February* 11, 1863.

Major-General DIX :

Pryor has been re-enforced somewhat. I cannot learn of any heavy
force at Zuni. As the Ninth Corps is for some ulterior end I fear promised forces will not be sent at this time.

JOHN J. PECK,
Major-General.

———

FORT MONROE, *February* 11, 1863

Major-General PECK :

Ninth Corps will remain except, it may be, apart. Can we do anything on the New London [Blackwater] by sending it to you, or would
it pay to drive Pryor off? We must economize in forces for great results hereafter.

JOHN A. DIX,
Major-General.

———

SUFFOLK, *February* 12, 1863.

Major-General DIX :

Your claim for the Ninth Corps is strong, and I hope it will remain.
If I had pontoons I would clear out Washington† and New London
[Blackwater] Bridge. In that event the presence of some old troops

———

* Some personal matter omitted.   † Franklin, Va.

from that command would be very essential.   One of the brigades here would enable us to move larger commands and make detachments with safety to them and this place.   How strong is the Ninth Corps?

JOHN J. PECK,
Major-General.

FORT MONROE, *February* 12, 1863.

Major-General PECK:
   The Ninth Corps is 15,000 strong.*

JOHN A. DIX,
Major-General.

HAMPTON ROADS, *February* 13, 1863—7.30 p. m.

General H. W. HALLECK,
      Commander-in-Chief U. S. Army, Washington, D. C.:
   I have just arrived from the South to obtain more heavy guns and ammunition.
   I have reconnoitered the whole coast from Charleston to the Ogeechee River, and can give full information of the state of affairs both naval and military.   While the ordnance is being loaded I can come to Washington to report in person, and with your permission I will do so.

J. G. FOSTER,
Major-General, Comdg. Eighteenth Army Corps.

FORT MONROE, *February* 13, 1863.

Major-General PECK:
   My man will return to Boston [Suffolk] to-night.   Facilitate him in getting through our pickets.   He is to be back in thirty days with important information.

JOHN A. DIX,
Major-General.

[FEBRUARY 13–18, 1863.—For correspondence between Halleck and Foster, in relation to return of the latter to South Carolina, see Series I, Vol. XIV, pp. 400, 402, 403, 408.]

FEBRUARY [16,] 1863.

Major-General FOSTER,
      Commanding Department of North Carolina:
   SIR: On the 5th of January, 1863, at 10.30 o'clock p. m., as Lieutenant Sanders was walking in company with three other men on the principal street in Elizabeth City, N. C., they were fired upon by a party of guerrillas from behind some brick walls, the ruins of burnt buildings.   One of the men was killed instantly.   My brother walked to his quarters and died in half an hour from the time he received the wounds.   The company immediately turned out and succeeded in capturing two of the murderers with their guns in their hands.   We captured several others, but without their arms.   They were placed in prison to await an investigation, which was held, and the innocent set free.

---

* Some details omitted from this dispatch.

The murder of Lieutenant Cox and family occurred on the morning of the 9th of February, 1863, in the following manner: He being a resident of Pasquotank County, and living 16 miles from town, went down for the purpose of moving his family to the city. On his return he was attacked by a gang of guerrillas, who came upon him from a thicket and fired a volley, killing him and a girl of four years old instantly and wounding the wife so that she died on the 13th instant. Three other men of my company were wounded, 1 mortally, 1 badly, 1 slightly.

The team ran to the city, but without any one to tell what had become of its riders, but the marks of blood on the carriage gave evidence of foul play. I immediately sent out an expedition, which returned in the evening with the bodies of Lieutenant Cox and child. This caused great excitement among the people, both civil and military, who urged that something be done to avenge, if possible, or at least to set an example to prevent the committing of such brutal outrages. I was asked by many to take all of those prisoners who could be proven guilty of being guerrillas and have them shot. I was not myself in favor of doing so; but when I thought the matter over deliberately I ordered one prisoner, by the name of A. White, to be brought out and shot, which was done by a brother of Lieutenant Cox, for which I hold myself personally responsible.

E. C. SANDERS,
Captain, Commanding Post at Elizabeth City.

SUFFOLK, VA., *February 16, 1863.*

Major-General DIX:

Major Stratton made a general reconnaissance in the direction of Blackwater, driving in the pickets about Carrsville, capturing 4 sabers, 1 Sharps' carbine, several blankets, and provisions. He examined contrabands who stated Pryor's force about Franklin at 11,000, and that 7,000 were at Black Creek Church with cavalry and "right smart artillery," making 18,000. These agree very nearly with the reports made some ten days since. Major [Stratton] and Captain Loomis credit the report as to the 7,000 and place Pryor's at 7,000 or 8,000 also. Captain Loomis made the captures.

JOHN J. PECK,
Major-General.

WAR DEPARTMENT,
Washington, February 16, 1863.

Major-General BURNSIDE, *Providence, R. I.:*

If agreeable to you to resume the command in North Carolina and of the Ninth Army Corps, please come to Washington.

H. W. HALLECK,
General-in-Chief.

PROVIDENCE, R. I., *February 17, 1863.*

Maj. Gen. H. W. HALLECK:

Your dispatch is received. I leave for Washington at once and will report to you in person.*

A. E. BURNSIDE.

---

* Burnside assumed command of the Ninth Army Corps March 17, 1863.

FORT MONROE, *February* 17, 1863.

Major-General PECK,
        Commanding at Suffolk:

I learn from a Surry County man, whom I think well informed and perfectly reliable, that Pryor's whole force, including a cavalry regiment at Philadelphia,* Albany,* and vicinity does not exceed 7,000 men. He says there is no force between vicinity of New York* and Georgetown* and only a small force at Black Creek Church.

JOHN A. DIX,
        Major-General.

WASHINGTON, D. C., *February* 18, 1863.

Brig. Gen. JOSEPH G. TOTTEN,
        Chief of Engineers:

GENERAL: In consequence of some changes that have been made it will not be necessary to send the pontoon equipage for which General Foster recently made a requisition. The General-in-Chief therefore requests you to retain it in New York until otherwise called for.

Very respectfully, your obedient servant,

G. W. CULLUM,
        Brigadier-General and Chief of Staff.

FORT MONROE, VA., *February* 18, 1863.

General JOSEPH G. TOTTEN,
        Chief Engineer U. S. Army, Washington, D. C.:

Very recent circumstances will prevent my going to the point where I expected to operate. I will therefore withdraw the application for the pontoon bridge to be sent there. I would, however, very much like to have it in North Carolina, if it is not wanted elsewhere.

J. G. FOSTER,
        Major-General, Volunteers.

SUFFOLK, *February* 18, 1863.

Major-General DIX:

Twenty men have deserted from Mounted Rifles since payment—many to the enemy.

What had better be done with goods confiscated from ladies?

JOHN J. PECK,
        Major-General.

HDQRS. DEPT. OF VIRGINIA, SEVENTH ARMY CORPS,
        Fort Monroe, Va., February 18, 1863.

Actg. Rear-Admiral S. P. LEE,
        Commanding North Atlantic Blockading Squadron:

ADMIRAL: The major-general commanding the department directs me to forward to you the inclosed list of vessels in Government employ

---

*Arbitraries peculiar to cipher used by Dix and Peck. Their names not determined.

at this place and vicinity, with the respective dates of assignment and numbers of the flags assigned to such vessels.*

I would also respectfully state that the omission to supply you with the list before was on account of my having supposed that due notice was also given you by the chief quartermaster, Lieutenant-Colonel Thomas, at the same time he furnished it to these headquarters.

I am, very respectfully, your obedient servant,

> **D. T. VAN BUREN,**
> *Assistant Adjutant-General.*

FORT MONROE, *February* 19, 1863.

Major-General PECK:

I am very much dissatisfied with Colonel Dodge and his management. He has allowed his men to plunder the country, and they are now deserting to the enemy. The President has recommended him to the Senate for brigadier-general. This ought not to be.

I think you had better sell Mrs. Portlock's goods at auction. Apply proceeds to public use.

> JOHN A. DIX,
> *Major-General.*

FORT MONROE, VA., *February* 19, 1863.

General H. W. HALLECK,
Commander-in-Chief U. S. Army, Washington, D. C.:

GENERAL: I have the honor to report that I have just had a conversation with Admiral Lee, in which he informed me that his gunboats in the sounds of North Carolina will soon be ready to operate up the Roanoke, Tar, and Neuse Rivers, for the purpose of destroying some iron clad gunboats reported to be building there.

He desires my co-operation, which I propose to give with all my available force. I can do this the more effectively if the Ninth Army Corps be ordered to assist.

If the disposable transportation be limited I think I could manage with the few remaining boats in the sounds to transport this force in detachments from Winfield, on the Chowan River, to the point where the force will be used.

I have the honor to be, very respectfully, your obedient servant,

> J. G. FOSTER,
> *Major-General, Volunteers.*

UNITED STATES FLAG-SHIP MINNESOTA,
Newport News, February 19, 1863.

Maj. Gen. JOHN A. DIX, U. S. A.,
Commanding Seventh Army Corps, Fort Monroe, Va.:

GENERAL: I have received from your assistant adjutant-general a communication dated February 18, inclosing a list of steamers in the employ of the Government at Fortress Monroe and vicinity. I beg to be informed if these are to be considered as additional to those included in the lists sent me in your letters of October 20 and 23. I fear that some irregularities have been occasioned by my not having been promptly

---

*The list, in which alterations were frequently made, is omitted.

supplied, agreeably to the arrangement agreed upon in October, with the names of steamers as they were added to or taken from the original list. Under this arrangement steamers may enter and pass out of the Roads without being recognized as in the employ of your department. To avoid any abuse which might arise out of this custom I have to request that you will issue orders that all steamers shall communicate with the guard vessel in passing between the hours of sunset and sunrise. I will instruct the outer guard vessel accordingly.

I have also to request that you will direct that the flag-of-truce steamers shall be required so to arrange their movements as not to pass the blockade at Newport News at night, as by doing so they are liable to be fired into.

I have the honor to be, general, very respectfully, yours,

S. P. LEE,
Actg. Rear-Admiral, Comdg. N. Atlantic Blockading Squadron.

NORFOLK, *February* 20, 1863.

Major-General DIX:

General Peck's information seems to tally with the reports brought to me that 15,000 men will move in this direction through Princess Anne County. I have examined three men to-night. They are very much frightened and believe all they say.

EGBERT L. VIELE,
Brigadier-General.

SUFFOLK, VA., *February* 20, 1863.

Major-General DIX, *Fort Monroe:*

General Viele has doubtless communicated the information received by him in respect to a contemplated raid or movement of the enemy in this direction. Reports come in from contrabands of re-enforcements from Richmond.

Major Stratton will go to Gatesville and South Mills to-morrow to watch that country.

JOHN J. PECK,
Major-General.

SUFFOLK, VA., *February* 20, 1863.

General VIELE, *Norfolk:*

Major Stratton will start in the morning for Gatesville and South Mills and will watch that section.

JOHN J. PECK,
Major-General.

HDQRS. DEPT. OF VIRGINIA, SEVENTH ARMY CORPS,
Fort Monroe, Va., February 20, 1863.

Actg. Rear-Admiral S. P. LEE,
Commanding North Atlantic Blockading Squadron:

ADMIRAL: I have just received your communication of yesterday. The list of steamers sent you by Colonel Van Buren yesterday shows the additions made to the list furnished you in October. These steamers should have been reported to you at the time they were respectively taken into the service of the Quartermaster's Department; but through a misapprehension in the assistant adjutant-general's office, explained in Colonel Van Buren's letter, they were not reported to me. I will see that no such mistake occurs hereafter, and that all changes are reported the day they are made. I think no inconvenience has resulted from it, as all these steamers have a flag number, and none others are passed without special permits.

All steamers in the service of the army communicate with the guard vessel now, both by night and day, when it is possible. If they are in the quartermaster's service they exhibit a flag with a number corresponding with that on the list which has been furnished. If not in his service they are passed under special permits.

There is a difficulty at night in distinguishing the guard vessel from others, and I respectfully suggest that the one here, as well as the one at Norfolk, may hoist a red light at night, so that our steamers may know and be able to communicate with them.

In regard to flag-of-truce boats, their purpose always is to reach here before night; but Colonel Ludlow is sometimes unavoidably detained, and it may happen, too, that our prisoners cannot be put on board the transports at City Point in time to reach your picket boat until after dark. The prisoners are generally miserably provided for, and a delay of a single night at Newport News would be inconvenient. I therefore propose that you suggest some signal, by whistle or lights, by which the flag-of-truce boats may advise you of their approach. It is not likely that it will be often necessary to use it.

I have the honor to be, very respectfully, your obedient servant,

JOHN A. DIX,
Major-General.

GENERAL ORDERS, } HDQRS. DEPT. OF VA., 7TH ARMY CORPS,
No. 13. } *Fort Monroe, Va., February* 20, 1863.

Lieut. Col. Louis H. Pelouze, assistant adjutant-general, Seventh Army Corps, having reported pursuant to orders from the War Department, is assigned to duty at these headquarters.

By command of Major-General Dix:

D. T. VAN BUREN,
Assistant Adjutant-General.

SUFFOLK, VA., *February* 21, 1863.

Maj. Gen. JOHN A. DIX, *Fort Monroe:*

I do not feel much apprehension about raids upon Norfolk and Portsmouth. Those places are very strong by nature. Tanner's Creek, Eastern, Southern, and Western Branches of the Elizabeth, with their arms, canals, and swamps, almost bar approach at any time, especially when everything is flooded. The rebel lines of defense are well selected, and by maps I have are only about 3 or 4 miles in extent—about one-third of mine. That swamp is a dangerous place for an ordinary force basing upon Blackwater. Had the enemy command of the Albemarle it would be another thing. The enemy must pass via South Mills. The bridges being destroyed, a small redoubt with a regiment and some artillery would bar up the approach.

The only inducement for a cavalry movement by that line would arise from combined operations against Suffolk, at least in the first instance.

JOHN J. PECK,
Major-General.

UNITED STATES FLAG-SHIP MINNESOTA,
Newport News, Va., February 21, 1863.

Maj. Gen. JOHN A. DIX, U. S. A.,
Commanding Seventh Army Corps, Fortress Monroe:

GENERAL: I have received your communication of February 20.

Have directed that the guard vessel off Fort Monroe and Norfolk shall have a red light hoisted between sunset and sunrise. When I wrote you about the flag-of-truce boat I had considered what you now suggest about a signal. The objection to that is this: Any such signal will be quickly understood through informers, and may be badly abused by the enemy. If the exchanged prisoners pass the night of their arrival at Old Point on board the steamer the inconvenience would probably be the same if the flag-of-truce boat should leave City Point at such an hour as would admit of her passing the blockade at daylight.

If this, which appears to me to be quite practicable, cannot be carried out, I will on hearing from you instruct the fleet captain to arrange variable signals with the flag-of-truce boat and the picket vessels.

I have the honor to be, general, very respectfully, yours,

S. P. LEE,
Actg. Rear-Admiral, Comdg. N. Atlantic Blockading Squadron.

HDQRS. DEPT. OF VIRGINIA, SEVENTH ARMY CORPS,
Fort Monroe, Va., February 23, 1863.

Actg. Rear-Admiral S. P. LEE,
Commanding North Atlantic Blockading Squadron ;

ADMIRAL: I have the honor to inclose a letter from Captain Edgar, of the steamer Thomas A. Morgan, the mail boat between this post and Yorktown, setting forth a forcible intrusion into his vessel by Lieutenant Blake, commanding officer of the Mahaska, the guard vessel at Yorktown, and the arrest of Mr. John E. Wilson, his clerk, who was taken on board the said vessel and kept in irons from 4 o'clock in the afternoon to 10 o'clock the next day. I have examined Mr. Wilson and a witness who saw a part of the transaction for which the former was arrested, and their testimony shows that the pilot, Mr. Green, had a quarrel with Mr. Wilson of a private nature, resulting in blows; and from all the facts I think there is no doubt that Mr. Green was the aggressor.

But whatever the merits of the case may be, the act of Lieutenant Blake in stopping the mail steamer in the service of the army and taking one of her officers out of her by force, instead of bringing the case before me, was an outrage which I do not doubt you will call on him promptly to redress.

The delay in bringing the case before you was caused by your absence and by accidentally mislaying Captain Edgar's letter.

I am, very respectfully, your obedient servant,

JOHN A. DIX,
Major-General.

UNITED STATES FLAG-SHIP MINNESOTA,
Off Newport News, Va., February 24, 1863.

Maj. Gen. JOHN A. DIX, U. S. A.,
Commanding Seventh Army Corps, Fortress Monroe, Va. :

GENERAL : I beg leave to acknowledge the receipt of your communication of February 23, covering a letter from Captain Edgar, of the steamer Thomas A. Morgan, in regard to an alleged forcible intrusion into that vessel by Lieutenant Blake, of the Navy, and the seizure and confinement by him of the clerk of that steamer.

This matter will receive prompt attention and the result will be communicated to you as soon as practicable.

I have the honor to be, very respectfully, yours,

S. P. LEE,
Actg. Rear-Admiral, Comdg. N. Atlantic Blockading Squadron.

HEADQUARTERS DEPARTMENT OF VIRGINIA,
Fort Monroe, Va., February 28, 1863.

Capt. W. E. BLAKE, *Provost-Marshal :*

CAPTAIN : You will on receipt of this send Mr. Newbould, the correspondent of the New York Times, out of the department. He has more than once misrepresented the condition of things here. I had last evening a dispatch from Major-General Peck informing me that one of Mr. Newbould's statements in regard to matters in his command was untrue. Representations in regard to a department in contact with the enemy should not only be prudent, but true; and Mr. Newbould in his zeal for the press with which he is connected has not taken pains to ascertain the truth of his statements, rendering corrections necessary, or creating uneasiness which no correction is in time to repair. He is obviously a sensationalist and this is no place for him.

I am, respectfully, yours,

JOHN A. DIX,
Major-General.

HDQRS. DEPT. OF VIRGINIA, SEVENTH ARMY CORPS,
Fort Monroe, Va., February 28, 1863.

Actg. Rear-Admiral S. P. LEE,
Commanding North Atlantic Blockading Squadron :

ADMIRAL : The officer in command of the guard vessel took from the captain of the steamer Planter, which arrived here this morning with troops, his original orders, handing him the copy, which I inclose. I respectfully ask that they may be returned to me. They constitute, with the indorsement of the quartermaster here, the evidence of the performance of the service for which the steamer was chartered, and are necessary for the adjustment of the captain's account with the Quartermaster's Department.

I respectfully ask that you will direct the commander of the guard vessel not to take from transient steamers arriving here with troops or supplies for the army their original orders, but to keep copies, if you require them.

I have the honor to be, very respectfully, yours,

JOHN A. DIX,
Major-General.

Abstract from Tri-monthly Return of the Department of Virginia (Seventh Army Corps), Maj. Gen. John A. Dix commanding, for February 28, 1863 (headquarters Fort Monroe, Va.).

Command.	Present for duty.		Aggregate present.	Aggregate present and absent.	Aggregate last return.	Pieces of field artillery.	Present for duty equipped.					
							Infantry.		Cavalry.		Artillery.	
	Officers.	Men.					Officers.	Men.	Officers.	Men.	Officers.	Men.
Headquarters Fort Monroe.—Maj. Gen. John A. Dix	17	......	17	18	18	....	....	....	....	....	....	....
Fort Monroe.—Col. S. M. Alford:												
Infantry	27	629	811	830	831	....	27	629	....	....	....	....
Attached garrison	....	....	28	28	25	....	....	....	....	....	....	....
Total	27	629	839	858	856	....	27	629	....	....	....	....
Camp Hamilton.—Col. Anthony Conk:												
Infantry	34	662	750	784	786	....	35	689	....	....	....	....
Cavalry	3	75	79	87	87	....	....	....	3	75	....	....
Artillery	12	324	373	388	364	....	....	....	....	....	13	32
Total	49	1,061	1,202	1,259	1,237	....	35	689	3	75	13	32
Norfolk.—Brig.Gen. E. L. Viele:												
Infantry	134	2,402	2,981	3,311	3,418	....	126	2,569	....	....	....	....
Cavalry	2	37	56	80	81	....	....	....	2	37	....	....
Artillery	4	139	154	190	187	6	....	....	....	....	4	18
Total	140	2,578	3,191	3,581	3,686	6	126	2,569	2	37	4	18
Suffolk.—Maj. Gen. J. J. Peck:												
Infantry	380	7,157	8,619	9,689	9,874	....	380	7,157	....	....	....	....
Cavalry	70	1,530	2,058	2,274	2,297	4	....	....	70	1,530	....	....
Artillery	27	818	950	1,336	1,345	30	....	....	....	....	27	84
Total	477	9,505	11,627	13,299	13,516	34	380	7,157	70	1,530	27	84
Yorktown.—Maj. Gen. E. D. Keyes:												
Infantry	191	2,872	3,568	4,207	3,356	....	191	2,872	....	....	....	....
Cavalry	48	1,014	1,244	1,421	1,141	....	....	....	48	1,014	....	....
Artillery	13	372	455	627	637	28	....	....	....	....	13	37
Total	252	4,258	5,267	6,255	5,134	28	191	2,872	48	1,014	13	37
Point Lookout, Md.—Maj. J. C. Brown:												
Infantry	6	150	182	197	197	....	6	150	....	....	....	....
Newport News.—Maj.Gen. William F. Smith:												
Infantry	870	14,406	17,820	25,143	25,431	....	828	14,322	....	....	....	....
Artillery	23	739	836	947	950	38	....	....	....	....	18	72
Total	893	15,145	18,656	26,090	26,381	38	828	14,322	....	....	18	72
Grand total	1,861	33,325	40,981	51,557	51,025	106	1,593	28,388	123	2,656	75	2,4

Abstract from Return of the Department of North Carolina, Maj. Gen. John G. Foster commanding, for the month of February, 1863 (headquarters, New Berne, N. C.).

Command.	Present for duty.		Aggregate present.	Aggregate present and absent.	Aggregate present and absent last monthly return.	Pieces of artillery.	
	Officers.	Men.				Heavy.	Field.
New Berne, N. C., Maj. Gen. John G. Foster, Eighteenth Army Corps.	10	....	10	19	19	......	......
New Berne, N. C., Brig. Gen. I. N. Palmer, First Division.	241	5,251	6,621	7,368	7,453	......	......
Port Royal, S. C., Brig. Gen. H. M. Naglee, Second Division.	....	....	....	6,653	6,778	......	......
Port Royal, S. C., Brig. Gen. O. S. Ferry, Third Division.	27	585	706	5,721	5,794	......	......
New Berne, N. C., Brig. Gen. H. W. Wessells, Fourth Division.	194	2,802	3,649	6,116	6,321	......	......
New Berne, N. C., Brig. Gen. Henry Prince, Fifth Division.	220	4,422	5,183	6,472	7,069	......	......
Port Royal, S. C., Brig. Gen. J. H. Ledlie, Artillery Brigade.	36	940	1,131	2,206	2,210	98	62
New Berne, N. C., Col. S. H. Mix, Third New York Cavalry.	38	620	762	931	927	......	2
Washington, N. C., Brig. Gen. E. E. Potter, First North Carolina (Union) Volunteers.	16	406	486	536	538	......	......
Grand total....................	782	15,026	18,548	36,022	37,109	98	64

REMARKS.—The divisions of Generals Naglee and Ferry are absent on detached service in the Department of the South, with the exception of the Fifty-eighth Pennsylvania Volunteers, of General Ferry's division.

The Twenty-fourth Massachusetts Volunteers and Tenth Connecticut Volunteers, of General Wessells' division, are absent on detached service in the Department of the South.

UNITED STATES FLAG-SHIP MINNESOTA,
Off Newport News, Va., March 1, 1863.

Maj. Gen. JOHN A. DIX, U. S. A.,
Comdg. Seventh Army Corps, Fort Monroe, Va.:

GENERAL: I received this evening your communication dated 28th ultimo. It is necessary that the guard vessel should have an original certificate to send in with the weekly return from the department in order to show the character of a vessel and cargo passing the blockade. The certificate of the quartermaster at Fortress Monroe will answer this purpose, which I respectfully request you will have given in all cases where it is desirable that the vessel should retain her original order. The guard vessel will be directed to return the order to which you refer, and hereafter merely to take the name of the transport having troops on board and afterward get a certificate from the quartermaster. This will be done in order not to detain the troops even to copy the order; but it will be very inconvenient to the guard vessel, in addition to her boarding duties—having no steam-tug to assist her—to do this except in case of troop ships. Even in case of troop transports it would be convenient if the quartermaster, who has tugs at his command, would send the certificate off to the guard vessel.

I have the honor to be, sir, very respectfully, yours,

S. P. LEE,
Actg. Rear-Admiral, Comdg. N. Atlantic Blockading Squadron.

Organization of the Eighteenth Army Corps, commanded by Maj. Gen. John
G. Foster (headquarters New Berne, N. C.), February, 1863.

FIRST DIVISION.

Brig. Gen. I. N. PALMER commanding.

First Brigade.	Second Brigade.
Col. T. J. C. AMORY commanding.	Col. H. C. LEE commanding.
17th Massachusetts.	5th Massachusetts.
43d Massachusetts.	25th Massachusetts.
45th Massachusetts.	27th Massachusetts.
51st Massachusetts.	46th Massachusetts.

SECOND DIVISION.

Brig. Gen. HENRY M. NAGLEE commanding.

First Brigade.	Second Brigade.
Brig. Gen. C. A. HECKMAN commanding.	Col. W. W. H. DAVIS commanding.
23d Massachusetts.	11th Maine.
9th New Jersey.	100th New York.
81st New York.	52d Pennsylvania.
98th New York.	104th Pennsylvania.
	Independent New York Battalion.

THIRD DIVISION.

Brig. Gen. O. S. FERRY commanding.

First Brigade.	Second Brigade.
Col. FRANCIS A. OSBORN commanding.	Col. J. B. HOWELL commanding.
39th Illinois.	56th New York.
62d Ohio.	58th Pennsylvania.
67th Ohio.	85th Pennsylvania.
176th Pennsylvania.	174th Pennsylvania.

FOURTH DIVISION.

Brig. Gen. H. W. WESSELLS commanding.

First Brigade.	Second Brigade.
Brig. Gen. L. C. HUNT commanding.	Brig. Gen. T. G. STEVENSON commanding.
85th New York.	10th Connecticut.
92d New York.	24th Massachusetts.
96th New York.	44th Massachusetts.
101st Pennsylvania.	5th Rhode Island.
103d Pennsylvania.	

FIFTH DIVISION.

Brig. Gen. H. PRINCE commanding.

First Brigade.	Second Brigade.
Brig. Gen. F. B. SPINOLA commanding.	Col. JAMES JOURDAN commanding.
132d New York.	3d Massachusetts Militia.
158th Pennsylvania.	8th Massachusetts Militia.
171st Pennsylvania.	158th New York.
175th Pennsylvania.	168th Pennsylvania.

ARTILLERY BRIGADE.

Brig. Gen. J. H. LEDLIE commanding.

3d New York Artillery.
23d Independent New York Battery.
24th New York Battery.
1st Rhode Island Artillery Battery F.
1st U. S. Artillery, Company C.

CAVALRY.

Col. S. H. MIX commanding.

3d New York Cavalry.

UNATTACHED.

Brig. Gen. EDWARD E. POTTER.

1st North Carolina (Union) Volunteers.

FORT MONROE, VA., *March* 2, 1863.

Maj. Gen. H. W. HALLECK, *Chief of Staff:*

A demonstration was made on the enemy's lines yesterday which brought out a considerable force. An attack was to have been made on one of his batteries last night, but was probably postponed for want of boats, to be brought from Norfolk. Every effort will be made to ascertain promptly his strength. I telegraphed General Peck on the subject last night, after my return from Suffolk, in consequence of a dispatch from General Butterfield stating that Hood's and Pickett's divisions were reported in Hooker's front. I have just received a dispatch from General Peck in which he says deserters from Pickett's division state that they saw Pickett yesterday and that no brigades have gone from Longstreet's command. They received orders to be ready to move last night, but the orders were countermanded. One of the deserters, a Texan, says that Hood was there yesterday. Jenkins' division is before Suffolk. I will direct General Peck to make a reconnaissance in force, and will be ready to make the movement referred to by you promptly.

JOHN A. DIX,
Major-General, Commanding.

HEADQUARTERS EIGHTEENTH ARMY CORPS,
New Berne, March 2, 1863.

Maj. Gen. H. W. HALLECK,
General-in-Chief U. S. Army, Washington, D. C.:

GENERAL: I have received information that the *corps d'armée* of Maj. Gen. D. H. Hill is within the limits of this State and that he commands this department. General Longstreet's corps, it is thought, has gone either to the southwest or to the vicinity of Charleston.

I referred in my last letter to some iron-clads being constructed on the Tar and Roanoke Rivers. It is understood that the one on the Roanoke River is nearly completed, and to prevent its being destroyed by our gunboats before it is ready for service the enemy have assembled a large force at Hamilton, said to be 7,000 infantry, 1,000 cavalry, and seven batteries of between six and eight pieces each.

The fortifications at Rainbow Bluff, just below Hamilton, destroyed by me last November, are being repaired and heavy guns being mounted from Weldon.   A considerable force is at Weldon and the enemy are busily engaged in fortifying that point.

My present force of artillery and the fact that my best troops have been sent to the Department of the South will not allow me to attack Hamilton with any reasonable prospect of success.

To prevent the enemy from putting their threat into execution of taking the town of Plymouth, taking the gunboats, or driving them out of the river, I propose to re-enforce that point, and at the same time I have prepared a strong reconnaissance, under General Prince, to move in the direction of Wilmington, and so prevent too great an accumulation of force on the Roanoke until such time as I shall be strong enough to attack with advantage.   The command is only waiting for a suitable condition of the roads to move, the recent rains having rendered them almost impassable.

I remain, general, very respectfully, your obedient servant,

J. G. FOSTER,
Major-General, Commanding.

UNITED STATES FLAG-SHIP MINNESOTA,
Newport News, March 3, 1863.
Maj. Gen. JOHN A. DIX, U. S. A.,
Commanding Seventh Army Corps, Fort Monroe, Va.:

GENERAL: I inclose Lieutenant Blake's explanation for your perusal, when please return it to me.   You will see that the circumstances of the case had not been fully and correctly represented to you.   Still the course pursued by this young officer, then in temporary command of the Mahaska, was irregular and injudicious.   I regret the occurrence, and am sure that no official discourtesy was intended.

I have the honor to be, general, very respectfully, yours,

S. P. LEE,
Actg. Rear-Admiral, Comdg. N. Atlantic Blockading Squadron.

SUFFOLK, VA., *March* 3, 1863.
Major-General DIX:

Colonel Spear has just reported the result of a reconnaissance toward Franklin.   From sources that he says are entirely reliable the enemy is reported at 20,000.

JOHN J. PECK,
Major-General.

MARCH 3.
Major-General PECK, *Suffolk:*

It is reported that a company of the Mounted Rifles have deserted to the enemy.   I cannot credit the report.   It is also reported that two of the companies refused to go on picket duty.   It is important that I should know the truth of these reports at once.

JOHN A. DIX,
Major-General.

SUFFOLK, *March 3, 1863.*

Maj. Gen. JOHN A. DIX:

The indorsement of Colonel Dodge is as follows:

Not one individual member of the Mounted Rifles has ever refused to do any duty. No company has deserted nor is there any possible probability of such an occurrence. About 20 men have deserted since 1st January—12 of them together; can satisfactorily explain why. The *morale* of the regiment was never better than it is to-day. My reasons for believing this are reliable, and will satisfy any one of the entire want of foundation for such rumors as are sent.

> CHARLES C. DODGE,
> *Colonel, &c.*

Have called for a report, which I will forward.

> JOHN J. PECK,
> *Major-General.*

SUFFOLK, *March 4, 1863.*

Major-General DIX:

Spear left at 11 last night, with the most profound secrecy, to cut off a guard on this side the bridge at Franklin. Two men deserted thirty minutes before he passed the pickets and carried the information to Franklin. All was ready for his reception—artillery, infantry, &c. He lost none but captured three. His last dispatch says Longstreet and Jackson are there with re-enforcements. Of the latter there can be but little doubt; as to those generals I cannot say. Longstreet has been reported in the West, which I do not believe.

> JOHN J. PECK,
> *Major-General.*

FORT MONROE, VA.,
March 4, 1863—9.20 a. m.

Maj. Gen. H. W. HALLECK,
General-in-Chief:

It is reported to me from Richmond that nearly all the insurgent army has left Fredericksburg, and are moving to North Carolina and the Blackwater. A deserter from Richmond also states that there were but 30,000 men at Fredericksburg a week ago. I have just received the following dispatch from General Peck:

SUFFOLK, VA., *March 3, 1863.*

Major-General DIX:

The news from Blackwater is that the Ninth Corps is here or arriving, on the supposition that the enemy has been re-enforced to 20,000. A relative of Jefferson Davis is in command where Pryor has been. The artillery is especially mentioned as being the best in the South. Some new cavalry reported. This comes from persons residing in different places, and Spear credits it. Spear is going out this evening.

> JOHN J. PECK,
> *Major-General.*

> JOHN A. DIX,
> *Major-General.*

SUFFOLK, VA., *March 5, 1863.*

Major-General DIX:

Colonel Spear has returned. He reports 20,000 on the Blackwater. General Colston is there. General Longstreet is at Petersburg with two divisions of his corps. He visits Blackwater once or twice every week; Jackson not there. Pryor has been to Richmond to give account of his operations before a court of inquiry and returned yesterday. Reports are contradictory that I get from prisoners.

> JOHN J. PECK,
> *Major-General.*

HDQRS. FIRST DIVISION, EIGHTEENTH ARMY CORPS,
New Berne, March 5, 1863.

Lieut. Col. SOUTHARD HOFFMAN,
Assistant Adjutant-General:

SIR: I have the honor to report, for the information of the commanding general of the department, the following facts relative to the arrest of certain citizens of Edenton by the military authorities in the Department of Virginia, and of the carrying away of certain horses by the same authority:

It appears that after the firing upon a party of Dodge's cavalry, and the killing of one of them by some guerrillas near Edenton, a military force was sent to that place and arrested some 8 or 10 persons. On my recent inspecting tour I had an interview with the mayor and principal citizens of Edenton for the purpose of ascertaining all the facts in the case. The citizens appear to be much outraged at the appearance of guerrilla parties in their vicinity, as of course they must suffer for it. They do not pretend to say anything in favor of some of those who were arrested, and say they are rejoiced that they have been carried away, as they are troublesome, bad men, and one or two of them are deserters from the rebel army.

Inclosed I send statement signed by those citizens concerning Joshua T. Stacy, Moses Hobbs, Seth Parker, John Coffield, John S. Leary, and J. S. Leary, jr., six of the persons arrested and carried to Suffolk.

The citizens who make these statements are said to be loyal men. My belief is that they have at least remained always, since Edenton has been in our possession, peaceable and quiet and desirous of doing no act against the United States authorities; and I think it nothing more than my duty to request you to bring the matter to the early attention of the commanding officer of the Department of Virginia in order that a fair investigation may be had in the several cases.

I am, sir, respectfully, your obedient servant,

> I. N. PALMER,
> *Brigadier-General Volunteers.*

SUFFOLK, VA., *March 6, 1863.*

Major-General DIX:

Three very intelligent non-commissioned officers have been out toward Blackwater looking for deserters. Last night they passed themselves for Confederates and had the freedom of the house of a leading rebel near Windsor, from whom they picked up many items. He said from 20,000 to 25,000 were on Blackwater; that a new general was there and they were coming over so soon as the river fell sufficiently. It was high and some bridges had been damaged. Their spies knew all about Suffolk; that we had 12,000, and two gunboats. These numbers agree very nearly with information I received from numerous quarters and from men of good judgment and general information.

> JOHN J. PECK,
> *Major-General.*

showing the position of the gunboat at A, and I request that she may be required to be removed and placed as far west as B, and that this fort and the anchoring ground between it and Hampton be left open to the access of vessels, as it was under Admirals Goldsborough and Wilkes, not only to such as have army supplies but such as come here for shelter, subject to the usual revenue and military inspection, which is never omitted.

There is an immense contraband traffic carried on between the York and Rappahannock Rivers, and the steamer which is blockading us might render a valuable service in that quarter instead of creating annoyance to the army here.

I have the honor to be, very respectfully, your obedient servant,

JOHN A. DIX,
Major-General.

SUFFOLK, *March* 7, 1863.

Major-General DIX, *Fort Monroe:*

The proposed exchange reminds me that the infantry force here is very low, considering its very recent organization. Bayonets of men for duty, 7,100; aggregate, 8,300. Should an attack be made during stormy weather, when communication is interrupted between Old Point and Norfolk, the enemy might possibly gain some advantage.

JOHN J. PECK,
Major-General.

FORT MONROE, VA., *March* 9, 1863.

Major-General HALLECK,
General-in-Chief:

I have just received the following dispatch from General Peck:

SUFFOLK, VA., *March* 9, 1863.

Major-General DIX:

Colonel Dodge has just returned from Blackwater beyond Windsor. His advance was fired upon by rebel cavalry. He charged them, following down Bridge road, and captured 4, with 5 horses and other equipments. The party crossed over. His information is corroborative of all we have of the force of the enemy. Prisoners give twenty-odd thousand on the river. General Hill had been there, but thought he was not there now. Additional cavalry regiments are mentioned; also new batteries. Pryor not in command.

JOHN J. PECK.

JOHN A. DIX,
Major-General.

FORT MONROE, VA., *March* 9, 1863.

Maj. Gen. H. W. HALLECK,
General-in-Chief:

The account of 20,000 men on the Blackwater is confirmed from many quarters. There is a large force at Petersburg and Drewry's Bluff. Very few troops at Richmond.

JOHN A. DIX,
Major-General.

FORT MONROE, VA., *March* 11, 1863.

Maj. Gen. H. W. HALLECK,
    General-in-Chief U. S. Army:

I have just received the following dispatch from General Peck:

SUFFOLK, VA., *March* 11, 1863.

General JOHN A. DIX:

The Fifty-second and Fifty-fifth North Carolina and two Mississippi regiments are among the late arrivals; deserters say large regiments; that General Longstreet has command, with headquarters at Petersburg. He sent a division to Charleston, which is returning to Petersburg for Fredericksburg. Two regiments, Virginians, under orders for Petersburg from Blackwater.

JOHN J. PECK,
    Major-General.

JOHN A. DIX,
    Major-General.

SUFFOLK, *March* 11, 1863.

Major-General DIX:

Charleston Mercury of 26th February has the following:

Longstreet's division of Lee's army is in motion. Some 15,000 passed through Richmond. They took the route pointing to the south side of the James.

This has been verified by the general reports since about that time. Of late, some reported a division going to South Carolina. To-day the deserters say it is back again, and will probably go to Fredericksburg.

JOHN J. PECK,
    Major-General.

HEADQUARTERS EIGHTEENTH ARMY CORPS,
    New Berne, N. C., March 11, 1863.

Maj. Gen. H. W. HALLECK,
    General-in-Chief U. S. Army, Washington, D. C.:

GENERAL: Referring to my letter of March 2 I have the honor to report that the reconnaissance of General Prince has returned and reported. General Prince proceeded up the south side of Trent River to Trenton, meeting with no opposition; he found the bridges over the Trent at that point not rebuilt. He then retraced his steps for Pollocksville; thence to Young's Cross-Roads; thence crossing the White Oak River to Onslow. The cavalry force under his command thoroughly scouted the country between White Oak and New Rivers, scattering all the small parties of the enemy in that vicinity. After obtaining all information possible he returned.

A reconnaissance, under command of Brigadier-General Potter, and consisting of a portion of the Fifty-first Massachusetts Volunteer Militia, a section of artillery, and detachment of cavalry, proceeded to Swansborough, on White Oak River. They met with no opposition.

A reconnaissance was sent up Trent road toward Kinston, consisting of the Twenty-fifth Regiment, under command of Colonel Pickett, and two companies Third New York Cavalry, under Captain Jacobs. A portion of this command proceeded to within 12 miles of Kinston, surprising an outpost of the enemy (two companies) at that point, capturing 5 prisoners, their camp equipage, &c.

Colonel Jones, commanding picket line, pushed a reconnaissance to Core Creek and drove the enemy back in that direction. A force was sent to Hyde County to catch certain guerrillas in that county and to break up a smuggling trade in corn and forage. This party was ambuscaded, and lost, before they dispersed the enemy, 4 killed and 13 wounded from the Third New York Cavalry. On their return, as I found the object had not been thoroughly accomplished, I sent a larger force, under command of Colonel Morris, One hundred and first Pennsylvania Volunteers. From this I have not yet heard.

The information derived from these various scouts is, briefly—

Thirty-eight thousand rations are issued daily from Goldsborough to troops within drawing distance. This in all probability includes the forces at Goldsborough, Kinston, Tarborough, Kenansville (west of Onslow, near the railroad), and possibly the force on the Roanoke River, leaving Weldon and Wilmington as separate points of issue.

The information given in mine of March 2, as to the force on Roanoke River, has been confirmed, both as to position and numbers. The iron-clad, also mentioned, is again reported as being now ready.

Owing to the dearth of transportation in this department at present I shall have to await the return of the expedition to Hyde County in order to send re-enforcements to Plymouth, which I propose to do, and also to erect a battery there capable of defending the town, holding the mouth of the river, and assisting the Navy in repelling the iron-clads.

Owing to the fact that so large a portion of my light artillery is now in the Department of the South (a picked force) it is necessary to mount two companies Third New York Artillery, and I have made the requisitions (to-day's mail) for two batteries of Napoleon guns, complete, and for the requisite number of horses. I trust this will meet your approval, and that the guns and horses will be at once ordered.

I omitted to mention that General Dix having kindly offered to scout from Norfolk and Suffolk, with his cavalry, in the direction of Edenton, Elizabeth City, and Winfield, I have embraced the offer, and shall concentrate the forces at these small posts, Plymouth, and Roanoke. The small posts above-named were difficult to re-enforce or support, and yet some force should be in this direction, and this relieves me of the weight.

Your favor of the 4th of March, on the subject of the Maine artillery, has just come to hand, and in obedience thereto I am taking the necessary steps to muster out such members of that organization as do not voluntarily join some other arm of the service.

I am, general, with great respect, your obedient servant,

J. G. FOSTER,
Major-General, Commanding.

SUFFOLK, *March* 12, 1863.

Maj. Gen. JOHN A. DIX:

There has been some mystery about Longstreet's moves, but the following from Charleston Mercury settles all doubt:

Longstreet has been appointed by the President to the department made vacant by the resignation of General Smith. This department includes South Virginia and North Carolina. General Longstreet's headquarters will be at Petersburg.

JOHN J. PECK,
Major-General.

SUFFOLK, *March* 12, 1863.

Major-General DIX:

Certain letters have this moment reached me to the effect that an attack upon Suffolk is to be made. One is from the signal officer of Norfolk. In it he says that every preparation is being made at Franklin to render the affair successful. The information he regards as from good sources.

Some person who has run the blockade gives it as the current report in Richmond.

JOHN J. PECK,
Major-General.

SUFFOLK, *March* 12, 1863.

Major-General DIX:

The reported increase on Blackwater has resulted from the movement of troops into your department. My impression has been that they were watching our moves. Longstreet's position with supports near Petersburg wears a threatening appearance, and may form the basis of the reports from Norfolk.

JOHN J. PECK,
Major-General.

FORT MONROE, *March* 12, 1863.

Major-General PECK,
    Commanding at Suffolk:

In view of reports you mention I shall send you 5,000 men, probably 2,000 to-morrow, from Newport News.

JOHN A. DIX,
Major-General.

SUFFOLK, *March* 12, 1863.

Major-General DIX:

Colonel Stetzel is 9 miles below Gatesville. Reports an attack by guerrillas some days ago, who were driven off by the troops and gunboat.

JOHN J. PECK,
Major-General.

FORT MONROE, VA.,
March 13, 1863—11 a. m.

Maj. Gen. H. W. HALLECK,
    General-in-Chief U. S. Army:

General Longstreet is in command of the forces at Richmond and on the Blackwater, in place of General Gustavus W. Smith, resigned. In view of the large re-enforcements on the Blackwater I have ordered Getty's division of the Ninth Army Corps to Suffolk. The rest are at Newport News.

JOHN A. DIX,
Major-General, Commanding.

HEADQUARTERS OUTPOSTS,
March 13, [1863]——6.30 p. m.

Lieut. Col. SOUTHARD HOFFMAN,
Assistant Adjutant-General:

SIR : The information of the attack on our Trent River posts reached me just now, on my return from an expedition to Core Creek, Street's Ferry, &c. My companies have not yet returned, but four of them are expected every minute; too tired, however, to move by the Tuscarora road and try the flank of any enemy that may be there. The best I can do will be to strengthen my posts and wait further intelligence and events. Three of my companies who were sent to examine the country near the Neuse River and Core Creek will not probably be back tonight.

Meanwhile I have no immediate use for the locomotive and send it in. If I had a few fresh troops I would move on the line indicated, Tuscarora and Red House road.

In the course of an hour or so I shall proceed to the Red House.

Very respectfully, your obedient servant,
J. RICHTER JONES,
Colonel, Commanding.

————

HEADQUARTERS OUTPOSTS,
March 14, 1863.

Lieut. Col. SOUTHARD HOFFMAN,
Assistant Adjutant-General :

SIR: I have the honor to report that from information received through Captain Willson, Company H, whom I sent on a reconnaissance at 3 p. m. this morning, I learn that a force of the enemy, not supposed large, are on Trent road near the Gully. My men are very tired, having marched 30 miles yesterday, and returned only at 11 p. m, but I shall move half my command by the Tuscarora road to re-enforce the Trent posts and, if opportunity be offered, attack the enemy's flank or front, according to circumstances.

Respectfully, your obedient servant,
J. RICHTER JONES,
Colonel, Commanding Outposts.

I propose holding this post to the last extremity, even to the risk of having to cut my way through, and then shall leave a garrison in my unfinished block-house.

————

HEADQUARTERS OUTPOSTS,
March 15, [1863]——8 o'clock p. m.

Lieut. Col. SOUTHARD HOFFMAN,
Assistant Adjutant-General :

SIR : I have just returned from a reconnaissance to Deep Gully, &c. I found no enemy there, nor within 3 miles beyond, and from information I obtained it would seem that the main body of their force moved away last evening and the residue early this morning, in full retreat.

From the examination I made they had eight pieces in battery in the field behind the Gully, and had a front of about 1,200 yards deployed, enveloping and turning our Deep Gully position on both flanks. From the signs on the ground made by the recoil of pieces, &c., tney fired but little.   They did not approach the Red House nor move on the Red House road.

   Very respectfully, your obedient servant,

         J. RICHTER JONES,
        Colonel Fifty-eighth Pennsylvania Volunteers.

     HDQRS. FIFTY-FIRST MASSACHUSETTS REGIMENT,
         Beaufort, N. C., March 15, 1863.

Lieut. Col. SOUTHARD HOFFMAN,
   Assistant Adjutant-General. :

 COLONEL : No train arriving yesterday, and receiving intelligence last night at 10 o'clock from Lieutenant-Colonel Studley that New Berne was attacked, I went up on hand-car after midnight to Newport Barracks, thinking there might be trouble there.   Found everything all right.   No signs of the enemy in that vicinity.   About 5 miles above, at the signal station, a single rail was removed from the track by a small party of rebel cavalry, 12 or 15 in number.   The number is verified by different persons.   I traced them several miles from the railroad.   They passed down last night within 2 miles of the track about 5 p. m. and returned at 8 p. m.   Our cavalry companies have been scouting, and no enemy is in that vicinity.   Are on the alert all along the line.

   Yours, truly,

        [A. B. R.] SPRAGUE,
        Colonel Fifty-first Massachusetts.

         SUFFOLK, *March* 16, 1863.

Major-General DIX :

 What will be done with General Dodge ?   I wish to make Spear chief of cavalry.   He will attempt the capture of the guard at Washington, with cavalry and infantry, about dawn, although roads are horrible.

         JOHN J. PECK.

     UNITED STATES FLAG-SHIP MINNESOTA,
       Off Newport News, March 16, 1863.

Maj. Gen. JOHN A. DIX, U. S. A.,
  Commanding Seventh Army Corps, Fortress Monroe, Va. :

 GENERAL : Commander Creighton has been informed that there are a number of wagons at Gloucester Court-House and the vicinity obtaining forage and provisions for the rebel forces ; that there are 500 rebel cavalry at Gloucester Court-House and 1,000 rebel cavalry at Saluda Court-House, and that their horses are in a very bad condition.

  I have the honor to be, sir, very respectfully, yours,

         S. P. LEE,
   Actg. Rear-Admiral, Comdg. N. Atlantic Blockading Squadron.

     WASHINGTON, N. C., *March* 16, 1863.

Lieut. Col. SOUTHARD HOFFMAN :

 COLONEL : I send with this a note from Lieutenant-Colonel Lyman, giving you all the information he has been able to obtain.   He seems to have no apprehension of attack, but if the rebels come we will try to give them a warm reception. I have sent my men to quarter on Grice's plantation.

Yours, with respect,

FRANCIS L. LEE,
Colonel Forty-fourth Regt. Massachusetts Vol. Militia.

[Inclosure.]

HEADQUARTERS,
Washington, N. C., March 16, 1863.

Lieutenant-Colonel HOFFMAN:

DEAR SIR: I have to report that I know nothing of the movements of the enemy except that we have heard from the direction of Plymouth and Williamston and nothing doing in that direction. I hear of nothing in the direction of Greenville beyond Tranter's Creek upon the opposite side of the Tar River. I hear nothing and of course have nothing to report. The enemy have not allowed any communications across the river for some days. Everything, so far as we know, about our lines remains the same as usual.

I am, in great haste, respectfully, yours,

LUKE LYMAN,
Lieutenant-Colonel, Commanding Post.

———

WASHINGTON, N. C., *March* 16, 1863.

Lieutenant-Colonel HOFFMAN,
Assistant Adjutant-General, Eighteenth Army Corps:

COLONEL: Since my first note I am informed by the provost-marshal that one of Mr. Grice's family slaves states that "massa says the d——d Yankees will smell hell here before next Saturday night."

The said Grice is preparing to move himself and family out to a plantation which he says is about 3 miles out. When I asked him why he moved he said, "Well, it is best for a family man to be in a quiet place, and when the lightning plays one can't tell where it will strike." I am informed several of the secesh families are moving from the place. I may feel called upon to detain these emigrants, but in regard to that I shall consult with Colonel Lyman.

Colonel Lyman thinks it unwise to close the lines to-night, but Grice's departure will depend upon what we may learn hereafter. I send the above for what it is worth, thinking you perhaps would be the better judge of that.

Your obedient servant,

FRANCIS L. LEE,
Colonel Forty-fourth Regt. Massachusetts Vol. Militia.

———

FORT MONROE, *March* 17, 1863.

Major-General PECK:

I do not intend that General Dodge shall command the cavalry force at Suffolk. I shall make some other arrangement if he is put on duty in my command.

JOHN A. DIX,
Major-General.

SUFFOLK, VA., *March* 17, 1863.

Maj. Gen. JOHN A. DIX, *Commanding Seventh Corps:*

You will be pleased to learn that Lieutenant Hill, of the New York Mounted Rifles, with a patrol of 10 men, captured the noted forager, Brown, and 6 men between Windsor and the Blackwater. Three of the rebels escaped in the woods. Brown has managed many of the supply trains of General Pryor. The tact and determination evinced by this officer and his party deserve the favorable notice of the Government.

JOHN J. PECK,
Major-General.

HEADQUARTERS EIGHTEENTH ARMY CORPS,
New Berne, N. C., March 17, 1863.

Maj. Gen. H. W. HALLECK,
General-in-Chief U. S. Army, Washington, D. C.:

GENERAL: I have the honor to most respectfully and earnestly request that the detachment of the Eighteeenth Army Corps now in the Department of the South be ordered to return here. My reasons for this request are the accounts from Port Royal show that there is no immediate prospect of a movement from that place, and the withdrawal of troops therefore would not be detrimental to the service; also the enemy are in large force in this State and becoming aggressive. General D. H. Hill is in immediate command, and the expressed determination of General Longstreet is to "clean out the Yankees from the State of North Carolina." Again, with the detachment of my troops returned I would be able to make some important movements in this State, cutting the railroad again, and, if a movement on the Blackwater were made simultaneously, perhaps reaching Weldon.

The enemy have a moving column 30,000 strong and with abundance of artillery. They should be met, and my picked troops and best artillery being absent I am utterly unable to do so.

I trust, general, that the above reasons given will be favorably received by you, and that in my request you will see a desire for the good of the service. I consider that we are perfectly able to act on the defensive here, but with the return of my detachment, from the lack of spirit displayed by the enemy in their recent demonstration, I feel confident that I can overpower the enemy here.

I have the honor to be, general, with great respect, your obedient servant,

J. G. FOSTER,
Major-General, Commanding.

FORT MONROE VA.,
March 17, 1863—4 p. m.

Maj. Gen. AMBROSE E. BURNSIDE, *Washington, D. C.:*

The First and Second Divisions are here. The Third Division, General Getty, has gone to Suffolk, viz, Ninth, Eighty-ninth, and One hundred and third New York; Tenth and Thirteenth New Hampshire; Eighth, Eleventh, Sixteeenth, and Twenty-first Connecticut; Fourth and Seventh Rhode Island, and Twenty-fifth New Jersey. The last left to-day, except the Ninth New York, which leaves to-morrow. General Willcox commands the corps; Ferrero the post of Newport News.

WM. H. FRENCH,
Captain.

SPECIAL ORDERS, } HDQRS. OF THE ARMY, ADJT. GEN.'S OFFICE,
No. 125.   }   Washington, March 17, 1863.

*   *   *   *   *   *   *

III. Brig. Gen. Henry M. Naglee, U. S. Volunteers, will report for duty to Major-General Foster, commanding Department of North Carolina.

*   *   *   *   *   *   *

By command of Major-General Halleck:

L. THOMAS,
Adjutant-General.

FORT MONROE, VA.,
March 18, 1863—8.30 p. m.

Maj. Gen. H. W. HALLECK, *General-in-Chief:*

General Peck has ascertained by very authentic testimony that the forces on the Blackwater are from 27,000 to 30,000, corresponding with my statement last evening. A portion has crossed the river and are intrenched on this side. Colonel Spear attacked one of their earthworks yesterday, but did not succeed in carrying it. Our loss is trifling. We captured a lieutenant, and, I understand, a few privates.

JOHN A. DIX,
Major-General.

FORT MONROE, VA., *March* 18, 1863.

Maj. Gen. H. W. HALLECK, *General-in-Chief:*

My man arrived from Richmond late last evening. He was at Staunton on the 7th. General Jones was in command with 35,000 men. Near Culpeper Court-House there were 1,800. He was at Fredericksburg on the 9th. The enemy had one hundred and seven regiments there, making, as he thinks, about 85,000. The regiments have been strengthened lately by conscripts. At Fort Darling there are about 7,000; between Fredericksburg and Richmond about 15,000; below Fredericksburg and on the Blackwater, 28,000. At Richmond there are not over 3,000. Wise, on the left bank of the James River, on the Chickahominy, at White House, and Diascund Bridge, has about 9,000. The enemy has reoccupied Fort Powhatan, on the right bank of the James River, with 4,000 men, and is fortifying strongly. This is a part of the 28,000 between Fredericksburg and the Blackwater. All my information confirms the belief that every man capable of bearing arms that could be reached in the insurgent States has been taken up by the conscription act.

JOHN A. DIX,
Major-General, Commanding.

FORT MONROE, VA.,
March 18, 1863—10 a. m.

Maj. Gen. AMBROSE E. BURNSIDE:

Received your dispatch of yesterday. Have reported to General Dix. He informs me that Getty's division has been sent to Suffolk. Willcox and Sturgis are still at Newport News. Shall I order Getty and Sturgis? It may cause a little delay to replace Getty at Suffolk by Willcox.

JNO. G. PARKE,
Major-General.

WASHINGTON, D. C., *March* 18, 1863.

Maj. Gen. JOHN G. PARKE:

General Halleck says to take Willcox's and Sturgis' divisions. Tell Getty he will follow very soon.

A. E. BURNSIDE,
Major-General.

FORT MONROE, VA.,
March 18, 1863—8 p. m.

Maj. Gen. AMBROSE E. BURNSIDE:

Willcox will commence the embarkation to-morrow. General Dix loaned the command a number of tents, and he wishes them returned. Both Willcox and Sturgis will require shelter-tents. I will get their requisitions and forward them to you. General Smith is absent. I will get a list of the staff belonging to the corps now on duty with it and send it to you for disposition.

JNO. G. PARKE,
Major-General.

NEWPORT BARRACKS, N. C., *March* 18, 1863.

Lieut. Col. SOUTHARD HOFFMAN:

COLONEL: I have learned from persons who have come from the vicinity of Peletier's Mills, about 17 miles from here, that there was a large force of cavalry at that place last Saturday night, but went away Sunday—some set the number as high as 1,500—and that General Robertson was in command. Their wagons were left at Smith's Mill on White Oak River. It is said there was a brigade in that vicinity, but nothing has been heard of them since Sunday. The two companies of cavalry stationed at this post are out in that direction (Peletier's) to-day, with instructions to learn if possible what troops they were.

Yours, &c.,

J. M. STUDLEY,
Lieutenant-Colonel, Commanding Post.

SUFFOLK, VA., *March* 19, 1863.

Maj. Gen. JOHN A. DIX:

One brigade of Pickett's division, commanded by General Bratton, is at Franklin (the First, Fifth, Sixth South Carolina, and First South Carolina Sharpshooters constitute a part of his command); General Colston's brigade of North Carolina and Mississippi troops is here—all under Longstreet, who is near Petersburg. The two other brigades of Pickett's are near the railway, some miles this side Petersburg. Baker's cavalry came from Raleigh, 1,000 strong. The servant of Colonel Baker says that General Hill would attack New Berne or had already done so. This he overheard.

JOHN J. PECK,
Major-General.

FORT MONROE, *March* 19, 1863.

Major-General PECK:

The two divisions at Newport News have been ordered out of the department. Getty's remains with you. New Berne has been feebly attacked. The rebels have retired.*

JOHN A. DIX,
Major-General.

FORT MONROE, VA.,
March 19, 1863—5.10 p. m.

Maj. Gen. AMBROSE E. BURNSIDE, *Commanding:*

One brigade of Willcox's division is embarked and part of the second; also a battery of artillery; but it is not proper that they should start. A severe snow-storm set in this morning and still continues, and as the steamers will have to wait until it is over I have ordered the embarkation to be postponed. Shall the ammunition and ambulance train of the First Division follow the division, or wait until the Second Division is embarked? General Smith is still absent. The chief quartermaster has not yet reported for duty; went west with General Burns. Captain Van Ness, acting, absent on leave. Dr. McDonald is absent with leave; all others present. Bowen, Coale, and Chambloss were assigned to the Ninth Corps, and Babcock to the Sixth, by orders from the War Department of March 1. It appears that these assignments are ordered by the President. Should not therefore those remain that are assigned to the Ninth Corps? The following list of officers composing the staff of the Ninth Corps was furnished me by Colonel Bowen, assistant adjutant-general: Lieut. Col. N. Bowen, assistant adjutant-general; Lieut. Col. O. E. Babcock, assistant inspector-general; Lieut. Col. John H. Coale, chief commissary; Colonel Chambliss, chief quartermaster; Dr. P. A. O'Connell, acting medical director; Dr. J. E. McDonald, medical inspector; First Lieut. O. M. Dearborn, ordnance officer; First Lieut. S. N. Benjamin, acting chief of artillery; Capt. T. B. Marsh, chief of ambulance corps.

JNO. G. PARKE,
Major-General.

FORT MONROE, VA.,
March 20, 1863—12 noon.

Maj. Gen. AMBROSE E. BURNSIDE:

The storm still continues and it is impossible to do anything. The transports cannot leave on account of the storm. As soon as it subsides I will start the transports and continue the embarkation. The men now on board are of course consuming rations, and provision should be made to replenish their stock in Baltimore.

JNO. G. PARKE,
Major-General.

(Copy to General Halleck.)

SUFFOLK, *March* 20, 1863.

Major-General DIX, *Fort Monroe:*

The storm is of great severity. In anticipation, I did all I could for the comfort of Getty's division. A deserter from Second Mississippi came in last night; belongs to General Davis' brigade of Mississippians

---

* Some matters of detail omitted.

which arrived recently from Goldsborough, N. C.   Second, Eleventh, and Forty-second Mississippi are part of brigade.   Says he is sure of four brigades.   Some North Carolina regiments are there also.   Has family in Pontotoc, Miss., and is tired of the war.

Have sent an order to Lieutenant James, as requested.

JOHN J. PECK,
Major-General.

HDQRS. FORTY-FOURTH REGT. MASS. VOL. MILITIA,
Washington, N. C., March 20, 1863.

Lieut. Col. SOUTHARD HOFFMAN,
Assistant Adjutant-General, Eighteenth Army Corps:

COLONEL : Since my note of March 16 I have deemed it prudent to keep the lines here closed.   The cavalry have made daily scouts upon the Jamestown and Greenville roads, and we have gathered only this : That it seems to be a general impression upon the minds of all the inhabitants, white and black, outside the rebel lines, that we are likely to be attacked at any time, and that the enemy have considerable forces in motion in this vicinity.

Lieutenant-Colonel Lyman does not seem to think there is much chance of an attack; still I have thought best to make every preparation in my power, and we will try to give them a warm reception if they come.

The last news we have heard of the enemy's movements was that Pryor's brigade was at Greenville on Monday and that Pettigrew's brigade was between Swift Creek and Greenville on Tuesday, moving slowly up toward that place, stripping the country of provisions of every description.

To-day we have a report of the supposed presence of a force (" right smart," be that large or small) at Tranter's Creek.   I will venture to suggest that if you have any reason to apprehend any immediate attack here a battery of artillery, say Belger's, and a company of cavalry would greatly strengthen the defense.   The rain has been heavy here to-day and yesterday, which it is thought may delay their attack if they still contemplate one.

I am, your obedient servant,

FRANCIS L. LEE,
Colonel, Commanding Post.

SUFFOLK, *March* 21, 1863.

Major-General DIX:

Nothing new.   Storm still continues.   Snow 4 inches.   Is it not time for your peddler [spy] to return?   He will be able to report much information, especially about matters on this side James River.

JOHN J. PECK,
Major-General.

UNITED STATES FLAG-SHIP MINNESOTA,
Off Newport News, Va., March 21, 1863—5 p. m.

Maj. Gen. JOHN A. DIX, U. S. A.,
Fortress Monroe, Va.:

Reconnaissance to-day shows no occupation of the old rebel forts at Day's Point and Burwell's Bay on the right bank of James River.

S. P. LEE,
Actg. Rear-Admiral, Comdg. N. Atlantic Blockading Squadron.

FORT MONROE, *March* 22, 1863.

Major-General PECK:

My man has been here and has gone to Baltimore. He says there are 28,000 men between New London* and the New York.* When they find the Ninth Army Corps withdrawn from Newport News they may reduce their force.

JOHN A. DIX,
Major-General.

HDQRS. FORTY-FOURTH REGT. MASS. VOL. MILITIA.,
Washington, N. C., March 23, 1863.

Lieutenant-Colonel HOFFMAN,
Assistant Adjutant-General:

COLONEL: On Saturday Lieutenant-Colonel Lyman notified me that he had received intelligence from what he considered "good authority" that the enemy had " moved away from our front"; that a large force was 10 miles from us last Monday, but had disappeared.

Of course that may or may not be correct, but I should judge by all we can learn that it is true. Yesterday Colonel Lyman learned at old Mr. Griert's that the Army of the Potomac, under Hooker, had crossed the Rappahannock; but we can get no papers, as the rebels allow no one to pass through their lines and no mail matter to pass out.

I would remind you that we left New Berne at two hours' notice and with no idea of a longer stay than ten days' rations implied. You told me that you should probably send a boat up to bring us back on Sunday, the 22d. We not only had no time to pack up our property which we left behind, but we brought nothing but a spare under-suit and the men not even that, as they were ordered to take only blankets. In this condition we are extremely uncomfortable, and the men will soon become sick on account of unavoidable filth. I would therefore venture to suggest that to avoid sickness the regiment should be recalled whenever it may be thought that this place is safe from attack.

I am, your obedient servant,

FRANCIS L. LEE,
Colonel, Commanding Post.

I send by this boat the men detailed for the census business.

LEE,
Colonel.

SPECIAL ORDERS, } HDQRS. OF THE ARMY, ADJT. GEN.'S OFFICE,
No. 136.   }   *Washington March* 23, 1863.

*   *   *   *   *   *   *

II. Brig. Gen. E. L. Viele, United States Volunteers, is hereby relieved from duty in the Department of Virginia, and will report in person without delay to Maj. Gen. D. Hunter, United States Volunteers, commanding Department of the South, for duty.

*   *   *   *   *   *   *

By command of Major-General Halleck:

L. THOMAS,
Adjutant-General.

---

* Cipher.

FORT MONROE, *March* 26, 1863.

Major-General HALLECK:
          General-in-Chief:

I have received the order relieving General Viele, but no one is assigned to the position of Military Governor of Norfolk. It is a place always, and especially at this moment, of the greatest importance and delicacy, and it needs a man of promptness, decision, prudence, integrity, and capacity to bear labor and annoyance. I am trying by a military commission incendiaries, blockade runners, and other malefactors, and though the sentences are not divulged, it is understood that they are very severe. I subjoin a dispatch from General Viele, just received:

NORFOLK, *March* 26, 1863.

Major-General DIX:

If the regiment you spoke of sending here could come at once I think it would be well. An attack was made last night on the pickets at Fort Norfolk. Dr. Green, the rebel surgeon, withdrew his parole at dark and requested to be confined. This excited suspicion, and the pickets were doubled. At the same time an attempt was made to fire the public stores in the city. I have taken stringent measures. I think the arrest and trial of Spence and Drummond and others has excited their friends to organize for their release. I have directed that all fire-arms shall be at once delivered to the provost-marshal, and shall allow no one in the streets after 9 o'clock.

          EGBERT L. VIELE,
                    Brigadier-General.

I have in my possession one of the combustibles with which it was attempted to fire the public stores, very artistically constructed. The theater is to be closed to-night, and the streets ordered to be cleared at 9 o'clock.

          JOHN A. DIX,
                    Major-General.

———

FORT MONROE, *March* 26, 1863.

Major-General HALLECK,
          General-in-Chief:

I will not leave until everything is quiet and until General Keyes returns. It is very important that he should come back as soon as possible. General Busteed asked my permission this morning to burn Williamsburg.

          JOHN A. DIX,
                    Major-General.

———

YORKTOWN, *March* 26, 1863.

Major-General DIX:

GENERAL: A telegram has just reached me that our pickets at Williamsburg were fired on this morning by a number of the enemy's infantry. A continual warfare of this character is kept up against us at and about the town. I am of the deliberate judgment that the only way of our immunity lies in the destruction of Williamsburg, and if you will approve it I would give the inhabitants notice that upon a repetition of these attacks the place should be destroyed. The town is a stronghold of rank traitors.

          RICHARD BUSTEED,
                    Brigadier-General, Commanding.

FORTRESS MONROE, VA., *March* 26, [1863].

General BUSTEED, *Yorktown:*

Our troops at Williamsburg must defend themselves as long as they can and drive off assailants. We must not destroy towns unless they are actually taken possession of by the enemy, and then not unless absolutely necessary for our own safety.

JOHN A. DIX,
Major-General.

———

HEADQUARTERS THIRD NEW YORK CAVALRY,
New Berne, March 26, 1863.

Lieut. Col. SOUTHARD HOFFMAN,
Assistant Adjutant-General, Eighteenth Army Corps:

COLONEL: I have the honor to report that in obedience to the accompanying order I left New Berne yesterday morning at 7 o'clock and arrived at Mill Creek at 10.45 a. m.; finding the bridge entirely destroyed, I awaited the arrival of the pioneer corps; the bridge not being completed until night, we remained in bivouac on this side of the creek until 6 o'clock this morning, when I moved the column to McDaniel's plantation, 4 miles beyond Pollocksville; arriving at which place I dispatched a squadron and one howitzer under Major Fitz Simmons to Young's Cross-Roads and a like command under Captain Pond to Trenton, giving each officer instructions in compliance with the order and verbal instructions from you. Between the hours of 11 and 12 the officers above named reported back to me, each reporting that there had been no vestige of Confederate troops in that vicinity for several days past. I immediately took up the line of march for New Berne, arriving here at 5 o'clock this evening.

It gives me pleasure to report that Lieutenant-Colonel McNary, in command of the One hundred and thirty-second and One hundred and fifty-eighth New York Volunteers, obeyed every request made by me.

I regret, colonel, my inability to perform the "big thing" you desired.

Very respectfully, your obedient servant,

G. W. LEWIS,
Lieutenant-Colonel, Third New York Cavalry.

[Inclosure.]

NEW BERNE, *March* 24, 1863.

Lieutenant-Colonel LEWIS,
Commanding Third New York Cavalry:

COLONEL: Information has been received that a pontoon train is *en route* for the White Oak River. You will therefore proceed with six companies cavalry and Allis' battery to-morrow a. m. to Pollocksville; gather all the information you can of any movements of this train; ascertain their purpose, if possible, and endeavor to intercept or catch them. Bring the train in, if practicable; if not, burn it.

You will necessarily use your own judgment in carrying out this movement. An infantry regiment will be sent toward and to Pollocksville.

The best way to take the train, if there be no evidence of trap, is the main object; the secondary one to ascertain what the object of the enemy is in sending the train to White Oak River.

By order of Brigadier-General Palmer:

SOUTHARD HOFFMAN,
Assistant Adjutant-General.

WAR DEPARTMENT,
Washington, March 27, 1863.

Major-General DIX, *Fort Monroe, Va.:*

General Viele was ordered south, by direction of the Secretary of War, under impression that General King was sufficient at Norfolk. General Hunter is much in want of generals. If you deem General Viele's services so necessary at present you can suspend the execution of the order.

H. W. HALLECK,
General-in-Chief.

FORT MONROE, VA., *March 27,* 1863.

Col. J. C. KELTON,
Assistant Adjutant-General:

The regiments and batteries of the Ninth Corps remaining under my command are as follows, and compose the Third Division of that corps, now at Suffolk, commanded by General Getty: First Brigade, consisting of Ninth New York, Eighty-ninth New York, One hundred and third New York, and Tenth New Hampshire; Second Brigade, consisting of Eighth, Eleventh, Fifteenth, and Sixteenth Connecticut; and Third Brigade, consisting of Twenty-first Connecticut, Thirteenth New Hampshire, Twenty-fifth New Jersey, and Fourth Rhode Island. Artillery consists of Battery A, Fifth United States, and A, First Pennsylvania.

JOHN A. DIX,
Major-General.

HDQRS. DEPT. OF VIRGINIA, SEVENTH ARMY CORPS,
Fort Monroe, Va., March 28, 1863.

Capt. C. B. WILDER,
Assistant Quartermaster, Superintendent of Contrabands:

Captain Wilder is authorized to take possession of the farm of Jefferson Sinclair, an absentee disloyalist, and the buildings thereon. If the present occupant, Mr. William H. Lynch, will take the oath of allegiance and agree to pay quarterly in advance such rent as Captain Wilder may deem fair for twenty acres of the land and such portion of the dwelling as he needs, Mr. Wilder may allow him to do so; the same also of the Fayette Sinclair farm and its occupant, Mr. Charles L. Collier; the same of Messrs. Hicks and Bowen, on the Booker Jones farm; the same of the farms of Benjamin Hudgins, Eliza Jones, John and Helen Moore, Levin Winder, John Winder, William Smith, Robert Hudgins; the George Booker farm—not, however, disturbing the Howard family; the Lowry farm, the Watts farm, the farm of B. Howard, called the Stakes farm, occupied by Mr. Host, and the Armstead farm, occupied by Hicks. The colored persons on these farms, if any, must come under Mr. Wilder's system of labor. The white tenants who will take the oath of allegiance and engage to pay rent as aforesaid are not to be expelled, but only to be limited to such portions of land and shelter as they require for their comfortable support, and are to be notified that any act of disorder or outrage will be visited with immediate removal as well as with legal penalties.

Captain Wilder will report to the provost-judge his proceedings under this order and will attend to the collection and payment into court of the rents. He will take and report an inventory of all personal property belonging to each estate, and not allow any property to be removed, except on his written permit, without General Dix's orders.

By command of Major-General Dix:

[JOHN A. BOLLES,]
Major and Aide-de-Camp, Provost-Judge.

SUFFOLK, VA., *March* 28, 1863.

Major-General Dix:

Have just returned from Western Branch by water. Found a deserter there. Several came in this morning. All agree with the statements made heretofore of not less than 12,000 or 15,000 immediately on the river; expecting more. General Longstreet was there last week and with Jenkins came over at Blackwater Bridge and recrossed near Zuni. Your new regiment of Virginia near Zuni. Cavalry force increased by another regiment.

JOHN J. PECK,
Major-General.

SUFFOLK, *March* 28, 1863.

Major-General Dix:

You are at liberty to say to General Halleck that I concur with your views touching the command of the cattle [cavalry?] as expressed in your telegram of this date.

JOHN J. PECK,
Major-General.

SUFFOLK, *March* 28, 1863.

Major-General Dix:

Have just returned from below the Western Branch with gunboat. Yesterday rode over the east side with my horse, devoting the day. Can be crossed most anywhere with three pontoons. Shall commence works at the point selected by the rebels for the new road. Their piles were down for the bridge. We have removed most of them. The position is half way, or 4 miles by water, while only two direct corn [roads]. One air [brigade] or two regiments there will make the line secure.

JOHN J. PECK,
Major-General.

SUFFOLK, VA., *March* 30, 1863.

Major-General Dix:

A sergeant of the engineers deserted Saturday night to the enemy. He has been on the works all the time and can give much valuable information. Sharp fellow, and probably has been bought.

JOHN J. PECK,
Major-General.

HDQRS. DEPT. OF VIRGINIA, SEVENTH ARMY CORPS,
Fort Monroe, Va., March 30, 1863.

Maj. Gen. J. G. FOSTER,
    Commanding Department of North Carolina :

GENERAL : I received your letter in regard to occupying the District of North Carolina north of Albemarle Sound and east of the Chowan River and forwarded it to the General-in-Chief, not being authorized to send troops out of this department except in cases of emergency and for temporary purposes.

I also received yours of the 25th, dated Chowan River, &c., and immediately telegraphed to the General-in-Chief a summary account of the expedition of Colonel Brown, of the Forty-second North Carolina Regiment, and its results.

It will afford me great pleasure to co-operate with you in every way possible in furtherance of the objects of the Government.

I am, very respectfully, your obedient servant,

JOHN A. DIX,
Major-General.

Internal and Coastwise Intercourse.

By the President of the United States of America.

A PROCLAMATION.

Whereas in pursuance of the act of Congress approved July 13, 1861, I did by proclamation, dated August 16, 1861, declare that the inhabitants of the States of Georgia, South Carolina, Virginia, North Carolina, Tennessee, Alabama, Louisiana, Texas, Arkansas, Mississippi, and Florida (except the inhabitants of that part of Virginia lying west of the Alleghany Mountains, and of such other parts of that State, and the other States hereinbefore named, as might maintain a loyal adhesion to the Union and the Constitution, or might be from time to time occupied and controlled by forces of the United States engaged in the dispersion of said insurgents) were in a state of insurrection against the United States, and that all commercial intercourse between the same and the inhabitants thereof, with the exceptions aforesaid, and the citizens of other States and other parts of the United States was unlawful, and would remain unlawful until such insurrection should cease or be suppressed, and that all goods and chattels, wares and merchandise coming from any of said States, with the exceptions aforesaid, into other parts of the United States without the license and permission of the President, through the Secretary of the Treasury, or proceeding to any of said States, with the exceptions aforesaid, by land or water, together with the vessel or vehicle conveying the same to or from said States, with the exceptions aforesaid, would be forfeited to the United States. And whereas experience has shown that the exceptions made in and by said proclamation embarrass the due enforcement of said act of July 13, 1861, and the proper regulation of the commercial intercourse authorized by said act with the loyal citizens of said States :

Now, therefore, I, Abraham Lincoln, President of the United States, do hereby revoke the said exceptions, and declare that the inhabitants of the States of Georgia, South Carolina, North Carolina, Tennessee, Alabama, Louisiana, Texas, Arkansas, Mississippi, Florida, and Virginia (except the forty-eight counties of Virginia designated as West Virginia, and except also the ports of New Orleans, Key West, Port Royal and Beaufort in North Carolina) are in a state of insurrection against the United States, and that all commercial intercourse, not licensed and conducted as provided in said act, between the said States and the inhabitants thereof, with the exceptions aforesaid, and the citizens of other States and other parts of the United States, is unlawful and will remain unlawful until such insurrection shall cease or has been suppressed, and notice thereof has been duly given by proclamation; and all cotton, tobacco, and other products, and all other goods and chattels, wares and merchandise coming from any of said States, with the exceptions aforesaid, into other parts of the United States, or proceeding to any of said States, with the exceptions aforesaid, without the license and permission of the President, through the Secretary of the Treasury, will, together with the vessel or vehicle conveying the same, be forfeited to the United States.

In witness whereof I have hereunto set my hand and caused the seal of the United States to be affixed. Done at the city of Washington this 31st day of March, A. D. 1863, and of the Independence of the United States of America the eighty-seventh.

By the President:

                                      A. LINCOLN.

WILLIAM H. SEWARD,
         Secretary of State.

                            SUFFOLK, VA., *March 31, 1863.*

Major-General DIX:

Yesterday the enemy came over to the vicinity of Carrsville with one or two regiments of infantry for the purpose of ambuscading our patrolling parties. They were secreted in woods on both roads, about 2 miles this side the place. Major Cornog, with some 160 men, was on his way to Carrsville to return by the Deserted House. His advance of 20 men, under a lieutenant, passed the center of the lines, when the enemy showed themselves; singular to say, all escaped save one.

Our cavalry pickets expected an attack last night, but all passed in quiet.

                                JOHN J. PECK,
                                  Major-General.

                      HEADQUARTERS FOURTH CORPS,
                          Yorktown, March 31, 1863.

Colonel LEWIS, *Commanding at Williamsburg:*

Let me hear at once all you know of the enemy's present force and position.

In case of an attack in force send down the public property. Hold Fort Magruder and shell the town the moment an armed enemy is known to be within it.

Let me hear from you frequently so long as the enemy remains in your neighborhood.

                                E. D. KEYES,
                                  Major-General.

Abstract from Tri-monthly Return of the Department of Virginia (Seventh Army Corps), Maj. Gen. John A. Dix commanding, for March 31, 1863 (headquarters Fort Monroe, Va.).

Command.	Present for duty. Officers.	Present for duty. Men.	Aggregate present.	Aggregate present and absent.	Aggregate last return.	Pieces of field artillery.	Present for duty equipped. Infantry. Officers.	Infantry. Men.	Cavalry. Officers.	Cavalry. Men.	Artillery. Officers.	Artillery. Men.
Headquarters Fort Monroe.— Maj. Gen. John A. Dix	16	......	16	18	18	....	......	......				
Fort Monroe.—Col. S. M. Alford:												
Infantry	20	522	710	828	828	....	20	522				
Attached garrison	......	......	28	28	28	....						
Total	20	522	738	856	856	....	20	522				
Camp Hamilton.—Col. Anthony Conk:												
Infantry	29	651	729	777	777	....	30	677				
Cavalry	3	69	78	84	86	....			3	69		
Artillery	10	314	364	379	374	....					14	326
Total	42	1,034	1,171	1,240	1,237	....	30	677	3	69	14	326
Norfolk.—Brig. Gen. E. L. Viele:												
Infantry	136	2,561	3,090	3,232	3,212	....	120	2,536				
Cavalry	2	49	60	88	88	....			2	49		
Artillery	4	138	154	167	167	6					4	138
Total	142	2,748	3,304	3,487	3,467	6	120	2,536	2	49	4	138
Suffolk.—Maj. Gen. J. J. Peck:												
Infantry	640	11,752	14,250	17,457	17,599	....	637	11,756				
Cavalry	66	1,510	2,015	2,255	2,257	4			66	1,510		
Artillery	28	1,001	1,142	1,254	1,257	40					28	1,012
Total	734	14,263	17,407	20,966	21,113	44	637	11,756	66	1,510	28	1,012
Yorktown.—Maj. Gen. E. D. Keyes:												
Infantry	199	2,920	3,566	4,168	4,174	....	199	2,920				
Cavalry	47	972	1,225	1,397	1,408	....			47	1,067		
Artillery	16	356	440	609	616	28					16	359
Total	262	4,248	5,231	6,174	6,198	28	199	2,920	47	1,067	16	359
Independent Battalion New York Volunteers.*	......	......	......		197	....						
Grand total	1,216	22,815	27,867	32,741	33,086	78	1,006	18,411	118	2,695	62	1,835

Organization of troops in the Department of Virginia, Maj. Gen. John A. Dix, U. S. Army, commanding, March 31, 1863.

FORT MONROE.

Col. S. M. ALFORD.

3d New York.

CAMP HAMILTON.

Col. ANTHONY CONK.

139th New York, Col. Anthony Conk.
11th Pennsylvania Cavalry, Company C, Capt. John Cassels.
3d Pennsylvania Artillery (battalion), Maj. John A. Darling.

---

* Maj. J. C. Brown commanding, left March 30 for Department of the South.

NORFOLK.

Brig. Gen. EGBERT L. VIELE.

148th New York, Col. William Johnson.
173d Pennsylvania, Col. Daniel Nagle.
177th Pennsylvania, Lieut. Col. H. J. Brady.
19th Wisconsin, Lieut. Col. C. Whipple.
11th Pennsylvania Cavalry, Company F, Capt B. B. Mitchell.
7th New York Battery, Capt. P. C. Regan.

SUFFOLK.

Maj. Gen. JOHN J. PECK.

PECK'S DIVISION.

Corcoran's Brigade.

Brig. Gen. MICHAEL CORCORAN.

69th New York, Col. M. Murphy.
155th New York, Col. William McEvily.
164th New York, Col. J. P. McMahon.
170th New York, Col. J. P. McIvor

Terry's Brigade.

Brig. Gen. H. D. TERRY.

99th New York, Col. D. W. Wardrop.
130th New York, Col. Alfred Gibbs.
1st New York Battalion Sharpshooters, Capt. Thomas Bradley.
167th Pennsylvania, Lieut. Col. J. D. Davis.

Foster's Brigade.

Col. R. S. FOSTER.

13th Indiana, Lieut. Col. C. J. Dobbs.
6th Massachusetts, Col. A. S. Follansbee.
112th New York, Col. J. C. Drake.
165th Pennsylvania, Col. C. H. Buehler.
166th Pennsylvania, Col. A. J. Fulton.

GETTY'S DIVISION.

Brig. Gen. GEORGE W. GETTY.

First Brigade.

Col. HARRISON S. FAIRCHILD.

10th New Hampshire, Col. M. T. Donohoe.
9th New York, Col. R. C. Hawkins.
89th New York, Capt. Joseph Morrison.
103d New York, Col. B. Ringold.

Second Brigade.

Col. EDWARD HARLAND.

8th Connecticut, Lieut. Col. John E. Ward.
11th Connecticut, Col. G. A. Stedman, jr.
15th Connecticut, Lieut. Col. Samuel Tolles.
16th Connecticut, Col. Frank Beach.

Third Brigade.

Col. A. H. DUTTON.

21st Connecticut, Maj. H. B. Crosby.
13th New Hampshire, Col. A. F. Stevens.
25th New Jersey, Col. A. Derrom.
4th Rhode Island, Lieut. Col. M. P. Buffum.

Artillery.

1st Pennsylvania, Battery A, Capt. J. G. Simpson.
5th U. S., Battery A, Lieut. James Gilliss.

UNASSIGNED.

1st New York Mounted Rifles, Lieut. Col. B. F. Onderdonk.
11th Pennsylvania Cavalry, Col. Samuel P. Spear.
7th Massachusetts Battery, Captain P. A. Davis.
3d Pennsylvania Heavy Artillery (battalion), Capt. John A. Blake.
4th U. S. Artillery, Batttery D, Capt. F. M. Follett.
4th U. S. Artillery, Battery L, Lieut. H. C. Hasbrouck.
2d Wisconsin Battery, Capt. Charles Beger.
4th Wisconsin Battery, Capt. John F. Vallee

YORKTOWN.

Maj. Gen. ERASMUS D. KEYES.

Busteed's Brigade.

Brig. Gen. RICHARD BUSTEED.

4th Delaware, Col. A. H. Grimshaw.
168th New York, Col. William R. Brown.
169th Pennsylvania, Col. Lewis W. Smith.
178th Pennsylvania, Col. James Johnson.
179th Pennsylvania, Col. William H. Blair.

Unassigned.

172d Pennsylvania, Col. Charles Kleckner.
2d Massachusetts Cavalry (First Battalion), Maj. C. Crowninshield.
6th New York Cavalry (Third Battalion), Maj. W. P. Hall.
5th Pennsylvania Cavalry, Lieut. Col. William Lewis.
1st New York Artillery, Batteries F and H, Capts. W. R. Wilson and C. E. Mink.
8th New York Battery, Capt. Butler Fitch.
1st Pennsylvania Artillery, Batteries E and H, Lieut. C. B. Brockway and Capt. Andrew Fagan.
5th U. S. Artillery, Battery M, Capt. James McKnight.

Abstract from Monthly Return of the Eighteenth Army Corps, Maj. Gen. John G. Foster commanding, for the month of March, 1863 (headquarters New Berne, N. C.).

Command.	Present for duty.		Aggregate present.	Aggregate present and absent.	Aggregate last monthly return.	Pieces of artillery.	
	Officers.	Men.				Heavy.	Field.
Eighteenth Army Corps, Maj. Gen. J. G. Foster.	20	....	20	20	19	....	......
First Division, Brig. Gen. I. N. Palmer.........	233	5,181	6,468	7,286	7,368	....	.....
Second Division, Brig. Gen. H. M. Naglee........				6,653	6,653		
Third Division, Brig. Gen. O. S. Ferry..........	26	553	698	5,708	5,721	....	......
Fourth Division, Brig. Gen. H. W. Wessells......	154	2,159	2,692	5,884	6,116	....	......
Fifth Division, Brig. Gen. H. Prince.............	213	4,310	5,090	6,220	6,472	....	......
Artillery Brigade, Brig. Gen. J. H. Ledlie.......	30	742	930	2,165	2,206	83	6
3d New York Cavalry, Col. S. H. Mix	38	619	752	914	981	....	2
1st North Carolina	12	382	455	561	536	....	......
Grand total	726	13,946	17,105	35,411	36,022	83	7

Organization of troops in the Eighteenth Army Corps, Department of North Carolina, commanded by Maj. Gen. J. G. Foster, for March, 1863. *

FIRST DIVISION.

Brig. Gen. INNIS N. PALMER commanding.

First Brigade.

Col. T. J. C. AMORY commanding.

17th Massachusetts, Lieut. Col. J. F. Fellows.
43d Massachusetts, Col. Charles L. Holbrook.
45th Massachusetts, Col. Charles R. Codman.
51st Massachusetts, Col. A. B. R. Sprague.

Second Brigade.

Col. H. C. LEE commanding.

5th Massachusetts, Col. George H. Peirson.
25th Massachusetts, Col. Josiah Pickett.
27th Massachusetts, Lieut. Col. Luke Lyman.
46th Massachusetts, Col. W. S. Shurtleff.

SECOND DIVISION.†

Brig. Gen. CHARLES A. HECKMAN commanding.

First Brigade.

Col. JACOB J. DE FOREST commanding.

23d Massachusetts, Lieutenant-Colonel Elwell.
9th New Jersey, Col. Abram Zabriskie.
81st New York, Lieut. Col. William, C. Raulston.
98th New York, Lieut. Col. F. F. Wead.

Second Brigade.

Col. W. W. H. DAVIS commanding.

11th Maine, Col. H. M. Plaisted.
52d Pennsylvania, Col. John C. Dodge, jr.
104th Pennsylvania, Lieut. Col. T. D. Hart.
Independent New York Battalion, Lieut. Col. Felix Comfort.

THIRD DIVISION.

Brig. Gen. ORRIS S. FERRY commanding.

First Brigade.‡

Col. J. B. HOWELL commanding.

56th New York, Lieut. Col. J. J. Wheeler.
58th Pennsylvania, Col. J. R. Jones.
85th Pennsylvania, Maj. Edw. Campbell.
174th Pennsylvania, Col. John Nyce.

Second Brigade.‡

Col. FRANCIS A. OSBORN commanding.

39th Illinois, Col. T. O. Osborn.
62d Ohio, Col. F. B. Pond.
67th Ohio, Col. A. C. Voris.
176th Pennsylvania, Col. A. A. Lechler.

FOURTH DIVISION.

Col. T. F. LEHMANN commanding.

First Brigade.

Col. J. S. BELKNAP commanding.

85th New York, Maj. R. V. King.
92d New York, Lieut. Col. Hiram Anderson.
96th New York, Maj. Charles H. Burhans.
101st Pennsylvania, Col. David B. Morris.
103d Pennsylvania, Lieut. Col. W. C. Maxwell.

Detachment Second Brigade.

Col. FRANCIS L. LEE commanding.

10th Connecticut (detachment), Lieut. W. W. Webb.
24th Massachusetts (detachment), Lieut. T. F. Edmands.
44th Massachusetts, Lieut. Col. E. C. Cabot.
5th Rhode Island, Col. H. T. Sisson.

---

* Compiled from division and brigade returns.
† Detailed in Department of the South.
‡ It appears from brigade return that these two brigades were consolidated into one by General Hunter's order of March 26, 1863. All these regiments except the Fifty-eighth Pennsylvania detailed in Department of the South.

FIFTH DIVISION.

Brig. Gen. HENRY PRINCE commanding.

First Brigade.	Second Brigade.
Brig. Gen. F. B. SPINOLA commanding.	Col. JAMES JOURDAN commanding.
158th Pennsylvania, Col. D. B. McKibbin. 168th Pennsylvania, Col. Joseph Jack. 171st Pennsylvania, Col. Everard Bierer. 175th Pennsylvania, Col. Samuel A. Dyer.	3d Massachusetts, Col. S. P. Richmond. 8th Massachusetts, Lieut. Col. J. Hudson. 132d New York, Lieut. Col. G. H. Hitchcock. 158th New York, Lieut. Col. W. H. McNary.

ARTILLERY BRIGADE (Eighteenth Army Corps).

Lieut. Col. CHARLES H. STEWART commanding.

3d New York, Lieut. Col. Charles H. Stewart.
23d New York Independent Battery, Capt. Alfred Ransom.
24th New York Independent Battery, Capt. Jay E. Lee.
1st Rhode Island, Battery F, Capt. James Belger.
1st U. S., Company C, Lieut. William K. Pollock.

HEADQUATERS EIGHTEENTH ARMY CORPS,
New Berne, N. C., April 1, 1863.

Brig. Gen. LORENZO THOMAS,
Adjutant-General U. S. Army, Washington, D. C.:

GENERAL : Being in temporary command at this point I have the honor to report that General Foster is at Washington, N. C., which point is probably now being attacked by the enemy in force.

There are two regiments in the town as garrison, and three regiments and one battery of artillery have been sent to General Foster, but have not been able as yet to get up, the enemy having a battery on the river below the town. Commander Davenport, U. S. Navy, has sent the only available gunboats from here to engage the battery.

The enemy are in large force in this State now and mean to act on the offensive. I will inform you whatever may arise.

I am, general, with great respect, your obedient servant,
I. N. PALMER,
Brigadier-General, U. S. Volunteers.

HEADQUARTERS EIGHTEENTH ARMY CORPS,
New Berne, N. C., April 1, 1863.

Maj. Gen. JOHN A. DIX,
Commanding Seventh Army Corps :

GENERAL : I have the honor to inform you that General Foster is at Washington, N. C., where an attack in strong force is probably now going on. Re-enforcements have been started to him, but as yet have not been able to get up to the town, the enemy having a battery on the river below the town. Two gunboats have gone up to engage the battery.

It is possible an attack may be made here whilst the general and his troops are kept at Washington. Our force is not very large, and I may have to call on you for a little aid. We have no transportation.

I write this for your information, and relying on your kind assistance if desirable.

I am, general, very respectfully, your obedient servant,

I. N. PALMER,
Brigadier-General Volunteers.

P. S.—There is a fair prospect of success for the rebels at Washington, and if they succeed this place ought to be attacked: I only suggest to you, general, as "food for thought," whether it would not be best to re-enforce this place with, say, 5,000 men temporarily? We are sadly in need of gunboats. Cannot you prevail upon Admiral Lee to re-enforce here temporarily? I have written to the admiral, or, rather, the senior naval officer here has done so.

Very respectfully,

I. N. PALMER.

FORT MONROE, *April* 2, 1863.
To the Editor of the New York Times:

Your Washington correspondent has attributed to me an opinion I have never expressed to any one here or elsewhere—that the enemy is about to evacuate Richmond. I have no information to warrant such a conclusion. I should not deem it necessary to contradict the statement if you had not made it the foundation of an elaborate editorial.

JOHN A. DIX,
Major-General.

NEW BERNE, N. C., *April* 2, 1863.
Maj. Gen. JOHN A. DIX,
Commanding Department of Virginia, Fort Monroe:

GENERAL: Captain Murray, of the Navy, who has been the senior naval officer here, will see you and explain the situation of affairs. His ideas of the kind of re-enforcements needed coincide with mine. Your letter to General Foster, in which you state that you will be obliged to consult the commanding general before sending forces to Elizabeth, was received this morning. I gather from that letter that you would not probably act upon my request of yesterday. Should you do so, however, and should the necessity for the re-enforcements be passed, I shall keep a small steamer on the lookout for any transports to turn them back. The commodore (Murray) will be able to inform you of matters generally.

There is a large force of the enemy in this State, and they appear to be determined to assume the aggressive.

Very respectfully, yours,

I. N. PALMER,
Brigadier-General, Commanding.

FORT MONROE, VA., *April* 3, 1863—8.30 p. m.
Maj. Gen. H. W. HALLECK,
General-in-Chief:

A division has arrived on the Blackwater from Petersburg and another division, under General Hood, is said to be coming. They have brought pontoons with them. This looks like a design to cross the Nansemond River, between Norfolk and Suffolk, where there is a weak spot. I directed General Peck to fortify it. He has done so, and besides the troops there we have three gunboats, one of which will be constantly in motion. Washington, N. C., has been attacked. General Foster is there and re-enforcements are going to him. He fears an attack on New Berne. A gentleman from Massachusetts, just arrived at Suffolk, says the railroad between Goldsborough and Weldon is lined with troops, he thinks 30,000; the rebels say from 50,000 to 75,000. They say they have between Blackwater and Wilmington 75,000 which can be concentrated in a short time. I will be in Washington on Monday morning.

JOHN A. DIX,
Major-General.

UNITED STATES FLAG-SHIP MINNESOTA,
Off Newport News, April 3, 1863.
Maj. Gen. JOHN A. DIX, U. S. A.,
Comdg. Seventh Army Corps, Fortress Monroe, Va.:

GENERAL: Mr. Hume, a citizen of New York, came to me this morning presenting a letter from General Viele in his behalf, asking permission to take a vessel to Suffolk to carry some staves thence to Norfolk. Having no authority to give such a permit, I told him that if he had a proper permit from General Dix he could pass. Since then I have considered that my instructions do not clearly indicate my authority to pass merchandise to or from Suffolk under your permit, and I have therefore instructed the commanding officer of the guard vessel in the Nansemond to allow no vessel with merchandise to pass, except under the specified permit from one of the three Secretaries.

I shall at once ask the Department for a definition of my authority in this respect, and hope that until I am instructed on the point in question you will abstain from giving permits allowing general traffic to or from Suffolk.

I have the honor to be, general, very respectfully, yours,

S. P. LEE,
Actg. Rear-Admiral, Comdg. N. Atlantic Blockading Squadron.

GENERAL ORDERS,) WAR DEPT., ADJUTANT-GENERAL'S OFFICE,
No. 88.   )   *Washington, April 3, 1863.*

The following orders in respect to the regulating of intercourse with the insurrectionary States, the collection of abandoned property, &c., are published for the information and government of the Army and of all concerned:

WAR DEPARTMENT,
Washington, March 31, 1863.

For the purpose of more effectually preventing all commercial intercourse with insurrectionary States except such as shall be authorized in pursuance of law, and of securing consistent, uniform, and efficient action in conducting such intercourse as shall be so authorized, and for the purpose of carrying out the provisions of an act of Congress entitled "An act to provide for the collection of abandoned property and for the prevention of frauds in insurrectionary States," approved March 12, 1863, it is hereby ordered—

I. That no officer of the Army of the United States nor other person connected therewith shall authorize or have any interest in the transportation of any goods, wares, or merchandise (except supplies belonging to or contracted for by the United States, designed for the military or naval forces thereof, and moving under military or naval orders, and except also sutlers' supplies and other things necessary for the use and comfort of the troops of the United States, and moving under permits of the authorized officers of the Treasury Department) into any State declared by the President to be in insurrection; nor authorize nor have any interest in the purchase or sale therein of any goods or chattels, wares or merchandise, cotton, tobacco, or other product of the soil thereof; nor the transportation of the same, except as aforesaid, therefrom or therein; nor shall any such officer or person authorize, prohibit, or in any manner interfere with any such purchase or sale or transportation which shall be conducted under the regulations of the Secretary of the Treasury, unless under some imperative military necessity, in the place or section where the same shall be conducted, or unless requested by an agent or some other authorized officer of the Treasury Department, in which case all commanders of military departments, districts, and posts will render such aid in carrying out the provisions of the said act, and in enforcing due observance of the said regulations of the Secretary of the Treasury, as can be given without manifest injury to the public service.

II. It is further ordered that every officer or private or person employed in or with the regular or volunteer forces of the United States who may receive or have under his control any property which shall have been abandoned by the owner or owners, or captured in any district declared to be in insurrection against the United States, including all property seized under military orders, excepting only such as shall be required for military use of the United States forces, shall promptly turn over all such property to the agent appointed by the Secretary of the Treasury to receive the same, who shall give duplicate receipts therefor.

And every such officer or private, or person employed in or with the regular or volunteer forces of the United States, shall also promptly turn over to such agent, in like manner, all receipts, bills of lading, and other papers, documents, and vouchers showing title to such property, or the right to the possession, control, or direction thereof; and he shall make such order, indorsement, or writing as he has power to make to enable such agent to take possession of such property or the proceeds thereof. Arms, munitions of war, forage, horses, mules, wagons, beef cattle, and supplies which are necessary in military operations, shall be turned over to the proper officers of the ordnance or of the quartermaster or of the commissary departments, respectively, for the use of the Army. All other property abandoned or captured or seized as aforesaid shall be delivered to the agent appointed by the Secretary of the Treasury.

The officer receiving or turning over such property shall give the usual and necessary invoices, receipts, or vouchers therefor, and shall make regular returns thereof, as prescribed by the Army Regulations. The receipts of the agents of the Treasury Department shall be vouchers for all property delivered to them, and whenever called upon by the agent of the Treasury Department authorized to receive such abandoned or captured or seized property as aforesaid, or the proceeds thereof, all persons employed in the military service will give him full information in regard thereto, and if requested by him so to do they shall give him duplicates or copies of the reports and returns thereof and of the receipts, invoices, and vouchers therefor.

And every officer of the Army of the United States hereafter receiving abandoned or captured or seized property, or the proceeds thereof, or under whose order it may be applied to the use of the military forces as aforesaid, shall, upon request of a duly authorized agent of the Treasury Department, render a written report, with invoices thereof, to said agent, in which he will specify the arms, supplies, or other munitions of war retained for the use of the military forces as aforesaid, and also, separately, the property turned over to said agent, or which may have been sold or otherwise disposed of.

And in case a sale of any such property shall be made under his authority or under the authority of any one subject to his order he will so state, and will describe the property so sold, and will state when and where and by and to whom sold, and the amount received therefor, and what disposition was made of the proceeds.

And all officers of the Army of the United States will at all times render to the agents appointed by the Secretary of the Treasury all such aid as may be necessary to enable them to take possession of and transport all such property, so far as can be done without manifest injury to the public service.

III. All commanders of military departments, districts, and posts will, upon receipt of this order, revoke all existing orders within their respective commands conflicting or inconsistent herewith, or which permit or prohibit or in any manner interfere with any trade or transportation conducted under the regulations of the Secretary of the Treasury; and their attention is particularly directed to said regulations, prescribed March 31, 1863, and they will respectively make such orders as will insure strict observance of this order throughout their respective commands.

All expenses of transporting property herein referred to will be reported by the officers of the Quartermaster's Department who furnish such transportation to the agents of the Treasury Department, and also, through the ordinary channels, to the Quartermaster-General at Washington, in order that the said expenses may be reim bursed from the proceeds of sales of such transported property.

EDWIN M. STANTON,
Secretary of War.

By order of the Secretary of War:

E. D. TOWNSEND,
Assistant Adjutant-General.

UNITED STATES FLAG-SHIP MINNESOTA,
Off Newport News, Va., April 4, 1863.

Maj. Gen. JOHN A. DIX, U. S. A.,
Commanding Seventh Army Corps, Fort Monroe, Va.:

GENERAL: I was not aware until making inquiries on receipt of your letter of the 2d instant that the ordnance storehouse was used as a domicile. I at once directed Lieutenant-Commander Phenix to have the family now there removed, and have forbidden the use of any fire or lights in the building except such lights in such lanterns as are actually necessary. The Bureau of Ordnance has established its depot at Fort ress Monroe, on shore, where it is supposed to be safe and most con venient, and desires to add to it. The subject of the purchase of another hulk or sailing-ship for ordnance stores is already before the Bureau.

I have the honor to be, general, very respectfully, yours,

S. P. LEE,
Actg. Rear-Admiral, Comdg. N. Atlantic Blockading Squadron.

APRIL 4, [1863].

Major-General KEYES,
Commanding, Yorktown:

I shall leave this afternoon for Washington.* I hope not to be absent more than ten days, though my leave is for fifteen. Nothing will be done in the department without your orders except the regular detail of duty. If in anything you cannot communicate satisfactorily by tele graph my chief of staff can go to Yorktown, or if you are able to leave to come here my quarters are at your service. I have promised General Peck in case he is attacked to send for the Ninth New York Volunteers which is at Camp Hamilton and belongs to Getty's division.

JOHN A. DIX,
Major-General.

HEADQUARTERS UNITED STATES FORCES,
Suffolk, Va., April 4, 1863.

Maj. Gen. JOSEPH HOOKER,
Commanding Army of the Potomac:

GENERAL: I am honored with your communication of the 2d touching the strength and position of my troops; also the strength and position of the enemy in my front. As these data may have an important bear ing upon your operations I most cheerfully proceed to give you the de sired information.

By the inclosed map you will perceive that a large district is under

---

* Left on the 5th.

my command, being, in general terms, all east of the Blackwater and Chowan. Several counties of North Carolina are nominally in General Foster's department, but really dependent upon me for protection. General Viele has a small force at Norfolk. My headquarters are at Suffolk, where I keep nearly the whole force, and from which point I move my columns according to circumstances. The service is hard and they are kept active when the weather permits. The enemy occupies the Blackwater in force down to the Chowan and probably below Winton.

From the fact that some 4,000 have been several weeks fortifying Fort Powhatan, on the James, I infer that Chipoak and Birchen Rivers, with Cypress Swamp, form the left of their line. (See military map of Southeastern Virginia from Coast Survey.)

All the fords, passes, and bridges are fortified and guarded. He occupies Surry Court-House and pickets a belt of 5 or 6 miles on this side of the river. The intermediate country is traversed by both and is the theater of many collisions.

On the 1st of March Hood's and Pickett's divisions left Fredericksburg for Petersburg, and General Longstreet assumed command about that time or a few days before. One division started for Charleston, but returned. General Longstreet made a reconnaissance, with General Jenkins commanding, on the river last week and returned to Petersburg. My information from numerous sources has been that Longstreet had within 20 or 30 miles of this place 15,000, and 15,000 along the railway this side of Petersburg which he could concentrate in twelve hours, and I was advised from headquarters a few days since that one of our spies had a list of the regiments and the strength, and they amounted to 28,000.

Deserters who left the Blackwater on the 1st say that General Corse's brigade of Virginia troops arrived at Zuni on the 23d; also that a large pontoon train came by rail. They state that Hood's division was expected to follow. A large brigade of Mississippians, under General J. R. Davis, arrived recently from Goldsborough; also a brigade of South Carolinians, under General Bratton. He is strong in cavalry and artillery.

Ever since my arrival the enemy has been impressed with the idea that an army would attempt this route, and they have watched very closely. Much of the time their force has been greatly in excess of mine. This has been in part due to the demonstrations I have made. My force has been greatly magnified by our people, and the rebels' was rated from 30,000 to 50,000, when I had less than 12,000.

Total infantry for duty	12,590
Total cavalry	1,683
Total artillery	893
Two divisions, total for duty	15,166

Four of my batteries are good and three are indifferent.

There is no foundation for the report of an intended evacuation of Richmond.

It will give me pleasure to advise you from time to time of any important changes made by the enemy and of the information brought to me from creditable sources.

Wishing you all success in your very responsible command, I remain, very truly, yours,

JOHN J. PECK,
Major-General.

NEW BERNE, *Sunday, April 5, 1863*—4 p. m.

Maj. Gen. J. G. FOSTER:

MY DEAR GENERAL: Your letter of the 4th, dated 1 a. m., was received about two hours since, and I am delighted to inform you that everything mentioned in that letter has been anticipated. You speak first of the matter of the ammunition—of the need of 6-pounder Wiard; that was sent yesterday by the Northerner, and a further supply goes in about one hour from this time by the Farina. You next inquire about sending a cavalry force across the river to harass the enemy's rear; that was anticipated by me, and I organized such an expedition on the 3d. Major Garrard, with a battalion of four companies and one howitzer, has started with orders to gain all the information possible about the position of the enemy at Swift Creek, and, if possible, to threaten the forces at Hill's Point. By the time you receive this he will be doing his best in those parts. He has also five companies of infantry at Street's Ferry in case he should wish to return that way. (He might find the enemy in his rear after he gets up the country, and he might wish to dash across to the ferry, as that is only 8 miles from Swift Creek.) The flats will go up to the ferry with a small steamer, with a gun on board.

In addition to the troops of Spinola's brigade already up near the Hill's Point Battery the Northerner yesterday took two regiments, the Fifth Massachusetts and One hundred and first Pennsylvania. To-day the Farina takes the Third Massachusetts and One hundred and third New York, and she will tow schooners with the Eighty-fifth New York and Ninety-sixth New York, making nine regiments. We will hold this place with the remainder of the troops; at any rate we will try. Here we are only thinking of you and the way of helping you.

You must bear in mind that ever since you left here we have had the most terrific weather; the wind has either blown the water all out of the river or it has been blowing such a gale that most of our transportation could not do anything. Our vessels have been either aground or wind bound. Such a time has never been known here since we took the place.

The Northerner yesterday took up a lot of small boats. By my order the harbor-master collected all these he could find to send up. There are three ship launches secured to us by Captain Davenport, which will be sent up just as soon as they can go.

Captain Davenport tells me that he has sent a bountiful supply of ammunition for all the gunboats.

General Prince writes to me by the same messenger who brings your letter. He read your letter to me and he says that as a matter of course he adopts your ideas and he will act upon them.

I am not surprised that you think that there is a want of promptness, but you have no idea what weather we have had. Nothing could be done by water for a great portion of the time.

Urge General Prince to send back all the steamers he can spare to this place, for now we have nothing left here in the way of transportation.

I sent to Colonel Pickett at Plymouth, informing him of the state of affairs generally, and I authorized him to evacuate the place if he was hard pressed there, but to hold on as long as he could.

My own opinion is that he had better come here at once with all his force and hold the mouth of the Roanoke by a gunboat for the present. I cannot, however, take the responsibility of this. Think of it and let me know how to advise him when I write again.

Captain Farquhar writes that he is getting along well with the field works. He knew nothing of the troubles when he wrote.

Lieutenant Wheaton will tell you more than I can write. Everything that you can suggest will be attended to at once by me.

Ever truly, yours,

I. N. PALMER.

FORT MONROE, VA., *April 6*, 1863.

Maj. Gen. JOHN A. DIX, *Washington, D. C.:*

General Palmer, under date of April 3, from New Berne, states, subsequent to special dispatch received here by Major Anderson, that General Foster feels tolerably strong in Washington for some days, but begs for re-enforcements. He wants 10,000, but will take any number that can be sent.

D. T. VAN BUREN,
Assistant Adjutant-General.

FORT MONROE, VA., *April 6*, 1863—10 p. m.

Maj. Gen. H. W. HALLECK,
General-in-Chief:

Brigadier-General Palmer writes, April 3, from New Berne, urgently asking General Dix for re-enforcements. Says General Foster is in Washington, N. C., and that the re-enforcements are needed to secure that place and New Berne. Why Foster did not write I know not. I am this moment in from Suffolk. General Peck thinks the enemy is still strong in front of him, but can, he thinks and I think, spare, say, three regiments a short time if North Carolina is in great danger. What shall be done? I return to Yorktown to-night. I have an expedition organized to start early to-morrow morning for Matthews County to destroy or bring in a lot of grain collected for the rebels.

E. D. KEYES,
Major-General.

HDQRS. DEPT. OF VIRGINIA, SEVENTH ARMY CORPS,
Fort Monroe, Va., April 6, 1863.

Actg. Rear-Admiral S. P. LEE,
Commanding North Atlantic Blockading Squadron:

SIR: In the absence of Major-General Dix, commanding the department, I have the honor to transmit herewith a copy of a communication this morning received from Brig. Gen. I. N. Palmer, commanding at New Berne, N. C.

I am, sir, very respectfully, your obedient servant,

D. T. VAN BUREN,
Assistant Adjutant-General.

[Inclosure.]

HEADQUARTERS EIGHTEENTH ARMY CORPS,
New Berne, N. C., April 3, 1863.

Maj. Gen. JOHN A. DIX,
Comdg. Seventh Army Corps, Fortress Monroe, Va.:

GENERAL: Since my communication of the 1st, sent by Major Anderson, I have received several dispatches from General Foster. General

Foster feels tolerably strong in Washington for some days, but the ultimate safety of that place depends on the batteries on the river being overcome. Our force to overcome them is not sufficient, and I therefore most respectfully but earnestly beg that if at all within your power re-enforcements be sent here. I should wish 10,000, but any will be acceptable, and the sooner the better, to save General Foster and perhaps to save North Carolina (*i. e.*, New Berne) by preventing or rendering it unnecessary to send more troops from New Berne.

I expect, decidedly, gunboats from Admiral Lee, and trust we can punish the enemy; but they are strong and we are weak.

I am, general, very respectfully, your obedient servant,

I. N. PALMER,
Brigadier-General.

A communication through the canal, informing me of the coming troops, will reach me before the troops will, and I can have such orders given as to their disposition as may be necessary. I have no transportation. These re-enforcements are of course only as a loan.

ORDERS, }
No. —.   }

HEADQUARTERS FOURTH ARMY CORPS,
Fort Yorktown, Va., April 6, 1863.

Major-General Dix being temporarily absent, the undersigned hereby assumes command of the Department of Virginia and of the troops therein.

All reports and returns for general headquarters will be addressed as heretofore to the department staff officers at Fort Monroe, and the regulations and orders established by Major-General Dix will remain in force unless otherwise specially ordered by the undersigned.

E. D. KEYES,
Major-General, Commanding.

WAR DEPARTMENT,
Washington, April 7, 1863—3.10 p. m.

Major-General KEYES, *Fort Monroe, Va.:*

The instructions to General Dix were to co-operate with General Foster as far as possible, sending him re-enforcements if they could be spared, he being the judge of that. In the absence of any advices from North Carolina I can give you no more definite instructions.

H. W. HALLECK,
General-in-Chief.

SUFFOLK, *April 7, 1863.*

Maj. Gen. JOSEPH HOOKER,
Commanding Army of the Potomac, Falmouth:

Answered your communication.* Just examined a man who left Petersburg on Wednesday; confirms my previous information. Longstreet moving troops this way last week.

JOHN J. PECK,
Major-General.

---

* See Peck to Hooker, April 4.

UNITED STATES FLAG-SHIP MINNESOTA,
Off Newport News, April 8, 1863.

Maj. Gen. JOHN A. DIX, U. S. A.,
Comdg. Seventh Army Corps, Fortress Monroe, Va.:

GENERAL: In your letter to me of April 5 you request that during your absence the signature of Capt. W. E. Blake, provost-marshal, might be respected by the guard vessel as conveying the same authority as your own. Immediately on the receipt of this request I referred the matter to the Navy Department for instructions, as I am especially directed in passing ships and merchandise to or from Norfolk for military purposes to recognize the signature of Major-General Dix, " and not of persons signing for him." Until, therefore, I am enabled to communicate the Department's decision to you I hope that such permits will not be given by Captain Blake, as the guard vessel must at present act under their original instructions. Permits to trade from the Secretary of the Treasury, War, or Navy will be of course always respected when presented here.

I have the honor to be, general, very respectfully, yours,
S. P. LEE,
Actg. Rear-Admiral, Comdg. N. Atlantic Blockading Squadron.

HEADQUARTERS DEPARTMENT OF VIRGINIA,
Fort Monroe, Va., April 8, 1863.

Maj. Gen. H. W. HALLECK,
General-in-Chief:

GENERAL: H. A. Gibbon, a deserter from the Fifty-seventh Regiment North Carolina, of Lee's army, came into our lines yesterday. He was conscripted from Chapel Hill College, N. C., and is remarkably intelligent. His relations corroborate many facts I have gleaned from less reliable sources, and seem worthy of the notice of the War Department. He says D. H. Hill with his division is in North Carolina; Pickett is near the Blackwater, and Hood near Petersburg. He confirms my former statement that Fitzhugh Lee, with four regiments of cavalry, came down to near Gloucester Point, having boasted he would take it. On his return he stopped at a Colonel Davis', where Gibbon learned the merriment caused by his failure. Lee's cavalry, he says, recently moved toward the left of the rebel lines.

Gibbon states that Lee has collected large pontoon trains and is ready to cross the Rappahannock; that he will attack Hooker soon if Hooker does not attack; that Lee's army is 80,000 strong, all well armed, and mostly with Enfield rifles. The men are in good condition and feel entire confidence that they will beat Hooker. Provisions are certainly very scarce, but there is no despondency.

Gibbon says the railroads north from Richmond are in a much worse condition than those south, and that railroad iron is very scarce.

The rebel generals from an army of 80,000 can keep more men in line of battle than Hooker and his generals can keep in line from an army of 100,000, and if Hooker has not more than that number he is in danger of being whipped.

I have not yet made a sufficiently close examination of this department to venture a positive opinion; but from the glance I took at Suffolk and the neighboring country I could see nothing there to tempt the enemy to make great sacrifices in that quarter which would weaken his attack on Hooker. I think I shall advise that with the works about Suffolk and the gunboats on the Nansemond Peck can hold the position with about half his present force. The railroads being in a bad condition north of Richmond Lee must guard them carefully. I would therefore collect every man not necessary to retain the strongholds in North Carolina and in this department into one body to threaten the railroads north of Richmond.

As the supplies of provisions in Matthews County, Gloucester County, and above are still plentiful, and as the rebels are taking steps to transport them to their army, I am doing all in my power to thwart their purpose. Eight hundred of my men came in last night after destroying a large amount of grain and bringing in many sheep and cattle and mules. I left Yorktown too early this morning to collect the figures. I have still 200 men out with the gunboats, and by the last accounts they were hard at work over in Matthews County. We have certainly destroyed about 30,000 bushels of grain within a week past. The enemy is undoubtedly busy about our picket lines, but I infer they are only masking other movements. My lines are so strong that I have no fear of small bodies, and can do more damage to large bodies than they can do to me. I shall therefore continue to hunt for his supplies.

I am, very respectfully, your obedient servant,

E. D. KEYES,
Major-General, Commanding.

UNITED STATES FLAG-SHIP MINNESOTA,
Off Newport News, Va., April 9, 1863.

Maj. Gen. JOHN A. DIX, U. S. A.,
Comdg. Seventh Army Corps, Fortress Monroe, Va.:

GENERAL: The bark Edisto, from Boston to Baltimore, claims demurrage for detention here while receiving repairs at the Gosport Navy-Yard, rendered necessary by a collision which took place on the 21st of March between her and the Wyandotte in Hampton Roads. It has been reported to me that this vessel, by your order of March 17 to Captain Millward, was sent to Hampton Roads and there detained.

I would be obliged if you would inform me, if practicable, of the circumstances which justified her being so ordered within the lines of this blockade, as in presenting the case to the Department it would be necessary to account for her presence here.

I have the honor to be, general, very respectfully, yours,

S. P. LEE,
Actg. Rear-Admiral, Comdg. N. Atlantic Blockading Squadron.

FORT MONROE, VA., *April* 9, 1863.

Maj. Gen. H. W. HALLECK,
General-in-Chief:

No communication has been received from General Foster, who, with 1,200 men, is shut up in Washington, N. C. Below him the Tar River is closed, I learn, by fourteen rebel batteries, against the possibility of our gunboats reaching him. He cannot be relieved except by an expedition by land. Palmer asks from New Berne for 10,000 men. Captain Murray, of the Navy, left here last night for Washington. He has the latest information from Foster's department. I will examine the subject further, and if I find it expedient will send such re-enforcements as can be spared.

E. D. KEYES,
Major-General.

WAR DEPARTMENT,
Washington, April 9, 1863—3 p. m.

Major-General KEYES, *Fort Monroe, Va.:*

If you can possibly assist General Foster do so in preference to anything else. Let me know what you have determined on.

H. W. HALLECK,
General-in-Chief.

HEADQUARTERS DEPARTMENT OF VIRGINIA,
Fort Monroe, Va., April 9, 1863.

Major-General H. W. HALLECK,
Commanding U. S. Army:

SIR: In consequence of the appeals of General Foster for relief (his letter of the 5th instant to you was forwarded) I have ready to move nigh 4,000 men—all that can be spared prudently from this department at the present moment. I have a rumor that Washington, N. C., has been burned and that the transports carrying troops from New Berne, not being able to reach Foster, had returned. I do not see the wisdom of General Foster's proposal to make a demonstration from Plymouth toward Washington with such a force as can be assembled there. Troops from Suffolk could only march to Gatesville, and I don't know of any transports to receive them there for Plymouth. I shall therefore limit myself, unless otherwise instructed, to sending re-enforcements to New Berne as transports can be had. None are here at present, and Colonel Thomas is not able to tell me when to anticipate them. I have this moment received a telegram from General Peck to state his working party at the ferry on the Western Branch of the Nansemond had been attacked. His people have had a successful skirmish near Isle of Wight, capturing 4 men, 9 horses, &c. The enemy on the Blackwater are reported ready to march; are building bridges, &c.

I have the honor to be, sir, your most obedient servant,

E. D. KEYES,
Major-General, Commanding.

HEADQUARTERS EIGHTEENTH ARMY CORPS,
New Berne, N. C., April 9, 1863.

Brig. Gen. LORENZO THOMAS,
Adjutant-General U. S. Army, Washington, D. C.:

GENERAL: The last steamer from here carried a letter from General Foster to General Halleck informing him of the situation of affairs in this department.

By referring to that letter you will see that the enemy had erected batteries on the river below the town of Washington and thus prevented re-enforcements or supplies from passing up. General Foster's first idea was to attempt, in conjunction with the naval forces, to take the batteries, but after a careful consideration of the matter he decided to have the forces which had already gone up to these batteries returned to this place, and with all the rest of the available force from here to march across the country to his relief. The expedition was by General Foster's order to be conducted by General Prince, but just at the point of starting (yesterday morning) General Prince was taken sick and the column started under the command of Brigadier-General Spinola.

This expedition consists of all the force that can possibly be spared from this place, and will number in the vicinity of 8,000 men. The force of the enemy around Washington and on the road between here and that place is estimated at something more than 20,000, under the command of Generals D. H. Hill, Pettigrew, and Garnett. There are roads leading into the route from here to Washington, down which the enemy can pour any number of troops, and several points on the route are fortified. A great portion of the country is swamp and exceedingly difficult to get over.

In a dispatch received this morning from General Spinola (who has proved himself, I think, an officer of energy, discretion, and good judgment) he informed me that from all the information he can get he concludes it impossible to force his way through to Washington without first taking the battery at Hill's Point, and he proposes to try that to-day. A success will place him in a better position, as he can then communicate with the gunboats on the river. Should he not have sufficient force, however, to take that position he will return here if he can. I have not given him orders to that effect, as I have only directed him to carry out the instructions of General Foster to the letter, if possible. New Berne, which should be held at all hazards, is threatened, and I have scarcely 3,000 men here.

There is no general officer with me, and the troops are mostly new— nine-months' men.

Of General Foster's policy in abandoning everything to the saving of Washington I have nothing to say, except that it meets with no favor from the military and naval officers who consider themselves privileged to speak of the matter. I obey General Foster's orders implicitly, trusting to holding this place.

Should the forces now *en route* get to Washington they will be there without supplies. It will take a large army to keep the road between that place and this. The river is lined with batteries, and the senior naval officer at the lower batteries, who has some of the finest gunboats in these waters under his control, informed me that he can make no impression on them.

I informed General Dix of the condition of affairs here by a special messenger, requesting a re-enforcement. I have only heard by the return of the officer sent that we could expect no re-enforcements here from the Army of Virginia, as they are now fully occupied there.

Admiral Lee has sent a small re-enforcement of gunboats, which in the absence of the troops make this place, of course, more secure.

I am, general, very respectfully, your obedient servant,
                                    I. N. PALMER,
                          Brigadier-General U. S. Volunteers.

HEADQUARTERS SEVENTH ARMY CORPS,
                                    Suffolk, April 9, 1863.
Major-General FOSTER,
        Department of North Carolina:

GENERAL: Although you have received more than 10,000 of my old and best troops within a few months without returning them, I am again contributing for your benefit. General Terry will join you with a considerable force, of which 3,000 from this point are the flower of my command.

General Longstreet has been in my front with not less than 28,000, for some weeks, that he could concentrate in a few hours of this place. For many days everything has indicated the offensive on his part, and I have confidently expected an attack.   Up to this time my own opinion and that of my commanders has been that no troops ought to leave this point, and you are indebted to me for them.

On the reading of Palmer's letter, in the hands of Major-General Keyes, on the 6th, I said send a strong brigade from this point at once and as many more as there was a probability of being replaced at short notice. The troops have been ready, waiting transportation and the orders of the department commander.

If Longstreet does not advance by the 12th I shall conclude that the exigencies at Charleston and other points have called for his reserves.

Wishing you all success in your contests with the rebels, I am, in haste, truly, yours,

JOHN J. PECK,
Major-General.

HDQRS. DEPT. OF VIRGINIA, SEVENTH ARMY CORPS,
Fort Monroe, Va., April 10, 1863.

Capt. C. B. WILDER,
Asst. Quartermaster and Superintendent of Contrabands:

SIR: In answer to your letter of March 31, which I answered orally at the time, and have since partially answered in writing, I would say:

1st. No rent need be exacted from tenants of farms under your care until the harvest is made.

2d. No oath is to be required of female tenants on such farms.

3d. Men holding as tenants under absentee disloyalists who will not take the oath of allegiance are not entitled to possession.

4th. No loyal tenant agreeing to pay a reasonable rent is to be disturbed.

5th. Very moderate rents only are in any case to be required, and where you and the tenant differ as to the amount please come with the tenant to me to fix the rate.

In conclusion I would say, generally, that it is very desirable that no Union man be subjected to inconvenience, and that a spirit of both fairness and kindness should be perfectly manifest in all the arrangements concerning the farms which are used in whole or in part by the Government.

Respectfully, yours,

JOHN A. BOLLES,
Major and Aide-de-Camp, Provost-Judge.

FORT MONROE, VA., *April 10, 1863.*

Maj. Gen. H. W. HALLECK,
General-in-Chief:

Your telegram urging re-enforcements for Foster was received here last night at 9 o'clock and by me at Yorktown at 11.   I gave immediate orders, and troops are now moving from Suffolk.   I can only send 1,800 or 2,000 at once, and that number every five days, by canal.   I have no means of transportation by sea, and the lack of such transportation prevented my sending aid to Foster on the 8th instant, when I first learned his situation, though the enemy was then attacking my line.   Peck says he is now threatened by a large force of rebels.

E. D. KEYES,
Major-General.

FORT MONROE, VA.,
- *April* 10, 1863—1 p. m.

Maj. Gen. H. W. HALLECK,
   General-in-Chief:

A great variety of information from prisoners, deserters, and from intercepted letters confirms the fact that the rebels are in great force on the Blackwater. They have built several bridges, issued four days' cooked rations, &c. An officer from City Point brought news that a great quantity of material had been sent down to the Blackwater. The testimony is too strong to be disregarded. I countermanded the orders for re-enforcements for Foster before any got off. I shall go to Suffolk in the morning.

          E. D. KEYES,
         Major-General, Commanding.

      FORT MONROE, VA., *April* 10, 1863.

Maj. Gen. H. W. HALLECK,
   General-in-Chief:

No news from Charleston since telegram of this morning referring to disaster to iron-clad Keokuk. No requisition for transports was made. Shortly after I concluded to re-enforce Foster a steamer came in; others were expected, and by diverting from fair-weather steamers I could send as many troops as I could spare. I telegraphed you that the information obtained to-day induced me to withhold all re-enforcements from Foster. Upon Peck's urgent call I have sent the Hawkins' Zouaves to Suffolk to-day.

          E. D. KEYES,
         Major-General, Commanding.

   HEADQUARTERS DEPARTMENT OF VIRGINIA,
      Fort Monroe, Va., April 10, 1863.

Maj. Gen. J. G. FOSTER, or
Brig. Gen. I. N. PALMER:

SIR: In consequence of your application for re-enforcements I have detached Brigadier-General Terry with a brigade of about 3,000 men— all that can possibly be spared from this department—with orders to proceed by sea to New Berne. A deficiency of vessels is causing delay in the departure of the troops. I would have sent them yesterday if possible, and the first installments are now embarking on steamers fit only for calm waters. I send these troops, which are so much needed in this department, for the purpose of relieving General Foster at Washington, N. C. If General Foster shall have been relieved or released, or if Washington shall have fallen on the arrival of General Terry at New Berne, I have directed him to return with his brigade forthwith to this place. In any event I shall anticipate their return in a very short time, as the enemy now threaten us on the Blackwater and elsewhere in great force.

One of the steamers sent is the Thomas A. Morgan, the mail-boat and transport between Fort Monroe and Yorktown. I desire that the Morgan may be returned here in the least possible time.

I have the honor to be, very respectfully, your obedient servant,
          E. D. KEYES,
         Major-General, Commanding.

HEADQUARTERS DEPARTMENT OF VIRGINIA,
Fort Monroe, April 10, 1863.

Major-General PECK, *Suffolk :*

General Halleck directs me to assist Foster if possible; so we will send Terry's brigade of 3,000, and I will, when the enemy advances on you, send Hawkins' Zouaves and other aid nearly equivalent. I shall order Terry to bring back his brigade the moment Foster is released or disposed of.

E. D. KEYES,
Major-General.

HEADQUARTERS DEPARTMENT OF VIRGINIA,
Fort Monroe, April 10, 1863.

Major-General PECK:

Vessels having arrived, Terry's brigade will go by sea. I have directed the quartermaster to keep you advised of the arrival of the transports.

I suppose his brigade does not exceed 3,000 men. No greater number can possibly be spared.

I will direct the quartermaster to send coal for your gunboats.

E. D. KEYES,
Major-General.

FORT MONROE, VA., *April 10, 1863.*

Major-General PECK, *Suffolk :*

We have been informed that the enemy have sent bridge material for five bridges from Petersburg, to be used in crossing the Blackwater in five places. This information is quite reliable. General Keyes is now at Old Point.

D. T. VAN BUREN,
Assistant Adjutant-General.

HEADQUARTERS STEAMER ESCORT, *April 10, 1863.*

Lieut. Col. W. H. LUDLOW :

COLONEL : By direction of General Palmer I beg leave to say, in answer to your dispatch of the 9th, that an expedition sent to raise the siege of Washington, and consisting of about 8,000 men, were repulsed at Blount's Creek, near the battery on Hill's Point.

The enemy are in force, about 22,000, and strongly posted. An effort will be made (troops on this boat) to run a regiment past the batteries to General Foster, so that he can make a more protracted defense of that place.

The only available transportation that can be sent to Gatesville is sufficient for 3,000 men; that amount of transportation will be at Gatesville the morning of the 13th, and will remain there forty-eight hours, hoping for troops.

Very respectfully, your obedient servant,

SOUTHARD HOFFMAN,
Lieutenant-Colonel and Assistant Adjutant-General.

NOTE.—Will Colonel Ludlow please forward this to the commanding general at Fort Monroe?

Very respectfully,

I. N. PALMER,
Brigadier-General, Commanding Department North Carolina.

WASHINGTON, *April* 10, 1863—6 p. m.

Brigadier-General PALMER,
  Commanding Forces, New Berne :

GENERAL : Your dispatches arrived this morning at 2 a. m. by the hands of Lieutenant-Colonel McChesney, who will return to-night.

I am directed by the major-general commanding to say that he could have wished that you had yourself come in command of the forces which moved yesterday from New Berne under General Spinola, notwithstanding the confidence you express in his activity and intelligence.

If General Wessells has arrived General Foster wishes you to take command in person of the advancing forces. Should General Naglee arrive he will be sent forward at once to take command.

In case you are not sufficiently strong at New Berne you will send for the regiment at Plymouth, leaving at that post three companies with three pieces of artillery as garrison for the fort if it be sufficiently completed.

The general wishes that a light-draught steamer, with her sides protected by hay-bales, should be sent here at once loaded with ammunition and provisions. Send also several schooners of light draught, protected and loaded in the same way.

The enemy have opened fire to-day from five batteries on the crest of the rising ground in rear of town. Their fire for a short time was very sharp, but no damage has yet been done.

The general expects, even if the expedition which has started be successful, that you will continue to make persistent efforts to send a force across to our relief.

Very respectfully, your obedient servant,
                        EDWARD E. POTTER,
                              Chief of Staff.

If anything goes to Washington before we return, a few thousand rations, some hay, and some 32-pound and 6-pound (Wiard) ammunition had better be sent if our supply is large at New Berne. McChesney says General Foster is in high spirits, &c.

                                        I. N. P.

HEADQUARTERS EIGHTEENTH ARMY CORPS,
                        New Berne, April 10, 1863.

Col. J. PICKETT,
  Commanding Post, Plymouth, N. C.:

COLONEL : I am instructed by General Palmer to inform you of the situation of affairs at present in this vicinity and at Washington.

Washington is completely or nearly invested by the enemy, so that it is impossible for the gunboats to proceed to General Foster's assistance. The attempt to re-enforce General Foster by sending troops to him by water had in consequence to be abandoned. The expedition sent from here across the country by way of Swift Creek has been obliged to return to this place on account of the greatly superior strength of the enemy.

The effective force at this place consists of about 9,000 men, and about 12,000 at Washington. The enemy's force is supposed to be about 20,000 in the immediate vicinity of Washington.

I am, very truly, your obedient servant,
                        WM. L. WHEATON,
                              Aide-de-Camp.

UNITED STATES FLAG-SHIP MINNESOTA,
Newport News, April 10, 1863.

Major-General PECK,
Commanding at Suffolk, Va.:

SIR: Herewith I respectfully return to you a permit given from your headquarters, December 29, to Edward Bust, to carry oysters in his sloop Jacob Marten to Suffolk, subject to the regulations of the naval authorities.

Edward Bust, with his sailing sloop and a large boat, was found in the Lower Nansemond day before yesterday morning by the picket boat Alert and brought on board this ship. As that region is infested by smugglers and rebel mail carriers I have found it necessary not only to prohibit the gathering of oysters in the Nansemond but to allow no boats there day or night where such illicit operations can be carried on, and to instruct the guard vessels to recognize no oyster permits after May 1 and until then only in open boats.

Edward Bust was sent back to the guard vessel to be released with his boats, with a warning in accordance with the above.

I have the honor to be, general, very respectfully, yours,
S. P. LEE,
Actg. Rear-Admiral, Comdg. N. Atlantic Blockading Squadron.

———

WAR DEPARTMENT,
Washington, April 11, 1863——11.24 a. m.

Major-General KEYES, *Fort Monroe, Va.:*

Your position should not be so weakened as to endanger its security. If you find the enemy in your front too strong to permit you to re-enforce General Foster you are right in not doing so; but you should not act upon mere rumors, which are always gotten up to influence the movements of troops on such occasions. Means should be taken to ascertain beyond doubt the strength of the enemy before you. You remember Napoleon's maxim, that no general should be ignorant of the strength and position of his enemy.

H. W. HALLECK,
General-in-Chief.

———

FORT MONROE, VA.,
April 11, 1863——12 noon.

Maj. Gen. H. W. HALLECK,
General-in-Chief:

Your telegram just received. My front is so extensive, the enemy are so busy, and the calls for assistance so general that I have not had time to examine Peck's position carefully. I have to rely on his and Viele's opinions to some extent more than my own. There is no doubt the enemy are pushing us all along from North Carolina to York River. As soon as I can look around I shall feel certain, and I will give no timid counsels. Our troops below Williamsburg were attacked by a large force this morning—4,000, 5,000, or 6,000. They have got below Fort Magruder and cut off communication with Colonel West, who has the One hundred and thirty-ninth New York Volunteers, Fifth Pennsylvania Cavalry, and one battery of field artillery. This moment they telegraph that Fort Magruder is safe and the enemy are retreating.

Two little forts on the right and left of it are occupied, and I have ordered them to hold the line against 10,000 rebels. Admiral Lee has ordered the Commodore Morris away from Yorktown. Her armament is only fit for service there, and I have urged the admiral to send her back from here at once to Yorktown.

> E. D. KEYES,
> *Major-General.*

> FORT MONROE, VA.,
> *April* 11, 1863—6 p. m.

Maj. Gen. H. W. HALLECK,
        General-in-Chief:

General Peck, at Suffolk, telegraphs just now enemy in large force are attempting to flank us on both sides; deserters say 50,000. General Keyes has just started for Suffolk. Williamsburg appears to be quiet. Our forces retain possession of Fort Magruder and have advanced pickets to outskirts of Williamsburg. The telegraph operator reports enemy are hanging around Williamsburg.

> D. T. VAN BUREN,
> *Assistant Adjutant-General.*

> HEADQUARTERS FOURTH CORPS,
> *Fort Monroe, April* 11, 1863—11.30 a. m.

Admiral S. P. LEE,
        On board Minnesota:

Our troops near Williamsburg have been driven by a large force of rebels down toward the mouth of Queen's Creek, and Colonel West calls for the aid of gunboats. The Crusader's armament will not answer, and I earnestly request that you will send the Commodore Morris back at once. If the gunboats are taken away even Yorktown may be lost. The enemy are now within 5 miles of Yorktown.

> E. D. KEYES,
> *Major-General.*

> HEADQUARTERS DEPARTMENT OF VIRGINIA,
> *Fort Monroe, Va., April* 11, 1863.

Actg. Rear-Admiral S. P. LEE,
        Commanding North Atlantic Blockading Squadron:

ADMIRAL: The enemy attacked Williamsburg early this morning, and by the last accounts were moving with a heavy force upon Fort Magruder, which is a mile and more below the city. They have also a force this side of Fort Magruder and have burned the camp of the Fifth Pennsylvania Cavalry.

It is possible the enemy have crossed troops from the south side of the James River; if so, and to ascertain the fact, I would be glad if you could send a gunboat up as far as Jamestown Island. Such a movement would also tend to diminish the pressure on our lines below Williamsburg.

The wires between Yorktown and Williamsburg have been cut. The enemy are represented as being in large force. The gunboats should therefore move up and down between Yorktown and Queen's Creek, and I trust you will be able to spare three gunboats to keep in sight of Yorktown.

I am, sir, very respectfully, your most obedient servant,

E. D. KEYES,
Major-General, Commanding.

FORT MONROE, VA., *April* 11, 1863.

Admiral S. P. LEE, *Newport News:*

The following just received from General Peck, at Suffolk, 5.35 p. m.:

Enemy is flanking us in large force on both sides.

General Keyes directs me to ask you, Can you send gunboats to mouth or up the Nansemond?

D. T. VAN BUREN,
Assistant Adjutant-General.

UNITED STATES FLAG-SHIP MINNESOTA,
Off Newport News, Va., April 11, 1863.

Maj. Gen. E. D. KEYES, U. S. A.,
Comdg. Department of Virginia, Fortress Monroe, Va.:

GENERAL: Yours of this date is received. With the force at my disposal I can only give partial support in James River to your outpost at Williamsburg by occupying that position instead of this, but this ship cannot go there.

As the two flag-of-truce boats arrived to-day from City Point do not report any rebel vessels in James River it is not probable that the enemy have crossed from the right to the left bank of the river at Jamestown Island.

I cannot assign the additional gunboat force you request for Yorktown, not having the means of doing so in consequence of the number of vessels required to assist the army in its occupation of several positions in the Sounds of North Carolina.

If the enemy have the means of crossing the Nansemond and wish to do so in force, under cover of their artillery, the two small navy and the small army vessels called gunboats (which are frail little river or harbor steamers, mounting in all but a few pieces of fixed artillery) should not be considered enough to prevent it. The Nansemond is a mere creek above the Western Branch, and musketry alone can command the decks and drive from their guns the crews of these little crafts, which are liable to be disabled in their exposed boilers, &c., by a few discharges from small and scattered field pieces.

Last fall I called the attention of General Dix to the policy of leveling the earthworks in this vicinity. Referring to my conversation with you on this subject at Yorktown last fall and on board this ship the other day, I respectfully renew my suggestion that the contrabands and other force, if necessary, should be employed to raze these works without delay.

Permit me to draw your attention to the inclosed extract* from a report I made to the honorable the Secretary of the Navy on the 24th of October last, immediately after my visit to Yorktown, referring to the

---

* See p. 442.

destruction of all military works in the vicinity of Norfolk and York-town which might encourage further efforts on the part of the enemy to reoccupy.

I have the honor to be, general, very respectfully, yours,

S. P. LEE,
Actg. Rear-Admiral, Comdg. N. Atlantic Blockading Squadron.

HEADQUARTERS DEPARTMENT OF VIRGINIA,
Fort Monroe, April 11, 1863—5 p. m.

Major-General PECK,
Commanding, Suffolk :

I have this moment received your telegram announcing that the enemy is moving upon you in large force.

I suppose the Hawkins' Zouaves are now with you. I shall start for Norfolk in a few minutes.

E. D. KEYES,
Major-General.

HEADQUARTERS DEPARTMENT OF VIRGINIA,
Fort Monroe, April 11, 1863.

Major-General PECK,
Commanding, Suffolk :

Wise and his whole command are at Williamsburg. The enemy got past Fort Magruder, destroyed the camp of the Fifth Pennsylvania Cavalry, and came down with a portion of their force to within 5 miles of Yorktown. I have ordered Colonel West to hold the line of Fort Magruder at all hazards. I may be obliged to send him re-enforce-ments and may have to recall Hawkins' Zouaves. I must look at your position to judge by comparison. How much time will I require to see your lines ?

E. D. KEYES,
Major-General.

GENERAL ORDERS, }   HDQRS. EIGHTEENTH ARMY CORPS,
No. 54.   }   *New Berne, April* 11, 1863.

It is hereby ordered that the divisions and brigades of the Eighteenth Army Corps now in this department resume their original organization and designation, agreeably to the provisions of General Orders, No. 11, Headquarters Eighteenth Army Corps, and all reports will be rendered accordingly.

The senior officers present will command in order of their seniority, and absent regiments will be accounted for as on detached service. The organization will be as follows :

The First, or General Palmer's, Division will consist of the brigade of Colonel Amory: Seventeenth Massachusetts Volunteers, Forty-third Massachusetts Volunteer Militia, Forty-fifth Massachusetts Volunteer Militia, Fifty-first Massachusetts Volunteer Militia; and the brigade of Col. H. C. Lee: Twenty-seventh Massachusetts Volunteers, Twenty-fifth Massachusetts Volunteers, Fifth Massachusetts Volunteer Militia, Forty-sixth Massachusetts Volunteer Militia.

The Fourth, or General Wessells', Division will consist of the brigade of General Hunt: Eighty-fifth New York State Volunteers, Ninety-second New York State Volunteers, Ninety-sixth New York State Volunteers, One hundred and first Pennsylvania Volunteers, One hundred and third Pennsylvania Volunteers; and the brigade of General Stevenson: Fifth Rhode Island Volunteers, Forty-fourth Massachusetts Volunteer Militia.

The Fifth, or General Prince's, Division will consist of the brigade of General Spinola: One hundred and thirty-second New York State Volunteers, One hundred and fifty-eighth Pennsylvania Militia, One hundred and seventy-first Pennsylvania Militia, One hundred and seventy-fifth Pennsylvania Militia; and the brigade of Colonel Jourdan: Third Massachusetts Volunteer Militia, Eighth Massachusetts Volunteer Militia, One hundred and fifty-eighth New York State Volunteers, One hundred and sixty-eighth Pennsylvania Militia.

By command of Brigadier-General Wessells commanding:

[———— ————,]
Major and Assistant Adjutant-General.

FORT MONROE, VA.,
April 12, 1863—12 noon.

Major-General DIX,
    No. 3 West Twenty-first street, New York, N. Y.:

General Peck telegraphs just now, "We are face to face. The attack is on the Somerton and Edenton front, and before this reaches you the fight will have commenced." I will have the Burden for you at Baltimore if you say so. I think you had better come down.

D. T. VAN BUREN,
Assistant Adjutant-General.

FORT MONROE, VA.,
April 12, 1863—4.30 p. m.

Maj. Gen. H. W. HALLECK,
    General-in-Chief:

The following dispatches received to-day from General Peck at Suffolk, at 12.30 p. m.:

The two armies are at this moment face to face. The attack is on the Somerton and Edenton road.

4 P. M.

The enemy, after advancing within a short distance of my front, has fallen back 2 or 3 miles, and is reported moving from the Somerton road toward the Edenton road.

D. T. VAN BUREN,
Assistant Adjutant-General.

NORFOLK, VA., *April* 12, [1863.]—7.30 p. m.
(Received 9.15 p. m.)

Maj. Gen. H. W. HALLECK,
    General-in-Chief:

The enemy approached our lines at Suffolk to-day and exchanged some cannon-shots and retired. The force of the enemy is great and I think they will make a serious attack. General Peck has just telegraphed that he has reason to believe Longstreet is receiving re-enforcements and heavy artillery. Wise with his whole force is certainly in front of Williamsburg and Fitzhugh Lee is said to be approaching Gloucester Point, and some persons anticipate rebel gunboats down James River. Information from all quarters concurs to establish a simultaneous movement against all portions of our lines. I have made the best disposition in my power of our troops and supplies, but I would be glad to receive heavy re-enforcements if they could be spared. We have seven small gunboats on the Nansemond, which I think renders Peck's right flank secure.

E. D. KEYES,
Major-General.

HEADQUARTERS DEPARTMENT OF VIRGINIA,
Norfolk, Va., April 12, 1863.

The proximity of the Confederate forces renders it proper, by virtue of the military and naval authority of the United States, to give the following notice:

All foreign consuls and their families, all women and children, and all other persons not in the service of the United States who prefer safety to the conflicts of war, are notified that on the approach of the enemy to any town or village within this department and the range of the Union guns, such town or village will be fired on without further consideration.

E. D. KEYES,
Major-General, Commanding Department of Virginia.

APRIL 12, 1863.

Major-General KEYES:

I believe Longstreet is receiving re-enforcements and heavy artillery by rail from Petersburg and Weldon.

PECK,
Major-General.

SUFFOLK, *April* 12, 1863.

Major-General KEYES:

A force is on the road leading to the Nansemond. How far they will come down remains to be seen; will keep you advised. The rails were removed by some of the Ninth Corps men through a misunderstanding of orders given by the commander of that front. I slept none in consequence of these affairs and of the responsibility.

PECK,
Major-General.

SUFFOLK, VA., *April* 12, 1863.

Maj. Gen. JOSEPH HOOKER,
Headquarters Army of the Potomac :

Longstreet is now before me with a very heavy force. The attack is on my front, which cuts off much of the aid of the gunboats on the flanks. Prisoners say 30,000 and more.

JOHN J. PECK,
Major-General.

(Copy to General Halleck.)

NORFOLK, VA., *April 12, 1863.*

Brigadier-General KING:

I see no objection to the withdrawal of Colonel West's pickets from the town of Williamsburg. Colonel West will, I trust, cause Wise to repent his rashness if he assails those forts.

E. D. KEYES,
Major-General.

FORT MONROE, VA., *April 12, 1863.*

Maj. Gen. JOHN A. DIX,
Eutaw House, Baltimore, Md.:

The Henry Burden left here at 11 o'clock this evening for Baltimore. The captain was ordered to report to you at the Eutaw House.

WM. H. LUDLOW,
Lieut. Col. and Asst. Insp. Gen.

FORT MONROE, VA., *April 12, 1863.*
(Received 10.45 p. m.)

Maj. Gen. H. W. HALLECK,
General-in-Chief:

A dispatch has just been received from Major-General Palmer stating that an expedition of 8,000 men sent to raise the siege of Washington was repulsed at Blount's Creek near the batteries on Hill's Point. The enemy was in force, about 22,000, strongly posted. An effort will be made to run a regiment past the batteries to General Foster, so that he can make a more protracted defense of that place. Transportation was to be sent to Gatesville hoping to receive re-enforcements of 3,000 men from this department. A dispatch has been sent to General Palmer informing him that no re-enforcements can be sent to him from this de partment. General Keyes is in Norfolk.

WM. H. LUDLOW,
Lieutenant-Colonel and Assistant Inspector-General.

NORFOLK, *April 12, 1863—5.30 p. m.*

Lieut. Col. SOUTHARD HOFFMAN,
Assistant Adjutant-General:

COLONEL: I am directed by the major-general commanding to acknowledge the receipt of your communication of the 10th instant, this moment placed in my hands, and to inform you that no re-enforcements can be sent to Major-General Foster from this department.

The enemy are now in large force this side of the Blackwater, under General Longstreet; are making an attack upon Suffolk. They occupy the country between Suffolk and Gatesville.

An attack is also making by them upon Williamsburg. Intelligence from deserters indicate a simultaneous movement upon the part of the enemy on all the lines in this department.

Twenty thousand additional troops are needed here.

I am, very respectfully, your obe ient servant,

WM. H. LUDLOW,
Lieut. Col. and Asst. Inspector-General, Seventh Army Corps.

HEADQUARTERS,
Plymouth, N. C., April 12, 1863.

Lieut. W. L. WHEATON,
    A. A. A. G., First Division, Eighteenth Army Corps:

Your communication of April 10, informing me of the situation of affairs in the vicinity of New Berne and Washington, has been received.

I have the honor to submit the following as the condition of affairs at this post:

The fort is nearly completed and is in condition to mount all the guns. One heavy gun arrived to-day from Roanoke Island and is being located in the fort. The wings of the fort are completed and small works constructed to protect its left flank. The woods upon all the main roads leading into Plymouth have been felled, and the guns when mounted will have excellent range.

From three ladies, said and believed to be of secession proclivities, the following facts were gleaned, viz: On Friday, April 10, they came from Williamston and passed, on the way between Williamston and Jamesville, infantry, artillery, and cavalry, said to be General Robertson's brigade.

From a prisoner whom our North Carolina cavalry took Thursday night, April 9, we learn that 11 miles from this place a squad of six cavalry pickets were stationed, with intervening couriers, to give the enemy at Washington notice of any attempted assistance from this direction.

From various sources we have heard of an iron-clad ram being built in the river above. Information this morning has been received to the effect that it is built to fit the prow of a steamer and that the enemy meditate an attack within a few days when it is completed. Apprehension is felt by the naval force that the two gunboats here, Perry and Underwriter, may not be able to resist it. With the present force here and with the constructed defenses it is believed we can hold this place against a large land force. Should the ram, however, succeed in getting opposite Plymouth the place would be untenable except with fearful loss. We have six or seven days' provisions on hand. Inclosed I send you a consolidated morning report of the land forces here.

I am, lieutenant, very respectfully, yours,
JOSIAH PICKETT,
Colonel, Commanding Post.

[Indorsement.]

The consolidated morning report will be sent in to-morrow morning.
GEORGE W. BARTLETT,
Acting Assistant Adjutant-General.

SPECIAL ORDERS, }   HDQRS. DEPARTMENT OF THE SOUTH,
    No. 190.   }   *Hilton Head, S. C., April* 12, 1863.

It having been officially represented to the major-general commanding by Brigadier-General Heckman, Maj. Solomon Giles, Third New York Artillery, and Capt. W. V. Hutchings, of the staff of Brigadier-General Stevenson, that Major-General Foster, commanding Department of North Carolina, is besieged and in danger of being captured by the enemy at Washington, N. C., Brigadier-General Heckman, U. S. Volunteers, is hereby ordered to proceed with his brigade, consisting of the following regiments: Ninth New Jersey, Twenty-third Massachusetts, Eighty-first New York, and Ninety-eighth New York, to New Berne, N. C., where he will report to Brigadier-General Palmer, or whoever may be the general in command, for service in the relieving of Major-General Foster.

This duty executed, or it being found that Major-General Foster has been already relieved, Brigadier-General Heckman will forthwith return with his command to this department.

By command of Major-General Hunter:

ED. W. SMITH,
Assistant Adjutant-General.

BALTIMORE, MD., *April* 13, 1863.

Major-General HALLECK:

Learning by telegraph yesterday that Suffolk was invested I came on from New York by the night train and am waiting for special boat to go to Fort Monroe.

JOHN A. DIX,
Major-General.

BALTIMORE, *April* 13, 1863.

Col. D. T. VAN BUREN:

I cannot help thinking that the attack on the Nansemond and Somerton road is a feint, and that the principal movement will be on the Nansemond, 8 miles from Suffolk. This should be looked to.

JOHN A. DIX,
Major-General.

FORT MONROE, VA., *April* 13, 1863.

Actg. Rear-Admiral LEE, *Newport News, Va.*:

General Peck telegraphs 11.50 a. m.:

Enemy is on three sides of us and advancing to cut the river communication. Ask the admiral to send light-draught vessels up.

D. T. VAN BUREN,
Assistant Adjutant-General.

VIA FORT MONROE, VA., *April* 13, 1863.
(Received 2.50 p. m.)

Maj. Gen. H. W. HALLECK,
General-in-Chief:

I am now in consultation with Major-General Peck. The enemy is in sight, and not far off. Artillery firing is going on slowly. Peck's position is strong, and will be vigilantly guarded. The only fear is that the enemy may cross the Nansemond. To prevent that, gunboats must be freely used. I will try to examine the river to-day. It is my opinion that the enemy's campaign is the recovery of the whole James River, and re-enforcements are arriving from various points, many of them from before Fredericksburg. The enemy's batteries have been open for some time. It is an imperative necessity that the Navy keep the Nansemond River open.

E. D. KEYES,
Major-General.

SUFFOLK, VA., *April* 13, 1863—5 p. m.
                                    (Received 6 p. m.)
Maj. Gen. H. W. HALLECK,
            General-in-Chief:

I have now completed a thorough examination of Major-General Peck's position except the river, which I am now going to examine to its mouth. I have been up and down both railroads to Norfolk and made the circuit of the lines. From every source it is made certain that upward of 40,000 rebels are in front and on the flanks of this position. The easiest way for the enemy to take it is to invest and starve us out. To prevent that I shall be able to give an opinion after going down the river. As most of the enemy are from the Rappahannock my present impression is that two divisions of Major-General Hooker's army ought to be sent here at once.

                                    E. D. KEYES,
                                Major-General, Commanding.

FORT MONROE, VA., *April* 13, 1863—11 p. m.
                                    (Received 14th, 12.10 a. m.)
Maj. Gen. H. W. HALLECK,
            General-in-Chief:

I have this moment returned from an examination of the Nansemond River. The enemy's sharpshooters line the left bank some distance down and all the passing steamers have been pelted to-day. Our pilot-house was struck seven times. The gunboats on that river are frail, wooden structures, which the enemy's field batteries can soon cripple or burn with hot shot. He can then without much exertion cross out of range of any of our works, get upon Peck's rear, and seize the two railroads, or attack his weakest side, which is from the Seaboard Railroad to the river, and along the river when the gunboats are out of the way. Once invested, it will be next to impossible to relieve Peck, and he would in a short time be starved into a surrender. The problem is a difficult one and requires the most able attention. Pickett's, Hood's, and Pryor's (now Davis') divisions are there. Pickett's left the Rappahannock February 15 and Hood's shortly after. The Southern Army is in fine health—soldiers made by poverty and hardships—and is perfectly armed. They have about fifty pieces of artillery and some cavalry. All or nearly all the horses are in poor condition. Coming down the river has increased, but not perfected, my knowledge of Peck's situation. I will need to observe it still more to-morrow. I will write more fully.

                                    E. D. KEYES,
                                Major-General, Commanding.

NORFOLK, *April* 13, 1863.
Admiral S. P. LEE:

Wise still threatens an attack on our forts just below Williamsburg and a gunboat on James River off College Creek would be of immense service to us. If a gunboat is not placed, Wise can be supplied by water. If you have no other boat to spare I would prefer to have that one at the mouth of the Nansemond sent up without delay, as an attack is anticipated.

                                    E. D. KEYES,
                                Major-General.

NORFOLK, *April* 13, 1863.

Acting Rear-Admiral LEE:

Another request has come for a gunboat off Williamsburg. The tower of the asylum is visible from the river; our line 1½ miles below that tower and the enemy's camp is above. I earnestly trust a gunboat may be sent up immediately if one has not gone.

E. D. KEYES,
Major-General.

UNITED STATES FLAG-SHIP MINNESOTA,
April 13, 1863.

Major-General KEYES,
Commanding Department:

Your two dispatches are received. I have no gunboat suitable to send off Williamsburg, and it would not be fit to send only one gunboat there if I had it.

S. P. LEE,
Acting Rear-Admiral.

SUFFOLK, VA., *April* 13, 1863—3.30 p. m.
(Received 4.20 p. m.)

Major-General HALLECK,
General-in-Chief:

Reliable information from intelligent deserters is to the effect that the enemy have 35,000 or 40,000 in our front, which have come from Fredericksburg, the condition of the roads rendering an attack there impossible. It is stated that D. H. Hill is advancing from North Carolina.

JOHN J. PECK,
Major-General.

FORT MONROE, VA., *April* 13, 1863—8.30 p. m.
(Received 10 p. m.)

Maj. Gen. H. W. HALLECK,
General-in-Chief:

Longstreet's advance division arrived in my front on Saturday and was followed by Pickett's, Hood's, and Anderson's yesterday. They advanced on my front and right flank about noon on the 12th, within extreme artillery range, and after much skirmishing fell back several miles. Early this morning they advanced on my front and rear with one division on the right flank. More or less artillery fire all day and much skirmishing. Colonel Foster's Light Troop handled the enemy's advance roughly, driving them back and retiring the picket line at dark. Anderson's division has been engaged on the water front with our gunboats and batteries. The firing has been brisk, and the enemy suffered. The command is in good spirits and will do its duty.

JOHN J. PECK,
Major-General.

SUFFOLK, VA., *April* 13, 1863—9 p. m.
(Received 10 p. m.)

Maj. Gen. H. W. HALLECK,
    General-in-Chief:

Longstreet's force is pretty well settled at 35,000. Co-operation of Hill expected. One division at least should be sent here, as they are fighting for the James River. He has one hundred and twenty pieces of artillery.

JOHN J. PECK,
Major-General.

SUFFOLK, *April* 13, 1863.

Major-General KEYES:

We have rations for about twelve days, including to-day. Please hurry up the stores as fast as possible.

JOHN J. PECK.

SUFFOLK, *April* 13, 1863.

Admiral S. P. LEE:

The enemy are said to be crossing at Sleepy Hole, below the mouth of the West Branch, where the river is wide. The river was left unprotected last night.

General Peck is at the front.

BENJ. B. FOSTER,
Assistant Adjutant-General.

SUFFOLK, VA., *April* 13, 1863—4 p. m.

Major-General HOOKER,
    Headquarters Army of the Potomac:

Intelligent and reliable deserters state that the force in my front, of 35,000 men, under Longstreet, has come from Fredericksburg in expectation of inaction on your part. D. H. Hill is said to be advancing from North Carolina.

JOHN J. PECK,
Major-General.

HEADQUARTERS ARMY OF THE POTOMAC,
April 13, 1863.

General PECK, *Suffolk:*

All of Longstreet's forces that have gone from here left in January and February last. None have left since. The enemy will be disappointed in the expectation you mention in your dispatch.

JOSEPH HOOKER,
Major-General.

SUFFOLK, VA., *April* 13, 1863—10 p. m.

Major-General HOOKER,
    Headquarters Army of the Potomac:

Three divisions have been more or less engaged all day. Early this morning one division advanced on the Somerton front, driving in the pickets, but was promptly repulsed, and our picket line was intact at dark. Some fine skirmishing by Colonel Foster's Light Troop and

Eleventh Pennsylvania Cavalry. On the rear or water line Anderson's force of 4,000 was held back by the gunboats and land batteries. The attack was vigorous and the result gratifying. Expect they will make a grand attack to-morrow. Longstreet has 35,000, some say 38,000, and from one hundred to one hundred and fifty pieces of artillery.

JOHN J. PECK,
Major-General.

(Copy to General Halleck.)

———

HEADQUARTERS,
Suffolk, Va., April 13, 1863.

Admiral LEE, *Newport News:*

The gunboats on the Nansemond in conjunction with the land batteries have been engaged through the day, repulsing Anderson's division very handsomely.

JOHN J. PECK,
Major-General.

———

YORKTOWN, April 13, 1863—9.30 a. m.

Major-General KEYES, *Norfolk:*

A dispatch just received from Colonel West reports all quiet at front. The picket lines are within 500 yards of each other. He is very anxious that a gunboat should be sent up James River to shell the enemy at Williamsburg. He says that the asylum tower is plainly visible from the James, and fire could be directed by the tower to the town; and the enemy's camp is north of town.

RUFUS KING,
Brigadier-General.

———

YORKTOWN, April 13, [1863]—9 p. m.

Major-General KEYES, *Norfolk:*

I have just received dispatch from West. He reports that a regiment of infantry and one of cavalry came into Williamsburg by Richmond road before sundown. Rumor places Wise's force at 6,000. Wagons loaded with furniture have been moving out of Williamsburg all day. The gunboat Morris tried to shell the enemy from York River this morning. Result not known. No gunboat yet in James River. Colonel West thinks that one should be there by morning with directions to shell the lower end of the town. He is prepared for attack at any time. No man hurt on our side to-day. Both our gunboats are off Queen's Creek to-night and will remain there.

RUFUS KING,
Brigadier-General.

———

FORT MONROE, April 13, 1863.

Brigadier-General CULLUM,
  Chief of Staff, Washington:

GENERAL: I leave at 12 m. Have you any orders for the Eighteenth Corps?

Palmer sent last night for re-enforcements, which General Keyes cannot send. Can any be sent from the Department of the South?

HENRY M. NAGLEE,
Brigadier-General.

WASHINGTON, *April* 13, 1863.

Brigadier-General NAGLEE:

Have no instructions. No re-enforcements can be sent from Department of the South.

G. W. CULLUM,
Chief of Staff.

———

SUFFOLK, VA., *April* 14, 1863—2.30 p. m.

Maj. Gen. H. W. HALLECK,
General-in-Chief:

I arrived here this morning. The post is closely invested with over 30,000 men. The report of the 1st instant, in the Adjutant-General's Office, will show our force. Two gunboats in the Nansemond are disabled; one is sunk. Our danger is that the enemy will cross the river and cut us off from Norfolk. I consider it necessary that an army corps, or at least two divisions, should be sent to Norfolk at once, so as to protect the Nansemond. The great superiority of the enemy makes it impossible to divide the force here with safety, and we cannot retreat on Norfolk without great sacrifice of property and life. This place must be held if possible.

JOHN A. DIX,
Major-General.

———

WAR DEPARTMENT,
Washington, D. C., April 14, 1863—7.15 p. m.

Major-General HEINTZELMAN, *Washington:*

GENERAL: You will immediately dispatch to Norfolk, reporting at Fort Monroe, 6,000 men or thereabouts. You will make requisitions on the Quartermaster's Department for transports. If necessary they will be recalled from Aquia Creek. This dispatch of troops must be made in preference to anything else and must be pushed with all possible haste, without regard to hours or to darkness.

H. W. HALLECK,
General-in-Chief.

———

SPECIAL ORDERS, }   HDQRS. DEPARTMENT OF WASHINGTON,
    No. 57.   }   *April* 14, 1863.

*   *   *   *   *   *   *

VII. The following troops will embark at daylight to-morrow morning for Norfolk, reporting at Fort Monroe:

The Second Brigade, General Abercrombie's division, with the exception of the Sixteenth Virginia Volunteers; the Third Brigade, General Abercrombie's division; the One hundred and seventeenth New York Volunteers, of Colonel Haskin's division; the Eleventh Rhode Island Volunteers, from the Convalescent Camp; the One hundred and sixty-ninth New York Volunteers, from General Martindale's command.

*   *   *   *   *   *   *

By command of Major-General Heintzelman:

C. H. POTTER,
Assistant Adjutant-General.

HEADQUARTERS FOURTH ARMY CORPS,
Yorktown, Va., April 14, 1863.

Maj. Gen. H. W. HALLECK,
    Commanding U. S. Army :

SIR : Major-General Dix arrived this morning and resumed command of the Department of Virginia.

During the nine days I was in temporary command of the department the approach of the enemy in great force down the Peninsula and upon Suffolk gave a serious aspect to affairs, and this paper is respectfully submitted as the result of my examinations and consequent conclusions while I was in command.

Of Peck's position and the surrounding country beyond Norfolk I had no ocular knowledge until the 6th instant, when I made a hasty visit to Suffolk by rail. Since that date I have made a careful examination of his defenses and passed over the other railroad from Norfolk and down the Nansemond River to Hampton Roads.

As I stated before in telegrams I consider our troops at Suffolk in a very critical situation, and it may be the rebels' boast that they have another Harper's Ferry affair on hand will be made good.

I have reflected on the following points :

1st. Is Peck secure against an attack, or is he able to resist an attack in his position ?

2d. Can the enemy cut his communication and invest him ?

3d. If the enemy should invest him have we the means to relieve him before he would be starved out?

4th. Can he retreat and take away his material ?

On the above points I conclude as follows:

1st. He is secure against an attack on any front now accessible to the enemy, and he will not be seriously attacked (feints will be made) until he is invested. After he is invested he is not secure from an attack.

2d. The enemy can cut his communications and invest him in spite of anything we can do to prevent him with the means north of Albemarle Sound and south of Hampton Roads and James River.

3d. If the enemy does invest him we could not break the investment after it had existed three days and relieve Peck with any available means within the command of the Government.

4th. I cannot give a positive opinion on this point. I have had no time to examine the line of retreat. The railroads are through the Dismal Swamp and are perfectly straight and the roadway narrow, and, on either side, an impracticable morass.

I assume that the Government knows Peck's strength and the amount of his supplies of provisions and ammunition. It is certain he has but a few days' supply of forage.

I have assumed all those facts of the last paragraph, and I have kept Napoleon's maxims in view (you called my attention to those maxims) in coming to my conclusions.

In regard to the Peninsula: If the line of Fort Magruder below Williamsburg is given up the enemy can go to Fort Monroe at once and possess everything outside the sand-spit on which the fort stands. Yorktown, owing to the ravines around it, would be nearly as uncomfortable as Fort Magruder now is, and of no great value to the Government. If the upper line is abandoned I trust this most sickly place (Yorktown) may be also abandoned. I recommended its abandonment in August last when called on for my views.

With one gunboat on James River, stationed opposite Williamsburg, and one additional regiment of infantry I could hold the line of Fort Magruder certainly. There being no gunboat there now Wise can have his supplies brought down there by water, and hold his camp there at his ease. Wise is now in a position to be easily captured, but I have not the force necessary. As I stated in my telegrams of yesterday and the day before, I thought re-enforcements necessary at once.

If any competent officer has examined and ascertained the difficulty the enemy would have to destroy the wooden gunboats and to cross the Nansemond, or to get round the left and cut the railroads, or to learn the roads and their capacity for retreat, I am ignorant of the fact. I did not simply because I had not the time. If Peck's 16,000 men and 4,000 horses, more or less, and his numerous artillery and supplies are surrendered I make no doubt that inquiry will be made on those subjects, but I shall not be able to answer.

I have the honor to remain, your most obedient servant,

E. D. KEYES,
Major-General, Commanding Fourth Corps.

FORT MONROE, VA.,
April 14, 1863—11.30 p. m.

Maj. Gen. H. W. HALLECK,
General-in-Chief:

I have just returned from Suffolk after going through the lines. General Peck is strong, but the danger of interception of his communications with Norfolk is imminent, as the gunboats are nearly all crippled. With two small divisions, say 5,000 each, we could repel the enemy. If we could have that number of men from the Army of the Potomac we could send them back in two weeks. General Peck has rations for twenty days and forage for ten. More forage goes up to-night. He must be relieved within twelve days at farthest.

JOHN A. DIX,
Major-General.

SUFFOLK, *April* 14, 1863.

Major-General DIX, *Fort Monroe:*

I am just informed that all the gunboats except the Smith Briggs have left the river, which is therefore almost entirely undefended.

JOHN J. PECK,
Major-General.

SUFFOLK, VA., *April* 14, 1863.

Major-General HALLECK, *General-in-Chief:*

Two gunboats have been disabled upon the Nansemond, and I fear I shall be unable to keep the river open.

JOHN J. PECK,
Major-General.

SUFFOLK, *April* 14, 1863.

Major-General DIX:

All the gunboats have left the river except mine. The West End went to Fort Monroe for ammunition. I most respectfully request that she be sent back as soon as she gets her ammunition on board.

JOHN C. LEE,
Captain, Commanding Smith Briggs.

SUFFOLK, VA., *April* 14, 1863.

General VIELE, *Norfolk:*

Send here at once every man you can spare.

JOHN A. DIX,
Major-General.

UNITED STATES FLAG-SHIP MINNESOTA,
Off Newport News, Va., April 14, 1863—11 a. m.

Major-General PECK,
Commanding at Suffolk, Va.:

On receipt of your dispatch last night I telegraphed the Department for light-draught, rifle-screened gunboats for the Nansemond, hoping there might be some of these in the Potomac Flotilla. The Department just replies that four boats are coming, but fear they cannot go far into the Nansemond. I shall apply at the fort for Nansemond pilots for them, and send them as far as they can go.

I shall have the light-draught tug Alert, just returned disabled from the Nansemond, repaired in a few hours. I have sent for some rifle-screening, and hope to increase to-day and to-morrow the force in the river.

S. P. LEE,
Actg. Rear-Admiral, Comdg. N. Atlantic Blockading Squadron.

UNITED STATES FLAG-SHIP MINNESOTA,
Off Newport News, Va., April 14, 1863.

Maj. Gen. JOHN A. DIX, U. S. A.,
Comdg. Seventh Army Corps, Fortress Monroe, Va.:

GENERAL: I am informed that the army transport Hunter Woodis, which can carry four or five pieces of field artillery, and have her light-draught, would be useful in the Nansemond. The transports might carry one or more field pieces with troops to fight them.

I have the honor to be, general, yours, respectfully,

S. P. LEE,
Actg. Rear-Admiral, Comdg. N. Atlantic Blockading Squadron.

YORKTOWN, *April* 14, 1863.

Actg. Rear-Admiral LEE,
Commanding North Atlantic Blockading Squadron:

General Dix is as anxious as myself to have a gunboat up James River opposite Williamsburg. I deem it absolutely necessary to save the line of Fort Magruder. If that is lost the whole Peninsula will be open to the enemy down to Fortress Monroe, and sharpshooters can render this place untenable. It would be better to lose two gunboats than to lose the Fort Magruder line. Whatever boat you send should have long-range guns, and should establish itself so as to fire by the line of the asylum tower.

E. D. KEYES,
Major-General.

YORKTOWN, *April* 14, 1863.

Colonel WEST, *Fort Magruder :*

I agree with you about the removal of the inhabitants from Williams-burg. They need not be interfered with, nor should fire be opened on the town except in case of another attack from that quarter.

I expect General Keyes here within an hour.

RUFUS KING,
Brigadier-General.

WASHINGTON, D. C., *April* 14, 1863.

Brigadier-General PALMER, *New Berne, N. C. :*

GENERAL: Your letter of the 9th instant is just received. I had hoped that General Keyes would send you 4,000 additional men, but his own condition was such that he deemed it necessary to counter-mand the order. At the present time it is impossible to send any other troops to you. Perhaps the circumstances may be different in a few days, but you must not rely upon receiving troops from any other department. Instead of sparing any, every general is pressing for more troops as though we had a cornucopia of men from which to supply their wants.

If any accident should occur to General Foster you will bear in mind that operations in North Carolina should be strictly defensive and the troops concentrated as much as possible. New Berne and Beaufort are the points of greatest importance.

Very respectfully, your obedient servant,

H. W. HALLECK,
General-in-Chief.

STEAMER HUNCHBACK,
Tuesday, April 14, 1863—1.30 p. m.

Maj. Gen. J. G. FOSTER, *Washington, N. C. :*

General Potter's letter of yesterday was received at 4 a. m. to-day. Fortunately every wish of yours indicated in that letter had been anticipated. By dint of labor, coaxing, threatening, stimulating with promise of reward, &c. (to the pilot and captain of the Escort), everything was arranged, and last night at dark the Escort started. Let me here remark that Colonel Sisson and officers of the Fifth Rhode Island Regiment aided the enterprise in every way. I have just made up my mind that the thing is a perfect success and that I was not mistaken in my belief that you could get any amount of men and supplies through the blockade. But I do not think Captain McCann is equal to this position. He ought to be above the blockade to reduce the batteries both at Hill's Point and Rodman's Point. It can be done, but it will not be done by the Navy unless we can get Flusser or some equally energetic officer here. I do not wish to do any injustice to any one; I only state my firm belief. Colonel Hoffman can explain something of my views to you.

General Potter, for you, expresses surprise that the Escort did not come through the night before, and that such lack of energy has been displayed in getting men and supplies to you. I would be glad if you would, after receiving all the information concerning these matters from

Colonel Hoffman, inform me where you think the blame lies. Don't spare me. When the history of "the siege of Washington" is written, if it is a disaster, a responsibility will rest somewhere; let it go where it belongs.

Lieutenant Wheaton goes immediately to New Berne for the North State, the shovels, and wheelbarrows, &c. He takes the Phœnix. Captain Gouraud remains here to perform the duties delegated to Colonel Hoffman. I hope to be with Captain Flusser not many hours after you receive this.

Your dispatches to General Halleck and General Dix will be forwarded immediately.

I sent transportation to Gatesville on the Chowan, to be there on the 13th, to receive any forces that may be sent by General Dix. Where will you have these re-enforcements if they arrive?

If the Escort returns here she will (unless you decide differently) take a return cargo.

This is written hastily, as there are many things to occupy me to-day.

Very respectfully, your obedient servant,

I. N. PALMER,
Brigadier-General, Commanding.

The signal officer here (Lieutenant Knox) has tried to signal to you to-day. He was on a small gunboat and the motion of the vessel prevented him from seeing properly. He is now out with the Southfield and I hope he will succeed. Don't fail to make the signal arrangement as perfect as possible.

WAR DEPARTMENT,
Washington, April 15, 1863—10.30 a. m.

Major-General DIX, *Fort Monroe, Va.:*

Six thousand men have been ordered to report to you at Fort Monroe. A portion embarked during the night; two gunboats have also been sent.

H. W. HALLECK,
General-in-Chief.

FORT MONROE, VA.,
April 15, 1863—8.30 p. m.

Maj. Gen. H. W. HALLECK,
General-in-Chief:

The enemy has not yet succeeded in crossing the Nansemond, though the pressure has been very heavy for several miles below Suffolk. The gunboats are holding a large force in check. A battery of 20-pounder rifled guns, which caused us much annoyance yesterday, was silenced to-day. The Smith Briggs, a newly-armed quartermaster's steamboat, was attacked in the river near General Peck's headquarters last night, but the assailants were driven off. Thus far the enemy has gained no advantage. He is pressing us at Williamsburg.

JOHN A. DIX,
Major-General.

SUFFOLK, VA., *April* 15, 1863—9 a. m.

Maj. Gen. H. W. HALLECK,
        General-in-Chief:

On Monday, with the aid of the gunboats, I was enab. ed to hold the line of the Nansemond, and things looked well, as I advised you, but yesterday 10,000 or 11,000 attacked the line of the river some miles down, and, with the aid of earthworks thrown up, cut off the water communication. All the gunboats except one were crippled and cut off many miles below. The enemy attempted to cross during the night but has not succeeded yet. I hope to hold him, although the river, by the curves, is some 12 miles in length before you reach the wide water, with an average width of 100 feet. At daylight I opened the Jericho Canal into the river and hope to fill up the marshes so as to impede their operations. A few troops at this time will make all secure. A large force in reserve is necessary, say 10,000, to take the initiative. If General Hill co-operates, more will be necessary. Prisoners state Washington has been taken.

JOHN J. PECK,
Major-General.

FORT MONROE, *April* 15, 1863.

Major-General PECK:

Troops are on their way to relieve you. Shall I order them to Bowers' Hill as fast as they arrive? Some must be here to-night unless the storm prevents.

JOHN A. DIX,
Major-General.

SUFFOLK, VA., *April* 15, [1863].

General DIX:

Hurry the troops here that first arrive, so that I can have enough to hold the river. All routes should be put in requisition. A day may be decisive. When their spies signal from Norfolk their arrival I fear they will attack.

JOHN J. PECK,
Major-General.

SUFFOLK, VA., *April* 15, [1863].

Brigadier-General VIELE, *Norfolk:*

It is just reported that the enemy, force and character unknown, have crossed at Sleepy Hole in spite of our gunboats. His attempt to cross in the narrow part of the river was defeated and his battery opposite silenced.

JOHN J. PECK,
Major-General.

FORT MONROE, *April* 15, 1863.

Major-General PECK, *Commanding, Suffolk:*

If the report be true would it not be inexpedient to carry out the suggestion in your last dispatch?

JOHN A. DIX,
Major-General.

April 15, 1863.

General Viele, *Commanding, Norfolk:*

If the enemy have crossed the Nansemond they may make a rapid movement on Norfolk for supplies. You must make the best disposition of your small force you can to oppose their entrance into the city. You will have re-enforcements to-night if the storm does not prevent.

JOHN A. DIX,
Major-General.

SUFFOLK, VA., *April 15, 1863.*

General Dix:

If the report be true the troops had better be massed at some point like that one mentioned by you. Will give you the very earliest intelligence. Sleepy Hole is the place named, half way down to the James, in the broad water, where the heavy boats go safely. As it is some miles from the track some trains will get through, especially on the Petersburg.

JOHN J. PECK,
Major-General.

SUFFOLK, VA., *April 15, 1863.*

Major-General Dix:

Only one regiment from Norfolk; another should be sent. We hold the Nansemond, although 11,000 were there yesterday and drove out the boats; much encouraged. Urge on supplies of forage and some heavy guns. One of my 20-pounder rifles burst on the Nansemond; it is our best gun. Can you send a few?

JOHN J. PECK,
Major-General.

FORT MONROE, *April 15, 1863.*

Major-General Peck:

General Viele has one regiment at Deep Creek, which is more important to you than to him. He has only two other regiments, with an aggregate of 1,300 men, of whom a part are at Bowers' Hill, 8 miles from Corinth, on the Seaboard road, with a section of artillery. The two other sections of his only battery are scattered. I will send you an old Vermont regiment from here, of 400 men, immediately. Telegraphed Halleck last night. Will send heavy guns.

JOHN A. DIX,
Major-General.

UNITED STATES FLAG-SHIP MINNESOTA,
Off Newport News, Va., April 15, 1863.

Maj. Gen. JOHN A. DIX, U. S. A.,
Comdg. Seventh Army Corps, Fortress Monroe, Va.:

GENERAL: I received your dispatch at 12.45 a. m., and will act accordingly.

S. P. LEE,
Actg. Rear-Admiral, Comdg. N. Atlantic Blockading Squadron.

APRIL 15, 1863.

Major-General PECK, *Commanding, Suffolk:*

I arrived at 10 last night and found your dispatch in regard to gun-boats. I ordered the West End back immediately. She was out of ammunition. I also telegraphed Admiral Lee, asking that his gunboats might go back. Received his answer after midnight that he would act as I requested.

JOHN A. DIX,
Major-General.

SUFFOLK, VA., *April* 15, 1863.

General DIX:

Up to this time I hold the line of the river and am satisfied nothing has passed over yet. The pressure has been heavy all along the river down to the West Branch. Gunboats there are holding a large force. My flanks are yet intact.

About noon we silenced the rebel battery of 20-pounder rifled, which caused so much trouble yesterday. The Smith Briggs was attacked near my headquarters in the night but drove off the rebels.

JOHN J. PECK,
Major-General.

UNITED STATES FLAG-SHIP MINNESOTA,
Off Newport News, Va., April 15, 1863—p. m.

Maj. Gen. JOHN A. DIX, U. S. A.,
Comdg. Seventh Army Corps, Fortress Monroe, Va.:

GENERAL: I sent two armed tugs into the Nansemond this morning, where I have two other small and armed vessels. The Mount Washington, a river steamer with fixed pieces on board, was towed out this morning much disabled from severe fighting in the Upper Nansemond yesterday.

You must not rely upon these few frail and open ferry-boats and river steamers, which you call gunboats, to keep the rebels from crossing the Upper Nansemond, which is long, narrow, and crooked, a mere creek, and from which we were driven yesterday. These craft are effective only from the gallantry with which they are fought, with their boilers, steam-pipes, and magazines all exposed to the concentrated fire of the rebel batteries, while the sharpshooters pick off with facility our unprotected gunners.

Reflect that these little vessels go into such a fight much in the exposed condition in which breached forts surrender when their magazines, &c., are exposed. I must call your attention to this in order that you may adapt your military dispositions to the necessities of your situation, which is not suitable to the operation of vessels.

General Keyes keeps calling for gunboats off Williamsburg. This ship cannot go there, and my force is not strong enough to detach from in view of the rebel naval force above.

The public interests here and even the communications of the Army of the Potomac depend on the security of this position.

I have the honor to be, general, very respectfully, yours,

S. P. LEE,
Actg. Rear-Admiral, Comdg. N. Atlantic Blockading Squadron.

P. S.—4 P. M.—Yours of this date, also a report from Lieutenant Cushing, dated 1.15 p. m., just received. Lieutenant Cushing says the enemy has not seen fit to renew the action of yesterday; that he had just received a dispatch from General Peck stating that the rebels had not crossed as yet, but believed they would try it this afternoon or to-night. Lieutenant Cushing says that the rebels intended to cross below the West Branch yesterday, but were beaten back by the fire of the gunboats. I had already instructed Lieutenant Lamson to do all he could to prevent the enemy from crossing the Nansemond. Lieutenant Lamson expects to go up the river on the arrival of the tug Alert, whose rudder has been repaired and is being shipped, with the assistance of a diver.

Lieutenant Cushing surmises that the rebels may be masking batteries to protect their crossing.

> S. P. LEE,
> *Acting Rear-Admiral.*

SUFFOLK, *April* 15, 1863.

Admiral LEE:

There has been a large force on the Upper Nansemond all day, but they have been prevented from crossing. I fear they will attempt this to-night. If your boats can arrive at once we shall be able to hold the river.

> PECK,
> *Major-General.*

ROANOKE ISLAND, *April* 15, 1863.

GENERAL: The inclosed letter was sent open to me yesterday at the blockade below Washington to be forwarded through General Dix. I immediately ran here to have them forwarded by the commanding officer here. Dispatches for Admiral Lee go at the same time.

The expedition under General Spinola, mentioned in General Foster's letter, returned to New Berne the third day after it left. General S. decided that his force was entirely too small to attempt to push its way to Washington.

As soon as I heard of his intention to return I determined that men and supplies could be sent through the blockade, and I placed one regiment, with a quantity of provisions and ammunition, on board a river steamer and went with them myself. After some little delay on account of weather and the fears of the pilot I succeeded by threatening, promising pecuniary reward, &c., to push the boat through. The navy gunboats ran up to the blockade to assist in case of accident. The steamer went through safely, I think. She was lying (as I am informed by a signal officer) safely at the wharf in Washington yesterday.

There are more troops and supplies near the blockade ready to be pushed in if General Foster wishes them.

General Wessells, who arrived in New Berne the day before I left, informs me in a dispatch of yesterday that the enemy are assembling a force at Swansborough. From there they threaten Beaufort, Morehead City, Fort Macon, and the railroad. This, I think, is only to prevent our sending too many of our forces from here toward Washington.

Lieutenant-Commander Flusser, a bold, energetic naval officer, has arrived to take command of the fleet below the blockade, and I think he will be able to reduce or cripple the batteries on the river.

A force (a brigade, one battery, and two companies of cavalry) has been sent by General Wessells again in the direction of Washington to divert the attention of the enemy from Washington.

The force at present at New Berne, effective strength, is in the neighborhood of 9,000. I can still send a force to General Foster and hold the place.

I am, general, very respectfully, your obedient servant,

I. N. PALMER,
Brigadier-General.

[Indorsement.]

HDQRS. DEPT. OF VIRGINIA, SEVENTH ARMY CORPS,
Fort Monroe, April 17, 1863.

Supposed to be for Major-General Halleck, and respectfully forwarded.

JOHN A. DIX,
Major-General.

STEAMER THOMAS COLYER, *April* 15, 1863.
Maj. Gen. J. G. FOSTER, U. S. V.,
Washington, N. C.:

GENERAL: Yesterday your dispatches for Admiral Lee and General Dix were received, and as soon as I was assured of the safe arrival at Washington of the Escort I determined to run to Roanoke and direct the dispatches forwarded from there. I wrote to General Dix, informing him of what had occurred since your letter was written. I also notified the admiral of the arrival of Lieutenant-Commander Flusser.

I received the dispatch from General Wessells informing of the assembling of the enemy of Swansborough. From there they threaten the railroad, Morehead City, &c. Give me your advice, if possible, as to the best mode of operating in that direction. It was my intention to run immediately back to the blockade, but I will return to New Berne to see the state of affairs there, in order to get more men and supplies in case you should need them.

Please inform me if you wish the forwarding of these to be continued. I think Captain Flusser will change the affairs at the blockade somewhat.

The Colyer needs a few hours' work on her, which she can have done while her cargo is getting ready. It is my impression that any amount of men and supplies can be sent through.

Four thousand men were ordered from the Fourth Army Corps to re-enforce here, and I sent transportation to Gatesville for them. The order was countermanded, and I expect the transports to return immediately. Fighting at Suffolk, where papers say that Longstreet has been driven back. Nothing positive, however, is known.

Very hastily, respectfully, yours,

I. N. PALMER,
Brigadier-General, U. S. Volunteers.

UNITED STATES FLAG-SHIP MINNESOTA,
Off Newport News, Va., April 15, 1863—4.30 p. m.

B. B. FOSTER,
Asst. Adjt. Gen. for General Peck, Suffolk, Va.:

Lieutenant Cushing reports that the enemy had not crossed at 1.15 o'clock to-day.

The tug which brought his report says all is quiet on the Lower Nansemond, and our boats moving between Hallowing Point and the obstructions at Western Branch.

The boats were driven disabled out of the Upper Nansemond yester day. The navy boats will do all in their power to assist you, but I fear those I could send this morning may not from their draught be able to cross the obstructions.

> S. P. LEE,
> *Acting Rear-Admiral.*

> SUFFOLK, VA., *April* 16, 1863—9.30 a. m.

Major-General HALLECK, *General-in-Chief:*

My lines, which extend along the Nansemond from mouth of West Branch to swamp on the left, are occupied, and are about 16 miles in length. The enemy has failed to turn either flank and has not dared an assault. Longstreet is resolved upon getting in if possible. He is cutting out extensive roads, destroyed and blocked. Parties were sent to blow up culverts, but failed. My roads are well guarded. If I hold my flanks, he will be compelled to assault after shelling from commanding ground. He has a great preponderance of artillery as well as other branches.

> JOHN J. PECK,
> *Major-General.*

> FORT MONROE, VA., *April* 16, 1863—10.30 a. m.
> (Received 11.30 a. m.)

Maj. Gen. H. W. HALLECK, *General-in-Chief:*

General Peck's dispatch, just forwarded, will inform you of the state of things this morning. I have given him every man that can be spared from Norfolk, and have taken care of the army supplies there, so that if the enemy should succeed in crossing the river and should move on that city he will find nothing except coal. No troops have arrived yet. If I had 10,000 men I could land at Smithfield, take the enemy in the rear, and make his movement on Suffolk a very disastrous one to him. Indeed, we should have that additional force under any circumstances, as the number of men and quality of material at Suffolk is too great to be put at hazard.

> JOHN A. DIX,
> *Major-General.*

> WAR DEPARTMENT,
> *Washington, April* 16, 1863—10 a. m.

Major-General DIX, *Fort Monroe, Va.:*

Have re-enforcements begun to arrive? Send back transports as rapidly as possible; they are greatly needed here.

> H. W. HALLECK,
> *General-in-Chief.*

> NORFOLK, *April* 16, 1863.
> (Received 12.10 p. m.)

Major-General HALLECK:

No troops arrived an hour ago when I left Fort Monroe. Not a moment shall be lost in the. return of transports. Wires are down to Suffolk. I hope it is accidental.

> JOHN A. DIX,
> *Major-General.*

WASHINGTON, D. C., *April* 16, 1863.

Major-General DIX:

Every transport that could be spared was sent with troops. When any of the vessels return it will be determined whether more troops can be sent to you.

H. W. HALLECK,
General-in-Chief.

SUFFOLK, VA., *April* 16, 1863.
(Received 7.20 p. m.)

Maj. Gen. H. W. HALLECK,
General-in-Chief:

My lines are still secure. Only one gunboat is here. Two are feeling their way up, in concert with my batteries. Deserters say Longstreet has been disappointed in his operations against Suffolk. He assured his troops they would be in this place last Monday.

JOHN J. PECK,
Major-General, Commanding.

SUFFOLK, VA., *April* 16, 1863.

Maj. Gen. JOHN A. DIX:

I hold the line of the river intact. Have urged the boats to feel their way up under our protection. All safe yet.

The enemy is cutting out extensive roads that we obstructed for miles and will perhaps move around more to the right. Push on the men and guns.

JOHN J. PECK,
Major-General.

SUFFOLK, *April* 16, 1863.

General DIX and
General VIELE:

I have doubled my patrols on both railroads. Individuals are trying to get in and blow up the culverts. One of my men was killed while guarding the wire.

PECK,
Major-General.

SUFFOLK, VA., *April* 16, 1863.

General DIX:

Have been on my lines all day. We hold the enemy's forces in check and I hope he will not be able to get over the river. Only the Smith Briggs is here. One or two boats are feeling their way up slowly in connection with the troops along the shore. Longstreet must be waiting for Hill, who can come by rail via Weldon. All parties distinctly state that such a combination was made. They want the whole line of the James a port for their iron-clads, and will ere long draw in their lines.

JOHN J. PECK,
Major-General.

UNITED STATES FLAG-SHIP MINNESOTA,
April 16, 1863—1 a. m.

General PECK:

Your dispatch is just received. We have now four vessels in the Nansemond with orders to do their best to prevent the enemy from crossing it. I fear that but one of these will be able to get above the obstructions. Two of our lightest draughts have returned disabled. The vessels expected from the Potomac have not arrived.

S. P. LEE,
Acting Rear-Admiral.

HDQRS. DEPT. OF VIRGINIA, SEVENTH ARMY CORPS,
Fort Monroe, April 16, 1863.

Admiral LEE:

Every disposable man has been put on the river. I have re-enforced General Peck to the extent of my ability. If your gunboats could feel their way up we could protect them from our side. The West End was disabled, but went up again at 6 last evening. Our line is intact as yet. I am just going to Norfolk to be back to-night.

JOHN A. DIX,
Major-General.

UNITED STATES FLAG-SHIP MINNESOTA,
Off Newport News, April 16, 1863.

Maj. Gen. JOHN A. DIX, U. S. A.,
Comdg. Seventh Army Corps, Fortress Monroe, Va.:

GENERAL: The master of the bark Edisto informed me, in his letter of March 22, that—

While lying at anchor in the mouth of the Potomac River, with a head wind, the captain of the port of Fortress Monroe came up and boarded my vessel and demanded my papers, as he suspected contraband goods, and after a careful overhauling of the same said they were all right, but ordered me into Hampton Roads.

Did Captain Millward order the Edisto here after he had ascertained that she was all right and had notified her master? If so, was the Edisto communicated with by the army authorities and notified that she could proceed on her voyage after her arrival outside the guard ship and before she attempted to run into the Roads? I ask the favor of a reply at your convenience, for my report of the case.

I have the honor to be, general, very respectfully, yours,

S. P. LEE,
Actg. Rear-Admiral, Comdg. N. Atlantic Blockading Squadron.

FORT MONROE, *April 16, 1863.*

Major-General PECK:

Just returned from Norfolk. Troops are arriving and will be sent over without delay.

JOHN A. DIX,
Major-General.

HEADQUARTERS FOURTH ARMY CORPS,
Yorktown, April 16, 1863.

Major-General DIX,
    Commanding Department of Virginia, Fort Monroe:

The enemy's pickets are in Williamsburg, and Governor Wise's troops have taken and paroled as prisoners of war two cavalrymen who were acting as nurses to the insane—to those whom Governor Wise styled Virginia's "little ones," and as belonging to a "hospital the most exempt of all from the least touch of war." I have ordered Dr. Wager and the two paroled cavalrymen to withdraw from the asylum.

E. D. KEYES,
Major-General.

FORT MONROE, VA., *April* 16, 1863.
(Received 6 p. m.)

Maj. Gen. H. W. HALLECK,
    General-in-Chief:

I send a dispatch from General Foster of the 12th. I have one from General Palmer of the 15th saying that a river steamboat, with supplies of provisions and ammunition and a regiment, had run the blockade, and was safe at the wharf at Washington the 14th:

FORT WASHINGTON, N. C., *April* 12, 1863.

Maj. Gen. H. W. HALLECK:

GENERAL: I have the honor to report that no very material change in the position of opposing forces around this town has taken place since the date of my letter of the 5th instant. The enemy has been constantly at work erecting batteries, and now has in full operation six batteries, mounting seven guns, on this side of the river, north side of the town, and three batteries, mounting six guns, on the south side of the river opposite the town. Added to these are the batteries erected to prevent boats coming up the river, some miles down. The guns are, however, mostly rifled, of small caliber, none being larger than 20-pounder Parrotts, except one 32-pounder smooth-bore. The works of the defensive have kept pace with the offensive, being always a little ahead, and the result of each day's firing has been the silencing of the enemy's batteries, forcing them to withdraw their guns from sight. The firing on both sides is quite sharp for a short time each day. No killed or wounded since my last letter. The force that I directed to march for my relief from New Berne has not as yet exhibited any result. General Palmer reports that the advance guard left New Berne on Wednesday under General Spinola. The latter general was under the impression that the whole force in his front was 16,000 men, double his own force. I have therefore to renew my application for re-enforcements, and that the number be increased to 10,000 men; also for General Naglee, who has been ordered to report to me. He hurried off as soon as possible to take command of the operating force. I am confident that I can hold out here provided I am supplied with ammunition and provisions from below. There is no great difficulty in supplying us by means of vessels and boats running the gauntlet of the batteries; and although the gunboats and our transports have not as yet fulfilled our expectations in this respect, yet I am informed by General Palmer that arrangements are now made to send me supplies of men and ammunition. I do not intend to yield one inch on any point if I can in any way prevent it, and shall therefore contest the occupation of this place until General Hill is forced to withdraw. I beg that you will look favorably upon my application for re-enforcements, unless the necessities of the service forbid it, for without them some disaster to our arms may occur in this department. The enemy's numbers are fully equal to the representations in my letters of last month, and from their movements I am confirmed in my opinion that as soon as the main army is forced to evacuate Virginia the field of operations will be this State; hence their efforts to obtain possession of the eastern counties, which are the most fertile in the State.

J. G. FOSTER,
Major-General, Commanding.

JOHN A. DIX,
Major-General.

NEW BERNE, N. C., *April 16*, 1863.
(Received April 17, 6.20 p. m.)

Maj. Gen. H. W. HALLECK,
   General-in-Chief:

 I left Washington, N. C., yesterday morning and run past the rebel batteries in the steamer Escort, which had reached Washington the previous night with the Fifth Rhode Island Volunteers and supplies on board. My object is to take the field at the head of the relieving forces and to fight a decisive battle, but I am not sure of the result. I have sent two dispatches for re-enforcements from the Department of Virginia, but understand none can be sent. General Naglee shows me General Cullum's dispatch of the 13th instant saying none can be sent from the Department of the South. I have to ask again, very respectfully, to have the detachment of the Eighteenth Army Corps, now in the Department of the South, ordered back as soon as possible, inasmuch as the rebel forces at Charleston, now liberated by the failure of the attack, will re-enforce the already large force in this State against which I am now contending. I left the troops in Washington in good spirits, the defenses good, and everything favorable for holding out as long as may be desired.

        J. G. FOSTER,
         Major-General.

NEW BERNE, N. C., *April 16*, [1863].
(Received April 18, 11.35 a. m.)

Maj. Gen. H. W. HALLECK,
   General-in-Chief:

 I have been obliged to concentrate my forces in sufficient numbers to meet the overpowering forces of the enemy and to evacuate Elizabeth City, Winfield, and Plymouth. This step was rendered necessary owing to information from Fort Monroe, showing that no re-enforcements could be expected from there, and from the telegram of General Cullum to General Naglee saying that no troops could be expected from the Department of the South.

        J. G. FOSTER,
       Major-General, Commanding.

NEW BERNE, N. C., *April 16*, 1863.
(Received April 18, 11.20 p. m.)

Maj. Gen. H. W. HALLECK,
   General-in-Chief:

 I have the honor to inform you that the advance of Heckman's brigade has arrived from the Department of the South. I am very grateful for this opportune re-enforcement, which will be of great service in the operations which, commencing to-morrow, will culminate in a battle in a few days. May I respectfully urge again the necessity of transferring the whole of the detachment of the Eighteenth Army Corps to North Carolina? My reason for reiterating this request is that re-enforcements are daily arriving to General D. H. Hill, and are supposed to be from vicinity of Charleston, though one of these regiments is known to be from Longstreet's force on the Blackwater. General Longstreet was with General Hill in conference the other day in front of Washington, N. C. The object and purpose of the consultation is not known, but must of course have been in regard to co-operation of the forces on the Blackwater and of North Carolina, and from the presence of a Virginia brigade and the one regiment recently arrived from the Blackwater I believe the feint to be on the Blackwater and the real attack to be here. These facts are submitted for your consideration. .

J. G. FOSTER,
Major-General, Commanding.

FORT MONROE, *April* 17, 1863.

Major-General HALLECK:

Is any general officer to come with the troops?

JOHN A. DIX,
Major-General.

WAR DEPARTMENT,
Washington, April 17, 1863—12 noon.

Major-General DIX, *Fort Monroe, Va.:*

You already have a larger proportion of general officers than we have here; nevertheless, if possible, I will send you another. Whether 4,000 more troops can be sent to you will depend upon the condition of affairs when the transports return. In any forward operations by you against the enemy, is not West Point the proper point? I will write you more fully by mail.

H. W. HALLECK,
General-in-Chief.

WASHINGTON, D. C., *April* 17, 1863.

Major-General DIX, *Fort Monroe, Va.:*

GENERAL: If the enemy has given up his attempt upon Suffolk and Norfolk it is probably on account of a movement of General Hooker. I think that Lee's main army will be massed between Richmond and the Rappahannock. This would of course give you an opportunity to operate in the direction of Hicks' Ford or Weldon, to destroy the railroads connecting with the South. But would that be a safe operation? Moreover, would it not be contrary to principle? The enemy would be between you and Hooker's army ready to strike at either Would he not in his central position have the same advantage over you and Hooker which he had last year over McClellan and Pope? It certainly seems so to me. Moreover, while you were operating south of James River might not the enemy recapture Williamsburg and Yorktown? Would it not be more in accordance with principles for you and Hooker to act as nearly together as possible and at the same time to secure your smaller force from the enemy's heavy blows? Suppose while General Hooker operates against the enemy's front you threaten his flank and rear by the Pamunkey and Mattapony in such a way as to secure your own retreat, would there not be greater chance of success? It seems to me that West Point furnishes you a most excellent base for such an operation. With the gunboats and a few heavy guns put in battery it could be made secure against greatly superior numbers. Moreover, while affording assistance to Hooker's operations it will serve as a protection to your line by Williamsburg and Yorktown. I am therefore of opinion that the moment you can safely withdraw troops from the south side of James River you should occupy West Point and operate as here suggested. The movement if made should be prompt and rapid, so as to force the enemy to give up all attempts upon Suffolk and Norfolk.

Please inform me by telegraph whether you adopt my views, but without stating what they are.

Very respectfully, your obedient servant,

H. W. HALLECK,
General-in-Chief.

FORT MONROE, VA., *April* 17, 1863.
(Received 9 p. m.)

Maj. Gen. H. W. HALLECK,
General-in-Chief:

We need field artillery at Suffolk by reason of the extent of our lines. If you can send two or three batteries it would be a great relief.

JOHN A. DIX,
Major-General.

FORT MONROE, *April* 17, 1863.

Major-General HALLECK, *General-in-Chief:*

Everything quiet last night. Some fighting yesterday. I am going up the Nansemond this morning. Six thousand men have arrived. Yesterday we captured the equipage of a regiment.

JOHN A. DIX,
Major-General.

FORT MONROE, *April* 17, 1863.

Major-General PECK:

I know nothing of the organization of the troops that have come and are coming. I have sent you, with the Nineteenth Wisconsin and Ninth Vermont, about 5,000 men; more coming. In order not to lose a moment I have not stopped them here. You must use them as you think best. I am not even advised whether a general officer is coming; hope to learn this morning.

JOHN A. DIX,
Major-General.

SUFFOLK, VA., *April* 17, 1863.

General DIX:

We are safe on the river. West End is probably below. One of the boats is working along up slowly in conjunction with the troops. I hold five points with artillery, and all the others are guarded. General Hood cannot force the river now.

JOHN J. PECK,
Major-General.

FORT MONROE, *April* 17, 1863.

Major-General PECK:

There are eight Navy gunboats on the Nansemond, six at and below West Branch. The enemy must cross if at all [high] up. The battery at West Branch was silenced after disabling the Teazer. Lieutenant Cushing is confident the railroad from Philadelphia* is reopened and the bridge rebuilt. If so, the enemy is at ease as to supplies.

JOHN A. DIX,
Major-General.

SUFFOLK, VA., *April* 17, 1863.

Major-General HALLECK, *Washington* :

It gives me great pleasure to say that I hold everything. The enemy maneuvered to throw me off my guard on the river below, which had the effect opposite to his wishes. Instead of withdrawing I re-enforced considerably. New troops have just arrived. Whether they arrived or not, no yielding or surrender would be permitted.

JOHN J. PECK,
Major-General.

SUFFOLK, VA., *April* 17, 1863.

Major-General DIX:

I have ordered Major Stratton with a force to South Mills to hold that outlet at all hazards and to watch General Hill's moves. He is directed to communicate with any troops at Elizabeth City. My line will be the Nansemond River, the Dismal Swamp to the Pasquotank River. General Viele will of course aid all he can with his men.

JOHN J. PECK,
Major-General.

SUFFOLK, *April* 17, 1863.

Major-General DIX:

Longstreet has not asked for the women and children. All communication is cut off for them, and they can get no supplies from without. In a short time they will have to be fed by us. I believe I shall call upon him to remove them or feed them.

PECK,
Major-General.

FORT MONROE, *April* 17, 1863.

Major-General PECK:

More troops have gone. I have now sent 7,400. Give me every morning a brief *résumé* of the preceding twenty-four hours, and I will advise the General-in-Chief. I think of going up the Nansemond this morning to West Branch; perhaps higher up.

JOHN A. DIX,
Major-General.

---

* Cipher.

FORT MONROE, April 17, 1863.

Major-General PECK:

Colonel Gurney is in command. He is just leaving. It is a regularly organized division. Foster being re-enforced, Hill cannot ———*
Can you not now act on the offensive? With your prudence I should fear no evil result. The enemy is full of stratagem and will need careful watching. I am just off for Nansemond.

JOHN A. DIX,
Major-General.

SUFFOLK, VA., April 17, 1863.

General VIELE:

We hold everything up to this time. Both my flanks are threatened. Longstreet is pressing on the river. He is building batteries at the mouth of the West Branch. Only one boat is with me. My impression is he cannot force a passage. Much skirmishing on all the avenues of approach.

Press on the men. Advise me of everything you hear.

JOHN J. PECK,
Major-General.

NEW BERNE, N. C., April 17, 1863.

Maj. Gen. H. W. HALLECK,
General-in-Chief:

Being about to start with a relieving force to raise the siege of Washington, I learned that the enemy had evacuated the batteries in front of Washington, and deserters say that the cause was that they were ordered to re-enforce the army in Virginia. I shall march myself with my force in pursuit and endeavor to overtake the enemy.

J. G. FOSTER,
Major-General.

SUFFOLK, VA., April 17, 1863.

General DIX:

I expect they will attempt to force a crossing somewhere in the darkness. Have taken great pains and every precaution. One of the railways is complete, so deserters say. All activity along the river. Their sharpshooters are very numerous. Have you any? We felt the enemy to-day on the South Quay and found his force large. Will more children [cavalry] arrive?

JOHN J. PECK,
Major-General.

SUFFOLK, April 17, 1863.

Major-General DIX:

Your message is not complete. It asks if I can act offensively; also says you fear evil will result, as enemy is full of stratagems. Will you repeat it? My opinion is that we shall have all we can do to hold the Nansemond and Dismal Swamp and Pasquotank. I am pressing them with light troops, and brisk firing is heard in several directions.

JOHN J. PECK,
Major-General.

---

* Message incomplete as sent. No record of it as received.

FORT MONROE, *April* 17, 1863.

Major-General PECK:

I said through your prudence there would be no evil result from your acting offensively, and that the enemy was full of stratagems and needed close watching. I have just returned from West Branch. Brought down General French's engineer. He was captured this morning by Lieutenant Cushing's picket. Will telegraph again.

JOHN A. DIX,
Major-General.

SUFFOLK, *April* 17, 1863—8.50 p. m.

Major-General DIX:

Until some men are executed in front of Fort Union for cowardice I shall not feel safe in my responsible command. Some companies have behaved very badly, and the example is highly pernicious. I must try them, and must be sustained when I act.

PECK,
Major-General.

FORT MONROE, *April* 17, 1863.

Major-General PECK, *Commanding, Suffolk:*

You will be sustained in any measures you may adopt for the punishment of cowardice or misbehavior in the face of the enemy. Try the miscreants at once. I have recommended Colonel Foster's promotion.

JOHN A. DIX,
Major-General.

YORKTOWN, *April* 17, 1863.

Major-General DIX, *Commanding:*

Yesterday I found a rebel battery of two rifled guns (Lieutenant Gillis thought they were Whitworths) on the left bank of the Pamunkey, 3 miles above West Point. They fired some twenty or thirty shots at us, which fell over and all around us, but none struck the gunboat. This morning at 4 o'clock I noticed the glare of camp fires on the clouds on the Gloucester side. The glare represented a large camp, but it was probably that of the 500 cavalry over there.

Governor Wise's pickets are now above Williamsburg. His boasting to take the forts has not yet been made good.

As it is represented the inmates of the asylum are on the borders of absolute starvation I have ordered up ten days' rations and sent back the paroled attendants.

E. D. KEYES,
Major-General.

HEADQUARTERS FOURTH ARMY CORPS,
OFFICE OF THE ASSISTANT ADJUTANT-GENERAL,
Fort Yorktown, Va., April 17, 1863.

Lieutenant-Colonel FARNSWORTH,
Chief Quartermaster Fourth Corps:

COLONEL: The commanding general is informed that notwithstanding the late occupation of Williamsburg by the rebel forces under General Wise and the consequent abandonment of the city by the Union troops, no provision whatever has been made for the support of the inmates of the lunatic asylum, tenanted as it is by their own kith and kin and by a class of patients demanding of all the civilized world the tenderest care and solicitude.

The commanding general is not willing that the imputation of inhumanity and want of civilization, so justly chargeable to these traitors to their country and enemies of their own blood, should rest, even with the lightest touch of seeming truth, upon himself or those in his command as representing in this section of the country the dignity and care of the Government of the United States.

Notwithstanding, therefore, that many of the servants of the asylum and nurses of its inmates were forcibly carried away by the rebels and the majority of the others have, of their own will, abandoned their charge; notwithstanding that two of our own soldiers placed as nurses to the lunatics were captured and paroled as prisoners of war, and notwithstanding that the city of Williamsburg and the asylum are not occupied by the forces of the United States and are beyond the picket lines of those forces, yet, in the name of humanity and Christianity, the commanding general directs that a ten days' supply of rations for 250 men (that being about the number of inmates at present in the asylum) be sent at once to Williamsburg to be delivered at once to the officer in charge of the asylum for the use of its inmates.

Very respectfully, your obedient servant,

C. C. SUYDAM,
Assistant Adjutant-General.

———

YORKTOWN, VA., *April 17, 1863.*

Col. R. M. WEST,
Commanding Advanced Brigade:

Johnson's regiment will remain with you for the present at least; they had better make camp, and shelter tents will be furnished them on requisition to-morrow. The general has urged the matter of a gunboat near you on James River, but Admiral Lee says that it cannot be furnished; consequently the whole left flank on the river from a short distance above Newport News is open and will need constant watching. A squadron of the Second Massachusetts Cavalry will report to you to-morrow; they will have shelter tents; they are about 100 strong. The general desires that Mr. Sweeny make an official written application for the protection asked for the asylum, stating on what it is based; he will then give it the proper consideration. Meantime he desires that Mr. Sweeny be furnished with a copy of my letter to Colonel Farnsworth in regard to sending the supplies to the asylum, that General Wise may learn in what estimation he is held. Major Hall has not seen the general, who directs that you picket your left as strongly as possible with the forces which will be at your command.

C. C. SUYDAM,
Assistant Adjutant-General.

———

FORT MONROE, VA., *April 17, 1863.*

Maj. Gen. J. G. FOSTER:

MY DEAR GENERAL: Your dispatch went to General Halleck last evening. A letter from General Palmer three days later (the 15th) informed us that you had received a regiment, with ammunition and provisions, through the blockade.

I am very sorry I cannot aid you. Suffolk is closely invested by Longstreet with over 30,000 men. The left bank of the Nansemond to the West Branch is occupied. Our gunboats hold the river and prevent the enemy from crossing, but he has disabled several of them. We have our hands full. I have just returned from the West Branch, where the enemy has a battery and rifle-pits, from which the firing is incessant.

We captured General French's engineer to-day.

Thus far the enemy has gained no advantage over us.

Trusting your gallant resistance may be successful, I am, sincerely, yours,

JOHN A. DIX.

UNITED STATES FLAG-SHIP MINNESOTA,
Off Newport News, Va., April 17, 1863.

Major-General FOSTER,
Commanding Military Department of North Carolina:

MY DEAR GENERAL: I am glad to hear by the steamer Spaulding that you are at New Berne. The experience attending your escape will give you a practical idea of the difference between the endurance and capabilities of frail, improvised wooden gunboats and earthworks. I saw in the papers that a brigade hesitated to land and attack, but waited for the little Lockwood to silence a battery of field artillery occupying earthworks which the enemy had abandoned last spring.

I mention this now that you are in less trouble, as in your private letter from Washington you speak of the gunboats as having too much veneration for such batteries. The Army places a complimentary but exaggerated opinion upon the capabilities of these gunboats.

In the Mississippi a scattered battery of six small field pieces did great damage to two regular Navy gunboats commanded by gallant officers. Here, at this time, on the narrow Upper Nansemond, a miserable creek, our frail, light-armed, light-draught steam-craft, called gunboats, with their powder and steam magazines and their machinery all so exposed and so vulnerable, are fighting the enemy's artillery and sharpshooters with great gallantry and sustaining much loss in killed, wounded, and injury to the vessels, which are much cut up, grounding, and having no water to work in.

The combat would be much more equal if our troops fought theirs with like means, as they should do, but somehow they don't see it.

The calls so numerous and so constant for gunboats to defend army posts are distressing, because so earnest and so much beyond my means to supply.

This important point (Newport News), upon the preservation of which the public interests in this quarter, the seat of Government, and even the communications of the Army of the Potomac depend, is weakened in its movable force to assist the army in its occupation of its many detached and assailable positions in the Sounds and here; but I will write you a brief official letter on this subject.

As I have before proposed to you, these detached and weak positions should be abandoned and our forces concentrated, then we can attack instead of being attacked in detail. This concentration cannot be effected as respects the naval force until it is done by the army, as the gunboats are required at the principal positions occupied by the army. Therefore the change depends upon you there and General Dix here.

Last spring we concentrated and defeated the enemy. Since then we have spread out and now the enemy is attacking us in detail. If not too late, I suggest, as I did last fall when my views were communicated by the Navy to the War Department, razing all their works. Their works are numerous in this vicinity, tempting a struggle for reoccupation and giving them a great advantage if reoccupied. I have and shall make every effort to co-operate with you.

The interest I feel in this great subject will be sufficient to excuse the freedom with which I communicate my views in reply to your private letter of the 12th instant, which I partly answered on the 16th instant.

Heartily wishing you success, I am, very truly, yours,

S. P. LEE,
Actg. Rear-Admiral, Comdg. N. Atlantic Blockading Squadron.

UNITED STATES FLAG-SHIP MINNESOTA,
Off Newport News, April 17, 1863.

Maj. Gen. JOHN A. DIX:

GENERAL: I send you a copy of a sketch received this evening by the Spaulding showing that the enemy has reoccupied his old earthworks at Washington, N. C. This experience sustains the views I have heretofore presented for your consideration.

I have the honor to be, general, respectfully, yours,

S. P. LEE,
Acting Rear-Admiral.

NEAR CORE CREEK, N. C.,
April 17, [1863]—1.45 p. m.

Lieutenant-Colonel HOFFMAN:

COLONEL: I have received your dispatch of this date, and shall observe its contents. The enemy's pickets were driven in on the railroad last night and at crossing of Dover road. They were driven from their intrenchments after the forcing of the creek. We have 1 man killed and 4 wounded and taken 4 prisoners. The position on the railroad has no weakness save that it may be turned.

Respectfully, yours,

HENRY PRINCE,
Brigadier-General, Commanding.

NEAR CORE CREEK, N. C.,
April 17, 1863—7.15 p. m.,

Lieutenant-Colonel HOFFMAN:

COLONEL: We have entertained the enemy very much to-day; during the entire day we have occupied his attention. My best information is that besides Nethercutt's 300 men there is a regiment, the Thirty-third [Sixty-third] North Carolina, at Wise's Cross-Roads; Ransom's brigade a mile or so this side of Kinston. We have observed evidences of a force on the railroad, 4 miles in our front, and we have rumors of a force at Sandy Ridge fortified. We are encamped on the east side of Core Creek, holding the railroad crossing and the Dover Crossing with pickets beyond the creek.

Yours, truly,

HENRY PRINCE.

FORT MONROE, VA., *April* 18, 1863.
(Received 1.30 p. m.)

Maj. Gen. H. W. HALLECK,
General-in-Chief :

Your dispatch, by Lieutenant Beaumont, is received. I have long been in favor of occupying the point referred to. Will write fully by mail. May go to Suffolk to-day. It is closely invested. I was up to the enemy's batteries on the Nansemond yesterday. They have re opened the railroad from the Blackwater and are redoubling their efforts. One gunboat was disabled yesterday.

JOHN A. DIX,
Major-General.

FORT MONROE, VA., *April* 18, 1863—8 p. m.
(Received 9.10 p. m.)

Maj. Gen. H. W. HALLECK,
General-in-Chief :

I have been all day in Suffolk. We have ascertained that the en emy's force is about 38,000. There are four divisions. The largest General Hood's, numbers 11,000. They have come for a campaign and not for a raid or a diversion. Hill's force in North Carolina, numbering 22,000, was to have joined them. Longstreet, French, Pickett, Hood and Anderson are before Suffolk. I telegraphed General Peck yester day to prepare to act on the offensive, and went over to-day to confer with him on the subject. He will attack a battery to-night, and if he succeeds he will attack one of the enemy's divisions to-morrow in force I will write you in full in a day or two in regard to this department and the views contained in your letter.

JOHN A. DIX,
Major-General.

FORT MONROE, VA., *April* 18, 1863.
(Received 11.50 p. m.)

Maj. Gen. H. W. HALLECK,
General-in-Chief :

Dispatches from General Foster state that General Hill has abandoned Washington. I have no doubt it is to carry out the plan of recapturing Suffolk and Norfolk. Our information, from a variety of sources, shows that this is the settled purpose of the enemy, and I am satisfied that nothing but a vigorous and successful movement on the part of General Hooker can prevent the intended co-operation of Hill and Longstreet with 60,000 men, on the Nansemond.

JOHN A. DIX,
Major-General.

SUFFOLK, VA., *April* 18, 1863.

Maj. Gen. H. W. HALLECK,
General-in-Chief :

General Longstreet has been made a lieutenant-general. Major-Gen eral French has joined him, and is in command of Southeast Virginia His chief engineer was taken yesterday laying out works. No change in the enemy's position, so far as can be ascertained. He is still pressing my right, and hopes to first destroy the gunboats and then cross under his batteries. He will not succeed.

> JOHN J. PECK,
> *Major-General.*

FORT MONROE, *April* 18, 1863.

Major-General PECK:

I sent a 12-pounder. I expect carriages from Washington to-day and will send you some Parrotts. I have asked General Halleck for some cavalry.

> JOHN A. DIX,
> *Major-General.*

SUFFOLK, VA., *April* 18, 1863.

Major-General DIX:

The capture of Major-General French's engineer indicates some connection with North Carolina. General French ranks many of these officers, and would hardly come without a command. What is the latest from North Carolina?

> JOHN J. PECK,
> *Major-General.*

SUFFOLK, VA., *April* 18, 1863.

Major-General DIX:

We are as yesterday. The enemy is pressing on the river. Made several attacks on the Edenton road last night. Richmond Sentinel of 16th says:

Longstreet cannot fail. He is a great general, and has all the means for great success. Suffolk is to fall.

We shall see.

> JOHN J. PECK,
> *Major-General.*

SUFFOLK, VA., *April* 18, 1863.

Major-General DIX:

We still hold the line of the Nansemond. During yesterday General Getty and the naval officers reported great activity on the part of the enemy in the lower part of the river, near West Branch; extensive works were being erected and everything indicated a purpose to cross under fire of their batteries. I re-enforced them to the extent of my ability, and sent down hay for the protection of the boats. The naval officers think one bridge is opposite Sleepy Hole, and works being erected.

The enemy was felt of smartly on all the roads yesterday and found in superior numbers at all points. Unless a diversion is made by General Hooker, or in some quarter, Longstreet will fortify a line and hold it as long as he can. I wish you would head a force at Smithfield. Hooker or Hunter should send you a corps.

> JOHN J. PECK,
> *Major-General.*

SUFFOLK, VA., *April* 18, 1863.

Admiral LEE, *Newport News:*

Men who have come in this evening say the rebels have eight iron boats in the James River that will come down so as to threaten the Nansemond, Norfolk, and other places. He will attack me to-morrow early, and will attempt to carry the line of the river. I hope you will be able to send me sufficient light boats to hold it.

JOHN J. PECK,
Major-General.

UNITED STATES FLAG-SHIP MINNESOTA,
Off Newport News, Va., April 18, 1863.

Maj. Gen. JOHN A. DIX, U. S. A.,
Commanding Seventh Army Corps, Fortress Monroe:

SIR: I do not see the propriety of continuing our small vessels in the Upper Nansemond, which is, above Western Branch, a mere creek or natural canal, and unfit for the operation of vessels, now that the enemy is establishing his artillery and rifle-pits in such strength as to command that communication.

The enemy is thus occupying in force the left bank of the Upper Nansemond with earthworks for his artillery and rifle-pits.

Our army, re-enforced since yesterday, may now oppose the enemy by occupying in like manner the right bank of that small stream. The same number of guns we now have on the Upper Nansemond would be better employed on shore.

I have directed Lieutenant Lamson not to remain in the Upper Nansemond any longer than his communications remain open, nor so long as to risk his ability to rejoin Lieutenant Cushing in the Lower Nansemond. Lieutenant Cushing reports that the enemy are fortifying below him.

I have the honor to be, general, very respectfully, yours,

S. P. LEE,
Actg. Rear-Admiral, Comdg. N. Atlantic Blockading Squadron.

HDQRS. DEPT. OF VIRGINIA, SEVENTH ARMY CORPS,
Fort Monroe, Va., April 18, 1863—6.30 p. m.

General FOSTER:

GENERAL: The following telegraphic dispatch has just been received:

WASHINGTON, D. C., *April* 18, 1863.

Major-General DIX:

Please inform General Foster by first opportunity that he must not expect re-enforcements at present, as none can be given to him. His part is simply a defensive one.

H. W. HALLECK,
General-in-Chief.

I am, very respectfully, yours,

JOHN A. DIX,
Major-General.

NEAR CORE CREEK, N. C.,
April 18, 1863—6.30 p. m.
Lieutenant-Colonel HOFFMAN:

COLONEL: My troops have been nearly all of them occupying positions in advance of Core Creek to-day, for the purpose of covering the operation of destroying the bridge at the Neuse-road Crossing.

I this moment learn the operation is successful, the enemy's pickets retiring at all quarters as our troops advance, we capturing but 4 cavalry soldiers, and orders have gone out to resume my position of last night in all respects. We have seen no indications of force to-day.

Very respectfully,

HENRY PRINCE.

I think they expect an advance on the railroad.

———

FORT MONROE, VA., *April* 19, 1863.
Maj. Gen. H. W. HALLECK,
General-in-Chief:

The following dispatch is just received at 2.15 o'clock:

SUFFOLK, VA., *April* 19, 1863.
Major-General DIX:

Admiral Lee has ordered the boats out of the river. This is fatal. It must be stopped from Washington or elsewhere.

JOHN J. PECK,
Major-General.

Major-General Dix has gone to the Nansemond and is expected back at 5 p. m.

LOUIS H. PELOUZE.

———

SUFFOLK, VA., *April* 19, 1863.
Admiral S. P. LEE, *Newport News:*

The withdrawal of all the boats above West Branch of the Nansemond at this crisis will be attended with great risk and may result in the enemy crossing. It will require me to detach many more regiments and guns, which I cannot afford. Earnest and continued co-operation of navy and army will beat General Longstreet in this campaign, and I beg you to reconsider the proposition. For two or three [very] good cover is afforded, and other works are being constructed.

JOHN J. PECK,
Major-General.

———

UNITED STATES FLAG-SHIP MINNESOTA,
Off Newport News, Va., April 19, 1863.
Major-General PECK,
Commanding at Suffolk, Va.:

Your telegraph is just received. Desire Lieutenant Lamson to await further orders from me. Our light draughts are much needed elsewhere West Branch Battery should be taken or silenced.

S. P. LEE,
Actg. Rear-Admiral, Comdg. N. Atlantic Blockading Squadron.

HDQRS. DEPT. OF VIRGINIA, SEVENTH ARMY CORPS,
Fort Monroe, Va., April 19, **1863.**

Actg. Rear-Admiral S. P. LEE,
Commanding North Atlantic Blockading Squadron :

ADMIRAL : I have just received your letter of the 18th in regard
the withdrawal of the gunboats from the Upper Nansemond. I shou
very much regret such a measure at this moment. I believe there a
only three of your gunboats above the West Branch, and their presen
is indispensable, for although I have re-enforced General Peck the
are 7 miles of river to guard and we have not troops enough to prote
every part of it and prevent the enemy from crossing. I have t
armed quartermasters' boats—the West End and the Smith Briggs
above the West Branch, and with your gunboats the defense of tl
part of the river is complete. We are establishing batteries, but f
want of heavy guns they are not yet in readiness Within the ne
forty-eight hours I hope to have them prepared for efficient servi
General Peck telegraphs me that the withdrawal of the gunboats
this time would be fatal.

I am, very respectfully, your obedient servant,

JOHN A. DIX,
Major-General

FORT MONROE, VA., *April* 19, 1863.

Maj. Gen. H. W. HALLECK,
General-in-Chief :

I have just returned from the Nansemond. Was on board of two
the gunboats which were engaged in shelling the enemy's batteri
One of the batteries was silenced this morning, but the enemy is ve
active, and is casemating another with heavy timber. He has co
here to stay, if possible, and will spare no effort to regain possession
the James River and the Nansemond.

JOHN A. DIX,
Major-General

FORT MONROE, *April* 19, 1863

Major-General PECK :

I sent you some Parrott guns last night; also over 100 artilleris
The latter are a part of the garrison of Fort Monroe, and should
sent back soon. I don't hear from you.

JOHN A. DIX,
Major-General

FORT MONROE, *April* 19, 1863

Major-General PECK :

Three batteries are here and will be with you to-morrow mornil
You will have three rifled 42-pounders the day after to-morrow. T
platforms wil be made here.

JOHN A. DIX,
Major-General

SUFFOLK, VA., *April* 19, 1863.

Major-General DIX:

General Getty, in conjunction with Lieutenant Lamson's boats, has ust stormed the heavy battery at the West Branch, and after severe ghting carried it. Captured six guns and 200 of the Forty-fourth Ala ama. Crossed in boats.

JOHN J. PECK,
Major-General.

FORT MONROE, *April* 19, 1863

Major-General PECK, *Commanding, Suffolk:*

I have received your gratifying dispatch. General Getty and th• ficers and men engaged in storming the battery have my warmest anks for their gallant conduct. It will be an example for the forces nder your command which cannot fail to give us the happiest results.

JOHN A. DIX,
Major-General.

SUFFOLK, VA., *April* 19, 1863.

Major-General DIX:

I see notices from Admiral Lee of doings here, but nothing that I have ported—the silencing of the ten-gun battery on Tuesday by the land atteries and the skirmishing of Colonel Foster.

JOHN J. PECK,
Major-General.

FORT MONROE, *April* 19, 1863.

Major-General PECK, *Commanding, Suffolk:*

I have regularly telegraphed all that has been done. I send a sum- ary this evening to General Halleck, which I trust will appear and ow that the army has not been idle.

JOHN A. DIX,
Major-General.

HEADQUARTERS OF THE ARMY,
Washington, April 19, 1863. (Received 8.20 p. m.)

Major-General HEINTZELMAN,
Commanding, &c.:

GENERAL: You will immediately prepare for embarkation, and send • General Dix at Fort Monroe about 4,000 infantry, so as to make in ll sent to him about 10,000 men. General Meigs will give you trans- ortation as rapidly as possible.

H. W. HALLECK,
General-in-Chief.

HEADQUARTERS EIGHTEENTH ARMY CORPS,
New Berne, N. C., April 19, 1863.

Major-General HALLECK,
General-in-Chief, Washington, D. C.:

GENERAL: By officers just in from Washington, N. C., I learn that e enemy have all gone from the vicinity of that place. The places occupied by their batteries on the rivers are all now in possession of our troops, who are able to hold them.   There is now no difficulty in passing into Washington with men and supplies.

General Foster left here yesterday with a force to march across the country. General Foster informed you in a letter of the 16th instant that he had directed Plymouth, Elizabeth City, and Winfield to be evacuated. He countermanded that order, too late, however, for Winfield; that has been abandoned, but the troops remain at the other places.

At Plymouth they are well fortified. Winfield is of little importance, and I shall not reoccupy the place, but leave it for General Foster to decide when he returns.

I am, general, very respectfully, your obedient servant,

I. N. PALMER,
Brigadier-General.

HDQRS. FIRST DIVISION, EIGHTEENTH ARMY CORPS,
New Berne, April 19, 1863.

Maj. Gen. J. G. FOSTER,
Commanding Eighteenth Army Corps:

GENERAL: General Prince himself a few miles beyond Core Creek and carrying out your instructions.

I last night informed you of the arrival of the other regiments of General Heckman's brigade, and asking the disposition to be made of them. General Halleck writes, in reply to my letter to him informing him of the state of affairs, that no re-enforcements can be spared to come here, and that "if any accident should occur to General Foster you will bear in mind that operations in North Carolina should be strictly defensive, and the troops concentrated as much as possible. New Berne and Beaufort are the points of most importance."

Farquhar is here from Plymouth. He will wait here for a day or two to see you. Winfield was abandoned before the order countermanding arrived. I saw to-day a large steamer with supplies for Plymouth. The Phœnix goes also with stores to Washington. I have written to General Halleck a history of affairs that have transpired since you wrote your last letter to him.

Very respectfully, your obedient servant,

I. N. PALMER,
Brigadier-General.

NEAR CORE CREEK, N. C.,
April 19, 1863—10.24 a. m.

Lieutenant-Colonel HOFFMAN:

COLONEL: I send by the train 4 prisoners, captured yesterday (with their arms and horses); all privates. The information gathered from these prisoners corroborates that I have already sent. The camp of the Sixty-third being at Wise's Cross-Roads and Ransom's brigade at Kinston.

Respectfully, yours,

HENRY PRINCE,
Brigadier-General Volunteers.

UNITED STATES FLAG-SHIP MINNESOTA,
Off Newport News, Va., April 20, 1863—noon.

Major-General DIX,
Comdg. Seventh Army Corps, Fortress Monroe, Va.:

SIR: A report from Lieutenant Cushing, dated at 8 a. m. to-day, informs me that the enemy has unmasked a new battery, containing some heavy pieces, by which and some infantry the Barney was sharply attacked yesterday. Supposing that the enemy is not in great force on the left bank of the Nansemond, I respectfully suggest to you the propriety of capturing this battery, as it commands the Lower Nansemond and cannot be materially affected by the firing from the flotilla.

I have the honor to be, very respectfully,

S. P. LEE,
Actg. Rear-Admiral, Comdg. N. Atlantic Blockading Squadron.

FORT MONROE, VA., *April* 20, 1863.

Major-General PECK, *Suffolk, Va.:*

The following just received from Admiral Lee, dated 2.40 p. m.:

Lieutenant Cushing reports that the enemy is retreating as fast as possible, and that the army, by a rapid movement, may cut off one of their brigades.

S. P. LEE,
Admiral.

Respectfully,

LOUIS H. PELOUZE,
Assistant Adjutant-General.

SUFFOLK, VA., *April* 20, 1863.

General DIX:

From all that can be gleaned Longstreet has asked for more troops Unless Lee wants them all he will get them. What is the total from Hooker?

JOHN J. PECK,
Major-General.

SUFFOLK, *April* 20, 1863.

Major-General DIX:

An examination shows that there is great suffering here for the necessaries of life. Traders must be allowed to bring flour, meat, and kindred articles. They will buy. Report of the provost has just reached me—since your departure. Will you order a change?

PECK,
Major-General.

SUFFOLK, VA., *April* 20, 1863.

Major-General DIX:

Major Stratton reports his visit to Elizabeth City. It had been abandoned on 18th, and the gunboats were shelling the banks as they moved down the river. Country full of guerrillas.

Longstreet's pickets at Sandy Cross. We stormed the West Branch

Battery just at dusk, and hold it now. One major, 1 captain, and ? officers were taken, with 6 guns, and between 100 and 200 soldiers. Eighty-ninth New York and Eighth Connecticut were the stormers.

JOHN J. PECK,
Major-General.

HEADQUARTERS,
Plymouth, N. C., April 20, 1863.

[Capt. J. A. JUDSON, A. A. G.:]

CAPTAIN: I have the honor to acknowledge the receipt of your communication inclosing and returning a report sent from here. I have reason to think another document has been forwarded in the same manner from these headquarters; if so, will you please return it that the mistake may be rectified? I will see that the error is not repeated hereafter. In reporting the situation here I directed my adjutant to call your attention to the necessity of our having supplies. That there should be no delay the post commissary had previously made his requisitions, which were approved and signed by me. He informs me they were sent forward. The steamer Long Island arrived to-day at 3 p. m. with rations, ammunition, horses, &c. Receipts will be duly forwarded to headquarters. Winfield has been abandoned and the works destroyed; one company of the garrison is here; the other has gone to New Berne, as I am informed, by orders from headquarters.

Respectfully, your obedient servant,

JOSIAH PICKETT,
Colonel, Commanding Post.

[Inclosure.]

HEADQUARTERS,
Plymouth, N. C., April 18, 1863.

Lieut. Col. SOUTHARD HOFFMAN,
Assistant Adjutant-General, Eighteenth Army Corps:

In accordance with Special Orders, No. 114, received at noon yesterday (17th), I made preparations to evacuate this post. I had made arrangements to transport the Forty-sixth Massachusetts Volunteer Militia, two sections of Lee's battery, and four detached companies, under command of Major Bartholomew, Twenty-seventh Regiment Massachusetts Volunteers, upon the Colyer and some small schooners I had taken possession of, and intended to hold the post with the Twenty-fifth Regiment Massachusetts Volunteers until the other transports arrived. Lee's two sections were aboard the transport and the Forty-sixth Regiment had struck their tents when the Massasoit arrived. Everything has been disembarked and will be arranged as before.

I sent word to the post at Winfield and gave them orders to evacuate the post, destroying block-houses, rifle-pits, &c. They had probably done so long before the Massasoit arrived, and are now on their way to Plymouth. I desire you to send me instructions as to whether that post is to be re-established.

We are almost entirely out of supplies, and must have a boat back immediately with rations or the men will suffer.

Everything is in good order here. We have the fort nearly finished, with one gun mounted and the rifle-pits completed, and can, if called upon, make a good fight. What we most want now is commissary stores, which I hope you will send at the earliest possible moment.

I have the honor to be, yours, &c.,

JOSIAH PICKETT,
Colonel, Commanding Post.

[Indorsement.]

HEADQUARTERS EIGHTEENTH ARMY CORPS,
New Berne, N. C., April 19, 1863.

Respectfully returned to Colonel Pickett. The signature attached is evidently not his own. This same communication will be properly signed and returned to this office.

By order of Brigadier-General Palmer commanding:

J. A. JUDSON,
Captain and Assistant Adjutant-General.

HEADQUARTERS FOURTH CORPS,
Yorktown, April 20, 1863.

Major-General DIX,
Commanding Department of Virginia, Fort Monroe :

It is reported at Williamsburg that General Wise has been retired, and that General Hood replaces him on this Peninsula with an additional regiment of cavalry. If so, I need two more regiments of infantry without delay and the replacement of the artillery sent from here to Norfolk two nights ago. My men are overworked now.

The rebels are anxious about their Merrimac No. 2; something seems to have gone wrong with them in that matter. If anything could add to the importance of holding the line of Fort Magruder it would be the appearance of the Merrimac.

E. D. KEYES,
Major-General.

SUFFOLK, *April 21, 1863.*

Major-General DIX:

It gives pleasure to say that General Getty is safe on this side with all the material of war and without loss. The prisoners were sent last night, and attempted to escape by uncoupling the cars, but did not succeed. I shall send out at once on the Swamp or E. road and assail Longstreet's right flank cautiously.

PECK,
Major-General.

SUFFOLK, VA., *April 21, 1863.*

Major-General DIX:

General Halleck seemed well pleased with affairs here, and I am very glad he made a visit. I hope you arrived all safe.

JOHN J. PECK,
Major-General.

SUFFOLK, VA., *April 21, 1863.*

Major-General DIX:

General Getty thinks the enemy has not fallen back. He thought so at one time yesterday. All over safe. Fires at night have not diminished.

JOHN J. PECK,
Major-General.

[FORTRESS MONROE,] *April* 21, [1863.]

Actg. Rear-Admiral S. P. LEE,
    Commanding North Atlantic Blockading Squadron:

I returned from Suffolk late last evening. Lieutenant Lamson having informed General Peck that you had ordered him to leave the Upper Nansemond with his gunboats, General Getty was directed to abandon the left bank, where we had captured one of the enemy's batteries, and bring away the guns. This has been done. When I left last evening the enemy was investing Suffolk as closely as ever, and there were no signs of his retiring. I regret exceedingly the withdrawal of the gunboats. If, as we have reason to believe, the enemy is very strong it will be difficult without their aid to prevent his crossing. We shall do the best we can with the two boats armed by my orders and manned by our troops.

JOHN A. DIX,
Major-General.

UNITED STATES FLAG-SHIP MINNESOTA,
Off Newport News, Va., April 21, 1863.

Maj. Gen. JOHN A. DIX, U. S. A.,
    Comdg. Seventh Army Corps, Fortress Monroe, Va.:

GENERAL: I am surprised by the statement in your dispatch of this date, just received, that the captured battery on the left bank had been abandoned because "Lieutenant Lamson had informed General Peck that you (I) had ordered him to leave the Upper Nansemond with his gunboats."

I inclose a copy of Lieutenant Lamson's report, showing that this is a mistake.

My letter of yesterday's date to General Peck (a copy of which is inclosed), written last night (but not sent to or forwarded by Lieutenant Lamson until this morning, after the battery was evacuated), affords no justification for the previous abandonment of the captured battery, which commanded the communications. As long as it was held our boats could pass above or below as it might be necessary. The responsibility of abandoning this position rests on other shoulders than mine. You must see that the representation you make does me injustice, and is not sustained by the facts of the case.

I have the honor to be, respectfully, yours,

S. P. LEE,
Actg. Rear-Admiral, Comdg. N. Atlantic Blockading Squadron.

[Inclosures.]

UNITED STATES FLAG-SHIP MINNESOTA,
Newport News, Va., April 21, 1863.

Actg. Rear-Admiral S. P. LEE,
    Commanding North Atlantic Blockading Squadron:

SIR: I have seen with much surprise the telegram of General Dix to yourself, in which he says that "Lieutenant Lamson having informed General Peck that you had ordered him (me) to leave the Upper Nansemond with the gunboats, General Getty was directed to abandon the left bank, where he had captured one of the enemy's batteries."

General Dix is laboring under a great mistake, for just the reverse of what he says is true. After the capture of the battery I received or ders from you to remain in the Upper Nansemond with the flotilla under my command, and so informed General Getty. I did not communicate with General Peck on the subject, but your order to me to remain was forwarded through him.

The only written orders I received from you on the subject were dated on the 18th and 20th instant; that of the 18th in these words: "You will not remain in the river (Upper Nansemond) any longer than your communications remain open, so that you can return and rejoin Lieutenant Cushing; not so long as to risk your ability to return."

On the 20th you repeated the same instructions.

When the first of the above orders was received it was already so dangerous to pass the rebel battery that I should not have attempted it unless I had been forced to do so, or had received positive orders, and Generals Peck and Getty had both agreed to put in execution a plan that I had proposed for capturing the battery, and which after two miscarriages on the part of the army was successfully accomplished.

On the 19th instant Fleet-Captain Crosby came up with discretionary orders, dated the 18th instant, in regard to the gunboats remaining in the upper river. That evening the battery was captured, and General Getty said he would move over troops and hold it if Captain Crosby would direct the gunboats to remain, which he did. That evening I received a telegram from you, through General Peck, directing me to remain on the upper river till further orders.

The next morning about 12 m. General Getty showed me his orders from General Peck to withdraw from the captured point, and later in the day an order to withdraw before night. I had received no orders from you which required me to withdraw from the Upper Nansemond, and so told General Getty, and earnestly expressed to him my entire disapprobation of the abandoning of the captured point. I told him repeatedly that I would remain in the Upper Nansemond as long as he held the point, but that if he evacuated it I should be obliged to go below it. My communications were perfectly safe as long as he held this key to the river. The position was an exceedingly strong one, and General Getty had crossed more than 1,000 men and had defended the rear by several lines of rifle-pits.

There was nothing in your instructions to me or in my communications to Generals Peck or Getty that rendered it necessary for them to abandon the work, but their movement made it absolutely necessary for me to move below.

Very respectfully, your obedient servant,

R. H. LAMSON,
Lieutenant, U. S. Navy, Commanding Flotilla.

UNITED STATES FLAG-SHIP MINNESOTA,
Off Newport News, Va., April 20, 1863.

[Major-General PECK:]

GENERAL: By dispatch received to-day from Lieutenant Lamson I am informed that the captured rebel battery at West Branch will be abandoned to-night. I hope that this work and all others on the left bank of the Nansemond will be completely razed, and not left to invite reoccupation and allow the enemy to annoy us and cut off our communications. If Suffolk is to be held I hope the present opportunity will be improved to construct such works on the right bank of the Upper Nansemond as its proper defense requires.

Our little gunboats, so much called for and relied on by the army, are not a suitable defense for that stream, and their services are really necessary elsewhere.

I have the honor to be, general, yours, respectfully,

S. P. LEE,
Actg. Rear-Admiral, Comdg. N. Atlantic Blockading Squadron.

[Indorsement.]

This was written last night and sent into the Nansemond under cover to Lieutenant Lamson this morning (21st) and forwarded to him. The battery was abandoned last night against the urgent remonstrances of Lieutenant Lamson.

L

SUFFOLK, VA., *April* 21, 1863

Major-General HOOKER,
     Army of the Potomac :

General Halleck has just left my headquarters. General Longstreet is here, waiting Hill or other troops. I hold everything yet. How do you get along?

JOHN J. PECK,
Major-General.

APRIL 21, 1863—10 p. m.

Major-General PECK, *Suffolk, Va. :*

Am glad to hear good tidings from you. You must be patient with me. I must play with these devils before I can spring. Remember that my army is at the bottom of a well and the enemy holds the top.

JOSEPH HOOKER,
Major-General, Commanding.

GENERAL ORDERS, }   HDQRS. EIGHTEENTH ARMY CORPS,
   No. 60.   }   *New Berne, April* 21, 1863.

The fort recently constructed at Plymouth, N. C., will be called Fort Williams, after Brig. Gen. Thomas Williams, killed in action at Baton Rouge, La., August 5, 1862, who was the first general officer commanding in this department.

By command of Maj. Gen. J. G. Foster:

[SOUTHARD HOFFMAN,]
Assistant Adjutant General.

SUFFOLK, VA., *April* 22, 1863.

Major-General DIX :

Everything is as yesterday. Since Hooker has not moved it will be requisite for the greatest caution here. There are reports that the rebels are sending troops north from Charleston. Stratton finds Longstreet's pickets on turnpike 10 miles this side of Sandy Cross and at

Hinton's Toll-Gate. He burned 7,000 bushels corn going to rebel army; knows that a rebel brigade or more is to occupy or move through Elizabeth City.

JOHN J. PECK,
Major-General.

HDQRS. DEPT. OF VIRGINIA, SEVENTH ARMY CORPS,
Fort Monroe, Va., April 22, **1863.**

Actg. Rear-Admiral LEE,
Commanding North Atlantic Blockading Squadron:

ADMIRAL: I received at midnight your letter of yesterday in regard to the battery captured at the mouth of the West Branch of the Nansemond River, inclosing one from Lieutenant Lamson, and cheerfully accept them as an explanation of the withdrawal of the gunboats. I supposed the order to withdraw them was absolute, and the impression was confirmed by your former dispatches, in which you said I "must not rely upon these frail and open ferry-boats and river steamers, which you (I) call gunboats, to keep the rebels from crossing the Upper Nansemond, which is long, narrow, and crooked, a mere creek, a natural canal, and unfit for the operations of vessels, now that the enemy is establishing his artillery and rifle-pits in such strength as to command that communication," and for this reason you said you did not see the propriety of continuing them there. From these and other expressions of the same character I supposed their withdrawal was definitely settled, although I had opposed it with all proper earnestness. My two armed steamers are to remain there. I know that there is danger that they will be fired into, injured, perhaps crippled; but this hazard must be incurred to prevent the rebels from crossing. Yours will be exposed to no more danger than mine. The position of the captured battery, though a commanding one, gives us no security against the crossing of the enemy except at that point. It would have been no obstacle to his crossing 1, 2, 3, 4, 5, or 6 miles above, and the troops we must have kept there to hold it would have been much more useful on the right bank of the river as a movable force to oppose him whenever he should have made an attempt to cross. Besides, its occupation would not have removed your objections to the employment of your gunboats in the narrow channel above. What we want is to have two or three gunboats moving up and down the Upper Nansemond for several miles to watch the enemy's movements and to aid in destroying his pontoon bridge if he should attempt to throw one across the river.

I have not time to enter into explanations, but if you will give to Lieutenants Lamson and Cushing (who have displayed so much gallantry) discretionary power, so that they may go up the Upper Nansemond when they think it safe, and permit them to act in conjunction with General Getty, who is charged with the defense of the right bank of the river, I feel confident we can defeat the enemy's purpose, and should he establish batteries below your gunboats I have no doubt they will be able to pass them without loss.

I know you will be happy to hear that the fleet above Vicksburg has passed that stronghold, as General Halleck informed me yesterday, without the loss of a single armed vessel, and I really think that your apprehensions in regard to your gunboats should be lessened when you consider that as yet not one of them has been permanently disabled.

I am, very respectfully, your obedient servant,

JOHN A. DIX,
Major-General.

HDQRS. FIRST DIVISION, EIGHTEENTH ARMY CORPS,
New Berne, N. C., April 22, 1863.

Lieut. Col. SOUTHARD HOFFMAN,
   A. A. G., Eighteenth Army Corps, New Berne, N. C.:

SIR: I have the honor to acknowledge the receipt of communication from the commanding general of this department of the 21st instant, and in reply to the interrogatory—

Why was not a large force sent to General Prince, in the Pamlico River, as ordered in my letter of April 1, 1863, and why was not greater alacrity displayed in getting troops to General Prince ?—

I have the honor to state that immediately on the receipt of the above instructions all the troops that could be possibly transported by the vessels then disposable in this harbor were put in readiness to leave to join General Prince. At that time a gale of wind was prevailing which had blown the water out of the river to such a degree that it was almost impossible for vessels to move around the harbor. The steamer Colyer, loaded with troops, was lying aground between this place and Washington, and the steamer Escort got fast aground in coming up to the dock here. However, four regiments were on board of vessels or about embarking here to join General Prince when the letter of the commanding general of April 5 was received. This letter notified me that he had changed his plans, and that two regiments were to be left at the blockade to be sent through, if possible, to Washington, by the way of the river, and that all the remaining force was to return to this place with General Prince, who was directed to take then all the available force from here and march across the country to Washington. It was my intention to obey the order or suggestion of the commanding general and to send to General Prince at least 5,000 men. The elements prevented this. There was no unnecessary delay on the part of any one. While waiting for the water in the river to rise I remained up nearly all night and visited the wharf twice after midnight, and while the troops were waiting to sail. Therefore I cannot see that there was a want of alacrity displayed in getting troops to General Prince.

In reply to the second interrogatory—

When my plan was changed, and orders were sent in my letter of April 5 to march across the country to raise the siege of Washington, why did you not go in command ?—

I will respectfully state that in the letter referred to, of April, 5 the commanding general says:

I have therefore ordered General Prince to send me two regiments, with a plentiful supply of ammunition for the heavy guns, then to return to New Berne, and with all the fighting force that can possibly be spared march across the country to Washington.

General Prince returned to this place on the 6th, followed by all the troops on the 7th, as the naval officer in command at the blockade said it was impossible to get any troops through by way of the river. On the 8th all the available force was in readiness to move. Only (about) 3,000 effective men were retained here. The movement of the troops across the river was carried on all through the night of the 7th and 8th. General Prince was notified on the morning of the 8th that the troops were ready, but he reported himself unable to start with them. One of his aides, Lieutenant Ordway, came to my headquarters to ask for a boat to be placed at the disposition of General Prince, who he said would follow the command. The steamer Allison was ordered to be placed at his disposition immediately.

I proceeded across the river, informed General Spinola of the state of affairs, and remained there until the whole command had started.

Immediately on my return I saw General Prince's aide, Lieutenant Ordway, who gave me to understand that General Prince had made every preparation to follow the command. I was told that an ambulance with his baggage was at his door. I then believed that he was going immediately.

I think it proper for me to state here that even had I known that General Prince was not going to join the command I should not then have gone myself, for I had determined in my own mind that General Foster needed only men and supplies of provisions and ammunition, and I felt assured that I could get them to him by the way of the river while the demonstration was being made by land. I had determined that if any officer should arrive to take command of New Berne I would take a steamer loaded with men and supplies and go to the blockade and see them through. General Wessells arrived here on the 9th and I left with the Escort on the next day. The delay in getting this steamer through the blockade was by no means unavoidable, but it was a delay for which I was in no way responsible. Three times the steamer was ready to move and she was stopped. The first time on the evening of my arrival at the blockade by the refusal of Lieutenant-Commander McCann (the senior naval officer there) to assist, at night; the second time, on the next morning, by the fog, which was so dense on the river that nothing could be seen at the proposed hour of starting; and the third time, the next night, by the mist and rain, that prevented any movement on the river.

The safe arrival eventually of the steamer at Washington accomplished, I was satisfied, more than could have been attained in any other way, and I was satisfied that my judgment was correct and that I had acted wisely in the matter.

With regard to the third interrogatory—

Was the question ever raised in any consultation or council of commanding officers as to my authority to give orders for movement of troops; if so, when, by whom, and under what circumstances?—

I will state that I never presumed to call any "council or consultation of officers" to discuss plain orders sent to me by the commanding general. His orders issued from Washington were just as much obeyed and respected by me as they would have been had they been issued from this place.

It is true, however, that I was an unwilling listener to several private conversations in which the "propriety" of sending too many troops away from this place, or the "policy" of abandoning everything to the saving of Washington, was spoken of, and doubts expressed as to who under the circumstances was in command of the department. I took no part in any such discussions any more than to inform every person that the orders of the commanding general would be obeyed, even if they were to abandon New Berne and everything in it.

I am, sir, very respectfully, your obedient servant,
I. N. PALMER,
Brigadier-General.

———

HEADQUARTERS EIGHTEENTH ARMY CORPS,
New Berne, N. C., April 22, 1863.
Rear-Admiral S. P. LEE,
Commanding North Atlantic Blockading Squadron:
ADMIRAL: I have the honor to acknowledge receipt of your letter of the 17th, on the subject of the occupation by our troops of too many

posts, recommending that those posts be abandoned for the purpose of concentration. This letter has unfortunately been mislaid, and so I can only answer the general tenor of the letter, confining myself to the reasons for the occupation of the posts and for continuing to hold them.

In regard to Fort Macon and the adjoining posts of Morehead City and Beaufort, there can, I think, be no question as to the necessity of holding them; likewise the forts at Hatteras, which hold the entrance to the Sounds; also Roanoke Island, which controls the navigation of Albemarle Sound. Then there only remain the towns of New Berne, Washington, and Plymouth. The former was occupied March 4, 1862, and has since been fortified and is held as a depot for supplies and as a basis for operations, possessing as it does the advantages of two lines of communication, one by railroad to Beaufort Harbor and one by the river to the Sounds.

The history of the occupation of Washington and Plymouth is that they were first held by gunboats lying opposite the towns. Afterward a picket guard of one company was sent to each place, as a picket guard for the gunboats on shore. This guard was afterward increased as demanded by circumstances and the necessities of service. Finally the importance of occupying the posts permanently was seen and recognized, and works were erected for this purpose. Some of the reasons which led to this determination were as follows:

1st. By not occupying these points—New Berne, Washington, and Plymouth—we permit their occupation by the enemy and their use by them as yards and arsenals in which to prepare rams and gunboats to operate against our gunboats in the Sounds.

2d. To permit egress of any lighter-draught gunboat that may be built in the rivers above; and, in fine, gives our gunboats the control of those rivers for offensive operations by water.

3d. These towns afford excellent landing places, at which our forces could be quickly and safely concentrated for offensive operations by land, having the towns as bases. This advantage is the more sensibly felt when any one town is besieged.

4th. These three strategical points retain within their power all the counties to the east of them, which is a matter of some importance, as they are the most fertile in corn, &c., of any in the State, and are so considered by the Confederate Government, as shown by the efforts of General Hill to repossess them.

In conclusion, I am strongly of the opinion that as long as I am strong enough to hold these points I should do so, and further think that if the exigency should compel me to abandon either that it would be a lost advantage, inasmuch as by holding the three I can operate more effectively with ——— force than I could with the same force concentrated at one or two of them, and the others held by the enemy.

In a naval point of view I of course yield and defer to your judgment, but it is my conviction that were either of these points held by the enemy, a larger, not a smaller, naval force would be necessary to hold the Sounds, irrespective of river navigation and the convoying of vessels.

These views are sent to you in, I assure you, the most friendly spirit, and in accordance with the harmony which has always existed between our two arms of the service, and merely that by exchanging ideas the result most to the interests of the service may be arrived at.

I have the honor to be, admiral, very respectfully, your obedient servant,

                                        J. G. FOSTER,
                                    Major-General, Commanding.

HDQRS. DEPT. OF VIRGINIA, SEVENTH ARMY CORPS,
Fort Monroe, Va., April 23, 1863.

General H. W. HALLECK,
General-in-Chief:

GENERAL: In my telegraphic dispatch of the 18th I said that I had been long in favor of occupying West Point. I should have taken possession of it if I had been able to spare 5,000 men, the smallest number requisite to make the occupation secure. My object was to cut off Gloucester and Matthews Counties as sources of supply to the insurgents, and to break up the system of contraband trade across those counties, and from the Piankatank River and the mouth of the Rappahannock. In your letter of the 17th instant you suggest the occupation of that position as a base for a movement in support of General Hooker, who I suppose is to move on Richmond from Fredericksburg. I have no doubt that it would be advisable if I could have a sufficient force. The White House would be a still better position, as it is 20 miles nearer the enemy's flank, but portions of the Pamunkey River are narrow, and the water communications might be interrupted or made insecure by batteries planted on its banks. Should the enemy withdraw from Suffolk I will occupy West Point with all the force I can spare.

I agree with you that a movement on Weldon would be hazardous, and it would be of little advantage unless we could go there in sufficient force to hold it. The destruction of the railroad bridge at Goldsborough, which cost us many lives, only interrupted the communication for about thirty days, a temporary inconvenience but not a serious disaster to the enemy. Our great error has been in occupying too many positions. There was an excuse for scattering our forces while there was reason to believe that the people of the South would rally around them as nucleus for the restoration of the Union. This hope is now gone, and as our only chance of success is by overpowering them by preponderance of force or wearing them out by cutting off their commerce with foreign countries, all interior positions, unless they have some special importance, should be abandoned.

In this department no useless positions are occupied. There are but two points of great importance—Fort Monroe and Norfolk—the former as a military position commanding the Chesapeake Bay and the rivers that enter into it, and the latter as a naval station for the repair of our gunboats and transports, which would otherwise be obliged to go to Baltimore or Washington on the occurrence of any ordinary casualty. Suffolk was occupied partly to cover Norfolk and partly in pursuance of the purpose, already referred to, of affording to the people a rallying point for the restoration of the Union. In the latter respect it has failed, and in view of the former there is a better position—the line of the Deep Creek and the West Branch of Elizabeth River—more defensible, and from which an army could retire on Norfolk with ease and safety. I am preparing to fortify it. Suffolk is weak from the long and narrow channel of the Nansemond, running 7 miles to the rear, with an average width of less than 100 yards. It requires a large force and incessant vigilance to prevent the enemy from crossing and cutting off our communications with Norfolk. But as it would be impossible to fall back on that city in the face of a superior force it must be held at all hazards.

Yorktown is occupied to keep the enemy at a distance from this post. He would not be likely to pass it while held by us. If it were abandoned he would push his forces down to Bethel or Hampton and shut us up in the fort. Williamsburg is only held as a picket station of Yorktown, to prevent the enemy from approaching the latter and harassing us in our intrenchments with rifled cannon and small-arms of long range. The troops in the vicinity of Williamsburg have orders to fall back on Yorktown if menaced by superior numbers.

I am, very respectfully, your obedient servant,

JOHN A. DIX,
Major-General.

SUFFOLK, *April* 23, 1863.

Major-General DIX:

As you well know, I have for many months performed more duties than is incident to any one army corps in the service. Now I am performing more than the commanders of two corps in the Army of the Potomac. I cannot do so longer in a proper manner without the rank and staff machinery. Please act upon this matter with the Secretary.

JOHN J. PECK,
Major-General.

SUFFOLK, VA., *April* 23, 1863.

Major-General DIX:

Yesterday was devoted to exploration in the Dismal Swamp. The impression was strong that, not succeeding in crossing the river, Longstreet was cutting a road through from the Edenton road. Duke states there is a ridge by which they can get through to the railway. A party is out now. In consequence of this and of the rain that demonstration was delayed. It is reported that their cars have been heard. Not satisfied of its correctness.

JOHN J. PECK,
Major-General.

SUFFOLK, *April* 23, 1863.

Major-General DIX:

Affairs stand as yesterday. I am employing all possible means to strengthen the river line. The boats of the Navy are below the Branch. Have sent troops into the swamp along the canal to watch the left flank. Major Stratton says the people report a force of 3,000 or 4,000 on this side the Chowan, drawing supplies from that section. He sent Mr. Hinton, of Hintonsville, in as a prisoner, a man of means and influence. Mr. Hinton says there is a force there, and that nineteen wagons with cavalry were up after forage. He says they are Hill's.

PECK,
Major-General.

OFF NEWPORT NEWS, *April* 23, 1863—8 a. m.

Hon. GIDEON WELLES,
Secretary of the Navy:

Lieutenant Cushing reports that yesterday afternoon with 90 men and a howitzer he went to the village of Chuckatuck, where a large cavalry force was reported to be. Encountered 40 cavalry in the village; defeated them; killed 2 and captured 3 of their horses, fully equipped. He lost 1 man killed. He thinks that his reconnaissance shows that the enemy are not in strong force near Suffolk.

S. P. LEE,
Acting Rear-Admiral.

UNITED STATES FLAG-SHIP MINNESOTA,
Off Newport News, Va., April 23, 1863.

Maj. Gen. JOHN A. DIX, U. S. A.,
    Comdg. Seventh Army Corps, Fortress Monroe, Va.:

GENERAL: I respectfully inform you that the proclamation of the President of the United States, dated March 31,* and the accompanying order of the Secretaries of War† and Navy of the same date, regarding commercial intercourse with inhabitants of the insurrectionary regions, which I understand as superseding the order of the President, dated November 12, 1862,‡ in reference to vessels and merchandise entering and departing from the port of Norfolk, have been communicated this day to the guard vessels for their guidance.

I have the honor to be, general, very respectfully, yours,

S. P. LEE,
Actg. Rear-Admiral, Comdg. N. Atlantic Blockading Squadron.

UNITED STATES FLAG-SHIP MINNESOTA,
Off Newport News, Va., April 23, 1863.

Maj. Gen. JOHN A. DIX, U. S. A.,
    Comdg. Seventh Army Corps, Fortress Monroe, Va.:

GENERAL: I send herewith 4 negroes, who went on board the Mount Washington in the Nansemond on the 15th instant, representing that they were free negroes, and that there was no enemy in sight; but scarcely a minute had elapsed when the Mount Washington was attacked and a long and severe engagement followed. I respectfully request that you will make such disposition of them as may seem proper under the circumstances of the case.

I have the honor to be, general, very respectfully, yours,

S. P. LEE,
Actg. Rear-Admiral, Comdg. N. Atlantic Blockading Squadron.

FORT MONROE, April 23, 1863.

Major-General KEYES,
    Commanding, Yorktown:

I have been every day since you were here to the Nansemond or to Suffolk. We cannot get more troops for you at present. I do not feel easy about our force at Fort Magruder. It would not be difficult to cut it off. If we remain there we must hold Williamsburg with our pickets. Please send the correspondence with Dr. Wager, late in charge of the asylum. I may write General Wise. If we get rid of the enemy at Suffolk I shall strengthen you for active work.

JOHN A. DIX,
Major-General.

---

* See p. 572.   † See General Orders, No. 88, April 3, p. 580.   ‡ See p. 452.

HEADQUARTERS FOURTH CORPS,
Yorktown, April 23, 1863.

Major-General Dix,
Commanding Department of Virginia, Fort Monroe:

Your telegram just received. We have had time to make such ar
rangements on the line of Fort Magruder as to be secure against surprise
We occupy seven redoubts in addition to that fort, and our troops say
they can and will hold the line against any force the enemy can bring
against them. They foiled Wise and are in high spirits. I can now
hold my ground without re-enforcements, but more troops are needed
to ease the great labors of those with me. We have a strong picke
line above the forts, with cavalry vedettes close up to the town. If the
enemy attacks we can damage him three or four times more than he can
damage us.

I will send the only letter received from Dr. Wager since the attack
by mail.

E. D. KEYES,
Major-General.

GENERAL ORDERS, }   HDQRS. EIGHTEENTH ARMY CORPS,
    No. 62.   }   New Berne, April 23, 1863.

In order that a more constant supervision may exist at the various
posts in this department, the following districts are hereby established
and will be commanded as follows:

I. The first will be known as the District of the Neuse.

This district will embrace that portion of the department lying be
yond the outside limits of the post of New Berne, the railroad and al
stations pertaining thereto, Morehead City, Carolina City, Beaufort, an
Fort Macon, and will be commanded by Brig. Gen. Henry M. Naglee
whose headquarters will be at Beaufort, N. C.

II. The second will be known as the District of the Albemarle.

This district will include the posts of Plymouth and Roanoke Island
and such other posts as may be hereafter established within the limit
of the district, and will be commanded by Brig. Gen. Henry W. Wes
sells, whose headquarters will be at Plymouth, N. C.

III. The third will be known as the District of the Pamlico.

This district will include the posts of Washington and Hatteras Inle
and such other posts as may be hereafter established within the limit
of the district, and will be commanded by Brig. Gen. Henry Prince
whose headquarters will be at Washington, N. C.

By command of Maj. Gen. J. G. Foster:

[SOUTHARD HOFFMAN,]
Assistant Adjutant-General.

SUFFOLK, VA., April 24, 1863.

Major-General Dix:

Major Stratton reports the Third Georgia Infantry in that quarte
and expects it will attempt to cut him off, but feels confident of defea
ing the purpose.

JOHN J. PECK,
Major-General.

SUFFOLK, VA., *April* 24, 1863.

Major-General DIX:

It is very muddy and much water on the ground, but I think it advisable to make a demonstration on the swamp flank. Shall be very glad to see you. If you come let me know the hour of leaving.

JOHN J. PECK,
Major-General.

SUFFOLK, VA., *April* 24, 1863.

Major-General DIX:

Six prisoners were taken this afternoon. They state no troops have left. A rumor was in circulation that troops were coming to both armies from Fredericksburg. Supplies come to them from Franklin. They say General French is much censured for losing the artillery. Hear nothing of troops leaving. Waiting to strike us outside.

General Getty just reports that the enemy are erecting works at new points on the river.

JOHN J. PECK,
Major-General.

SUFFOLK, VA., *April* 24, 1863.

Major-General HOOKER,
Headquarters Army of the Potomac:

Richmond papers state that Longstreet has been re-enforced. They are despondent about his campaign. This afternoon I made a demonstration on his right, resting on the Edenton road. Thus far my operations have been successful.

JOHN J. PECK,
Major-General.

(Copy to General Halleck.)

FORT MONROE, VA., *April* 24, 1863—9.30 p. m.

Maj. Gen. H. W. HALLECK,
General-in-Chief:

I went to Suffolk this morning and returned this evening. General Corcoran was sent with a strong force at 1 o'clock. General Peck, whose excellent arrangements I cannot too highly commend, just sent the following dispatch:

SUFFOLK, VA., *April* 24, 1863.

Major-General DIX:

We made a successful demonstration on Longstreet's right flank in a heavy rain. The enemy was routed out of all his advance rifle-pits and driven back to his main defenses at Darden's Mill Dam in a very handsome manner, where several batteries are posted, and it is thought that a large force is massed between the Edenton and Somerton roads. Our loss was only 35, and the object of the movement was fully attained. Corcoran, Foster, and Spear were out. The bayonet was used with effect.

JOHN A. DIX,
Major-General.

HDQRS. DEPT. OF VIRGINIA, SEVENTH ARMY CORPS,
Fort Monroe, Va., April 25, 1863.

Actg. Rear-Admiral S. P. LEE,
Commanding North Atlantic Blockading Squadron :

ADMIRAL : I received in New York City your letter of the 9th instant, advising me that the Navy Department, under date of April 8, declines to authorize certain articles for the Smith Briggs to be furnished from the Navy supplies, &c.; also that you are directed hereafter to refer my requisitions for ordnance for gunboats to the Navy Department, to enable it to inquire of the War Department if such requisitions are authorized or sanctioned by it.

The difficulty of procuring from the Navy gunboats of light draught decided me some months ago to arm one or two quartermasters' boats for the defense of the Upper Nansemond. The propriety of the measure is vindicated by the existing condition of things there, your gunboats being withdrawn and the Smith Briggs, one of the boats armed by me, being one of our chief supports at Suffolk. These boats were armed by me by virtue of my general authority, as commanding officer of the department, to do whatever is essential for the safety of my command in the face of the enemy. I did not hesitate, therefore, without any special authority from the War Department, to ask you for certain articles required for the boats referred to, not doubting that you would promptly respond, as you always have done, to any requisition for co-operation in maintaining the authority of the Government against the common enemy. In the same spirit our tugs, our army wagons, our ammunition, and whatever else you needed have always been placed at your disposal without inquiring into your authority to ask for them.

Though the Navy Department has decided to respond to no more requisitions from me, as commander of the department, for ordnance for the gunboats, whatever may be the urgency of the case, without inquiring whether they are authorized or sanctioned by the War Department, I beg to say that in reference to you, as commanding officer of the blockading squadron, I shall act on a totally different principle, and that any material of war of any sort under my control which you may need in the discharge of your responsible duties will be most cheerfully furnished on your requisition without stopping to inquire whether they are authorized or approved by the Navy Department.

I have the honor to be, very respectfully, your obedient servant,

JOHN A. DIX,
Major-General.

SUFFOLK, VA., *April 25, 1863.*

Major-General DIX:

The enemy clearly meditated a crossing last night between Jericho Creek and Fort Conn. There was great activity on his part. He was shelled from Fort Onondaga and the vigilance of the troops defeated his intentions.

Have re-enforced Major Stratton, who is fearful of being cut off.

JOHN J. PECK,
Major-General.

SUFFOLK, VA., *April 25, 1863.*

General EGBERT L. VIELE :

Major Bovey will report to you. Longstreet is still at work. He cut a road down to the river last night and fully intended to cross. Our batteries command the road. We made a successful demonstration on his right flank yesterday, driving in all his advanced parties from their rifle-pits, nearly three-quarters of a mile, to their main line at Darden's Mill Dam.

> JOHN J. PECK,
> *Major-General.*

SUFFOLK, *April* 25, 1863—4.30 p. m.

Major-General DIX:

Several regiments are here whose terms expire in a few days. What shall I do with them?

Two deserters state clearly that General Garnett's brigade has joined within three days from North Carolina; also that troops are expected from Fredericksburg.

> JOHN J. PECK,
> *Major-General.*

FORT MONROE, *April* 25, 1863.

Major-General PECK,
> *Commanding, Suffolk:*

On Tuesday two heavy guns, drawn each by 10 horses, passed down the Blackwater on the way to Suffolk.

> JOHN A. DIX,
> *Major-General.*

SUFFOLK, VA., *April* 25, 1863.

Major-General DIX:

It only goes to show that they have no idea of leaving. The impression is that new troops are arriving. One brigade is certainly here from North Carolina. Several bands of music were playing last evening on the high ground. When will the other 10-pounder Parrotts be up? We need more in the field-works in order to release the horse batteries. Not less than twenty pieces are requisite for General Getty's line, which reduces our stock.

> JOHN J. PECK
> *Major-General.*

[APRIL, 25, 1863.]

General HOOKER:

One brigade has just joined Longstreet from Carolina. He is bringing very heavy artillery. He means to take his time.

> JOHN J. PECK,
> *Major-General.*

HEADQUARTERS EIGHTEENTH ARMY CORPS,
Dept. of North Carolina, New Berne, April 25, 1863.

Maj. Gen. JOHN A. DIX,
> *Commanding Department of Virginia:*

MY DEAR GENERAL: I have received your letter of the 24th, and in accordance with your request am now starting as strong force as I can spare to make an attack on D. H. Hill, at Kinston.

I shall continue this demonstration for four or five days, and if in the mean time you do not defeat Longstreet I will make a new demonstration in another direction.

Please keep me constantly advised of what you wish, and I will aid you to the extent of my power. If I only had my troops back from South Carolina I should be able to make such an attack up the Roanoke River as would make Longstreet retire or leave Weldon. I was half tempted to run up to Suffolk and look at your defenses. If they are properly constructed and well laid out General Peck ought to be able to hold out against five times his number. At Washington we were unassailable (after the first day) with ten times our number around us.

Our outposts taunted the rebels with the inquiry why they did not come in and take Little Washington.

Egotism apart, however, every line of defenses should have at about 800 yards (dependent upon the natural features of the ground) a self-sustaining work, perfectly inclosed, which cannot be taken even if the enemy penetrated the lines on the right or left. These works should be able to fire even to the rear. Each of these works should be mounted with heavy guns (long 32-pounders, firing shell, are very good) and completely manned. The garrisons should be instructed to hold the works to the last extremity, and made to feel their entire independence of any mishaps to other portions of the line.

These works should be of a strong profile, with a wide and deep ditch without, and a palisade in the middle of the ditch or a good abatis in front of it. Between these works should extend a line of infantry intrenchments, with a good ditch and parapet flanked by the fires of the strong works.

If there be time, the infantry intrenchments (along which embrasures for light field pieces may be roughly made) may be supplied with loop-holes for infantry, formed of rods and high enough to protect the heads of those firing. If you have any timber send me, and at once, and I will do all that I can.

My advance toward Kinston are already in front of the rebels at Core Creek, and will engage them to-morrow.

Ever yours, most truly,

J. G. FOSTER,
Major-General, Commanding.

HEADQUARTERS EIGHTEENTH ARMY CORPS,
Dept. of North Carolina, April 25, 1863.

Admiral S. P. LEE,
Comdg. North Atlantic Blockading Squadron,
U. S. Flag-ship Minnesota, off Newport News, Va.:

ADMIRAL: I have the honor to acknowledge the receipt of your letter of the 24th in relation to the occupying of Smith's Island, at the mouth of the Cape Fear River, by our forces. The idea is a good one, and should, in my opinion, be carried out as soon as other operations will permit or render it advisable.

When the plan of operations against Wilmington was decided on, and my preparations were making, this point (Smith's Island) was selected as the first point on which to land and make an establishment to cover a depot of supplies. I am glad that Captain Case sees the importance of it now, for there is no reason why it may not be used in the [manner] he suggests, and thus relieve the blockading vessels at the west entrance of the Cape Fear River.

There may, however, at this time be some trouble in occupying the island, for I have heard that the rebels have recently planted a battery on the island to prevent this very thing. The island can nevertheless be taken by a determined effort at any time that it is absolutely required. I will be most happy to co-operate in any way as soon as I have the force.

If the 8,000 men belonging to this department, now lying at Port Royal, were sent back to me, with the abundant supply of siege guns, ammunition, and artillery that I took down with me to the Department of the South, I will at once engage to occupy Smith's Island with batteries to command the channel, to annoy Fort Caswell, and also as far as practicable to command the New Inlet Channel. Unless this return of my troops be made, which is now refused by the Government, I can do nothing to aid you, inasmuch as nearly 1,000 of the two-years' men have to be discharged in a few weeks and eight regiments of nine-months' men within two months. This will very seriously deplete my already small force, and although I can hold my own I cannot undertake to do more than act strictly on the defensive.

Whatever may be decided on by the Government you can rely upon my ready and energetic co-operation.

Very respectfully and truly, your obedient servant,

> J. G. FOSTER,
> *Major-General, Commanding.*

P. S.—I am now moving on Kinston.

> FORT MONROE, VA.,
> *April 26, 1863—7.30 p. m.*

Maj. Gen. H. W. HALLECK,
    General-in-Chief:

I have just returned from Suffolk. I went to the top of the signal station, 80 feet high, and saw two forts which the enemy is building— one in front of Fort Nansemond and the other across the river, below General Peck's headquarters. Garnett's brigade, which arrived on Friday, consists of five regiments. One of my spies, who arrived last evening, reports Powhatan not yet armed, but 600 contrabands at work. Two thousand troops, who were there a fortnight ago, have come to Suffolk. The Navy could easily have prevented the enemy from intrenching at Fort Powhatan. Everything indicates that the movement on Suffolk is a campaign and looks to Norfolk. The gauge of the railroad from Petersburg to the Blackwater has been altered to correspond with ours this side. If you can spare a few thousand more troops they will no doubt be needed, and can be sent back the moment the exigency is over. The extent of our river line absorbs a large number. The enemy has cut a broad road down to the river, and indicates a determination to cross.

> JOHN A. DIX,
> *Major-General.*

> SUFFOLK, VA., *April 26, 1863.*

Major-General DIX, *Norfolk:*

Major Stratton had some skirmishing with the enemy yesterday; the particulars I have not learned.

> JOHN J. PECK,
> *Major-General.*

FORT MONROE, *April* 26, 1863.

Major-General PECK,
          Commanding, Suffolk:

I send you to-day by mail a brigadier-general's commission for
Colonel Harland. General Gordon was here yesterday and has gone
back for his staff. He will return in a few days. I am not quite sure
whether I shall be with you to-day. The enemy has no artillery where
General Getty captured the battery. Lieutenant Rowe, of the West
End, volunteers to pilot the Commerce down. Shall he try ?

                              JOHN A. DIX,
                                   Major-General.

SUFFOLK, VA., *April* 26, 1863.

Major-General HOOKER,
          Army of the Potomac:

Longstreet is still here. Heavy artillery is coming to him from
Petersburg. The storm has ceased; mud drying up. Advise me in
cipher of as much as you deem proper of your operations.

                              JOHN J. PECK,
                                   Major-General.

APRIL 26, 1863.

Major-General PECK, *Suffolk, Va.:*

Your dispatch received. I have been delayed in my operations by
the severe storm. I have communicated to no one what my intentions
are. If you were here I could properly and willingly impart them to
you. So much is found out by the enemy in my front with regard to
movements that I have concealed my designs from my own staff, and
I dare not intrust them to the wires, knowing as I do that they are so
often tapped.

                              JOSEPH HOOKER,
                                   Major-General.

SUFFOLK, VA., *April* 27, 1863.

Major-General DIX :

Major Stratton reports that he destroyed a new ferry-boat at Camden, opposite Elizabeth. Three hundred guerrillas at Elizabeth, called
Fifty-sixth North Carolina. He is advised of 500 cavalry and four pieces
in that vicinity, with a regiment of infantry at Woodville. Union men
are the sources. The Fifth Virginia Infantry has left Woodville for
Suffolk.

A party attempted to cross near Sleepy Hole last night in boats.

                              JOHN J. PECK,
                                   Major-General.

SUFFOLK, *April* 27, 1863.

Col. D. T. VAN BUREN, *Fort Monroe:*

The engineer and captain of the Commerce refuse to run her. Will
a payment of $50 to a volunteer engineer be authorized?

                              JOHN J. PECK,
                                   Major-General.

FORT MONROE, *April 27*, 1863.

Major-General PECK :

General Dix says you can offer the $50 to a volunteer.

D. T. VAN BUREN,
Assistant Adjutant-General.

FORT MONROE, *April 27*, 1863.

Major-General PECK :

The Commerce and Swan have arrived safely. Somewhat peppered, but all right. Lieutenant Rowe deserves great credit.

JOHN A. DIX,
Major-General.

WASHINGTON, D. C., *April 27*, 1863.

Major-General FOSTER,
Commanding, &c., New Berne, N. C. :

GENERAL : The Navy Department has requested that your attention be called to the importance of the military occupation of Smith's Island at the mouth of Cape Fear River. It is said that by the occupation of this island both channels may be closed, and thus prevent the entrance of contraband goods to Wilmington.

I informed Mr. Fox that no additional forces could be given to you at the present time, but that possibly you might accomplish this object, which he deems most important. He says that at this season, while the water is smooth, there will be no difficulty in landing.

If you should be able to occupy this island as many contrabands as possible should be used in fortifying and holding the position. I understand from the Secretary of War that a Colonel Wild, of Boston, has been directed to report to you to organize one or more negro regiments. If this should be done it is suggested that they can be used to the best advantage on Smith's Island.

It is regretted that we cannot give you more troops for active operations in the field, but at this time it is impossible to do so.

Very respectfully, your obedient servant,

H. W. HALLECK,
General-in-Chief.

SPECIAL ORDERS, }   HDQRS. OF THE ARMY, ADJT. GEN.'S OFFICE,
No. 190.   }   *Washington, April 27,* 1863.

I. Brig. Gen. George H. Gordon, U. S. Volunteers, will report for duty without delay to Maj. Gen. John A. Dix, commanding, &c., Fort Monroe, Va.

*   *   *   *   *   *   *

By command of Major-General Halleck :

E. D. TOWNSEND,
Assistant Adjutant-General.

GENERAL ORDERS, }   HDQRS. EIGHTEENTH ARMY CORPS,
No. 64.   }   *New Berne, April 27,* 1863.

General Orders, No. 62, are hereby amended as follows:

The first district will be called the District of Beaufort, and will include the posts which are or may hereafter be established in that portion of the county of Craven lying south of a line drawn from Evans' Mill due east to the Neuse River and including Evans' Mill, and in the counties of Jones and Carteret with the exception of the post of Portsmouth.

The second district, or the District of the Albemarle, will include all the posts which are or may hereafter be established in the counties of Washington and Tyrrell, and in all the counties of this State northwest of those counties whose waters flow into the Albemarle Sound.

The third district, or the District of the Pamlico, will include all the posts which are or may be hereafter established in that portion of Craven County north of Neuse River, excepting the post of Fort Anderson, and in the counties of Pitt, Beaufort, and Hyde, as well as the post of Portsmouth.

By command of Maj. Gen. J. G. Foster:
[SOUTHARD HOFFMAN,]
Assistant Adjutant-General.

WAR DEPARTMENT,
Washington, April 28, 1863—4.55 p. m.
Major-General DIX, *Fort Monroe, Va.:*
The two artillery companies at Fort Delaware will be sent to you.
H. W. HALLECK,
General-in-Chief.

UNITED STATES FLAG-SHIP MINNESOTA,
Off Newport News, Va., April 28, 1863.
Maj. Gen. JOHN A. DIX, U. S. A.,
Commanding Seventh Army Corps, Fortress Monroe, Va.:
GENERAL: I have received your communication of the 22d. You therein refer to some general views which I had expressed, and from which you draw the conclusion that I had withdrawn the flotilla from the Upper Nansemond.

When General Keyes a fortnight since informed me on current reports obtained from rebel deserters and fugitives all along the line that Longstreet was approaching Suffolk with 40,000 men, heavy artillery, and pontoons, and earnestly preferred requests for gunboats to protect the line of the river, the greater part of the light-draught force of this squadron was engaged co-operating in defense of the military positions on the Sounds of North Carolina, and I was in receipt of urgent requests from that quarter also for an additional gunboat force. There was a similar pressure for additional gunboats for Williamsburg and Yorktown. Here I had but one available gunboat, the Commodore Barney, which I at once detailed for duty in the Lower Nansemond. The Nansemond was already occupied by one light ferry-boat (mounting four field howitzers), which had been used for naval guard ship there. There remained here two river steamboats and four tugs (mounting two light pieces each) belonging to the naval service and used for transport, tender, mail, and picket duties. All of these, save one of the tugs for picket, I immediately equipped with detachments of men and such appliances as I had at my disposal for their protection from rifle shot, arming one of the river steamers with four field pieces on field carriages from this ship, and sent them up the Nansemond in accordance with the request I had received. One of the river steamers I reserved for trans port of ammunition, coal, and dispatches at the service of the vessels in the Nansemond. The embarrassment thus occasioned here by the absence of tenders was partially relieved by the kind loan of the quartermaster's tug Du Pont. In further response to urgent calls from General Peck and yourself I applied to the Department for an additional force of light draughts to meet the demands on the Navy in these waters. Four vessels were then detached from the Potomac Flotilla, this being half of Commodore Harwood's steam force. They arrived here on the 16th and were sent into the Nansemond the same evening. Lieutenants Cushing and Lamson, who had in charge the two divisions of the flotilla in the Nansemond, were instructed to do everything in their power to assist the army.

The upper part of the river, in which most of the slight vessels thus hastily equipped were ordered to operate, is but a canal or ditch, of width so insignificant that the boats are obliged to touch one bank with their bows that their sterns may swing clear of the other. This narrow and tortuous stream winds between banks covered with woods, where riflemen or artillery can at any time conceal themselves and open a murderous and concentrated fire on our men on the open decks of the vessels at short range, shifting from place to place or masking batteries above and below, cut off our communications at will, and destroy or capture the flotilla.

Had the enemy in force really determined to cross the Nansemond how long could such vessels effectually oppose the movement? It was obvious to me that the few light field pieces we had (mostly on field carriages) would in the event of contesting a crossing have done better service behind earthworks than on open decks over magazines of powder and steam; for the boilers, machinery, and ammunition of these light-draught vessels, unlike those of regular men-of-war, are near or above water and exposed to shot and shell.

The line which these frail and vulnerable vessels were called upon to protect, and in front of which they were expected to patrol and draw the enemy's fire, was purely a military line, whose natural defenses should have been earthworks on our side against earthworks on the other—riflemen, scouts, communications, and proper disposition of troops to oppose similar demonstrations on the part of the enemy. Was it therefore justifiable for you to impose or for me to undertake, without a word of warning to you regarding its utter impracticability, a naval defense of your military line, which defense, if fairly tried, must have failed, to the grief of the nation and the probable reproach of the Navy?

I beg to remind you that while thus straining every effort to meet these demands on the part of the army, though I was under the conviction that it was an anomalous and improper use of naval means, I suggested to you, having in view the confidence so flatteringly reposed in such means by you and General Peck, to arm and equip with field pieces and men for this service on the Nansemond, as I had done with the Mount Washington and Stepping Stones, one of the numerous tugs and transports at your disposal, of which, as shown by your official notices to me, you have about forty. I have not been informed that the suggestion was adopted. In your letter of the 22d you say, alluding to the gunboats, "I know there is danger that they will be fired into, injured, perhaps crippled; but this hazard must be incurred to prevent the rebels from crossing. Yours will be exposed to no more danger than mine."

A newspaper correspondent from Fortress Monroe and professing to derive his inspiration from the "highest authority"—a great breach of military and professional decorum—accuses me of withholding the necessary services of the gunboats and of desiring to keep them out of danger by putting them in glass cases.

I have not learned that for this gross and indecent assault, this wicked misrepresentation of an honest and earnest performance of duty under high responsibilities, the anonymous correspondent has in any way been corrected. These things constrain me to quote from a report by Lieutenant Lamson, under date of Sunday, April 19:

We have fought the rebels every day since last Saturday except to-day, with a heavy loss compared to our force, and the army have laid on their bank or in their earthwork without a man hurt, and have utterly failed to render me the assistance and support they ought to have given.

During this time the Mount Washington and Alert had been disabled and withdrawn for repairs, the former in a serious contest with the enemy's battery at West Branch, having had her boiler exploded, her gallows-frame destroyed, and having been otherwise much cut up while helpless and aground on the bar commanded by that battery, without the use of her steam. Our loss in this and subsequent unequal contests amounted to one of our vessels entirely disabled and three of the other four partially so, and 24 men killed and wounded, a very large proportion of our small number of men engaged. The interval of two days between the disabling of some vessels and the arrival of others on the Upper Nansemond, together with the absence of any naval demonstration on the part of the enemy in James River, seemed to indicate that it was not his intention to cross the Nansemond. Your re-enforcements giving you as I am told a strong army of 22,000 men at Suffolk, enabling you, as you have just done, to erect works and to defend the line of the river; the inability of our little vessels, as shown by subsequent contests with the rebel batteries, to raise the blockade of the Upper Nansemond, whilst my transports and tenders were being cut up without being adequate to the main object of protecting that line; my orders to return the vessels from the Potomac Flotilla as soon as the emergency was over, and a requisition upon me to convoy and protect Major-General Hooker's supply vessels going into the Pamunkey, combined to dispose me to withdraw the light draughts from the Upper Nansemond, and I accordingly sent Fleet Captain Crosby to Suffolk to ascertain facts and to bring them down if practicable, giving due notice to the army. But at your and General Peck's instance I kept them in the river, as shown in my dispatches of the 19th to General Peck before and to General Getty after the capture of the battery on the West Branch, which capture opened our communications. The former dispatch went through your headquarters.

I am further constrained to say that it was not until after two failures on the part of the army to support Lieutenant Lamson that that young officer was finally enabled to put into execution (with the gallant and effectual co-operation of the troops under General Getty) the plans which he had made and urged to capture the battery at West Branch.

A due regard for the facts should have prevented the reflection implied in your letter. The readiness and zeal which the officers and men under my command have exhibited in these unequal contests, in which our vessels have been "fired into, injured, and crippled;" the gallantry with which they have incurred "hazard to prevent the rebels from crossing," these did not tempt me selfishly to misuse the means and lives with which I am intrusted for the public welfare to undertake without proper explanation an enterprise which is military and not naval—which is practicable in the former sense and impossible in the latter. Hence

I have taken pains to apprise the military authorities of the insufficiency of these means to the ends proposed and urged by them.

Lieutenants Cushing and Lamson are still in the Nansemond and still under instruction to give all the assistance in their power to the army. The orders which I have given Lieutenant Lamson not only do not restrain but direct his going into the Upper Nansemond when necessary and practicable at his discretion.

I have the honor to be, general, very respectfully, yours,

S. P. LEE,
Actg. Rear-Admiral, Comdg. N. Atlantic Blockading Squadron.

FORT MONROE, VA., *April* 28, 1863.

Maj. Gen. H. W. HALLECK,
    General-in-Chief: .

Admiral Lee has withdrawn all his gunboats from the Upper Nansemond, against my remonstrance and General Peck's, leaving us to take care of ourselves. We had two unarmed transports at Suffolk, which were much wanted, and yesterday I ordered them down. Two of our officers, who have been commanding on a gunboat I armed myself, volunteered to pilot them, and they have this morning performed the service successfully. Both boats received some cannon-shot and a good many rifle-balls, but that we expected. Neither sustained any injury worth mentioning, though they were fired on by three batteries and from a good many rifle-pits. I have just received the following dispatch from General Peck, from which you will see that the enemy is in earnest:

SUFFOLK, VA., *April* 28, 1863.

Maj. Gen. JOHN A. DIX:

The force reported by Stratton on the Chowan was Garnett's six regiments of infantry, one of cavalry, and some artillery, which has joined Longstreet. Garnett commanded at Little Washington. The enemy were very active all night, and we kept several batteries in play on chopping parties. General Getty reported movement of troops down the river with artillery, indicative of crossing.

JOHN A. DIX,
Major-General.

FORT MONROE, VA.,
April 28, 1863—9.30 p. m.

Maj. Gen. H. W. HALLECK,
    General-in-Chief:

I have been on the Nansemond to-day. No movements there. General Garnett's brigade, from North Carolina, has joined Longstreet. Two heavy guns, drawn each by 10 horses, passed through Surry County to Suffolk on Tuesday evening, reaching there yesterday. We shall no doubt soon hear from them.

JOHN A. DIX,
Major-General.

SUFFOLK, VA., *April* 28, 1863.

General DIX:

The enemy opened a new battery with three guns on the river last night. Lieutenant Rowe deserves great credit for his exploit. When will the guns we talked about be sent?

JOHN J. PECK,
Major-General.

FORT MONROE, *April* 28, 1863.

Major-General PECK:

Captain Baylor already preparing the guns, and they will be sent as soon as possible.   You will have twelve.

JOHN A. DIX,
Major-General.

SUFFOLK, VA., *April* 28, 1863.

Major-General DIX:

A man who was at Franklin on the 20th says the railway bridge was being built; also that he saw two trains of troops coming from Weldon.

The people told him that 45,000 men were under Longstreet and more coming from Carolina.

•   JOHN J. PECK,
Major-General.

FORT MONROE ARSENAL, VA., *April* 28, 1863.

Lieut. A. B. JOHNSON, *Suffolk, Va.* :

I will send you to-morrow 1,000,000 cartridges, caliber .57, and the remainder soon after.   I will forward the 24 and 12 pounder ammunition as soon as it can be prepared.   I have telegraphed for the 18-pounder ammunition.   Your requisitions are large.   Have you storage for it?

T. G. BAYLOR,
First Lieutenant, Arsenal, Fort Monroe.

SUFFOLK, *April* 28, 1863.

Lieut. T. G. BAYLOR,
Commanding Arsenal, Fortress Monroe, Va.:

I am aware that my requisitions are large, but not as large as the general suggested.   He thinks we shall soon have use for it all.

My storage is not sufficient, but am assured that more shall be provided.

The amount of daily consumption of ammunition now is not small, although reports say "all quiet at Suffolk."

A. B. JOHNSON,
Lieutenant, Ordnance Officer.

HDQRS. DEPT. OF VIRGINIA, SEVENTH ARMY CORPS,
Fort Monroe, Va., April 28, 1863.

General HENRY A. WISE,
Or Commanding Officer of the Troops on the Chickahominy:

SIR: The town of Williamsburg has been occupied, as you are aware, by the troops under my command as a picket station or outpost of Yorktown.   A large portion of the inhabitants are known not to be well disposed to the Government of the United States.   They have nevertheless been quietly pursuing their domestic avocations, been unmolested, and have been permitted to supply themselves with the necessaries and comforts of life at Yorktown and Fort Monroe.   The insane asylum at Williamsburg has been put under the superintendence of an army surgeon, and its 300 helpless inmates supplied, at the expense of the United

States, with everything necessary to their comfort and with the remedial treatment they require. While exercising these offices of humanity the troops at Williamsburg have been several times attacked by your forces, not with a view to gain and hold possession of the place and to assume the guardianship which has been extended to the inhabitants and the tenants of the asylum by us, but for the purpose of harassing those who were performing this generous service. On the 31st ultimo your forces entered and endeavored to take possession of the town, occupying several houses and firing upon the troops, and in this, as I am informed, they were aided by some of the inhabitants, who have been living for nearly a year under our protection. More recently your forces entered the town and took possession of it, placing our employés in the insane asylum under parole, carrying off some of the servants, and depriving its inmates of the care to which they have been accustomed and which their helpless condition renders indispensable. You have by withdrawing your forces left the asylum again to our charity and compelled Major-General Keyes, the commanding officer of the troops at Yorktown and Fort Magruder, to supply it with food to save the patients from starvation. These raids, under the peculiar circumstances, are in violation of every dictate of humanity. Having no result and apparently no object but annoyance and a useless sacrifice of life, they are also in violation of every principle of honorable warfare. I have directed Major-General Keyes to reoccupy the town; and that the aggressions referred to may cease I give you notice in case of any repetition of them—

1st. That the inmates of the asylum will be sent to Richmond and the United States relieved of the burden of their support;

2d. That any house which may be taken possession of for the purpose of firing upon the troops stationed there will be razed to the ground; and,

3d. That any citizen of Williamsburg not belonging to a regularly organized corps who shall be found co-operating in these attacks and rising in arms against the occupying troops will be put to death as a violator of the laws of civilized warfare.

I am, very respectfully, your obedient servant,

JOHN A. DIX,
Major-General.

————

HDQRS. FIRST DIVISION, EIGHTEENTH ARMY CORPS,
Core Creek, Dover Road, April 28, 1863.

Lieut. Col. SOUTHARD HOFFMAN,
Assistant Adjutant-General, Eighteenth Army Corps:

COLONEL: The troops of this command were all in position last night. On account of the limited number of cars it took several trips to bring everything up. Colonel Amory's brigade I sent to the railroad crossing at Core Creek. He took possession of the bridge and sent a force immediately across the creek and as far as the switch. There was nothing there.

I marched here (about 12 miles) from Colonel Jones' camp, arriving a little after midnight. I brought with me the brigade of Colonel Lee, the section of artillery, and one company of cavalry, with Colonel Jones and his regiment. Plank was brought from Colonel Jones' camp to repair the bridge here, and it was at the bridge at 1 this morning. A force was sent immediately across the creek here, which went out some distance on the road, but found nothing. This force still remains across the creek. The cars were running to the creek till late last night, and the noise of the whistles was constant and imposing.

At midnight it commenced to rain very heavily, and now the whole country is under water. The men are patient and trying to keep warm and dry. One shower succeeds another very quickly, and we are waiting patiently for a lull in the storm. I communicate with Colonel Amory, who is about 2 miles from here.

It is my impression that everything has retired to Kinston; that is, every force of any size.

With the best care that could be taken a good portion of the men's rations will be soaked, and to-morrow we will have to get a supply. These should be sent to Core Creek by rail. We need 2,500 to 3,000 rations daily, and the cavalry horses have no forage. There are two companies of them here.

This I shall send by Captain Harris, commissary of Colonel Amory's brigade.

I am, colonel, very respectfully, your obedient servant,

I. N. PALMER,
Brigadier-General.

UNOFFICIAL.—P. S.—A ration of whisky ought to be sent for the men if provisions are to be sent.

I. N. P.

UNITED STATES FLAG-SHIP MINNESOTA,
Off Newport News, Va., April 29, 1863.

Maj. Gen. JOHN A. DIX, U. S. A.,
Commanding Seventh Army Corps, Fort Monroe, Va.:

GENERAL: On the 21st of this month, by the exhibition of a white flag on shore by a person in citizen's dress, a boat from the Stepping Stones was lured ashore, fired on by troops in ambush, one of its crew killed, and the following-named men taken prisoners, viz: James Coleman, J. McNiclety, F. Hopkins, and J. Reed. This was a base transaction and the men should be surrendered and not exchanged as prisoners of war. Lieutenant Lamson verbally informed me that in a recent communication by flag of truce at Suffolk the enemy expressed a purpose to return these three men. Please have this done.

I have the honor to be, sir, very respectfully, yours,

S. P. LEE,
Actg. Rear-Admiral, Comdg. N. Atlantic Blockading Squadron.

HDQRS. DEPT. OF VIRGINIA, SEVENTH ARMY CORPS,
Fort Monroe, Va., April 29, 1863.

Maj. Gen. H. W. HALLECK,
General-in-Chief:

GENERAL: Major-General Peck, as you are aware, is performing very arduous duties, greater, I presume, than any commander of an army corps who has not a separate department.

Would it be practicable to create an army corps for him from the troops under his command? I could designate the regiments to compose it without interfering with my own corps—the Seventh. He is greatly in need of the additional staff which such an organization would give, and no officer deserves more for his vigilance, discretion, and devotion to his duties.

I am, very respectfully, your obedient servant,

JOHN A. DIX,
Major-General.

FORT MONROE, *April* 29, 1863.

Major-General PECK:

Captain Baylor has sent you seven guns and 200 rounds of ammunition for each. He has also sent four mortars and 1,000,000 cartridges for small-arms. His men are very much overworked, and will keep fast to-morrow.* The other five guns will be sent the next day.

JOHN A. DIX,
Major-General.

SUFFOLK, VA., *April* 29, 1863.

Major-General HOOKER,
Headquarters Army of the Potomac:

I think I can hold Longstreet here for some time, which will favor your operations very materially. When he retires it will only be to his two railroads, where he can go to Lee or strike at me, according to circumstances. You and I will have plenty of work. He is bridging the Blackwater for railroad purposes. The impression is strong that Hill will leave North Carolina and join Longstreet.

JOHN J. PECK,
Major-General.

(Copy to General Halleck.)

APRIL 29, 1863.

Major-General PECK or DIX, *Suffolk, Va.:*

I have fully commenced my operations here. The result may be to draw from your front and afford you an opportunity to push or hold them.

JOSEPH HOOKER,
Major-General, Commanding.

APRIL 29, 1863.

Major-General HOOKER,
Army of the Potomac:

No change of note here. Heavy rain. Governor Seward was here to-day.

JOHN J. PECK,
Major-General.

HDQRS. DEPT. OF VIRGINIA, SEVENTH ARMY CORPS,
Fort Monroe, April 29, 1863.

General J. G. FOSTER, *New Berne, N. C.:*

MY DEAR GENERAL: I have just returned from Suffolk. There is a constant interchange of shots from rifle-pits and occasionally from batteries. The enemy has about 40,000 men.

---

* The day of national humiliation, fasting, and prayer enjoined by the President's proclamation of March 30, 1863.

The weak points at Suffolk are the Nansemond, running to the rear 7 miles, with an average width of less than 100 yards, and a range of heights which overlook a portion of our defenses.

All your suggestions have been anticipated, and it will require a large force to dislodge us. Our line is a long one, but with a reserve force in position to be moved promptly to any point of attack I feel confident that we are secure. The enemy is bringing siege guns from Petersburg and is constructing forts. He has three batteries on the Nansemond, and is constructing casemated forts there. All indicate that he has come to stay. I visit Suffolk every other day. I have entire confidence in General Peck, whose prudence, watchfulness, and good judgment leave nothing to be desired.

I am greatly indebted to you for the diversion you are making, and if you can keep General Hill where he is you will render us a great service.

General Hooker has moved with his whole army. It is large, well disciplined, and amply provided with all the *matériel* of war; great and confident hopes are entertained of the success of his movement on Rich-mond. I have never thought it the right way to that capital, but join in the general hope.

We have a cavalry force at South Mills and shall keep open the canal route as long as we can. It would be well, however, to exercise some caution in using it and arrange so as to secure the destruction of the dispatches with which a messenger is charged if he should chance to be intercepted.

I am, dear general, truly, yours,

JOHN A. DIX,
Major-General.

Please keep me advised of your movements.

———

HEADQUARTERS BRIGADE,
Washington, N. C., April 29, 1863.

Lieut. Col. SOUTHARD HOFFMAN,
Asst. Adjt. Gen., Eighteenth Army Corps:

COLONEL: Major-General Foster, commanding Eighteenth Army Corps, informed me that Washington, N. C., had been made a military post, and that my brigade had been ordered there, and that I was to command the post while General Prince was to command the District of the Pamlico, and that Washington would be included in that district and form part of his command. I also received very full verbal instruc-tions from General Foster in regard to the management of the post, as well as to what he desired should be done to strengthen its defenses. I accordingly (after reporting on my arrival here to General Wessells, who was in command at that time) fully complied with all of General Foster's verbal instructions so far as they applied to the south side of the river by disposing of part of the troops at Hill's Point and Rodman's farm, at the cross-roads, Red Hill, &c., in exact conformity with the general's instructions; but after General Prince's arrival I discovered that his views did not correspond with those of General Foster. He informed me that he had received no written orders defining his duties or mine; but he issued the annexed (General Orders, No. 2) from his headquar-ters on the afternoon of April 28, 1863, and on April 29, 1863, at 6.45 o'clock p. m., I was served with General Orders, No. 3, from the head-quarters of General Prince, a copy of which is also hereto attached.

If I have misunderstood General Foster, I deeply regret it; but it is utterly impossible that I could do so, as the conversation was too definite and explicit. *I write now for the purpose of asking that my duties as commander of the post may be defined by an order.* My desire is to serve my country to the best of my ability, but I can be of no benefit to the service in my present position unless I either have some instructions to guide me or I am allowed to proceed according to my own judgment.

By General Orders, No. 2 (hereto annexed), the defenses of the post were placed under my command. This morning I commenced throwing up an earthwork at a point to the right of Block-house No. 3, where General Potter indicated that General Foster desired it should be done; but, as the order of General Prince defining my duties and placing the defenses of the post under my command has been rescinded, I do not feel at liberty to proceed with this or any of the other works necessary for the defense of the place until I shall receive an explicit order to do so, as Orders No. 2 placed me not only in command of the defenses of the post but also of the troops stationed here. That being now rescinded it leaves me without any command.

I did feel a desire to aid in driving back the enemy that now seems to be hovering around this place. In fact I was in hopes that I would be able to make it too warm for them to have even a picket within 20 miles of Washington, much less to be allowed to remain in force within 6 or 7 miles of this place.

A Mrs. Lucinda Willard, from the neighborhood of Beaver Dam, and who says that General Potter knows her very well, came to our lines to-day on the Plymouth road and informed me that the enemy was encamped in large force at Tranter's Creek, and that they intended making another attack upon the place, both by land and with a floating battery which they are to bring down the river, and that their object this time is to burn the town. She says that the rebel soldiers have been writing this to their families in her vicinity for the past three or four days. I make the statement for what it is worth. If General Potter knows her he can tell whether any reliance should be put in what she says. Her statement in regard to the troops and their location is confirmed from other sources. However, I think it would be well to have a strong work erected on the extreme left of our lines, as in case they should take it in their heads to approach the place by the river and at a time when the gunboats might be engaged below the bridge they could give us some trouble unless we have everything ready for their reception.

I am, colonel, very respectfully, your obedient servant,

F. B. SPINOLA,
Brigadier-General Volunteers.

[Inclosures.]

GENERAL ORDERS, } HEADQUARTERS DISTRICT OF THE PAMLICO,
No. 2.   }   *Washington, N. C., April 28, 1863.*

I. The military post of Washington consists of the immediate defenses of that place. The town and citizens are not included in the military post. The command of those defenses and of the troops will devolve upon Brigadier-General Spinola. The town is in charge of the provost-marshal, whose authority emanates from headquarters of the district.

II. No interference with private property excepting by or through the provost-marshal will be sanctioned.

III. The slashings and abatis about the defenses of works in this district will be carefully protected by the troops and preserved; no interference with them will be permitted.

By order of Brig. Gen. Henry Prince:

S. W. WALDRON, JR.,
Captain and Assistant Adjutant-General.

GENERAL ORDERS, } HEADQUARTERS DISTRICT OF THE PAMLICO,
    No. 3.   }   *Washington, N. C., April 29, 1863.*

Paragraph I of General Orders, No. 2, Headquarters District of the Pamlico, Washington, N. C., April 28, 1863, is hereby rescinded.

By command of Brig. Gen. Henry Prince, commanding district:

S. W. WALDRON, JR.,
Captain and Assistant Adjutant-General.

HEADQUARTERS DISTRICT OF THE PAMLICO,
Washington, N. C., April 29, 1863.

Lieut. Col. SOUTHARD HOFFMAN,
    Assistant Adjutant-General, Eighteenth Army Corps:

COLONEL: I have the honor to report the following interesting facts showing how by timely orders to a grand guard I probably saved it from capture:

On visiting the pickets over the river day before yesterday, the day on which I took command here, I found a grand guard (1 captain, 2 lieutenants, and 70 enlisted men of infantry, and 2 cavalry soldiers) stationed at the cross-roads. Considering them so much out of place as to be a mere invitation to the enemy to come and take them, I ordered all the vedettes to be called in at once, so that no time should be lost, and that the force should retire with all dispatch to inside of Red Hill, defining the position to be occupied. This was at 11 o'clock a. m.

I have to-day the most perfectly reliable intelligence that at 12 m day before yesterday, Daniel's brigade (five counted regiments and some cavalry) arrived near the chapel which is 1 mile from the cross-roads toward Greenville. They halted half a mile before reaching the chapel and " made ready for a fight and sent forward the cavalry to the cross-roads." But the informant does not know why the cavalry soon returned, when the brigade immediately marched back on the Greenville road and made their headquarters at Taft's Store, 15 miles from here.

Respectfully, your obedient servant,

HENRY PRINCE,
Brigadier-General Volunteers, Commanding.

N. B.—A reliable man on the Greenville road this evening sent me this message: "They are all gone from Taft's Cross-Roads, but I do not know which way." Probably Taft's Store and Cross-Roads refer to same place, and that Daniel has gone to Virginia.

On the 26th the Fifty-ninth North Carolina, a cavalry regiment in good condition employed on the north side throughout the siege, was relieved at its camp, 10 miles this side of Greenville, by the broken-down regiment of Claiborne. The former " went off for Suffolk." This informant is Private Ferris, a deserter from the Fifty-ninth.

GENERAL ORDERS,　}　　HDQRS. EIGHTEENTH ARMY CORPS,
　No. 68.　　　}　　　　　　*New Berne, April 29, 1863.*

The general commanding desires to express to the officers and men of the Third New York Volunteer Cavalry his appreciation of their gallant conduct and efficiency in the various actions and skirmishes in which they have been engaged with the enemy during their year's service in the Department of North Carolina.

The regiment will inscribe upon its standard and the several companies upon their guidons the names of battles and skirmishes as previously directed in orders.

The battle-flag of the Seventh Confederate (Claiborne) Cavalry, which was captured from the enemy in the gallant charge by a detachment of Companies A and E against superior numbers near Little Washington on the 18th day of April instant, is presented to the regiment as a distinguished mark of the favor and appreciation in which the gallant services of this command are held.

By command of Major-General Foster:

[SOUTHARD HOFFMAN,]
Assistant Adjutant-General.

———

FORT MONROE, VA.,
April 30, 1863—3.30 p. m.

Maj. Gen. H. W. HALLECK,
　　General-in-Chief:

The Ninth Regiment New York Volunteers is, I find, determined to leave on Sunday. It is one of the best regiments I have and I cannot afford to lose it at this moment. Can you give me another regiment in place of it? If not, can I have the company of heavy artillery at Fort McHenry belonging to Colonel Roberts' regiment here? I am told General Morris did not need it and thought of mounting it. With this and the two companies you have ordered from Fort Delaware I will try to manage, if you cannot give me another regiment.

JOHN A. DIX,
Major-General.

———

SUFFOLK, *April 30, 1863.*

Major-General DIX:

What does General Halleck say about the corps? One is due for my services, which have long been more arduous and responsible than most corps commanders.

JOHN J. PECK,
Major-General.

———

FORT MONROE, VA., *April 30, 1863.*

Maj. Gen. JOSEPH HOOKER,
　　Commanding Army of the Potomac:

We are invested at Suffolk by a superior force, but are getting stronger every day. I returned from there last evening. If the enemy attacks he will fare badly. A successful movement on your part, for which we are all most anxious, will be of great service to us by preventing Longstreet from being further re-enforced and may compel him to withdraw.

JOHN A. DIX,
Major-General.

APRIL 30, 1863—12.30 noon.

Major-General DIX, *Fort Monroe:*

The enemy has need of every man here.   He has his hands full.   Rely
on this.   I can say no more.

JOSEPH HOOKER,
Major-General, Commanding.

(Copy to General Peck.)

———

SUFFOLK, *April* 30, 1863.

Major-General HOOKER,
Commanding Army of the Potomac :

The enemy opened upon the Commodore Barney this afternoon with
one Whitworth, one 30-pounder, and one 35-pounder Parrott.   The
Barney and Captain Morris' battery, in Fort Stevens, silenced the battery very handsomely.   Heavy rain for two days and much mud.

JOHN J. PECK,
Major-General.

———

SUFFOLK, VA., *April* 30, 1863.

Maj. Gen. JOHN A. DIX,
Department of Virginia : .

The enemy opened early this morning from near Le Compte's house
with one Whitworth gun, one 30 and one 35 pounder Parrott.   This
afternoon they opened on the Commodore Barney, and the battery was
silenced by the Barney and Captain Morris' battery, in Fort Stevens.
We hold Hill's Point again.

JOHN J. PECK,
Major-General.

———

FORT MONROE, *April* 30, 1863.

Major-General PECK:

I have asked a corps for you and will advise you the moment I hear
JOHN A. DIX.

———

SUFFOLK, VA., *April* 30, 1863.

General DIX:

Our gunboats ought not to leave Elizabeth City, as they can command the lowest approach from Carolina by Camden.   That route turns
South Mills.

JOHN J. PECK,
Major-General.

———

FORT MONROE, VA.,
April 30, 1863—6 p. m.

Brigadier-General RIPLEY:

General Dix requests that six 30-pounder Parrott guns, implements
and equipments be sent to him as soon as possible.   The enemy are
bringing up heavy guns against the works at Suffolk, and these guns
with some 100-pounders that I will get from the forts here, are deemed
necessary to meet them.

T. G. BAYLOR,
First Lieutenant of Ordnance.

SUFFOLK, VA., *April 30, 1863.*

Major-General DIX:

Have had a party at Lake Drummond to-day. They went up the Jericho Canal and then moved up the Washington until they met the rebel pickets. Everything is looking well.

JOHN J. PECK,
Major-General.

FORT MONROE, *April 30, 1863.*

Major-General KEYES,
Commanding, Yorktown:

Has my letter gone to General Wise? Do you think it would be advisable for us to let the Confederates take charge of the insane asylum? They would be sending in and going out for supplies and it seems to me it would be a means of communication with the rebels. Douglass can come back as steward, if you think proper, under our superintendence.

JOHN A. DIX,
Major-General.

HEADQUARTERS FOURTH CORPS,
Yorktown, April 30, 1863.

Major-General DIX,
Commanding Department of Virginia, Fort Monroe:

Your letter to Governor Wise was sent from Williamsburg yesterday at 5 p. m.

Our picket line now embraces that town. The case of the insane asylum is a difficult matter in our hands or with the Confederates. If they have it, it would afford a standing pretext for visits from their emissaries, which evil must be balanced by our troubles with the institution. I would like to have you decide the question. Douglass I regard as a pretty bad rebel.

E. D. KEYES,
Major-General.

UNITED STATES FLAG-SHIP MINNESOTA,
Off Newport News, April 30, 1863.

Maj. Gen. JOHN A. DIX, U. S. A.,
Comdg. Seventh Army Corps, Fortress Monroe, Va.:

GENERAL: Your letter of the 25th is received. Whilst I have, by assuming authority, promptly complied with your requisitions for *matériel* of war for quartermasters' vessels, the reference of all your requisitions, especially those for general outfits for such vessels, to the Department was strictly obligatory upon me. Among these articles which, had I approved your requisition, I would have been obliged to have had purchased in Baltimore for you were sixty hammocks, which now cost $5.75 each. The officer who brought your requisitions in answer to my questions why the quartermaster did not make these purchases replied because they would not be allowed in his accounts. Could I properly do for that Department what it could not properly do for itself? The necessities of the war have obliged the Navy to use Fortress Monroe as a temporary depot. This has afforded the Army the opportunity to extend to the Navy very considerable facilities, and this has always been kindly done and gratefully received. There is a difference, however, between lending a spare tug or wagon already provided for the use of the Army and buying such a tug to be given to the Navy without proper authority to do so. In vindication of your policy of providing an army-navy for the defense of the Upper Nansemond you speak of your gunboat, Smith Briggs, as being one of your " chief supports at Suffolk in consequence of our gunboats being withdrawn;" and in your letter to me of the 22d you say: "My two armed steamers are to remain there. Yours are to be exposed to no more danger than mine," and you encourage me by a reference to the safe running by the Vicksburg batteries of our iron-clads under cover of night with high water and a swift current.

As to the withdrawal of the gunboats, Lieutenant Lamson was obliged to drop down below the bar, that is to say, from the Upper to the Lower Nansemond, on account of the abandonment, against the earnest remonstrance of Lieutenants Cushing and Lamson, of the captured rebel battery by our troops after it had been held by the cross-fire of the gunboats, whilst the troops so strengthened it in the rear with rifle-pits, intrenchments, embrasures, and artillery as to make it almost impregnable, and which, while occupied by the enemy, had harassed the gunboats considerably and cut off their communications by commanding the bar, over which but one of them could pass at or near low water.

Had this battery been held it, with our battery nearly opposite, would have afforded the gunboats a cover above the bar, whence they might at any time of tide have moved up in front of our earthworks, which Lieutenant Lamson informs me now line the right bank of Nansemond Creek. Your gunboat West End dropped below the bar when our gunboats did so, but Lieutenant Lamson informed me it refused to stop to ferry back your troops.

As to your other gunboat, the Smith Briggs, I am informed she never engaged the batteries, but has laid at Suffolk expending navy ammunition, which has been freely supplied to her, in shelling the woods. I cannot see how she or any other gunboat could have proved a " host at Suffolk." It would seem better to have the guns mounted in batteries ashore than on gunboats floating in the ditch before the battery or fort. The West Branch Battery not having been reoccupied by the enemy, it was picketed by you or us. Some of the navy gunboats were to go above the bar yesterday. I suppose when the boats get above the battery the enemy, if in force, will reoccupy it.

I hope you will see in this only a purpose to put myself and my command right on the record. I close with the earnest assurance that I will always be, as I always have been, happy to co-operate with you, and that whatever means are at my command shall be at your service within the extent of my authority.

I have the honor to be, general, very respectfully, yours,

S. P. LEE,
Actg. Rear-Admiral, Comdg. N. Atlantic Blockading Squadron.

HEADQUARTERS,
Elizabeth City, April —, 1863.

Assistant Adjutant-General HOFFMAN:

SIR: I make the following report of the forces under my command at this post to this date:

I was sent here by General Palmer February 28. I have one company of Eighth Massachusetts, 80 men; one of the Third Massachusetts, 75 men; one North Carolina company of about 20 men; two armed schooners, with 26 men each, and about 100 negroes as laborers.

March 12 I sent a party of soldiers from the North Carolina company into the woods for wood with 12 negroes. After being there a short time they were attacked by about 40 guerrillas and 1 negro killed and 2 wounded and 3 of the soldiers taken and carried away prisoners. Soon as the alarm was given I sent a company in pursuit, but they having taken up the bridge were not overtaken by our forces.

I have kept the negroes employed lately in throwing up an intrenchment and have it nearly finished. I shall then send those that are not needed here to New Berne.

Nothing more occurred until the 6th of April. Captain Sanders, of the North Carolina company, with a detail of 7 soldiers and 10 negroes, was sent down the river in a schooner after wood; the wind blowing, they were not able to land that day; he returned home and left the men on board; in the evening they went on shore to see their families, and were all taken and carried away to Richmond prisoners, leaving that company now with only 14 men for duty. Had we a company of cavalry here I think we might rid this section of the country from the guerrillas. As it is now, unless we go out in a large force, we are liable to be picked off. We have now six horses and one yoke of oxen, enough to do our teaming. Previous to your last instructions, under General Palmer's order I had returned to the persons taken from 10 horses and 13 mules, and have given receipts for the rest.

We have received no rations since I arrived here, although I have sent two requisitions, and I have been obliged to forage upon the citizens, and if the Government is to pay for them it will be much more expensive than if sent from New Berne, as provisions are scarce and high.

The negroes are very much in need of clothing, not having received any pay or clothing from the Government and have been employed seven months.

Yours, respectfully,

J. W. WALLIS,
Major, Commanding Post, Elizabeth City, N. C.

Abstract from Tri-monthly Return of the Department of Virginia (Seventh Army Corps), Maj. Gen. John A. Dix commanding, for April 30, 1863 (headquarters Fort Monroe, Va.).

Command.	Present for duty.		Aggregate present.	Aggregate present and absent.	Aggregate last return.	Pieces of field artillery.	Present for duty equipped.					
							Infantry.		Cavalry.		Artillery.	
	Officers.	Men.					Officers.	Men.	Officers.	Men.	Officers.	Men.
Headquarters of Department, Maj. Gen. John A. Dix.	17	......	17	18	18	...	......	......	...	...	...	...
Fort Monroe, Col. S. M. Alford	15	416	593	852	857	...	15	416	...	...	...	...
Camp Hamilton, Maj. J. A. Darling.	19	574	680	702	501	...	......	......	3	77	19	542
Norfolk, Brig. Gen. E. L. Viele..	120	2,228	2,556	2,698	2,728	6	99	2,092	2	54	3	136
Suffolk, Maj. Gen. J. J. Peck ..	1,153	22,822	26,731	32,038	20,879	252	1,038	19,980	63	1,453	43	1,422
Yorktown, Maj. Gen. E. D. Keyes.	287	5,054	6,012	6,717	6,739	30	230	3,706	42	1,032	13	386
Grand total..............	1,611	31,094	36,589	43,025	31,722	288	1,382	26,194	110	2,616	78	2,486

NOTE.—The Monthly Return for April gives the "Aggregate present" as 39,095.

Organization of troops in the Department of Virginia, Major-General Dix commanding, April 30, 1863.

SUFFOLK.

Maj. Gen. JOHN J. PECK.

FIRST DIVISION, SEVENTH ARMY CORPS.

Brig. Gen. MICHAEL CORCORAN.

*Terry's Brigade.**	*Foster's Brigade.*
Brig. Gen. H. D. TERRY.	Col. R. S. FOSTER.
99th New York [N. G. A.].	6th Massachusetts.
130th New York.	13th Indiana.
New York (Battalion) Sharpshooters.	112th New York.
167th Pennsylvania.	169th New York.
11th Rhode Island.	165th Pennsylvania.
	166th Pennsylvania.

Murphy's Brigade.

Col. MATHEW MURPHY

10th New Jersey.
69th New York.
155th New York.
164th New York.
170th New York.

GETTY'S DIVISION.

Brig. Gen. GEORGE. W. GETTY.

First Brigade.	*Third Brigade.*
Col. R. C. HAWKINS.	Col. A. H. DUTTON.
10th New Hampshire.	21st Connecticut.
9th New York.	13th New Hampshire.
89th New York.	25th New Jersey.
103d New York.	4th Rhode Island.
117th New York.	

Second Brigade.

Brig. Gen. EDWARD HARLAND.

8th Connecticut.	
11th Connecticut.	*Artillery.*
15th Connecticut.	1st Pennsylvania, Battery A.
16th Connecticut.	5th U. S., Battery A.

GURNEY'S DIVISION.

Col. WILLIAM GURNEY.

Porter's Brigade.	*Hughston's Brigade.*
Col. B. PORTER.	Col. ROBERT S. HUGHSTON.
40th Massachusetts.	127th New York.
22d Connecticut.	142d New York.
141st New York.	143d New York.
	144th New York.

*On the Monthly Return the Twenty-sixth Michigan and the One hundred and fifty-second New York appear in this brigade instead of the Ninety-ninth New York and —— New York Battalion.

RESERVE BRIGADE.

Col. D. W. WARDROP.

99th New York.*
118th New York.
9th Vermont.
19th Wisconsin.

UNATTACHED.

1st New York Mounted Rifles.
11th Pennsylvania Cavalry.
1st Delaware Battery.
7th Massachusetts Battery.
3d Pennsylvania Artillery.
16th New York Battery.
19th New York Battery.
4th U. S. Artillery, Battery D.
4th U. S. Artillery, Battery L.
2d Wisconsin Battery.
4th Wisconsin Battery.

YORKTOWN.

Maj. Gen. ERASMUS D. KEYES.

King's Brigade.	*Advance Brigade.*
4th Delaware.	**Col. R. M. WEST**
168th New York.	
169th Pennsylvania.	139th New York.
179th Pennsylvania.	172d Pennsylvania.
	178th Pennsylvania.
	5th Pennsylvania Cavalry.
	Artillery detachment.

Unattached.

2d Massachusetts Cavalry, First Battalion.
6th New York Cavalry, Third Battalion.
1st New York Artillery, Batteries H and F.
8th New York Battery.
1st Pennsylvania Artillery, Batteries E and H.
5th U. S. Artillery, Battery M.

NORFOLK.

Brig. Gen. EGBERT L. VIELE.

148th New York.
173d Pennsylvania.
177th Pennsylvania.
11th Pennsylvania Cavalry (one company).
7th New York Battery.

FORT MONROE.†

Col. S. M. ALFORD.

3d New York.

CAMP HAMILTON.

Maj. JOHN A. DARLING.

3d Pennsylvania Artillery (five companies).
11th Pennsylvania Cavalry (one company).

---

*Appears also in Terry's brigade, First Division, Seventh Army Corps.
† Department Headquarters.

Abstract from Tri-monthly Return of the Eighteenth Army Corps, Maj. Gen. John G. Foster commanding, for April 30, 1863 (headquarters New Berne, N. C.).

Command.	Present for duty.		Aggregate present.	Aggregate present and absent.	Aggregate last return.
	Officers.	Men.			
Eighteenth Army Corps, Major-General Foster	20	....	20	21	21
First Division, Brigadier-General Palmer	146	2,923	3,765	7,170	7,216
Second Division, Brigadier-General Naglee	103	1,861	2,382	6,503	6,514
Third Division, Brigadier-General Ferry	25	544	695	5,609	5,609
Fourth Division, Brigadier-General Wessells	192	2,604	3,286	5,568	5,824
Fifth Division, Brigadier-General Prince	200	3,967	4,881	6,148	6,192
Artillery Brigade, Brigadier-General Ledlie	33	609	816	2,077	2,091
Cavalry, Col. S. H. Mix	25	347	463	874	905
First North Carolina (Union) Volunteers, Lieutenant-Colonel McChesney.	10	391	477	544	544
Grand total	754	13,246	16,785	34,514	34,916

Organization of the Eighteenth Army Corps, Department of North Carolina, Maj. Gen. John G. Foster, U. S. Army, commanding, April 30, 1863.

FIRST DIVISION.

Brig. Gen. INNIS N. PALMER.

First Brigade.

Col. T. J. C. AMORY.

17th Massachusetts.
43d Massachusetts.
45th Massachusetts.
51st Massachusetts.

Second Brigade.

Col. H. C. LEE.

5th Massachusetts.
25th Massachusetts.
27th Massachusetts.
46th Massachusetts.

SECOND DIVISION.

Brig. Gen. HENRY M. NAGLEE.

First Brigade.

Brig. Gen. CHARLES A. HECKMAN.

23d Massachusetts.
9th New Jersey.
81st New York.
98th New York.

*Second Brigade.**

Col. W. W. H. DAVIS.

11th Maine.
100th New York.
52d Pennsylvania.
104th Pennsylvania.
Independent New York Battalion.

THIRD DIVISION.*

Brig. Gen. O. S. FERRY.

First Brigade.

Col. J. B. HOWELL.

56th New York.
58th Pennsylvania.
85th Pennsylvania.
174th Pennsylvania.

Second Brigade.

Col. FRANCIS A. OSBORN.

39th Illinois.
62d Ohio.
67th Ohio.
176th Pennsylvania.

*Detached, in Department of the South, with the exception of the Fifty-eighth Pennsylvania.

FOURTH DIVISION.

Brig. Gen. HENRY W. WESSELLS.

First Brigade.	*Second Brigade.*
Brig. Gen. LEWIS C. HUNT.	Brig. Gen. THOMAS G. STEVENSON.
85th New York.	10th Connecticut.*
92d New York.	24th Massachusetts.*
96th New York.	44th Massachusetts.
101st Pennsylvania.	5th Rhode Island.
103d Pennsylvania.	

FIFTH DIVISION.

Brig. Gen. HENRY PRINCE.

First Brigade.	*Second Brigade.*
Brig. Gen. F. B. SPINOLA.	Col. JAMES JOURDAN.
158th Pennsylvania.	3d Massachusetts.
168th Pennsylvania.	8th Massachusetts.
171st Pennsylvania.	132d New York.
175th Pennsylvania.	158th New York.

ARTILLERY.

Brig. Gen. J. H. LEDLIE.

3d New York (twelve companies).
23d New York Battery.
24th New York Battery.
1st Rhode Island, Battery F.
1st U. S., Battery C.

UNATTACHED.

3d New York Cavalry, Col. S. H. Mix.
1st North Carolina (Union).

WAR DEPARTMENT,
Washington, May 1, 1863—1 p. m.

Major-General DIX, *Fort Monroe, Va.:*

We find it impossible to send you another regiment now. Every available man is employed. I think the siege of Suffolk will very soon be raised.

H. W. HALLECK,
General-in-Chief.

MAY 1, 1863—7.30 p. m.

Major-General PECK, *Suffolk, Va.:*

Hood's and Pickett's divisions, of Longstreet's corps, are in our front; so reported by deserters and prisoners captured to-day. This will leave nothing of Longstreet's command in your front but Ransom, if he is there.

DANL. BUTTERFIELD,
Major-General, Chief of Staff.

The larger portion of regiment detached in the Department of the South.

SUFFOLK, VA., *May* 1, 1863.

General D. BUTTERFIELD, *Army of the Potomac:*

There may be portions of Longstreet's troops with your opponents. If so, they are the first installments. Deserters and contrabands who came in yesterday from Hood's and Pickett's divisions agree in all points with others that have fallen into our hands. The pickets of Corse, Garnett, and Law are on all the roads now. There have been heavy rains here for a few days. Longstreet had two railroads in about 16 miles of his line.

JOHN J. PECK,
Major-General.

(Sent by General Butterfield to General Hooker 11.45 p. m.)

FORT MONROE, *May* 1, 1863.

Maj. Gen. JOHN J. PECK:

Among the many marvels of this war are the impossibility on ou) part of getting information as to the enemy and the facility with which he ascertains everything as to us. I allude especially to General Butterfield's dispatch to you stating that Hood's and Pickett's divisions are in front of the Army of the Potomac.

JOHN A. DIX,
Major-General.

SUFFOLK, VA., *May* 1, 1863.

General DIX:

There may be some regiments of Longstreet's on their way. Probably they are the first installments. His line was only about 15 or 16 miles from his two railways. If so, it shows that the rebels knew of Hooker's moves before we did. Deserters and contrabands came in yesterday, giving the same reports as heretofore, and appear entitled to full credit. If Lee has called for him his necessities must be pressing.

JOHN J. PECK,
Major-General.

SUFFOLK, *May* 1, 1863.

Major-General DIX:

Have just examined one of the deserters of Garnett's brigade, recently from North Carolina. He says about what all have said from the outset as to the force and design. His captain said Longstreet would try to take Suffolk, and that he had telegraphed for re-enforcements.

JOHN J. PECK,
Major-General.

UNITED STATES FLAG-SHIP MINNESOTA,
Off Newport News, Va., May 1, 1863.

Maj. Gen. J. G. FOSTER, U. S. A.,
Commanding Department of North Carolina:

GENERAL: I beg leave to acknowledge the receipt at the hands of Captain Gouraud of your communication of April 25.

The proposition regarding Smith's Island has been submitted to the

Navy Department, which has expressed its approval, providing the necessary co-operating force is furnished from the army. The Department informs me that it has unofficial information that Major-General Halleck promises to suggest to you to assist in any way you can, with the force under your command, in carrying out this object. I have ventured to send a copy of your letter to the Navy Department, with the expression of my hope that the War Department would find it expedient to furnish you with means sufficient to undertake and successfully accomplish so desirable a work. I hope that you will soon be supplied with the necessary means to enable you to communicate to me your readiness to put the project into execution. I will be prompt as far as my means will allow to render all proper naval assistance.

With many thanks for the cordial manner in which you have met the proposition, and with many hopes for your success in the movement on Kinston, I have the honor to be, general, very respectfully, yours,

S. P. LEE,
Actg. Rear-Admiral, Comdg. N. Atlantic Blockading Squadron.

UNITED STATES FLAG-SHIP MINNESOTA,
Off Newport News, Va., May 1, 1863.

Maj. Gen. J. G. FOSTER, U. S. A.,
Commanding Department of North Carolina:

GENERAL: I had the honor to receive on the 27th ultimo your interesting and instructive communication of the 22d ultimo, giving your views respecting the occupation of posts within the limits of your command.

It was only in connection with the occupation of such posts by the Navy, as a part of their defense, that the subject claimed my official attention.

I meant in my communication of the 17th to refer only to positions in the Sounds of North Carolina, and not to Fort Macon and Beaufort Harbor, the defense of which, and of Hatteras Inlet, is of obvious necessity.

As to Roanoke Island, I suppose it best that the abandoned rebel works there should be razed and the obstructions in Croatan Sound removed. Then such observation or police as would prevent any attempts at reconstruction might answer; but even if reoccupied by the enemy we could, if there were not too many other places to guard, concentrate and dislodge them. But this position does not receive naval occupation at present, and therefore is only referred to in view of future demands. Your views in respect to New Berne, Washington, and Plymouth possess great force. They would require considerable military defenses, however, to accomplish all you have in view. They are sickly places; Plymouth especially.

The enemy can build gunboats on the Tar above Washington, and on the Roanoke above Plymouth, though their facilities would be better at the towns if they held them.

The question with us is how many places can we profitably hold, comparing the advantages with the expense of possession. We do not hold Elizabeth City, Edenton, Hertford, Winfield, &c., nor does the enemy derive any visible advantage from having access to them.

My general view of our policy is to take places which the enemy has fortified; to level his works of defense, and then to leave these places as they were before the rebellion, unless they are of particular military im portance, in which case they would require and justify proper defenses.

Where a place is held it seems to me that the military occupation ought to be as complete as practicable in itself; and when this cannot be done the occupation becomes one of questionable propriety to the extent that gunboats are permanently needed for its defense.

I do not desire or attempt to interfere with your military plans, and I fully appreciate the good spirit in which you favor me with your views. It is certainly my wish and purpose to co-operate heartily with you. I shall be glad if this interchange of ideas will lead to such an examina- tion of the subject as will show in connection with each necessary mili- tary occupation precisely what kind and extent of naval force is re- quired in the Sounds. It appears to me that the naval part of our policy there is to have such a force as can co-operate in expeditions with the army, and in the mean time, by cruising and as guard vessels, preserve the blockade and the police of the waters.

Should the enemy build gunboats on the rivers above the towns the naval force should be sufficient to destroy his vessels before they unite or after they have combined.

I have the honor to be, general, very respectfully, yours,

S. P. LEE,
Actg. Rear-Admiral, Comdg. N. Atlantic Blockading Squadron.

GENERAL ORDERS, } HEADQUARTERS DISTRICT OF THE PAMLICO,
No. 5. } *Washington, N. C., May* 1, 1863.

I. Pursuant to orders from the Headquarters of the Department of North Carolina it is hereby announced that the lines are closed. No ingress or egress can be permitted, and no trade whatever with persons living beyond the lines.

All persons who have taken the oath of allegiance are hereby warned against any unauthorized communication with persons residing within the enemy's lines, by letter or otherwise.

* * * * * * *

By order of Brig. Gen. Henry Prince:

S. W. WALDRON, JR.,
Captain and Assistant Adjutant-General.

WAR DEPARTMENT,
Washington, D. C., May 2, 1863—10 a. m.

Major-General DIX, *Fort Monroe, Va.:*

Measures should be taken to ascertain the force of the enemy in front of Suffolk. If, as is supposed, the mass of Longstreet's troops has joined Lee, the demonstration agreed upon should be immediately made.

H. W. HALLECK,
General-in-Chief.

MAY 2, 1863.

Major-General HALLECK, *General-in-Chief:*

A demonstration was made on the enemy's line yesterday, which brought out a considerable force. An attack was to have been made on one of the batteries last night, but was probably postponed for want of boats to be brought from Norfolk. Every effort will be made to ascertain promptly his strength. I telegraphed General Peck on the subject last night, after my return from Suffolk, in consequence of a dispatch from General Butterfield stating that Hood's and Pickett's divisions were reported on General Hooker's front. I have just received a dispatch from General Peck in which he says deserters from Pickett's division state that they saw Pickett yesterday and that no brigades have gone from Longstreet's command. They received orders to be ready to move last night, but the orders were countermanded. One of the deserters—a Texan—says that Hood was there yesterday. Jenkins' division is before Suffolk. I will direct General Peck to make a reconnaissance in force and will be ready to make the movement referred to by you promptly.

JOHN A. DIX,
Major-General.

HEADQUARTERS ARMY OF THE POTOMAC,
May 2, 1863—11.30 a. m.

General E. D. KEYES, *Yorktown, Va.:*

Our cavalry ought yesterday or to-day to have been in rear of enemy, on the Richmond and Fredericksburg road, at its crossing of the Pamunkey or in that vicinity, and have destroyed it. Use every possible means to get any information, and telegraph it to us and oblige. Things are very lively here now.

DANL. BUTTERFIELD,
Major-General and Chief of Staff.

MAY 2, 1863.

Major-General HOOKER, *Army of the Potomac:*

Deserters from Pickett's division state that they saw Pickett on the 1st and that no brigades have gone from Longstreet's command. They received orders to be ready to move last night, but the orders were countermanded. One of these is a Texan, who states that Hood was here yesterday. Jenkins' division is here.

JOHN J. PECK,
Major-General.

HEADQUARTERS ARMY OF THE POTOMAC,
May 2, 1863—11.10 a. m.

Major-General PECK, *Suffolk, Va.,* and
Colonel KELTON, *Assistant Adjutant-General, Washington, D. C.:*

Two deserters here from Pickett's division. Left him on the Blackwater April 30, and no signs of a movement then.

DANL. BUTTERFIELD,
Major-General, Chief of Staff.

MAY 2, 1863.

General BUTTERFIELD, *Army of the Potomac:*

Let me ask explanation of the last clause—no signs of a movement then. Does that refer to Longstreet's move or General Hooker's?

JOHN J. PECK,
Major-General.

MAY 2, 1863—6.40 p. m.

Major-General PECK:

The last clause referred to movements of their divisions in front of you, meaning that there were no signs of these divisions in your front moving, as we understood it. The deserters have gone to Washington. We are in full movement and have been for some time.

DANL. BUTTERFIELD,
Major-General, Chief of Staff.

FORT MONROE, *May* 2, 1863.

Maj. Gen. JOHN J. PECK:

The children [cavalry] of the Army of the Potomac were to have cut the railroad at the Pamunkey, half way from Fredericksburg to Richmond, yesterday. Watch the enemy closely to-night and make a reconnaissance in force to-morrow morning.

JOHN A. DIX,
Major-General.

SUFFOLK, VA., *May* 2, 1863.

Major-General DIX:

I organized a command before the reception of your dispatch covering your suggestions. But the telegram from Butterfield to the effect that no movement had been made here on the 30th agrees with all the evidences up to this time. Did they cut the line?

JOHN J. PECK,
Major-General.

HEADQUARTERS ARMY OF THE POTOMAC,
May 2, 1863—8.15 p. m.

Major-General PECK, *Suffolk, Va.:*

Our latest and most reliable information from Richmond is as follows. Am inclined to the belief that this will prove true:

Our friend just returned. The works around Richmond are most formidable. At Meadow Bridge and Mechanicsville route they are intended for field artillery. No guns in position. At Richmond are the City Battalion and some artillery. Twenty-seven hundred rations issued to troops in Richmond in active service. General Wise has 5,000 on the Peninsula. Longstreet has three divisions at Suffolk. When they left Lee they were each 8,000 strong. Their effective force, all told, not over 15,000 men D. H. Hill is ordered from Washington to re-enforce Longstreet's corps. He may, however, take Longstreet's place at Suffolk and Lee may be re-enforced by Longstreet.

DANL. BUTTERFIELD,
Chief of Staff.

SUFFOLK, VA., *May* 2, [1863,]
Via Fort Monroe, Va., May 4, 1863—12.30 a. m.

General BUTTERFIELD,
Chief of Staff, Headquarters Army of the Potomac:

It is important to arrive at correct conclusions regarding Longstreet's force. You say three divisions left Fredericksburg with 24,000. My information from more than 100 individuals has been that his force was

28,000 to 30,000. One of the spies, who has spent weeks in their camps, supplied a list of that army, as well as Lee's, and 28,000 was the figure on April 1. He has enforced the conscription most vigorously in several counties, not heretofore visited, on this side of the Blackwater. He has been joined by 4,000 from Hill, and perhaps more; but the advance of Hooker will soon force him to the river. His men are ready to go at a moment's warning.

JOHN J. PECK,
Major-General.

(Copy to General Halleck.)

MAY 2, 1863.

General DIX:

The papers from the other line have the idea that Longstreet is up there and this was a foraging expedition. This correction proves that my limited sources of information have been better than General Hooker's for many weeks. General Longstreet has his own campaign and will not give it up until compelled to do so. The people at Washington should understand the nature of this siege of twenty-two days.

JOHN J. PECK,
Major-General.

SUFFOLK, VA., May 2, 1863—8.50 p. m.

General DIX:

By a later dispatch from General Butterfield it is now understood that no troops have left my front. It is now reported to me that a train arrived at sunset and that troops were seen about the railway station.

JOHN J. PECK,
Major-General.

MAY 2, 1863.

General DIX:

Richmond Enquirer of 30th has a column on Hooker's advance and the adjunct by way of Suffolk. It thinks that "Longstreet has broken up the camp of negro-stealing Yankees, destroyed the command, and thereby inflicted a fatal blow to Hooker, involving a change of his plans."

JOHN J. PECK.
Major-General.

HDQRS. DEPT. OF VIRGINIA, SEVENTH ARMY CORPS,
Fort Monroe, Va., May 2, 1863.

Actg. Rear-Admiral S. P. LEE,
Commanding North Atlantic Blockading Squadron:

ADMIRAL: Your letter of the 29th ultimo contains some references to affairs on the Nansemond which concern the immediate commander there more nearly than myself, and a copy will be forwarded to him.

I desire to acknowledge, as I always have, the readiness with which my calls on you for aid have been answered. In regard to differences of opinion between us concerning our respective duties I have done all in my power to confine the knowledge of them to those immediately around me and my official superiors. How difficult it is to carry out such a purpose in this country of free discussion I need not suggest to you. My own public conduct in this department has in more instances than one been criticised in a most unjust and offensive manner by a ———— correspondent whom I knew, but as it did not affect any public interest I did not notice it, although I have sent three out of the department—two for giving military information and one for interference with officials. In regard to the newspaper article referred to by you, the moment my attention was called to it (for I rarely read correspondents' letters) the reputed author was advised that he had been guilty of a great impropriety in using the words "highest authority," which was explained to be a common phrase among newspaper correspondents, importing that the statement was made on undoubted information. He was also advised that the remarks in regard to yourself were strongly disapproved by me, and on both points I was assured that there would be no cause for complaint hereafter.

The last paragraph of your letter, advising me that Lieutenants Lamson and Cushing were authorized in their discretion to go into the Upper Nansemond and co-operate with my forces there against the enemy, is all I can ask, and I know that the spirit and gallantry those officers have exhibited on all occasions will insure to us all the aid it is possible to afford.

I have the honor to be, very respectfully, your obedient servant,

JOHN A. DIX,
Major-General.

SPECIAL ORDERS, }   HDQRS. OF THE ARMY, ADJT. GEN.'S OFFICE,
No. 200.   }   *Washington, May 2, 1863.*

*   *   *   *   *   *   *

III. Brig. Gen. Isaac J. Wistar, U. S. Volunteers, will report to Major-General Dix, commanding, &c., Fort Monroe, Va., for assignment to duty at Suffolk, Va.

By command of Major-General Halleck:

E. D. TOWNSEND,
Assistant Adjutant-General.

FORT MONROE, VA., *May* 3, 1863—8 p. m.

Maj. Gen. H. W. HALLECK,
        General-in-Chief:

I have just returned from Suffolk. General Getty crossed the Nansemond, near General Peck's headquarters, to-day, with 5,000 men. He was in front of the enemy's intrenchments, 2 miles back. A strong demonstration will be made on the enemy's right flank to-morrow morning. In the action in front of our center the day before yesterday we lost 7 killed and 20 wounded. The enemy acknowledge 33 killed and a large number wounded. We cannot ascertain and do not think any of his troops have been withdrawn. To-morrow we shall be able to judge better of his strength.

JOHN A. DIX,
Major-General.

YORKTOWN, *May* 3, 1863—12 noon.

Major-General BUTTERFIELD:

I learn that the enemy have left the White House on the Pamunkey. They have planted torpedoes there in the river. I cannot learn whether the bridge has been destroyed.

E. D. KEYES,
Major-General.

MAY 3, 1863.

General DIX:

Garnett's and Benning's brigades joined, from Carolina, and Kemper's is on the way from near Gatesville. Longstreet's plans and arrangements were all for permanent occupation. He designed to push the siege, and Hooker's move and my preparation only prevented. His force was over 30,000. When he can he will return with the same end in view.

Wounded yesterday.

PECK,
Major-General.

FORT MONROE, *May* 3, 1863.

Maj. Gen. JOHN J. PECK:

I saw Admiral [Lee] last evening on the Nansemond. He expressed the opinion that there had at no time been a large force at Suffolk—not over 20,000—and that the enemy had only a few movable guns. I have no doubt it is from him that the views which seem to prevail in Washington have been derived. I think I shall be with you to-day. Will advise you as soon as I get my mail.

JOHN A. DIX,
Major-General.

FORT MONROE, VA., *May* 3, 1863.

Maj. Gen. H. W. HALLECK,
General-in-Chief:

I have just received the following dispatch from General Peck. From my personal observation to-day I am satisfied that the conclusion he and the other general officers named came to is right. Our loss will probably reach 60 in killed and wounded:

The reconnaissance in force has been pushed up very close to the enemy's main line of intrenchments, which is strong and flanked by artificial and natural obstructions. It is evident that he has considerable force massed there, and means to make a strong fight if pressed. It cannot be attacked without a greater loss than I can afford at this time. My position is secure now, and in crossing the river on a single bridge to fight a battle on his ground much risk is assumed. These views are entertained by Generals Getty and Gordon. The troops have been under fire nearly all day, and behaved with great spirit and gallantry, and I shall withdraw them probably during the night. At this time 42 wounded are reported. I regret to say that Colonel Ringold, of the One hundred and third New York, was twice wounded. He is an officer of much merit.

JOHN A. DIX,
Major-General, Commanding.

SUNDAY, *May* 3, 1863.

Major-General FOSTER:

MY DEAR GENERAL: My official letter, May 1, briefly and rather hastily gives my views on the public points noticed in your unofficial favor of the 22d ultimo.

I am sure you will not misunderstand my motives. I am subject to so many calls for aid which I have not to give and for service which I cannot render that I must try and find out just what is or should be required of me and to try to do it. If I had only time to lay before you the quantity and kinds of demands made on me here you would laugh outright if they were not so earnest and provoking.

One point requires a word of explanation from me to you. My impression is that I twice had some conversation with you respecting naval occupations (resulting from army occupations) in the Sounds. Some of the views you now write you expressed to me at New Berne. I expressed my views fully to Townsend and I think to Davenport and Flusser. This Townsend recollects, and says Davenport thinks he recollects some conversation between you and myself about it. It may be that I said less to you than to others after hearing your views, for then as now I was impressed by what you said.

If the occupation of Washington and Plymouth would facilitate instead of clogging your operations, of which you are the best judge, you are right to hold them. But I should like to have the military occupation made as complete as possible so as to lessen or dispense with the stationary naval force at each point.

I meant to add to my official letter to you that I hope you will be at liberty with the Dirigo to have the obstructions in the river at Washington removed. Such impediments should be removed everywhere. The army is less hampered by limits than the navy I believe, especially in war.

I was sorry to hear you were not quite well. Hope your ailment was slight. Please present my most respectful compliments to Mrs. Foster, and believe me, very truly, yours,

S. P. LEE.

P. S.—General Halleck cannot give you the troops for that island. I am very sorry it is so.

I have been obliged to write in great haste to save this good chance for Beaufort. We place no dependence in the canal mail now.

FORT MONROE, VA.,
May 4, 1863—10.30 a. m.

Maj. Gen. H. W. HALLECK,
            General-in-Chief:

A few hours after the fight yesterday the enemy commenced his retreat. We are in pursuit. He was re-enforced on Saturday by Benning's brigade from North Carolina and Kemper's is on the way, having crossed the Chowan near Gatesville. I shall make the movement agreed upon with you at once. Longstreet has over 30,000 men.

JOHN A. DIX,
Major-General.

FORT MONROE, VA., *May* 4, 1863.

Maj. Gen. H. W. HALLECK,
    General-in-Chief:

General Peck says Longstreet's line of rifle-pits and batteries is not less than 10 miles in extent. Batteries are arranged with embrasures and parapets of 12 or 15 feet thickness. His line was of immense strength. It encircled Suffolk from the Edenton road to the Nansemond.

JOHN A. DIX,
Major-General

FORT MONROE, VA.,
May 4, 1863—9 p. m.

Maj. Gen. H. W. HALLECK,
    General-in-Chief:

Major-General Foster is applying for cavalry, and I understand for some of mine. I have but 2,600, and can spare none. I have 1,500 at Suffolk, 900 at Williamsburg, and 200 at Norfolk; besides, General Hill is on the Blackwater. General Foster will be undisturbed.

JOHN A. DIX,
Major-General.

FORT MONROE, VA.,
May 4, 1863—9 p. m.

Major-General HOOKER,
    Headquarters Army of the Potomac:

Following just received from General Keyes:

Lieutenant-Commander Gillis, just returned from near West Point, has learned that the rebel force from White House and below, and opposite on the Pamunkey, have been withdrawn to Hanover Court-House. There are troops on this Peninsula, but how many is not known. Nothing has been learned about bridges except that the railroad bridge at the White House still stands.

JOHN A. DIX,
Major-General.

FORT MONROE, VA.,
May 4, 1863—3.30 p. m.

Maj. Gen. H. W. HALLECK,
    General-in-Chief:

I have just received the following dispatch from General Peck:

I have in my possession the communication of Maj. Gen. D. H. Hill to General Longstreet, reporting his arrival at Carrsville, with his entire division 4 miles this side of Carrsville on the 2d, and awaiting his orders.

A telegram from Major Stratton, just received, confirms this. He says:

The troops from Carolina were ordered to Suffolk on the 2d, and the wagons to Franklin. Have just returned from a portion of their center line, which would have cost us not less than 2,000 men to have carried. All their lines are strictly in accordance with the rules of a besieging army. Hill may commence operations unless demanded elsewhere.

JOHN A. DIX,
Major General.

MAY 4, 1863.

Major-General DIX:

A brigade is on this side the Chowan and Longstreet was re-enforced on Saturday morning (2d) by General Benning, with five regiments and fifteen pieces, who crossed the Chowan and marched from Gatesville. Hood commanded yesterday, and had his division and other troops. Longstreet was 2 miles back. Providence Church was filled with wounded. At 9.30 p. m. all his forces save picket lines moved for Blackwater. He had seven hours the start. Colonel Foster started with a brigade, battery and some cavalry, and turned up at Leesville at 6 a. m., where he has found the enemy. I have cautioned him repeatedly against being led off too far. Before troops can reach him they will be over. He will do all that can be done on that route.

JOHN J. PECK,
Major-General.

SUFFOLK, VA., *May* 4, 1863.

Major-General DIX:

A telegram from General Getty to the effect that Hood and Anderson had seven brigades on the river yesterday, and that at 8.30 orders were given to retire. We should have had a warm time.

JOHN J. PECK,
Major-General.

FORT MONROE, *May* 4, 1863.

Major-General PECK:

The enemy having gone I must have 5,000 men at once, either Montgomery's [?] division or any other you choose. Send them to Norfolk.

JOHN A. DIX,
Major-General.

SUFFOLK, VA., *May* 4, 1863.

General DIX:

It will hardly be advisable, it seems to me, while they are on this side the river and the results of the pursuit are unknown. It would be signaled to Franklin in an hour or two. Let me have your views. Have to send Corcoran.

JOHN J. PECK,
Major-General.

[MAY 4, 1863.]

Major-General DIX:

It is my opinion that General Hill is to take Longstreet's place on the Blackwater.

If any one goes it must be Gordon, and with the number you stated That number is all that ought to be taken under any circumstances.

JOHN J. PECK,
Major-General.

FORT MONROE, VA., *May* 4, 1863.

Major-General PECK, *Commanding, Suffolk:*

It is not best to interrupt the pursuit of the enemy; but our troops should be recalled the moment the enemy crosses the Blackwater. I would rather have Gordon or Getty. The movement to be made is an important one and needs experience in command. But your safety must be consulted.

The enemy will not be likely to return unless Hooker fails.

JOHN A. DIX,
Major-General.

FORT MONROE, *May* 4, 1863.

Major-General PECK, *Commanding, Suffolk:*

Do you mean to say that all the forces before Suffolk have moved for the Blackwater, including Pickett's division? Advise me as soon as possible. I do not quite understand your dispatch.

JOHN A. DIX,
Major-General.

FORT MONROE, *May* 4, 1863.

Major-General PECK:

Defer till to-morrow.

JOHN A. DIX,
Major-General.

FORT MONROE, *May* 4, 1863.

Major-General PECK, *Commanding, Suffolk:*

Let General Gordon be ready with 6,000 men. The movement must commence to-morrow. I will advise you. Let General Getty take 110 of the Ninth New York. I may want the rest to save the Third New York—one of the finest regiments in service. Will know in two or three days.

JOHN A. DIX,
Major-General.

MAY 4, 1863—about 7 a. m.

Major-General PECK, *Suffolk, Va.:*

Nothing of positive nature with regard to Hood and Pickett. Among 800 or 1,000 prisoners yesterday statements to any one talking to them was to effect that Hood and Pickett were due here last night, and we should soon hear from them. The most reliable information I have had is from a deserter, a resident of Orleans County, New York, conscripted in a Louisiana regiment, who stated that on Saturday, while detailed to the rear, their columns engaged to cook provisions, a force about equal to two brigades marched by. Conversing with the troops he asked whose they were. They said they were Hood's division. They are being re-enforced in some measure from below—whether from your

front or General Keyes' of course I do not know.   They had nothing at
Richmond to send here.   We have had heavy fighting her for two or
three days.

DANL. BUTTERFIELD,
Major-General, Chief of Staff.

HEADQUARTERS ARMY OF THE POTOMAC,
May 4, 1863—10.45 a. m.

Major-General PECK, *Suffolk, Va.:*

Our cavalry bring information of 15,000 or 20,000 of Longstreet's
forces getting off from the cars at Gordonsville.

DANL. BUTTERFIELD,
Major-General, Chief of Staff.

SUFFOLK, VA., *May 4,* 1863.

Major-General HOOKER,
Commanding Army of the Potomac:

Longstreet was re-enforced by General Benning with five regiments
and fifteen pieces on the 2d.   He crossed the Chowan with pontoons.
General Kemper, with another brigade, has also crossed, making three
in all.   Hood commanded yesterday, and Longstreet was 2 miles in the
rear with reserves. They suffered.   At 9.30 p. m. all his forces moved
by different interior routes for the Blackwater.   He has several hours
the start.   All his arrangements were for a continual siege of Suffolk.
I was fully prepared for that.

JOHN J. PECK,
Major-General.

(Copy to General Halleck.)

MAY 4, 1863.

Maj. Gen. JOSEPH HOOKER,
Commanding Army of the Potomac:

I have a communication of General Hill to General Longstreet, of
May 2, 1863, in which he reports his arrival with his entire division at
or near Carrsville, and asks for orders.   His command was then only
14 miles from Suffolk.   This is confirmed by telegraph from South Mills,
N. C.   All the troops that crossed the Chowan were ordered to Suffolk
and the supply trains to Franklin, the depot of the railroad from North
Carolina.   Every arrangement was made by the enemy that is called
for by the rules governing a besieging army.

JOHN J. PECK,
Major-General.

MAY 4, 1863.

Major-General KEYES,
Commanding, Yorktown:

The enemy commenced his retreat from Suffolk at 9.30 last evening.
We are in pursuit.   We had a sharp fight yesterday, driving him to his
intrenchments.   Our loss about 60.

JOHN A. DIX,
Major General.

YORKTOWN, VA., *May 4, 1863.*

Major-General DIX:

The following received a few moments ago from Colonel West:

FORT MAGRUDER.

Colonel SUYDAM:

Intelligence comes to me that cannot be disregarded that the enemy will attack at daylight or before. I have taken every precaution against surprise.

R. M. WEST.

Shall I go down to Fort Monroe in the morning? Please reply immediately.

E. D. KEYES,
Major-General.

[General KEYES:]

Come, if the attack is not made.

J. A. D.

HEADQUARTERS,
South Mills, N. C., May 4, 1863—8.30 a. m.

Maj. Gen. JOHN J. PECK,
Commanding at Suffolk, Va.:

GENERAL: The rebel forces have left all the country between this and the Perquimans River. Captain Reynolds was at Sandy Cross at 3 o'clock this morning. Known Union citizens there informed him that the rebel infantry left Saturday night at sundown and the cavalry at daylight on Sunday morning. The infantry had orders to report at Suffolk, the cavalry at Sunbury, and the wagon train was ordered to be at the Blackwater to-day (Monday). A man who had come through from Sunbury stated that the cavalry on arriving at Sunbury received orders to report at Suffolk. The citizens near Sandy Cross thought that the rebels were still at Suffolk on Sunday night, say at sundown.

Captain Roberts and command reached Woodville this morning at 2 o'clock. The enemy (Third North Carolina Cavalry) left there on Saturday night at 9 o'clock. They left two or three sick behind, who, together with several other soldiers were captured by Captain Roberts. Captain Roberts says:

They seem to have gone in the direction of Gatesville. I shall immediately push forward toward Newby's Bridge and ascertain further particulars.

The bearers of the dispatches from Captain Roberts say that the enemy left Woodville apparently in considerable haste, according to reports of citizens.

Very respectfully, your obedient servant,

FRANKLIN A. STRATTON,
Major, Commanding Detachment at South Mills.

UNITED STATES FLAG-SHIP MINNESOTA,
Off Newport News, Va., May 4, 1863.

Maj. Gen. JOHN A. DIX, U. S. A.,
Comdg. Seventh Army Corps, Fortress Monroe, Va.:

GENERAL: In view of Major-General Hooker's present movements and of the fact that you have a very considerable army in this department, say 20,000 troops, and understanding to-night that the enemy has disappeared from before Suffolk, I respectfully and earnestly propose to you a joint expedition to take Fort Powhatan, Petersburg, and perhaps Richmond. I am ready to move at a moment's notice and will co-operate with you in any and every way possible. My gunboats and a few companies will hold your posts at Suffolk and Yorktown.

The opportunity for striking a great blow is such as rarely presents itself in the history of nations. I am confident you will improve it.

I have the honor, general, to be, very respectfully, yours,

S. P. LEE,
Actg. Rear-Admiral, Comdg. N. Atlantic Blockading Squadron.

UNITED STATES FLAG-SHIP MINNESOTA,
Off Newport News, Va., May 4, 1863.

Maj. Gen. JOHN A. DIX, U. S. A.,
Comdg. Seventh Army Corps, Fortress Monroe, Va.:

GENERAL: I have received your communication of the 2d instant. Unfounded and unjust newspaper attacks on the Navy Department and myself by a known correspondent at the fort under your command are certainly injurious to the public service, whether they are contradicted and repelled in the same manner, thus creating controversy between public officers and exposure of public affairs, or whether they are allowed to remain unanswered. The discipline of the Navy does not sanction a resort to newspapers to remedy a wrong thus wantonly done. It is wholly inexcusable to resort to newspaper attacks in cases where an appeal can be taken to and a remedy applied by the Government to matters affecting the public interests.

The only order I gave for the withdrawal of the gunboats from the Upper Nansemond was on the 19th, when I sent the fleet captain to Suffolk to communicate with the authorities and withdraw the gunboats if practicable. This order was revoked the same day at the instance of General Peck by an order sent by me through your headquarters in a dispatch to General Peck. When that order was given you had been re-enforced largely; you had just provided military defenses for the right bank of the Upper Nansemond; the improvised little gunboats were not a sufficient or necessary defense there and were much wanted elsewhere and their communications were interrupted by a battery in a strong earthwork, which had cut up several of them badly, killed or wounded a large per cent. of their small crews, whilst two detachments of troops according to the official reports to me had failed to co-operate with Lieutenant Lamson to take the battery and raise the blockade.

On the afternoon of the 19th efficient support (by General Getty in person) was given to Lieutenant Lamson's plan, and he landed the 300 troops close to and in rear of the battery, and, aided by them, got his four navy field-pieces up the bank and taking the enemy's battery in reverse stopped their attempt to turn it on our troops, who gallantly dashed in and easily took it. The surprise was complete.

Next day, the 20th, General Peck abandoned this earthwork, the rear to which in the mean time had been strengthened by our troops. This evacuation was earnestly resisted by Lieutenants Cushing and Lamson, and obliged the latter to drop down a few hundred yards from the battery and just below the bar which it commanded. Thus General Peck and not myself caused the gunboats to withdraw.

My subsequent orders to Lieutenant Lamson did not prevent but required this gallant and willing young officer to render the army all practicable assistance. I should mention that I not only revoked my order of the 19th to Captain Crosby before it was executed and before the battery was taken (as General Peck well knows, because it was in my telegram to him in answer to one from him), but when the battery was taken I immediately informed General Getty that I cordially allowed the boats to remain. In view of the exertions I had made to equip and maintain a little flotilla to aid you whilst you were perfecting your defenses, of the service that flotilla had rendered you, and your knowledge that its withdrawal from above the battery, though necessary and proper, was not by my order, you must feel that the assault made on me by the well-known correspondent at the fort, who gave point to his attack by declaring that he was reflecting your feelings, was most unwarrantable.

This correspondent, in the same inspired communication (for in that light he has presented his reflections to the public), also charges me with being at fault for the reoccupation by the rebels of their abandoned earthworks, called Fort Powhatan, in the upper part of James River. This reoccupation was a military act done in your department. When Colonel Ludlow informed me of it on his return down James River in a flag of truce I did not wait for you to ask me to co-operate, but I went immediately to confer with you on the subject. Your reply was that you could do nothing; that the enemy was on this side of the Blackwater in greater force than yourself; but you asked me if I could not shell them out. I confess that I was a little surprised at this expectation, in view of the failure, from want of army co-operation, of a better force than I had to shell the enemy out of Fort Darling, which had no rebel navy to support it.

The reoccupation of Fort Powhatan was the easy and natural effort of the enemy, who had remained in possession of the Blackwater in front of Suffolk (between Suffolk and Fort Powhatan) for the last eight months. Where an active enemy holds military possession of a country in force he may not only reoccupy his forts on his river front, but he may, where there is no military interference, build forts on the bluffs of the river where he had none before. One of our gunboats, as proposed, or several of them, aided by the one iron-clad I then had, could not have driven him from Fort Powhatan after he had reoccupied it.

Under the circumstances of this case the unfounded and injurious assaults made by a correspondent at the fort, who is under your immediate authority and who professedly writes from military intelligence communicated to him there, it seems both proper and decent that his unfounded charges against the Navy Department and myself should be publicly corrected by the same authority under which he claimed and is understood by the public to write.

The current duties of the squadron require and receive my first attention. It is only when they are disposed of that I can give attention to matters even of this interest.

I have the honor to be, general, very respectfully, yours,

S. P. LEE,
Actg. Rear-Admiral, Comdg. N. Atlantic Blockading Squadron.

HDQRS. DEPT. OF VIRGINIA, SEVENTH ARMY CORPS,
Fort Monroe, May 4, 1863.

Maj. Gen. J. G. FOSTER:

MY DEAR GENERAL: General Naglee is here. I have no cavalry to spare, as I have an important movement to make.

We had a sharp fight at Suffolk yesterday; our loss nearly 70; the enemy's not known.

Last night Longstreet's whole force fell back to the Blackwater.

General D. H. Hill arrived on the Blackwater at Carrsville the day before yesterday. General Peck has his communication of the 2d instant reporting his arrival there to General Longstreet.

You can have scarcely anything left to oppose you in North Carolina. Garnett's brigade arrived at Suffolk more than a week ago.

Hooker has moved and has been fighting.

The enemy will concentrate his whole force between Richmond and Fredericksburg.

In haste, very truly, yours,

JOHN A. DIX,
Major-General.

HDQRS. OUTPOSTS, CAMP FIFTY-EIGHTH REGT. PA. VOLS.,
May 4, 1863.

Lieut. Col. SOUTHARD HOFFMAN,
Assistant Adjutant-General, Tenth Army Corps:

SIR: I have the honor to report, on the information of my patrol, that the enemy have re-established their posts on Core Creek; also that they were burning or endeavoring to burn the railroad bridge yesterday afternoon.

Very respectfully, your obedient servant,
J. RICHTER JONES,
Colonel Fifty-eighth Regiment, Commanding Outposts.

UNITED STATES FLAG-SHIP MINNESOTA,
Off Newport News, Va., May 4, 1863.

Maj. Gen. JOHN A. DIX, U. S. A.,
Comdg. Seventh Army Corps, Fortress Monroe, Va.:

GENERAL: In view of the recent sudden and extraordinary calls made upon me for naval defense of military lines and positions I consider it to be my duty to request you to inform me what military posts or occupations in your department require, in your judgment, naval defense, for what reason, and to what extent.

I have the honor to be, general, very respectfully, yours,
S. P. LEE,
Actg. Rear-Admiral, Comdg. N. Atlantic Blockading Squadron.

UNITED STATES FLAG-SHIP MINNESOTA,
Off Newport News, May 5, 1863.

Maj. Gen. JOHN A. DIX, U. S. A.,
Comdg. Seventh Army Corps, Fortress Monroe, Va.:

GENERAL: In your communication to me of the 2d instant you say:

In regard to differences of opinion between us concerning our respective duties I have done all in my power to confine the knowledge of them to those immediately around me and my official superiors.

I will thank you to let me know what are the "differences of opinion between us concerning our respective duties," to which you refer.

I have the honor to be, general, very respectfully, yours,
S. P. LEE,
Actg. Rear-Admiral, Comdg. N. Atlantic Blockading Squadron.

HDQRS. DEPT. OF VIRGINIA, SEVENTH ARMY CORPS,
Fort Monroe, Va., May 5, 1863.

Actg. Rear-Admiral S. P. LEE,
Commanding North Atlantic Blockading Squadron:

ADMIRAL: I have the honor to acknowledge the receipt of your letter of the 4th instant requesting me to inform you what "military posts or occupations" in my department, require, in my judgment, "naval defense, for what reason, and to what extent."

I have the pleasure of furnishing the desired information:

1st. Fort Monroe, the importance of which as a key to the Chesapeake Bay and its tributaries it is unnecessary to state to you. We need no naval defense there beyond what might be furnished in case of emergency by your fleet at Newport News.

2d. Norfolk. This position was occupied, and I will say also every other position held by me was in the occupation of our forces before I took command of this military department. The especial object in view on the part of the Government in holding Norfolk I suppose to be to deprive the enemy of a means of annoyance. He might build vessels there and send them out at favorable moments to molest us, as he did on former occasions. Two other very essential objects are to keep open our internal line of communication between the departments of Virginia and North Carolina, and to have a naval depot where our numerous steamers on the Lower Chesapeake and its tributaries can be repaired without being sent to Baltimore or Washington on any sudden emergency or in case of any common casualty. I think there should be two gunboats in Norfolk Harbor.

3d. Suffolk is held to cover Norfolk, insure the inland communication to Albemarle Sound, and to keep the enemy at a distance. We have had two gunboats there, the Stepping Stones, one of yours, and the West End. I have armed the Smith Briggs, and if the Stepping Stones is needed elsewhere her services can be dispensed with.

4th. Yorktown. This post is considered important to give us the control of the Peninsula up to that point, keeping the enemy from coming below it, and commanding the York River in case we need it for the movement of troops. It would be desirable to have two gunboats there, as the occupation of Gloucester, on the other side, follows that of Yorktown.

5th. Williamsburg is occupied as an outpost of Yorktown for the purpose of preventing the enemy from approaching the latter and annoying us with field guns and small-arms of long range and of watching his movements as tightly as possible up the Peninsula. This position is not susceptible of naval defense, and it is only referred to from its relation to Yorktown to give you a complete view of the subject.

6th. I am about to occupy West Point to cut off the enemy's communication with Matthews and Gloucester Counties, and as a position from which a flank movement can be made, in case of emergency, on the enemy's forces at Richmond if he should be assailed from the north or south. It is at the confluence of two rivers, and two gunboats are very desirable.

I have the honor to be, very respectfully, your obedient servant,

JOHN A. DIX,
Major-General.

HDQRS. DEPT. OF VIRGINIA, SEVENTH ARMY CORPS,
Fort Monroe, Va., May 5, 1863.

Actg. Rear-Admiral S. P. LEE,
  Commanding North Atlantic Blockading Squadron:

ADMIRAL: I have had the honor to receive your letter of yesterday, proposing a co-operation of the army and navy forces under your command and mine, "to take Fort Powhatan, Petersburg, and perhaps Richmond," supposing that your gunboats and a few companies can hold the posts of Suffolk and Yorktown. My movable force is comparatively small and entirely inadequate to the great object referred to, nor would it be safe to depend on your gunboats and a few companies to hold Suffolk and Yorktown. Only the river front at Suffolk could be protected by your guns, leaving the other lines, several miles in extent, to be defended by a few companies. The same observation is applicable in a more forcible manner to Yorktown. Neither of these positions, with the large amount of guns and ordnance stores in both, can be safely left without a strong garrison.

I may add in regard to Suffolk that the enemy is in force on the Blackwater; that his abandoned works are very heavy and extensive, showing his designs to be permanent occupation, and that we may expect the investment to be renewed as soon as the emergency which has led to his withdrawal shall have passed by.

You will remember that I called your attention in an interview with you several weeks ago to the fact that the enemy were at work at Fort Powhatan, and expressed an earnest desire that some of your gunboats should drive him away before any guns were mounted. My last advices are that he is now occupying it with considerable force. I should be most happy to co-operate with you if I had a sufficient number of disposable men under my control to insure the object, but all the troops I can spare are required for another movement, which has already commenced.

If Fort Powhatan could be reduced I could not be assisted by you in an attack on Petersburg or Richmond, except to cover my supplies to City Point, as the Appomattox is not navigable up to the former city, and from thence to the latter the movement would be made at a distance from the James River, the most important part of which is in possession of the enemy and so obstructed as not to be available for your vessels without great delay. Moreover my advices are that every mile of the country between Petersburg and Richmond is strongly fortified, so much so that a very large force would be necessary to reach Richmond in that direction.

In the movement I have above referred to as commenced I will in another communication ask your aid.

I have the honor to be, very respectfully, your obedient servant,

JOHN A. DIX,
Major-General.

UNITED STATES FLAG-SHIP MINNESOTA,
Off Newport News, May 5, 1863—evening.

Maj. Gen. JOHN A. DIX, U. S. A.,
  Comdg. Seventh Army Corps, Fortress Monroe, Va.:

GENERAL: I received this evening your communication of this date. I have made Lieutenant-Commander Gillis, of the Commodore Morris, now at Yorktown, acquainted with your object, and instructed him to give you all the assistance in his power.

Lieutenant-Commander Babcock, in the Morse, accompanied by the Mystic, is instructed to inform you by 10 a. m. to-morrow of his readiness to accompany the troops to York River, where he will report to Lieutenant-Commander Gillis.

I have the honor to be, general, very respectfully, yours,

S. P. LEE,
Actg. Rear-Admiral, Comdg. N. Atlantic Blockading Squadron.

FORT MONROE, VA.,
May 5, 1863—10.30 a. m.

Maj. Gen. H. W. HALLECK,
General-in-Chief:

I have just received the following from General Peck. I am going to Suffolk to send off the expedition referred to heretofore:

Major Stratton's information, from entirely reliable sources, Union and rebel, is that Longstreet had over 30,000 before he was joined by any of Hill's forces. The enemy had three entire lines of works where we were on Sunday, and could not have been carried.

JOHN A. DIX,
Major-General.

SUFFOLK, VA., *May* 5, 1863.

Major-General DIX:

During the investment of Longstreet's and Hill's forces we have captured five pieces of artillery, about 400 prisoners, much camp equipage, and some rifles. Not less than 400 or 500 have deserted from the rebels; probably his loss in killed and wounded is about 600, making his total loss about 1,500.

Our killed is 34; wounded, 201; and missing, 14. Total, 249.*

All the morale, prestige, glory, and victory of the twenty-three days belong to our patient and brave men. Besides, they have held the masses of the enemy around Suffolk, in order to enable General Hooker to secure a crowning victory for the Union, and are entitled to a share of the glory that may accrue to his arms.

JOHN J. PECK,
Major-General.

FORT MONROE, *May* 5, 1863.

Major-General PECK:

I am just leaving for Suffolk.

JOHN A. DIX,
Major-General.

NEW BERNE, N. C., *May* 5, 1863.

General HALLECK,
Commander-in-Chief U. S. Army, Washington, D. C.:

GENERAL: There are several contingencies likely to occur in the affairs of this department which should I think be brought to your notice more fully than I have or can in fact do in correspondence. I would like

---

* But see revised statement, p. 288.

therefore to run off for a day and lay the whole matter before you, which I can do very briefly should it meet your wishes to permit me to do so.

Please to telegraph your reply to General **Dix**, at Fortress Monroe, where I will have an officer to bring it to me.

Very respectfully and truly,

J. G. FOSTER,
Major-General.

HEADQUARTERS EIGHTEENTH ARMY CORPS,
New Berne, N. C., May 5, 1863.

Maj. Gen. H. W. HALLECK, *General-in-Chief U. S. Army:*

GENERAL : I have the honor to acknowledge receipt of your letter of April 27.

My idea of an attack on Wilmington was to take and hold Smith's Island as a basis of supplies, &c., and I still incline to so doing, though information shows that it cannot now be done as easily as it could have been then, the enemy having established a post there and erected a battery. (This information is not deemed certain.) I will attempt anything I am directed to, but my opinion is that my force is utterly inadequate to accomplish any outside work, and is merely sufficient for present defense. Information shows that General Hill is still in our front with his forces (barring one brigade, Garnett's, which I have no information of), and is threatening. Troops from Wilmington threaten Morehead City (our depot of supplies) and the line of the railroad, the defense of which I have given to General Heckman and his brigade, 2,100 men (my old troops), recently arrived from the Department of the South. General Heckman has as much as he can do to protect that line, and I have ordered him to stay and do so. Intercepted correspondence shows the plans somewhat of the enemy and shows the sending of a pontoon train for crossing the White Oak and New Rivers, necessary to an attack on Morehead. In fact we are threatened at all points, and though I feel perfectly confident at every point I know that constant vigilance is required and also the presence of every man now here. If I had 5,000 disposable men I would undertake Smith's Island, and I think with success; and in that light let me respectfully say, though at the risk of seeming importunate (which intention, at least, I disclaim), that if the brigade of Brig. Gen. T. G. Stevenson could be ordered back to me I would be in a position to attack Smith's Island. General Stevenson's brigade consists of two regiments of my old brigade and three other veteran regiments, and is now in the Department of the South. Of course to occupy and fortify a post my guns, ordnance tools, &c., would be necessary, and all that I took down for the Charleston expedition are yet afloat and untouched in Beaufort Harbor. These would have to be ordered back.

I must in this connection recall to your mind that by the 1st day of July the effectives in this department will not be more than 5,000 men, as 500 artillery are now being mustered out, their term of service (two years) having expired, and in June twelve of my fullest regiments are to be mustered out, their term of service then expiring (nine months). This fact shows what I can do with my effective force, and my reasons for urging the return of some of my troops.

I have the honor to be, general, very respectfully, your obedient servant,

J. G. FOSTER,
Major-General, Commanding.

FORT MONROE, VA.,
May 6, 1863—10 a. m.

Maj. Gen. H. W. HALLECK,
                General-in-Chief:

I embarked 5,000 men yesterday and last night at Norfolk, and hope to have them at their destination to-morrow morning. We had a heavy blow last night, and it is yet too rough for some of our transports. I was at Suffolk yesterday. Over 200 prisoners had been brought in. They represented forty regiments, three batteries, two independent battalions, and one cavalry regiment. It is not at all probable that in these captures all the regiments before Suffolk were represented. The enemy's works, which are very extensive and heavy, indicate continued occupation. He was building stables. General Peck sends out a cavalry force to the Blackwater to-day.

JOHN A. DIX,
Major-General.

FORT MONROE, *May* 6, 1863.

Major-General PECK:

I have no news from Washington. This is not encouraging, as the wires were in operation last night. The enemy have doubtless left the Blackwater. Trains 3 miles long reached Petersburg last night.

JOHN A. DIX,
Major-General.

WAR DEPARTMENT,
Washington, May 6, 1863—3.30 p. m.

Major-General DIX, *Fort Monroe, Va.:*

The operation agreed upon between us will not be made till further orders. Everything will remain as it is till you hear further from Washington.

H. W. HALLECK,
General-in-Chief.

YORKTOWN, *May* 6, [1863].

Major-General DIX:

Colonel Davis, of the Twelfth Illinois Cavalry, with the advance of his regiment, has arrived at Gloucester Point, having accomplished fully the orders of General Stoneman. I have sent a cavalry scout up the Richmond road to get information of any of our cavalry which may be coming down. General Stoneman seems not to have been aware that the enemy have all along had troops on this Peninsula, and Colonel Davis encountered a regiment of infantry and three pieces at Tunstall Station. There is still a battery of eight pieces, by all accounts, at or near New Kent Court-House. Colonel Davis is very anxious to have a gunboat go up to the Mattapony to look for a detachment of his regiment under Major Bronson.

E. D. KEYES,
Major-General.

FORT MONROE, May 6, 1863.

General GORDON, *Atlantic Hotel, Norfolk:*

I think it important, on reflection, that you go up with the troops. They will leave at daylight. If anything should delay me it would be very awkward. The troops should be pushed on to their destination, landed, and intrenched immediately. The engineer will not be here in time to leave before 9 or 10 o'clock. The cavalry will be all ready. Captain Ludlow will furnish a tug at any time you name. I will telegraph him.

JOHN A. DIX,
Major-General.

MAY 6, [1863.]

Major-General KEYES,
Commanding, Yorktown:

I think you had better send up a cavalry force toward Diascund Bridge, but not a gunboat in the direction now.

JOHN A. DIX,
Major-General.

UNITED STATES FLAG-SHIP MINNESOTA,
Off Newport News, May 6, 1863.

Maj. Gen. JOHN J. PECK, U. S. A.,
Commanding Suffolk, Va.:

GENERAL: Your communication dated the 21st ultimo,* in reply to mine of the 20th, was received on the 26th.

Squadron duties have prevented an earlier reply to your communication, which I regret to find is very deficient in candor and professional comity proper in official correspondence, and reasonably to be expected from an officer educated at West Point. When naval defense is necessary for military works a timely requisition from the War or Navy Department for the number and kind of vessels needed therefor should be made, that they may be built or purchased and equipped.

I am not responsible, as you seem to suppose, for the defense of the military post at Suffolk, as dependent on the defense of the military line of the Upper Nansemond, which is a mere creek, unsuited to the operations of vessels and obviously requiring military defense. Nor was it my fault that such necessary military preparations were not already made. Heretofore I had a small vessel—the Stepping Stones—resembling a Norfolk ferry-boat, carrying field pieces on field carriages, patrolling that small stream to preserve the blockade and intercept rebel communications, trade, mails, &c.

When Suffolk was threatened, as General Keyes informed me, by the enemy, 40,000 strong, with pontoons and heavy artillery (as reported by deserters all along the lines), urgent calls were made upon me for gunboats. This call was preceded by equally earnest calls for gunboat assistance to repel the enemy, who was attacking one and threatening another military post in the Sounds of North Carolina, which required all the light draughts provided by the Government for other naval duty not needed to answer demands at other points, except the Commodore Barney, which I sent to the Nansemond, together with my two transports, one armed with field pieces and manned by a detachment from this vessel, the other as a tender, with ammunition, coal, &c., and three of my small tugs (each armed with two light pieces), thus leaving

---

* Not found.

the squadron without a transport, tender, dispatch, mail, or picket boat, save one tug. When on the 14th of April you telegraphed me that three of the improvised gunboats were disabled, and asked for more, I obtained temporarily and sent to the Nansemond four tugs, half the Potomac steam flotilla.

This recital shows what earnest efforts were made to relieve you. It must be very apparent to every candid and intelligent professional mind that had General Longstreet really intended to force a crossing of the Upper Nansemond with the reputed means at his command these few light pieces, mostly field pieces, on the open decks of a few merchant vessels could not have prevented his doing so there. The same number of field pieces would have made a better resistance behind earthworks ashore than on frail little steamers afloat. Hence in my instructions of the 13th ultimo, sent to Lieutenants Cushing and Lamson that day and night, these views were expressed by me to be communicated to you. Your theory therefore that this conviction was the result of the rough handling the boats received in fighting the enemy's earthworks on the 14th falls to the ground. It was my manifest duty to let you know that the Navy had not the means to make the military defense expected of it. Had I undertaken the defense imposed without a word of warning as to the sufficiency of the naval means as a substitute for military defense to protect your rear from a real attempt by the enemy to cross the Nansemond Creek, the failure that must have ensued, so disastrous to the army and nation, would have been charged upon the Navy. I did send Fleet Captain Crosby to Suffolk on the 19th to withdraw the boats if practicable from the Upper Nansemond.

The situation was this : You had been largely re-enforced, and had a gallant army, 22,000 strong, at Suffolk. You had just erected earthworks and rifle-pits along the right bank of the Nansemond suitable to its defense. The enemy had made no attempt to cross Nansemond Creek, the blockade of which he had established. His earthwork at West Branch, which commanded the bar at the mouth of Nansemond Creek, had cut off the communications of the gunboats whilst yours were open ; had thoroughly disabled one and seriously damaged three other boats, besides killing and wounding a large proportion of their small crews. The enemy's rifle-pits and artillery on the left flank were a serious annoyance to the boats but did not seem to threaten the safety of the post. Your detachments had twice failed to support Lieutenant Lamson and capture this battery and raise the blockade (which was afterwards so easily done), and our transports and tenders were sustaining in an unequal and unnecessary contest with the enemy's earthworks much damage. Nevertheless, when you that day (the 19th) by telegraph desired the retention of the gunboats in the Upper Nansemond I promptly replied by telegraph and directed Lieutenant Lamson through you to remain with the boats. You most unfairly omit this from your statement of the case and go on to charge me with having withdrawn the gunboats, when the fact is I gave no such orders to do so after the one I just revoked at your instance and through you.

On the 20th you ordered this earthwork, which our troops had held under the cross-fire of the gunboats and had greatly strengthened, to be abandoned. Lieutenant Lamson reported to me that this evacuation, earnestly opposed by him, obliged him to withdraw the boats from the Upper to the Lower Nansemond from just above to just below the bar, under West Branch Battery and commanded by it a distance of half or three-quarters of a mile. Thus your orders and not mine occasioned the withdrawal of the gunboats. In your communication of the 21st you admit your ability to hold the Nansemond without the boats.

Your reference to what you term Longstreet's "present campaign," as occasioned by his reoccupation over two months since without interruption of Fort Powhatan, thus "establishing most firmly his left flank on James River," is scarcely intelligible.   Fort Powhatan is 50 miles in an air line from Suffolk, whilst the enemy have been permitted to occupy for the last half year the line of the Blackwater immediately in front of Suffolk and less than half way in the general direction of Fort Powhatan. Of course it was easy enough for them to reoccupy their fort in their rear.

It may instruct you to know that as soon as I learned from Colonel Ludlow that the enemy had reoccupied and was strengthening Fort Powhatan, a military act performed within the military lines of this military department, without waiting for General Dix to ask me for naval co-operation I promptly called on and conferred with him on the subject, and received his assurance that he could not act, as the enemy was on the Blackwater in greater strength than he had.   It was obvious from the failure from want of military co-operation in the attack on Fort Darling, with an iron-clad and gunboat force quite equal to that at my command, that I could not without military co-operation prevent the enemy from holding and extending a fort on his river front when he held in force undisputed military possession of the country around it.

Respectfully, yours,

S. P. LEE,
Actg. Rear-Admiral, Comdg. N. Atlantic Blockading Squadron.

YORKTOWN, VA., *May* 7, 1863.
(Received 8.55 a. m.)

Maj. Gen. H. W. HALLECK, *General-in-Chief:*

I am on my way to West Point, where all the troops must have arrived with the exception of a battery which has been delayed for transportation and which will be there before night.   They would have gone up last night but for the weather, which was too rough for some of the small transports.   General Keyes and General Gordon are with them. I ordered the small cavalry force with the expedition to be sent, as soon as landed, to the White House to try and destroy the railroad bridge. Colonel Davis, who led the cavalry raid to the neighborhood of Richmond, arrived at Gloucester Point yesterday.   Generals Jenkins, Davis, and Wilcox are on the Blackwater, with their headquarters at Franklin. We have not yet heard what force is at Zuni and Ivor, but hope to learn to-day.   None of Longstreet's force could well have been at Fredericksburg on Sunday.   It may be now, but if so, by forced marches, the railroad communication having been broken.

JOHN A. DIX,
Major-General.

UNITED STATES FLAG-SHIP MINNESOTA,
Off Newport News, May 7, 1863

Maj. Gen. JOHN A. DIX, U. S. A.,
Commanding Seventh Army Corps, Fort Monroe, Va.:

GENERAL: I have directed Lieutenant-Commander Gillis to detail the United States steamers Morse and Mystic to give all possible assistance in respect to your proposed occupation of West Point.

Very respectfully, yours,

S. P. LEE,
Acting Rear-Admiral.

YORKTOWN, VA., *May* 7, 1863.
(Received 9.35 a. m., May 8, 1863.)

Maj. Gen. H. W. HALLECK,
   General-in-Chief:

I ordered a reconnaissance up the Peninsula, above Williamsburg, yesterday. The enemy have withdrawn from Diascund Bridge, 15 miles above, where they had 2,000 men, and crossed the Chickahominy. They have doubtless gone to Richmond.

JOHN A. DIX,
Major-General.

SUFFOLK, *May* 7, 1863.

Major-General DIX:

Have ordered a court of inquiry in the Corcoran-Kimball affair.
Generals Jenkins, Davis, and Wilcox have the Lower Blackwater, headquarters at Franklin, with a full division. What is above at Blackwater Bridge, Zuni, and Ivor I am not advised, but probably one of Hill's divisions. All the people outside state that the generals told them the army would remain all summer, and raising crops was out of the question near the lines.

JOHN J. PECK,
Major-General.

FORT MONROE, VA., *May* 7, 1863.

Major-General KEYES,
   Commanding, Yorktown:

The batteries are on board the John Rice; the spades and pickaxes on board a tug towing a float for a temporary wharf; materials and workmen for repairing the old wharf accompany the expedition, with 25,000 rations, forage, &c.
- Everything has been provided for. Push on the moment the transports arrive. Land and send your cavalry out at once to destroy the railroad bridge over the Pamunkey at White House. They should move rapidly, but circumspectly, as there may be enemy's troops after the dispersed Illinois cavalry. The Spaulding, with General Gordon, will be behind. Do not wait for her; she is faster than some of the other transports and will overtake you.
You should leave Yorktown by 8 o'clock if possible.

JOHN A. DIX,
Major-General.

FORTRESS MONROE, VA., *May* 7, 1863.

Major-General KEYES:
   Commanding, Yorktown:

Five thousand infantry have gone, besides the batteries. I fear one of the latter will not be up till 3 p. m. You had better push on the moment the infantry gets up.

JOHN A. DIX,
Major-General.

FORT MONROE, *May* 7, 1863.

General GORDON, *Yorktown:*
    (To be sent on board the Spaulding the moment she arrives.)

The cavalry will have gone ere you reach Yorktown. Push on to your destination. General Keyes has gone on to send off the cavalry at once to destroy the railroad bridge of which I spoke, and will see to the landing till you arrive. He will command the movement at present. I hope to be up by 3 p. m. After you left I found it was necessary to push up rapidly. A float for temporary wharf, materials for repairing the old one, intrenching tools, and all necessary supplies have gone. I am anxious that you should reach the point of landing as soon as the mass of your division.

JOHN A. DIX,
Major-General.

YORKTOWN, VA., *May* 7, 1863—7 p. m.

Maj. Gen. H. W. HALLECK, *General-in-Chief:*

The forces sent up the York River this morning have effected a landing at West Point without opposition. No appearance of any enemy in that quarter.

RUFUS KING,
Brigadier-General, Commanding Post.

WEST POINT, VA., *May* 7, 1863—7 p. m.

Maj. Gen. H. W. HALLECK, *General-in-Chief.*

Our troops are all landed and in position. A small party of rebel cavalry was found here. We took 5 prisoners and lost 1 of our lieutenants, killed. On one of the prisoners found Richmond papers this morning. Railroad communication between Fredericksburg and Richmond was re-established yesterday (6th), a train of wounded having arrived at Richmond from Guiney's Station, 12 miles from Fredericksburg. They acknowledge a loss of 7,000 or 8,000. It is officially stated that General Hooker is at United States Ford, holding a strong position, well intrenched, and receiving heavy re-enforcements. General McGowan reported severely wounded. Generals Hill and Heth are on duty again. Ninety-two of Colonel Davis' (Stoneman's) cavalry are with him at Gloucester. Dispatch from Tullahoma (5th), says that General Forrest has captured 1,600 Yankees near Rome, Ga., arms, horses, &c.

JOHN A. DIX,
Major-General.

YORKTOWN, VA., *May* 7, 1863.

Hon. E. M. STANTON, *Secretary of War:*

Colonel Kilpatrick, with the Harris Light Cavalry and Twelfth Illinois Cavalry, have just arrived at Gloucester Point, having accomplished the object of their mission fully and most gallantly. They pursued the enemy to within 3 miles of Richmond, and destroyed a large amount of property and bridges. General Dix and General Keyes left this morning for West Point.

RUFUS KING,
Brigadier-General.

HDQRS. DEPT. OF VIRGINIA, SEVENTH ARMY CORPS,
On the York River, above Yorktown, May 8, 1863—10 a. m.

Major-General HALLECK, *General-in-Chief:*

I received your dispatch of the 6th at 2 o'clock this morning. The rapidity of my movements had, as you were advised, anticipated it. But I will hold my transportation subject to your orders, and no inconvenience can result, as the troops can move more rapidly from their present position than from Suffolk if they are needed on the Rappahannock or even on the James River.

The enemy left Suffolk Sunday night. Our troops were in pursuit on Monday. On Monday night I ordered the movement agreed on. The troops were thrown across the railroad to Norfolk and embarked, and had reached Fort Monroe on Wednesday morning, with the exception of two batteries which marched. Wednesday we were detained by a heavy blow. On Thursday the troops were pushed up to West Point, the wharf repaired, and they were in position and partially intrenched before dark. I sent up materials for repairing the wharf and intrenching tools with the expedition. Nothing was omitted. Brigadier-General Gordon was in command of the troops before Wednesday night. I ordered Major-General Keyes to take 100 cavalry—all he could spare— and go up himself. He conducted the landing with good judgment and great promptness, and I joined him with Major Stewart, my chief engineer, before the landing was completed and shortly after he and General Gordon had commenced putting the troops in position $1\frac{1}{2}$ miles from the wharf on a well-chosen and very defensible line.

The cavalry, under Major Hall, of the Sixth New York, agreeably to my previous order, pushed on at once to White House and destroyed the railroad bridge over the Pamunkey, in the night, under fire from the opposite side. It was very dark, and none of his party were injured. The movement was so prompt that he was only five minutes behind the messenger, who arrived at the White House from the —— at West Point with the information of cur landing. On his return he encountered and captured a party escorting Lieutenant Estes, aide to Colonel Kilpatrick, and 20 of his men to Richmond. Lieutenant Estes had previously, with his small party, captured and paroled 3 officers and about 20 men, but had been surrounded by the militia, which had turned out *en masse.*

Major Hall deserves great praise for his promptitude and gallantry. Lieutenant Estes will make a written report to his proper commander. He refused a parole for himself and men when captured. Colonel Kilpatrick has arrived with 700 men at Gloucester Point, 400 of his own and 300 of Colonel Davis' Illinois regiment. He says none of Longstreet's men had left Richmond on Sunday morning. The colonel captured an aide of General Winder within the fortifications, 3 miles from Richmond. He does not believe the railroad connection to Fredericksburg was re-established on Wednesday.

I have 5,000 infantry, two batteries, and 100 cavalry at West Point.

I am, very respectfully, your obedient servant,

JOHN A. DIX,
Major-General.

———

YORKTOWN, *May* 8, 1863.

Lieut. Col. LOUIS H. PELOUZE,
Assistant Adjutant-General, Fort Monroe, Va.:

I am at this place with my staff and only one regiment of my brigade; the other two regiments are with General Gregg's division. I expected

after destroying the bridges near Richmond to return to General Stone
man's headquarters, but was forced to seek safety within your lines. I
am here with my entire staff and without a command. I respectfully
ask for instructions.

> J. KILPATRICK,
> *Col. Comdg. First Brigade, Third Division, Cavalry Corps.*

YORKTOWN, VA., *May* 8, 1863.

Maj. Gen. H. W. HALLECK,
   General-in-Chief:

Colonel Kilpatrick, with his regiment (the Harris Light Cavalry) and
the rest of the Illinois Twelfth, has just arrived at Gloucester Point
opposite this fort. They burned the bridges over the Chickahominy
destroyed three large trains of provisions in the rear of Lee's army
drove in the rebel pickets to within 2 miles of Richmond, and have lost
only 1 lieutenant and 30 men, having captured and paroled upward of
300 prisoners. Among the prisoners was an aide to General Winder
who was captured with his escort far within the intrenchments outside
of Richmond. This cavalry have marched nearly 200 miles since the 3d
of May; were inside of the fortifications of Richmond on the 4th; burned
all the stores at Aylett's Station, on the Mattapony, on the 5th; de
stroyed all the ferries over the Pamunkey and Mattapony and a large
commissary depot near and above Tappahannock, and came here in good
condition. They deserve great credit for what they have done. It is
one of the finest feats of the war.

> RUFUS KING,
> *Brigadier-General.*

WAR DEPARTMENT,
May 8, 1863.

General RUFUS KING, *Yorktown:*

Thanks for your telegram. Please give me any further information
you have. We are all anxious to hear from the gallant officers and sol
diers who have performed an achievement unsurpassed for daring and
success. Give my congratulations and compliments to them.

> EDWIN M. STANTON.

YORKTOWN, VA., *May* 8, 1863—12 p. m.

Hon. E. M. STANTON,
   Secretary of War:

Your dispatch of this day has been received, and will be communi
cated in general orders to the Harris Light Cavalry and the Twelfth
Illinois to-morrow. The officers and men will be rejoiced to know that
their brilliant exploit is fully appreciated at headquarters. They are in
good condition, and after a day's rest will be fit, as they are anxious, for
further active service. All quiet on our front and nothing new here.

> RUFUS KING,
> *Brigadier-General, Commanding*

WAR DEPARTMENT,
Washington, May 8, 1863—4 p. m.

Major-General DIX, *Fort Monroe, Va.:*

Your movement is all right. Hold on to what you have got. I only wished delay for General Hooker.

H. W. HALLECK,
General-in-Chief.

SUFFOLK, VA., *May* 8, 1863.

Major-General DIX:

I see by the papers that the Richmond press states that Longstreet's troops were not with Lee; only Longstreet in person. This I apprehend is the true version.

JOHN J. PECK,
Major-General.

WASHINGTON, D. C., *May* 8, 1863.

Major-General DIX,
(*For General Foster, Fort Monroe, Va.*):

General Foster at the present time should not be absent from his command. Moreover no interview can now give him re-enforcements by any possibility.

H. W. HALLECK,
General-in-Chief.

WAR DEPARTMENT,
Washington, May 8, 1863.

Major-General HOOKER, *Falmouth, Va.:*

General Dix had moved his troops before he received my order to suspend his operations, and probably occupied West Point in force yesterday.

H. W. HALLECK,
General-in-Chief.

UNITED STATES FLAG-SHIP MINNESOTA,
Off Newport News, May 8, 1863.

Maj. Gen. JOHN A. DIX, U. S. A.,
Comdg. Seventh Army Corps, Fortress Monroe. Va.:

GENERAL : On the morning of the 4th instant I proposed to you a joint expedition against Fort Powhatan, Petersburg, and Richmond. This was in consequence of information that the enemy had left Suffolk; that General Hooker was between Richmond and the rebel army at Fredericksburg, and that you had 30,000 troops here. Your reply, dated May 5, received on the 6th instant, gives your reasons for not being able to co-operate in the proposed movement. In this reply you remark :

You will remember that I called your attention, in an interview with you several weeks ago, to the fact that the enemy were at work at Fort Powhatan, and expressed an earnest desire that some of your gunboats should drive him away before any guns were mounted. My last advices are that he is now occupying it with considerable force.

This statement I am sorry to say is extremely inaccurate and injurious to me. You seem to have overlooked my correct statement of this matter in another communication to you of the 4th instant, to which you promised in another communication of the 5th instant to reply "when relieved from the pressure of (your) present very urgent duties."

On Wednesday, the 18th of March, Colonel Ludlow, returning with a flag of truce from City Point, in a note dated Tuesday, informed me that the "rebels are very much strengthening their works at Old Fort Powhatan and seem to have a large force in garrison there." Notwithstanding this reoccupation was a military act performed within the military lines of your department, I did not wait for you to call on me for co-operation, but went to see you the next day on the subject. You stated that the enemy was already on this side of the Blackwater with 28,000 men, a larger force than yours, and that you could not act in the matter. You showed me the position of Fort Powhatan (not laid down on my chart) about 10 miles from Harrison's Point. You asked me, with the usual complimentary opinion of the army as to the ability of the gunboats not only to protect but to take forts, if my gunboats could not "shell them out."

In view of the failure for want of military co-operation of a better iron-clad and gunboat force than I then had to "shell them out" of Fort Darling, I explained to you why your suggestion was impracticable and left you, as I supposed, satisfied on that point.

This occurred seven instead of several weeks ago, nor did I then understand you as "expressing an earnest desire that some of our gunboats should drive him away before any guns were mounted," for the reason that, with the facts then fresh in your memory, you knew as well as I did from Colonel Ludlow's report of the previous day that the enemy had a large force in garrison there, and you could not possibly have supposed that he would have garrisoned his fort with a large force when it was without guns.

I trust, general, there can be no settled purpose to do me injustice, and therefore ask you to correct this error.

I have the honor to be, general, very respectfully, yours,

S. P. LEE,
Actg. Rear-Admiral, Comdg. N. Atlantic Blockading Squadron.

SUFFOLK, *May* 9, 1863.

General DIX:

From all the information I can get, about two divisions are on the Blackwater. Spear is very sick. When he recovers I shall feel of something.

JOHN J. PECK,
Major-General.

YORKTOWN, *May* 9, 1863.

Maj. Gen. JOHN A. DIX:

General Gregg was ordered to destroy the bridges referred to. I only burned those over the Chickahominy. I do not know that he succeeded, but was told by prisoners that he did.

J. KILPATRICK,
Colonel, &c.

WASHINGTON, D. C., *May* 9, 18€3.

Major General FOSTER, *New Berne, N. C.:*

GENERAL : Your report, dated April 30, of the defense of Washington is just received. Both the President and Secretary of War have spoken in the highest praise of the gallantry of yourself and your troops in the defense of Washington against the superior forces of the enemy. It will rank among the most glorious operations of the war.

I have also just received your letters of the 5th instant asking for reenforcements. I regret it is at present utterly impossible to give you any. Every available man was sent to Suffolk and to co-operate with General Hooker. I have the positive orders of the President to withdraw no troops at present from General Hunter's command. There is no other place from which troops can now be withdrawn. As you know, I have from the beginning had no hopes of success at Charleston, but the Navy insisted upon making the attack. It is unfortunate that so many things are undertaken at the same time; but this I cannot avoid. I think you will agree with me that our operations on the Mississippi River are much more important at the present time than any that can be carried on in North Carolina.

In regard to matters in Virginia we have our hands full. Troops cannot be withdrawn from there without great danger. Moreover, the President directed some months ago that no troops be taken from General Hooker's army. I hope we may soon get recruits by draft. It will be made very soon; but we cannot yet calculate positively upon the result.

Had General Hooker been successful on the Rappahannock it would have helped us very much in carrying out the conscription. Now we may possibly have some difficulty; but this will be overcome.

General Hooker failed to accomplish his main object on the Rappahannock but he met with no disaster. He believes the loss of the enemy to be much greater than his own and will immediately renew operations.

Very respectfully, your obedient servant,
H. W. HALLECK,
General-in-Chief.

HDQRS. DEPT. OF VIRGINIA, SEVENTH ARMY CORPS,
Fort Monroe, Va., May 10, 1863.

Maj. Gen. H. W. HALLECK,
General-in-Chief U. S. Army, Washington, D. C. :

GENERAL : The troops at Suffolk have been hard at work demolishing the enemy's works, which are very substantial and extended. They could have been constructed during the three weeks of the investment by less than 30,000 or 40,000 men. I have ordered General Peck to take up all the rails on both roads from the Blackwater to Suffolk and send them to this fort. The enemy had already removed them from the first 3 miles beyond Suffolk, on the Weldon road, and had loosened the spikes on 6 miles more, either to carry them off for use on other roads or to construct iron-clad batteries in front of ours.

I desire to present to you some views in regard to holding Suffolk, and ask your decision in regard to them. Suffolk is no longer of any use to us as a position for making friends of the secessionists. The population there and in the surrounding country are bitter and implacable. The only object in holding it is to render the inland connection with North Carolina by the canals on the eastern side of the Dismal Swamp somewhat more secure. Is this object of sufficient importance to warrant the cost and the hazard of maintaining the position? The connection is convenient during the months of December, January, February, and March, when the communication by sea is liable to interruption by storms; but during the other eight months it is of little importance. We only use it for dispatches, a semi-weekly mail, and for the transportation of officers, and occasionally a few men. They may as well go outside. It does not follow that we shall lose this connection by withdrawing from Suffolk, but we shall make it less secure. Suffolk is strong with a large force, and very weak with a small one. In the face of an enemy it is impossible to fall back on Norfolk. It must be held at all hazards. We have over one hundred guns there. Its capture would be the greatest disaster of the war. It has a very narrow river running back 7 miles to the rear, always endangering the loss of our communication with our supplies. The enemy can approach it rapidly by two railroads. It can never be safely left without 15,000 men, and if invested by a large force it must have 25,000.

The line of Deep Creek is 8 miles from Norfolk. It is a better line in all respects. The communication with the rear cannot well be cut. It will always be possible, even in the face of an enemy, to fall back on Norfolk. It can be defended by 10,000 men. There is but one objection to the change—the moral effect. We fall back 12 miles; but on the other hand we advance 40 on the York River and place ourselves at West Point, within 35 miles of Richmond. By occupying the line of Deep Creek we should save from 10,000 to 15,000 troops, and the transportation of supplies up the Nansemond, and gain a more secure position. The change can be made now while the great body of the enemy is away. It will be impossible when he returns. If the change should be approved, I should place General Peck in command of the new line and make him Military Governor of Norfolk, where his vigilance and promptitude would be of great advantage, sending General Viele into the field. I should also take up the rails on both roads between Suffolk and Deep Creek and deprive the enemy of the power of using them either for roads or for constructing iron batteries.

I am, very respectfully, your obedient servant,

JOHN A. DIX,
Major-General.

[Indorsements.]

MAY 14, 1863.

Respectfully referred to General Totten, Chief Engineer, General Barnard, and General Cullum for the expression of their views in regard to General Dix's general plan.

H. W. HALLECK,
General-in-Chief.

WASHINGTON, D. C., *May* 14, 1863.

We concur in the general views of General Dix respecting the abandonment of Suffolk, Va., the determination of the strength and direction of the new line of defense at Deep Creek being left to General Dix and his engineers.

J. G. TOTTEN,
Brigadier-General, Chief of Engineers.
J. G. BARNARD,
Brigadier-General, &c.
GEO. W. CULLUM,
Lieutenant-Colonel Engineers and Brigadier-General.

HEADQUARTERS OUTPOSTS,
Camp Fifty-eighth Regt. Pa. Vols., May 10, 1863.

Lieut. Col. SOUTHARD HOFFMAN,
Assistant-Adjutant General, Eighteenth Army Corps:

SIR: I have the honor to report that the enemy have occupied the
line of Core Creek in greater force than heretofore, how great I have
not yet ascertained.   They made a reconnaissance this side the Dover-
road bridge on Thursday with a troop of cavalry (of the Sixty-third
North Carolina) and some infantry.   They have leveled the works I
had commenced this side the bridge (at Dover-road Crossing), and have
erected field works with two embrasures beyond the creek.   Also the
bridge itself seems to have had additional work on it since we retired.
Very respectfully, your obedient servant,

J. RICHTER JONES.

UNITED STATES FLAG-SHIP MINNESOTA,
Off Newport News, Va., May 11, 1863.

Maj. Gen. JOHN A. DIX, U. S. A.,
Comdg. Seventh Army Corps, Fortress Monroe:

GENERAL: In the communication from you dated the 5th and received the 7th instant you state your expectation that the siege of Suf
folk will be renewed.

Soon after assuming this command I had the honor to propose to you
that all the abandoned rebel earthworks within your lines should be
razed.   Standing as they do, hardened by age, they tempt the reoccupation by the enemy, to whom it would be but the work of a night to reoccupy them, to mount and casemate guns enough to command the
channel, and cut off the communications of the gunboats.

Last fall Commodore Livingston, at my suggestion, leveled the work
at Helena which commands the navy-yard.

I respectfully suggest to you that it would be of great advantage to
naval operations if you would have the abandoned rebel earthworks on
the Lower Nansemond, Elizabeth River, and at Sewell's Point thoroughly
leveled, excepting, of course, such as you may deem necessary for military purposes.

I have the honor to be, general, very respectfully, yours,

S. P. LEE,
Actg. Rear-Admiral, Comdg. N. Atlantic Blockading Squadron.

HEADQUARTERS EIGHTEENTH ARMY CORPS,
Department of North Carolina, May 11, 1863.

Maj. Gen. H. W. HALLECK,
Commander-in-Chief U. S. Army, Washington, D. C.:

GENERAL: I have the honor to acknowledge the receipt of your telegram of the 8th instant.

I beg leave to say that it was not mainly to obtain re-enforcements
that I wished to see you, although I desire above all things, as I am
free to confess, the return of the brave men whom I took from this de-

partment to that of the South, and who are there subject to mortification and discomfort and a situation apparently of no benefit to the public service.

My object related to contingencies that might arise (and which have now arisen) and what should be my action under the circumstances. I am pleased, personally, that the trip will not now be needed, and that I can now give my whole attention to the necessary preparation. I have made up my mind to meet the enemy at every point and to contest every step so obstinately that its attainment will be made by him with sorrow. I have no fears of any disaster in this department (and with 3,000 more men I could obtain a small victory), but I beg you to believe that whatever efforts may be made against us we will try to give you a satisfactory report.

I have the honor to be, very respectfully, your obedient servant,

J. G. FOSTER,
Major-General, Commanding.

YORKTOWN, *May* 11, [1863.]
Major-General DIX:

I am just down from West Point. The works there are now strong in front, and I left General Gordon at work on batteries near the Point, where at least four 20-pounder Parrotts are necessary, and if you can send back all that were taken from here I can supply them. What I shall recommend for the positions under my immediate command will depend in a great degree on the condition of the Army of the Potomac, which I do not know.

E. D. KEYES,
Major-General.

SUFFOLK, *May* 12, 1863.
Major-General DIX:

Line from Bowers' to Southern Branch that is shortest and offers an impassable flank rests upon the arm of the Branch near Hodge's, on Martin's place. By Heine's map, 7 miles of Deep Creek would be thrown out, as well as approaches along Dismal Canal. Deep Creek is narrow and would have to be guarded. Please look particularly. Five miles difference, which is very great.

JOHN J. PECK,
Major-General.

FORT MONROE, VA., *May* 13, 1863.
Hon. E. M. STANTON:

I send you by this evening's mail two Charleston papers of the 9th and 11th, handed to me by the captain of Her Britannic Majesty's steamship Rinaldo, just arrived from that city in forty-five hours. No news except the death of Stonewall Jackson, telegraphed from Richmond on Monday. News from Vicksburg to the 9th. Landing of Federal troops at Young's Point is announced.

JOHN A. DIX,
Major-General.

HDQRS. DEPT. OF NORTH CAROLINA, EIGHTEENTH A. C.,
New Berne, N. C., May 13, 1863.

Rear-Admiral S. P. LEE,
  Comdg. N. Atlantic Blockading Squadron, Hampton Roads, Va.:

SIR: I have the honor to acknowledge the receipt of your letter of May 1, repeating some of your views on the subject of posts on the Sounds in this department, and, as always, your views claim my careful consideration.

In, as it were, a joint department like this it is a matter of discrimination what points to hold as of greater benefit to both arms of the service. The points on the coast are of course equally important for all parties. Roanoke Island is of great advantage to us as a strategical point; would be to the enemy. If the island were abandoned and the works were razed I have no doubt that it would be occupied by the enemy via Nag's Head and across Roanoke Channel. At this point, from the shallowness of the water, gunboats could not prevent the occupancy and could not prevent the erection of batteries, even were it known that it would be attempted; whereas that position could be held by a small force on the island against a large one crossing.

Experience has shown us the facility with which sand batteries can be erected, and also proved that their power of withstanding fire is greater than stone. It would require but a few weeks to again fortify Roanoke Island (should the enemy have it), and probably the taking of it has shown them the falsity of their previous line of defense; and I believe the division might lose more men than were withdrawn from my force as garrisons.

As to Washington and Plymouth my views were given in my letter of the 22d ultimo. While I have force sufficient it seems to me important to hold the rich grain-growing counties lying in the pockets held by these towns, and also as strategical points for harassing the enemy so long as I have force sufficient for any offensive movements; but such may not be the case long.

Again, if the enemy should construct gunboats up the Tar and Roanoke Rivers they probably could not be made sufficiently formidable to defeat the naval forces at Washington and Plymouth; the naval as well as land batteries could assist in the defense. It is not likely, however, that naval vessels crossing through the Sounds would be in force equal to encounter the combined forces at Washington and Plymouth, in which case (the enemy always being in a position to make concerted movements) a concentration of the vessels from several might be made for attacking detached vessels, in which case the result might be disastrous. Of these probabilities you of course are the best judge. But merely in accordance with our mutual desire to exchange ideas for the general good I give it as my opinion that were the towns of Washington and Plymouth abandoned the mouths of the rivers so situated would be the right and best places for the guard-boats, and that the presence of the assistance on land would necessitate the presence of a large naval force to be as effective as the present guarding force. Would the class of boats in service here be of much use in outside service?

I inclose herein a slip cut from a Raleigh paper, which shows the views held by the enemy upon the subject of our abandonment of the counties of Albemarle, the advantage gained by them of food, &c.

I have the honor to remain, admiral, very respectfully, your obedient servant,

J. G. FOSTER,
Major-General, Commanding.

HEADQUARTERS OUTPOSTS,
Camp Fifty-eighth Regt. Pennsylvania Vols., May 13, 1863.

Lieut. Col. SOUTHARD HOFFMAN,
 Assistant Adjutant-General:

SIR: I have the honor to report that a civilian who came down the Neuse road yesterday informs me that he found no posts at Core Creek, and has been told that there are none this side of Moseley Creek. Also the sergeant in charge of my daily patrol informs me that a man who came down the Dover road stated to him that there are no Confederate troops this side of Gum Swamp. These reports I shall endeavor to verify in the course of the day.

 Very respectfully, your obedient servant,
         J. RICHTER JONES,
   Colonel Fifty-eighth Regiment, Commanding Outposts.

SUFFOLK, *May* 14, 1863.

Major-General DIX:

Major Wentz thought he would be ready on Monday evening. Yesterday he said he would be at Carrsville before sunset. Colonel Foster went yesterday, and writes that the train is not through. He decided to try that road first after examination. Time is precious, but I hope we shall succeed. After taking up several miles he might change roads.

         JOHN J. PECK,
          Major-General.

HDQRS. DEPT. OF VIRGINIA, SEVENTH ARMY CORPS,
Fort Monroe, Va., May 14, 1863.

Maj. Gen. E. D. KEYES,
 Commanding, Yorktown:

GENERAL: I have forwarded your letter to the Adjutant-General, and suggested that Major-General Ord should have a command better suited to his rank than that of West Point, if one can be given to him. But he has behaved so handsomely I deemed it due to him to suggest also that his wishes should be consulted.

On the maturest consideration I have decided to make West Point an independent command. Your own is a very extensive and important one, embracing Gloucester Point, Yorktown, Williamsburg, and indeed the whole Peninsula. I do not think your attention should be divided between this command and another. You need nothing but troops to make it the most important in the department, as it brings you nearer to Richmond than any other except West Point, and regarding your limits as now extended to the neighborhood of the White House you are even nearer. Should the enemy reappear at Diascund Bridge I will do all I can to afford you the means of assailing him, as I proposed more than two months ago. It is very doubtful whether there will be an advance from West Point with a sufficient force to accomplish anything. If there should be I shall take the command myself.

You cannot doubt my desire to do all in my power to meet your wishes, and also to do justice to your rank. Circumstances have made the command at Suffolk during the last two months more important than any other, but events may at any moment render it necessary to throw the principal part of my force into your own command. I desire under all circumstances that you should retain it, and I suggest whether now you may not repeat Colonel West's reconnaissance, pushing it farther on.

I am told there is only a small cavalry force at the White House. The expedition, if you think it advisable, from the information in your possession, to undertake it, should be organized under your personal superintendence.

I am, very respectfully, your obedient servant,

JOHN A. DIX,
Major-General.

[FORT MONROE], *May* 14, 1863.

Major-General KEYES,
Commanding, Yorktown:

Your dispatch arrived this morning while I was away. I wrote you a few hours ago, stating that on full reflection I had decided to make West Point an independent command.

I have suggested a movement up the Peninsula. Please make the change you desire in the cavalry and I will endeavor to give it back to you in a few days with an addition of the same arm.

I have forwarded your letter to the Adjutant-General, as I have explained in mine, which you will receive to-morrow; but I cannot concur in your removal to another department.

JOHN A. DIX,
Major-General.

HDQRS. DEPT. OF VIRGINIA, SEVENTH ARMY CORPS,
Fort Monroe, Va., May 14, 1863.

Actg. Rear-Admiral S. P. LEE,
Commanding North Atlantic Blockading Squadron:

ADMIRAL: I have the honor to acknowledge the receipt of your letter of the 11th instant proposing that all the rebel earthworks within my lines, except such as are necessary for military purposes, should be razed.

All the troops at Suffolk have been constantly occupied since the retreat of the enemy in leveling his intrenchments, which are very extended and solid. When this is completed they will be occupied with not less urgent labors for the next month.

At Norfolk and Fort Monroe I have barely force enough for guard duty, but I will personally examine as soon as practicable all the earthworks in this vicinity and meet your wishes as far as I can. Elizabeth City is in North Carolina and not under my control.

I have the honor to be, very respectfully, your obedient servant,

JOHN A. DIX,
Major-General.

WASHINGTON, D. C., *May* 14, 1863.

Major-General DIX:

The matter of your letter of the 10th is approved. I write you to-day.

H. W. HALLECK,
General-in-Chief.

WASHINGTON, *May* 14, 1863.

Major-General DIX, *Fort Monroe:*

GENERAL: Your letter of the 10th is received. I fully agree with you that the line of Deep Creek is much better for the defense of Norfolk than the line of the Nansemond. Suffolk is a most ill-chosen position for defense, and is unimportant in any other respect than security of Norfolk. Why it was ever occupied I do not know.

Although fully concurring in your views I felt unwilling to approve the change without first submitting the matter to a board of able and experienced officers and afterward to the Secretary of War. All confirm your views. Before making the change the new line should be well fortified and prepared for the batteries. It should for the present be considered the second line, and the intended change kept a profound secret. The arrangements for the defense of this line should be made under the direction of your chief engineer, Major Stewart.

When abandoned, the works of Suffolk should be destroyed.

Yours, truly,

H. W. HALLECK,
General-in-Chief.

———

FORT MONROE, *May* 14, 1863.

Major-General PECK:

I have a dispatch from the General-in-Chief approving my suggestions as to changes I named to you. The second line and the dismantling of the railroads must be pushed to completion.

JOHN A. DIX,
Major-General.

———

SUFFOLK, VA., *May* 14, 1863.

General DIX:

At 5 p. m. Colonel Foster had driven the enemy back to his intrenchments and the working party was doing well; within 2½ miles of Blackwater.

JOHN J. PECK,
Major-General.

———

SUFFOLK, VA., *May* 15, 1863.

Major-General DIX:

The working party are now just this side of Carrsville; getting along well. Have sent rations to Colonel Foster. The enemy are running cars very actively in view of advance on that line.

JOHN J. PECK,
Major-General.

———

HEADQUARTERS OUTPOSTS,
Camp Fifty-eighth Regt. Pennsylvania Vols., May 15, 1863.

Lieut. Col. SOUTHARD HOFFMAN,
Assistant Adjutant-General:

SIR: I have the honor to report that the facts which I communicated to headquarters yesterday respecting the line of Core Creek are confirmed by my patrol, and that the enemy have now no force on that line.

I also learn from various sources, so that I count on it as reliable to a reasonable degree, that the enemy's force in Kinston is now very small, not exceeding five regiments, and that there are few troops at Goldsborough. Of the five regiments, one is at Gum Swamp and one at Wise's Forks, and the regiment at Gum Swamp is open to a movement on its rear and might be cut off. If it is thought desirable under existing circumstances to seize Kinston and Goldsborough I would request to be allowed to strike the railroad somewhere north of Goldsborough, in order to intercept re-enforcements, &c. With one good infantry regiment added to my own and three or four troops of cavalry and a section of artillery I feel confident I could reach that railroad with little or no opposition and break it up extensively, that is, provided the intention be kept entirely secret.

The enterprise would justify some labor and risk in reference to the capture of Goldsborough only, but as connected with a simultaneous movement from Suffolk on Weldon it might materially interrupt the enemy's communications and influence the war.

Very respectfully, your obedient servant,

J. RICHTER JONES,
Colonel Thirty-eighth Pennsylvania Vols., Comdg. Outposts.

FORT MONROE, VA.,
May 16, 1863—1 p. m.

Maj. Gen. H. W. HALLECK,
General-in-Chief:

Colonel Foster is covering our work, which is in good progress, on the railroad near Carrsville. Has been engaged with the enemy more or less for two days. A lively artillery fire has been kept up on our workmen. Yesterday the enemy advanced within canister-range, but was driven back with considerable loss. On our side a caisson was riddled, a horse killed, and 9 men wounded. The iron is arriving in Norfolk. When we get on the other road we shall probably have some sharp fighting.

JOHN A. DIX,
Major-General.

FORT MONROE, *May* 16, 1863.

Major-General PECK,
Commanding, Suffolk:

A report has just reached me, not on the best authority, that the enemy has 5,000 men at Scott's factory and 10,000 at Colonel Thomas'. Where these places are I do not know, but somewhere between the Blackwater and the Nansemond, I believe.

JOHN A. DIX,
Major-General.

SUFFOLK, VA., *May* 16, 1863.

Major-General DIX:

Scott's factory is at Smithfield, but the other place I cannot locate exactly. That is a good country for supplies, and from it they flank all moves on Blackwater. If there, it looks like assuming the offensive, for there is a considerable force on the river massed near Franklin.

JOHN J. PECK,
Major-General.

FORT MONROE, *May* 17, 1863.

Major-General PECK,
      Commanding, Suffolk:

My man is here from New Haven [Richmond]. He says none of Long-street's force have gone beyond New Haven, and that they are on the New London* and head of Washington.* Heard that there was some trap to draw out the troops at Boston [Suffolk]. It would be well to ascertain truth of yesterday's report. Foster must be very vigilant.

                                        JOHN A. DIX,
                                            Major-General.

FORT MONROE, *May* 17, 1863.

Major-General PECK:

No pains should be spared to sustain Foster. He should be re-enforced, if necessary. Was the enemy seen near Alexandria?

                                        JOHN A. DIX,
                                            Major-General.

HDQRS. DEPT. OF VIRGINIA, SEVENTH ARMY CORPS,
                              Fort Monroe, May 17, 1863.

Maj. Gen. H. W. HALLECK,
      General-in-Chief:

GENERAL: Your letter of the 14th is received and your wishes have all been anticipated. The moment I received your telegraphic dispatch saying that you approved my views, I sent Major Stewart to examine the new line, and it will be fortified under his direction. It has been given out that we are to fortify it as a second line, and a show of strengthening the defenses at Suffolk is to be kept up until it is ready.

I have just returned from Suffolk; the enemy is on this side the Blackwater and in considerable force. Colonel Foster is between him and our working party with 8,000 men. We hope to finish our work on the Weldon road by Wednesday. When we go to Zuni we shall send a still larger force.

My man came in from Richmond to-day. He says that only one division of Longstreet's force went north of Richmond, and that it returned to Petersburg, being too late for the battle of Fredericksburg. He confirms my former statements that the force before Suffolk was near 40,000, and he says this whole force is at Petersburg, on the Blackwater, and back of Franklin, on the Weldon road.

The Richmond has met with an accident; he could not ascertain precisely what, but thinks it was some damage to her machinery. The two iron-clads on the stocks are getting on slowly. He thinks they cannot be completed before August, but he judged from what he saw that workmen had been transferred from one to the other, indicating an intention to bring one out as soon as possible.

He is satisfied that troops have recently been brought to Richmond from Georgia and South Carolina and sent on to Fredericksburg. It was said at Richmond that Lee was to attack Hooker and drive him back to the Potomac.

I am, very respectfully and truly, yours,

                                        JOHN A. DIX,
                                            Major-General.

---

* Cipher.

HEADQUARTERS FOURTH ARMY CORPS,
Fort Yorktown, Va., May 17, 1863.

Lieut. Col. L. H. PELOUZE,
Assistant Adjutant-General, Department of Virginia :

COLONEL : I have the honor to forward to you (according to instructions from Headquarters Army of the Potomac) instructions given me from the same headquarters. I expect my command will have all arrived by this evening. While it is my great desire to literally carry out the orders of my chief, I intend also to act in compliance with the wishes and instructions of the major-general in whose department I am to temporarily remain. Any advice, suggestion, or instruction that the major-general commanding the department may do me the honor to forward I shall be pleased to receive and promptly to execute.

Very respectfully, your obedient servant,

J. KILPATRICK,
Colonel, Commanding Cavalry Brigade.

[Inclosure.]

HEADQUARTERS ARMY OF THE POTOMAC,
May 13, 1863.

Colonel KILPATRICK,
Commanding Cavalry Brigade :

COLONEL : The major-general commanding directs that you assume command of the regiments of cavalry now with you at Yorktown ; that you will hold your force well in hand, inflicting whatever damage the legitimate rules of war sanction upon the enemy, his supplies, and his communications. You will observe his movements as far as possible. You will take with you from this camp the dismounted men of both regiments and remount them there with captured animals. You will report by letter and telegraph as occasion requires, holding your command ready to co-operate with this army in its operations.

You will furnish General Keyes, or the commanding officer in whose department you may temporarily remain, with copies of your instructions that you may receive from time to time.

Very respectfully, your obedient servant,

S. WILLIAMS,
Assistant Adjutant-General.

———

DISTRICT OF THE ALBEMARLE,
Plymouth, N. C., May 17, 1863.

Lieut. Col. SOUTHARD HOFFMAN,
Asst. Adjt. Gen., Department of North Carolina :

COLONEL : I have the honor to report the condition of affairs in the district as follows :

The lines in front of this town are in progress toward completion. The parapet of Fort Williams is now well sodded on its exterior slope, as also three sides of the superior slope and palisades, ready for the ditch.

The breastworks on the right and left are being strengthened by a substantial revetment of timber and the ditch considerably widened, as also the epaulement on the left of the Columbia road.

The excavation and revetment of the redoubt near Boyle Creek is nearly complete, and will be ready for the gun by the last of this week. The redoubt above, intended for the protection of river obstructions, is progressing favorably, but the frame for magazine has not been received, and preparations are now made to construct it on the ground.

This work, constructed by the Ninety-sixth New York Volunteers, I have named Fort Gray, in memory of Col. C. O. Gray of that regiment, killed in battle at Kinston, subject to the approval of the commanding general. The obstructions at the head of the island have been commenced. There have been many difficulties on account of repairs to the pile-drivers and density of the substratum, but it is believed that work will progress hereafter more rapidly.

Light guns are required for Fort Williams and for the redoubt near the Columbia road.

At Roanoke Island working parties are employed in getting out palisades for Forts Reno and Parke. The north face of the latter is in danger of being seriously washed, as also the easterly face of Fort Foster, both of which require attention.

A few guerrillas are skulking within the limits of this county, but in small numbers, and a company of cavalry is reported to be in the neighborhood of Jamesville, but thus far have made no hostile demonstrations.

Respectfully, your obedient servant,

H. W. WESSELLS,
Brigadier-General Volunteers, Commanding.

SUFFOLK, VA., *May* 18, 1863.

General DIX:

A contraband from Franklin says General Jenkins states that we are fortifying at Carrsville and relaying the road from this end with the rail from that end with the view of advancing. The mail-boats are at or below Franklin. Stratton reports Lieutenant Titus with 47 men having a skirmish near Newby's Bridge with 150 guerrillas. An ambuscade was prepared to capture all his party, but he cut his way through; Lieutenant Beatty and 2 privates severely and 1 sergeant slightly wounded; 1 rebel killed, 2 prisoners, several wounded. No loss of horses, some having been taken by us. Stratton approves the conduct of Lieutenant Titus.

JOHN J. PECK,
Major-General.

SUFFOLK, VA., *May* 18, 1863.

General VIELE:

The boats were taken down to the Albemarle Sound and into the Chowan. They are at Franklin probably. Major Stratton sent out a party to the Pasquotank with a view of intercepting them.

JOHN J. PECK,
Major-General.

FORT MONROE, *May* 18, 1863.

Major-General PECK:

Do I understand that the railroad connection between Boston * and Baltimore * is now complete; and, if so, how many miles of iron this side the former are taken up and removed?

JOHN A. DIX,
Major General.

---

* Cipher.

SUFFOLK, *May* 18, 1863.

Major-General DIX:

Engine now running. Iron removed for about 3½ miles this side Carrsville.

JOHN J. PECK,
Major-General.

SUFFOLK, *May* 18, 1863.

Major-General DIX:

If Hooker is reduced as reports state, Lee does not require Longstreet o leave Blackwater.

JOHN J. PECK,
Major-General.

GENERAL ORDERS, }   HDQRS. EIGHTEENTH ARMY CORPS,
No. 79.   }   *New Berne, May* 19, 1863.

In obedience to orders from the War Department Brig. Gen. E. A. Wild, U. S. Volunteers (a gallant and accomplished soldier and gentleman), has arrived in this department for the purpose of raising a brigade of colored troops. General Wild will establish recruiting offices t such points as he may select, and all district commanders, commanding officers of posts, and other officers and men, are hereby enjoined nd ordered to afford to General Wild, his officers and men, every facility and aid in the performance of their duties and in carrying out ully and in good faith the orders of the Government.

The commanding general expects that this order will be sufficient to sure the prompt obedience (the first duty of a soldier) of all officers nd soldiers in this department to the orders from the War Department.

By command of Maj. Gen. J. G. Foster:

[SOUTHARD HOFFMAN,]
Assistant Adjutant-General.

FORT MONROE, *May* 20, 1863.

Major-General PECK:

The Baltimore Sun of Monday says we are taking up the track of he Seaboard and Roanoke Railroad from Carrsville to the junction of he Norfolk and Petersburg Railroad. The writer of this letter is not ere; when he returns I shall see to it. The rails on the Seaboard road eigh 158 tons per mile; those on the Petersburg road 246 tons per ile. Of course it will require time to remove them. The operation n the latter road will amount to a campaign and we must look for some arp fighting, for I do not believe 5,000 tons of railroad iron will in he present emergency be given up without a contest.

All quiet at West Point. Gordon needs more guns, and one of his giments goes shortly   How are you getting on?

JOHN A. DIX,
Major-General.

SUFFOLK, VA., *May* 20, 1863.

General DIX:

The papers do our cause almost as much harm as the rebel armies. Hooker's moves were all read in the papers long before the hour for Lee to strike, and he knew both sides of the game.

Wentz commenced as he did to save time. He has not reported this morning, but I believe I will transfer the work at dark.

A deserter says between 20,000 and 30,000 on Blackwater under Longstreet. Have not believed it.

JOHN J. PECK,
Major-General.

SUFFOLK, VA., *May* 20, 1863.

Major-General DIX:

I ordered Windsor to be occupied at dusk as a base of operations, which you fully understand. Work is to be rushed vigorously. Fortifications of Suffolk are in progress.

JOHN J. PECK,
Major-General.

SUFFOLK, *May* 20, 1863.

Major-General DIX:

Wentz is now within 3 miles of Suffolk. The programme is all arranged for the matter spoken of.

JOHN J. PECK,
Major-General.

HEADQUARTERS OUTPOSTS,
Camp Fifty-eighth Regt. Pennsylvania Vols., May 20, 1863.

Lieut. Col. SOUTHARD HOFFMAN,
Assistant Adjutant-General:

SIR: I have the honor to report that I propose sending the Fifty-eighth Regiment Pennsylvania Volunteers to-morrow morning (Thursday) to seize the crossings of Core Creek, to rebuild the bridges, and to capture, if practicable, the enemy's post at the railroad switch; to raise up at all events the latter enterprise as a cover and pretext for our ulterior movements.

To carry on the movement without losing time and opportunity I ought to have the re-enforcements by rail or otherwise at Core Creek to-morrow afternoon or evening; the earlier, the more time for the men to rest and sleep. I contemplate moving from Core Creek about 10 p. m., so as to reach my position just before daylight.

I might effect our object just with two regiments, but to guard against possibilities I wish six; also three companies of cavalry, two pieces of artillery (though the artillery is not likely to be used), and the men had better have three days' rations. For cavalry I should prefer Pond's company and Jacob's, who have been with me before; and I shall take Wilson's (now on the line) for the third.

As regards your suggestion respecting the Trent road I shall carry out by ordering one of the cavalry companies now on that end of the line, or both, with two companies of the infantry now there, to make

econnaissance on Friday on the Trent road, at least as far as Trenton
'orks, and, if the cavalry can cross the river at the ford above the town,
o capture any small parties that may be there.

For the bridge fifteen to twenty or twenty-five 2-inch plank, not less
han 12 feet long, will be sufficient, poles with dirt on them answering
or the ends near the banks, as far out as earth can conveniently be cast
vith a shovel; and a team had better be sent with them to report this
vening to the office at Batchelder's Creek bridge and there to await my
rders. If I succeed I shall need the team in addition to my own, to
ransport captured arms, &c., and at all events to bring along lame
oldiers.

If there are any further explanations required or suggestions to be
aade please communicate.

If I have a really good marching regiment in addition to my own I
hall prefer the path to the left as a surer course, though it will involve
ome fording of small streams, mud, &c., and will probably oblige field
fficers to move on foot.

Very respectfully, your obedient servant,

J. RICHTER JONES,
Colonel, Commanding Outposts.

FORT MONROE, VA.,
May 21, 1863—12 noon.

Maj. Gen. H. W. HALLECK,
General-in-Chief:

The rails will all be up on the Weldon Railroad beyond Suffolk to-day.
Co-morrow we commence on the Petersburg Railroad. The troops were
n position last night. We hope to save 7,000 tons of iron, but expect
o fight for it.

JOHN A. DIX,
Major-General, Commanding.

FORT MONROE, *May 21, 1863.*

Major-General PECK :

The articles relating to removing rails came from the correspondent
f the Associated Press and not from the correspondent of the Herald.
Mr. Thompson will call on you to-day. I think him a reliable man.

JOHN A. DIX,
Major-General.

SUFFOLK, *May 21, 1863.*

Maj. Gen. JOHN A. DIX:

General Getty writes me that a report is current throughout the
 country that Suffolk is to be abandoned. He was informed that it origi-
aated with the adjutant of the One hundred and forty-eighth New York
Volunteers. Stories of the greatest absurdity are circulated by officers,
nd I think this one should be investigated, as a caution to officers.

JOHN J. PECK,
Major-General.

FORT MONROE, VA., *May 22, 1863.*

Maj. Gen. H. W. HALLECK,
            General-in-Chief:

Eighty contrabands were sent last week to Franklin from Richmond to take up the iron on the Weldon road. Four of them are in Suffolk. We have now all the iron safe. We have commenced on the Petersburg road, near Zuni, and shall take up the track back to Windsor by to-night. We commenced dismantling these roads at the right time.

JOHN A. DIX,
Major-General.

SUFFOLK, *May 22, 1863.*

Major-General DIX:

Will be at Windsor before night on the return. I have 10,000 there to protect workmen. General Dodge is just from Windsor. He says 45-pound rail is just as good as the heavy one, and the Government can save much.

JOHN J. PECK,
Major-General.

FORT MONROE, *May 23, 1863.*

Major-General PECK:

I incline to the belief that there are few troops on the Blackwater. From two sources I learn that troops in large numbers have gone from New Haven to New York and to the Southwest by Danville. We have no artillerists. You must take them from your cavalry regiments.

JOHN A. DIX,
Major-General.

SUFFOLK, VA., *May 23, 1863—8.45 p. m.*

General DIX:

General Dodge at Antioch Church was attacked at 6.15 p. m. No particulars.

JOHN J. PECK,
Major-General.

RED HOUSE, PICKET STATION, *May 23, 1863.*

Col. J. RICHTER JONES,
            Commanding Outposts:

COLONEL: I have the honor to report that in accordance with your orders to me of the 21st instant I moved my company, together with Company L of my regiment and two companies of the One hundred and fifty-eighth New York Regiment from Captain —— command, on the Trent road, at 5 o'clock yesterday morning. On arriving at the Trenton Forks, which point was reached without our seeing more of the enemy than a half dozen who scattered into the woods at our approach, I sent one of the infantry companies down the Trenton road to reconnoiter the crossing of the river, and left the other at the forks. I proceeded with the cavalry up the Kinston road, and on reaching the edge of Noble's plantation, 6 miles from the forks, found it barricaded, and a small earthwork thrown up to the right of the road. Passing this obstruction I found at the distance of a quarter of a mile a long earthwork with two embrasures for cannon, extending about 200 yards on each side of the road. There were also huts erected for a regiment. Two rebel cavalrymen were seen as we approached in rear of the earthwork, and I was informed by Mrs. Noble that 12 comprised the whole force of the enemy at this point. These eluded our pursuit, which was continued for about a mile. From Noble's a road runs to the Trent River. The bridge has been burned, and I learned that the river was unfordable at this point. I therefore countermarched and proceeded by the road which unites the Trent and Kinston roads, 4 miles beyond the forks, to Trenton Bridge. A few of the enemy's cavalry dismounted fired upon us from the town, but retreated too rapidly to permit their capture, although I forded the river immediately and chased them 3 miles, by the road which leads out of Trenton, up the river.

Not more than a dozen of the enemy were seen, and this appeared to be the force of pickets maintained in Trenton, which is relieved daily from Tuckahoe, 16 miles distant. While I was in Trenton two small unoccupied buildings were burned by some one of my command without orders.

I bivouacked at the forks of the roads and this morning sent out a platoon, 4 miles by the Kinston road, which saw no signs of the enemy. After waiting for further orders until 4 o'clock p. m. at the Forks I returned to camp.

I am, colonel, very respectfully, your obedient servant,

N. HALL,
Captain Company G, Third New York Cavalry.

HEADQUARTERS ARMY OF THE POTOMAC,
May 25, 1863.

Major-General DIX, *Commanding, &c.*:

Have you it in your power to obtain reliable information of the transfer of troops from Charleston to Richmond? From recent indications it is of great importance that this fact should be ascertained as early as practicable.

JOSEPH HOOKER,
Major-General, Commanding.

FORT MONROE, *May* 25, 1863—3 p. m.

Major-General HOOKER:

I am informed from three different sources, and do not doubt, that troops have gone from South Carolina and Georgia, but whether to Bragg or Lee not quite certain. The greater part of Longstreet's forces, recently on the Blackwater, are near Richmond, ready to move either on Fredericksburg or West Point.

JOHN A. DIX,
Major-General.

FORT MONROE, VA.,
May 26, 1863—11 p. m.

Maj. Gen. H. W. HALLECK,
General-in-Chief:

Major-General Ord, who has come down this evening from West Point, recommends, with the concurrence of General E. D. Keyes and

General Gordon, the withdrawal of our troops from that position, unless he can have 4,000 more infantry, 28 guns in addition to those already there, and a pontoon bridge 1,200 yards long. The recommendation is founded on the altered state of things since the occupation took place: First, the retreat of General Hooker; second, the very recent concentration of troops in the vicinity of Richmond from the Blackwater and North Carolina line; third, the probability of an attack in force at an early day, as I am advised by General Gordon by telegraph since General Ord left; and, fourth, the apprehension that our communication with the supplies will be interrupted by their erection of heavy batteries on the York, the enemy having already with his light guns fired with some effect on our mail-boat, so as to render an armed convoy necessary for our transports. In the uncertainty as to General Hooker's movements I have thought proper to communicate with you at once. I have discharged three regiments. More are soon to follow, and from appearances I suppose I cannot hope to have their places supplied. In that case my force will soon be reduced below the minimum necessary for my extended command. Averse as I am to any retrograde movement, I should be disposed to concur with my three general officers, unless from your more extended view of the whole ground you can afford me a hope of being strengthened either by fresh troops or by early movements in Virginia, which will keep the enemy fully occupied.

JOHN A. DIX,
Major-General.

HDQRS. DEPT. OF VIRGINIA, SEVENTH ARMY CORPS,
Fort Monroe, Va., May 26, 1863.
Maj. Gen. E. D. KEYES,
Commanding, Yorktown:

GENERAL: I have until to-day been prevented by urgent engagements from replying to Colonel West's letter to your assistant adjutant-general, of the 14th instant, with your indorsement of the 15th.

The colonel refers to the meritorious conduct of the troops at Williamsburg and Fort Magruder, when assailed by a superior force under General Wise, and regards my omission to speak of them in my order concerning the recent investment of Suffolk as forcing "the unpleasant conclusion that there was something left undone which should have been done."

In your indorsement you say you "regard Colonel West's complaint as just," with an intimation that I have been guilty of "partiality."

I regret very much that Colonel West should have drawn from my omission to refer to his command in the order alluded to the inference that he and his troops had not done all that brave and devoted men could do, and he will see from a statement of facts that there is no ground for such an inference.

The operations at Suffolk, after the third day of the investment of three weeks, were carried on under my own observation, as I was every alternate day either there or on the Nansemond.

On the other hand the operations at Williamsburg and its vicinity commenced and ended during my absence and while you were in command of the department. This fact would, however, have made no difference with me if the meritorious services of the troops had been properly represented to me by a report from you or from Colonel West. But no such representation has ever been made to me. Nothing was left by you at the headquarters of the department, either in the form of a report or statement of the services of Colonel West and his troops; nor could I find among the telegraphic dispatches a single one giving any but the most meager account of the advance and retreat of the enemy. Thus you will perceive if there is a fault anywhere it is not due to the "partiality" unjustly imputed to me, but to your omission to leave on the files of the department the data necessary to enable me to do justice, as I would most cheerfully have done at the proper time, to Colonel West and his command.

You will please send to him a copy of this letter, with a request that it may be communicated to his officers.

I am, very respectfully, your obedient servant,

JOHN A. DIX,
Major-General.

GENERAL ORDERS, } HDQRS. DEPT. OF N. C., EIGHTEENTH A. C.,
No. 81.   }   *New Berne, May* 26, 1863.

The commanding general, in common with the officers and men of this command, is called upon to mourn the loss of a most gallant officer, Col. J. Richter Jones, Fifty-eighth Pennsylvania Volunteers, who fell at the head of his regiment on the evening of May 23, whilst repelling an attack on the outposts.

Colonel Jones won the admiration of all in this department by the indefatigable, able, and gallant manner with which he filled the arduous duties of commander of the outposts. He died whilst yet enjoying the triumph of a victory won by his valor and counsel. To the service, to this department, and to his regiment this death has been a sad loss; and to all here, and to those at home whom he loved, the commanding general offers his most sincere sympathy. May his bright example lead many to tread the arduous path of duty with as pure an appreciation of duty and with as firm unswerving tread as he.

All the flags in this department will be carried at half-mast for the three days following the receipt of this order, and at this post half-hour guns will be fired from Forts Totten and Rowan from sunrise to sunset to-morrow, May 27.

By command of Maj. Gen. J. G. Foster:

[SOUTHARD HOFFMAN,]
Assistant Adjutant-General.

FORT MONROE, *May* 27, 1863.

Major-General PECK:

We are threatened with an attack at West Point, and I shall be obliged to call on you for some troops and guns. General Ord is on his way here. He took command there yesterday.

JOHN A. DIX,
Major-General.

SUFFOLK, *May* 27, 1863.

Major-General DIX:

Will the Provisional Brigade answer? Wardrop and Wistar are in it. Wardrop is one of my best officers. The Ninety-ninth is equal to thrice its number of ordinary men.

JOHN J. PECK,
Major-General.

FORT MONROE, *May* 27, 1863.

Major-General PECK:

The Provisional Brigade will do. Have it ready to move at a moment's warning. I am waiting dispatches from Washington. Unless Hooker does something the question of retaining West Point becomes a doubtful one.

JOHN A. DIX,
Major-General.

SUFFOLK, *May* 27, 1863.

Major-General DIX:

Will have brigade ready. Unless Hooker moves, that position will be very hazardous indeed.

JOHN J. PECK,
Major-General.

MAY 27, 1863—12 m.

Maj. Gen. E. D. KEYES,
Commanding, &c., Yorktown:

Do you know of any force of the enemy to prevent Colonel Kilpatrick with his two regiments from crossing the country from Gloucester to Urbana, and are his horses in suitable condition to make the march? All of the enemy's cavalry in my front are at Culpeper, and he has no infantry below Port Royal. From Urbana Colonel Kilpatrick's command could be ferried over the Rappahannock, under cover of the gunboats, should it be necessary. Please reply without delay.

JOSEPH HOOKER,
Major-General, Commanding.

FORT MONROE, VA., *May* 27, 1863.

Maj. Gen. JOSEPH HOOKER,
Commanding Army of the Potomac:

I send below a dispatch from Major-General Keyes in reply to yours. I have received a dispatch from General Gordon advising me of a force on the Mattapony and that he is threatened with an attack. About 200 of Colonel Kilpatrick's men are not mounted. I wish you would leave them with me at present. I need them very much at West Point, where I have only 200 cavalry. I will endeavor to get horses for them in Gloucester County.

JOHN A. DIX,
Major-General.

[Inclosure.]

Major-General HOOKER,
Commanding Army of the Potomac:

I know of no force to prevent Colonel Kilpatrick crossing to Urbana, if he can cross the Rappahannock safely; their horses in fair condition

E. D. KEYES,
Major-General.

WASHINGTON, *May* 28, 1863.

Major-General DIX, *Fort Monroe:*

My information is that Lee is massing all his forces on the Rappahannock. As General Hooker reports directly to the President I know

not what he intends to do. I can give you no re-enforcements whatever. If under these circumstances your position at West Point is
deemed unsafe you will withdraw from it.

H. W. HALLECK,
General-in-Chief.

UNITED STATES FLAG-SHIP MINNESOTA,
Off Newport News, Va., May 28, 1863.
Maj. Gen. J. G. FOSTER,
Comdg. Eighteenth Army Corps, New Berne, N. C.:

GENERAL: Your interesting communication of the 13th instant was
received during my absence at Washington, where I saw General Halleck and urged him to give you more men. He informed Secretary Fox
and myself that it would be utterly impossible to do so until conscripts
are got. Still I pressed the matter in another interview, and left at
the Department a report on the subject, which I was informed would
be communicated to the Secretary of War.

I hope you may get the troops which you so greatly need for the
occupation of Smith's Island and the attack on Wilmington.

Your views respecting the occupation of Plymouth, Roanoke Island,
and Washington are certainly very forcible. I will at all times use
every effort to sustain you in holding your positions, and especially
while you are supported by so few troops. I have instructed Commander Davenport to make every exertion to support you at this critical period.

If you can make the military occupation of New Berne, Plymouth,
and Washington complete, so as to require little or no gunboat defense,
fewer vessels will be required in the Sounds, and yet allow a sufficient
movable force there to keep the police of its waters, prevent such es-
capes as those of the Arrow and Emily up the Chowan, and prevent
violations of the blockade. Though the vessels in the Sounds are not
adapted to outside cruising a portion of them would be very useful for
blockade and other duty here.

I have just written urgently to the Navy Department to try and get
you more troops and artillery.

I have the honor to be, general, very respectfully, yours,
S. P. LEE,
Actg. Rear-Admiral, Comdg. N. Atlantic Blockading Squadron.

UNITED STATES FLAG-SHIP MINNESOTA,
Off Newport News, Va., May 30, 1863—12 m.
Maj. Gen. JOHN A. DIX, U. S. A.,
Comdg. Seventh Army Corps, Fortress Monroe, Va.:

Your dispatch is just received. I have but one gunboat here, attending a court-martial, and one at Norfolk, repairing with dispatch for important duty. Five other gunboats are now in the vicinity of Yorktown.

Please inform me fully what service is required, that I may know
what dispositions to make and what instructions to give to promote the
public interest.

S. P. LEE,
Acting Rear-Admiral.

WAR DEPARTMENT,
Washington, May 30, 1863.

Major-General DIX, Fort Monroe, Va.:

The troops withdrawn from West Point are greatly needed here. Can they not be spared?

H. W. HALLECK,
General-in-Chief.

FORT MONROE, VA.,
May 30, 1863—1 p. m.

Maj. Gen. H. W. HALLECK,
General-in-Chief:

I went with Major-Generals Peck and Keyes to West Point yesterlay, and on consultation with General Gordon it was unanimously decided to withdraw the troops, throw them up the Peninsula above Williamsburg, and, in conjunction with the force under Keyes, attack the enemy at Diascund Bridge, which is as near Richmond as West Point. There are at West Point only 4,700 men, and they will be reduced to 4,000 shortly by the discharge of a regiment. General Keyes has only 5,000 men at Gloucester Point, Yorktown, and Williamsburg, and it is very desirable that he should have this re-enforcement. I have lost three regiments and shall lose fourteen more by expiration of service.

JOHN A. DIX,
Major-General.

FORT MONROE, May 30, 1863.

Major-General KEYES:

Send word to General Gordon as quickly as possible that the gunboats have failed me, and that they cannot be ready till to-morrow. I will send up the transportation to-morrow night.

JOHN A. DIX,
Major-General.

MAY 31, 1863—10 a. m.

Major-General DIX, Fortress Monroe:

Agreeably to your request directions have been given for the dismounted men of Colonel Kilpatrick's cavalry to report to you. Will you please have me furnished with a map of the position of your forces at West Point, and also the position and approximate strength of the enemy's forces in that vicinity? We have concurrent evidence that Hood's division is posted between Gordonsville and Louisa Court-House, and Pickett's at Taylorsville (near Sexton's Junction). Longstreet is in front of me. I conclude that General Lee must be absent, as I have received no communication from him in reply to mine since a week ag) yesterday.

JOSEPH HOOKER,
Major-General, Commanding.

FORT MONROE, *May* 31, 1863.

Major-General HOOKER,
    Commanding Army of the Potomac :

It has been decided to withdraw from West Point and throw the force there up the Peninsula toward the White House. I can get no satisfactory information as to the enemy's force. There was last week a considerable body massed north of Richmond, on the railroad, ready to support Lee at Fredericksburg or Wise at White House. I can hear nothing of them since Wednesday. I will advise you of all my movements. My force is small.

JOHN A. DIX,
Major-General.

DISTRICT OF BEAUFORT,
Morehead City, N. C., May 31, 1863.

Lieut. Col. SOUTHARD HOFFMAN,
    Assistant Adjutant-General, Eighteenth Army Corps:

COLONEL: I have the honor to communicate that I assumed command of the district on my arrival here yesterday.

I have put 250 men at work on the fort in front of this city to-day.

I have also started things up at Newport Barracks and vicinity, where I found matters very loose. I am in hopes I shall have everything in fine working order in a day or two.

I am, most respectfully, your obedient servant,

F. B. SPINOLA.

Abstract from Tri-monthly Return of the Department of Virginia (Seventh Army Corps),
Maj. Gen. John A. Dix commanding, for May 31, 1863 (headquarters Fort Monroe, Va.).

Command.	Present for duty.		Aggregate present.	Aggregate present and absent.	Aggregate last return.	Pieces of field artillery.	Present for duty equipped.					
							Infantry.		Cavalry.		Artillery.	
	Officers.	Men.					Officers.	Men.	Officers.	Men.	Officers.	Men.
Headquarters Department, Maj. Gen. John A. Dix.	17	......	17	17	17	....	......	......	....	......	....	......
Fort Monroe, Col. S. M. Alford.	15	432	582	663	698	....	15	432	....	......	....	......
Camp Hamilton, Maj. J. A. Darling.	15	497	594	623	611	....	......	...	3	74	15	394
Norfolk, Brig. Gen. E. L. Viele.	120	2,172	2,546	2,692	2,694	6	102	1,975	2	54	5	132
Suffolk, Maj. Gen. John J. Peck.	966	18,068	22,386	26,821	27,724	100	849	15,773	76	1,391	30	1,326
Yorktown, Maj. Gen. E. D. Keyes.	295	5,050	5,996	6,555	6,563	30	238	3,668	3	902	13	448
West Point, Brig. Gen. G. H. Gordon.	217	4,533	5,351	6,277	6,299	...	196	4,121	6	93	8	282
Grand total..............	1,645	30,752	37,172	43,348	44,606	136	1,400	25,969	12	2,514	77	2,582

Organization of troops in the Department of Virginia, Maj. Gen. John A. Dix, U. S. Army, commanding, May 31, 1863.

FOURTH ARMY CORPS.

Maj. Gen. ERASMUS D. KEYES.

FIRST DIVISION (Yorktown).

Advance Brigade.

Col. R. M. WEST.

139th New York, Col. Anthony Conk.
6th New York Cavalry (battalion), Maj.
   W. P. Hall.
178th Pennsylvania, Col. James Johnson.
5th Pennsylvania Cavalry, Lieut. Col.
   William Lewis.

King's Brigade.

Brig. Gen. RUFUS KING.

4th Delaware, Col. A. H. Grimshaw.
168th New York, Col. William R. Brown.
169th Pennsylvania, Col. Lewis W.
   Smith.
179th Pennsylvania, Col. William H.
   Blair.

SECOND DIVISION (West Point).

Brig. Gen. GEORGE H. GORDON.

First Brigade.

Col. WILLIAM GURNEY.

127th New York, Lieut. Col. S. L. Woodford.
142d New York, Col. N. M. Curtis.
143d New York, Col Horace Boughton.
144th New York, Lieut. Col. David E.
   Gregory.

Second Brigade.

Col. BURR PORTER.

22d Connecticut, Col. George S. Burnham.
40th Massachusetts, Maj. Joseph M. Day.
141st New York, Lieut. Col. William K.
   Logie.

Artillery.

2d Wisconsin Battery, Capt. Charles Beger.
4th Wisconsin Battery, Capt. John F. Vallee.

RESERVE ARTILLERY (Yorktown).

Capt. JAMES MCKNIGHT.

1st New York, Batteries F and H, Capts. Willliam R. Wilson and Charles E. Mink.
8th New York Battery, Capt. Butler Fitch.
1st Pennsylvania, Batteries E and H,* Capts. T. G. Orwig and Andrew Fagan.
5th U. S., Battery M, Capt. James McKnight.

UNASSIGNED INFANTRY.

172d Pennsylvania, Lieut. Col. James A. Johnson.

SEVENTH ARMY CORPS.

Maj. Gen. JOHN A. DIX.

PECK'S DIVISION (Suffolk).

Brig. Gen. MICHAEL CORCORAN.†

First Brigade.

Brig. Gen. H. D. TERRY.

26th Michigan, Col. J. S. Farrar.
1st New York Battalion Sharpshooters,
   Capt. Joseph S. Arnold.
130th New York, Col. Alfred Gibbs.
152d New York, Col. Alonzo Ferguson.
167th Pennsylvania, Col. J. D. Davis.
11th Rhode Island, Col. Geo. E. Church.

Second Brigade.

Col. R. S. FOSTER.

13th Indiana, Lieut. Col. C. J. Dobbs.
112th New York, Col. J. C. Drake.
169th New York, Lieut. Col. John Mc-
   Conihe.
165th Pennsylvania, Col. C. H. Buchler.
166th Pennsylvania, Col. A. J. Fulton.

---

* One section of Battery E with West's brigade and another at West Point.
† Maj. Gen. John J. Peck commanding the post of Suffolk.

Third Brigade.

Col. MATHEW MURPHY.

10th New Jersey, Colonel Ryerson.
·   69th New York, Lieutenant Colonel Reid.
155th New York, Colonel McEvily.
164th New York, Colonel McMahon.
170th New York, Colonel McIvor.

GETTY'S DIVISION (Suffolk).

Brig. Gen. GEORGE W. GETTY.

First Brigade.	*Third Brigade.*
Col. W. R. PEASE.	**Col. A. H. DUTTON.**
25th New Jersey, Col. Andrew Derrom.	21st Connecticut, Lieut. Col. T. F. Burpee.
89th New York, Lieut.Col.T. L. England.	10th New Hampshire,* Colonel Donohoe.
103d New York, Col. William Heine.	13th New Hampshire, Col. A. F. Stevens.
117th New York, Lieut. Col. A. White.	4th Rhode Island, Lieut. Col. M. P. Buffum.
Second Brigade.	*Reserve Brigade.*
Brig. Gen. EDWARD HARLAND.	Brig. Gen. I. J. WISTAR.
8th Connecticut, Col. John E. Ward.	99th New York, Col. D. W. Wardrop.
11th Connecticut, Col. G. A. Stedman.	118th New York, Lieut. Col. O. Keese, jr.
15th Connecticut, Col. C. L. Upham.	9th Vermont, Lieut. Col. E. H. Ripley.
16th Connecticut, Col. Francis Beach.	19th Wisconsin, Col. H. T. Sanders.

Artillery.

1st Pennsylvania, Battery A, Capt. John G. Simpson.
5th U. S., Battery A, Lieut. James Gilliss.

UNASSIGNED (Suffolk).

Cavalry.

1st New York Mounted Rifles, Col. B. F. Onderdonk.
11th Pennsylvania,† Col. S. P. Spear.

Artillery.

Capt. F. M. FOLLETT.

1st Delaware Battery, Capt. B. Nields.
7th Massachusetts Battery, Capt. P. A. Davis.
16th New York Battery, Capt. F. L. Hiller.
19th New York Battery, Capt. W. H. Stahl.
3d Pennsylvania Heavy Artillery (2d battalion), Capt. J. S. Stevenson.
4th U. S., Battery D, Capt. F. M. Follett.
4th U. S., Battery L, Lieut. H. C. Hasbrouck.

NORFOLK, VA.

Brig. Gen. EGBERT L. VIELE.

148th New York, Col. William Johnson.
173d Pennsylvania, Col. Daniel Nagle.
177th Pennsylvania, Col. G. B. Wiestling.
 11th Pennsylvania Cavalry (Company F),Capt. B. B. Mitchell.
 7th New York Battery, Capt. P. C. Regan.

---

* Transferred from First Brigade.   † Two companies on detached service.

FORT MONROE.

Col. S. M. ALFORD.

3d New York, Col. S. M. Alford.

CAMP HAMILTON.

Maj. JOHN A. DARLING.

3d Pennsylvania Artillery (1st battalion), Maj. John A Darling.
11th Pennsylvania Cavalry (one company).

Abstract from Tri-monthly Return of the Eighteenth Army Corps, Department of North Carolina, Maj. Gen. John G. Foster, U. S. Army, commanding, for May 31, 1863.

Command.	Present for duty.		Aggregate present.	Aggregate present and absent.
	Officers.	Men.		
General staff	21	....	21	21
Palmer's division	227	4,708	6,349	7,718
Jourdan's brigade	79	1,605	2,155	3,140
Lee's brigade	67	1,104	1,405	1,839
Mix's cavalry brigade	18	319	378	859
Artillery	41	1,103	1,306	1,721
Total at New Berne	453	8,839	11,614	15,298
District of Beaufort	83	1,718	2,353	3,041
District of the Albemarle	121	1,567	1,892	2,259
District of the Pamlico	137	2,781	3,318	3,619
Detached (Department of the South)	......	....	....	10,065
Grand total	794	14,905	19,177	34,300

Organization of the Eighteenth Army Corps, Department of North Carolina, Maj. Gen. John G. Foster, U. S. Army, commanding, May 31, 1863. *

FIRST DIVISION (New Berne).

Brig. Gen. INNIS N. PALMER. †

First Brigade.†	Second Brigade.†
Col. T. J. C. AMORY.	Col. HORACE C. LEE.
17th Massachusetts, Maj. Jones Frankle.	5th Massachusetts, Col. George H. Peirson.
43d Massachusetts, Lieut. Col. John C. Whiton.	25th Massachusetts, Col. Josiah Pickett.
45th Massachusetts, Col. Charles R. Codman.	27th Massachusetts, Maj. W. G. Bartholomew.
51st Massachusetts, Col. A. B. R. Sprague.	46th Massachusetts, Col. William S. Shurtleff.

---

* According to corps return for the month of May, 1863, discrepancies between that return and those of the subordinate commands for same period noted. The names of regimental and battalion commanders taken from subordinate returns.

† The division return reports Colonel Amory commanding the Division, Col. C. L. Holbrook commanding First Brigade, and Col. George H. Peirson commanding the Second Brigade.

INDEPENDENT BRIGADES, ETC. (New Berne).

Jourdan's Brigade.

Col. JAMES JOURDAN.

3d Massachusetts, Col. S. P. Richmond.
8th Massachusetts, Col. F. J. Coffin.
158th New York, Lieut. Col. W. H. Mc-
Nary.
58th Pennsylvania, Lieut. Col. C. B.
Curtiss.

Artillery.

3d New York, Maj. T. J. Kennedy.
1st Rhode Island, Battery F, Capt. James
Belger.

Lee's Brigade.

Col. FRANCIS L. LEE.

44th Massachusetts, Col. Francis L. Lee.
92d New York, Capt. T. A. Merriman.
5th Rhode Island, Col. Henry T. Sisson

Cavalry.

Col. S. H. MIX.

3d New York, Lieut. Col. G. W. Lewis.
12th New York, Lieut. Col. P. G. Vought.
23d New York Battalion, Capt. Emory
Cummings.

Outpost.

132d New York, Col. P. J. Claassen.

DISTRICT OF THE ALBEMARLE. *

Brig. Gen. HENRY W. WESSELLS.

85th New York, Col. J. S. Belknap.
96th New York, Col. E. M. Cullen.
101st Pennsylvania, Col. David B. Morris.
103d Pennsylvania, Lieut. Col. W. C. Maxwell.
  8th Massachusetts (three companies), Capt. F. E. Porter.
  1st North Carolina (Union), Company L, Lieut. G. W. Graham.
  3d New York Cavalry, Company D, Capt. H. W. Brown.
24th New York Battery, Capt. J. E. Lee.

DISTRICT OF BEAUFORT.

Brig. Gen. HENRY M. NAGLEE.†

23d Massachusetts, Col. A. Elwell.
  9th New Jersey, Col. A. Zabriskie.
81st New York, Maj. D. B. White.
98th New York, Lieut. Col. F. F. Wead.
  3d New York Cavalry, Companies B and C.
  1st U. S. Artillery, Battery C.

DISTRICT OF THE PAMLICO.‡

Brig. Gen. HENRY PRINCE.

158th Pennsylvania, Col. D. B. McKibbin.
168th Pennsylvania, Col. Joseph Jack.
171st Pennsylvania, Col. E. Bierer.
175th Pennsylvania, Col. S. A. Dyer.
  1st North Carolina (Union), Lieut. Col. J. M. McChesney.
  5th Massachusetts, Company G, Capt. W. T. Grammer.
  3d New York Cavalry (two companies), Capt G. F. Jocknick.
  1st North Carolina Artillery (Union), Company A.
23d New York Battery, Capt. A. Ransom.

---

*Organized May 3, 1863. According to district return the Eighty-fifth and Ninety-
sixth New York and the One hundred and first and One hundred and third Pennsylvania constituted a brigade, under Col. T. F. Lehmann.
†According to district return Brig. Gen. F. B. Spinola was in command, and he was
assigned to that command May 29, 1863. The district return reports the infantry as
brigaded under Colonel De Forest.
‡On district return the Pennsylvania regiments appear as the "Keystone Brigade,"
under Col. D. B. McKibbin.

DETACHED. *

10th Connecticut, Col. John L. Otis.
11th Maine, Col. H. M. Plaisted.
24th Massachusetts, Col. F. A. Osborn.
39th Illinois, Col. Thomas O. Osborn.
56th New York, Col. Charles H. Van Wyck.
100th New York, Col. George B. Dandy.
—— New York Battalion.
62d Ohio, Col. Francis B. Pond.
67th Ohio, Col. Alvin C. Voris.
52d Pennsylvania, Col. J. C. Dodge, jr.
85th Pennsylvania, Col. Joshua B. Howell.
104th Pennsylvania, Lieut. Col. T. D. Hart.
174th Pennsylvania, Col. John Nyce.
176th Pennsylvania, Col. A. A. Lechler.

UNITED STATES FLAG-SHIP MINNESOTA,
Off Newport News, June 1, 1863.

Maj. Gen. JOHN A. DIX, U. S. A.,
   Comdg. Seventh Army Corps, Fortress Monroe, Va.:

GENERAL: I had the honor verbally to inform you, shortly after the receipt of my instructions in the matter, which were dated January 3, that I was prohibited from admitting supplies within this blockade for foreign men-of-war, themselves allowed here only by courtesy, and to afford such vessels when they were in distress for coal with only enough to enable them to get to Annapolis, where their wants could be satisfied. I availed myself of the opportunity when Commander Thrupp, R. N., commanding H. M. S. Desperate, was here yesterday morning to communicate this information to him, and to tell him that the admission of a collier for H. M. S. Rinaldo, on the 19th ultimo, during my recent absence, was allowed by the officer left in command in ignorance of my order on the subject. In the course of conversation he informed me that he had been in the habit of getting coal from Colonel Thomas, quartermaster of this post, and that Colonel Thomas in such cases sent for more coal to supply the vacancy thus occasioned, apparently not being informed of the requirement of the blockade in this respect.

I would respectfully observe that it is a violation of the blockade (under my instructions from the Department for its preservation) to turn over to foreign men-of-war supplies of any kind which have been introduced within its lines for the United States troops, and I would suggest that instructions be issued to prevent such violation in future.

I have the honor to be, general, very respectfully, yours,
                                                S. P. LEE,
   Actg. Rear-Admiral, Comdg. N. Atlantic Blockading Squadron.

FORT MONROE, VA., *June* 2, 1863—3.30 p. m.
                                (Received 4.30 p. m.)

Maj. Gen. H. W. HALLECK,
   General-in-Chief :

I have just received the following dispatch from General Peck. Will you please communicate it to General Hooker?

I have a man who left Richmond last week. He says Pickett's division passed through, the day before he left, for Fredericksburg. It had been there and partici-

---

* For service in Department of the South.

pated in the funeral of Jackson.　General Elzey commands in the city.　Citizens and soldiers talk of Lee's moving into Maryland with 85,000 men.　Says the most of Longstreet's troops that left Blackwater stopped about Richmond in consequence of the alarm resulting from the raids.　General Ewell made lieutenant-general.

> JOHN A. DIX,
> *Major-General.*

Copy of this has been sent to Major-General Hooker.

> THOS. T. ECKERT,
> *Major, &c.*

YORKTOWN, VA., *June* 2, 1863—12.30 p. m.

Major-General HOOKER,
　Headquarters Army of the Potomac:

It seems apparent from the rumors that reached me that a movement of rebel troops is going on from south to north, and that the idea prevails over the lines that an invasion of Maryland and Pennsylvania is soon to be made.　I have heard nothing definite, but all the rumors concur to produce the impression stated.

> E. D. KEYES,
> *Major-General.*

(Copy to General Halleck.)

HDQRS. DEPT. OF VIRGINIA, SEVENTH ARMY CORPS,
Fort Monroe, Va., June 2, 1863.

Actg. Rear-Admiral S. P. LEE,
　Commanding North Atlantic Blockading Squadron:

ADMIRAL: When I received your letter of the 23d of April advising me that you considered the President's proclamation of the 31st March as superseding his order of the 11th November last I had no information on the subject to warrant me in giving it a definite answer.　I have recently, and in several instances, seen letters from the Treasury Department informing individuals in reply to inquiries made by them that the whole matter of trade with Norfolk was still under my control by virtue of the order referred to.　I would respectfully suggest under these circumstances that you ascertain from the President himself, through the Navy Department, whether the order is in force, unless you are satisfied with the view taken by the Treasury Department, which is constantly granting permits on my certificates as heretofore.

I have the honor to be, very respectfully, your obedient servant,

> JOHN A. DIX,
> *Major-General.*

HDQRS. DEPT. OF VIRGINIA, SEVENTH ARMY CORPS,
Fort Monroe, Va., June 2, 1863.

Capt. C. B. WILDER,
　Asst. Quartermaster and Superintendent of Contrabands:

The major-general commanding directs me to acknowledge the receipt of your communication of this date relating to certain contra bands awaiting transportation to Norfolk, &c., and in reply to state that he has referred so much of said communication as relates to the said contrabands to Lieutenant-Colonel Thomas, chief quartermaster, for report thereon.

As to the definition of your powers and duties under your instructions from the War Department, dated January 28, 1863, I am also requested to state that colored persons (contrabands or otherwise) who are employed and paid by the several chiefs of the staff departments as laborers are entirely under the control of the said chiefs of departments, and that no passes to these persons can be given by you except as may be authorized by the said chiefs of departments; that passes to others (contrabands or colored vagrants) not employed as mentioned above may be given by you to Hampton, Fox Hill, and other places within the lines this side of Yorktown, but cannot be given by you either to come inside Fort Monroe or any other military post, or to go on board public transports from one place to another in this department, or to go out of the department, and that all passes for such purposes must be submitted to and receive the indorsement of the proper military authority before they can be used or become valid.

I am, very respectfully, your obedient servant,

D. T. VAN BUREN,
Assistant Adjutant-General.

———

FORT MONROE, VA.,
June 3, 1863—2 p. m.

Maj. Gen. H. W. HALLECK,
General-in-Chief :

From all that can be gathered a good many conscripts have gone to General Lee. Beauregard's troops have not gone in that direction. They have probably gone to Vicksburg, as well as the troops from Georgia. Longstreet was at Petersburg last week. It is reported to-day that he dined at South Quay, below Franklin, on the Blackwater, yesterday.

JOHN A. DIX,
Major-General, Commanding.

———

SPECIAL ORDERS, } HDQRS. OF THE ARMY, ADJT. GEN.'S OFFICE,
   No. 249.   }   *Washington, June* 3, 1863.

*   *   *   *   *   *   *

II. Brig. Gen. Hector Tyndale, U. S. Volunteers, will report for duty to Maj. Gen. John A. Dix, U. S. Volunteers, commanding Department of Virginia.

*   *   *   *   *   *   *

By command of Major-General Halleck :

E. D. TOWNSEND,
Assistant Adjutant-General.

———

UNITED STATES FLAG-SHIP MINNESOTA,
Off Newport News, June 3, 1863.

Maj. Gen. JOHN A. DIX, U. S. A.,
Comdg. Seventh Army Corps, Fortress Monroe, Va. :

GENERAL : I have received your letter of yesterday regarding permits for Norfolk trade, and have referred the case to the Navy Department with your suggestions.

I would be much obliged to you if you would cause me to be advised by telegraph or otherwise, as most convenient, when opportunities occur for sending mails, dispatches, or passengers by the quartermaster's boats from Fortress Monroe to New Berne or Beaufort. I am often much embarrassed for means of communicating with this squadron on the coast off Wilmington and in the Sounds of North Carolina, and not unfrequently steamers leave for the above-mentioned ports before I can avail myself of the opportunities they afford.

I beg leave to acknowledge the willingness and courtesy with which dispatches, passengers, and sometimes stores have been taken and delivered for the Navy by the army transports.

I have the honor to be, general, very respectfully, yours,

S. P. LEE,
Actg. Rear-Admiral, Comdg. N. Atlantic Blockading Squadron.

UNITED STATES FLAG-SHIP MINNESOTA,
Off Newport News, June 13, 1863.

Maj. Gen. JOHN A. DIX, U. S. A.,
Comdg. Seventh Army Corps, Fortress Monroe, Va.:

GENERAL : In reply to your letter of June 2 on the supposed superseding of the President's order of November 11, 1862, by the President's proclamation of March 31, 1863, with respect to Norfolk trade, I beg to inform you that according to your suggestion I referred the matter to the Department on the 3d, and in reply, under date of the 9th, received this morning, I am instructed that the order of November 11, 1862, is not considered suspended. I have instructed the guard vessels accordingly.

I have the honor to be, general, very respectfully, yours,

S. P. LEE,
Actg. Rear-Admiral, Comdg. N. Atlantic Blockading Squadron.

CONFEDERATE CORRESPONDENCE, ETC.

PETERSBURG, VA., *August* 28, 1862.

General S. COOPER :

The Federal fleet (nine gunboats) which came up the river yesterday has gone down James River to its out-anchorage off Westover and come to. No Federal vessels in James River above that point (Westover). The fleet landed a small force at City Point last night; also a small party on the Appomattox River in order to flank one of my signal stations. They were disappointed in their object. The post, not being armed, fell back. Is there no possible means of arming the signal corps, at least with revolvers? I understand the Navy Department has a number.

Your obedient servant,

J. F. MILLIGAN,
Captain, &c.

PETERSBURG, VA., *August* 29, 1862.

General S. COOPER,
Adjutant [and Inspector]-General :

The Federal fleet off Berkley (nineteen gunboats, including the monitor Galena) got under way this morning at 10 a. m. and stood down the river. At 12 m. one of my signal men telegraphed from Berkley that the fleet [was out] of sight from that point, heading down the river.

J. F. MILLIGAN.

GENERAL ORDERS, }   HEADQUARTERS,
    No. 1.   }   *Richmond, Va., August 30, 1862.*

I. By direction of the War Department Maj. Gen. G. W. Smith assumes command of the defenses of Richmond and its approaches.

II. The officers whose names are herein announced constitute the staff: Maj. Samuel W. Melton, assistant adjutant-general; Surg. E. S. Gaillard, medical director; Maj. A. F. Cone, chief quartermaster; Maj. B. McKennie, assistant quartermaster; Maj. S. B. French, chief commissary; Maj. R. F. Beckham, ordnance officer; Lieut. James Howard, C. S. Artillery, aide-de-camp.

                              G. W. SMITH,
                                  Major-General.

THREE MILES FROM TUNSTALL'S STATION,
        Cross-Roads, New Kent, August 30, 1862.

Maj. SAMUEL W. MELTON:

MAJOR: The enemy advanced to-day to New Kent Court-House and to Forge Mill, on the Diascund road. At the latter place 150 cavalry reported. My scouts were fired upon by 40 or 50 men just this side of New Kent Court-House. New Kent is about 9 miles from me, and Forge Mill about 7 or 8 miles. I send scouts out again to-night. I understand that the Yankees are about leaving Williamsburg, and these parties may be assuring their rear.

Very respectfully, your obedient servant,
                              W. P. SHINGLER,
                                  Lieutenant-Colonel, &c.

                              AUGUST 31—8.30 p. m.

GENERAL: The above note has just been received. I expect some thing more definite by to-morrow morning.

Yours, respectfully,

                                      G. W. S.

                              HEADQUARTERS,
            Petersburg, Va., September 8, 1862.

Hon. GEORGE W. RANDOLPH,
        Secretary of War :

SIR: In pursuance to your instructions by indorsement on back of a letter of John Goode, jr., I have the honor to report that the complaints made by owners of negroes at work here on the defenses are founded on misrepresentations. The negroes are well taken care of.

2d. The work is in the main part completed from the Appomattox River to near where it will cross the Jerusalem road. About four-fifths of the work is therefore finished.

3d. Could the engineer department procure, say, 150 negroes, these might be discharged on Saturday next, notwithstanding.

4th. That General Hill promised with his force to obstruct the Roanoke River, because it can be done by the engineer force and such as I can procure voluntarily in that section of country.

Very respectfully, your obedient servant,
                              S. G. FRENCH,
                                  Brigadier-General.

SPECIAL ORDERS, } ADJT. AND INSPECTOR GENERAL'S OFFICE,
   No. 211.   }   *Richmond, Va., September 9, 1862.*

*   *   *   *   *   *

XXV. Brig. Gen. G. J. Rains will turn over his submarine defenses in James River to Lieut. Hunter Davidson, C. S. Navy.

*   *   *   *   *   *

By command of Secretary of War:

JNO. WITHERS,
Assistant Adjutant-General.

ENGINEER BUREAU,
Richmond, Va., September 10, 1862.

Col. J. F. GILMER,
   Chief Engineer Department of Northern Virginia:

COLONEL: Inclosed I send you a communication* from the Secretary of War, directing the construction of a passage-way through the obstructions for the iron-clad steamer Richmond. I inclose you also a tracing of a drawing in my possession, showing the two upper lines of obstructions, with depths of water at ebb-tide. I have studied the question with some care, and think the opening, if made, should be on the north side of the river as near the bank as possible. The gateway may be arranged as shown below, although further study may greatly improve the idea:†

The bottom of the passage-way would of course have to be kept leveled with *pierres perdues,* so that the lighter when sunk would come to the low-water level. There is some difference of opinion as to the propriety of making the passage-way, and it would certainly seem of doubtful policy to send below an iron-clad vessel with an inferior single-acting engine, at least if we are to form any judgment from recent disasters. The whole question is now naturally referred to you as chief engineer of the Department of Northern Virginia. It would seem an easy matter to raise the crib of the second line of obstructions, which one is too low, to the level of low water. It is here mentioned as a matter of importance.

Very respectfully, &c.,

ALFRED L. RIVES,
Acting Chief of Engineer Bureau.

HEADQUARTERS,
Richmond, Va., September 15, 1862.

Major-General S. G. FRENCH,
   Commanding, &c., Petersburg, Va.:

GENERAL: Your letter of yesterday was received at 12 m. to-day. I handed it to the Secretary, with the remark that unless he objected I would send the regiments. He told me to use my own discretion, and handed me a letter which he received a few moments before from ——. [Original torn.] I inclose the letter* with this. Colonel Daniel takes with him two of his best regiments and a fine battery. If the Second North Carolina Cavalry will be of use to you in this expedition suspend the order sending them forward until after you get back. I have directed

---

* Not found.   † Drawing omitted.

Colonel Daniel to return with his command as soon as the expedition is over. Strike the hardest blow you can. Communicate with me as often as practicable.

With full confidence in your judgment, and wishing you every success, I remain yours, truly,

G. W. SMITH,
Major-General, Commanding.

HEADQUARTERS,
Wakefield, Va., September 17, 1862.

General S. G. FRENCH:

GENERAL: I fear very much that unless the business of building the bridge and repairing the railroad be pushed our expedition will be a very discreditable failure to us all. Capt. [Charles H.] Dimmock has returned to Petersburg without my seeing him, so I do not know what arrangement he has made; but there are no materials whatever here—no timber, no tools, and no car-logs to haul the timber. The bridge can best be built somewhere on the railroad, and when this is finished transported down to Zuni; but if the enemy choose to they can prevent it until they are driven away. Whatever we are to do must be done quickly, or all our trouble will be in vain.

Very respectfully, your obedient servant,

J. J. PETTIGREW,
Brigadier-General.

P. S.—This was written before I received your note at night, but it may as well go.

WEDNESDAY NIGHT, [*September* 17, 1862.]

General S. G. FRENCH:

GENERAL: I have just received your note. You say nothing about Daniel, but I suppose your note to him gives all the requisite directions. I inclose a note from Ferebee just come in. The captain you saw in my tent said he thought some artillery had gone up by the river. Nevertheless I am surprised at the amount, for I was told that a lady arrived at Franklin with dates up to Monday, and said there were only six pieces. I shall order Burroughs to withdraw his pickets Saturday night and rendezvous his force at Isle of Wight Court-House early on Sunday morning, and proceed thence to the river opposite to Suffolk, upon the supposition that we are to advance Sunday unless you make a different disposition. Do send a courier to hunt up Lieutenant Iredell, my ordnance officer, and send him down here. I hope Morey will have forage collected for us at Franklin. I think it would be well to order down some extra surgeons. I am very poorly off in that line. Upon the strength of the eighteen pieces I inclose an order for the two iron 32s and a very good company. Moseley has not men enough in his command to justify more guns. If they are to come to me here it must be by rail, and I wish you would give an order for transportation. But I rather think they had better go by land, and if you agree with me please alter the inclosed order so as to make them report at Franklin instead of Wakefield and send it out to Moseley's camp.

Very truly, yours,

J. J. PETTIGREW,
Brigadier-General.

[Inclosure.]

HEADQUARTERS,
Franklin, Va., September 17, 1862—11 a. m.

Brig. Gen. J. J. PETTIGREW:

GENERAL: My bridge across the Blackwater will be completed with certainty in five hours. It will be strong enough to support the heaviest artillery. The damage to the village from the guns of the enemy on Monday last is of trifling importance—no damage in fact. The strength of the enemy at Suffolk on Monday last was 1,900 cavalry, five regiments of infantry, and eighteen pieces of artillery. This is reliable.

I am, general, most truly, yours,

D. D. FEREBEE,
Colonel, Commanding.

HEADQUARTERS BAINS' FARM,
Wakefield, Va., September 17, 1862.

Major-General FRENCH, *Commanding:*

GENERAL: I have the honor to acknowledge the receipt of yours of this date. I herewith inclose the letter of instructions to Colonel Owens, commanding Fifty-third Regiment North Carolina Infantry, whose regiment I wish to join me. The instructions in regard to the route I shall leave with you to give according to your suggestions.

Very respectfully, &c.,

JUNIUS DANIEL,
Colonel, Commanding Brigade.

COLERAIN, N. C., *September* 18, 1862.

Hon. ZEBULON B. VANCE, *Raleigh, N. C.:*

SIR: Some of the leading farmers and citizens of Bertie County had a consultation on the 15th instant in Windsor, it being Monday of superior court, for the purpose of making representations to Your Excellency in regard to the condition of affairs in this county and to ask some executive action in their behalf. Lewis Thompson, esq., was appointed to visit Raleigh and see you in person, but he not being able to go until about October 1, I was requested in the mean time to lay before you in writing the points agreed to be presented and the reasons which induced the gentlemen present to ask some action upon them.

This county is almost entirely surrounded by the waters of the Albemarle Sound and the Roanoke and Chowan Rivers, all of which are navigable to the largest of the enemy's steamers, while the Caskie River and Salmon Creek, running into the very heart of the county, are navigable to his steamers of highest draught. Upon these water-courses lie the main body of the excellent farming lands of the county, and several thousand slaves are upon these lands. The gunboats of the enemy are traversing these waters almost daily. Occasionally the enemy land a few troops at unexpected points, but so far have committed very little depredation. The military post at Plymouth is upon the very border of the county and is accessible by the water-courses above named. There is not a Confederate soldier here, and not the least show of protection extended to the citizens. They are completely at the mercy of the enemy and nothing but his clemency prevents their total ruin. The people are for the most part loyal to the Confederacy and have acted with surprising prudence and faithfulness. But how long is it prudent to suffer these people to depend entirely upon the enemy for safety and feel that they are neglected, if not abandoned, by their own Government? The greater part of the able-bodied men of the county have volunteered in companies raised in this and the adjoining counties and are now in the army. Some have been taken out by the conscript law, and the attempted execution of that law has driven many of not very reliable character to the enemy at Plymouth, and many more of little better character are in readiness to repair to Plymouth or to the gunboats if its further execution is attempted. The loyal citizens have more to dread from these deserters than from the regular enemy. By the census of 1860 it appears that there are 8,000 slaves in this county and only 6,000 whites. They have as yet lost comparatively few slaves, but it is with great difficulty that the few men left here, unsupported by a show of military force, are able to guard the avenues of escape and keep up efficient police regulations. If they should attempt to remove the slaves the most of them would run off at once, and any general attempt to remove them would produce an almost universal stampede, resulting in the loss of the negroes and endangering the lives of the few citizens. But if the removal could be effected, how could so large a number be fed elsewhere, and what would become of the property necessarily left behind? But as Southern men they take another view of the consequences of such a removal. If the slave-holders, being men of means, flee upon the approach of danger and leave the poorer classes, who are unable to move, and the families of soldiers in the army exposed not only to the enemy but to the gangs of runaway slaves, it will produce a state of things and of feeling much to be dreaded. Is it not the duty of the influential slave-holder to remain and to exert himself to preserve social order and to prevent an entire disruption of society? It is hoped that the enemy will soon be driven away, and these people are bearing up under their troubles sustained by that hope, feeling that they have been and still are neglected, but yet willing to believe that the best has been done that circumstances would allow. Several months spent in this state of constant danger and anxiety has enabled the thinking men of this county to see what was necessary to be done more clearly, perhaps, tnan can be seen by those at a distance, even in authority, who must judge from reports only.

They met in Windsor on the 15th instant and agreed to ask the influence of Your Excellency with the Confederate authorities to adopt the following measures and such others as may be deemed most expedient:

1st. That two companies of cavalry be quartered in Bertie County permanently, and they desire especially the two companies commanded by Captains Randolph and Eure, which are now somewhere on the Seaboard and Roanoke Railroad. They ask these two officers because they know them to be men of great discretion, having the entire confidence of the people of this section. They think a force under an indiscreet officer would be of more injury than benefit. For instance, should an officer exhibit any troops upon water-courses in sight of the enemy it would cause a shelling of the whole neighborhood, and if near any dwelling would insure its destruction. They deem the character of the officer sent in this emergency of the very greatest importance, and would prefer no force 'o one under an officer of doubtful judgment. With this cavalry to back them the citizens left could preserve order and prevent any great number of slaves from escaping. The very presence of such a force would intimidate the enemy and embolden the loyal citizens to speak and act with freedom and zeal. The loyal citizens of this county ought to have some support. The interest of the Confederacy in this section requires it.

2d. That the President be requested by Your Excellency to exercise the discretion vested in him by the late act of Congress to exempt this county from further execution of the conscript law. There are not now men enough in the county for efficient police duty, and any further attempt at executing the law instead of getting soldiers for our army would run recruits to the enemy, for the correct-minded men subject to the law have already gone to camp. The substantial men of the county dread to see the others made their enemies. If the conscript law is extended to forty-five years its execution would complete the ruin of this county.

3d. That no military order requiring slaves to work on fortifications or serve in the army be sent to this county. Its effect would be to make the slaves run off and very few could be obtained under the order, for it would be idle to attempt to hunt negroes in this section now.

But another reason why such an order should not be sent here, and why the counties bordering on the enemy's lines should be especially exempted by name, is this: If the Confederate authorities commence taking these exposed slaves, or any part of them, the enemy will then have a military excuse to take those that are left, and they will not be slow to do so. Mr. Thompson will be in Raleigh about October 1 to communicate verbally with Your Excellency upon this subject and to make more full and specific statements than can be well done within the limits of a letter.

I have written under the instructions of the meeting of Bertie gentlemen, as mentioned above, but allow me to add that for the most part I approve their recommendations and think it is the best that could be done under the circumstances. Perhaps so small a force as two companies might be in danger of being cut off by the enemy, but I think in an emergency the citizens would rally with such arms as they could get to repel an attack. If the Confederate authorities are not able to do something it might be well to authorize the raising of a State force to operate in this section. It could be done without difficulty under a proper officer, and would be efficient after awhile; but something ought to be done for this section of the State at once.

Allow me personally to assure you of my esteem and readiness to render you all the service in my power in any measures deemed best for the interests of the State.

Yours, most respectfully,

JOHN POOL.

———

HEADQUARTERS,
Richmond, Va., September 18, 1862.

Maj. Gen. S. G. FRENCH,
Commanding, &c. :

GENERAL : If you are not entirely satisfied that your force is ample, and that prompt and complete success can be attained, your movement should be suspended and the troops should promptly return to their original positions. A good deal of time has elapsed in preparing, and I am satisfied that the enemy are well informed of our intentions and that they are prepared. Besides, the indications are that they would avail themselves of any advantage they might gain and follow us up. They have reoccupied Williamsburg in force and are extending their lines again in this direction from that point. An attempt was made last night to burn the bridges over the river here. It is not wise at this time to bring on a doubtful conflict so far from our lines and so close to their strongholds. Unless you are certain of great advantages suspend your operations and let the greater part of the troops resume their former positions.

Respectfully and truly, yours,

G. W. SMITH,
Major-General, Commanding.

HEADQUARTERS DEPARTMENT OF NORTH CAROLINA,
Richmond, Va., September 18, 1862.

Maj. Gen. S. G. FRENCH:

Your letter of yesterday is received. If you are not entirely satisfied that you have ample means for accomplishing the object promptly and successfully you had better suspend the movement. I have already furnished you more than could well be spared. There are indications that the enemy has notice of our intentions and is prepared to meet us, and also to take advantage of the fact that the troops are absent from the defenses of this city.

G. W. SMITH,
Major-General, Commanding.

GENERAL ORDERS, ⎰ ADJT. AND INSPECTOR GENERAL'S OFFICE,
No. 69.   ⎱   *Richmond, Va., September* 19, 1862.

*   *   *   *   *   *   *

III. Hereafter the command of Maj. Gen. G. W. Smith will embrace that part of the country lying south of the line of operations under General R. E. Lee, including the Department of North Carolina. All commanders within these geographical limits will report to and receive their orders from Major-General Smith.

*   *   *   *   *   *   *

By order:

S. COOPER,
Adjutant and Inspector General.

SEPTEMBER 19, 1862.

I have information from Suffolk as late as Wednesday afternoon. The force is two full regiments and three skeleton regiments of infantry numbering 3,800, 1,900 cavalry, and six pieces of artillery. The Yankee merchants are packing up their goods preparatory to a move. Yankee cavalry to the number of 140 now encamped in 5 miles of us to watch our movements. The bridge complete.

D. D. FEREBEE,
Colonel, Commanding.

HEADQUARTERS,
Richmond, Va., September 27, 1862.

Maj. Gen. S. G. FRENCH,
Comdg. Dept. of North Carolina, Petersburg, Va.:

GENERAL: Your report of movements in the direction of Suffolk and the causes which induced you to suspend operations was duly received. You acted wisely in returning under the circumstances as developed; there was too great doubt of success to justify an engagement in that quarter at this time.

I received your note of the 23d, inclosing pencil report of agent from Suffolk. It seems to have been delivered to the Secretary of War, and by him handed to General Magruder to be given to me. Magruder did not meet me, and forgot the note. Not having heard from you since, I infer that the report has not been confirmed. I think it important that you should as far as [practicable] and consistent with other duties and necessities hold your forces in North Carolina in condition and position to move promptly in this direction at any and all times. General Lee is far off, and we may be called upon suddenly without aid from him to repel an attack in force. The Secretary of War has several times suggested the withdrawal of Major Burroughs' companies of cavalry. He intends uniting [them] with others upon this side and forming a regiment. I request that you at the earliest moment have these Virginia companies under Major Burroughs relieved by other cavalry and ordered to report to Major Melton, adjutant-general of my command, in this city. We have found here large numbers of men left behind, sick or unfit to march, in the different camps at the time General Lee's forces left. These men have been collected and sent forward to their commands. I would be glad if any such remain in your vicinity to have you collect and organize them in detachments, under control of officers and non-commissioned officers, and send them forward by the cars. On arriving here they will be taken charge of by Colonel Walker's guard, which is under General [Winder], and dispatched to Winchester.

Large quantities of arms, clothing, tents, * * * the camps in this vicinity, and I presume something of the same kind, but to a less extent, occurred near Petersburg; if so, have measures taken to remedy the evil. I hope that you are getting the detached companies and irregular forces into satisfactory shape.

Have you heard from Col. J. O. Long, sent to inspect Partisan Rangers in Western North Carolina?

Respectfully and truly, yours,

G. W. SMITH,
Major-General.

I have just received your note of this morning since writing the above.

STATE OF NORTH CAROLINA, EXECUTIVE DEPARTMENT,
Raleigh, N. C., September 28, 1862.

General GUSTAVUS W. SMITH,
Commanding Department of North Carolina:

GENERAL: I learn that the troops (cavalry) in Eastern North Carolina are to be brigaded, which is proper enough; but the very first order calls all of them to Garysburg, leaving the whole coast of North

Carolina without protection. Without the protection of the cavalry the finest provision region in the State can be desolated by the enemy in a few days. It is not to be thought of for a moment, and I earnestly protest against it. If it is not the intention of the President to protect us we must protect ourselves. Major Evans will speak more particularly.

Respectfully, your obedient servant,

Z. B. VANCE.

EXECUTIVE OFFICE,
Richmond, Va., September 29, 1862.

Col. J. R. DAVIS,
 Aide-de-Camp, Richmond, Va.:

COLONEL: You will proceed to Petersburg, Va., and confer with General French respecting the general condition of his command, and especially as to the number, organization, and efficiency of the partisan troops serving, or being proposed for service, in that district; also as to the number, position, and movements of the enemy in the country on the south side of the James River and eastern coast of North Carolina. Should it be requisite you will visit the encampments of the partisans and the camp of instruction near to Raleigh; but it is desired that you should return by or before Thursday next.

Very respectfully, yours,

JEFFERSON DAVIS.

Abstract from Return of the Department South of James River, commanded by Brig. Gen. S. G. French, for September, 1862.

Command.	Present for duty.		Aggregate present.	Aggregate present and absent.	Horses serviceable.	Horses unserviceable.	Artillery.	
	Officers.	Men.					Heavy.	Field.
Petersburg, Va.:								
Brig. Gen. J. J. Pettigrew, brigade	158	3,021	3,821	4,519	....	..	......	...
Capt. J. F. Milligan, Signal Corps	4	110	122	125	....	....	......	..
Capt. S. T. Wright, artillery	1	39	49	123	43	2	......	1?
District of North Carolina, Brig. Gen. J. G. Martin.	177	2,854	3,721	4,327	....	...	...	...
Franklin, Va., Col. J. K. Marshall, two regiments and two sections of artillery.	50	918	1,110	1,390	....	...		
Port Walthall, Captain Sturdivant, artillery	3	64	79	96	56	....	.....	
Fort Clifton, Capt. J. C. Coit, infantry and artillery.	8	238	285	343	96	1	.....	
Richmond turnpike, Captain Murchison, cavalry..	2	30	96	105	102	3	.....	
Prince George Court-House, Capt. D. Bell, cavalry.	4	66	79	81	....	...		
Total	407	7,340	9,362	11,109	297	6	......	2?
Wilmington, N. C., Brig. Gen. G. J. Rains, District of the Cape Fear.	222	3,559	4,921	5,595	252	16	55	1?
Grand total	629	10,899	14,283	16,704	549	22	55	3?

Abstract from Field Return of troops commanded by Maj. Gen. G. W. Smith, October 1, 1862 (headquarters, Richmond, Va.).

Commands.	Present for duty.		Effective total.	Aggregate present.	Aggregate present and absent.
	Officers.	Men.			
Maj. Gen. S. G. French, commanding:					
Troops in North Carolina (Wilmington and Kinston).....	420	7,117	7,515	9,265	10,756
Troops in Virginia (Petersburg)......................	242	4,498	4,686	5,569	6,657
Brig. Gen. H. A. Wise's brigade, Chaffin's farm	111	1,660	1,765	2,214	2,780
Col. T. J. Page, Chaffin's Bluff............................	23	265	329	413	481
Brig. Gen. J. Daniel's brigade, near Drewry's Bluff	191	2,908	3,044	3,893	4,922
Lieut. Col. W. P. Shingler's cavalry, picketing the Peninsula.	11	147	168	223	261
Richmond defenses, light and heavy batteries around Richmond.	89	1,693	1,825	2,238	2,983
Near Brook Run, on Brook turnpike:					
54th Regiment North Carolina State Troops.............	27	377	405	502	764
57th Regiment North Carolina State Troops.............	30	591	602	767	978
59th Regiment Georgia Volunteers......................	28	622	638	789	991
42d Regiment Mississippi Volunteers....................	33	443	470	633	741
Brigadier-General Winder, Department of Henrico (includes Camp Lee, city guard, &c.)	40	1,742	1,751	2,097	2,522
Colonel Chambliss, on Rappahannock:					
61st Regiment Virginia Volunteers....................	17	393	408	454	741
13th Regiment Virginia Cavalry *	......	......	......	......	......
2d Regiment North Carolina Cavalry *	......	......	......	......	......
Capt. S. S. Lee, C. S. Navy, Drewry's Bluff*................	......	......	......	......	......
Grand total...	1,262	22,456	23,606	29,057	35,577

* No report received.

RICHMOND, VA., *October* 1, 1862.

General JONES, *Winchester, Va.:*

Inform General Lee that a fleet of one hundred and twenty-five to one hundred and thirty transports moved up toward Alexandria on the 29th ultimo; that the enemy had blown up the fortifications at Evansport and Cock Pit Point; that 300 cavalry occupied Warrenton on the same day, paroled the sick and wounded and left at night; that two regiments of infantry, one of cavalry, and a battery of four pieces are moving toward Warrenton and the Rappahannock. These are all the facts. It is reported that Sigel on the 27th ultimo moved on Centreville with 30,000 men, mostly new regiments (destination Gordonsville), and that a large force was to advance immediately toward Richmond via Fredericksburg. We have pretty reliable information that the force at Suffolk has been increased to about 18,000 men.

G. W. SMITH,
Major-General.

HDQRS., *Richmond, Va., October* 2, 1862.

Maj. Gen. S. G. FRENCH,
Comdg. Department of North Carolina, Petersburg, Va.:

GENERAL: Yours of yesterday is received. I think it advisable to order up the two regiments proposed, *i. e.*, one from Wilmington and one from Kinston, immediately. I would then feel that we had two brigades immediately available for any point, at the same time leaving a respectable force at Petersburg, at Drewry's Bluff, and at Chaffin's Bluff.   The accumulation of force at Suffolk is such that in case they should land below the obstructions on James River a force from their large fleet of transports, we would need all the available force from North Carolina.   Please have the two regiments that will be left at each of the points named—Wilmington and Kinston—ready to move whenever called upon.   In case the enemy makes a very strong demonstration upon Gordonsville and General Lee is not in position to meet it, I shall have to move some of the forces from here in that direction; and as both Richmond and Petersburg must be guarded, this might require that all the troops except the heavy artillery, some cavalry, and a few infantry companies for guards of bridges, &c., should be withdrawn from North Carolina.   Be ready.   I directed the adjutant-general to send you the information received here upon which the telegram of yesterday was based.   How far down the James River does your signal line extend now?   Give us the earliest practicable accurate information of the movements of the enemy.   I am much obliged to you for sending General Rains' letter.   I directed it to be returned, thinking you would prefer to file it in your own office.   Let me have Burroughs' cavalry companies as soon as you can.   They are much needed above.   If the particular company you refer to from the vicinity of Suffolk cannot be spared now, keep it for the present; send on the others Say to General Pettigrew, please, that it is contemplated that his brigade will be called in this direction for active service.   I know he will be ready Communicate with me freely and in full all your views and wishes.

I remain, respectfully and truly, yours,

G. W. SMITH,
Major-General, Commanding.

HEADQUARTERS DISTRICT OF NORTH CAROLINA,
Raleigh, N. C., October 5, 1862.

Hon. SECRETARY OF WAR:

SIR: When I was assigned to the command of this district by the direction of General Lee I assumed the general control of the conscription or recruiting business in the State.   So, after doing so, deemed it advisable to issue the inclosed order, in connection with the order and proclamation of Governor Vance.   The good effect of that order has been very perceptible.   Your telegram* to Major Mallett of yesterday's date will set aside this order and cause great complaint I respecfully suggest that men be not forced into regiments, but be allowed the choice assured in my order, Major Mallett only using such influence as he can to direct their choice.   Should a sudden emergency require the use of 400 or 500 men in the vicinity of Richmond it would be better, in my judgment, to order the camp guard there for a week or so than to compel conscripts to go to those regiments.

I am, very respectfully, your obedient servant,

J. G. MARTIN,
Brigadier-General.

[Indorsement.]

Write to General Martin that it was deemed necessary, in order to insure uniformity in the execution of the law for the enrollment of conscripts, that it should be conducted under the control of the department, and it was so ordered on April 28 last in General Orders, No.

---

* Not found.

30.   Experience thus [far] has confirmed the views then taken, and it has been found that to place the enrollment of conscripts under the control of the general commanding a department, subjects it to change with every change of a department commander.   General Lee's orders were not intended to conflict with the policy and express order of the department, but merely to secure the valuable aid of the adjutant-general of the State in carrying that policy out.   The only objection to the order proposed by General Martin is that it conflicts with the conscript act in restricting the maximum of infantry companies to a smaller number than is allowed by that act.   The right to volunteer before enrollment is reserved by law, and the order to Major Mallett only applies to enrolled men.   Orders have been given for the immediate filling up of the Virginia and North Carolina regiments at Richmond, because the enemy are preparing to attack the city with a heavy force.

G. W. RANDOLPH.

[Inclosures.]

GENERAL ORDERS,   }   STATE OF N. C., EXECUTIVE DEPT.,
No. 7.   ADJT. GENERAL'S OFFICE (MILITIA),
                    Raleigh, N. C., September 13, 1862.

I.   Colonels and other officers in command of the Militia of North Carolina are hereby ordered to bring all men liable to conscription in their commands and all soldiers absent from their regiments without leave to the camp of instruction at Raleigh.   All power necessary for the enforcing of this order is hereby given them.

II.   A failure or refusal to comply with this order will subject the offender to the penalties of a court-martial and consequent reduction to the ranks.

III.   The executive, through its own officers, having thus undertaken to collect all persons liable to militia duty instead of allowing Confederate officers to do so, it is earnestly hoped that all will come up promptly to the performance of their duty.

By order of Governor Vance:

J. G. MARTIN,
Adjutant-General.

A proclamation by Z. B. Vance, Governor of North Carolina.

EXECUTIVE DEPARTMENT OF NORTH CAROLINA,
September 18, 1862.

Whereas information has reached me that certain persons, unmindful of the calls of patriotism and forgetful of the duties of good citizens, are using their influence to prevent obedience to the law of Congress known as the conscription law, and that others are attempting to organize an open resistance to its execution ; and whereas such conduct being not only in direct violation of law, but also detrimental in the highest degree to the cause of our country, it becomes my sacred duty to prevent and repress the same by all the means in my power :

Now, therefore, I, Zebulon B. Vance, Governor of North Carolina, do issue this my proclamation warning all such persons to desist from such unpatriotic and criminal conduct, earnestly hoping that all who are disinclined to defend their homes themselves, either by reason of age, infirmity, or cowardice, will cease to dissuade those who are willing, and notifying positively all persons contemplating an armed resistance to the law, if there really be any such misguided and evil-disposed persons in our midst, that they will commit the crime of treason according to the laws of Congress, and must not expect to escape its penalties. While thousands upon thousands of our best and bravest have cheerfully obeyed the law, and by their patriotic valor have driven the enemy back to the Potomac, it would be an intolerable outrage upon them to permit others to shirk or evade the law, or worse still, to resist it by open violence. Let no one, therefore, be deceived. The law will be enforced, and I appeal to all loyal and patriotic citizens to sustain those who are charged with its execution.

Given under my hand and attested by the great seal of the State. Done at the city of Raleigh the 18th day of September, 1862.

Z. B. VANCE.

By the Governor:
    R. H. BATTLE, JR.,
       Private Secretary.

GENERAL ORDERS,   HDQRS. DISTRICT OF NORTH CAROLINA,
    No. 2.   *Raleigh, N. C., September 9, 1862.*

I. All persons liable to military duty under the conscription law are hereby required to come to the camp of instruction near this city at once. Those doing so will be allowed to select the infantry regiments they wish to join, and unless full they will be assigned accordingly.

II. The regiments of infantry and artillery on duty in this State are authorized to enlist conscripts to increase each company of infantry and heavy artillery to 100 men, but not exceeding it, and light batteries to 150 men.

By command of Brig. Gen. J. G. Martin:

A. GORDON,
Assistant Adjutant-General.

STATE OF N. CAROLINA, EXECUTIVE DEPT., A. G. O.,
Raleigh, N. C., September 22, 1862.

The $50 bounty will be paid to all men who come into camp under this call before they leave to join their regiments.

J. G. MARTIN,
Adjutant-General.

ENGINEER BUREAU,
Richmond, Va., October 9, 1862.

Col. WALTER GWYNN, *Richmond, Va.:*

SIR: By direction of the honorable Secretary of War you are hereby assigned, as an agent of the Department, to make an examination of the navigable water-courses in the eastern part of the State of North Carolina, viz, the Neuse, Tar, Roanoke, and Chowan Rivers, with a view to their defense against a naval and land attack. It is desirable to control the rivers as far down as possible, and thus afford all the protection in our power to plantations and other property along their borders. To be effective the defense in each case will consist of two distinct parts: First, the placing of strong obstructions in the channel of the river; second, batteries (with works of proper strength for defense against land attack) so placed on the bank as to have a complete command of the obstructing works. As the garrison that can be furnished for each fort will have to be small, the facilities for sending prompt succor to each position occupied must be carefully studied. The strength of profile to be given to the works along the land fronts will of course be governed by the same consideration. It is hoped that it will be found practicable to occupy a point on the Neuse at least as low as Kinston, on the Tar as low as Greenville, and on the Roanoke as low as Hamilton. This can only be determined upon, however, after making the examination intrusted to you. As to the Chowan River, it is probably at present so entirely under the control of the enemy as to prevent us from holding any point along its banks. In the progress of events this occupation may become practicable, in which case you will make the desired examination. In the selection of sites for batteries to command rivers high points should be preferred, and the open range of river below should not be greater than that of our own guns. As soon as you have decided upon the positions to be held and the general character of the works, namely, obstructions, batteries, forts, &c., you will report at once to this Bureau, sending such sketches, maps, and plans as will give a full understanding of your projects. At the same time you will make preparations for procuring all necessary materials and labor for construction, reporting the results at once to this office. Application will be made to the major-general commanding at Richmond for instructions to be given to the commanders in North Carolina to furnish troops, when needed, for protecting the operations now committed to your charge. At the earliest day practicable two assistants will be assigned to you, with the hope that by their aid you can press the defenses the more rapidly to a state of efficiency. You will please to proceed to North Carolina at once and enter upon the duties assigned you. You will notify this Bureau as early as possible as to the point at which the assistants shall be ordered to report to you. Prompt arrangements will be made for paying the necessary expenses.

I am, sir, very respectfully, your obedient servant,

J. F. GILMER,
Lieutenant-Colonel and Chief of Engineer Bureau.

HEADQUARTERS,
Richmond, Va., October 10, 1862.

Maj. Gen. S. G. FRENCH,
Comdg. Department of North Carolina, Petersburg, Va.:

GENERAL: The Secretary of War says that although we cannot form the Partisan Rangers into a brigade regularly there is no reason why the regiments of Colonel Claiborne, Colonel Ferebee, Colonel Griffin, and Colonel Evans should not all be required to report to Brigadier-General Robertson. He requests that this be done and that General Robertson be assigned to command the pickets and outposts of these regiments as well as the camp of instruction, and that the picket and outpost duty be performed by details, so that all may share instruction in camp. If General Robertson will request the adjutant and inspector general to assign an assistant adjutant-general or quartermaster and a commissary to his command it will be done, and his wishes I am sure will be complied with in regard to the particular officers he may designate for these places, if it is practicable to do so.

Very respectfully and truly, yours,

G. W. SMITH,
Major-General, Commanding.

ENGINEER BUREAU, *Richmond, Va., October* 11, 1862.

Maj. SAMUEL W. MELTON,
    Assistant Adjutant-General, Richmond, Va.:

MAJOR : By direction of the Secretary of War I have assigned to Col. Walter Gywnn, civil engineer, the duty of examining the Neuse, Tar, Roanoke, and Chowan Rivers, including their tributaries, with a view to their defense by obstructions placed in the rivers and batteries commanding the same. Colonel Gwynn is instructed to proceed with the works at once, if practicable. To aid him and give the necessary protection to his operations I have to respectfully request Major-General Smith, commanding, to give orders to the commanders in North Carolina and at Petersburg, Va., to act in concert with Colonel Gwynn, and afford him every assistance possible with the troops under their respective commands. I will, if possible, assign two engineer officers to assist in pressing forward the contemplated works. It is hoped the planters along the rivers will be able to furnish the requisite labor for constructing the defenses.

I am, very respectfully, &c.,

J. F. GILMER,
Lieutenant-Colonel and Chief of Bureau.

P. S.—Please furnish a copy of the general's orders to this Bureau for the use of Colonel Gwynn.

———

ENGINEER BUREAU,
Richmond, Va., October 11, 1862.

Capt. C. R. COLLINS,
    Corps of Engineers, C. S. Army, Smithville, N. C.:

CAPTAIN : Your letter of the 2d instant was received three or four days ago, but a pressure of current business in this office has prevented an earlier reply. In reference to the construction of casemates in Fort Caswell I have to say that it is, in my judgment, impracticable to do so, but as a protection to the artillerists thick and high traverses should be constructed between the guns and the parapet raised on the right and left so as to form half embrasures, giving only such field of fire as may be necessary to cover the channels of approach. The parapet ought to have a height of not less than $5\frac{1}{2}$ even feet above the level of the terre-plein, and the intermediate traverses should have a thickness of not less than 18 feet at the base. If the guns are too near each other to allow space for traverses of the requisite dimensions then every alternate one should be removed and mounted at new points selected so as to give the best fire possible on the approaches. For revetting the traverses the turf or sod from the low, marshy ground adjacent will probably answer, also for the increased height to be given to the parapet on the right and left of each gun. If possible, you should form bomb-proofs within the work for sheltering the artillerists not engaged in serving the guns. At the rear end and under the intermediate traverses may be a proper place for the bomb-proofs. If possible, additional long-range guns will be provided for Fort Caswell. As soon as the new appropriations become available funds will be placed to your credit, as promised by Captain Rives. It is out of the power of this Bureau, owing to the many calls for engineer officers, to furnish you with an assistant at this time. If the works will be delayed for the want of one you must employ a competent civil engineer.

Very respectfully, your obedient servant,

J. F. GILMER,
Lieutenant-Colonel and Chief of Engineer Bureau.

HEADQUARTERS,
Richmond, Va., October 13, 1862.

Major-General FRENCH,
  Commanding Department of North Carolina :

GENERAL : In giving instructions for replacing incompetent men on signal duty by other details the major-general commanding designed to restrict such details to your command proper, his authority over men from other armies who may be in hospital only continuing so long as they are properly retained as inmates. He directs that you will regard General Lee's orders in reference to Sergt. H. M. Cottingham, Company B, Second Georgia Battalion, and Private Thomas F. Holly, Company H, Third Alabama Regiment, as imperative, and remand these men to their respective commands. Their places in the Signal Corps will be supplied by details from your own command. An order has been issued to-day (a copy of which has been furnished you) assigning Col. Walter Gwynn, civil engineer, to the duty of examining the Neuse, Tar, Roanoke, and Chowan Rivers, with a view to their defenses, and directing you to assist as far as possible with the forces under your command. If possible, two other engineer officers will assist in pressing the works forward. It is very desirable that measures be taken to procure labor from the planters along these rivers, and the major-general commanding desires that whatever may be necessary to that end be done promptly. If the people will furnish the assistance reasonably expected of them the works can be completed at an early day.

  Very respectfully, general, your obedient servant,
SAML. W. MELTON,
Major and Assistant Adjutant-General.

ENGINEER BUREAU,
Richmond, Va., October 14, 1862.

Lieut. W. G. BENDER,
  Corps of Engineers, Provisional Army, Richmond, Va. :

SIR : Herewith I hand you an order to proceed to Goldsborough, N. C., and report to Col. Walter Gwynn, civil engineer, for duty. As an assistant in the operations committed to Colonel Gwynn, in addition to the ordinary duties of the engineer, you are charged with the disbursements of all funds to be expended in payment for materials and workmanship applied in the construction of defenses along the rivers of Eastern North Carolina and for surveys of the country bordering thereon. For this purpose funds will be placed to your credit with the treasurer of the Confederate States at Richmond, Va. You will keep and render this Bureau, for transmission to the Treasury, the monthly and quarterly statements and accounts as required by the Army Regulations. On your application to this office the necessary blank forms will be supplied.

  I am, respectfully, your obedient servant,
J. F. GILMER,
Lieutenant-Colonel and Chief of Bureau.

EXECUTIVE OFFICE,
Richmond, October 17, 1862.

His Excellency ZEBULON B. VANCE, *Governor of North Carolina :*

MY DEAR SIR : The resolutions adopted at a meeting of the citizens of Onslow County, North Carolina, referred to me by you, were duly received, and have occupied my serious attention.

I have not been unmindful of the condition of the eastern portion of your State, and can make allowance for the anxiety felt by those who reside there. Efforts are industriously made to organize and instruct the new levies of mounted troops, that force being most relied on to protect your exposed districts, and you may be assured that the Government will do everything in its power to defend the citizens of Onslow against the depredations of the enemy. With this view General French has received orders to send thither as soon as practicable a force to prevent marauding expeditions and afford protection to private property.

The large and increasing numbers of the enemy at Suffolk, whence he threatens North Carolina and Virginia as well as our principal line of communication, has rendered it necessary to concentrate our forces at a point where they can offer the most effective resistance; and in the success of that resistance I am sure that the intelligent citizens of Onslow County, as well as of the rest of North Carolina, will perceive how deeply they are interested.

I gratefully acknowledge the earnest and patriotic manner in which, since your assumption of the executive authority in North Carolina, you have labored to fill her battle-thinned regiments and recruit our armies in the field. I am happy in the confidence that you will continue to afford this Government your valuable co-operation, and beg to assure you of the deep interest I feel in all that relates to the security and welfare of your State.

Very respectfully and truly, yours,

JEFFERSON DAVIS.

STATE OF NORTH CAROLINA, EXECUTIVE DEPARTMENT,
Raleigh, October 20, 1862.

His Excellency President DAVIS:

DEAR SIR: Pardon me for addressing you in regard to a matter that should ordinarily come before the Quartermaster-General, but its importance justifies me in bringing the matter directly to your notice.

Large quantities of harness are made in this State by contract with the Confederate Government agents. The prices paid being more remunerative, almost two-thirds of our leather is made into harness instead of shoes. As shoes are now our greatest need I respectfully suggest that the Quartermaster-General cease to contract for leather harness and allow the whole product of our tanneries to go into the manufacture of shoes. Harness sufficiently strong for all reasonable purposes can be made of heavy cotton goods. Much of it is in use in this State, and is found to answer every end. So far as my observation goes it would enable us to double the amount of shoes produced.

I need not remind you of the importance of this item for the army nor of the great difficulty we are realizing in getting a supply.

Hoping you may think favorably of the suggestion, I remain, very respectfully, your obedient servant,

Z. B. VANCE.

ENGINEER BUREAU,
Richmond, Va., October 20, 1862.

Col. WALTER GWYNN, *Kinston, N. C.:*

COLONEL: I am in receipt of your letter of the 17th instant, in which you describe the position of the defensive works on the Neuse River, 3 miles below the town of Kinston, constructed by Maj. W. B. Thompson 'he selection of a better position for defending the river is desirable, specially if one can be found below.   Much must be left to your judg- 1ent and experience in making the change, but when you have chosen new site you will as soon as possible furnish this office with a full de- cription and sketch of the ground and the approaches. If you need he service of Major Thompson as an assistant you can retain him.   His)cal knowledge will give him advantages that will no doubt make his ervices the more valuable. I presume Lieuts. [W. G.] Bender and Randolph, Provisional Engineers, have reported to you by this time as ssistants.   You have the authority to employ agents to collect the nec- ssary negro force to construct the work committed to your charge, and)remen or overseers to direct their labors to the best advantage.   With he services of Major Thompson and Lieutenants Bender and Randolph s assistants it is hoped that you will not find it necessary to employ •ersons in the capacity of superintendents.   It does not appear from he records of the Adjutant and Inspector General's Office that Major 'hompson holds the appointment of major in the Provisional Army of he Confederacy.   Is he an officer in one of the North Carolina regiments ow in the Confederate service?   I fear that there will be much difficulty n procuring a sufficient number of chains and anchors for securing eavy rafts, such as you propose for obstructions in place of cribs sunk ith the stone or in place of piling.   You will please to make every ffort to procure such materials as will be needed for the works you may ecide upon.   You will purchase all the shovels and spades you can and n the best terms they can be procured; also such other tools as may be ecessary.   If you fail to get as many as you may need the Bureau may •e able to aid you to a limited extent.

I am, sir, very respectfully, your obedient servant,

J. F. GILMER,
Colonel and Chief of Bureau.

Abstract from Field Return of troops commanded by Maj. Gen. G. W. Smith, October 20, 1862 (headquarters, Richmond, Va.).

Commands.	Present for duty.		Aggregate present.	Aggregate present and absent.
	Officers.	Men.		
•epartment of North Carolina	650	11, 537	14, 805	17, 767
haffin's Bluff:				
Brigadier-General Wise's brigade	116	1, 699	2, 266	2, 887
Col. T. J. Page	23	265	413	481
•rewry's Bluff, Brigadier-General Daniel's brigade	198	3, 359	4, 475	5, 437
'icketing Peninsula, Holcombe Legion (cavalry)	11	147	223	261
tichmond defenses	87	1, 679	2, 128	2, 845
•n Brook Run:				
42d Regiment Mississippi Volunteers	27	340	490	565
54th North Carolina Troops	29	540	726	873
57th North Carolina Troops	25	562	737	971
•n Rappahannock:				
61st Virginia Infantry	28	404	500	571
59th Georgia Volunteers *				
13th Virginia Cavalry *				
2d North Carolina Cavalry *				
redericksburg, 15th Virginia Cavalry *				
•rewry's Bluff, Capt. S. S. Lee, C. S. Navy *				
•epartment of Henrico *				
Grand total	1, 194	20, 532	26, 763	32, 658

* No report received.

HEADQUARTERS,
Petersburg, Va., October 22, 1862.

[Governor VANCE, *Raleigh, N. C.*:]

DEAR GOVERNOR: I have the honor to acknowledge the receipt of your letter of yesterday.

Let me first assure you that you have not the interest and welfare of the people of your State more at heart than I have.

2d. That after the departure of General Lee to Northern Virginia North Carolina was stripped of all her available forces to meet the enemy on the Potomac.

3d. That on the threatening advance of the enemy at Warrenton and Lower Potomac I was directed to hold all the regiments at points on the line of the railroads to move up here, and in this condition they now mostly remain. It was my wish to rapidly mass my forces and strike blows at different points where the enemy were in small force in different parts of your State, but the requirements of General Lee have, together with the accumulation of the troops of the enemy at Suffolk, prevented my doing so.

4th. Finding the enemy not disposed to advance, some days since I sent orders to Col. [W. F.] Martin (Seventeenth Regiment) to hold his troops ready to move on Plymouth; that Colonel Cantwell would join him, &c., and not to disclose the movement to any human being. I did not know the colonel was on leave. The orders to both him and Cantwell were on the outside marked "Private," lest some staff officer should open them. The result was Martin's "Private" letter and Cantwell's must have been forwarded to them, and neither being with their regiments nothing has been heard from them.

5th. On the 20th, Radcliffe's regiment was ordered up in place of Cantwell's, and Colonel Radcliffe has been directed to move with his regiment and Martin's on Plymouth, to drive out the enemy and give the people of Martin, Washington, and Tyrrell Counties an opportunity to bring out their provisions, &c. As secrecy is the soul of success in cases of this kind, I told no one except one officer on my staff, who did part of the writing for me. I presume Radcliffe will move the last of this week or early next week, on Plymouth, and I hope with successful results. About this you had better say nothing, for between gossip and the newspapers nothing can be done without the enemy finding it out before it can be executed.

6th. There were some complaints came to me respecting the withdrawal of forces from Onslow County. The same cavalry force is there under Captain Ward that has been there since the fall of New Berne except two companies of Partisan Rangers. When these rangers are disciplined in the camps of instruction at Garysburg we will have a force for the position that can move rapidly from point to point.

7th. I have been anxious to have the rivers obstructed, but have had no means to do it. Finally engineers have been sent to examine them. Had they been ordered to report to me I should now have had them on the Roanoke River at work. I can only say, in conclusion, that I will do all that can be done to protect the people, at the same time confront the threatening forces of the enemy where they are in large force. The forces in Suffolk now are 25,000. [This] holds most of my troops, from necessity, here and at Franklin.

I will be most happy to confer with you at any time and will thank you to write to me freely your views on any matters concerning our common welfare.

Yours, very truly,   S. G. FRENCH,
                                        Brigadier-General, Commanding.

ENGINEER BUREAU, *October* 25, 1862.

Maj. SAMUEL W. MELTON,
    Assistant Adjutant-General:

I have respectfully to state that this Bureau is particularly anxious to act in concert with the commanders of the troops in the military districts of the Department of Northern Virginia. As chief engineer of that department, and at the earnest solicitation of the congressional delegation from North Carolina, I sent Col. Walter Gwynn, a civil engineer of great experience and a graduate of West Point, to examine promptly the question of obstructing and defending the rivers of Eastern North Carolina, with authority to engage negro labor and materials for the works; to report his action at once to this Bureau; also to Brigadier-General French, commanding, &c., and ask of him protection and support, if needed.

On the 11th instant I asked of Major-General Smith that instructions be given to the district commanders to give every assistance and protection possible with their troops in furtherance of the works—works for which I as chief engineer of the department am responsible. I feel sure Colonel Gywnn will keep Brigadier-General French informed of all his selections of sites, the character of the works proposed, their progress, &c., as he has been directed. As the question of defending the rivers of Eastern North Carolina is strictly one for the engineer, I must have the control and direction of the officers engaged in the labor, but in such direction I have and will order them to act in full concert with Brigadier-General French and other district commanders.

Very respectfully,

J. F. GILMER,
Colonel of Engineers and Chief of Bureau.

EXECUTIVE DEPARTMENT, C. S. A.,
Richmond, Va., October 27, 1862.

His Excellency Gov. ZEBULON B. VANCE:

SIR: I am directed by the President to inform you that your letter of the 20th instant, suggesting the employment of heavy cotton stuffs for army harness and the devotion of leather to the exclusive manufacture of shoes was referred to the Quartermaster-General, who reports that very inconsiderable contracts are made by the Quartermaster's Department for harness in North Carolina. The contracts to which you refer are probably for the Ordnance Bureau. The suggestion is a good one, that the practice of using leather be discontinued as far as possible for the manufacture of anything else than shoes; but the Quartermaster-General thinks that while cotton serves very well for plantation harness it is unfit for the wear and tear to which harness is necessarily subjected in the army.

Your letter has been forwarded to the Secretary of War with directions to secure the leather of the country as far as practicable for shoes.

I have the honor, sir, to present you the compliments of the President.

Your obedient servant,

BURTON N. HARRISON,
Private Secretary.

HEADQUARTERS, *Richmond, Va., October* 29, 1862.

Maj. Gen. S. G. FRENCH,
 Comdg. Department of North Carolina, Petersburg, Va.:

GENERAL: Your private note of the 25th was duly received. I have succeeded in getting authority to order Lieut. Col. [R.] Lindsay Walker, of the artillery, to report to you, to take charge of the artillery defenses of Petersburg and vicinity. You will find Colonel Walker an energetic and determined officer. He has served with marked distinction in the field, and I am satisfied will be of great service to you. When Colonel Walker reports to you, in case the services of Major Moseley are no longer essentially necessary the previous order directing him to report to General Pendleton for duty in General Lee's army should be carried into effect. If it is necessary in your judgment to retain Major Moseley inform me of the fact in order that further instructions in regard to him may be given. I am trying to get up a battery of heavy rifled guns on field carriages, to use either at Petersburg or here as necessity may require. Please say to General Rains that General Lee is much pleased with the manner in which the enemy were beaten off by the Whitworth guns, but he says that he cannot spare the two Whitworths he has at present. I wrote to General Lee asking him to let General Rains have these guns but he declines.

I hope that your arrangements for opening up the counties of Martin, Washington, and Tyrrell will be successful. Everything practicable should be done to effect this important object, and I entirely approve of all your efforts to do so. General Wise had started with his command for Williamsburg and Jamestown Island when your telegram of Sunday morning reached me. I ordered the infantry to return to Chaffin's Bluff, but the cavalry has gone down to arrest and punish negroes for murders committed by them in that vicinity. There is no one available but Brigadier-General Clingman for Kinston. He is at present on leave of absence, and the President thinks that Clingman prefers to go to General Lee's army. You ought to have a brigadier at that point, and if General Martin does not desire to continue in that command, exclusive of his present duties in Raleigh as adjutant-general—which are in my opinion incompatible with the first—I request you to suggest or recommend a good officer for the position. I will lay the subject before the Secretary and endeavor to get a brigadier-general there.

I have requested Colonel Gilmer to send you an engineer. I am satisfied that, besides the general engineers [who] are under his control, as [commander] of a department you have use for [an engineer] under your own orders. If you can recommend one that would suit you I will take pleasure in aiding to get him appointed and ordered on duty with you. Yours of yesterday in reference to Colonel Gwynn has been referred to Colonel Gilmer, Chief Engineer. Colonel Gwynn should have reported to you at once, showing you his orders, and asking assistance and securing co-operation. I hope he has now done so.

 Respectfully and truly, yours,

       G. W. SMITH,
        Major-General.

———

       HEADQUARTERS,
     Petersburg, Va., October 30, 1862.

Hon. ZEBULON B. VANCE,
 Governor of North Carolina, Raleigh, N. C.:

GOVERNOR: I have the letter written by Mr. Nanns to you from Tarborough, which was indorsed to me by your aide-de-camp. I would most cheerfully send three regiments and a corresponding force of artillery to the vicinity of Leechville but for two considerations : First, I have not got them to spare ; secondly, with the power of the enemy to throw heavy re-enforcements from New Berne into Washington it would be extremely hazardous ; they might be cut off.   You will readily perceive under what embarrassments I labor.   With my small force I have to hold in check 25,000 at Suffolk, 2,000 at Washington, 12,000 perhaps now in New Berne, and a large force represented at Beaufort. The force I sent last week to Plymouth I hope is now on the borders of Beaufort and Washington Counties, and may bring out some supplies. You will readily perceive I cannot handle my small force as I would wish, because if I were to withdraw them from any point to operate on another for any length of time it would be but to expose that point from which they were withdrawn.   If I take the troops from Kinston to operate toward Beaufort County it exposes Goldsborough and Wilmington.   If I send them from here it leaves 25,000 in front of me with only a march of 40 miles from Zuni.   I am doing all I can to draw supplies from the eastern parts of the State, and even in this much depends on the cheerful co-operation of the people.

Yours, very truly,

S. G. FRENCH,
Major-General, Commanding.

ENGINEER BUREAU, *October* 30, 1862.

Col. WALTER GWYNN, *Goldsborough, N. C.*:

COLONEL : I have to acknowledge the receipt of your letters of the 22d and 24th instant.   In accordance with your wish your son has been applied for, and as soon as the detail is granted he will be ordered to report to you in Tarborough for duty.

I have just learned from a letter of General S. G. French to General G. W. Smith that 100 negroes are ordered to assemble at Hamilton. You will therefore take immediate steps to receive and set them to work.

In your letter of the 24th, alluding to the defenses of Neuse River, you write the works embrace the river batteries and will require 10,000 men for their defense.   You further estimate that an armament of thirty-four guns in all will be necessary.   These are works of vastly greater magnitude than I have ever contemplated or can approve.   In my letter of instructions of the 9th instant I particularly called your attention to the fact that the garrisons of such forts as you might construct would be necessarily small.   Instead, therefore, of building forts defending the river, in turn to be defended by covering works, I decidedly prefer, as a general thesis, and without special and controlling circumstances, one work commanding the river with strong land as well as water fronts, defiled, if necessary, to protect it from attacks on commanding ground. I most earnestly therefore call your special attention to prompt studies and actions to carry out these views.   In my judgment, with rare exceptions, a permanent garrison for each position of one regiment is the utmost that can be reasonably hoped for.

Very respectfully,

J. F. GILMER,
Colonel and Chief of Engineer Bureau

Abstract from Field Return of troops commanded by Maj. Gen. G. W. Smith, October 31, 1862 (headquarters Richmond, Va.).

Commands.	Present for duty.		Effective total.	Aggregate present.	Aggregate present and absent.
	Officers.	Men.			
Maj. Gen. S. G. French, Department of North Carolina.....	573	10,045	10,858	13,524	16,100
Brig. Gen. H. A. Wise's brigade, Chaffin's farm............	126	1,621	1,760	2,242	2,809
Col. T. J. Page, Chaffin's Bluff...........................	21	246	341	417	487
Brig. Gen. J. Daniel's brigade, near Drewry's Bluff........	195	3,255	3,468	4,387	5,412
Holcombe Legion (cavalry), picketing the Peninsula........	13	125	153	196	264
Richmond defenses	93	1,717	1,824	2,140	2,703
Brook turnpike:					
42d Regiment Mississippi Volunteers....................	30	298	307	426	496
54th Regiment North Carolina Troops.........	34	466	505	657	784
57th Regiment North Carolina Troops...................	25	545	561	762	1,042
59th Regiment Georgia Volunteers......................	38	593	619	761	966
Capt. S. S. Lee, C. S. Navy, Drewry's Bluff (in part)	12	220	300	359	395
Department of Henrico......................................	107	2,124	2,428	3,146	5,228
61st Regiment Virginia Infantry*..........................					
Colonel Chambliss, on Rappahannock:					
2d Regiment North Carolina Cavalry*.................					
13th and 15th Regiments Virginia Cavalry*.............					
Grand total..	1,267	21,255	23,124	29,017	36,686

* No reports.

SUBSISTENCE DEPARTMENT, C. S. A.,
Richmond, November 2, 1862.

His Excellency Gov. ZEBULON B. VANCE, *Raleigh, N. C.:*

SIR: It is very desirable to exhaust the hogs, beeves, pease, beans, and potatoes of that part of North Carolina which lies within the lines of the enemy or accessible to them. The President called my attention to information derived from you on the subject, and the representations made in response to inquiries have been of a discouraging nature. I venture to apply to you for action thereon. It is obvious that those charged with such an undertaking should be reliable business men, whose integrity and energy should be personally known to those among whom they are to operate. Neither myself nor any one in my office has such knowledge of the country or the people of lower North Carolina as to enable me to make the proper selections and the necessary arrangements to the above end. That being the case I write to ask if you will allow your agency to be used in this matter by having the whole devolve upon you, except so far as existing arrangements go. They run thus far: Mr. Jacob Parker has a contract for packing hogs at Warrenton, and has the following counties allotted to him for purchase, viz: Franklin, Warren, Nash, and Halifax. In addition, Maj. W. H. Smith has made certain arrangements with Mr. H. Hayes, of Harrellsville, which he will detail to you. The balance of the district spoken of it is proposed to put under your charge, with these remarks:

1st. That as this Bureau has already more captains and majors than it ought to have it is not expedient to appoint more, except in case of absolute necessity, but to operate by agents, whose agencies can cease when their business with the Department closes.

2d. That the points of delivery of the hogs should be fixed with reference to the packing-houses, both in and out of the State of North Carolina, so that such as can go conveniently to the packeries, which Major Smith has established or will establish, may do so, and such as are more convenient to Petersburg can go to that point, whence they can be brought to this place.

3d. That it may be necessary to procure both bags and transportation to get out the pease and potatoes and any bacon that may be attainable. As to the transportation, Mr. Hayes, in a letter to Major Ruffin, says that a few teams and wagons can be bought in his region. If they can be bought at prices satisfactory to yourself you will be authorized to buy them, and when they are done with they can be disposed of in some satisfactory manner. As to the bags, it would be very desirable to secure the services of some of the factories of North Carolina in order to get them, and as they have not been called on up to this time it is to be hoped that they will now be able to serve the needs of this Bureau. One of the greatest difficulties now is to get bags, and there are not half enough. Can you not get them? Please try.

I have been induced to ask you to undertake the above service in consequence of your communication to the President, and my notice of your address to the people of your State, indicating a readiness to help the cause in general.

I have the honor to be, very respectfully, your obedient servant,

L. B. NORTHROP.

———

ENGINEER BUREAU, *November 3, 1862.*

Col. WALTER GWYNN,
   In charge of Defenses in Eastern North Carolina:

COLONEL : I have to acknowledge the receipt of your letter of the 29th instant relating to the defenses, disbursements, &c., in Eastern North Carolina. A requisition for $30,000 in favor of Lieut. W. G. Bender has been made.

I am glad to hear that so satisfactory a position for the defense of the Roanoke River has been found at Rainbow Bend. The line of infantry to cover 1½ miles to the pond, causing the enemy to make a detour of 15 miles, seems a good suggestion. It is not possible at present to furnish all the armament required, still platforms and positions should be prepared for formidable river batteries (a part of these platforms should be prepared for siege carriages). You will most probably have to exercise your ingenuity in mounting the guns, as the supply of guns is very limited. There are only two pile-drivers in this vicinity, both steam, with 2,000-pound hammers, and in constant use; they are, moreover, mounted on boats. They should be sought for in the section where you are, and if they cannot be found seek to have them made where you are; and failing in that, if you will send on drawings of the hammers, &c., required, I will order them to be executed at the Tredegar Works. While our founderies and machine-shops are so overtasked, and the price of labor and iron so high, I do not think screw-piles at all advisable. Before approving the suggestion of repairing the steamboat Cora, it is necessary for the Bureau to have an approximate estimate of the cost. Communicate with Maj. Gen. S. G. French respecting provisions and transportation and request his co-operation. Capt. C. H. Dimmock, engineer in charge at Petersburg, will be requested without delay to forward you the required amount of intrenching tools. Your call for stationery will be promptly attended to.

When convenient, please send a fair, legible copy by a clerk of your communications to this Bureau.

Very respectfully, your obedient servant,

J. F. GILMER,
Colonel and Chief of Engineer Bureau.

SUBSISTENCE DEPARTMENT, C. S. A.,
Richmond, November 3, 1862.

His Excellency ZEBULON B. VANCE,
Governor of North Carolina, Raleigh:

SIR: By order of Col. L. B. Northrop, Commissary-General of Subsistence, who has written to you fully in regard to purchase of certain articles to be made for the Subsistence Department of the Confederate States, I send Mr. Jacob Parker to see you in the hope you have accepted the position which Colonel Northrop has felt warranted in calling upon you to undertake, not less from a desire to avail of your advantage of position than from a conviction of your patriotism and energy. Mr. Parker wishes to know what price to pay for hogs, and I refer to you and Major Smith, especially yourself, as the best source of information on that head. He also represents that speculators are ready to dog his steps as soon as he moves and asks how he is to get rid of them. I reply that whatever plan you may recommend will have the respectful consideration of this Bureau. If approved, as it is presumed it will be, the most strenuous efforts will be used to get for it the active sanction of the War Department.

Very respectfully, your obedient servant,

FRANK G. RUFFIN,
Major and Commissary of Subsistence.

NAVY DEPARTMENT, C. S. A.,
Richmond, November 4, 1862.

His Excellency ZEBULON B. VANCE,
Governor of North Carolina:

SIR: Commander Cooke, sent by me to North Carolina to obtain iron for plating the gunboats being built in and for the defense of the State, has returned without having accomplished this object. He reports that you have the control of a quantity of railroad iron, and I therefore address myself to you upon the subject.

To enable the boats to resist the guns of the enemy their armor must be at least 4 inches thick, placed at an angle of at least 36°. This armor, from the limited power of our mills, we are compelled to roll into plates 2 by 7 inches and 10 feet long, and to put them on the vessels in two courses.

If you will let the Department have the rails, and facilitate its transportation to Richmond, they will be immediately rolled into plates for the vessels in question and for such other defenses as we may build in the waters of your State.

Commander Cooke will remove the iron if you consent to its transfer, and will arrange the compensation according to his instructions.

Please telegraph your reply.

I am, respectfully, your obedient servant,

S. R. MALLORY,
Secretary of the Navy.

ENGINEER BUREAU, *November 4*, 1862.

Capt. JAMES W. COOKE,
  C. S. Navy, White Hall, N. C.:

CAPTAIN: Col. Walter Gwynn sends the following extract from a letter of yours to him:

According to the understanding with you in Richmond I have commenced work at White Hall, and if you think the river cannot be defended in time to protect the work I will thank you to inform me of the fact through Colonel Gilmer or the Secretary of the Navy.

To which Colonel G. replies in his letter to me:

My opinion is that with a sufficient force the obstructions we are placing in the Neuse River can be defended against any force the enemy are likely to send against it. They, as well as the land defenses, will be completed, I think, in six weeks; but unless the south side of the Neuse is occupied, if the enemy possesses any enterprise at all they will most assuredly destroy the gunboat which Commander Cooke is building at White Hall. A force stationed at White Hall might, however, prevent such a disaster. You will please communicate this opinion to Commander Cooke.

If further information with regard to troops for defense be desired it is respectfully suggested that Maj. Gen. S. G. French, commanding at Petersburg, be addressed on the subject.

Very respectfully, yours,

        J. F. GILMER,
    Colonel and Chief of Engineer Bureau.

ENGINEER BUREAU,
Richmond, Va., November 4, 1862.

Col. WALTER GWYNN,
  Dept. of Eastern North Carolina, Goldsborough, N. C.:

COLONEL: I have to acknowledge your letter of October 31, just received. Your views regarding the safety of the Roanoke River and the propriety of continuing the construction of a gunboat at Hamilton shall be promptly communicated to Commander James W. Cooke, of the Navy. I am of the decided opinion that the cost of screw-piles and the difficulty of obtaining them renders their use injudicious. With regard to the two pile-drivers called for by you I would suggest that definite descriptions and plans should be prepared, and that they should be executed in Petersburg. The Bureau cannot attend to such details, and the workshops of Richmond are so crowded with work for the Ordnance Department that they should be the last called on for other work. Three thousand pounds each strikes me as an excessive weight for your hammers; 1,200 pounds would be far better. If you need another assistant it is suggested that you employ Glaucus E. Olds, a member of Capt. William W. Carraway's company (unattached), of the Forty-first Regiment North Carolina Troops. The company is now at Kinston. His services can probably be secured at once by communicating with his captain, and in the mean time, should you desire it, an application will be made to the Secretary of War for his regular detail.

Very respectfully, yours,

        J. F. GILMER,
    Colonel and Chief of Engineer Bureau.

HEADQUARTERS,
Richmond, Va., November 5, 1862.

Maj. Gen. S. G. FRENCH,
      Comdg. Department of North Carolina, Petersburg, Va. :

GENERAL Your letter of yesterday in reference to the movements of
the enemy to cut off Colonel Radcliffe is received. It was shown to the
Secretary of War, and with his approval I telegraphed General Lee at
Culpeper Court-House :

General French urgently asks that a brigade be sent to him at once. Can you send
it immediately ? It is needed. I think a division should in addition be sent here, but
this is not so immediately urgent.

I inclose with this a copy of a note addressed to me by Major Beckham, ordnance officer, in reference to arms for General Robertson's
troops. We will do everything we can for you. Keep me informed
fully upon all movements of importance.

Respectfully and truly, yours,

G. W. SMITH,
Major-General.

P. S.—I have written to the Postmaster-General, requesting him to
establish a telegraph station at Rocky Mount, between Goldsborough
and Weldon.

ENGINEER BUREAU, *November 6, 1862.*

Col. WALTER GWYNN, *Goldsborough, N. C. :*

COLONEL: I have just received your letter of the 2d instant and
hasten to reply to the points therein presented. In reference to the extent of the works for land defense on the Neuse River I have to say that
the lines as proposed by you will form an intrenched camp, and as such
are I doubt not well located. But this is not the character of the defense indicated by your instructions. Owing to the great call for troops
to meet the enemy where he is in great strength the force that can be
assigned to the defense of the Neuse, Tar, and Roanoke Rivers must be
comparatively small. The proper defense therefore for these rivers is the
one named in the instructions heretofore sent from this Bureau to you
for your government, viz: One work with batteries bearing on the river
and the obstructions therein, with water and land fronts of sufficient
strength of profile to resist an assault, thus enabling the small garrisons
(as small they must be) to hold out until a succoring force can relieve
them. Such works as a general thing can be enfiladed from surrounding heights. This kind of work must be first established. If time be
allowed for occupying the surrounding hills afterward it may be judicious to do so. Intrenched camps may have to be made by the troops
when they are concentrated for the defense of a particular point. The
ground at Rainbow Bend, as you describe it (being defended in part by
an extensive pond and swamp) is particularly favorable. The line you
are extending across to rest its right flank on these natural defenses is
no doubt judiciously chosen, but you will not lose sight of the importance of a work even at this position which can be held by a small
garrison, say one regiment. I will call the attention of Major-General
Smith, commanding the southern portion of the Department of Virginia,
to what you report in reference to want of concert in the operations of
the troops in your vicinity. I approve your proposition to visit the city
of Petersburg for the purpose of getting pile-drivers and hands skilled
in their use as soon as you shall have made all the arrangements for
the prosecution of the works. When in that city you will please call on

Major-General French and confer fully with him on the subject of defenses for the rivers of Eastern North Carolina.

I do find some difficulty in reading your letters, and when possible I must ask you to have fair copies made for transmission to this Bureau. The engagement of the assistant you met with at Tarborough must be but temporary, as application has been made for the detail of your son for service at that place; this at your request.

It has occurred to me that much can be done to aid in the defense of the rivers in North Carolina by taking favorable points below your forts and felling a large number of trees along the banks and getting them in the stream in such a manner as to lodge and form irregular rafts extending long distances up and down stream, and then at favorable points along the banks make rifle-pits for sharpshooters, who can protect the obstructions. I will make every effort to get guns to arm the forts you are building, but it will not be possible to get them of the heaviest caliber, and such as we can get will probably be mounted on siege-carriages.

I am, sir, your obedient servant,

J. F. GILMER,
Colonel and Chief of Engineer Bureau.

ENGINEER BUREAU, *November 8, 1862.*

Col. J. GORGAS, *Chief of Ordnance:*

COLONEL: Defensive works are in course of construction on three of the most important rivers of Eastern North Carolina—on the Roanoke, in the vicinity of Hamilton; on the Tar, near Tarborough, and on the Neuse, at Kinston. Anticipating the early completion of these works I have the honor to make a requisition for the armament. This in each case should consist of five rifled guns on siege-carriages of such caliber as can be most promptly supplied. Of these fifteen guns those required for the Roanoke will probably be first needed. As soon as any of these are ready I respectfully request to be notified of the fact.

Very respectfully, your obedient servant,

J. F. GILMER,
Colonel and Chief of Engineer Bureau.

STATE OF NORTH CAROLINA, EXECUTIVE DEPARTMENT,
Raleigh, November 8, 1862.

Col. L. B. NORTHROP:

DEAR SIR: Your communication to Governor Vance has been received, in which you propose to avail yourself of his agency in procuring a speedy removal of the hogs, beeves, pease, beans, and potatoes from that portion of the State "within the lines of the enemy or accessible to them." His Excellency directs me to say in reply that he will most cheerfully undertake the task which you propose to assign to him. He is of opinion that the energies of the Department should be directed to the removal of those articles from the counties which are threatened with immediate invasion. All the counties west of this place are at present safe, and if a supply of salt can be procured the hogs will be cured into bacon, which can be procured at any time.

Yours, very respectfully,

DAVID A. BARNES,
Aide-de-Camp to Governor Vance.

SPECIAL ORDERS, }   ADJT. AND INSPECTOR GENERAL'S OFFICE,
      No. 262.   }   *Richmond, Va., November* 8, 1862.

*   *   *   *   *   *   *

VI. Brig. Gen. W. H. C. Whiting is assigned specially to the defense of the Cape Fear River. He will proceed to Wilmington, N. C., and enter upon that duty.

*   *   *   *   *   *   *

By command of Secretary of War:

JNO. WITHERS,
Assistant Adjutant-General.

ORDNANCE BUREAU,
Richmond, November 10, 1862.

Hon. ZEBULON B. VANCE,
        Governor of North Carolina:

SIR: Colonel Gorgas requests me to state in reply to your favor of the 8th instant that the Secretary of War has given general directions in regard to the equipment of forts, and that Wilmington will not be forgotten.

Very respectfully, your obedient servant,

T. S. RHETT,
Colonel, Inspector of Ordnance.

RICHMOND, VA., *November* 11, 1862.

Governor VANCE, *Raleigh, N. C.:*

Yours of the 9th and 10th received. The re-enforcements sent. Evans' brigade is all that is now disposable. It is not practicable at this time to reduce the command in Tennessee. The vigilance of deepest interest watches affairs in North Carolina. We will try to anticipate the enemy.

JEFFERSON DAVIS.

HEADQUARTERS,
Richmond, Va., November 11, 1862.

Maj. Gen. S. G. FRENCH,
        Commanding, Petersburg, Va.:

The Secretary of War directs that you send four regiments to the vicinity of Wilmington immediately—the two recently withdrawn from there and two others to be selected by yourself. He suggests that General Clingman be assigned to command them, reporting to the commander of the defenses of Cape Fear River, Brig. Gen. W. H. C. Whiting.

G. W. SMITH,
Major-General.

HEADQUARTERS,
Richmond, Va., November 12, 1862.

Maj. Gen. S. G. FRENCH,
        Commanding, &c., Petersburg, Va.:

GENERAL: Since my telegram of yesterday, directing that four regiments be sent to the vicinity of Wilmington with orders to report to Brig. Gen. W. H. C. Whiting, commanding defenses of Cape Fear River, the Secretary of War has requested me to ask your views in re

ard to the proper geographical boundary of the district about Wilmington. General Whiting, I understand, is to be ordered to report
directly here. I sent you a telegram to-day informing you that the
place for delivering paroled prisoners was changed to City Point, and
directed the adjutant-general (Major Melton) to send a letter of instructions. The commissioner (Major Ould) will go over to-morrow, and I
send an officer of my staff to confer with your officers in your absence
and endeavor to assist in making the necessary arrangements. General Lee, under date of the 10th instant, writes that when the regiments
are filled by conscripts—

they could surely, in addition to those you now have, enable you to secure the forage, beef, and pork in the eastern part of the State. This is not only important, but
will be necessary, in my opinion, to insure a supply of provisions for the army, and
hope you will use every effort to accomplish it.

This he writes me in answer to my letters to him in regard to matters
in your department. There can be no question in regard to the importance of securing the supplies referred to, and I am perfectly aware of
the fact that you are and have been for a long time of this opinion. At
the same time always keep an eye to Petersburg and Weldon and the
railroad. It is a difficult question to solve and a hard task to perform
with small means. The division I asked for has not been sent, but keep
me informed of the exact condition of affairs, and I will do everything
in my power to support and assist you. I hope to be able to send you
the heavy guns asked for at the obstructions. Will write you more
fully upon this to-morrow. Colonel Gwynn called upon me with
Colonel Gilmer to-day. He was requested to see you in person without
delay, and to carry out your views and instructions. He said that he
would do so cheerfully.

Respectfully and truly, yours,

           G. W. SMITH,
              Major-General.

STATE OF NORTH CAROLINA, EXECUTIVE DEPARTMENT,
              Raleigh, November 12, 1862.

His Excellency President DAVIS:

MY DEAR SIR: I have accepted the proposition of Colonel Northrop, Commissary-General, to collect with my own agents all the supplies
possible in Eastern North Carolina, and my agents are already down
there at work. Two of the richest counties in the State are Gates and
Hertford, and I am extremely anxious to strip them first. It is necessary, however, to have some protection and assistance from the troops.
I therefore earnestly request that you will order General French to
send Colonel Ferebee's Regiment, Fifty-ninth (who were raised in that
section), with a section of artillery to Winton, on the Chowan. By so
doing the whole county of Hertford could be stripped in their rear and
much brought across the Chowan from Gates. It seems to me this can
be done with great advantage to the service.

Respectfully, &c.,

           Z. B. VANCE.

STATE OF NORTH CAROLINA, EXECUTIVE DEPARTMENT,
              Raleigh, November 12, 1862.

His Excellency President DAVIS:

MY DEAR SIR: Will you do me the favor to read the inclosed letter?
is from a highly intelligent and patriotic gentleman in the mountains

of North Carolina, and gives a touching description of things in that region about which I spoke to you when in Richmond—in regard to the propriety of exempting it from any further call. The greater portion thereof I am convinced would form a proper object for the exercise of the discretion vested in you by the law. Should you not think so I would be glad to be allowed the privilege of receiving all such as organized companies for the defense of our coast this winter.

   Very respectfully,

             Z. B. VANCE.

[Inclosure.]

          NEAR FRANKLIN, *November* 3, 1862.

Governor VANCE:

 DEAR SIR: There are about enough men in Macon County between the ages of thirty-five and forty to make one company. We have an opportunity, as I understand, of getting into Colonel Folk's battalion. This is preferable to going as conscripts. I am requested by a number of our most respectable citizens, who are between these ages, to ask you whether in your opinion any other alternative will be presented than conscription or going to that battalion. We have no hesitation in believing that it is our duty to stay here and provide for the helpless while it is in our power to do so. Consultations were held, and it was agreed in family councils who should go and what ones should stay. Those on whom the lot fell to stay in many instances made the greater sacrifice of feeling. But we have taken upon us charges and responsibilities that we cannot throw off until compelled to do so, or until there is a certainty that we will be so compelled. Having acted conscientiously in the matter we feel that we have done nothing to deserve the punishment of going to the army discredited by conscription. Before we are taken to a camp of instruction discredited and scattered to the four winds we ask the privilege of doing what we should have done long ago had it not been for the earnest appeals of brothers who have fallen in the service to stay and take care of those left to our charge. I shall venture on a suggestion, though it may seem to come from a party interested. For every able-bodied man taken from this county there ought to be an able-bodied man retained. We have a number of men in the field now falling very little below the number of voters in the county. Our people, having poor facilities for communication with other sections, have learned to subsist mainly on the immediate production of their own labor. Deprive us of that labor and the innocent and helpless must perish, though their pockets were filled with current money. You know all about men and their powers of endurance for their wives and children. They can turn away from the graves of comrades and brothers firm in the resolve to die, as they have died, for the sake of objects coming to their recollection with thoughts of home. But what consolation or encouragement can come to a man's heart in an hour of trial from a home where the helpless are perishing for want of his hands to provide?

 We have but little interest in the value of slaves, but there is one matter in this connection about which we feel a very deep interest. We are opposed to negro equality. To prevent this we are willing to spare the last man, down to the point where women and children begin to suffer for food and clothing; when these begin to suffer and die, rather than see them equalized with an inferior race we will die with them. Everything, even life itself, stands pledged to the cause; but that our greatest strength may be employed to the best advantage and the strug gle prolonged let us not sacrifice at once the object for which we are fighting.

I have not thought it worth while to dwell in argument upon the question as to whether the mountain people can subsist after taking out every man between the ages of eighteen and forty. It will be sufficient for any one acquainted with this section to pass in imagination through almost any neighborhood and consider the matter over. In a short distance of where I now write there are seven families, living on adjoining lands, and the only man to be left for them all is ninety years old. I have mentioned this case to no one who has not been able to point out one similar to it. The usual means of subsistence seems to be cut off from great numbers.

I shall only ask you to reply to the questions presented in the first few sentences. Knowing the press of important matters that must be upon you, it is with reluctance that I have written at all, and was only induced to bring matters to your notice which are not immediately under your control by the request of a number of citizens that I should do so.

With great respect, yours, truly,

D. W. SILER.

RICHMOND, VA., *November* 13, 1862.

Brig. Gen. S. G. FRENCH,
　　Commanding, Petersburg, Va.:

Brig. Gen. W. H. C. Whiting having been assigned to Wilmington, N. C., for the defense of the Cape Fear, will report directly to Maj. Gen. G. W. Smith. The Secretary of War desires your opinion as to what should constitute the boundaries of the proposed Wilmington District.

Very respectfully, &c.,

JASPER S. WHITING,
　　Assistant Adjutant-General.

CAPE FEAR DISTRICT,
Warsaw, N. C., November 14, 1862.

Maj. Gen. GUSTAVUS W. SMITH,
　　Commanding, &c., Richmond, Va.:

GENERAL: My first and last request will be for troops the instant they are available. The Department is undoubtedly aware of the imminent need for them for the defense of Wilmington. The fever is abating rapidly and there will shortly be no danger to apprehend as to the health of the men. Then it is that I anticipate trouble from the enemy, who, aware of the undefended condition of this important place, are likely to strike before we can collect our resources. The peculiar features of the site of Wilmington as regards the ocean, the harbor at a distance of 24 miles with its two entrances, the river and the surrounding country, make the presence of a strong maneuvering force, in addition to the stationary batteries, indispensable. Not less than 10,000 effective men should be collected as soon as possible, together with five or six field batteries. I hope the Department will be able to comply with this requisition, which, as the difficulty of the position is so well known, will not be considered too great. The batteries might be drawn from the reserve artillery of the army, which, in my opinion, was always in larger force than required. If any troops are on hand to start they may be sent at once to Northeast Station, on the Wilmington and Weldon Railroad.

2d. There is now on the Cape Fear upward of 300,000 bushels of excellent rice in the barns of the planters between the city and the lower rice lands. The crop has not been thrashed, owing to various obstacles. It will be very valuable to us in every way, both for food and forage, and should not be suffered to fall into the hands of the enemy; should there be danger of that I shall destroy it. In the mean time I suggest the purchase of the whole or a greater portion by the Commissary and Quartermaster's Departments. The planters will sell to the Government now at a far more reasonable price than to private purchasers, and as rice, like everything else, is rising in value it will be well to secure this important article of food at once. Please to call the attention of the Secretary of War and Commissary-General to this.

3d. Please to send me the authority, which from time to time has been issued to generals in command, relative to the securing or destruction of private property to prevent its falling into the hands of the enemy. I refer especially to crops—cotton, naval stores, lumber, &c., of which he stands so much in need. I require this, as I shall at once take all means in my power to secure these things on the Cape Fear.

4th. Instructions as to the proclamation of martial law in districts menaced by the enemy.

Please address me at Wilmington.

Very respectfully and obediently,

W. H. C. WHITING,
Brigadier-General, Commanding.

CAPE FEAR DISTRICT,
Warsaw, N. C., November 14, 1862

Hon. GEORGE W. RANDOLPH,
Secretary of War, Richmond, Va.:

SIR: I beg leave to call the attention of the Department to the position of Wilmington and its vital importance in this war. There are now but three great harbors on our coast not in possession of the enemy—Charleston, Mobile, and Wilmington. Of these, Charleston, though its capture would be a severe blow to us and an occasion of great triumph to the enemy and have serious effect on the war at home and abroad, is not a point of such strategic importance in the present position of affairs as the other two. Their capture destroys two great arteries of communication now more than ever necessary since the loss of the Mississippi; cuts two great lines of telegraph; renders Charleston of little avail to us, should it prove impregnable, as an importing point for war material, and affords by rivers and roads most effective basis by which the enemy may extend their power to the interior, endangering at once the armies of the east and the west, on which now the hopes of the country rest. These two points, Mobile and Wilmington, are, from local circumstances, exceedingly difficult to defend, the latter especially.

I speak advisedly, from long service at all of these cities in the engineer service of the late United States. Though nearly all that may be said on this subject in regard to Wilmington will apply locally as well as generally to Mobile, it is with the former I now have to do. It is of the last importance to hold the port. In the fall and winter the blockade is exceedingly difficult, owing to Cape Fear, a dangerous point on the coast, which, with its extensive shoals, extends far to seaward between the two entrances to the harbor. The prevalence of southeast weather at the main entrance, while it is very dangerous for vessels outside, forces them to the northward of the Cape and gives easy access to vessels running the blockade. In like manner the northeast gales drive the enemy to shelter to the southward of the Cape and clears the new inlet or upper entrance. The river affords great facilities for building gunboats. Two are already there ready for their iron. Their completion ought not to be left to chance, for either of them would compel most extraordinary preparations on the part of the enemy and undoubtedly enable us to hold the port for a great length of time, and time is much with us now. Once in service and there is nothing to prevent the building of a fleet of similar vessels. Along the Sound, in the immediate vicinity of the river, are extensive works producing 3,000 bushels of salt daily. This important supply depends entirely on our holding the port. I mention these considerations as worthy of attention, but subordinate to the great strategic importance of the plan in relation to the progress of the war.

As to its defense and the difficulties of the problem, it will be seen by reference to the map that the two entrances, 7 miles apart, separated by Smith's Island, are isolated from mutual support by the river itself. As the works defending them (not, by the way, of strength commensurate with the object) are liable to separate attacks both by sea and land from the northward and southward, the supporting force is liable to be divided. This difficulty would not be so formidable were our means of boat transportation greater, but as we stand it is very much so. The series of swamp lands and bayous which separate Oak Island for a considerable distance from the mainland form an additional and serious obstacle to the relief of Fort Caswell, the work designed to protect the main entrance. The fall of one, though so far apart, will necessarily result in that of the other, and thus, without mutually assisting in the defense of either, the safety of either of these important positions depends on the other. This is owing to the fact that the Cape Fear from 8 to 10 miles from the mouth spreads over extensive shoals, with the channel so far from the land that artillery can scarcely be placed so as effectually to prevent the access to the upper river from being cut off, and with it the river communications to the forts. In addition, though the forts command the entrances, which are comparatively narrow, neither of them have any control over the harbor nor the inside anchorages, while we are prevented by want of means from increasing our batteries on the mainland so as to render the harbor unsafe for the enemy after a successful passage of the entrances. The distance of the city is an unfavorable element in the matter—21 miles to Fort Fisher and 28 to Fort Caswell, with the three routes, the river and the roads by either bank. The roads are extremely heavy, passing through tracts of deep sand. The city, again, though 24 miles from its harbor, is but 6 miles from the sea, and may be attacked from the Sounds by way of Topsail and Swansborough without any attempts on the forts, and this in the present position of the enemy is not unlikely. In event of his success the forts must fall without resistance. In this condition of things the presence of a strong maneuvering force is indispensable and its necessity immediate, no matter how strong we may be able to make the forts or how perfect the arrangements for obstruction; and as both our means and time are limited the supporting army must be in readiness. That granted, though the odds are more favorable to the attack than the defense, the enemy may be afraid to undertake it. I have mentioned the difficulties of the defense to show how urgent is the necessity of the force. There is another consideration which deserves attention. The fact that once in his possession all the circumstances now so favorable to us are of advantage to him, and the means to drive him out must be so extraordinary and so disproportionate to those now needed to defend it, that I fear we should be altogether unable to regain the place. The Cape Fear, navigable to Fayetteville, gives him a barrier on the south impassable to us, near the city especially, where the river, separating into several channels, forms directly opposite the broad and swampy rice lands of Eagle's Island. The Northeast Branch, on the other hand, with the great Holly Shelter Swamps extending along its east bank for 20 or 30 miles and close to the Sounds, would entirely defend him (taken in connection with his inexhaustible means of support and re-enforcement from the seaward) against attack from the northward. All the means in our power, therefore, or rather all that can be spared from points equally menaced, though perhaps not so important, should be put forward at once. To retain this position 10,000 effective men, with four to six field batteries, is the least force I can recommend as the supporting corps for its defense. If this cannot be had we must trust to God in what we have, small as it is, and the blindness of the enemy. Why he neglected this place and struck at New Berne is more than I can tell. I may add that the danger of its reduction is more imminent from the disorders consequent on the pestilence which has desolated the unfortunate city. Preparations have been suspended, the garrison reduced and withdrawn, the workshops deserted, transportation rendered irregular and uncertain, provisions, forage, and supplies exhausted. Unless therefore more speedy measures for re-enforcement and relief be adopted I have great apprehensions of a successful *coup de main* on the part of the enemy. Even a lodgment or the successful passage of one of the forts by even one or two of his gunboats would be a most serious matter, and as things now stand there is little to prevent such disaster. Having been assigned to this important charge but a few days since I am not yet prepared to say whether the dispositions adopted are altogether such as I would recommend. No doubt in general they are the best which circumstances would permit. It is now, however, too late to undertake changes, perhaps also to make additions, unless in the all-important matter of the supporting troops, and that I have hurriedly endeavored to set forth.

In conclusion I beg leave to refer you to a communication of this date to Major-General Smith relative to the securing of the large amount of rice, &c., in the vicinity.

Respectfully urging these remarks upon your attention, and requesting their consideration by the President, I remain, very respectfully, your obedient servant,

W. H. C. WHITING,
Brigadier-General, Commanding.

[Indorsements.]

NOVEMBER 20, 1862.

Referred to Maj. Gen. G. W. Smith.
By order of the Secretary of War:

JOHN A. CAMPBELL.

Respectfully returned.

It is certainly desirable to increase the force at Wilmington, but at present I have not the means of doing it. An extract from General Whiting's letter to me has been forwarded to General Lee, but under present circumstances I have reason to believe that he has no force to spare. General Whiting's remarks about the rice in his vicinity have been submitted to the commanding general. When the pressure of the enemy on the north will permit, forces should, and I have no doubt will, be detached south of James River. Until such time I do not see how the permanent force at Wilmington can be materially increased; but in emergency all disposable force within reach would be sent at once to the support of this or any other important point in imminent danger of immediate attack by superior forces.

> G. W. SMITH,
> *Major-General.*

This has been adequately attended to by General Smith.

> J. A. SEDDON,
> *Secretary of War.*

———

> HEADQUARTERS,
> *Richmond, Va., November 14, 1862.*

Maj. Gen. S. G. FRENCH,
　Comdg. Department of North Carolina, Petersburg, Va.:

GENERAL: Your two letters in regard to boundary of the Wilmington District and report of your recent movement against the enemy, with inclosed note to Secretary of War, are received. I will lay them before the Secretary in the morning.

A letter from Governor Vance to the President, dated the 12th, was referred to me to-day. The Governor requests the President to order that certain points on the Chowan be occupied by troops. I recommended that the letter be sent you; that you would, without further instructions, do everything for the best interests of the service. I congratulate you upon preventing their forward movement, and only regret that they retired before giving you an opportunity to punish them. Three guns on their way here from Wilmington have been ordered to be turned over to you for use in the works at the obstructions. This order was given, I understand, by the Ordnance Bureau. I hope to be able to get more guns for you soon.

The Secretary of War, on the application of the Commissary-General, has directed that no permits are to be given allowing flour to be shipped out of Virginia for private use.

Colonel Ball, from Fredericksburg, telegraphs to-night that the enemy are moving upon him in some force and asks help. Things seem to be quiet in front of General Lee. General Johnston has reported for duty. It is understood that he will be ordered to the army in Tennessee and Mississippi.

Respectfully and truly, yours,

> G. W. SMITH,
> *Major-General.*

———

> EXECUTIVE DEPARTMENT,
> *Raleigh, November 15, 1862.*

Hon. S. R. MALLORY,
　Secretary of the Navy:

DEAR SIR: His Excellency Governor Vance has received your letter stating that he had the control of a quantity of railroad iron and asking his consent to have the same rolled into plate to be used upon boats now being built in this State.

His Excellency presumes that your informant, Commander Cooke, alludes to the iron of the Atlantic road. The State is but a stockholder in the road, a large portion belonging to private individuals. A meeting of the directors of the company has been called and your proposition will be submitted to them. Their decision will be made known to you.

Yours, very respectfully,

DAVID A. BARNES,
Aide-de-Camp to the Governor.

HEADQUARTERS,
Petersburg, Va., November 16, 1862.

His Excellency ZEBULON B. VANCE,
Governor of North Carolina:

GOVERNOR: Your letter to the President of November 11* has been referred to me, in which you represent that some forty persons were arrested in the eastern part of North Carolina and sent to Salisbury for confinement. I have invariably instructed officers on the frontier not to molest any citizen unless they had positive proof of his having committed offense against our Government or violated its ordinances, and this because I found it resulted in no good, for often, however guilty, nothing could be proven against them, and when liberated they went home more embittered. Besides, the enemy can arrest any number of our friends for each one we may arrest, and it cannot now be prevented. I regret that Colonel Radcliffe should have brought them beyond Tarborough. I will write to Colonel Radcliffe to have him make out charges against such as have committed offenses, and that the others at least be sent back under guard by way of Goldsborough to Greenville, to return to their homes under such obligations as you may impose on them. These obligations will readily suggest themselves to you. If, however, you wish to have nothing to do with them I will instruct the commandant of the post of Salisbury what to do with those against whom no charge is made; but this will take some little time.

Yours, very respectfully,

S. G. FRENCH,
Major-General, Commanding.

HEADQUARTERS,
Petersburg, Va., November 17, 1862.

Maj. Gen. GUSTAVUS W. SMITH,
Commanding Army, &c., Richmond, Va.:

GENERAL: When I was on the Roanoke River the other day I passed over the route for several miles by which the army under General Foster advanced and saw many evidences of their wanton destruction of private property and heard related many of their acts of cruelty to inoffensive citizens. At Hamilton they burned from sixteen to eighteen private dwellings, and in nearly every house in the town they made a forcible entry and destroyed all the furniture, broke all the crockery, and demolished the doors and windows. They entered houses by the roadside and in the presence of the inmates destroyed everything in the dwellings. They burned all bedding, all the ladies' dresses, and stole, in one instance, money from the bosom of an aged lady by force. They, in pure wantonness, shot cattle and hogs by the roadside and in the fields. In Williamston they quartered their horses in the parlors of dwellings, and in that place also destroyed the jail and other buildings

---

* See Series IV.

Under this condition of affairs I write you, and request you to lay the matter before His Excellency the President to enable him to consider the propriety of having Foster and his officers declared to be no longer entitled to be regarded as soldiers, and that they have forfeited all claim to the benefit of the cartel, &c. I have written to Ex-Governor Clark at Tarborough to collect the facts in regard to this malicious destruction of private property. I saw two carriages which they had stolen and left in their camps and which they could take no farther, stripped of curtains and otherwise rendered useless.

Yours, very respectfully,

S. G. FRENCH,
Major-General, Commanding.

[Indorsement.]

Respectfully referred to General French.

It is better that General French should address a letter to General Foster inquiring whether these outrages were committed with his knowledge and sanction, informing him that such outrages are considered as forfeiting the right to be treated as prisoners of war, and that the action to be taken in the case will depend on the answer received from him. If no answer is received within — days it will be considered that he admits and holds himself responsible for the acts charged.

By command of Maj. Gen. G. W. Smith :

SAML. W. MELTON,
Major and Assistant Adjutant-General.

State of North Carolina, Executive Department,
Raleigh, N. C., November 17, 1862.

General GUSTAVUS W. SMITH,
Acting Secretary of War :

DEAR SIR : His excellency Governor Vance received a communication from your immediate predecessor, Hon. G. W. Randolph, in which he states that in consequence of the threatened attacks upon the railroad connections in the eastern portion of North Carolina and Virginia, and our inability at present to withdraw from the Army of Northern Virginia re-enforcements sufficiently large to secure those connections, it is considered very important to complete the Danville and Greensborough connection as speedily as possible, and asking him to aid in procuring hands to work upon that improvement. His Excellency instructs me to say that he will most cheerfully give whatever assistance he can consistently with his sense of duty to further the speedy completion of this work, but at the same time he hopes it will not be improper to remark that the Government should at all hazards and at all times defend our present railroad connections at Weldon. That section of the country is of the utmost importance to the Government, abounding in abundant supplies for the army. His Excellency must decline authorizing or recommending the Legislature to authorize the drafting slaves for this purpose. Vast numbers of slaves are leaving our eastern counties, threatened with invasion, and their owners are anxiously seeking employment. The contractors upon the work can, without the intervention of the public authorities, obtain the most abundant supply of hands if they will offer fair and remunerating prices.

Yours, very respectfully,

DAVID A. BARNES,
Aide-de-Camp to the Governor.

HEADQUARTERS,
Wilmington, N. C., November 18, 1862.

Maj. Gen. GUSTAVUS W. SMITH,
        Commanding, &c., Richmond, Va. :

GENERAL: It appears now to be pretty certain that the enemy have withdrawn from their late movement toward Tarborough and Weldon. What may be their next move is only matter of conjecture. Early in the fall, as we have definitely ascertained by spies in New Berne, an expedition against Wilmington was organized, the attack to be made from the direction I have always been apprehensive of—to land with transports at Topsail Inlet, 22 miles from the city; there at high water (10 to 12 feet) [troops] may enter and march by the plank road directly on the city. This plan of attack is the most to be feared, and the one of all others which promises success to the enemy, if in force. Unless we are able to meet and beat them in battle all the forts and batteries on the river fall, without the necessity of firing a gun, with the fall of the city. After these movements commence it will be too late to re-enforce. Within 10 or 12 miles of the point of landing they would cut the railroad bridges on the northeast branch of the Cape Fear, a wide and deep river; that gone, while succor is cut off, retreat is also, and the garrison of Wilmington must either conquer or surrender. My want of troops you know. I hope at least six field batteries may be spared me, which I think might be done from the immense reserve artillery of the Army of the Potomac, a train seldom, if ever, used in our late campaign. I have also great need of cavalry. A very large extent of country has to be picketed and I have not exceeding 100. They are especially necessary to prevent communication with the enemy's blockaders, who skirt the coast daily 20 or 30 miles on each side of the harbor. A regiment would be none too many. I have already represented the number of infantry which I think is the least should be on hand. I will forward you as soon as possible a report and sketch showing our means of defense and their location. I find everything in confusion, owing to the pestilence, and works in many cases stopped or left unfinished.

It is a matter of great importance that a telegraph office should be established at Magnolia, half-way between Goldsborough and Wilmington; this on account of running the trains with troops over the Wilmington and Weldon Railroad (the distance to Goldsborough from here being 82 miles, too far without a station), and also because at this point (Magnolia) we can procure from the pickets the earliest information of the movements of the enemy from New Berne and Beaufort. Will you ask accordingly?

        Very respectfully,

                        W. H. C. WHITING,
                        Brigadier-General, Commanding.

_____

HEADQUARTERS,
Wilmington, November 19, 1862.

Brig. Gen. THOMAS JORDAN,
        Chief of Staff, Charleston :

GENERAL: I have to-day sent over to Charleston three negroes belonging to Nassau, W. I. They formed part of the crew of a small schooner which, loaded with salt, was endeavoring to run the blockade on Monday last, but being cut off from Wrightsville Inlet was beached.

The enemy sent a party on shore, of whom a lieutenant, 2 midshipmen, and 10 sailors were captured by our pickets, together with the negroes, whom the enemy had taken. The captain of the vessel was also rescued. I think they should be placed at the disposal of the British consul.

They certainly were endeavoring to help us. I have therefore sent them over to Charleston, where there may be a chance for them to return to Nassau.

Very respectfully,

W. H. C. WHITING,
Brigadier-General, Commanding.

[Indorsement.]

HDQRS. DEPT. OF SOUTH CAROLINA AND GEORGIA,
Charleston, S. C., November 20, 1862.

Cannot Messrs. John Fraser & Co. find employment for these negroes on their steamers?

Respectfully,

THOMAS JORDAN,
Chief of Staff.

HEADQUARTERS,
Richmond, Va., November 19, 1862.

Maj. Gen. S. G. FRENCH,
Commanding, &c., Petersburg, Va.:

GENERAL: Your letter of this date has been received. I have sent you to-day a battery of two 30-pounder Parrott guns, fully furnished with horses and men. They will arrive to-morrow.

Respectfully and truly, yours,

G. W. SMITH,
Major-General.

HEADQUARTERS,
Wilmington, N. C., November 20, 1862.

Maj. Gen. GUSTAVUS W. SMITH,
[Acting] Secretary of War, Richmond, Va.:

GENERAL: I have been informed that at least a week since you directed five regiments to be sent here, including the two (Radcliffe's and Cantwell's) formerly here; but one (Cantwell's) has arrived; the others are said to be retained by order of Major-General French. Time is pressing. I cannot more clearly explain the necessity for troops than I have done to the late Secretary, nor can I diminish the estimate I conceive the necessity of the case requires, viz, 10,000 infantry and six batteries. My information from New Berne and from the examination of prisoners leads to the belief that the enemy, fully aware of the defenseless state of Wilmington against a land attack, intends a speedy movement, knowing that on account of the force we shall be found unprepared. Against a naval attack I am not so apprehensive, but it is now easily in their power to neutralize all our sea-coast and river defenses. A small detachment can but prove a bait and must necessarily be sacrificed. It would be better, if troops are not to be or cannot be sent, to do without rather than lose the few here and the place too, as must inevitably be the case should the attack be made by the land approach; for the garrison of Wilmington in that event there is no retreat. I earnestly hope, if it is intended that this important point be held, that dispatch will be used in providing a sufficient number of troops. You are doubtless aware that within a few hours of the landing of the enemy at Topsail Inlet (should he attack by land) communication with any point north of this will be cut off entirely by his destroying the railroad bridge on the northeast, not far from abreast of his landing, and I cannot hope for any aid from south of this. I have only then to assure you that after his demonstration commences and attack here is indicated it will, unless providentially otherwise ordered, be too late to re-enforce.

Very respectfully,

W. H. C. WHITING,
Brigadier-General, Commanding.

[Indorsements.]

Referred to General Smith.

J. A. SEDDON,
Secretary of War.

RICHMOND, VA., *November* 26, 1862.

Respectfully forwarded with suggestion that the Governor of North Carolina be requested to furnish all the aid that he can to General Whiting, at Wilmington, and that the substance of this letter be laid before General Lee for his consideration and such action on his part as the exigency demands, so far as it may be in his power to furnish assistance. There are no available troops for such a purpose in and about this city, and there are too few in North Carolina to successfully resist a determined attack in force upon any one of its many important points within easy reach of the enemy. I send a copy of this letter and indorsement to General Lee.

G. W. SMITH,
Major-General.

HEADQUARTERS,
Wilmington, N. C., November 21, 1862.

Maj. Gen. GUSTAVUS W. SMITH,
    [*Acting*] *Secretary of War, Richmond, Va.:*

GENERAL: In the event of the general movements of the enemy in the winter's campaign bringing about a concentration of the Army of the Potomac near to Richmond and the transfer of a portion of the troops to North Carolina, I respectfully apply for the brigade of General Pender's North Carolina Troops and that of General Law, now consisting of three North Carolina regiments and the Fourth Alabama; also for Captain Reilly's battery to be included in the number to be sent here. Will you please to refer this to the Secretary of War? General Clingman, who reported for duty yesterday, informs me that nearly ten days ago you ordered the two regiments lately taken from here, together with two others, to be moved back to this place. Only one has arrived (Cantwell's). Radcliffe's and the other two have been detained by Major-General French near Kinston. I can add nothing more forcible to my explanations heretofore given of the weakness and necessities of this point. I am sure the Department and yourself are fully aware of all the circumstances. Information has been received from a spy that the enemy have concentrated quite a large force of troops (upward of 20,000, it is said) on Roanoke Island, part of which came from New York and part from the vicinity of Suffolk, intended for an expedition, according to camp talk, against this place. However that may be, Roanoke Island is certainly a favorable point for preparing and fitting out the requisite transportation for such an expedition, and considering the difficulty we should have in obtaining early information of any movement from Roanoke Island its selection shows judgment. If such an attempt is to be made from there our first intimation of it will probably be from the pickets at Topsail, 22 miles off, too late for efficient support. As things stand now I could hardly hope to offer opposition enough to enable me to destroy the city. By examining the maps of this vicinity you will see that attack coming along the plank road from the Sounds, the garrison of the town and the two sides of the river have no mode of escape. The river and its branches are wide and deep and our water transportation is not sufficient to allow of the escape of even the field batteries. The forward condition of one of the gunboats now building here; the large amount of valuable property in crops, machinery, &c., all of which ought to be destroyed rather than that the enemy should get them, makes me perhaps importunate in my appeal. As things stand it is my intention, unless otherwise ordered, in case of attack in force by land previous to the arrival of the troops estimated as necessary, to destroy all I can, even to burning the city to the ground.

Very respectfully,

W. H. C. WHITING,
Brigadier-General, Commanding.

CHARLESTON, *November* 21, 1862.

Brig. Gen. THOMAS JORDAN:

SIR: We have received and read General Whiting's letter, addressed to you, in reference to some negroes captured from the enemy. We have no knowledge of them, and are sorry to say have no steamer here, having recently lost one on the Cape Fear.

Thanking you for your kind attention we beg to say that we will cheerfully carry out your wishes hereafter and by first opportunity.

Yours, very respectfully,

JNO. FRASER & CO.

HEADQUARTERS,
Wilmington, N. C., November 22, 1862.

Maj. Gen. GUSTAVUS W. SMITH,
Commanding, &c., Richmond, Va.:

GENERAL: Several days since I called the attention of the Secretary of War to the very important matter of the crops of rice in this vicinity. I advised the purchase by the Commissary Department of the lot. I have had no reply. The planters will sell to the Government for $2, a most reasonable price, considering especially the shortness of the crops and the relative value of corn and rice, the former having reached $1.75, while its customary value is not more than half that of rice. To speculators they ask a higher price. The result will be that unless taken now we must eventually either destroy it or the Government will have to pay two or three prices. I shall be compelled, I fear, to destroy it, and also much other valuable property. It is two weeks since my first representation of the critical condition of this important point, second now only to Mobile in its effects upon the war, and so far one regiment has been sent to me. I have asked but a moderate number (10,000 men and six batteries) wherewith to oppose from 15,000 to 20,000 men concentrating in New Berne and Roanoke, with at least the reported, certainly the probable, purpose of attacking this place. No answer has been given me in the premises. I have explained also the defenseless condition of the place against the attack sure to come. By water we may be regarded as tolerably secure. Unfortunately the enemy will not take that way, or will only approach that way. My antagonist is soldier enough, and in addition has been stationed here long enough to know the best way to attack the city, the batteries, the harbor, and the forts. He will adopt that way—the attack from the Sound. Against that advance I have now but 700 infantry and about 300 heavy artillery, with two or three companies of Partisan Rangers. In opposing this attack the garrisons of Forts Fisher, Caswell, Saint Philip, and other batteries cannot be taken into account. They must man the batteries whether the enemy attack the river or not. If the Government intends to send me troops, please let me know. If it cannot, I will endeavor to save what can be saved from him, and as there is no mode of retreat from this position I will also make preparation to destroy the city. The enemy may then find the garrison among the ruins.

Very respectfully,

W. H. C. WHITING,
Brigadier-General, Commanding.

HEADQUARTERS ARMY OF NORTHERN VIRGINIA,
November 23, 1862.

Maj. Gen. GUSTAVUS W. SMITH,
Commanding, &c., Richmond, Va.:

GENERAL: My letter of yesterday to the Adjutant and Inspector General* contains all the information I possess relative to General Burnside's army. There are no indications of his future movements or plans. His apparent present inaction leads me to apprehend that he may be preparing to transfer his army to some other quarter, as his position is such as to render it extremely difficult to obtain information as to what may transpire in his rear. Scouts are on the watch, but they have to make so large a circuit, both right and left, that great delay necessarily occurs in receiving the information they obtain. I have therefore thought it advisable to request that you will endeavor to obtain accurate information of what may be transpiring south of James River and to take measures, if possible, to be informed as early as practicable of the approach to our waters of any transports or vessels. I shall endeavor to have watch kept on the Potomac of the movements of vessels down that river, as it is very difficult to approach Aquia Creek.

I am, very respectfully, your obedient servant,

R. E. LEE,
General.

HEADQUARTERS,
Petersburg, Va., November 24, 1862.

Gov. ZEBULON B. VANCE, *Raleigh, N. C:*

DEAR SIR: When I joined our forces that were assembled near Tarborough I was very forcibly struck with the want of positive and accurate information as respected the force of the enemy under General Foster as well as to the roads along which he was advancing, and which important information I think could and should have been conveyed to General Martin by the inhabitants residing along the line of his march. To remedy such, or rather to provide for the ascertaining of all movements of the enemy on any future advance, permit me to sug-

---

* See Series I, Vol. XXI, p. 1026.

gest that you cause in all the eastern counties, as far as practical, the enrollment of all persons capable of bearing arms into companies (that are not conscripts), whose duty it shall be to watch the enemy, and on any movements taking place to hover on his line of march and give information and join our forces as guides and skirmishers; these, on being enrolled, to meet occasionally for drill and consultation under their officers as to what each shall do on the occasion and arrangement of places of rendezvous; the rolls of such companies to be sent to Richmond to put them in the Confederate service, but not to serve unless such occasion for local service be required; the sole object of putting them in the Confederate service being that should any be taken prisoners they can be exchanged. No troops in the service of any State when taken prisoners can be exchanged, the United States Government only dealing with the Confederate Government. These men can and must remain at home just as though not in service until their officers call them out on the approach of the enemy. All the details of these duties can be arranged by the men and officers when they assemble, the whole being more particularly to gain and give information and act as guides when necessary. Such a company as this for local purposes I commanded in Mississippi long before secession and for domestic tranquillity at home. A very heavy penalty was attached to any member who did not assemble with his gun and ammunition at one of the rendezvouses, or at the nearest rendezvous to the point where his services might be required, on notice from any member of the company; consequently each knew he would meet the others there. By such a system as this all approach of the enemy could be made known and all preparation be made to meet him more successfully by our army. I deem it much preferable to calling out militia and taking them from their homes. Besides, this is a revolution of the people, and those out of the army are as deeply interested as those mustered into the service. All good citizens must aid. It has been truly said that "when a people are suddenly called upon to fight for their liberty and are sorely pressed upon, the last field of battle is the floors upon which their children have played; the chambers where the family of each man has slept; upon and under the roofs of which they have been sheltered; in the gardens of their recreations; in the streets or in the market-place; before the altars of their temples and among their congregated dwellings, blazing and uprooted;" and if the people cannot do all or part of this, they can organize and ambush the enemy by the wayside and dog his steps and harass him at every swamp and crossing in those counties. Some of the best and most influential citizens should by their presence and example be with the parties engaged in obstructing the rivers, and not sit idle, smoking the pipe of peace by their family firesides and calling solely on our poor soldiers to do all. We must all unite against a common and barbarous enemy, who disregards most of the customs of civilized war.

Yours, very truly,

S. G. FRENCH,
Major-General, Commanding.

HEADQUARTERS,
Wilmington, N. C., November 26, 1862.

Major-General FRENCH,
    Commanding District, Petersburg, Va.:

GENERAL: Yours of the 23d instant is received. I hope Radcliffe's regiment will be on shortly as well as Faison's. The attack on Wilmington will be by land from Topsail. Possibly a feint or diversion simultaneously may be attempted with gunboats on the outer harbor. I have reported to the Department 10,000 infantry, six batteries of artillery, and one regiment of cavalry, as the very least force by which Wilmington can be rendered secure against an advance from the Sound. While the Department agrees with me in this necessity, we are so pressed everywhere that doubtless it will be unable to comply. You remark, in regard to co-operativeness, "if Wilmington is attacked, will send you assistance." It must be observed that if the attack is waited for it will be too late to send assistance. With their advance from the Sound they would of course cut off the railroad bridge over the W——— E———, and the garrison here can neither be relieved nor can it retreat against such an approach. The artillery on the river cannot be counted an element in the defense. In any case they must remain at their batteries. Clingman's brigade (when complete), Young's small battalion, and one battery is all that is here for the defense of the place.

Very respectfully,

W. H. C. WHITING,
Brigadier-General, Commanding.

HEADQUARTERS,
Wilmington, N. C., November 26, 1862.

Maj. Gen. GUSTAVUS W. SMITH,
Commanding District, Richmond, Va.:

GENERAL: Yours of the 21st is received to-day. I regret as you do the inability to supply the troops I deem necessary to secure this place. I was afraid of it, but it was necessary to represent exactly the state of affairs and the necessity in the premises. We must do the best we can. I have been in hopes that possibly a few thousand men might be spared from the western army for the winter on this coast if not from General Lee. The river defenses here are in pretty good order, and seem to be well designed. Fort Caswell is weak. If the river was the only route of the enemy to this city I think he would find it difficult. Day before yesterday a steamer entered New River and steamed up several miles. I ordered the only light battery I have to attack her. Have not yet heard from it. General French seems to be under the impression that I am under his command. Will you please to inform him that by the express direction of the War Department I report to you for orders? I shall, of course, keep him advised of everything that attains, with a view to cordial co-operation, but I am not under his orders.

Very respectfully,

W. H. C. WHITING,
Brigadier-General, Commanding.

HEADQUARTERS,
Richmond, Va., November 26, 1862.

General R. E. LEE,
Comdg. Army of Northern Va., Fredericksburg, Va.:

GENERAL: Your letter of the 23d was received at the Point of Rocks on Monday afternoon. Instructions were given to General French and Brigadier-Generals Wise and Daniel to take effective measures for procuring the earliest practicable information.

In the absence of perfectly conclusive and definite information everything tends to confirm the impression that the enemy are preparing to strike determined blows south of the James River. I feel grave apprehensions for the safety of Wilmington. Besides the artillery garrisons of the forts and batteries there are only four regiments of infantry at that point. Evans' brigade is at Kinston, with a superior force of the enemy at New Berne, threatening Goldsborough. At Weldon there are only about two cavalry regiments, under General Robertson, being instructed. The enemy are pressing upon the Blackwater to such an extent that General French has ordered down to that line four regiments of infantry, in addition to the two of cavalry, and sent all his available artillery, including the two 30-pounder Parrott guns with Dabney's company, from here. This leaves two regiments in Petersburg besides one regiment local guard in the town. In accordance with your letter the Fifty-ninth Georgia and the battery were withdrawn from the South Anna Railroad Bridges after the 20th instant. I would be glad to have the four Mississippi companies of infantry ordered to rejoin their regiment here, and would suggest that Colonel Ball's cavalry, and the battery attached, be relieved at Fredericksburg and placed on the line between the mouth of the Pamunkey and your right. There is a great deal of contraband trade and unauthorized communication across that line to the enemy. I hope you will soon be enabled to send me the Sixty-first Virginia and the Thirteenth Virginia Cavalry for service on the south side of James River. We are extremely weak in numbers at all points from Richmond to Wilmington inclusive. To be prepared, detachments should be made from your army as soon as it is at all safe to do so. I have directed some of General Whiting's letters to be forwarded for your information. Please do not forget to send me the Norfolk Light Artillery Blues as soon as you can spare them. Generals Whiting and French are both calling for artillery and both need it. We have about 3,300 of the 4,500 negroes called for working on the obstructions, fortifications, and roads. I have requested a call to be made for 5,000 more negroes. I rode over the country and lines between here and Petersburg on Monday, spent Tuesday around Petersburg with General French and returned last night. The works at Petersburg are necessarily progressing slowly, nearly all the troops being absent. I have directed a force of negroes to be sent there as soon as they are received. Upon your refusal to part with General Early, Maj. Gen. Sam. Jones, who was to have been assigned to the local command here, was ordered to Northwestern Virginia, and I am still necessarily confined closely to this place. I am very anxious to visit North Carolina, but up to this time have not been able to do so.

Respectfully and truly, yours,

G. W. SMITH,
Major-General.

HEADQUARTERS,
Wilmington, N. C., November 28, 1862.

CITIZENS OF WILMINGTON:

I request all those citizens of Wilmington who are willing to take arms in defense of their homes (and I well know there are many such) to organize themselves into a body, with such weapons as they may have and with those I can supply, and I suggest that they select a leader and such officers as their numbers will require. I address this request to many gallant gentlemen who, from age and according to law in the exercise of many duties, are not otherwise called on to bear arms in this war. I and my staff will be glad to afford them instruction at such times and places as may be most convenient. They will be called on when the enemy is at our doors. I am confident, from my long and intimate association with the men of Wilmington and vicinity, that they are not only willing but eager to fight the invader, and am sure they will do their utmost to the last.

W. H. C. WHITING,
Brigadier-General, Commanding.

HEADQUARTERS,
Richmond, Va., November 29, 1862.

Maj. Gen. S. G. FRENCH,
Comdg. Department of North Carolina, Petersburg, Va.:

GENERAL: For your information I herewith forward you copy of a letter just received from Brigadier-General Whiting, dated Wilmington, November 18. I request that General Evans be ordered to support General Whiting at Wilmington with his whole force if necessary whenever called upon by General Whiting, provided the support can be given without endangering too much the points guarded by General Evans. You will please send to General Whiting a copy of your instructions to General Evans. I will write to General Whiting instructing him to give to General Evans all the support within his power consistent with his defense of Wilmington in case General Evans should be pressed by the enemy. I fear, however, that until General Whiting shall be re-enforced he will not be able to render much assistance to General Evans now that the fever has abated in Wilmington. The object of this is that in case of an attack by the enemy upon either command there will be perfect co-operation between the commanders.

Very respectfully, yours, &c.,

G. W. SMITH,
Major-General.

Abstract from Return* of the Department of North Carolina, commanded by Maj. Gen. S. G. French, for November, 1862.

Commands.	Present for duty.		Aggregate present.	Aggregate present and absent.	Horses serviceable.	Horses unservice-able.	Artillery.	
	Officers.	Men.					Heavy.	Field.
Petersburg, Va.:								
Brig. Gen. J. J. Pettigrew, brigade	189	3,465	4,417	5,256				
Col. J. K. Connally, Fifty-fifth Regiment North Carolina Troops.	26	466	684	814				
Capt. J. F. Milligan, Signal Corps	3	107	122	125				
Fort Clifton, Capt. F. M. Wright, infantry and artillery.	10	222	300	351	34	2	6	6
Garysburg, N. C., Brig. Gen. [B. H.] Robertson, cavalry brigade.	81	1,327	1,744	2,321				
Prince George Court-House, Capt. D. Bell, cavalry.	4	69	82	84	91			
Port Walthall, Captain Sturdivant, artillery	4	73	85	96	58			4
Grand total	317	5,729	7,434	9,047	183	2	6	10

* No reports from District of North Carolina, District of the Cape Fear, Franklin, Va., and Kinston, N. C.

NAVAL COMMANDANT'S OFFICE,
Wilmington, N. C., December 2, 1862.

To the SECRETARY OF WAR,
Richmond, Va.:

SIR: Adjutant-General Cooper sometime since informed me that men in the ranks of the army who were mariners by profession would by your predecessor be detailed, on application, for the naval service, provided they were not in the face of the enemy.

As commander of the naval defenses of North Carolina I submitted last month to General French, at Petersburg, and to Governor Vance, at Raleigh, a plan for defending the inland water-courses of North Carolina against marauding expeditions of the enemy by means of movable batteries of heavier caliber than howitzers. Both promised co-operation, but without the sanction and interposition of the authority of your Department there is no hope of success.

My purpose is to raise men accustomed to the water—for at times it may be necessary to take to the water—divided into three companies, with two light 32-pounders each, to be posted, respectively, at intermediate points between the Chowan and the Roanoke, the Roanoke and the Tar, and the Tar and the Pamlico Rivers—the inland position to be as near as possible and equidistant to the two streams between which it lies; the roads to be kept in good condition both to the rivers and for some distance down their banks, and lines of signals, consisting of red, white, and black canvas balls, to be established by isolation of trees denuded of their branches, from central positions to remotest look-out points. By this means, upon first intelligence of the enemy ascending one of the rivers, two of the batteries, one on each side, could be transported to that river's bank to defend it. These movable batteries, unlike fixed ones, will not require protecting forces; and in the event of a flank movement by the enemy it is proposed to have roads from central positions to the railroads for transportation of batteries; and as the soil of North Carolina between the delta and the mountains is sandy it by consequence becomes more indurated than softened by the winter rains. There are many men now in the camps who from their former pursuits are admirably fitted for such an undertaking, and I respectfully ask your permission to procure their names and, they consenting, your authority for their transfer to the rolls of the Navy. It would be mere platitude to speak of both professions being embarked in one common cause, &c. Your intelligence will decide what is practicable, and its decision will be enforced by patriotism.

I have the honor to be, very respectfully, your obedient servant,

W. F. LYNCH,
Flag-Officer, C. S. Navy.

———

HEADQUARTERS,
Wilmington, N. C., December 2, 1862.

Maj. Gen. GUSTAVUS W. SMITH,
Commanding, &c., Richmond, Va.:

MY DEAR GENERAL: I fully appreciate your situation, and have for some time realized that until it was decided one way or another between Generals Lee and Burnside we could hardly hope for increase of force here now needed. My chief aim and hope, after attempting to demonstrate the necessity of the case and amount of troops required to give promise of a successful resistance in this position, has been to show also that after attack it will be too late to re-enforce. I have also been somewhat restive under the delays which have been made in complying with your orders and with the change in designated regiments made by your juniors in rank, apparently without your sanction. General French writes me a note explaining the delay, but not the change in the regiments. I needed, also, very much more field artillery, and that was an arm which I presumed, from my knowledge of the Army of the Potomac, there could be no difficulty in supplying. I have received, both from Richmond and General Beauregard, telegrams relative to the starting of the enemy's fleet. They do not so far seem to be intended for me; most probably, in my opinion, for Mobile. They have had ample time to reach Charleston or this place. I think that we can make a pretty fair fight against a naval attack, but as I have frequently explained, my force is utterly inadequate on land. The report shows quite a large aggregate of heavy artillery, but that cannot be included at all in the estimate for the land defense, nor indeed can the heavy artillery defend itself against land attack. I wish you could come and see me. In two hours' observation you would learn more of the situation than from a dozen of my letters, though I do not think you would differ materially from me.

Very truly, yours,

W. H. C. WHITING,
Brigadier-General, Commanding.

HEADQUARTERS FORCES ON THE BLACKWATER,
December 4, 1862.

General BEAUREGARD:

MY DEAR GENERAL: My position in command of the forces at this advanced post places me in frequent and full communication with friends within the enemy's lines. They afford me information which I generally find correct. From a letter, dated yesterday, written by my most reliable correspondent in Suffolk, I think proper to furnish you the following extract:

I would further state that I also learn a simultaneous attack will be made on Fredericksburg, Weldon, and Charleston. They will attack Charleston, they say, with 200 vessels, and that very soon.

This you will take for what it is worth. In the New York Times of the 28th, in the local column, is a paragraph to the effect that Banks' expedition of 300 vessels is about to start, with the design of inflicting a destructive blow on the heart of the rebellion. Perhaps it means Charleston. In abundance of precaution I have thought proper to possess you of these rumors.

Confident in your ability to repel any assault, I have the honor to be, truly, your friend,

ROGER A. PRYOR.

HEADQUARTERS,
Wilmington, N. C., December 6, 1862.

Governor VANCE, *Raleigh, N. C.:*

SIR: I send you herewith a copy of letters addressed to the War Department since my assignment to the defense of the Cape Fear, touching the importance of the matter in hand and the men and means re quired. I believe the Department to be fully impressed with the urgency of the case and aware of its necessities; but pressed so heavily at so many points it has so far been unable to supply here but a very small part of the number of troops I consider indispensable to a successful defense of Wilmington. In the mean time I am endeavoring to make the best use I can of the means at my disposal. In view of my small force and the undoubted intention of the enemy to attack this place at no distant day, I recommend Your Excellency to take speedy and strong measures to secure to your people the large supply of salt now on hand in the city. It should at once be placed, at the expense of the owners, out of the chance of capture by the four routes—Wilmington and Manchester Railroad, Charlotte and Rutherford Railroad, Cape Fear River, and Wilmington and Weldon Railroad. Should the place fall (and I cannot say it will not, unless I am heavily and speedily re-enforced) the salt-works must be lost. I should do all in my power to aid in securing it. The accompanying letter will explain to you the difficulty of this position.

Very respectfully,

W. H. C. WHITING,
Brigadier-General, Commanding.

CHARLESTON, S. C., *December* 7, 1862.

Brig. Gen. W. H. C. WHITING,
Wilmington, N. C.:

Look out for Weldon, if they are not going to James River.

G. T. BEAUREGARD.

HEADQUARTERS,
Wilmington, N. C., December 8, 1862.

Maj. Gen. GUSTAVUS W. SMITH,
Commanding, &c., Richmond, Va.:

GENERAL: I understand that your first order directing four regiments to be sent here to me assigned the two which had been taken from here by General French, viz, [Paul F.] Faison's and Radcliffe's. Neither of the latter have arrived. It is reported that Colonel Jordan's regiment, which has come, was substituted for Colonel Faison's by General French, on the ground that Colonel Faison's was too good a regiment for him to spare and he preferred sending an indifferent one; but as I have but very few troops with which to perform or attempt a great work I much prefer they should be as good as can be had. I therefore respectfully request that you will cause General French to carry out the original order. General Clingman is my authority for the circumstance of the substitution. So far three regiments have arrived here—Cantwell's, Shaw's, and Jordan's. Should it be in your power to forward at any time additional troops, and I cannot have any of my old Mississippi regiments, I should like to have Colonel Leventhorpe's North Carolina regiment sent here.

I have not so far been able to ascertain the destination of the fleet reported to have left New Berne. It has not to our knowledge passed to the southward.

Very respectfully,

W. H. C. WHITING,
Brigadier-General, Commanding.

[Indorsement.]

RICHMOND, VA., *December* 11, 1862.

Respectfully referred to General French.

I am disappointed and surprised to learn that only three regiments had arrived at Wilmington on the 8th instant. I would be pleased to have all the facts stated in reference to the change of regiments and the cause of delay or non-arrival of the fourth regiment.

G. W. SMITH,
Major-General.

WAR DEPARTMENT, C. S. A.,
Richmond, Va., December 9, 1862.

Maj. Gen. GUSTAVUS W. SMITH:

GENERAL: The inclosed letter of Governor Vance, of North Carolina, and the reply* of this Department upon the subject of the destruction of certain staple productions of that State in the contingency of the danger of their falling into the hands of the enemy, will inform you of the views of the Department as to your own conduct in that contingency. Much property has been sacrificed improperly in the Southwest under the act of Congress of March 17, 1862, to regulate the destruction of property under military necessity, and anxiety is naturally felt whenever there is any prospect of an exercise of the powers intrusted to the military authorities. While the Department is persuaded of the propriety of destroying property rather than it should be captured to aid the enemy in the prosecution of the war, it is solicitous that the destruction should not take place unless there is imminent danger that such a contingency will happen. You will instruct the generals and other officers of your department conformably to the views herein expressed.

With consideration and respect, your obedient servant,

By order of the Secretary of War:

J. A. CAMPBELL,
Assistant Secretary of War.

[Inclosure.]

STATE OF NORTH CAROLINA, EXECUTIVE DEPT.,
Raleigh, N. C., December 6, 1862.

Hon. JAMES A. SEDDON, *Secretary of War:*

DEAR SIR: The State of North Carolina is purchasing some 15,000 or 20,000 bales of cotton and storing in the interior for purpose of obtaining credit abroad, &c. The order to burn all not removed west of the Weldon and Wilmington Railroad by the 16th instant will embrace a large lot bought by the State. Can you not order General French to respect all such where the holder exhibits a contract of sale to the State? If so, I will make arrangements to destroy it myself on the approach of the enemy. I would respectfully suggest that the execution of that order will have a very unhappy effect on that portion of the country, not only producing great dissatisfaction but even distress in many instances, where people have lost negroes and stock and have nothing left but their cotton to live upon. I respectfully recommend that the order be generally delayed.

Very respectfully, your obedient servant,

Z. B. VANCE.

---

* Not found.

HEADQUARTERS,
Petersburg, Va., December 9, 1862.

General GUSTAVUS W. SMITH,
   Commanding Army, &c., Richmond, Va.:

DEAR SIR: I sent you a copy of my letter to General J. G. Foster, U. S. Army; inclosed you have his reply.* You will perceive he conveniently disavows that the acts were done with his knowledge and consent. I cannot well go behind that, and unless instructed otherwise by Saturday next shall reply without further reference.

   Yours, very truly,

S. G. FRENCH,
Major-General, Commanding.

P. S.—I have not yet received the affidavits sent you of the outrage in Craven County on women. Send it as soon as possible. I forwarded them to you.

SPECIAL ORDERS, }   ADJT. AND INSPECTOR GENERAL'S OFFICE,
   No. 288.   }   *Richmond, Va., December 9, 1862.*

*   *   *   *   *   *   *

XVII. By direction of the President the privilege of the writ of *habeas corpus* is hereby suspended at Salisbury, N. C., and for 10 miles around said place.

*   *   *   *   *   *   *

By command of the Secretary of War:

JNO. WITHERS,
Assistant Adjutant-General.

Abstract from Field Return of troops commanded by Maj. Gen. G. W. Smith, December 10, 1862 (headquarters Richmond, Va.).

Command.	Present for duty.		Aggregate present.	Aggregate present and absent.
	Officers.	Men.		
Maj. Gen. S. G. French, Department North Carolina	716	11,254	14,103	19,141
Brig. Gen. W. H. C. Whiting, District of the Cape Fear	174	2,804	3,911	4,826
Brig. Gen. John H. Winder, Department of Henrico	85	1,486	2,017	2,680
Brig. Gen. H. A. Wise, brigade	136	1,628	2,229	2,962
Brig. Gen. J. Daniel, brigade	192	3,080	4,128	5,253
Brig. Gen. J. R. Davis, brigade	136	2,341	2,944	3,943
Col. [T. S.] Rhett, Richmond defenses	97	1,481	1,955	2,457
Col. T. J. Page, Chaffin's Bluff	23	279	415	488
Capt. S. S. Lee, C. S. Navy, Drewry's Bluff	17	245	377	391
Col. W. P. Shingler, cavalry Holcombe Legion	8	119	218	259
Grand total	1,584	24,717	32,297	42,400

---

* See French to Foster, November 27, and Foster's reply, December 4, pp. 466 470, 471.

HEADQUARTERS,
Wilmington, N. C., December 12, 1862.

Maj. Gen. GUSTAVUS W. SMITH, *Richmond, Va.*:

The following dispatch has just been received from Col. James Radcliffe:

The enemy in large force is within 2 miles of Trenton, on the north side of the Trent River; reported advancing, direction either Kinston or Magnolia. The fleet is reported to have left New Berne to attack Wilmington.

W. H. C. WHITING,
Brigadier-General.

CIRCULAR.]   HEADQUARTERS,
Richmond, Va., December 12, 1862.

GENERAL: Major-General Elzey having reported to me for duty is assigned to the command of the Richmond defenses and that portion of my command lying north of James River. Drewry's Bluff and the works around Manchester being a part of the Richmond defenses proper will be under the command of General Elzey. It is difficult to prescribe exact geographical boundaries between the commands of Generals Elzey, French, and Whiting, but even were these lines definitely drawn they would necessarily be disregarded in emergency, and, in case of active operations against the enemy, department or district lines would be set aside and a combined effort made to beat the foe. I desire to impress upon you the importance of co-operation and a thorough understanding of the condition of affairs in the respective commands. Information concerning the movements of the enemy should be promptly sent to the nearest commander at the same time that it is communicated to this office. It is my desire that you should exercise within your respective commands all the authority which the regulations, usage, and orders confer upon geographical military commanders in war in the presence of the enemy. I shall endeavor to give you all the assistance and support within my power and will be with you in person whenever practicable. The duties of Brigadier-General Winder being of a peculiar character, and more or less connected directly with the War Department, he will continue to make his report to this office and to the Secretary of War or Adjutant and Inspector General of the army as heretofore; but as regards the military operations proper, and the defenses of the city, all will, when called upon, be under the direction of the senior officer present.

Respectfully and truly, yours,

G. W. SMITH,
Major-General, Commanding.

GENERAL ORDERS,)   .   HEADQUARTERS,
No. 15.   )   *Richmond, Va., December* 12, 1862.

I. Maj. Gen. Arnold Elzey is assigned to the command of the Richmond defenses, and of such other portions of this command as are not included in the Cape Fear District and the Department of North Carolina. He will establish his headquarters in the city of Richmond.

II. Capt. John W. Riely, assistant adjutant-general, is temporarily assigned to duty with Major-General Elzey.

By command of Maj. Gen. G. W. Smith:

SAML. W. MELTON,
Major and Assistant Adjutant-General

BRIGADE HEADQUARTERS,
Chaffin's Farm, Va., December 13, 1862.

Maj. Gen. GUSTAVUS W. SMITH,
        Commanding, &c.:

GENERAL: I report to you the condition of things in the Chickahominy and York Peninsulas, below this post: [W. P.] Shingler's and
[L. J.] Hawley's cavalry were not sufficient for pickets or for posts.
They had been badly disciplined. The pickets were negligent and were
cut off, and the posts not sufficiently guarded to prevent the enemy from
making very dangerous dashes. I have deemed it proper and necessary
to send Lieutenant-Colonel Councill, of the Twenty-sixth Virginia Regiment, in command of about 100 effective infantry and the re-enforcements of Major Robertson's cavalry. He has taken post at Sherman's,
on the Diascund road, 2 miles below Forge Bridge. Yesterday evening
he sent to me the accompanying field return, which shows:

SHINGLER'S COMMAND [HOLCOMBE LEGION].

Commissioned officers	9
Non-commissioned officers	20
Privates	148
Aggregate	177
Sick	26
[Effective total]	151
Extra duty	29
Fit for field duty	122

ROBERTSON'S COMMAND.

Officers	6
Non-commissioned officers	9
Privates	100
Aggregate	115
Sick	1
[Effective total]	114
Extra duty	8
Fit for field duty	106

HAWLEY'S COMMAND.

Officers	4
Non-commissioned officers	8
Privates	42
Aggregate	54
Sick	7
[Effective total]	47
Extra duty	3
Fit for duty	44
Total cavalry fit for duty	272

INFANTRY PRESENT.

Officers 10
Non-commissioned officers 15
Privates 93

        Aggregate 118
Sick 6

        [Effective total] 112
Extra duty 1

Fit for duty 111
Add total effective force of cavalry 272

        Total effective force, infantry and cavalry 383

The accompanying report from Colonel Councill and my reply will give details of duties reported upon and in hand. You will see that I have informed him how to get forage. The suggestion to take the corn in shucks might be well to observe. It saves labor, saves corn from shelling, and gets long forage as well as short in the most compact form for transportation.

Deserters in New Kent were not found; they were straggling conscripts; I have ordered their arrest. I ask that printed forms for company morning reports may be sent. My quartermaster cannot get any. I send you a report from Lieutenant Harman, who is my scout in Isle of Wight. From his messages I infer that the enemy are massing their forces, via Norfolk, in and below Suffolk. I have as yet received no dispatches or messages from the scouts sent to Matthews and Gloucester. Have any been received at department headquarters from them? My men have nearly completed their winter quarters and the outer line of our field breastworks. The camp hospital is progressing, but this building and all others have been delayed by want of lumber. We are now cutting and hauling our own lumber from Cox's woods and Aiken's Mill. As soon as sufficient is obtained a part of the hospital buildings can be completed and the storehouse for provisions can be commenced. The latter can soon be put up. Thus I have endeavored to picket and guard our outposts, to provide for them, to construct the necessary winter hospital and other buildings, and to complete our intrenchments. In another week the whole will be well on the way to completion. I therefore make a timely application for leave of absence for nine days from Wednesday, December 24 instant, in order that I may meet my family the second time since April last, and attend to some necessary and important private business. The first leave, you will remember, was cut off by a sudden recall to duty. I make this application now because danger is seemingly somewhat distant and I might perhaps be better spared sooner than at the time I ask for. My family is still at Dover Mills, only 20 miles above Richmond, and a courier can bring me back to my post at any time in eight hours from the moment he leaves your headquarters, and I will hurry back at the first notice, day or night; but, as before, I beg you will not grant this request if you doubt the propriety of doing so.

Very respectfully, your obedient servant,

                                        HENRY A. WISE,
                                        Brigadier-General.

HDQRS. FORCES OPERATING ON THE PENINSULA,
Sherman's Farm, Va., December 12, 1862.

Brig. Gen. HENRY A. WISE:

GENERAL: Your dispatch* of December 10, forwarded from Chaffin's at 5 o'clock, reached me at 1.30 a. m., December 11. Yesterday morning I ordered a commissioned officer to visit the courier stations as far as Crenshaw's, and directed him to notify the couriers as far as that place that I required of them to travel with dispatches at the rate of 8 miles an hour; that in case of failure to do so I would have the delinquents punished, if it could be ascertained who they were. Information reached me yesterday, through an officer who had been down to our pickets, that the negroes below reported that the enemy would come up again yesterday, and would afford an opportunity to all negroes who wished to avail themselves of the chance to return with them. Coming, as the information did, from negroes, I scarcely credited it, but it is a notable fact, I am informed, that heretofore when the negroes have announced their coming they have actually come. I at once ordered the cavalry and infantry to move, directing the latter to occupy a position at Sherman's Mill, and accompanied the cavalry myself on to the Diascund, crossed the Diascund, and proceeded as far as our pickets at James' gate, and returned by the way of Barhamsville. My object was to be near at hand in the event our pickets needed any support, and if nothing else was effected our visit could at least give them confidence. I could hear nothing from the enemy. From what I can learn there is no doubt that they have heard that this post has been re-enforced, and I am inclined to think they will not come up again shortly. After mature reflection, I have abandoned for the present the plan I submitted in my last dispatch of ambuscading the enemy at James' gate. In the first place there is no certainty as to their coming at any particular time, and we might, even if they came up at all, be compelled to lie there for several days and then not have a sight of them. Secondly, as I stated in my communication to you, I think it is not prudent to operate so far down with a mere detachment of infantry and in a country entirely unknown to them. The detachment of cavalry that you ordered to be sent to the upper portion of New Kent returned last night. Mr. Hopkins knew nothing of any deserters in that section, and informed the officer in charge that the information which he had imparted to the department was with reference to conscripts and not deserters. There are no doubt many of them in that locality. My forage-master succeeded in procuring forage at Mr. Selden's, on James River, and I think more can be had there. I think the distance from Hopewell to Crenshaw's too far for a courier to ride, and would recommend that a post be established at Gill & Ladd's shop. Is it your wish that Major Robertson, as the ranking officer of cavalry at this post, shall exercise a command over the whole cavalry force, or must his command be confined to his own cavalry?

We need forms for company morning reports. Forward me a supply if you can conveniently. This cavalry force does not seem to have been much accustomed to returns of any kind. I herewith forward a tri-monthly return of the command. It is the best that I can do with them for the present.

My last dispatch was hurriedly written, and I regret that I should

---

* Not found.

have sent it without my signature. The fact is there is considerable annoyance and difficulty to encounter with this command, and I scarcely have a moment's leisure from morning until night.

I am, general, very respectfully, your obedient servant,

J. CALVIN COUNCILL,
Lieutenant-Colonel, Commanding Post.

BRIGADE HEADQUARTERS,
Chaffin's Farm, Va., December 12, 1862.

Lieut. Col. [J. C.] COUNCILL,
Commanding, &c.:

COLONEL: Your movement to meet the enemy is approved. I have no doubt the negroes are in constant and regular communication with the enemy, and it may be that the latter, whenever they desire to disappoint your movements or to make their own unmolested will cause the former to give it out that they are coming upon a given day. I suggest that you might possibly deceive the deceivers sometimes by going, seeming to return to your camp, and going back to your advance position suddenly and secretly, say at night. I would never advance openly if I could do it by night or stealthily at any time. By watchfulness you can catch them certainly. Is Sherman's Mill not too far off for the infantry to aid your cavalry? I would advance them to Diascund Bridge at least, or not at all, whenever I expected the enemy to come up. It is desirable to have conscripts arrested and made to serve as well as deserters. Have everyone you can reach arrested and sent to Richmond.

Lieut. Col. Randolph Harrison, of the Fourth, informed me to-day that his father has, he supposes, 500 barrels of corn, which is being gathered at the place called the Row, below the Charles City Court-House. I suggested that it would be best to haul the corn in the shucks to your camp at the forge or Sherman's. It would save the labor of shucking to the farm and would give you both long and short forage, and the corn would be cheaper and more compact to haul than corn and shucks apart. He seemed willing to sell in that way, and promised me to write to you. I would not wait to hear from him, but would send at once all my wagons and stop the shucking of the corn. Even at near the same price you would save all wastage by shelling in hauling.

Let a courier's post be established at Gill & Ladd's shop. You will send a trusty trooper or two there. You will observe that Robertson's cavalry, at the suggestion of General Smith, are to be kept separate and apart from Shingler's. This, I understood, was to prevent Major Robertson from taking command of the whole cavalry. Major Robertson is to be kept as a kind of reserve. I am sure I inserted this in your orders. Let the respective corps report to you separately. Whenever they are called to act together in marches or service the ranking officer will of course then, under your orders, command.

I have ordered forms of company morning reports to be forwarded to you.

Your force is stronger than I supposed, and with a good supply of forage on hand I shall expect you to advance whenever you can or whenever the enemy threatens. I recommend you by all means to reach down as far as you safely can after forage. My scouts' last reports from far down James River are that there is no appearance as yet of any gunboats coming up the river. The enemy have in the last two days crossed the Rappahannock below Fredericksburg.

The adjutant informs me that just at this moment he has no printed forms of company morning reports, but he will get them for the whole command as early as possible. I send you a few envelopes.

Very respectfully, colonel, your obedient servant,

HENRY A. WISE,
Brigadier-General.

WAR DEPARTMENT, C. S. A,
Richmond, Va., December 13, 1862.

General GUSTAVUS W. SMITH, *Petersburg, Va. :*

General Lee telegraphs that the enemy attacked this morning at **several** points; that there was fighting all day, but at night the enemy were repulsed on all points of attack. A renewal of the battle expected by him to-morrow. His troops behaved (he says) admirably.

J. A. SEDDON,
Secretary of War.

[DECEMBER 13, 1862.—For Seddon to Beauregard, in reference to reenforcements for Wilmington, N. C., and resulting correspondence, see Series I, Vol. XIV, p. 711.]

HDQRS. FORCES OPERATING ON THE PENINSULA,
Sherman's Farm, Va., Saturday Night, December 13, 1862.

Brig. Gen. HENRY A. WISE:

GENERAL: One of our scouts who went below about five days ago returned this evening. He brings no intelligence of any importance concerning the enemy. He was within 5 miles of Williamsburg and had not a sight of any Yankees. He met with a lady from Williamsburg, who informed him that the Yankees reported to Williamsburg that a fleet was in readiness to ascend the James with a view of attacking the works at Drewry's. He thinks from what he could gather that the post of Yorktown was more of a school for instruction than anything else. Mrs. Vaiden applied to me to-day for a permit to allow her to pass our picket at James' gate to see her sick daughter, who resides some 6 miles below the picket. I inquired who would accompany her, and was informed her servant. I refused to grant the request upon the ground that I had positive orders from you to allow no one to pass our pickets either way, up or down, without your permission. I told her she must await your decision. Mrs. Vaiden is the mother of Major Vaiden, of this county, and I reckon is a loyal lady, but I do not think it prudent to allow her servant to accompany her even if you grant her request.

If we move our camps to Diascund Bridge, as I proposed this morning, I think, upon reflection, it would be better to change the location of our pickets and advance them nearer to the enemy—say a little below the Burnt Ordinary—and let our inside pickets occupy the ground that our outside ones do now. We have heard severe cannonading nearly the whole day; there must have been hard fighting at Fredericksburg. Please send me a paper with particulars, if you can do so conveniently.

A Dr. Taylor, who had been one of our scouts, was captured by the enemy, with his horse and cart, about the time I came to this post. He is not in the service, as I am informed. The enemy has released him and he has returned, I learn, with his horse and cart. I want to understand something about his case. Would it not be best to send for him, and if he refuses to come have him arrested and brought here? I had determined at one time to send for him without consulting you, but have concluded it would be advisable to confer with you in reference to his case. He may have taken the oath, for all I know, and I ought to see him. Coming back with his horse and cart looks suspicious, indeed.

I have supplied the post at Gill & Ladd's with two men from Robertson's command [Thirty-second Battalion Virginia Cavalry]; they come to me as reliable men. I was positive with Robertson in my direction not to send any but trusty men. I am afraid I shall not be enabled to correct the dilatory habits of this line of couriers without personally visiting each post. I sent an officer along the line yesterday to Crenshaw's with positive directions to the men at each post. His visit has not had the effect that I desired; they are still as slow as ever. It is not important that this shall go before the morning; I may have something to add by then.

I am, general, very respectfully, your obedient servant,
J. CALVIN COUNCILL,
Lieutenant-Colonel, Commanding Post.

Sunday morning.—I shall send for Dr. T. without waiting to hear from you.

HEADQUARTERS,
Richmond, Va., December 13, 1862.

Major-General ELZEY, *Commanding, &c.:*

GENERAL: The major-general commanding directs that you will forthwith place General Davis' brigade in position south of the James River to support Generals Daniel or Wise or to take the cars for Petersburg as circumstances may require. Let the brigade move at once. The brigade will bring rations (of which they have six days on hand), and their camp equipage should follow them to their position over the river. Their rations may be cooked after arriving at their position.

Very respectfully, general, your obedient servant,
SAML. W. MELTON,
Major and Assistant Adjutant-General.

BRIGADE HEADQUARTERS,
Chaffin's Farm, Va., December 14, 1862.

Lieut. Col. J. C. COUNCILL,
Commanding, &c.:

COLONEL: Yours of last night reached me within this hour. You have done right to examine Dr. Taylor. Be careful how you trust any of the timid occupants of a section held by the enemy. Some are traitors, some love their property better than public liberty. Do not trust Dr. Taylor any more, but make him serve. Be particular as to your couriers; they are improving at this end of the line. Major Robertson must be held responsible for the discipline and conduct of his men. Be positive, firm, and unyielding to all the cavalry; they all need the strictest discipline. I will endeavor to visit your whole line of couriers, posts, and pickets during the next week; let this be known. If I cannot, the expectation of it may do good. I am confident the enemy are now weak on the Williamsburg Peninsula. As soon as possible arrange your vedettes, couriers, and pickets as you proposed in your last, and as I approved, and advance your whole force as far as your judgment will approve. Let them come to Drewry's; we are ready. Do not allow Mrs. Vaiden or servant—no one—to pass your lines downward. She is a daughter of Mrs. Piggott, an arch traitoress. Move your camp and advance your pickets if you can get forage. I think you can. News has just come that General Lee has beaten the enemy at all points near Fredericksburg. Now is your time to make a rapid demonstration. Do it, if you dare. We have no paper of particulars as to Fredericksburg. Be unceasing in moving.

Yours, truly,

HENRY A. WISE,
Brigadier-General.

GOLDSBOROUGH, N. C., *December* 14, 1862.
General FRENCH:

After severe fighting all day General Evans retired this evening across the river and destroyed the bridge. The enemy are now shelling Kinston, and General Evans will make another stand on heights overlooking the town. He reports their strength at 22,000. Our loss severe; enemy's very great.

Z. B. VANCE.

WAR DEPARTMENT, C. S. A.,
Richmond, Va., December 14, 1862.
General GUSTAVUS W. SMITH, *Weldon, N. C.:*

General Lee telegraphs, in reply to the substance of your letter, as follows:

I think it best to draw re-enforcements you propose, and all available from North and South Carolina. Keep guards to batteries on James River.

By the re-enforcements you propose, General Lee means such as you propose to draw from here.

J. A. SEDDON,
Secretary of War.

PETERSBURG, VA., *December* 14, 1862.
Hon. JAMES A. SEDDON:

We have nothing from Kinston since my note sent by courier. General Whiting reports Banks' fleet at Beaufort. Is there any news from Fredericksburg? I expect to leave at 8 o'clock to-night, and would like to hear from there before I start.

G. W. SMITH,
Major-General.

WILMINGTON, N. C., *December* 15, 1862.
Brig. Gen. S. R. GIST, *Florence, S. C.:*

There will be an officer to meet you on the other side of Cape Fear River. I have a room for you, Clem, and Colquitt. The enemy had

fallen back 1 mile from Kinston last night. To-day no communication
with Kinston. Have not heard from there to-day. We have driven
the enemy some 2 miles in Virginia.

J. H. HILL,
Assistant Adjutant-General.

HEADQUARTERS,
Wilmington, N. C., December 15, 1862.

Maj. Gen. GUSTAVUS W. SMITH,
Commanding, Goldsborough, N. C.:

GENERAL: If compelled to fall back from Goldsborough I think the
best line to take will be toward Raleigh a short distance. If Foster has
conceived the idea of marching on Wilmington from Goldsborough, as
is said by prisoners, his communication will be cut by your people when
he moves. I can be aided by Beauregard with the hope of stopping
him on the northeast bank of Cape Fear River. If, on the other hand,
he is disposed to go toward Weldon you can play the same move.

Very respectfully,

W. H. C. WHITING,
Brigadier-General.

HEADQUARTERS,
Richmond, Va., December 15, 1862.

Major-General ELZEY, *Commanding, &c.:*

The major-general commanding directs that the three Mississippi
regiments of Davis' brigade, with the batteries, and three select regiments of Daniel's brigade, with the battery, be put on the march for
Goldsborough at once by railroad. I have notified General Daniel and
Colonel Stone to provide their commands with five days' rations and be
in readiness. Colonel Walker, commanding city guard, has been directed to return to their commands the companies in the city belonging
to the above-mentioned brigades. You will direct six companies of the
Fifty-ninth Georgia Regiment (Col. Jack Brown) to report to Colonel
Walker at once in place of the companies so relieved. Each regiment
will carry with it one first-rate ammunition wagon and team.

Very respectfully, your obedient servant,

SAML. W. MELTON,
Major and Assistant Adjutant-General.

WAR DEPARTMENT, C. S. A.,
Richmond, Va., December 15, 1862.

General R. E. LEE, *Fredericksburg, Va.:*

General G. W. Smith, by courier from Petersburg, reports the enemy,
22,000 strong, to be pressing Evans at Kinston. The railroad connection and Raleigh must, he fears, be lost without further support. He
proposes to withdraw re-enforcements from this vicinity and the Blackwater, trusting to you to sustain the city if absolutely necessary. As
I see no instant prospect of attack here I approve his purpose, but
deem it proper to inform you.

J. A. SEDDON,
Secretary of War.

RICHMOND, VA., *December* 15, 1862.

To the PRESIDENT, *Montgomery, Ala.:*

General R. E. LEE:

I arrived here (Goldsborough, N. C.) at 3 p. m.   The telegraph with General Evans is cut off.   By latest information he was at Falling Creek, 6 miles this side of Kinston. Enemy now estimated at 30,000, and scouts report re-enforcements constantly arriving from New Berne.   Governor Vance is here.   All accounts agree that our troops behaved admirably in the engagement yesterday.

G. W. SMITH,
Major-General.

The above just received at 8.30 p. m.   We have sent all the re-enforcements to be spared here, from the Blackwater, and in North Carolina.   General Beauregard has promised 5,000, which I hope will arrive in time.   I have ordered here, if possible to be spared, two regiments from General Samuel Jones and two from General Humphrey Marshall.

J. A. SEDDON,
Secretary of War.

DECEMBER 16, 1862.

Maj. Gen. GUSTAVUS W. SMITH, *Goldsborough, N. C.:*

The line being cut by the enemy, can I help you by moving up to any point on the railroad, or shall I wait?   Glad my last train reached you.

W. H. C. WHITING,
Brigadier-General.

GOLDSBOROUGH, N. C., *December* 16, 1862—8 p. m.

Maj. Gen. S. G. FRENCH, *Moseley Hall, N. C.:*

GENERAL: I shall send down five trains to-night, and I think it would be well to have the men sleep on board in case the enemy move upon the railroad and county bridges.   General Clingman should be re-enforced at once or we lose all chance of taking the offensive when our forces arrive.   It might be very important to have a battery promptly brought up.   How many pieces have you?   None of the troops from Richmond have arrived yet, and the batteries are behind the infantry. The two 30-pounders got here to-day, but without horses.   They are almost useless, if not in the way.   Large number of trains have been sent up, and I hope to be able to bring down some horses and wagons for the command.   One regiment (the Fifty-second North Carolina) has just arrived.   I shall send it over the river.   I think if it is practicable that General Pettigrew had better come up in the first train with Burgwyn's regiment, and that his troops should follow.   Let General Robertson hold position at Spring Bank Bridge with, say, two regiments and two pieces, and let General Evans, with his brigade, take position to cover the town on this side, support Robertson if it should be necessary, and be in place to support the troops beyond the bridges if required.   There are five field pieces now at and beyond the bridges, with Col. [S. D.] Pool's battalion of artillery and Clingman's two regiments.   The almost entire absence of information and the conflicting nature of what is brought in make it very difficult to determine upon anything understandingly.   If General Pettigrew's brigade crosses over I desire that you should take command of the forces on that side; that is, of Clingman and Pettigrew.   When my six regiments get here, if the movement is made on the other bank, we will, I hope, be strong enough to leave a sufficient force to protect this place from any movement they may make from the other side of the river by their pontoon bridge, and still be strong enough on that bank to beat them. Such is an outline of my present intention, as far as the present information enables me to judge of the probable views and intentions of the enemy. If you receive no further instructions, let Pettigrew's brigade come up to this place at daylight and Evans fall back in this direction, as above, Robertson taking position at Spring Bank Bridge, leaving outlying guards below upon the river and roads for the purpose of giving information.

     Very respectfully and truly, yours,

G. W. SMITH,
Major-General.

P. S.—Your note of 9.30 p. m. was received just after the above was signed. We have not yet been in condition to cross the river at this point and move forward, but must await the arrival of the troops from Richmond and horses to mount the cavalry before we can hope to act with effect in the presence of such a force.

HEADQUARTERS,
White Hall Bridge, N. C., December 16, 1862—4.30 p. m.

[Maj. Gen. S. G. FRENCH:]

GENERAL: About two hours since it was reported that the enemy, after leaving the bridge, moved up the river, but the news was not confirmed. Their ambulance and wagon trains are now passing White Hall, going in the same direction. They are undoubtedly making direct for the railroad, which I have suspected since yesterday evening. Hurry up the ammunition for Leventhorpe. Firing has nearly ceased.

     In haste, most respectfully,

B. H. ROBERTSON,
Brigadier-General.

WILMINGTON, N. C., *December* 16, 1862.

General GUSTAVUS W. SMITH, *Goldsborough, N. C.:*

Two regiments and a battery have arrived from Beauregard. Telegraph your orders.

W. H. C. WHITING,
Brigadier-General.

SPRING BANK, N. C.,
December —, 1862—sundown.

Maj. Gen. S. G. FRENCH, *Commanding, &c.:*

GENERAL: Two hundred of the Thirty-first Regiment were left on guard at White Hall. They had no rations. I think a force of 30 men, with 2 mounted couriers, enough to guard that point, considering the present position of the enemy.

     Most respectfully,

B. H. ROBERTSON,
Brigadier-General, Commanding.

SPRING BANK BRIDGE, N. C.,
December 17, 1862.

Maj. Gen. S. G. FRENCH,
Commanding, &c., Goldsborough, N. C.:

GENERAL: Please send the rations to this point. My men are, some of them, much in need of them.

Most respectfully,

B. H. ROBERTSON,
Brigadier-General, Commanding.

P. S.—Rest assured I will hold the ferry to the last extremity. I wish you could send Colonel Leventhorpe to me.

GOLDSBOROUGH, N. C., *December* 18, 1862.

Hon. JAMES A. SEDDON,
Secretary of War:

One of my best officers returned at 2 o'clock, having followed the enemy 13 miles on the road toward New Berne. He is satisfied that they are rapidly moving for that place.

G. W. SMITH,
Major-General.

WAR DEPARTMENT, C. S. A.,
Richmond, Va., December 19, 1862.

General R. E. LEE:

A telegram from General Smith last evening announces that from the report of one of his best officers, who followed the enemy 13 miles, he is satisfied they are rapidly returning to New Berne. There is no reliable intelligence of any movements of the enemy either in the Peninsula or on the Blackwater. Your glorious victory has probably broken up all their plans and frustrated their hopes. No official intelligence of movements in the West.

J. A. SEDDON,
Secretary of War.

WILMINGTON, N. C., *December* 19, 1862.

General BEAUREGARD, *Charleston, S. C.:*

I have the following from G. W. [Smith]:

The enemy's next move will be here. Think they will go back to New Berne and Beaufort, though they may march direct. The enemy burned the railroad bridge yesterday. We crossed over the forces at hand by the county bridge, drove them back, and saved the county bridge. The enemy retired during the night, supposed toward Wilmington. They were here in very large force, supposed more than 20,000. My artillery and cavalry have not yet arrived from Richmond and Petersburg; expected to-day or to-morrow. Have not transportation sufficient even for ammunition. Will move as soon as possible.

W. H. C. WHITING.

WILMINGTON, N. C., *December* 19, [1862.]

Colonel SIMONTON, *Magnolia, N. C.:*

COLONEL: Return with your brigade as soon as the train reaches you. If the cavalry are there direct them to look out for approach of enemy. Retire on their advance toward Wilmington, sending me courier. Enemy have retired from before Goldsborough; supposed to be moving in the direction of Wilmington.

Answer that you receive this.

W. H. C. WHITING,
Brigadier-General.

WILMINGTON, N. C., *December* 19, 1862.

Maj. Gen. GUSTAVUS W. SMITH:

On receipt of your dispatch I recalled the troops at Magnolia. If enemy approaches Wilmington it must be by the coast east of Northeast Branch of Cape Fear River.

W. H. C. WHITING,
Brigadier-General.

DECEMBER 19, 1862.

General BEAUREGARD, *Charleston, S. C.:*

I received the following dispatch from General Smith yesterday:

The enemy's army have gone to New Berne rapidly.

W. H. C. WHITING.

CHARLESTON, S. C.,
December 19, 1862—10.30 a. m.

Brig. Gen. W. H. C. WHITING,
Wilmington, N. C.:

Enemy have fallen back in haste to New Berne; probably for James River; but still look out for Wilmington.

G. T. BEAUREGARD,
General, Commanding.

CHARLESTON, S. C.,
December 19, 1862—10 a. m.

Maj. Gen. GUSTAVUS W. SMITH,
Goldsborough, N. C.:

Can't enemy be pursued hotly with 40 rounds of ammunition and five days' provisions in haversacks? They are probably going to James River.

G. T. BEAUREGARD.

Abstract from Field Return of troops at Goldsborough, N. C., commanded by Maj. Gen. G. W. Smith, for December 20, 1862.

| Command. | Present for duty. | | | | | | Effective total. | Aggregate present. | Aggregate present and absent. |
| | Infantry. | | Cavalry. | | Artillery. | | | | |
	Officers.	Men.	Officers.	Men.	Officers.	Men.			
Clingman's brigade	111	1,614					1,662	1,987	
Daniel's brigade	108	1,603					1,625	1,749	2,633
Davis' brigade	108	1,518					1,561	1,743	2,716
Evans' brigade	102	1,269					1,269	1,371	
Pettigrew's brigade	192	3,096					3,131	3,715	
Burwell's provost guard	2	63					65	67	
Mallett's battalion	6	201					201	207	
Robertson's cavalry (dismounted)			64	662			667	743	1,057
Badham's [William] (North Carolina) battery.					8	109	116	135	158
Bunting's [S. R.] battery					3	72	66	81	95
Cumming's [James D.] battery					4	71	71	88	94
Dabney's [W. J.] battery (heavy artillery)					2	31	34	38	53
Starr's [J. B.] battery						66	66	68	88
Grand total	629	9,364	64	662	17	349	10,534	11,992	6,888

Abstract from Field Return of troops commanded by Maj. Gen. A. Elzey, December 20, 1862 (headquarters Richmond, Va.).

| Commanding officer and troops. | Present for duty. | | Effective total. | Aggregate present. | Aggregate present and absent. |
	Officers.	Men.			
Brig. Gen. H. A. Wise	158	1,889	2,222	2,620	3,387
Brig. Gen. J. Daniel	127	1,727	1,925	2,412	3,327
54th Virginia Regiment, Col. [R. C.] Trigg	44	639	647	721	987
27th Virginia Battalion, Col. [H. A.] Edmundson	21	250	252	283	565
50th Virginia Regiment, Col. [Thomas] Poage	29	471	484	521	821
29th Virginia Regiment, Col. [A. C.] Moore	20	366	385	408	943
63d Virginia Regiment, Col. [J. J.] McMahon	21	272	286	311	870
Col. [T. S.] Rhett	100	1,521	1,676	1,995	2,466
Col. T. J. Page	25	259	354	411	486
Drewry's Bluff, Major Smith	15	242	289	372	390
Grand total	560	7,636	8,520	10,054	14,242

SPECIAL ORDERS, }   ADJT. AND INSPECTOR GENERAL'S OFFICE,
    No. 298.   }   *Richmond, Va., December 20, 1862.*

*   *   *   *   *   *   *

XVI. Brig. Gen. R. E. Colston, Provisional Army, will report to Maj. Gen. Arnold Elzey, commanding, &c., in this city, for duty in command of a brigade, to be composed of the following regiments, &c.:

Twenty-ninth Regiment Virginia Volunteers, Fiftieth Regiment Virginia Volunteers, Fifty-fourth Regiment Virginia Volunteers, Sixty-third Regiment Virginia Volunteers, Twenty-seventh Battalion Virginia Volunteers.

*   *   *   *   *   *   *

By command of the Secretary of War:

                                        JNO. WITHERS,
                                    Assistant Adjutant-General.

HEADQUARTERS,
Wilmington, N. C., December 21, 1862.

Captain NEWKIRK, *Commanding Cavalry :*

CAPTAIN : In case of an advance of the enemy from New River or landing at Topsail you will direct one company to retire by Holly Shelter road, advising them that we have infantry pickets at Island Creek. The remainder will join you and keep close observation on the enemy's movements. Scouts should be frequently sent toward the enemy to obtain information.

W. H. C. WHITING,
Brigadier-General, Commanding.

DECEMBER 22, 1862.

Major-General SMITH, *Goldsborough N. C. :*

I would like Clingman's brigade (including Radcliffe's and Faison's regiments) sent back, if you can spare them. General Rains is in Richmond before now. I burst my best gun at Fort Fisher yesterday against enemy's steamer. Please give all possible facility for 10-inch gun from Richmond.

W. H. C. WHITING.

GOLDSBOROUGH, N. C., *December* 23, 1862.

Hon. JAMES A. SEDDON,
Secretary of War :

General Evans' brigade reoccupied Kinston yesterday. The bridge at that point is being rebuilt. General Pettigrew's brigade and Leventhorpe's regiments were ordered to Weldon and Petersburg last night, but they were detained by a collision, in which two engines were disabled; no lives lost. The brigade started this afternoon. General French has returned to Petersburg. The cars are running regularly from Wilmington to the Neuse River, and the railroad bridge at that point being reconstructed.

G. W. SMITH,
Major-General.

BURWELL'S BAY, *December* 23, 1862.

Brig. Gen. HENRY A. WISE :

GENERAL : No change at Newport News; yesterday misty; could not see down to the Point; the day before only three vessels in port. On Monday 45 Yankees came to Smithfield to see about the election; on the same night General Pryor visited the same place. Report says the enemy came to Isle of Wight Court-House yesterday.

WILLIAM HARMAN.

GOLDSBOROUGH, N. C., *December* 27, 1862.

Hon. JAMES A. SEDDON,
Secretary of War :

I returned this evening from Wilmington. Have ordered Clingman's brigade to General Whiting and the two siege guns (30-pounder Par rotts) to General French for the Blackwater. All is reported quiet in the direction of New Berne. Your letter of the 23d is just received.

G. W. SMITH,
Major-General.

BURWELL'S BAY, *December* 29, 1862.

Brig. Gen. HENRY A. WISE:

GENERAL: Yesterday was the first time I could get a view of Newport News since my note of the 20th instant; it has been hazy all the time. Found only two vessels in sight to-day. A small sloop passed down from Mulberry Island; she had the United States flag flying.

On the night of Christmas eve a party of negroes came over from the other side and robbed a gentleman by the name of Branch of meat and other things to the value of over a thousand dollars. Branch lives 6 miles above my station. This is the second time they have come over since I came here. These negroes are said to be camped in nearly every vacant farm house from Jamestown Island to Newport News. If I had 30 men and a sufficient number of boats I believe I could capture a number of these negroes.

WILLIAM HARMAN.

CLAREMONT, *December* 30, [1862].

GENERAL: I received two dispatches to-day, one indirect; the other has been delayed several days.

Yours, respectfully,

WM. DICKINSON.

Abstract from Field Report* of the troops of the District of the Cape Fear, commanded by Brig. Gen. W. H. C. Whiting, for December, 1862.

Troops.	Present for duty.		Effective total.	Aggregate present.
	Officers.	Men.		
Brigadier-General Clingman's brigade	111	1,858	2,031	2,409
Colonel Harrison's brigade	70	1,071	1,144	1,415
24th Regiment South Carolina Volunteers	35	587	614	688
Field artillery (four companies)	18	357	361	395
10th Battalion North Carolina Artillery	13	175	203	213
City guard (two companies)	7	117	119	156
Bridge guard	1	31	31	32
Light-House Battery (one company)	4	71	71	85
Fort Caswell (six companies)	19	258	353	483
Fort Fisher (nine companies)	28	540	673	794
Fort French (one company)	4	47	47	61
Fort Johnson (two companies)	9	105	109	132
Fort Saint Philip (four companies	11	162	204	268
Grand total	339	5,379	5,960	7,131

*This report does not include seven companies of cavalry. It is forwarded without this to prevent further delay.

Abstract from Field Return of troops commanded by Maj. Gen. A. Elzey, December 31, 1862 (headquarters Richmond, Va.).

Command.	Present for duty.		Effective total.	Aggregate present.	Aggregate present and absent.
	Officers.	Men.			
Brig. Gen. H. A. Wise	152	1,817	2,098	2,501	3,400
Col. E. C. Brabble	127	1,611	1,804	2,274	3,311
Col. T. S. Rhett	96	1,424	1,677	1,983	2,467
Col. T. J. Page	26	252	340	404	489
Capt. S. S. Lee	16	266	306	383	395
Grand total	417	5,370	6,225	7,545	10,062

WAR DEPARTMENT, C. S. A.,
Richmond, Va., January 1, 1863.

General R. E. LEE:

I have information that there is in Hampton Roads a large fleet, said to be one hundred transports. General Smith has just returned from North Carolina; apprehends very seriously invasion on a large scale in that State. Either that or a surprise of this city may be meditated. Would it not be judicious to have a considerable detailment of your army either here or within supporting distance?

J. A. SEDDON,
Secretary of War.

HEADQUARTERS PROVISIONAL FORCES, C. S. A.,
Warm Springs, N. C., January —, 1863.

His Excellency ZEBULON B. VANCE,
Governor of the State of North Carolina:

SIR: I have the honor to inform Your Excellency that upon full investigation I am convinced that the late attack on Marshall was made by a band of men numbering about 50 only, who were instigated by desire of plunder, and that there is no treasonable organization of citizens of North Carolina in the mountain region having in view the injury of the Government of the Confederate States or the giving aid to that of the United States. Having an ample force of Confederate soldiers I have informed Colonel McElroy that he can disband his militia, who will be no doubt of more service at home attending to their own domestic affairs, there not being any necessity for keeping them longer in the field. I am pleased to hear that they have been active and zealous in searching for the outlaws, and would no doubt have been very efficient had the trouble been as serious as reported. I have directed all the citizen prisoners to be turned over to the civil authorities of Madison, requesting Colonel McElroy to guard them to such safe jail as they may be committed to. You will be furnished, I suppose, by Colonel McElroy with a list of the prisoners and the evidence against them. They are all implicated in the [burning of the] town of Marshall. I have placed Maj. [W. N.] Garrett, Sixty-fourth North Carolina Volunteers, in charge of a force of about 200 of his regiment, one company of cavalry, and 30 Indians, which force is now on Laurel Creek. Major Garrett has orders to pursue and arrest every man in the mountains, of known bad character, whether engaged in any of the late outrages or not. He will be aided by six companies of cavalry, scouring the mountain regions in Washington, Carter, and Johnson Counties, Tennessee. Col. W. H. Thomas, with 200 whites and Indians of his legion, is operating in Madison, and will go into Haywood, Jackson, and Cherokee Counties, North Carolina, and Clay County, Georgia, with orders to arrest all deserters and recusant conscripts and all tories who have been engaged in unlawful practices on the Tennessee line of the mountains. He will be aided by cavalry and infantry. I have ordered Major Garrett to arrest all deserters he may find and to clear the counties lying adjacent to the mountains of them before he returns to his command. I am satisfied they are leagued with disloyal men frequently and perpetrate many of the crimes which are committed in this part of the State. Believing that it will be of service to your State to get rid of such a population as that inhabiting the Laurel region I have proposed to allow all who are not implicated in any crime to leave the State and to aid them in crossing into Kentucky. I am informed that nearly the whole population are desirous of accepting this offer. They will be driven to do so from necessity, as I learn our troops have consumed all the corn and meat in the settlement. If the people alluded to agree to emigrate I will cause them to be paid for their property used by our troops. Those who are of good character and who have not been guilty of any offense have not been molested by our troops, and will not of course be included among the number who are to be induced to emigrate as mentioned. I propose to give all tories of bad character who may be arrested the option of going to prison (unless they find security for good behavior) or of enlisting in the army. If they enlist they will be sent to Mississippi, from whence they will not find it so easy to desert. I am in hopes the measures adopted will secure peace and security to the families of our soldiers and to the good citizens living in this region of the State. I feel gratified in being able to assist in producing such results, and shall at any future trial be glad to serve your State, which has become endeared to the army by the patriotism exhibited by her children at home and the valor of her soldiers in the field.

I have the honor to be, very respectfully, Your Excellency's obedient servant,

W. G. M. DAVIS,
Brigadier-General, Commanding.

WAR DEPARTMENT, C. S. A.,
Richmond, Va., January 2, 1863.

General G. T. BEAUREGARD, *Charleston, S. C.:*

General Smith seriously apprehends renewed invasion in North Carolina, directed most probably on Wilmington. Can you not again send assistance, and, as General Smith desires, if the attack be made, give the potent aid of your presence?

J. A. SEDDON,
Secretary of War.

RICHMOND, VA., *January 2,* 1863.

Major-General FRENCH:

The troops recently sent from here under Brigadier-General Colston and one regiment of cavalry will be left to protect Petersburg, Va.,

Weldon, and the Blackwater. You will move with the rest of your troops as soon as possible to Goldsborough and take command there until my arrival.

G. W. SMITH,
Major-General.

WAR DEPARTMENT, C. S. A.,
Richmond, Va., January 2, 1863.

General G T. BEAUREGARD, *Charleston, S. C.:*

Further, more reliable intelligence indicates very strongly the purpose of the enemy to move with force (supposed to be 30,000 men) in North Carolina, probably on Wilmington, landing at New Berne or Morehead City, marching to Swansborough; thence along the coast. Aid as soon and as far as you can with safety.

J. A. SEDDON,
Secretary of War.

WAR DEPARTMENT, C. S. A.,
Richmond, Va., January 2, 1863.

General R. E. LEE, *Fredericksburg, Va.:*

Information of fleet in the Roads derived from two different gentlemen residing on the bay, represented (but not known to me) as reliable. Information of expected movement in North Carolina and probable intent to advance on Wilmington from private sources at New Berne vouched by past experience to be trustworthy. I have telegraphed General Beauregard requesting aid, as far as safe to himself, for Wilmington. He had withdrawn his late re-enforcement. General Smith nearly strips Richmond, leaving only about 2,500 men.

J. A. SEDDON,
Secretary of War.

WAR DEPARTMENT, C. S. A.,
Richmond, Va., January 2, 1863.

General R. E. LEE, *Fredericksburg, Va.:*

Reliable information satisfies me there has been in the bay a large fleet. Their movements are puzzling. They brought some troops to Gloucester Point and Yorktown, probably new levies, and carried off others. The fleet, containing at the least 7,000 or 8,000 men, sailed up the bay at least as far as New Point. Whether this was a ruse and they returned and passed the capes at night I cannot learn. I think it probable, for from all items of intelligence I conjecture an expedition meditated on North Carolina. General Bragg's victory more complete and its fruits greater than at first supposed. The enemy in retreat, with our cavalry in his rear.

J. A. SEDDON,
Secretary of War.

FREDERICKSBURG, VA., *January* 2, 1863.

Hon. JAMES A. SEDDON,
Secretary of War:

Your dispatches of 1st and 2d just received. Is the information of the presence of the transports true? They have not passed down the Potomac, nor is there any indication in General Burnside's army to show a purpose of moving.

R. E. LEE.

———

WAR DEPARTMENT, C. S. A.,
Richmond, Va., January 2, 1863.

Col. J. F. GILMER,
  Chief of Engineer Bureau:

SIR: By a contract made by my predecessor (General Randolph) with the Richmond and Danville Railroad Company, they undertook the construction of the connection between Danville and Greensborough, in North Carolina, and were to receive bonds of the Confederate Government, bearing 8 per cent. interest, for $1,000,000 (the amount appropriated by the act of Congress), less by the sum of $75,000, which was advanced them. This contract was made on May 6 last, and the railroad company, having given the bond and executed the securities required for the future repayment of the amount, are entitled to receive the bonds for $925,000, to be issued as of May 6 last. You are requested to draw a requisition upon the Secretary of the Treasury for the amount of bonds to which the company is entitled, and to hand them to Lewis E. Harvie, esq., president of the road, or his authorized agent, taking a receipt for them.

Your obedient servant,

J. A. SEDDON,
Secretary of War.

———

CHARLESTON, S. C., January 2, 1863.

Maj. Gen. GUSTAVUS W. SMITH,
  Goldsborough, N. C.:

War Department anticipates [attack] in force on Wilmington, but I believe their real objective point is Weldon; therefore look out in that quarter. But their troops once afloat may be landed anywhere on the coast. Bragg has gained brilliant victory; driven enemy at all points.

G. T. BEAUREGARD.

———

CHARLESTON, S. C., January 2, 1863.

Hon. JAMES A. SEDDON,
  Secretary of War, Richmond, Va.:

I fear real point of attack is Weldon, not Wilmington. Will render all assistance possible, but to send troops hence far as Weldon might endanger Charleston. Enemy's troops once afloat can be landed anywhere. Railroad to Wilmington in wretched condition; 1,000 men forty-eight hours on way. Please see return, transmitted three days since, for effective force in whole department.

G. T. BEAUREGARD.

———

ENGINEER BUREAU, January 2, 1863.

Col. WALTER GWYNN, Greenville, N. C.:

COLONEL: I am in receipt of your letter of the 30th instant [ultimo], informing me that you would go over to the Tar River the following day to lay off works at a point 5 miles above Greenville and obstruct the river, in obedience to orders from Maj. Gen. G. W. Smith. These works must be pressed forward with great energy. You will at once report fully to Major-General French all your operations for the defense of the Tar and Roanoke Rivers, receive his orders as to the points to be occupied, and act in all things in full concert with the troops under his command. Substantial obstructions should be placed at once in the two rivers. You will give these works your immediate and constant attention. If a pile-driver is necessary to the building of the obstructions have one completed at the earliest moment practicable.

Your obedient servant,

J. F. GILMER,
Colonel of Engineers and Chief of Bureau.

WAR DEPARTMENT, C. S. A.,
Richmond, Va., January 3, 1863.

General R. E. LEE:

SIR: I write to give you rather fuller information than the telegraph readily allows of the various items of intelligence we have of the movements of the enemy on the bay and in North Carolina, and of the surmises they give rise to. For some days past from various sources, represented as reliable but communicated at second hand and in rather a vague form, I have been informed that there was a large fleet of transports in the bay, estimated by one as 100 in number, by another as being fully as numerous as when McClellan's army was being transported to the Peninsula. As I did not know the informants, and the accounts, I felt sure, must be exaggerated, I thought it prudent to give you notice, but did not attach much weight to them. Last night, however, there was handed me by Mr. Jones, the delegate in the Virginia Assembly from Gloucester, a letter from his brother, whom I knew well, giving not only what he had collected but what had been reported by two of General Wise's scouts. That letter* I inclose. Its substantial accuracy may be, I think, relied on. I infer from it that there is some decided movement in contemplation by the enemy. They may be bringing down troops from Washington and Annapolis and carrying others back, or they may be bringing troops from Burnside's army. Mr. Dudley, the president of the York River Railroad, has just called to inform me that a man living in Matthews County, near New Point, whom he believes perfectly reliable, reports more than 100—indeed, than 200—vessels were seen by him a few days ago to come from toward the mouth of the Potomac and proceed toward Old Point. I cannot believe in any such number, especially as you are sure Burnside has not sent off any considerable force, and that no large number of transports have proceeded down the Potomac. I have no information of any considerable number now in the bay. I have also intelligence that the forces at Suffolk were lately largely re-enforced, and that a force of some 5,000 have preceded them by Gatesville toward North Carolina. I learn that immediately after the return of the late Federal expedition to New Berne General Foster proceeded to Old Point; then, after a short delay, proceeded to Washington, and very soon returned and set off at once for New Berne. We have, too, information from the same person who gave very accurate information from New Berne of the late foray of the enemy from there, that another expedition is being

---

* Not found.

prepared there, to be accompanied by a feint on Goldsborough but really intended for Wilmington. General Smith is fully possessed, from all he has learned, with the conviction of such design; and General French, without being so decided that Wilmington is to be aimed at, shares the conviction that some serious blow in North Carolina is meditated. I think it very probable that on his late expedition Foster obtained information that encouraged him to some serious operation, and that he returned to Washington to urge and arrange for it.

There is said to be between political parties in North Carolina at this time much bitterness, and that no little disaffection to the Confederacy exists, and that adverse military events just now in the State might eventuate in very grave efforts to separate from the Confederacy and arrange with the Federal Government. I cannot credit this danger, but all accounts agree as to the existence of great discontent and complaint of desertion by the Government. This renders more important all means in our power to repel promptly any serious invasion. Under this feeling I have telegraphed General Beauregard to render all aid in his power to Wilmington. He has promised to do so, but thinks Goldsborough or Weldon more apt to be aimed at, and says in the present state of transportation on the Wilmington and Weldon road he does not deem it safe to send his troops farther than Wilmington. I have also allowed General Smith almost to strip this city, leaving here only some 2,500 or 2,700 men, of whom there are only 500 at Drewry's Bluff. I have counseled him instead of taking all the forces he is collecting (amounting to 10,000 or 12,000) to Goldsborough, as he intended, to have there only a brigade and concentrate the residue either at Weldon or Rocky Mount, so as to be ready to move readily either back toward Petersburg or on toward Goldsborough and Wilmington, as the enemy may move. With Beauregard's aid Wilmington could resist successfully, he (General Smith) thinks, until he could arrive from Weldon. I think he will pursue this course, but he laments much the paucity of his numbers and wishes earnestly to be re-enforced. I feel no serious apprehension about this place, and yet, considering its importance, feel bound to guard against the contingency of a surprise. Your gallant officers, Stuart and Hampton, have shamed the enemy into more enterprise, as shown by their recent successful raid on the railroad at Bristol. A sudden dash of the forces on the Peninsula or from Suffolk might endanger us here. I should therefore feel better satisfied if we had a portion of your force, say some 5,000 or 10,000 men, here, or even as near as the Junction, whence by two roads they could be speedily brought in case of need. Having informed you, however, fully, I trust the decision to your judgment, as your command extends over the city and you are fully aware of the necessity of watching over and defending it.

I ought not to conclude without adding that General Samuel Jones has written to urge the return of a force to him equivalent to what he sent here under my late orders. The number was about 2,500. He would prefer other forces, as he thinks those sent by him would be more useful at a greater distance from their homes. The late spirit of enterprise manifested by the Federals in the attack on the railroad has alarmed him for exposed portions of Greenbrier and Monroe, which fertile counties will be almost indispensable to him in the spring. He thinks, too, that there will be an earnest effort to obtain possession of all the counties embraced in the newly-admitted State of West Virginia. I fear there is little prospect of returning his forces or their equivalent unless you can feel safe to spare them, at least until after the result of the threatened movements in North Carolina.

General Pemberton telegraphs to-day that the enemy at Vicksburg, being repulsed in several attacks on our positions, have apparently relinquished their enterprise and have re-embarked. No further dispatch from General Bragg.

With high consideration and esteem, most respectfully, yours,

J. A. SEDDON,
Secretary of War.

RICHMOND, VA., *January 3, 1863.*

General S. G. FRENCH,
Commanding, Petersburg, Va.:

Concentrate all your forces near Weldon and Rocky Mount ready to move in any direction, except Colston's brigade and one regiment of cavalry, which will be left to guard Petersburg and the Blackwater. I expect General Beauregard will re-enforce Wilmington, and that General Lee will place troops in position to guard Richmond and Petersburg from being taken during our absence. You had, I think, better take Weldon or Rocky Mount for your headquarters at present. The cipher telegram of yesterday directed you to move to Goldsborough. This has been changed as above, pending certain information of actual movements of the enemy. Please have the troops of Daniel's brigade which were sent from here to Petersburg last night forwarded to Goldsborough as soon as possible. I am endeavoring to obtain additional troops from General Lee's army for service in North Carolina, and will probably know by to-night or to-morrow morning the result of my efforts, and I shall thereupon return to North Carolina. Please write me fully by return of messenger.

Very respectfully and truly, yours,

G. W. SMITH,
Major-General.

CHARLESTON, S. C., *January 3, 1863.*

Brig. Gen. W. H. C. WHITING,
Wilmington, N. C.:

Here is Smith's telegram:

General Beauregard has been requested by Secretary of War to assist you in resisting the threatened attack. I will concentrate as soon as possible.

G. T. BEAUREGARD,
General, Commanding.

CHARLESTON, S. C., *January 3, 1863.*

Brig. Gen. W. H. C. WHITING,
Wilmington, N. C.:

Cannot translate all Smith's telegram, but it refers to following from Secretary of War:

Enemy's intelligence indicates strongly his purpose to move with force (supposed 30,000), probably on Wilmington, landing at New Berne or Morehead City, marching to Swansborough; thence along coast.

I must aid soon and far as can with safety, but I cannot do much beyond leaving forces still with you, for railroads are too slow, not knowing where enemy are going to strike.

G. T. BEAUREGARD.

CHARLESTON, S. C., *January* 3, 1863.

Brig. Gen. H. W. MERCER, *Savannah, Ga.*:

Harrison's brigade will be delayed for a time at Wilmington. Please send to it cooking utensils and change of clothing.

THOMAS JORDAN,
Chief of Staff.

CHARLESTON, S. C., *January* 3, 1863.

S. COOPER,
Adjutant and Inspector General, Savannah, Ga.:

Five Whitworth 12-pounder guns have lately arrived at Wilmington. Cannot two be sent here and two to Savannah for Genesis Point? They are much required to drive off blockaders.

G. T. BEAUREGARD.

RICHMOND, VA., *January* 3, 1863.

General G. T. BEAUREGARD,
Charleston, S. C.:

The guns have been already disposed of by the Secretary of War—one retained at Wilmington, one sent to Charleston, one to Mobile, and one to Vicksburg. The fifth belongs to the Navy Department.

S. COOPER,
Adjutant and Inspector General.

HEADQUARTERS ARMY OF NORTHERN VIRGINIA,
January 3, 1863.

Hon. JAMES A. SEDDON,
Secretary of War:

SIR: I replied by telegraph to your dispatches of the 1st and 2d, but as the line does not seem to be in operation I think proper to write by mail to-day. It is very important to ascertain the correctness of the information conveyed in your dispatches, and if transports are in Hampton Roads their purpose and cargoes. It is customary at this season of the year for coasters to take refuge in those waters from impending or apprehended storms. I have myself counted over one hundred vessels that had taken shelter there at one time. I can discover no indications of any movement of General Burnside's army, and feel very confident that the transports mentioned did not descend the Potomac, nor do I think any considerable portion of General Burnside's army could have been embarked without my knowledge. I have scouts on the right and left flanks of the enemy, which extend to the Potomac, and receive information of all movements of importance. On the 31st ultimo I dispatched General Stuart with a large detachment of cavalry to penetrate the rear of the enemy, with a view of ascertaining his position and purpose. He followed his line of communication from Dumfries to the Little River turnpike, passing between Fairfax Court-House and Alexandria, returning through Aldie and Warrenton. He reports all quiet and could learn nothing of any projected operation. In addition to obtaining information my object was to create anxiety for his communications and cause him, if possible, to discover his intentions. He threw out large bodies of troops in the direction of the Orange and

Alexandria Railroad, which they reached and tore up a portion of. The destruction of the road might have been caused by my having the bridge at Rappahannock Station reconstructed and a train of cars sent to Warrenton Junction during General Stuart's expedition. General Stuart captured over 200 prisoners, destroyed several wagons, cavalry camps, &c., and caused the destruction by the enemy of several depots of provisions on the routes.

I have the honor to be, your obedient servant,

R. E. LEE,
General.

P. S.—All the detachments of the enemy toward the railroad have returned within their lines.

[JANUARY 3, 1863.—For Gist's report of movements to re-enforce Wilmington in December, 1862, see Series I, Vol. XIV, p. 741.]

HEADQUARTERS ARMY OF NORTHERN VIRGINIA,
Camp near Fredericksburg, Va., January 4, 1863.

Maj. Gen. GUSTAVUS W. SMITH,
Commanding, Richmond, Va.:

GENERAL: Your letter of the 1st instant has been received. As you seem to be certain that the enemy are re-enforcing Suffolk and passing troops from that point to New Berne I would recommend that you collect a force at Goldsborough and within supporting distance of it adequate to oppose them. I do not think that the enemy can bring into the field in that region at present a large or stable force—their troops must be new and not very reliable—nor have they any officer there that I am aware of in whom much confidence is reposed by his Government. It is as impossible for him to have a large operating army at every assailable point in our territory as it is for us to keep one to defend it. We must move our troops from point to point as required, and by close observation and accurate information the true point of attack can generally be ascertained. I may be mistaken, but I have thought that the troops at your disposal would be sufficient to drive back the threatened incursions of the enemy south of James River until he is re-enforced from some of his armies now in the field. General Burnside has all his army between Fredericksburg and Aquia Creek, with the addition of Sigel's corps. His own headquarters are near Brooke's Station, nor is there any indication of an embarkation or retrograde movement or going into winter quarters. I think it dangerous to diminish this army until something can be ascertained of the intentions of that opposed to it, and I hope you will be able by judicious arrangement and concentration of the troops under your command to protect the frontier line of North Carolina. Partial encroachments of the enemy we must expect, but they can always be recovered, and any defeat of their large army will reinstate everything. From information received from the Secretary of War I yesterday put Ransom's division in motion to Hanover Junction, and will continue him to Richmond unless I receive other information. You will find it necessary in North Carolina to dispose your troops so that they can march to the points required instead of trusting to the railroads, otherwise it will be impossible to collect your troops as speedily as necessary. The railroads must be reserved for transporting munitions of war. I would recommend that you take the field in person and endeavor to get out troops from the State of North Carolina for her defense. Wilmington should be defended at all hazards.

I have the honor to be, with great respect, your obedient servant,

R. E. LEE,
General.

HEADQUARTERS ARMY OF NORTHERN VIRGINIA,
January 5, 1863.

Hon. SECRETARY OF WAR, *Richmond, Va.:*

SIR: I have to thank you for your long explanatory letter of the 3d instant in relation to operations in North Carolina. Owing to the position of the enemy, the features of the country, and the strength of our army in that State we can only at present expect to act upon the defensive. I hope we shall be able to obtain troops for that purpose. I have relied much on the troops of that State turning out for its defense, and have heretofore found that they have cheerfully and promptly done so when necessity required. If you think any benefit will be derived by sending an officer to Raleigh to inspirit or encourage the people I will detach from this army Maj. Gen. D. H. Hill, a native of North Carolina, and a most valuable officer, for the purpose. By co-operating with the Governor and State authorities great advantage might be gained. At this distance I do not see how offensive operations could be undertaken with advantage, as the most we could hope for would be to drive the enemy to his gunboats, where he would be safe. The assignment therefore of any of our active forces to North Carolina would be to withdraw them from the field of operations, where, as far as I can yet discover, they may be much needed. General Burnside's army is increasing rather than diminishing. The troops from in front of Washington and the Upper Potomac that have not made a junction with him have been moved down toward Stafford. General Slocum's division is at Occoquan and Dumfries. General Sigel's corps is at Stafford Court-House. General Milroy has moved down as far as Martinsburg. From the letter of Mr. Jones, which you sent me, it seems that re-enforcements from Yorktown and Gloucester are being forwarded to him. I have not, however, yet heard of their arrival. It is very clear that General Burnside will not advance toward Richmond unless he is re-enforced. If he determines to go into winter quarters I think it probable that a part of his force may be sent south of James River; but if he does not he must be strengthened rather than weakened. Before the battle of the 13th I think his force could not have been less than 120,000 men; it may have been more. Since then Generals Sigel's, Slocum's, and Geary's forces have joined him. Taking the lowest number, his force is double that of this army. You can judge then of the propriety of weakening it if it is to keep the field. I have always believed that General Foster's force has been much overrated. The reports from citizens, however intelligent and honest, cannot be relied on. Had General Foster received all the re-enforcements that have been reported since this army recrossed the Potomac he ought to have the largest Federal army now in the field. I am not certain that he will attempt any expeditions except those of a predatory character. I think he will rather be deterred than encouraged by the result of his late expedition, especially when he considers the probability of re-enforcements being sent to North Carolina. It is as natural that he should be preparing for defense as offense. It is proper, however, that we should be prepared, and we ought to concentrate there as large a force as possible, and to be successful in our operations our officers must be bold and energetic. Information should be obtained by our own scouts—men accustomed to see things as they are and not liable to excitement or exaggeration.

After receiving your dispatch of the 2d instant I put General Ransom's division in march for Richmond on the morning of the 3d. He has orders to report to General Smith. I hope it may not be necessary to advance him beyond Drewry's Bluff. I think it very hazardous to divide this army. Much labor has been expended in its organization. It is now in excellent condition, physically and morally, and I wish to maintain it so if possible. If I get further intelligence to-day rendering it advisable I will place another division near Hanover Junction, but until I can learn something definite of General Burnside's intentions I do not think it advisable to send it farther. I think it very certain that General Burnside's whole army is between this place and the Potomac, and that as yet he has made no movement to put it into winter quarters or to transfer it elsewhere. The glorious victory obtained by General Bragg will, I think, produce a pause in the military operations of the Federal Army everywhere. New organizations and new combinations will have to be made before much of importance can be attempted. In the mean time we should prosecute our preparations with the greatest energy and vigor.

I have the honor to be, with great respect, your obedient servant,

R. E. LEE,
General.

HEADQUARTERS,
Wilmington, N. C., January 5, 1863.

Flag-Officer LYNCH,
Commanding C. S. Navy:

COMMODORE: I have received your note of yesterday, placing the naval forces under your command at my disposal for the defense of this place and requesting information as to their disposition. I am much obliged. Regarding the security of the gunboats as of the first importance, and indeed, in case of disaster here the most efficient, if not the only, means of reprisal upon the enemy to regain the place, I do not think their safety should be risked. In the event of a formidable attack they should be carried out of the way up the Cape Fear River. For further security I have caused batteries at three points on the river to be located, and the guns and crew of the Arctic should be disposed to occupy and hold these batteries against any attempt by the enemy's boats to ascend the river. This is obvious to me as the proper arrangement under the circumstances, and indeed those guns are nearly all that I have to depend upon for this important service. I will in addition if possible assign a small Whitworth gun to your command.

Very respectfully,

W. H. C. WHITING,
Brigadier-General, Commanding.

HEADQUARTERS,
Wilmington, N. C., January 5, 1863.

Col. JOHN A. BAKER,
  Comdg. Forty-first [North Carolina Troops or Third] Cavalry ·

COLONEL: Colonel Stevens, commanding Twenty-fourth South Carolina Regiment, with Preston's battery of four pieces, has been directed to occupy the vicinity of Island Creek, on the Holly Shelter road, in advance of Northeast Bridge, as outpost there. He is erecting works of defense at that point. In like manner, on the plank road at Sudberry's, about 17 miles from here, an outpost has been established, to which Colonel Harrison, commanding Third Brigade, has been ordered with two batteries. On the advance of the enemy in force for the attack of Wilmington you will endeavor to ascertain the route he takes with his main column. A part of your cavalry should fall back on the Holly Shelter road and report to Colonel Stevens, and a portion on the plank road, reporting to Colonel Harrison. The division of your command and the route you yourself take will of course depend on the circumstances of the enemy's approach, and is left to you. The enemy's advance should be delayed by every means in your power. The Magnolia couriers and troops most advanced in that direction might annoy their rear, retreating, if compelled, by the west side of the Northeast Branch and rejoining the command by the ferry in rear of Colonel Stevens. Colonel Harrison being in the vicinity of Captain Newkirk's camp, that officer will for the present report to the colonel for special orders, continuing of course his routine reports to you.

Very respectfully,

W. H. C. WHITING,
Brigadier-General.

CHARLESTON, S. C., *January 5, 1863.*

Brig. Gen. W. H. C. WHITING,
  Wilmington, N. C.:

Send the Whitworth gun soon as possible. Carriage may be made here.

G. T. BEAUREGARD.

STATE OF NORTH CAROLINA, EXECUTIVE DEPARTMENT,
Raleigh, N. C., January 5, 1863.

Hon. JAMES A. SEDDON,
  Secretary of War:

SIR: I beg to trouble you in regard to a matter of great importance to the army—the increase of desertion. In most of the midland and lowland counties of this State I shall be able to make arrests and prevent serious combinations of them by means of the local militia, with the occasional assistance of the regiment of conscripts at this place; but in the mountains of the west the case is different. The enforcement of the conscript law in East Tennessee has filled the mountains with disaffected desperadoes of the worst character, who, joining with the deserters from our army, form very formidable bands of outlaws, who hide in the fastnesses, waylay the passes, rob, steal, and destroy at pleasure. The evil has become so great that travel has been almost suspended through the mountains. The militia has become too feeble to resist them, as that section has turned out its proportion for the war with the greatest patriotism and unanimity. I propose to organize about 200 men, put them under the command of experienced officers, arm and equip them at State expense, if the President will accept them into Confederate service and pay them only when actually engaged. I hope the Department will accede to the proposition. The impunity which the deserters enjoy and the contagion of their example is operating most ruinously upon the efficiency of the army, to say nothing of the injury to property and citizens of that section. I am now maturing a vigilant system of general police for the whole State for the prompt arrest of deserters and conscripts, which my adjutant-general will submit for your approval soon and perhaps ask your assistance. I also intend to urge upon our Legislature, soon to reassemble, the passage of a law disfranchising all who illegally avoid their duty in the public defense.

I am, sir, very respectfully, your obedient servant,

Z. B. VANCE.

CHARLESTON, S. C., *January* 6, 1863.

Hon. JAMES A. SEDDON,
    Secretary of War, Richmond, Va.:

I have one brigade and three batteries in Wilmington; have ordered one brigade from Savannah here and transportation ready to Wilmington, but it is dangerous to weaken forces here too much, considering difficulty of getting back in case of sudden attack by the enemy. I think General Evans must overestimate latter.

G. T. BEAUREGARD.

CHARLESTON, S. C., *January* 6, 1863.

Brig. Gen. W. H. C. WHITING,
    Wilmington, N. C.:

Reported force at New Berne must be greatly exaggerated. No troops appear to have left the Chesapeake lately for that point. Will prepare for rapid transportation of all troops I can possibly spare in plain emergency but fear slowness of railroad.

G. T. BEAUREGARD.

RICHMOND, VA., *January* 6, 1863.

Governor VANCE:

Could you not give aid against the invasion of your State by calling out the militia which would embrace the exempts as well as those over forty-five? We are straining to send force to you.

J. A. SEDDON,
    Secretary of War.

WELDON, N. C., *January* 6, 1863.

Hon. SECRETARY OF WAR:

General Evans reports Generals Peck, Davis, and Naglee at New Berne with 50,000 men; says one column will move on Wilmington, the other on Kinston and this place. They have no tents; are supplied with hard bread and beef-cattle from Yorktown. I have also information from the Chowan. Yesterday there was a large force in Gates County reported *en route* for New Berne; thirteen gunboats and transports in the Chowan, apparently to take them to New Berne. We have between here and Wilmington only about 12,000 available men; it must be doubled. Can you send us immediately 15,000 more men? I will write you in detail by this evening's mail. This has been shown to Major-General Smith.

S. G. FRENCH.

[Indorsement.]

Read and returned to the Secretary of War. Have you asked Governor Vance to furnish militia? What of the troops to come from Western Virginia?

J. D.

WELDON, N. C., January 6, 1863.

Hon. JAMES A. SEDDON,
Secretary of War, Richmond, Va.:

SIR: Immediately after the fall of New Berne I was ordered to the District of the Cape Fear and the defenses of Wilmington, which city I fortified by a vast amount of labor; thence in July I was called to Petersburg in command of the Department of North Carolina. Petersburg then had no works of defense except a trifling work on the Appomattox. This left me a line to defend from Drewry's Bluff to South Carolina, with the enemy occupying an inland frontier line from the James River to Beaufort, N. C. My force then was scarcely adequate to the task, when, on the last of August, I was summoned to Richmond by your predecessor, and cheerfully—to strengthen the Army of the Potomac—reduced the force to about ten regiments, and some of them very small ones. With this small force the Blackwater has been successfully defended against three attempts by the enemy with large force to cross it, and Foster's advance on the Roanoke and their various gunboat excursions have been defeated, and lastly, without a soldier sent from Richmond to Goldsborough being brought into action, General Foster was again obliged to retire to New Berne. But to meet Foster, in the first instance I took all the infantry force from Wilmington and all but a city guard from Petersburg; in the latter instance General Smith did the same, to the virtual abandonment of those cities by the forces of this department. Now, again, there is but one available regiment in Petersburg, and the force on the Blackwater is very much reduced, and we cannot bring over 12,000 effective for the defense of the line between here and Goldsborough. During all this time the enemy have been steadily increasing their forces, until now I believe they have at least 40,000 men in New Berne, supported by an undue proportion of artillery and a large fleet of gunboats. They also have about 5,000 infantry in Suffolk. As we must act on the defensive, it will not be possible with our means of transportation on the railroad to concentrate them in front of the enemy should he advance even on one line ere he reaches the railroad, much less should he divide and threaten Wilmington and Weldon. I mention all this to give you a brief account of the progress of the operations in North Carolina and to show you how it constantly causes the change of troops. Now, every infantry soldier and officer who have built up the defenses of Petersburg and the Blackwater and are familiar with the topography of the country are gone. This is a military error, in my opinion; but it could not have been avoided, yet it may be remedied. But my object chiefly is to inform you of the condition of affairs on the line and to ask for re-enforcements. As I have stated, there are at least 40,000 men in New Berne, say 5,000 in Suffolk, and small forces in other towns. We have but about 12,000 men and other 2,000 on the Blackwater to meet them. Would it not be better to send the timely aid of at least from 12,000 to 15,000 men? Should the fortunes of war be averse to us it will require double that number to restore our line where it now is. Therefore it is and because I have labored assiduously to maintain the line so long from the James to Wilmington, that now that it is imperiled I ask timely aid, which I trust you may be able to send. I mentioned to General Smith I should write you, and as our views of the necessity for aid are the same, he approved my doing so. The State of North Carolina is in danger. I inclose you some communications just received.

I have the honor to be, yours, most respectfully,

S. G. FRENCH,
Major-General, Comdg. Department of North Carolina.

[Inclosure No. 1.]

NEAR BARFIELD, N. C., *January 5, 1863.*
Col. [D. D.] FEREBEE:

SIR: There are 12,000 Yankee troops in the counties of Gates and Chowan on their way to re-enforce General Foster at New Berne. Thirteen gunboats and transports made their appearance at Colerain, in Bertie County, this morning. It is thought that they are going to take on the 12,000 Yankee troops at Holly Wharf, or Dillard's farm. Others think they are gone by the way of the new canal down to Plymouth and from there to New Berne. There is no doubt in the world of their going to New Berne. I have seen several gentlemen who have seen them, and they all agree that New Berne is certainly their destination. There are a good many desertions from their army, and they all say that they are going to re-enforce New Berne.

D. W. LEWIS,
Lieutenant, Comdg. Pickets on the Chowan River.

[Indorsement.]

WELDON, N. C., *January 7, 1863.*

I respectfully forward this note, but I have some doubts about the correctness of the information.

S. G. FRENCH,
Major-General.

[Inclosure No. 2.]

KINSTON, N. C., *January 6, 1863.*
Maj. Gen. S. G. FRENCH:

Captain Whitford reports fifty steamers at New Berne; about 50,000 troops; Generals Naglee, Peck, and Davis. Naglee, he supposes, will march on Wilmington, while Foster will attack this place and Weldon. Naglee's division is 15,000 strong. The prisoners state that the troops have no tents. Hard bread and beef cattle all brought from Yorktown. The enemy says that he will destroy the railroad between Weldon and Wilmington to prevent re-enforcements reaching Wilmington.

N. G. EVANS,
Brigadier-General, Commanding.

FREDERICKSBURG, *January 6, 1863.*

Hon. JAMES A. SEDDON:

Ransom should be in Richmond to-night. Advance him, if necessary, troops from Richmond, Petersburg, &c.

Let me know what is done and what more is wanted.

I do not believe the force at New Berne is as large as reported.

R. E. LEE.

———

HEADQUARTERS,
Wilmington, January 7, 1863.

General BEAUREGARD, *Charleston:*

Your dispatch received. Special messenger from G. W. [Smith] just arrived. G. W. writes General Lee says Wilmington must be defended at all hazards. Enemy are concentrating very heavily at New Berne. Don't you think movements of your troops ought to begin? It will make great difference in my maneuvers if they are here in time.

W. H. C. WHITING.

———

CHARLESTON, S. C., *January 7, 1863.*

Brig. Gen. W. H. C. WHITING, *Wilmington, N. C.:*
Maj. Gen. GUSTAVUS W. SMITH, *Goldsborough, N. C.:*

I cannot read telegram. I send by mail a new copy of cipher. I may be able to send 5,000 in all to Wilmington, provided rapid transportation can be had. If enemy divide his forces we must concentrate on one point, sacrificing less important one, and then defeat him everywhere in succession.

G. T. BEAUREGARD.

———

ENGINEER BUREAU,
Richmond, January 7, 1863.

Capt. E. T. D. MYERS,
   Chief Engineer Piedmont Railroad, Danville, Va.:

CAPTAIN: Inclosed is sent authority from the Secretary of War recently granted for you to take possession of 50 per cent. of the unlaid iron belonging to the Western North Carolina Railroad, the Raleigh and Gaston Railroad, the Atlantic and North Carolina Railroad, and the Virginia Central Railroad; also authority to take possession of all the iron in the Clarksville and Keysville road, the Port Walthall road, and the York River road beyond the Pamunkey.

I presume, captain, it is unnecessary to urge upon you the importance of appointing promptly energetic agents to secure this iron without delay. The enemy seem to be systematically threatening our great lines of communication, and your link may in consequence become one of vital consequence.

Very respectfully,

J. F. GILMER,
Colonel of Engineers and Chief of Bureau.

HEADQUARTERS,
Weldon, N. C., January 7, 1863.

Hon. JAMES A. SEDDON,
        Secretary of War :

SIR : I have the honor to inclose you a copy of a letter recently received from Maj. Gen. J. G. Foster, U. S. Army; also a copy of a letter from Edward Stanly addressed to General Foster, and a copy of my reply to him.* As I may expect an answer from General Foster I should be pleased to know in advance if these negroes will be returned to their owners provided this Government will return those they have abducted. I have received several letters and have written him several touching the outrages that have been committed by his troops.

Very respectfully, your obedient servant,

S. G. FRENCH,
Major-General, Commanding.

I hope my letter will meet your approval.

ADJUTANT AND INSPECTOR GENERAL'S OFFICE,
Richmond, Va., January 8, 1863.

General G. T. BEAUREGARD,
        Charleston, S. C.:

Throw into Wilmington the number sent before, say, as we suppose, 5,000 men in all. Beyond that exercise your own judgment in contingencies. The Secretary has telegraphed to urge the additional transportation you desired in your late dispatch.

S. COOPER,
Adjutant and Inspector General.

CHARLESTON, S. C., *January 8, 1863.*

Brig. Gen. W. H. C. WHITING,
        Wilmington, N. C.:

I will send you same amount of troops as before. First regiment will leave to-morrow morning; then rapidly as possible.

G. T. BEAUREGARD.

CHARLESTON, S. C., *January 8, 1863.*

General S. COOPER,
        Adjutant and Inspector General, Richmond, Va.:

Will send same number of troops to Wilmington as supposed by Department. First regiments will leave to-morrow morning; others rapidly as possible.

G. T. BEAUREGARD.

---

* See Foster to French, December 31, 1862, p. 497, and French's reply of January 6, 1863, p. 505.

WAR DEPARTMENT, C. S. A.,
Richmond, Va., January 8, 1863.

His Excellency ZEBULON B. VANCE,
Governor of North Carolina, Raleigh, N. C.:

SIR: I have the honor to inclose the copy of a letter addressed to the Governor of Virginia, which will indicate to you the measures which have been agreed upon between His Excellency and the Department to meet the existing emergency. May I not suggest to Your Excellency the importance of similar action in North Carolina to aid in repelling the threatened movement of the enemy upon the railroad connections of your State?

With high consideration, your obedient servant,

J. A. SEDDON,
Secretary of War.

[Inclosure.]

WAR DEPARTMENT, C. S. A.,
Richmond, Va., January 7, 1863.

His Excellency JOHN LETCHER,
Governor of Virginia:

SIR: In view of the menacing movements of the enemy in North Carolina with the intent of striking at the railroad connections in that State, and perhaps of invading Virginia, I am instructed by the President respectfully to suggest to your consideration the propriety of calling out the militia in all the counties near to the North Carolina line, in preparation to aid in repelling any such enterprise. The call might be limited to those of the exempted classes and those above the age of forty at the same time. This Department will call on all subject to the conscript law in such counties to come forward and report at suitable places of rendezvous. Thus the whole arms-bearing population may be promptly commanded for temporary emergency.

With high consideration and esteem, most respectfully, yours,

J. A. SEDDON,
Secretary of War.

HEADQUARTERS,
Wilmington, N. C., January 8, 1863.

[General G. T. BEAUREGARD:]

MY DEAR GENERAL: I send you an incomplete sketch, which you can have copied and returned. It will help you to some idea of my position. I also send G. W. Smith's note, received last night. These will be handed you by Mr. Hazell, of my headquarters, a young gentleman from South Carolina, who has already borne a brave part in eleven battles. I think General Lee's remark somewhat funny. To turn to the map. We should consider, in attacking Wilmington, the enemy having his base in New Berne and Beaufort he may make his choice of two modes of attack—one to send on his iron-clads in advance and attempt, by the reduction of the forts, to clear the way for his transports into the lower harbor, whence he could advance upon the city both by fleet and land; the other to march either from Swansborough or Topsal Inlet, take the forts and river batteries in reverse, and attempt the town, with the fall of which that of the forts would ensue. The latter course is not probable. To Swansborough he can come either overland from New Berne or by railroad to Beaufort, and then overland or by water from Beaufort through the Sounds in light-draught steamers.   He would probably use all these.   If he came to Topsail [Inlet] he would be compelled to have a sea-going fleet of transports, and until or unless he were sure of his harbor he would scarcely attempt that.   Suppose him on the advance and on the line of New River, distant by the road between 40 and 50 miles from the city.   There are two roads, one called the Holly Shelter road, which follows the Northeast Branch of the Cape Fear, and the other the Sound or Plank road near the coast. These fork a short distance from Onslow, which is 50 miles from here and separated by the great Holly Shelter Swamp.   There is no communication between them until within 15 miles of the city.   Except for cavalry and for the purpose of destroying the Northeast Railroad Bridge I do not think he will use Holly Shelter road in force.   Every consideration would keep him to the coast.   Communication all along with his gunboats, supplies, &c., would all influence him, together with the fact that he would have no bridges and rains would not hurt the sandy road.   But it is of the first importance that I should be able to check him on this road at a distance of one day's march, say, from the city (I would not put it farther on account of my own troops, supplies, &c.), and because I should be enabled to hold the Northeast Bridge to delay his advance until I could be supplied with re-enforcements sufficient to enable me to prevent him from attacking the town and Fort Fisher and river batteries in the rear at the same time, which he would assuredly do were I compelled from paucity of force to fall back at once upon my intrenchments.   The longer he can be kept off the more uncertain he is as to our weakness, and time is given to G. W. [Smith] to effect with his troops a heavy diversion in my favor, either by crossing or heading the Northeast Branch of Cape Fear (see map—there is a bridge over Cape Fear near Bannerman and South Washington); or, supposing me to have saved the Northeast Bridge, to throw his force in the city and, combined, attack instead of defending.   If Foster presses on to the close neighborhood of town, my troops being within the outer line, he with his force can keep us in (if, indeed, with my present numbers we can keep him out) while he at his leisure by the Old Brunswick road (see sketch) takes Fort Fisher and the river batteries in reverse.

It is this difficulty which makes so necessary the presence of a movable column to maneuver in defense of Wilmington, especially against a land attack, and to force the enemy to a choice in his operations—one or the other.   The immediate vicinity presents no strong features and no obstacles—open, piney woods, where numbers must tell.   The extent of the outer line of intrenchments, which, by the way, are not formidable in people, is too great entirely for the troops I have here now.   We are using such time as will be allowed us to strengthen the outpost positions.   I have Stevens at the Northeast Bridge and Island Creek with two batteries and Harrison on the plank road about 16 miles from the city with two batteries.   At the latter point, had Gist his troops here, we might trouble the enemy greatly.   I send you these maps.

Please have a tracing made of the country lying between the Trent, the Wilmington and Weldon Railroad, and the Cape Fear, and send back as soon as possible.   Gist says you have no map.   You will see what a terrible effect the taking of Wilmington will have on Charleston and your whole department by examining this map; also that if beaten the relics of my force, if any escape, will have a very troublesome route. If satisfied that the enemy are approaching me with a very heavy force perhaps I may have to see you in person to work out the problem whether Foster, with 30,000 or 40,000 Yankees, is equal to three old engineers, with 7,000 or 8,000 Southrons. I am very much obliged for Gist. He is cool, sensible, and brave. Do not forget to send back that map. I cannot spare it. You might in a short time have the State east of Wilmington and Weldon Railroad traced off. You will perceive some notes on the sketch in pencil. The Brunswick River has been strangely neglected heretofore. Only a few rows of piles have been placed to obstruct it. I have for the purpose neither material nor machinery. Have erected as many batteries as I had guns to spare, and shall put a number of Rains' torpedoes down. What they will do I do not know. The town can be approached, supposing the enemy in possession of the lower river and batteries, by the way of Brunswick River, cutting the railroad bridge of the Manchester Railroad without crossing under fire. This was a great oversight during the past year. You will observe the pencil-marked position of Fort Saint Philip. The position is good and the work pretty well made, but the guns are too light, and what is worse are unbanded—those that are rifled. It forms the left of a line of works put up to command the Smithville and Wilmington road. (See map.) These works force the enemy, unless he could carry them around Green Swamp. But he would never take that side of the river, and I do not attach much importance to them. I have mentioned the importance I attach to have sufficient force to compel the enemy to make his choice between Fort Fisher and the town; that is, the one or the other, not both at once. Or to explain: I ought to have a force the presence of which at Wilmington would compel an attacking enemy to reduce the town by itself first, not having it in his power to sit down before the town and at the same time be able to move on Fort Fisher and thus make an easy entrance for his fleet. You will see on consulting the sketch that the presence of a maneuvering force resting on Wilmington would make a march to Confederate Point or a division of the enemy's forces hazardous. The absence of such a force puts everything in his power. If forced from paucity of men simply to man my lines why, of course, the whole vicinity east of the town is open to him, and he can send at his leisure and take the river batteries.

I would like to have a talk with you. Maps and hurriedly-written letters give so little idea as compared with sight and hearing. The yellow fever has been a terrible obstacle to the works about this place. On my arrival here six weeks ago everything had been at a stand-still for a long time and almost all had to be reorganized. Fort Caswell, being a fort of the old United States, seems to have been considered finished and perfect (probably out of regard for General Totten), and was not strengthened. I am building iron casemates as fast as I can. A battery which I put up eighteen months ago to command the bar was taken down, I believe, for fear it might be taken and used in the fort.

It is a hard place to defend, this, and a hard position. I hope you will not think me importunate. I have demonstrated over and over again to the War Department the importance of the place to the whole country, the war, to Richmond, and to Charleston; shown how it affects the blockade—for it is the easiest place on the coast for the runners and hardest for the enemy—and asked for what I thought necessary. I do not complain. I suppose they could not aid me or they would have done it. Since you and [General] G. W. [Smith] have come to my assistance I feel much better. The gunboats are not near completion. They would be invaluable, if ready. The fever again stopped them or they would now be ready. As they are they increase my embarrassments, for I have to provide for sending them up the river in case of disaster and protect them after they are moved. If they were only ready, one at Fort Fisher and one at [Fort] Caswell, then let them come. One is launched and has her wooden shield on, the other on the ways. I have steamers ready to tow them up the river, and have already constructed batteries on the high bluff of the Cape Fear below the point to which the gunboats can go. Can you send over an engineer officer whose judgment could be relied on for throwing up temporary field works and obstructions? I have just received your telegrams relative to strategic matters. I do not think Raleigh enters into the matter for the present, nor do I regard either of them in the light of cities; that is to say, so much property. The enemy having already possession of Tybee and Pulaski, I cannot regard Savannah as of any strategic importance. It is a place, to be sure, and one which we hope to hold; but it is an extremity, not an artery. To me it appears plain that for the winter the main operations of the enemy will take place in North Carolina, whether their object be Richmond or Charleston. The enemy will not divide his attack on all three of the places you suggest; he will take one or the other. If he goes toward Weldon and Petersburg it is plain that Foster's large concentration is to co-operate with Burnside, and Richmond is the point. If here, it is a separate invasion, though collaterally affecting Richmond and Charleston, and the Carolinas are the object. I have always been of the opinion that Wilmington would be attacked before Charleston, if the enemy have any sense. If it is saved, Charleston will not be troubled; if it falls, Charleston will not be long in following, though locally it might hold out for a time. Look at the map. It is for you to decide whether you will risk your troops, as also the relative value of different points. I have no more time just at this present, but am, truly, yours,

[W. H. C.] WHITING,
[Brigadier-General.]

[Inclosure.]

GOLDSBOROUGH, N. C., January 7, 1863.

[Brig. Gen. W. H. C. WHITING:]

GENERAL: I returned last night. General Lee advises that we draw troops from the State of North Carolina for her defense, and adds that Wilmington must be defended at all hazards. I have just inquired of you by telegraph, asking what number of Beauregard's troops you have and in what contingency you will have to give them up. I have here Daniel's and Davis' brigades. Pettigrew is at Rocky Mount; French, with a brigade, at Weldon. Pryor has four regiments on the Blackwater, and Ransom, with two brigades, arrived in Richmond last night. The enemy are concentrating at New Berne, and there is a force (reported 12,000) in Gates County threatening Weldon, or ready to be transported by water to New Berne or other points. I still have hopes that we will receive additional troops from General Lee's army, but if they are not faster they will be too late. If Beauregard can furnish you with troops enough to hold them at bay long enough for us to come to your relief, all will be well. If he cannot I will, if possible, send enough to enable you to hold on until more troops can be brought from above. Write me fully.

Very truly, your friend,

G. W. SMITH,
Major-General.

WAR DEPARTMENT, C. S. A.,
Richmond, Va., January 8, 1863.

His Excellency ZEBULON B. VANCE,
Governor of North Carolina:

SIR: I send you herew'th an extract from a letter of General Robert
E. Lee, just received.* It explained his views in relation to the threatened movements of the enemy on your State and his inability to supply
the re-enforcements which would be desirable for your defense. You
will observe that he, like myself, relies, in the existing deficiency of
regular troops, on the patriotism and valor of the citizens of your State,
and seeks to know whether the presence of one of his most distinguished
generals (General D. H. Hill of your State) might not prove advantageous in rousing and stimulating the people and in counseling and co-
operating with the State authorities. On this subject I wish to defer to
your judgment and wishes, of which I should be pleased to be advised.
Before receiving this letter from General Lee I had taken the liberty
respectfully to suggest for your consideration a call I had made on the
Governor of Virginia for the aid of the militia, and to request, if it met
your approbation, that a similar call should be made in North Carolina
by the State on its militia, and by the Confederate Government on the
conscripts. By such means I hope adequate aid may be obtained to
repel the threatened invasion of your State.

With high respect and esteem, very truly, yours,

J. A. SEDDON,
Secretary of War.

———

HEADQUARTERS,
Wilmington, N. C., January 9, 1863.

Colonel HARRISON, *Commanding Brigade:*

COLONEL: Having secured your immediate position on the road and
cleared away the brush in front of the works, proceed to the full extent
of your implements and force to the construction of obstacles and defensive works to the right of your position, at all points where the enemy
might endeavor to turn your right, just as if you were to have 5,000 men
instead of only your present command. For one species of obstacles I
would recommend parties of ax-men, under intelligent officers, to follow
the course of the little miry runs on the low ground to the left and
right of the old field, to fell trees and make a difficult abatis on this side
of the crests or rises on this side—a continuous line of log breastworks
for skirmishers and riflemen; clear out brush and undergrowth in the
field of fire on the opposite side, and fell trees in line and at random to
throw opposing movements into confusion, taking care to have our own
side masked. For road-cutters, press the negro and salt-workers generally. With a little instruction and under superintendence of intelligent
officers they will soon learn. As well as I recollect the little sketch here
is something like the old field.†

I would here a little in advance of the road throw up two *crémaillère*
lines, selecting the most commanding ground, one following somewhat
the direction *a o* toward the pond, the other that of *c a*, thrown well to
your rear. On the right of the pond, again, similar works might be
made where sufficiently open country occurs. The cover also for the
batteries heretofore proposed for Sudberry's Crossing may also be constructed, together with infantry cover. I must leave a great deal to your

---

* See Lee to Seldon, January 5, p. 819.   † Omitted as unimportant.

judgment, not being able to be on the ground myself, and to that of Lieutenant Obenchain. It is possible that reconnaissance in front of your position and a short distance beyond the road which leads from the plank road to Holly Shelter may afford a good site for a small outpost or advanced work for pickets. All of the troops here with General Gist commenced leaving Charleston to-day; so you will soon have your full command and be assured of able support. It behooves us therefore to work very hard and rapidly; and although I did not at first glance think very well of that position, yet with some labor and a strong supporting force we shall be able materially to check, if not defeat, the enemy's advance. General Gist will visit your shortly.

Very respectfully,

W. H. C. WHITING,
Brigadier-General, Commanding.

GOLDSBOROUGH, *January* 9, 1863.

Hon. JAMES A. SEDDON, *Secretary of War :*

I returned this evening from Raleigh, which place I visited at the solicitation of Governor Vance. I sent you telegram from there last night, saying it was not advisable to call out the militia at this time, and I will add that I do not think it ever will be advisable to do so. I telegraphed at the same time that I purposed ordering Ransom's division into North Carolina. I would have done this whilst at Richmond had I felt at liberty to act in the case upon my own judgment, and will do it from here at once as soon as a movement of the enemy in force is known. But as my general views have been laid before the Department and General Lee, and the latter only detached Ransom's division for the protection of Richmond and Petersburg, I refrain from ordering it farther on mere anticipated action of the enemy; but it is needed here, and many more troops will be required to put us on anything like equality of numbers with the enemy.

General Beauregard has left two regiments and a battalion at Wilmington. This, in addition to Clingman's brigade, which is about 2,000 effectives, makes General Whiting's force too small for maneuver far from his interior line of intrenchments and materially lessens the chances of his being effectively aided by a force from here. General Beauregard evidently considers it hazardous to place any large number of his troops in Wilmington when there is any prospect of the iron-clads taking possession of the Cape Fear. There is much reason in this view of the case.

From information received from Beaufort and New Berne it is not only certain that the enemy is concentrating rapidly at New Berne through the Sound and by sea through Beaufort, but that had not their principal iron-clad vessel been lost and others injured they would in all probability ere this have made a combined attack by land and sea upon Wilmington. I have no great confidence that either Fort Caswell or Fort Fisher can prevent the passage of heavy iron-clad steamers into the river. If either of these forts are passed by such vessels both forts will fall. A storm at sea has deferred the time of attack. We have, I hope, still time enough to get ready for them.

General Lee's letter to me, which I showed you the night before I left Richmond, has almost deterred me from referring further to the subject of re-enforcements from that end of the line; but I beg that you will bear in mind that it is far more easy to hold Wilmington than to retake it. The same is true of other points in this State and true of the State itself.

I send you with this copies of communications just received from General Whiting and General Beauregard. I may have to re-enforce Wilmington from here. I have one brigade at Kinston, about 1,200; two here, one of 1,300, the other about 3,000. Ransom's two brigades should have been sent at once and should be rapidly following. Please let me know as soon as possible whether General Lee can look after Richmond and Petersburg if Ransom's troops are ordered here, and decide what additional forces if any are to be sent. It is very important that I should know what force I am to have and that I have it in hand as soon as possible.

Very respectfully and truly, yours,

G. W. SMITH,
Major-General.

[Inclosures.]

HEADQUARTERS,
Wilmington, January 7, 1863.

Maj. Gen. GUSTAVUS W. SMITH:

MY DEAR GENERAL: Yours just received. I would have been all right had Beauregard allowed his troops to remain. As it is, he stopped taking all away, leaving me Stevens' regiment, Harrison's regiment, and a battalion. These with Clingman's brigade, three of Beauregard's batteries, and my three, make my present disposable force. It is not enough to hold the enemy, in such a country as the plank road, at a distance from town, if he comes in the force represented or even half of that. And to keep him at a distance is all important, because that is my only way to save the Northeast Bridge. I send you Beauregard's telegraph to me. But if Wilmington is the point menaced and I believe it is, those troops ought to be here to enable me to maneuver. General Lee's remarks about drawing troops from North Carolina, and then adding that Wilmington must be defended at all hazards, rather crowds me. If I could possibly have those 5,000 here I could stop the enemy 15 miles from here and keep his hands full, besides saving the Northeast [Bridge], which is important to your movement whether you intend to strike him in flank or rear; and of course very important to Wilmington. I shall write Beauregard and also telegraph him. Hadn't you better telegraph him that the movement of his troops should commence at once. I know he had them all ready to move, but transportation is so fearfully slow.

Very tired; just off a 40-mile reconnaissance to eastward.

Yours, truly,

W. H. C. WHITING.

CHARLESTON, *January* 8, [1863.]

Major-General WHITING:

Should enemy's iron-clads or other steamers enter Cape Fear River would not my troops at Wilmington be cut off from possibility of return? If so, ought Charleston and Savannah to be endangered for that city? Weldon, Raleigh, and Wilmington are three objective points of enemy; first two are decisive objectives. If all three cannot be defended together with strong probability of success, enemy's movements and our available forces must determine which to sacrifice in timely succession for defense of most important one. Such is my view of present military operations in North Carolina. Please answer.*

G. T. BEAUREGARD.

---

*Same to Cooper and Smith.

[Indorsement.]

JANUARY 10, 1863.

[Note in pencil on Smith's letter.]

The exempts for Confederate service should be fitted out for emergency. The Government has, I suppose, the power.

J. D.

HEADQUARTERS,
Kinston, N. C., January 9, 1863.

Maj. Gen. S. G. FRENCH,
    Comdg. District of North Carolina, Weldon, N. C.:

GENERAL: I received your letter last night and telegraphed what I learned from our underground railroad. "Reliable" says that on Monday, the 4th instant, Foster was shipping his Napoleon guns all day, but could not learn their destination. He reports also that a long black steamer, with light Dahlgren guns and two pivot guns, one each in the bow and stern, [had arrived.] She is intended for Wilmington and is to enter the harbor as the Alabama, the enemy firing at her as she passes. She is to sail under Confederate colors. This I think probable. I have my pickets within 8 miles of New Berne, who keep me advised of every movement. I have learned that the enemy will attack Weldon, Wilmington, and this place at the same time. Foster will probably come this way, Heintzelman go to Wilmington, Peck and Corcoran to Weldon. Troops have been again sent to Suffolk, or were to leave when Corcoran left Yorktown. I am convinced Foster will not attack me again on the south side of the Neuse, but will march up the left bank to co-operate with the force (if necessary) that attacks Weldon. With the two brigades now at Goldsborough I think I can prevent his junction by attacking him as far down as Contentnea Creek, which he will be obliged to cross if he marches out from New Berne to attack Goldsborough. I can also, if he passes Snow Hill, easily attack his rear. My scout thinks every precaution should be taken to guard the Weldon bridge, as the enemy are trying to bribe citizens to burn it. I will keep you advised.

Very respectfully, your obedient,

N. G. EVANS,
Brigadier-General, Commanding.

EXECUTIVE DEPARTMENT,
Richmond, January 9, 1863.

Hon. JAMES A. SEDDON,
    Secretary of War of the Confederate States:

SIR: Your letter of the 7th instant, directed to the Governor, has been received. He requests me to inform you that the requisition for the militia has been complied with, by the issue of the necessary orders to the adjutant-general of this State, a copy of which is herein inclosed.

Very respectfully,

GEORGE W. MUNFORD,
Secretary of the Commonwealth.

[Inclosure.]

The adjutant-general will issue to the proper officers orders calling out immediately for a service of six months, unless sooner discharged, the militia of the counties hereinafter named, not called for under the conscript law of the Confederate States, embracing all the able-bodied men between the ages of forty and forty-five years.

Employés of railroad and transportation companies and officers of banks, and other persons who are exempt by the laws of the State and Confederate States, are not liable to duty.

The rendezvous will be at Petersburg.

When arrived at the rendezvous the troops will be reorganized into companies, battalions, and regiments. The oldest commissioned officers present, of the respective grades required, will be assigned to duty, and supernumeraries will be reduced to the ranks.

The troops will be supplied with arms and ammunition when they arrive at Petersburg.

The officers in command of detachments will cause the men to be furnished with necessary provisions until mustered into service of the Confederate States, and for this purpose may purchase or impress necessaries and transmit the accounts therefor to the auditing board.

The counties upon which the call is made are the counties of Greenville, Dinwiddie, the city of Petersburg, the counties of Brunswick, Lunenburg, Mecklenburg, Halifax, Charlotte, Pittsylvania, Henry, Patrick, Franklin, Nottoway, Prince Edward, and Campbell, including the city of Lynchburg.

This call is made by the War Department by order of the President of the Confederate States. It is of great importance that the force called for be promptly furnished and organized.

—

SPECIAL ORDERS, }   ADJUTANT-GENERAL'S OFFICE, VA.,
No. —.   *January 9, 1863.*

The commandants of the Fiftieth Regiment, Greenville County; Eighty-third, Dinwiddie; Thirty-ninth, Petersburg; Sixty-sixth and Ninety-sixth, Brunswick; Seventy-third, Lunenburg; Twenty-second and Ninety-eighth, Mecklenburg; Sixty-ninth, Eighty-fourth, and One hundred and seventy-second, Halifax; Twenty-sixth, Charlotte; Forty-second, One hundred and first, and One hundred and sixty-eighth, Pittsylvania; Sixty-fourth, Henry; Eighteenth and One hundred and fifty-sixth, Patrick; Forty-third, One hundred and tenth, and One hundred and ninety-fifth, Franklin; Forty-ninth, Nottoway; Sixty-third, Prince Edward; Fifty-third and One hundred and seventeenth, Campbell, and Thirty-first, Lynchburg, will immediately call out, for a service of six months, unless sooner discharged, all the militiamen not called for under the conscript laws of the Confederate States, embracing all able-bodied men between the ages of forty and forty-five years.

Officers and employés of railroad and transportation companies, officers of banks, and other persons who are exempt by the laws of the State and Confederate States, are not subject to this call.

Where there are no field officers in a regiment the senior captain is commandant; where no captains, the senior lieutenants of highest rank command; and all such are peremptorily required to execute this order without a moment's delay. They will cause the men to be assembled at the most convenient places within the respective regiments and marched thence to Petersburg, the point of general rendezvous, in charge of the officer highest in rank in the regiment. Require the men to bring with them clothing and blankets.

Officers commanding detachments will procure subsistence for them, until mustered into service of the Confederate States, by purchase, if practicable; if not, by impressment, and certify such purchases or impressments to the auditing board at Richmond.

Officers commanding detachments will report as fast as they arrive at Petersburg to such officer in the service of the Confederate States as may be appointed to receive and muster them into service. The troops will there be organized into companies, battalions, and regiments, and supplied with arms and ammunition. They will, as far as practicable, obtain railroad transportation for the detachments to the place of general rendezvous, giving certificates of the number of men transported, which will be paid by the State.

By command:

WM. H. RICHARDSON,
Adjutant-General.

CHARLESTON, S. C., *January* 10, 1863.

Brig. Gen. W. H. C. WHITING,
Wilmington, N. C.:

Maps received. Your views of enemy's mode of attack on Wilmington are doubtless correct, and I fully agree to best point for meeting him, provided he can land no considerable force in your rear. I send all forces I can spare from this department; same as before. Will return maps.

G. T. BEAUREGARD.

CHARLESTON, S. C., *January* 10, 1863.

Maj. Gen. GUSTAVUS W. SMITH,
Goldsborough, N. C.:

I am sending Whiting same forces as before. Do not let them be taken. Why don't you apply for Lovell? He is in Richmond, anxious for the field.

G. T. BEAUREGARD.

WAR DEPARTMENT, C. S. A.,
Richmond, Va., January 10, 1863.

Maj. Gen. GUSTAVUS W. SMITH,
Goldsborough, N. C.:

We think it desirable the militia of North Carolina should be called out. Can you not encourage it? General Lee urges that Ransom's division should not be ordered beyond Drewry's Bluff. The President thinks that division likely to be specially serviceable in North Carolina, but would approve of an equal force being returned to Drewry's Bluff. No late news of special interest.

J. A. SEDDON,
Secretary of War.

GOLDSBOROUGH, N. C., *January* 10, 1863.

General G. T. BEAUREGARD,
Commanding, Charleston, S. C.:

MY DEAR GENERAL: Your telegram of the 8th instant was received last night on my return from Raleigh. I answered by telegraph that your opinions were well founded, but that I thought the difficulty you suggested in getting the troops back in case the iron-clads pass the forts and get into the Cape Fear could be obviated. It is very important for the Confederate Government to hold Wilmington, and it is almost absolutely necessary to this State. They cannot take Wilmington by land, I think, if General Gist with the troops he had there before is in the place in time to maneuver in front and check their approach. I have here and at Kinston a little over 5,000 men. There are three regiments at Rocky Mount, half-way from Goldsborough to Weldon, and three at Weldon. I hope that General Lee will yet see in time the necessity for transferring a portion of the forces now in front of Fredericksburg to this State, which I feel assured is to be the theater of active operations this winter and spring. If we can hold Wilmington and Weldon the enemy, if they penetrate the interior of the State, cannot hold themselves there. But if they succeed at Wilmington, and once get possession of it, we will never get it away from them. My opinion is that but for the storm at sea which sent the Monitor to the bottom, disabled the Passaic, and sent the Galena no one knows where, they would before this time have made a combined attack by sea and land upon Wilmington, and would probably have succeeded in passing the forts with their iron-clads; and if we had been caught with inadequate forces to resist and check them on land they would have had a comparatively easy time of it. But the iron-clads are foiled so far, and if advantage is taken of the delay they will find themselves headed off in every direction.

I cannot close this hurried letter without thanking you for the prompt and efficient assistance you so generously gave in December when we were seriously threatened, and hope that you will be able to continue it to us now. I know you will do all you can. We must combine and contrive to beat them. I am always glad to hear from you and will endeavor to write to you often.

Very respectfully and truly, yours,

G. W. SMITH,
Major-General.

Since writing this I have received your cipher sent to War Department October 16, 1862. The copy sent me dated January 7, 1863.

HEADQUARTERS,
Wilmington, N. C., January 10, 1863.

Maj. Gen. GUSTAVUS W. SMITH,
Commanding, &c., Goldsborough, N. C. :

MY DEAR GENERAL : I send you the inclosed note,* although it is doubtless exaggerated; still the very report indicates that the war is rapidly being transferred from Virginia to this State. I trust our authorities are equally active. You may depend upon it that Burnside, smarting under his terrible defeat at Fredericksburg, recollecting his successes in North Carolina, the plans he had made to invade upset by the Richmond battles, has induced Lincoln to transfer the war, and sensibly, too, a winter campaign in Northern Virginia being out of the question. I have no doubt that for the last month troops have been moving from Burnside's army through by Suffolk and from outside.

*Not found.

Foster's name and "to re-enforce Foster" are words retained only as a blind because they know that the designation of any prominent general would indicate their plans. I should not be surprised if you wake up and find yourself in front of Burnside or "Little Mac," and Lee far off up yonder. The same circumstances which point the enemy to this field of war prevent Lee from moving on Washington. Indeed that magnificent army should be hastening southward. Tell me your opinion and what you think will be done. How it will turn out here I cannot tell. We shall have a fight and a heavy one. I fear your own hands will be so full that you can hardly help me, but I hope not.

Very respectfully,

W. H. C. WHITING,
Brigadier-General.

HEADQUARTERS,
Wilmington, January 10, 1863.

Maj. Gen. GUSTAVUS W. SMITH, *Goldsborough:*

They must be moving troops from Burnside's army through by way of Suffolk. Fifty-five transports and twenty-one gunboats are reported at Beaufort. If true, this means outside work. A very large force is concentrated at Morehead City. Depend upon it Burnside has induced them to change their programme from Virginia to this State.

W. H. C. WHITING.

GOLDSBOROUGH, N. C., *January* 11, 1863.

Hon. JAMES A. SEDDON,
Secretary of War:

The following telegram just received from General Whiting at Wilmington:

Have information from [Lieut John S.] Fairly, of my staff, at Swansborough. He sent a man into the lines, who reports that the enemy are moving their troops to New Berne as fast as possible; that their numbers now amount to 75,000 at New Berne and 15,000 at Morehead City, the former to advance on Weldon by Kinston, the latter on Wilmington; reports that on yesterday and to-day they will get all their troops to New Berne, and that the move on Kinston will commence Tuesday or Wednesday. You will need all the forces that can be got from northward. Yankee fleet is assembling here.

The numbers are exaggerated, but there is no doubt but they have been largely re-enforced. They have, I think, over 30,000 and less than 40,000 men. The troops at Petersburg should be placed at my disposal at once and others brought there or to Richmond.

G. W. SMITH,
Major-General.

CHARLESTON, S. C., *January* 11, 1863.

Brig. Gen. W. H. C. WHITING,
Wilmington, N. C.:

Enemy cannot be 90,000 strong under Foster, who had 15,000 before, and he may have received as many more. I will send with your maps my system for calculating enemy's forces. It seldom fails.

G. T. BEAUREGARD.

CHARLESTON, S. C., *January* 11, 1863.
Brig. Gen. W. H. C. WHITING, *Wilmington, N. C.:*

Few enemy's blockaders in sight this morning. Have you fortified your advanced position by rifle-pits and abatis?

G. T. BEAUREGARD.

CHARLESTON, S. C., *January* 11, 1863.
Brig. Gen. W. H. C. WHITING,
　　Commanding at Wilmington, N. C.:

MY DEAR GENERAL: Your favor of the 8th instant and accompanying drawings were duly received. I telegraphed you my coincidence in your views relative to the meditated attack of the enemy on Wilmington and its proposed defense by you. We differ, however, in this respect—that should he have any iron-clads to operate with he will first pass and take or silence your forts on the river, and then land his forces immediately before the city to make a land and water attack on its defenses, thereby cutting off your retreat across the river to prevent you from re-enforcing Charleston. Should it become necessary, your communications at the same time with Goldsborough would be cut off by a strong movable column, which would destroy all the rail and common road bridges in that direction. He would also make a demonstration against Goldsborough or Weldon to keep Smith's [forces] there inactive, and so operate as to compel him to sacrifice the least important positions in succession for the protection of the most important ones. This is what I meant in my telegram, and not that they would attack Wilmington, Raleigh, and Weldon at one and the same time. Wilmington would certainly be a great loss to the Confederacy, but not as much so as Raleigh and Weldon, which would give the enemy both lines of communication between the South and Richmond. Moreover, the capital of any State, which to us signifies nothing, is an event of great importance in Europe. I will repeat here a French proverb, which is as true in war as in the ordinary walks of life, " *Qui trop embrasse mal etreint.*" You all seem to be very much in the dark about the enemy's movements and forces, exaggerating the latter terribly. This must have a depressing effect upon your troops. I always make mine believe we are stronger and the enemy is weaker by about one-third than is actually the case. After a battle I reverse this. With a proper system of spies all the enemy's important movements ought to be known to you, and by counting his generals you ought generally to know pretty nearly what his forces are; for instance: One brigade (four regiments of 500 effective men), 2,000; one division (four brigades), 8,000; one corps (four divisions), 32,000; cavalry brigade, 2,000; artillery (about three pieces for 1,000 infantry), ninety-six pieces. This would give 1 general commanding, 4 major-generals, and 17 brigadier-generals, or 22 in all; but the Abolitionists have generally colonels commanding brigades for the sake of economy. I have my doubts whether Foster commands at this moment more than the above force, although it may be increased greatly ere long. By using this table you will find that Burnside's army of three corps and a reserve at Fredericksburg amounted to about 125,000 or 130,000 men, with about three hundred pieces of cannon. Now that the iron-clads are played out for the present, I feel less nervous at having sent you my best available troops; but I hope they will be returned in time should they be required for the defense of this department.

Wishing you the amplest success, I remain, sincerely, yours,

G. T. BEAUREGARD.

WAR DEPARTMENT, C. S. A.,
Richmond, Va., January 11, 1863.

Gov. ZEBULON B. VANCE, *Raleigh, N. C.:*

With the President's concurrence I recommend the calling out of the militia in North Carolina to such extent as we can arm—say 5,000 men. The Governor of Virginia will call out the militia from the counties near North Carolina, and the Department at the same time calls for conscripts from those counties to rendezvous at Petersburg. We send every man to North Carolina who can be spared from points not vital, but have no further regular troops at command. We must rely on irregulars for any further force.

J. A. SEDDON,
Secretary of War.

GOLDSBOROUGH, N. C., *January* 11, 1863.

Maj. Gen. S. G. FRENCH,
Commanding, &c., Weldon, N. C.:

DEAR GENERAL: Yours of the 9th is received. In regard to Ransom's division there is some conflict of opinion. General Lee ordered it to Richmond. I ordered it to move to Petersburg without stopping in Richmond, take position in that immediate vicinity and be held constantly in readiness to move in any direction on the shortest notice. General Lee objects to their being this side of Drewry's Bluff. I object to their returning to Drewry's Bluff unless that place is attacked, and have asked to be allowed to order them into North Carolina. This is objected to at present. I consider this division *in transitu* and can determine nothing in regard to it at present. Fifty telegrams and letters have passed, I think, about this division from quartermasters, railroad, State, and General Government officers. Have you determined where you desire the four 32-pounders to be placed? As far as I am now advised it seems to me that Weldon and Halifax would be suitable positions for them, relying upon lighter guns and rifles for the defenses of points lower down. Have you seen Colonel Gwynn? I directed him to report to you at Weldon and carry out your instructions. The four 32-pounders from Charleston (ready to be put in position complete) are here on the cars. As soon as you determine where to place them they will be sent forward. General Whiting seems satisfied that Wilmington will be attacked, and thinks that they will occupy our attention at Weldon and Goldsborough at the same time. I have written again to the War Department in reference to sending re-enforcements, and have warned them that they are losing time. I hope that we will not be too late; but we will do the best we can with the means we have and can get together. I am always glad to hear from you. Write as often and fully as you can.

Very respectfully and truly, yours,

G. W. SMITH,
Major-General.

P. S.—Can you not have a bridge constructed over the Roanoke at Halifax? I think it is very important, and will, if you require it, try to send you some one to take charge of it.

GOLDSBOROUGH, N. C., *January* 12, 1863.

Maj. Gen. S. G. FRENCH,
    Commanding, &c., Weldon, N. C.:

GENERAL: You are unquestionably in command of the forces on the Blackwater, those belonging to Petersburg, and General Pettigrew's command at Rocky Mount, &c.; and there is no order relieving Evans from your command, nor have I intended there should be, so far as reports, returns, &c., are concerned. I mean the last to apply to Evans. But as long as I am so much closer to him will give him direct orders in regard to his movements. Ransom is considered *in transitu*. General Lee wishes him to return to Drewry's Bluff. I wish to bring him to North Carolina. In case he comes on at all, if he stops short of [this place] I will order him to report to you. I will direct the adjutant-general to return any reports, returns, &c., which may be forwarded by your command without being transmitted through your office. In regard to the official reports, no original reports had been received in my office previous to your leaving here. They were only copies sent for my information, and they were returned. The reports were handed to me by Evans the day before I left for Richmond, except that of the chief engineer. My own report was written hurriedly, and I am not certain what is in it, but remember distinctly making up my mind neither to blame nor praise any one, nor go into particulars, but to make the report in the barest outline and refer for particulars to the sub-reports. I am sorry that any omissions have given you concern, but allow me to say, first, that Evans' report should have been made to you, and you should have reported to me. It is perhaps my fault that I allowed him to hand me his report while I was visiting at Kinston. I will have copies of the reports sent to you that were handed me by Evans, and would be glad if you would get General Pettigrew to make out a report, and I will transmit them to the adjutant and inspector-general, to be filed with the others. This is but just and right.

Very respectfully and truly, yours,

G. W. SMITH,
    Major-General.

P. S.—Try a simple order on and test the question of command practically. The idea of an officer stationed at Petersburg saying that he is not under your command borders on trifling.

EXECUTIVE DEPARTMENT, NORTH CAROLINA,
    ADJUTANT-GENERAL'S OFFICE (MILITIA),
        Raleigh, N. C., January 12, 1863.

COLONEL: You will forthwith assemble all able-bodied men fit for military duty not called for as conscripts up to this date, and who are liable to militia duty under existing laws and orders, in your regiment, and organize them into one or more companies of 75 men each. Should the number of men in any regiment equal or exceed 120 they will be formed into two equal companies. Detachments of 40 men will be allowed a captain and second lieutenant; 25 men a first lieutenant, and 15 men a second lieutenant. A full company of 75 will be allowed all these officers, to be in all cases selected by the rank and file. The militia having been so much reduced by recent calls for conscripts, and this call including all who are fit for duty, renders it necessary that the commissioned officers should be now included, except the field officer of highest grade and captain or senior officer of each district. When the companies are formed the colonels will immediately report the fact to this office by letter, inclosing roll of company and the probable number and kind of arms in the regiment.

2d. Companies, when thus formed, will assemble each Saturday for drill and inspection at a place to be designated by the captain, who will report to this office each week the condition of the company, which will always be held in readiness for active duty at the shortest notice.

3d. This organization and drill is for the purpose of being prepared to repel an expected advance of the enemy, and will remain in force until further orders from the Governor. The utmost promptness is expected in the execution of this order, and ten days from its reception is deemed sufficient to complete the organization herein directed.

By order of Governor Vance:

J. G. MARTIN,
Adjutant-General.

WILMINGTON, [N. C.,] *January* 12, 1863.

Colonel [WILLIAM] LAMB, *Fort Fisher:*
Lieutenant-Colonel GWATHMEY, *Fort Caswell:*

From information received here it is probable the enemy will move to attack this place, both by land and sea, on Wednesday. Have everything ready to receive them.

B. W. FROBEL,
Chief of Artillery.

WILMINGTON, N. C., *January* 13, 1863.

General G. T. BEAUREGARD, *Charleston, S. C.:*

General Gist has asked for six wagons to a regiment. Can they not be sent me at once?

Five of the enemy's steamers are engaging Fort Caswell. Fort replying slowly. No other fleet off.

W. H. C. WHITING.

CHARLESTON, S. C., *January* 13, 1863.

Brigadier-General WHITING, *Wilmington, N. C.:*

Do not think Abolitionists will make much if any attack without ironclads. Latter are not much to be feared at present on account of condition. I send maps to-day.

G. T. BEAUREGARD.

WILMINGTON, N. C., *January* 13, 1863.

General BEAUREGARD:

Firing has just ceased.

W. H. C. WHITING.

HEADQUARTERS,
Wilmington, N. C., January 13, 1863.

Lieut Col. GWATHMEY,
    Commanding Fort Caswell, N. C.:

COLONEL: We have reports from the enemy's lines which indicate that the enemy will commence a movement upon this place both by land and water to-morrow. Though our works are by no means as forward as we could wish, I am sure that everything has been done in our power and with our limited time, especially by your command. You will hold your position to the last extremity. If attacked by iron-clads upon which you can make no impression or which succeed in passing you, endeavor to save some of your guns for fire upon the wooden ships or transports. As soon as the enemy make their appearance send off your negro force. For this purpose a steamer will be sent you; but in case a steamer should not arrive soon enough you are authorized in the mean time to impress and hold at the fort all the sail-boats and small vessels about Smithville. Should it unfortunately, from want of provisions or destruction of your armament, become necessary to abandon the work, make arrangements to blow it up and destroy it as far as practicable. Send out an intelligent officer to select the best point in such an event for crossing the marsh to the mainland and endeavor to bring off your command. The time for putting down the submarine shells is left to your judgment. The keys would seem to be the best position. I sincerely wish that the direction relative to destruction will not be tested, but relying upon God, our cause, and your brave command I hope for victory. If we are beaten it will be through no fault of yours.

    Very respectfully,

                W. H. C. WHITING,
                Brigadier-General, Commanding.

———

HEADQUARTERS,
Wilmington, N. C., January 13, 1863.

Col. [WILLIAM] LAMB,
    Commanding Fort Fisher, N. C.:

COLONEL: I have received reports from the enemy's lines which indicate that an attack will be made both by land and water upon this place, the movement to commence to-morrow. I need not repeat the expressions of my confidence in you and your garrison and in your determination to hold your position to the last. Some contingencies may arise in which you may require instruction. Should you find that iron-clads are too much for you and succeed in passing, endeavor to save and reserve some of your guns for fire on the wooden ships and transports. You will report by telegraph every hour the progress of events. I do not think ships alone can drive you out, though it is possible that iron-clads may be able to dismount your guns. You will therefore, even if the iron-clads pass you, continue to hold the fort as long as you are supplied with provisions. Instruct your vedettes to patrol for any indications of an attempt to land in force below Masonborough Sound and give me instant information. As soon as the enemy's fleet makes its appearance send off your negro force; a steamer will be sent for that purpose; but should it not appear in time you will send them off on foot under charge to make a forced march, say to the Riverside Salt-Works or other point where a steamer can be sent, at the same time letting this office know the point. With a firm reliance on Divine Providence, I bid you and your brave garrison Godspeed. Fight as well as you have labored and I have no fears for the result.

Very respectfully,

W. H. C. WHITING,
Brigadier-General, Commanding.

WAR DEPARTMENT, C. S. A.,
Richmond, January 13, 1863.

General R. E. LEE, *Fredericksburg, Va.*:

Without fully crediting I send the following dispatch from General G. W. Smith for your information:

GOLDSBOROUGH, *January 12, 1863.*

Hon. JAMES A. SEDDON:

I have just received from General Whiting the following dispatch, dated to-day: " Have received further information from Lieutenant Fairly, confirmatory of that sent to-day." Adds that General Dix, at Shepherdsville Friday last, reports that many of the enemy are from Burnside's army ; reports the enemy at New Berne from 50,000 to 70,000 men ; 15,000 at Morehead City, with forty-two steamers, and that they move on Kinston by Dover road ; that they intend landing a force on the Sound and attacking the force here at the same time, and all the movements will commence on Wednesday.

G. W. SMITH,
Major-General.

The following dispatch just received from General Smith:

GOLDSBOROUGH, *January 12, 1863.*

Hon. JAMES A. SEDDON:

General Beauregard telegraphs that he has reliable information from New York that General Naglee's land force was but 12,000 strong.

G. W. SMITH,
Major-General.

J. A. SEDDON,
Secretary of War.

HEADQUARTERS,
Wilmington, N. C., January 13, 1863.

Col. JOHN A. BAKER,
Comdg. Forty-first Regiment [N. C. T., or Third Cavalry]:

COLONEL : Unless General Robertson has given you special instructions as to your movements, you will, in case of a land advance of the enemy in this direction, send one company to fall back upon Colonel Harrison and with the remainder of your force watch their flank, moving, if forced back, across the Cape Fear (Northeast Branch) to afford as much protection as you can to the railroad and telegraph. If they land below the mouth of New River watch their rear and follow them up.

Very respectfully,

W. H. C. WHITING,
Brigadier-General, Commanding.

WAR DEPARTMENT, C. S. A.,
Richmond, Va., January 13, 1863.
General R. E. LEE, *Commanding, &c.* :

SIR : At the suggestion of the President I inclose for your consideration a letter from General Smith, covering another from Brigadier-General Pryor. They were received day before yesterday, but under the
impression that the greater needs of the army in North Carolina would
require all the re-enforcements you could safely spare, I had forborne
to press them on your attention.

With high esteem, most respectfully, yours,

J. A. SEDDON,
Secretary of War.

[Inclosure.]

GOLDSBOROUGH, N. C., *January* 9, 1863.
(Received January 10, 1863.)

Hon. JAMES A. SEDDON,
Secretary of War :

I have the honor to inclose copy of letter from Brigadier-General
Pryor, and to request that either Colonels Ball's or Chambliss' regiment
of Virginia Cavalry, and the Sixty-first Virginia Infantry (properly
belonging to the Richmond command, but now with General Lee's
army), be sent to General Pryor. I have not the force to spare, but am
satisfied that General Pryor should be furnished with the little aid he
asks for to enable him to accomplish such important results.

Very respectfully and truly, yours,

G. W. SMITH,
Major-General.

[Sub-inclosure.]

HEADQUARTERS FORCES ON BLACKWATER,
January 6, 1863.

Maj. Gen. [GUSTAVUS W.] SMITH:

GENERAL : It is just a month since I assumed command of the forces
on the Blackwater. The day before I arrived within sight of headquarters the enemy routed a portion of our forces, captured a section of artillery, and carried away a number of prisoners. We never thought
then of crossing the line with any aggressive purpose, and our utmost
exertions were devoted merely to the maintenance of our position on
this side the Blackwater. The enemy had absolute control of the
country between this point and Suffolk. I am happy to assure you,
general, that such is not now the case. A most formidable attack upon
one point of my line I repulsed with a handful of men and drove the
enemy back to Suffolk. I assumed the offensive, and, as you know,
with a very inferior force I have repeatedly driven in the enemy's pickets
almost within sight of his stronghold. The result is that I have shut
up the enemy in Suffolk. I have delivered all the intervening country
from their desolate sway. When I arrived here forage and provisions
were all drawn from Petersburg. Since I assumed command not a
pound of meat nor a grain of corn, not a bundle of fodder, has been derived from that source. I have subsisted my own command within the
enemy's lines and have furnished General French's quartermaster 5,000
pounds of beef and 50,000 pounds of salted pork, all procured from within
the enemy's lines. Meanwhile I have strengthened my line throughout

its length by obstructing ponds, digging rifle-pits, throwing up intrench-ments, and by other artificial means of defense. I consider my position perfectly secure, even with the small force under my command. But there are certain results to be achieved by an aggressive policy, to the successful prosecution of which a small increase of strength is essential. To be brief, if you will furnish me with another regiment of cavalry (I have but one, and that extremely weak) and another strong regiment of infantry, so as to give me an available force of 3,000 men for the field, I will engage, general, to accomplish three things, viz : 1st, to shut the enemy up in Suffolk, and so to threaten the place as to prevent any de-tachment of troops to the army in North Carolina; 2d, to intercept communication between Suffolk and the Chowan across the county of Gates, and so compel the enemy to a most circuitous route ; 3d, to realize for our army within the enemy's lines 300,000 pounds of pork and a still larger proportion of corn over and above the wants of my command. It may appear hardly possible to do this with so small a force as I request, but the nature of the country is such as to neutralize disparity of numbers and to make 3,000 men equivalent to twice their number. The cavalry I have is not sufficient to picket my line—300 men scattered along 50-odd miles. A few days ago General French found it necessary to transfer my other cavalry regiment to North Carolina. One regiment of the infantry of my command is de-tained in Petersburg. Would it not be possible to spare me that ?

The suggestions I have hazarded are most respectfully submitted to your superior judgment.

Very respectfully, your friend and obedient servant,

ROGER A. PRYOR,
Brigadier-General, Commanding.

PETERSBURG, VA., *January* 14, 1863.
General S. COOPER:

General Pryor reports the enemy 6,000 strong at Windsor, near Ivor. Should they try to force the Blackwater the regiment now here could move, but then the guard for city, &c., would have to come from Ran-som's brigade; or can two of his regiments move there if needed?

S. G. FRENCH.

JANUARY 14, 1863.
General FRENCH:

Send the regiment referred to in your dispatch just received; or, if the emergency, in your judgment, should require, the two regiments of Ransom's brigade, as suggested by you.

S. COOPER.

FREDERICKSBURG, VA., *January* 14, 1863.
Hon. JAMES A. SEDDON:

Your dispatch just received. Advance Ransom and any other avail-able troops in Richmond or Petersburg. See my dispatch of 6th instant

R. E. LEE.

SPECIAL ORDERS,   HDQRS. ARMY OF NORTHERN VIRGINIA,
No. 14.   *January 14, 1863.*

I. Maj. Gen. D. H. Hill, Provisional Army of the Confederate States, will immediately proceed to Richmond, Va., and report to the Adjutant and Inspector General, C. S. A.

*   *   *   *   *   *   *

By order of General Lee:

W. H. TAYLOR,
Assistant Adjutant-General.

General S. COOPER,
Adjutant and Inspector General, C. S. A.

GOLDSBOROUGH, *January 14, 1863.*

Hon. JAMES A. SEDDON,
Secretary of War, Richmond:

MY DEAR SIR: I have sent several telegrams within the last three or four days all tending to show that the enemy are re-enforcing rapidly in North Carolina and actively preparing for an offensive campaign. The force here is, as I have often stated before, inadequate for the protection of the important points from Wilmington to Richmond, inclusive, and we have no force as a reserve ready to take the offensive and meet the enemy whenever they come out in force. I have asked that Ransom's force be placed at my disposal, and have urged that additional troops be sent. Of course if this cannot be done we must get along the best we can without them. But it is my business to speak plainly upon these subjects and to continue to speak thus so long as there is any probability that the necessary measures for preparing to resist successfully the invasion that is now impending will be adopted. I remember well what force we had last winter in the Army of the Potomac holding position farther north than that now held by General Lee, and it was then not only decided to be impracticable to re-enforce the Army of the Potomac but detachments were made from it and sent here. What I mean to say is this, that General Lee in command of an army at Fredericksburg is not in the same point of view, and evidently does not see things precisely as they appeared to him when General Johnston commanded that army, and he (General Lee) was overlooking and judging of the whole general operations from Richmond. This is natural, and perhaps could hardly be avoided by any one. But it is for the Government to decide whether when active operations are evidently commenced in force against important points in this State it is not necessary to diminish somewhat the army under General Lee at Fredericksburg.

Before I was reduced in relative rank in this army it was a question whether General Lee or myself should command the active forces in Northern Virginia, the other to command in Richmond, &c. Now I would like this subject brought up for a moment and considered under the supposition that I commanded in Fredericksburg and General Lee here. Would he allow me to retain the army at Fredericksburg whilst the attack in force was preparing against Wilmington? You are aware that my visit to Richmond in the latter part of December was for the purpose of conveying to the Government and to General Lee my convictions in regard to the condition of affairs in this State and to prepare in time. You saw my letter to General Lee and his reply. I received a telegram from you on the 10th instant stating that General Lee opposed

Ransom's division being brought this side of Drewry's Bluff. I have received nothing since from the Department and, I think, nothing but this telegram since I left Richmond on the 5th instant. I fear your telegrams to me have again miscarried.

I remain, very respectfully and truly, yours,

G. W. SMITH,
Major-General.

[Indorsement.]

JANUARY 16, 1863.

Read and returned to Secretary of War. The question of forces has been considered. The question of rank of Major-General Smith is not for action.

J. D.

HEADQUARTERS,
Wilmington, N. C., January 15, 1863.

Maj. [JOHN J.] HEDRICK,
    Comdg. Fort Saint Philip, N. C. :

MAJOR : I need not tell you to hold your position as long as possible. If, however, many of the enemy's fleet should succeed in passing your batteries and proceeding up the [river], or compel you to withdraw, you are directed to proceed to the railroad bridge on Brunswick River for its protection, placing a strong picket at the obstruction on that river. You should in this event take with you all the provisions, &c., you can carry, taking teams for the purpose. Please to recollect that for one, two, or even three steamers passing you, you will not necessarily leave ; but a large fleet sufficient to overcome the upper batteries after getting by might remove the obstructions and destroy the bridge. Further orders will be sent you.

W. H. C. WHITING,
Brigadier-General.

HEADQUARTERS,
Wilmington, N. C., January 15, 1863.

General S. COOPER,
    Adjutant and Inspector General, Richmond, Va. :

GENERAL : Assigned to take charge of defense of Wilmington, I arrived here November 17, 1862. The yellow fever, which had desolated the city and stopped all work, had not yet ceased. The condition, importance, and necessities of the place were immediately set forth and have since been repeatedly urged to the department. I found the defensive works generally imperfect and many important points neglected ; a partial line of earthworks, well constructed but weak in profile, had been thrown up between the two mill-ponds on the east and south of the city 1½ miles in extent. They had twelve pieces of artillery mounted, mostly naval 24s and 32s, of the old pattern. These batteries, mounting eight guns, had been placed just below the upper jetty lights, and two to command an imperfect obstruction, composed of logs and chains, near Mount Tirza. An attempt had been made to build an iron battery for this purpose, but so defective in design and position that I directed it to be stopped. On the opposite side of the river, 14 miles from the city, Battery Saint Philip had been erected, well constructed, mounting eleven guns, but defective in the quality and caliber of its ordnance and in the location of proper protecting traverses from enfilade and even reverse fire. On Confederate Point, to protect New Inlet, had been constructed the earthwork known as Fort Fisher. Here the skill, ingenuity, and perseverance of, successively, Maj. [John J.] Hedrick, of the artillery, Maj. [R. K.] Meade, of the engineers, for a short time, and especially of Col. [William] Lamb, now commanding, and his men, have been signally displayed. The fort is a strong sea-coast work, partly casemated and partly barbette. It would not, however, be tenable for any length of time against a formidable land attack. Fort Caswell, commanding the main entrance, appeared to have had little or nothing done to increase its efficiency; numerous guns of little or no efficiency had been crowded together without any protection by traverse or embrasure for either guns or men. The advanced batteries nearest the bar previously arranged had from some unknown reason been leveled. I regarded it, and still do, as one of the weakest points on the system. In the very important matter of river obstructions little had been done, nor had preparations been made for obstructing the approaches to the city in case of attack. Brunswick River is an important branch, forming the island known as Eagle's Island, directly opposite the city, affording, out of fire, an easy access to the Upper Cape Fear River, and opportunity for an enemy in the lower river to destroy the Wilmington and Manchester Railroad Bridge and cut off all communications south of Wilmington. In this branch the only obstruction was a few rows of piles not protected by any effective fire. In the city itself, as if it was to be abandoned at the first appearance of a hostile gunboat, not a single work had been put up, though many admirable sites presented themselves. On the gunboats the pestilence had stopped labor; both were on the stocks and no provision whatever had been made or even projected for saving them in case of disaster or providing for them during attack. During the two months' grace the enemy have given us it is not for me to say what has been done to remedy the defects here stated. I have to give my warmest praise to the manner in which officers and men have labored day and night. Colonel Lamb and Lieutenant-Colonel Gwathmey, of the Navy, Major Forrest, of the Navy (until his unfortunate illness), Major Young and Captain Andrews, and Captain James and Lieutenant Obenchain, of the Engineers, have been indefatigable with their excellent commands in strengthening the defenses. Their value, incomplete as they still are (necessarily from want of time, implements, and material), must shortly be tested. If they succeed, these officers and men should have great praise; if they fail, it is not their fault. I have now, in addition to the works, a movable column of a little more than 7,000 men, with five smooth-bore field batteries. Of these, all but Clingman's brigade and two batteries have been furnished me from the defense of Charleston by General Beauregard, under command of General Gist. I have stated too often the importance of this place to the country to repeat it here, but I will repeat what I have said before—that from here there is no route or retreat, and once taken by the enemy it cannot be retaken by the means belonging to the Confederacy. Strong diversions and powerful aid should be at once started. While we will do all we can do and will hold and defend the place while it is possible, every endeavor should be used to relieve it. The Charleston garrison ought not to be vainly sacrificed.

The above statement has been made because I think it is due to the officers and men of this army and to myself. The enemy are moving in very heavy force, and there is no time to be lost.

Very respectfully,

W. H. C. WHITING,
Brigadier-General.

JANUARY 15, 1863.

General BEAUREGARD :

G. W. [Smith] says the real attack is probably on Wilmington, with their whole force. He inquires how he can best aid me, whether by reenforcing or falling on his reserve. The best way is the speediest junction. Asks how many men I have and whether I can withdraw if ironclads pass the forts. I shall not withdraw except by order. If 50,000 men are thrown on Wilmington you must stir up troops in the north. They ought to have hurried before this, unless they expect impossibilities.

W. H. C. WHITING

CHARLESTON, S. C., *January* 15, 1863.

Brig. Gen. W. H. C. WHITING,
    Wilmington, N. C.:

Good plan attacking monitor is to board in small boats at night, throwing bottles burning fluid in tower and bags powder in funnel or chimney.

G. T. BEAUREGARD.

HEADQUARTERS,
Wilmington, N. C., January 16, 1863.

Col. JOHN A. BAKER,
    Comdg. Forty-first [N. C. T. or Third] Cavalry:

COLONEL: Impede the enemy's advance by every device within your means; destroy all bridges in his route, however trifling. Keep on the alert, and as he draws nearer to our lines dispatch frequent couriers. Accustom your men to skirmish with his advance, to ambuscade, &c.

Very respectfully,

W. H. C. WHITING,
Brigadier-General, Commanding.

HEADQUARTERS,
Wilmington, N. C., January 16 1863.

General GUSTAVUS W. SMITH,
    Commanding, Goldsborough:

Scouts report just received. Still no enemy this side of Trent yesterday or night before last, but very large force on opposite bank making toward Kinston. Citizens report two regiments of Indian with them.

W. H. C. WHITING.

WAR DEPARTMENT, C. S. A.,
Richmond, Va., January 16, 1863.

General GUSTAVUS W. SMITH,
    Goldsborough, N. C.:

General Lee has placed Ransom's division at your control. I telegraphed you to that effect two days ago.

J. A. SEDDON,
Secretary of War.

ROCKY MOUNT, *January 17, 1863.*

General S. COOPER,
      Adjutant and Inspector-General:

On 15th a large fleet left Beaufort, N. C., to attack Wilmington by water; also a large force (70,000) started by way of Swansborough to co-operate with them by land. They are arming the negroes to garrison Washington, N. C.

W. F. MARTIN,
Commanding District of the Tar River.

WAR DEPARTMENT, C. S. A.,
Richmond, Va., January 17, 1863.

His Excellency ZEBULON B. VANCE,
      Governor of North Carolina:

SIR: Maj. Gen. D. H. Hill, of your State, who is so favorably known to yourself, as indeed to the whole Confederacy, for his distinguished services with the army in Virginia, has, to the regret of the Department, been constrained to retire from his late command by ill health. He has consented for the present not to resign, but will be for a time at home in North Carolina. It has occurred to me that from the appreciation of the Department of his proven valor and skill it might be pardonable in me to suggest that in view of the dangers from the enemy now menacing your State the benefits of his counsel and co-operation might be obtained by you on conference with him. His deserved influence with the people of North Carolina might prove advantageous in animating and encouraging them to effort and endurance, and his experience and judgment give valuable suggestions as to the best mode of commanding and guiding the means of the State for defense.

Trusting to be excused for the liberty of such suggestion, I have the honor to be, with very high consideration and esteem, most respectfully, yours,

J. A. SEDDON,
Secretary of War.

HEADQUARTERS,
Wilmington, January 18, 1863.

Colonel HARRISON, *Commanding Outpost:*

Send the following order to Colonel Baker:

Your dispatch of 10.30 p. m., 18th, received. Your outposts must not be too precipitate. I want accurate information of the route and advance of the enemy. They must therefore neither fall back too far nor too rapidly. Advance by Tuckahoe, on the railroad, toward Kenansville should be communicated to the telegraph office there; on the Jacksonville road should be forwarded here.

W. H. C. WHITING.

HEADQUARTERS ARMY OF NORTHERN VIRGINIA,
January 19, 1863.

Hon. JAMES A. SEDDON,
      Secretary of War:

SIR: I have received your letter of the 13th instant inclosing one from General Smith and another from General Pryor. I am pleased to hear of the successful operations of the latter below Petersburg. I will send some cavalry down when I can spare it. As he is operating in front of Petersburg I think he might be re-enforced by the regiment of which he speaks in that city or any other available troops near that place, leaving a sufficient garrison there.

I have the honor to be, very respectfully, your obedient servant,

R. E. LEE,
General.

WILMINGTON, N. C., *January* 20, 1863.

Governor VANCE:

Information just received would indicate a formidable movement of the enemy against this place or Goldsborough. Do what you can at Richmond to have troops sent south.

T. L. CLINGMAN.

HEADQUARTERS,
Wilmington, N. C., January 20, 1863.

Major-General FRENCH,
Commanding Division, Kenansville, N. C.:

MY DEAR GENERAL: I send you a map, in case you should have none at hand. My advanced post in Holly Shelter is at Island Creek, 4½ miles above the ferry at the railroad bridge, and fortified. On the Sound road my advance is about 17 miles from the city, also fortified, and additional works under construction as fast as possible. An advance by the enemy in force by land will most probably come by the Sound road, for many reasons, but a column might come down the Holly Shelter. It would be all-important to prevent the position on the Sound road from being turned on my left, which they would undoubtedly try to do. It would become, then, a question of consideration, in case you support, whether you would move directly in Holly Shelter, crossing at Bannerman's bridge (supposing the enemy did not burn it), or at South Washington, to fall in their rear, or march at once to the ferry and operate from Island Creek in their front. My opinion inclines to the latter course for your troops, leaving to the main body, under the general commanding, to operate in the rear. In case the enemy adopt the plan of endeavoring to land somewhere between my advanced position and Confederate Point, the latter course suggested would undoubtedly be your best course and would, indeed, become very necessary to insure the security of Fort Fisher and the iron batteries from reverse attack. As any such movement of the enemy would undoubtedly be accompanied by a corresponding advance on the Sound road, which it would become necessary to check, I have directed the greater portion of the cavalry in advance, in case of being forced back, to retire on Kenansville. Their intelligence is communicated by both ways. They will, of course, come under your immediate control, and you will obtain information of the enemy's movements sooner than I shall, and in time to adopt either alternative, as General Smith may direct. If their attack is ascertained to be really on Wilmington, and you have to cross the ferry, I would suggest that your force keep abreast and a little in advance of their motion to enable you to take position on their front. To save trouble of correspondence, if you approve of these suggestions, I send a copy of this note to General Smith, with whom you can consult by telegraph. My weakest point is the forts. The passage of them and occupation of the lower harbor will require new and different combinations.

Very respectfully,

W. H. C. WHITING,
Brigadier-General, Commanding.

WAR DEPARTMENT, C. S. A.,
Richmond, Va., January 20, 1863.

GILBERT ELLIOTT, Esq., *Halifax, N. C.:*

SIR: Your letter of the 2d instant relative to the defenses of Roanoke River was referred to the Chief of Engineers, who replies that every exertion has been made to procure guns for the defense of that river. Four guns have been ordered to be sent, one of which is a rifled, banded 32-pounder.

Respectfully,

J. A. SEDDON,
Secretary of War.

HEADQUARTERS DEPARTMENT OF EAST TENNESSEE,
Knoxville, Tenn., January 21, 1863.

His Excellency Gov. ZEBULON B. VANCE:

GOVERNOR: Inclosed please find an extract from a letter received this morning from Brig. Gen. W. G. M. Davis. From his statement I think the outbreak in Madison has been greatly exaggerated, and, as telegraphed you this morning, I think there is no present need of the State force called out by you. The outbreak has, I think, been suppressed, but an adequate force will be kept in the mountains as long as necessary for the protection of loyal citizens and their property.

I am, Governor, very respectfully, your obedient servant,

H. HETH,
Brigadier-General, Commanding.

[Inclosure.]

HEADQUARTERS,
Greenville, Tenn., January 20, 1863.

GENERAL: As I informed you by telegraph on yesterday, Captain Nelson has returned and reports that his company went into Laurel Valley, N. C., and had a brush with the tories, in which he killed 12 and subsequently captured 20. From information I have received from all quarters from men of intelligence and reliable character, I am satisfied there is no organization in the mountains of armed men banded together for the purpose of making efforts to destroy bridges or to burn towns or property of Confederate officers and soldiers. I think the attack on Marshall was gotten up to obtain salt, for want of which there is great suffering in the mountains. Plunder of other property followed as a matter of course. Col. [L. M.] Allen's Sixty-fourth North Carolina Regiment and the men of his command are said to have been hostile to the Laurel men and they to the former for a long time—a kind of feud existing between them. Of the men killed by Nelson's cavalry all but one or two were deserters from Colonel Allen's regiment. They formed part of the expedition against Marshall and no doubt plundered Allen's house.

There has been no [attack] made on parties traveling on the Asheville road; the stage has not been destroyed and no acts of hostility committed that I can hear of but the plunder of Marshall and of Allen's house. The whole force that went to Marshall did not exceed 50 men. All the reports stating the existence of organized bands of armed men numbering 300 or 400 are false beyond a doubt. The attack on Marshall has given rise to wild rumors of organizations of armed tories throughout the mountains, bent on sacking towns and the plunder of loyal men. The reports, greatly magnified as they went to Raleigh, have no doubt led the Governor of North Carolina to call on the Confederate Government for a protecting force. I think you can safely assure him that the militia are not needed.

*   *   *   *   *   *   *

Very respectfully, your obedient servant,
                                        W. G. M. DAVIS,
                                            Brigadier-General.

                                RALEIGH, N. C., *January* 21, 1863.
General [HENRY] HETH, *Knoxville, Tenn.*:
    Yours received. I hope you will not relax until the tories are crushed. But do not let our excited people deal too harshly with these misguided men. Please have the captured delivered to the proper authorities for trial.
                                        Z. B. VANCE.

                            GOLDSBOROUGH, N. C., [*January*] 21, 1863.
Maj. Gen. S. G. FRENCH, *Commanding*:
    When Griffin's cavalry arrives use such couriers as may be necessary, but except in case of emergency I prefer that the regiment should be kept concentrated as much as possible and under the orders of General Robertson. A train has been sent to Tarborough for supplies. Get all you can from the country you are in.
                                        G. W. SMITH,
                                            Major-General.

                                GOLDSBOROUGH, *January* 21, 1863.
Hon. JAMES A. SEDDON,
            Secretary of War:
    MY DEAR SIR: The reports from the front to-day are that the enemy in some force, exact numbers not known, was last night within 3 miles of Jacksonville, Onslow County—cavalry, artillery, and infantry; probably the same force that appeared at Trenton some three days since.
    I have had no information through our secret agent in New Berne later than the 16th, which was received on the 18th. I am still clearly of the opinion that their forces at New Berne and Beaufort, &c., number from 20,000 to 40,000. But our latest advices go to show that the effect of the storm upon their iron-clads, the opposition to the proclamation of Lincoln freeing the negroes, and the rapid retreat of Foster from this place in December have together caused great discontent and shaken the *morale* of their army. I suppose there is really some truth in these reports. That their plans have been interfered with to some extent is certain, and I think but for the disaster to the monitor and

the recent storms on the coast they would have been out in force before now.

There is at this time only one battery behind; it is expected to-night and is intended for Kinston, which place has been fortified since the recent raids, and the bridge rebuilt. I think Evans can now hold it for several days against almost any force that may be brought against it. He, however, calls loudly for re-enforcements upon any collision of the extreme pickets. His brigade has been recently strengthened by returning soldiers; some 500 or 600, I understand.

Governor Vance sent me a copy of his order reorganizing the militia and offering to call them out whenever I wanted them. I sent him a telegram immediately asking him to order them out at once and when reorganized and ready for service to let me know. In the new shape they will probably be of some service. But he tells me that there is no law for the reorganization, and the whole subject will, I expect, be brought up for discussion in the Legislature.

I have written Governor Vance, sending him copies of the letter of instructions to recruiting officers and of a recent order published from here in regard to deserters and all absent without proper authority, requesting the Governor to issue a proclamation and appeal to the people. He told me when he was here on Sunday last that he would do so. The Governor has shown the utmost willingness to co-operate with us in all matters here affecting transportation, supplies, recruiting, and general efficiency of the command.

General French is at Kenansville, Warsaw, and Magnolia, with Pettigrew's, Ransom's, and Cooke's brigades. Daniel's and Davis' brigades are here. Robertson is covering the front.

My forces in this part of the State, all told, amount to about 13,000. This does not include the garrison of Wilmington. There are fortifications, with heavy guns, and one regiment of infantry at Weldon; one regiment at Hamilton and Greenville, besides the forces at Petersburg and the Blackwater. I shall endeavor to concentrate upon the enemy and beat them whichever way they may come. If their main attack is against Wilmington and the iron-clads don't succeed in passing the forts we will, I think, beat them badly. It is a long line to defend; they are in very superior numbers, but we expect to win. My health is not as good as I would wish, but I won't break down if they will only come on.

Very respectfully and truly, yours,

G. W. SMITH,
Major-General.

HEADQUARTERS,
Wilmington, January 21, 1863.

General SMITH, *Goldsborough:*
General FRENCH, *Magnolia:*

Enemy encamped last night 2 miles from Jacksonville; 1,000 cavalry, six pieces of artillery; said to be waiting for their infantry force, which is reported very large. Information comes from scouts and a man at whose house enemy stopped. General Robertson at Jacksonville.

W. H. C. WHITING.

JANUARY 22, 1863.

Major-General FRENCH:

Report from the front states that the enemy has withdrawn from Jacksonville beyond White Oak.

W. H. C. WHITING.

CONFIDENTIAL.]   CAMP FREDERICKSBURG, *January* 23, 1863.

Mr. PRESIDENT : I have thought it my duty to give you all information in my possession which might enable you to form a correct estimate of the character of the principal officers of the army. I have
thought this due to yourself and called for by the momentous contest in
which we are engaged. In that spirit I inclose a letter from General
Ransom addressed to General Chilton. It is without the knowledge
of the former but with the assent of the latter. I beg you will make
the same allowance for the feelings of the writer that I do. He is evidently, as he states, smarting under a supposed degradation of position;
cannot be supposed therefore to take the most favorable view of affairs,
yet he narrated circumstances which if true are not calculated to cause
anticipations of happy results. You have the means of obtaining
information which I have not. I have no fear therefore of injustice
being done to General Smith. I have not only the kindest feelings but
have conceived the highest opinion of this officer, not so much from my
own observation as from the estimate of all the officers under whom he
has served. I confess, however, that the letter of General Ransom
makes me more anxious that General Kirby Smith should be in command in North Carolina, and as I fear you may find difficulty in changing his assignment I have determined to write to you. I think it probable that General G. W. Smith's state of health makes him apprehensive
of exertion or excitement, and a more quiet command may be necessary
for his condition. If so, the service or position may require a change.
It may be better, if General Kirby Smith cannot be obtained, that
General Elzey should take the field and General Smith resume his position at Richmond. I had supposed that General Ransom would have
liked the tour of duty in North Carolina, and I wished him to have had
the opportunity of filling the ranks of his regiments. I am sorry it
was found necessary to break up his division, though it was a small
one. I was surprised to learn from General A. P. Hill on my return
that the other two North Carolina brigades, Pender's and Lane's, which
had been ordered off, were delighted at the suspension of their order.
They did not wish to go to North Carolina. Please destroy General
Ransom's letter after perusal.

Wishing you all health and happiness, I remain, with great esteem,
your obedient servant,

R. E. LEE.

STATE OF NORTH CAROLINA, EXECUTIVE DEPARTMENT,
Raleigh, N. C., January 24, 1863.

General GUSTAVUS W. SMITH, *Goldsborough, N. C. :*

MY DEAR SIR : Yours, accompanying the orders, &c.,* received this
morning. My proclamation will appear in the morning papers, and
everything that I can do shall be done. I received information this
morning from Wilmington that General Whiting had seized all the
teams, hands, and boats belonging to the State salt agent and completely stopped the works. This is a great calamity to our people to
stop the making of 350 bushels of salt per day right in the midst of the
pork-packing season. I can scarcely conceive of any such emergency
as would justify it. A little trouble on the part of General Whiting's
quartermaster would have enabled him to press teams in the adjacent
counties, and a requisition upon me for labor would have furnished as

---

* Not found.

much as he wanted, as was done with Colonel Stevens. Let me ask you to have these hands and teams restored to the agent, unless it be impossible to supply their places in time. It is almost as important to the State as the safety of the city, as our people cannot live without the salt.

Most truly, yours,

Z. B. VANCE.

HEADQUARTERS,
Wilmington, N. C., January 24, 1863.

Maj. Gen. GUSTAVUS W. SMITH,
Goldsborough, N. C.:

GENERAL: I am in receipt of information from within the enemy's lines which bears an appearance of probability. It is that they are now only waiting for favorable weather to attempt the reduction of the forts by the iron-clads, and that their main force will not march on this place until that shall be accomplished. The draught of the iron-clads is stated at 9 feet 2 inches. Their success will depend greatly on the weather. Supposing that they gain the entrance and harbor, entirely new combinations will be necessary and the question becomes one of much difficulty. They will move their force by transports in that event, or at least the greater part of them, and will endeavor to secure a base upon the mainland either at Smithville or on the left bank, perhaps both. I have ordered a line of defenses from the river to the Sound between here and Fort Fisher on the other side. We have already the line resting at Fort Saint Philip. Leaving out for the present the assault of the river by the iron-clads alone, the other side in Brunswick County, looking to the communication south and the security of the Upper Cape Fear River, becomes very important and forces may be required over there to hold them in check. Whether the iron-clads come up or not to endeavor to cut the communication, we must be prepared with movable batteries to stop transportation. Your battery of 20-pounder Parrotts will be invaluable. Three more iron-clads—the Weehawken, Nahant, and Patapsco—are on their way to Beaufort. We must have as many of the heaviest guns as we can possibly get. Unless the submarine mortars can do something, I do not see how the iron-clads can be kept out, though we may stop the fleet.

Very respectfully,

W. H. C. WHITING,
Brigadier-General, Commanding.

HEADQUARTERS,
Wilmington, N. C., January 24, 1863.

Col. [WILLIAM] LAMB,
Commanding Fort Fisher, N. C.:

COLONEL: A probable plan of the enemy will be the reduction of the forts by iron-clads preparatory to movement in force. From their invulnerability and the great range of their guns it is not likely that they can be much affected by your shot. You should endeavor to preserve your guns and men as much as possible from damage to enable you to stop the wooden vessels. Fire should be given very deliberately from your heaviest metal and the Whitworth upon the iron-clads. Supposing her to close her ports and come in, you should provide parados or reverse traverses to keep your casemate batteries from bei.1g destroyed. I will send some submarine mortars down to be placed on the keys, near Letel[?] Island. They may be of service.

Very respectfully,

W. H. C. WHITING,
Brigadier-General.

HEADQUARTERS,
Golding Place, January 25, 1863.

Major HILL, *Assistant Adjutant-General:*

A dispatch sent by Major Nethercutt to General Robertson (and brought here by mistake), dated 10 o'clock p. m. to-day. states that the enemy had passed Trenton on their way toward Kinston. Nothing is said as to the force. The cavalry had passed before Nethercutt wrote.

JOHN A. BAKER,
Colonel, Comdg. Forty-first North Carolina Infantry.

[Indorsement.]

JANUARY 26, 1863.

General SMITH:

The above just received.

W. H. C. WHITING,
Major-General, Commanding.

NAVAL COMMANDANT'S OFFICE,
Wilmington, N. C., January 26, 1863.

Hon. JAMES A. SEDDON,
Secretary of War:

I have the honor to acknowledge receipt of your letter of 22d instant, and in compliance with its request inclose extract copy of my communication of 2d December, 1862.*

The threatening attitude of the enemy has confined me to this place, where we have great naval interests at stake; but if the men were furnished they might undergo preparatory training at the battery erected on the right bank of Cape Fear River for the protection of the iron-clad gunboats we are constructing, and, as part are drilled, detailed for the movable batteries to which my letter refers.

I am, very respectfully, your obedient servant,

W. F. LYNCH,
Flag-Officer.

GOLDSBOROUGH, *January 26, 1863.*

Hon. JAMES A. SEDDON,
Secretary of War, Richmond:

MY DEAR SIR: Since writing you last I have visited Wilmington, Magnolia, and Kinston. The fortifications at the former place are very strong and we will be enabled to make very effective resistance against an attack by land. With the troops from General Beauregard, General Whiting can hold them until our forces from Magnolia and this place can be brought to his relief. The matter to be apprehended at Wilmington is the passage of the iron-clads past the forts, which would

---

* No inclosure found. See letter from Lynch to Seddon, December 2, 1862, p. 789.

not only give them the outer harbor but would seriously embarrass and endanger the defense of the city. Two 10-inch guns in addition to the one recently sent would add greatly to our chances against the iron-clads. These guns have been applied for. I hope that the Ordnance Department will be able to furnish them. It is very important, and there is no time to spare. In placing the three brigades near Kenansville under Major-General French they are in position to move against the flank or rear of the enemy in case they attack Wilmington; can effectually prevent their turning General Whiting's advanced position, which is on the Sound road, 16 miles from the town; and we can, if required, move to the front on Trenton or take them in flank or rear if they move on Kinston. These three brigades are in good position to meet any movement of the enemy from New Berne or Beaufort on the south side of the Neuse.

But the shortest and best road from New Berne to Kinston crosses to the left or north bank of the Neuse some 10 or 12 miles below Kinston. I scarcely think they will cross the river; if they do I have two brigades here ready to move by railroad toward Weldon, Kinston, or Wilmington, and will endeavor to beat them, let them come as they may. Railroads are an uncertain reliance; they will worry me out of my life yet I think. But I must say in simple justice to Mr. Whitford, president of the North Carolina and Atlantic Railroad, who was appointed Government agent of railroad transportation at this point by General Holmes, and of Mr. Harvey, his subordinate, that no men could be more willing, attentive, and obliging and none more efficient than they have shown themselves. At all hours, night and day, they have served me; within five minutes they were always ready to comply with any requirement of mine. The State of North Carolina owns two-thirds of the stock in all the railroads within the State except one, and has placed everything possible at my disposal. The only trouble heretofore has been in the condition of the roads and their fixtures. Colonel Wadley left here about two weeks ago for Charleston and told me that Mr. Whitford would represent him in his absence, and all has gone on smoothly until to-day. Mr. Whitford and his subordinate or assistant, Mr. Harvey, resigned when Colonel Wadley first arrived here, but he urged them to retain their positions, which they consented to do, at least for the present. I am informed that their arduous and valuable services have been rendered the Government without compensation. The communication from Quartermaster-General dispensing with Mr. Whitford's services from the 20th instant has crippled me, as far as railroad transportation is concerned, for the present. At the moment Mr. Whitford's note, a copy of which is sent herewith,* was handed me I received a telegram saying that the pickets reported the enemy advancing in force from Trenton upon Kinston. I immediately telegraphed you, and hope that the Quartermaster-General has reversed his action, or, if not, that in future he will consult with or notify me before taking a step so vitally affecting the interest and safety of my command.

The works at Kinston are strong against attack from the south side and the enemy will find it a very different place to take from what it was before, even with the same force only there.

The papers I sent forward in General Evans' case (charges preferred against him by one of his colonels) I would like to have acted upon in some way. Please notice that General Evans had preferred charges against the colonel previously, a fact not known to me for some two

---

* Not found.

weeks after the charges preferred against him by the colonel had been forwarded. If I had known that General Evans had preferred charges against the colonel those of the colonel against him would not have been entertained until at least after the colonel had been tried, which trial I would have ordered at once. If nothing else can be done in the case I would suggest that the papers in the case be returned to me in order that I may do something with them.

The enemy have put on double guards around New Berne and Beaufort, and our usual channels of communication with the interior of their lines have been cut off or delayed for ten days; but we continue to get information that their force and fleet are both large; that all preparations have been made for a movement, and that there is much dissatisfaction in their army.

I remain, very respectfully and truly, yours,

G. W. SMITH,
Major-General.

[Indorsements.]

Read and returned. The heavy guns asked for should be furnished as soon as practicable.

J. D.

The guns have been ordered as soon as those before directed for Vicksburg and Atchafalaya shall have been furnished.

J. A. S.,
Secretary.

———————

[JANUARY 26, 1863.]

A PROCLAMATION.

Whereas it has been made known to me that a large number of soldiers from our armies are absent from their colors without proper leave in this hour of our greatest need, and it is being confidently believed that a large majority of such were impelled to this by a natural and almost irresistible desire to see their friends and homes once more, after so long an absence, and not because of a cowardly determination to leave their brave comrades to share all the dangers and hardships of the field alone; and whereas Maj. Gen. G. W. Smith, in command of the Department of North Carolina, by consent of the Secretary of War, has published an order declaring that all who may voluntarily return to duty by the 10th day of February next shall be received into their several commands with no other punishment than a forfeiture of their pay for the time they have been absent without leave; and declaring further that all who do not so return by the said 10th day of February shall, when apprehended, be tried for desertion and upon conviction be made to suffer death:

Now, therefore, I, Zebulon B. Vance, Governor of the State of North Carolina, do issue this my proclamation to all soldiers from the State serving in the army of the Confederacy who are now illegally absent from their colors, commanding them to return to duty with their comrades, and exhorting them to avail themselves of this opportunity of saving their friends from the disgrace and infamy which will cling forever to the name of a deserter from his country's cause and themselves from a felon's death. Many, after carrying their country's flag in triumph through various bloody conflicts and making for themselves a name of which their children's children might have been justly proud, have forfeited it all by absenting themselves at a moment when their own State is invaded and about to be desolated by a brutal, half-savage foe. Now is the time to reinstate themselves by a prompt return to duty. I appeal to them to stand by their country yet a little longer, and not to sully by desertion the bright and glorious reputation of the State which they have helped to win on a hundred hard-fought fields ; and I appeal to all good and loyal citizens throughout the State to give their influence to induce these men to return. Let no one, unmoved by this appeal to his patriotism and honor, suppose that he can remain at home with impunity; the full powers of the State authorities, aided, if need be, by the Confederacy, shall be put in force to arrest him and bring him to punishment after the 10th day of February next, and there shall be no rest for the deserter in the borders of North Carolina. And let none excuse their desertion by declaring that they go home to take care of their families; they will add nothing to the comforts of their families by hiding like guilty men in the woods by day and plundering their neighbors by night; they only bring shame and suffering upon the heads of the innocent, and their little children, when gray-headed old men, will have the finger of scorn pointed at them and the bitter taunt will ring in their ears, "Your father skulked in the woods to keep from fighting for his country." The State is now trying to provide food for your families and each county is making a similar provision, and as your chief magistrate I promise you that the wives and children of the soldiers who are in the army doing their duty shall share the last bushel of meal and pound of meat in the State. Let every patriot in the land assist with all his influence in the execution of this proclamation and our victorious ranks will again be filled and our country soon be rid of the enemy.

In witness thereof Zebulon B. Vance, our Governor, captain-general, and commander-in-chief, hath signed these presents and caused the great seal of the State to be affixed. Done at our city of Raleigh on the 26th day of January, in the year of our Lord 1863.

Z. B. VANCE.

By the Governor:

    R. H. BATTLE, JR.,
       Private Secretary.

WAR DEPARTMENT, C. S. A.,
Richmond, Va., January 27, 1863.

General D. H. HILL, *Charlotte, N. C.:*

The President desires to know if the command of the army in North Carolina would be acceptable to you?

J. A. SEDDON,
Secretary of War.

RICHMOND, VA., January 27, 1863.

Maj. Gen. S. G. FRENCH:

General Smith has been called to this city. You will proceed with the least possible delay to Goldsborough and assume the command.

S. COOPER.

HEADQUARTERS,
Wilmington, N. C., January 28, 1863.

Hon. JAMES A. SEDDON, *Secretary of War, Richmond, Va.:*

SIR: I send you a sketch* showing the lines about Wilmington. Though not of a formidable kind, yet, manned by brave troops, they will make a stout resistance. My last information, received this morning from Beaufort, is that during the past week large bodies of troops have been moved by railroad from New Berne and put on board the transports, twenty or thirty of which have swung out into the stream preparatory to mooring. They are mostly sailing craft. There are no blockaders off the harbor this morning, which indicates that they have been called off to assist the transportation. Seven steamers from the southward arrived at Beaufort last Friday. My great trouble is the possibility of the monitors forcing their way in the outer harbor and destroying the forts, thus opening an easy and admirable base for their future operations against the city and the interior. The attack by land, if such is made, I do not fear, by reason of our advanced positions and the dispositions of his army by Major-General Smith; but the tremendous ordnance possessed by the enemy makes me apprehensive of the results of an action with the forts should wind and weather enable him to cross the bars. I have strengthened Fort Caswell by iron-clad casemates; 450-pounder shot, however, are hard to fend off, either for forts or monitors. It is much to be regretted that a judicious system of obstruction has not been made for this important harbor during the two years past, time enough for executing any work of the kind. One similar to the Charleston boom (impracticable there) could readily have been placed and maintained here on the "keys" or inner bulkheads, near [Fort] Caswell and New Inlet, and in the narrow river near the city, where this would be invaluable. Such means of obstruction as I have been able to gather in the last two months I have employed; that is, scows laden with stone and two small vessels, the only ones to be had. Obstructions of this nature are objectionable here from the shifting nature of the bottom and the great extent of shoal. A channel is soon formed around them to restore the equilibrium which they disturb. Strong, open framework or *chevaux-de-frise* of timber, iron, and chain, which would not interfere with the water-way, is the best for this coast; but that is work for which I have not been able to find the time, the workmanship, or the material. The submarine mortars of General Rains may aid us. They are placed to the best of my judgment. Though the number of guns at [Forts] Caswell and Fisher is considerable, their quality is bad and caliber small. Many of the rifle guns are not banded and not to be trusted. We have but one 10-inch gun and but one rifle as large as 42 in the district. I have great hopes in the inefficiency of the monitors at sea and in the difficulty of the channel. A scoundrel of a pilot has managed to go over to the enemy in the past three weeks and is now on board their fleet. I cannot disguise the fact that the consequences of a successful passage will be very serious. In this respect I refer to my letter to the Secretary of War of November 14 last, previous to my assuming command here, and to a consideration of the map of this section. Major-General Smith, being now in Richmond, will be able fully to inform the Department in this matter, our views being, I am happy to say for my part, identical.

Very respectfully,

W. H. C. WHITING,
Brigadier-General.

---

* Not found.

WILMINGTON, N. C., *January 28, 1863.*

General FRENCH:

Information received from Beaufort that during past week large bodies of troops have been moved from New Berne by railroad and put on board transports. Twenty transports loaded and swung out into the stream. They are mostly sailing vessels.

W. H. C. WHITING,
Brigadier-General.

———

HEADQUARTERS,
Wilmington, N. C., January 28, 1863.

Flag-Officer [W. F.] LYNCH,
Commanding C. S. Navy, Wilmington, N. C.:

COMMODORE: Yours of yesterday relative to protection of the gun-boats is received. The subject of troops to support the batteries on the upper river has been duly considered for the disposition of the forces for the defense. It is not, however, thought necessary to post them immediately, their movement depending on contingencies which may or may not arise. No difficulty is anticipated in placing troops at that point. In the mean time every possible preparation in the way of obstruction is recommended to be got ready. Combined with sinking of the Arctic, trees with the branches on held with chains will form a formidable and easily-made obstacle. Very few obstructions, however, will be able to withstand the spring freshets, which in this river are very heavy. I do not advocate the immediate obstruction of the river, but that preparations should be made for it. Positions and pits for riflemen should be selected and made in every suitable place.

Very respectfully,

W. H. C. WHITING,
Brigadier-General, Commanding.

———

HEADQUARTERS CAVALRY BRIGADE,
Salem, Va., January 28, 1863.

His Excellency ZEBULON B. VANCE,
Governor of North Carolina:

SIR: I desire to call your attention to a matter of much concern to the public interest. In order to enable the armies at Fredericksburg, Richmond, and other points having railroad communication with this section to obtain the necessary supplies of corn, &c., all the horses, mules, &c., of this department have been sent to a considerable distance, to be foraged until spring, from the line of this railroad (Virginia and Tennessee road). In thus distributing these animals, and after overstocking almost every part of Virginia, it became a matter of necessity to send some of them to portions of North Carolina, where both grain and long forage were abundant. But, unfortunately, there is a great indisposition on the part of people there to sell their produce for Confederate money at any price, and I desire to ask relief at your hands in the form of authority of some kind for impressment. This authority you can limit with such restrictions as will make it entirely certain that no injustice will be done to your people. If some step of this sort is not taken promptly and we should be compelled in this portion of South-western Virginia to bring the horses in the service of the Government back to this section, and thus consume the forage which is essential to the wants of our armies elsewhere, it is manifest that most serious detriment to the public service must occur.

Knowing your disinterested patriotism, not only from your public character but also from a personal acquaintance which I had the pleasure of having while we were both members of the old Federal Congress, and your full and entire devotion to our cause (which is not the cause of a State, but of the whole South), I have taken the liberty of addressing you upon this subject. I shall forward this to you after having referred it for the consideration of the general commanding this military department.

I am, sir, respectfully, your obedient servant,

A. G. JENKINS,
Brigadier-General.

GOLDSBOROUGH, N. C., *January* 28, 1863.

General S. COOPER:

I came up here this morning and assumed command. It is rumored the troops have embarked. It needs confirmation.

S. G. FRENCH.

GOLDSBOROUGH, N. C., *January* 30, 1863.

General S. COOPER:

General Whiting reports twenty-four regiments on transports at Beaufort ready to sail, and 25,000 troops still in New Berne, under Sigel, to move by land.

S. G. FRENCH.

WILMINGTON, N. C., *January* 31, 1863.

General GUSTAVUS W. SMITH, *Richmond:*

A portion of the enemy's fleet left Beaufort yesterday. Five steamers and seventeen transports passed Swansborough last night. Recollect that should they pass below me, either to feint or make a real attack on Charleston, Beauregard may recall his troops. Their presence, or at least an equal number, should be always here, and if you supply their place you must have more from the North. Sigel is at New Berne with (reported) twenty-five regiments. Greater part of the force at Morehead City and on board transports.

W. H. C. WHITING,
Brigadier-General, Commanding.

Abstract from Return of the Department of North Carolina, commanded by Maj. Gen. S. G. French, for January, 1863.

Command	Present for duty. Officers.	Present for duty. Men.	Aggregate present.	Aggregate present and absent.	Pieces of artillery. Heavy.	Pieces of artillery. Field.
Brig. Gen. R. E. Colston, forces at Petersburg, Va..........	95	1,465	1,741	2,338		14
Brig. Gen. J. J. Pettigrew, French's division, at Magnolia, N. C.	444	7,270	8,509	12,503	8	18
Brig. Gen. W. H. C. Whiting, District of the Cape Fear....	650	8,951	11,719	11,719		
Brig. Gen. N. G. Evans, one brigade, at Kinston, N. C...	167	1,840	2,269	3,399		
Brig. Gen. J. Daniel, one brigade, at Goldsborough, N. C.	176	2,969	3,656	4,624	2	8
Brig. Gen. J. R. Davis, one brigade, at Goldsborough, N. C.	121	1,756	2,094	2,605		6
Maj. J. C. Haskell, four batteries, at Goldsborough, N. C.	11	318	362	433		4
Capt. J. B. Starr, one light battery, at Goldsborough, N. C.	4	91	96	110		16
Col. J. A. J. Bradford, post of Goldsborough, N. C......	27	415	455	504		6
Col. J. A. J. Bradford, four artillery companies, at Goldsborough and near New Berne.	14	237	295	385		
Col. George C. Gibbs, one regiment, at Weldon, N. C....	30	603	828	1,045		
Capt. W. J. Dabney, one heavy battery, at Weldon, N. C..	2	48	53	67	2	
Col. William F. Martin, one regiment and one battery, at Hamilton, N. C.	46	754	925	1,077		6
Brig. Gen. B. H. Robertson, three regiments cavalry, at Kinston, N. C.						
Grand total..	1,787	26,717	33,002	40,809	12	78

Abstract from Report of the Troops of the District of the Cape Fear, commanded by Brig. Gen. W. H. C. Whiting, for January 31, 1863.

Command	Present for duty. Officers.	Present for duty. Men.	Effective total.	Aggregate present.	Aggregate present and absent.	Pieces of artillery.
Brigadier-General Clingman's brigade.............	135	1,811	2,065	2,633	3,380	....
Colonel Colquitt's brigade.	176	2,412	2,534	2,916	3,747	4
Colonel Harrison's brigade............	87	1,344	1,446	1,707	2,208	10
Colonel Wilson's brigade...........	109	1,497	1,583	1,801	2,369	8
41st Regiment North Carolina Troops (cavalry)...........	24	354	365	423	550	....
3d Battalion North Carolina Artillery...............	11	216	217	237	272	....
Fort Caswell (six companies)...............	20	278	357	500	537	....
Fort Fisher (nine companies)...............	34	534	667	791	885	....
Fort Johnson (two companies)...........	7	98	104	130	142	....
Fort Saint Philip (four companies)...........	14	194	233	268	288	....
10th Battalion North Carolina Artillery...........	13	183	201	231	265	....
Fort French (one company)...........	4	55	58	66	78	....
Light-House Battery (one company)...........	4	105	105	129	158	....
Company F, Tenth Regiment North Carolina Troops..	4	41	47	65	93	....
Company B, Sixty-first Regiment North Carolina Troops.	2	10	12	19	48	....
Captain Buie's company, North Carolina Troops........	4	20	23	32	33	....
Clark Artillery...........................	3	55	54	79	107	....
Bridge guard............................	1	31	31	32	32	....
Signal Corps............................	1	22	22	23	23	....
Grand total...........................	653	9,260	10,124	12,082	15,215	22

Organization of Troops in the District of the Cape Fear, commanded by Brig. Gen. W. H. C. Whiting, for January 31, 1863.

GENERAL GIST'S DIVISION.*

Brigadier-General Clingman's Brigade.

8th North Carolina.
31st North Carolina.
51st North Carolina.
61st North Carolina.

Colonel Wilson's Brigade.

25th Georgia.
29th Georgia.
30th Georgia.
Humphry Troop.
Detachment artillery.
Preston's, [W. C., South Carolina] light battery.
Waties' light battery.

Colonel Colquitt's Brigade.

46th Georgia.
7th Battalion South Carolina Volunteers.
16th South Carolina.
24th South Carolina.
25th South Carolina.
Culpeper's light battery.

Colonel Harrison's Brigade.

32d Georgia.
47th Georgia.
4th Louisiana Battalion.
Adams', [Z. T., North Carolina] light battery.
Paris', [A. B., Virginia] light battery.

MISCELLANEOUS.

Unattached.

41st North Carolina (cavalry).
Fort Caswell (six companies).
Fort Fisher (nine companies).
Fort Johnson (two companies).
Fort Saint Philip (four companies).

City and River Defense.

Lieut. Col. [C. E.] THORBURN commanding.

10th Battalion North Carolina Artillery.
Fort French (one company).
Light-House Battery (one company).

City Garrison.

Company F, Tenth Regiment North Carolina Troops.
Company B, Sixty-first Regiment North Carolina Troops.
Captain Buie's two companies North Carolina Troops.
Clark Artillery.

Unattached.

3d Battalion North Carolina Artillery.

Signal Corps.

Bridge Guard.

Detachment Capt. Bradberry's company.

Abstract from Field Return of Troops, Maj. Gen. A. Elzey commanding, for February 1, 1863 (headquarters Richmond, Va.).

Command.	Present for duty.		Effective total present.	Aggregate present.	Aggregate present and absent.
	Officers.	Men.			
Brig. Gen. H. A. Wise	161	2,002	2,115	2,503	3,445
Col. T. J. Page	25	322	388	432	510
Col. T. S. Rhett	82	1,428	1,588	1,879	2,319
Col. Jack Brown	33	624	700	908	1,153
Maj. F. W. Smith	16	246	322	365	385
Grand total	317	4,622	5,113	6,087	7,812

* Report leaves it in doubt whether any or all brigades given below constitute this division.

FEBRUARY 2, 1863.

General GUSTAVUS W. SMITH, *Richmond :*

I think the attack on Savannah can only be a feint by gunboats to draw troops from North Carolina; impossible they can mean otherwise with the very large force at New Berne and Morehead City. Take care that troops are not withdrawn from here. Wilmington and Charleston are now worth ten Savannahs, especially in view of our late naval success. Let us secure this place until the gunboats are done beyond peradventure.

W. H. C. WHITING.

STATE OF NORTH CAROLINA, EXECUTIVE DEPARTMENT,
Raleigh, N. C., February 2, 1863.

General W. G. M. DAVIS, *Warm Springs, N. C.:*

SIR : Yours, giving an account of operations in your command in the mountains of this State, has been received. The result is quite satisfactory, and I am especially pleased to learn that there appears to be no regular organization of enemies to the Government in that country. I was loath to believe so, and from the first was of the opinion that the raid was only for plunder and that the whole matter was probably exaggerated. I hope now that quiet and order are restored in that region, and have to return you my thanks for the very prompt and energetic aid afforded by your command in producing this state of things. I was fearful in the great excitement prevailing among our people that the misguided people of Laurel might be dealt too harshly with, and warned the officers to be civil and just. I was therefore sorry to learn this morning that Colonel Allen had hanged several of the captured prisoners. I hope this is not true, as it would be much better to have them dealt with by the law. In regard to running them into Kentucky I approve of the plan, provided they desire to go. I would not wish, however, to exile the women and children or old men if they desire to remain, as the law ought to be strong enough to keep them in subjection. I hope Colonel McElroy will take proper steps to prevent the escape of his prisoners.

With sentiments of regard, I am, sir, your obedient servant,

Z. B. VANCE.

WAR DEPARTMENT, C. S. A.,
Richmond, Va., February 3, 1863.

Brig. Gen. [W. H. C.] WHITING :

General Beauregard expects an early attack on Charleston. Send him one of the brigades he forwarded you—Gist's, if you can spare it. Hold another ready to be forwarded. I will telegraph General French at Goldsborough as far as practicable to re-enforce you.

J. A. SEDDON,
Secretary of War.

WAR DEPARTMENT, C. S. A.,
Richmond, Va., February 3, 1863.

Maj. Gen. [S. G.] FRENCH, *Goldsborough, N. C.:*

General Beauregard expecting early attack at Charleston, I must return the troops sent by him to Wilmington. I order one brigade to be forwarded at once and another to be held in readiness for transportation. You must re-enforce General Whiting as far as you can venture to weaken your line.

J. A. SEDDON,
Secretary of War.

HEADQUARTERS,
Wilmington, N. C., February 3, 1863.

Maj. Gen. [S. G.] FRENCH,
  Goldsborough, N. C.:

MY DEAR GENERAL: The question of traverse against reverse fire at [Forts] Fisher and Caswell has already been amply provided for. Another heavy casemate has been erected at Fisher, a little to the right of the detached battery Bolles. Were my guns of heavier caliber I should be much at ease as to that work. When the 10-inch columbiads get as far as Goldsborough push them through. At Fort Caswell, which was the weakest point of the system, I have six guns in iron casemates of good construction. With a little more time will have the whole channel guns iron-covered. Heavy sand traverses separate them. On the reverse faces most of the guns looking inward have been placed on the cornice-way, for fire on the anchorage, and their place terre-plein occupied by huge traverses, which defilade the reverse of the casemates and cover the citadel. The casemates in the channel fronts also cover the citadel. Guns of the heaviest caliber are also mounted there. In Brunswick River strong obstructions have been placed, covered by a strong battery, 1½ miles below Fort French upon a high hill. The railroad bridge to Wartherton [Lumberton] Railroad is covered by a battery of three 24-pounders and by rifle-pits. [*Sic.* The railroad bridge over the Lumber River is covered by a battery of three 24-pounders and by rifle-pits.] The bluffs in the city from old Robert Brown's house, near the shipyard, down to Frolick's sword factory, below the foundery, are occupied by several strong batteries. Another above the Wilmington and Weldon Railroad Wharf commands the thoroughfare. The movements of the enemy puzzle me. Unless they are gone mad they cannot mean to attack Savannah. It could have no possible effect on the war if they were to take it. Wilmington, Charleston, or Mobile is worth forty Savannahs to us and to them. They may mean to try and withdraw troops from here and North Carolina for they still have a very heavy force at Beaufort; but that should be resisted. I fear Beauregard will take alarm and recall his troops from here. I have let G. W. [Smith] know my views on the matter. Nothing new this morning. Heavy gale of wind from northward.

Very respectfully,

W. H. C. WHITING,
Brigadier-General, Commanding.

HEADQUARTERS,
Wilmington, N. C., February 3, 1863.

Colonel GORGAS,
  Chief of Ordnance, Richmond, Va.:

COLONEL: I wish to call your attention to the necessity for guns of the heaviest caliber within the means of the department for the successful defense of this place. I learn with great pleasure that one 10-inch columbiad is now on its way. One more is absolutely necessary. The heavy rifled guns for the Navy gunboats ought, if possible, to be sent forward, as they might be mounted until required on board. I presume, however, that your Department has nothing to do with them. Secretary Mallory offers the co-operation of the Navy in guns and men. No doubt your recommendation to the founderies on the importance of completing these guns would hasten them. The vital points of the Confederacy now are Richmond, Wilmington, Charleston, Mobile, and Vicksburg. Let us hold these, and whatever else goes we are safe.

Very respectfully,

W. H. C. WHITING,
Brigadier-General, Commanding.

HEADQUARTERS,
Wilmington, N. C., February 3, 1863.

Maj. Gen. GUSTAVUS W. SMITH,
Commanding Department:

GENERAL: I need not urge upon you the necessity of our having here as many heavy guns as we can get; the heavier the better. Please to urge it upon the Department. I am happy to learn that a 10-inch columbiad is on the way. One more of the caliber is absolutely needed and I hope may be procured. I prefer the 10-inch smooth-bore to rifle-guns as against iron-clads. We can use the 120-pound bolt in them with effect. In the mean time, taking the offer of the Secretary of the Navy, the heavy guns and ammunition destined for the gunboats building here should be sent forward at once. Pending the completion of the boats they can be placed in battery to do effective service. Colonel Stevens has sent me an engineer experienced in submarine galvanic batteries. If we can arrange the material I am sure there is no better locality for such than this, and to blow up one or two monitors is perhaps the best and cheapest way to procure a few 15-inch guns. I shall send this officer (Lieut. [Henry] Bolton) to Richmond to get up the machinery. Please to give him your countenance and recommend the matter to the attention of the Secretary of War. Richmond, Wilmington, Charleston, Mobile, and Vicksburg are five vital and most important points to our country and cause. Hold them, no matter what else goes, and the republic is safe. In this view I cannot regard expeditions and attacks upon places of minor importance as other than feints to draw off forces from the defense of those positions, unless, indeed, the enemy is struck with judicial blindness and does not know what we know. I hope that their security will be placed beyond peradventure, first, by the posting of a sufficient permanent garrison or infantry force for any sudden descent of the enemy—this to be always on hand; and, secondly, by the system you have adopted in your command of a movable army, which can act in any part of the department according to circumstances. Here now I have no more than are absolutely necessary; yet this garrison, withdrawn from the next southern department, is liable to be recalled and leave Wilmington open. I beg you will urge what I have so often brought forward—the necessity of the presence here of a movable column of my own, ready to act either upon a land or sea approach or both, until relief should come from your *corps d'armée.* Many previous letters set forth and explain this necessity by reference to the topographical features of this district.

Very respectfully,

W. H. C. WHITING,
Brigadier-General, Commanding.

HEADQUARTERS,
Goldsborough, N. C., February 3, 1863.

Maj. Gen. GUSTAVUS W. SMITH,
Richmond, Va. :

DEAR SIR : If the information be true that the iron-clads (monitors) are now at Port Royal, and that some thirty transports and a number of gunboats have left Beaufort and gone south, I think the attack on Wilmington is abandoned, if it was ever seriously entertained. Now, it appears to me the United States Government has two great objects in view—first, the capture of Richmond, and, second, the opening of the navigation of the Mississippi River by the reduction of Port Hudson and Vicksburg. Taking this for granted, and that unless they think their army ample for the accomplishment of the first, might we not suppose that the forces under General Foster, now at Beaufort, may when the proper time arrives embark and proceed up the James River ? In this case we would have no knowledge of his movements, or rather destination, until he showed himself on the banks of the river, all the coast being in the enemy's possession. If they sail south it appears to me they would go to the Mississippi rather than waste their strength in attacking minor points. It may be, however, that they may land near Savannah. I write this to call your attention to the unprotected state of the James River, and to say that as soon as ever I find positively that the fleet have sailed I wish to move a part of my forces toward Petersburg. If you deem these suggestions worthy of consideration you may forward this letter to the War Department.

Yours, very truly,

S. G. FRENCH,
Major-General, Commanding.

[Indorsements.]

HEADQUARTERS,
Richmond, Va., February 6, 1863.

Respectfully forwarded as requested for the information of the Secretary of War.

G. W. SMITH,
Major-General, Commanding.

RICHMOND, VA., *February* 6, 1863.

Respectfully referred to the President.

J. A. SEDDON,
Secretary of War.

SECRETARY OF WAR :

The suggestion of forces in position to defend the approach of James River is worthy of attention. If the enemy has gone toward the south the destination is most probably the coast of South Carolina, and requires that Charleston and the railroad to Savannah should be covered with a larger force than heretofore. There are many reasons to anticipate an attempt against Charleston, and the inducements to capture any other point on the coast south of Wilmington are so small that a concentration of force is clearly indicated at Charleston and on its approaches. There should be simultaneously the greatest activity in Eastern North Carolina, and coupled with military operations there should be vigorous and well-directed efforts to get out the supplies of forage and subsistence remaining in that region.

JEFFERSON DAVIS.

General GUSTAVUS W. SMITH:

Would it not be well to send from troops around Goldsborough further re-enforcements to Wilmington and forward thence all the force that can possibly be spared for defense of Charleston? I do not apprehend attack on Petersburg or Richmond, nor do I see how, consistently with the other objects referred to by the President, forces can be drawn back in this direction. All subsistence supplies that are attainable should be collected and sent from North Carolina to this city.

J. A. SEDDON,
Secretary of War.

RICHMOND, VA., February 10, 1863.

Respectfully referred to General French, calling his attention to the indorsements of the President and Secretary of War.

G. W. SMITH,
Major-General.

[FEBRUARY 3–6, 1863.—For correspondence between President Davis, the Secretary of War, and General Lee, in reference to re-enforcements from Army of Northern Virginia for North and South Carolina, see Series I, Vol. XIV, pp. 759, 762–764, 766.]

HEADQUARTERS,
Wilmington, February 4, 1863.

General BEAUREGARD, <i>Charleston, S. C.:</i>

Dispatch received from Secretary of War ordering me to send you a brigade and to hold another in readiness. Troops will accordingly move to-day, as fast as transportation will admit, commencing with Colquitt's brigade. Has been a smash on the railroad. Charleston mail not in. What news from the enemy? Are they threatening Charleston? Do you want Gist? Do not think the enemy intend Savannah at all.

W. H. C. WHITING,
Brigadier-General.

[FEBRUARY 4–7, 1863.—For Beauregard to Whiting, see Series I, Vol. XIV, pp. 762, 764, 767, 768.]

RICHMOND, VA., February [March?] 5, 1863.

Lieutenant-General LONGSTREET,
       Commanding, &c.:

GENERAL: The Secretary of War requested me to write to you and say that he desires you to have a close reconnaissance made of Suffolk with the view of attacking and carrying it, if you think it advisable and it can be done with advantage. If, however, the works are found too strong, he does not propose to carry it out. I think you had better come over and see him yourself if you can spare the time.

Very truly and respectfully, your obedient servant,

ARNOLD ELZEY,
Major-General.

WILMINGTON, *February* 7, 1863.

Hon. JAMES A. SEDDON:

Have sent General Beauregard two of his brigades. If I send more off must have another brigade here.

W. H. C. WHITING,
Brigadier-General.

RICHMOND, VA., *February* 7, 1863.

Maj. Gen. S. G. FRENCH,
Commanding, Goldsborough, N. C.:

MY DEAR GENERAL: Inclosed I send the map of fortifications of New Berne and the description accompanying it, and also inclose memoranda of roads furnished by Colonel Pool and another by two of my staff officers.* Your suggestions in regard to the probability of attack by the James and the possible necessity for a prompt move in this direction are in accordance with my own views of the probable contingencies that must be anticipated. I have long thought that the whole organization of my command ought to be rearranged, and looked to the chances of my being permanently assigned as major-general to command Richmond and its immediate defenses, in which case I hoped to have had Daniel's and Davis' brigades as part of the permanent garrison here as before, and perhaps to have you again at Petersburg; not in my command, but as a neighbor, closely identified with the defense of Richmond, and that our friend, General Pettigrew, if not promoted would be with you. Of course it was taken for granted that active operations in North Carolina would require the presence of a commander of higher rank than a division commander, and as I had made up my mind not to serve under any of the lieutenant-generals who were my juniors as major-generals it was tolerably clear to my mind that I would have to retire from that field before the struggle was over. It seems that the Government first intended to send E. K. Smith and then D. H. Hill to command, but something went wrong and * * * to have settled down upon the * * *, excepting I was to remain in the * * * in Goldsborough. I have to-day [determined] to send in my resignation, and thus * * * my plans at least for the present.

To yourself and General Pettigrew and all the officers and men of your command I tender my best wishes. May success and prosperity always attend you. To-day I am not in the mood to write, even if I had time.†

I remain, very truly, your friend,

G. W. SMITH.

SPECIAL ORDERS, }   ADJT. AND INSPECTOR GENERAL'S OFFICE,
No. 32.   }   *Richmond, Va., February* 7, 1863.

＊   ＊   ＊   ＊   ＊   ＊   ＊

XXX. Maj. Gen. D. H. Hill is assigned to the command of the troops in the State of North Carolina, and will report by letter to Maj. Gen. G. W. Smith, in this city.

＊   ＊   ＊   ＊   ＊   ＊   ＊

By command of the Secretary of War:

JNO. WITHERS,
Assistant Adjutant-General.

---

* Not found.   † Portions of original illegible.

RICHMOND, VA., *February* 8, 1863.

General FRENCH, *Goldsborough, N. C.:*

General Whiting has been telegraphed to return to General Beauregard all the force received from his command.

S. COOPER,
Adjutant and Inspector General.

HEADQUARTERS,
Wilmington, N. C., February 10, 1863.

Col. [H. L.] BENBOW,
Commanding Brigade, Sudberry, N. C.:

COLONEL : Your brigade will take the position at Sudberry lately occupied by Colonel Harrison's brigade. You will complete the works commenced and indicated by the engineer officers. You will examine the dispatches brought from the front by couriers from the outposts, and learning their contents forward them to me by telegraph. Persons passing in the direction of the enemy are required to have a special pass from these headquarters. Market carts and provisions are allowed to pass the lines. You will reconnoiter and make yourself thoroughly acquainted with the vicinity of your post, its approaches, and defenses, and require all your mounted officers to do the same. Cause strict discipline to be maintained ; drills, parades, and all camp duties to be regularly and properly performed You are required to protect private property from depredation.

Very respectfully,

W. H. C. WHITING,
Brigadier-General, Commanding.

WAR DEPARTMENT, C. S. A.,
Richmond, Va., February 10, 1863.

His Excellency ZEBULON B. VANCE,
Governor of North Carolina :

SIR : In the present state of the roads, and with the deficient means of transportation afforded by the railroads, the subsistence of General Lee's army is seriously endangered and may become actually dependent on the means of commanding the forage and provisions which have been and are now being collected by the Bureaus of this Department in your State. The vital importance of the subject will, I trust, excuse me in your estimation for invoking your attention to the subjoined copy of a telegram just received from Colonel Wadley, the agent of the Government for railroad transportation, and asking your co-operation with him in so managing and controlling the transportation on the line of roads within your State as to render them most efficient in forwarding promptly and regularly the supplies so essential to our main army. Colonel Wadley or his leading assistant is now in Raleigh, and will gladly avail himself of the privilege of conferring with you on your call, and I would bespeak your favorable consideration of the suggestions his experience may dictate.

With high esteem, most respectfully, yours,

J. A. SEDDON,
Secretary of War.

[Inclosure.]

RALEIGH, *February* 10, 1863.

Hon. JAMES A. SEDDON,
        Secretary of War :

Everything is in the utmost confusion on the North Carolina Rail-road, and I can get no satisfactory answer from the Wilmington and Weldon road about transportation of corn. The State holds a controlling interest in both. Cannot some arrangement be made with the Governor by which a more efficient management can be had?

W. M. WADLEY,
Assistant Adjutant-General.

HEADQUARTERS DEPARTMENT OF NORTH CAROLINA,
        Goldsborough, N. C., February 12, 1863.

Hon. JAMES A. SEDDON,
        Secretary of War :

SIR: I have the honor to acknowledge the receipt of your letter of the 10th instant, inclosing a letter written to you by Maj. C. S. Carrington in relation to forage at Tarborough and the sources from which I am to draw supplies for my forces. I have had many years of experience in the quartermaster's department, and foreseeing last summer that the Army of the Potomac would have to depend on the supplies from North Carolina, gave implicit instructions to all my quartermasters accordingly. Before the crop was ripe enough to shell I ordered it to be brought in the shuck in box cars, and from that time to the present have sent it forward to Petersburg and Richmond as fast as cars could be procured. The quartermasters at Weldon and Tarborough have been furnished by me with every means necessary to collect the forage, but the greatest difficulty I have had to encounter has been with the railroad companies. I have caused many letters to be written and have had interviews with the officers asking their aid to get the forage out of the country, and have gone so far as to impress trains to send grain to your city. Several weeks since I directed Captain Venable to force the cars, whenever they were about to return empty from Weldon to Petersburg, to proceed to Halifax for grain for the Army of the Potomac. In a letter addressed to W. T. Joynes some time since I earnestly solicited his aid as president of the Petersburg and Weldon Railroad in this matter, and have urged this also on Colonel Frémont of the Wilmington and Weldon Railroad. Storehouses have been built and large wagon trains sent to Tarborough by my orders to secure grain; and I was not before aware that Major Carrington had much control over these supplies, which have claimed the particular attention of my chief quartermaster as well as myself. Without exception, I have always directed that supplies for all commands should be drawn from the surrounding country, except on the Blackwater and other extreme frontier lines, when they were required, as far as possible, to forage within the lines of the enemy. I am apprehensive that Major Carrington is not well informed respecting the resources of the State, or he would not have thought it possible for the troops south of Goldsborough to find supplies in that part of the country. I am getting all that can be found, especially from Sampson County; but there is only a little that can be purchased. In Onslow County some could be found, but it will all be required for the cavalry on duty there before the crop of oats mature. Before the receipt of your letter I ordered General J. J. Pettigrew with his brigade to march via Greenville to Washington County to drive the enemy out of the town of Plymouth and from the counties adjoining Washington, so as to enable us to get the supplies out of that part of the State and to give protection to the people and induce them to plant largely for the coming season. A force has also been sent into Bertie County for a similar purpose, and to operate in Gates and Chowan Counties. The people of the eastern part of the State have some cause of complaint for want of protection, because the small force I have had in my command precluded my advancing them far east of the railroad. Now for the first time I have an available force to send east and attack the enemy and give some protection to the citizens. To-day finds the enemy not advanced a foot from where he was in July last, when I was placed in charge of this department. I inclose with this a letter from the quartermaster at Tarborough in reply to one from my chief quartermaster. You may rest assured I shall draw all my supplies as far as possible from the surrounding country. The requirements for Wilmington are 10,000 bushels per month.

Yours, very respectfully,

S. G. FRENCH,
Major-General, Commanding.

[FEBRUARY 12, 1863.—For Beauregard to Whiting, see Series I, Vol. XIV, p. 774.]

NAVY DEPARTMENT, C. S. A.,
Richmond, Va., February 13, 1863.

His Excellency ZEBULON B. VANCE,
Governor of North Carolina, Raleigh, N. C.;

SIR: I am informed by Flag-Officer Lynch that there are at Lawrenceburg, N. C., 4,224 bars, or about 707 tons, of railroad iron, and that all operations upon the extension of the railroad beyond that point have been suspended and will not be renewed during the war. I have the honor to request that this iron may be turned over to this Department to be rolled into plates for protecting the gunboat and battery under construction on the Roanoke River. The iron will be paid for at its market value, or the Department will agree to return it six months after a declaration of peace. All efforts made to obtain iron in North Carolina and elsewhere have failed, and I beg leave to urge upon your consideration the expediency of turning over the lot of iron referred to, with the understanding that it will be used exclusively for plating gunboats and batteries now nearly ready for it in your State.

I am, respectfully, your obedient servant,

S. R. MALLORY,
Secretary of the Navy.

FREDERICKSBURG, *February* 13, 1863.

General S. COOPER:

I think a division under Ransom, as well as I can judge at this distance, can be sent. I refer to my letters to the President and Secretary.

R. E. LEE,
General.

[FEBRUARY 13, 1863.—For Seddon to Whiting, see Series I, Vol. XIV, p. 776.]

HEADQUARTERS,
Fredericksburg, February 14, 1863.

Hon. JAMES A. SEDDON,
        Secretary of War :

SIR : I think it proper to report, for the information of the Department, that I have received this morning a letter dated Heathville, 10th instant, from Lieut. C. Littleton Upshur, signing himself enrolling officer, stating that on the 9th and 10th transports of the enemy loaded with troops, horses, &c., passed down the Potomac. I do not know Lieutenant Upshur, but he states that he is directly on the river and can see all their movements. If they are anything more than convalescents returning to their commands south I think it probable they are re-enforcements for General Foster. I do not think that they were embarked at Aquia Creek, inasmuch as I have received a letter of the same date from a scout watching that position in which he states that a large number of the enemy is encamped at that point, and no mention is made of embarkation or transports. Other scouts on the Potomac have as yet reported no passage of troops down that river.

Capt. E. P. Bryan, signal officer, whom I had directed to cross over into Maryland for the purpose of watching the Potomac on that side, I fear may not now be on that duty, as an order has been received here (Special Orders, No. 20, Paragraph XX, Adjutant and Inspector General's Office) directing him to report to General Beauregard, and he may have reported accordingly without my knowledge.

I have the honor to be, with great respect, your obedient servant,

R. E. LEE,
                General.

HEADQUARTERS ARMY OF NORTHERN VIRGINIA,
February 14, 1863.

Hon. JAMES A. SEDDON,
        Secretary of War :

SIR : After dispatching my letter to you this morning I received information from one of my scouts on the enemy's left that a small steamer with troops had on Sunday passed down the Potomac ; that since that time seven large steamers and five or six transports, towed by the steamers and laden with troops, had also descended the Potomac.

On the 11th and 12th instant no movements had been observed.

This evening I received information from scouts on the enemy's right up to the 12th instant. Two report that the Ninth Army Corps of General Hooker's army had embarked at Belle Plains and sailed for Suffolk ; that a large fleet of transports was at Aquia Creek, and there was other evidence of a general move. Their cavalry had been withdrawn from the Spotted Tavern and Hartwood Church toward the railroad, leaving pickets in their stead. Sigel's corps is still at Stafford Court-House. Three brigades had reached Washington. The infantry at Union Mills Ford (Bull Run) were leaving for Washington, and the cavalry for Stafford Court-House Prisoners captured by General Hampton report that General Hays, with three regiments of infantry, seven pieces of artillery, and a squadron of cavalry, was to leave Union Mills Ford yesterday for Washington.

I have directed General Pickett's division to march to-morrow for Richmond and General Hood's division to be held in readiness. One of the scouts reported that it was the Second Army Corps which had embarked for Suffolk. Although it is stated that their destination is

Suffolk, should no other troops follow I think it probable that this corps is intended to re-enforce their army in South Carolina; but should its real destination be Suffolk, General Pickett's division will be ample to resist it.

I have the honor to be, with great respect, your obedient servant,

R. E. LEE,
General.

WAR DEPARTMENT, C. S. A.,
Richmond, Va., February 15, 1863.

General R. E. LEE:

I subjoin a telegram just received from General Pryor; likewise the closing paragraph of a telegram by order of General French, at Goldsborough, calling for large supplies of ammunition. I consider the latter the result of similar intelligence from General Pryor. I doubt the Newport News report. Have you information to determine it? Would you advise delay in sending troops to Charleston from North Carolina?

J. A. SEDDON,
Secretary of War.

FRANKLIN, VA., *February* 14, 1863.

Two persons from Norfolk Thursday (one a lady and the other a gentleman), where there had been no concert, inform me that thirty-six regiments landed at Newport News Wednesday. They say it is Hooker's army. Within the past week Suffolk largely re-enforced.

ROGER A. PRYOR,
Brigadier-General, Commanding.

An attack is expected here.

Meaning at Hamilton, N. C.

[J. A. S.]

WAR DEPARTMENT, C. S. A.,
Richmond, Va., February 15, 1863.

General R. E. LEE:

General French telegraphs that he must, on the call of General Pryor, send re-enforcements to him. General Davis with a brigade is ordered. A brigade has also been ordered from Wilmington to Charleston. Colonel Tabb reports considerable fleets of steamers and transports at mouth of James River as coming from a reliable source. The President thinks you had better move an adequate force at or toward Hanover Junction to aid here if required.

J. A. SEDDON,
Secretary of War.

WAR DEPARTMENT, C. S. A.,
Richmond, Va., February 15, 1863.

General R. E. LEE, *Commanding, &c.:*

SIR: I send you herewith full copies of the telegram from General French and letter from Colonel Tabb, to which I have referred in a telegram I have just sent you.* In the letter you will perceive a mistake, either in regard to the York or James River. I concluded in my telegram that the James was meant in both places, though it may be well doubted if the York, as first named, was not designed throughout. It matters not, however, as the danger could not be materially different in

---

* Not found.

the event of a landing in force on either. I cannot believe that a serious blow at this city is contemplated at this season, and if the approach is to be from the York River I am satisfied it will not be ventured. Still, it is well to be guarded fully and in time, and the President thinks if you do not apprehend immediate attack, which, with the present state of the roads he does not think practicable, that you had better move what you may deem an adequate force to protect this city in supporting distance, say at Hanover Junction. We have not, I fear, more than some 3,000 effective troops here and at Drewry's Bluff. On the receipt of General French's dispatch General Davis, with his brigade, was ordered to the Blackwater to re-enforce General Pryor. The intelligence of an expected attack on Charleston, and the removal of nearly all the troops, together with General Foster and his staff, south from North Carolina, induced the President likewise to order a brigade (Clingman's) from Wilmington to Charleston, and another from General Daniel's division to replace it, and be held prepared to move forward likewise to Charleston if events required, to be itself replaced by a further brigade from General [Junius] Daniel's division. The other forces in North Carolina have been for the present ordered to be disposed by General French as he deems best for the protection of Weldon, Goldsborough, and the line of the railroad. Not having the key to your cipher, and a mistake having been committed by the telegraph operator in the first two words in cipher, I have been much puzzled to make out your telegram received this morning; and though I had the aid of Maj. [William] Norris, of the Signal Corps, it was not until after my telegram this evening was sent that, by trying other words, I succeeded in deciphering it. The march of Pickett's division to Richmond may, very probably, suffice at present to guard against any sudden attack on this city. I will keep you advised of any further intelligence received. General Pryor promised, by telegram of the 14th instant, to give by to-night certain intelligence, both in relation to the reported forces on the James and the re-enforcements at Suffolk. As yet the intelligence has not come.

> With high esteem, very truly, yours,
>
> J. A. SEDDON,
> *Secretary of War.*

> WAR DEPARTMENT, C. S. A.,
> *Richmond, Va., February* 15, 1863.

Maj. Gen. GUSTAVUS W. SMITH,
Commanding, &c.:

SIR: After consultation with the President I desire that you will order Brigadier-General Davis, with his brigade, to re-enforce General Pryor, on the Blackwater, and Clingman's brigade from Wilmington to Charleston; that you will send a brigade of Daniel's division at once to Wilmington to replace Clingman's and hold another ready to move in the same direction, so that in case events require it likewise may be forwarded to Charleston and be itself replaced at Wilmington—perhaps afterwards followed to Charleston by another brigade of Daniel's division. The residue of his force General French will dispose as he deems most judicious for the defense of Weldon, Goldsborough, and the line of the railroads.

> With high esteem, very truly, yours,
>
> J. A. SEDDON,
> *Secretary of War.*

HEADQUARTERS,
Wilmington, N. C., February 15, 1863.

His Excellency the GOVERNOR, *Raleigh, N. C.:*

SIR: I send for your information a letter* just received from Lumberton, in Robeson County, respecting a deplorable condition of things in that section, due to the presence and depredations of deserters. Accordingly, I have ordered Capt. J. R. McDonald, Fifty-first North Carolina, and his company (all Robeson County men) to proceed there and either capture or, if necessary, destroy these freebooters. A copy* of his orders is herewith. The statement of the inadequacy of the militia force and the disaffection of the free negroes renders this action on my part necessary, and I think it will meet your approval.

Very respectfully, your obedient servant,

W. H. C. WHITING,
Brigadier-General, Commanding.

Abstract from Field Report of the Troops of the District of the Cape Fear, commanded by Brig. Gen. W. H. C. Whiting, February 15, 1863.

Troops.	Present for duty. Officers.	Present for duty. Men.	Effective total.	Aggregate present.
Brigadier-General Evans' brigade	134	1,854	2,028	2,288
Brigadier-General Ransom's brigade	160	2,791	2,906	3,151
Forts Caswell, Fisher, Johnson, and Saint Philip (twenty-one companies).	65	1,228	1,504	1,800
City and river defense (one battalion artillery and three companies)...	21	416	461	558
Three unattached companies	11	144	159	188
3d Battalion North Carolina Artillery	10	134	135	158
Four light batteries	18	446	460	487
Three companies of cavalry	8	203	205	225
Signal Corps	1	17	17	20
Bridge guard	1	24	24	27
Grand total	429	7,257	7,899	8,902

NOTE.—Aggregate present and absent not reported.

WAR DEPARTMENT, C. S. A.,
Richmond, Va., February 16, 1863.

General R. E. LEE, *Fredericksburg, Va.:*

General Pryor reports:

Scout from opposite Newport News reports transports landing there since Wednesday evening. Knows nothing of the number. Saw eleven steamboats at one time.

J. A. SEDDON,
Secretary of War.

---

* Not found.

HEADQUARTERS CAMP FREDERICKSBURG,
February 16, 1863.

Hon. JAMES A. SEDDON,
    Secretary of War, Richmond, Va.:

SIR: I informed you on the 14th that General Pickett's division was on the march to Richmond. It is directed to halt on the Chickahominy, where it can find shelter in woods and procure from Richmond provisions and forage.

General Pickett will send forward an officer to select a position and make arrangements. Will you be kind enough to afford him the necessary facilities? Should circumstances require him to be further advanced, I must request you to give him orders. He can take position below Richmond on the right or left bank of the river as you may designate.

Upon the reception last night of your dispatch of yesterday I directed Hood's division to move to Hanover Junction. It will halt there unless required to advance.

I am, with great respect, your obedient servant,

R. E. LEE, .
General.

YADKINVILLE, N. C., *February* 16, [1863].

Governor VANCE:

DEAR SIR: It is my painful duty to inform you of a most melancholy affair which occurred in this county on last Thursday. I sent out a squad of 14 men in search of conscripts. They found a number of them (now supposed to be between 20 and 30) lodged in a school-house and attacked them. The conscripts were well armed and resisted most stubbornly. They shot through cracks and windows at our men, and killed two of the best citizens of this county—James West, a magistrate, and John Williams, a most excellent man. These men were shot dead in their tracks. Two of the conscripts were killed and the balance escaped, though two of them are seriously wounded. The conscripts known to have been in it and who have escaped are William Dobbins, Jesse Dobbins, Benjamin Willard, Lee Willard, Thomas Adams, Enoch Brown, Jack Douglas, Anderson Douglas, Sandford Douglas, Hugh Sprinkle, and Horace Allgood, though we have since captured the Douglases and Hugh Sprinkle and lodged them in jail. The four first named are the leaders of the band; and I am informed that they will probably try to make their way to Tennessee. I leave it to Your Excellency whether or not a sufficient reward shall be offered for these four bad and dangerous men to insure their apprehension. Robert Hutchins, William Willard, James Wooten, Elkana Willard, and others are believed to have been in it. If a reward had no other effect it would I think deter others from resisting the execution of the law, seeing that the Governor of the State had taken the matter in hand. If they do not leave the county they will rally their crowd (as I understand some of them are trying to do) and fight again. They are much better armed than the militia, having been preparing for it for months. We have arrested and sent out of this county within three months past over 100 men, and yet we have a considerable number left. Inasmuch as we have scarcely any arms or ammunition I would suggest that Your

Excellency send us as soon as possible a detachment of 40 or 50 men to scour the county. It would not only enable us to execute speedily but might save some valuable lives. We intend at all hazards to execute the law.

Very respectfully, your obedient servant,

W. A. JOYCE,
Lieutenant-Colonel, &c.

ASHEVILLE, N. C., *February* 16, 1863.

GOVERNOR : Your letter of the 9th instant is just received. I beg to assure you that I shall at the next term of the court prosecute vigorously such of the prisoners to whom you direct my attention as may be turned over to the civil authorities. The late expedition to Laurel sent only four prisoners to jail, and one of them was admitted to bail on yesterday by Judge Bailey. I understand there are no more to send. I have no knowledge of my own touching the shooting of several prisoners in Laurel. I have learned, however, from a most reliable source that 13 of them were killed ; that some of them were not taken in arms but at their homes ; that all the men shot (13, if not more) were prisoners at the time they were shot ; that they were taken off to a secluded cave or gorge in the mountains and then made to kneel down and were thus shot. One man was badly and mortally shot in the bowels, and while he was writhing in agony and praying to God for mercy a soldier mercilessly and brutally shot him in the head with his pistol. Several women were whipped ; this I learned from one who got his information from some of the guilty parties. I learned that all this was done by order of Lieut. Col. James A. Keith. I know not what you intend doing with the guilty parties, but I suggest they are all guilty of murder. I do not suppose they had any order to do so barbarous a deed ; but if they had the order was void absolutely, no matter by whom issued. Such savage and barbarous cruelty is without a parallel in the State, and I hope in every other. I am gratified that you intend to take the matter in hand. I will make such investigation as I can, but I have no means of compelling any one to disclose facts to me. It will not be difficult, I learn, to prove that the prisoners were killed. I assure you that I will prosecute all persons who have committed criminal offenses in this circuit at the next term of the court, and in the mean time I will do all in my power to suppress crime and violence. These are fearfully on the increase in this section of the State. A report might be made that would astonish you. I have done all I could in reference to the complaints made to you from Jackson and Cherokee Counties.

*   *   *   *   *   *   *

I am, &c., yours, truly,

A. S. MERRIMON.

SAVANNAH, GA., *February* 16, 1863.

Brig. Gen. W. H. C. WHITING,
Wilmington, N. C.:

Order brigade to report to Jordan. Received at Pocotaligo same report about Foster.

G. T. BEAUREGARD.

HEADQUARTERS ARMY OF NORTHERN VIRGINIA,
February 17, 1863.

Maj. Gen. GUSTAVUS W. SMITH,
         Commanding, &c.:

GENERAL: Please retain in Richmond all men belonging to Generals Pickett's and Hood's divisions, Longstreet's corps, who are on their way to join them, until the arrival of these divisions within your reach and then I would thank you to send them immediately to them. They are in march for Richmond and will be joined by General Longstreet.

Very respectfully, your obedient servant,

R. E. LEE.

WAR DEPARTMENT, C. S. A.,
Richmond, Va., February 17, 1863.

General R. E. LEE, *Commanding, &c.:*

GENERAL: I have the honor to acknowledge the receipt of your letters of the 14th and 16th instant. They give me interesting information but correspond only partially with the accounts I receive here of the movements of the enemy. An officer of the Signal Corps, much trusted as a scout, has just returned from within a few miles of Fort Monroe and Newport News. He reports as certain that about 20,000 men have been landed and are encamped at Newport News. They were brought there by transports in tow of steam-tugs. They are building tent-chimneys and bake-ovens, and seem settling themselves for a time at least. They, as the scout learned, reported themselves as part of Hooker's army, being Burnside's old division, and believed they were again to be placed under Burnside's command. In addition to these troops at Newport News, 8,000 or 10,000 were reported (as the scout believes truly) to have been sent to Suffolk. In front of Newport News were five iron-clads, with steam kept constantly up and occasionally moving about. They professed to expect an attack from our gunboats coming down the James, and do not intend to be taken by surprise as at Charleston. On the bay there were some twenty-five or thirty transports. They had come down the bay with these troops, or a part of them; but whether down the Potomac or not the scout could not learn. He passed on up the York River on his return. There were no transports in that river, nor had any additional troops been moved to or landed at Yorktown or Gloucester Point. Such is pretty fully all that is material in the reports of the scout.

I send inclosed a copy of the only dispatch received to-day from General Beauregard. There is no later intelligence from either Generals Pryor or French. All the troops sent by General Beauregard to Wilmington have been returned, and two brigades from North Carolina (Clingman's and Cooke's) have been sent from Wilmington. General Ransom's other brigade will very probably likewise be ordered in the same direction, and he replaced in command of his division. As yet, however, the brigade under him is only ordered to be held in readiness. I am pleased to learn that with characteristic vigilance you are forwarding Pickett's and Hood's divisions to keep ward here. As you have confided in my discretion the location to which, until further orders, they shall be assigned, I shall order Pickett's on the other side of the river, so as to be in a position, if necessary, more readily to support Pryor and defend Petersburg. I am inclined to think the enemy's movements too serious for a feint or a diversion and that Hooker really designs withdrawing from the Rappahannock and changing his whole plan. He seemed fully committed to an advance on the Rappahannock, but, very fully trusted by his Republican or Abolition "confreres," he can venture to advance and do what Burnside could not. We must, however, await developments, for as yet information is too scant for confident judgment.

With great esteem, truly, yours,

J. A. SEDDON,
Secretary of War.

GREENVILLE, N. C., *Tuesday*, [*February*] 17, 1863.
Maj. Gen. D. H. HILL:

I did not receive the letter to which you refer in your note of to-day, but I got the information about the re-enforcements from Whitford's men. I start to-morrow and will proceed across Tranter's Creek; shall move around in front of Washington so as to threaten the Plymouth road. This may prevent re-enforcements going out of Washington. But the danger is that if I am attacked in front of Washington Garnett cannot possibly come to my assistance nor can I to his if he is attacked from Plymouth, so that we are in very bad military position, each liable to be attacked separately. An immense swamp will be between us; to march to him I must either go down the Plymouth road and abandon my line of communication, which is utterly out of the question in this country, or pass around behind this swamp, probably a three-days' journey. I will take my position without much apprehension from the enemy, but I think he had better withdraw himself before any danger on his left flank and rear. I fear they will bounce out upon Kinston some day when we are all off and handle Daniel roughly.

Very respectfully, your obedient servant,

J. J. PETTIGREW,
Brigadier-General.

HEADQUARTERS ARMY OF NORTHERN VIRGINIA,
February 18, 1863.
Lieut. Gen. JAMES LONGSTREET,
Commanding Corps:

GENERAL: The transfer of a portion of the Federal Army of the Potomac to Hampton Roads has rendered it necessary to move two divisions of your corps towards James River. I desire you to join them and place them in position where their comfort will be secured and whence they can be readily moved to resist an advance upon Richmond by the enemy from his new base. It is reported that he has been largely re-enforced at Suffolk. It will therefore be prudent for you to change the present order for General Pickett to halt on the Chickahominy, and to let him proceed to Falling Creek, on the south side of James River, or to some better point, from which you can readily defend Petersburg, &c. Should the movement of the enemy from the Potomac render it expedient your other divisions will be ordered to join you. I desire therefore you be prepared to receive them and to select encampments for their comfortable accommodation. You will be advised of their approach. I need not remind you of the importance of selecting sheltered positions, where there is plenty of wood, and which may be convenient to supplies. It is also desirable that these positions be, as far as possible, not liable to prove injurious to the agricultural interests of the country. You will require at least two battalions of your artillery and probably one of your reserve corps. The horses are in such a reduced state and the country so saturated with water that it will be almost impossible for them to drag the guns. They might be transported by railroad, by which route all heavy baggage, if possible, should also be conveyed and the battery horses be led. I wish you to inform me where I can communicate with you.

To inform yourself of the movements of the enemy in your front and to keep me advised I suggest that you report to the Secretary of War, on your arrival in Richmond, as he will have information and possibly some orders to communicate.

It will be well to have Lane's battery at some favorable point on the James River, to destroy the enemy's transports if they should ascend.

I am, with much respect, your obedient servant,

R. E. LEE.

RICHMOND, VA., *February* 18, 1863.

Maj. Gen. GEORGE E. PICKETT, *Commanding, &c.:*

GENERAL: The Secretary of War directs that on your arrival with your division you take position on the south side of the James River in immediate vicinity of Drewry's Bluff, and there await further orders. You will have in view the defense of Chaffin's and Drewry's Bluffs, keeping yourself advised and ready to move if necessary to repel advances from the Blackwater and to defend the city of Petersburg.

Very respectfully, &c.,

S. COOPER,
Adjutant and Inspector General.

ENGINEER BUREAU,
Richmond, Va., February 18, 1863.

Lieut. Col. W. H. STEVENS,
Corps of Engineers, C. S. A., Richmond, Va.:

COLONEL: His Excellency the President has been informed that the works for the defense of Weldon Bridge are being built on a scale that will require a large force, say several thousands of men, to defend them, and has sent to this Bureau to ascertain if such is the fact. In my original instructions to Colonel Gwynn he was directed in all cases to give the works for defending points in the rivers of North Carolina a development such that they could be held by a small force, say 400 or 500 men, until relieved by a succoring force. These instructions are fully approved by the President. If defenses of a different character have been laid out at Weldon and are in progress you will please to have my original directions carried out as far as the nature of the ground will, in your judgment, permit.

Very respectfully, yours,

J. F. GILMER,
Colonel and Chief of Bureau.

ENGINEER BUREAU,
Richmond, Va., February 18, 1863.

Col. WALTER GWYNN, *Weldon, N. C.:*

COLONEL: In reply to your communication of the 14th instant I have to state that it is important that the works in progress for the defenses of East North Carolina should be under the control of Lieut. Col. W. H. Stevens, chief of construction, and for this reason you were instructed to report to him directly. The local engineers at Goldsborough, Kinston, the works on Tar River, and at Rainbow Bend should, and will hereafter, report to Colonel Stevens. For the present your duties are limited to the works at Weldon, N. C., under the direction of the chief of construction. I will take occasion to read your report to Colonel Stevens in regard to the works for the defense of Weldon Bridge.

Very respectfully, your obedient servant,

J. F. GILMER,
Colonel of Engineers and Chief of Bureau.

HEADQUARTERS DEPARTMENT OF NORTH CAROLINA,
Goldsborough, N. C., February 18, 1863.

Maj. Gen. J. G. FOSTER, U. S. A.,
Commanding Eighteenth Army Corps, New Berne, N. C.:

GENERAL: In a communication addressed to me, and written by Maj. Gen. J. G. Foster, U. S. A., and dated at New Berne on the 31st day of December last, he desired that a watch which was taken from the person of Surgeon Hunt, who was killed in a skirmish near the town of Washington, should be returned, to be placed in the possession of his relatives. On the publication of General Foster's letter the man who had the watch voluntarily sent it to me, and it now affords me much pleasure to be able to return it to you, that it may be placed in the hands of his relatives. Will not this act of a private in our army, voluntarily returning this watch, offer a noble example to some of your generals and to their wives, who have taken (I will not say stolen) pianos, bedsteads, dining sets, works of art and virtu, horses, carriages, &c., and carried them to their homes in the North, to return them to their owners? I regret to make such charges against your officers, and above all against their wives; but when such acts are committed by men in high position, or by women of intelligence and refinement, it deserves condemnation. I refrain from naming them, but if you wish it names shall be sent and the alleged acts specified and the whole sent you for publication to show the world that neither rank nor position nor religion nor female loveliness can resist the temptation to violate the commandments when what they covet is the property of a rebel. These remarks, general, are not personal to you, and are intended only for those to whom they truly apply. I send you a letter which has been handed me mentioning some instances where private property has been taken in New Berne.*

I am, general, yours, very respectfully,

S. G. FRENCH,
Major-General, Commanding.

WAR DEPARTMENT, C. S. A.,
Richmond, Va., February 19, 1863.

Brig. Gen. R. A. PRYOR:

Ascertain as early and as far as possible the proposed movements of the enemy at Newport News and Suffolk. Is there reason to believe they are intended for North or South Carolina?

J. A. SEDDON,
Secretary of War.

---

* Not found.

HEADQUARTERS,
Diascund Bridge, February 19, 1863—8 p. m.

Brig. Gen. HENRY A. WISE, *Commanding :*

GENERAL : Lieutenant Harman [Company B, Fifty-ninth Virginia Infantry] has just returned from his expedition to Burwell's Bay, in Isle of Wight County. Dense fogs prevented his seeing across the river to Newport News, but having obtained what he regards as entirely satisfactory and reliable information he did not wait for the weather to clear, but returned at once to communicate it. From Captain Drummond, of Norfolk, and from Captain Nelson, of Isle of Wight, he learned that the enemy have landed a considerable force at Newport News under the command of General Burnside. The Galena, the Minnesota, two monitor boats, and ten gunboats are lying off Newport News. The troops were landed from large side-wheel bay steamers, each with a sloop in tow. Up to the time that the fog prevented further observation of their movements ten of these steamers came up daily, commencing on the 12th instant. As soon as the troops disembarked the steamers returned to Norfolk for coal, and having supplied themselves put back toward the Potomac. No re-enforcements have been sent to Norfolk or Suffolk. It is generally understood that the expedition consists of Franklin's corps and is destined for Charleston. Lieutenant Harman returns to-morrow and will report any further movements.

Very respectfully, your obedient servant,

W. B. TABB,
Colonel, Commanding.

YADKINVILLE, N. C., *February* 19, 1863.

DEAR SIR: We have had a startling occurrence in this county, of which you have doubtless heard before this time, which has greatly exasperated every intelligent and good citizen of the county. I mean the murder of two of our best citizens, magistrates of the county, by a band of deserters and fugitive conscripts. The circumstances are these: There has been a strong feeling against the conscript law among the uninformed part of the citizens here ever since its passage. Many of that class swore that they would die at home before they would be forced off, and when the time came for them to go perhaps nearly 100 in this county took to the woods, lying out day and night to avoid arrest; and although the militia officers exerted themselves with great zeal, yet these skulkers have always had many more active friends than they had and could always get timely information of every movement to arrest them and so avoid it. The militia officers have been able to arrest very few of them. This state of affairs has encouraged the dissatisfied in the army from this county to desert and come home, until, emboldened by their numbers and the bad success of the militia officers in arresting them, they have armed themselves, procured ammunition, and openly defied the law. They have even sent menacing messages to the militia officers, threatening death to the most obnoxious of them and all who assist them. Last Thursday 12 of the militia officers came on 16 of these desperadoes in a school-house about 4 miles from this town, armed, fortified, and ready for the fight. The firing immediately commenced; which side first fired is not positively certain, but from the best information I can get I believe it was those in the school-house. They finally fled, leaving 2 of their number dead and carrying off 2 wounded, after killing 2 of the officers. In the school-house were found cartridges of the most deadly and **murderous** quality, made of home-made **powder** (one of the men known to have been among them has been engaged in making powder). Four of the conscripts who were in the fight have since come in and surrendered and are now in jail here, but the leaders and the most guilty of them are still at large; and the section of the country in which they lurk is so disloyal (I grieve to say it), and the people so readily conceal the murderers and convey intelligence to them, that it will be exceedingly difficult to find them, even if they do not draw together a larger force than they have yet had and again give battle to the sheriff and his posse. But my principal object in writing this letter is to ask you what we shall do with those four murderers we have and the others if we get them? Suppose we try them for murder, do you not believe that our supreme court will decide the conscription act unconstitutional and thus leave these men justified in resisting its execution? I believe they will, and tremble to think of the consequences of such a blow upon the cause of our independence. It would demoralize our army in the field and bring first the horrors of civil war to our own doors and then perhaps subjugation to the enemy, which no honorable man ought to want to survive. I think I know Judge Pearson's opinion on the conscription act, and I believe that he is just itching to pronounce it unconstitutional. Suppose these men get out a writ of *habeas corpus* and have it returned before him and he releases them (which he would be bound to do if he holds that they were only resisting the execution of an unconstitutional law with such force as was necessary to repel force from their persons), do you not believe it would produce a mutiny in the army of the Rappahannock; and if it did not, how would you get another conscript to the field or keep those there who have already gone, or who could keep the loyal and indignant citizens at home from executing vengeance on these infamous murderers and traitors to the country? These are considerations which alarm me, and I would like to know what you think of them. Please write to me, and I will receive your opinion as confidentially as you may desire and ask. Could these men, and ought they if they could, be turned over to the Confederate courts to be tried for treason? Could the military authorities, and ought they to, deal with them? I hope you know I am conservative and for the rights of the citizens and the States, but for my country always, and for independence at all hazards.

Your obedient servant,

R. F. ARMFIELD.

HEADQUARTERS,
Wilmington, N. C., February 20, 1863.

Governor VANCE, *Raleigh, N. C.:*

I received your orders of the 9th instant directing the militia officers in Robeson, Cumberland, and Richmond to turn over all able-bodied free negroes between eighteen and forty-five. None such have yet arrived. Robeson and Cumberland have heretofore done well and supplied much free and slave labor. They have certainly done their share. A vast deal of work is still required here, and the labor of 400 to 500 negroes is essential to complete our works as rapidly as possible. I respectfully request that you provide me with this labor as soon as possible. Every advantage must be taken of the enemy's movements in other directions to strengthen this place.

Very respectfully,

W. H. C. WHITING,
Brigadier-General.

RICHMOND, VA., *February* 20, 1863.

Maj. Gen. A. P. HILL,
      (*Care of General R. E. Lee:*)

GENERAL: In reply to yours of the 7th instant, inquiring as to the source from whence the commissions for officers of the North Carolina State troops should issue, I am directed by the Secretary of War to say that the question is before the Attorney-General of the Confederate States for decision. In the mean time the right to commission appears in several instances to have been conceded to the Governor of North Carolina. There is not much doubt that the decision of the Attorney-General will be that the Governor has the right to appoint, as he has so decided in similar cases in other States.

                Very truly, &c.,

                              E. A. PALFREY,
                              Assistant Adjutant-General.

Abstract from Field Return of Troops, commanded by Maj. Gen. S. G. French, February 20, 1863 (headquarters Goldsborough, N. C.).

Troops.	Present for duty.		Aggregate present.	Aggregate present and absent.
	Officers.	Men.		
Davis' brigade	115	1,602	1,946	2,589
Pettigrew's brigade	136	2,570	2,851	3,709
Ransom's brigade	150	2,553	2,904	4,022
Cooke's brigade [ordered to Charleston]				
Robertson's (cavalry) brigade [no report]				
Colston's command	270	4,879	6,028	8,257
Daniel's command	194	3,375	4,081	5,597
Troops at and near Goldsborough	40	541	710	794
Troops at Hamilton	51	778	984	1,121
Reserve artillery	13	336	379	444
Grand total	969	16,634	19,883	26,533

                          FRANKLIN, *February* 21, 1863.

Hon. JAMES A. SEDDON,
        Secretary of War:

Troops still landing at Newport News. Impression in Norfolk that 30,000 arrived, and that movement against Richmond. All communications with Suffolk cut off evidently to conceal some movement. Large numbers of horses landed at Newport News and wagon trains moving some miles up the river.

Gold in New York 161 and rising.

Bill to employ privateers passed United States Senate. McDougall said war with France before fall.

        Respectfully,

                              ROGER A. PRYOR,
                              Brigadier-General, Commanding.

FRANKLIN, *February* 21, 1863.
Hon. JAMES A. SEDDON,
    Secretary of War:

Two persons, perfectly reliable, whom I sent to Suffolk Monday and who remained there several days, satisfy me that former reports exaggerated the re-enforcements in Suffolk. The whole force there does not exceed 15,000. They are enrolling and organizing the negroes.

Nothing is revealed of the enemy's designs at Newport News. The force visible from this side is not very large, apparently 15,000 or 20,000. Citizens say a portion negro recruits.

ROGER A. PRYOR,
Brigadier-General, Commanding.

SPECIAL ORDERS, }   ADJT. AND INSPECTOR GENERAL'S OFFICE,
    No. 44.   }   *Richmond, Va., February* 21, 1863.
    *   *   *   *   *   *   *

XXI. Maj. Gen. G. E. Pickett, Provisional Army of the Confederate States, will report without delay to Lieut. Gen. J. Longstreet, commanding Department of Virginia and North Carolina.
    *   *   *   *   *   *   *

By command of the Secretary of War:

JNO. WITHERS,
Assistant Adjutant-General.

WAR DEPARTMENT, C. S. A.,
    Richmond, Va., February 22, 1863.
General R. E. LEE, *Commanding, &c.:*

GENERAL: I inclose a telegram* from General Pryor, which gives the latest intelligence I have of the numbers of the enemy concentrating at Newport News and Suffolk. It agrees substantially with the reports I have from scouts sent to the vicinity of Old Point by General Elzey and from an intelligent officer just exchanged, who had been allowed to recover from his wounds, received at Sharpsburg, in Baltimore, and on his return was detained some days at Fort Monroe. He says as far as he could collect about 25,000 men had been sent to Newport News, and in addition some 2,000 or 3,000 were sent up the York River to Yorktown and Gloucester Point. They gave out (it is said by our scouts, not by the officer) that they are going to Charleston and expect to be commanded by General Burnside. The officer could learn nothing of their designs, but from unmistakable manifestations is satisfied great dissatisfaction and demoralization prevail and that they extend to many officers as well as to the men. He represents the feeling of our friends in Maryland as increasing in confidence and those of the Unionists as sinking into despondency. The prospects North are certainly encouraging and may lead to decisive results unless we sustain several reverses in the next few months. I have no late intelligence of movements from Wilmington or Charleston. I still expect an attack in great force on Charleston, but cannot understand the causes of delay in making it. Some controversy about rank between the commanders may

---

* Probably that of February 21.

perhaps afford the explanation; but I think it more likely that it has resulted from the dissatisfation of the troops recently sent South at finding themselves associated with negro regiments. A brief period must, however, afford a solution. Pickett's and Hood's divisions have passed through, and their general appearance, spirit, and cheerfulness afforded great satisfaction. General Longstreet is here, and under his able guidance of such troops no one entertains a doubt as to the entire safety of the capital.

With great esteem, cordially, yours,

J. A. SEDDON,
Secretary of War.

GOLDSBOROUGH, N. C., *February* 23, 1863.
Hon. JAMES A. SEDDON,
 Secretary of War, C. S. A.:

Will you permit me to give a frank statement of the condition of things in this district and hear a few suggestions made with the utmost deference? Wilmington is the point of great importance, and Fort Caswell, a small, antiquated structure, is the key to the position. It is of brick, without casemates, and has in its limited area a large brick building covered with slate. It is easy to see that a concentrated fire would be most murderous to the garrison. No work seems to have been done there until the arrival of General Whiting. He has casemated the guns bearing on the sea and has just begun casemating those on the face bearing on the inner channel. He is also raising the parapet on the harbor front so that an iron-clad, having run into the channel, cannot have a reverse fire on the water front. This work will be completed in two or three weeks. Should an attack be made earlier the fort must fall, or at least the destruction of life would be very great in it. But even when the work is done the caliber of the guns is so light that vessels might run past with but little risk. I most earnestly ask to be furnished with an 8-inch, a 10-inch, and an 11-inch gun. The works around Wilmington to resist a land attack are too slight. It is difficult to imagine what the troops employed themselves at for the last two years. I feel concerned about Wilmington. The Yankees seem to have become alarmed at the magnitude of the task before them at Charleston and may first try their hand at Wilmington by way of encouraging their troops, just as they captured Arkansas Post to get up heart for Vicksburg; or it may be that they will attack Wilmington after the fall of Charleston or the failure there. In the first case, inspirited by success, the attack would be with enthusiasm; in the latter case it would be to cover the mortification of failure and disgrace. In either event of success or reverse at Charleston we may confidently expect a fight at Wilmington; and as the enemy believe Wilmington to be the weakest of the three points threatened he may begin with it in order to remove the demoralization of the troops. I fear that we cannot make a successful resistance without more guns of heavy caliber. As soon as the movement begins at Charleston I want to threaten New Berne, Washington, and Plymouth, and possibly Morehead City, in order to keep Hunter from getting re-enforcements from this State; but I cannot make the proposed expeditions without at least one more brigade. The works at Kinston are unfortunately on the wrong side of the river, and can only be held by a brigade. Goldsborough needs fully a brigade for its protection, as it has no works at all except a bridgehead. I have now in the department only the infantry brigades of Evans, Pettigrew, and Daniel, and the wonderfully inefficient brigade of Robertson. With one more brigade I could harass the enemy, detain his troops in this State, possibly force him to send others here; could bring out a vast quantity of bacon, pork, and corn from the counties on the coast, and could increase our ranks by numerous conscripts. The department commissary—an energetic and efficient officer—tells me that the western part of the State is exhausted, and unless he can draw from the east he will soon be unable to supply the troops. There are millions of pounds of bacon in Hyde and Tyrrell which can be brought out with a proper force, and the question of supply is getting to be a very alarming one. The troops on the Rappahannock must be inactive for some time and could be well employed here. There is still another view of it, which is important in its future bearing: The planters on the Neuse, Tar, and Roanoke have sent large numbers of negroes into the interior and do not propose to raise a crop for another year. The Confederacy cannot afford to lose the planting interest, and a brigade judiciously disposed would afford such protection as is necessary to secure confidence and encourage the farmers to plant. I learn that Hampton is now idle at Gordonsville, recruiting his horses. He would find more forage in Beaufort, Washington, and Hyde than in the whole of Virginia, and he would protect the planting interest. Such a man as Hampton is much needed here; but if a brigade is needed at Gordonsville could not Robertson, with his rangers, who are not partisans, be swapped for Hampton? If the latter were in this State the Yankees would hug their gunboats everywhere. To sum up the whole matter: We need more heavy guns at Wilmington; we need another brigade of infantry to harass the Yankees, to detain their troops from Charleston, to protect the planting interest in the rich counties of the east, and to bring out supplies and conscripts; we need an efficient brigade of cavalry to keep the Yankees close shut up in their fortifications.

I hope that you have had the patience to read this long letter, and that the suggestions will receive your consideration. Whatever weight you may attach to them I am so impressed with them myself that I could not feel satisfied until I had communicated them.

  With great respect,

          D. H. HILL,
           Major-General.

[Indorsements.]

            FEBRUARY 27, 1863.

Respectfully referred to the President.

These views strike me as sensible and timely. Would it not be well to order another brigade? Perhaps with General Longstreet's force where it now is General Colston's brigade might be spared from Petersburg.

          J. A. S.,
          Secretary of War.

The brigade now being removed from Goldsborough to a point on the railroad from Petersburg to Suffolk would, with the least derangement to organization, serve the first purpose. I proposed some time since the proposed disposition of Hampton's brigade to General Lee, but he dissented. It may be that the views of General Hill will prevail over his objections. It is proper to add that that brigade is idle because the norses are unfit for immediate service. I have entertained the opinio . expressed as to an attack on Wilmington, and therefore my recommen- dation for an increase of heavy guns, especially at Fort Fisher. I am glad to see that General Hill's attention is directed to procuring supplies from Eastern North Carolina and to promoting the cultivation of the next crop. His views are generally approved, and he should by all practi- cable means be aided and encouraged to execute them. General Long- street can take care of the routes to and from Suffolk by detachments from his command.

J. D.

HEADQUARTERS,
Wilmington, N. C., February 23, 1863.

Hon. JAMES A. SEDDON,
  Secretary of War, Richmond, Va.:

SIR: The inadequacy of the armament for the defense of this impor- tant district has been frequently set forth. The urgent necessities of other positions threatened by the enemy have divided many of the req- uisitions intended for this place, and I am well aware of the difficulty of procuring in the present state of our resources a sufficiency of guns of heavy caliber; but in the mean time can you not give me a battery of 30 or 20 pounder Parrotts for the river defenses? They would be of great service here, and their mobility would add to their efficiency. I beg also that, as soon as possible, three 10-inch columbiads and three 7-inch rifles may be sent me. These guns are absolutely necessary to defend the outer harbor, the point of all others we must endeavor to keep.

Very respectfully,

W. H. C. WHITING,
Brigadier-General, Commanding.

[FEBRUARY 24, 1863.—For D. H. Hill to Beauregard, and reply of March 1, see Series I, Vol. XIV, pp. 789, 798.]

KENT COURT-HOUSE,
February 24, 1863.

Capt. J. H. PEARCE,
  Assistant Adjutant-General:

CAPTAIN: I deem it proper to report that a deserter from the Yankee forces, who has just been sent in by Captain Hill, reports that there are some 6,000 troops at Yorktown and that fresh troops are constantly being landed there. This deserter seems to have passed the cavalry pickets and fallen in with some of Captain Hill's men. It is proper for me also to report that there are four cases of small-pox in Captain Hill's company, who have been placed in hospital near Barhamsville.

R. T. W. DUKE,
Colonel.

[Indorsement.]

Respectfully forwarded to Maj. Gen. A. Elzey for his information.

HENRY A. WISE,
Brigadier-General.

ASHEVILLE, N. C., *February* 24, 1863.

[Hon. ZEBULON B. VANCE:]

GOVERNOR: In obedience to your directions so to do, I have made inquiries and gathered facts such as I could in reference to the shooting of certain prisoners in Laurel Creek, in Madison County. I have to report to you that I learned that the militia troops had nothing to do with what was done in Laurel. Thirteen prisoners, at least, were killed by order of Lieut. Col. J. A. Keith. Most of them were taken at their homes, and none of them made resistance when taken; perhaps some of them ran. After they were taken prisoners the soldiers took them off to a secluded place, made them kneel down, and shot them. They were buried in a trench dug for the purpose. Some two weeks since their bodies were removed to a grave-yard. I learned that probably 8 of the 13 killed were not in the company that robbed Marshall and other places. I suppose they were shot on suspicion. I cannot ' arn the names of the soldiers who shot them. Some of them shrank from the barbarous and brutal transaction at first, but were compelled to act. This is a list of the names of those killed: Elison King (desperate man); Jo Woods (desperate man); Will Shelton, twenty years old (of Pifus); Aronnata Shelton, fourteen years old (was not at Marshall); James Shelton (old Jim), about fifty-six years old; James Shelton, jr., seventeen years old; David Shelton, thirteen years old (was not in the raid); James Madcap, forty years old; Rod Shelton (Stob Rod); David Shelton (brother of Stob Rod); Joseph Cleandon, fifteen or sixteen years old; Helen Moore, twenty-five or thirty years old; Wade Moore, twenty or twenty-five years old. It is said that those whose names I have so marked did not go to Marshall. The prisoners were captured on one Friday and killed the next Monday. Several women were severely whipped and ropes were tied around their necks. It is said Col. L. M. Allen was not in command and that Keith commanded. Four prisoners are now in jail, sent here, as I learned, by order of General Davis. These are Sipus Shelton, Isaac Shelton, William Morton, and David Shelton, son of Sipus. I think the facts stated are about true. One thing is certain, 13 prisoners were shot without trial or any hearing whatever and in the most cruel manner. I have no means of compelling witnesses to disclose facts to me, and I do not know that I shall be able to make a fuller report to Your Excellency at any early day. I hope these facts will enable you to take such steps as will result in a more satisfactory development of the true state of the matter.

I am, &c., yours, truly,

A. S. MERRIMON.

———

GOLDSBOROUGH, N. C., *February* 25, 1863.

[General WHITING:]

GENERAL: I have written to the Secretary of War in reference to heavier armament at Wilmington. A letter from you to me on the same subject, to be forwarded to him, might be of service. In the mean time it seems to me that your channel front at Caswell ought to be strengthened by the columbiads near town. The exterior works should first be cared for. Ransom's men ought to be employed in thickening the curtains and completing the circle around town. Evans, too, should be at work at Sudberry in making that position impregnable. I do not feel satisfied that the Yankees will not return to Wilmington. They seem to be demoralized at Charleston, and may try the smaller job by way of

encouraging their men, just as they reduced Arkansas Post to get up
heart for Vicksburg. At any rate, we ought to spare no effort and lose
no time in getting ready. I have referred the matter of Cogdell's company to General Daniel.

   With great respect,

               D. H. HILL,
                Major-General.

                  HEADQUARTERS,
         Goldsborough, N. C., February 25, 1863.

The undersigned has been placed in charge of the troops in North
Carolina. In assuming command he would address a few words of ex-
hortation to his forces :

Soldiers! Your brutal and malignant enemy is putting forth efforts
unexampled in the history of the world. Having failed to subjugate
you, he is maddened with the thirst for vengeance, and is pushing forward his foreign mercenaries to plunder your property and lay waste
your homes. But his marauding hosts have been so often beaten and
baffled that they are now discouraged and demoralized. Should you be
able to check them everywhere for the next sixty days the 300,000 whose
time expires in May will not re-enlist, and the war will end before July.
Should the scoundrels, however, gain a single substantial success at any
one point the war will be prolonged during the entire administration
of Lincoln. It becomes a solemn duty then to labor and fight during
the next two months as we have never done before. We must make
the war unpopular with the mercenary vandals of the North by harassing and annoying them. We must cut down to 6 feet by 2 the dimensions of the farms which these plunderers propose to appropriate. You
will have to endure more hardships and to fight more desperate battles
than you would have done were your ranks properly filled. Our cities,
towns, and villages are full of young and able-bodied skulkers, wearing the semblance of men, who have dodged from the battle-field under
the provisions of the exemption bill. The scorn of the fair sex and the
contempt of all honorable men have not been able to drive these cowardly miscreants into the ranks, so long as they can fatten upon the
miseries of the country and shelter their worthless carcasses from Yankee bullets; but they are insensible to shame. But a day of retribu-
tion awaits these abortions of humanity. Their own descendants
will execrate their memory when the finger of scorn is pointed and the
taunt is uttered, " He is the son, or grandson, or great-grandson of an
exempt and extortioner." Do your full duty, soldiers, and leave these
poltroons and villains to the execration of posterity.

All commanding officers are hereby enjoined to furnish the names of
officers and men who distinguish themselves in pitched battles and skirmishes. Those so distinguishing themselves will be recommended for
promotion and their names published in the principal papers of their
respective States.

The infantry have to bear the brunt of every battle and to endure
special hardships in every campaign. The post of danger and of suffering
is the post of honor. If our liberty be ever won it will be due mainly
to the indomitable pluck and sturdy endurance of our heroic infantry.

The Confederate artillery has behaved most nobly, and the wonder is
that with inferior guns and ammunition it has been able to cope successfully with the splendid armament of the enemy. It has been a mistake, however, to contend with the Yankee artillery. Reserve your
fire, as at Fredericksburg, for the masses of infantry, and do not with

draw your guns just when they are becoming effective. It is glorious to lose guns by fighting them to the last; it is disgraceful to save them by retiring early from the fight.

The cavalry constitute the eyes and ears of the army. The safety of the entire command depends upon their vigilance and the faithfulness of their reports. The officers and men who permit themselves to be surprised deserve to die, and the commanding general will spare no efforts to secure them their deserts. Almost equally criminal are the scouts who through fright bring in wild and sensational reports. They will be court-martialed for cowardice. Many opportunities will be afforded to the cavalry to harass the enemy, cut off his supplies, drive in his pickets, &c. Those who have never been in battle will thus be enabled to enjoy the novel sensation of listening to the sound of hostile shot and shell, and those who have listened a great way off will be allowed to come some miles nearer, and compare the sensation caused by the distant cannonade with that produced by the rattle of musketry.

D. H. HILL,
Major-General.

———

STATE OF NORTH CAROLINA, EXECUTIVE DEPARTMENT,
Raleigh, N. C., February 25, 1863.
Hon. JAMES A. SEDDON,
Secretary of War:

SIR: I had the honor some three weeks or a month ago to address you respectfully, asking the removal of a lot of broken-down cavalry horses from the northwestern counties of this State, of General Jenkins' command, which were devouring the substance of a people threatened with famine. I have not had the pleasure of receiving a reply to that letter. I beg leave to inform you that their depredations are still continued and that they have become not only a nuisance but a terror to the community, and to inclose you a letter* from Colonel Forkner, of Seventy-third North Carolina Militia, giving evidence of their behavior. With every possible disposition to aid in the support of the army, I have the strongest reasons conceivable—the existence of my own people—for declining to permit those horses to remain in that section of the State. When the question of starvation is narrowed down to women and children on the one side and some worthless cavalry horses on the other I can have no difficulty in making a choice. Unless they are removed soon I shall be under the painful necessity of calling out the militia of adjoining counties and driving them from the State. I hope, however, to be spared such a proceeding.

Very respectfully, your obedient servant,

Z. B. VANCE.

———

RICHMOND, VA., *February* 25, 1863.

Lieut. Gen. JAMES LONGSTREET,
Petersburg, Va.:

You are, by special orders, this day assigned to the command of the department recently made vacant by the resignation of Maj. Gen. G. W. Smith.

S. COOPER,
Adjutant and Inspector General

———

* Not found.

HEADQUARTERS, *February* 26, 1863.

General R. E. LEE, *Fredericksburg, Va.:*

The following is just from General Pryor:

Scouts just in report arrivals of transports daily.   Number now estimated at 50,000. Gradually moving up the river.   Persons from Norfolk report Hooker at Fort Monroe.

My scout reports the force at Newport News at 40,000 or 50,000, but has none of the other items.

JAMES LONGSTREET,
Lieutenant-General.

HDQRS. DEPT. OF VIRGINIA AND NORTH CAROLINA,
Petersburg, Va., February 26, 1863.

In obedience to authority from the War Department the undersigned hereby assumes command of this department.   Department headquarters are for the present established at this point, to which all reports will be directed.   The following-named officers are announced as composing the general staff, and will be obeyed and respected accordingly: Maj. G. M. Sorrel, assistant adjutant-general; Maj. Thomas J. Goree and Lieut. R. W. Blackwell, aides-de-camp; Majs. J. W. Fairfax and O. Latrobe, inspectors-general; Maj. S. P. Mitchell, chief quartermaster; Maj. R. J. Moses, chief commissary of subsistence; Maj. Thomas Walton, commissary of subsistence; Lieut. Col. P. T. Manning, chief of ordnance; Surg. J. S. D. Cullen, medical director; Surg. R. Barksdale, medical inspector; Col. J. B. Walton, chief of artillery; Capt. J. H. Manning, signal officer.

JAMES LONGSTREET,
Lieutenant-General, Commanding.

HEADQUARTERS,
Wilmington, N. C., February 27, 1863.

Maj. Gen. D. H. HILL, *Goldsborough, N. C.:*

MY DEAR GENERAL: I have sent one 10-inch columbiad to Fort Caswell.   I may also send the one now mounted at the city.   I wrote to the Secretary some days since with regard to armament.   They are no doubt fully aware of the necessities of this place, which I have earnestly endeavored to set forth ever since I was assigned to this command. Please write to the Governor and urge the speedy sending here of 500 or 600 negroes.   I have spoken and written to him about it.   I have moved Evans' brigade to camp near Masonborough.   Faison's regiment, of Ransom's [brigade], occupies Harrison's lines at Sudberry's, and another regiment Stevens' lines on northeast.   The remaining three regiments are south of the city, outside the Greenfield Pond.   I send you a letter* from my man Sharp, whom I keep in front as my "cavalry."   It contains some interesting information.   Evans had an underground communication with New Berne.   I presume Daniel may have the same.   There was a battery of four 20-pounder Parrotts at Goldsborough, for which, or a similar one, I applied.   It would make a formidable addition to our means of defense, especially on the river, from its mobility.   I do not know whether you have it now or not.   It was General Smith's intention to send it to me.

Very respectfully,

W. H. C. WHITING,
Brigadier-General.

---

* Not found.

WILMINGTON, N. C., *February 27, 1863.*

Hon. JAMES A. SEDDON,
  Secretary of War, Richmond, Va.:

SIR: I think it necessary in the present aspect of matters on this coast to have another brigade. It should be placed in Brunswick County. If the attack should be made definitely on Charleston it can be readily thrown to re-enforce General Beauregard. With it should be sent a battery of long-range guns. The field batteries in my command are very indifferent, being mostly 6-pounders, smooth, and 12-pounder howitzers. A cavalry force in Brunswick would also be of great service. It is reported that the enemy make boat expeditions about the inlets (Shallotte and Little River), to attack the steamers running the blockade. They are armed with the Dahlgren boat howitzer, and it is said some of these have captured the Wave Queen, with a very valuable cargo of saltpeter and powder. I am not certain of the truth of this for I do not see how row-boats can take a steamer at sea; but it may be so. Foster has certainly left New Berne on his way from Washington to Port Royal. I have information that he impressed and carried with him all the pilots he could get in Beaufort, N. C., familiar with the North Carolina coast. This is ominous, and the design may be that, having failed to surprise Charleston, they may attempt this as the weakest place, as after their Vicksburg failure they went to Arkansas Post. The moment any heavy guns can be sent me I hope they will be forwarded with dispatch. My armament is sadly inadequate.

  Very respectfully,
                        W. H. C. WHITING,
                             Brigadier-General.

———

STATE OF NORTH CAROLINA, EXECUTIVE DEPARTMENT,
                        Raleigh, N. C., February 27, 1863.

Brigadier-General DAVIS, *Knoxville, Tenn.:*

GENERAL: In my last letter to you I referred to a report that a number of prisoners taken on Laurel had been shot in cold blood, and expressed the hope it might not prove true. I fear, however, that it is even worse than was first reported. I beg leave to ask your attention to the copy inclosed of a part of a letter* from A. S. Merrimon, esq., attorney for the State in that district, and to respectfully request you to make inquiry into the truth of the statements within, with a view to proceedings against the guilty parties. While expressing again my thanks for the prompt aid rendered by your command in quieting the troubles in that region, I cannot reconcile it to my sense of duty to pass by in silence such cruel and barbarous conduct as is alleged to have characterized a portion of them, and more especially as the officers mentioned are citizens of this State.

  Very respectfully, your obedient servant,
                        Z. B. VANCE.

———

STATE OF NORTH CAROLINA, EXECUTIVE DEPARTMENT.,
                        Raleigh, N. C., February 28, 1863.

Hon. JAMES A. SEDDON, *Secretary of War:*

SIR: Some six months since a disturbance occurred in Madison County, North Carolina, near the Tennessee border, by some disloyal persons cap-

———

* See p. 881; see also p. 893.

turing the little county town and seizing a lot of salt and other plunder. An armed force was promptly sent from Knoxville, under command of General Davis, to suppress the insurrection, which was accomplished before the local militia could get there, though ordered out immediately. But in doing so a degree of cruelty and barbarity was displayed, shocking and outrageous in the extreme, on the part of Lieut. Col. J. A. Keith, Sixty-fourth North Carolina Troops, who seems to have been in command, and to have acted in this respect without orders from his superiors, so far as I can learn. I beg leave to ask you to read the inclosed letter* (copy) from A. S. Merrimon, State's attorney for that judicial district, which you will see discloses a scene of horror disgraceful to civilization. I desire you to have proceedings instituted at once against this officer, who, if the half be true, is a disgrace to the service and to North Carolina. You may depend upon the respectability and fairness of Mr. Merrimon, who made an investigation officially by my order. I have also written General Davis.

Very respectfully, your obedient servant,

Z. B. VANCE.

HEADQUARTERS,
Petersburg, Va., February 28, 1863.

Maj. Gen. D. H. HILL,
Goldsborough, N. C.:

GENERAL: From the reports that we have of the enemy's strength at and near New Berne it would seem practicable for us to concentrate from Wilmington and your forces and cut the New Berne garrison off from the sea-coast. Please have this in your mind and collect such information on the subject as may be useful, and at the same time make such other arrangements for such an expedition as may be necessary, but let no one know that you have anything of the kind in view. We should make every effort to get supplies from the counties near the enemy's position. I hope that you will collect all information upon the subject of supplies also. I hope to be able to make you a visit soon, but hope that you will send me all the information in the mean time. The cavalry was ordered to Bertie for the purpose of getting supplies as much as for any other purpose. If the cavalry is particularly important where it is it can remain for the present. Pickett's and Hood's divisions, of my corps, are here. The enemy is reported quite strong at Newport News, but no present indications of active operations.

I remain, very respectfully, your obedient servant,

JAMES LONGSTREET,
Lieutenant-General.

HEADQUARTERS,
Fredericksburg, Va., February 28, 1863.

Lieut. Gen. JAMES LONGSTREET,
Commanding North Carolina Department:

GENERAL: I have received your letter of the 24th† and dispatch of 25th.† I have as yet heard of but three army corps of General Hooker's army descending the Potomac. A scout who has been on the river for the last ten days reports on the 26th that everything has been quiet on

---

*See p. 893.   †Not found.

the Potomac during the past week, only two or three steamers passing up and down during the day. Numerous sail vessels with large amount of hay descended. From the number and size of transports he estimates that from 15,000 to 20,000 troops have descended the river since the 9th. The army in front of us is still very strong, compactly located along the railroad from Falmouth to Aquia, with cavalry on either flank, extending from river to river. It is now so difficult to get in or out of his lines that I had to send Fitz Lee's cavalry to force an entrance. With 400 men he broke through 5 miles north of Falmouth, found them in strong force, fell upon their camps, and brought off 150 prisoners, including 5 commissioned and 10 non-commissioned officers.

Major Moses took his departure yesterday.

I will give directions about Hood's guns, if they have not gone. Make them take care of all the horses.

With great respect, your obedient servant,

R. E. LEE,
General.

———

HEADQUARTERS,
Wilmington, N. C., February 28, 1863.

Hon. JAMES A. SEDDON,
Secretary of War, Richmond, Va.:

SIR: The chief object I propose to gain in my application for a battery of 30-pounder or 20-pounder Parrotts and for a brigade to occupy Brunswick County is to strengthen Fort Caswell, always the weakest point in the system of defenses here. Its inherent weakness, that is due to its construction and armament, I am endeavoring to overcome by increasing its defenses and its armament as fast as our means will permit. A memoir detailing the design and progress of these works will be shortly submitted for your information. But its isolated position, cut off as it is from relief from the mainland, renders necessary the establishment of interior positions to arrest, at any rate materially to delay, the advance of the enemy beyond gaining an entrance, supposing him to succeed in reducing the fort. For this purpose, in addition to the very few guns I am able to command for permanent location on the Smithville Bluff, there are no better means than those proposed—a good battery of four or six Parrotts, supported by a column of troops able to make a formidable resistance to an attempt at lodgment on the main. Such an attempt would undoubtedly be the first object of the enemy should they succeed in entering the outer harbor. It would furnish them with a depot. They would strongly fortify it. It would give them a base for future operations exceedingly embarrassing to us, and would effectually prevent any possibility of relief to Caswell. The facility with which such a battery might be moved to different points commanding the anchorage or the channels, and its well-known effect upon steamers and transports would give at the smallest outlay the greatest available accession to our strength. I know no position where such a battery is more needed. Nothing that is possible to procure should be omitted in endeavoring to preserve the outer harbor from the enemy. I have directed the construction of lines to repel landings and cover these guns in their field of operations, a work which has heretofore only been postponed, partly from works of perhaps more immediate necessity and partly from the small-pox pestilence which has raged in that vicinity. The troops required are necessary in addition to what I already have, my force not been large enough to divide. In this connection I refer to my letters to your predecessor of November last and to my correspondence with Major-General Smith, in which the necessity of a covering or movable column of troops is fully set forth. Will you please to submit these considerations to the President? I shall shortly be able to forward for his information maps and sketches which will show the whole system of defense for this important post.

Very respectfully, your obedient servant,

W. H. C. WHITING,
Brigadier-General.

HEADQUARTERS,
Petersburg, Va., February 28, 1863.

General S. COOPER,
Adjutant and Inspector General:

GENERAL: I wrote several days ago asking for generals of cavalry. General Robertson, now commanding the cavalry in this department, was sent here to organize and instruct it. He was not deemed a very efficient officer in the field and was therefore relieved from duty with the Army of Northern Virginia. The cavalry is now considered in proper condition for field service, and could be used to great advantage, in proper hands, in getting supplies from North Carolina in and near the enemy's lines. I write to you upon the subject again, in order that the Department may fully understand the importance of having the cavalry in proper hands, and to renew my recommendation of General Ransom for promotion to the cavalry. It may be important, too, that we should act promptly if we hope to collect any great quantity of the supplies in Eastern North Carolina.

I am, sir, most respectfully, your obedient servant,

JAMES LONGSTREET,
Lieutenant-General.

Abstract from Field Return of Troops commanded by Maj. Gen. S. G. French, for February 28, 1863.

Command.	Present for duty.		Aggregate present.	Aggregate present and absent.
	Officers.	Men.		
Forces on Blackwater	318	4,823	5,904	8,123
Twenty-ninth Regiment Virginia Volunteers	36	604	642	862
Moseley's artillery battalion	8	140	160	182
Bradford's battery	3	75	86	92
Sturdivant's battery	3	74	86	100
Confederate Guard	3	63	68	96
Hargrove Blues	3	96	105	123
Moise's cavalry company	2	23	28	29
Signal Corps	4	124	133	140
Camp paroled prisoners	14	152	173	216
Grand total	394	6,174	7,385	9,963

Abstract from Report of the Troops of the District of the Cape Fear, commanded by Brig. Gen. W. H. C. Whiting, for February, 1863.

Command.	Present for duty.		Effective total.	Aggregate present.	Aggregate present and absent.
	Officers.	Men.			
Brigadier-General Evans' brigade	138	1,743	1,853	2,078	2,887
Brigadier-General Ransom's brigade	164	2,656	2,673	2,987	3,825
Forts Caswell, Fisher, Johnson, and Saint Philip (twenty-one companies).	52	1,153	1,426	1,718	1,925
City and river defenses (one battalion and three companies) ..	22	402	446	538	625
Three unattached companies	10	130	146	170	208
Third Battalion North Carolina Artillery	11	194	205	234	267
Four light batteries	16	441	443	479	538
Three companies of cavalry	5	180	181	206	278
Signal Corps	1	22	22	23	23
Bridge guard	1	24	24	27	31
Grand total	420	6,945	7,419	8,460	10,607

Abstract from Field Return of Troops, Maj. Gen. A. Elzey commanding, for March 1, 1863 (headquarters Richmond, Va.).

Command	Present for duty.		Effective total present.	Aggregate present.	Aggregate present and absent.
	Officers.	Men.			
Brig. Gen. H. A. Wise	128	2,029	2,182	2,519	3,405
Col. Thomas S. Rhett	78	1,451	1,585	1,868	2,168
Col. Jack Brown	31	714	766	926	1,136
Col. T. J. Page	22	320	384	433	520
Capt. S. S. Lee, C. S. Navy	13	311	367	405	434
Grand total	272	4,825	5,284	6,151	7,663

Abstract from Field Return of the Department of North Carolina, commanded by Maj. Gen. D. H. Hill, for March 1, 1863.

Command.	Present for duty.		Aggregate present.	Aggregate present and absent.
	Officers.	Men.		
Whiting's command [not reported]				
Pettigrew's brigade	169	3,068	3,582	4,476
Daniel's brigade	216	3,513	4,247	5,680
Reserve Artillery	13	335	380	447
Hamilton, N. C	47	832	1,036	1,132
Weldon, N. C	32	653	879	1,113
Goldsborough, N. C.	40	541	710	794
Robertson's cavalry brigade	105	1,378	1,703	2,177
Grand total	622	10,320	12,537	15,819

WAR DEPARTMENT, C. S. A.,
Richmond, Va., March 1, 1863.

His Excellency ZEBULON B. VANCE,
Governor of North Carolina:

SIR: I regret to learn from your letter of the 25th ultimo that such serious opposition is entertained by you to the continuance of the horses of a portion of General Jenkins' command in the western counties of North Carolina. I had commended your previous letter to the attention of the general commanding that department with the hope that the evil complained of would be inquired into, and, if found remediable, would be corrected. Doubtless it has been continued only from the necessity of the case. The truth is, that the large number of cavalry in the mountainous regions of East Tennessee and Virginia could not be subsisted there during the winter, and it was deemed imperatively necessary that most of the men should be dismounted and the horses sent to more distant regions, less exhausted by being ravaged or drained by the struggling armies, for subsistence and preparation for the approaching campaign. It was supposed, and indeed strongly represented, that the counties on the eastern slopes of the mountains in North Carolina would afford abundant supplies and early pasturage for them, and that benefit would result from sending them there, not only to the horses, but to the people around, in affording them a market for their surplus grain and forage. Only a moderate number, however, were sent there, and more were scattered about in the various more distant counties of Virginia, along the valley and mountainous districts. Complaints similar to those addressed to you have come up from various counties of this State, where they have been collected, for the products of the last season were scant almost everywhere, and some irregularities are but too apt to occur with the rather irregular and partially disciplined cavalrymen sent with the horses. But our authorities have been content with the effort to redress them by appeal to the officers or commanding generals, and no effort has been made or intimated of a purpose to expel them by force. They are, it will be recollected, not, as Your Excellency supposes, broken-down horses, nor can they be considered as Virginia cavalry, though lately engaged in that State. They are horses of the cavalry of the Confederate States, engaged for the common defense, as well for North Carolina as for every other State, and placed where they are to preserve them in a state of efficiency for our further struggles in a common cause. I trust therefore Your Excellency will forbear from any forcible expulsion of them, should their still longer stay be deemed indispensable. Your letter, however, shall be sent to the general commanding the department where these horses were sent, and his attention especially invoked to your remonstrances.

With high esteem, very truly, yours,

J. A. SEDDON,
Secretary of War.

———

HEADQUARTERS,
Petersburg, Va., March 1, 1863.

Maj. Gen. D. H. HILL,
Goldsborough, N. C.:

GENERAL: Your letter of the 25th is this instant received. Your views are almost precisely those that I wrote you two or three days ago.

I do not know that I expressed the idea that a forward movement would be a diversion in favor of Charleston, but I had it in my mind. I will send orders to General Whiting to prepare himself to re-enforce you, say 4,000 men. This, with the cavalry and what you have, ought to run your force up to 14,000 or 15,000 men. At least this is my calculation. With this force I think you could cut the railroad behind New Berne and probably force the enemy out to fight. From here, though, it looks as if most of the cavalry could operate to greater advantage on the north side of the river, so that we can forage at the same time that the forces are displayed in front of the enemy's works. General Whiting might bring you 5,000 men, I should think, but I cannot promise so many until I am better posted. If there is a chance of doing anything we should not be idle. We are much more likely to succeed by operating ourselves than by lying still to await the enemy's time for thorough preparation before he moves upon us. I have been confined with a terribly sore throat since I have been here, but hope to be out in a few days more, when I shall make a visit to your headquarters. In the mean time please make your preparations quietly for a forward movement. Cannot you persuade the good people in charge of the railroads to work a little more and with more system, in order that freight, &c., can be brought through promptly? Our people have been so accustomed to have all kinds of labor at their hands that they seem at a loss for resources when emergencies arise. " Where there is a will there is a way" of overcoming all human obstacles. It is left for us to find it out. All suggestions are thankfully received, and as I know that all of your ideas are good you need not hesitate about expressing them.

I remain, most respectfully, your obedient servant,

JAMES LONGSTREET,
Lieutenant-General.

———

HEADQUARTERS,
Petersburg, Va., March 1, 1863.

General R. E. LEE,
Fredericksburg, Va. :

GENERAL: Your letter of the 28th is received. I shall keep you advised of matters here that you may, by comparing notes, satisfy yourself of the enemy's position, &c. I shall be guided by the information that I may receive from you of the enemy's movements more than by what I hear here, for the present at all events. The force now here I think quite sufficient to overcome that of the enemy at any time that I may be able to meet him, and shall act accordingly until I find that he is moving additional troops from your front. I do not think, however, that he will withdraw any force that he now holds in your front, but may possibly send back the force now at Newport News. Deserters, however, report that this force is intended to operate in North Carolina.

I remain, sir, very respectfully, your most obedient servant,

JAMES LONGSTREET,
Lieutenant-General.

P. S.—I have parties on each bank of the river to watch the force at Newport News.

HEADQUARTERS,
Wilmington, N. C., March 2, 1863.
Hon. JAMES A. SEDDON,
    Secretary of War, Richmond, Va.:

SIR: If it is not practicable to send me the heavy Parrott guns lately requested may I not have a field battery of 12-pounder Parrotts or other rifled guns, for the purpose specified in my previous letters on this matter? I should like to have Reilly's, both from the skill of that officer, his thorough acquaintance with the country (especially the locality in which he would operate), and the quality of his guns. The matter of the brigade asked for is becoming daily more important. My information from the enemy's lines confirms my opinion heretofore expressed that the Abolitionists, having utterly failed to surprise Charleston, and [being] very unwilling to attempt it, believing it almost impregnable, will endeavor to move against some weaker point. Unless Hunter should overrule Foster and try Savannah they must come here. I do not see that they would gain much, even should they take Savannah, since they already hold the port of that city and Fort Pulaski, while they might lose a great deal. At any rate, should they come here, the attack this time would be from the southward, that is, Cape Fear and the Frying-Pan Shoals. A corresponding advance by land from New Berne, as at first designed, would be supported by fresh troops drawn from the North. The fact of Foster's taking with him all the North Carolina pilots he could find especially marks this place as the point selected. I urged it as essential to our success that I should be provided with a brigade, to be placed on the south side of the river. All the time they give me is devoted to strengthening Fort Caswell, the weakest point in the system. The proposed disposition would greatly strengthen it.

    Very respectfully,

W. H. C. WHITING,
Brigadier-General.

HEADQUARTERS,
Wilmington, N. C., March 2, 1863.
Maj. Gen. D. H. HILL,
    Commanding, &c., Goldsborough, N. C.:

MY DEAR GENERAL: I quite agree with you that the Yankees, having failed to surprise Charleston and finding it very strong, will make an attempt on some weaker point. That will be undoubtedly Wilmington, unless Hunter should object and overrule Foster. The latter's carrying off the North Carolina pilots with him to Port Royal is ominous as to this. I have received notice that a 10-inch columbiad is started from Richmond for me and another will soon be sent. Please to hurry them through. Time now is all-important. Cannot you stir me up some labor—negro labor? I need very much fully 500, not so much for the city as for Caswell, Smithfield, and Fisher. I have applied to the Secretary for another brigade. In my opinion now, the attack coming as it will from the southward, it is essential that a brigade be stationed in Brunswick County, to maneuver against any attempt to land, and it is especially in case of any of their vessels passing Caswell that I need both the troops and a battery of Parrott guns. My field batteries are very defective, being mostly smooth-bores and howitzers. This is very important, and I trust you will give the matter all the aid in your power. A brigade might, I think, readily be spared from about Richmond. The negro force lately raised and armed about New Berne has been, as I hear, disarmed, in consequence of disagreement on the subject between Stanly and Lincoln.

With great respect, yours,

W. H. C. WHITING,
Brigadier-General.

HEADQUARTERS,
Petersburg, Va., March 2, 1863.

General G. T. BEAUREGARD,
Commanding, Charleston, S. C.:

GENERAL: Scouting parties just come in from around New Berne report that General Foster, on his way back to Charleston, took with him pilots for Cape Fear River and North Carolina inlets. The scouts also report that the Yankees think Charleston impregnable. In consequence of this General Whiting anticipates a return of General Foster's force and an attack at Wilmington. The difficulty between Generals Hunter and Foster may have induced General Foster to advise against Hunter's attack, and possibly may have induced the United States Government to change the point of attack. This difficulty, I think, insures your victory if the attack is made. When generals quarrel their troops will not fight; that is, they will not fight a severe battle. I hope that you will keep your eye upon Foster, and advise me if he should turn around and come back to his first love. I hope, though, that you may have your opportunity, for I am quite satisfied that vou will be able to beat back any attack that may be made upon you.

I remain, very respectfully and sincerely, yours,

JAMES LONGSTREET,
Lieutenant-General, Commanding.

HEADQUARTERS,
Petersburg, Va., March 2, 1863.

Maj. Gen. W. H. C. WHITING,
Wilmington, N. C.:

GENERAL: I desire that you will make preparations for sending the half of your force and as many more as can be spared from Wilmington garrison to re-enforce Major-General Hill for foraging service. If your services may be spared from Wilmington I would like to have you on this service also, as some important service may grow out of it. Please make your arrangements as quietly as possible, giving no one an indication that any serious service is expected. Advise me as early as possible of the force that you can send or take out.

I remain, sir, very respectfully, your obedient servant,

JAMES LONGSTREET,
Lieutenant-General.

P. S.—If your forts in the harbor are not ordered to be held at all hazards and for all time up to starvation, such orders should be given in writing. If operations should become extensive in North Carolina it may at some time be necessary to abandon Wilmington for a time to operate elsewhere; but if we hold the harbor we can at any time retake the city. I do not know anything of the plan of defenses, and have taken it for granted that the harbor defenses are independent of those of the city, &c. Further orders will be sent before a movement is made.

HEADQUARTERS,
Petersburg, Va., March 3, 1863.

In reference to the inclosed letter* of General R. A. Pryor, and which the lieutenant-general has referred to me, I have to remark: General R. A. Pryor was sent by me to the Blackwater, as desired by General G. W. Smith. A considerable force was then on this line, under a most able officer, who had twice·repulsed the enemy in force when he attempted to cross the river. I allude to Col. C. Leventhorpe. When the enemy began to assemble a force at New Berne in December last I found it obligatory to withdraw all the North Carolina regiments from the Blackwater, and on January 5 last left Petersburg to take command of them for the defense of Wilmington. A few days previous to this General Colston arrived at this place with a brigade. I directed him to proceed with all his command (except one regiment), and dispose of it for the defense of the line on the Blackwater, and to leave the brigade there under the immediate command of General Pryor, and that he should then return and remain in Petersburg during my absence. He was to defend the James, Blackwater, and Weldon while I was near Wilmington. After the sailing of the enemy from Beaufort, and when disposing of the troops, I ordered General J. R. Davis, with his brigade, to the Blackwater, and on my arrival here, as will be seen by the inclosed order,* sent General Colston to command these two brigades and the line of the Blackwater. General Pryor was under General Colston all the time since I left here, and the only change is General Colston has moved down on the line. General Pryor still has the command of a full brigade, just as he had before. Had General Colston gone down and taken his own brigade it would have left General Pryor without a command. But he does not, and leaves his own brigade under General Pryor as he did in the first instance. And I do not think General Pryor has any cause of complaint. He came here without any troops, and he now has the command of Colston's brigade just as he has had for the last two months. I cannot say that General Pryor has been superseded in command. It was necessary to send there a second brigade, and with that increased force General Colston was sent as the immediate commander of the line of the Blackwater and of both brigades. One of the bridges referred to was built by Colonel French, and a second one I directed Colonel Claiborne to build. As regards supplies they have been always directed to be drawn from the enemy's lines. During the summer, pork could not well be cured, and it was not until after General Pryor went down there that the farmers commenced killing hogs. Indeed, they were not then in condition to kill and the weather was too warm.

S. G. FRENCH,
Major-General.

HEADQUARTERS ARMY OF NORTHERN VIRGINIA,
March 3 [30], 1863.

Lieut. Gen. JAMES LONGSTREET,
Commanding, &c., Petersburg, Va.:

GENERAL: Your letter of the 27th has been received.† I have heard nothing of the Sixth Army Corps being united with the Ninth. Reports from our scouts on the Lower Potomac as late as the 28th instant give no indication of a movement of troops from Aquia. On the contrary it is stated that within the last fortnight re-enforcements have been re-

---

ceived. At that time there were not more than five or six steamers at Aquia and Potomac Creeks, and the number of vessels and transports passing up the Potomac is reported to be less than usual. I fear that the enemy, by a systematic propagation of falsehood, has been able to deceive us, and that the report of troops from Newport News going to North Carolina was purposely spread to conceal their movement west. The weather here is so bad as to preclude any military movement, and the enemy's pickets are so closely posted on their right, being within 50 steps of each other, that our scouts find it impossible to get within their lines, and we have to rely upon citizens, who are easily gulled. The ground is again covered with snow and a northeast rain is prevailing. The enemy's positions in North Carolina have always appeared to me to be taken for defense, and if driven from them they can easily escape to their gunboats. Unless therefore they will come out into the country I do not know how you can advantageously get at them. You will probably find Suffolk fortified as New Berne is. If the line you propose, cutting the Blackwater near Mayfield, is necessary to enable you to draw supplies from the counties east of the Chowan it becomes important, as those supplies are necessary to us. But except to draw provisions from North Carolina at this distance I do not see that you can accomplish much. You need not, however, be restrained by my operations, as at present I can do nothing. I cannot advance and the enemy will not, though all reports agree that he is ready to cross the Rappahannock and waits only for the weather. I fear you can expect no co-operation from the Navy, nor do I know that they can give any, as boats are not of a character to contend with the enemy's iron-clads.

I am, general, very respectfully, your obedient servant,

R. E. LEE,
General.

HEADQUARTERS,
Petersburg, Va., March 4, 1863.

General S. COOPER,
Adjutant and Inspector General:

GENERAL : I have the honor to send herewith a dispatch just received from Maj. Gen. D. H. Hill. General Hill thinks, from the information that he has received, that the enemy may abandon his attack upon Charleston and concentrate for an attack upon Wilmington. In view of this I suggest that General Beauregard be advised to send back the forces to Wilmington, should he find the enemy moving back to that point. It is possible that the disaffection in the ranks of the enemy may force him to make some such effort. I shall not have the force to resist it without re-enforcements from Charleston. I shall leave for Goldsborough on the 6th if the intelligence is confirmed. Burnside's force must have been drawn from Newport News, but we have no information of a movement from that point.

I remain, sir, very respectfully, your obedient servant,

JAMES LONGSTREET,
Lieutenant-General.

HEADQUARTERS,
Wilmington, N. C., March 4, 1863.

Lieutenant-General LONGSTREET,
Commanding Department, Petersburg, Va.:

GENERAL : I have received your letter of the 2d instant. From your postscript I perceive you are not acquainted with this vicinity and the relations which subsist between the city, the outer harbor, the defenses and the interior. I earnestly beg you, before taking any such action as your letter indicates, to refer to my correspondence with the War Department and with Major-General Smith, in which this matter is fully set forth, and that you will refer to the Secretary. So far from considering myself able to spare troops from here I have applied for and earnestly urged that another brigade be sent here immediately. The works here are by no means completed and I need the services of every man I can raise. This necessity is so well understood that when the attack on Charleston was imminent the troops sent from here to re-enforce General Beauregard were immediately replaced by order of the Secretary. Information received from the enemy's lines leads me to think that they have by no means abandoned their designs on this place, of so vital importance to the Confederacy. Major-General Hill informs me that his spies report the arrival of Burnside and a very heavy force at New Berne. Mine report that Foster has returned. I send out again to-day for further information, of which I will give you immediate notice.

With great respect, your obedient servant,

W. H. C. WHITING,
Brigadier-General, Commanding.

HDQRS. DEPT. OF VIRGINIA AND NORTH CAROLINA,
Petersburg, Va., March 4, 1863.

Maj. Gen. S. G. FRENCH, *Commanding, &c. :*

GENERAL : General Longstreet desires a work constructed on the James River for a field battery of four or six guns, of which some are 20-pounder Parrotts. He has no engineer officer at present serving with him and asks that you will send yours to select a suitable point somewhere in the vicinity of Fort Powhatan. As soon as the site is chosen if your officer will report at this office he will be furnished with such working details as he will require for a rapid prosecution of the work.

I am, general, very respectfully, your obedient servant,

G. MOXLEY SORREL,
Assistant Adjutant-General.

PETERSBURG, VA., *March* 4, 1863.

Maj. Gen. D. H. HILL,
Commanding, &c., Goldsborough, N. C. :

Yours of 2d received. If the information contained therein be confirmed the general will start to join you on the 6th instant. He asks you to keep him promptly advised by telegraph of any confirmation or additional information.

G. MOXLEY SORREL,
Assistant Adjutant-General.

[MARCH 5, 1863.—For correspondence between Longstreet and Beauregard, see Series I, Vol. XIV, p. 810.]

HEADQUARTERS,
Petersburg, Va., March 5, 1863.
General S. COOPER,
    Adjutant and Inspector General:

GENERAL: Maj. Gen. D. H. Hill reports a large force landing at New Berne, N. C. This force must be part of the command intended for the attack upon Charleston, which seems to have been abandoned.

I inclose herewith a letter* from Brigadier-General Whiting, commanding at Wilmington. He is anxious to have his armament increased, as also his laboring force. I hope that the Department may do all that is in its power to give him the aid that he desires.

I remain, sir, very respectfully, your obedient servant,
                JAMES LONGSTREET,
                       . Lieutenant-General.

RICHMOND, VA., March 5, 1863.
Lieut. Gen. JAMES LONGSTREET,
        Petersburg, Va.:

GENERAL: The President desires that the troops which were drawn from Generals Samuel Jones' and H. Marshall's commands in Western Virginia should be returned to these commands, and that the brigade of General Joe [J. R.] Davis, which moved a short time since from Goldsborough, N. C., to the Blackwater in Virginia should be returned to Goldsborough. You will please issue the necessary orders in these cases.

Very, respectfully, &c.,
                    S. COOPER,
             Adjutant and Inspector General.

WAR DEPARTMENT, C. S. A.,
Richmond, Va., March 5, 1863.
His Excellency ZEBULON B. VANCE,
    Governor of North Carolina, Raleigh, N. C.:

SIR: I have received your letter of the 28th ultimo, in reference to the conduct of Lieut. Col. J. A. Keith, Sixty-fourth North Carolina Regiment, and have directed General [D. S.] Donelson, commanding at Knoxville, to investigate the matter and report the facts to the Department.

Very respectfully, your obedient servant,
                J. A. SEDDON,
              Secretary of War.

SPECIAL ORDERS, } HDQRS. DEPT. VIRGINIA AND N. CAROLINA,
   No. 39.   }   Petersburg, Va., March 5, 1863.

*   *   *   *   *   *   *

II. Jenkins' brigade is relieved from further duty with Major-General Pickett's division and will proceed to the Blackwater and relieve the brigade of Brig. Gen. R. E. Colston.

III. Brig. Gen. R. E. Colston, with his brigade, is assigned tempora-

---

* See p. 904.

rily to Major-General Pickett's division and will report accordingly on being relieved by General [M.] Jenkins.

IV. The Fifty-fifth North Carolina Troops is relieved from duty with Colston's brigade and is temporarily assigned to the brigade commanded by Brig. Gen. J. R. Davis.

*   *   *   *   *   *   *

By command of Lieutenant-General Longstreet:

G. MOXLEY SORREL,
Assistant Adjutant-General.

HEADQUARTERS,
Petersburg, Va., March [*April*]* 6, 1863.

Hon. JAMES A. SEDDON,
Secretary of War:

SIR: I desire to cross the Blackwater on Saturday for the purpose of driving the enemy into his intrenchments at Suffolk while we draw out the supplies of subsistence and quartermaster's stores from the counties east of that river. If the Navy Department can co-operate with us we may be able to capture Suffolk and its garrison. All that I desire at present is that such vessels as may be ready pass the obstructions, so that they may be able to join us in case it should find a favorable opportunity for them. I believe that there is but one ironclad of the enemy in the James River. If this is the case I presume that we could with our vessels and batteries on the river bank drive the enemy off, cut off any re-enforcements, and possibly capture the garrison.

I remain, sir, very respectfully, your most obedient servant,

JAMES LONGSTREET,
Lieutenant-General, Commanding.

HDQRS. DEPT. VIRGINIA AND NORTH CAROLINA,
Petersburg, Va., March 6, 1863.

Maj. Gen. ARNOLD ELZEY, *Richmond, Va.:*

GENERAL: I have the honor to acknowledge receipt of your note of the 5th instant, in reference to the proposed movement on Suffolk. General Longstreet left last night for Goldsborough, to be absent a few days. Your communication will be forwarded to him by this evening's mail.

I am, general, very respectfully, your most obedient servant,

G. MOXLEY SORREL,
Assistant Adjutant-General.

HEADQUARTERS, *Wilmington, N. C., March* 6, 1863.

Maj. Gen. D. H. HILL,
Commanding, &c., Goldsborough, N. C.:

GENERAL: The Whitworth guns are all we have to depend on to keep the blockaders at such a distance as will enable the steamers to run the blockade. One is at [Fort] Caswell, one at Fort Fisher, and one about 5 miles above [Fort] Fisher, on the beach. We have now four British and one Confederate steamer in port daily expecting to leave, and several steamers are expected to arrive. We have had an engagement

---

* Misplaced.

with the enemy over each one of these vessels, the enemy's sloops of war fiercely attacking the forts while their smaller vessels attempt to cut off the steamers. This has happened at both forts. Without the disposition alluded to at Fort Fisher we should have lost the Cornubia inevitably three days ago. She had been thrice chased off the coast and became short of coal; running into the land at Masonborough she communicated with Colonel Lamb, and the disposition being offered, boldly made for the bar, a fleet of five vessels firing into her. She had the most valuable cargo of powder and arms she has yet brought. Under these circumstances, unless for a matter of greater and pressing importance, I should not like to take the responsibility of detaching the gun from the coast defense. What is this expedition of which you speak? General Longstreet wrote me something about it, but wanted me to send off half my force and half my garrisons.

With great respect, your obedient servant,

W. H. C. WHITING,
Brigadier-General.

HEADQUARTERS ARMY OF NORTHERN VIRGINIA,
March 7, 1863.

Lieut. Gen. JAMES LONGSTREET,
Commanding Department of North Carolina, &c.:

GENERAL: I have received your letters of the 4th and 5th instant. I have as yet seen nothing to indicate a change of purpose in the enemy to attack Charleston. If Wilmington is their object, as supposed by General Whiting, it will be disclosed by the return of their mailed gunboats and army. General Beauregard will no doubt communicate the withdrawal of the enemy from his department, and then, as soon as possible, if Wilmington should be pointed at, our troops should be drawn to that point. I see that General Foster has returned to New Berne, but, as far as I can learn, without his troops. I supposed this might be in consequence of his disagreement with General Hunter, and that leaving his forces with the latter officer was an additional sign that the attack on Charleston or Savannah was not abandoned. General Burnside was reported a few days since to be in Washington City. As far as I can form an opinion only three corps have been sent from General Hooker's army to Newport News, and by the last reports they were still there and the indications showed that they did not contemplate an immediate departure. I have estimated their force at 21,000. All of our scouts agree (those from the enemy's line as well as those on the Potomac) that only three corps have left; seven remain. They also report that some disaffected regiments have been sent away on the plea of preventing contagion. These latter are reported to have gone to Washington and to their States for the purpose of recruiting, and their places to have been supplied by other regiments, so that their strength is equal to what it was before the battle. Their cavalry force has been greatly augmented recently, and the report still is that they intend to advance by this route. It is also stated that the corps sent to Newport News is intended for Burnside and that he will operate in North Carolina. General Hooker has his headquarters on the Potomac Creek near Brooke's Station. His army is located along the railroad from Falmouth to Aquia, but the greater part near Aquia. There are no signs of further embarkation of troops or collection of transports. The only steamers descending the Potomac are those apparently conveying supplies, towing barges, sail vessels, &c., on which troops are seen, but not more than returning absentees, convalescents, &c., would justify. Where the large force said to be landing at New Berne comes from I cannot conceive. I hope you will be able to get accurate information and put yourself in communication with General Beauregard, so as to be prepared for all emergencies. You had better keep yourself advised of the movements of the force at Newport News.

Very truly, yours,

R. E. LEE,
General.

WAR DEPARTMENT, C. S. A.,
Richmond, Va., March 7, 1863.

Brig. Gen. W. H. C. WHITING,
Commanding, Wilmington, N. C. :

GENERAL : I have received your letters of the 23d and 28th ultimo, stating the need for additional guns at Wilmington. Colonel Rhett, inspector of ordnance, reports, under date of the 2d instant, that "one 10-inch gun will probably leave Richmond to-day for Wilmington. On Friday or Saturday a 4.62-inch rifled gun will be ready for that point, and early next week another, and probably a 10-inch also on Monday. A 30-pounder will be ready, I hope, on Tuesday next." Every exertion shall be made, as far as the resources of the Ordnance Bureau will allow, to meet the calls for guns necessary for the defense of Wilmington. I still believe the leading point of attack designed by the enemy is Charleston ; but they may recoil from that and make the attack you apprehend. All preparation therefore possible should certainly be made for such a contingency.

Your obedient servant,

J. A. SEDDON,
Secretary of War.

STATE OF NORTH CAROLINA, EXECUTIVE DEPARTMENT,
Raleigh, N. C., March 7, 1863.

Hon. S. R. MALLORY,
Secretary of the Navy :

SIR : You can have the iron requested by your letter of the 13th ultimo, to be replaced, if you will permit it to be exchanged for the old iron on the different roads of the State. They are rapidly running down and are applying for the same iron. I suppose their worn-out rails would answer the same purpose for rolling.

Very respectfully, your obedient servant,

Z. B. VANCE.

HEADQUARTERS CAVALRY BRIGADE,
March 7, 1863.

Maj. Gen. D. H. HILL,
Comdg. Department of North Carolina, Goldsborough, N. C. :

GENERAL : I regret that your courier should have missed those stationed between this point and Goldsborough, thus rendering it necessary for him to come all the way through. He came a different road from the one usually traveled. I have directed him which way to go in the morning and hope no mistake will occur in future. Your dispatches were received and your orders will be carried out. I have one of my best squadrons (Captain Harris') on picket between Jacksonville and White Oak. Considering the present position of the enemy's main cavalry force (being in the vicinity of Deep Gully), and the fact that the bridge over New River was burnt by Colonel Baker, would it not be advisable to withdraw Captain Harris? Unless you object, I shall do so, as I am much in need of more cavalry and desire to send an additional force to the neighborhood of Kinston.

Most respectfully, your obedient servant,

B. H. ROBERTSON,
Brigadier-General, Commanding.

HEADQUARTERS,
Wilmington, March 7, 1863.

General S. COOPER,
Adjutant and Inspector General, Richmond:

GENERAL: I request you to define the limits and responsibility of this command. No difficulty but some little confusion now obtains in the staff departments from misapprehension.

When I was assigned to duty here I was directed by the Secretary of War to report to the War Department, through the commanding general, then Maj. Gen. G. W. Smith, now Lieutenant-General Longstreet. This was constituted a separate district—in no sense considered a part of the department command of North Carolina.

In many respects, the nature of the command being considered—its object the special defense of a very important place and post, and the necessity which exists for direct communication between the officer in command here and the Department—I think it best that the arrangement heretofore existing should be maintained and that I should be directed to consider myself under the command of the lieutenant-general commanding and report direct to him.

I do not, however, wish to be understood as making any question or objection to any arrangement which may be considered best. I simply desire to have the command defined one way or another, expressing at the same time my opinion that it is best here to have communication as direct as possible.

Very respectfully,

W. H. C. WHITING,
Brigadier-General.

Respectfully forwarded through Lieutenant-General Longstreet, commanding.

[Indorsement.]

HEADQUARTERS, *March* 12, 1863.

Respectfully forwarded.

If any change has been made I am not aware of it. I hope that the matter may be settled as early as possible.

JAMES LONGSTREET,
Lieutenant-General, Commanding.

RICHMOND, VA., *March* 9, 1863.

Lieut. Gen. JAMES LONGSTREET, *Petersburg, Va.:*

GENERAL: It is highly important to know the strength, organization, and position of the forces under your command, and you are desired to give this information with the least delay practicable, extending your report so as to embrace the forces on the line of North Carolina, Wilmington included.

Very respectfully, &c,

S. COOPER,
Adjutant and Inspector General.

HDQRS. DEPT. OF VIRGINIA AND NORTH CAROLINA,
Petersburg, Va., March 9, 1863.

General S. G. FRENCH, *Commanding, &c.:*

GENERAL: I am instructed by the commanding-general to direct that you order one of the regiments of cavalry now serving on the Blackwater down to Greenville, N. C., to operate with a brigade of infantry to be sent to Tarborough in covering and protecting foraging expeditions. The regiment should start with at least three days' rations, and on its reaching Greenville the commander will notify General Hill, at Goldsborough, by telegraph, of the arrival of his command. The commanding general desires it to move with promptness and dispatch.

I am, general, very respectfully, your obedient servant,

G. MOXLEY SORREL,
Assistant Adjutant-General.

HEADQUARTERS,
Kinston, N. C., March 9, 1863.

Maj. Gen. D. H. HILL,
Commanding at Goldsborough, N. C.:

GENERAL: I have the honor to inclose communications* from Captain Whitford. Major Nethercutt desires me to say that he ascertained that the works at Shepherdsville or Newport can be turned on the left, through a bad road of swamp land for 4 or 5 miles; on the right, cannot be turned except by going around by Carolina City and crossing Newport River at railroad bridge. The enemy have pickets there and there is a block-house. Persons traveling the Sound road can be seen from the Sound in passing from Swansborough to Carolina City. The Sound road comes into the road that leads from Smith's Mill to Carolina City immediately above Broad Creek; Fifty-first Massachusetts Regiment and five companies of cavalry are on duty at Shepherdsville.

William F. Bell, called the 3d (now at Warsaw, a refugee), can give you more reliable information of that country than any one else. The latest information of the enemy I forwarded you by telegraph. The negro alluded to in one of the telegrams is here a prisoner. He is intelligent, and his story as to their numbers is corroborated by the rumors Majors Nethercutt and McNeill had from citizens. There is no enemy,

---

*Not found.

I think, between here and 12 or 15 miles of New Berne. Scouts were sent out yesterday but have not yet been heard from. My pickets are where they were when you were here. They were ordered there yesterday at 1 o'clock. Heard from Colonel Lewis this morning. He makes no report of the enemy. I am trying to get information from New Berne. Will certainly keep you advised of everything I can hear of importance. The telegram sent you last night about the enemy at White Oak River was to General Robertson, from one of his captains, on picket on the opposite side. Maj. [J. H.] McNeill says he is reliable. The information was that from the noise he thought they were building a bridge there. The country was such that they could not see the enemy. I will open communication from there to General R. and will telegraph you anything that is important.

Very respectfully, &c.,

JUNIUS DANIEL,
Brigadier-General.

Abstract from Field Return of Pickett's division, Department of Virginia and North Carolina, commanded by Maj. Gen. G. E. Pickett, March 9, 1863.

NEAR PETERSBURG, VA.

Troops.	Present for duty.				Aggregate present.	Aggregate present and absent.
	Infantry.		Artillery.			
	Officers.	Men.	Officers.	Men.		
Garnett's brigade	117	1,440			1,851	3,079
Armistead's brigade	137	1,590			2,150	3,492
Kemper's brigade	115	1,459			1,836	3,310
Corse's brigade	90	934			1,229	2,004
Artillery battalion			13	274	312	434
Grand total	459	5,423	13	274	7,428	12,319

Abstract from Field Return of Hood's Division, Department of Virginia and North Carolina, commanded by Maj. Gen. John B. Hood, March 9, 1863.

Troops.	Present for duty.				Aggregate present.	Aggregate present and absent.
	Infantry.		Artillery.			
	Officers.	Men.	Officers.	Men.		
Texas brigade	110	1,404			1,902	3,036
Law's brigade	131	1,650			2,204	3,570
Anderson's brigade	123	1,734			2,246	3,440
Toombs' brigade	96	1,413			1,726	2,448
Artillery battalion			12	292	342	362
Grand total	460	6,201	12	292	8,420	12,780

Abstract from Field Return of Troops commanded by Maj. Gen. S. G. French, March 10, 1863.

PETERSBURG, VA.

Troops.	Present for duty.		Aggregate present.	Aggregate present and absent.
	Officers.	Men.		
Brig. Gen. R. E. Colston's command	328	5,217	6,422	8,188
29th Regiment Virginia Volunteers	40	618	694	874
Moseley's artillery battalion	8	146	166	180
Bradford's battery	4	79	94	99
Sturdivant's battery	4	76	87	100
Confederate Guard	4	63	70	98
Hargrove Blues	4	103	114	124
Detachment of cavalry	1	23	27	28
Signal Corps	7	125	137	145
Camp paroled prisoners	16	191	222	308
Grand total	416	6,641	8,033	10,144

Abstract from Field Return of Troops commanded by Maj. Gen. D. H. Hill, March 10, 1863.

GOLDSBOROUGH, N. C.

Troops.	Present for duty.		Aggregate present.	Aggregate present and absent.
	Officers.	Men.		
Whiting's command [see Department return]				
Garnett's brigade [see Department return]				
Pettigrew's brigade	153	2,947	3,399	4,158
Daniel's brigade	226	3,760	4,517	5,791
Robertson's (cavalry) brigade	90	1,557	1,899	2,146
Reserve artillery	13	335	380	447
Hamilton, N. C.	46	823	1,014	1,141
Weldon, N. C.	26	814	955	1,242
Post of Goldsborough, N. C.	36	557	729	806
Grand total	590	10,793	12,893	15,731

Abstract from Return of the Department of Virginia and North Carolina, commanded by Lieut. Gen. James Longstreet, C. S. Army, for March 10, 1863.

Command.	Present for duty.		Aggregate present.	Aggregate present and absent.
	Officers.	Men.		
Major-General Elzey's command	277	4,825	6,156	7,668
Pickett's division	472	5,697	7,428	12,319
Hood's division	472	6,494	8,420	12,780
Major-General French's command	416	6,641	8,033	10,144
Major-General Hill's command	590	10,793	12,893	15,731
Brigadier-General Whiting's command	434	6,949	8,478	10,626
Lane's (North Carolina) battery	2	131	141	174
Grand total	2,663	41,530	51,549	69,442

Troops in the Department of Virginia and North Carolina, commanded by Lieut. Gen. James Longstreet, for March 10, 1863.

MAJ. GEN. A. ELZEY'S COMMAND.

(Headquarters Richmond, Va.)

Col. T. S. Rhett's command.
Col. Jack Brown's command.

Col. T. J. Page, Chaffin's Bluff.
Captain Lee, Drewry's Bluff.
Wise's Brigade.

MAJ. GEN. S. G. FRENCH'S COMMAND.

(Headquarters, Petersburg, Va.)

Brigadier-General Colston's command.
29th Virginia Regiment.
Detached cavalry.
Confederate Guard.
Hargrove Blues.

Moseley's artillery battalion.
Bradford's battery.
Sturdivant's battery.
Camp of paroled prisoners.
Signal Corps.

MAJ. GEN. D. H. HILL'S COMMAND.

(Headquarters Goldsborough, N. C.)

Daniel's brigade.
Pettigrew's brigade.
Robertson's cavalry brigade.
Reserve artillery.

Troops at Goldsborough, N. C.
Troops at Hamilton, N. C.
Troops at Weldon, N. C.

BRIG. GEN. W. H. C. WHITING'S COMMAND.

(Headquarters Wilmington, N. C.)

Evans' brigade.
Ransom's brigade.
Company F, Tenth North Carolina Troops.
Company B, Sixty-first North Carolina Troops.
Captain Buie's company, North Carolina Troops.
Captain Moore's cavalry.
Captain Newkirk's cavalry.
Captain Smith's cavalry.
3d Battalion North Carolina Artillery.
10th Battalion North Carolina Artillery.
Clark Artillery (heavy).
Captain Adams' light battery.

Capt. [R.] Boyce's (South Carolina) light battery.
Capt. [J. R.] Branch's light battery.
Captain Paris' light battery.
Fort Caswell (six companies).
Fort Fisher (nine companies).
Fort French (one company).
Fort Johnson (two companies).
Fort Saint Philip (four companies).
Light-House Battery (one company).
Bridge guard (Weldon and Wilmington Railroad).
Signal Corps.

MAJ. GEN. J. B. HOOD'S DIVISION.

(In camp near Richmond, Va.)

Anderson's brigade.
Law's brigade.
Robertson's brigade.
Toombs' brigade.

[W. K.] Bachman's (South Carolina) battery.
[H. R.] Garden's battery.
[James] Reilly's battery.

MAJ. GEN. G. E. PICKETT'S DIVISION.

(In camp near Petersburg, Va.)

Armistead's brigade.
Corse's brigade.
Garnett's brigade.

Jenkins' brigade.
Kemper's brigade.

UNATTACHED.

Captain Lane's battery.

NOTE ON ORIGINAL.—Since the date of this report Jenkins' brigade of Pickett's division has been ordered on the Blackwater and Colston's brigade assigned to Pickett's division.

TARBOROUGH, N. C., *March* 10, 1863—11 a. m.

Maj. Gen. D. H. HILL, *Goldsborough, N. C.:*

GENERAL: I was ordered to report to you for orders by telegraph on my arrival at this place, but there is no office nearer than Rocky Mount. I left Petersburg yesterday evening with 800 men; the rest of my brigade, some 600 men, were to follow this morning. I was told the quartermaster of General Longstreet's corps would make arrangements for the transportation of my troops, which was not done, so that I have been able to bring with me only 160. I do not think my command will get here till to-morrow night, if then. I have left all my baggage at Petersburg except cooking utensils. Had I better send for all my camp and garrison equipage? I hope to receive your instructions very soon.

R. B. GARNETT,
Brigadier-General, Commanding.

HEADQUARTERS,
Petersburg, Va., March 12, 1863.

Maj. Gen. ARNOLD ELZEY,
Commanding, Richmond, Va.:

GENERAL: Your letter of —, expressing the views of the honorable Secretary of War with regard to a movement against Suffolk, is received.* Will you do me the favor to explain to the honorable Secretary that I do not think that it would be a prudent move, while the enemy holds twenty-odd thousand men at Newport News, within a few hours' sail of the city of Richmond? To give the move the probability of success a large force should move, and to move a large force would leave Richmond in the power of the enemy should he be quick enough to avail himself of the opportunity. I am erecting some works on the James River below this with a view to keep back transports. When they are completed I desire to operate with my forces; but in order that I may have reasonable hopes of success I should have cavalry. The difficulty that I shall have to contend against with regard to cavalry I have already explained in a previous letter to the War Department. A move against Suffolk, properly aided by cavalry, might be very successful and complete, but without this aid would be but a partial success, which would hardly pay for the movement of the troops. I do not consider it prudent under any circumstances to explain fully my plans, for the reason that if no one knows them but myself the enemy will surely not hear of them. If they are made known to any one but myself that person might in his sleep speak of them and they might reach the enemy.

I am, general, your most obedient servant,
JAMES LONGSTREET,
Lieutenant-General, Commanding.

HEADQUARTERS,
Petersburg, Va., March 12, 1863.

General S. COOPER,
Adjutant and Inspector General:

GENERAL: Your letter directing that the troops from Western Virginia be returned to their proper commands and that General Davis

---

* See p. 871.

brigade be sent to Goldsborough is received. Please designate what troops are here from Western Virginia, as I have no record to show it. I had ordered General Garnett's brigade to North Carolina before your letter was received, and hope that this may supersede the necessity of the move of Davis' brigade. General Davis is on the Blackwater and occupies one of the most important positions in the department. He is familiar with the country where he is and if taken from there a brigade would be sent there which would be placing them and General Davis in positions which are strange to all parties. Another reason for sending Garnett's brigade was that it was thought that it might have a good effect to send some Virginia troops to that State. If it is necessary to move General Davis' brigade, however, it will be done with pleasure.

I remain, sir, very respectfully, your obedient servant,

JAMES LONGSTREET,
Lieutenant-General.

NAVY DEPARTMENT, C. S. A.,
Richmond, March 13, 1863.

Maj. Gen. D. H. HILL, C. S. A.,
Headquarters, Goldsborough, N. C. :

DEAR SIR : Having directed Flag-Officer Lynch to invoke your aid to procure iron in North Carolina for the completion of gunboats, I beg leave to say that the water defenses of Wilmington would, I think, be regarded with satisfaction if the two iron-clad sloops under his charge there were completed. Covered with 4 inches of iron, placed at an angle of 36°, and mounting each four heavy guns they would be floating forts of the most formidable character. We have obtained from Georgia and South Carolina sufficient iron for one of these vessels.

The demands for armor for vessels under construction in those States preclude us from obtaining more iron there at present, and unless we can get supplies from North Carolina for the rolling-mill at Atlanta, Ga., we shall be unable to complete the second vessel at present.

We can construct boats for Albemarle and Pamlico Sounds, which, in my judgment, will expel or destroy the enemy if we can obtain the iron to plate them.

Ten or 12 miles of railroad iron will meet these immediate wants and in taking it rails unfit for service on the roads could be selected. Iron thus taken from the roads of North Carolina would be rolled into plates at Richmond or Atlanta and returned for the defenses of that State.

May I therefore ask you to aid Flag-Officer Lynch in this important service ?

I am, respectfully, your obedient servant,

S. R. MALLORY,
Secretary of the Navy.

DISTRICT HEADQUARTERS,
Richmond, Va., March 14, 1863.

Lieutenant-General LONGSTREET, *Commanding :*

GENERAL : I explained your views to the Secretary of War and showed him your letter. He said you were perfectly right, and he approves your course. General Lee reached here yesterday. No other news.

With great respect, your obedient servant,

ARNOLD ELZEY,
Major-General.

BRIGADE HEADQUARTERS,
Chaffin's Farm, Va., March 14, 1863.

Maj. Gen. ARNOLD ELZEY,
    Commanding, &c., Richmond, Va.:

GENERAL : I respectfully beg to submit the following tabular statement of this command, in accordance with the circular from the Adjutant and Inspector General's Office, March 10, 1863 :

The Fourth Virginia Heavy Artillery, Col. J. Thomas Goode ;
Twenty-sixth Virginia Infantry, Col. P. R. Page ; Forty-sixth Virginia
Infantry, Col. R. T. W. Duke ; Fifty-ninth Virginia Infantry, Col. W.
B. Tabb ; cavalry, Holcombe Legion (four companies), Col. W. P.
Shingler ; Thirty-second Battalion Virginia Cavalry, Maj. J. R. Robert-
son ; Company D, Tenth Virginia Cavalry, Capt. L. J. Hawley ; Com-
pany A, Light Artillery Battalion, Capt. A. D. Armistead ; Company
B, Light Artillery Battalion, Capt. D. A. French—battallion com-
manded by Maj. A. W. Stark.

Very respectfully, your obedient servant,
HENRY A. WISE,
Brigadier-General.

———

HEADQUARTERS, *March* 15, 1863.

Brig. Gen. W. H. C. WHITING,
    Commanding, [*Wilmington*], *N. C.:*

GENERAL: Your letter of the 4th instant was received on my return
to this place.   You will need more troops for the defense of Wilmington
when there is a probability of attack there, but I do not agree with you
in your desire to mass troops there in order to have them for the attack.
On the contrary, I think that every soldier should be kept busy.   If
the troops at Wilmington are not constantly employed there they should
be in the field, annoying the enemy whenever and wherever it may be
done.   They should not, however, be so far removed from Wilmington
as to be out of supporting distance should they be needed there.   I
should think that a brigade was quite enough for sudden emergencies,
particularly in case those used in the field are placed between you and
the enemy.   If we hold isolated positions by detachments the enemy
will at his pleasure move upon the different points and take them in
detail.

I remain, very respectfully, your most obedient servant,
JAMES LONGSTREET,
Lieutenant-General.

———

HEADQUARTERS,
Petersburg, Va., March 15, 1863.

Maj. Gen. D. H. HILL, *Goldsborough, N. C.:*

GENERAL: If your observation upon your expedition leads you to
suppose that any important results may obtain by a stronger expedition
against New Berne advise me at once, and I will endeavor to assist you
in making more complete arrangements.   I can spare the Whitworth
that I have here as soon as I can get "Long Tom" and "Charlie," as
they are called, in my battery at Fort Powhatan.   I have established a
battery at Fort Powhatan for the purpose of intercepting transports
should they attempt to pass up James River.   If the reduction of New
Berne is practicable in field operations, I submit the following as my

plan, and the only one that I can see, viz: Have three brigades, with one Whitworth, down on the south side of the Neuse; one of Whiting's brigades and one Whitworth up to join you near New Berne, and one brigade down on the north side of the Neuse, with the Whitworth that I have here. If we can drop a ball into the fort every minute from these directions the troops may become frightened and surrender. If the matter is practicable, I will either join you myself or, remaining here, will make a strong diversion against Suffolk. I shall start for the Blackwater on the day after to-morrow and expect to be absent six days. If you wish to telegraph me, do so at Franklin; that is, if you wish to do so in the next four days.

I remain, very respectfully, your most obedient servant,

JAMES LONGSTREET,
Lieutenant-General.

N. B.—This must not go beyond yourself.

HDQRS. FORCES NEAR DREWRY'S BLUFF, VA.,
March 15, 1863.

Maj. T. O. CHESTNEY,
Assistant Adjutant-General, Richmond, Va.:

MAJOR: In compliance with orders received from Major-General Elzey's headquarters, I respectfully submit to you the following tabular report of my command, viz:

Maj. B. H. Gee, commanding Fifty-ninth Georgia Infantry Regiment; Capt. W. A. Graham,* commanding Second Squadron, Second North Carolina Cavalry.

I am, major, very respectfully, your obedient servant,

JACK BROWN,
Colonel, Commanding Post.

SWIFT CREEK, *March* 15, [1863]—9 p. m.

General D. H. HILL:

A scout from Street's Ferry, sent down for the purpose, reports that there is no doubt of the landing of a large force, and from the noise he thinks they are fixing a pontoon over the Neuse to bring their infantry over. Captain Whitford is convinced that we shall have it to-morrow. It seems so to me. Send me a regiment of cavalry immediately and come yourself. My danger is on my right flank and rear; by marching from Greenville you can protect both. Bring your provisions and ammunition. Send them soon, directly to Kinston. I have no couriers.

J. J. PETTIGREW,
Brigadier-General.

HEADQUARTERS ARMY OF NORTHERN VIRGINIA,
March 16, 1863.

Lieut. Gen. JAMES LONGSTREET,
Commanding, &c., Petersburg, Va.:

GENERAL: As far as can be ascertained from my own observation, from the reports from our scouts on the opposite side of the Rappahannock, and from what the citizens say, I am led to believe that none of

*Since ordered to Petersburg.

the army of General Hooker have left the vicinity of Aquia, except the corps of General Smith, which went to Newport News. It is also reported that it is General Hooker's intention to cross the river and advance as soon as the state of the roads will permit, and that in fact he has issued repeated orders to that effect. I am not fully informed as to their apparent intentions, strength, &c., on the south side of the James River, but we should be prepared to concentrate to meet him wherever he should advance in force. From present indications it is fair to presume that we shall be called upon to engage him first on the Rappahannock, and I desire you to be prepared for this movement, and make endeavors to keep yourself advised of the disposition and preparations of the enemy on our front for moving the troops recently detached from the First Corps, or such of them or others as may be necessary in that direction. As our numbers will not admit of our meeting him on equality everywhere we must endeavor, by judicious dispositions, to be enabled to make our troops available in any quarter where they may be needed, after the emergency passes in one place to transfer them to any other point that may be threatened. Please let me hear from you on this subject.

R. E. LEE.

HEADQUARTERS,
Wilmington, N. C., March 16, 1863.

General S. COOPER,
    Adjutant and Inspector General, Richmond, Va. :

GENERAL : I send you to-day a tabular statement of my command, as required by the letter of Maj. [S. W.] Melton, of the 10th instant. I call your attention to the following list of unattached companies of heavy artillery : Captain McBryde's company, 92 strong, Fort Caswell ; Capt. W. A. Holland's company, 54 strong, Fort Johnson ; Capts. A. McRae's company, 143 strong, and George Tait's company, 84 strong, Fort Fisher ; Capt. Calvin Barnes' company, 61 strong, Fort Saint Philip ; Capts. D. M. Beuie's company, 78 strong, R. G. Rankin's company, 116 strong, city garrison ; W. B. Lewis, Company A, 86 strong, H. M. Barnes, Company B, 90 strong, and C. [M.] T. McCauley, Company C, 94 strong. Total, 898. The last three constitute the Tenth North Carolina Battalion, and under the command of Maj. W. L. Young. These companies are in service for three years or the war; are well drilled and armed. They are heavy artillery, and have been raised in the district for the defense of the Cape Fear and Wilmington. I think it will be better on all accounts and that the efficiency of these troops will be promoted by organizing them into a regiment. Should a move from here become necessary this will have to be done. I propose that the ten companies as they stand in order of the rank of captains shall be constituted or accepted as a regiment of Confederate troops; and as they are already in service I recommend for appointment the following field officers: To be colonel, Robert Tansill, captain, C. S. Army ; to be lieutenant-colonel, John J. Hedrick, major battalion of artillery, C. S. Army, and to be major, W. L. Young, major battalion of artillery, C. S. Army. Capt. [Robert] Tansill, C. S. Army (Regular Army), formerly an officer of Marines and late colonel First [Second] Virginia Artillery, is a Virginian, is now acting inspector-general, and has been frequently recommended for promotion. His knowledge of the profession is thorough and extensive. I know no officer whom I should prefer to command a regiment. Maj. John J. Hedrick is from this town and

State, and is a most active and indefatigable officer. He is now in command of Fort Saint Philip. The works he has constructed both there and at Fort Fisher entitle him to great credit. He is an artillery officer of rare promise and an excellent disciplinarian. Major Young is also from this State, and commands a battalion of three companies. He is a young officer of great energy, and has displayed great zeal in the defense of this place. These officers are all on duty here and with the troops it is proposed they shall command. If you approve of this suggestion please to let me know and lay this matter before the President for his action.

Very respectfully,

W. H. C. WHITING,
Brigadier-General.

HEADQUARTERS, *March* 17, 1863.
Maj. Gen. D. H. HILL, *Goldsborough, N. C.*:

GENERAL: Your telegram of report of the scout Harrison is received. If it is confirmed you had better move Garnett's brigade near enough to you to be in easy supporting distance and keep me advised, that I may send you other re-enforcements. I shall hold three other brigades ready for you. Meantime get all the provisions together that you can and have your supply of ammunition well looked to. If you do not get satisfactory information otherwise put your cavalry together and send it with a battery toward the enemy's rear and learn what the enemy is going to do.

I remain, very respectfully, your most obedient servant,

JAMES LONGSTREET,
Lieutenant-General, Commanding.

HEADQUARTERS, *March* 17, 1863.
General M. JENKINS, *Franklin, N. C.*:

GENERAL: General D. H. Hill telegraphs the arrival of re-enforcements at New Berne. Those at Suffolk are probably intended for New Berne.

JAMES LONGSTREET,
Lieutenant-General, Commanding.

HEADQUARTERS, *March* 17, 1863.
General R. E. LEE,
Commanding, &c., Fredericksburg, Va.:

GENERAL: Your letter of the 16th is just received. I have Hood's division on the railroad ready for a move in any direction, and have kept him there with the view to some such emergency as indicated in your letter. The order for the return of the troops from Western Virginia to their old positions and some movements that I thought best to make in order to draw the enemy out into some development of his plans have made it necessary to detach some of General Pickett's division. I shall be ready to join you with Hood's division at any moment unless there is a fine opportunity to strike a decided blow here, in which case I think I had better act promptly and trust to your being able to hold the force in your front in check until I can join you. The force at Newport News is reported to-day as moving to re-enforce Suffolk. I fear that the real object is to join Foster at New Berne. If this is the intention I shall be obliged to move all of Pickett's division down to Goldsborough. I have tolerably accurate information of this force and put it down at 20,000 full, but its condition is such that I do not regard it as certain to succeed in any desperate undertaking. The prisoners taken at Arkansas Post are expected here to-day. If they arrive they will be organized and armed at once, and will help us along wonderfully. I am about to start out for the Blackwater, and will write to you more fully on my return.

I am, general, most respectfully, your obedient servant,

JAMES LONGSTREET,
Lieutenant-General.

HEADQUARTERS,
Kinston, N. C., March 17, 1863.

Maj. Gen. D. H. HILL,
Commanding at Goldsborough, N. C.:

GENERAL: I herewith inclose dispatches* from Generals Garnett and Pettigrew; they came directed to you; I opened them for the purpose of gaining information of the enemy's movements. I have not heard from General Pettigrew since I saw you. I think, however, that he is not in any immediate danger, or I should have heard from him or Captain Whitford. I have sent a courier to Captain Whitford to find out the state of affairs there and will let you know as soon as I hear. General Robertson I have not yet heard from. Mr. J. C. Washington has a contract with the Confederate Government for the delivery of a large amount of iron, and he has a lot of corn here to enable him to feed his operatives. He has offered to exchange this corn for the same quantity in the vicinity of Tarborough, and as it is more abundant there than here I think it would be well to make the exchange. Will I be allowed to make the exchange? The quartermaster there could give him the quantity that he turns over to the quartermaster at this post. I have received no report this morning from my pickets.

Very respectfully,

JUNIUS DANIEL,
Brigadier-General.

HEADQUARTERS,
Petersburg, Va., March 18, 1863.

General R. E. LEE,
Commanding, &c., Fredericksburg, Va.:

GENERAL: Your letter of 10.30 p. m. yesterday is received. I do not think it would be well to draw off any portion of Pickett's division at present. All of it cannot well be taken from here as long as the enemy holds this force of his so near Richmond. The force at Newport News and Suffolk cannot be less than 26,000. We shall have to meet that with hardly a third, including Pickett's division; but there are three brigades of Pickett's division near here, which may possibly be thrown up by rail; that is if the enemy makes no effort to advance by the south side. I think, however, that he will make a diversion from Suffolk, and as strong as is in him.

Your letter,† in relation to supplies, of yesterday is this moment re-

---

*Not found.   †Not found; but see Longstreet to Hill, same date.

ceived. All things considered I now think that our better plan would have been to fight the enemy on the Rappahannock with the force that you have there, or slightly diminished even, and to leave the force that was here to drive back the enemy in North Carolina and draw out the supplies there. I cannot divest myself of the opinion that an obstinate resistance on the Rappahannock will hold that line, and the force that I had here would then do to drive the enemy out of North Carolina, where it seems we must get our supplies. With the force left here by the with-drawal of Hood's division nothing can be done more than to hold our fortified positions and railroads, and the latter is somewhat doubtful. If it is necessary to give ground anywhere it seems to me that it would have been better to retire your force across the Anna, and to keep possession of all that part of North Carolina where we may be able to get supplies. From your report of the scarcity of supplies with you I fear that Hood's division may be more than you can supply, and I doubt if it can reach you in time by marching. I shall therefore try and have it sent by railroad, unless I get authority by telegraph to stop it. I shall go to Richmond this afternoon and await there further intelligence.

I remain, general, your most obedient servant,

JAMES LONGSTREET,
Lieutenant-General.

P. S.—The enemy is re-enforcing at New Berne and at Suffolk. His intentions it is presumed are to make diversions on both points when he moves to cross the Rappahannock. Success at either point will be pushed, of course, unless he fails again on the Rappahannock.

HDQRS. DEPT. OF VIRGINIA AND NORTH CAROLINA,
March 18, 1863.

Maj. Gen. D. H. HILL,
Commanding, &c., Goldsborough, N. C.:

GENERAL: The commanding general has received your letter of last night. He leaves this afternoon for Richmond. He wrote you fully this morning, and the letter is sent you with this. By his direction I have telegraphed you that you might go as you propose and use Ransom's brigade. I have also telegraphed to General Whiting to respond to your call for that brigade. The enemy seems to be pressing on the Rappahannock. It looks as if a battle must soon be fought there.

I am, general, very respectfully, your obedient servant,

G. MOXLEY SORREL,
Assistant Adjutant-General.

HEADQUARTERS, *March* 18, 1863.

Maj. Gen. D. H. HILL:

GENERAL: I have just received a letter from General Lee, calling for Hood's division back upon the Rappahannock. The enemy is reported across with cavalry and artillery at Kelly's Ford and attempting with infantry at United States Ford. General Lee calls for myself also and Pickett's division. The latter, I think, cannot be spared; at all events not till we ascertain what is likely to be the disposition of the force lately held at Newport News. I shall start back to Rappahannock to-morrow unless other news is received. If the enemy moves against you you will have to try and hold your positions by obstinate resistance. The force [lately] at Newport News is supposed to be at Suffolk, and a part of it is supposed to be the re-enforcements reported at New Berne. Tr/ and be well advised of the troops in your front, and if any re-en-forcements come from Charleston call on General Beauregard for some of his forces, advising him, of course, that the enemy is re-enforced in your front from his. If you find that you cannot hold and protect your railroad, then Wilmington must be looked to and held at all hazards. It cannot be long before we will be able to help you from the Rappahan-nock. I doubt now if we will be able to give you any further aid from there until the battle is fought on the Rappahannock. The en-emy may advance by the Blackwater with his re-enforcements or they may be moved down to re-enforce the garrison at New Berne. What-ever arrangement he makes it seems now that we must first overcome his force at Fredericksburg.

I remain, general, your obedient servant,

JAMES LONGSTREET,
Lieutenant-General.

RICHMOND, VA., *March* 19, 1863.

General R. E. LEE,
Commanding, Fredericksburg, Va.:

GENERAL: I wrote you hastily yesterday, which partially answered your letter of the 17th instant. In one of your letters you ask what I can do toward procuring supplies in North Carolina. I can, I think, get all of the supplies in that State if I can use my forces; but if the two divisions are to be held in readiness to join you, or even one of them, I can do nothing. The enemy has 40,000 men, at the lowest esti-mate, between York River and the Cape Fear. I have about the same, but almost every available man for active operations must be held to re-enforce you; therefore I cannot use them. If the divisions of Pickett and Hood are to be withdrawn whenever the enemy on the Rappahan-nock advances we shall leave a force of twenty-odd thousand near Suffolk, with no force to oppose it, except Davis' brigade, and on this side of the James River the usual garrison of the city. A tolerably respectable move from Suffolk would give the enemy possession of Pe-tersburg fortified. He could take it without the loss of a man. That point in his possession North Carolina would soon be at his command from the railroad east. That line would cut off most of the supplies that we depend upon for our sustenance. I know that it is the habit with individuals in all armies to represent their own positions as the most important ones, and it may be that this feeling is operating with me; but I am not prompted by any desire to do, or to attempt to do, great things. I only wish to do what I regard as my duty—give you the full benefit of my views. It seems to me to be a matter of prime necessity with us to keep the enemy out of North Carolina in order that we may draw out all the supplies there, and if we give him ground at all it would be better to do so from the Rappahannock. It is right, as you say, to concentrate and crush him; but will it be better to concen-trate upon his grand army rather than on his detachments and then make a grand concentration on the grand army? If we draw off from the front of his grand army we ought to be able to crush rapidly his detachments, and at the same time hold the grand army in check as far back as the South Anna at least, particularly while the roads are so very bad, then concentrate on the grand army and try and dispose of that. We have been ready to fight for the last three months, and have only failed to do so because we could not reach his force on the Rappahannock, and because it was not convenient to touch him elsewhere. If we delay until he is again ready to give battle we give him all that he can desire, besides we fail to avail ourselves of the opportunity to produce a favorable political impression at the North, or rather we fail to reap the rewards of that impression already produced. If we cripple him only, a little at one place and then another, we may mutually produce grand results. I hope that I have gone into details sufficiently to give you my views, but I am always ready to do and to say all that I can.

I remain, general, most respectfully, your most obedient servant,

JAMES LONGSTREET,
Lieutenant-General, Commanding.

General Hood is ordered back to his old camp.

ADJT. AND INSP. GEN.'S OFFICE, WAR DEPT., C. S. A.,
Richmond, Va., March 19, 1863.

Lieut. Gen. JAMES LONGSTREET,
Commanding, &c., Richmond, Va.:

GENERAL: The Secretary of War directs me to say to you that in accordance with the telegram received from General Lee you are directed to recall the divisions of Generals Hood and Pickett and to retain them in their former positions or such others as you may select. In your absence, and for the sake of expedition, similar orders were issued directly to Generals Hood and Pickett yesterday.

I am, very respectfully, your obedient servant,

JOHN WITHERS,
Lieutenant-Colonel and Assistant Adjutant-General.

HEADQUARTERS ARMY OF NORTHERN VIRGINIA,
March 19, 1863.

Lieut. Gen. JAMES LONGSTREET,
Commanding, &c.:

GENERAL: On my arrival here yesterday I learned that the cavalry force of the enemy which crossed at Kelly's Ford had subsequently retired, and that the reported attempt to force a passage at the United States Ford had not been made. I therefore sent a telegram to General Cooper, requesting that the divisions ordered up here might be stopped and returned to their former positions. I need not remind you that it will be necessary to maintain great vigilance in your front as well as here, and to hold the troops at both points ready to co-operate whenever it is correctly ascertained where the attack of the enemy will fall. I hope you will be able to act on the suggestions contained in my letter from Richmond relative to obtaining all the supplies possible of forage and subsistence from North Carolina and turn all the energies of your department in that direction.

With great respect, your obedient servant,

R. E. LEE,
General.

STATE OF NORTH CAROLINA, EXECUTIVE DEPARTMENT,
Raleigh, N. C., March 19, 1863.

General R. E. LEE:

His Excellency Governor Vance has received information that certain soldiers belonging to the brigades of Generals Ramseur and Hoke are now under arrest and are being tried for desertion. His Excellency is deeply pained to learn this, and directs me to communicate to you the facts and circumstances connected with the return of these men to the army. While Maj. Gen. G. W. Smith was in command of this department he caused an order to be issued extending a full pardon (except forfeiture of pay for the period of unauthorized absence) to all enlisted men absent without leave who should voluntarily return to their respective commands on or before February 10. Upon consultation between General Smith and the Governor it was thought that a proclamation by His Excellency, appealing to the patriotism and State pride of absentees, would induce their speedy return to duty. A proclamation was accordinglly issued, and the reasonable expectation as to its effect was fully realized and hundreds were induced to return to their colors. The period at first limited was so brief that numbers in remote parts of the State were unable to comply. With a knowledge of this fact, and in conformity with an order of General French, another proclamation was issued extending the time to March 5. It is true that General Smith's order could only extend to his own department, but His Excellency thought it right to extend it to all North Carolina soldiers. Copies of the order of General Smith and the proclamation of the Governor are herewith inclosed.* In the opinion of His Excellency the punishment of these men would be a gross violation of justice and good faith, and he enters his most solemn protest against it. In issuing these proclamations he was actuated by a sincere and earnest desire to promote the interest of the public service and he had reason to believe that his course would meet the approbation of the Confederate authorities, and he trusts and believes that in this reasonable hope he will not be disappointed. He will not allow himself to doubt that your sense of justice and right will induce you to cause all such soldiers to be immediately discharged from arrest.

With sentiments of the highest respect, your obedient servant,

DAVID A. BARNES,
Aide-de-Camp to the Governor.

ENGINEER BUREAU,
Richmond, Va., March 19, 1863.

Maj. W. T. ALEXANDER,
Quartermaster and Inspector of Transportation:

MAJOR: I have the pleasure to inclose a tabular statement of the distances from the Capitol to the batteries around Richmond. The distances both by the road and by air-line are given.

---

* General Smith's order and the Governor's second proclamation not found.

Distances of the batteries around Richmond from the Capitol.

No. of battery.	Location.	Distance by road.	Distance by air-line.
		Miles.	*Miles.*
1	On James River, opposite Drewry's Island	3¼	2⅜
2	Marion Hill	3¼	2⅝
3	Mount Erin	3	2½
4	Blakey's Mill road	2¼	1¾
5	Stoney Run	2½	1¾
6	Mechanicsville turnpike	2¼	1⅝
7	Mount Comfort Central Railroad	2⅜	1¼
8	Mitchell's track	2¼	1¾
9	Brooke turnpike	2¼	1⅞
10	Fair Ground	2¼	2¼
11	Wertham plank-road	2½	2
13	Danville Railroad	2¼	1½
14	Danville Railroad	3½	2¼
15	Coal-Pit turnpike	3	2½
16	Broad Rock Island	3¾	2¾

Very respectfully, &c.,

J. F. GILMER,
Colonel Engineers and Chief of Bureau.

Abstract from Field Return of Pickett's division, Department of Virginia and North Carolina, temporarily commanded by Brig. Gen. J. L. Kemper, March 19, 1863.

NEAR PETERSBURG, VA.

Troops.	Present for duty.				Aggregate present.	Aggregate present and absent.
	Infantry.		Artillery.			
	Officers.	Men.	Officers.	Men.		
Garnett's brigade						
Armistead's brigade	93	1,279			1,695	2,712
Kemper's brigade	94	1,227			1,585	2,900
Corse's brigade	78	922			1,209	2,012
Artillery battalion			17	374	434	537
Grand total	265	3,428	17	374	4,923	8,161

NOTE FROM RETURN.—Fifty-seventh Virginia Regiment, aggregate present last report, 528; on detached duty at Fort Powhatan. First Virginia Regiment, aggregate present last report, 206; on detached service at Fort Powhatan. Bradford's battery assigned to duty with the division since last report. [Garnett's brigade] on detached duty in North Carolina.

Abstract from Field Return of troops commanded by Maj. Gen. S. G. French, March 20, 1863.

Troops.	Present for duty.		Aggregate present.	Aggregate present and absent.
	Officers.	Men.		
Brig. Gen. M. Jenkins' command [no report]				
29th Regiment Virginia Volunteers	36	696	732	915
Moseley's artillery battalion	8	140	166	179
Sturdivant's battery	3	75	87	100
Confederate Guard	4	62	72	98
Hargrove Blues	4	103	114	125
Detachment of cavalry	1	23	24	25
Signal Corps	9	124	137	146
Camp paroled prisoners	11	190	218	302
On duty in hospitals, Petersburg	22		80	80
Grand total	98	1,413	1,630	1,970

HEADQUARTERS,
Petersburg, Va., March 20, 1863.

General S. COOPER,
Adjutant and Inspector General, Richmond, Va.:

GENERAL: I have the honor to forward herewith a rough statement*
of the cavalry force in this department. As soon as I can get accurate
statements of the regiments and detached companies I propose to organize the force into two brigades, and desire General Ransom's promo
tion as major-general, to command the cavalry. Col. E. D. Hall is highly
recommended by Maj. Gen. D. H. Hill for brigadier-general of cavalry.
I hope that he may be appointed to take the Second Brigade. If this
force cannot be formed into a division of cavalry I desire authority to
transfer General Ransom from his position in the infantry to the charge
of the cavalry as a brigade. I have already explained to the Department the difficulties in the way of efficient operations of the cavalry, and
desire that some action may be had which will increase its efficiency.

I remain, sir, very respectfully, your most obedient servant,
JAMES LONGSTREET,
Lieutenant-General, Commanding.

HEADQUARTERS,
Kinston, N. C., March 20, 1863.

Maj. Gen. D. H. HILL,
Commanding at Goldsborough, N. C.:

GENERAL: I send up names of those who acted well in skirmishes on
the 7th instant. The names of those who acted well last week I will
send up as soon as the commanders can make them out. The charges
against Forstler, the deserter, go up in the morning. Major Guion reported this morning, and I directed him to examine the country with a
view of making a line from the work around the obstructions to Washington's Hill. I will report as soon as it can be made. I would like
very much to have Coleman or some good engineer officer. The regi-

---

* Not found.

ment is ready to make the demonstration upon Core Creek. The weather is still bad, and by starting to-morrow it will make the attack upon Sunday, and I would prefer that the men should rest on that day if any other day will answer as well. Please telegraph me whether you desire the move to be made to-morrow.

Very respectfully, &c.,

JUNIUS DANIEL,
Brigadier-General.

HEADQUARTERS,
Petersburg, Va., March 20, 1863.

Maj. Gen. D. H. HILL, *Commanding, &c.* :

GENERAL : General Kemper's brigade is on the road to co-operate with Garnett in an expedition against Washington. I will send General Pickett to take charge of the expedition. I desire that you will collect and give General Pickett such information, guides, and written instructions as you deem proper, and to telegraph me what number of batteries will be required for the expedition and the kind of pieces. I shall give General Pickett general instructions but subject to such changes as you may see fit to make. I will send you a copy of them. Meanwhile I wish you to continue your arrangements, and if the expedition had better be made immediately do not allow this to delay it. I send General Pickett to take charge of it, because I think it prudent that you should be at Goldsborough with all the force now there to watch the enemy and prevent any movement against the expedition from New Berne. If there is no probability of such a move nor of trouble at Goldsborough from the force at New Berne you had better proceed at once on the expedition against Washington if it is already prepared.

I remain, very respectfully, your most obedient servant,

JAMES LONGSTREET,
Lieutenant-General, Commanding.

P. S.—In your letter of the 16th, giving some account of your expedition against New Berne, you intimate that there may have been some desire on the part of the Department " to perpetrate a swindle " upon you in putting you in command in North Carolina. I presume that this was not intended as an official communication and have not forwarded it. I hope that you will send up another account of you trip.

RICHMOND, *March* 21, 1863.

General J. H. WINDER,
Commanding Department of Henrico, &c. :

GENERAL : I am instructed by the Secretary of War to ask that you will strengthen the night guard of this building by adding another sentinel.

He will report for orders to Mr. Peebles, disbursing clerk of the War Department.

Very respectfully, &c.,

JOHN WITHERS,
Assistant Adjutant-General.

HEADQUARTERS,
Petersburg, Va., March 21, 1863.

General D. H. HILL,
    Commanding, &c., Goldsborough, N. C. :

GENERAL : Your letters of the 19th and 20th are received. If Ransom's brigade is brought to Goldsborough you will not need Kemper's, and it had better be returned at once, and Ransom's being at Goldsborough will relieve me of all anxiety about that place and save the necessity of sending General Pickett down. I have ordered my Whitworth gun to be sent you for the expedition, but I cannot let it go any farther, as General Lee regards it as part of his command, and will require it if he recalls me to his aid. The snow is 10 or 12 inches deep, and the Whitworth at Fort Powhatan. I fear therefore that I will not be able to get it here in time to ship it to-morrow afternoon, but it shall go as soon as it is possible to get it off. Send some one to meet it and conduct it to you. It will be ordered to Tarborough from here.

I desire you to move from Greenville as quickly as possible. The success of such expeditions depends altogether upon their promptness and action. If you need Kemper at any point in your rear keep him for the time, but send him back as soon as possible. General Pickett will not be sent down, as General Ransom's presence at Goldsborough will satisfy all conditions. You must always have an eye to drawing out the supplies from the country in which you move. You will not confine yourself to the prices fixed by the Department in purchasing supplies, but give the market price and liberal prices for transportation whenever you purchase near the enemy's lines ; and when you purchase and find that you can draw off the supplies, take every pound that is in the market, and when you find it necessary impress at the market prices. If it is necessary, you can leave Garnett's brigade to protect trains, &c., while hauling. I suppose that you will need General Pettigrew's at Goldsborough. If not, you can also use it in aiding you to get out supplies.

I remain, very respectfully, your most obedient servant,
JAMES LONGSTREET,
Lieutenant-General.

HEADQUARTERS,
Kinston, N. C., March 21, 1863.

Maj. Gen. D. H. HILL,
    Commanding at Goldsborough, N. C. :

GENERAL : Your note of this date has been received. From its contents I presume you intend me to await Kemper's arrival, should he be accidentally detained beyond Monday. I understand Blount Hall to be the place you desire me to go to. I think it a more suitable position than Snow Hill for the reason you assign. The place I refer to is, I presume, the one you mean ; it is on one of the roads leading from this place to Greenville, about 18 or 20 miles from here, between the Contentnea and Greenville, and some 6 or 8 miles from the Neuse. I shall take with me three days' rations. I have but four pieces of artillery now belonging to my brigade, General Pettigrew not having returned the two rifle guns. I wish to take one of the four-gun batteries here ; there will then be left twelve pieces besides those Kemper will bring with him. I would like to have the troops I leave behind on picket duty relieved as soon as possible. I think they can be relieved on Wednesday, and wish you would so order it. Nethercutt's people will be here and they know the country thoroughly. I will not send the regiment to Core Creek on Monday, as it could not join me before Thursday or Friday, would leave my brigade very much scattered, and would very much impair its efficiency. Kemper can make the demonstration if you still desire it. Colonel Lewis will remain in command of the outposts until my men are relieved, and he can give all the information. The regiment that I should have sent knew nothing at all of the country. With Nethercutt's people there will be no lack of guides.

I am, general, very respectfully, &c.,

JUNIUS DANIEL,
Brigadier-General.

HEADQUARTERS,
Petersburg, Va., March 21, 1863.

General R. E. LEE, *Commanding, &c.* :

GENERAL: Your letter of the 19th is received. I am doing all that I can to draw the supplies from the eastern portion of North Carolina, but have been obliged to detach portions of General Pickett's division for that purpose. My operations must be very limited, as I do not feel authorized to use Hood's division for any purpose, as it would take him so [far] from you that he would not be able to join you at Fredericksburg. In this connection I would suggest that the troops should be taken up by rail instead of the artillery. I think that you will need the infantry more than the artillery. When I arrived at Richmond I found that the troops were moving up to join you by marching and the battalion of artillery shipping by rail. The movement of the latter had better be delayed than that of the former.

I remain, general, most respectfully, your obedient servant,

JAMES LONGSTREET.

P. S.—I send you a report just received. Reports reach me from various directions leading to the same conclusion. The commander on the Blackwater has reported the arrival of large re-enforcements at Suffolk. I believe that an advantageous battle could be made at Suffolk in the next fifteen days, but at least one division in addition to what we have would be necessary.

Most respectfully,

J. L.

HEADQUARTERS ARMY OF NORTHERN VIRGINIA,
March 21, 1863.

Lieut. Gen. JAMES LONGSTREET,
Commanding Department, &c., Petersburg, Va.:

GENERAL: I have received your letter of the 19th instant. I had hoped that you would have been able with the troops in North Carolina to have accomplished the object proposed in my letter of the 17th* and did not suppose that you would have required Pickett's and Hood's divisions, as from information I received the enemy between the Roanoke and Tar is feeble. I still think if you can retain them in reserve, to be thrown on any point attacked or where a blow can be struck, it will be the best disposition of them. If, however, you see an opportu-

---

* Not found.

nity of dealing a damaging blow, or of driving him from any important positions, do not be idle, but act promptly. If circumstances render it impossible or disadvantageous for you to rejoin this army when attacked we must withdraw toward you, if we cannot resist alone.

In operating against any point accessible to the enemy's gunboats be prepared for them. I am confident that at all times and in all places you will do all that can be done for the defense of the country and advancement of the service, and are ready to co-operate or act singly as circumstances dictate. I only wish you therefore to keep me advised of your movements that I may shape mine accordingly, and not to feel trammeled in your operations other than is required by the general plan of operations when an opportunity offers for you to advance the object of the campaign.

I am, with great respect, very truly, yours,

R. E. LEE,
General.

STATE OF NORTH CAROLINA, EXECUTIVE DEPARTMENT,
Raleigh, N. C., March 21, 1863.

Hon. JAMES A. SEDDON,
Secretary of War :

SIR : Yours of 7th instant, inclosing letters from Lieutenant-Colonel Cook and General Jones, in relation to impressment of forage by a detachment of General Jenkins' cavalry, has been received. I am sorry to see that the charge of impressment is denied upon the authority of Sergeant Hale. The concurrent testimony of the citizens of about twenty counties with at least fifty letters to that effect in my office would seem to be sufficient to establish a fact of general notoriety. Those men were in several detachments, operating in as many different counties, and Sergeant Hale hardly could know what they were all doing at the same time. Their method was to go to a farmer's house and tell him they wanted corn at $1.50 per bushel, and if he did not sell it they would take it. In some instances their quartermaster attended public sales and publicly notified the assemblage (most of them families of absent soldiers) that they need not bid for the corn; that they were determined to have it. Yielding where resistance would have been useless they (the cavalry) took the corn at such price as they saw proper to pay, and this is not impressment ! I beg leave also to assure you that the imputations indulged in by General Jones and Lieutenant-Colonel Cook against the loyalty of the people of that region (I suppose also upon the authority of Sergeant Hale) are entirely without foundation in fact, the refusal to take Confederate money, if such was the case, originating solely in the fact that they did not have the corn to sell. Neither North Carolina money nor gold could buy an article which was not in the country. That country, to my personal knowledge, may safely challenge any similar region in the South to show a better muster-roll in the army. But that is not the matter at issue. I complain that a large body of broken-down cavalry horses are in North Carolina, eating up the subsistence of the people in a region desolated by drought and reduced to the verge of starvation ; impressing it at prices about one-half the market rates. The people or the horses must suffer. I ask for the removal of the horses. Is it denied or refused? That is the question. I beg leave to disabuse your mind of the impression which it seems to entertain, that I objected to these impressments because they were for Virginia cavalry. By no means. I did not term them such, at least did not so intend to term them. I have no prejudice against the troops from any State engaged in defending the common cause, but I am unwilling to see the bread taken from the mouths of women and children for the use of any troops, when those troops might be easily removed to regions where there is corn to sell, and I earnestly request once more that they may be so removed.

Very respectfully, your obedient servant,

Z. B. VANCE.

[Indorsements.]

MARCH 25, 1863.

Respectfully referred to Maj. Gen. S. Jones for information and report; also for reference to Brigadier-General Jenkins' command. It is a matter of much concern to this Department that there is so much of evil spoken of General Jenkins' bands of cavalry.

By order of the Secretary of War:

J. A. CAMPBELL,
Assistant Secretary of War.

HEADQUARTERS DEPARTMENT OF WEST VIRGINIA,
April 6, 1863.

Respectfully returned to the War Department with the report of Col. W. H. French of the 3d instant. My own remarks on this letter were given in my letter* of the 2d instant to the Secretary of War.

SAM. JONES,
Major-General.

[Inclosure.]

HEADQUARTERS CAVALRY BRIGADE,
Salem, Va., April 3, 1863.

Maj. Gen. SAMUEL JONES,
Commanding Department of Western Virginia:

GENERAL: A communication from His Excellency Governor Vance, of North Carolina, referred by the Secretary of War to you and by you to myself, has just been received. In reply I would state on the subject of impressment that no orders have ever been issued to any officer or agent of this command to impress forage prior to your communication* of the 22d ultimo, authorizing Capt. [M. B.] Porteaux, assistant quartermaster, to do so. If any impressments have been made not included in that authority the party making them rendered himself liable to charges, and on proper notification from any aggrieved person in North Carolina they would have been promptly preferred and the complaint fully investigated; and I beg leave to state that, notwithstanding the fifty letters received by Governor Vance and the notoriety of the offenses of Jenkins' bands of cavalry, not one single specific charge has ever been sent to these headquarters from that or any other source since I have been in command of this brigade (nearly a month), nor before General Jenkins left, as I am informed by a member of his staff.

On another point touching the character of this command I feel called upon to state that the larger portion of it has been quartered here in this county nearly four months, and I would invite investigation to the fact that no serious complaints have been made by any citizens; and while officers and agents sent out by us under your orders on detached service at remote points to arrest deserters and forage horses may have

---

* Not found.

been guilty of improper conduct, such offenders have, on due notice, always been brought to justice. It seems hardly reasonable that the reputation of a whole command should suffer on account of the offenses of a few members, removed from the eye of its commander, when the offenses are not reported and no opportunity is afforded him to render justice. It was from no desire to impeach the loyalty of the citizens of North Carolina that it was stated they would not receive Confederate money, but frequent instances which have occurred seem to indicate that the dissatisfaction arose not so much from scarcity of corn as an unwillingness to receive the only money which our agents had to offer. I will mention two, reported by Capt. [W. W.] Parsons, of the Seventeenth Regiment Virginia Cavalry: Two farmers on the Yadkin, in Davies County, had each from 500 to 1,000 bushels of corn, which they were offering for sale, but refused it to our agents because they could pay neither gold or silver nor North Carolina money, and the same officer stated that if he had had gold and silver he could have bought as much corn as he wanted.

It is recommended that the horses be removed from North Carolina to some portion of your department. South of the railroad there are already as many of our horses as can be barely subsisted. In this county the horses of officers and those used for transportation are at this time receiving only half rations of corn and no hay, using straw instead. In Botetourt the Government requires all surplus forage to be reserved for the use of the iron-works. In Rockbridge we already have the horses of six companies, and I understand that General Stuart has sent thither three regiments of his command to remain for some time. In Craig we have the horses of two companies living on hay alone for the last three weeks, besides many of the transportation horses of this command and a large number under charge of Major McMahon, quartermaster. Even hay is become very scarce there and almost impossible to procure. The counties north of the last mentioned were, you are aware, overrun by the enemy, and on account of this and the unfavorable season the corn crop was very light and very little grass was cut.

Another fact of great importance is that there is not enough forage between this point and our horses in North Carolina (from 100 to 300 miles) to subsist them on their route hither, and they cannot consequently be moved until grass begins to afford pasturage. This is the information we receive from our agents. But even if they could be subsisted on their way hither they would still have to be subsisted on grain here until grass season or perish.

The above report includes, I believe, every fact of importance desired by you, and I leave the whole subject for your determination, awaiting such orders as you may think best to give, stating merely that I am willing to move the horses at the earliest period when the grass will afford them subsistence—probably about May 1.

I am, general, very respectfully, your obedient servant,

WM. H. FRENCH,
Colonel, Commanding Brigade.

[Indorsement.]

Hdqrs. Department of Western Virginia,
Dublin, Va., April 6, 1863.

Respectfully forwarded through the Adjutant and Inspector General to the Secretary of War. Colonel French's views in regard to moving the horses from North Carolina coincide with mine, expressed in my letter of the 2d instant to the Secretary of War. Colonel French says correctly that no serious complaints have been made against the brigade in the counties where the chief part of it has been stationed for the last three months. The numerous complaints have come from localities where detached companies have been sent to collect conscripts and arrest deserters—a delicate duty, well calculated to cause complaints— and from North Carolina, where horses were sent to forage. It happens that the complaints have come from sections of the country remote from the scenes of military operations, and where troops have not heretofore been, and the people in those localities do not bear patiently one of the necessary evils of the war. In regard to the complaints of the consumption of forage in North Carolina, Captain Porteaux, assistant quartermaster, whom I sent to North Carolina some time since to pay outstanding claims, reports that he had an interview with Governor Vance, "and from the tenor of his remarks I (Porteaux) judged that it was not the consumption of grain or forage that was complained of, but that the parties were not paid for what had been used; that was what the grumbling was about." I have heard no complaints since an officer was sent to North Carolina to pay for forage consumed.

SAM. JONES,
Major-General.

HEADQUARTERS, March 22, 1863.

General R. E. LEE,
    Commanding, &c., Fredericksburg, Va.:

GENERAL: Your letter of yesterday is received. The enemy's force, as you say, is feeble between Roanoke and Tar Rivers, but he has facilities for throwing other troops there to re-enforce or to cut off our trains, &c. I think therefore a sufficient force should be there to meet any such emergency. Two of Pickett's brigades are now on their way, and General D. H. Hill is ordered to use all possible dispatch in the execution of the plans for drawing out supplies and, if it is possible, to take the garrison at Washington. Hood's division will be held ready to join you unless I find a most favorable opportunity to strike an important blow. I will advise you of any movement of that division. I will also make every effort to have Pickett's division concentrated rapidly.

I remain, general, very respectfully, your most obedient servant,

JAMES LONGSTREET,
Lieutenant-General, Commanding.

HEADQUARTERS, March 22, 1863.

Maj. Gen. D. H. HILL, <i>Goldsborough, N. C.:</i>

GENERAL: Your letter of the 21st is received, and I have made the effort to telegraph you to go, but the wires are down. I hope, however, that this letter may reach you in time to prevent any delay. It seems to me that you would be able to move more promptly if you put Kemper at Snow Hill, instead of relieving Daniel at Kinston in order to place Kemper there, and let Kemper support either point. Besides you will save time when Kemper is to return here. The arrangement then should be: Daniel at Kinston, Ransom at Goldsborough, Kemper at Snow Hill, Garnett and Pettigrew operating against Washington, but if your plans are already made and this would be likely to delay your movements a day do not wait; the grand thing is to get Washington and its garrison. You can not only give it out that the move is against New Berne, but you can seriously threaten it if an effort should be made to re-enforce Washington from New Berne. I think that your movement would thus be made doubly secure. The moment this is accomplished you can move your entire force against New Berne. It will not do to wait this move for the operations against Charleston, because I believe that an attack upon Charleston will not be made until the army on the Rappahannock is ready to advance; then we shall want every man that we can get to meet the grand army. I do not think that there can be any doubt but we can keep re-enforcements from leaving Suffolk for the succor of Washington. The way seems to me to be clear if we can only be prompt. If your health is likely to fail you advise me and I will go down myself. I can send you General Pickett if you desire. I tried to send a telegram to General Whiting to send you Ransom's brigade, but the wires being down I could not. I inclose one to be sent him if the wires are operating between Goldsborough and Wilmington.

I remain, very respectfully, your obedient servant,

JAMES LONGSTREET,
Lieutenant-General, Commanding.

P. S.—Retain the Whitworth that I have sent you if you can move promptly against New Berne, and you will need all the troops for that purpose.

HEADQUARTERS,
Wilmington, N. C., March 23, 1863.

Hon. JAMES A. SEDDON,
Secretary of War, Richmond, Va.:

SIR: I wish to call your attention to the evil of permitting private parties to ship cotton except for the purpose of bringing in articles useful for the conduct of the war. It is a crying evil. It fosters and increases speculation in the wildest manner. The burden falls exclusively upon the soldier and his family in the enormously increased prices of every necessary. He has a fixed and moderate stipend. The non-combatant engaged in mercantile pursuits has facilities for procuring what he needs and can pay any price from the enormous profits. I believe the cotton is in great part exchanged at Nassau with Yankee merchants for Yankee goods. The goods at least that come here are mostly of Yankee manufacture, and houses have been established in Nassau by men of Northern birth, who have left this city since the war and still have partners here. Lastly and especially, those engaged in this trade from this port to the largest extent or interest are partly Yankees outright and partly of Union sentiments.

Very respectfully,

W. H. C. WHITING,
Brigadier-General, Commanding.

HEADQUARTERS,
Wilmington, N. C., March 23, 1863.

Hon. JAMES A. SEDDON,
Secretary of War. Richmond, Va.:

SIR: The steam-tug Mariner, formerly the most powerful tug in this river, has come in from Nassau, her owners having put her to blockade running. She is not suitable for this purpose, carrying but very little cargo, while, her boilers and engines being very good, she is absolutely necessary here for the navy first and then for us. She can readily be fitted into a powerful gunboat. I consider her essential for the defense here, especially in connection with the gunboats building, as a tender, and also in connection with the valuable cargoes now arriving in Government steamers. With her we shall be able to save much in case of accidents which might happen to any of our vessels from the enemy's fire. She is also needed for army transportation. Please to show this to the Secretary of the Navy who will, I hope, at once order her pur chase. Flag-Officer Lynch concurs with me in the necessity of this and will doubtless report at once. If the Navy Department does not want the boat we certainly do. I shall not permit her to leave unless ordered. Great efforts no doubt will be made to procure a permit, but I beg to refer you to my letter of this date relative to blockade running. The boat could carry but very few bales. Her engines, boiler, and hull are too valuable to permit them to be sacrificed in order that a party of speculators should make money.

Very respectfully,

W. H. C. WHITING,
Brigadier-General, Commanding.

HEADQUARTERS,
Wilmington, N. C., March 23, 1863.

Hon. JAMES A. SEDDON,
Secretary of War, Richmond, Va.:

SIR: I will add to my letters of this date some considerations on the subject of the blockade running, to show how this matter of private exportation of cotton is affecting our currency. Vessels owned abroad come in with cargo, which sells for nearly $1,000,000 Confederate currency, and for $50,000 Confederate currency they buy a load of cotton, as much as they can carry, to take back. The balance of proceeds they can afford to expend for exchange and gold at enormous prices, and still make a handsome profit. Each vessel that comes in instead of producing the effect by increase of supply of diminution of prices actually increases prices and the current value of gold. I can illustrate this by an example, a small one, but showing the whole business, which has come to my knowledge: A man brought in six demijohns of gin, which cost him in Nassau $24. He sold them here for $900. This man could afford to give $9 for $1 of specie in gold, which he did, and then make $76 profit, a good business for a common sailor. The profits made by these people are not expended here; they are invested in gold and abroad. Every single bale of cotton that goes abroad on other than Government account to establish Government credit abroad does us injury at home. I know there is a law prohibiting the exportation of cotton. I am not aware of its being repealed on the statute book. Until so informed I shall not permit a bale to be shipped, except by special orders, other than Government cotton.

Very respectfully,

W. H. C. WHITING,
Brigadier-General, Commanding.

HEADQUARTERS,
Wilmington, N. C., March 23, 1863.

Col. [L. B.] NORTHROP,
Commissary-General, Richmond, Va.:

COLONEL: I think it necessary to call your attention to the accompanying papers,* not for any purpose of complaint, but as illustrating the growing scarcity, and especially because, in my opinion, the strongest and promptest efforts ought to be made to furnish the forts which guard this harbor with at least thirty days' rations, to be kept on hand as reserve, the daily consumption to be supplied as usual. These forts are liable to be attacked at any time and may become isolated without being taken. I have endeavored ever since I have been here to procure the supply. I do not now think it can be done except you especially direct it; at any rate, unless some changes be made in the rate of procuring meat.

Very respectfully,

W. H. C. WHITING,
Brigadier-General, Commanding.

HEADQUARTERS FORCES ON BLACKWATER,
March 24, 1863.

GENERAL: I have made inquiries concerning young Ford, as you desired. There is only one of that name in the Hampton Legion—Stephen Ford, from Georgetown, S. C.

Your note concerning movements on the Rappahannock was received yesterday. I confess that I was but little satisfied with the affair, even as stated by our papers. I regret much the loss of Major Pelham. However, we must accept with gratitude, notwithstanding our loss, the indication that our cavalry will fight and subject themselves to severe loss, *i. e.,* what would be termed severe for them. If the war continues much longer we will come to the conclusion that it is better to use our cavalry on occasion even against infantry on the battle-fields, especially after the shock of infantry.

I was very greatly disappointed at your not coming at the time of General French's visit. I sincerely hope and think it important that you should pay a visit here. I am working hard to make the line here impregnable, and in ten days it would give me pleasure to receive a visit on the lower part of my line. I have scouts out all the time and of course get numerous and conflicting reports. I received yesterday reports of the enemy's forces at Suffolk being re-enforced to some 30,000, but I cannot believe that they can exceed at an outside limit 20,000, and think 15,000 will cover their effective force. I expect to get more precise and definite intelligence in a day or so. The sharpshooters gave

---

* Not found.

Spear and his crack regiment a very rough handling a few days since, of which you have heard by General French. They carried off four 4-horse ambulances filled with wounded, their legs hanging out in front and rear, and their caisson-boxes were also crowded with wounded and a number also on horseback. They acknowledged at the time a loss of 70. I would like your judgment of the two following plans which I have matured and concluded to try in a few days: First, to move out at night and place a regiment of infantry in ambush between Carrsville and Suffolk and a regiment in ambush where the South Quay road intersects the other road from Carrsville to Suffolk, and move out with artillery and infantry (some three or four regiments) to Councils Cross-Roads, to support, if necessary, and try and annihilate Spear's regiment; then follow this with a dash of Baker's regiment of cavalry upon the enemy's cavalry camp on the Windsor road (some 4 or 5 miles this side of Suffolk), moving out on the Windsor road with all the forces I can spare from the exposed points on the line and taking a strong position beyond Windsor, give them battle if they will come out with their forces. I am anxious to have the other companies of Baker's regiment here and hope you will not replace his regiment by another, as he is a fine officer, and with his absent companies I think I could, after breaking up Spear with infantry, keep the enemy close in Suffolk.

Very respectfully, your obedient servant,

M. JENKINS,
Brigadier-General, &c.

HEADQUARTERS, *March* 24, 1863.

Maj. Gen. D. H. HILL,
Commanding, &c., Goldsborough, N. C.:

GENERAL : Your letter of the 23d* and General Garnett's of the 22d,* through you, are received. I believe that I understand the positions of your troops. I suppose General Kemper, with one regiment of General Daniel's brigade and one of Ransom's, to be at and near Kinston; Daniel's brigade, less one regiment, at Blount Hall, in readiness to threaten New Berne or support you; Garnett and Pettigrew to operate against Washington if practicable; if not, to draw off supplies for our entire army. I did telegraph to stop the movement of Ransom's brigade and substitute that of Kemper's, but I afterward suggested that it would be well to have Ransom's at Goldsborough, in addition to the others, that you might, if you had occasion to do so, threaten New Berne while operating against Washington. Ransom is not necessary at Wilmington and might greatly aid you in your operations by strengthening your force at Goldsborough so as to enable you to seriously threaten New Berne in case that garrison should be disposed to succor the one at Washington. General Whiting has been ordered to send Ransom to you should you call for him for this purpose. He has acknowledged the receipt of the order, and you can have Ransom's brigade at Goldsborough if you will telegraph for it.

General Garnett's transportation has been ordered to him and ought to be at Tarborough now unless it has been detained by high water, &c. Great results depend more or less upon the rapidity of your movements. I am likely to be called upon for Garnett's and Kemper's bri-

---

*Not found.

gades on the Rappahannock at any moment, but think that the enemy will not be able to make a move there before April 10. I hope that you may be able to reduce the garrisons at Washington and New Berne before that time, the former at least. If you deem the latter not ad- visable, return the two brigades of General Pickett's division as soon as you have accomplished the former and gotten out the meat supplies. I do not expect you to take Washington, of course, if it is found to be more difficult than you anticipated. Exercise your own good judgment in the matter. The important question is to draw in all of the meat rations that can be had. I have already written you not to confine yourself strictly to the prices fixed by the Subsistence Department if you find that a higher price will facilitate your operations. Every vehicle in the country should be put in use and at liberal rates of trans- portation so as to haul in supplies for our armies. I wish you would advise me of the probable quantity of meat that you may be able to get as soon as you can get the proper data. We may have to make an advance move up here so as to get out the supplies from the counties east of the Chowan. If you are likely to get enough from Hyde, &c., the latter move will not be necessary. I hope that my Whitworth gun has reached you ere this. The party is tolerably well experienced in the use of it.

I remain, general, very respectfully, your most obedient servant,

JAMES LONGSTREET,
Lieutenant-General, Commanding.

HEADQUARTERS, *March* 24, 1863.

General R. E. LEE, *Commanding, &c.:*

GENERAL: I have the honor to inclose a report of Major Moses on the subject of subsistence for our armies. He has just returned from a tour through Virginia and North Carolina and from a visit to the Commissary-General. This report is the result of his observations. The particular counties referred to by him as containing abundant supplies for our armies are now in the enemy's lines. We can occupy that coun- try and draw the supplies out with another division of my old corps, but I do not think it would be prudent to attempt such a move with a less force. The divisions of Generals Pickett and Hood, with one other bri- gade (Davis'), are all the troops that I can command for this service. The enemy has at Suffolk and in supporting distance 27,000 men— 21,000 that came down from General Hooker's army and 6,000 that were at Suffolk before. I think that a move against Suffolk would draw off re-enforcements from General Hooker's army unless we can act promptly enough to prevent it. I submit the case for your determination. If we can supply our army otherwise the expedition should not be made. If it is a case of necessity we should lose no time. I fear that our ne- cessities may be exposed by the expeditions that are now out in Eastern North Carolina for the same purpose, and when it becomes known to the enemy he will make a great effort to prevent us from moving to those important counties. If we find it necessary to make this move I desire to have a consultation with you before it sets out.

I remain, very respectfully, your obedient servant,

JAMES LONGSTREET,
Lieutenant-General, Commanding.

HEADQUARTERS,
Wilmington, N. C., March 25, 1863.

Lieut. Gen. LONGSTREET,
Commanding, Petersburg, Va.:

GENERAL: Your orders to send off Ransom's brigade to report to Major-General Hill have been received and carried out. Let me hope that the removal of these troops is only temporary and that they may hereafter be assigned to me, or at least until all danger of attack here is past, as the stationary brigade of this district. There certainly should always be one brigade here; in my opinion more, but one at least. This one, about 3,000 strong, takes off two-thirds of my available force, and all that is disciplined and efficient. I place but little reliance on Evans' brigade, which certainly is in worse condition than any I have ever seen. It has but about 1,500 men for duty, a very large number of field officers absent or under arrest, and it requires careful attention and strict discipline to bring it to the efficiency which should belong to troops who have been so long in the service as they have.

Very respectfully, your obedient servant,

W. H. C. WHITING,
Brigadier-General.

HEADQUARTERS, *March 25, 1863.*

Maj. Gen. D. H. HILL, *Commanding:*

GENERAL: Your letter of the 24th is received. General Garnett's transportation started from here some ten days ago. If there is telegraphic communication between this and Tarborough I wish you would keep some one there to take any dispatches that we may have to send you. If there is not, name some point nearest you where we may telegraph you. Spare no pains to haul off all meats that you may be able to secure.

I remain, very respectfully, your most obedient servant,

JAMES LONGSTREET,
Lieutenant-General, Commanding.

HEADQUARTERS,
Fredericksburg, Va., March 27, 1863.

Gen. JAMES LONGSTREET, *Commanding, &c.:*

GENERAL: I received by the last mail your letter of the 24th instant accompanying the report of Major Moses on the subject of subsistence to be obtained in North Carolina. I do not know whether the supplies in that State are necessary for the subsistence of our armies, but I consider it of the first importance to draw from the invaded districts every pound of provision and forage we can. It will lighten the draught from other sections and give relief to our citizens. As to the force necessary for this purpose I cannot so well decide. As far as I am informed the force of the enemy south of James River and north of the Cape Fear is small. It can be re-enforced speedily from the troops encamped at Newport News, but if you operate discreetly, concealing your movements and only occupying the country from which you are drawing, I think much may be done before your purpose is discovered and time be gained to develop the plans of the enemy, when we can act more understandingly. You have about 40,000 effective men; the enemy can bring out no more. I feel assured that with equal numbers you can go where you choose.

If this army is further weakened we must retire to the line of the Annas and trust to a battle nearer Richmond for the defense of the capital. It throws open a broad margin of our frontier and renders our railroad communications more hazardous and more difficult to secure. Unless, therefore, a retrograde movement becomes necessary I deem it advantageous to keep the enemy at a distance and trust to striking him on his line of advance. A sudden, vigorous attack on Suffolk would doubtless give you that place. Of the propriety of this step you can best judge. To hold it you must control the navigation of the Nansemond or the troops from Newport News could soon be thrown upon you. There is a point about 6 miles below Suffolk where we once had a four-gun battery that was said to be a good position, and other points lower down. A battery, I should think, would also have to be just below Smithfield and one at Manny's Neck, unless there is some better point at the head of the Chowan. If operations in that quarter should draw re-enforcements from General Hooker, more troops could be spared from this army; but I hope you now have available troops in North Carolina sufficient for the purpose. Should you find it advisable to have a personal conference with me at any time I will be happy to see you here, or it may be that I could meet you in Richmond.

I am, with great esteem, very truly, yours,

R. E. LEE,
General.

HEADQUARTERS, *March* 27, 1863.

General R. E. LEE, *Fredericksburg, Va.* :

GENERAL : A gentleman, professing to be reliable, informs us that it has been determined at Washington to bring the Sixth Army Corps down to Suffolk to unite with the Ninth. I send you this that your scouts may be on their guard and report such movement at the earliest moment. I expect to move Hood's division down toward Surry County in a few days and to run my line across from the Blackwater to the James, or to some of the streams flowing into the James. My line will then cut the Blackwater at some point near Mayfield. My left will be somewhat exposed to the enemy's iron-clads. If I can have the aid of the Navy on the James I think that such a position would hold the enemy in check whatever his force may be. I do not expect aid from the Navy unless you can get it for me. As my arrangements should depend very much on your plans it is proper that I should advise with you and ask your views. The new position will throw me far away from you, but if we hope to draw supplies from the counties east of the Chowan I think it indispensable.

I remain, very respectfully, your obedient servant,

JAMES LONGSTREET,
Lieutenant-General.

HEADQUARTERS,
Blount Hall, N. C., March 27, 1863.

Maj. Gen. D. H. HILL,
Commanding at Greenville, N. C. :

GENERAL: Major Guion furnished me with his map and report of the Contentnea Creek. I ordered Captain Barrows, Engineers, as soon as he reported to commence immediately to lay off the work proposed, and that I would send an officer and working party to execute it. Your call for shovels will leave me only about 40 shovels. I send all the picks the quartermaster has here—only 4. I had but about 15 at Kinston. Have sent an order to Captain Divine, quartermaster, for 100 shovels and 20 picks. When they arrive the working party of 40 shovels will be increased by that number, and the work here will go on as laid off by Captain Barrows and Major Guion. Colonel Washington, with his regiment and two pieces of artillery, took up a position on Core Creek early Monday morning. He found it impracticable to cross the artillery, and sent two companies and a detachment of Nethercutt's over, under Captain Davis, to drive in their pickets. Captain Davis attacked their pickets in about 8 miles of New Berne, killing some 3 or 4. He reports after this Colonel Washington opened with artillery, and by felling trees and other noise made a demonstration of building the bridge and crossing in force. About night, after our troops had withdrawn, they ran their monitor car some 1 or 2 miles from their picket post and shelled the woods furiously, but did not venture nearer than 5 or 6 miles of the creek.

Very respectfully, &c.,

JUNIUS DANIEL,
Brigadier-General.

———

HEADQUARTERS,
Petersburg, Va., March 27, 1863.

General W. H. C. WHITING,
Commanding, Wilmington, N. C.:

GENERAL: Your letter of the 25th is received. General Ransom's brigade is only temporarily at Goldsborough. It will return to you as soon as General Hill can draw out the subsistence stores in the eastern counties. During the absence of Daniel's and Pettigrew's brigades from Goldsborough it is thought the brigade of General Ransom can be well employed in protecting the railroad at Goldsborough, and at the same time give quite effectual protection to Wilmington by threatening New Berne in case of a movement from there against Wilmington. General Evans reported his brigade 3,500 strong when here a few days ago. I hope that you are doing well in your labors. The Postmaster-General promised me a few days ago to put Fort Caswell in telegraphic communication with your headquarters.

I remain, very respectfully, your obedient servant,

JAMES LONGSTREET,
Lieutenant-General.

———

HEADQUARTERS,
Weldon, N. C., March 28, 1863—8 p. m.

Lieutenant-General LONGSTREET,
Comdg. Department of Virginia and North Carolina:

GENERAL: I am this moment in receipt of an order by courier from Maj. Gen. D. H. Hill, copy of which order I annex. Three companies of my regiment (D, E, F) are on detached service, under Lieut. Col. [John E.] Brown, and have been on the Chowan River. On the 23d and 24th they fought the enemy, official report of which engagement I sent to General Hill's headquarters to-day. Subsequently Colonel Brown notified me by courier that the enemy were coming up Roanoke River in force to get in his rear and thus cut off his command, and that he had fallen back 10 miles this side of Colerain, and asking for re-enforcements. I had ordered two companies to march at daylight to his assistance when I received orders from General Hill to move to Hamilton. My men were being drilled at the 32-pounder guns (mounted) and officers were being made acquainted with the topography of the country.

I have the honor to be, general, very respectfully, your obedient servant,

GEO. C. GIBBS,
Colonel Forty-second North Carolina Regt., Comdg. Post.

[Inclosure.]

GREENVILLE, N. C., *March 27, 1863.*

Col. GEORGE C. GIBBS, *Forty-second North Carolina:*

COLONEL: The reports from our scouts indicate an advance upon Hamilton. I wish you to move down there immediately, and if necessary call on Lieutenant-Colonel Brown to aid you. I have written to Lieutenant-General Longstreet to guard Weldon during your absence. Hamilton must be held at all hazards.

Respectfully,

D. H. HILL,
Major-General.

———

FREDERICKSBURG, VA., *March 28, 1863.*

General JAMES LONGSTREET:

General W. E. Jones reports the Ninth Corps (Burnside's) started West last Sunday by the Pennsylvania Central and Baltimore and Ohio, supposed for Kentucky. Are the troops still at Newport News?

R. E. LEE.

[Indorsement.]

Respectfully referred to Major-General French, with request that he direct his scouts to be more particular and minute in reports.

JAMES LONGSTREET,
Lieutenant-General, Commanding.

———

HEADQUARTERS FORCES ON BLACKWATER,
March 28, 1863.

GENERAL: I returned yesterday from a visit to Broadwater Bridge, &c. I met General Corse at Ivor, and we rode over the whole neighborhood and line together. Upon close examination of the country he concluded to take position with his brigade at Tucker Swamp Church, about 1½ miles from Ivor, putting one regiment near Broadwater Bridge to picket that point and Proctor's Bridge, and send a guard of four men each to Wall's and Birch Island Bridges. Another regiment at my request he placed a mile from his headquarters toward Seacock Swamp, to cover and picket Joiner's Ford. This arrangement, in my judgment, renders the line of Blackwater perfectly secure. My reason for desiring him to picket Joiner's Ford was that it was a very critical point to his position, and that while I picketed it, Seacock Swamp being difficult to cross even with the bridge, might prevent supports to the picket arriving in time; also if he moved either up or down he would gather his brigade as he went, and thus would have all the advantages of concentration.

At the present season there is no crossing the Blackwater with facility between Blackwater Bridge (a very uncertain one) and Wall's Bridge, some 20 miles up. I would therefore suggest that instead of increasing the force at Ivor you place a brigade near Wakefield, when, by crossing at Birch Island Bridge and taking by Cypress Creek, they cover between the Blackwater and James Rivers by a short line and give us time to concentrate and cut off any small force or to attack in flank and rear any large one moving from Suffolk. After passing by Proctor's Bridge an enemy would not cross the Blackwater in moving upon Petersburg, as the river trends westward toward Petersburg.

I would like to move forward the cavalry picket now along Cypress Creek and make a line across from Broadwater or Proctor's Bridge to the head of Pagan Creek, which runs by Smithfield to the James and is impassable. I would have some 14 miles of open country to picket and far enough in advance to get information to a force at Wakefield, near Birch Island Bridge, and to get my command ready to attack the flank. I think it important to have a force to check any movement in that direction, as the river is difficult of crossing at this season. I think that the picket line across to Pagan Creek would answer much better than the one at Cypress Creek, as the latter is so much to my rear. I hope you may be able to come down, as I think you will be able to give me many points, and I think you will like the line of defense I have marked out and suggested above.

I am, general, very respectfully, yours,

M. JENKINS,
Brigadier-General.

P. S.—Do you get Northern papers regularly?

PETERSBURG, Va., *March 29, 1863.*

General W. H. C. WHITING,
  Wilmington, N. C.:

Have Ransom's brigade, including his battery, at Goldsborough.

JAMES LONGSTREET,
Lieutenant-General.

HEADQUARTERS, *March 29, 1863.*

Maj. Gen. D. H. HILL, *Commanding, &c.:*

GENERAL: Your dispatches of the 21st are received. We have a report that 1,000 infantry have passed down to Edenton. It is probably the force that is strengthening Plymouth. I wish you would send a regiment of cavalry into Bertie if you have not already done so. General Ransom was placed at your disposal some time ago, and I believe that he is now at Goldsborough As it is possible that he may not be, I will telegraph General Whiting to send him at once. I shall send Major Sorrel out to join Colonel Gibbs with special instructions. I think that I can cut off any move against Weldon by a force from Franklin. I send Colonel Alexander down to examine into our ordnance arrangements, ammunition particularly.

I remain, very respectfully, your most obedient servant,

JAMES LONGSTREET,
Lieutenant-General.

PETERSBURG, VA., *March* 29, 1863.

General R. E. LEE, *Fredericksburg, Va.:*

The troops are reported at Suffolk and Newport News still.

JAMES LONGSTREET,
Lieutenant-General.

PETERSBURG, VA., *March* 29, 1863.

Lieutenant-General LONGSTREET:

GENERAL: I have had many reports informing me that all or a part of Burnside's army corps was in Suffolk. New York Herald (20th and 21st) says Burnside was at Fortress Monroe. Same paper of 24th instant has a dispatch from Cincinnati (23d) saying Burnside was expected there to-morrow (24th). On the 24th instant it is announced that he had gone West to relieve General H. G. Wright, whose nomination was not confirmed. Nothing is said about troops. The troops that were sent to Suffolk are still there, and had any large number been embarked near Newport News I think I would have been advised of it. It may be that General Jones is mistaken about the Ninth Army Corps. I am having chills or I would come and see you. I will write to the Blackwater to endeavor to find out if anything can be learned in regard to the matter.

Yours, truly,

S. G. FRENCH,
Major-General.

HEADQUARTERS, *March* 30, 1863.

General R. E. LEE,
Commanding, Fredericksburg, Va.:

GENERAL: The troops have left Newport News; embarked on Friday and Saturday; supposed to have gone to North Carolina. My informant says they sailed for North Carolina.

JAMES LONGSTREET,
Lieutenant-General, Commanding.

HEADQUARTERS, *March* 30, 1863.

Maj. Gen. D. H. HILL, *Greenville, N. C.:*

I have just learned that the force at Newport News has sailed for the coast of North Carolina. They embarked on Friday and Saturday, probably 12,000.

JAMES LONGSTREET,
Lieutenant-General, Commanding.

HEADQUARTERS, *March* 30, 1863.

Maj. Gen. D. H. HILL, *Commanding, &c.:*

GENERAL: I have just received information that the troops at Newport News have sailed; it is supposed to be for North Carolina. They left Friday and Saturday. I presume that your move is discovered and the enemy has had time to discover it. The force gone south is probably 10,000; possibly more. If your information corroborates this you will probably be obliged to act on the defensive. Advise me as soon as possible, that I may be duly informed.

Most respectfully,

JAMES LONGSTREET,
Lieutenant-General, Commanding.

HEADQUARTERS,
Petersburg, Va., March 30, 1863.

General W. H. C. WHITING, *Wilmington, N. C.:*

GENERAL: My scout reports that the enemy's force from Newport News embarked on Friday and Saturday for the coast of North Carolina. I presume that this is true, and that the re-enforcements may have gone to New Berne. I advise you that you may caution your scouts to be particular and keep you advised. This force of the enemy has been drawn off by the operations of General Hill, I presume.

I remain, general, very respectfully, your most obedient servant,

JAMES LONGSTREET,
Lieutenant-General, Commanding.

HEADQUARTERS,
Petersburg, Va., March 30, 1863.

Brig. Gen. R. RANSOM, [Jr.], *Goldsborough, N. C.:*

GENERAL: General Whiting has been ordered to send your battery to you, and if you find that your field officers are likely to be wanted with their regiments you can telegraph him to send them to you. If you find yourself the senior officer, take charge of the defense of Goldsborough and the railroad. If you are not the senior, report to the officer who is. The command at Goldsborough will also look to the protection of Wilmington, the latter being the essential point; but a force at Goldsborough threatening New Berne ought to prevent any advance from that point against Wilmington. I have just been informed that the enemy has embarked his force from Newport News for the coast of North Carolina. If this is the case—and I have good reason to believe it—the force is intended to re-enforce New Berne. This will give the enemy an additional force of 10,000 or 12,000. He will not be able to begin any operations, however, until you can be advised. If the re-enforcements arrive at New Berne you must have General Hill advised of it in due time.

I remain, general, very respectfully, your most obedient servant,

JAMES LONGSTREET,
Lieutenant-General, Commanding.

P. S.—The troops from Newport News embarked on Friday and Saturday.

HEADQUARTERS ARMY OF NORTHERN VIRGINIA,
March 30, 1863.

Lieut. Gen. JAMES LONGSTREET,
Commanding, &c., Petersburg, Va.:

GENERAL: One of our scouts reports, under date of 29th instant, that he was in Washington and Baltimore the first of last week, and that Burnside's corps left Newport News at that time for the West. He does not state whether the information was derived from his own observation or from others. The New York Times of the 25th and the Washington Chronicle of the 26th state that Burnside was in Cincinnati on the 24th and is charged with the defense of Kentucky, but do not mention his troops. Can you not ascertain definitely whether these statements are correct?

I am, general, very respectfully and truly, yours,

R. E. LEE,
General.

HEADQUARTERS,
Petersburg, Va., March 30, 1863.

General R. E. LEE, *Commanding:*

GENERAL: Your letter of the 25th instant is received. My letter forwarding report of Major Drummond was very carelessly written. The report was sent merely to indicate the movement of the enemy, not that I gave any credit to the reported strength. I thought that my desire to move in the direction of Suffolk would indicate to you that I put no faith in the report of numbers. There are no particular advantages in giving battle at Suffolk, except that we might do so by rapid movements, with a greater force than the enemy could have. This to me would be a novelty and something of a luxury. I am quite satisfied that the enemy could be drawn from his intrenchments by threatening his rear. Then, with a superior force, we ought to get the entire force this side of Norfolk. I do not believe that the enemy will advance from Suffolk with a view to give battle unless this force is very greatly reduced. In that event he will have a short and not very difficult route to Richmond. I cannot well concentrate from North Carolina, as the enemy has a force of 10,000 at New Berne, a considerable force at Washington and Plymouth. With his facilities for transportation he can move his troops, and, aided by his gunboats, move against any portion of our railroad; besides, I am obliged to keep all the spare troops in the field hauling in bacon and other supplies. I think it utterly impossible for the enemy to move against your position until the roads are sufficiently dry for him to move around you and turn your position. By re-enforcing here we might destroy the enemy and get our forces together again in time to resist him at the Rappahannock. But if we succeed in destroying him here and have to retire to the Annas before we can give him a general battle we will accomplish a great deal and really have the enemy in a better position for our operations than the one he now occupies. We can cross the Blackwater at any point, as we still hold both banks of the river. It is a very strong defensive line, but can be turned as soon as the roads become dry enough for the enemy to move up the James River with his fleet and army; but I think that a very strong offensive and defensive position could be taken by letting the line cut the Blackwater and rest its left flank on the James, but this would require some aid on the part of our Navy in order to strengthen our left flank.

I remain, general, very respectfully, your most obedient servant,

JAMES LONGSTREET,
Lieutenant-General.

P. S.—I have just received intelligence by one of my scouts that the enemy sailed on Friday and Saturday from Newport News for the coast of North Carolina. In arranging our forces to protect supply trains into the eastern counties of North Carolina we had hoped to make a diversion upon New Berne and surprise the garrison at Washington. The high waters have washed away the bridges and detained us a week, and it is probable that the enemy has discovered our movements. It is possible, however, that this force may have returned to the Army of the Potomac.

WAR DEPARTMENT, C. S. A.,
Richmond, March 30. 1863.
Brig. Gen. W. H. C. WHITING,.
Commanding, Wilmington, N. C.:

GENERAL: In reply to your letter of the 23d instant I have the honor to say that it is not perceived how prices are increased by the export of cotton. As necessaries, to some extent at least, are brought in in return, the trade ought to diminish the prices; but apart from this the existing law allows the export, and the Department is not authorized, except under military exigencies, to obstruct or stop the trade.

Your obedient servant,

J. A. SEDDON,
Secretary of War.

HEADQUARTERS,
Swift Creek, Va., March 31, 1863.
Maj. Gen. D. H. HILL,
Commanding at Cross-Roads:

GENERAL: Your letter of this date, directing me to march with all my force to Yankee Hall, has been received. I will move early to-morrow with [William A.] Owens' [Fifty-third North Carolina] and [Thomas S.] Kenan's [Forty-third North Carolina] regiments by way of the cross-roads. Col. [E. C.] Brabble, [Thirty-second North Carolina], with the other troops, will march directly across, and I presume will be able to reach there to-morrow night. I learn from Lieutenant Barrington that Yankee Hall is on the Tar River, 7 miles above Washington. I will write to Kemper immediately.

Very respectfully,

JUNIUS DANIEL,
Brigadier-General.

RICHMOND AND DANVILLE R. R., PRESIDENT'S OFFICE,
Richmond, Va., March 31, 1863.
Hon. JAMES A. SEDDON,
Secretary of War:

SIR: I regret to have to report to you that the condition of this road is such as to make it indispensable that there should be at least 5 miles of iron procured for it. There are between 4 and 5 miles of road at Amelia Court-House that is unsafe and cannot be rendered safe without it is laid with new rail. With the exception of that portion of the road we may continue to run it, with great care and caution, for some time to come. No caution or care can make safe the portion of the track above referred to. We have had various and frequent accidents, caused by the condition of that part of the road, and, being unable to procure iron, I am driven with great reluctance to appeal to the Government for help. The old iron now on the track is the flat bar, which we will exchange with the Government, yard for yard, for T or U rail, we paying for the difference in weight if the Government can furnish the new iron. I know very well the difficulty that it will have to encounter in order to furnish this road with the iron asked for, but it has become indispensable to the continued use of the road, in my judgment and that of the superintendent, and, it not being possible for us to get the iron, no alternative is left but to appeal to the Government for aid. Without the use of this road I do not see how the necessary transportation for the army can be done, and it therefore becomes my duty to apprise you of its condition. The constant increase of prices paid in the Government shops for mechanics makes it impossible for us to procure and keep machinists enough to keep in repair our rolling-stock. That and the deterioration of the track for want of material presents a gloomy condition and calls for some action on its part. Every effort on the part of the management of the road has been made and will be continued to enable it to answer the calls made on it by the Government and community. I beg that you will give this matter your early and serious attention, as the exigency does not admit of delay.

Respectfully,

LEWIS E. HARVIE,
President.

[Indorsement.]

ENGINEER BUREAU, *April* 7, 1863.

Respectfully returned to the Honorable Secretary of War.

The condition of the Richmond and Danville Railroad, as represented, seems to demand that a portion of the iron taken from other roads (if it be decided to take it) should be applied to its wants. The removal of the rail from the York River road is now in progress, and it is hoped some will soon be obtained from the Norfolk and Petersburg road. In exchange for good iron the Government should have an amount of worn iron equivalent in value.

J. F. GILMER,
Colonel of Engineers and Chief of Bureau.

Abstract from Field Return of Troops, Maj. Gen. Arnold Elzey commanding, for April 1, 1863 *(headquarters Richmond, Va.).*

Command.	Present for duty.		Effective total present.	Aggregate present.	Aggregate present and absent.
	Officers.	Men.			
Brig. Gen. H. A. Wise	157	2,025	2,144	2,498	3,445
Col. T. S. Rhett	85	1,523	1,639	1,952	2,191
Col. Jack Brown	32	602	634	768	863
Lieut. Col. J. M. Maury	25	325	398	445	526
Capt. S. S. Lee	15	311	374	427	451
Grand total	314	4,786	5,189	6,090	7,476

RICHMOND, VA., *April* 1, 1863.

Lieut. Gen. JAMES LONGSTREET:

The enemy have abandoned Newport News. Burnside, with his corps (the Ninth), passed through Baltimore a few days since to re-enforce Rosecrans. Other troops have been sent from Hooker's army into Tennessee. One iron-clad reported at the mouth of the James River. The above may be relied on.

ARNOLD ELZEY,
Major-General.

HAMILTON, N. C., *April* 1, 1863.

Maj. Gen. D. H. HILL, *Commanding, &c. :*

GENERAL : Colonel Lamb started this morning five of his companies in the direction of Plymouth for a reconnaissance, and I propose to join them with him to-morrow. It will probably, however, be unnecessary to send this force any distance down the river, as Lieutenant-Colonel Towns, with four companies, is to-night reported as having just returned from within 1½ miles of Plymouth. The force there is said to be unchanged and no evidences of a movement in the direction of Weldon. Colonel Gibbs is now sending over to Lieutenant-Colonel Brown to ascertain if his position is the same and if any movements have taken place in his front. I have been to-day expecting to hear your guns at Washington but have heard nothing. The force at Plymouth is reported 800 men and two gunboats.

I am, general, very respectfully, your most obedient servant,

G. MOXLEY SORREL,
Major and Assistant Adjutant-General.

GENERAL ORDERS, ⎰ ADJT. AND INSPECTOR GENERAL'S OFFICE,
    No. 34.   ⎱   *Richmond, Va., April* 1, 1863.
*   *   *   *   *   *   *

II. The geographical limits of the command of Lieutenant-General Longstreet, embracing the defenses of Richmond and extending south to include the State of North Carolina—the whole under the supervision and general direction of General R. E. Lee—will be divided into three military departments, as follows: All north of the James River for the defense of Richmond will constitute the Department of Richmond, under Major-General Elzey, headquarters Richmond; all that portion of Virginia south of the James River and east of the county of Powhatan will constitute the Department of Southern Virginia, under Major-General French, headquarters at some central point near Blackwater; the State of North Carolina will constitute the Department of North Carolina, under Maj. Gen. D. H. Hill, headquarters Goldsborough.
*   *   *   *   *   *   *

By order :

S. COOPER,
Adjutant and Inspector General.

HEADQUARTERS ARMY OF NORTHERN VIRGINIA,
April 2, 1863.

Lieut. Gen. JAMES LONGSTREET,
   Commanding Corps, Petersburg, Va.:

GENERAL: Your letters of 29th and 30th ultimo have been received. I fear that the enemy, by propagation of consistent falsehood and persistent reports of intended advance, are deceiving us, and that while acting on the defensive on the Rappahannock and Blackwater they may be re-enforcing their armies west, with a view to offensive operations. I do not think Burnside's corps is in North Carolina but in Kentucky; all the information that I get confirms the truth of this. General Burnside reached Cincinnati on the 24th and has assumed command of the Department of the Ohio. His corps is intended to operate in Kentucky, where their papers state that a large rebel force is expected. It may be intended, however, that it shall re-enforce Rosecrans. You are, at any rate, relieved of half the force that has been opposed to you. You will therefore be strong enough to make any movement that you may consider advisable; but, as stated in former letters, so long as the enemy choose to remain on the defensive and covered by their intrenchments and floating batteries I fear you can accomplish but little, except to draw provisions from the invaded districts. If you can accomplish this it will be of positive benefit. I leave the whole matter to your good judgment. If your troops cannot be advantageously employed in North Carolina they will be very useful here, for unless General Hooker soon takes the aggressive I must endeavor to operate to draw him out. All the reports of our scouts and citizens north of the Rappahannock show that they are impressed with the belief that he will advance against us so soon as the weather and roads permit. Several periods in the past month were appointed by him to advance, and in every case he was prevented by storms.

I am, with great respect, very truly, yours,

R. E. LEE,
General.

HEADQUARTERS,
Greenville, N. C., April 2, 1863—8 p. m.

Maj. Gen. D. H. HILL,
   Commanding at Kinston, N. C.:

GENERAL: Your dispatch to General Pettigrew and myself has been received. I will move to Hookerton to-morrow morning. The rifle 4.62-inch and 32-pounder gun and ammunition, and a good deal of other ammunition, I understood, had been removed to Tarborough before my arrival here. I have sent an officer to Tarborough to remove the rifle gun to Falkland; the 32-pounder I presume you prefer having at Tarborough. Colonel Brabble is at Taft's Cross-Roads with two pieces of [J. B.] Starrs' battery. I have directed him to move to this point at daybreak. He will be left here, and I would prefer his keeping the two pieces of artillery with him until the rifle gun is in position. If you do not object to it I think it would be well for him to keep these pieces with him as long as he remains. I will leave them until I hear from you. Please let me know in your next if he can keep them. The rifle gun will be in position to-morrow evening, Major Haskell thinks. Upon the receipt of your three notes directing me to be ready to move to the assistance of General Ransom I sent the different battery commanders to examine the ammunition here and was informed that it was not suited to field guns—that most of it was ammunition that had been missent. As it was utterly impossible for me to remove the commissary stores and this ammunition, and be in a condition to go to the assistance of General Ransom, I concluded it would be best to send the ammunition to Tarborough. My transportation is so limited that it is with much difficulty that I can feed my troops when moving about unless hard bread is the issue. I hope, general, that this disposition will meet with your approval, as the ammunition is not, I understand, suited for field guns, and had I removed it and the commissary stores I would not have been ready for two days or more to have gone to the assistance of General Ransom. Colonel Ferebee I presume you wish to remain here until he hears from you, as I understand from General Robertson that you informed him that he would be sent to the Blackwater when he left here. I have heard nothing from him since the dispatch I forwarded you stating that he had been informed by citizens that there were a good many wagons in Washington and some 4,000 or 5,000 troops, and he thought they would march somewhere to-day. I will, unless I receive further instructions, encamp in the vicinity of Hookerton to-morrow night.

Very respectfully, &c.,

JUNIUS DANIEL,
Brigadier-General.

There has been no movement on the Washington road since day before yesterday.

HEADQUARTERS GARNETT'S COMMAND,
Two miles from Washington, N. C., April 2, 1863.

[Maj. Gen. D. H. HILL:]

GENERAL: I have directed the engineer officer (Lieutenant Stevens) to proceed to build the bridge immediately (he has charge of the pontoneers sent with Colonel Singeltary), and he is now engaged on that work. He reported to me in person and I impressed upon him to use all possible dispatch. You state in one of your dispatches that General Daniel has been sent to my assistance. Please let me know what disposition you wish made of his troops. If you apprehend that re-enforcements will be sent from Plymouth he had better be ordered in that direction, I should think, unless you design that he shall, in concert with me, assault Washington. I do not understand what your particular plans are. I would be glad to act under your personal directions, if that can be done consistent with your judgment.

Very respectfully, your obedient servant,

R. B. GARNETT,
Brigadier-General, Commanding.

HEADQUARTERS GARNETT'S COMMAND,
Near Washington, N. C., April 2, 1863.

[Maj. Gen. D. H. HILL:]

GENERAL: I have the honor to acknowledge the receipt of two dispatches from you. I very much regret that my communications to you should have been so irregular as well as late in reaching you. I did not know where you would establish your headquarters or the arrangement made of the line of couriers to communicate with you. I sent two messengers to Swann's Point, who returned and reported they could find no means of crossing. This occasioned considerable delay. My forces are in front of and below the town. I deemed these the best positions to threaten the enemy and prevent his escape. My battery (four smooth bores) is from half to three-quarters of a mile from the enemy's works. I have not yet opened, because the guns are partially concealed, and the Yankees can concentrate on my artillery from ten to twelve guns of superior metal, some, if not all, rifled pieces. It is impossible to contend successfully with smooth-bores against guns intrenched and of superior range.

In accordance with your instructions to look well to my rear and strongly guard the Williamston, Jamestown, and Plymouth roads, I have placed Colonels Washington and Singeltary on these routes. This leaves me an infantry force but slightly superior to that of the enemy, as far as I can learn from careful inquiry. The Yankee works are strongly constructed, with artillery to sweep the front and enfilade the ditch extending along the whole line, 12 feet wide and from 4 to 5 feet deep. The fallen timber in advance of the line of fortification, within range of canister and grape, makes the construction of rifle-pits almost impossible. I have no evidence that the enemy has been demoralized by our presence, there having been no desertions or messages from them. I therefore infer they will make a good resistance if attacked. I will look into the practicability of using cotton bales as you suggest. I am truly anxious to forward your views, but I am satisfied that without long-range artillery to silence the enemy's batteries I cannot assail the town without great sacrifice of men, with doubtful hope of success.

Very respectfully, your obedient servant,

R. B. GARNETT,
Brigadier-General, Commanding.

P. S.—I have made arrangements to send you couriers by a shorter route. Please order the arrangements to be completed on your side of the river.

HEADQUARTERS,
Ivor, Va., April 2, 1863.

Maj. Gen. D. H. HILL, *Commanding, &c.:*

GENERAL: I think that the force recently at Newport News has gone West, except the re-enforcements left at Suffolk. From the accounts that I get the force at Suffolk varies from 18,000 to 50,000. The former estimate is probably about right, though I cannot satisfy myself that there can be more than 16,000. This is considerably more than I can put into the field. I must therefore call for the brigades of Kemper and Garnett, of General Pickett's division, and I also desire that you send the two Whitworth guns—all to Franklin. It may be necessary for you to suspend operations in North Carolina until I can send you another force. I desire particularly to haul from the counties east of the Chowan the subsistence and quartermasters' supplies there. We may not have so favorable an opportunity, and it is important that we should get the supplies from those counties. The enemy's cavalry force is more than double that which I can put into the field. I am particularly anxious to get a regiment of cavalry to put with our present force. If the cavalry has gone to Bertie I wish you would order it up to Franklin, except a regiment for Bertie and to look after gunboats. If the cavalry is still with you please make prompt arrangements with it to meet these views. I hope that you will lose no time in putting the brigades of General Pickett's division at Franklin, and the two Whitworth guns, unless one is indispensable to you. Let the cavalry report at the same point. I would like to be advised of the time necessary to accomplish this, as this alone will delay my operations. I sincerely hope that you may have succeeded at Washington.

I remain, general, respectfully, your obedient servant,

JAMES LONGSTREET,
Lieutenant-General, Commanding.

BRIGADE HEADQUARTERS,
Goldsborough, N. C., April 2, 1863.

Maj. Gen. D. H. HILL,
Commanding in the Field:

GENERAL: Yesterday I received a note from General Longstreet stating that 10,000 or 12,000 men of the enemy had left Newport News, Va., for the coast of this State. General L. stated that he had good reason to think they were intended for New Berne. He has directed me to look after the enemy in the direction of New Berne and Wilmington, preferring the safety of the latter to this place. I have directed General Kemper to get the earliest information from New Berne and if any movement be commenced to send you intelligence at once, as General Longstreet directed you should be informed. Everything quiet at last accounts. Kemper made his demonstration on Monday. I sent to him a regiment. It is still there. As Evans' cavalry has been taken away, there must be some cavalry in front, and I have directed Robertson to supply it. I pray by this time you have the enemy as you wish them.

Very respectfully and truly,

R. RANSOM, JR.,
Brigadier-General.

ENGINEER DEPARTMENT, DISTRICT OF THE CAPE FEAR,
Wilmington, N. C., April 2, 1863.

His Excellency ZEBULON B. VANCE,
Governor of the State of North Carolina:

DEAR SIR: The army commissary here finds it extremely difficult to keep up a supply of provisions to meet the wants of the army, and the negroes sent by you at work on defenses under my charge have in consequence been on short rations since their arrival here. I respectfully suggest that if you will induce the owners, or others interested in the negroes, to send here a suitable supply of meat and bread I will pay the highest market rates for it and see that the negroes are properly fed.

I am, very respectfully, your obedient servant,

W. H. JAMES,
Captain and Chief Engineer.

WAR DEPARTMENT, C. S. A.,
Richmond, Va., April 2, 1863.

His Excellency ZEBULON B. VANCE,
Governor of North Carolina, Raleigh, N. C.:

SIR: On the receipt of your telegram with regard to the condition of affairs in Western North Carolina I directed General Donelson to send a force to Asheville * and vicinity to repress the disorders existing there. I have just received from him the following dispatch:

KNOXVILLE, TENN., *April* 1, 1863.

Hon. JAMES A. SEDDON.

In compliance with your order a regiment of cavalry will leave this place for Asheville, N. C., to-morrow morning, with orders to sweep the mountains in its vicinity of marauders, conscripts, and deserters.

D. S. DONELSON,
Brigadier-General Commanding.

With high regard, your obedient servant,

J. A. SEDDON.

RICHMOND, *April* 2, 1863.

W. S. MORRIS, Esq.,
    President Telegraph Company:

I am desired by the Secretary of War to request that you will permit nothing relative to the unfortunate disturbance which occurred in the city to-day to be sent over the telegraph lines in any direction for any purpose.

Very respectfully, &c.,

JNO. WITHERS,
Assistant Adjutant-General.

RICHMOND, *April* 2, 1863.

To the Richmond Press:

GENTLEMEN: The unfortunate disturbance which occurred to-day in this city is so liable to misconstruction and misrepresentation abroad that I am desired by the Secretary of War to make a special appeal to the editors and reporters of the press at Richmond, and earnestly to request them to avoid all reference directly or indirectly to the affair. The reasons for this are so obvious that it is unnecessary to state them, and the Secretary indulges the hope that his own views in this connection will be approved of by the press generally. Any other course must tend to embarrass our cause, and to encourage our enemies in their inhuman policy.

Very respectfully, &c.

JNO. WITHERS,
Assistant Adjutant-General.

HEADQUARTERS, *April* 3, 1863.

General R. E. LEE, *Commanding:*

GENERAL: Your letter of the 27th is just received. On Monday I started down for the Blackwater for the purpose of making arrangements for crossing a force for foraging in the counties east of the Chowan. I hope to be able to concentrate a force and have good bridges prepared by Wednesday next. My scout reported on Monday that the enemy at Newport News had embarked—it was supposed for North Carolina. There are some reports in this section that the enemy lately at Newport News has gone West. According to the best information that I can get he has a force at Suffolk of at least 17,000 men, well fortified. However, I hope to be able to cross with about the same force and to forage all the counties east of the Chowan. I do not deem it practicable to make movements concealed in any portion of this country.

---

* See Seddon to Donelson, Series I, Vol. XXIII, Part II, p. 726.

In the first place I do not suppose the enemy so very careless as to admit of it; second, there are many people in the eastern counties who sympathize with the opposite cause; third, our transportation is the most indifferent, rendering slow movements almost impracticable; rapid movements out of the question. Your transportation I thought indifferent. If you could see such as there is in this section you would be delighted at the contemplation of those large, fine teams of your own. The vehicle almost universal here is what our soldiers call the ox sulky. I will send you a sketch of one of them as soon as I can get a good draughtsman. I believe with you that a sudden vigorous attack upon Suffolk would give me that place, but I see no chance of getting the garrison unless I can get assistance from the Navy. Besides, it would cost me 5,000 men; but with another division I can do more and at a third the sacrifice. I have thought since about January 23 last (when I made the same suggestion to you) that one army corps could hold the line of the Rappahannock while the other was operating elsewhere. I cannot now appreciate the necessity of your retiring to the Annas in case you send off more troops from the Rappahannock. There you are fortified on the river and on the heights; on the Annas you would have neither. Besides, you would lose *morale* and encourage the enemy. If I move out to make the attack upon Suffolk I shall attack a position which ought to be well fortified, and I have information that it is. That position can be re-enforced from the Army of the Potomac in three days. I might get re-enforcements from you possibly in two days. I doubt, too, the policy of giving time to develop the plans of the enemy, but would prefer to act before his plans are matured. Our plans must be made to suit the emergency, so they might be more effective if made and executed before the enemy's were matured. I shall move, as I have said, across the Blackwater as soon as I can get substantial crossings, and at least make a forced reconnaissance while I endeavor to draw off subsistence and quartermasters' stores. If more can be done without great sacrifice I shall do it. My chief object in wishing a consultation was to endeavor to get your aid in securing co-operation on the part of the Navy. With that I should hope to capture the force at Suffolk and re-enforcements from the army of the Rappahannock.

I remain, general, very respectfully, your most obedient servant,

JAMES LONGSTREET,
Lieutenant-General, Commanding.

HEADQUARTERS,
Petersburg, Va., April 4, 1863.

General R. E. LEE,
Commanding, Fredericksburg, Va. :

GENERAL : I have the honor to acknowledge the receipt of your letters of the 27th and 31st ultimo and of the 2d instant. General Hill has succeeded in cutting off the enemy's position at Washington from his gunboats and has surrounded it, but he fears that time alone will reduce the garrison. He complains of want of artillery. It is thought that there are no iron-clads on the coast of North Carolina, and if I am correctly informed there is but one in the James River. General Hill is ordered and urged to be prompt in his operations. If he finds that too much time will be consumed in reducing the garrison at any point he is to draw off as soon as he gets out the supplies from the eastern counties. I hope to be able to cross the Blackwater on Wednesday or

Thursday next and to get what supplies there are east of that stream and, if I find it possible, to make an effort to get that garrison. There seems but little room to doubt but the enemy is inclined to make his great effort in the West, but we may break him up in the East and then re-enforce in the West in time to crush him there. It may be necessary in this view to suggest to the commander in the West to decline battle there until we can re-enforce, unless he finds a favorable opportunity. I hope to be able to finish with the operations in this section in time to join you as soon as the roads are in condition for you to begin to operate. I have not thought that the enemy could advance on either this or your line until the roads were better; on this, not at all, unless he sent other than the forces that he has had here. The forces that have gone West may have been sent there to keep down trouble. It is possible, too, that he has deceived himself with regard to the forces sent by us West. The three regiments that were sent from here may have been magnified into a great force. Their papers have frequently mentioned movements of our troops toward Kentucky.

I remain, very respectfully, your most obedient servant,
JAMES LONGSTREET,
Lieutenant-General, Commanding.

P. S.—All of my information is to the effect that half at least of Burnside's command is still at Suffolk.

HEADQUARTERS, *April* 4, 1863.
General R. E. LEE,
Commanding, Fredericksburg, Va.:

GENERAL: I send you a letter just received from General Hill. I have ordered six rifled guns instead of only four. As he has undertaken Washington it is important that he should reduce it; otherwise it will give the enemy great confidence. I doubt if New Berne is worth the trouble and time it would take to reduce it. General H. asks for two weeks; in addition to these two weeks it will require two to move out to Suffolk and draw the supplies from there. Can we afford to consume this time and reach you before the enemy can move? It depends on your roads more than anything else. If you can spare me two more brigades and artillery I can operate at once. I think that I might do with one brigade and a battalion of artillery. If we succeed in getting one of the positions of the enemy the others may not be so difficult.

I remain, very respectfully, your most obedient servant,
JAMES LONGSTREET,
Lieutenant-General, Commanding.

You might telegraph in such a way as to indicate your wishes without making them understood to operators.

HEADQUARTERS,
Kinston, N. C., April 4, 1863.
Lieut. Gen. JAMES LONGSTREET,
Comdg. Department of Virginia and North Carolina:

GENERAL: Your letter of the 30th was duly received. Kemper made a demonstration on New Berne. The enemy kept within his works. Hill has been around Washington since Tuesday. He has called one of my regiments to his vicinity. To-morrow Kemper goes to Franklin. I shall be here with four regiments and enough artillery for my infantry. I have but one squadron of cavalry. If an opportunity offers I shall strike; but with only 2,500 men I shall have to be circumspect. Hill has directed me not to go to Whiting under any circumstances unless the latter states that the enemy's fleet is directly off the forts below. In this official note let me ask a favor. If it be possible to prevent it do not let me be kept only to watch when others are doing better. I am not partial to service where there has been so little done and where there are poor opportunities to render real good.

Very respectfully, your most obedient servant,

R. RANSOM, Jr.,
Brigadier-General.

HEADQUARTERS, *April 4*, 1863.

General R. RANSOM, [Jr.,]
Commanding at Goldsborough, N. C.:

In case you are likely to give battle, telegraph for Colonel Ransom; otherwise let him remain on the coast. I do not know where General Robertson is. Please send an order to him to send three companies of cavalry to General Whiting. Explain to him why I send the order through you.

JAMES LONGSTREET,
Lieutenant-General Commanding.

HEADQUARTERS, *April 4*, 1863.

General W. H. C. WHITING,
Commanding at Wilmington, N. C.:

Keep Col. [M. W.] Ransom unless his regiment is going into battle, when General Ransom will telegraph for him. Three companies are ordered in the place of Colonel Barbour. I hope that the monitor off the bar will not be able to weather the storms. If she attempts to cross have a party ready to board her.

JAMES LONGSTREET,
Lieutenant-General Commanding.

HEADQUARTERS FORCES ON BLACKWATER,
April 4, 1863.

Lieutenant-General LONGSTREET,
Commanding Department:

GENERAL: I send you the map of roads. The enemy have not gotten over the fright of my move to Carrsville and are on the alert, expecting an attack from us. My scouts report the cars running day and night from Norfolk. I learn from Mr. Hofman, just from Suffolk, that when he left the forces consisted only of some sixteen to eighteen regiments inclusive, say some 13,000 men. Thirteen regiments have been there, and either three or five of the Ninth Army Corps are there. He thinks that fortifications run from Suffolk to Dismal Swamp, but I think he is mistaken and will have an examination made. If this be so it may be difficult to get between Suffolk and Norfolk. He says the plan of Suffolk and fortifications I sent you is correct. The troops at Suffolk are not reliable. I am preparing to rebuild the Joiner Bridge. I will hear to-night, I think, from a gentleman in Suffolk and will write you by next mail.

Very respectfully, your obedient servant,

M. JENKINS,
Brigadier-General, Commanding.

HEADQUARTERS,
Petersburg, Va., April 4, 1863—2 p. m.

Maj. Gen. D. H. HILL, *Commanding, &c.:*

GENERAL: In asking you to send me the cavalry, leaving a regiment in Bertie, I only wished the cavalry over and above the force that you need on your picket line. Three companies should be kept with General Whiting at Wilmington. The enemy seems to be re-enforcing in the West with a view to operating actively there, and only on the defensive in the East. We should therefore act promptly here with the purpose of pushing some of our forces West as soon as we may be able to do so. If you find that you are likely to be detained any time in reducing Washington it will probably be better to abandon it and confine yourself to drawing out the supplies from the eastern counties. This you can do with the force properly belonging in North Carolina. The cavalry I will send back as soon as we can get the supplies from the country east of the Chowan. I want the brigades of Generals Garnett and Kemper at Franklin, Va., as soon as you find that you cannot reduce the garrison at Washington without consuming too much time; or, if you are successful, I want them returned to me at Franklin; also my Whitworth, if it is not the one that was burst. Give me the earliest information of the time that these troops can be put at Franklin.

I remain, very respectfully, your obedient servant,

JAMES LONGSTREET,
Lieutenant-General

I suppose that you know that we have not the ammunition to fight an artillery battle against the enemy's fortifications.

WILMINGTON, N. C., *April 5, 1863.*

Lieutenant-General LONGSTREET:

Beauregard informs me eight monitors off Charleston Bar. Enemy have landed four regiments on Cole's Island. He desires telegraph kept open.

W. H. C. WHITING.

WAR DEPARTMENT, C. S. A.,
Richmond, Va., April 5, 1863.

General W. H. C. WHITING,
Wilmington, N. C.:

The movements of the enemy seem to threaten an approaching attack on Charleston. Hold Ransom's brigade in readiness for movement in the event their forces should be concentrated for a land attack.

J. A. SEDDON,
Secretary of War.

GOLDSBOROUGH, N. C., *April 5, 1863.*

Maj. G. MOXLEY SORREL, *Assistant Adjutant-General:*

I have no cavalry to send to Wilmington; all available actively employed. Claiborne's horses broken down. Will send the companies as soon as possible.

B. H. ROBERTSON,
Brigadier-General, Commanding Cavalry.

HDQRS. FORCES ON BLACKWATER, *April 6, 1863.*

Lieut. Gen. JAMES LONGSTREET:

GENERAL: I have postponed for a few days my attempts upon the enemy's advanced post, having found him much on the alert. In view of your designs I have taken steps to have them think you are gone to the West with the greater portion of your force to meet Burnside's movement. I will send an intelligent officer or scout to-night to discover whether it will be possible to throw a force by the south side between Suffolk and Norfolk. He will have no idea, of course, why I wish to know, as I will lead him to suppose it is merely for a cavalry raid to tear up the railroad, &c. If it cannot be done we might effect the same object by crossing the Nansemond River by pontoon. My last estimate of the forces at Suffolk I think correct—say 12,000 to 15,000. If you succeed in capturing them it will be the most brilliant affair of the war and would be attended by glorious results to the cause. Part of Lane's battery has arrived, but the most important gun for our purposes is not with it, and the ammunition is defective. I hope the Whitworth gun will be here in time for the gunboat; at any rate I will make the attempt with the guns I have the next trip they make.

I am, general, your obedient servant,

M. JENKINS,
Brigadier-General.

HEADQUARTERS, *April 6, 1863.*

General M. JENKINS, *Commanding at Blackwater:*

GENERAL: I desire that you have your command in readiness to cross the Blackwater on Friday. The divisions of Generals Pickett and Hood will not be able to cross before Saturday; but if the force at Suffolk is no larger than stated in your letter of the 4th you will be able to cross with the two brigades on the day before them and take up some strong position between the Blackwater and Suffolk. You will probably cross at the Franklin Bridge. I hope to join you on Thursday at your headquarters and will then give detailed instructions. The regiment of Colonel Baker should be ready to move with you. You should have four days' rations cooked. The squadron of Captain Graham is ordered to be at Blackwater Bridge, to cross at that point, and move on the flank via Windsor. The pickets that you have on the other side of the Blackwater had better be left there, provided with the number of rations already mentioned. You can take them on to join you after crossing. You will require tools for intrenching. The cavalry should be provided with wires to stretch across the roads in case the enemy's cavalry should attack it, particularly for any cavalry charge.

Please acknowledge receipt of this by telegraph.

I remain, very respectfully, your most obedient servant,

JAMES LONGSTREET,
Lieutenant-General, Commanding.

HEADQUARTERS,
Petersburg, Va., April 6, 1863—1 p. m.

Maj. Gen. D. H. HILL, *Commanding, &c. :*

GENERAL : From your letter of the 4th instant I infer that your cavalry is picketing continually from Roanoke to Wilmington. This, it seems to me, is superfluous labor. I should think three companies quite enough for General Whiting. Six ought to be enough at and around New Berne and three near Washington. Then a cavalry force—say Claiborne's regiment—in Bertie ought to be more than enough to watch that country while their horses are resting. The balance of the force ought to be kept at some suitable point for other operations and for foraging the animals. If, however, you cannot make such arrangements I must do without him. I am satisfied that we have a much greater cavalry force than the enemy. That being the case I cannot see how we should be obliged to use but part of a regiment on the other side of the Blackwater against two of the enemy. The enemy is reported to be ready to commence his attack upon Charleston, so he cannot re-enforce from that quarter. My move across the Blackwater will secure you against any re-enforcement from that quarter, so you will be free to operate with your other forces, which (not including Generals Garnett and Kemper) will exceed the force of the enemy. The two regiments at Hamilton ought to be enough to keep up your investment without Garnett, and they will then be in position to cut off any force that might be so indiscreet as to venture up to Weldon. You could at least keep the enemy inside his works and draw out the supplies from the eastern portion of the State. Your letter of the 2d instant expressed confidence in entire success if you could get four other rifle guns. I ordered them to you at once, but you now say that nothing but heavy artillery will answer. I hope, therefore, that you will return the guns under Capt. [James] Reilly to me at Franklin. I hope to cross the river on Saturday, and as they are the only long-range guns belonging to one of my divisions they will be essential to me. The enemy will surely be in condition to begin his operations on the Rappahannock in a month more, and we should at least be ready to defend in this department and re-enforce on the Rappahannock by that time. I was so much encouraged by your letter of the 2d that I sent you the artillery that you called for and asked if the time (two weeks) could be given you with Garnett's and Kemper's brigades. From your letter of the 4th I conclude that it is still a matter of doubt whether you will then reduce the garrison at Washington. It must be better, therefore, for me to get my forces together at once and move across the Blackwater and secure such provisions and forage as may be in that portion of Virginia and North Carolina.

I remain, very respectfully, your most obedient servant,
JAMES LONGSTREET,
Lieutenant-General, Commanding.

It may be that after I have finished on the other side that I can send you some other force, but I presume that I shall be obliged to return to the Rappahannock.

HEADQUARTERS,
Petersburg, Va., April 6, 1863.

General D. H. HILL, *Commanding:*

GENERAL: In writing for the cavalry I only wanted such as would not be in use in your line as pickets. Three companies should go to

General Whiting. I wish you would establish an infantry and cavalry force in Bertie to guard the Chowan and give notice at Franklin if any of the enemy's gunboats ascend the river. I think there can be no need of troops at Weldon except such as may be necessary to guard the bridge. I sent you four rifle guns and two Napoleons. I shall need them as soon as you may be able to dispense with them. When they are returned send them to Franklin by rail. Let me know by telegraph when they will start back.

Most respectfully, your obedient servant,

JAMES LONGSTREET,
Lieutenant-General, Commanding.

P. S.—I have this moment received your letter of the 4th. I wrote you yesterday, suggesting that you might keep Garnett's brigade if it would be of much use to you. You now say, however, that heavy artillery alone can be useful, so I suppose there is no prospect of a successful termination of your expedition. I sent authority to you to keep General Garnett and sent you six of my best field guns. As they will be of no service to you I hope you will send them back to Franklin as soon as possible. You can at least keep the enemy inside his works and haul off all supplies that may be in the counties east of you. This will be a great thing, and we may yet be able to render you such aid as you desire. You know, though, that we cannot afford to fight artillery against them, particularly when they are behind their works. The order for the return of the troops was given under the impression drawn from your letters that there was no prospect of reducing the garrison at Washington. A letter from you yesterday seems to give some hope of success and you were then authorized to retain Garnett. Now, again, you seem to have but little hope except from heavy artillery. The enemy is reported about to commence operations at Charleston, so you can go on, at least, hauling off supplies from any portion of the State. If I can get through in time or find that I can render other assistance to you I will do so promptly. I regret very much that matters have so turned out as to delay me, but we must hope for better fortune hereafter.

HEADQUARTERS DEPARTMENT OF RICHMOND,
April 6, 1863.

Lieut. Gen. JAMES LONGSTREET, *Commanding:*

GENERAL: I received your note this evening and hasten to answer it. The proposed diversion on the Peninsula can be made. Owing to the continually threatened riots in Richmond it would not do to move any of Rhett's command. It must be done with Wise's brigade. He has on the Pamunkey 380 men guarding and supporting the engineers in tearing up the railroad iron from West Point to White House. This cannot be disturbed. He has then left 1,563 infantry and 412 cavalry and two light batteries, making a force of 1,975 and two batteries. This, deducting camp guards to be left at Chaffin's farm, will constitute the expedition under General Wise. I shall start him down the Peninsula Wednesday morning unless I receive contrary instructions from you by telegraph. There is a force at Yorktown of from 3,000 to 5,000 men. Of course Chaffin's and Drewry's Bluffs will be left without any infantry. I do not think it will be well to go far beyond Yorktown unless the force up to that point is met and whipped. Fort Magruder, you are aware, will have to be carried or the garrison forced to retire before proceeding to

Yorktown. Wise has been chafing for a chance and I am glad he has got it. He knows the country thoroughly and no doubt will do well.

I have the honor to be, with great respect, your obedient servant,

ARNOLD ELZEY,
Major-General.

HEADQUARTERS ARMY OF NORTHERN VIRGINIA,
April 6, 1863.

Maj. Gen. ARNOLD ELZEY,
Commanding at Richmond, Va.:

GENERAL: General Longstreet contemplates a move across the Blackwater and thinks he may require more infantry and artillery than he now has. In that event, can you spare him either Wise's brigade or your artillery battalion, armed as infantry, with a light battery or two? As he will be in front of Richmond, and as there are now no Federal troops on the James River, except those in his front, I think you could re-enforce him with advantage. Please see the Secretary on the subject and communicate with General Longstreet.

I am, with great respect, your obedient servant,

R. E. LEE,
General.

HEADQUARTERS ARMY OF NORTHERN VIRGINIA,
April 6,. 1863.

Lieut. Gen. JAMES LONGSTREET,
Commanding, &c., Petersburg, Va.:

GENERAL: I have received your two letters of the 4th instant, inclosing one from General D. H. Hill, of the 2d instant. General Hill seems to be operating judiciously and you have given him all that he requires. I hope therefore he may be successful and may not be obliged to storm the enemy's intrenchments, which might cause the loss of many of our brave men. I was in hopes he might have had enough troops in the Department of North Carolina for his military operations, and regret that he has to use Kemper's and Garnett's brigades for such work. You know how much depends on your divisions, and I wish to reserve them as much as possible. As to your own operations you must push them according to your own judgment, and I would recommend careful reconnaissances before attacking Suffolk or any other fortifications of the enemy, and that you endeavor to draw his forces out by threatening his communications. I think you will find none of Burnside's corps opposed to you. The troops in your front are those which have been at Norfolk and Old Point. Burnside's corps has certainly gone West. At the first intimation of its departure from Newport News a scout was dispatched to watch the Baltimore and Ohio Railroad. He proceeded as far as Ellicott's Mill and learned that the troops had been brought up the bay and were encamped around Baltimore. He saw them on their way over the Baltimore and Ohio Railroad and counted some fifty-seven trains. He conversed with the men at some of the stations, who expressed great dissatisfaction at being transferred West; were fearful of the climate, their health, &c., and deserted on every opportunity that offered. The troops conveyed over this road were altogether infantry. If any artillery was taken West it was carried on the Pennsylvania Central road, which, I learn from other sources, was also used in the transportation of Burnside's corps.

The roads in this section have dried astonishingly, but the storm of Saturday has again surrounded us with mud and water.   I cannot say whether General Hooker will advance or not, though, as before stated, all the information I receive from every source goes to show that it is his intention to do so, and that he is prepared.   It may be a part of their general plan to deceive us while re-enforcing their western armies; but as soon as I can move I will endeavor to find out.   In the mean time I do not think it prudent to weaken the force here, but should you require more strength I think it better that you call on General Elzey for Wise's brigade and such artillery as can be sent you from Richmond.   I have written to General Elzey on the subject.

I am, very respectfully, your obedient servant,

R. E. LEE,
General.

DIVISION HEADQUARTERS,
April 6, 1863.

Lieut. Gen. JAMES LONGSTREET:

MY DEAR GENERAL: I sent up yesterday some Yankees taken by Dearing.   From what I could gather from the sergeant a good many enlistments would soon expire, and he seemed to think the men would not re-enlist and thought they would not be forced in.   Schriver is here yet.   I would have sent him down yesterday to Suffolk, but he will have to go to Newport News; thence to Norfolk and Suffolk.   He says he will have no difficulty in reaching Suffolk by that route, but much by any other.   In order to send him that way some little money will be necessary.   I have none except Confederate money, which will not pass.   I think $40 of State money would answer and would be well expended.   He could return (by starting on Wednesday) on Sunday or Monday next, and could bring back accurate information if he chooses.   I think it worth trying, and if you have any funds on hand for such purposes and wish the venture made please send down by first train.   If not I will immediately return Schriver to his company.

I am, general, your obedient servant and friend,

GEO. E. PICKETT.

P. S.—Mr. Riddick hears from Chuckatuck that the Yankees have not crossed the river at Reed's Bridge, but are repairing the bridge; will take probably three days.   When completed it gives them a chance to sweep the country.   Shall I send expedition down after forage and at same time burn bridge?

WAR DEPARTMENT, C. S. A.,
Richmond, Va., April 7, 1863.

Lieut. Gen. JAMES LONGSTREET, *Commanding, &c.:*

GENERAL: Your letter of the 6th instant* reached me this morning. Gratified to learn that you contemplate an important movement at so early a day.   I was anxious to aid in making it as effective as possible and lost no time in conferring with the Secretary of the Navy to secure the co-operation of such vessels as could be commanded to cut off the enemy from retreat and effect their capture.   The Secretary had every disposition to meet your views, and thought at first that the iron-clad

---

* See p. 910.

gunboat Richmond, with another light steamer, might be ventured to aid your operations. He had, however, to consult his naval officers and likewise to learn whether the obstructions could be removed or widened in time to allow the ships to pass. Unfortunately, it has been ascertained that the vessels could not pass without such removal of the heavy obstructions as to render it very doubtful whether the work could be accomplished in time. At the same time the replacement of the obstructions after the termination of the expedition, it is estimated, would require much time and expenditure. I have required a fuller report than I yet have to satisfy me of the inexpediency of attempting the present removal; but Colonel Gilmer, the head of the Engineer Bureau, expresses himself so strongly against the feasibility of the speedy removal that I fear that portion of your plan will have to be relinquished. Should I conclude otherwise I will promptly inform you; but you had better proceed without counting on naval co-operation. I have arranged with Major-General Elzey to make an expedition down the Peninsula with some 2,000 men, as if to threaten Yorktown and Fort Monroe, and at the same time to have a few companies of cavalry threaten the enemy at Gloucester Town, as if there was a purpose, by combined attack, to carry all the posts of the enemy on the Peninsula. These movements, it is hoped, will agitate and alarm the enemy, so as to make their resistance to your real attack less serious and effectually preclude their drawing any re-enforcements from this side.

With my best wishes for the success of your operations, I remain, with high respect, very truly, yours,

> J. A. SEDDON,
> *Secretary of War.*

HEADQUARTERS, *April* 7, 1863.

Major-General ELZEY, *Commanding:*

GENERAL: In giving instructions to General Wise you had better direct that he should not pass Yorktown any considerable distance with his entire force unless he finds that he will by doing so draw out the force at Yorktown, but that instructions must not prevent him taking advantage of any favorable opportunity that may occur.

I remain, sir, very respectfully, your obedient servant,

> JAMES LONGSTREET,
> *Lieutenant-General, Commanding.*

P. S.—It would probably be well to magnify his command as much as he can. The enemy likes to be deceived, or rather to have good excuses for reverses. People who play tricks are always the easiest tricked. He might give it out that you are behind him with any number of troops. I want half a dozen 20-pounder Parrotts for my expedition. I have the men and horses for them if you cannot spare them.

> HEADQUARTERS,
> *Petersburg, Va., April* 7, 1863.

Maj. Gen. D. H. HILL, *Commanding:*

GENERAL: Your letter of the 5th instant is just received. You should remember that my orders are based upon information that I receive. Up to the 2d instant you gave me no reason to hope that you could accomplish anything at Washington; on the contrary, you seemed to have but little hope in your own letter, and frequently forwarded letters from General Garnett which always argued the utter impossibility of your being able to accomplish anything. Under these circumstances I called for the troops to be returned to me that I might put them at other work, for we have already been idle too long. Then came your letter of the 2d, which was full of encouragement and hope. I sent you, instead of four guns, as you desired, six, and sent you authority to retain General Garnett's brigade. After your letter of the 2d came one of the 4th, which, I believe, was more desponding than your previous letters, and expressing the opinion that nothing but heavy artillery would answer any good purpose. I then sent my order for Garnett's brigade to return and the six pieces of artillery. Your letter of the 5th revives much hope again, and I now authorize you to retain General Garnett and the six field pieces if they are important to you. I fear from the tone of General Garnett's letters that he was so well satisfied that Washington could not be taken that he was not even willing to make the effort. Because things are not laid down in the book it does not follow that things cannot be done. You mention for the first time that General Foster is below you with a succoring force. If that be so New Berne must be weak and General Ransom might get a position below it, which will leave it in the same condition as Washington. I would have been glad to have left General Kemper at Kinston to aid in such a purpose had I been advised. You have enough force for this and your own work without him, however; that is, if you have not sent General Garnett back. If there is a good point below New Berne where a battery can be placed which will cut off the garrison from succor you had better have it fortified at once. You will readily see the advantage of this without my going into details. The Secretary of War telegraphed General Whiting yesterday that he should hold General Ransom ready to go to South Carolina. General Whiting telegraphed me to know what he should do. He is ordered to leave General Ransom where he is, but the Secretary is advised that General Evans may be spared, but it is the only brigade at Wilmington. Communicate with me at Franklin, either by telegraph or otherwise. Anything of the ordnance department send to Col. P. T. Manning at this place. If General Ransom can get a good position below New Berne which he can fortify I think Colonel Manning can send him some heavy guns.

I remain, very respectfully, your most obedient servant,

JAMES LONGSTREET,
Lieutenant-General, Commanding.

P. S.—I fully appreciate the importance of your success. Besides the bacon and corn that you speak of it ought to give us the coast of North Carolina as far as the mouth of the Chowan at least.

HEADQUARTERS,
Petersburg, Va., April 7, 1863.

General R. E. LEE, *Commanding:*

GENERAL: Your letter of the 5th is received. General Hill reports the enemy in the river below him with a considerable succoring force under General Foster; that his fort, some distance below, keeps the force back, and that the enemy will have to come out and give him battle before he can reach Washington, unless he succeeds in reducing the fort. He has not yet been able to make any impression upon our fort. General Hill is now ordered to endeavor to establish a like fort below New Berne to prevent this succoring force returning to New Berne. He expresses every confidence in being able to overcome the enemy should he land for the purpose of relieving Washington. If he reduces Washington and succeeds in getting a good point on the river below New Berne I hope that all of the State (North Carolina) below the Chowan will soon be relieved of the presence of the enemy. I shall not be able to cross the Blackwater before Saturday, possibly not before Sunday. If I find it practicable I shall get around the enemy's position at Suffolk and endeavor to cut off re-enforcements by batteries on the river, &c. I do not propose to do anything more than draw out the supplies from that country unless something very favorable should offer. I have ordered General Wise, with such of his force as can be spared from Richmond, to make a strong diversion on the Peninsula. If I find that I can do no more than haul off supplies I shall hurry one of my divisions (Hood's) back, so as to be within reach of you, unless the force is much stronger at Suffolk than you suppose it to be.

I remain, very respectfully, your obedient servant,

JAMES LONGSTREET,
Lieutenant-General.

HEADQUARTERS,
Petersburg, Va., April 7, 1863.

Hon. JAMES A. SEDDON,
Secretary of War:

SIR: Major-General Hill is now operating against Washington, N. C., with the purpose of reducing that garrison and opening thereby the counties east of that to our subsistence and quartermasters' departments. The town of Washington is completely invested, and a fort that we have constructed below that cuts off re-enforcements. General Foster is said to be in the mouth of the river with re-enforcements, but unable to get them to Washington until he can reduce our fort. He has not as yet been able to make any impression on the fort, and we hope that he may be obliged to land and give battle or give up the garrison. In the mean time General Hill is ordered to throw a force below New Berne and fortify some good position so as to prevent General Foster returning to New Berne. To make this last move secure it may be necessary for General Hill to use the brigade of General Evans, the only one left at Wilmington. I deem it proper to advise you of the condition of affairs in North Carolina that you may better judge of the propriety of ordering General Evans' brigade to Charleston. I have received no intimation from the department that any of the troops of this command would be called for to re-enforce Charleston and could not therefore be expected to be ready for such emergency. If the safety of Charleston depends upon such re-enforcements, however, we can resume defensive arrangements and spare even more than this brigade.

I remain, sir, very respectfully, your obedient servant,

JAMES LONGSTREET,
Lieutenant-General, Commanding.

APRIL 7, 186 —7.30 p. m.

[Maj. Gen. D. H. HILL:]

GENERAL: I have examined the positions in front of Washington for rifled pieces with Capts. [Samuel R.] Bunting and Starr, of the artillery, and am of the opinion that those occupied by the smooth-bores of Captain Starr's battery, six in number, are the most favorable that can be found. They are on the east and front of the town and would command the block-house and new earthwork (lately erected by the Yankees to fire, I presume, on Rodman's Point) and the fort, as it is called, about the center of line of intrenchments. I shall strengthen the earth about them to-night and will be ready for them whenever they may be sent.

Very respectfully, your obedient servant,

R. B. GARNETT,
Brigadier-General, Commanding.

HEADQUARTERS BRIGADE,
Contentnea Creek Bridge. April 7, 1863.

Maj. Gen. D. H. HILL:

GENERAL: I got here at 12 o'clock to-day with my three regiments and battery. General Robertson has gone to the front. I hear nothing from Swift Creek to-day. Direct your couriers to bring dispatches by the cross-roads some 8 or 10 miles this side of your headquarters, where the Greenville road crosses the Birney place and Boyd's Ferry road, and thence direct to this place and not by Snow Hill. General Robertson has ordered an officer to fix this line of couriers. If the enemy attempt to move on Greenville we will try to give a good account of ourselves.

Yours, &c.,

R. RANSOM, JR.,
Brigadier-General.

HEADQUARTERS,
Kinston, N. C., April 7, 1863.

Maj. Gen. D. H. HILL,
Commanding North Carolina:

DEAR SIR: Your favor of yesterday is to hand. Whitford had sent me word of the advance of the enemy. I shall be ready to obey your instructions. Some days ago I sent a force to the Contentnea to throw up batteries, rifle-pits, &c., to protect those passes. I wrote you last evening. The couriers seem to travel too slowly. I will direct them to go 8 miles the hour. Order yours in coming this way to do the same. I have just gotten yours of yesterday, and it is 7 o'clock.

Yours, very respectfully,

R. RANSOM, JR.,
Brigadier-General.

WAR DEPARTMENT, C. S. A.,
Richmond, April 7, 1863.

General W. H. C. WHITING,
Wilmington, N. C.:

General Evans' brigade must be held prepared to move to Charleston.

J. A. SEDDON,
Secretary of War.

HEADQUARTERS,
Wilmington, N. C., April 7, 1863.

Maj. Gen. D. H. HILL,
    Cross-Roads, 3 *miles south of Washington, N. C.:*

GENERAL: I wish I had some 10-pounder Parrotts for you, but we have never had any of those guns though I have frequently applied for them. My field artillery is wretched, being mostly smooth-bore and howitzers. I hope you will be successful, but fear they will be enabled to re-enforce. Beauregard reports all the monitors off the bar at Charleston. Secretary of War ordered me to hold Ransom in readiness to move. I referred the dispatch to Longstreet.

    Very respectfully,

W. H. C. WHITING,
Brigadier-General.

WILMINGTON, N. C., *April* 7, 1863.

Lieutenant-General LONGSTREET:

    Secretary of War has ordered Evans' brigade to be ready to move. Action commenced at Charleston. I must have some troops to replace them if they go; it will not do to leave this place bare.

W. H. C. WHITING,
Brigadier-General.

WAR DEPARTMENT, C. S. A.,
Richmond, April 8, 1863.

General JAMES LONGSTREET, *Petersburg, Va.:*

    I would not have you abstain from offensive operation. They may effect as much by diversion as more direct aid. Still if you can arrange to spare one brigade (say Evans') for Wilmington I should be much pleased. The arrangement to send one forward in case of necessity was known to General Beauregard and General Whiting prior to your command, and I supposed had been communicated to you.

J. A. SEDDON,
Secretary of War.

HEADQUARTERS, *April* 8, 1863—3 p. m.

Maj. Gen. D. H. HILL, *Commanding, &c.:*

    GENERAL: Let me suggest that you have your fort so arranged that you will be able to put your guns out of fire from the gunboats if it should become necessary. By having your platforms high you can put your guns on them when in action, and if the enemy's guns have a longer range than yours you can run your guns down under the parapet so as to get them out of fire; or you might have pits alongside your platforms so as to run your guns out of fire. We must not expect to contend against the enemy in ammunition, so it may become necessary for you to occupy the fort merely to keep back the enemy's transports or only to play upon the gunboats when they are in close range. If you can cut General Foster off from New Berne by using Evans' brigade at Wilmington, do not hesitate to do so. Your force in North Carolina must be superior to that of the enemy. If you can only get his garrison at one position you will be able to concentrate to great advantage upon the next.

I remain, very respectfully, your most obedient servant,

JAMES LONGSTREET,
Lieutenant-General.

HEADQUARTERS,
Petersburg, Va., April 8, 1863.

Maj. Gen. D. H. HILL, *Commanding, &c.:*

GENERAL : I wrote you yesterday to endeavor to get a point below New Berne to prevent General Foster's return there with his re-enforcements. If you cannot make such arrangements at once have it in your mind, and should Foster land and give you battle be prepared to cut him off from New Berne by land and water, if you are so fortunate as to beat him back. Please send couriers and letters to me at Franklin until otherwise advised. The War Department has arranged it so that your command is a department and includes all the troops in the State. The Secretary has ordered General Evans' brigade to be ready to go to Charleston. I hope that it will not be necessary to send him there.

I remain, very respectfully, your obedient servant,

JAMES LONGSTREET,
Lieutenant-General, Commanding.

HEADQUARTERS,
Petersburg, Va, April 8, 1863.

Brig. Gen. W. H. C. WHITING,
Wilmington, N. C.:

I wrote the Secretary of War yesterday. He knows your situation. I hope that there may be no occasion for Evans to move.

JAMES LONGSTREET,
Lieutenant-General, Commanding.

HEADQUARTERS,
Petersburg, Va., April 8, 1863.

Brig. Gen. W. H. C. WHITING,
Commanding, &c., Wilmington, N. C.:

GENERAL : Colonel Long has just made his inspection report. I am much gratified at the favorable account that he gives of your condition and your progress in your difficult labors. I have ordered the chief of subsistence to have you supplied with provisions for at least a month at your forts. It seems to me that you have hardly enough ammunition in your forts. I have written the Secretary of War, giving him, I think, very good reasons why your garrison should not be reduced below its present force, yet I think that that force can be spared for a few days better than any other. General Hill is now at Washington. He has invested the place and has thrown up a fort below which cuts out re-enforcements. General Foster is below with re-enforcements, but cannot get in unless he can reduce the fort. General Hill thinks that he will be compelled to land and give battle or give up the garrison. If he lands we hope to destroy him. General Hill is ordered to try and throw a force below New Berne and erect a battery on the river, which will prevent Foster from returning to New Berne. I have explained the condition of affairs to the Secretary, suggesting that if you could keep Evans you could so co-operate as to make the last move completely successful. I wish you to have this in your mind, and if, in communicating with General Ransom, you find a favorable opportunity you should not fail to take advantage of it. I leave to-night for Franklin to cross Blackwater and cut off re-enforcements for North Carolina, and at the same time haul off all provisions, &c., from the counties east of the Blackwater.

I remain, very respectfully, your obedient servant,

JAMES LONGSTREET,
Lieutenant-General Commanding.

CONFIDENTIAL.]   HDQRS. ARMY OF NORTHERN VIRGINIA,
April 9, 1863.

Hon. JAMES A. SEDDON,
Secretary of War:

SIR: General Longstreet proposes to cross the Blackwater with a view to obtaining supplies from the counties of Nansemond, Isle of Wight, &c. He is apprehensive that the enemy may move up James River and get in his rear, and asks whether he cannot obtain some co-operation from the Navy. I am not aware that the Navy can operate below the obstructions at Drewry's Bluff. If, however, any of their steamers could go down as low as Hardy's Bluff, at which point General Longstreet might place some batteries on the land, they could observe the river below, and I do not think the enemy would venture to throw a land force ashore above Day's Point. They might also enable the Quartermaster's Department to use boats on the river to transport supplies, which would prove more expeditious than hauling them by land.

I am, with much respect, your obedient servant,

R. E. LEE,
General.

HEADQUARTERS,
Cross-Roads, April 9, 1863.

Maj. Gen. D. H. HILL, *Commanding, &c.:*

GENERAL: General Pettigrew reports that the enemy are advancing upon him (1.15 p. m.; reached here about 3 p. m.). I immediately ordered the Fiftieth to him. Since then two dispatches have been received. The first stated that the part of the column seen by Major Ross was half a mile long, but he did not see the rear of it. The next states that there were three brigades of infantry and two regiments, and that there were eighteen pieces of artillery. I have ordered the Fiftieth Regiment and Second Battalion (seven companies) down to him. The last two dispatches were sent by General P. They were from Leventhorpe's officers. Nothing has been received from General P. since his first dispatch, asking me to send a part of my troops to him. Since then I have sent him the dispatch from Morehead, stating that they were within 4 miles of Swift Creek. Nothing has been received from Swift Creek since the first dispatch (2.30 p. m.). I do not think there will be an advance from Swift Creek, but I may be mistaken. The last courier from General Pettigrew said they were fighting at Blount Creek Mill.

Very respectfully, &c.,

JUNIUS DANIEL,
Brigadier-General.

APRIL 9, 1863—11.45 o'clock.

[Maj. Gen. D. H. HILL:]

GENERAL: I have sent the battery which came with Colonel Martin's regiment (it arrived this morning) back to its station. I have more light artillery than I can use. Forage is getting very scarce, and Colonel M. says it is needed in the defense of Rainbow Banks. I would also suggest in this connection that Captain Starr's battery be also ordered to Greenville, or any other point you may deem best. The batteries of Captains Reilly and Bunting are sufficient, I should think, for my command. The enemy strengthen their works every night. Their line of intrenchments is now as strong as it can well be made, as far as I can judge with my glass. My wagon train started down to Pungo yesterday morning.

Very respectfully, your obedient servant,

R. B. GARNETT,
Brigadier-General, Commanding.

HEADQUARTERS,
Petersburg, Va., April 9, 1863—9 a. m.

Maj. Gen. D. H. HILL,
Commanding Department of North Carolina:

GENERAL: If you can operate without the aid of Evans' brigade the commanding general desires you to order it to be in readiness to move to Charleston at a moment's notice. If you need it and cannot get along without it he desires you to retain it. General Longstreet left last night for Franklin. Your communication by courier of the 7th instant is received. It will be forwarded at once to the general.

I am, general, very respectfully, your obedient servant,

G. MOXLEY SORREL,
Assistant Adjutant-General.

BRIGADE HEADQUARTERS,
Diascund Bridge, Va., April 9, 1863—3.30 p. m.

Maj. Gen. ARNOLD ELZEY,
Commanding, &c.:

GENERAL: I moved yesterday morning at 9 a. m. with my whole force except the several guards. Arrived here in person with the artillery about 12.30 p. m. My men marched well and in fine spirits, and did well in weather and bivouac and roads. The infantry are delayed at Forge Bridge by the high water. I ordered the baggage wagons to be emptied to take them across dry-footed. As soon as I arrived I called the chief officers of this post together for reports. Here they report:

Holcombe Legion, fit for action	175
32d (Virginia) Battalion, Maj. [J. R.] Robertson, fit for action	40
Total cavalry to be relied on in a fight	215
One section of artillery	39
One battalion of infantry	239
At Diascund, of all arms	493

At Diascund, of all arms 493

    Re-enforcements brought by me:

Artillery (one battery and two sections) 174
Infantry (71 officers and 1,040 enlisted men).......................... 1,111
Hawley's cavalry, about.. 35

    Total of all arms brought by me 1,320

    Total of all arms..................... 1,813
Deduct for error in cavalry report....................................... 40

    Total................. 1,773

SUMMARY.

Total of cavalry... 210
Total of artillery.. 213
Total of infantry 1,350

    Grand total.. 1,773

If my men are not too much broken down I will move upon Williams-burg near enough to attack to-morrow evening or by daylight next morning. I send you a note* from Colonel Tabb, which met me on the way. Infantry or no infantry, enemy re-enforced or not, I will certainly attack them Saturday morning as early as my men can take aim. I find the forces here deficient in ammunition, and beg you to forward some, according to the accompanying requisitions, with dispatch.

    Very truly, your obedient servant,

                          HENRY A. WISE,
                           Brigadier-General.

                   NAVY DEPARTMENT, C. S. A.,
                    Richmond, April 10, 1863.

Hon. JAMES A. SEDDON,
      Secretary of War:

    SIR: I have the honor to request that the James River obstructions be opened at the earliest practicable moment, to permit the Richmond to pass below them.

    I deem it very important that our armed vessels in the river should be able to pass the barrier at any time, and I respectfully suggest that this be provided for. The large schooner Galego may perhaps be used in connection with this measure.

    I am, respectfully, your obedient servant,

                          S. R. MALLORY,
                       Secretary of the Navy.

          [Indorsements.]

                            APRIL 11, 1863.

Respectfully referred to the President for his consideration.

                              J. A. S.,
                              Secretary.

It would be well, before action, to have a report and opinion of the Chief Engineer.

                                   J. D.

---

                  * Not found.

APRIL 12, 1863.

To the ENGINEER BUREAU:

Note the President's suggestion of a report. It is desirable to know among other things how far the permanence and security of the remaining works would be endangered by making the required opening; how long it would require to remove; whether the opening could be so arranged as still to make the obstructions effective to arrest and keep under fire hostile vessels attempting to pass, and also whether a passage might not more easily or advantageously be made by cutting a canal around through the low ground on one side of the river at the point of obstruction.

J. A. S.,
Secretary.

ENGINEER BUREAU, *April* 20, 1863.

Respectfully returned to the honorable Secretary of War.

A report in reply to the above questions has been forwarded to-day.*

J. F. GILMER,
Colonel of Engineers and Chief of Bureau.

WAR DEPARTMENT, C. S. A.,
Richmond, April 10, 1863.

General W. H. C. WHITING,
Wilmington, N. C.:

General Beauregard telegraphs that clear indications denote an early attack by land from Bull's Bay on Charleston, as likewise contemporaneous assaults on other parts of his line, and urges earnestly the forwarding of re-enforcements. If you can venture the risk, send forward any troops (Evans' brigade or less). The movement, however, is rested on your discretion, with only an expression of the desire of the Department. If you send, inform General Longstreet, whose address I do not know.

J. A. SEDDON,
Secretary of War.

FRANKLIN, VA., *April* 10, 1863.

Hon. JAMES A. SEDDON:

It will probably occupy two weeks of time to haul out the subsistence and quartermaster's supplies. This would probably give abundance of time for the co-operation.

JAMES LONGSTREET,
Lieutenant-General, Commanding.

EXECUTIVE DEPARTMENT OF VIRGINIA,
April 10, 1863.

Hon. JAMES A. SEDDON,
Secretary of War:

SIR: The mayor of this city has called upon the Governor for a military force in aid of the civil authority in suppression of an outbreak

---

* See Gilmer to Seddon, April 20, p. 1008.

which his honor has been informed may be expected during the coming night. In addition to the force Brigadier-General Winder has placed at His Excellency's command, Major-General Elzey has been requested to bring into the city two of his battalions. To this request the major-general from Chaffin's Bluff has promptly replied:

> The two battalions asked for have been ordered to hold themselves in readiness under arms; but it would be well for His Excellency (the Governor) to apply to the Secretary of War in the mean time for the force under my command. I am inspecting, but will be in the city by sundown.

Accordingly, by direction of His Excellency, I have the honor to ask that the order suggested by General Elzey may be given.

I am, most respectfully, your obedient servant,

S. BASSETT FRENCH,
Colonel and Aide-de-Camp.

APRIL 10, 1863—11 a. m.

[General HILL:]

GENERAL: My wagon train will be here from Pungo at 7 p. m., the quartermaster writes me who is in charge of it. Captain Reilly opened on the enemy this morning, but can produce but little effect, except to make him keep close. They returned his fire with four 32-pounders. I trust to God all is going well with you. Let me know what I shall do. My quartermaster at Tranter's Bridge has forage for some four days, after which he says he knows not where to procure it. No recent news from Bath.

Very respectfully, your obedient servant,

R. B. GARNETT,
Brigadier-General, Commanding.

Abstract from Field Return of Troops commanded by Maj. Gen. S. G. French, April 10, 1863.

Troops.	Present for duty.		Aggregate present.	Aggregate present and absent.
	Officers.	Men.		
Forces on Blackwater	382	5,456	6,744	....
32d Virginia Regiment	19	92	177	251
Moseley's artillery battalion	8	146	164	179
Sturdivant Battery	4	86	95	101
Hargrove Blues	3	76	85	125
Detachment cavalry	1	23	24	25
Signal Corps	9	143	154	161
Camp paroled prisoners	15	832	861	920
On duty in hospitals, Petersburg	21	55	76	76
Grand total	462	6,909	8,380	1,838

BURWELL BAY, *April* 11, 1863.

Maj. WILLIAM NORRIS,
    Chief of Signal Corps:

SIR: I have the honor to report my return from my first trip across the river. There are few Abolitionists on the Peninsula. No addition to the number at Yorktown.   Two (lieutenants) only at Newport News. Hawkins' Zouaves at Camp Hamilton (Segar's farm) and Third New York in garrison at Fort Monroe.   None have gone to Suffolk since the 15th or 20th of March.   Their number there is estimated at 20,000.   I will endeavor to learn the exact force there to-morrow night, when I shall procure papers, &c.   The usual fleet at the mouth of the river.

Very respectfully, your obedient servant,

C. H. CAUSEY,
Captain, Confederate States Army.

HEADQUARTERS ARMY OF NORTHERN VIRGINIA,
April 11, 1863.

Maj. Gen. ARNOLD ELZEY,
Commanding at Richmond:

GENERAL: Your letter of 7th has been received.   The diversion you project in the direction of Yorktown will serve to distract the enemy and prevent re-enforcements being sent to Suffolk, and I hope will afford more aid to General Longstreet than the additional troops you could give him.   I approve, therefore, of your course, and hope it will be carried out boldly and energetically.

I am, very respectfully, your obedient servant,

R. E. LEE,
General.

WAR DEPARTMENT, C. S. A.,
Richmond, Va., April 11, 1863.

General JAMES LONGSTREET, *Franklin, Va.:*

General Beauregard is so urgent for re-enforcements that I request you will send Ransom's brigade, or some other, to Wilmington to replace Evans', which I shall order to Charleston.

J. A. SEDDON,
Secretary of War.

HEADQUARTERS,
Seven miles of Suffolk, Va., April 11, 1863.

Hon. JAMES A. SEDDON,
Secretary of War:

SIR: Your telegram is received.   The most that we can possibly spare to re-enforce General Beauregard would be a brigade.   It would hardly be worth the while to send it.   I hope that General Hill may in a few days be able to send more.   I have advised him of General Beauregard's necessities.   It must occupy the enemy several days to begin to make any impression at Charleston; meanwhile we may do much more good here and in North Carolina.   General Hill's address by telegraph is Rocky Mount, N. C.; from that point your dispatches will be forwarded to him.   His orders and arrangements were complete as far as I could make them when I left Franklin.   Please send him such orders or instructions as you think proper.

May I ask that you pardon this pencil note?   My writing materials have not yet come up.

I remain, most respectfully, your obedient servant,

JAMES LONGSTREET,
Lieutenant-General, Commanding.

WAR DEPARTMENT, C. S. A.,
Richmond, Va., April 11, 1863.

General W. H. C. WHITING,
    Wilmington, N. C.:

I have requested General Longstreet to send Ransom's or some other brigade to Wilmington to replace Evans' brigade.

J. A. SEDDON,
    Secretary of War.

HEADQUARTERS,
Wilmington, N. C., April 11, 1863.

Hon. JAMES A. SEDDON,
    Secretary of War, Richmond, Va.:

SIR: I received your telegram referring to General Beauregard's apprehension of an attack by Bull's Bay. If well founded this is a very serious demonstration, and, combined with the fact that the enemy is in force in the Sounds below Charleston, where his base is, it will make the successful defense of the city and surrounding country a very difficult problem with the force at General Beauregard's command. The object of a demonstration by Bull's Bay might either be the establishment in force on the Haddrell's Point side, isolation of Sullivan's Island, and bombardment of the city, or an attempt to cut the North Carolina Railroad, or both. With regard to my power to assist General Beauregard, you are aware that my force is already much reduced by the absence of General Ransom's brigade for the operations against Foster about New Berne and Washington, in which also General Longstreet, by letter of 8th instant, desires me to co-operate if possible. The only available force here is Evans' brigade, not a very strong one. Of this I must take the responsibility, upon your telegram, of sparing three regiments to General Beauregard, though I must earnestly urge that their place be supplied at once, with the double view of giving him, in case of necessity, further and much needed aid and of preventing all risk here where I am by no means as strong as I desire to be and where the presence of troops is at all times necessary as well for labor as for defense. With regard to the water defenses, I hope you will be able to let me have at least two Brooke rifles, one for each entrance, those guns appearing to have been most effective against monitors.

Very respectfully,

W. H. C. WHITING,
    Brigadier-General.

HEADQUARTERS DISTRICT OF THE CAPE FEAR,
Wilmington, N. C., April 11, 1863.

Hon. JAMES A. SEDDON,
    Secretary of War, Richmond, Va.:

SIR: A letter of Flag-Officer [William F.] Lynch to Secretary of the Navy, with accompanying letter of Senator [George] Davis, of North Carolina, has been referred to me as relating to the defense of the Cape Fear. There are several points in both letters (mistakes as well as improprieties) upon which I might remark with some animadversion. I will simply refer to them : In the first place, the battery to which Flag-Officer Lynch refers, March 13, has not been discontinued, but (although the guns will be needed for the North Carolina) is prepared for mounting others; second, the river obstructions are not only much further advanced than when " I (he) first came on the station," but nearly all that has been done in this matter has been done since I assumed command ; is rapidly progressing as satisfactorily as the means at my command and the nature of the problem will permit.   In this connection permit me to refer you to my report on the defenses of the Cape Fear, section headed " Obstructions," and generally.   Many projects of obstructions, mostly impracticable, have been presented to me.   There is, thirdly, "no uneasiness felt in the community" with which the Department has not been fully (through myself, when well founded) made acquainted, and upon which I have perhaps equal facilities with Senator Davis to enlighten it.   Flag-Officer Lynch says, fourthly, " Under these circumstances I pray you to obtain authority for me to obstruct the river, which in twelve days I will be ready to defend with the North Carolina under one coat of plating."   I am competent to give the authority asked and most cheerfully concede it in the same spirit in which I have always assisted and co-operated with the Navy and always shall, though I most respectfully suggest that I think the completion of the gunboats will be quite as much as the Navy authorities can attend to, the North Carolina not yet being ready for the purpose proposed on the 13th March.   As to the defense, that is my affair.   I will not further allude to the manifest impropriety of these letters than to notice a remark in that of Senator Davis, that he has " reason to believe that General D. H. Hill has been painfully disappointed in the defense of Wilmington."   If General Hill had any such feeling it was doubtless in relation to the deficiency of the armament—a feeling shared by the department and by myself and due to the straitness of our resources and the pressing demands upon us everywhere, and not to any measures I have taken.   Senator Davis in a natural, proper anxiety upon a matter of the greatest importance to himself and people, and not familiar with the subject, has no doubt misunderstood General Hill.   I request that you will permit Senator Davis, if not inconsistent with the public service, to read the report upon the defenses of the Cape Fear which I had the honor to submit for the information of the President, with his permission, and that you will refer this letter to the Secretary of the Navy, to whom Flag-Officer Lynch's letter was originally addressed.

Very respectfully,

W. H. C. WHITING,
Brigadier-General.

HEADQUARTERS, *in Camp, April* 11, [1863].
(Via Franklin April 12.)

Hon. JAMES A. SEDDON :

I hope that we shall have plenty of time to re-enforce General Beauregard.   It will take much time for the enemy to accomplish anything, even after his attack is begun.

I telegraphed General Hill to re-enforce as soon as he possibly can.

JAMES LONGSTREET.

HEADQUARTERS,
Kinston, N. C., April 12, 1863.

Maj. Gen. D. H. HILL,
Commanding in North Carolina :

GENERAL: I have received your two notes of yesterday and have put on foot the men on the railroad.   Shall act vigorously in getting the conscripts. Have also started a party to put up the Core Creek Bridge. I hold the force I took with me to Contentnea so that I may move to any point from here. Unless the enemy should again strip New Berne a demonstration only in that direction could do little good. I hardly think old man Wessells will try to march to Wilmington; if he does he will never get back. May God grant you a speedy success at Washington. If I go toward New Berne I desire to enter the town. If your scouts gain no more information than mine you must be embarrassed; but the short line between the rivers makes it very difficult to pass.

Inclosed I send a letter from Mr. Washington, perhaps the richest man in the county. The corn he speaks of is indispensable to us. He has carried off his own entire crop, and this corn was bought last fall. If one man be permitted to take it away we will be able to get none. It is with difficulty that we get on now. I have refused every one, no matter how small the quantity. Mr. Washington has a mill, and claims that because he has sold to us since last fall some $1,500 or $2,000 worth of meal that he should be exempt, and also because he has the iron contract. His slaves were hired up the country principally, and in my judgment he should not have permission to carry off one bushel. There is hardly a man in the Confederacy who has done less for the Government. As to the corn in Warren County I simply said to Mr. Washington he could find it there. As to the nature of his contract I know nothing; he has been reticent on that point. I do not consider that I am bound by the permits of my predecessors, for I do not know how far they may have been taken advantage of. Until I get your positive orders to let the corn go it will remain, unless necessity compels me to use it. I shall apply to Mr. Washington the same rules I do to others.

Everything quiet.

Very respectfully, your obedient servant,

R. RANSOM, JR.,
Brigadier-General.

WILMINGTON, N. C., *April 12, 1863.*

Maj. Gen. D. H. HILL, *Commanding:*

MY DEAR GENERAL: I have your note this afternoon. Have telegraphed you. By reason of the urgent dispatches of the War Department, General Beauregard, together with General Longstreet's instructions, and the importance of the case, I have felt obliged to let General Evans and three regiments go to Charleston. I keep two here. Suppose you let either Colonel Ransom's or Col. [L. M.] McAfee's regiment (Forty-ninth North Carolina), from General Ransom's brigade, come down here. I shall not then feel uneasy as to any temporary attack or feint of the enemy. Colonel Ransom is here on a court-martial. That brigade is so strong, and [being] composed of five regiments, would not, I think, greatly miss one, while the presence of one here would be much for me. Your movements as against Washington and Foster appear to me to be admirably designed, and I hope you will bag him. My scouts report great alarm in New Berne. We have a refugee who has escaped them to our lines. He describes the impression there that you will destroy Foster. I have applied for the First and Third North Carolina Regiments, now in Virginia, to be sent here as a garrison of Wilmington. **These regiments are not brigaded in any North Carolina brigade, and** might perhaps suit. It would be a very good thing; I wish you would urge it. It would greatly help all of our operations to have a couple of independent regiments.

Very truly, yours,

W. H. C. WHITING,
Brigadier-General.

WAR DEPARTMENT, C. S. A.,
Richmond, Va., April 13, 1863.

General D. H. HILL, *Rocky Mount, N. C.:*

General Evans' brigade being sent from Wilmington to Charleston, replace it with a brigade. General Longstreet is informed of this.

J. A. SEDDON,
Secretary of War.

WAR DEPARTMENT, C. S. A.,
Richmond, Va., April 13, 1863.

Lieut. Gen. JAMES LONGSTREET, *Franklin, Va.:*

General Whiting still urges re-enforcements. Send force to replace Evans' brigade.

J. A. SEDDON,
Secretary of War.

WAR DEPARTMENT, C. S. A.,
Richmond, Va., April 13, 1863.

Lieut. Gen. JAMES LONGSTREET :

GENERAL : Your letter of the 11th instant has been delivered by your courier. General Whiting calls still so urgently for re-enforcements to replace General Evans' brigade (sent on to Charleston) that the matter has been laid before the President, and his judgment is that it would be unsafe to leave Wilmington without such re-enforcements. Therefore I telegraphed you this morning that such should be sent. I will now, having learned General Hill's address through your letter, telegraph him directly to the same effect. I regret very much to interfere in any way with your concerted arrangements, but an engagement was previously given to send forward a brigade when required to Charleston, and I did not feel at liberty to disregard it. As explained to you in a previous letter, I had supposed you acquainted with that arrangement. I do not propose that more than one brigade be sent to Charleston to be supplied at Wilmington. That will not, I trust, materially interfere with the plans of General Hill or yourself.

Very respectfully, your obedient servant,

J. A. SEDDON,
Secretary of War.

P. S.—The above letter was returned by the same courier.

WAR DEPARTMENT, C. S. A.,
Richmond, Va., April 13, 1863.

Brig. Gen. W. H. C. WHITING, *Wilmington, N. C.:*

General Hill has been ordered to send a brigade to replace Evans', to be forwarded to Charleston.

J. A. SEDDON,
Secretary of War.

APRIL 13, 1863.

[Maj. Gen. D. H. HILL:]

GENERAL: I am in receipt of your dispatch of April 13, 7:30 a. m. My ordnance officer has gone to Boyd's Landing for the Parrott ammunition. When I have completed all the breastworks for batteries and placed guns in them I shall require more troops to support them, otherwise my command will be too much scattered. Col. [W. F.] Martin had better be sent over, I think. Your instructions will be communicated to Captain Reilly. I do not know at what point on this side your boat will land to establish the courier line you speak of. Three Yankee prisoners were brought up this morning by the cavalry from Bath. These men deserted from the troops at New Berne and went over to Hyde County, where they delivered themselves to two of Captain Swindell's men. One is an orderly sergeant, and seems to be an intelligent man. He reports 10,000 troops at New Berne under the command of Palmer; says many of these troops are disaffected and those who are to be discharged in May will not serve longer. I have sent the deserters to Greenville subject to your further orders. They are very anxious that their names should not appear in the papers as deserters for fear it may bring punishment upon them when they return and work to their prejudice at their homes. I therefore hope you will give the necessary instructions should you order them to Richmond.

Very respectfully, your obedient servant,

R. B. GARNETT,
Brigadier-General.

P. S.—The deserters are from the One hundred and first Pennsylvania.

APRIL 13, 1863—5 p. m.

[General D. H. HILL:]

GENERAL: I have given the instructions to Captain Reilly about opening on the Yankee barracks, in accordance with your orders in dispatch of 7.30 a. m. to-day. Colonel Ferebee has been ordered to collect conscripts and also to watch the roads you speak of. He says that General Robertson, who was here yesterday, spoke of relieving Colonel Ferebee's men by Griffin's cavalry. I presume he means those on the Jamesville and Plymouth roads. I have frequently impressed upon Colonel F. to guard those roads well, and he informs me that the necessary steps have been taken to do so. My ordnance officer went for the ammunition to Boyd's Ferry this morning. I mentioned, in reply to your note this morning, that I thought it better for Colonel Martin's regiment to join me here, and will send him the order to-night. I can learn nothing of the condition of the enemy inside, but I fear that they can keep themselves supplied by fishing with seines, as fish are very plentiful in the river at this season. I sent up the Jamesville road this morning about 7 miles and found Griffin's pickets on it, so I presume it is all right in that direction.

Very respectfully, your obedient servant,

R. B. GARNETT,
Brigadier-General.

APRIL 13, 1863—7 p. m.

[Maj. Gen. D. H. HILL:]

GENERAL: I inclose you a note from Colonel Cantwell relative to the seizure of a vessel bound to New Berne. I have ordered the property of the Widow to be removed and the captain and crew to be arrested and sent to me; also the vessel to be burned should there be any danger of her falling into the hands of the enemy. I wish you would give me instructions as to what I shall do with the arrested persons and the schooner. I think she should be burned, but will not give the order until I hear from you to that effect. The ordnance officer I sent for ammunition reports that the road which was ordered to be repaired leading to Boyd's Ferry will not admit of artillery or even many wagons passing over it without cutting it up very much. As they be an important work, I deem it proper to mention this fact to you.

Very respectfully, your obedient servant,

R. B. GARNETT,
Brigadier-General.

HEADQUARTERS,
Raleigh, N. C., April 13, 1863.

Maj. Gen. HILL,
Comdg. Dept. of North Carolina, Goldsborough, N. C.:

GENERAL: If you have any command for me I have the honor to request that I may be ordered to it at once. The position of commanding officer here is, in my opinion, a necessary one, but the duties can be performed by an officer unable to do field service. Col. [W. L.] De Rosset, now in the State, could easily take my place here. A general officer is not required here, and the circumstances of my situation, which are known to you, make it desirable to me to leave the State, and under any contigencies to leave the city of Raleigh. Should you have no command to offer me, please approve, recommend, and forward the inclosed application.

I am, general, very respectfully, your obedient servant,

J. G. MARTIN,
Brigadier-General.

[APRIL 13, 1863]—12 m.

Maj. Gen. D. H. HILL:

GENERAL: Yours of 10.30 just received. I would like to have all the movable rifle artillery or rather "anti-gunboat," that I can get. The ground on the enemy's side of the mouth of the creek does certainly command ours, and unless we can drive the gunboats away they can cross; but how they are to march to Fort Hill afterward will puzzle them, provided our forces are ready to concentrate. They must concentrate to attack. Everything depends upon our being able to do the same is my opinion. I think the guns in question had better come down.

Yours, respectfully,

J. J. PETTIGREW,
Brigadier-General.

HEADQUARTERS,
Kinston, N. C., April 13, 1863.

Maj. Gen. D. H. HILL, *Commanding:*

GENERAL: Your two notes of to-day are just received. Of course I will cheerfully do whatever is for the good of our service; but I hope my brigade may be kept together. Faithfully have I striven to get it to a first-rate state of efficiency, and it would be a proud moment for me to take it a unit into a battle. You are well aware how soon the best troops can become demoralized. But recently, during a very short absence from my brigade, I had reason to regret that I had left it. I beg you will do what you can not to split my command to pieces and cause it to become of little use. If you could see it together I know you would award it a place second to no other. Whatever may be your orders I will obey with zeal and faithfulness.

I wrote to Major Anderson to-day. Everything as quiet as possible. I can get no news from New Berne; have tried hard, and am still making efforts.

Very respectfully, your obedient servant,

R. RANSOM, JR.,
Brigadier-General.

HEADQUARTERS,
Kinston, N. C., April 13, 1863.

Maj. Gen. D. H. HILL:

GENERAL: I inclose a note* from General Whiting by a courier, whom I sent with your letter to him. It has just come in. I hear that the enemy is landing heavy forces below Charleston. Whiting will doubless give you the news.

Very respectfully,

R. RANSOM, JR.,
Brigadier-General.

KINSTON, N. C., *April* 14, 1863.

General D. H. HILL,
Commanding in North Carolina :

GENERAL: Your note of yesterday was received early to-day. I had sent off about a dozen conscripts. Will retain the others. With no evidence except against one of the 14 sent up by your order from Beaufort I can make but a poor investigation. Major Kennedy sent me only one letter from Ed. Stanly, addressed to a United States naval officer, that commits partially one of the parties. He too, I should say, was over forty years old. The rest had best be sent to Richmond or directly to the Rappahannock. My Quakers are obstinate. They have withstood hunger and thirst for over four days. I sent down Major Guion, of the Engineers, to superintend the building of the bridge over Core Creek. To-day I find it completed, but so low to the water that a slight rise would wash it away. My scouts report a larger force now in New Berne than for some weeks past. They say re-enforcements have arrived within the past few days. If so, an advance will be attempted toward this place and an attack by the gunboats be made on Wilmington. They will thus hope to prevent your sending any one to Wilmington, and perhaps to pass over us before you can get here, or it may be they will be content to hold us all here. If you do not order the demonstration on New Berne I shall not make it. With half the number of my force in the town I cannot take it. Two demonstrations have already been made upon the place, and, with respect, I suggest that a repetition of these feints tend to weaken us and give courage and importance to the enemy. If the enemy go out again I will be as rapid as man can be to take his place ; and if in your better judgment it be wise to make the demonstration let me know and it shall be promptly

---

* Not found.

executed. I have been told that you had heavy firing this morning and last night. I earnestly pray you have again repulsed them. Your note relative to the engineers has just reached me. I will attend to its commands.

6 p. m.—Lieutenant Connor has just gone off in the direction you speak of and will be near you by the time you get this. Lieutenant Foy, whom I sent scouting near New Berne, has returned within the hour. He states that a day or two ago some twenty iron-clads and other gunboats left Beaufort—that a strong re-enforcement came up from there to New Berne. The officer I sent to break up the railroad has not yet reported. He has hardly had time, as I wished the bridge near Shepherdsville destroyed, if possible.

Very respectfully and truly,

R. RANSOM, Jr.,
Brigadier-General.

HEADQUARTERS,
Wilmington, N. C., April 14, 1863.

Maj. Gen. D. H. HILL,
Commanding near Washington, N. C.:

GENERAL: I have just received yours of the 12th,* inclosing a telegram * from Longstreet. I have received so many orders and counter-orders from so many different sources that really I am puzzled how to answer. The War Department has been directing me to re-enforce General Beauregard. The lieutenant-general commanding orders co-operation with you, while from his headquarters at Petersburg I get directions to aid Beauregard if the latter is urgent. Finally, General Beauregard suspends the movement of Evans' brigade. My position is then this: One regiment of Evans' brigade is in Charleston, having got off before the movement was stopped; the general himself is there; I have four here. I do not think the enemy have in the least given up their designs on Charleston. It is incredible that after such monstrous preparations they should give up ——— † of that performance of the monitors. Nor am I apprehensive immediately of any demonstration on Wilmington, though such might be attempted. If, as you surmise, any feint should be made by land, your cavalry ought to let Ransom know the moment it is discovered, that he need not wait for me to call upon him. If your estimate of Foster's troops, viz, 8,000, is correct, and as Longstreet says he has received no more re-enforcements, he will neither dare to attack you nor to move on me. I know him too well. Still I must keep on the lookout. I only fear that my armament is not heavy enough to keep a monitor out. For one to get inside would be a very serious embarrassment; but it will hardly be tried, I think, until the defenses of Charleston are more thoroughly tested; and surely unless they abandon their great expedition altogether before that first repulse they will not divert any portion of their land or naval forces for an attempt on a subordinate position. If I should hear that the fleet and transports had all passed the Charleston bar going northward I should think they were coming here and call for all the aid I could get. If they abandon their Charleston move Beauregard could aid me. In the mean time I do not like to think that your operations should be in any manner crippled to aid me unless at the last extremity. Your operations there are in fact my great security here, unless an additional expedition should be fitting out

---

* Not found.   † Illegible.

in the North of which we know nothing. I therefore hope you will be able to press Foster hard. He is not the man, nor Wessells either, to fight you and me both at once.

Very truly,

W. H. C. WHITING,
Brigadier-General.

SPECIAL ORDERS, }   HDQRS. DEPT. VIRGINIA AND N. CAROLINA,
No. —.   }   *Near Suffolk, Va., April* 14, 1863.

Maj. Gen. S. G. French is temporarily assigned to the command of all the artillery serving with the forces on the Blackwater. It will be under his control and direction, and commanding officers will accord due observance of his orders and dispositions.

By command of Lieutenant-General Longstreet:

G. MOXLEY SORREL,
Assistant Adjutant-General.

HEADQUARTERS DISTRICT OF THE CAPE FEAR,
Wilmington, N. C., April 15, 1863.

Hon. JAMES A. SEDDON,
Secretary of War, Richmond, Va.:

SIR: I beg leave, in the short lull afforded by the enemy, to urge my need of more heavy guns, especially the 8 or 10-inch columbiads and the Brooke rifle. The enemy, I think, now will either renew a desperate effort on Charleston, or, fearful of that place, try one they suppose to be weaker. If injury to us be an object they ought scarcely to attempt this place. You are aware of the inadequacy of our armament here, and that many guns intended for Wilmington have been diverted to meet what have been required as more pressing necessities elsewhere. I am much in want now of at least two heavy rifles and four columbiads (8 or 10-inch), with their ammunition.

Very respectfully,

W. H. C. WHITING,
Brigadier-General.

APRIL 15, 1863—9.30 a. m.

[Maj. Gen. D. H. HILL:]

GENERAL: My train has just arrived from the Pungo River. It brings up 65 barrels of corn and about 8,000 pounds of bacon. Of this lot 2,000 pounds came from Hyde. Captain Swindell, who sent agents into Hyde, reports that most of the bacon remaining in that country is in the hands of persons who have taken the oath of allegiance, and they will not sell it unless it is impressed. I have ordered my train to go to Tranter's Creek Bridge. You do not say in your last dispatch how the surplus meat at Tranter's Bridge is to be transported. I suggested that it should be sent to Greenville or Tarborough by steamboat from Boyd's Landing. Please let me have definite instructions in this matter, as I do not think my train can haul the meat in question should we have to move the wagon train all at once. I have no control over the steamboat, and have therefore reported the above facts to you in order that you might give the necessary directions should you deem this mode of transportation preferable. I judge from the spirited reply the enemy make to our fire that their ammunition has been replenished.   We have had quite a heavy fall of rain.   Whether it will endanger our bridges I am unable to say.

Very respectfully, your obedient servant,

R. B. GARNETT,
Brigadier-General.

APRIL 15, 1863—7.25.

[Maj. Gen. D. H. HILL :]

GENERAL : Lieut. [James A.] Reid has just delivered your note.   He reports the water very high on the route, and as we have had a very heavy fall of rain since his arrival I fear my artillery ammunition will all be wet in crossing the creeks.   My infantry ammunition will have to be renewed at Tranter's Creek, as I am sure that it is all spoiled by the violent rain-storm, the men having no tents or flies to protect against the weather.   My command will be in a very bad condition to march farther than Tranter's Creek Bridge, as they will have to wade almost up to their waists and without rest.   They have been on picket duty every other night for a long time.   I will make every possible effort to join you, but you must make allowance for pitch darkness and deep streams to march through.

Very respectfully, your obedient servant,

R. B. GARNETT,
Brigadier-General.

HEADQUARTERS, *April* 15, 1863.

Maj. Gen. S. G. FRENCH, *Commanding, &c.:*

GENERAL : Your letter and its inclosure are received.   I think that you had better reduce the charge of the big guns and try them.   The full charge seems to burst them all.   I think that Major Henry had better be relieved by Capt. [R. M.] Stribling to-night.   Cannot the parapet at the battery where Major Henry is be so arranged as to protect the pieces from the fire on the opposite side and at the same time allow our pieces to play upon the gunboats?   If it can be done I would like to have it.   General Hood will give you such detail as you need to work.   If you keep Captain Stribling's battery you should send him the other that —— took; that is Bradford's.   He has but two on our right, and that seems the only point where the enemy will venture out.   He has been out with strong lines of skirmishers there twice to-day.   I was called up there in consequence and could not therefore go over to see you.   I ordered Captain Clarke to you this morning to examine and place batteries or breastworks wherever you thought best.   Direct as you think best, and order him to call for such details as he needs in my name.

Most respectfully,

JAMES LONGSTREET,
Lieutenant-General, Commanding.

HEADQUARTERS, *April* 15, 1863.

Maj. Gen. D. H. HILL, *Commanding :*

GENERAL : Information reaches me to-day that the enemy is landing on the Chowan, in Gates County, from your part of the country.   I wish you would keep your Yankees to yourself; or if you find them pushing up here from New Berne you must send me some more troops. I hope that you will send me Garnett and Reilly as soon as it can be done; and if you find other troops coming from New Berne you had better try and make some arrangement by which you can re-enforce me further.

I remain, most respectfully, your obedient servant,

JAMES LONGSTREET,
Lieutenant-General, Commanding.

I am greatly in need of cavalry. Have but seven companies of Colonel Baker's regiment. What can it be doing? General Whiting complains that he can get none and you say that it is worthless. I have been trying to get some ever since I have been in the department and think that I could make it very useful if I could ever get hold of it.

APRIL 15 (OR 18), 1863—8.30 a. m.

Maj. Gen. D. H. HILL:

GENERAL: I received your note last night inclosing one from Brown and one from Whitford. If the dispatch mentioned by Brown was really sent to the commander of the expedition it was very kind of him to communicate it; but what becomes of General Longstreet's effort to keep the enemy in Suffolk if they thus march across his face? My opinion is what it was last night—concentrate. If you are going to fight in the rear of the road leading from Blount's farm to the Swift Creek road I am opposed to exposing any one at the Blount's Creek, for I should consider them sacrificed unless I stationed a regiment at the farm, and that would increase the dispersion of our forces, which already exceeds reasonable limits. I send you Captain McCrady's dispatch, by which it appears that the same steamer ran down by both batteries this morning. So passes away the blockade. As somebody remarked this morning, with more truth than agreeability, "The entertainment will now conclude with the laughable and amusing farce of ' Running the Blockade.' Parents may send their children with the assurance that the exhibition is perfectly innocent." It is a mystery to me that the one battery should not have seen her and the other should not have sunk her.

Very respectfully,

J. J. PETTIGREW,
Brigadier-General.

HEADQUARTERS,
Near Suffolk, Va., April 15, 1863.

Maj. Gen. D. H. HILL,
     Comdg. Dept. of North Carolina, near Washington, N. C.:

GENERAL: Your letter of the 10th to the commanding general is received. I am directed to write as follows:

We cannot afford to keep the large force that you have watching the garrison at Washington. It would seem that you could, by fortifying the positions that you hold around Washington, keep the garrison securely inside with 3,000 men. If you should order the two regiments that were at Hamilton in the place of Garnett's brigade, and let them fortify, they could keep the garrison in on the north side. Pettigrew's brigade on the south side ought to be able to keep the enemy in on that side. Indeed, it seems that half of this brigade is enough on the south side. By such an arrangement you will have treble the force of the garrison. Garnett then could come here; Daniel go to Kinston, and Ransom to Wilmington. If you cannot effect such an arrangement the investment had better be abandoned. If you prefer, it is suggested that the two regiments at Hamilton be sent to Wilmington; then Ransom's brigade can remain where it is, and you will thus have Daniel and Pettigrew at Washington, which ought to be abundant. There can be no great force to succor Washington, and it must come from New Berne. If it comes from that point you can support by Daniel's brigade and replace it by part of Ransom's.

Two of your letters reported the enemy evacuating New Berne. If this be done you will require little or no force at Kinston. A portion of the troops from North Carolina are reported landing in Gates County for Suffolk. It thus appears that the force that you are to contend against is being drawn in this direction. Send Garnett's brigade and Reilly's battery here as soon as possible, but endeavor to continue the siege. When the enemy had all his force in North Carolina you had no trouble in driving back his succoring force; now that part of it is here you can surely keep back the little force that he may possibly be able to bring against you.

It is suggested that excessive charges may account for the repeated disasters to your guns. If they were reduced it is thought that not so many would burst.

The enemy is re-enforcing here from his reserves in Baltimore and other points. His accessions, however, are not believed to be large. Not a gun has been fired here at the enemy's works. We have no ammunition to throw away in this manner.

I am, general, very respectfully, your most obedient servant,

G. MOXLEY SORREL,
Assistant Adjutant-General.

APRIL 15, 1863.

Maj. [L. M.] SHUMAKER,
Chief of Artillery:

Withdraw the batteries and go into camp, and do not attack the gunboats unless they move up; in that case attack them. I wish you to remain here to-night with the batteries. I go up to assist Major Henry. Keep a watch and let no boats pass down.

S. G. FRENCH,
Major-General.

APRIL 16, 1863.

[Maj. Gen. D. H. HILL:]

GENERAL: I have had my courier line removed already. I applied for the boat to-day, but the captain said he was specially under your orders, and if he went up to Greenville he could not return without going a considerable distance above that town to get wood. I therefore concluded to try to move my stores with my own wagons. It will require some two days to send the meat, meal, and corn I have at Pactolus to Greenville. I will leave Colonel Ferebee to defend Tranter's Creek Bridge when I leave. The steamer is loading the flats with large guns. Two are already on board. This will prevent the boat from taking my men over. If what the captain says is correct the steamer will have to run some distance above Greenville to get wood, and will not be able to return until late to-morrow morning to Boyd's Ferry, I should judge. I am in great perplexity how to manage to get over before some time in the day to-morrow. I thought it would not be safe to leave the bridge until I heard from you after Colonel Ferebee's report of an advance of the enemy. Subsequent reports do not confirm an advance, though it is likely they will do so if they are re-enforced at Washington. Please let me hear from you as soon as possible.

Very respectfully, your obedient servant,

R. B. GARNETT,
Brigadier-General.

APRIL 16, 1863—9.30.

[Maj. Gen. D. H. HILL:]

GENERAL: I have received your dispatch of this morning and will take the steps you desire. My men are very much worn out by constant picketing, and the wet and the somewhat long march of last night. It took my command until daylight to make it. I have a quantity of commissary stores and some corn. I will send these up by boat to Greenville provided your orders do not conflict with this arrangement. The boat can take them up and return to-night or early to-morrow. Should there be any delay in removing my stores I will direct Colonel Ferebee to protect them.

Very respectfully,

R. B. GARNETT,
Brigadier-General.

TRANTER'S CREEK BRIDGE,
April 16, 1863—8.30 p. m.

[Maj. Gen. D. H. HILL:]

GENERAL: I have received your dispatch by Lieutenant Reid; also yours of 5.30 p. m. I shall withdraw to-morrow morning at daylight. I have directed Colonel Ferebee to remain here, and to take up the bridges at this point and at Gaines. I shall get off all my stores, except a quantity of corn that I am having ground at Pactolus. I think Colonel F. can hold the enemy long enough in check to have it ground and sent to Greenville. I sent Captain Reilly off this morning to Tarborough, according to your orders. Captain Bunting is still here, but I do not apprehend I shall require his services. I can get along better without the boat. The road to Boyd's Ferry is impassable for wagons, and even couriers have a very hard time at night.

Very respectfully, your obedient servant,

R. B. GARNETT,
Brigadier-General, Commanding.

TRANTER'S CREEK BRIDGE,
April 16, 1863—12.10 p. m.

[Maj. Gen. D. H. HILL:]

GENERAL: Colonel Ferebee has retired with his brigade to this point. He reports that he left his position near Washington between 8 and 9 o'clock this morning; also that their cavalry and a body of infantry followed them some distance. The information is indefinite, but the enemy may advance upon me at this point. It would not do, I should think, to leave this position open. The destruction of the bridge would not detain the enemy long. I cannot depend upon the steamboat to take up my stores. She is loading at Boyd's Ferry and I cannot tell what she will be able to transport. I shall try to get my stores up by wagons, but it will take some days to do so. The road to Boyd's Ferry on this side is said to be exceedingly bad, impassable to wagons. The last rain has made it very much worse.

Very respectfully, your obedient servant.

R. B. GARNETT,
Brigadier-General.

HEADQUARTERS DAVIS' BRIGADE,
Before Suffolk, Va., April 16, 1863.

Maj. GRAHAM DAVES,
Assistant Adjutant-General:

MAJOR: I respectfully request to know if my brigade belongs to the division commanded by Major-General French; and, if so, am I to continue to receive orders and instructions from an intermediate commander, or from the major-general commanding?

I am, major, your obedient servant,

JOSEPH R. DAVIS.
Brigadier-General, Commanding.

[Indorsement.]

HDQRS. DEPARTMENT OF SOUTHERN VIRGINIA,
April 17, 1863.

Respectfully forwarded to the lieutenant-general commanding.

I apprehend there is no difficulty in this question. While I regard this brigade, of course, a part of my command as well as General Jenkins' brigade, yet, as I must be absent much of my time, the division must be under command of the senior officer present.

S. G. FRENCH,
Major-General, Commanding.

SIGNAL OFFICE,
Richmond, Va., April 16, 1863.

Maj. WILLIAM NORRIS, *Chief Signal Corps:*

SIR: Pursuant to your orders I left Richmond on the 8th instant and proceeded to Day's Neck, on the James, nearly opposite to the mouth of Warwick River, which place I reached on the 10th. On the 11th at night succeeded in crossing to Mallicote's house on the opposite shore, about 4 miles from Newport News. Obtained but little information that night, but delivered the letters intrusted to me to a reliable person, who placed them in the Federal post-office at Fort Monroe. Attempted to cross on Sunday night, but owing to the intense darkness, and having no compass or glasses, got lost, and after many hours' hard labor at the oars found myself on the same side from which I started. Made another attempt the next night and ran over in full view of the blockading fleet, consisting of the Minnesota, an iron-clad of the Monitor model, and three or four small wooden gunboats. Obtained files of papers to the 9th ultimo, and the subjoined note from a friend, dated the 13th instant:

There has been great excitement here during the past few days owing to the action of our troops at Williamsburg and on the south side of the James River. On Saturday night the long bridge across Hampton Creek was lined with sentinels, and so great was the fear that the rebels would make a descent that long piles of combustibles were placed on the eastern end to facilitate its intended destruction if they came in sight. In consequence of disasters present and likely soon to occur, military men exhibited great despondency, and are unanimous in speaking most disparagingly of Uncle Sam's prospects. General Dix is absent in New York, trying to persuade Governor Seymour to furnish him men enough to hold the Peninsula from Williamsburg down, which he admits his inability to do unless strongly re-enforced, and that right speedily. To conciliate the Governor he is using pleas of Democratic fellowship, &c.; with what success has not yet transpired. Foster, in North Carolina, is in a most critical condition; nor can one man be sent him, either from this point or from Suffolk.

After reaching the south side on Tuesday morning a heavy cannonade began, which continued until nightfall. The next morning I met a man who was acting as a guide the day of the firing, and he informed me that he had been almost entirely around Suffolk; that the Norfolk and Petersburg road was then in our possession, and two brigades were pushing rapidly on to the Seaboard and Roanoke road; that our light batteries were lining both banks of the Nansemond, and had sunk one gunboat and disabled two others. Rifled 32s were being brought up and a pontoon bridge thrown across to facilitate their passage. If his information is entirely reliable (and I see no reason for doubting it) Suffolk is completely isolated.

C. H. CAUSEY,
Captain, C. S. Army.

BRIGADE HEADQUARTERS,
Near Williamsburg, Va., April 16, 1863.

Maj. Gen. ARNOLD ELZEY, *Commanding, &c.:*

GENERAL: This is now Thursday morning; all is quiet, and I shall begin to fall back at 3 o'clock this evening. This is the fifth day after our attack upon the enemy, and they have shown no disposition to advance. We have all the forage and provisions that can be obtained in the neighborhood and sent them behind us. About Saturday or Sunday next I expect to reach Diascund Bridge by falling back slowly and posting my cavalry close up to Williamsburg. I wish you would say by courier whether I shall leave the forces at Diascund as they were before my advance (Colonel Tabb's command), or what number of forces I shall leave there, and also please say whether I am to fall back to Chaffin's farm with my force. I must beg of you to order forward Captain Doby's company of cavalry immediately, the cavalry force here being very insufficient and inefficient.

Very respectfully and truly,

HENRY A. WISE,
Brigadier-General.

HEADQUARTERS,
Six Mile Ordinary, Va., April 16, 1863—6.30 p. m.

Maj. Gen. ARNOLD ELZEY, *Commanding, &c.:*

GENERAL: After getting all the forage and provisions in Williamsburg and its immediate neighborhood I left Casey's, 2 miles from Williamsburg, at 3.30 p. m. to-day and reached this place about 5 p. m.   Before I moved, Surgeon Wager, the enemy's surgeon at the lunatic asylum, sent through Major Garrett a letter addressed to him by acting Brigadier-General West, his commander at Fort Magruder, to withdraw from that institution and surrender it to the commander of the Confederate forces in and around Williamsburg.   I ordered Major Garrett to make no reply to this notice; but I had anticipated some such ruse, and yesterday had arranged with Talbot Sweeny, esq., the only State of Virginia officer left with the asylum, to attend to and provide for its wants. I will also send to it Dr. Martin, a resident practicing physician of this county, to superintend its hygeia.   It is pretty certain, too, the enemy have drawn in their lines, and the report is that they have informed the inhabitants that they consider the town itself surrendered.   For two days they have made no demonstration and have not disturbed my forces in gathering all the plunder we could find and in moving out the inhabitants and their effects.   It is worthy of attention, too, that while exchanging these communications under the flag of truce their officers were emphatic and even urgent in persuading my officers that Fort Magruder is impregnable to any force short of 20,000 men.   In other words, they are very desirous to get rid of our presence in their front. Another evidence of this is that they ran gunboats up both James and York Rivers yesterday and to-day.   Indeed, this evening after we began to move two gunboats ran up York River as high as Mount Folly and shelled the shore.   This was evidently intended to hurry our departure. I have therefore not moved back my cavalry pickets and main force of cavalry at all, but have halted here with my artillery and infantry to get more forage and to render further assistance to the citizens.   I have placed a strong infantry guard on my right at Centreville, the Fifty-ninth between this and Centreville, the Twenty-sixth and Fourth here with the artillery, and a strong infantry guard at Deneufville's Store, on the York River road, thus covering every road with strong flankers right and left.

The day after to-morrow morning I will fall back farther and retire a portion of the command quite to Diascund, moving my cavalry farther back to supporting distance, and completing my return to Diascund by Sabbath at noon.   I am thus obeying your instructions to fall back slowly, and particularly in order that you may modify your instructions according to your better judgment.   We have but few sick men.   They stand the service admirably and behave well in all respects.

I am, general, very truly, your obedient servant,

HENRY A. WISE,
Brigadier-General.

SPECIAL ORDERS, }   HEADQUARTERS FRENCH'S COMMAND,
     No. 2.   }   *April* 16 (*or* 17), 1863.

*   *   *   *   *   *

III. The following artillery companies are assigned to duty in General Pickett's division, and will report to Maj. James Dearing, chief of artillery: Macon's battery, Stribling's battery, Blount's battery, Caskie's battery.   The artillery companies on duty with the division will draw rations and forage from their divisions respectively.   ·

IV. The following artillery companies are assigned to duty with General Hood's division, and will report to Major Henry, chief of artillery: Lane's battery, Bachman's battery, Garden's battery.   The artillery companies on duty with the divisions will draw forage and rations from their divisions respectively.

*   *   *   *   *   *   *

By command of Maj. Gen. S. G. French:

GRAHAM DAVES,
Assistant Adjutant-General.

HEADQUARTERS ARMY OF NORTHERN VIRGINIA,
April 17, 1863

Lieut. Gen. JAMES LONGSTREET,
Commanding, &c.:

GENERAL: Your letter of the 13th has been received. I am glad that you are steadily progressing in your operations. I wish I could give you any aid, but I feel every confidence that you will do all that can be done.

I wrote to Richmond to ask assistance for you, from the Navy, if possible. I have had no reply. Should you know of any assistance which could be given you had better write direct to Richmond for it, and state that it is at my request.

The enemy's cavalry are again on our left. They presented themselves Tuesday evening at Kelly's Ford, Rappahannock Bridge, and Beverly's Ford in large force. Their attempts to cross the river have been so far repulsed. Stuart thinks the movement is intended to cover a change of base or some other operation of the grand army. Nothing, however, has been ascertained.

Yesterday three gunboats appeared in the Rappahannock below Port Royal, and are reported to be ascending the river. Their character, description, and intentions are not yet known.

I am, very respectfully, and truly yours,

R. E. LEE,
General.

HEADQUARTERS,
Near Suffolk, Va., April 17, 1863.

Hon. JAMES A. SEDDON,
Secretary of War:

SIR: I have the honor to acknowledge the receipt of your favor of the 13th. I regret the necessity of sending troops from this department to South Carolina, and still think that we should have abundance of time for such re-enforcement after the enemy had really begun his attack. Wilmington is without a garrison, yet I think there is less need of one there than at any other point in the command. I think that it will not be attacked at all unless we shut up the troops there so that the enemy cannot get at us anywhere else. One regiment I think enough for its garrison, but have suggested to General Hill the propriety of sending two there.

From the reports in newspapers I fear that some anxiety may be felt for us at Suffolk. We have not fired again at the enemy's stronghold nor do I expect to do so. I am very well convinced that we could reduce it in two or three days, but doubt if we can afford to expend the powder and ball. To take it by assault would cost us 3,000 men. This would be less excusable than the other mode. There is but one other means—that of turning it. This cannot be done by the river in consequence of the gunboats in the river. On our right it could be done by taking Norfolk, but we cannot hold Norfolk twenty-four hours without the aid of the Navy or heavier guns than we now have. I do not think that we should have much trouble getting both places with the aid of the Richmond. Suffolk would surely fall if the Richmond would only come down and anchor in the mouth of the Nansemond. The principal object of the expedition was to draw out supplies for our army. I shall confine myself to this unless I find a fair opportunity for something more. The reports of bacon and corn are very favorable thus for. In some instances I have heard of bacon being bought at 12½ cents per pound. General Hill is expecting the enemy's force at Charleston to return to North Carolina and make their operations there. It looks to me more sensible for the enemy than South Carolina.

I remain, sir, very respectfully, your obedient servant,

JAMES LONGSTREET,
Lieutenant-General, Commanding.

HEADQUARTERS, *April* 17, 1863—9 p. m.

Maj. Gen. S. G. FRENCH, *Commanding, &c.:*

GENERAL: Your note of 7th is received. I regret to learn that Lieutenant Rogers is probably captured. I hope that we are more troublesome to the gunboats than they are to us. I think that you had better send the whole of Colonel Connally's regiment down early in the morning. The long guns from Fort Powhatan will probably be ready the day after to-morrow. I have two cavalry companies below the Western Branch, which ought to keep off the Yankee pickets. Colonel Brown is at Smithfield; I will order him down to the Nansemond.

Yours, respectfully,

JAMES LONGSTREET,
Lieutenant-General, Commanding.

HDQRS. DEPARTMENT OF SOUTHERN VIRGINIA,
Petersburg, Va., April 17, 1863.

[Maj. Gen. S. G. FRENCH:]

GENERAL: I inclose you a note* from Captain Milligan, to hand this morning, as I cannot attend to it here, and he is by this time nearer your present headquarters than these. I telegraphed Major Daves last night that Colonel Brown's entire command had left Fort Powhatan, probably for Smithfield, as Major Sorrel ordered six companies through Captain Riely to move at once with Dabney's battery to that place. I telegraphed to Fort Powhatan yesterday to know if the four companies had moved, and learned there was no one there, when I went to see Captain Riely, who told me of Major Sorrel's order to him. I hope there is no mistake about this matter, and the four companies will reach Franklin in good time; but under the existing state of affairs I cannot feel myself responsible for any miscarriage of orders, as Colonel Brown's command either is or is not under your immediate command. No news here and but little doing in the office.

Hoping for your safe and speedy return, I am, yours, sincerely,

CHAS. D. MYERS.

P. S.—I sent you a New York Herald of the 13th instant on yesterday.

---

*Not found.

HEADQUARTERS,
Near Suffolk, Va., April 17, 1863—6.30 p. m.

Maj. Gen. S. G. FRENCH, *Commanding, &c.:*

GENERAL: The commanding general desires me to say that you may use the North Carolina regiment (Fifty-fifth) of General Davis' brigade on the river for the protection of your batteries. I am just writing to Colonel Brown, and tell him, as I also did this morning, to send his four companies, if he has not already sent them, to Franklin by the nearest route. The balance of his regiment will be at Smithfield to-night. The guns are behind; he will wait for them there.

I am, general, very respectfully,

G. MOXLEY SORREL,
Assistant Adjutant-General.

———

HEADQUARTERS ARMY OF NORTHERN VIRGINIA,
April 18, 1863.

Hon. JAMES A. SEDDON,
Secretary of War:

SIR: An officer reported to-day, bringing from Captain Pannill, pro-vost-marshal of Petersburg, six disloyal citizens of North Carolina, captured by General D. H. Hill. The three younger ones will be assigned to the North Carolina regiments, as conscripts, by your order. I think it would be better, however, to send them somewhere into the interior of the country. They will be worth nothing as soldiers, and the facilities for desertion to the enemy are very great here. They will of course carry to the enemy all the information which they have obtained in North Carolina, Richmond, and elsewhere, and communicate any intended movement of this army of which they may chance to hear.

There have already been frequent desertions from the North Carolina regiments, and the enemy claim that many have come to them. The three men who are over the conscript age I will send back by the train to-morrow, as they are evidently not included in your order. General Hill states that he will send the charges against these men to Petersburg. I would suggest that in order not to create any ill-feeling it might be better to try them within the limits of the State from which they come.

I am, very respectfully, your obedient servant,

R. E. LEE,
General.

———

WAR DEPARTMENT, C. S. A.,
Richmond, Va., April 18, 1863.

Lieut. Gen. JAMES LONGSTREET,
Commanding, &c.:

GENERAL: I am gratified by the receipt of your letter of the 17th instant. The successful repulse of the enemy's marine attack at Charleston appears to have so deranged their plans and discouraged them that, in General Beauregard's opinion, they are withdrawing as well a portion of their land forces as their iron-clads. He is in consequence returning the troops sent from Wilmington. I have telegraphed him in doing so to exchange Cooke's brigade for Evans', retaining the latter and sending back the former. Fearing that, baffled at Charleston, the enemy might seek to retrieve his disaster by a sudden attack on Wilmington, I have not ventured to stop any troops moving from General Hill to re-enforce General Whiting, until assured of the return of Cooke's brigade. When that is restored, any troops parted with by General Hill in the interim might, if in your judgment deemed safe, be restored to him.

Your proceedings in regard to Suffolk are deemed judicious and fully approved. I concur in thinking the object not worth the sacrifice to be entailed by an attack. I regret not having been able to receive the co-operation of the Navy, but the President has not deemed it wise to open the obstructions without fuller information as to the effect on the remaining obstructions, and the consequence that might ensue in case of sudden attack. The subject is still under investigation by the engineers, and their report is awaited before a final decision. If it be decided to send out the Richmond, you shall be promptly informed. Meantime it is not unlikely the enemy may pour in re-enforcements to Suffolk and give you some chance of action with them in the open field. They are greatly agitated and alarmed by reports of the operations of youself and General Hill. The main object of your expedition is, I am happy to believe, being fully accomplished. It will, however, be difficult for you to bring out with dispatch the subsistence supplies you can command. The transportation we can afford is lamentably deficient. I would recommend the impressment of all wagons on both sides of the Blackwater, with their teams, to get the subsistence supplies to a safe point on this side. I need not, however, make suggestions on the subject, as doubtless your own attention, with fuller information, has been engaged in securing the utmost dispatch and efficiency in this business.

With high esteem, very truly, yours,

J. A. SEDDON,
Secretary of War.

HEADQUARTERS ARMY OF NORTHERN VIRGINIA,
April 18, 1863.
Lieut. Gen. JAMES LONGSTREET,
Commanding, &c.:

GENERAL: Your provost-marshal in Petersburg (Mr. Pannill) to-day forwarded some disloyal North Carolina citizens as conscripts to this army, on a suggestion of General D. H. Hill, approved by yourself and the Secretary of War. The facilities for desertion are so great here that these men cannot be kept a week. They will be worth nothing as soldiers and will convey all the information they can to the enemy. Will it not be better always to try disloyal citizens in their own State, in order to avoid jars and all ill-feeling? They had best be sent to the interior somewhere, as they will do us but little harm, unless they can communicate with the enemy. Three of these men I send back, as they are not of the conscript age.

I am, very respectfully, your obedient servant,

R. E. LEE,
General.

HEADQUARTERS, *April* 18, 1863.
Maj. Gen. S. G. FRENCH Commanding, &c.:

GENERAL: It is a question with me whether it is best to put the long guns in battery below Western Branch or above it. Please give me your views.

Most respectfully,

JAMES LONGSTREET,
Lieutenant-General, Commanding.

HEADQUARTERS,
Kinston, N. C. April 18, 1863—2.30 p. m.

[Maj. Gen. D. H. HILL:]

GENERAL : Nothing has happened since last night. The enemy hold Core Creek and appear to be at work there. Their force would require all mine to dislodge them quickly and with success. The move was to cover a more general one this evening or to-morrow, or it may be a feint. As your courier told me you would be here this evening I shall delay any action until you arrive. It is not necessary to pass the regiment up. I have a telegram from Whiting which may be of importance to you, and has had weight in causing me to defer acting until you arrive.

Very respectfully,

R. RANSOM, JR.,
Brigadier-General.

HEADQUARTERS DISTRICT OF THE CAPE FEAR,
Wilmington, N. C., April 18, 1863.

Col. T. S. RHETT, *Chief of Artillery, Richmond, Va.:*

COLONEL : Since the failure of the reconnaissance on Charleston I am inclined to think they may try this place. You know my armament, though much improved, is still greatly inadequate. I beg that you will do all in your power to increase my supply of 8 and 10 inch columbiads and heavy rifles as many as can possibly be sent me, for none will be superfluous at such a point as this. I should be much pleased if you would come down here and assure yourself both of the nature of the problem of defense here and the necessities I have. The heavy calls on the Department for other places have diverted many of the guns intended for me. I think we can now be supplied. I would not be so urgent were it practicable for me to obstruct the harbor entrances. That, however, may be regarded as out of the question, and hence we must obtain the most formidable concentration of fire possible. Both Forts Caswell and Fisher should have Brooke rifles in addition to columbiads. I can make good use of ten or twelve 32-pounder iron bands, many of my 32-pounders being unbanded and therefore not reliable. Please when you send guns to send with them at least 100 rounds.

Very respectfully,

W. H. C. WHITING,
Brigadier-General.

APRIL 19, 1863.

Maj. [L. M.] SHUMAKER:

I will have the matter of forage attended to. I hope you may succeed in sinking those infernal gunboats that have shown no consideration for women or children. If you cripple one and can use the field batteries against her do so. I felt too ill from the medicine I took to come down this morning. Keep me advised.

Yours, truly,

S. G. FRENCH,
Major-General, Commanding.

HEADQUARTERS, *April* 19, 1863.

Major SHUMAKER :

Let me know what is the result of the heavy cannonade now going on. Show this to Colonel Connally and have him post his regiment to repel any landing of infantry against the batteries.   They had better move down near the battery of Stribling's.   The countersign is "Morgan" for to-night.

Yours, truly,

S. G. FRENCH,
Major-General, Commanding.

HEADQUARTERS GARNETT'S BRIGADE,
Near Greenville, N. C., April 19, 1863.

[Maj. Gen. D. H. HILL:]

GENERAL: I shall move with all the haste possible, but no route was indicated, and I have to make inquiries about the best route, arrange about rations, &c.   I am ignorant of the country and where supplies could be obtained if I left with an insufficient quantity.   My supply train was at Pactolus when I got your order, and that could only rejoin me late this afternoon.

With many kind wishes for your success,

I am, general, very respectfully, your most obedient servant,

R. B. GARNETT,
Brigadier-General, Commanding.

HEADQUARTERS, *April* 19, 1863.

Maj. Gen. S. G. FRENCH, *Commanding, &c.:*

GENERAL: The two guns from Powhatan have not yet arrived.   I am expecting to hear of their arrival at Smithfield every hour.   I do not know if they had not better be placed near Smithfield, on the James, to prevent transports passing up, should the enemy take a notion to send troops from the Army of the Potomac.   Turn the whole matter over in your mind and let me know what you think best.

Most respectfully,

JAMES LONGSTREET,
Lieutenant-General, Commanding.

HEADQUARTERS, *April* 19, 1863.

Maj. Gen. S. G. FRENCH, *Commanding, &c.:*

GENERAL: Your note and inclosure are received.   Please let me know the result of the furious cannonade now going on as soon as you learn.   Have you the regiment of infantry so placed as to support the batteries in time should the enemy attempt to land an infantry force against them ?   I have ordered more ammunition for the large guns.

Most respectfully,

JAMES LONGSTREET,
Lieutenant-General, Commanding.

Please order the gunners of Capt. [D. L.] Smoot's [Alexandria Light Artillery, Va.] to fire with great deliberation and care.

HEADQUARTERS, *April* 19, 1863.

Maj. Gen. S. G. FRENCH, *Commanding, &c.:*

GENERAL: General Hood has moved a brigade down to where the battery was. It will be better not to move any more troops in the darkness.

Most respectfully,

JAMES LONGSTREET.

Try and ascertain as soon as possible the circumstances and why the North Carolina regiment was not at the support of the battery. Your note is received. I think that you had better hurry down. Robertson's brigade is on the way via Norfleet's house. General Hood can advise you of the route it took.

———

HEADQUARTERS, *April* 19, 1863.

Maj. Gen. S. G. FRENCH, *Commanding, &c.:*

GENERAL: General Hood writes me that General Law sends him word that the enemy landed below the battery and charged it. I fear that our infantry has not been doing its duty properly. Please ascertain the facts in the case and apply the remedy. If it is true that the enemy is on this side he should be driven into the river. General Hood has ordered General Robertson's brigade down. If you need it you had better send Davis' brigade also and have the infantry so placed in future as to guard against any such contingency. I am fearful that some such attempt may be made at the other batteries.

Most respectfully,

JAMES LONGSTREET,
Lieutenant-General, Commanding.

———

HEADQUARTERS,
Near Suffolk, Va., April 19, 1863.

Hon. JAMES A. SEDDON, *Secretary of War:*

SIR: From present appearances we shall be occupied some two weeks longer in drawing off the supplies from the counties east of the Chowan. If the Richmond would pass the obstructions she would be of great service by being in position to threaten any move that the enemy might be inclined to make toward my rear. If the enemy knew that she was outside of the obstructions he would not venture within her reach. I do not desire that she should move down the river at all.

I am somewhat apprehensive that if we should prove to be very troublesome here the enemy may move a considerable force from the Army of the Potomac in behind me. I have no great dread of any force that may come in my front, but a move on my flank may compel me to retire. I believe that we are doing very well in drawing in supplies, but some difficulty exists in consequence of having too many purchasers in the field. The citizens at first agreed that 50 cents was enough for their bacon, but some agents of the Commissary-General have come over and are, I understand, giving $1. So we are obliged now to pay 75 cents, and I suppose that it will advance to $1 in a few days.

I remain, sir, with great respect, your most obedient servant,

JAMES LONGSTREET,
Lieutenant-General, Commanding.

P. S.—The enemy's troops from the counties south of this are reported to have fled to Roanoke Island.

PETERSBURG, VA., *April* 19, 1863.

Maj. Gen. S. G. FRENCH, *Comdg. Department of Virginia :*

GENERAL : I received your order of the 15th instant to abandon the line of signals from Fort Powhatan to Smithfield, at Hog Island, on the 16th instant at 2.30 p. m., and started at once for Ivor, where I found Captain Small had already preceded me. The work is very heavy along the line of railroad in erecting stations. Added to that, our resources are limited, and the line is not as efficient as it could be made had we glasses. We ought to have two glasses at each intermediate station. As it is now we have but one, and hard work to get them at that. My reconnaissance along the line of James River has been thorough and complete, and I think the line will be very serviceable when located to communicate to Smithfield should we keep a force there. I return in the morning to Ivor, and if the line is completed from there to General Longstreet's headquarters I will at once proceed to again locate posts on the James River as far as Boykins' old —— (Fort Boykins), just above the mouth of Pagan Creek and about 3 miles from Smithfield, which can be supplied by vedette, the woods and the character of the country generally precluding all possibility of running a line of signals direct to Smithfield unless we had undisputed possession of the river and the creek (by James River and Pagan Creek).

I find Hog Island a delightful pasturage for 1,000 horses, the clover now upon it being ankle-deep ; also herd-grass and timothy. Would it not be well enough to place a guard upon it and put our broken-down horses there to recuperate ? All through Surry, Isle of Wight, Sussex, and Prince George where I have been is scarce of forage and high.

Please send me written instructions what you desire me to do, and order me in detail what you desire should be done. The work of cutting out is very heavy, and I would most respectfully suggest that some company be ordered to report to me to act as guard to exposed posts and pioneers.

Your obedient servant,

J. F. MILLIGAN,
Captain, Comdg. I. S. C. [Independent Signal Corps ?].

———

HEADQUARTERS, *April* 20, 1863.

Maj. Gen. S. G. FRENCH, *Commanding, &c.:*

GENERAL: Your note per courier is received just after daydawn. Have a careful examination of the enemy made and let me know his dispositions as soon as possible. I shall be prepared to re-enforce you if the enemy is inclined to give battle below.

Most respectfully,

JAMES LONGSTREET,
Lieutenant-General, Commanding.

———

HEADQUARTERS, *April* 20, 1863.

Major-General FRENCH, *Commanding, &c.:*

GENERAL : From what Captain Clarke says of the creek on your right it would be much easier to make a ford there than a bridge. Please have it examined and attended to as soon as possible.

Yours, respectfully,

JAMES LONGSTREET,
Lieutenant-General, Commanding.

HEADQUARTERS PETTIGREW'S BRIGADE,
Hookerton, N. C., April 20, 1863—12 m.

Maj. Gen. D. H. HILL:

GENERAL: Yours of 7 o'clock this morning is just received. A half hour before I received a note from General Daniel, dated yesterday, containing the same information. As I hear nothing from him to-day I suppose the Yankees are not serious. I am 20-odd miles from Greenville. If I am to support Greenville and Kinston it is absolutely necessary that the depot commissaries at these two points should have enough to issue to troops arriving, for in this country it is utterly impossible to support troops while they are marching. I have just received a report that there is nothing at Kinston. The weather is very hard on troops on the march, and it is trying them too hard to add hunger to their other sufferings. I think that General Robertson should be ordered to establish the necessary courier lines. There must be maps of this country. I have some of the north of the Tar and south of the Neuse but none between. Please order your engineer to have a copy made and sent to me.

I received your letter about the Seventeenth [North Carolina] some time after it was written, but I was unable to learn their whereabouts until I received your note of this morning. Major Haskell having no orders I brought him and one battery with me; the remainder was left behind with Generals Daniel and Garnett. I have just ordered his battery back to General Daniel.

Very respectfully, your obedient servant,

J. J. PETTIGREW,
Brigadier-General.

HEADQUARTERS,
Kinston, N. C., April 20, 1863—6 a. m.

[Maj. Gen. D. H. HILL:]

GENERAL: Your note of yesterday is just received. I shall at once set to work to fortify Southwest Creek, as I presume you mean that stream. Batchelder's Creek is only 10 miles from New Berne. The enemy was quiet yesterday. Now that they find their move on the north side was fruitless I presume they will be for trying the old route. Martin's regiment and Moore's battery arrived late yesterday. Shall I keep them here? I suppose they can be of as much service here as anywhere else.

Yours, truly,

R. RANSOM, JR.,
Brigadier-General.

HEADQUARTERS,
Near Suffolk, Va., April 20, 1863.

Maj. Gen. S. G. FRENCH, *Commanding, &c. :*

GENERAL: I have the honor to communicate to you the desire of the commanding general that you forward with as little delay as practicable a report of the affair yesterday, involving the capture of Stribling's battery.

I am, general, very respectfully, your most obedient servant,

G. MOXLEY SORREL,
Assistant Adjutant-General.

HEADQUARTERS,
Wilmington, N. C., April 20, 1863.

Hon. JAMES A. SEDDON,
  Secretary of War, Richmond, Va.:

SIR : The circumstances developed in the late engagement between the monitors and batteries at Charleston have confirmed me in certain opinions treated in my report on the defenses of this place, especially as regards Fort Caswell. If you will refer to that report under the section treating of Fort Caswell and the lower harbor you will see that I strongly recommend as auxiliary to Fort Caswell the occupation of Smithville both by troops and guns to prevent, as there urged, the establishment of the enemy in the harbor. I would modify this only to press the point still further by recommending a powerful permanent battery at Smithville. This I am constructing, and I only write to the Department now to endeavor to obtain the most powerful guns for it. Glancing at the maps you will see the range of the proposed battery opposite Battery Island, and that it would cover the channel there besides materially aiding Fort Caswell should the monitors endeavor to pass the fort and take position inside to act on the reverse of our defenses. I should want guns that would be formidable to iron-clads and which could render the anchorage unsafe for them. These should be Brooke guns—rifled 42s or 8 or 10 inch columbiads. In addition to the position at Smithville I shall occupy with a battery (see maps) a high bluff at the mouth of Price's Creek. This would have a strong fire on the Narrows, a difficult passage in the channel shown by the shoal soundings on the map opposite Price's Creek, besides controlling the anchorage above Smithville. Farther up the river, at the point immediately above Governor's Creek, I would place another battery for action upon the eastern anchorage. These works, constructed of sand, I am sure would require land forces on the part of the enemy to reduce them and would be of the utmost importance to us in the event of a forced entrance into the harbor. The only difficulty will be in procuring the guns.

Recollect the problem of obstructions here is one very difficult of solution, if not impracticable, and our main reliance must be on our batteries. You know we have an armament here vastly less powerful than that at Charleston. The place itself is little less important to us; is far more so than Savannah or any unoccupied seaport. I hope I may be able to obtain at least eight or ten more powerful guns. Heretofore I have been driving at the strengthening of our outer works first. Those are still deficient in heavy guns, but are much stronger than they were.

The importance of holding the outer harbor here is so very great that I must be excused for continuing to press this matter. It involves both Caswell and Fisher, all our importation of arms through this place, as well perhaps as the place itself, and nothing should be left undone that can be done.

Very respectfully,

W. H. C. WHITING,
Brigadier-General.

[Indorsement.]

It is not possible to defend Wilmington with its present inadequate armament. I have reason to believe that forces are being withdrawn from Charleston to support Foster. Wilmington and the railroad will be the next Yankee move.

D. H. HILL,
Major-General.

BRIGADE HEADQUARTERS,
Diascund Bridge, Va., April 20, 1863—2.30 p. m.

Major-General ELZEY, *Commanding, &c.:*

GENERAL: My infantry and artillery have reached here within this hour. I delayed to get long forage, which is very scarce in this section, and have effected much good in assisting the citizens of Williamsburg in removing their persons and effects from the reach of the enemy. The Yankee rascals tried to throw the hospital on my hands to embarrass and pump me as to my purpose of permanent occupation. I declined to have anything to do with it, and they retired their superintendent, nurses, &c. I then gave it up to the State civil authorities, who, by my counsel, obtained from them ten days' provisions without compromising our dignity or claiming from them any protection. I will send to Governor Letcher, through you, copies of all the correspondence as soon as I return to Chaffin's Bluff. You may assure the Governor that the patients will not suffer, as I know they will take charge of the asylum again now that I have retired. I could not draw them out of their intrenchments. They made no move, and I left all quiet, though they were in the last two or three days considerably re-enforced. I have picketed the cavalry in two lines—an inner and outer line, the latter running across from the Chickahominy to James River Church, below Centreville; thence to Centreville; thence to the Six Mile Ordinary, and to a fork in the Telegraph road below; thence to the crossroads at Deneufville's store; thence to Austin's store; thence to Albert Hankins', on the York River; the inner line running from Bush's Mill to Mrs. Piggott's gate; thence to Garrett's gate; thence to Richardson's lane, and thence to Mount Folly, on the York River. Established a depot for forage and Colonel Shingler's headquarters at Hickory Neck Academy, extending the quarters thence to Burnt Ordinary and Olive Branch Church.

Before I leave for Chaffin's I will move the cavalry headquarters up to Barhamsville and draw in the pickets across from Albert Hankins', on York River, west bank of Scimmino Creek, to Whitaker's Mill, and thence across to Bush's Mill and the Chickahominy.

Rodgers' cavalry have scarcely any men besides couriers for duty, from desertion to the enemy. They cannot be trusted for any duty, and Doby's and Hawley's companies barely supply their places in number, and the necessity for Hawley here leaves the Chickahominy without pickets on the Charles City side. I beg you to take the Holcombe Legion and Robertson's battalion away and to restore to me my old regiment of cavalry, which I raised and mustered (the Tenth Virginia Cavalry), with one company (the James City Cavalry, belonging to the Fifth Virginia Cavalry) added. Thus I could have good men, familiar with the paths of James City, York, Charles City, New Kent, and Henrico. The present strangers to our roads need guides to every post. I have saved the records of York, Warwick, and Elizabeth City Counties and forwarded them to you to be handed over to Governor Letcher for safe-keeping. It is important I should know how long I am to remain here, as, if long, my men must send for changes of clothing. I await your orders, and am, very truly, your obedient servant,

HENRY A. WISE,
Brigadier-General.

HEADQUARTERS BRIGADE,
Hookerton, April 20, 1863.

Maj. Gen. D. H. HILL:

GENERAL: Not knowing what to do with Major Haskell I ordered him to accompany us. He bears this himself to receive your orders. In addition to my two batteries, he has another here and you have ordered Captain Moore's. To command this battalion, it would be very agreeable to me if you would assign him to me. In that event Captain McCreery should be assigned to other duty, as his rank is inferior to some of the officers he commands.

Would it not be proper for General Robertson to establish a line of couriers between this place and Kinston?

Very truly, your obedient servant,

J. J. PETTIGREW,
Brigadier-General.

————

CHARLESTON S. C., *April* 20, 1863

Maj. Gen. D. H. HILL, *Goldsborough, N. C.:*

No troops or iron-clads have left here to support Foster as yet.

G. T. BEAUREGARD.

————

GOLDSBOROUGH, N. C., *April* 20, 1863.

General G. T. BEAUREGARD, *Charleston:*

GENERAL: For the last four weeks I have been around Washington and New Berne with three objects in view: To harass the Yankees, to get out supplies from the low country, and to make a diversion in your favor. In the first two objects we succeeded admirably, whipping the enemy in every skirmish and fight. Washington was closely besieged for sixteen days, but they succeeded in getting two supply boats into town, furnishing about twenty days' rations to the garrison. I then abandoned the siege.

I have failed to get information from New Berne for some days. The usual channel of communication is cut off, and I am very much in the dark as to what is going on. My last information was that a brigade had gone up from Morehead City. This must have come from Charleston. I send Captain West specially to you to ascertain whether any troops have left your point. I am inclined to think that the rascals have abandoned all idea of attacking Charleston and that Wilmington will be their next move. Should this be so I hope that you will be able to give us back our North Carolina troops. We have now but four brigades in the State. I have rejoiced greatly at your success, and trust that you may continue to enjoy the smiles of a protecting God. Our hope must be in Him.

Yours, truly,

D. H. HILL,
Major-General.

————

HEADQUARTERS, *April* 20, 1863.

Maj. Gen. D. H. HILL,
Comdg. District of North Carolina, Goldsborough:

GENERAL: I inclose you Major Kennedy's report, and also letter from

Colonel Griffin, together with communication from Lieutenant Harvie, whom I sent down to inspect the courier line.*

The conduct of Captain Nichols' company on two different occasions has been disgraceful in the extreme, and I must either have authority to appoint competent officers to this and other companies in Griffin's as well as Claiborne's regiments, or the companies requiring them must be disbanded. It is not entirely the fault of the men, and I feel sure with proper commanders I would not again be subjected to the mortification and disgust occasioned by the misbehavior and cowardice of these men, who have been taught nothing by their officers unless it be to run from the enemy. The proceedings of boards of examination forwarded to Richmond have never been heard from and probably never will be. In such cases (I mean where officers are found incompetent and inefficient) please inform me what I must do when no action is taken by higher authority.

Nichols has tendered his resignation and his other officers are incompetent. Can I not appoint officers to this company? I should like to put Captain Wright in command of it at once. Situated as I am I should be permitted to act promptly when occasion requires, and I should like to be informed if you will sustain me in taking the steps necessary to place these two regiments in a state of efficiency without loss of time—without waiting to hear from the Department at Richmond. In case all the officers of a company are worthless the power to appoint is admitted; but the action of the Department is first necessary as regards those reported incompetent. If nothing is ever heard from their decision surely no charge can be made according to the requirements of the law. I send the small courier as requested.

With the mounted men of the three disbanded companies I am forming a company of couriers as arranged. If upon examination they do not appear sufficiently intelligent I shall substitute it for one of Claiborne's more suitable for such duty. Unless you object I shall relieve Captain Pitt and order Colonel Griffin to take charge of that line as heretofore. It is very important that Claiborne's whole regiment should be disciplined.

Owing to the scarcity of forage and the arrival of Pettigrew's brigade I shall have to move in a few days. Where shall I go? As soon as I can straighten the command I now have here, finish with an examining board now in session, &c., I shall report to General Longstreet, as I presume Ferebee is on his way to Blackwater, although you did not tell me.

Please answer at your earliest convenience.

Very respectfully, your obedient servant,

B. H. ROBERTSON,
Brigadier-General, Commanding Cavalry.

WAR DEPARTMENT, ENGINEER BUREAU, C. S. A.,
Richmond, Va., April 20, 1863.

Hon. JAMES A. SEDDON,
        Secretary of War:

SIR: I have the honor to make the following report as suggested by His Excellency the President, and requested by you in a recent indorsement on a communication by the honorable Secretary of the Navy,† re-

---

* Not found.   † Of April 10, 1863, p. 976.

questing that an opening be made in the James River obstructions at Drewry's Bluff for the passage of the C. S. steamer Richmond.

Col. W H. Stevens, chief of construction department of Northern Virginia, in a recent letter to this Bureau, after careful examination and consideration, expresses the opinion that a satisfactory opening for the passage of vessels may be made in ten days. While this opinion as to time seems rather too sanguine, I think it clear, however, that the undertaking is not one necessarily requiring much delay for its realization.

This opening can be so arranged as to be closed on short notice by sinking a vessel at its lower extremity and keeping ready at points higher up rafts for the same purpose. The barrier, however, will be neither so perfect nor so safe after as before the completion of the opening.

I do not think it advisable to cut a canal through the low grounds on account of the treacherous nature of the soil. Such a canal, by the influence of successive freshets, might enlarge to dangerous dimensions.

In conclusion, considering the fact that there are two bars in James River between Drewry's Bluff and City Point over which the Richmond can pass only in time of freshets, and further that her machinery and speed are so defective, I most respectfully but earnestly represent that it will be judicious to make an opening in the James River obstructions only when a second iron-clad is on the eve of completion.

I have the honor to be, very respectfully, your obedient servant,

J. F. GILMER,
Colonel of Engineers and Chief of Bureau.

[Indorsement.]

The view in relation to the propriety of waiting for an additional iron-clad vessel is concurred in.

J. D.

HEADQUARTERS ARMY OF NORTHERN VIRGINIA,
April 21, 1863.

Hon. JAMES A. SEDDON,
Secretary of War, Richmond, Va. :

SIR: I have just received a letter from General Longstreet, dated the 20th instant, stating that the enemy crossed below Hill's Point on the evening of the 19th; attacked and captured Stribling's battery at that point operating against the gunboats. He again expresses a desire that the Richmond would only show herself in the James River, and thinks that alone would strengthen his left by 10,000 men. I do not know that anything can be done by the Navy and only express his wishes.

I am, with great respect, your obedient servant,

R. E. LEE,
General.

HEADQUARTERS, *April* 21, 1863.

Maj. Gen. S. G. FRENCH, *Commanding:*

GENERAL: The commanding general desires to know what arrangements or dispositions you have made for watching the gunboats or other movements of the enemy on the river. If you have made none he wishes you to take steps at once to have them carefully observed. The last report that we have from the river is that General Hood is in possession of the old fort.

I am, general, very respectfully, your obedient servant,

G. MOXLEY SORREL,
Assistant Adjutant-General.

HEADQUARTERS, *April 21, 1863.*

Maj. G. MOXLEY SORREL,
    Assistant Adjutant-General:

DEAR SIR: I am in receipt of your communication asking what arrangements or dispositions I have made for watching the gunboats or other movements of the enemy on the river. When the lieutenant-general commanding placed the artillery under my orders I found a battery in Henry's work and another at Hill's Point, and I placed the two heavy guns in a work which I caused to be erected. The general is aware that the guns at Hill's Point were taken by the enemy, and that Bradford's guns were ordered by General Hood to be withdrawn last night, and that he ordered the heavy guns to Providence Church. The only infantry force that belonged to my command was the Fifty-fifth North Carolina Troops, which he ordered down there to support the batteries, and that has been ordered back to its brigade. I had a few sharpshooters down on the Western Branch of the Nansemond, but those I ordered back, thinking it unnecessary to keep such a small force on the left of General Hood, whose line extends to near by its mouth. When the general ordered the heavy guns to Providence Church I took it for granted he designed them for other service. Inasmuch as the troops of General Hood extended to Hill's Point I did not think the watching of the movements of the enemy devolved on me. I will thank the general to state what should be the number and character of the forces he wishes me to send there, and if he wishes it done to-night, and I will order them at once. As I observed, General Hood's forces extend to the mouth of the Western Branch of the Nansemond River.

Yours, very respectfully,

S. G. FRENCH,
Major-General, Commanding.

HEADQUARTERS, *April 21, 1863—11.15 p. m.*

Maj. Gen. S. G. FRENCH, *Commanding, &c.:*

GENERAL: Your communication of this evening is received and will be fully considered to-morrow. Meantime the commanding general desires you to make some arrangements to-night to keep at least a lookout on the river to discover what may be going on. More extended and systematic dispositions may be effected to-morrow.

I am, general, very respectfully, your obedient servant,

G. MOXLEY SORREL,
Assistant Adjutant-General.

[Indorsement.]

HEADQUARTERS FRENCH'S COMMAND,
April 22—1 a. m.

In accordance with the directions contained herein Brigadier-General Jenkins will dispatch a force of 25 men to take post near Riddick's farm, who will observe closely all movements of the enemy and give timely notice of the same. Two mounted men are sent to act as couriers. Please acknowledge and return this paper.

By order of Major-General French:

GRAHAM DAVES,
Assistant Adjutant-General.

CHARLESTON, S. C., *April* 21, 1863.

Brigadier-General WHITING, *Wilmington, N. C.:*

Three thousand feet submarine wire will be sent you. By authority Secretary of War, Cooke's brigade will be sent you in place of Evans'. Shall send Hall's regiment soon. Please send back Evans' regiments by the transportation.

G. T. BEAUREGARD.

GOLDSBOROUGH, N. C., *April* 21, 1863.

His Excellency ZEBULON B. VANCE,
Governor of North Carolina:

DEAR SIR: I think that infantry would be of little service in Moore County without the co-operation of cavalry. I wish to send 25 horsemen and 50 infantry. This is, however, a bad time to weaken my force. I learn that there are one hundred vessels now at Morehead City, and that troops are pouring in from Charleston. The Charleston expedition is abandoned, and Wilmington and the railroad are the next object of Yankee cupidity.

General Longstreet wrote me to ask you to call out the militia. I do not know that any good could result from it except the exposure of the skulkers. The men staying at home now are consumers and not producers. They ought to be kicked into the ranks by some means. One of your stirring appeals would do good. Your scathing rebuke of deserters and skulkers makes even cowards blush. I fear that the discontent and demoralization of the troops have been mainly caused by unwise ebullition of temper on the part of our local press. Would to God that our editors could fight the common enemy and let their private quarrels lie over. If conquered by the Yankees our doom will be the most miserable known in history. There is no insult and no indignity which these infernal wretches will not inflict upon us. I earnestly hope that you will call out every able-bodied man in the State, but especially that you will issue a proclamation in regard to deserters and skulkers.

Yours, truly,

D. H. HILL,
Major-General.

HEADQUARTERS,
Greenville, N. C., April 21, 1863—4 p. m.

Maj. Gen. D. H. HILL, *Commanding, &c.:*

GENERAL: The force that came up on the Washington road yesterday will not exceed 300 or 400 men and two pieces. The force at the cross-roads evening before last was represented as being very large; a large number of ambulances and wagons. They retired last evening. I sent the cavalry down the road to look after them. I sent a small mounted force on the roads to Swift Creek. I have not yet heard from the one that comes by Black Jack Church and into the Washington road at Taft's. From the upper road the captain reports that he saw Whitford, who was near the enemy as late as 2 o'clock in the morning. They were then in possession of Swift Creek and were cutting and working a good deal. Whitford represents this force at 4,000. Should they advance I will make the main fight 3 miles from town, the best position this side of the Swift Creek road, but still much in favor of the enemy. General Pettigrew is at Adams' Bridge. I will endeavor to keep you advised.

Very respectfully, &c.,

JUNIUS DANIEL,
Brigadier-General.

HEADQUARTERS,
Greenville, N. C., April 21, 1863—5.30 p. m.

Brig. Gen. J. J. PETTIGREW, *Commanding, &c.:*

GENERAL: There will be no necessity of your marching here to-night. I have not yet heard from the force I sent in the direction of Washington, but they (the enemy) must still be near Washington, or I should have heard from them. My information from Swift Creek is that they still occupy it and are at work upon something. In regard to attacking them I do not see how we can do so unless we attack the force at Swift Creek, or those at Washington should come out again.

I will write you again when I get reports from below.

Very respectfully,

JUNIUS DANIEL,
Brigadier-General.

WAR DEPARTMENT, C. S. A.,
Richmond, April 22, 1863.

General G. T. BEAUREGARD, *Charleston, S. C.:*

General Hill telegraphs that New Berne has been strongly re-enforced from Charleston; that heavy force is marching on Kinston, and that he needs help. General Whiting confirms the transfer of troops and gunboats to New Berne. Render all the aid you safely can.

J. A. SEDDON,
Secretary of War.

CHARLESTON, *April 22, 1863.*

Maj. Gen. D. H. HILL, *Goldsborough:*

Send you Cooke's brigade, although much needed, enemy being still in force at Port Royal and North Edisto; his six monitors in latter bay.

G. T. BEAUREGARD.

[Same to Brigadier-General Whiting.]

CHARLESTON, S. C., *April 22, 1863.*

Brig. Gen. W. H. C. WHITING, *Wilmington, N. C.:*

Evans returns immediately to Wilmington. Soon as enemy's fleet shall leave Port Royal and North Edisto will send you another brigade besides Cooke's.

G. T. BEAUREGARD.

CHARLESTON, S. C., *April 22*, 1863.

Brig. Gen. W. S. WALKER, *Pocotaligo, S. C.*:

Cooke's brigade must return to Wilmington soon as possible. Regiment will be sent you from Savannah. Use transportation to send on Cooke's troops. Answer.

THOMAS JORDAN,
Chief of Staff.

___

CHARLESTON, S. C., *April 22*, 1863.

JAMES A. SEDDON,
Secretary of War, Richmond, Va.:

Have already ordered Cooke's brigade to report to General Whiting; Evans to remain in North Carolina until further orders. I will hold Clingman's ready to move so soon as I can ascertain what enemy's forces intend doing here.

G. T. BEAUREGARD.

___

ADAMS' BRIDGE, *April 22*, 1863—6.30 a. m.

Major-General HILL:

GENERAL: Your special courier has just arrived with your dispatch of 9.30 p. m., 21st instant.

I have already sent a dispatch to you at Kinston announcing that I am going to Hookerton, there to await orders. But I shall now proceed from that point to Kinston by the direct road, whatever that may be.

I have forwarded your previous dispatches to me to General Daniel, so I suppose he knows what to do. I have given him no instructions from myself.

Yours, very truly,

J. J. PETTIGREW,
Brigadier-General.

You know I am ignorant of the topography around Kinston. Please have a guide and a map for me if I am to go into position.

___

GUM SWAMP, N. C., *April 22*, 1863.

[Maj. Gen. D. H. HILL:]

GENERAL: Capt. [B.] Lane has just returned from the reconnaissance on which he went early this morning. He went to within half a mile of Core Creek and sent a lieutenant ([M.] Lee) and 3 men over the creek, who went half a mile beyond the creek, to the late encampment of the enemy. It appears like the encampment of a brigade. They left this morning before day. An old family near that place say there was 4,000 or 5,000. Nothing has been done lately to the railroad bridge, but it can easily be prepared for use, being only about 25 feet long. The track was destroyed by being overturned, the sills still adhering to the rails, and you will at once see that it can be rendered fit for use by simply turning the superstructure back to its original position, which can be done rapidly when sufficient force can be brought to bear. The enemy have righted up the track for about 3 miles this side of the creek. The track has been upturned in the manner described from a point about 1½ miles beyond this. Thence upward the sills or cross-ties have been burned and the iron bent, and it will require time to reconstruct the track.

Very respectfully, your obedient servant,

WM. J. CLARKE,
Colonel [Twenty-fourth North Carolina Troops], Comdg.

HEADQUARTERS,
Near Suffolk, Va., April 22, 1863.

Hon. JAMES A. SEDDON,
        Secretary of War:

SIR: I have the honor to acknowledge the receipt of your favor of the 18th. If the enemy has abandoned the intention of reducing Charleston it would be well to have all the troops sent from North Carolina returned as soon as practicable, and indeed some of those comprising the regular garrisons. Generals Clingman's and Evans' brigades could be placed at Wilmington and General Cooke's at Goldsborough.

We were so unfortunate as to meet with a serious disaster on the 18th in losing Captain Stribling's battery, 55 of his men, and 70 of General Law's brigade. The enemy succeeded in making a complete surprise by moving down the river with one of his gunboats until he got nearly under the fire of the battery, as though it was the intention to run by the battery, then he opened fire upon our fort at or upon Hill's Point from gunboats and land batteries as though his desire was to draw our attention from the gunboat which seemed to be trying to get by our battery. Under this fire and the seeming desire of the boat to pass the enemy landed probably 200 or 300 men in the vicinity of our fort and captured it by complete surprise. I have not made any report of the facts before this because I had hoped to have General French's report of the facts officially. It has been so long delayed, however, that I have thought it proper to mention this much that you may be apprised of the facts so far as they have come to light. As well as I can judge at present the misfortune is due to the entire want of vigilance on the part of the troops in the fort. The fort is on the Nansemond, just above the mouth of Western Branch. The 70 infantrymen were, I understand, sharpshooters selected for the service. A regiment (about 700 strong) had been stationed by General French in supporting distance of the battery, but no call was made upon it for aid. One of our scouts just from Fort Monroe reports the enemy re-enforcing him to a considerable extent, and that the enemy's intention now is to effect a surprise by landing the Army of the Potomac on both sides of the James above us. His late successful dash at our battery and the limited time for which he holds many of his soldiers may induce him to attempt some extraordinary movements. Please keep me advised of any important information that you may receive.

I remain, with great respect, your most obedient servant,

JAMES LONGSTREET,
Lieutenant-General, Commanding.

Since writing this letter I have received dispatches from Generals Hill and Whiting reporting the arrival at Beaufort, N. C., of the enemy's forces and fleet from Charleston. I hope that General Beauregard may be ordered to re-enforce General Hill sufficiently to enable him to resist the advance of the enemy in North Carolina. I do not apprehend any immediate move against Wilmington, but the enemy may attempt to break up our line of railroad.

Most respectfully,   J. L.

[Indorsements.]

APRIL 25, 1863.

Respectfully submitted to the President for information.

General Beauregard is returning the troops sent from North Carolina. In presence of General Hill's force I do not apprehend any serious movement of the enemy toward our railroad. They will probably be content to hold their fortified places.

J. A. SEDDON,
Secretary.

APRIL 30, 1863.

Respectfully returned by the President to the honorable Secretary of War.

G. W. C. LEE,
Colonel and Aide-de-Camp.

NEAR SUFFOLK, VA., *April* 22, 1863.
(Received at Richmond, Va., April 23, 1863.)

SECRETARY OF WAR:

Dispatches from Generals Hill and Whiting report the expedition against Charleston abandoned by the enemy and that the army and the fleet have arrived at Beaufort, N. C. May I ask that General Beauregard be ordered to return to North Carolina the troops that came from there last winter? Please acknowledge receipt of this.

Respectfully,

JAMES LONGSTREET,
Lieutenant-General.

HEADQUARTERS FRENCH'S DIVISION,
April 22, 1863.

Maj. G. MOXLEY SORREL,
Adjutant-General, Dept. of North Carolina and Virginia:

MAJOR: In accordance with instructions from the lieutenant-general commanding a detachment from one of the companies of the Fifty-fifth North Carolina Troops was sent last night to do picket duty near Hill's Point. It is respectfully suggested that these men be relieved, inasmuch as they went off hurriedly late at night and took no rations.

I am, major, very respectfully, &c.,

S. G. FRENCH,
Major-General, Commanding.

HEADQUARTERS, *April* 22, 1863.

Maj. Gen. S. G. FRENCH, *Commanding, &c.:*

GENERAL: I have notified General Hood of the detachment of the Fifty-fifth North Carolina Troops doing duty on the river and asked him to relieve it.

Very respectfully, yours,

G. MOXLEY SORREL,
Assistant Adjutant-General.

WAR DEPARTMENT, C. S. A.,
Richmond, Va., April 22, 1863.

Maj. Gen. D. H. HILL, Goldsborough, N. C.:

I have telegraphed General Beauregard to send you all the aid he can safely spare. We can spare none here or at Petersburg. You have doubtless informed General Longstreet.

J. A. SEDDON,
Secretary of War.

HEADQUARTERS,
Near Suffolk, Va., April 22, 1863.

Maj. Gen. S. G. FRENCH, Commanding, &c.:

GENERAL: In reply to your letter of the 21st the lieutenant-general commanding directs me to say that he desires to know what sharp-shooters you had on the Western Branch which you ordered in, inas-much as you state that you had no infantry other than the Fifty-fifth North Carolina in your command. He ordered the heavy guns back to Providence Church during the occupation of the left bank of the river by the enemy, and while the men of that battery were occu-pied in bringing off the ammunition that had been left behind in their hasty withdrawal from their position on the river. The battery at Fort Henry was withdrawn during the night of the 20th to prevent a chance of a surprise. The enemy retired from this side of the river yesterday, and the lieutenant-general commanding expects that you will resume the responsibilities of the river batteries and their protection, if it is agreeable to you; otherwise he expects you to advise him that he may make other arrangements.

The commanding general is somewhat surprised at your idea of the heavy guns being intended for other service because they were ordered to Providence Church, inasmuch as there was no ammunition for either of the guns when they were ordered back. In assigning to you the charge of the artillery, and particularly the river defenses, the commanding general had every confidence in your ability to select positions for bat-teries and to assign proper infantry supports for their protection. He has not given himself any anxiety upon the subject further than to in-sist upon your taking to the support of the batteries the whole of the Fifty-fifth North Carolina Regiment instead of only the three companies proposed by you. In your note of the evening of the 19th you reported to the commanding general that you had three companies of this regi-ment in the old fort. This seems to have been a mistake. The com-manding general expects you to make such arrangements as you deem necessary to secure the river from another surprise, and to have such batteries placed upon it as may be required to prevent the passage of gunboats. He will be glad to offer suggestions upon any particular points on which you may have doubts.

I am, general, very respectfully, your most obedient servant,

G. MOXLEY SORREL,
Assistant Adjutant-General.

HEADQUARTERS, April 22, 1863.

Maj. G. MOXLEY SORREL,
Assistant Adjutant-General:

DEAR SIR: I am in receipt of your letter of this morning. The sharpshooters referred to were 25 men detailed from General Jenkins' brigade. By the general commanding placing the artillery under my charge I cannot admit that I was charged particularly with the river defenses. That embraces what was being performed by other troops than mine. In answer to the general's kind inquiry if it will be agreeable to me to resume the responsibilities of the river batteries and their protection, I reply it will not be. General J. B. Hood's command on the left extends far down the river to Hill's Point, and as the working parties, tools, and the main protection must come from him, while my command is about 9 miles distant, there will be a want of unity of action. If the brigades of Generals Jenkins and Davis were on the left I would take charge of the batteries with pleasure and the defense of the river.

Yours, very respectfully,

S. G. FRENCH,
Major-General, Commanding.

WAR DEPARTMENT, C. S. A.,
Richmond, April 22, 1863.

General R. E. LEE, *Fredericksburg, Va.:*

General Hill telegraphs that large re-enforcements have been brought by the enemy from Charleston to New Berne; that they are marching in force on Kinston, and that he needs help. I have telegraphed General Beauregard to send all he can safely spare.

Reliable information is just received that on Sunday night last eleven large transports with troops landed at Yorktown, each believed to contain not less than 750 men. A good deal of field artillery also landed at Yorktown. Seventeen large transports likewise passed the York River on the way to Fortress Monroe or Norfolk.

J. A. SEDDON,
Secretary of War.

CHARLESTON, S. C., *April 23, 1863.*

Maj. Gen. W. H. C. WHITING, *Wilmington, N. C.:*

Cannot now spare heavy guns from here. Six monitors are still in North Edisto. Savannah also loudly calls for some heavy guns.

G. T. BEAUREGARD.

CHARLESTON, S. C., *April 23, 1863—9.30 p. m.*

JAMES A. SEDDON,
Secretary of War, Richmond, Va.:

Am informed four heavy Whitworth guns have arrived at Wilmington on Merrimac. Cannot two be sent here? They are much needed.

G. T. BEAUREGARD.

HDQRS. DEPT. SOUTH CAROLINA, GEORGIA, AND FLORIDA,
Charleston, S. C., April 23, 1863.

Maj. Gen. D. H. HILL,
Commanding, &c., Goldsborough, N. C.:

GENERAL: Your letter of the 20th instant, through Captain West, has been received. I thank you for your timely move on Washington, and regret much the circumstances which prevented the capture of Foster's forces. I hope you will still be able to do so before long.

I am not yet able to tell precisely what has become of all Hunter's forces in my front, but it is probable a part has been sent to re-enforce Foster. I have in consequence ordered Cooke's brigade to report at once to Whiting and General Evans' brigade to remain in North Carolina until further orders. Clingman's will be sent also as soon as it may be absolutely required and I can ascertain more positively that Hunter has weakened himself too much to be dangerous to this place or Savannah. You may rely that I will afford you and Whiting all the assistance in my power, for the enemy must not be allowed any success within the reach of our available forces.

Wishing you ample good luck, I remain, yours, truly,

G. T. BEAUREGARD,
General, Commanding.

HDQRS. DEPARTMENT OF SOUTHERN VIRGINIA,
April 23, 1863.

General M. JENKINS, *Commanding, &c.*:

GENERAL: I shall assume the immediate command of the division composed of your brigade and that of General Davis. Will you please let your assistant adjutant-general give to Major Daves, assistant adjutant-general, the names of the regiments now on picket duty? The details will hereafter be made by Major Daves. My chief commissary could not leave Petersburg, and the same commissary will have to act for the command. Maj. [John B.] Morey, chief quartermaster, will take prompt measures to forward all necessary supplies.

Yours, very truly,

S. G. FRENCH,
Major-General, Commanding.

HEADQUARTERS ARMY OF NORTHERN VIRGINIA,
April 23, 1863.

Lieut. Gen. JAMES LONGSTREET,
Commanding, &c., Petersburg, Va.:

GENERAL: There is great need of more cavalry in this army. Our cavalry has been reduced by hard and long service, and the enemy's recently has been very much increased. They have drawn from Maryland the cavalry which has been serving on the left bank of the Potomac, in the interior, and the counties on the Eastern Shore, in addition to the re-enforcements they have received from the North. They now have six brigades, formed into three divisions, composing a corps, under General Stoneman, and in recent operations on the Rappahannock General Stuart reports that they ride over him by sheer force of numbers. It therefore has become necessary to strengthen that arm of the service, and I desire to know whether there is not more cavalry in North Carolina than you require. There are two North Carolina regiments of cavalry in this army, and if I could get three more I could form a North Carolina brigade. Can you spare three regiments or a brigade, or what can you spare? Please let me know at your earliest convenience, or order such regiments forward as you can spare.

Very respectfully, your obedient servant,

R. E. LEE,
General.

STATE OF NORTH CAROLINA, EXECUTIVE DEPARTMENT,
Raleigh, N. C., April 23, 1863.

Maj. Gen. D. H. HILL,
  Commanding, Goldsborough, N. C.:

GENERAL: Yours of yesterday is just received. In view of the alarming information it conveys of this probable invasion of the State, I will not press for the troops to be sent to Moore County at present. I will at once issue an appeal to the people to send in the deserters and absentees and do everything I can to bring up every man to his post. I do not think, general, that the militia ought to be called out, for various reasons: Their help would be little, their consumption of rations great, and beyond any sort of doubt their removal now from their crops would be followed by the most disastrous consequences. If you think it necessary when the enemy's movement is fully developed I will call out the militia officers, of whom there are some 2,000 or 3,000, which will be a larger number, I fear, than we can arm and make available. I can bring them to Raleigh at once by an order. I earnestly hope, however, that such a thing will not be necessary. In accordance with a previous request, I have addressed a note to the city editors, urging them to avoid exciting any panic among the people and to be cautious not to speak of the movements of troops, &c.

Very respectfully,

Z. B. VANCE.

BRIGADE HEADQUARTERS,
Chaffin's Farm, Va., April 23, 1863.

Maj. Gen. ARNOLD ELZEY, *Commanding, &c.:*

GENERAL: Yesterday morning I issued all the necessary orders, as you instructed me, and moved back all the forces which I took down from this place. They will reach here this morning, or some time to-day, as the weather permits. We left all quiet, the enemy making no demonstration, and still re-enforcing and fortifying at Fort Magruder. I placed the headquarters of the cavalry at Barhamsville, as better for them in all respects than Diascund, having shorter transportation of forage and a closer eye on the Pamunkey and York Rivers. I ordered Hawley's company back to its position on the Lower Chickahominy, below Diascund Creek. The pickets are arranged in inner and outer lines, with infantry scouts all in and about Williamsburg.

And now, general, again I urgently appeal to you to send to the Fifty-ninth and Forty-sixth Regiments their companies, detailed for police duty at Richmond. The two of the Fifty-ninth and five of the Forty-sixth are absolutely required on the Peninsula, if we are to protect the people in making crops this year. They are near Richmond, and produce there is most convenient to the city. We can maintain no forces down below without making there something to eat, and that object is more important than the police of Richmond. Will the city battalion never be organized?

I am confident that if the iron-clad boat (the Richmond) was sent down the river it would yet make General Longstreet's attempt a success.

Very respectfully, yours, truly,

HENRY A. WISE,
Brigadier-General.

SPECIAL ORDERS, } ADJT. AND INSPECTOR GENERAL'S OFFICE,
No. 99. } *Richmond, Va., April 23*, 1863.

* * * * * * *

XXII. The defenses at Drewry's Bluff and Manchester will be included in the Department of Richmond, under the command of Major-General Elzey.

* * * * * * *

By command of the Secretary of War:

JNO. WITHERS,
Assistant Adjutant-General.

TRANTER'S BRIDGE, N. C.,
April 24, 1863—3 p. m.

GENERAL: Grey Ligget is near Washington. I will send for him forthwith. Forty men will be sent with Captain Graham's battery as directed. Colonel Griffin's pickets are in that direction. I can rely, however, on my own men. Capts. [J. B.] Cherry and [William] Sharp, whom I sent to the vicinity of Plymouth, are in. They report, on what they regard as reliable authority, that there are 5,000 Yankees in Plymouth and expecting an attack from us. They are fortifying the place. The force in Washington two days since numbered 8,000; they were the same that came up the right bank of the river. Two thousand of them returned yesterday for New Berne with wagons on the transports. This information is from Mr. J. Randall, just from W. But why the wagons on transports? I inclose you General Potter's order, which please forward to Maj. Gen. D. H. Hill. A large number of persons in consequence of this order have left town and are now on the hill near Mrs. Ellerdee with their effects, and suffering greatly. Would it not be well to send a flag of truce, protest against the rascally conduct, and ask leave to remove the suffering women and children? I learn they are in great distress. I can rebuild the Tranter's Creek Bridge if you wish it, and will furnish transportation for the plank, which are 5 miles off. I would be glad to learn your wish on the subject. I send, as you requested, the names of the men who captured the deserter for you: Corpl. W. A. Allen, Alfred Redfern, Stephen Myers, John Edwards, E. R. Simons, and W. H. Boggan.

I am, general, most truly, your obedient servant,

D. D. FEREBEE,
Colonel Fifty-ninth North Carolina Troops.

HEADQUARTERS, *April* 24, 1863.

Maj. Gen. S. G. FRENCH, *Commanding, &c.:*

GENERAL: I hope that you will try and have the battery at the right fixed to-night, if possible, and the bridge across the run at your right flank fixed to-morrow, if it is not already done. It is important that these things should be attended to promptly. Have your artillery harnessed and hitched by daylight in the morning. The battery on the railroad should be arranged at once, else the enemy may move out and erect a battery that would sweep along the railroad embankment.

Most respectfully,

JAMES LONGSTREET,
Lieutenant-General, Commanding.

Caution your front line to be particularly on the alert in the morning.

HEADQUARTERS, *April* 24, 1863—4 p. m.

Maj. Gen. S. G. FRENCH, *Commanding Division:*

GENERAL: The commanding general directs that you have the batteries on your line hitched up at once.

Very respectfully, your obedient servant,

G. MOXLEY SORREL,
Assistant Adjutant-General.

General Pickett reports that the enemy have opened heavily on his front with artillery, with strong infantry support.

HEADQUARTERS, *April* 24, 1863—5 p. m.

Maj. Gen. S. G. FRENCH, *Commanding Division*:

GENERAL: The commanding general directs that you get your troops under arms as soon as you can.

Very respectfully,

G. MOXLEY SORREL,
Assistant Adjutant-General.

GENERAL PICKETT'S HEADQUARTERS,
April 24, 1863.

Maj. Gen. S. G. FRENCH, *Commanding, &c.:*

GENERAL: The effort of the enemy this evening proves to have been nothing more than a strong reconnaissance. It is all over now and your troops may return to their bivouacs. The commanding general directs you to have everything ready early in the morning and your batteries hitched up.

Respectfully, yours,

G. MOXLEY SORREL,
Assistant Adjutant-General.

The commanding general desires you to order Bradford's battery to report to Major Dearing at General Law's headquarters early to-morrow morning.

CHARLESTON, S. C., *April* 25, 1863.

Maj. Gen. D. H. HILL, *Kinston, N. C.:*

Scouts are mistaken. Five monitors are in Edisto and one at Port Royal. Only one supposed gone North disabled. Some troops are still on Folly Island, Edisto, and Port Royal. Probably some gone to North Carolina.

G. T. BEAUREGARD.

HEADQUARTERS, *April* 25, 1863.

Maj. Gen. S. G. FRENCH, *Commanding, &c.:*

GENERAL: Capt. [Thomas J.] Goree thinks that he saw distinctly new works about 600 yards in rear of the old line of works and near the tents. Did your examination extend as far back as this? If you have time you had better have a minute examination made to-night and let us know.

Most respectfully,

JAMES LONGSTREET,
Lieutenant-General, Commanding.

HEADQUARTERS DISTRICT OF THE CAPE FEAR,
Wilmington, N. C., April 25, 1863.

Maj. Gen. D. H. HILL,
Commanding, &c., Goldsborough:

GENERAL: Yours of the 23d received. General Cooke and his troops are arriving, but General Beauregard has received General Evans in his stead, so I have only made an exchange, but am a gainer by the swap. Beauregard says the enemy are still in force in his front, but that the moment I am menaced he will aid me. I do not think a land attack can be made upon me here with you in position at Kinston. I should of course require more troops than I have now, but should expect them from Beauregard. In the mean time we are daily growing stronger as against a sea attack.

The Merrimac, Charleston, Margaret, and Jessie all came in day before yesterday. We had quite a spirited engagement over the two former. As you expected, my 30-pounder Parrott burst in the engagement. The Merrimac brings me three splendid Blakely guns, 8-inch rifled 130-pounders. Two of them are for this place, one gone to Mississippi. I shall place one at Caswell and one at Fisher. I have three 10-inch columbiads at Caswell.

I wrote you about torpedoes. I have only a few here, hardly enough for the obstructions. You had better apply to Rains, chief of Conscript Bureau. I think there are any number of them in Richmond.

Inclosed please find a letter from my scout,* which may give you some intelligence.

As to telegraph, use the cipher for important words. I have both the War Department cipher and Beauregard's.

Very respectfully,

W. H. C. WHITING,
Brigadier-General.

KINSTON, N. C., *April 26, 1863.*

Maj. J. N. WHITFORD, *Swift Creek Village:*

DEAR SIR: I learn that my scout Kinsly has lost the confidence of the Yankees and that George Smith is suspected. It seems, then, a difficult task to put Foster on a wrong scent again. B. and C. tell me that our deserters are also suspected, and that the last two sent down are in irons. I wish, therefore, to arrange a plan with you for chasing the deserters and firing upon them until you run them into their lines. This would relieve all suspicions and enable me to stuff Foster to my heart's content. Come up to-morrow or next day and we will arrange the plan.

I was at Core Creek, on the Dover road, on Friday. The mills are not destroyed as reported. I wish you to have the scouts arrested who

---

* Not found.

gave the false report. We must have true information, and the careless and sensational scout deserves punishment. General Ransom is unwell and may be detained here four or five days, but I would prefer you to come to-morrow. I think that you can break up the negro nest on Goose Creek Island. I will draw Foster off towards Plymouth while you are operating there.

The Big Pine tories must be cut off, but I fear a fight with them lest you kill some of my spies among them. Could you not manage through Smith to give them notice in a quiet way to get off somewhere. You can't be too cautious in this matter. Suspicion might be excited and the whole thing prove a failure.

Send F. Riggs down to-morrow, and let me have a full report from that section by the 1st of May at furthest.

I cannot too emphatically caution you that your men must not trust to the report of others, but must see with their own eyes everything they report.

The accounts of the Yankee treatment of Spinola amuse me very much. He made his escape in good time, however, and deserves credit for his foot-race if not for his fight.

If you cannot come up to-morrow send up Lieutenant Barrington or Lieutenant Whitford, now I believe a captain.

The note of mine found at Hill's Point was not important, at least I think not.

Respectfully,

> D. H. HILL,
> *Major-General.*

> HEADQUARTERS,
> *Near Suffolk, Va., April 26, 1863.*

Maj. Gen. ARNOLD ELZEY,
    Commanding Department of Richmond, Va.:

GENERAL: The commanding general desires you to cause the wharves and landing places on your side of the river wherever the enemy might effect a landing to be burnt or otherwise destroyed. Please direct their destruction to be thorough and complete.

I am, general, very respectfully, your obedient servant,

> G. MOXLEY SORREL,
> *Assistant Adjutant-General.*

> NAVY DEPARTMENT, C. S. A.,
> *Richmond, April 27, 1863.*

Hon. JAMES A. SEDDON,
    Secretary of War:

SIR: Your letter of the 25th instant, inclosing a letter from General Whiting, has been received, and in reply I inclose herewith copy of my letter to General Whiting on the subject to which he refers in his letter to you.

General Whiting's letter is herewith returned.

I am, respectfully, your obedient servant,

> S. R. MALLORY,
> *Secretary of the Navy.*

[Inclosures.]

NAVY DEPARTMENT, C. S. A.,
Richmond, April 25, 1863.

Brig. Gen. W. H. C. WHITING, C. S. A.,
Commander-in-Chief, Wilmington, N. C. :

GENERAL : Your letter of the 21st instant has been received. Knowing your want of heavy guns I would have sent you the Raleigh's battery before had it been ready. But two of the guns designed for her are anywhere near ready. They will be sent with ammunition and equipments in a few days. They are two 11,000 pound double-banded Brooke 6.4 guns, whose penetration, as shown by our iron targets, equal that of the 7-inch. Their bolts weigh 90 pounds.

Very respectfully, your obedient servant,
S. R. MALLORY,
Secretary of the Navy.

HEADQUARTERS,
Wilmington, April 21, 1863.

Hon. JAMES A. SEDDON,
Secretary of War, Richmond :

SIR : Please to ask the Secretary of the Navy if he will lend me the armament of the Raleigh, especially the Brooke rifles, until she is ready to use them. She will not be ready for at least three months, and during that time I may be attacked and those guns would be of incalculable service in the defense.

Very respectfully,
W. H. C. WHITING,
Brigadier-General.

———

HEADQUARTERS ARMY OF NORTHERN VIRGINIA,
April 27, 1863.

Lieut. Gen. JAMES LONGSTREET, *Commanding, &c. :*

GENERAL : I received last night a dispatch from Maj. [William] Norris, chief of signal corps in Richmond, stating that a special scout to Washington City had returned Saturday night. After giving the strength of General Hooker's army, which he had put down very heavy (between 150,000 and 160,000), and that he had been re-enforced from Baltimore, Washington, Alexandria, and Harper's Ferry, he says that 10,000 or 12,000 men had been sent to Suffolk which were not taken from Hooker's army. Although I think his statement very much exaggerated, yet all accounts agree that Hooker has been re-enforced, and that troops from the rear have been brought forward to the Rappahannock. This looks as if he intended to make an aggressive movement, but by what route I cannot ascertain.

A dispatch from Stuart, of the 26th, received last night, states that Stoneman is in force in the neighborhood of Warrenton; that a brigade of infantry is guarding the Rappahannock Bridge and the fords each side; that the trains are running regularly on the Orange and Alexandria Railroad to Bealeton, but that he does not learn they bring up any troops.

I am glad to learn by your letter received yesterday by special courier that you are getting everything out of North Carolina as rapidly as possible. Can you give me any idea when your operations will be completed and whether any of the troops you have in North Carolina can be spared from there? As regards your aggressive movement upon Suffolk, you must act according to your good judgment. If a damaging blow could be struck there or elsewhere of course it would be advantageous; but if the place was taken I doubt whether we could spare a garrison to hold it, and storming of his works might cost us very dear.

I am, very respectfully, yours,

R. E. LEE,
General.

P. S.—Is not the Eighth Corps, which you mention in your front, Keyes', from Yorktown?

HEADQUARTERS,
Near Suffolk, Va., April 27, 1863.

Hon. JAMES A. SEDDON,
Secretary of War:

SIR: If the reports of officers of the quartermaster's and subsistence departments are to be relied upon, it will require a month to haul out the supplies of this portion of the country. If it is desirable that we should remain for that purpose the Richmond would be of great assistance to us; it would at least secure Richmond City against any sudden move of the enemy and protect my left. Unless a part of this force is necessary on the Rappahannock it would probably be well for us to hold our line as it now is instead of giving up the country back to the Blackwater again. I learned yesterday that there are a number of guns in the old river forts that were abandoned by us when this country was given up. I have sent Captain Clarke (engineers) down to examine the old works and guns and report their condition. I presume that many of these guns may be made useful if we can have carriages made for them.

I remain, sir, very respectfully, your most obedient servant,
JAMES LONGSTREET,
Lieutenant-General, Commanding.

HEADQUARTERS, *April 27, 1863—1 p. m.*

Lieutenant-General LONGSTREET,
Commanding, &c.:

GENERAL: I started this morning at 8 a. m., and, with Generals Jenkins and Davis, have walked the margin of Spikes' Run from where the right of my line strikes the run to where General Garnett is defending the ford, on the old Somerton road. The distance is over three-quarters of a mile, and the run, while it is an obstacle, is no barrier to infantry. It can be crossed at any point throughout its length between those points by infantry. There are several log crossings in the interval. I have your note, and will have an examination made with a view to have a ford for artillery. I mention the condition of Spikes' Run that it may be duly considered as a part of the general line.

Very truly,

S. G. FRENCH,
Major-General, Commanding.

HEADQUARTERS,
Near Suffolk, Va., April 27, 1863.
Maj. Gen. S. G. FRENCH, *Commanding, &c.:*

GENERAL: The commanding general desires you to cause the earth in front of the rifle-pits on your line to be so increased in thickness as to enable it to resist the fire of artillery. He also wishes you to cause the interval between your works and the brush or abatis in front to be filled up with the same kind of brush or abatis, the whole when completed to cover 60 or 70 yards in front of the works.

I am, general, very respectfully, your obedient servant,

G. MOXLEY SORREL,
Assistant Adjutant-General.

STATE OF NORTH CAROLINA, EXECUTIVE DEPARTMENT,
Raleigh, N. C., April 27, 1863.
Hon. JAMES A. SEDDON,
Secretary of War, Richmond, Va.:

SIR: I received a message from you by Judge Ruffin in regard to supplies for the army and desiring to know if I could not turn over to the Confederacy the stores on hand belonging to the State. It affords me great pleasure to assure you that the crisis in regard to provisions in this State has passed over, and the conviction is now firm in all minds that there is not only enough but to spare. The passage of the impressment act and the near approach of a harvest, which promises to be abundant, have brought to light many hoards that the fear of famine kept out of the market. The call for aid to the army has met with a liberal response from our generous people, and I trust all fears may be dismissed. The quantity of provisions on hand was not large belonging to North Carolina. They were purchased under authority of an act of our Legislature to prevent suffering in the families of soldiers and consequent disquiet and desertion in the army. The demand has been much less than I expected, and in a few weeks I shall be able to see what can be dispensed with. I hope to be able to turn over some 250,000 pounds of bacon and some corn to the Confederacy, precisely how much I cannot now say. The purchases of Government agents can also be increased when the State and most of the private individuals cease to be in the market.

Very respectfully, your obedient servant,

Z. B. VANCE.

TUESDAY NIGHT, *April* 28, 1863.
(Received May 1, 1863.)
[Maj. WILLIAM NORRIS:]

The enemy on the Peninsula have not been re-enforced by a man since I last reported (April 22). There is only a camp guard at Newport News; three companies of the Third New York on garrison duty at the fortress, and Robertson's battalion (six companies) at Camp Hamilton; Keyes, with one brigade (and that a small one) and a few cavalry, is at Yorktown and Fort Magruder. I have positive information that rations are regularly drawn for 40,000 men at Suffolk. Beef-cattle are butchered at Newport News and the meat sent direct to Suffolk. Dix has called for 10,000 more men. This information was thus obtained: A friend of ours was at the fort and saw the post commissary of subsistence of Newport News, who informed him that he sent 40,000 rations of beef. Great fear is manifested because of the rumored coming of our gunboats. All Government material at Newport News is ready to be moved at a moment's warning. The usual fleet is in the river.

Very respectfully, your obedient servant,

C. H. CAUSEY,
Captain, C. S. Army.

HOOKERTON, N. C., *April* 28, 1863—9 p. m.

Maj. Gen. D. H. HILL:

GENERAL: Yours of 6.15 p. m. is just received. I will be ready, but I am very doubtful of their coming to Goldsborough if they say they are coming; though if this be a demonstration, and they have sent their re-enforcements back from Washington, I know not where the real attack can be. Unless General Longstreet has more hope of doing something at Suffolk than I have, I wish him back on the railroads. I hope the commissary will be ready for us at Kinston when we come, for the commissariat question is my great bother.

Yours, very truly,

J. J. PETTIGREW,
Brigadier-General.

EXECUTIVE DEPARTMENT, NORTH CAROLINA,
Raleigh, April 28, 1863.

Hon. JAMES A. SEDDON,
Secretary of War:

SIR: From the best information to be obtained it seems now pretty certain that the enemy has abandoned further attempts upon Charleston and will direct his attention principally to the invasion of North Carolina during this season. I desire to say that coast of North Carolina is very poorly defended indeed. The Roanoke, the Tar, and the Neuse, embracing the richest corn-growing region of the State, upon which the army of General Lee has been subsisting for months, have no heavy artillery for their defense. The attack on Washington recently failed through the defect of artillery and the very alarming inferiority of the ammunition. I very much fear that region will not be planted, so disheartening is the prospect of defense. One-fifth of the care taken in rendering Charleston impregnable would be well bestowed in strengthening the defenses of Wilmington, which are now confessedly weak. It is a point equally important in a military view in every respect, and calls as loudly for the protection of the Government, and yet nearly all the heavy guns of the Confederacy seem to have been sent to Charleston, and other points are left to take the chances. An attack upon Wilmington by half of the number of iron-clads which assaulted Charleston would be equivalent to the capture of the city. Can nothing be done to strengthen that point?

From Roanoke Island to the late siege of Washington the history of the war has been a succession of calamities in North Carolina which none but the ungenerous and untruthful can charge to a want of bravery and patient endurance on the part of her people. I shall not pretend to say that our defense is intentionally neglected, but that it is very poorly provided for is a fact too patent to deny, and that it can be better provided for I hope is true, from the fact, which I am assured is true, that every sea-port in our possession is stronger than Wilmington. It is discouraging to know this when we consider what North Carolina has done for the cause in men and means. We certainly ought to fare no worse than our sisters.

I am again called on by General Hill to call out the militia. Considering that our white male population is already taken to the age of forty; that nearly twenty of our richest counties have been stripped of their slaves; that over 1,500 are yet at work on the fortifications, it seems a physical impossibility to prevent a famine should all the balance of our labor be abstracted from the farms in the middle of the planting season, yet I could call them out with less reluctance, and put raw plowmen to contend with iron-clad ships of war with less regret, if I were honestly convinced that everything possible to do had been done, and that such a course was unavoidable. What the resources of the Ordnance Department are of course I do not know. But may I hope that now that the attack upon Charleston is over, the defenses of Wilmington and navigable rivers of the State will receive the earnest attention of the War Department, and the requisitions of the generals in command will meet with every possible fulfillment? Permit me to assure you in the candor which I usually employ in addressing you, that an earnest and vigorous effort to defend these exposed points would work a most happy effect in the dissatisfied public mind of the people.

I am, sir, most respectfully, your obedient servant,

Z. B. VANCE.

RICHMOND, VA., *April* 29, 1863.

Maj. Gen. S. G. FRENCH, *Petersburg, Va.:*

GENERAL: The Secretary of War directs that you send here all the available forces at your command in and around Petersburg with the least delay practicable. In order not to interrupt railroad transportation this force will move by marching.

Very respectfully, &c.,

S. COOPER,
Adjutant and Inspector General.

RICHMOND, VA., *April* 29, 1863.

Maj. Gen. D. H. HILL,
    Commanding, &c., Goldsborough, N. C.:

GENERAL: The following telegram has just been received from General Lee:

The enemy is crossing below Deep Run, about the same place as before. The fog has been so thick during the night and morning that we can only see a few yards. Taken with the reports received from our left, it looks like a general advance; but where his main effort will be made cannot say. Troops not wanted south of James River had better be moved in this direction and all other necessary preparations made.

R. E. LEE.

This renders it important that such forces as you deem judicious should be concentrated at Richmond, to be in supporting distance. General Lee may telegraph you. In absence of instructions from him make such arrangements with above view as your judgment shall dictate. A like dispatch has been sent to Lieutenant-General Longstreet.

I am, general, very respectfully, your obedient servant,

S. COOPER,
Adjutant and Inspector General.

[APRIL 29, 1863.]

[General LONGSTREET:]

The following dispatch has just been received from General Lee:

FREDERICKSBURG, VA., *April* 29, 1863.

The enemy is in large force on north bank of Rappahannock, opposite the railroad, at Hamilton's Crossing. He is crossing troops below the point at which he crossed in December, and extends lower down the river. I have discovered nothing lower than the mouth of Massaponax Creek. He is certainly crossing in large force here, and it looks as if he was in earnest. I hear of no other point at which he is crossing, except below Kelly's Ford, where General Howard has crossed with his division, said to be 14,000, six pieces of artillery, and some cavalry. Stoneman will probably cross about the Warrenton Springs, and I fear will make for Gordonsville and may destroy our roads. I have nothing to oppose to all that force up there except the two brigades of cavalry under General Stuart. All available troops had better be sent forward as rapidly as possible by rail and otherwise.

R. E. LEE.

S. COOPER,
Adjutant and Inspector General.

RICHMOND, VA., *April* 29, 1863.

General LONGSTREET,
Franklin, Va., near Blackwater:

I have sent dispatch to you by messenger more in detail. Be prepared to move your command in accordance with that dispatch with the least practicable delay.

S. COOPER,
Adjutant and Inspector General.

ADJUTANT AND INSPECTOR GENERAL'S OFFICE,
Richmond, Va., April 29, 1863.

Lieutenant-General LONGSTREET:

The following telegram just received since the one already communicated to you:

If any troops can be sent by rail to Gordonsville under a good officer I recommend it. Longstreet's division, if available, had better come to me, and the troops for Gordonsville and the protection of the railroad from Richmond and North Carolina if practicable. General Howard, of the enemy's forces, making toward Gordonsville, has six batteries with him. Please order the forwarding of supplies.

The Secretary, in view of the above, directs the return of your command, or at least such portions of it as can be spared without serious risk; also any surplus force that can be spared from General D. H. Hill. Rhett's command has been sent to Gordonsville. These movements are required to be made with the utmost dispatch.

Respectfully, &c.,

S. COOPER,
Adjutant and Inspector General.

KINSTON, N. C., *April* 29, 1863.

General G. T. BEAUREGARD, *Charleston, S. C.:*

GENERAL: I see it stated in the New York papers that Hunter had but 7,000 men who could be spared to co-operate with Du Pont. How true this is I do not know, but all the papers concur in the statement the land force was small. I have force enough here, if concentrated, to fight Foster successfully, but the troops are necessarily scattered over near 100 miles. With the Neuse, Tar, Roanoke, and Chowan running nearly up to the railroad, it is an easy matter for the Yankees to make raids into the richest agricultural portion of North Carolina and of the South and carry off hundreds of negroes and destroy an incalculable amount of property. It is impossible to protect the farmers' interests of this fertile region without a division of force and consequent weakness. I learn from General Whiting that Evans' brigade has gone back to Charleston, and the object of this is to ask if you could send me Clingman's brigade. If the attack should be renewed at Charleston I could return it rapidly, as I would encamp it on the railroad at Magnolia Depot. General Longstreet has got all my cavalry worth a sou, and a sudden cavalry raid on the railroad might be successful in destroying the bridges and trestle-work below Magnolia.

With great respect,

D. H. HILL,
Major-General.

KINSTON, N. C., *April* 29, 1863.

General G. T. BEAUREGARD, *Charleston, S. C.:*

GENERAL: I send you report of a trustworthy scout. I am satisfied that Foster has applied for and is getting back the twenty regiments furnished to Hunter. This will give him a force more than double of mine, and troops, too, which have seen more service. The Yankees have shown unusual boldness lately, and this with them always indicates the presence of a large force. Yesterday my outposts were pushed back to within 5 miles of this place and they are near me in heavy force. I cannot bring my three brigades to this point lest a sudden movement be made from Washington on Greenville and Tarborough. I am very desirous to get Clingman's brigade at Wilmington, that Cooke might be on the railroad. Clingman's troops have been much demoralized, and I learn can only be trusted behind earthworks. I have no idea that the Yankees under Hunter will make a land advance. Foster, however, is bold, but ambitious and fanatical. I have obtained a copy of a letter from him to Dix last winter (December), in which he proposes to destroy the railroad at Kinston and march upon Wilmington. The defeat of Burnside arrested that pretty little plan. I hope that you can send me Clingman's brigade.

With great respect,

D. H. HILL,
Major-General.

[Inclosure.]

SWANSBOROUGH, N. C., *April* 27, 1863.

Maj. JAMES H. HILL:

MAJOR: The highest estimate that any one in whom I can rely has made of the number of troops sent up to New Berne is 5,000. Of the number of vessels I have been unable to learn anything further than has been already dispatched you. Through a scout of General Ransom's I learned that on Saturday at 3 p. m. Heckman's brigade passed down the road through Shepherdsville, as the scout believed, to Beaufort, but I have learned from another source that their destination was more probably Carolina City. The enemy, I am informed, are fortifying at or near that point on Newport River, extending to the Sound, a distance of 4 miles. For this purpose they have been pressing the negroes. This movement of Heckman's brigade was sent to General Ransom last Saturday night at 2 a. m. I would have sent it immediately to you, but, knowing that it would reach you almost as soon by that route as by this I concluded to await news from my usual source, by which I would get something more, or at least confirmatory. In this I was in part disappointed. The conductor did not visit the road himself, but through him from another man, who saw the cars pass, said that they were loaded with troops from New Berne. With this dispatch you will find the Express of the 14th instant, a very interesting paper.

Please send me a half quire of paper and a pack of envelopes.

Very respectfully, yours, &c.,

R. J. SHARP.

HEADQUARTERS, *April 29, 1863.*

Maj. Gen. D. H. HILL,
Commanding North Carolina Department:

GENERAL: Your letter of the 26th is received. I am somewhat relieved to find you are not threatened with anything immediate from the enemy. They always move slowly, and must do so in North Carolina, where they have no railroad for their transportation. I hope that all the troops sent to South Carolina will soon be returned to you. I doubt, though, if the enemy intends any decided move in North Carolina or here. The enemy will try any dodge or trick, however, which gives any promise of success. Re-enforcements have been sent here (to Suffolk) but I am not satisfied as to the extent. I am of the opinion, however, that I can hold my position against any attack from the front. We shall be here at least two weeks longer hauling out supplies. I expect you to keep General Foster's forces off of me and I shall consider myself quite safe. There are no other forces to accumulate against me. We have recovered some twenty-odd siege-guns that were left near here when we gave up this county last year, which I hope that we may be able to send you as soon as we can get carriages for them. This is all that I can promise you in artillery. I can get nothing in Richmond, or little at best. If you cannot keep General Foster's forces off of me you must be prepared to join us with part of your force in case General Foster should move in this direction from North Carolina. Have your scouts out and keep yourself well advised of the enemy's movements. We are in telegraphic communication with you now via Petersburg.

I remain, very respectfully, your most obedient servant,

JAMES LONGSTREET,
Lieutenant-General, Commanding.

RICHMOND, VA., *April 30, 1863.*

General G. T. BEAUREGARD, *Charleston, S. C.:*

Send a full brigade immediately to North Carolina to report to General Hill.

S. COOPER,
Adjutant and Inspector General

RICHMOND, VA., *April* 30, 1863.

Maj. Gen. D. H. HILL, *Kinston, N. C.:*

Send a brigade immediately to this place; Ransom's preferred, if no loss of time is involved.

S. COOPER,
Adjutant and Inspector General.

RICHMOND, VA., *April* 30, 1863.

Lieut. Gen. JAMES LONGSTREET, *Suffolk, Va.:*

Move without delay with your command to this place to effect a junction with General Lee.

S. COOPER,
Adjutant and Inspector General.

SUFFOLK, VA., *April* 30, 1863.

General S. COOPER,
　　Adjutant and Inspector General:

GENERAL: You can send General Wise's brigade to Gordonsville and telegraph General D. H. Hill for a brigade and replace it, and General Beauregard for Clingman's brigade for General Hill.

JAMES LONGSTREET,
Lieutenant-General, Commanding.

HEADQUARTERS, *April* 30, 1863.

Maj. Gen. D. H. HILL:

GENERAL: Your letter of the 27th is received. The battery on the Chowan will hardly be needed, as the probabilities are that this command will soon be moved to the Rappahannock. If this is done one of the brigades in North Carolina will be needed here to hold the line of the Blackwater. But I presume that Generals Evans and Clingman will return to you before the brigade is called for. I very much doubt the policy of holding all the points of your line or of attempting to do so. Two points, with your forces so arranged as to meet an advance against either, I should think your better arrangement. The greater the number of points that the enemy holds the better, inasmuch as he increases his line and diminishes the number of available troops. When the enemy does advance I think that it would be well to let him get well out from his base before giving him battle. Then, if you can get a strong position behind him, you will force him to attack you and will be almost certain to destroy him. I regret that you have ordered so much of the cavalry here. I only wanted one regiment and called particularly for Colonel Claiborne's, because I thought it was in such a condition as to be of little use to you, and could scout the counties south of this and at the same time help to consume forage that we might not be able to haul off. I desire that you recall all the cavalry that you have ordered except one regiment. If my troops are recalled to the Rappahannock I expect to return with them; but no move will be made for several days yet.

I remain, very respectfully, your most obedient servant,

JAMES LONGSTREET,
Lieutenant-General, Commanding.

RALEIGH, N. C., *April* 30, 1863.

Maj. Gen. D. H. HILL,
Comdg. Dept. of North Carolina, Goldsborough, N. C. :

GENERAL: I received to-day your letter of the 28th instant. You are right in saying I would not like the command of the defenses of the Roanoke, including Hamilton and Weldon. While this is true, I prefer it to my present position and will gladly take it rather than remain here. Please give the order at once. I beg, however, that you will not consider this as giving up any chances I may have for some more important position, and should another be offered you must not consider me changeable if I take it. I hope you will give me the two regiments now in the State not belonging to brigades—the Seventeenth and Forty-second. The Fifty-fifth North Carolina, now near Suffolk, has never been regularly brigaded. General Longstreet might be willing to send that back to the State. Leventhorpe's regiment has been recently attached to Pettigrew's brigade and Faison's Fifty-sixth more recently to Ransom's. All of them have never been under my command. I do not now know a position that would be agreeable to me, and can therefore make no suggestions. I am, however, much obliged to you for the kind offer to do what you can to accommodate me.

Very truly, yours,

J. G. MARTIN.

HEADQUARTERS, *April* 30, 1863.

Maj. Gen. S. G. FRENCH, *Commanding, &c. :*

GENERAL: General Hood reports that the enemy is again attempting a landing on this side the river near the old fort. The commanding general desires you to have your troops in readiness to move to the point threatened.

Very respectfully,

G. MOXLEY SORREL,
Assistant Adjutant-General.

[Indorsement.]

HEADQUARTERS FRENCH'S DIVISION,
April 30, 1863.

In accordance with the within information, General Jenkins will hold his brigade in readiness to move at a moment's warning.

By order of Brigadier-General French :

GRAHAM DAVES,
Assistant Adjutant-General.

Please return this.

HEADQUARTERS,
Near Suffolk, Va., April 30, 1863.

Maj. Gen. S. G. FRENCH, *Commanding, &c.:*

GENERAL: I am directed to ask that you will relieve to-night the pickets of General Anderson's brigade by a portion of Brig. Gen. J. R Davis' command.

I am, general, very respectfully, your obedient servant,

G. MOXLEY SORREL,
Assistant Adjutant-General.

SPECIAL ORDERS, }   HDQRS. DEPT. OF S. C., GA., AND FLA.,
    No. 95.   }   *Charleston, S. C., April* 30, 1863.

     *   *   *   *   *   *   *

VIII. Brigadier-General Clingman is relieved from duty in this department and will report with his brigade to Brigadier-General Whiting, at Wilmington, N. C. The commanding general parts with this fine brigade with the hope that in losing it from his command the good of the service will be subserved and an opportunity afforded for distinction and substantial service against the enemy of the Confederate States.

     *   *   *   *   *   *   *

By command of General Beauregard:

JNO. M. OTEY,
Assistant Adjutant-General.

RICHMOND, *May* 1, 1863.

General R. E. LEE, *Fredericksburg, Va.:*

Orders were sent on Wednesday to General Longstreet to move forward his command to re-enforce you. He replied he would do so immediately, but expected to be a little delayed in gathering up his transportation train to prevent its falling into the hands of the enemy, then in sight. General D. H. Hill, at Kinston, was also directed to send forward a brigade (Ransom's), and from his reply it may be expected here to-night, when it will be immediately pushed forward. You have already been informed by the President of the 1,400 troops sent from here to Gordonsville. I do not look for the arrival of Longstreet's command here before to-morrow evening, on account of difficulty in collecting his train, which may be employed in collecting subsistence in the counties in North Carolina (East).

S. COOPER,
Adjutant and Inspector-General.

RICHMOND, *May* 1, 1863.

General R. E. LEE, *Fredericksburg:*

The following dispatch has just been received from General Hill:

KINSTON, *May* 1, 1863.

Two strong regiments have left in train for Petersburg; remainder of Pettigrew's brigade will start when trains can be gotten. Could not disabled soldiers take the place of the negligent operators on the line? Your telegram of yesterday reached me 9 a. m. to-day.

D. H. HILL.

S. COOPER,
Adjutant and Inspector General.

RICHMOND, VA., *May* 1, 1863.

Lieut. Gen. JAMES LONGSTREET,
    Near Suffolk, Va.:

Since my dispatch to you last night I have received your letter of 30th. The order sent you was to secure all possible dispatch without incurring loss of train or unnecessary hazard of troops.

S. COOPER,
Adjutant and Inspector General.

MAY 1, [1863.]

General BEAUREGARD, *Charleston :*

Please send Clingman. Enemy have crossed Rappahannock. Fighting commenced.

W. H. C. WHITING.

HEADQUARTERS DISTRICT OF THE CAPE FEAR,
Wilmington, May 1, 1863.

Mr. J. H. FLANNER, *Present:*

SIR: The affair of the steamer Lizzie is entirely in the hands of the War Department and has been ever since her arrival in this port, at which time I stated the circumstances of the steamer, the objections to her being permitted to leave, which in my opinion are very strong, and the necessity, in both a military and naval point of view, which I conceived to exist for her remaining in the river for Government service, concluding with the statement that I should not permit her to leave without the orders of the Department. To this letter I have received no reply, nor to subsequent letters, nor to my telegraph sent previous to your own application. To the latter I fully expected you would have before this received an answer. I will, however, telegraph again to-day, requesting an immediate reply.

I do not know that any distinction should be made between a native and a foreign owner when the latter may be either an enemy or belonging to a nation which does not choose to recognize us and whose Government has prohibited the business in which she is engaged; if any, perhaps in favor of the native. I am sorry if the owners have suffered in common with many others from some of the inconveniences of a state of war. But with reference to this trade which this vessel and others are engaged in, I must say that I have advised the Government to take possession of them all. The telegram I have referred to is as follows:

MAY 1, 1863.

Colonel GORGAS, *Richmond :*

What decision has the Department come to in case of steamer Lizzie, formerly Mariner? Answer as soon as possible.

I presume the Government would remunerate the owners for any damages sustained by them as engaged in a legitimate trade, on account of the action of the military authorities.

Very respectfully,

W. H. C. WHITING,
Major-General.

CHARLESTON, S. C., *May* 1, 1863.

Brig. Gen. W. H. C. WHITING,
Wilmington, N. C. :

Clingman received orders yesterday to report to General Hill. Will leave to-day and following. Iron-clads still as before reported.

G. T. BEAUREGARD.

BRIGADE HEADQUARTERS,
Chaffin's Farm, Va., May 1, 1863.

Maj. Gen. ARNOLD ELZEY, *Commanding, &c. :*

GENERAL: I received your order respecting the burning of all the wharves and landings on this side of James River late last evening. At

9 a. m. this morning I proceeded to execute the order, and have destroyed two wharves—Cox's and Aiken's. The destroying of landings, as ordered by General Longstreet, I do not understand. To-morrow the working party will proceed to Deep Bottom, Curtis' Neck, Turkey Island, and Ladd's, destroying all the wharves as low down as we can reach. Will you please say by return courier how low down I must go? The order embraces all the wharves on this side of James River. It will require more force than I have under my command to execute it. Shall I proceed as far as I safely may to the mouth of the Chickahominy?

General, permit me to say this is a vain expenditure of labor. The enemy can land any 5 miles as well without as with the wharves. I say this under a sense of duty.

Very truly and respectfully, your obedient servant,

HENRY A. WISE,
Brigadier-General.

Abstract from Field Return of Troops, Department of Richmond, Maj. Gen. Arnold Elzey commanding, for May 1, 1863.

Command.	Present for duty.		Effective total present.	Aggregate present.	Aggregate present and absent.
	Officers.	Men.			
Brig. Gen. H. A. Wise	172	2,155	2,284	2,707	3,530
Lieut. Col. J. M. Maury	24	339	403	452	530
Capt. S. S. Lee	16	324	378	434	458
Grand total	212	2,818	3,065	3,593	4,518

HDQRS. DEPT. SOUTH CAROLINA, GEORGIA, AND FLORIDA,
Charleston, S. C., May 2, 1863.

Maj. Gen. D. H. HILL, *Commanding, Kinston, N. C.:*

GENERAL: Your favor of the 29th ultimo has been received. Two regiments of Clingman's brigade left here yesterday for Wilmington; the other two will probably leave to-day. You have also been telegraphed to that effect. I will also be happy to assist you to the extent of our means, so soon as I shall know positively the departure of the balance of Foster's troops still on Folly Island, near the mouth of the Stono, and on Seabrook's Island, North Edisto. The enemy's iron-clads are still as already reported—one in Port Royal and five in North Edisto. What he proposes doing with them is more than can now be determined; probably he has not done so himself.

Wishing you ample success in your future operations, I remain, yours, very truly,

G. T. BEAUREGARD,
General, Commanding.

[MAY 2-7, 1863.—For correspondence and orders, in reference to raid from Army of the Potomac, see Series I, Vol XXV.]

RICHMOND, VA., *May* 2, 1863.

Lieut. Gen. JAMES LONGSTREET:

GENERAL: It will not be possible to furnish transportation from Franklin for any of your command. March to Ivor Depot, where the railroad, with such limited transportation as can be commanded, will be placed at your disposal. Capt. E. B. Branch, assistant quartermaster at Petersburg, has been telegraphed to inform you at Franklin of this arrangement. Please inform Captain Branch, assistant quartermaster at Petersburg, at the earliest moment you may want the cars.

S. COOPER,
Adjutant and Inspector General.

SUFFOLK, VA., *May* 2, 1863.

General S. COOPER:

I cannot move unless the entire force is moved, and it would then take several days to reach Fredericksburg. I will endeavor to move as soon as possible.

JAMES LONGSTREET,
Lieutenant-General, Commanding.

[Copy telegraphed to General Lee same date.]

HEADQUARTERS, *May* 2, 1863.

Maj. Gen. S. G. FRENCH, *Commanding, &c. :*

GENERAL: Your note is received. As many as six or eight couriers have been sent Major Mitchell and Colonel Baker to use the utmost exertions to [move] everything across the Blackwater to-[night], and I hope that everything may be before night to morrow. But we [must] be prepared to wait in case everything should not get over. I have no particular objections to a fight should the enemy pursue us. General Hood will take care of everything in his vicinity until all is over the river.

Most respectfully,

JAMES LONGSTREET,
Lieutenant-General, Commanding.

HEADQUARTERS, *May* 2, 1863.

Maj. Gen. S. G. FRENCH, *Commanding, &c.:*

GENERAL: Your note is received. I am glad to hear that the Fifty-fourth New York was well punished. We will move back to-morrow night. You ought to advise your signal line on the James River to what point it should retire to-morrow. You need not tell that we are going to move back, but only order them back to some point that will be safe for them.

With respect,

JAMES LONGSTREET,
Lieutenant-General, Commanding.

SPECIAL ORDERS, }   HEADQUARTERS,
     No. —.   }   *Suffolk, Va., May 2, 1863.*

This command will move back to the right bank of the Blackwater immediately after dark to-morrow night: Major-General French's command by the South Quay road, Major-General Pickett's by the Somerton road, and Major-General Hood's by the Blackwater road, the last crossing the Blackwater at Franklin. These commanders will make all arrangements that may be necessary to facilitate the movement and will be careful to give instructions to every portion of their commands. The rear guards will be composed of at least two good regiments and a battery of artillery. General Armistead's brigade will be withdrawn from the White Marsh road at sunset, leaving his line of pickets, which will be withdrawn at dark and then move on to rejoin the brigade. The picket lines in front of General Pickett's main position, General French's, and General Hood's will be withdrawn at 11 o'clock at night as quietly as possible, and will march rapidly until they rejoin their commands. All batteries will be moved back at sunset to some point where their movements cannot be heard after dark, and will there await the orders of their division commanders. General French will halt his command at the intersection of the Somerton and South Quay roads, and General Pickett will leave a brigade and battery near Holy Neck Church to guard any of our trains that may not be able to cross the river before the troops reach there. Major-General Hood will move on and cross the river with his entire command, when he will have the pontoon bridge removed and the other bridges so nearly destroyed as only to allow persons on foot to pass. A party of select axmen will be left with each rear guard with orders to fell such large trees in the streams and swamps as may assist in delaying pursuit on the part of the enemy. Should the enemy's cavalry attempt to annoy our rear, every effort will be made to destroy it by ambuscade or otherwise, but too much time must not be lost in endeavoring to do so. Discreet officers will be selected to relieve and conduct the picket lines. Captain Barham's cavalry will report to General French at sunset to-morrow. General Pickett will give orders to the cavalry now temporarily serving with him, and General Hood to Captain Graham's cavalry. All vehicles not absolutely necessary with the troops will be sent back as early to-morrow as possible.

By command of Lieutenant-General Longstreet:

                                          G. MOXLEY SORREL,
                                          Assistant Adjutant-General.

GENERAL ORDERS, }   DIVISION HEADQUARTERS,
     No. 4.   }   *Near Suffolk, Va., May 2, 1863.*

I. This division will be in readiness to move toward Franklin to-morrow night, immediately after dark, on the South Quay road.

II. All teams and vehicles not absolutely necessary will be sent forward to-morrow and will cross the Blackwater and go into camp about 3 miles from Franklin, all stopping near Colonel Baker's cavalry camp.

III. General J. R. Davis' brigade will move in advance (left in front), to be followed by General M. Jenkins' brigade.

IV. General Jenkins will detail two regiments of his brigade as a rear guard, and with these regiments Capt. George Ward's battery of artillery will march, forming a portion of the guard. A suitable number of ambulances will go with the rear guard. Should the enemy pursue, especially with his cavalry, strenuous efforts will be made to destroy it, by ambuscade particularly, unless such ambuscades should cause too much delay. With the rear guard will be left a select number of axmen, who will in the swamps, at the crossings of streams, and other places fell large trees across the road to retard the pursuit of the enemy. A part of these men might move in advance to partly fell the trees before the rear guard passes. Captain Barham's cavalry will also form part of the rear guard.

V. The field batteries will be harnessed up and move to the rear about a mile from these headquarters at sunset to-morrow, and their position in line of march will be in advance of the infantry, and General Davis will, with his infantry, aid them in crossing any bad places in the road, so that no delay will be caused.

VI. The pickets in front will be withdrawn at 11 o'clock to-morrow night in the most quiet and secret manner possible, and will then march rapidly to join their respective regiments. The withdrawal of these pickets will be entrusted to careful and prudent officers, selected for the purpose, and the general commanding wishes General Jenkins to give them careful instructions in this respect. Teamsters are forbidden to crack their whips or shout at their animals.

VII. This command will halt at the junction of the South Quay and Somerton roads until any wagons that may be out foraging shall have returned.

By order of Maj. Gen. S. G. French:

GRAHAM DAVES,
Assistant Adjutant-General.

WAR DEPARTMENT, C. S. A.,
Richmond, Va., May 3, 1863.

Lieut. Gen. JAMES LONGSTREET, *Ivor Depot, Va.:*

We have information that two detachments certainly, perhaps three, of enemy's cavalry, with some light artillery, are converging on Richmond. Their distance at present is not more than 12 or 14 miles from the city. Hurry as fast as possible re-enforcements.

J. A. SEDDON,
Secretary of War.

HEADQUARTERS, *May 3, 1863.*

Maj. Gen. S. G. FRENCH, *Commanding:*

GENERAL: I shall start in about noon to try and look at the ground on this side before night. Major Mitchell hopes to get the wagons over to-night. If he succeeds in this, General Pickett is ordered to move on over with his command and send Colonel Baker to report to you. You will remain on this side until we see if the enemy means any pursuit. Generals Pickett and Hood are ordered to act with you in case of emergency in my absence. This was not necessary really, but I thought best to give the order that there should be no misunderstanding. I shall leave three fresh couriers at Holland's Shop. Anything important send there and it will be taken over by a fresh man—that is, up to sunset; after that they will go on and join me. My headquarters after night will be at the house where General Jenkins was before we crossed over. I am sorry to find this side of the sheet so badly soiled.

Most respectfully,

JAMES LONGSTREET,
Lieutenant-General, Commanding.

HEADQUARTERS, *May* 3, 1863.

Maj. Gen. FRENCH, *Commanding, &c.:*

GENERAL: General Hood reports a regiment of the enemy landed at the old fort. He may give us battle to-day; but unless his movements are decided we must not be detained in ours.

Most respectfully,

JAMES LONGSTREET,
Lieutenant-General, Commanding.

HEADQUARTERS, *May* 3, 1863.

Maj. Gen. S. G. FRENCH, *Commanding, &c.:*

GENERAL: General Hood reports the enemy displaying force in front of General Law. Have your two brigades and your artillery ready to support on the left, or to re-enforce either your own pickets or those of General Hood. Let General Hood's picket line know that you are to support them in case an attack is made, so that they may know where to send for support.

Very respectfully,

JAMES LONGSTREET,
Lieutenant-General, Commanding.

HEADQUARTERS, *May* 3, 1863—3 p. m.

Maj. Gen. S. G. FRENCH, *Commanding, &c.:*

GENERAL: Your note is received and General Pickett is ordered to draw his troops to the left, leaving a regiment and battery only on the White Marsh road. As General Pickett moves on toward the position you have, you can move on to the left; only a little, however, so as to be able to support Hood should the battle become hot.

Most respectfully,

JAMES LONGSTREET,
Lieutenant-General, Commanding.

Davis' brigade can be moved a mile or so to the left at once.

HEADQUARTERS, *May* 3, 1863.

Major-General FRENCH, *Commanding, &c.:*

GENERAL: Your note is received. The force at Chuckatuck cannot be more than a few hundred men from vessels. It is impossible that more could be put over in transports as yet. Possibly the enemy may put cavalry over to annoy us to-night. If the left is seriously threatened move in that direction, but not until it is certain that General Hood is severely pressed. I think his force fully able to sustain itself. Advise General Pickett if the matter becomes serious and he will move two brigades to where you are.

Most respectfully,

JAMES LONGSTREET,
Lieutenant-General, Commanding.

I shall not start back until things become more settled.

HEADQUARTERS PETTIGREW'S BRIGADE,
April [*May*] 3, 1863.

Maj. T. O. CHESTNEY, *Assistant Adjutant-General :*

MAJOR: From what General Elzey tells me it is very probable that the Eleventh Regiment North Carolina troops, now here, and the Fifty-second and Forty-fourth, expected, will be sent up to me at Hanover Junction to-night. Please order wagons to carry their ammunition to them (railroad depot), and let your quartermaster point out to them where their baggage can be stored, for they have no wagons.

Yours,

J. J. PETTIGREW,
Brigadier-General.

HEADQUARTERS,
Near Suffolk, Va., May 3, 1863.

Maj. Gen. S. G. FRENCH, *Commanding Division :*

GENERAL: The commanding general desires you to be extremely careful in the selection of officers to relieve and conduct your picket lines to-night. Let only those be chosen who are thoroughly acquainted with the roads they are to take. Generals Hood and Pickett are instructed to communicate freely with each other and to you such matters of note as may occur. Will you also keep them advised of anything that may come under your observation?

I am, general, very respectfully,

G. MOXLEY SORREL,
Assistant Adjutant-General.

HEADQUARTERS,
Wilmington, N. C., May 3, 1863.

Major-General HILL, *Commanding, &c., Kinston, N. C.:*

I send you a letter* from Shays, containing some interesting reports, which, though he does not vouch for them, may have something in them. He writes from Swansborough, which you know is at the mouth of White Oak. No doubt the enemy is fortifying at Carolina City to protect the terminus of the railroad in case of retreat and against raids. He may have a design also of putting some works on White Oak, being perhaps alarmed by the activity of our troops lately and fearing a descent upon their communications. Any advance toward Swansborough would be doubtless with that view or to harry the country. In that case cavalry would move toward Smith's Mill to prevent the force from being cut off.

I am sorry you insist upon Cooke's brigade going to Magnolia. The importance of this place and the very limited number of troops at my command indicate that those few should be the best possible, not the worst. It must be said in addition that when threatened, no matter from what quarter, I am expected to hold the enemy in check until assistance can be sent me. To do this I must not sit down behind breastworks, but must maneuver. It was to get reliable troops that I consented to exchange Evans for Cooke. However, I will go to work on Clingman's brigade and get it into shape. If it were not for some of the officers I dare say there would be but little difference. Two Brooke rifles belonging to the Raleigh are on their way for me. Please give orders to hurry

---

* Not found.

them along as fast as possible with their ammunition. Clingman's regiments are beginning to arrive. Some of Cooke's will, I dare say, be able to go this evening.

Very respectfully,

W. H. C. WHITING,
Major-General.

DIVISION HEADQUARTERS, *May* 3, 1863.

[Maj. Gen. S. G. FRENCH:]

GENERAL: All I desire you to do is to support two regiments, which I have on picket, until to-night.

Respectfully, general, your obedient servant,

J. B. HOOD,
Major-General.

P. S.—They have formed in a heavy line in Law's front, and have set the woods on fire to try and smoke out his skirmishers. They have also formed in front of my two regiments near you. Please be ready to support them.

FRANKLIN, *May* 4, 1863.

Hon. JAMES A. SEDDON,
Secretary of War:

I am left here with two brigades, or 4,000 men, to defend a line of 40 miles in length, from Fort Powhatan to South Quay, with 25,000 of the enemy in front.

I protest against being left with an inadequate force. I must have at least three brigades.

S. G. FRENCH,
Major-General.

FRANKLIN, *May* 4, 1863.

Hon. JAMES A. SEDDON,
Secretary of War:

I can send troops from here now if cars can be sent for them.

JAMES LONGSTREET,
Lieutenant-General, Commanding.

IVOR, VA., *May* 4, 1863.

Hon. JAMES A. SEDDON,
Secretary of War:

We had a sharp skirmish yesterday. If the enemy does not molest us again, General Hood's division will be at Ivor early to-morrow.

JAMES LONGSTREET,
Lieutenant-General.

FRANKLIN, *May* 4, 1863.

Hon. JAMES A. SEDDON,
Secretary of War:

Hood's division will be at Ivor at 8 o'clock to-morrow morning.

JAMES LONGSTREET,
Lieutenant-General.

FRANKLIN, *May 4, 1863.*

Lieutenant-General LONGSTREET, *Richmond:*

I must insist on having three brigades left here, on a line 40 miles in length, from Fort Powhatan to South Quay. I have telegraphed the Secretary of War.

S. G. FRENCH.

HEADQUARTERS,
South Quay, N. C., May 4, 1863—2 p. m.

General JENKINS:

General Jenkins will take charge of crossing the division to the right bank of the Blackwater and the removal of the pontoon train.

S. G. FRENCH,
Major-General, Commanding.

HEADQUARTERS,
South Quay, N. C., May 4, [1863]—2 p. m.

Lieutenant-General LONGSTREET:

GENERAL: My whole force is on the other side. I cannot well withdraw it and leave down the pontoon bridge, and there are none of Lieutenant-Colonel Pool's pontoneers here. Please send them at once. I can make a good defense on the other side. Will the pontoneers be here soon? I will call and see you as soon as I cross.

Yours, truly,

S. G. FRENCH,
Major-General, Commanding.

Where are the teams for the pontoon wagons? I can take the bridge up with my men to-night.

HEADQUARTERS
South Quay, N. C., May 4, 1863.

Maj. G. MOXLEY SORREL,
Assistant Adjutant-General:

SIR: In regard to your note of this morning, I reply that I did comply with the general's orders, and I think did even more than comply. On the 3d instant the general wrote me, "You will remain on this side until we see if the enemy means any pursuit." And it was arranged that instead of stopping in position at the intersection of the roads I was to form line of battle nearer the river than at the intersection of the roads, on better ground. When I found General Pickett not at the intersection I guarded the road on which I fell back with two regiments and a battery until he passed. My orders were to defend the passage until we found if the enemy pursued, and in compliance with this order I kept all my command on the other side. Besides, the contingency of my remaining at the intersection was to do so if Mitchell's wagons had not passed. General Longstreet gave his assent to me and General Jenkins that we should take a position nearer the river than that mentioned in the order of retreat. The intersection of the roads is marked but 1 mile from the river on the sign-board. I presume the general will remember agreeing with us that we should hold the position which General Jenkins named just before he was ready to leave on the 3d instant.

Yours, respectfully,

> S. G. FRENCH,
> *Major-General.*

I might add that when I reached the intersection of the roads General Pickett's wagons had passed and his artillery was passing, and before the head of his columns made their appearance my command moved to position and there remained until they were ordered to cross on this side—in fact are crossing now.

> HEADQUARTERS,
> *Near Franklin, Va., May 4, 1863.*

Maj. Gen. S. G. FRENCH, *Commanding Division :*

GENERAL: Colonel Ferebee's regiment of cavalry has been ordered to Ivor to await orders there from you. The commanding general desires you to relieve the four companies of the Fifty-ninth Georgia Regiment in time for them to rejoin their regiment as it passes, which will be tomorrow. He also wishes you to relieve General Benning's brigade at once, and to establish your guards on the Blackwater by to-night.

I am, general, very respectfully, your obedient servant,

> G. MOXLEY SORREL,
> *Assistant Adjutant-General.*

> MAY 4, 1863—5 p. m.

Major-General ELZEY :

GENERAL: Amid the thousand contradictory statements of respectable citizens, cavalry, scouts, &c., the following seems to be the condition of things: On my arrival here yesterday at sunset I learned that the enemy were at Ashland and had captured a train. I think this was only one regiment (Twelfth Illinois), from which we have captured several stragglers. It thence proceeded to Hanover Court-House, burnt property, &c.; thence a portion went off inquiring the road to the White House; the rest came back by the South Anna Bridge at night and passed up the country. The best intelligence (which I believe) is that there are none now at Fredericksburg, but they have gone in large force south. Some are still on the Fredericksburg Railroad below Ashland. The prisoners say they started with eight days' rations, now nearly exhausted. Cannot the force in Richmond, here at Gordonsville, and under Hampton co-operate to catch them?

The news from General Lee's army continues very favorable. Passengers say that the bridges behind the enemy at Chancellorsville are sunk, and we hope to capture that portion; that they have Marye's Hill, but we will retake it to-day. Firing suddenly ceased at 12 m.

Very respectfully, your most obedient servant,

> J. J. PETTIGREW,
> *Brigadier-General.*

WAR DEPARTMENT, C. S. A.,
Richmond, Va., May 4, 1863.

Governor VANCE, *Raleigh, N. C.:*

General Hill and yourself can either better appreciate the position of things in North Carolina and the propriety of calling out the militia. In my judgment it would require strict necessity to induce the call of the militia at this season. I do not advise it.

J. A. SEDDON,
Secretary of War.

———

HEADQUARTERS,
Wilmington, N. C., May 4, 1863.

Maj. Gen. D. H. HILL, *Kinston, N. C.:*

Yours of 3d received. I wrote you yesterday, I think. Cooke and most of his force will be at Magnolia this evening; balance follow in next thirty-six hours. I presume your aide in speaking of my scouts alluded to my cavalry. I place no reliance upon them whatever. Have but two scouts (Fairly and Shays), and they by no means depend on rumors or talk. As for cavalry I saw too much of them in Virginia and here too. I have just received dispatch from Fredericksburg. Enemy badly whipped with heavy loss; retreating over the Rappahannock. Jackson severely wounded; Heth and A. P. Hill slightly; Paxton killed.

Very respectfully,

W. H. C. WHITING,
Major-General.

———

SPECIAL ORDERS, }
No. —.   }

HEADQUARTERS,
Near Franklin, Va., May 4, 1863.

I. Major-General French will proceed at once to arrange his troops for the defense of the line of the Blackwater.

II. The divisions of Major-Generals Pickett and Hood will proceed as rapidly as possible via Ivor to the city of Richmond, where further instructions will meet them.

III. The battalions of artillery under Majors Dearing and Henry will march by dirt road to Petersburg, where orders will meet them.

By command of Lieutenant-General Longstreet:

G. MOXLEY SORREL,
Assistant Adjutant-General.

———

PETERSBURG, *May 5, 1863.*

Hon. JAMES A. SEDDON:

Your telegram of to-day is received. I leave at 7 o'clock this evening for Richmond.

JAMES LONGSTREET,
Lieutenant-General.

———

GORDONSVILLE, *May 5, 1863.*

Hon. JAMES A. SEDDON:

A courier arrived from Baltimore, sent by Mr. Edmund Law Rogers, relative of mine, brings information that on Wednesday evening Foster's and Hunter's troops were on board transports bound for Chesapeake Bay. They are either to co-operate with General Hooker on the Rappahannock or land at White House in case our army is forced back from Fredericksburg. But small force left in North Carolina. Please do not publish the name of Mr. Rogers. Please acknowledge receipt by telegraph.

W. H. F. LEE,
Brigadier-General.

PETERSBURG, VA., *May 5, 1863.*

Maj. Gen. S. G. FRENCH, *Franklin :*

The enemy's cavalry is reported to be in large force north and west of Richmond. Endeavor to have all roads blockaded by felled timber to prevent the escape of the enemy's cavalry to any other force of his south of James River. Trees felled across the roads in [all crossings of] streams would be most likely to effect this. Is General Pickett's division on the march for this place? He should march by the Jerusalem pike and keep with him Dearing's and Henry's battalions of artillery and get here as soon as it is possible. Send him this advice if he has not already received it. Have roads by which the enemy may approach you blocked, except such as you must use yourself, and have those well guarded.

JAMES LONGSTREET,
Lieutenant-General, Commanding.

PETERSBURG, VA., *May 5, 1863.*

Maj. Gen. D. H. HILL, *Goldsborough :*

The enemy's cavalry is reported north and west of Richmond. It is supposed to be a very large force. Try and have notice given to the citizens in all directions of this, and get them to go to work and block every road by which the enemy may try to effect a junction with his other forces in North Carolina. Fell trees in all crossings of streams, particularly.

JAMES LONGSTREET,
Lieutenant-General, Commanding.

HEADQUARTERS,
Kinston, N. C., May 5, 1863.

Maj. Gen. D. H. HILL,
Commanding at Goldsborough :

GENERAL : I will move to-morrow to carry out the verbal instructions you gave me before leaving. I propose to leave the Second Battalion on this side, near the obstructions; to leave Colonel Martin on the Wilmington road to carry on the work there, as I think it should be completed, and to leave a regiment at Wise's Fork, and to send one regiment on the Neuse road to Moseley Creek, and with the remainder of my own and Ransom's brigade to move to Core Creek. The distance is too great for a day's march; I will therefore encamp to-morrow night some 12 or 15 miles from here.

I inclose dispatches* received relating to the movement of the enemy about Pollocksville and on the road to Shepherdsville. I am afraid Captain Wharton has been captured.

Your dispatch from the Secretary of War has been received.

I have no information from New Berne since you left.

Very respectfully,

JUNIUS DANIEL,
Brigadier-General.

HEADQUARTERS,
Richmond, Va., May 6, 1863.

Maj. Gen. D. H. HILL:

GENERAL: Your letter of the 5th was received but a few moments ago.

We have reports from scouts and persons from Maryland that Hunter's and Foster's armies are to come to Virginia.

The repulse of Hooker's force does not yet appear to be entirely decided. He has been driven back at all points, but holds still a position on this side the Rappahannock, near the United States Ford.

Your views regarding our policy I think sound, particularly as I urged the same course as yourself, and it must have been at the same time. Burnside's failure on account of mud was quite evidence enough to me that we had abundance of time to operate wherever we chose.

I shall endeavor to have forces sent you from South Carolina, and shall in all probability call for your forces as the enemy moves north. Watch his movements carefully and keep us advised.

The enemy's cavalry is still at Columbia, Va., and may try to effect his escape by uniting with Foster. Have all routes that he would most likely take blocked well (for as great a distance as time will admit of) with felled trees. This the citizens must do, as their only means of saving their horses and slaves. They can delay the enemy until we may have time to overtake him and destroy him. I am trying to get a mount for Hood's division to send in pursuit. I wish that you would impress every horse that you may be able to find not in necessary use on farms. This is no time to have horses for pleasure; all such must be put into service. If you do not need them send them here.

I remain, general, yours, most respectfully,

JAMES LONGSTREET,
Lieutenant-General, Commanding.

WAR DEPARTMENT, C. S. A.,
Richmond, May 6, 1863.

General D. H. HILL, *Goldsborough, N. C.:*

General Lee urges you should send him Ransom's division. Do so if you can with any safety. Hooker remains on the south side of the Rappahannock in a strong position at the Mine Ford. General Longstreet arrived here last night. His forces are yet in Petersburg.

J. A. SEDDON,
Secretary of War.

---

* Not found.

GOLDSBOROUGH, N. C., *May* 6, 1863.

Hon. JAMES A. SEDDON,
 Secretary of War, C. S. A. :

The troops reported on the transports could scarcely have come from North Carolina. If my scouts and spies can be relied upon, Foster has a large force in this State, some forty-five regiments. One or two of these were expected to leave about the 1st May, term of service having expired. These may be the troops seen on the transports.

I have written several times in regard to the utter worthlessness of the cavalry—Partisan Rangers—in this State. Yesterday a company was surprised and captured. They will neither fight nor watch.

I earnestly repeat my request to have authority to dismount and conscript all who are surprised and who run. Unless you clothe me with this authority I can do nothing with them, and would prefer to have them sent out of the State.

In the whole brigade of cavalry there has been but 1 man killed in the war. I propose to have a magnificent monument erected to his memory.

With great respect,

D. H. HILL,
 Major-General.

HEADQUARTERS,
 Wilmington, N. C., May 6, 1863.

Maj. Gen. [D. H.] HILL,
 Commanding, Goldsborough, N. C. :

GENERAL : I am sorry to hear of the loss of a cavalry company at White Oak. I think our cavalry is the poorest in the world. I only depend on Major [George] Jackson, Fairly, and Shays, who are worth a whole regiment. I have not yet received a report of this affair; will probably hear to-night. One regiment of Clingman's is at the advanced lines; one of Cooke's ought to be near Bannerman's, where are works. You will see it on the map. The remainder of Clingman's are on the road, on hand for need. I do not think Foster is in a hurry to advance. He has certainly got some troops from South Carolina, but not yet, I think, all; Jackson is of opinion about 5,000. If he tries the Sound road he ought to be a lost Foster; but I should have another brigade to insure holding him at bay long enough to destroy him. The news is very good from Lee; he has certainly given Hooker a terrible thrashing. That last battle, driving Sedgwick over the Rappahannock and reoccupying Fredericksburg, is masterly. But what is Stuart doing, allowing that band of scamps to harry the country? Not one should escape. I am much concerned about Jackson.

I send you a return of field and siege guns. Your chief of ordnance ordered field and heavy armament of this command which he is not entitled to. I wrote you about it.

Very respectfully,

W. H. C. WHITING,
 Major-General.

[Inclosure.]

ORDNANCE OFFICE, *Wilmington, N. C., May 6, 1863.*

Consolidated Report of siege guns and field artillery in the District of the Cape Fear.

	Ordnance.					Carriages.				Caissons.			Forges &c.	
	24-pounders.	6-pounders, brass.	3-inch rifles.	12-pounder howitzer, iron.	12-pounder howitzer, brass.	24-pounder siege.	6-pounder.	3-inch rifle.	12-pound howitzer.	6-pounder.	3-inch rifle.	12-pounder howitzer.	Battery wagon.	Forges.
Maj. W. L. Young	3					3								
Captain Adams		2		2			2		2	2		2		
Captain Paris		3	1	2			3	1	2	3	1	2	1	1
Captain Ellis, 3d North Carolina Battalion		3	1				3	1		3	1		1	1
Company B [Moore's Battalion], 3d North Carolina Battalion		2			2		2		2	2		2	1	
Capt. J. G. Moore, 3d North Carolina Battalion		2			2		2		2	2		2		
Total	3	12	2	4	4	3	12	2	8	12	2	8	3	2

NOTE.—The siege carriages are without limbers.

Respectfully submitted.

JNO. M. PAYNE,
Lieutenant, Ordnance.

[Indorsement.]

HEADQUARTERS,
Wilmington, May 6, 1863.

Respectfully forwarded.

I wish the caliber of the field batteries, the small number and the great want of rifled and entire want of Napoleon guns, to be noted.

W. H. C. WHITING,
Major-General.

HEADQUARTERS ARMY OF NORTHERN VIRGINIA,
May 7, 1863.

Lieut. Gen. JAMES LONGSTREET, *Commanding, &c.:*

GENERAL: I have just received yours of 2d instant upon my return to my former camp.

My letter of the 1st instant, to which you refer, was intended to apprise you of my intended movement and to express the wish rather than the expectation that one of your divisions could co-operate in it.

I did not intend to express the opinion that you could reach me in time, as I did not think it practicable. The emergency that made your presence so desirable has passed for the present, so far as I can see, and I desire that you will not distress your troops by a forced movement to join me, or sacrifice for that purpose any public interest that your sudden departure might make it necessary to abandon. The only immediate service that your troops could render would be to protect our communications from the enemy's cavalry and assist in punishing them for the damage they have done.

Very respectfully, your obedient servant,

R. E. LEE,
General.

HEADQUARTERS,
Richmond, May 7, 1863.

Maj. Gen. D. H. HILL,
    Commanding, &c., Goldsborough :

GENERAL : We have reports from different sources that the plans of the enemy are to concentrate Hunter's and Foster's armies for a general attack upon Richmond. Make all needful arrangements to prevent such a contingency.

Your force will, of course, be obliged to come up here; so with the chief force at Charleston. If you find such movements in progress you will so shape your own to meet them without awaiting further orders from these headquarters.

I remain, very respectfully, your obedient servant,
                    JAMES LONGSTREET,
                        Lieutenant-General.

HEADQUARTERS,
Richmond, Va., May 7, 1863.

Hon. JAMES A. SEDDON,
    Secretary of War :

SIR : His Excellency the President expressed the desire last night that I should join General Lee at Fredericksburg at once.

I regard the opening and securing the communication of General Lee's army with this city of the first importance, and fear that this may not be accomplished if I leave it unfinished. There are some indications, too, that the enemy may bring one or two other columns against this city, with the hope of getting possession by a sudden dash. I think it more important that these things should be considered and that we should have our forces so in hand as to meet any such contingency. I propose, therefore, to remain here until I can so arrange and dispose of my forces as to free General Lee's army of the force which now threatens his communications.

I remain, sir, with great respect, your most obedient servant,
                    JAMES LONGSTREET,
                        Lieutenant-General.

GOLDSBOROUGH, N. C., *May* 7, [1863]—10 a. m.

Hon. JAMES A. SEDDON,
    Secretary of War, C. S. A.:

Inclosed are the last reports* from scouts. Foster has sent out of New Berne and Washington the citizens who have hitherto furnished information. I think that these papers clearly establish that the Charleston expedition is abandoned, and that the few troops leaving New Berne are more than replaced by others. I have believed ever since the failure at Charleston that Foster would demand and get back the twenty regiments furnished to Hunter.

General Daniel has gone down with two brigades (his own and Ransom's) to feel the enemy about Core Creek. If they fall back without show of fight it is clear that Foster is not strong there and that he is massed upon the railroad between New Berne and Morehead, fearing that the Confederates will cut it. Unfortunately this is a difficult task. There are but three approaches to it through the swamps and these are fortified. I have but three brigades outside of Wilmington (Daniel,

---
* Not found.

Ransom, and Cooke); two are at Kinston, and the third has one regiment at Weldon and three below, at Magnolia Depot, 50 miles above Wilmington. If you think that one more should be sent, I will send Cooke.

I feel confident that Ransom and Daniel can whip Foster. But with Foster's superiority of numbers and great water facilities he can cut the railroad and make most destructive raids on the Roanoke, Chowan, and Tar, and it will be impossible to prevent them.

There is nominally a large force in the State, but there is a heavy garrison in Wilmington, and the four regiments of cavalry are not worth four companies of inferior infantry. In fact, did we not need a large number of couriers over this 300 miles of coast, I would prefer them to be ordered off.

I have laid the facts before you in regard to the Confederate strength and that of the Yankees as far as can be ascertained, and must leave it to your discretion whether to order off more forces or not.

Most respectfully,

D. H. HILL,
Major-General.

HEADQUARTERS,
Tarborough, N. C., May 7, 1863.

Maj. Gen. D. H. HILL,
Comdg. Dept. of North Carolina, Goldsborough, N. C.:

GENERAL: Upon my arrival here last night I found that Colonel Evans had gone toward Greenville instead of Rocky Mount, as we supposed. I immediately recalled him.

Claiborne's regiment has, strange to say, not yet arrived. As soon as possible I shall relieve the companies of the Sixty-third (Evans) below Kinston, and also the couriers between Goldsborough and Greenville and between Snow Hill and Kinston, as all the men belong to Ferebee's command.

Please inform me by Captain Worthington (who will deliver this) how many men those lines will require under existing circumstances. There are a great many more at present than are needed on that duty since the withdrawal of the troops from Hookerton and Greenville.

While on the railroad I should very much like to send the dismounted men of Claiborne's regiment to procure horses, and if this request meets your approbation instruct Captain Worthington to telegraph me at once before the men leave here. You can readily perceive, general, the necessity for the step proposed, which I hope you will approve. Colonel Claiborne is absent from his regiment, I understand. Was the authority granted from your headquarters?

Very respectfully, your obedient servant,

B. H. ROBERTSON,
Brigadier-General, Commanding.

Where had Claiborne's regiment better encamp? About Greenville forage is scarce and Griffin is there.

HEADQUARTERS, *May 8, 1863.*

Hon. JAMES A. SEDDON,
Secretary of War:

SIR: I have the honor to return herewith a letter and dispatch from General Lee. All of our reports represent the enemy's main cavalry force returning to the Rappahannock by the same or nearly the same route as that he came. I fear that no effort has been made by our forces or citizens to obstruct his routes.

I am, sir, with great respect, your most obedient servant,

JAMES LONGSTREET,
Lieutenant-General, Commanding.

I received a dispatch from General R. E. Lee asking the arrangements that I have ordered in reference to his communication with this city.

HEADQUARTERS DEPARTMENT OF RICHMOND,
May 8, 1863.

General J. J. PETTIGREW:

General Hood's division is *en route* for Hanover Junction. General Lee desires the wagon road from there to Fredericksburg repaired. If you move ahead of Hood, see to it; if not, he will attend to it. I send by first train to the Junction 100 shovels, 50 picks, and 25 axes to care of your quartermaster.

Respectfully,

ARNOLD ELZEY,
Major-General, Commanding.

HEADQUARTERS DISTRICT OF THE CAPE FEAR,
Wilmington, May 8, 1863.

Maj. Gen. D. H. HILL,
Commanding, &c., Goldsborough:

GENERAL: Yours of 2 p. m. yesterday received. I am sorry Cooke has to go. Beauregard is sending off two strong brigades to Pemberton, and the coast will be very greatly weakened. We are all, from Savannah to Weldon, mutually dependent on each other. I do not think Ransom should be removed, unless at the last emergency. But I do not know the exact position of affairs in Virginia. The enemy seems to have received a terrible thrashing. But his numbers, according to their own account 158,000, may give us great trouble yet, unless they are too demoralized to fight well. I suppose Lee has 60,000 at least. It will be a difficult matter to defend Wilmington and the railroad with three brigades. Longstreet will have to help. I will send you a statement of heavy ordnance. The enemy would not cross at Snead's Ferry; the river is too wide, over 1,000 yards, and with any wind or —— flats are not practicable. We have a picket there, as also at Swansborough, in advance.

I cannot very well spare Major Cameron. Should he be absolutely necessary to you I should have to supply his place.

Very truly, yours,

W. H. C. WHITING,
Major-General.

GOLDSBOROUGH, N. C., *May* 9, 1863.

Hon. JAMES A. SEDDON,
Secretary of War, C. S. A.:

Your letter and order in regard to deserters has been received.* Desertion is alarmingly on the increase in my own command.

---

* Not found.

There is a powerful faction in the State poisoning public sentiment and looking to a reconstruction. The soldiers are induced by these traitors to believe that this is an unjust war on the part of the South and that their State soldiers and citizens have been slighted and wronged by the Confederate States Government.

Unless the Government will boldly take this matter in hand and arrest the editors and speakers who are daily uttering treason, the crime of desertion will go on, and I fear that there will be thousands in armed resistance to the Government. The teaching of one paper in this State is treasonable in the highest degree, and the editor certainly is a tory at heart and almost openly.

Respectfully,

D. H. HILL,
Major-General.

[Indorsement.]

MAY 10, 1863.

SECRETARY OF WAR:

It might be well to correspond with the Governor of North Carolina in relation to the subject matter of the within.

J. D.

———

GOLDSBOROUGH, N. C., *May* 10, 1863.

Hon. JAMES A. SEDDON,
Secretary of War, C. S. A.:

Inclosed you will find a letter from Major Whitford, commanding battalion guerrillas. His spelling is rather original, but he is a good, brave, and truthful man. The other letter is from Mr. Marshall, until recently our only reliable source of information in New Berne. Foster has expelled him, however, and my information is very vague. We have an employé in Foster's military family who is as true to the South as President Davis. But unfortunately all the communications from this person came through Mr. Marshall, and I have now no agent working in town. With Foster's control of the waters and railroad from Morehead City to New Berne, he has been able to deceive my scouts by movements of troops backward and forward. Our troops have been incessantly harassing them day and night for two months, and the soldiers whose enlistment will expire soon are in a very pleasant state of mind to stay. The Yankees hold the whole county of Carteret, but except to make raids confine themselves to Plymouth, Washington, and New Berne. They do not venture out more than a mile from the first, 3 miles from the second, and 8 from the third, except in the direction of Morehead City.

There are but three approaches to the railroad from New Berne to Carolina City, and these are strongly fortified. The Yankees have been engaged for three weeks in fortifying line from Newport River to Bogue Sound. This looks like an evacuation of New Berne in case of a strong pressure. Ought not that squeeze to be given?

I would not ask for more infantry, but would like to have good rifle guns, not of Richmond make.

Since Foster's disgraceful whipping at Blount Creek by General Pettigrew he has shown no disposition to give a field fight, though the most insinuating methods were used by General Daniel to coax him on.

With great respect,

D. H. HILL,
Major-General.

[Inclosures.]

SWIFT CREEK, *May* 9, 1863.

GEN'L: To-day when your courrier came with your dispatch to me I was off trying to get information from the enemy. My scouts on Tar River report seven or eight steamers went down Tar River on the nights of the 7th and 8th instant. Those steamers are not at New Berne, or was not yestiday evening; they had not passed up Nuse River. The Yankees at Mrs. Grice's place, this side Washington, told the citerzens at Cross-Roads yestiday that Yankee General Palmer's brigade and Yankee General Naglee's brigade has gone to re-enforce Hooker. They said Spinola was yet in Washington with his brigade. The movements about New Berne is now on the railrode. I can't get any person in their lines under no pretence; they turn all back from this side Nuse River. My two men that was crossing Nuse to and from is both sick. I understand persons from south side Nuse River can go in town and return. I don't know whether they can or not. If some citerzens that could be reliad upon, that lives below Pollocksville, in Jones County, [would go,] that is the best way now, as they will not allow any person from the north side to go in town. If they would I would soon know what Foster is up to. I don't know the people on the other side Nuse, or I would go in Jones County and get up a line of communication soon. I think Major Nethercutt could get some person to go in, as he knows every man in Jones County. I have scouts in every direction below here to find out there movements all I can. I think a demmonstration in front of New Berne would stop Foster from sending off his troops to Hooker. I am glad to hear of Hooker's defeat. I will get that to the Yankees soon. They know in Washington and New Berne that Hooker is whiped.

Yours, very respecufully, and obediant servant,

JOHN N. WHITFORD,
Major, Comdg. Outpost, Swift Creek.

SWIFT CREEK, *May* 8, 1863.

[Maj. Gen. D. H. HILL:]

DEAR GENERAL: Rumor informs us at this place that thirty families have been sent up on the railroad from New Berne in the direction of Kinston three days ago; other rumors say that the Yankees have not decided whether to send them to Street's Ferry or to Core Creek. I am now waiting to hear from my letter to Foster; and should they send them out, and I down here, do me the favor to have my wife informed that I have engaged quarters for her and our effects with Mrs. Virginia Dudley, in Kinston. I should also take it as a great favor to be informed by the first courier if my family should be sent in that direction.

Several persons have tried to get to New Berne from this place, and all have failed except one lady that crossed the river and went down on the railroad. She came up Wednesday, and says they were all packed up to start, but were afraid (the Yankees) that the train or boat would be captured by our forces, as there was no flag of truce, &c.

I know of no better way than to stay here until they move in the matter, as there is no telling what they will do. They have paroled a prisoner and sent him out, who states that they are sending great quantities of negroes away on transports. Others that have left New Berne and gone to Bay River tell the same tale, and all agree, too, as to their fortifying Morehead City. They let no person go to town from the north side of the river; I think it indicates some mysterious move on their part. They have been practicing, too, with very heavy guns, something that has not been done by them for six months before. From their great secrecy about everything, and pretending to be on the eve of sending out the citizens and failing each day to do it, looks to me like an evacuation of the place. I think it is all done to keep up appearances, and could I be certain as to the fortifying of Morehead City I should feel confident.

There has been an order issued by Foster to the effect that no more goods be brought to New Berne by their merchants; that is so. I am certain that the taking and holding it has not done much in the way of restoring the Union, and has been rather a failure than anything else; and as they have stolen all that is in their reach I think they have concluded to leave New Berne and make arrangements to hold Fort Macon and Hatteras and perhaps Roanoke Island.

I think I shall be able soon to open a direct communication to New Berne should they leave any of the citizens there. They have got the news of their defeat at Fredericksburg and acknowledge that Hooker is whipped. Several ladies were down to Barrington yesterday and say that the colonel told them that Hooker was whipped and asked them if we had heard it. They knew nothing about General Jackson being wounded. I hope that General Jackson may recover from his wounds, as the country would lose one of her noblest sons, besides his great services as one among the greatest generals of the age. I pray God he may recover from his wounds.

Very truly, yours,

W. H. MARSHALL.

RICHMOND, *May* 10, 1863.

Maj. WILLIAM NORRIS, *Chief of Signal Corps:*

SIR: I returned from the enemy's lines, in the vicinity of Newport News, yesterday morning before daylight, bringing the following intelligence:

Troops from every quarter are hurrying toward the discomfited army of Hooker. Many have been withdrawn from Suffolk, and only 400 or 500 are left at Fortress Monroe. General Dix, with 5,000 men, 500 wheelbarrows and intrenching tools, left the fortress on Wednesday, it is reported, for the White House. Five hundred cavalry left Yorktown the same day. It is my belief that Dix will not now proceed so far, as I think he was only to occupy that position provided Hooker was victorious, and then this much-coveted city was to have been assailed on all sides. Depredations are daily committed on the defenseless citizens near Suffolk by Dodge's cavalry. I bring a paper of the date of the 7th, which I have sent to the honorable Secretary of War.

Very truly, your obedient servant,

C. H. CAUSEY,
Captain, C. S. Army.

Abstract from Field Return of troops commanded by Maj. Gen. S. G. French, for May 10, 1863. (*No station given.*)

Command.	Present for duty.		Aggregate present.	Aggregate present and absent.
	Officers.	Men.		
General staff	9	......	9	13
Jenkins' brigade	247	2,267	2,846	4,036
Davis' brigade	171	2,335	2,893	3,470
Boggs' battalion artillery	21	304	388	484
Coit's battery	3	115	136	143
Bradford's battery	4	76	96	100
Baker's cavalry regiment [no report]	......	......	......	......
Grand total	455	5,097	6,368	8,246

HEADQUARTERS ARMY OF NORTHERN VIRGINIA,
May 11, 1863.

Brig. Gen. J. J. PETTIGREW,
  Commanding, &c., Hanover Junction:

GENERAL: General Pickett informs me, on what he deems reliable authority, that a regiment of infantry, one battery of artillery, and 200 cavalry of the enemy are at West Point, the confluence of the Pamunkey and Mattapony Rivers. He thinks it possible that they may ascend the north bank of the Pamunkey and attempt to reach Hanover Junction. I give you this notice that you may be on your guard.

I am, very respectfully, your obedient servant,

R. E. LEE,
General.

HEADQUARTERS DISTRICT OF THE CAPE FEAR,
Wilmington, May 11, 1863.

H. P. WALKER,
  H. M. Actg. Consul for the States of N. C. and S. C. at Charleston:

SIR: I have received your letter of this date relating to the schooner Harkaway, alleged to belong to a British subject engaged in running the blockade, and seized in this port by the military authorities of the Confederate States of America.

I am not aware that my Government has recognized you as the representative of Her Britannic Majesty. Her Britannic Majesty's Government has certainly not recognized the Government of the Confederate States. I decline, therefore, to discuss the subject with you or to release the vessel, but will forward your communication to the Secretary of State and await orders.

In the mean time, as Her Britannic Majesty's Government does not recognize the jurisdiction of the Confederate States here, and the United States Government claims it, perhaps it would be as well to apply to the latter.

Very respectfully,

W. H. C. WHITING,
Major-General.

HEADQUARTERS,
Kinston, N. C., May 12, 1863.

Maj. Gen. D. H. HILL,
Commanding at Goldsborough :

GENERAL : Yours of this date has been received. Colonel Martin moved to-day for Greenville. Brabble takes his place on picket.

As soon as Captain Coleman returns, or I am well enough to make the examination, I will have the work extended as you desire.

I am much obliged to you for your kind offer to relieve me by General Cooke, and if everything is quiet here I would like very much to go home for a week or ten days, as my health is poor and I have some business, giving in my taxes, &c., which can only be done by myself, as I am the only male member of my family in the State; and as I have paid no attention to my affairs in more than two years I would not be able to do so without an examination. I will be in a mile or two of the telegraph office in Weldon and could return any day should anything occur.

I expected to have had some information from Lieutenant Foy to-day, but have not heard from him.

Our scouts report the enemy's picket posts some 6 or 7 miles below Core Creek. They had not to-day relaid the track torn up 4 miles below Core Creek.

I was very much grieved to hear of the death of General Jackson, and think that our victory was a dearly-bought one.

Very respectfully,

JUNIUS DANIEL,
Brigadier-General.

———

HEADQUARTERS,
Near Fredericksburg, May 12, 1863.

Maj. Gen. D. H. HILL:

GENERAL: Your letters of the 8th and 10th, with inclosures, are received.* I think that there is every probability that the enemy intends fortifying somewhere near the coast below New Berne, and leaving small garrisons in North Carolina to occupy the forts, with the purpose of sending all the rest of his force here. I have already heard that Suffolk is only occupied now by a small force, some 18,000 having come to re-enforce Hooker's army. The same thing will be done with the forces in North Carolina. In view of this, I have suggested that Clingman's and Evans' brigades be brought to North Carolina and that Ransom's and Cooke's be brought here; also the troops from the Blackwater, and that you have command of Petersburg and everything south of that and north of South Carolina. This I presume will be the arrangement for the summer. By threatening the enemy's capital we will be able to draw all of his available force here, and as our strength here increases his must do the same.

I remain, general, very respectfully, your most obedient servant,

JAMES LONGSTREET,
Lieutenant-General, Commanding.

———

* Not found.

WAR DEPARTMENT, C. S. A.,
Richmond, May 12, 1863.

General W. H. C. WHITING, *Wilmington, N. C.:*

Let me know what force you have and what aid you can, in case of necessity, lend to Charleston.

J. A. SEDDON,
Secretary of War.

WILMINGTON, N. C., *May* 12, 1863.

Hon. JAMES A. SEDDON,
Secretary of War, Richmond :

I have Clingman's. On a pinch, can send three regiments of that, but General Hill should be notified. Arrangements should be made to transfer them back should point of attack be changed.

W. H. C. WHITING,
Major-General.

MAY 12, 1863.

General BEAUREGARD, *Charleston :*

Anything threatening in your front? Secretary wants to know what I can spare you. Let me hear direct. Will do all in my power.

W. H. C. WHITING,
Major-General.

MAY 12, 1863.

Major-General HILL, *Goldsborough :*

Secretary wants to know what I can do for Charleston in need. Can let three regiments go on a pinch, but told him you must be notified. Have you heard anything?

W. H. C. WHITING.

BURWELL'S BAY, *May* 13, 1863.

Maj. WILLIAM NORRIS, *Chief Signal Corps :*

SIR : Major-General Keyes, with one division of infantry and a brigade of cavalry, is at or near the White House, unless he has fallen or been driven back since Monday. The cavalry are from Stoneman's division. There are few troops at Suffolk, none at Newport News, and a very small garrison at Fortress Monroe. Blockading squadron consists of two iron-clads of the Monitor model—the Galena and Minnesota.

Respectfully, your obedient servant,

C. H. CAUSEY,
Captain, C. S. Army.

HEADQUARTERS DEPARTMENT OF RICHMOND,
May 13, 1863.

General S. COOPER,
Adjutant and Inspector General :

SIR : In compliance with the wishes of the Secretary of War, I have the honor to make the following report of the forces in and about Rich-mond for his information:

DEPARTMENT OF RICHMOND.

Brigadier-General Wise's brigade, now occupying the Peninsula. Colonel Rhett's command (artillery, for defenses) has been ordered back, and supposed to be on its way.

Garrisons at Chaffin's and Drewry's Bluffs.

City of Richmond.—Brigadier-General Winder's command—City Bat-talion, seven companies; Wren's battalion of cavalry, two companies; Col. H. H. Walker's guard forces, seven companies.

Major-General Pickett's division—South side, near Manchester.

One regiment and one battery of Brigadier-General Pettigrew's bri-gade, near Richmond.

One regiment of Brigadier-General Robertson's cavalry, near Rich-mond.

RECAPITULATION.

Department of Richmond, including Colonel Rhett's command: Effective total	4,288
Brigadier-General Winder's command	1,300
Major-General Pickett, say	8,000
Regiment and battalion of Pettigrew	750
Regiment of Robertson (cavalry)	500
Aggregate	14,838

I have the honor to request that this communication be laid before the Secretary of War at your earliest convenience.

Very respectfully, your obedient servant,

ARNOLD ELZEY,
Major-General, Commanding.

WAR DEPARTMENT, C. S. A.,
Richmond, May 13, 1863.

General D. H. HILL, *Goldsborough, N. C.:*

Necessity compels me to reduce the force at Charleston very low. General Whiting, on inquiry, informs me that on a pinch he can send to the aid of Charleston in case of attack three regiments. I inform you of this, and in addition suggest if, as I believe, the enemy have nearly withdrawn, let your arrangements be made to allow in case of necessity the transfer of a larger force.

J. A. SEDDON,
Secretary of War.

CAVALRY CAMP,
Near Williamston, May 13, 1863.

Maj. ARCHER ANDERSON,
Assistant Adjutant-General, Goldsborough:

MAJOR: I have just returned from Jamesville, the lowest point occu-pied by our cavalry pickets on the Roanoke.

I met Lieutenant-Colonel Towns, of the Sixty-second Georgia Regi-ment, on the road, who had been absent two days visiting his picket stations. He saw to-day a man from Plymouth day before yesterday.

From him he learns that General Wessells is certainly in command there with two New York regiments, not exceeding 500 men each, and one battery; no cavalry. The cavalry and some other troops had left the town—supposed toward Suffolk.

The enemy is throwing up some intrenchments on a high point near Plymouth, either for the purpose of changing his camp, which is represented to be very filthy, or protecting some fisheries at the point. Colonel Towns considers this information entirely trustworthy.

I examined Fort Branch yesterday and feel satisfied, if properly garrisoned and provisioned, it can repel any attack of the enemy by land or water less than a regular siege. The supply of ammunition is good, and provisions for 1,000 men for thirty days are being placed in as rapidly as present circumstances permit. Coniho Creek, of which the general spoke to me, will be a very serious obstacle to a land attack on Fort Branch. The three roads crossing it near and below the fort are being effectually impeded. One of them has been closed entirely and the bridge destroyed. At one of the others intrenchments have been prepared and at the third are being prepared. This creek, however, is no impediment to an advance on Tarborough.

If the troops of my brigade are to be used exclusively to close Plymouth and Washington between the Tar and Roanoke, my impression is they should be moved nearer and occupy a line beginning from Jamesville or Gardner's Creek, near that town, and running toward Tranter's Creek, thence to the Tar River at or near Pactolus. On this subject I feel some hesitation in yet expressing a positive opinion.

If my brigade is to be held with a view to protect Weldon or some other point, it should not be removed beyond Hamilton or Greenville, except for picket guard.

Will you please inform me if any troops are to be stationed at Weldon and if they are to be under my command?

I shall go to-morrow to Greenville and thence to Tarborough, where I shall spend a day or two examining the quartermaster's and commissary departments.

The order substituting Colonel Griffin's cavalry regiment for Colonel Evans' has been received.

I am, major, very respectfully, your obedient servant,

J. G. MARTIN,
Brigadier-General.

P. S.—Since writing the above the pickets have brought in 2 Yankee prisoners, who say that both General Wessells and General Hunt are in Plymouth with five regiments—the Eighty-fifth, Ninety-second, and Ninety-sixth New York, and One hundred and first and One hundred and third Pennsylvania; that the troops which left there recently went to New Berne, and they think General Wessells' brigade is going to Suffolk soon.

———

HANOVER JUNCTION, *May* 14, 1863—1 p. m.

Major-General ELZEY, *Commanding, Richmond:*

GENERAL: Tuesday night I sent a company of cavalry out, with instructions to go as near West Point as they could and find out what was going on there. I received a report dated 12 m. yesterday, "King William County, 4 miles outside of the enemy's pickets." From what they heard, the enemy had landed on Thursday last some 3,000 infantry, a regiment of cavalry, and some light artillery. They were fortifying across the Peninsula, a mile or so from the Point. It was thought that the post was intended as a refuge for stealing parties, runaway slaves, &c., but I fear they will give us more trouble than that, for they can march up in force, threaten the railroad north of North Anna, perhaps attack it, or cross suddenly at Hanover Court-House, do the same on the south side, and return by the White House. As for finding out the strength of any such party, my experience of the cavalry and citizens during the last raid has convinced me it is impossible. As Richmond is so much nearer the White House and West Point you have much better means of obtaining intelligence than I have, and I think ought to be able to give me such information as may be necessary. It seems to me that this triangle between the railroad and the North and South Anna Rivers should be fortified. Had I the tools I could do it myself, but I might be ordered away in the midst, and it would be a great deal better to send an engineer from Richmond, who could continue until the work was done. Works would be required on the North Anna at the crossing of the Telegraph road, the Fredericksburg Railroad, Morris' Bridge, and Bear Island Ford; on the South Anna, at the crossing of the Central Railroad, of the Fredericksburg Railroad, and the Telegraph road; at the two crossings on Little River, and perhaps at the Junction.

Very respectfully, your obedient servant,

J. J. PETTIGREW,
Brigadier-General.

————

HEADQUARTERS, *May* 14, 1863.

Maj. Gen. D. H. HILL,
   Commanding, North Carolina:

GENERAL: Your letter of the 8th is just received. The impressment of horses was ordered at the time that the Yankee cavalry was in position to threaten a raid through North Carolina. It is not necessary therefore to impress further, but all horses that you may have impressed, and that are not necessary to the support of families or used in tilling the soil, had better be retained for our purposes if you are in need of them.

I think that the enemy will probably abandon North Carolina and Southern Virginia, except some posts occupied by small garrisons, and concentrate his great force in front of our army here. If he does I think that a brigade at Goldsborough and one at or near Petersburg will be all of the infantry force that you will need. As I know of no other reliable officer whom we can place in that command I have suggested your name, knowing that you would prefer it to a position here.

I remain, very respectfully, your most obedient servant,

JAMES LONGSTREET,
Lieutenant-General, Commanding.

————

RICHMOND, *May* 15, 1863.

Maj. Gen. D. H. HILL, *Goldsborough, N. C.:*

GENERAL: I have received your letter of yesterday's date, and in answer to the several suggestions therein I am authorized to state:

1st—in reference to the bridge and provost guards within your command. If these guards have been mustered in for local defense it will be necessary to refer to the terms entered into with them at the time of their muster, and if they have not secured service at a particular spot they would have to be discharged, if found useless, when their places may be supplied by the militia or by disabled soldiers, as suggested by you. In the event of their discharge such of them as are liable to conscription should be immediately enrolled for general service.

2d. You will consider the guard to the prisoners at Salisbury as subject to your orders, to be disposed of in such manner as in your judgment the interests of your command shall require, first sending the prisoners by proper escort to this city to report to General Winder.

3d. In the cases of such of the cavalry of your command as may permit themselves to be surprised or may behave badly in the presence of the enemy, you will make special reports of the facts to this office, in order that authority may be given you to dismount, and where such behavior is repeated, disband the men whose conduct may be so reported; those ordered to be disbanded and who may be subject to conscription to be enrolled to serve as infantry.

4th. You will cause an inspection to be made of Colonel Wheeler's regiment, and if the organization is found unwarranted by the number of troops you will report the fact to this office for orders in the case.

5th. In respect to the exchange of full brigades of your command with skeleton brigades in General Lee's army, I have to state that as General Lee is now in this city a conference will be had with him on the subject of such exchanges, when you will be informed of the result.

I am, general, &c.,

S. COOPER,
Acting Inspector-General.

SPECIAL ORDERS, }   ADJT. AND INSPECTOR GENERAL'S OFFICE,
No. 116. }   *Richmond, May* 15, 1863.

*   *   *   *   *   *   *

VIII. Maj. Gen. G. E. Pickett will move forward immediately with his command and take position at Hanover Junction.

*   *   *   *   *   *   *

X. The artillery battalion attached to Drewry's Bluff and the officers and crew of the gunboat Richmond recently ordered to this city will return immediately to their former commands.

*   *   *   *   *   *   *

By command of the Secretary of War:

JNO. WITHERS,
Assistant Adjutant-General.

HEADQUARTERS,
Kinston, N. C., May 16, 1863.

Maj. Gen. D. H. HILL, *Goldsborough:*

GENERAL: Your dispatch of this date directing me to proceed with my brigade to Richmond has been received. Two of the regiments will be ready to leave by 10 o'clock a. m. The others will be ready so soon as transportation can be furnished. The two regiments would have been ready sooner, but all except one were on picket duty at the time the order was received.

Very respectfully, &c.,

JUNIUS DANIEL,
Brigadier-General.

RICHMOND, VA.,
May 16, 1863.

Maj. Gen. D. H. HILL,
   Commanding Department of North Carolina:

GENERAL: In reply to your letter of the 14th instant, I will state that the extent of the re-enforcements you can send to the Army of Northern Virginia must necessarily depend upon the strength of the enemy in your front.

The plan you propose of exchanging your full for its reduced brigades I fear will add but little to its real strength. It would increase it numerically but weaken it intrinsically by taking away tried troops under experienced officers and replacing them with fresh men and uninstructed commanders. I should therefore have more to feed but less to depend on.

I can exchange Daniel's brigade with one of those you propose, but cannot designate which until I return to camp, as I am not sufficiently acquainted with their condition to make the selection. You can therefore put Daniel in motion at once. Ransom and Cooke I consider as belonging to the Army of Northern Virginia and have relied upon their return.

As far as I am able to judge, the plan of the enemy is to concentrate as large a force as possible to operate in Virginia. Whether he will unite the whole under General Hooker on the Rappahannock or operate with different columns I cannot say, but from the information I receive he is withdrawing troops from South Carolina and the country south of James River.

It is of course our best policy to do the same and to endeavor to repel his advance into Virginia. If he weakens his force in North Carolina I think you will be able, by using all your local troops, such portion of your regular cavalry and regular brigades as may be necessary, to repulse and restrain his marauding expeditions and protect the railroads and the farming interests of the country you now hold. Every man not required for this purpose I desire you to send to me and rely upon your good judgment to proportion the means to the object in view.

I think it now too late for any important expedition to be undertaken by the enemy in the Carolinas. They will, I think, place themselves on the defensive in those States, endeavor to deceive us by threatening our communications, &c., and send their available troops where they can operate to more advantage. I have no fear that they will be able to mislead you.

I hope you will be able to collect and secure for the use of the army all the provisions and forage in the districts in which you are operating.

   I am, with great respect, your obedient servant,

R. E. LEE,
General.

HEADQUARTERS MARTIN'S BRIGADE,
Tarborough, May 16, 1863.

Maj. ARCHER ANDERSON,
Assistant Adjutant-General, Goldsborough, N. C.:

MAJOR: I returned here last night from Greenville. I found Captain Coleman had laid out a line of defenses around the town. They do not fulfill all the conditions necessary to a good defense, but I thought it the best the ground would permit. I understood the captain to say General Hill had decided to put the line of defense at Greenville, and I did not examine any other point.

Colonel Griffin was absent from his headquarters visiting his pickets, and I did not see him. The adjutant showed me the picket stations on the map, and they seemed to be well selected.

The telegraph operator at Rocky Mount is said not to understand the English language. It seems to me very desirable that this line should be extended to Tarborough at once. I also think it would be less expensive than to keep a line of couriers on the road.

I shall leave here to-day for Hamilton, where my headquarters will be established till I can become well acquainted with the roads or General Wessells shall move from Plymouth. The presence of this general in Plymouth with his brigade made it advisable, in my judgment, to move Colonel Martin's regiment to Hamilton. I found also that on account of the scarcity of tools the working detail from the Forty-seventh Regiment would not be heavy.

I am, major, very respectfully, your obedient servant,

J. G. MARTIN,
Brigadier-General.

HEADQUARTERS MARTIN'S BRIGADE,
Hamilton, May 17, 1863.

Maj. ARCHER ANDERSON,
Asst. Adjt. Gen., General Hill's Hdqrs., Goldsborough:

MAJOR: I returned here last night. Another prisoner from the Ninety-sixth New York Regiment was brought in yesterday. I examined him carefully to-day. He confirms in all essential points the information derived from the two whom I examined at the cavalry camp near Williamston. He says the Ninety-second New York, one of Wessells' brigade, was left in the fort opposite New Berne, but a Massachusetts regiment took its place in the brigade at Plymouth. The regiments are small; only nine companies in the Ninety-sixth New York; all the officers of Company G in that regiment having resigned—the men were transferred to other companies. The prisoner's company had not more than 25 for duty and the regiment did not exceed 300. He thought all the others were rather larger, but could not say positively. General Hunt had been in Plymouth and in command of Wessells' brigade during the absence of the latter on account of the death of his wife, but had returned to New Berne.

I think I have made such arrangements as will give me information from Plymouth through our own people in a few days.

The Seventeenth reached Hamilton yesterday. Colonel Griffin reports that there are 500 of the enemy's infantry at Hill's Point and the same number at Rodman's farm; ten regiments of infantry, several pieces of light artillery, and about 40 cavalry (Jocknick's), besides a company of 40 cavalry, now in Washington. It is thought there is no other cavalry on the south side of Tar River. The enemy has infantry and cavalry pickets 1½ miles from Washington on the Plymouth, James-ville, and Williamston road, and fences across the two first named. He has strengthened his earthworks near the town, the work having been done by negroes. Also that there is no direct communication with Washington on either side of the river. Enemy not active and the cit-izens have not been much troubled on the north side. Bacon is still brought over the lines. This I believe is extensively done, and I think it advisable to permit its continuance and allow the persons doing so to return without difficulty.

I am, major, very respectfully, your obedient servant,

J. G. MARTIN,
Brigadier-General.

HEADQUARTERS ARMY OF NORTHERN VIRGINIA,
May 19, 1863.

Brigadier-General PETTIGREW,
Commanding Forces at Hanover Junction:

GENERAL: Your letter of the 14th instant is received.

The commanding general desires me to inform you that he thinks it best that you should dispose of all your cavalry to the east and south of the railroad and depend upon the cavalry of this army to cover you in the direction of the Rappahannock and Gordonsville, your cavalry being disposed so as to watch the enemy in the direction of West Point and the Peninsula. The general further desires that you will always keep your command well in hand, so as to be able to operate in any direction with the greatest promptness.

You will find inclosed the order regulating the transportation of bag-gage of the army. You are desired to regulate the transportation of your command according to this order.

I am, very respectfully, your obedient servant,

A. L. LONG,
Colonel and Military Secretary.

HAMILTON, N. C., *May 18, 1863.*

General HILL, *Commanding, &c., Goldsborough:*

GENERAL: I regret I should not have understood your wishes about the Seventeenth North Carolina Regiment, as I would not then have moved it to this point. As it is here, and the officers and men are well acquainted with the roads and swamps of this vicinity, due from a tour of field service, I shall order Colonel Gibbs to Greenville.

I shall leave for Greenville to-morrow to make it my headquarters.

Your letter of the 17th was received at 1 o'clock. This will be sent by return courier.

I am, general, very respectfully, your obedient servant,

J. G. MARTIN,
Brigadier-General.

None of the unattached companies have arrived here, and nothing has been heard of any of them in answer to the Governor's order.

HEADQUARTERS,
Fredericksburg, May 20, 1863.

Hon. JAMES A. SEDDON,
    Secretary of War, Richmond, Va.:

SIR: The services of General Longstreet will be required with this army. Upon his leaving the department south of James River I had supposed its command would have devolved upon General D. H. Hill as the senior major-general. He informed me this morning that he directed the three major-generals in command of the several districts to report directly to the War Department. I would recommend, therefore, that General D. H. Hill be assigned to the command of the department between James River and the Cape Fear. The battery at Drewry's Bluff, if considered more convenient, could be embraced within the command of General Elzey. I wish General Hill to make such disposition of his troops as to give me all the force that can be spared from North Carolina. Jenkins' brigade, belonging to Pickett's division, is still on the Blackwater, and I do not like to order it up until I hear whether proper dispositions are made to relieve it. It is much wanted with its division. Our scouts report that General Heintzelman, with his corps from Washington, has joined General Hooker, Governor Curtin having promised to defend Washington City with 20,000 State troops. I have not heard yet of any fleet of transports ascending the Potomac. Single transports are frequently seen coming up the river. Yesterday forty transports were counted at Aquia Creek. Regiments of the two years' men are being discharged, I learn, as their time expires, and it is thought are sent off at night.

I am, with great respect, your obedient servant,
                                R. E. LEE,
                                    General.

HEADQUARTERS ARMY OF NORTHERN VIRGINIA,
May 20, 1863.

Maj. Gen. ARNOLD ELZEY,
    Commanding Department of Richmond, Va.:

GENERAL: A party of deserters from the North Carolina regiments of this army left camp last night, taking their arms and equipments with them. Some of them are supposed to be making for Ashe County, North Carolina, and many, it is said, cross the James River at Lumberton, about 45 miles above Richmond, and Roanoke at Horse Ford Mill. General Lee directs me to request that your guards be instructed to be on the alert for them, and if practicable the points indicated be watched and guarded.

Very respectfully, your obedient servant,
                                W. H. TAYLOR,
                                Assistant Adjutant-General.

Abstract from Field Return of troops commanded by Maj. Gen. S. G. French, May 20, 1863. (Ivor, Va.)

Troops.	Present for duty.		Aggregate present.	Aggregate present and absent.
	Officers.	Men.		
Jenkins' brigade	250	2,394	2,965	4,120
Davis' brigade	163	2,414	2,971	3,455
32d Regiment Virginia Volunteers*	21	89	161	260
41st North Carolina Cavalry †	7	194	224	252
Boggs' artillery battalion	27	510	598	708
Moseley's artillery	4	56	65	71
Bradford's battery	4	76	88	92
Fort Powhatan ‡			360	612
Camp Paroled Prisoners §	13	137	193	286
Battalion pontoniers ‖				
Grand total	489	5,870	7,625	9,836

* One company detached.   † A portion only.   ‡ Not classified.
§ Does not include exchanged prisoners.   ‖ No report.

BURWELL'S BAY, *May* 21, 1863.

Maj. WILLIAM NORRIS, *Chief of Signal Corps:*

SIR: I have the honor to report my safe return, with dates of the 20th instant. The Yankees at West Point have been re-enforced, but from the best information I can obtain they do not, I think, number more than 10,000. Five or six light batteries and all the spare horses and mules at Fortress Monroe were sent to Yorktown on Monday. The force at Suffolk still numbers about 15,000.

Respectfully, your obedient servant,

C. H. CAUSEY,
Captain, C. S. Army.

RICHMOND, *May* 21, 1863.

General D. H. HILL, *Goldsborough:*

You had better wait for receipt of General Lee's letter to you. I have telegraphed him to send a copy. The President says the letter refers the matter to your discretion according as you may find the strength of the enemy to be.

S. COOPER,
Adjutant and Inspector General.

STATE OF NORTH CAROLINA, EXECUTIVE DEPARTMENT,
Raleigh, May 21, 1863.

His Excellency President DAVIS:

DEAR SIR: Captain Elliott, commanding a company of State troops, captured last Saturday two steamers in the Albemarle and Chesapeake Canals, one of them carrying a large mail. Upon overlooking the mail, in addition to various items of intelligence, we found a letter from a man by the name of Montgomery, in Washington City, to General Foster, at New Berne, proposing a general negro insurrection and destruction of all railroad bridges, &c., in the South. I inclose you a copy of the letter, giving all the minutia of the damnable scheme. You can of course make such use of it as you may think best. The necessity for increased diligence in guarding our bridges, &c., is apparent.

The letter has not yet been made public.

Very respectfully, &c.,

Z. B. VANCE.

[Inclosure.]

WASHINGTON, D. C., *May* 12, 1863.

Major-General FOSTER,
    Comdg. Department of North Carolina, Beaufort, N. C.:

GENERAL: A plan has been formed for a simultaneous movement to sever the rebel communications throughout the whole South, which has been sent to some general in each military department in the seceded States, in order that they may act in concert and thus secure success. The plan is to induce the blacks to make a concerted and simultaneous movement or rising, on the night of the 1st of August next, over the entire States in rebellion; to arm themselves with any and every kind of weapon that may come to hand and commence operations by burning all railroad and country bridges and tearing up railroad tracks and destroying telegraph lines, &c., and then take to the woods, the swamps, or the mountains, whence they may emerge, as occasion may offer, for provisions and for further depredations. No blood is to be shed except in self-defense. The corn will be in roasting-ears about the 1st of August, and with this and hogs running in the woods, and by foraging upon the plantations by night, they can subsist. This is the plan, in substance, and if we can obtain a concerted movement at the time named it will doubtless be successful. The main object of this letter is to state the time for the rising, that it may be simultaneous over the whole South. To carry the plan into effect in the department in which you have a command, you are requested to select one or more intelligent contrabands, and after telling them the plan and the time (night of the 1st of August) you will send them into the interior of the country, within the enemy's lines, and where slaves are numerous, with instructions to communicate the plan and the time to as many intelligent slaves as possible, and requesting of each to circulate it far and wide over the country, so that we may be able to make the rising understood by several hundred thousand slaves by the time named.

When you have made these arrangements please inclose this letter to some other general commanding in the same department with yourself—some one whom you know or believe to be favorable to such movement—and he in turn is requested to send it to another, and so on until it has traveled the entire rounds of the department, and each command and post will in this way be acting together in the employment of negro slaves to carry the plan into effect.

In this way the plan will be adopted at the same time and in concert over the whole South, and yet no one of all engaged in it will learn the names of his associates and will only know the number of generals acting together in the movement. To give this last information, and before inclosing this letter to some other general, put the numeral I after the word "Approved" at the bottom of this sheet, and when it has gone the rounds of the department the person last receiving it will please reinclose it to my address, that I may thus know and communicate the fact that the plan is being carried out at the same time.

Be assured, sir, that I will inform every department in the seceded States of the plan and the time, that the movement may thus be general and simultaneous.

Very respectfully, your obedient servant,

AUGUSTUS S. MONTGOMERY.

NOTE.—This letter may be sent to other departments farther south after having gone the rounds of yours, which will show to all that the plan is being generally adopted.

DEPARTMENT OF NORTH CAROLINA.

Approved.

C. MARSHALL,
Major and Aide-de-Camp.

HEADQUARTERS DEPARTMENT SOUTHERN VIRGINIA,
Ivor, May 22, 1863.

Maj. Gen. ARNOLD ELZEY, *Richmond, Va.:*

GENERAL : I have received your telegrams respecting Smoot's battery. Ever since I have been here (after leaving Richmond) we have been occupied with the enemy. They appeared at Carrsville with 12,000 men, thirty pieces of artillery, and cavalry, and commenced taking up the railroad. They were driven back 2 miles to where they were strongly intrenched. Last night information came that there were three gunboats coming up the Chowan and that they were not far below the Meherrin, and to-day they are in strong force within 8 miles of this place; nevertheless I ordered back the guns, though much wanted to protect the steamers we have at Franklin and for the defenses of the river.

Yours, very respectfully,

S. G. FRENCH,
Major-General, Commanding.

HEADQUARTERS ARMY OF NORTHERN VIRGINIA,
May 22, 1863.

Maj. Gen. D. H. HILL,
Commanding District of North Carolina :

GENERAL : I am informed by telegram from General Cooper that you have received my telegram but not my letter from Richmond of the 16th.* I herewith inclose you a copy of the letter. I have nothing in addition to say, further than our scouts have not reported the passage of any large fleets of vessels (transports) from Suffolk up the Potomac, but have reported a number of individual vessels bearing troops. Re-enforcements of 30,000 men have also reached Hooker from the direction of Washington since the late battles. Four gunboats are reported ascending the Rappahannock below Urbana, and a scout who has just returned from the enemy's lines reports that every indication leads to the belief that he is preparing for an early move.

Your particular attention is called to the inclosed letter, and you are desired to push forward re-enforcements from North Carolina as rapidly

---

* See Lee to Hill, of that date.

as circumstances will permit. I wish to be able to oppose the full strength of this army to the enemy when it becomes necessary to meet him again.

I am, very respectfully, your obedient servant,

R. E. LEE,
General.

CAMP FREDERICKSBURG, *May* 22, 1863.

General ARNOLD ELZEY, *Commanding, &c.:*

GENERAL: Captain Capps, Fifteenth Virginia Cavalry, on duty in King William County, reports that Mr. Davis, whose home is at West Point, and who at this time is employed in the Confederate Navy, has been noticing the movements of the enemy, and states that they have left in part. Three transports left on the 15th loaded with troops. There appears now to be there two squadrons of cavalry, one company artillery, and a small portion of infantry. About 1,000 negroes are at work on the intrenchments. All the gunboats and transports have left except two. They appear to be ferry-boats. Have you received intelligence corroborating this, or can you ascertain what is the condition of things? It was reported yesterday that four gunboats were ascending the Rappahannock and had come within 12 miles of Tappahannock. Milroy has recrossed the mountains and returned to the valley. Our scouts north of the Rappahannock report indications of another move on the part of General Hooker. Seven pieces of artillery and some infantry have reached Stafford Court-House from Dumfries. Heintzelman is said to have joined him. Reports from Alexandria state that 30,000 new troops are to be sent to him. May I ask you to report these circumstances to the Secretary of War for his information?

Very respectfully, your obedient servant,

R. E. LEE,
General.

SPECIAL ORDERS, } ADJT. AND INSPECTOR GENERAL'S OFFICE,
No. 122. } *Richmond, May* 22, 1863.

* * * * * * *

X. Major Wren will proceed with his battalion in the direction of Lynchburg, Va., to guard the passes on the James River. Quartermaster's and commissary departments will provide forage and rations.

* * * * * * *

XX. Brig. Gen. George H. Steuart, Provisional Army of the Confederate States, will proceed without delay to Fredericksburg, Va., and report to General R. E. Lee for assignment to duty.

* * * * * * *

By command of the Secretary of War:

JNO. WITHERS,
Assistant Adjutant-General.

HEADQUARTERS,
Wilmington, May 23, 1863.

Major-General HILL, *Commanding, &c., Goldsborough:*

GENERAL: I send you a note from Shays.* They seem over the lines to be busy fortifying themselves. I do not think they will shortly

---

*Not found.

advance, though the manner in which we are stripped of troops from Savannah up must be a great bait for them.

I am in hopes we may hear something more favorable about the Southwest. Pemberton is said to have had over 60,000. What can he be about? * * *

Very truly, yours,

W. H. C. WHITING,
Major-General.

HEADQUARTERS,
Fredericksburg, May 25, 1863.

General D. H. HILL,
Commanding Department South of James River:

GENERAL: I have received by courier your letter of the 21st. I am much gratified to learn that the enemy has been so harassed and punished during the past months, and wish that your force was sufficient to drive them from the State. If your information is correct that their troops are moving from the State I hope you will be able to spare the brigades belonging to this army. They are very essential to aid in the effort to turn back the tide of war that is now pressing south.

Since the battle of Chancellorsville the enemy has made a lodgment at West Point, the confluence of the Pamunkey and Mattapony Rivers, and are fortifying that neck. Whether it is a feint or preparation for a new base of operations I do not know. I have thought it probable that the troops from your department may be in process of transference to that point. I therefore desire that you direct Brigadier-General Jenkins to join his division (Pickett's) at Hanover Junction, and Brigadier-General Ransom to repair to Richmond. Should it be necessary to move him farther he will receive orders from General Elzey, to whom he will report. You can retain Brigadier-General Cooke for the present, or until you can more fully ascertain the intentions of the enemy, and see what dispositions you can best make for the protection of your department. I think, if necessary, troops may be drawn from South Carolina and Georgia to re-enforce you, as I can hardly suppose that the enemy contemplates any serious invasion of that department this summer. I think, too, the season has passed for making any movement in North Carolina more than raids of devastation or attempts to retain there our troops in idleness. I hope you will be able to frustrate and punish all such efforts.

I am very much in need of cavalry, and if you can spare another regiment, as you suggest, I will be much obliged to you to order it to repair to Orange Court-House and report to General Stuart. I am told there is a regiment on the Blackwater, whose horses are in good condition, which, if you could replace by another, it might be well to send.

If you require General Robertson to command or organize the cavalry in your department I will return him to you.

I am, with great respect, your obedient servant,

R. E. LEE,
General.

NAVAL COMMANDANT'S OFFICE,
Wilmington, N. C., May 25, 1863.

Lieutenant-General LONGSTREET,
Commanding Military Department, Petersburg, Va.:

GENERAL: I have serious misgivings as to the safety of the gunboat and floating battery building near Scotland Neck, upon the Roanoke.

Unless there be a cavalry force on the left bank to give notice of the enemy's approach, by a sudden raid across from Winston, our work can be destroyed by a night's raid, thus crushing all our hopes of repossessing Albemarle Sound.

It is not for me to suggest any course to you, who are so much better qualified to determine what should be done, and I simply express my anxiety for the vessels, upon which we are working with all possible rapidity, and ask you to protect them, for I have not men sufficient to compose the crew of the iron-clad almost completed here.

Very respectfully, your obedient servant,

W. F. LYNCH,
Flag-Officer, Commanding Naval Defenses, North Carolina.

[Indorsement.]

HEADQUARTERS, *June* 7, 1863.
Respectfully referred to Major-General Hill.

JAMES LONGSTREET,
Lieutenant-General.

HEADQUARTERS ARMY OF NORTHERN VIRGINIA,
May 26, 1863.

His Excellency ZEBULON B. VANCE,
Governor of North Carolina, Raleigh :

GOVERNOR: I have the honor to acknowledge the receipt of your letter of the 21st instant, with its inclosures, for which I return you my thanks.

I think the course pursued by you with reference to the letter of Montgomery, in withholding it from publication, judicious and proper. I would suggest that measures be taken to advise all the State authorities and military commanders privately of the proposed insurrection, in order that they may be upon their guard and take the necessary precautions to prevent the movement and protect public and other property.

I thank you for the copy of the order showing the regiments of nine months' men that go out of service, and hope your adjutant-general may succeed in ascertaining the number of regiments in the Department of North Carolina. The information would be useful, and I should like to have it.

Very respectfully, your obedient servant,

R. E. LEE,
General.

HEADQUARTERS ARMY OF NORTHERN VIRGINIA,
May 26, 1863.

The Hon. SECRETARY OF WAR:

SIR: I have the honor to inclose to you a copy of a letter forwarded to me on the 21st instant by His Excellency Governor Vance, of North Carolina.* Governor Vance states that it is a copy of an original letter addressed to General Foster, and recently taken in a Federal mail, captured by some of our troops in the State service. The Governor also says that he has not given publicity to the letter, a course which I have advised him that I consider prudent and judicious. I have suggested

---

* See inclosure to Vance's letter, p. 1063.

to Governor Vance to cause the State and military authorities to be confidentially advised of the proposed movement, that proper precautionary measures may be adopted. Without knowing anything of the letter or the writer, further than may be inferred from the apparent indications of the connection of the latter either with those in authority or with others who have united to carry out this diabolical project, I deem it my duty to lay the matter before you for such action as you may see fit to take in the premises.

I am, very respectfully, your obedient servant,

R. E. LEE,
General.

———

GENERAL ORDERS, }   HDQRS. DEPT. OF NORTH CAROLINA,
No. 20.   }   *Goldsborough, May 26, 1863.*

The department commander announces the well-known fact of the death of the great and good Jackson, not merely in order to pay a tribute to the illustrious dead, but also to incite the troops to imitate his example. His name has been identified with almost all the great battles of the war, and his genius and courage have been the chief elements in Southern success and Yankee discomfiture. The eagle glance and iron will of the great commander were happily united in him with the patient, uncomplaining endurance of the common soldier.

His wonderful battles have contributed largely to our independence, and his great fame has shed a halo of glory over his beloved South. But his virtues as a man will be as fondly remembered by his countrymen as the brilliant deeds of his military career. He has taught us that he who most fears God the least fears man; that the most exalted courage may be associated with the modesty of the shrinking girl; that the lips which were never defiled with ribaldry and profanity could cheer on most loudly amidst the roar of cannon and the clash of arms. His whole life was a rebuke to the intriguing, the selfish, the cowardly, the vulgar, and the profane.

The pure man will be loved as much as the heroic soldier will be admired in the future ages of the republic.

Let us drop our laurel upon his bier, but remember that we may best honor him by striving day and night, and with his unwavering trust in God, to secure the independence for which he gave his life.

D. H. HILL,
Major-General.

———

GOLDSBOROUGH, N. C., *May 27, 1863.*

Major-General WHITING:

GENERAL: Ransom has been ordered to Virginia. His first regiment leaves to-day. This makes us very weak. The mail captured by the guerrillas showed the astonishing fact that there are thirty-one regiments at New Berne, and that instead of sending off they have been receiving troops. Nine regiments are there mentioned which were not in my original list and of which I have never seen any mention in their papers. Take care that we are not all bagged some of these days.

Jones, the great brigand, was really killed in my chase of him the other day. He was a bold, dangerous, bad man. His work has been that of the Comanche.

I am afraid that our scouts knew nothing of the strength of the Yan kees; they have been relying entirely upon what the citizens tell them, and now that the blockade is strict they know nothing. I hope that your works are strong on Sound and Holly Stretch road.

Direct to Petersburg.

Very respectfully,

D. H. HILL,
Major-General.

HEADQUARTERS,
Goldsborough, N. C., May 27, 1863.

[General A. H. COLQUITT:]

GENERAL: This will be handed you by Major Nethercutt, who has a battalion of Partisan Rangers on the Upper Trent road.

General Ransom is leaving at a very unfortunate time, as the Yankees are certainly in large force at New Berne, and neither you nor Cooke know the country.

You will find Major Nethercutt a very trustful, reliable, and worthy man. He is thoroughly posted in regard to the country. Major Nethercutt has about 500 men. Capt. C. G. Wright is there with a battalion of 300 men. Maj. J. N. Whitford is at Coward's Bridge with some 400 men. He should be ordered up in case of an advance upon Kinston. You can thus bring into battle upward of 5,000 men. General Martin is at Greenville with two regiments and could be sent for in case anything serious should occur. He is your senior, and after General Ransom has left he will be in charge of this State. Telegraph to me promptly at Petersburg should there be a serious movement.

Do not attempt to fight farther out than the Southwest. You can whip any force upon the Neuse and Lower Trent road; but should the Yankees swing round on the upper road—the Upper Trent and Wilmington road—you may cross over to attack their rear or fall back across the river. It will never do to fight in the earthworks just over the bridge.

Have the new bridge finished rapidly; clear away all the trees on the other side for at least 500 yards and have strong batteries and rifle-pits to protect the bridge. After you have finished the bridge the old bridge could be destroyed in case of an advance. Those silly works near the bridge on the other side could then be destroyed, as the Yankees would use them as batteries against the town.

I hope that you may have great success in your new field. Study the roads and country rapidly.

With great respect,

D. H. HILL,
Major-General.

GOLDSBOROUGH, N. C., *May* 27, 1863.

General R. E. LEE, *Commanding Army:*

GENERAL: I wrote to you two days ago that the information through the captured mail showed that there were thirty-one regiments in New Berne and possibly six more, as six others, not mentioned in the letters, were known to be there before the battle of Chancellorsville. I received your order last night to remove Ransom. My transportation is very limited, and it will take three days to get him off. I hope that you will replace Ransom by one of the shattered brigades, else the railroad can be cut and possibly Wilmington be taken. The removal of Ransom I regard as hazardous at this time unless you move soon. I go on to-day to Petersburg to be provost-marshal there.

As soon as I know where Brigadier-General Jenkins is I will order him to join General Pickett.

With great respect,

D. H. HILL,
Major-General.

P. S.—I have sent you about 9,500 on paper, possibly 8,000 effectives, if the partisan cavalry can be called effectives. I have received in return about 1,500 effective men, really good and true.

I am much obliged to you for the offer of Brigadier-General Robertson, but he has been once in this department.

HEADQUARTERS ARMY OF NORTHERN VIRGINIA,
May 28, 1863.
Maj. Gen. D. H. HILL,
  Commanding, &c., Kinston, N. C. :

GENERAL : Your letter of the 25th instant is received. I regret to hear of the occurrence reported by you, and fear that the regiment allowed itself to be surprised. I am gratified, however, that you drove the enemy back so promptly to his intrenchments and did all in your power to retrieve the disaster.

With reference to the Federal force in North Carolina, I have observed that the department has been divided into three districts, a list of which, with the names of the commanders, I inclose. The name of General Foster is not mentioned. He may still command the department or he may have been withdrawn. I am at a loss to account for the troops that have appeared at West Point, unless they came from North Carolina; I do not think they were taken from the Army of the Potomac. All the information received indicates that none have gone down the Potomac. On the contrary, troops have been reported coming up the river, and Hooker has received re-enforcements since the late battles. I supposed that the troops at West Point might have come from North Carolina and that General Foster may be in command or that he will be. The division of the department into districts would indicate that active operations on an extensive scale were not contemplated, but rather the occupancy of the country.

I think your view with regard to the letters correct, and that the writers addressed them to their correspondents in ignorance of their having left North Carolina, a fact that would of course be withheld as long as possible from the knowledge of the public.

My letter of the 25th instant will have already apprised you that I desire Jenkins to be ordered to rejoin his division at once at Hanover Junction, and Ransom to proceed to Richmond, where he will receive further orders through General Elzey, if it be necessary. The same letter will have advised you that you can retain General Cooke for the present, until you have better ascertained the enemy's intentions and made the best provision for the defense of your department.

When General Longstreet left the south side of the James a considerable amount of transportation remained, from which Colonel Corley has directed Colquitt's brigade to be supplied. I thought this better than to send the transportation he left here, as the distance is great.

I inclose you a statement of the artillery on the Blackwater and near Petersburg.* The heavy batteries of Dabney and Smoot are intended to operate on the rivers and are best for that purpose. I wish you to send me a report of the field batteries in North Carolina, and would be glad to know whether you have any surplus of good ones.

R. E. LEE,
General.

WAR DEPARTMENT, C. S. A.,
Richmond, Va., May 28, 1863.

Maj. Gen. D. H. HILL, *Commanding, &c.:*

GENERAL : Your letter of to-day has been just sent me by the Adjutant-General, and I learn with some surprise that both Ransom's brigade and that of General Jenkins have been ordered from your department to join General Lee. I received on yesterday a telegram from General Lee, recommending that Cooke's brigade should be ordered to this city, and suggesting that in case of need General Beauregard should re-enforce you. On conference with the President, to whom this telegram was exhibited, it was resolved before giving a positive order for such movement to consult you as to its effect on the safety of your command. General Lee must have concluded this recommendation had not been complied with when he ordered up Ransom's and Jenkins'. From your exhibition of the forces of the enemy in North Carolina I am of the same opinion with yourself, that with a knowledge of the facts both brigades would not have been ordered from you. The best plan will be, as you have started Ransom's brigade, to send that on and retain both Jenkins' and Cooke's, at least until further communication can be had with General Lee and his counsel taken on the new aspect presented by your statement of the enemy's forces in North Carolina.

General Lee evidently supposes that the forces of the enemy have been largely withdrawn from both North Carolina and Suffolk and have been concentrated on the Rappahannock and at West Point. He states in his telegram that Foster has been withdrawn, and he presumes with his force has been sent to one or other of the last-named points. It will certainly be better that he should have fuller information before you carry out his instructions fully.

With high esteem, very respectfully, yours,

J. A. SEDDON,
Secretary of War.

HEADQUARTERS DISTRICT OF THE CAPE FEAR,
Wilmington, May 28, 1863.

Maj. Gen. D. H. HILL,
Commanding, &c., Petersburg:

GENERAL : I have your letter, and don't like the news either of Ransom's departure or the force of the enemy. What can we do ? Cooke cannot defend Kinston by himself and I cannot aid him. I should find hard work to hold Wilmington by my force, and he cannot aid me. I don't think Beauregard can help me now. Do try and get some troops down here. They will surely make a raid on the railroad as soon as they learn you are gone, and the scoundrels hear almost everything.

---

*Not found.

The Governor is calling back his negroes, which troubles me greatly. You know I am not yet ready and have not yet guns enough. The labor of the past two months has been immense.

Very respectfully,

W. H. C. WHITING,
Major-General.

SPECIAL ORDERS, } ADJT. AND INSPECTOR GENERAL'S OFFICE,
No. 127.   }   *Richmond, Va., May 28,* 1863.

*   *   *   *   *   *   *

II. The Department of North Carolina will hereafter include the Department of Southern Virginia as far north as to embrace the city of Petersburg and its environs, and including the Appomattox River. All the troops within this department, thus extended, will be under the command of Maj. Gen. D. H. Hill. The arrangements for the parole and exchange of prisoners by the Appomattox River will, as heretofore, be under the control of the agent for exchange (Colonel Ould), and the disposal of the prisoners, after paroled or exchanged, will be directed by the orders of Brig. Gen. [J. H.] Winder, commanding the Department of Henrico.

III. Maj. Gen. S. G. French is relieved from the Department of Southern Virginia, and will proceed without delay to Mississippi, where he will report for duty to Gen. Joseph E. Johnston.

*   *   *   *   *   *   *

By command of the Secretary of War:

JNO. WITHERS,
Assistant Adjutant-General.

RICHMOND, *May 29,* 1863.

General R. E. LEE, *Fredericksburg, Va.:*

GENERAL: Hill says he has reported to you as to condition in North Carolina.

To withdraw Ransom's, Cooke's, and Jenkins' brigades is to abandon the country to the enemy, if last information be correct.

Jenkins' brigade was exchanged for the one which had previously guarded the approach across the Blackwater, and which is understood to have gone up with General Pickett.

Ransom has been promoted, to relieve General French, ordered to Mississippi

JEFFERSON DAVIS.

RICHMOND, VA., *May 30,* 1863.

His Excellency ZEBULON B. VANCE:

SIR: I have the honor to acknowledge the receipt of your letter of the 21st instant, conveying a copy of a letter captured from the enemy, in which a plan is proposed to General Foster for a general insurrection of the slaves on the night of August 1, to destroy railroad bridges, &c. Please accept my thanks for the information conveyed. The matter has been referred to the special attention of the Secretary of War, who will communicate a warning to generals commanding armies in the field.

JEFFERSON DAVIS.

CONFIDENTIAL.]   HEADQUARTERS,
                                    Fredericksburg, May 30, 1863.

His Excellency JEFFERSON DAVIS:

Mr. PRESIDENT: I hope you received my reply to your dispatch of yesterday.

When in Richmond I gave General D. H. Hill discretionary instructions, stating my belief that the contest of the summer would take place in Virginia, to apportion his force to the strength of the enemy, and send me every man he could spare. He declined to act under those instructions and requested positive instructions. He now offers objections which if previously presented I should not have issued the latter. You will see that I am unable to operate under these circumstances, and request to be relieved from any control of the department from the James to the Cape Fear River. I have for nearly a month been endeavoring to get this army in a condition to move to anticipate an expected blow from the enemy. I fear I shall have to receive it here at a disadvantage or to retreat. The enemy will either make a combined movement to force me back or transfer his army to the James River. If I was stronger I think I could prevent either and force him back.

You will perceive by the return of the 20th, forwarded to the Adjutant and Inspector General, the effective strength of the army. If I could use it altogether or had only to oppose General Hooker's army I should be content. But my wish has been to organize a force to defend Richmond against the army apparently collecting on the York River. I can get no positive information as to its strength. I have no knowledge of the scouts sent in that direction. General Longstreet when on the Blackwater sent a person to Washington. He could get no farther than Baltimore. No one but the military was allowed on the cars from Baltimore to Washington. He said while in Baltimore troops were constantly passing to Washington, said to be Mitchel's, from the West, going to General Hooker. At Old Point, on his return, he saw some of Foster's troops, and was informed that Generals Dix, Keyes, and Foster were at West Point. There were only three companies at Fort Monroe. I receive this information with some allowance, but it may be taken as evidence that troops are being thrown into Virginia.

I only directed Ransom's brigade to be sent to Richmond; Jenkins' to Hanover Junction; Cooke's to wait till movements of the enemy could be further ascertained.

General Longstreet says Pickett has no brigade in the place of Jenkins'. He had temporarily a brigade formed of two regiments from General Sam. Jones and two from General Marshall. It was first under Pryor and afterward under Colston. Three of the regiments were sent back to the West; one is still in Petersburg, or rather one that was exchanged for it.

This army has been diminished since last fall by the brigades of Jenkins, Ransom, Cooke, and Evans. It has been increased by Pettigrew's. I consider Colquitt's exchanged for Daniel's. General Hill has retained in North Carolina a regiment from Pettigrew and Daniel. General Hooker's army, as far as I can form an opinion, has been increased.

I have given Your Excellency all the facts in my possession to enable you to form an opinion as to what is best to be done. I fear the time has passed when I could have taken the offensive with advantage. From the indications that reach me, the enemy is contemplating another movement. I have not discovered what it is. There may be nothing left for me to do but fall back   General Hill has in North Carolina Jenkins',

Davis', Cooke's, Ransom's, Clingman's, and Martin's brigades, a large amount of field artillery, and three regiments of cavalry; one of the latter, in addition to the two sent, he has offered to send me. I have directed him to suspend the execution of the orders from me and await orders from the Adjutant and Inspector General.

I am, with great respect, your obedient servant,

R. E. LEE,
General.

HEADQUARTERS ARMY OF NORTHERN VIRGINIA,
May 30, 1863.

Maj. Gen. D. H. HILL,
Commanding Department South of James:

GENERAL : Your letter of May 27 has been received. I telegraphed to you this morning to suspend the execution of my order of the 25th instant. The President will give you such orders as he may see fit. I know nothing of the force in your front, but I attach no importance to the estimate of the enemy's forces in New Berne based on the captured mail. These letters only go to show that the writers thought these regiments were in New Berne at the time they wrote.

One of Longstreet's scouts, in whom he places some confidence, has just returned from Fortress Monroe. He reports some of Foster's forces at that point, and that Foster, Dix, and Keyes are at Yorktown and West Point.

From the returns of Pettigrew's and Daniel's brigades the effective force of the two is 5,844. Two cavalry regiments give 1,068 effectives. Estimating the third regiment of cavalry at 500, this will give a total effective of 7,500 sent from your department. Each of the two brigades is reported to have left one regiment in North Carolina.

I am, very respectfully, your obedient servant,

R. E. LEE,
General.

RICHMOND, *May 30, 1863.*

General D. H. HILL, *Petersburg, Va.:*

What force can you spare to General Lee on the basis of his proposition to you ? Was a regiment of Pettigrew's and another of Daniel's brigade left in your department ? What became of the force on the Blackwater which was substituted by Jenkins' brigade ? Did it join Pickett's division and was it a brigade ?

S. COOPER,
Adjutant and Inspector General.

WAR DEPARTMENT, C. S. A.,
Richmond, May 30, 1863.

Maj. Gen. D. H. HILL, *Commanding, &c.:*

GENERAL: I inclose you a copy of a confidential letter just received from General Lee.* You will perceive he anticipates a serious effort on the part of the enemy by a sudden inroad to possess themselves of Richmond, and urges timely preparation. This impression on General Lee's part accounts in a measure for his orders for the removal of troops

---

* See Lee to Davis, p. 1078.

from North Carolina, for he had recommended a brigade, at least, to be held here.

My latest intelligence from the Peninsula is that the force there is not very large and is thought either to be removing or to be concentrating at Yorktown. If the design of sudden attack on Richmond be really contemplated I think it not unlikely that instead of resorting to the Peninsula route, on which they have hitherto failed, a sudden advance from Suffolk by way of Petersburg may be preferred. It would be well, therefore, that you should keep yourself as well advised as possible of the movements of their troops in that direction, and it might be advisable, quietly but effectively, to accomplish such organization of the arm-bearing population remaining in that city as General Lee recommends here. I shall endeavor to carry out his suggestions in this city; but of course such force can be little relied on; and in view of the importance, in every point of view, of defending this city, I shall be compelled to have the aid of one of your brigades. That of Ransom's, a part of which has already reached and been detained here, had better for the present be placed here or so near as to be in supporting distance in case of emergency. I must rely on you to make such dispositions as you deem judicious to render any other assistance in your power should it be needed, or at least to give timely notice of any hostile movements from the south side. I incline myself to think the enemy have work enough before them on the Rappahannock to demand all their forces, and that such intimations as have reached General Lee are intended to mislead. Still, he is very cautious and judicious in forming his conclusions, and his advice renders every precaution possible incumbent on us.

With high esteem, very respectfully, yours,

J. A. SEDDON,
Secretary of War.

HEADQUARTERS DISTRICT OF THE CAPE FEAR,
Wilmington, May 30, 1863.

Maj. Gen. D. H. HILL, *Commanding, &c., Petersburg*:

GENERAL: I will try to put a small force at Magnolia, though it pinches me. It cannot be possible that Cooke is to leave too. Ransom's going is hard, but to strip the whole line in the face of the large force in front of us is giving up the railroad. I hope you have represented the condition of affairs, especially your discovery of the increase of force at New Berne. The Northern papers are full of accounts of the sending on all the North Carolina troops to General Lee, and urging Foster to attempt Wilmington, representing that now is the time. No doubt the rascally blockade runners carry information also. Recollect that if they drive Colquitt from Kinston they will also take Goldsborough, destroy the bridge once more, as they did before, and no aid can reach me. I can't look for any from Beauregard, who has been depleted to all he can bear. Please to urge this. It seems to me that one of the small brigades of the Virginia army might be spared. The risk of stripping this whole line is very great. I don't understand Pemberton's arrangement; never did; but still have great faith and much hope in Old Joe. It will be a dreadful disaster to us if Vicksburg is lost.

Very truly,

W. H. C. WHITING,
Major-General.

P. S.—The troops at Kinston, it seems to me, ought to, if beaten back, retreat this side the Neuse to make a junction with me. If the bridge is burned and they separated from me, I could not, should Foster turn his whole force upon me, hope to save the place, except by a miracle. However, you will judge of that. I have written to the Secretary.

————

HEADQUARTERS,
Wilmington, May 30, 1863.

Hon. JAMES A. SEDDON,
    Secretary of War, Richmond:

SIR: Though the Department must be aware of the general danger to which this line is now exposed there are some considerations which I beg leave to urge without, I hope, impropriety.

Major-General Hill informs me that he captured a mail from the enemy by which it appears that he has in New Berne thirty-one regiments, an increase of nine over any previous estimates in our possession. A very moderate count will give between 12,000 and 15,000 men. Against this we have but two small brigades; that is, if General Cooke is under orders, and I understand he is. The danger which I anticipate is the destruction of the railroad at Goldsborough, as was done before. But on the previous occasion I was assisted by General Beauregard to such an extent that Wilmington was comparatively secure. Should this recur I cannot expect anything from General Beauregard, who has probably detached all he can to the West. With the bridges down between here and Petersburg I could not receive troops from above, and Foster would be at liberty to concentrate his whole force upon me by land. He would not need iron-clads, for I would not have force enough to man my works. The whole subject of the maneuvering and of the line of attack has been pointed out and discussed in many previous communications. I am now only pointing out the dangers that now threaten, in the hope that you may be able to provide some re-enforcement.

All the Northern dates during this month contain advices of the stripping of this line to re-enforce General Lee, and urge Foster to make the attempt on Wilmington while in its present condition and before the sickly season sets in. My scouts in the front give me the same information.

In view of the great responsibility which rests upon me I have felt it my duty to advise you of this state of things and what may possibly occur here.

I have no doubt that in spite of all my precautions—much more stringent, as I am told, than anywhere else in the country—this miserable blockade running by private parties furnishes the enemy with all the information they require.

I respectfully urge the consideration of the above and its reference to the President.

Very respectfully,

W. H. C. WHITING,
Major-General.

[Indorsements.]

Respectfully referred to the President.

It is feared serious hazard is run, but I see no mode to avoid it. Local organizations, which I will press, are the only resources at command.

J. A. SEDDON,
Secretary of War.

SECRETARY OF WAR:

Is this not the same information which was before you when discussing the distribution of troops with General Hill when he was last in this city? If the evidence of force at New Berne, &c., has not been sent to General Lee, it would be well to forward copies of these letters.

J. D.

JUNE 3, 1863.

ASSISTANT SECRETARY:

Let copies of these letters be made out and sent with a letter to General Lee, stating that at the suggestion of the President they are sent for his information and that his attention is respectfully invited to them.

J. A. S.,
Secretary.

———

PETERSBURG, *May* 30, 1863.

General S. COOPER:

All five of Pettigrew's regiments and battery have gone to him. Four regiments, a battalion, and battery of Daniel's have been sent, leaving one regiment behind. I do not know what troops General Jenkins relieved. I could exchange Cooke's for Ransom's brigade.

D. H. HILL,
Major-General.

———

RICHMOND, *May* 30, 1863.

Maj. Gen. D. H. HILL, *Petersburg, Va.*:

Let one of the regiments come here and retain the other two at Petersburg.

S. COOPER,
Adjutant and Inspector General.

———

BUREAU OF CONSCRIPTION, C. S. A.,
Richmond, Va., May 30, 1863.

Maj. Gen. D. H. HILL, *Commanding, &c.*:

DEAR GENERAL: You must have received my letter in answer to yours for subterra shells before this. I have instructed Major Cross in the use of both subterra shells and submarine mortar shells. The latter, I think, you can get here already cast, and from sad experience at Charleston in accidentally sinking one of our own vessels, which negligently was suffered to drift upon one of the latter (she sunk in twenty seconds), no doubt can exist of their efficacy; and I learn this morning it was one of the same which sunk the enemy in Yazoo River.

I wrote a book with drawings, &c., and gave it to the President. It caused him to enter with zest into the schemes, and behold I find myself ousted from my position as superintendent of Bureau of Conscription and ordered to Vicksburg. I protested, knowing General Johnston's opinion, but it was no go, and he ordered the Secretary of War to write the following:

WAR DEPARTMENT, C. S. A.,
Richmond, Va., May 27, 1863.

General JOSEPH E. JOHNSTON, *Commanding:*

GENERAL: Brig. Gen. G. J. Rains having been detailed for duty in connection with torpedoes and subterra shells, has been ordered to report to you. The President has confidence in his inventions, and is desirous that they should be employed both on land and river, if opportunity offers, at Vicksburg and its vicinity. Should communication allow, you are desired to send him there; but if otherwise, to employ him in his devices against the enemy where most assailable in that way elsewhere. All possible facilities and aid in the supply of men and material for the fair trial of his torpedoes and shells are requested on your part. Such means of offense against the enemy are approved and recognized by the Department as legitimate weapons of warfare.

With high esteem, very truly, yours,

J. A. SEDDON,
Secretary of War.

Adieu, my dear general.

G. J. RAINS.

P. S.—A requisition upon Lieut. Col. George W. Rains, at Augusta, Ga., will get whatever sensitive priming-tubes you want. I went there and instructed in their make, and they have been furnished Mobile, Savannah, Charleston, &c., by the thousand.

RICHMOND, *May 31, 1863.*

General R. E. LEE,
Commanding, &c., near Fredericksburg, Va.:

GENERAL: Yours of the 30th was delivered to me last night. Before it was received General Cooper had sent a dispatch to General D. H. Hill, which opened the correspondence of which you will find copies* inclosed.

I had never fairly comprehended your views and purposes until the receipt of your letter of yesterday, and now have to regret that I did not earlier know all that you had communicated to others. I could hardly have misunderstood you, and need not say would have been glad to second your wishes, confiding, as I always do, as well in your judgment as in your information.

The reports in relation to the enemy at West Point are not, I fear, quite reliable; but in the uncertainty of the case it had appeared to me that it might be well to bring up a brigade of General Hill's force and place it on the south side of James River sufficiently near to the pontoon bridge to be used in any operations which a movement of the enemy on the north side might require. The recommendation of General Hill in relation to Ransom's brigade, though not quite the same, may answer the purpose, and I have confidence in the cordiality and alacrity with which Ransom would meet such requirement. General Hill having mentioned Cooke's brigade as one which he is disposed to exchange, it seemed best to order it up and rely upon his supplying its place, at least partially, by the organization of the various guards and the battalion at Salisbury, which he had asked for authority to embody in his army. To complete Heth's division without creating complaint on the part of North Carolinians it seemed to me desirable that there should be but one North Carolina brigade in it. To observe that condition we had to choose between Jenkins' South Carolina brigade and Davis', of Mississippi; as Jenkins had been commanding on the Blackwater and was supposed to be acquainted with the country, and Davis was temporarily absent, it was thought for that and minor reasons better to detach Davis' brigade. If General Hill's force should prove inadequate as the season advances we should be able to draw further from the troops in South Carolina and Georgia. Mr. Seddon, however, thinks nothing more is to be obtained there. You will perceive that no destination is given by the Adjutant-General to the brigades drawn

---

* Not found.

from General Hill. Please send your orders to this place, so that the troops may be moved in conformity to your wishes.

By the proposed arrangement you will have lost, without receiving anything in exchange, the brigade of Evans', as, being able to get no trace of the troops for which Jenkins' brigade was reported to have been exchanged, I can only wonder as to what constituted the command on the Blackwater before the troops from Western Virginia went there. From the account which General Hill gave of a part of his cavalry, I do not think you would be benefited by receiving that which he proposes to send you. He asked for and received conditional authority to dismount a portion of that force.

I note your request to be relieved of the command of the troops between the James River and the Cape Fear. This is one of the few instances in which I have found my thoughts running in the opposite direction from your own. It has several times occurred to me that it would be better for you to control all the operations of the Atlantic slope, and I must ask you to reconsider the matter. I wish I knew how to relieve you from all anxiety concerning movements on the York or James River against Richmond while you are moving toward the north and west; but even if you could spare troops for the purpose, on whom could you devolve the command with that feeling of security which would be necessary for the full execution of your designs? I readily perceive the disadvantage of standing still, and sorely regret that I cannot give you the means which would make it quite safe to attempt all that we desire. That any advantage should have been lost by delay is sad enough where the contest at best was so very unequal as to give little room for the exercise of what General Charles Lee called "that rascally virtue," prudence. I do not know what success we shall have in organizations for local defense, but should it be all that I can hope you know how far our army will still fall short of the numerical strength of the enemy. Missouri, Kentucky, the most populous portions of Tennessee and Louisiana, are contributing nothing to recruit our army. If General Kirby Smith should have success on the west side of the river he will soon have a large force by volunteers from Missouri and Southern Louisiana. General Johnston did not, as you thought advisable, attack Grant promptly, and I fear the result is that which you anticipated if time was given. The last intelligence indicates that Grant's army is concentrating on the Yazoo, where he connects with his gunboats and river transportation and threatens the line of communication between Jackson and Vicksburg. The position, naturally strong, may soon be intrenched, and, with the heavy guns which he can bring by water, will require to be reduced by some other means than a direct attack. It is useless to look back, and it would be unkind to annoy you in the midst of your many cares with the reflections which I have not been able to avoid. All the accounts we have of Pemberton's conduct fully sustain the good opinion heretofore entertained of him, and I hope has secured for him that confidence of his troops which is so essential to success.

Very respectfully, and truly, your friend,

JEFFERSON DAVIS.

RICHMOND, *May* 31, 1863.

General D. H. HILL,
    Comdg. Department of North Carolina, Petersburg, Va.:

GENERAL: I have received your dispatch and letter both, dated 30th instant. It has been determined that Major-General Ransom be put in command of the district of your department which includes the Appomattox and Blackwater, and that his force consists of his former brigade and Jenkins' brigade; Davis' and Cooke's brigades to be detached from your department and directed to report to General Lee. This arrangement will take place with least practicable delay, and you will give the necessary orders. The two regiments of Ransom's old brigade now here will be directed to report to you at Petersburg for your instructions. It is believed and hoped that, as this arrangement will leave you five brigades and three regiments of cavalry and such additional force as you will be able to get from the bridge and provost-marshal guards and the guard of prisoners at Salisbury, your force will be equal to the wants of the service in your department. Should the enemy move up from South Carolina you can in that event be reenforced from that quarter.

Very respectfully, &c.,

S. COOPER,
Adjutant and Inspector General.

KINSTON, *May 31, 1863.*

General D. H. HILL, *Commanding:*

GENERAL: There is nothing of special interest to communicate. My time since my arrival has been spent upon the roads, and I hope to be thoroughly acquainted with the country soon.

The line of defense along the Southwest is too long as a fighting line for this small force. Regiments scattered at the different crossings could not be readily concentrated. On the Neuse and Dover roads we could resist successfully the enemy's advance, but men could not be spared for the other roads. If the enemy should advance upon either of the other roads—that is, the Upper Trent and Wilmington—do you not think it would be hazarding too much if we should cross over to assail him in rear without having a force sufficient to check him in front? If we should whip him it would of course cure any imperfections in the plan; but if in the chances of war it should be otherwise the result might be disastrous. Whatever your skill and experience may suggest as the best course I shall endeavor to execute with all my power, and I trust you will give me your views in full and specifically.

The new bridge will be completed in a day or two. Details are at work on the batteries and rifle-pits. Other details will be made to cut the roads and fell the timber as soon as the engineer is ready for them. When the work is done I think the town can be held against a much superior force. From the most reliable information that I have received I think that the force in New Berne does not exceed 7,000 or 8,000 effective men. None of the regiments there have yet gone out of service. Major Whitford has sent in 10 Yankees captured and 3 deserters. As he desired to see you on business I have consented that he conduct them to you.

If nothing more important demands my attention I shall keep enterprises on foot to destroy the railroad bridge or damage the road between New Berne and Morehead City, and other things that may be harassing and troublesome.

For the sake of the country and for my own character I trust that no disaster or unpleasant circumstance will occur in this hitherto unfortunate section while the responsibility rests upon my shoulders. You may rest assured that I will exert myself to prevent it.

Very truly, your obedient servant,

A. H. COLQUITT,
Brigadier-General.

Abstract from Monthly Return of the Department of North Carolina, Maj. Gen. D. H. Hill, commanding, for May 31, 1863 (headquarters Petersburg, Va.).

Command.	Present for duty.		Effective total present.	Aggregate present.	Aggregate present and absent.	Pieces of field artillery.	Aggregate present and absent last return.
	Officers.	Men.					
General staff	15	2	2	17	17		14
District of the Cape Fear:							
Permanent force	153	2,504	2,537	3,450	3,984		3,746
Clingman's brigade	120	2,085	2,105	2,551	3,328		
Colquitt's brigade	148	1,706	1,711	2,077	2,998		3,019
Cooke's brigade*	153	2,179	2,198	2,638	3,505	4	3,462
Martin's brigade†	118	1,995	2,025	2,388	2,874		2,893
Jenkins' brigade	250	2,394	2,401	2,965	4,120		
Ransom's brigade‡	182	2,885	2,897	3,274	4,019	6	4,164
Davis' brigade§	163	2,414	2,418	2,971	3,455		
Unattached infantry‖	109	1,452	1,452	1,646	2,643		
Field artillery outside of the District of the Cape Fear¶	68	1,451	1,463	1,678	1,951	55	
Cavalry	70	920	940	1,182	1,575	5	
Grand total	1,549	21,987	22,149	26,838	34,469	70	

* June 12. Cooke's brigade has joined the Army of Northern Virginia since May 31. Includes battery attached.
†Includes infantry of Martin's brigade and not Sixty-second Georgia Cavalry.
‡ Includes battery attached; 149 captured.
§June 12. Davis' brigade has joined the Army of Northern Virginia since date of return.
‖ Consists of two partisan battalions, provost and prison guards, and garrison at Fort Powhatan.
¶June 12. One of these batteries moved to Richmond since date of report.

Abstract from Field Return of troops, Department of Richmond, Maj. Gen. Arnold Elzey commanding, for May 31, 1863.

Command.	Present for duty.		Effective total present.	Aggregate present.	Aggregate present and absent.
	Officers.	Men.			
Brig. Gen. H. A. Wise	197	2,333	2,500	2,902	3,579
Brig. Gen. J. J. Pettigrew	203	3,482	3,630	4,089	4,992
Col. T. S. Rhett	94	1,496	1,636	1,930	2,190
Lieut. Col. J. M. Maury	24	336	397	466	531
Capt. S. S. Lee	18	281	370	429	459
Grand total	536	7,928	8,533	9,816	11,751

HEADQUARTERS FORCES ON BLACKWATER,
June 1, 1863.

Maj. GRAHAM DAVES, *Assistant Adjutant-General:*

MAJOR: I have the honor to report everything quiet. There are indications that the enemy contemplate withdrawing from Suffolk. It is reported that they are fortifying a line with the left on Deep Creek, some 6 or 7 miles this side of Portsmouth, and have been removing their heavy guns, &c., from Suffolk to that point.   Also that they are sending away valuables, &c.

The scouts report that a brigade was sent away in transports some five days ago.   The Yankee soldiers thought they were going to join Hooker.

I hope to obtain more definite information in a few days.

I am, major, with great respect, your obedient servant,

M. JENKINS,

Brigadier-General, Commanding.

HEADQUARTERS MARTIN'S BRIGADE,
Greenville, June 1, 1863.

Maj. ARCHER ANDERSON,
Assistant Adjutant-General, Petersburg, Va. :

MAJOR : Colonel Martin writes to me that he has received information from a gentleman just arrived from Edenton, N. C., that a cavalry expedition is being fitted out at that place, destination unknown, and that all communication from there to Plymouth has been cut off.   His informant is a trustworthy man.

Colonel Martin further reports the enemy still fortifying at Plymouth. General Wessells' full brigade there, supposed to be 2,500 men.

I am, very respectfully, your obedient servant,

J. G. MARTIN,

Brigadier-General.

GREENVILLE, N. C., *June 1, 1863.*

Maj. Gen. D. H. HILL, *Petersburg, Va. :*

GENERAL : Since writing to you this morning I have heard through a person employed to collect information from the people on this river the following :

On Friday last one steamer loaded with troops came up the river to Washington ; on Saturday two, also with troops ; one of these was Foster's boat.   During the nights of Friday and Saturday several boats went down the river ; no troops seen.   The general impression made on the people on the river was that they were changing troops.   Some of them, however, thought the enemy was re-enforcing preparatory to a raid.   He has been very strict for several days in not allowing any communication with Washington.

I am inclined to the opinion that he is organizing a formidable force at Edenton with a view to Weldon, from Colerain or Winton, on the Chowan.   The Colerain route to Weldon has always been considered by our people the most dangerous one to us the enemy could take to approach Weldon.

I have yet heard nothing of the movement of Moore's battery or Nethercutt's battalion.   Have they been ordered to Bertie ?

I think the best disposition to make of Colonel Griffin would be to place him in command of all the troops beyond the Roanoke.   Could the company of his regiment now at Franklin be sent to him in Bertie or Hertford ?

Please let me know if you intended that I should act on the applications for leave of officers.   I supposed so, from several being returned to me without indorsement.

I understand General Ransom has left the State.

Did you intend by your letters to me that I should assume command of all outside the District of Cape Fear, or will you give an order to that effect? In either case please designate the place you prefer for headquarters.

I have heard nothing from General Ransom since you left.

Communicate with me by mail at Tarborough, where a line of couriers meets the mail. By telegraph I should hear sooner from Goldsborough, unless it is just in time at Rocky Mount for the Tarborough train, at 7 o'clock in the evening.

I am, general, yours, with respect,

J. G. MARTIN,
Brigadier-General.

HEADQUARTERS ARMY OF NORTHERN VIRGINIA,
June 2, 1863.

His Excellency JEFFERSON DAVIS,
President of the Confederate States, Richmond, Va.:

Mr. PRESIDENT: I have had the honor to receive yesterday your letter of the 31st ultimo.

I am well aware of the difficulties pressing upon all parts of the country and of your great anxiety to relieve them. The question which seems always to be presented is a wise choice of difficulties.

I think Cooke's brigade had better be halted on the Chickahominy for the present, and Davis' brigade sent forward to this place to complete Heth's division. I regret to lose Ransom and Jenkins, both good and tried officers, with veteran troops. As well as I now recollect, Pettigrew's brigade was on the line of the Blackwater when the regiments from the West were brigaded there under Pryor.

Upon the arrival of General Longstreet he made some changes, detaching Jenkins, in whom he had confidence, from Pickett's division, in order to place him in command. The Western brigade was placed subsequently under General Colston, and afterward the brigade was broken up and the regiments sent back to Generals Jones and Marshall.

I do not know the condition of the cavalry proposed by General Hill to be sent to this army. He offered a regiment and I accepted it, but if it is of the character described by you it had better be retained. I understand there is a good regiment on the Blackwater as regards men and horses, but it is at present in an unfortunate condition on account of a difficulty between the colonel and officers. If that could be reconciled they would be very serviceable.

I think it would be better if General Robertson were in command of the cavalry within the State, as he is a good organizer and instructor, but General Hill does not appear to require him. I would then brigade the North Carolina regiments in this army, under Colonel Baker, from that State, who is said to be a good officer.

I requested to be relieved from command of the troops between the James and the Cape Fear Rivers because I did not see that I could advantageously exercise it, but, on the contrary, to continue in it might be productive of harm. I could only exercise it beneficially by relying upon the judgment of General D. H. Hill, who declined to act upon discretionary orders, and I thought it best for the service to leave him to his own discretion. The only object of command, in my opinion, is the benefit of the service.

I hope the forces we can place near Richmond will be able to secure it against attack from the York or James River. The local troops of the city should be organized promptly and be kept in readiness for service at any moment. With Cooke and Wise advanced, the one to the north and the other to the east, under Elzey, we will have a sufficient out-guard, and for the present I will leave Pickett and Pettigrew at the Junction. If I am able to move I propose to do so cautiously, watching the result, and not to get beyond recall until I find it safe.

If a brigade of cavalry under a good officer could be placed north and east of the city to repress the marauding expeditions of the enemy and prevent reconnaissances, I should feel it was safe. In case of emergency I think General Hill's troops could be brought up from North Carolina and be replaced there by some from General Beauregard.

I still hope that General Johnston will be able to demolish Grant, and that our command of the Mississippi may be preserved. The enemy may be drawing to the Yazoo for the purpose of reaching their transports and retiring from the contest, which I hope is the case. General Kirby Smith ought, if possible, to collect a sufficient force and occupy Helena or some better point on the west bank of the river.

As far as I can ascertain the enemy seems to be quiet in Western Virginia and the troops of General Sam. Jones are idle. They could also be brought to Richmond or to Eastern Virginia if occasion require it.

I am, with great respect, your obedient servant,

R. E. LEE,
General.

GREENVILLE, N. C., *Tuesday, June* 2, 1863—a. m.
Major-General HILL, *Petersburg :*

GENERAL: I received this morning yours of the 31st. Colonel Griffin is now in Bertie looking after his picket posts. I will send for him at once and hope to have him ready to march promptly. Please recollect that this will leave me entirely without cavalry.

No negro laborers have yet reported. A company of the Seventeenth is still out for deserters. Would it not be better to return Captain MacRae to the camp of instruction, to be used for this purpose, and the company of the Seventeenth take his place at Weldon?

There have been a good many desertions from the Forty-second. The deserters of that regiment to be shot are here. Shall I send to Richmond to the penitentiary the men so sentenced or to Fort Caswell? I think I could manage the Conscript Bureau, but I did not report myself incapable of field service. I can and am willing to stand the increased suffering if it is necessary and whenever necessary.

Very truly, yours,

J. G. MARTIN,
Brigadier-General.

GREENVILLE, *June* 2, 1863.
Maj. Gen. D. H. HILL,
Comdg. Dept. of Virginia and N. Carolina, Petersburg, Va.:

GENERAL: Your letter of the 29th of May came here to-day by the mail about 2 o'clock. I have persons employed trying to get information of the enemy's force and movements in and about Washington and Plymouth. As yet no decided success has resulted.

The horses taken by Griffin and Claiborne were ordered to be returned some days since. I have not heard how many, if any, they now have. I think, however, I can make the arrangement you suggest about using infantry as couriers, &c., in place of Griffin's men.

Colonel Griffin has been spoken to once about answering your letter;

he said he had prepared an answer which he would soon send, but it has not come in. I wrote you this morning that he was now in Bertie.

You said nothing about Moore's battery. What is to be done with Griffin's artillery company? It seems to me a dead waste of horses to put an artillery company in one of our regiments of cavalry.

Reports in town to-day from the country people on the other side of the river that the enemy is reducing his force in Washington. No fact mentioned showing this to be the case.

One of the men sent toward Plymouth reported to Colonel Martin to-day that only three regiments remain in and near Plymouth—Eighty-eighth Pennsylvania and Ninty-sixth and One hundred and third New York. The Ninty-sixth is at Warren's Neck, still intrenching there, and also immediately around the town. It may be necessary for me to keep one company of Griffin's regiment for some days, whilst I am making the arrangement for the infantry to take their places as cavalry or couriers.

I have sent parties out on the Chowan to try to find out something of what is going on there. Will keep you informed of everything I hear.

I am, general, very truly, yours,

J. G. MARTIN,
Brigadier-General.

The enemy is evidently increasing his intrenchments at Washington as well as Plymouth. I infer from this he intends to reduce his force.

WAR DEPARTMENT, C. S. A.,
Richmond, June 2, 1863.

General R. E. LEE, *Near Fredericksburg :*

Reliable intelligence informs that the enemy have evacuated West Point, and probably to a great extent Yorktown and Gloucester Point, and are marching in a column of 2,000 or 3,000 men on both sides of the Piankatank northwest. This may be meant to cover some movement of Hooker to the Lower Rappahannock, and across or up the Piankatank, or it may be a mere diversion. You can best judge. I telegraph the above to the commander at Hanover Junction for his information.

J. A. SEDDON,
Secretary of War.

HEADQUARTERS DIVISION,
Taylorsville, June 2, 1863.

Maj. Gen. ARNOLD ELZEY, *Commanding, &c., Richmond :*

GENERAL : I received last night about 12 o'clock a telegram addressed to the commanding officer at Hanover Junction and from the Secretary of War, to the effect that a strong cavalry force of the enemy was reported upon reliable authority advancing up King and Queen County, and to guard the railroad bridges over the Mattapony. This being more in General Pettigrew's line, and he being under your command, at least so considered by me, I immediately sent a staff officer to communicate with him. He placed little or no credence in the report; said that he had a cavalry scout already out in the direction indicated; that all the railroad bridges are guarded. He did not seem to know, however, anything regarding Milford Depot. I attempted to telegraph Milford to ascertain what, if any, force was there, but failed. I advised him to send to Hanover Court-House a guard, but he replied he had no force to spare. I therefore, considering it important, started one of Arm istead's regiments for that point at 4 a. m. this morning. I suppose, however, General P. has communicated the steps he may have taken.

I received a telegram yesterday from General Lee to send 8 wagons and a guard to Newton for bacon. I know of no such place. Telegraphed immediately to find out what place was meant. As usual from those headquarters, received no reply. There is a place called Newtown in King and Queen County; that may be the one intended. I detailed the guard, but have not ordered the train off on account of the news of the cavalry raid. Please communicate with the Secretary of War in regard to these matters, letting him know what steps I have taken, and telegraph me at once should anything have been developed.

I send this by my aide-de-camp, Captain Baird, who will go in on horseback, neither myself nor staff being allowed to travel on the Fredericksburg cars without an order from General Lee. This circumstance and its great detriment to the facilities of expediting military movements of importance I have reported three times to General Lee's headquarters (first communication two weeks since), but cannot obtain even the scratch of a pen in reply. It would be well, general, to mention this fact to the Secretary of War, asking for some authority for you and myself to communicate directly with each other and by this train. I sent my assistant adjutant-general down by the Fredericksburg train the other day on duty and he was summarily ejected at Ashland.

Captain Baird has just returned from a scout to the Rappahannock and can probably give you some information concerning that portion of the country. I am under orders to be ready to move at a moment's notice with three days' rations; no route indicated.

If there is nothing to prevent it, and you think it not injudicious, I will come in on the Central train and meet you at your office this evening about 6.30.

I am, general, very respectfully, your obedient servant,

GEO. E. PICKETT,
Major-General.

[Indorsements.]

WAR DEPARTMENT, *June 2, 1863.*

This paper was forwarded by General Pickett through me to General Elzey, who requested me to lay it before the honorable Secretary of War, as he was unable from sickness to see him personally.

Respectfully submitted,

E. R. BAIRD,
Aide-de-Camp.

For conference with General Elzey 3d June, 1863.

J. A. S.,
Secretary.

SOUTH ANNA BRIDGE, *June 3, 1863.*

[Hon. JAMES A. SEDDON:]

The enemy encamped last night at Norman's Ferry, on the Pamunkey, and are now advancing, I think, to South Anna Bridge. Until further developments I shall keep one regiment and one gun at North Anna; the balance I have concentrated here. I am glad you are sending more men. One more regiment will be enough. Reports vary as to their strength from 3,000 to 10,000. My position at South Anna is strong, and unless the enemy turn me I have no fear. I will do my best.

E. D. HALL,
Colonel, Commanding.

PETERSBURG, VA., *June* 3, 1863.

Hon. JAMES A. SEDDON,
    Secretary of War, C. S. A.:

I hope that I will not be regarded as intrusive for again urging that Ransom be sent to North Carolina.

The political reasons are still stronger than the military. I am satisfied that if the Yankees get on the railroad there will be an amount of toryism developed not now dreamed of. Mr. Warren, of Beaufort, one of the Governor's council, said in a speech in the Legislature that if the enemy got possession of the railroad it would be time for North Carolina to decide to whom her allegiance was due, the United States or Confederate States Government. Holden and his followers are ready to go to Goldsborough to meet the Yankees and welcome them to the State.

The Forty-second and Seventeenth North Carolina regiments are large and strong, and I would be willing to give up either of them to secure Ransom, and I presume either has as many men as his brigade.

Very respectfully,

D. H. HILL,
Major-General.

HEADQUARTERS FORCES LOCAL DEFENSE,
Third Line of Defenses, Darbytown Road, June 3, 1863.

Maj. T. O. CHESTNEY,
    Assistant Adjutant-General, &c., Richmond, Va.:

MAJOR: I have the honor to report that in obedience to instructions the forces for local defense are distributed on the Charles City, Darbytown, and New Market roads, viz, about 600 on the former, under Lieutenant-Colonel Brown; about 600 on the second, under Major Waller; about 350 on the third, under Lieutenant Minor (Navy). One thousand of the militia were reported on the way last night, and were directed to be posted on the Varina road.

Everything quiet here.

Very respectfully,

G. W. C. LEE,
Brigadier-General.

P. S.—I omitted to mention that there is one boat howitzer on the New Market road and none on the other two roads of which I have charge. If there is danger of attack on these roads artillery is necessary.

WAR DEPARTMENT, C. S. A.,
Richmond, June 3, 1863.

General R. E. LEE:

Information fully confirmed as to the evacuation of West Point and movement of column of 4,000 or 5,000 of the enemy, flanked by a circling cavalry detachment, probably as scouts, on the north and west side, to the Rappahannock, in Essex, near Tappahannock.

J. A. SEDDON,
Secretary of War.

APPENDIX.

Embracing documents received too late for insertion in proper sequence.

UNION CORRESPONDENCE, ETC.

Organization of troops in the Department of Virginia, Seventh Army Corps, commanded by Maj. Gen. John A. Dix, January 31, 1863.

Camp Hamilton, Va.

Col. ANTHONY CONK.

139th New York, Col. Anthony Conk.
11th Pennsylvania Cavalry, Company C, First Lieut. Augustus H. D. Williams.
Battalion Pennsylvania Heavy Artillery (four companies), Maj. Joseph Roberts.

Fort Monroe, Va.

Col. SAMUEL M. ALFORD.

3d New York, Col. Samuel M. Alford.

NORFOLK, VA.

Brig. Gen. EGBERT L. VIELE.

99th New York, Col. David W. Wardrop.
148th New York, Lieut. Col. George M. Guion.
173d Pennsylvania, Col. Daniel Nagle.
19th Wisconsin, Lieut. Col. Charles Whipple.
11th Pennsylvania Cavalry, Company M, Capt. Gerard Reynolds.
New York Light Artillery, 7th Battery, Capt. Peter C. Regan.

SUFFOLK, VA.

Maj. Gen. JOHN J. PECK.

Corcoran's Irish Legion.

Brig. Gen. MICHAEL CORCORAN.

69th New York, Capt. Jasper M. Whitty.
155th New York, Col. William McEvily.
164th New York, Lieut. Col. James C. Burke.
170th New York, Lieut. Col. James P. McIvor.

Terry's Brigade.

Brig. Gen. HENRY D. TERRY.

130th New York, Col. Alfred Gibbs.
167th Pennsylvania, Col. Charles A Knoderer.
177th Pennsylvania, Col. George B. Wiestling.

Provisional Brigade.

Col. ROBERT S. FOSTER.

13th Indiana, Lieut. Col. Cyrus J. Dobbs.
6th Massachusetts, Col. Albert S. Follansbee.
112th New York, Col. Jeremiah C. Drake.
165th Pennsylvania, Col. Charles H. Buehler.
166th Pennsylvania, Col. Andrew J. Fulton.
7th Company U. S. Sharpshooters, Capt. Joseph S. Arnold.

(1093)

Unassigned.

1st New York Mounted Rifles, Col. Charles C. Dodge.
11th Pennsylvania Cavalry, Col. Samuel P. Spear.
Massachusetts Light Artillery, 7th Battery, Capt. Phineas A. Davis.
4th U. S. Artillery, Battery D, Capt. Frederick M. Follett.
4th U. S. Artillery, Battery L, Capt. Robert V. W. Howard.
Wisconsin Light Artillery, 2d Battery, Capt. Charles Beger.
Wisconsin Light Artillery, 4th Battery, First Lieut. George B. Easterly.

YORKTOWN, VA.*

Maj. Gen. ERASMUS D. KEYES.

Busteed's Brigade.	*Reserve Artillery, Fourth Corps.*
Brig. Gen. RICHARD BUSTEED.	Lieut. Col. EDWARD H. FLOOD.
4th Delaware, Col. Arthur H. Grimshaw.	New York Light Artillery, 8th Battery, Capt. Butler Fitch.
169th Pennsylvania, Col. Lewis W. Smith.	1st Pennsylvania Light Artillery, Battery E, Capt. Thomas G. Orwig.
178th Pennsylvania, Col. James Johnson.	1st Pennsylvania Light Artillery, Battery H, Capt. Andrew Fagan.
179th Pennsylvania, Col. William H. Blair.	5th U. S. Artillery, Battery M, Capt. James McKnight.

Unassigned.

172d Pennsylvania, Col. Charles Kleckner.
6th New York Cavalry (3d Battalion), Maj. William P. Hall.
5th Pennsylvania Cavalry, Lieut. Col. William Lewis.
1st New York Light Artillery, Battery F, Capt. William R. Wilson.
1st New York Light Artillery, Battery H, Lieut. Charles E. Mink.

CONFEDERATE CORRESPONDENCE. ETC.

HEADQUARTERS. *Petersburg, Va., March 12, 1863.*
His Excellency ZEBULON B. VANCE, *Governor of North Carolina:*

SIR: Your favor of the 4th instant was received at Wilmington on the 8th. The removal of General Pryor from the Blackwater was made necessary by other movements of troops. I can assure you and the good people in whose behalf you write that the change will in no way disparage their interest. The officer now in command on the Blackwater is one of our most energetic and enterprising brigadiers. I can safely assure you that yourself and the citizens will be quite well satisfied with the change after the officer is known. General Pryor's command was only in this department for the winter. It will soon return to the command where it properly belongs—Western Virginia. I hope that this may be a satisfactory explanation of the recent change on the Blackwater.

I thank you sincerely for your kind expressions about myself, and trust that I may be able to fulfill your expectations. We have many difficulties to contend with, and one of the most serious is the want of system and order in our transportation. If you can assist us in regulating this, I think that we can promise you important results in our operations.

---

* Includes troops at Gloucester Point and Williamsburg, Va.

It was my intention to have done myself the honor to make you a flying visit, but I find that I cannot well quit my post.

With the greatest respect, I am, your most obedient servant,

JAMES LONGSTREET,
Lieutenant-General, Commanding.

GENERAL ORDERS, } ADJT. AND INSPECTOR GEN.'S OFFICE,
No. 112.   }   *Richmond, August 15, 1863.*

I. A court of inquiry having been convened at Richmond on the 29th of July, 1863, pursuant to Paragraph XVII, Special Orders, No. 176, Adjutant and Inspector General's Office, current series, to examine into certain charges preferred against Maj. William Norris, chief of the signal corps, and having made the required examination, the report of facts proven, with the opinion of the court thereon, is published for the information of all concerned.

REPORT OF FACTS.

1. Major Norris was not intoxicated on the 31st of May, 1863.
2. He did not reveal the alphabet of the signal corps on the 31st of May, 1863.
3. The enemy knew, or had opportunity to know, the locality of the signal stations between City Point and Clairmont before the 31st of May, 1863, none of which were disclosed to him by Major Norris on that day.
4. The dispatch shown to Captain Mulford by Major Norris was a private dispatch, conveying a report of successes at Vicksburg.
5. There was no improper intercourse between Major Norris and any officers or persons in the service of the enemy, on the 31st of May, 1863.

OPINION.

I. The court is of opinion that the charges in this case have been loosely made, and without due care and investigation, and should not be further entertained. The court is also of opinion that the private and official character of Major Norris remain unaffected by this proceeding.

II. The charges, of which Major Norris has been thus fully exonerated by the court, were made without that consideration which their serious character demanded, and in a manner that subjects the prosecutor, Lieut. R. A. Forbes, Second Company Independent Signal Corps, to the grave censure of the department. The personal and official character of an officer is not to be lightly assailed. The accuser will be held to support his charges by evidence; and in an especial manner is he required to avoid creating the impression that the loose, unofficial statements of others are facts within his own knowledge. The greatest care and consideration should be manifested by those preferring charges, particularly when the reputation, personal and professional, of a superior is called in question.

III. The court of inquiry, of which Lieut. Col. George Deas, Adjutant-General's Department, was president, is hereby dissolved.

By order:

S. COOPER,
Adjutant and Inspector General.

ALTERNATE DESIGNATIONS OF ORGANIZATIONS MENTIONED IN THIS VOLUME.*

Adams' (Zachariah T.) **Artillery.** See *North Carolina Troops, 2d Regiment, Battery D.*

Alexander's (Aldon) **Artillery.** See *Montgomery True Blues Artillery.*

Alexandria Artillery. See *Virginia Troops.*

Alford's (Samuel M.) **Infantry.** See *New York Troops, 3d Regiment.*

Allen's (L. W.) **Cavalry.** See *Wren's Cavalry.*

Allen's (L. M.) **Infantry.** See *North Carolina Troops, Confederate, 64th Regiment.*

Allen's (William A.) **Infantry.** See *North Carolina Troops, Confederate, 51st Regiment.*

Allis' (James A.) **Artillery.** See *New York Troops.*

Amory's (Thomas J. C.) **Infantry.** See *Massachusetts Troops, 17th Regiment.*

Anderson's (Hiram, jr.) **Infantry.** See *New York Troops, 92d Regiment.*

Angel's (James R.) **Artillery.** See *New York Troops, 3d Regiment, Battery K.*

Armistead's (A. D.) **Artillery.** See *Virginia Troops.*

Armor's (David M.) **Infantry.** See *Pennsylvania Troops, 101st Regiment.*

Arnold's (Job) **Infantry.** See *Rhode Island Troops, 5th Regiment.*

Arnold's (Joseph S.) **Sharpshooters.** See *New York Troops, 1st Battalion.*

Ashby's (George E.) **Artillery.** See *New York Troops, 3d Regiment, Battery E.*

Avirett's (John Alfred, jr.) **Infantry.** See *Alabama Troops.*

Bachman's (W. K.) **Artillery.** See *German Artillery.*

Badham's (William, jr.) **Artillery.** See *North Carolina Troops, Confederate, 3d Battalion, Battery B.*

Baker's (John A.) **Cavalry.** See *North Carolina Troops, Confederate, 3d Regiment.*

Ball's (William B.) **Cavalry.** See *Virginia Troops, 15th Regiment.*

Barham's (Theo. G.) **Cavalry.** See *Virginia Troops.*

Barnes' (Calvin) **Artillery.** See *North Carolina Troops, Confederate.*

Barnes' (H. M.) **Artillery.** See *North Carolina Troops, Confederate, 10th Battalion, Company B.*

Bartholomew's (Walter G.) **Infantry.** See *Massachusetts Troops, 27th Regiment.*

Barton's (James) **Infantry.** See *Massachusetts Troops, 3d Regiment.*

Beach's (Francis) **Infantry.** See *Connecticut Troops, 16th Regiment.*

Beger's (Charles) **Artillery.** See *Wisconsin Troops, 2d Battery.*

Belger's (James) **Artillery.** See *Rhode Island Troops, 1st Regiment, Battery F.*

Belknap's (Jonathan S.) **Infantry.** See *New York Troops, 85th Regiment.*

Bell's (D) **Cavalry.** See *North Carolina Troops, Confederate, 4th Regiment.*

Bierer's (Everard) **Infantry.** See *Pennsylvania Troops, 171st Regiment.*

Blair's (William H.) **Infantry.** See *Pennsylvania Troops, 179th Regiment.*

Blake's (John A.) **Artillery.** See *Pennsylvania Troops, 3d Regiment, Heavy.*

Blount's (J. G.) **Artillery.** See *Virginia Troops.*

Boggs' (Francis J.) **Artillery.** See *Virginia Troops, 12th Battalion.*

Boughton's (Horace) **Infantry.** See *New York Troops, 143d Regiment.*

Bowler's (George) **Infantry.** See *Massachusetts Troops, 46th Regiment.*

Boyce's (R.) **Artillery.** See *Macbeth Artillery.*

Brabble's (E. C.) **Infantry.** See *North Carolina Troops, Confederate, 32d Regiment.*

Bradberry's (John J.) **Infantry.** See *North Carolina Troops, Confederate.*

Bradford's (W. D.) **Artillery.** See *Confederate Guards Artillery.*

Bradley's (Thomas) **Sharpshooters.** See *New York Troops, 1st Battalion.*

Brady's (H. J.) **Infantry.** See *Pennsylvania Troops, 177th Regiment.*

Branch's (J. R.) **Artillery.** See *Virginia Troops.*

Brockway's (C. B.) **Artillery.** See *Pennsylvania Troops, 1st Regiment, Battery E.*

Brown's (H. W.) **Cavalry.** See *S. H. Mix's Cavalry.*

Brown's (Jack) **Infantry.** See *Georgia Troops, 59th Regiment.*

* References are to index following.

Brown's (John C.) **Infantry.** See *Enfans Perdus Infantry.*

Brown's (John E.) **Infantry.** See *North Carolina Troops, Confederate, 42d Regiment.*

Brown's (William R.) **Infantry.** See *New York Troops, 168th Regiment.*

Brown's (W. Leroy) **Infantry.** See *Virginia Troops, 5th Battalion, Local Defense (Arsenal).*

Buehler's (Charles H.) **Infantry.** See *Pennsylvania Troops, 165th Regiment.*

Buffum's (Martin P.) **Infantry.** See *Rhode Island Troops, 4th Regiment.*

Buie's (Duncan M.) **Artillery.** See *North Carolina Troops, Confederate.*

Bunting's (S. R.) **Artillery.** See *North Carolina Troops, Confederate.*

Burgwyn's (H. K., jr.) **Infantry.** See *North Carolina Troops, Confederate, 26th Regiment.*

Burhans' (Charles H.) **Infantry.** See *New York Troops, 96th Regiment.*

Burke's (James C.) **Infantry.** See *New York Troops, 164th Regiment.*

Burnham's (George S.) **Infantry.** See *Connecticut Troops, 22d Regiment.*

Burpee's (Thomas F.) **Infantry.** See *Connecticut Troops, 21st Regiment.*

Burroughs' (Edgar) **Cavalry.** See *Virginia Troops, 15th Regiment.*

Burwell's (Philip L.) **Infantry.** See *North Carolina Troops, Confederate.*

Cabot's (Edward C.) **Infantry.** See *Massachusetts Troops, 44th Regiment.*

Cady's (A. Lester) **Artillery.** See *Jay E. Lee's Artillery.*

Camden Guerrillas. See *Willis B. Sanderlin's Infantry.*

Campbell's (David) **Cavalry.** See *Pennsylvania Troops, 5th Regiment.*

Campbell's (Edward) **Infantry.** See *Pennsylvania Troops, 85th Regiment.*

Cantwell's (J. L.) **Infantry.** See *North Carolina Troops, Confederate, 51st Regiment.*

Cape Fear Artillery. See *North Carolina Troops, Confederate.*

Carroll's (Gray) **Artillery.** See *Stribling's Artillery.*

Caskie's (William H.) **Artillery.** See *Hampden Artillery.*

Cassel's (John) **Cavalry.** See *S. P. Spear's Cavalry.*

Chambers' (John G.) **Infantry.** See *Massachusetts Troops, 23d Regiment.*

Chambliss' (John R., jr.) **Cavalry.** See *Virginia Troops, 13th Regiment.*

Chesterfield Artillery. See *South Carolina Troops.*

Church's (George E.) **Infantry.** See *Rhode Island Troops, 11th Regiment.*

Claassen's (Peter J.) **Infantry.** See *New York Troops, 132d Regiment.*

Claiborne's (W. C.) **Cavalry.** See *Confederate Troops, Regulars, 7th Regiment.*

Clark Artillery. See *North Carolina Troops, Confederate, Rankin's Artillery.*

Clarke's (William J.) **Infantry.** See *North Carolina Troops, Confederate, 24th Regiment.*

Clark's (John D.) **Artillery.** See *New York Troops, 3d Regiment, Battery H.*

Clopton's (Thomas C.) **Cavalry.** See *Wren's Cavalry.*

Codman's (Charles R.) **Infantry.** See *Massachusetts Troops, 45th Regiment.*

Coffin's (Frederic J.) **Infantry.** See *Massachusetts Troops, 8th Regiment.*

Cogdell's (D. A.) **Infantry.** See *John N. Whitford's Partisans.*

Coit's (J. C.) **Artillery.** See *Chesterfield Artillery.*

Cole's (George W.) **Cavalry.** See *S. H. Mix's Cavalry.*

Comfort's (Felix) **Infantry.** See *Enfans Perdus Infantry.*

Confederate Guard Infantry. See *Virginia Troops.*

Confederate Guards Artillery. See *Mississippi Troops.*

Conk's (Anthony) **Infantry.** See *New York Troops, 139th Regiment.*

Connally's (John K.) **Infantry.** See *North Carolina Troops, Confederate, 55th Regiment.*

Cornog's (George T.) **Cavalry.** See *S. P. Spear's Cavalry.*

Crabb's (George W.) **Artillery.** See *Union Troops, Regulars, 5th Regiment, Battery A.*

Crosby's (Hiram B.) **Infantry.** See *Connecticut Troops, 21st Regiment.*

Crowninshield's (Casper) **Cavalry.** See *Massachusetts Troops, 2d Regiment.*

Cullen's (Edgar M.) **Infantry.** See *New York Troops, 96th Regiment.*

Culpeper's (J. F.) **Artillery.** See *Palmetto Battalion, Battery C.*

Cumming's (James D.) **Artillery.** See *Cape Fear Artillery.*

Cumming's (Emory) **Cavalry.** See *New York Troops, 23d Battalion.*

Curtis' (N. M.) **Infantry.** See *New York Troops, 142d Regiment.*

Curtiss' (Carlton B.) **Infantry.** See *Pennsylvania Troops, 58th Regiment.*

Dabney's (W. J.) **Artillery.** See *Virginia Troops.*

Dandy's (George B.) **Infantry.** See *New York Troops, 100th Regiment.*

Darling's (John A.) **Heavy Artillery.** See *Joseph Roberts' Artillery.*

Davis' (Hasbrouck) **Cavalry.** See *Illinois Troops, 12th Regiment.*

Davis' (James E.) **Artillery.** See *Montgomery True Blues Artillery.*

Davis' (Joseph D.) **Infantry.** See *Pennsylvania Troops, 167th Regiment.*

Davis' (Phineas A.) **Artillery.** See *Massachusetts Troops, 7th Battery.*

Davis' (William W. H.) **Infantry.** See *Pennsylvania Troops, 104th Regiment.*

Day's (Joseph M.) **Infantry.** See *Massachusetts Troops, 40th Regiment.*

Day's (Samuel C.) **Artillery.** See *Joseph J. Morrison's Artillery.*

De Forest's (Jacob J.) **Infantry.** See *New York Troops, 81st Regiment.*

Denny's (J. Waldo) **Infantry.** See *A. B. R. Sprague's Infantry.*

Derrom's (Andrew) **Infantry.** See *New Jersey Troops, 25th Regiment.*

Devane's (W. S.) **Infantry.** See *North Carolina Troops, Confederate, 61st Regiment.*

Dobbs' (Cyrus J.) **Infantry.** See *Indiana Troops, 13th Regiment.*

Doby's (James) **Cavalry.** See *Holcombe Legion.*

Dodge's (Charles C.) **Mounted Rifles.** See *New York Troops, 7th Regiment, Cavalry*

Dodge's (John C., jr.) **Infantry.** See *Pennsylvania Troops, 52d Regiment.*

Donohoe's (Michael T.) **Infantry.** See *New Hampshire Troops, 10th Regiment.*

Drake's (Jeremiah C.) **Infantry.** See *New York Troops, 112th Regiment.*

Drennan's (James M.) **Infantry.** See *A. B. R. Sprague's Infantry.*

Duke's (R. T. W.) **Infantry.** See *Virginia Troops, 46th Regiment.*

Durkee's (Charles) **Infantry.** See *New York Troops, 98th Regiment.*

Dyer's (Samuel A.) **Infantry.** See *Pennsylvania Troops, 175th Regiment.*

Easterly's (George B.) **Artillery.** See *Wisconsin Troops, 4th Battery.*

Edmands' (T. F.) **Infantry.** See *Massachusetts Troops, 24th Regiment.*

Edmundson's (H. A.) **Cavalry.** See *Virginia Troops, 27th Battalion, P. R.*

Elliott's (John Thompson) **Infantry.** See *North Carolina Troops, Confederate.*

Ellis' (Andrew J.) **Artillery.** See *North Carolina Troops, Confederate, 3d Battalion, Battery A.*

Elwell's (Andrew) **Infantry.** See *Massachusetts Troops, 23d Regiment.*

Enfans Perdus Infantry. See *New York Troops.*

England's (Theophilus L.) **Infantry.** See *New York Troops, 89th Regiment.*

Eure's (M. L.) **Cavalry.** See *North Carolina Troops, Confederate, 2d Regiment.*

Evans' (P. G.) **Cavalry.** See *North Carolina Troops, Confederate, 5th Regiment.*

Ewer's (Barnabas, jr.) **Infantry.** See *Massachusetts Troops, 3d Regiment.*

Fagan's (Andrew) **Artillery.** See *Pennsylvania Troops, 1st Regiment, Battery H.*

Faison's (Paul F.) **Infantry.** See *North Carolina Troops, Confederate, 56th Regiment.*

Farrar's (Judson S.) **Infantry.** See *Michigan Troops, 26th Regiment.*

Fauquier Artillery. See *Virginia Troops.*

Fellows' (John F.) **Infantry.** See *Massachusetts Troops, 17th Regiment.*

Ferebee's (D. D.) **Cavalry.** See *North Carolina Troops, Confederate, 4th Regiment.*

Ferguson's (Alonzo) **Infantry.** See *New York Troops, 152d Regiment.*

Fitch's (Butler) **Artillery.** See *New York Troops, 8th Battery.*

Fitz Simmons' (Charles) **Cavalry.** See *S. H. Mix's Cavalry.*

Flemming's (J. A.) **Infantry.** See *North Carolina Troops, Confederate, 49th Regiment.*

Follansbee's (Albert S.) **Infantry.** See *Massachusetts Troops, 6th Regiment.*

Follett's (Frederick M.) **Artillery.** See *Union Troops, Regulars, 4th Regiment, Battery D.*

Folk's (George N.) **Cavalry.** See *North Carolina Troops, Confederate, 7th Battalion.*

Foster's (Robert S.) **Infantry.** See *Indiana Troops, 13th Regiment.*

Frankle's (Jones) **Infantry.** See *Massachusetts Troops,* 17th *Regiment.*
French's (D. A.) **Artillery.** See *Virginia Troops.*
Fuller's (Thomas C.) **Artillery.** See *J. B. Starr's Artillery.*
Fulton's (Andrew J.) **Infantry.** See *Pennsylvania Troops,* 166th *Regiment.*
Garden's (H. R.) **Artillery.** See *Palmetto Artillery.*
Garrard's (Jeptha) **Cavalry.** See *S. H. Mix's Cavalry.*
Garrett's (W. N.) **Infantry.** See *L. M. Allen's Infantry.*
Gee's (B. H.) **Infantry.** See *Georgia Troops,* 59th *Regiment.*
German Artillery. See *South Carolina Troops.*
Gibbs' (Alfred) **Infantry.** See *New York Troops,* 130th *Regiment.*
Gibbs' (George C.) **Infantry.** See *North Carolina Troops, Confederate,* 42d *Regiment.*
Gibson's (A. A.) **Artillery.** See *Pennsylvania Troops,* 2d *Regiment, Heavy.*
Gilliss' (James) **Artillery.** See *Union Troops, Regulars,* 5th *Regiment, Battery A.*
Goode's (J. Thomas) **Artillery.** See *Virginia Troops,* 4th *Regiment, Heavy.*
Graham's (Edward) **Artillery.** See *Petersburg Rocket Artillery.*
Graham's (G. W.) **Infantry.** See *North Carolina Troops, Union,* 1st *Regiment.*
Graham's (J.) **Artillery.** See *North Carolina Troops, Confederate,* 1st *Regt., Bat'y C.*
Graham's (W. A.) **Cavalry.** See *North Carolina Troops, Confederate,* 2d *Regiment.*
Grammer's (W. T.) **Infantry.** See *Massachusetts Troops,* 5th *Regiment.*
Gray's (Charles O.) **Infantry.** See *New York Troops,* 96th *Regiment.*
Gregory's (David E.) **Infantry.** See *New York Troops,* 144th *Regiment.*
Griffin's (Joel R.) **Cavalry.** See *Georgia Troops,* 62d *Regiment.*
Grimshaw's (Arthur H.) **Infantry.** See *Delaware Troops,* 4th *Regiment.*
Guion's (George M.) **Infantry.** See *New York Troops,* 148th *Regiment.*
Hall's (E. D.) **Infantry.** See *North Carolina Troops, Confederate,* 46th *Regiment.*
Hall's (Newton) **Artillery.** See *S. H. Mix's Cavalry.*
Hall's (William P.) **Cavalry.** See *New York Troops,* 6th *Regiment.*
Hampden Artillery. See *Virginia Troops.*
Hampton Legion. See *South Carolina Troops.*
Hargrove Blues, Infantry. See *Virginia Troops.*
Harris Light Cavalry. See *New York Troops,* 2d *Regiment.*
Harris' (Thomas W.) **Cavalry.** See *P. G. Evans' Cavalry.*
Harrison's (George P., jr.) **Infantry.** See *Georgia Troops,* 32d *Regiment.*
Hart's (T. D.) **Infantry.** See *Pennsylvania Troops,* 104th *Regiment.*
Hasbrouck's (Henry C.) **Artillery.** See *Union Troops, Regulars,* 4th *Regiment, Battery L.*
Hawkins' (Rush C.) **Infantry.** See *New York Troops,* 9th *Regiment.*
Hawley's (Louis J.) **Cavalry.** See *Virginia Troops,* 10th *Regiment.*
Haynes' (Thomas W.) **Cavalry.** See *Virginia Troops,* 9th *Regiment.*
Heckman's (Charles A.) **Infantry.** See *New Jersey Troops,* 9th *Regiment.*
Heine's (William) **Infantry.** See *New York Troops,* 103d *Regiment.*
Hill's Company. Official designation unknown. See *Captain Hill.*
Hill's (James C.) **Infantry.** See *R. T. W. Duke's Infantry.*
Hiller's (Frederick L.) **Artillery.** See *New York Troops,* 16th *Battery.*
Hinds' (George W.) **Infantry.** See *New York Troops,* 96th *Regiment.*
Hitchcock's (George H.) **Infantry.** See *New York Troops,* 132d *Regiment.*
Holbrook's (Charles L.) **Infantry.** See *Massachusetts Troops,* 43d *Regiment.*
Holcombe Legion. See *South Carolina Troops.*
Holland's (W. A.) **Artillery.** See *North Carolina Troops, Confederate.*
Hook's (Cornelius, jr.) **Artillery.** See *Union Troops, Regulars,* 1st *Regiment, Battery C.*
Howard's (R. V. W.) **Artillery.** See *Union Troops, Regulars,* 4th *Regiment, Battery L.*
Howell's (John H.) **Artillery.** See *New York Troops,* 3d *Regiment, Battery M.*
Howell's (Joshua B.) **Infantry.** See *Pennsylvania Troops,* 85th *Regiment.*
Hudson's (James, jr.) **Infantry.** See *Massachusetts Troops,* 8th *Regiment.*
Humphrey Troop, Cavalry. See *John A. Baker's Cavalry.*

Hunt's (Lewis C.) Infantry.   See *New York Troops*, 92d *Regiment*.
Jack's (Joseph) Infantry.   See *Pennsylvania Troops*, 168th *Regiment*.
Jacobs' (Ferris, jr.) Cavalry.   See *S. H. Mix's Cavalry*.
James City Cavalry.   See *Virginia Troops*, 5th *Regiment*.
Jenney's (Edwin S.) Artillery.   See *New York Troops*, 3d *Regiment, Battery I*.
Jocknick's (George F.) Cavalry.   See *S. H. Mix's Cavalry*.
Johnson's (James) Infantry.   See *Pennsylvania Troops*, 178th *Regiment*.
Johnson's (James A.) Infantry.   See *Pennsylvania Troops*, 172d *Regiment*.
Johnson's (William) Infantry.   See *New York Troops*, 148th *Regiment*.
Jones' (John A.) Infantry.   See *Alabama Troops*, 44th *Regiment*.
Jones' (John Richter) Infantry.   See *Pennsylvania Troops*, 58th *Regiment*.
Jordan's (John V.) Infantry.   See *North Carolina Troops, Confederate*, 31st *Regiment*.
Jourdan's (James) Infantry.   See *New York Troops*, 158th *Regiment*.
Keese's (Oliver, jr.) Infantry.   See *New York Troops*, 118th *Regiment*.
Kenan's (Thomas S.) Infantry.   See *North Carolina Troops, Confederate*, 43d *Regiment*.
Kennedy's (T. J.) Artillery.   See *New York Troops*, 3d *Regiment*.
Kilpatrick's (Judson) Cavalry.   See *New York Troops*, 2d *Regiment*.
King's (Reuben V.) Infantry.   See *New York Troops*, 85th *Regiment*.
Kleckner's (Charles) Infantry.   See *Pennsylvania Troops*, 172d *Regiment*.
Kleinz's (Christopher) Cavalry.   See *Pennsylvania Troops*, 5th *Regiment*.
Knoderer's (Charles A.) Infantry.   See *Pennsylvania Troops*, 167th *Regiment*.
Kurtz's (John) Infantry.   See *Massachusetts Troops*, 23d *Regiment*.
Lamb's (John C.) Infantry.   See *North Carolina Troops, Confederate*, 17th *Regiment*.
Lane's (James S.) Artillery.   See *North Carolina Troops, Confederate*.
Lechler's (A. A.) Infantry.   See *Pennsylvania Troops*, 176th *Regiment*.
Ledlie's (James H.) Artillery.   See *New York Troops*, 3d *Regiment*.
Lee's (Francis L.) Infantry.   See *Massachusetts Troops*, 44th *Regiment*.
Lee's (Horace C.) Infantry.   See *Massachusetts Troops*, 27th *Regiment*.
Lee's (Jay E.) Artillery.   See *New York Troops*, 24th *Battery*.
Lee's (John C.) Infantry.   See *New York Troops*, 99th *Regiment*.
Leggett's (Robert) Infantry.   See *Connecticut Troops*, 10th *Regiment*.
Leventhorpe's (C.) Infantry.   See *North Carolina Troops, Confederate*, 11th *Regiment*.
Lewis' (George W.) Cavalry.   See *New York Troops*, 3d *Regiment*.
Lewis' (W. B.) Artillery.   See *North Carolina Troops, Confederate*, 10th *Battalion, Company A*.
Lewis' (William) Cavalry.   See *Pennsylvania Troops*, 5th *Regiment*.
Littleton's (John K.) Cavalry.   See *Wren's Cavalry*.
Logie's (William K.) Infantry.   See *New York Troops*, 141st *Regiment*.
Lyman's (Luke) Infantry.   See *Massachusetts Troops*, 27th *Regiment*.
Lyon's (C. A.) Infantry.   See *North Carolina Troops, Union*, 1st *Regiment*.
McAfee's (L. M.) Infantry.   See *North Carolina Troops, Confederate*, 49th *Regiment*.
Macbeth Artillery.   See *South Carolina Troops*.
McBryde's (M. H.) Artillery.   See *North Carolina Troops, Confederate*.
McCandless' (William G.) Cavalry.   See *Pennsylvania Troops*, 5th *Regiment*.
McCauley's (C. M. T.) Artillery.   See *North Carolina Troops, Confederate*, 10th *Battalion, Company C*.
McChesney's (Joseph M.) Infantry.   See *North Carolina Troops, Union*, 1st *Regiment*.
McClees' (N.) Artillery.   See *J. W. Moore's Artillery*.
McConihe's (John) Infantry.   See *New York Troops*, 169th *Regiment*.
McDevitt's (Martin) Artillery.   See *John F. Vallee's Artillery*.
McEvily's (William) Infantry.   See *New York Troops*, 155th *Regiment*.
McIntire's (A.) Cavalry.   See *P. G. Evans' Cavalry*.
McIvor's (James P.) Infantry.   See *New York Troops*, 170th *Regiment*.
McKibbin's (David B.) Infantry.   See *Pennsylvania Troops*, 158th *Regiment*.
McKnight's (James) Artillery.   See *Union Troops, Regulars*, 5th *Regiment, Battery* **M**.

McMahon's (James P.) **Infantry.**   See *New York Troops, 164th Regiment.*
McMahon's (J. J.) **Infantry.**   See *Virginia Troops, 63d Regiment.*
McNary's (William H.) **Infantry.**   See *New York Troops, 158th Regiment.*
Macon Artillery.   See *Georgia Troops.*
Macon's (M. C.) **Artillery.**   See *Richmond Fayette Artillery.*
MacRae's (A.) **Artillery.**   See *North Carolina Troops, Confederate.*
Madison Light Artillery.   See *Mississippi Troops.*
Magruder's (John Bowie) **Infantry.**   See *Virginia Troops, 57th Regiment.*
Mallett's (Peter) **Infantry.**   See *North Carolina Troops, Confederate.*
Manchester's (H. A.) **Artillery.**   See *New York Troops, 1st Regiment, Marine Artillery.*
Marshall's (J. K.) **Infantry.**   See *North Carolina Troops, Confederate, 52d Regiment.*
Martin's (S. Taylor) **Artillery.**   See *Virginia Troops.*
Martin's (W. F.) **Infantry.**   See *North Carolina Troops, Confederate, 17th Regiment.*
Maxwell's (Wilson C.) **Infantry.**   See *Pennsylvania Troops, 103d Regiment.*
Mercer's (William E.) **Artillery.**   See *William J. Riggs' Artillery.*
Merriman's (T. Adams) **Infantry.**   See *New York Troops, 92d Regiment.*
Mink's (Charles E.) **Artillery.**   See *New York Troops, 1st Regiment, Battery H.*
Minor's (R. D.) **Infantry.**   See *Virginia Troops, 4th Battalion, Local Defense (Naval).*
Mitchell's (B. B.) **Cavalry.**   See *S. P. Spear's Cavalry.*
Mix's (John) **Cavalry.**   See *New York Troops, 3d Regiment.*
Mix's (Simon H.) **Cavalry.**   See *New York Troops, 3d Regiment.*
Mizell's (Jonathan T.) **Infantry.**   See *North Carolina Troops, Union, 1st Regiment.*
Moise's (E. W.) **Cavalry.**   See *Confederate Troops, 7th Regiment.*
Montgomery True Blues, Artillery.   See *Alabama Troops.*
Moore's (A. C.) **Infantry.**   See *Virginia Troops, 29th Regiment.*
Moore's (A. D.) **Artillery.**   See *North Carolina Troops, Confederate, 1st Regt., Bat'y E.*
Moore's (J. G.) **Artillery.**   See *North Carolina Troops, Confederate, 3d Battalion, Battery C.*
Moore's (Julius W.) **Cavalry.**   See *John A. Baker's Cavalry.*
Moore's (J. W.) **Artillery.**   See *North Carolina Troops, Confederate, 3d Battalion.*
Morris' (David B.) **Infantry.**   See *Pennsylvania Troops, 101st Regiment.*
Morrison's (Joseph) **Infantry.**   See *New York Troops, 89th Regiment.*
Morrison's (Joseph J.) **Artillery.**   See *New York Troops, 3d Regiment, Battery B.*
Moschell's (John F.) **Cavalry.**   See *S. H. Mix's Cavalry.*
Moseley's (E. F.) **Artillery.**   See *Virginia Troops, 1st Regiment.*
Murchison's (Alexander) **Cavalry.**   See *North Carolina Troops, Confederate, 3d Regt.*
Murphy's (Mathew) **Infantry.**   See *New York Troops, 182d Regiment.*
Murray's (Albert M.) **Artillery.**   See *Union Troops, Regulars, 5th Regiment, Battery A.*
Nagle's (Daniel) **Infantry.**   See *Pennsylvania Troops, 173d Regiment.*
Nelson's (William B.) **Cavalry.**   See *Thomas Legion.*
Nethercutt's (J. H.) **Rangers.**   See *North Carolina Troops, Confederate, 8th Battalion.*
Newkirk's (Abram F.) **Cavalry.**   See *John A. Baker's Cavalry.*
Nichols' (J. W.) **Cavalry.**   See *J. R. Griffin's Cavalry.*
Nields' (Benjamin) **Artillery.**   See *Delaware Troops, 1st Battery.*
Norfleet's (Hamlin) **Cavalry.**   See *North Carolina Troops, Confederate.*
Norfolk Blues, Artillery.   See *Virginia Troops.*
Nyce's (John) **Infantry.**   See *Pennsylvania Troops, 174th Regiment.*
Onderdonk's (Benjamin F.) **Cavalry.**   See *New York Troops, 7th Regiment.*
O'Neil's (John) **Artillery.**   See *William J. Riggs' Artillery.*
Orwig's (Thomas G.) **Artillery.**   See *Pennsylvania Troops, 1st Regiment, Battery E.*
Osborn's (Francis A.) **Infantry.**   See *Massachusetts Troops, 24th Regiment.*
Osborn's (Thomas O.) **Infantry.**   See *Illinois Troops, 39th Regiment.*
Otis' (John L.) **Infantry.**   See *Connecticut Troops, 10th Regiment.*
Owens' (W. A.) **Infantry.**   See *North Carolina Troops, Confederate, 53d Regiment.*
Page's (P. R.) **Infantry.**   See *Virginia Troops, 26th Regiment.*

Palmetto Artillery. See *South Carolina Troops.*
Palmetto Battalion Artillery. See *South Carolina Troops.*
Palmetto Sharpshooters. See *South Carolina Troops.*
Pardee's (Benjamin S.) Infantry. See *Connecticut Troops, 10th Regiment.*
Paris' (Andrew B.) Artillery. See *Staunton Hill Artillery.*
Pasquotank Guerrillas, Infantry. See *Elliott's Infantry.*
Patton's (Alexander G.) Cavalry. See *New York Troops, 7th Regiment.*
Pease's (William R.) Infantry. See *New York Troops, 117th Regiment.*
Peirson's (George H.) Infantry. See *Massachusetts Troops, 5th Regiment.*
Perkins' (Elisha A.) Cavalry. See *John A. Baker's Cavalry.*
Petersburg Rocket Artillery. See *Virginia Troops.*
Pickett's (Josiah) Infantry. See *Massachusetts Troops, 25th Regiment.*
Plaisted's (Harris M.) Infantry. See *Maine Troops, 11th Regiment.*
Poage's (Thomas) Infantry. See *Virginia Troops, 50th Regiment.*
Pollock's (W. K.) Artillery. See *Union Troops, Regulars, 1st Regiment, Battery C.*
Pond's (Francis B.) Infantry. See *Ohio Troops, 62d Regiment.*
Pond's (Nathan P.) Cavalry. See *S. H. Mix's Cavalry.*
Pool's (Stephen D.) Artillery. See *North Carolina Troops, Confederate, 1st Regiment.*
Porter's (Francis E.) Infantry See *Massachusetts Troops, 8th Regiment.*
Potter's (Edward E.) Infantry. See *North Carolina Troops, Union, 1st Regiment.*
Preston's (William C.) Artillery. See *South Carolina Troops.*
Radcliffe's (J. D.) Infantry. See *North Carolina Troops, Confederate, 61st Regiment.*
Randolph's (John) Cavalry. See *North Carolina Troops, Confederate, 2d Regiment.*
Rankin's (R. G.) Artillery. See *North Carolina Troops, Confederate.*
Ransom's (Alfred) Artillery. See *New York Troops, 23d Battery.*
Ransom's (M. W.) Infantry. See *North Carolina Troops, Confederate, 35th Regiment.*
Raulston's (William C.) Infantry. See *New York Troops, 81st Regiment.*
Regan's (Peter C.) Artillery. See *New York Troops, 7th Battery.*
Reid's (Thomas M.) Infantry. See *New York Troops, 182d Regiment.*
Reilly's (James) Artillery. See *Rowan Artillery.*
Reinhart's (H. W.) Cavalry. See *John A. Baker's Cavalry.*
Reynolds' (Gerard) Cavalry. See *Pennsylvania Troops, 11th Regiment*
Rhett's (A. Burnet) Artillery. See *South Carolina Troops.*
Richardson's (Colin) Cavalry. See *S. H. Mix's Cavalry.*
Richmond Fayette Artillery. See *Virginia Troops.*
Richmond's (Silas P.) Infantry. See *Massachusetts Troops, 3d Regiment.*
Richter's (Henry M.) Infantry. See *Massachusetts Troops, 25th Regiment.*
Riggs' (William J.) Artillery. See *New York Troops, 3d Regiment, Battery H.*
Ringold's (Benjamin) Infantry. See *New York Troops, 103d Regiment.*
Ripley's (Edward H.) Infantry. See *Vermont Troops, 9th Regiment.*
Roberts' (Joseph) Artillery. See *Pennsylvania Troops, 3d Regiment, Heavy.*
Roberts' (W. Dewees) Cavalry. See *S. P. Spear's Cavalry.*
Robertson's (J. R.) Cavalry. See *Virginia Troops, 32d Battalion.*
Rodgers' (Andrew J.) Cavalry. See *J. R. Robertson's Cavalry.*
Rogers' (S. H.) Infantry. See *North Carolina Troops, Confederate, 47th Regiment.*
Rowan Artillery. See *North Carolina Troops.*
Ryerson's (Henry O.) Infantry. See *New Jersey Troops, 10th Regiment.*
Sanderlin's (Willis B.) Infantry. See *North Carolina Troops, Confederate.*
Sanders' (Enos C.) Infantry. See *North Carolina Troops, Union, 1st Regiment.*
Sanders' (Horace T.) Infantry. See *Wisconsin Troops, 19th Regiment.*
Schultz's (Carl) Artillery. See *Charles Beger's Artillery.*
Shaw's (H. M.) Infantry. See *North Carolina Troops, Confederate, 8th Regiment.*
Shingler's (W. P.) Cavalry. See *Holcombe Legion.*
Shurtleff's (William S.) Infantry. See *Massachusetts Troops, 46th Regiment.*
Slaten's (C. W.) Artillery. See *Macon Artillery.*

Sikes' (J. H.) Cavalry. See *W. C. Claiborne's Cavalry.*
Simpson's (John G.) Artillery. See *Pennsylvania Troops, 1st Regiment, Battery A.*
Simpson's (Thomas) Artillery. See *James Belger's Artillery.*
Sisson's (Henry T.) Infantry. See *Rhode Island Troops, 5th Regiment.*
Small's (Nathaniel W.) Signal Corps. See *Confederate Troops.*
Smith's (Benjamin G.) Cavalry. See *John A. Baker's Cavalry.*
Smith's (Lewis W.) Infantry. See *Pennsylvania Troops, 169th Regiment.*
Smoot's (D. L.) Artillery. See *Alexandria Artillery.*
Spear's (Samuel P.) Cavalry. See *Pennsylvania Troops, 11th Regiment.*
Sprague's (Augustus B. R.) Infantry. See *Massachusetts Troops, 51st Regiment.*
Stahl's (William H.) Artillery. See *New York Troops, 19th Battery.*
Stark's (A. W.) Artillery. See *Armistead's and French's Batteries.*
Starr's (J. B.) Artillery. See *North Carolina Troops, Confederate, 2d Regt., Bat'y B.*
Staunton Hill Artillery. See *Virginia Troops.*
Stedman's (Griffin A., jr.) Infantry. See *Connecticut Troops, 11th Regiment.*
Stevens' (Aaron F.) Infantry. See *New Hampshire Troops, 13th Regiment.*
Stevens' (C. H.) Infantry. See *South Carolina Troops, 24th Regiment.*
Stevenson's (John S.) Artillery. See *Joseph Roberts' Artillery.*
Stevenson's (Robert H.) Infantry. See *Massachusetts Troops, 24th Regiment.*
Stewart's (Charles H.) Artillery. See *New York Troops, 3d Regiment.*
Stone's (Henry M.) Artillery. See *New York Troops, 3d Regiment.*
Storer's (Jacob J.) Infantry. See *New Hampshire Troops, 13th Regiment.*
Stribling's (Robert M.) Artillery. See *Fauquier Artillery.*
Sturdivant's (N. A.) Artillery. See *Virginia Troops.*
Swindell's (Edward S.) Rangers. See *North Carolina Troops, Confederate.*
Tabb's (William B.) Infantry. See *Virginia Troops, 59th Regiment.*
Tait's (George) Artillery. See *North Carolina Troops, Confederate.*
Taylor's (Alexander W.) Infantry. See *Pennsylvania Troops, 101st Regiment.*
Tevis' (C. Carroll) Infantry. See *Delaware Troops, 4th Regiment.*
Tew's (George W.) Infantry. See *Rhode Island Troops, 5th Regiment.*
Thomas' (George W.) Artillery. See *New York Troops, 3d Regiment, Battery I.*
Thomas' (W. H.) Legion Infantry. See *North Carolina Troops, Confederate.*
Thorp's (Thomas J.) Infantry. See *New York Troops, 130th Regiment.*
Tolles (Samuel) Infantry. See *Connecticut Troops, 15th Regiment.*
Trigg's (Robert C.) Infantry. See *Virginia Troops, 54th Regiment.*
Troxel's (Elias S.) Infantry. See *Pennsylvania Troops, 158th Regiment.*
Upham's (Charles L.) Infantry. See *Connecticut Troops, 15th Regiment.*
Vallee's (John F.) Artillery. See *Wisconsin Troops, 4th Battery.*
Van Wyck's (Charles H.) Infantry. See *New York Troops, 56th Regiment.*
Voris' (A. C.) Infantry. See *Ohio Troops, 67th Regiment.*
Vought's (Philip G.) Cavalry. See *New York Troops, 12th Regiment.*
Wall's (John) Artillery. See *New York Troops, 3d Regiment, Battery G.*
Wallace's (G. A.) Infantry. See *W. B. Tabb's Infantry.*
Waller's (Richard P.) Infantry. See *Virginia Troops, 2d Battalion, Local Defense (Quartermaster's Department).*
Ward's (George) Artillery. See *Madison Light Artillery.*
Ward's (John E.) Infantry. See *Connecticut Troops, 8th Regiment.*
Wardrop's (David W.) Infantry. See *New York Troops, 99th Regiment.*
Washington's (J. A.) Infantry. See *North Carolina Troops, Confederate, 50th Regt.*
Waties' (John) Artillery. See *Palmetto Battalion, Battery B.*
Wead's (Frederick F.) Infantry. See *New York Troops, 98th Regiment.*
Webb's (Louis H.) Artillery. See *North Carolina Troops, Confederate.*
Webb's (W. W.) Infantry. See *Connecticut Troops, 10th Regiment.*
Wellman's (Abijah J.) Infantry. See *New York Troops, 85th Regiment.*
Wheelan's (James N.) Cavalry. See *Charles C. Dodge's Cavalry.*

Wheeler's (John J.) Infantry.   See *New York Troops*, 56*th Regiment*.

Wheeler's (S. J.) Cavalry.   See *North Carolina Troops, Confederate*, 12*th Battalion*.

Whipple's (Charles) Infantry.   See *Wisconsin Troops*, 19*th Regiment*.

White's (Alvin) Infantry.   See *New York Troops*, 117*th Regiment*.

White's (David B.) Infantry.   See *New York Troops*, 81*st Regiment*.

Whitford's (John N.) Partisans.   See *North Carolina Troops, Confederate*.

Whitney's (Stephen) Artillery.   See *Frederick M. Follett's Artillery*.

Whiton's (John C.) Infantry.   See *Massachusetts Troops*, 43*d Regiment*.

Whitty's (Jasper M.) Infantry.   See *New York Troops*, 69*th Regiment*.

Wiestling's (George B.) Infantry.   See *Pennsylvania Troops*, 177*th Regiment*.

Wilkins' (Edward) Infantry.   See *Maryland Troops, Union*, 2*d Regiment, Eastern Shore Home Guards*.

Williams' (Augustus H. D.) Cavalry.   See *Pennsylvania Troops*, 11*th Regiment*.

Williams' (Robert) Cavalry.   See *Massachusetts Troops*, 1*st Regiment*.

Willson's (John M.) Cavalry.   See *S. H. Mix's Cavalry*.

Wilson's (William R.) Artillery.   See *New York Troops*, 1*st Regiment, Battery F*.

Winans' (Ira) Infantry.   See *New York Troops*, 99*th Regiment*.

Woodford's (Stewart L.) Infantry.   See *New York Troops*, 127*th Regiment*.

Wren's (John F.) Cavalry.   See *Virginia Troops*, 40*th Battalion*.

Wright's (C. G.) Infantry.   See *North Carolina Troops, Confederate*.

Wright's (S. T.) Artillery.   See *Virginia Troops*.

Wyatt's (James W.) Artillery.   See *Virginia Troops*.

Young's (W. L.) Artillery.   See *North Carolina Troops, Confederate*, 10*th Battalion*.

Zabriskie's (Abram) Infantry.   See *New Jersey Troops*, 9*th Regiment*.

INDEX.

Brigades, Divisions, Corps, Armies, and improvised organizations are "Mentioned" under name of commanding officer; State and other organizations under their official designation. (See Alternate Designations, pp. 1096–1104.)

(1105)

1118

INDEX.

1128 INDEX.

---

* Originally called 2d Partisan Rangers. Co. H served as artillery.

1158   INDEX.

* Became 23d and 24th New York Batteries in Sept., 1862.
† Howitzer battery, attached to 3d New York Cavalry.
‡ Batteries designated when practicable.
§ First Mounted Rifles.

1162 INDEX.

Page.

New York Troops. Mentioned—Continued.

Infantry—*Regiments:* **85th,** 60, 92, 95–98, 100, 249, 259, 377, 487, 500, 548, 577, 584, 599, 679, 737, 1060; **89th,** 271, 276, 286, 302, 304, 305, 308, 312, 314, 317, 562, 570, 575, 640, 676, 735; **92d,** 60, 95–97, 99, 100, 104, 172, 184, 377, 487, 500, 548, 577, 599, 679, 737, 1060, 1064; **96th,** 18, 56, 59, 60, 92, 95–98, 100, 101, 103, 104, 248, 249, 377, 487, 500, 518, 548, 577, 584, 599, 679, 722, 737, 1060, 1064, 1090; **98th,** 487, 501, 548, 577, 603, 678, 737; **99th,** 272, 277, 287, 292, 293, 299, 359, 376, 377, 468, 487, 499, 501, 575, 676, 677, 729, 735, 1093; **100th,** 33, 49, 50, 487, 501, 548, 678, 738; **103d,** 278, 286, 301, 302, 305, 306, 308, 312, 316, 562, 570, 575, 584, 676, 735, 1090; **112th,** 125, 133, 135, 137, 279, 286, 289, 293, 294, 487, 575, 676, 734, 1093; **115th,** 124, 496, 497, 499, 508, 515, 529; **117th,** 271, 278, 286, 303–306, 309–311, 318, 608, 676, 735; **118th,** 272, 287, 294, 299, 359, 677, 735; **127th,** 287, 294, 323, 676, 734; **130th,** 35, 37, 125, 132–137, 139, 286, 292, 293, 392, 487, 575, 676, 734, 1093; **132d,** 168, 173, 225, 249, 459, 487, 548, 569, 578, 599, 679, 737; **139th,** 468, 487, 499, 574, 595, 677, 734, 1093; **141st,** 287, 323, 676, 734; **142d,** 287, 323, 357, 676, 734; **143d,** 287, 294, 306, 313, 323, 676, 734; **144th,** 287, 306, 323, 676, 734; **148th,** 468, 487, 575, 677, 735, 1093; **152d,** 272, 286, 299, 676, 734; **155th,** 125, 126, 132, 134, 135, 137–141, 286, 289, 296–298, 487, 575, 676, 735, 1093; **158th,** 173, 225, 249, 454, 468, 470, 487, 499, 548, 569, 578, 599, 679, 726, 737; **164th,** 125, 126, 135, 141, 286, 289, 296–298, 487, 575, 676, 735, 1093; **168th,** 576, 677, 734; **169th,** 272, 286, 294, 295, 608, 676, 734; **170th,** 286, 289, 296, 297, 306, 313, 487, 575, 676, 735, 1093; **175th,** 487; **182d,** * 132–135, 137, 138, 140, 286, 296, 298, 487, 575, 676, 735, 1093.

Nichols, J. W. Mentioned 1008
Nicoll, James R. Mentioned 10
Nicoll, Sylvester D. Mentioned 5–7
Nields, Benjamin. Mentioned 735
Nixon, Richard. Mentioned 280
Nixonton, N. C. Skirmish at, April 6, 1863.
  Co-operation of Navy, U. S., with Army 259, 260
  Report of Enos C. Sanders 259
Noble, Mrs. Mentioned 727
Nolan, Patrick. Mentioned 134, 139
Non-combatants. Communications from
  Dix, John A 405, 409
  Keyes, Erasmus D 600
  Lee, S. P 404–406, 411
  Peck, John J 626
      See also *Eastern Insane Asylum, Va.*
Norcom, James. Mentioned 526, 527, 552
Norfleet, Hamlin. Mentioned 19
Norfleet House, Va. Engagements near the.
  April 14, 1863. See *report of Peck,* p. 274.
  April 15, 1863. See *reports of Getty,* p. 301; *Peck,* p. 274.
Norfolk, Va.
  Affair at, March 25, 1863. Communications from
    Dix, John A 568
    Viele, Egbert L 568
  Blockade of. See *Blockade.*
  Election of member of Congress. Communications from
    Dix, John A 474
    War Department, U. S 472
  Emancipation celebration at 501, 502

* Also called 69th New York National Guard Artillery.

---

*From Sept. 19, 1862, to April 1, 1863, embraced in the Department of Virginia and North Carolina.

North Carolina Troops. Mentioned. (Confederate.)

Artillery, Heavy—*Battalions:* **10th,*** 786, 809, 865, 866, 917, 922 ; (*Companies*) **A, B, C,** 922. *Companies :* Barnes', 922 ; Buie's, 865, 866, 917, 922; Holland's, 922; McBryde's, 922; MacRae's, 922; Rankin's, 865, 866, 917, 922; Tait's, 922; Webb's, 142. *Regiments:* **3d**† (*Companies*) **F,** 120.

Artillery, Light—*Battalions:* **3d,**‡ 121, 122, 865, 866, 879, 901, 917 ; (*Batteries*) **A,** 1049 ; **B,** 807, 1049 ; **C,** 1049. *Batteries :* Bunting's, 113, 807, 975 ; Cape Fear, 807 ; Lane's, 335, 884, 916, 917, 963, 995 ; Rowan, 782, 904, 917, 975, 991. *Regiments :* **1st,**§ 110, 113, 118, 120, 457, 803 ; (*Batteries*) **C,** 190–192, 1020; **E,** 255, 1004, 1007, 1087, 1090 ; **F,** 865, 866, 917 ; **2d** ‖ (*Batteries*) **B,** 111, 113, 115, 117–121, 807, 954, 971, 975 ; **D,** 34, 866, 917.

Cavalry—*Battalions:* **7th,** 772 ; **12th,** 255, 1062. *Companies:* Norfleet's, 19; Swindell's Rangers, 984. *Regiments :* **2d.** 743, 746, 751, 759, 764, 921, 963, 1038 ; **3d,** 34, 111, 112, 529, 564, 693, 750, 767. 865, 866, 917, 941, 963, 990, 1056, 1067 ; **4th,** 19, 121, 122, 197, 457, 670, 750, 755, 771, 984, 1044, 1051 ; **5th,** 121, 122, 160, 197, 198, 631, 638, 713, 755, 913, 957, 1051, 1060.

Infantry—*Battalions:* Mallett's, 113, 807 ; Whitford's, 192, 194, 253, 508, 883, 894 ; Wright's, 1074 ; **2d,** 974, 1046; **8th,** 72, 154, 225, 240, 255, 631, 932, 933, 945, 1074, 1087. *Companies:* Bradberry's, 809, 865, 866, 879, 901, 917 ; Burwell's, 807 ; Elliott's, 356, 1067 ; Sanderlin's, 356. *Regiments:* **1st, 3d,** 982 ; **8th,** 117–119, 457, 791, 866 ; **11th,** 113, 121, 122. 791, 808, 1033, 1041 ; **17th,** 47, 49, 146, 199, 457, 760, 975, 984, 1004, 1033, 1064, 1065, 1089, 1092 ; **25th,** 364 ; **26th,** 192, 193, 457, 803; **31st,** 121, 122, 441, 457, 791, 804, 866 ; **32d,** 951 ; **35th,** 170, 961, 982 ; **42d,** 201, 202, 945, 946, 1033, 1089, 1092 ; **43d,** 160, 951 ; **44th,** 192, 1041: **45th,** 163 ; **46th,** 1011 ; **47th,** 113, 1064; **49th,** 226, 240, 255, 982 ; **50th,** 945, 974 ; **51st,** 117–119, 457, 760, 781, 782, 791, 866, 879 ; **52d,** 18, 19, 111, 117–120, 556, 803, 1041 ; **53d,** 745, 951 ; **54th,** 751, 759, 764 ; **55th,** 325–328, 332, 338–340, 556, 788, 910, 997, 998, 1002, 1010, 1015, 1016, 1033 ; **56th,** 364, 658, 785, 791, 808, 896, 1033 ; **57th,** 751, 759, 764 ; **58th,** 362 ; **61st,** 113, 115, 118, 119, 760, 781, 782, 785, 791, 808, 865, 866, 917 ; **64th,** 810, 853.

Miscellaneous—Thomas' Legion, 811, 853.

North Carolina Troops. Mentioned. (Union.)

Infantry—*Regiments :* **1st,** 6, 7, 9, 13, 14, 47–49, 157, 201, 202, 212, 213, 216, 217, 259, 260, 533, 547, 549, 576, 675, 678, 679, 737.

North Carolina and Southern Virginia, Department of. See *Virginia and North Carolina, Department of.*

Northerner, Steamer. Mentioned 145, 147, 181, 182, 223, 224, 584

Northern Virginia. Operations in,

Sept. 3–Nov. 15, 1862. Communications from Gustavus W. Smith 751

Nov. 15, 1862–Jan. 25, 1863. See *Dumfries and Fairfax Station, Va. Raid on, Dec.* 27–29, 1862.

April 27–May 6, 1863. *Chancellorsville Campaign.*

Northern Virginia, Army of. (Confederate.)

Orders, Special, series 1863 : **No. 14,** 847.

Re-enforcements for. Communications from

Adjutant and Inspector General's Office, C. S. A 1079, 1082

Daniel, Junius 1062

Davis, Jefferson 1083

---

* Companies designated when practicable.

† Called also 40th Regiment.

‡ Batteries designated when practicable.

§ Called also 10th Regiment. Batteries designated when practicable.

‖ Called also 36th Regiment.

1178

INDEX.

* Formally constituted April 1, 1863.

---

[*] Company A, 1st Heavy Artillery.   [†] Formally constituted April 1, 1863.

---

* Geographical command of Smith, afterward Longstreet.

Page.

Virginia Troops. Mentioned—Continued.

Artillery, Light—*Batteries:* Petersburg Rocket (continued), 35, 36, 42; Richmond Fayette, 334, 995; Staunton Hill, 866, 917; Sturdivant's, 900, 916, 917, 930, 978; Wright's, 142, 145; Wyatt's, 190, 191. *Regiments:* 1st, * 900, 916, 917, 930, 978, 1067.

Cavalry—*Battalions:* 27th, 142, 807; 32d, 795, 798, 800, 920, 975, 1006; 40th, 341, 1059, 1070. *Companies:* Barham's, 1038, 1039. *Regiments:* 5th, 341, 1006; 9th, 342; 10th, 795, 920, 976, 1006, 1019; 13th, 751, 759, 764, 787, 845; 15th, 749, 752, 759, 764, 787, 845.

Infantry—*Battalions:* City, 684, 1059; 2d, Local Defense (*Q. M. Dept.*), 1092; 4th, Local Defense (*Naval*), 1092; 5th, Local Defense (*Arsenal*), 1092. *Companies:* Confederate Guard, 900, 916, 917, 930; Hargrove Blues,† 900, 916, 917, 930, 978. *Regiments:* 1st, 929; 5th, 658; 8th, 215; 14th, 340; 17th, 289; 26th, 920, 995; 29th, 341, 807, 900, 916, 917, 930; 32d, 978, 1067; 46th, 208, 342, 343, 892, 920, 1019; 50th, 142, 145, 519, 807; 54th, 142, 145, 807; 57th, 929; 59th, 207, 208, 209, 920, 995, 1019; 61st, 751, 759, 764, 787, 845; 63d, 142, 145, 807.

Militia—*Regiments:* 18th, 22d, 26th, 31st, 39th, 42d, 43d, 49th, 50th, 53d, 63d, 64th, 66th, 69th, 73d, 83d, 84th, 96th, 98th, 101st, 110th, 117th, 156th, 168th, 172d, 195th, 835.

Voliva, Thomas. Mentioned ... 181
Voorhees, B. F. Mentioned ... 433
Voris, Alvin C. Mentioned ... 577, 738
Vought, Philip G. Mentioned ... 737
Wadley, William M.
  Correspondence with War Department, C. S ... 874
  Mentioned ... 859, 873
Wadsworth, James S. Mentioned ... 409
Wageley, Louis. Mentioned ... 26, 30
Wager, Peter H. Mentioned ... 622, 651, 652, 995
Waldron, S. W., jr. For correspondence as A. A. G., see *Henry Prince.*
Wale's Head, N. C. Destruction of Salt-Works at, Feb. 2, 1863. Report of
  Francis E. Porter ... 148
Wales, Thomas B., jr. Mentioned ... 350
Walker, George H. Mentioned ... 257, 258
Walker, H. H. Mentioned ... 749, 802, 1059
Walker, H. P. Correspondence with W. H. C. Whiting ... 1056
Walker, Lindsay R. Mentioned ... 762
Walker, W. S. Correspondence with G. T. Beauregard ... 1013
Wall, Richard. Mentioned ... 90
Wallace, G. A.
  Mentioned ... 207
  Report of skirmish at Williamsburg, Va., March 29, 1863 ... 208
Waller, Richard P. Mentioned ... 1092
Wallick, William F. M. Mentioned ... 294
Wallis, J. W. Correspondence with John G. Foster ... 674
Walton, J. B. Mentioned ... 896
Walton, Thomas. Mentioned ... 896
War Department, C. S. Correspondence with
  Baird, E. R ... 1091
  Beauregard, G. T ... 799, 811–813, 816, 822, 1012, 1013, 1017
  Campbell, J. A ... 1082
  Davis, Jefferson ... 803, 823, 834, 848, 860, 870, 891, 976, 1009, 1015, 1053, 1081, 1082

---

* Four batteries serving at Petersburg, Va.   † Originally Company I, 12th Virginia Infantry.

Page.

     *Joseph E. Johnston's geographical command.